MKTG

A South-Asian Perspective

Charles W. Lamb
Texas Christian University

Joseph F. Hair, Jr.
Kennesaw State University

Dheeraj Sharma
Indian Institute of Management Rohtak

Carl McDaniel
University of Texas—Arlington

Cengage

Australia • Brazil • Canada • India • Mexico • Singapore • United Kingdom • United States

Cengage

MKTG

Charles W. Lamb
Joseph F. Hair, Jr.
Dheeraj Sharma
Carl McDaniel

Cover Image:
© indiatodayimages.com

MKTG5, SE Package

This edition is reprinted with license from, Brooks-Cole, a part of Cengage Learning, Inc., for sale in India, Pakistan, Bangladesh, Nepal, Bhutan, Sri Lanka and Maldives.

ISBN-13: 978-81-315-2034-5
ISBN-10: 81-315-2034-X

Cengage Learning India Pvt. Ltd.
T-303, 3rd Floor
DAV Complex, Plot 3
Mayur Vihar Phase 1
Delhi 110091

Disclaimer:
This book contains link to resources which are a part of the international edition. The same may not be available with the Indian edition. The buyer needs to purchase a copy of the international edition to have full access to those resources. In no event the publisher shall be liable for any limitation or performance due to unavailability of these resources.

Printed by:
Saurabh Printers Pvt. Ltd.
67A-68, Ecotech Ext-I, Greater Noida,
Tel-0120-2341180

Printed in India
Print Number: 05 Print Year: 2025

Preface

4LTR Press, a Cengage Learning product, is a widely acclaimed concept of learning with a simple approach—creating an innovative teaching and learning solution built around today's learners and teachers. The idea behind bringing out this series of books is to introduce students and teachers in South Asia to an innovative concept in management studies. Since the launch, 4LTR Press has helped more than 1,800,000 college students at over 2,000 schools succeed worldwide. Every book in the series is built on the findings based on the inputs from discipline-specific focus groups, conversations, and surveys.

The books in this series present visually engaging page layouts and succinct yet thorough topical coverage and are designed from the ground up to meet the needs of teachers and students. These books help increase students' classroom engagement and improve learning outcomes.

The books address a number of concerns, including the reality of the reading habits of the majority of today's students. 4LTR Press offers information in the formats students find engaging, while still providing the high-quality content instructors need. The chapters in these books are short and understandable. The text is easier to pay attention to, and the books are actually enjoyable to read. Everything is much more inviting than a regular textbook. The review cards at the end of each chapter serve a unique purpose: Students first go through the review card to preview the new concepts, then they read the chapter to understand the material, and finally they go through the review card again to make sure they have registered the key concepts.

We are sure that this series, a first of its kind in the South Asian market, will revolutionize the way students approach and become familiar with the concepts of management.

LAMB | HAIR | SHARMA | MCDANIEL

MKTG

Brief Contents

Contents

PART 1
THE WORLD OF MARKETING

FGM

3 Ethics and Social Responsibility 56

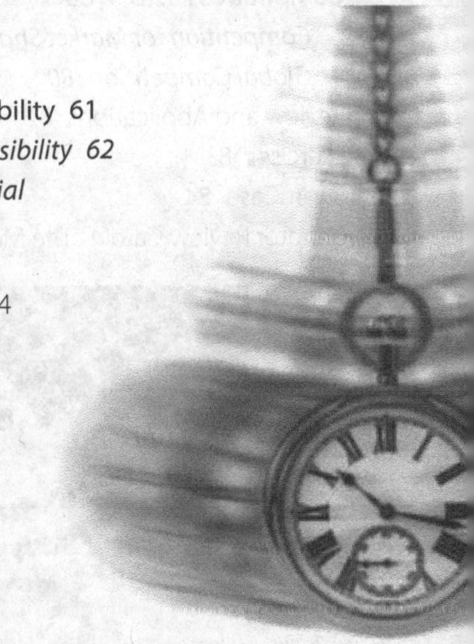

4 The Marketing Environment 70

Retirement
Plan
Date:

7 Business Marketing 168

9 Decision Support Systems and Marketing Research 218

PART 3 PRODUCT DECISIONS

10 Product Concepts 262

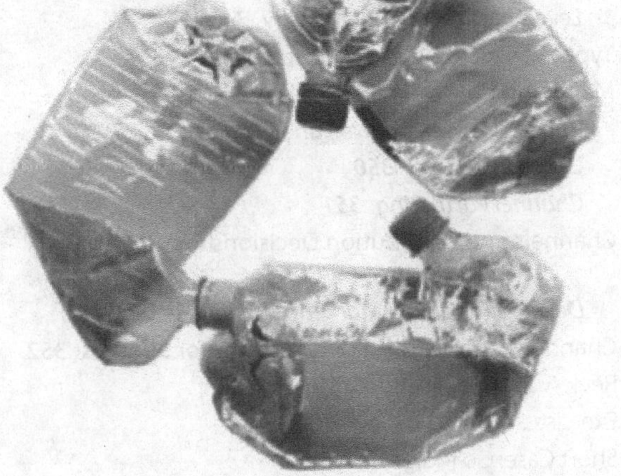

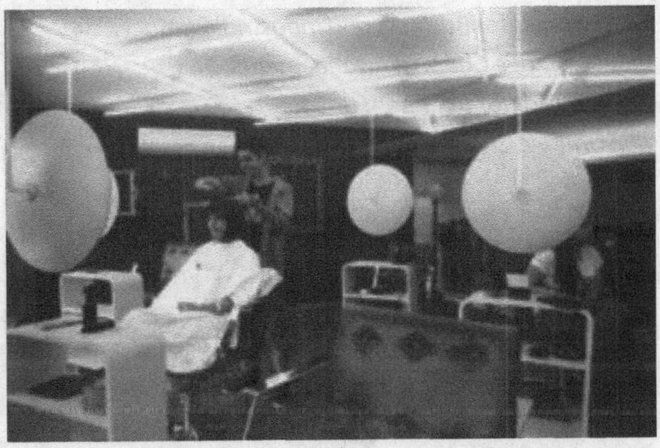

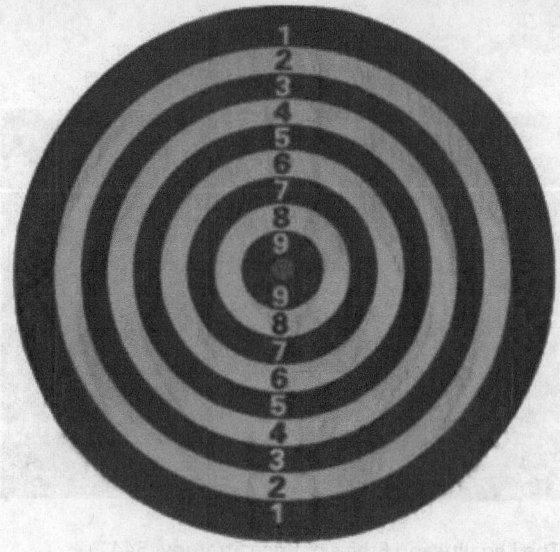

PART 8 NEW FRONTIERS OF MARKETING

CHAPTER 1

An Overview of Marketing

Learning Outcomes

LO 1 Define the term *marketing*

LO 2 Describe four marketing management philosophies

LO 3 Discuss the differences between sales and market orientations

LO 4 Describe several reasons for studying marketing

"Marketing is too important to be left only to the marketing department."
—David Packard

LO1 What Is Marketing?

What does the term *marketing* mean to you? Many people think it means the same as personal selling. Others think marketing is the same as advertising. Still others believe marketing has something to do with making products available in stores, arranging displays, and maintaining inventories of products for future sales. Actually, marketing includes all of these activities and more.

marketing the activity, set of institutions, and processes for creating, communicating, delivering, and exchanging offerings that have value for customers, clients, partners, and society at large

Marketing has two facets. First, it is a philosophy, an attitude, a perspective, or a management orientation that stresses customer satisfaction. Second, marketing is an organization function and a set of processes used to implement this philosophy.

The American Marketing Association's definition of marketing focuses on the second facet. **Marketing** is the activity, set of institutions, and processes for creating, communicating, delivering, and exchanging offerings that have value for customers, clients, partners, and society at large.[1]

Marketing involves more than just activities performed by a group of people in a defined area or department. In the often-quoted words of David Packard, co-founder of Hewlett-Packard, "Marketing is too important to be left only to the marketing department." Marketing entails processes that focus on delivering value and benefits to customers, not just selling goods, services, and/or ideas. It uses communication, distribution, and pricing strategies to provide customers and other stakeholders with the goods, services, ideas, values, and benefits they desire when and where they want them. It involves building long-term, mutually rewarding relationships when these benefit all parties concerned. Marketing also entails

***Note:** All the figures in U.S. dollars are converted into rupee using the value $1 = ₹45.*

EMPLOYEES AS COMPETITIVE ADVANTAGE

Rewarding employees for outstanding job performance (sales, meeting development goals, etc.) reinforces positive behaviors, such as great customer service, and maintains employee (and by extension, customer) satisfaction. Recognizing an individual doesn't have to cost a fortune. For example, trusting an outstanding employee with important clients or including an excellent team on the next big deal not only encourages employees to work harder, but helps ensure that customers receive the company's best talent and effort. A good workplace environment translates to the customer through employees, which ultimately benefits the business by making the customer comfortable, confident, and happy.[5]

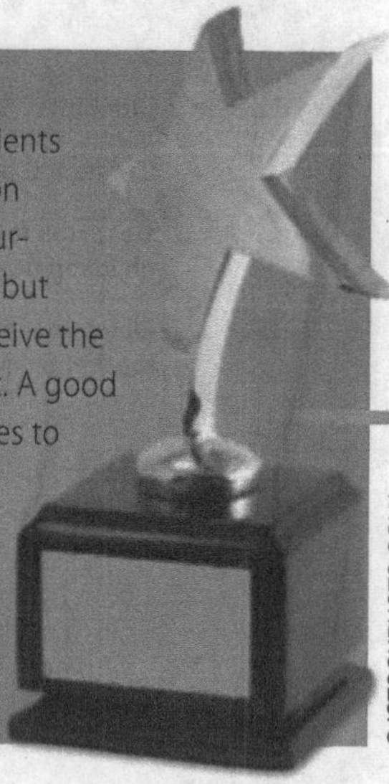

an understanding that organizations have many connected stakeholder "partners," including employees, suppliers, stockholders, distributors, and others.

Research shows that companies that reward employees with incentives and recognition on a consistent basis are those that perform best.[2] TATA Steel's employment philosophies have always been based on the recognition that its people are its primary source of competitiveness. In fact, the core principles enlisted in its human resources policies are equality of opportunity, continuing personal development, fairness, mutual trust, and teamwork.[3] The group is of the view that employee loyalty can be earned by offering challenging jobs, development opportunities and competitive compensation and benefits schemes.

One desired outcome of marketing is an **exchange**; people giving up something in order to receive something they would rather have. Normally, we think of money as the medium of exchange. We "give up" money to "get" the goods and services we want. Exchange does not require money, however. Two people may barter or trade such items as baseball cards or oil paintings. An exchange can take place only if the following five conditions exist:

1. There must be at least two parties.
2. Each party has something that might be of value to the other party.
3. Each party is capable of communication and delivery.
4. Each party is free to accept or reject the exchange offer.
5. Each party believes it is appropriate or desirable to deal with the other party.[4]

exchange people giving up something in order to receive something they would rather have

Exchange will not necessarily take place even if all these conditions exist. They are, however, necessary for ex-change to be possible. For example, you may place an advertisement in your local newspaper stating that your used automobile is for sale at a certain price. Several people may call you to ask about the car, some may test-drive it, and one or more may even make you an offer. All five conditions are necessary for an exchange to exist. But unless you reach an agreement with a buyer and actually sell the car, an exchange will not take place. Notice that marketing can occur even if an exchange does not occur. In the example just discussed, you would have engaged in marketing even if no one bought your used automobile.

LO 2 Marketing Management Philosophies

Four competing philosophies strongly influence an organization's marketing processes. These philoso-

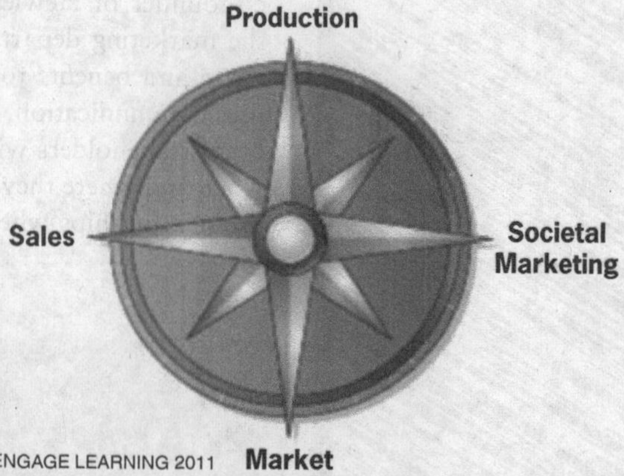

phies are commonly referred to as production, sales, market, and societal marketing orientations.

Production Orientation

A **production orientation** is a philosophy that focuses on the internal capabilities of the firm rather than on the desires and needs of the marketplace. A production orientation means that management assesses its resources and asks these questions: "What can we do best?" "What can our engineers design?" "What is easy to produce, given our equipment?" In the case of a service organization, managers ask, "What services are most convenient for the firm to offer?" and "Where do our talents lie?" Some have referred to this orientation as a *Field of Dreams* orientation, from the well-known movie line, "If we build it, they will come."

There is nothing wrong with assessing a firm's capabilities; in fact, such assessments are major considerations in strategic marketing planning (see Chapter 2). A production orientation falls short because it does not consider whether the goods and services that the firm produces most efficiently also meet the needs of the marketplace. Sometimes what a firm can best produce is exactly what the market wants. Apple has a history of production orientation, creating computers, operating systems, and other gadgetry because they can, and hoping to sell the result. Some items have found a waiting market (early computers, iPod, iPhone). Other products, like the Newton, one of the first versions of a PDA, were simply flops. In other situations, as when competition is weak or demand exceeds supply, a production-oriented firm can survive and even prosper. More often, however, firms that succeed in competitive markets have a clear understanding that they must first determine what customers want and then produce it, rather than focusing on what company management thinks should be produced.

© AP IMAGES/PAUL SAKUMA

production orientation a philosophy that focuses on the internal capabilities of the firm rather than on the desires and needs of the marketplace

sales orientation the ideas that people will buy more goods and services if aggressive sales techniques are used and that high sales result in high profits

marketing concept the idea that the social and economic justification for an organization's existence is the satisfaction of customer wants and needs while meeting organizational objectives

Sales Orientation

A **sales orientation** is based on the ideas that people will buy more goods and services if aggressive sales techniques are used and that high sales result in high profits. Not only are sales to the final buyer emphasized, but intermediaries are also encouraged to push manufacturers' products more aggressively. To sales-oriented firms, marketing means selling things and collecting money.

The fundamental problem with a sales orientation, as with a production orientation, is a lack of understanding of the needs and wants of the marketplace. Sales-oriented companies often find that, despite the quality of their sales force, they cannot convince people to buy goods or services that are neither wanted nor needed.

One of the dangers of a sales orientation is failing to understand what is important to the firm's customers. When that occurs, sales-oriented firms sometimes use aggressive incentives to drive sales. For example, after Toyota recalled lakhs of vehicles due to acceleration problems and other safety concerns, the company implemented aggressive incentives to bring customers back. Zero-percent financing, increased cash back, and free maintenance packages, as well as other incentives, enabled some customers to lease new Rav 4s for ₹7,605 a month, whereas before they would have paid ₹12,555 a month.[6]

Market Orientation

The **marketing concept** is a simple and intuitively appealing philosophy that articulates a market orientation. It states that the social and economic justification for an organization's existence is the

market orientation a philosophy that assumes that a sale does not depend on an aggressive sales force but rather on a customer's decision to purchase a product; it is synonymous with the marketing concept

societal marketing orientation the idea that an organization exists not only to satisfy customer wants and needs and to meet organizational objectives but also to preserve or enhance individuals' and society's long-term best interests

satisfaction of customer wants and needs while meeting organizational objectives. What a business thinks it produces is not of primary importance to its success. Instead, what customers think they are buying—the perceived value—defines a business. The marketing concept includes the following:

- Focusing on customer wants and needs so that the organization can distinguish its product(s) from competitors' offerings
- Integrating all the organization's activities, including production, to satisfy these wants
- Achieving long-term goals for the organization by satisfying customer wants and needs legally and responsibly

The recipe for success is to consistently deliver a unique experience that your competitors cannot match and that satisfies the intentions and preferences of your target buyers.[7] This requires a thorough understanding of your customers and distinctive capabilities that enable your company to execute plans on the basis of this customer understanding, and delivering the desired experience using and integrating all of the resources of the firm.[8]

Firms that adopt and implement the marketing concept are said to be **market oriented**, meaning they assume that a sale does not depend on an aggressive sales force but rather on a customer's decision to purchase a product. Achieving a market orientation involves obtaining information about customers, competitors, and markets; examining the information from a total business perspective; determining how to deliver superior customer value; and implementing actions to provide value to customers.

What are the names of some firms known for delivering superior customer value and satisfaction? Maruti Suzuki has topped the JD Power customer satisfaction survey for 12 consecutive years in the auto dealer service category.[9] It was followed by Honda Siel cars at the second spot and General Motors and Volkswagen jointly at the third place.

Understanding your competitive arena and competitors' strengths and weaknesses is a critical component of a market orientation. This includes assessing what existing or potential competitors might be intending to do tomorrow as well as what they are doing today.

Kinetic took the Indian two wheeler industry by storm through its two key offerings – luna (moped) and gearless scooter. These two names, in fact, became the generic names of their respective product categories and were market leaders. However, with changing times, the brand failed in catching the pulse of the market and meeting the customer expectations. The brand no longer exists in the market, thus bringing an end to an era.

Societal Marketing Orientation

The **societal marketing orientation** extends the marketing concept by acknowledging that some products that customers want may not really be in their best interests or the best interests of society as a whole. This philosophy states that an organization exists not only to satisfy customer wants and needs and to meet organizational objectives but also to preserve or enhance individuals' and society's long-term best interests. Marketing products and containers that are less toxic than normal, are more durable, contain reusable materials, or are made of recyclable materials is consistent with a societal marketing orientation. The American Marketing Association's definition of marketing recognizes the importance of a societal marketing orientation by including "society at large" as one of the constituencies for which marketing seeks to provide value.

Although the societal marketing concept has been discussed over 30 years, it did not receive widespread support until the early 2000s. Concerns such as climate change, the depleting ozone layer, fuel shortages, pollution, and raised health concerns have caused consumers and legislators to be more aware of the need for companies and consumers to adopt measures that conserve resources and cause less damage to the environment. Studies, conducted in U.S., reporting consumers' attitudes toward, and intentions to buy, more environmentally friendly products show widely varying results. One study that helps explain some of this contradiction found that 44 percent of consumers were "theoretically" interested in buying environmentally friendly products, but the proportion doing so was much less.[10] The top three reasons customers gave for not following through by purchasing and using these more environmentally friendly products were doubts about effectiveness, expense, and lack of availability at convenient outlets.[11] In another study, 35 percent of consumers say they would pay more for environmentally friendly products.[12] One study found that while half of its respondents thought a company's environmental record was important, only 7 percent could name an environmentally friendly product they had purchased.[13]

Many marketers have made substantial commitments to either producing products using more environmentally friendly processes or making more environmentally friendly products. Coca-Cola has made a long-term commitment to recover and reuse 100 percent of bottles and cans placed in the market. In 2008, Coca-Cola opened the largest bottle-to-bottle recycling plant in the world, located in South Carolina.[14] Nokia India, Panasonic India, Wipro, MRF Tyres are some of the leaders in the industry in the "eco-friendly" movement.[15]

What will the future bring? The current trends are that more customers are becoming concerned about the environment each year, more customers are trying to buy environmentally friendly products and support more environmentally friendly companies, and more companies are joining the movement by developing processes and products that do less damage to the environment than in the past. The green market grew 41 percent from 2004 to 2009 in the United States, and despite the recession, the green market outperformed the rest of the economy in 2009, showing flat growth rather than decline. India too has witnessed a rise in green marketing campaigns undertaken by the companies. NDTV-Toyota launched the Greenathon campaign supporting the cause of "Lighting a billion lives" that works toward providing solar power to such villages that have no electricity. HUL also came up with its "Save water" campaign and launched products that consumed less water.[16]

LO 3 Differences between Sales and Market Orientations

The differences between sales and market orientations are substantial. The two orientations can be compared in terms of five characteristics: the organization's focus, the firm's business, those to whom the product is directed, the firm's primary goal, and the tools used to achieve those goals.

The Organization's Focus

Personnel in sales-oriented firms tend to be "inward looking," focusing on selling what the organization makes rather than making what the market wants. Many of the historic sources of competitive advantage—technology, innovation, economies of scale—allowed companies to focus their efforts internally and prosper. But that same inward focus characteristic of the sales orientation has also led to the demise of a firm.

Today, many successful firms derive their competitive advantage from an external, market-oriented focus. A market orientation has helped companies such as Mahindra Tractors and Cavin Care outperform their competitors. These companies put customers at the center of their business in ways most companies do poorly or not at all.

Customer Value **Customer value** is the relationship between benefits and the sacrifice necessary to obtain those benefits. Customer value is not simply a matter of high quality. A high-quality product that is available only at a high price will not be perceived as a good value, nor will bare-bones service or low-quality goods selling for a low price. Instead, customers value goods and services that are of the quality they expect and that are sold at prices they are willing to pay. Value can be used to sell a Mercedes-Benz as well as a Nirma washing powder.

Lower income consumers are price sensitive, but they will pay for products if they deliver a benefit that is worth the money.[17] The shampoo sachet revolution is a prime example proving this theory right. By offering low quantities of shampoo in sachet packaging at affordable price points of ₹1, the customers were presented with great value.

Value is not about pricing alone, however. Crossword has relied on its comfortable, upscale bookstores to add more value to its book offerings than its competitors offer. For example, Crossword's brightly lit stores have got seating facility for the customers so that customers can sit and leisurely browse through books. They also keep holding events like book launch and book reading sessions and send personalized mails to customers about latest offerings.

Marketers interested in customer value:

- *Offer products that perform:* This is the bare minimum requirement. After grappling with the problems associated with its Vista operating system, Microsoft listened to its customers and made drastic changes for Windows 7,

customer value the relationship between benefits and the sacrifice necessary to obtain those benefits

customer satisfaction customers' evaluation of a good or service in terms of whether it has met their needs and expectations

which has been receiving greatly improved reviews.

- *Earn trust:* A stable base of loyal customers can help a firm grow and prosper. Despite the evolution of modern retail in India, the neighbourhood mom-n-pop grocery stores still hold a lion's share of the total retail market for the simple reason that owners of these stores have developed strong relations with their customers over time and earned their loyalty in return.
- *Avoid unrealistic pricing:* E-marketers are leveraging Internet technology to redefine how prices are set and negotiated. With lower costs, e-marketers can often offer lower prices than their brick-and-mortar counterparts. The enormous popularity of auction sites such as eBay illustrates that online customers are interested in bargain prices. Many are not willing to pay a premium for the convenience of examining the merchandise and taking it home with them. Others will gladly pay a premium for an experience that is not only functionally rewarding, but emotionally rewarding as well. Executives at Taj Hotels Resorts and Palaces believe that they are able to make an emotional connection with their guests by anticipating and delivering on their unexpressed expectations with panache, warmth, and graciousness.
- *Give the buyer facts:* Today's sophisticated consumer wants informative advertising and knowledgeable salespeople. It is becoming very difficult for business marketers to differentiate themselves from competitors. Rather than trying to sell products, salespeople need to find out what the customer needs, which is usually a combination of products, services, and thought leadership.[18] In other words, salespeople need to start with the needs of the customer and work toward the solution.
- *Offer organization-wide commitment in service and after-sales support:* Private sector banks such as HDFC, HSBC, and ICICI played a pivotal role in changing the service standards of the banking industry in India. Being tech-savvy and having expertise in their domain, these banks transformed the entire banking industry and made banking transactions efficient and customer friendly. By offering multiple services such as ATMs, banking facilities, insurance, loans, etc., the banks offered great value to customers.
- *Co-creation:* Some companies and products allow customers to help create their own experience. Dell allows its customers to create their own laptop as per their requirements. It offers the customers with the opportunity to customize their laptops and delivers the same at their doorstep, thereby offering flexibility and convenience to the customers. Thus, the customer is freed from the strategy of "one size fits all".

©INDIATODAYIMAGES.COM

Customer Satisfaction **Customer satisfaction** is the customers' evaluation of a good or service in terms of whether that good or service has met their needs and expectations. Failure to meet needs and expectations results in dissatisfaction with the good or service. Some companies, in their passion to drive down costs, have damaged their relationships with customers. Firms that have a reputation for delivering high levels of customer satisfaction do things differently from their competitors. Top management is obsessed with customer satisfaction, and employees throughout the organization understand the link between their job and satisfied customers. The culture of the organization is to focus on delighting customers rather than on selling products.

Coming back from customer dissatisfaction can be tough—particularly for enormous firms like Walmart. In 2008, the retail giant had a 45.5 percent customer satisfaction rating in the MSN *Money* survey conducted in the United States. By 2010, however, customers' satisfaction with Walmart had climbed to 56.9 percent, the largest gain in the survey. How did Walmart improve so dramatically? The company targeted recession customers by re-vamping its stores to offer a more enjoyable shopping experience, and it increased its offering of upscale products at low prices. Even Walmart's new slogan reflects its focus on customer satisfaction: "Save money, live better."[19]

Building Relationships Attracting new customers to a business is only the beginning. The best companies view new-customer attraction as the launching point for developing and enhancing a long-term relationship. Companies can expand market share in three ways: attracting new customers, increasing business with existing customers, and retaining current customers. Building relationships with existing customers directly addresses two of the three possibilities and indirectly addresses the other.

Relationship marketing is a strategy that focuses on keeping and improving relationships with current customers. It assumes that many consumers and business customers prefer to have an ongoing relationship with one organization rather than switch continually among providers in their search for value. Maruti Suzuki is a good example of a company focused on building long-term relationships with customers. In an annual Customer Service survey conducted by J.D. Power, Maruti has been the only company to be ranked in the top spot for 12 years running. This success rate is largely attributed to performing the service work correctly the first time and providing high value at lower service costs.[20]

relationship marketing a strategy that focuses on keeping and improving relationships with current customers

Most successful relationship marketing strategies depend on customer-oriented personnel, effective training programs, employees with authority to make decisions and solve problems, and teamwork.

Customer-Oriented Personnel For an organization to be focused on building relationships with customers, employees' attitudes and actions must be customer oriented. An employee may be the only contact a particular customer has with the firm. In that customer's eyes, the employee is the firm. Any person, department, or division that is not customer oriented weakens the positive image of the entire organization. For example, a potential customer who is greeted discourteously may well assume that the employee's attitude represents the whole firm.

Isadore Sharp, founder, chair, and CEO of the Four Seasons hotel chain says, "Personal service is

THE ESSENCE OF MARKETING

A theme that you will find running throughout this text is the critical importance of providing a good customer experience. When one strips away all of the functions, plans, and strategies of marketing and asks the simple question, "What is this all about?" the answer is the customer experience. Think about it—whether you buy something a second or third time or become loyal to a brand depends on the experience that you had while purchasing and consuming the product or service. Most products need to be sold to a customer more than once in order for the company to start making money. Your favorite places rely on repeat business: a favorite grocery store, the local record shop/bookstore, the best stand in the food court. By considering the product, convenience, prices, and customer service, those places give you a good customer experience, all so you will come back.

© INDIATODAYIMAGES.COM

empowerment delegation of authority to solve customers' problems quickly—usually by the first person the customer notifies regarding a problem

teamwork collaborative efforts of people to accomplish common objectives

not something you can dictate as a policy. It comes from the culture. How you treat your employees is how you expect them to treat the customer."[21]

Some companies, such as Coca-Cola, Kellogg, and Yatra.com, have appointed chief customer officers (CCOs). These customer advocates provide an executive voice for customers and report directly to the CEO. Their responsibilities include ensuring that the company maintains a customer-centric culture and that all company employees remain focused on delivering customer value.

The Role of Training Leading marketers recognize the role of employee training in customer service and relationship building. Sales staff at Shoppers' Stop receive an annual training of 52 hours a year.

Empowerment In addition to training, many market-oriented firms are giving employees more authority to solve customer problems on the spot. The term used to describe this delegation of authority is **empowerment**. Employees develop ownership attitudes when they are treated like part-owners of the business and are expected to act the part. These employees manage themselves, are more likely to work hard, account for their own performance and that of the company and take prudent risks to build a stronger business and sustain the company's success.

Empowerment gives customers the feeling that their concerns are being addressed and gives employees the feeling that their expertise matters. The result is greater satisfaction for both customers and employees.

© ISTOCKPHOTO/THINKSTOCK

Teamwork Many organizations that are frequently noted for delivering superior customer value and providing high levels of customer satisfaction, such as Walt Disney World assigns employees to teams and teaches them team-building skills. **Teamwork** entails collaborative efforts of people to accomplish common objectives. Job performance, company performance, product value, and customer satisfaction all improve when people in the same department or work group begin supporting and assisting each other and emphasize cooperation instead of competition. Performance is also enhanced when cross-functional teams align their jobs with customer needs. For example, if a team of telecommunications service representatives is working to improve interaction with customers, back-office people such as computer technicians or training personnel can become part of the team with the ultimate goal of delivering superior customer value and satisfaction.

The Firm's Business

A sales-oriented firm defines its business (or mission) in terms of goods and services. A market-oriented firm defines its business in terms of the benefits its customers seek. People who spend their money, time, and energy expect to receive benefits, not just goods and services. This distinction has enormous implications. As a senior executive of Coca-Cola noted, Coke is in the hydration business.[22]

Because of the limited way it defines its business, a sales-oriented firm often misses opportunities to serve customers whose wants can be met through a wide range of product offerings instead of specific products. For example, in 1989, 220-year-old Britannica had estimated revenues of ₹2925 crores and a worldwide sales force of 7,500. Just five years later, after three consecutive years of losses, the sales force had collapsed to as few as 280 representatives. How did this respected company sink so low? Britannica managers saw that competitors were beginning to use CD-ROMs to store

"IF I HAD LISTENED TO THE MARKETPLACE, I WOULD HAVE BUILT A FASTER, CHEAPER HORSE."

—Henry Ford

huge masses of information but chose to ignore the new computer technology as well as an offer to team up with Microsoft.

WHAT IS THIS FIRM'S BUSINESS?

Answering the question "What is this firm's business?" in terms of the benefits customers seek, instead of goods and services, offers at least three important advantages:

- It ensures that the firm keeps focusing on customers and avoids becoming preoccupied with goods, services, or the organization's internal needs.
- It encourages innovation and creativity by reminding people that there are many ways to satisfy customer wants.
- It stimulates an awareness of changes in customer desires and preferences so that product offerings are more likely to remain relevant.

Having a market orientation and a focus on customer wants does not mean offering customers everything they want. It is not possible, for example, to profitably manufacture and market automobile tires that will last for 1,60,935 kilometers for ₹1125. Furthermore, customers' preferences must be mediated by sound professional judgment as to how to deliver the benefits they seek. As Henry Ford once said, "If I had listened to the marketplace, I would have built a faster, cheaper horse."[23] Consumers have a limited set of experiences. They are unlikely to request anything beyond those experiences because they are not aware of benefits they may gain from other potential offerings. For example, before the Internet, many people thought that shopping for some products was boring and time consuming but could not express their need for electronic shopping.

Those to Whom the Product Is Directed

A sales-oriented organization targets its products at "everybody" or "the average customer." A market-oriented organization aims at specific groups of people. The fallacy of developing products directed at the average user is that relatively few average users actually exist. Typically, populations are characterized by diversity. An average is simply a midpoint in some set of characteristics. Because most potential customers are not "average," they are not likely to be attracted to an average product marketed to the average customer. Consider the market for shampoo as one simple example. There are shampoos for oily hair, dry hair, and dandruff. Some shampoos remove the gray or color hair. Special shampoos are marketed for infants and elderly people. There are even shampoos for people with average or normal hair (whatever that is), but this is fairly small portion of the total market for shampoo.

A market-oriented organization recognizes that different customer groups want different features or benefits. It may therefore need to develop different goods, services, and promotional appeals. A market-oriented organization carefully analyzes the market and divides it into groups of people who are fairly similar in terms of selected characteristics. Then the organization develops marketing programs that will bring about mutually satisfying exchanges with one or more of those groups. Chapter 8 thoroughly explores the topic of analyzing markets and selecting those that appear to be most promising to the firm.

The Firm's Primary Goal

A sales-oriented organization seeks to achieve profitability through sales volume and tries to convince potential customers to buy, even if the seller knows that the customer and product are mismatched. Sales-oriented organizations place a higher premium on making sale than on developing a long-term relationship with a customer. In contrast, the ultimate goal of most market-oriented organizations is to make a profit by creating customer value, providing customer satisfaction, and building long-term relationships with customers. The exception is so-called nonprofit organizations that exist to achieve goals other than profits. Nonprofit organizations can and should adopt a market orientation. Nonprofit organization marketing is explored further in Chapter 12.

Tools the Organization Uses to Achieve Its Goals

Sales-oriented organizations seek to generate sales volume through intensive promotional activities, mainly personal selling and advertising. In contrast, market-oriented organizations recognize that promotion decisions are only one of four basic marketing mix decisions that have to be made: product decisions, place (or distribution) decisions, promotion decisions, and pricing decisions. A market-oriented organization recognizes that each of these four components is important. Furthermore, market-oriented organizations recognize that marketing is not just a responsibility of the marketing department. Interfunctional coordination means that skills and resources throughout the organization are needed to create, communicate, and deliver superior customer service and value.

© ISTOCKPHOTO.COM/P-WEI

Word of Caution

This comparison of sales and market orientations is not meant to belittle the role of promotion, especially personal selling, in the marketing mix. Promotion is the means by which organizations communicate with present and prospective customers about the merits and characteristics of their organization and products. Effective promotion is an essential part of effective marketing. Salespeople who work for market-oriented organizations are generally perceived by their customers to be problem solvers and important links to supply sources and new products. Chapter 18 examines the nature of personal selling in more detail.

MARKETING POTENTIAL IN SOCIAL MEDIA

Social media is increasingly being used for sharing views and exchanging opinions. With the huge potential for user growth, companies are also looking for ways to use the networking sites for marketing activities like increasing brand awareness, maintaining customer relations, and gaining customer feedback. With nearly 50 lakh and 4 crore users on Twitter and Facebook respectively, the social networking sites are serving as interactive platforms for consumers. According to a survey by MindShift, Twitter is the most used site for airing views with a share of 49 percent, followed by Facebook with 33 percent, and other forums and blogs with 9 percent. This gives an ideal platform to companies to reach out to their consumers and engage with them.[24]

© ISTOCKPHOTO.COM/MATT JEACOCK

LO 4 Why Study Marketing

Now that you understand the meaning of the term *marketing*, why it is important to adopt a marketing orientation, how organizations implement this philosophy, and how one-to-one marketing is evolving, you may be asking, "What's in it for me?" or "Why should I study marketing?" These are important questions whether you are majoring in a business field other than marketing (such as accounting, finance, or management information systems) or a nonbusiness field (such as journalism, education, or agriculture). There are several important reasons to study marketing: Marketing plays an important role in society, marketing is important to businesses, marketing offers outstanding career opportunities, and marketing affects your life every day.

Marketing Plays an Important Role in Society

The total population of India exceeds 120 crore people.[25] Think about how many transactions are needed each day to feed, cloth, and shelter a population of this size. The number is huge. And yet it all works quite well, partly because the developed Indian economic system efficiently distributes the output of farms and factories. The share of food basket in total consumption expenditure stands at 57% and 44% for rural and urban India respectively.[26] Marketing makes food available when we want it, in desired quantities, at accessible locations, and in sanitary and convenient packages and forms (such as instant and frozen foods).

Marketing Is Important to Businesses

The fundamental objectives of most businesses are survival, profits, and growth. Marketing contributes directly to achieving these objectives. Marketing includes the following activities, which are vital to business organizations: assessing the wants and satisfactions of present and potential customers, designing and managing product offerings, determining prices and pricing policies, developing distribution strategies, and communicating with present and potential customers.

All businesspeople, regardless of specialization or area of responsibility, need to be familiar with the terminology and fundamentals of accounting, finance, management, and marketing. People in all business areas need to be able to communicate with specialists in other areas. Furthermore, marketing is not just a job done by people in a marketing department. Marketing is a part of the job of everyone in the organization. Therefore, a basic understanding of marketing is important to all businesspeople.

Marketing Offers Outstanding Career Opportunities

Marketing offers great career opportunities in such areas as professional selling, marketing research, advertising, retail buying, distribution management, product management, product development, and wholesaling. Marketing career opportunities also exist in a variety of nonbusiness organizations, including hospitals, museums, universities, the armed forces, and various government and social service agencies.

Marketing in Everyday Life

Marketing plays a major role in your everyday life. You participate in the marketing process as a consumer of goods and services. For every rupee you spend, a major share pays for marketing costs, such as marketing research, product development, packaging, transportation, storage, advertising, and sales expenses. By developing a better understanding of marketing, you will become a better-informed consumer. You will better understand the buying process and be able to negotiate more effectively with sellers. Moreover, you will be better prepared to demand satisfaction when the goods and services you buy do not meet the standards promised by the manufacturer or the marketer.

Review and Applications

Define the term *marketing*. Marketing is the activity, set of institutions, and processes for creating, communicating, delivering, and exchanging offerings that have value for customers, clients, partners, and society at large.

1.1 What is the AMA? What does it do? How do its services benefit marketers? **www.marketingpower.com**

Describe four marketing management philosophies. The role of marketing and the character of marketing activities within an organization are strongly influenced by its philosophy and orientation. A production-oriented organization focuses on the internal capabilities of the firm rather than on the desires and needs of the marketplace. A sales orientation is based on the beliefs that people will buy more products if aggressive sales techniques are used and that high sales volumes produce high profits. A market-oriented organization focuses on satisfying customer wants and needs while meeting organizational objectives. A societal marketing orientation goes beyond a market orientation to include the preservation or enhancement of individuals' and society's long-term best interests.

2.1 Your company president has decided to restructure the firm to make it more market oriented. She is going to announce the changes at an upcoming meeting. She has asked you to prepare a short speech outlining the general reasons for the new company orientation.

2.2 Donald E. Petersen, former chairman of the board of Ford Motor Company, remarked, "If we aren't customer driven, our cars won't be either." Explain how this statement reflects the marketing concept.

2.3 Give an example of a company that might be successfully following a production orientation. Why might a firm in this industry be successful following such an orientation?

Discuss the differences between sales and market orientations. First, sales-oriented firms focus on their own needs; market-oriented firms focus on customers' needs and preferences. Second, sales-oriented companies consider themselves to be deliverers of goods and services, whereas market-oriented companies view themselves as satisfiers of customers. Third, sales-oriented firms direct their products to everyone; market-oriented firms aim at specific segments of the population. Fourth, although the primary goal of both types of firms is profit, sales-oriented businesses pursue maximum sales volume through intensive promotion, whereas market-oriented businesses pursue customer satisfaction through coordinated activities.

3.1 A friend of yours agrees with the adage "People don't know what they want—they only want what they know." Write your friend a letter expressing the extent to which you think marketers shape consumer wants.

3.2 Your local supermarket's slogan is "It's your store." However, when you asked one of the stock people to help you find a bag of chips, he told you it was not his job and that you should look a littler harder. On your way out, you noticed a sign with an address for complaints. Draft a letter explaining why the supermarket's slogan will never be credible unless the employees carry it out.

3.3 How does Philip Morris handle the sensitive issues associated with marketing tobacco? What kind of information does its Web site at **www.philipmorris.com/** provide about smoking and its negative effects on health? How do you think Philip Morris is able to justify such marketing tactics? After checking around the site, do you think that approach makes the company more or less trustworthy?

Describe several reasons for studying marketing. First, marketing affects the allocation of goods and services that influence a nation's economy and standard of living. Second, an understanding of marketing is crucial to understanding most businesses. Third, career opportunities in marketing are diverse, profitable, and expected to increase significantly during the coming decade. Fourth, understanding marketing makes consumers more informed.

4.1 Write a letter to a friend or family member explaining why you think that a course in marketing will help you in your career in some field other than marketing.

Exercises

APPLICATION EXERCISE

Understanding the differences among the various marketing management philosophies is the starting point for understanding the fundamentals of marketing.[27] From reading the chapter, you may be convinced that the market orientation is the most appealing philosophy and the one best suited to creating a competitive advantage. Not all companies, however, use the market orientation. And even companies that follow it may not execute well in all areas.

Activities

1. Visit your local grocery store and go through the snack-food, staples, and hair care aisles. Go up and down each aisle slowly, noticing how many different products are available and how they are organized on the shelves.

2. Count the varieties of product in each product category. For example, how many different kinds of biscuits are on the shelves? How many different sizes? Do the same for staples and shampoo.

3. Now try to find a type of product in the grocery store that does not exhibit such variety. There may not be many. Why do you think there are enough kinds of biscuits to fill an entire aisle (and then some), but only a few different types of, say, soya milk? Can this difference be explained in terms of marketing management philosophy (soya milk manufacturers do not follow the marketing concept) or by something else entirely?

4. Have you ever wanted to see a particular kind of snack food on the shelf? Think of product varietals (like orange flavoured toothpaste or chocolate covered popcorn) that you have never seen on the shelf but would be interested in trying if someone would make it. Write a letter or send an e-mail to an appropriate company, suggesting that it add your concept to its current product line.

ETHICS EXERCISE

In today's business environment, ethics are extremely important. In recent years, there have been numerous scandals and trials that stem from a lack of ethical judgment. For this reason, we are including an ethical exercise in every chapter. A brief scenario will present you with a situation in which the right thing to do may or may not be crystal clear, and you will need to decide the ethical way out of the dilemma.

Rani Pharmaceuticals is the maker of several popular drugs used to treat high blood pressure and arthritis. Over time, the company has developed a positive relationship with many of the patients who use its medications through a quarterly newsletter that offers all the latest information on new medical research findings and general health and fitness articles. The company has just been acquired by a group of investors who also own Soothing Waters Hot Tubs and Spas. The marketing director for Soothing Waters would like to use Rani's mailing list for a direct-mail promotion.

Questions

1. What should Rani Pharmaceuticals do?
2. Do you think it is ethical to use customer information across multiple divisions of the same company? Explain.
3. To which marketing management philosophy do you think the marketing director for Soothing Waters subscribes? Explain.

MARKETING PLAN EXERCISE

You can use many of the basic concepts of marketing introduced in this book to get the career you want by marketing yourself to a prospective employer. This exercise and the Career Appendix at the end of this chapter can help you plan that particular marketing campaign. Build a marketing plan for yourself in a one-page document or table with these elements:

1. *What is your mission?* Are you looking for part-time or temporary experience to enhance your résumé, a career stepping stone, or a full-time, long-term career choice? (This mission will help you set the stage for the rest of your plan.)

2. *What are your strengths and weaknesses?* Make an honest self-assessment, because these issues often come up during job interviews. What about opportunities and threats in the marketplace? Who are your competitors? Do you have a competitive advantage? List any special leadership skills, international travel, computer experience, team projects, communications efforts, and other attributes. (Any competitive advantages you possess should be noted in the cover letter of your résumé and in your job interview.)

3. *What are your objectives?* Do you need to find a job within the next thirty days, or are you more flexible? Are there specific job activities that you would like to perform? (These job activities could be stated in the objectives portion of your résumé. Be sure the objectives are very specific: general objectives are of little use to you or an employer.)
4. *What is your target market?* Are you looking only for jobs with big, established organizations or small entrepreneurial firms? Are you looking at companies in a particular industry? Do you have any geographic preferences? When you figure out your target, compile a list of firms that meet your requirements and describe them. (The more you know about your target-market potential employers, the more prepared you will be in an interview.)
5. You are the product. *How can you best present yourself?* Think of your own packaging with regard to dress, appearance, mannerisms, and speech.
6. What about place? *Are you willing to travel or relocate?* Or do you need an employer close to home? How will you travel to the employer? Is telecommuting an option?
7. *How will you promote yourself?* A carefully constructed cover letter, résumé, business card, and personal Web site can all help communicate your skills to a potential employer.
8. Think carefully about pricing issues, including salary, commission, bonuses, overtime, flexible time, insurance, and other benefits. *What is a fair price for you?* What is a normal price for a company of that size in that industry to offer?
9. And finally, *how will you implement your plan?* That is, what is your plan for applying to companies? How will you contact them for potential interviews? How will you prepare your wardrobe and work on your interviewing skills? When job offers come in, how will you evaluate them? If job offers don't come in, can you find out why and control for these aspects?

The Appendix at the end of this chapter introduces various aspects of a career in marketing, such as types of marketing jobs, pay scales, preparation for interviewing, and what to expect the first year on the job.

Short Case: MARUTI SUZUKI

Prepared by
Dr. Dheeraj Sharma,
Indian Institute of Management, Ahmedabad

Marketing is all about providing a good experience to the consumer after using the product. Hence, it can customize its offering according to the consumer preferences.

Example: It has been a long journey for Maruti Udyog Limited (MUL) in India. MUL was re-christened as Maruti Suzuki India Limited in 2007. It was the first company in India to sell 1 crore cars. It continues to be a market leader in the Indian automobile India. Maruti 800 was the first car launched by MUL. It was a major success in Indian market and continued to be the largest selling car in India till 2004. MUL had a few other offering in its initial years. It offered two variants of Maruti Omni van and Maruti Gypsy jeep-styled vehicle in India. One variant of Omni was targeting large families and second variant was devoid of seats in the back and was targeting cargo carriers. Gypsy targeted adventurers and driving enthusiasts, who would travel in difficult terrain or off-roading. However, Gypsy became very popular with law enforcement agencies. Both Omni van and Gypsy were highly successful in their respective market segments. In 1995, MUL launched Zen. Zen became very popular because it had low noise engine and bigger capacity compared to Maruti 800. Subsequently, MUL introduced Alto, Wagon R, Swift, Esteem, among others. MUL continued to provide reliable, robust, and economical vehicles.

Liberation era began in 1991; however the flowers of liberation started to blossom in mid to late 1990s. The second wave of liberation from late 1990s to middle of 2000s created a new class of upper middle class with significantly large disposable income. Recent reports indicate that passenger vehicles segment grew over 25% in India 2010, miles ahead of Japan, Brazil, and in and the USA. Passenger vehicle market is expected to continue to grow at a fast rate for the next decade.[28] Particularly, there has been a huge growth in the luxury car segment in India. This segment is over Rs 5000 crore and is expected to grow 40 percent annually. According to a report by McKinsey and Co. there are over 20 lakh households in India with an income of over Rs 1.5 lakhs per month and it expected that by 2015 there will be over 80 lakh household with income of over Rs. 1.5 lakhs.[29]

In an attempt to enter and capture this segment MUL offered new line vehicles that were in semi-luxury to luxury segment. MUL launched Baleno, Grand Vitara, Swift DZire, Versa, among others. However, MUL faced challenges capturing this segment. The semi-luxury and luxury segment is an attractive segment as it offers higher profitability.

Despite several operational and marketing attempts to position its vehicle in non-economy segment, MUL did not achieve significant success. Swift and Swift Dzire were successful in diesel variants but did not have similar success in petrol version. MUL has a strong brand equity and loyalty in the economy segment.

MUL today offers a car in almost all categories of consumer price-range with varied success. It has become a challenge for MUL to offer good experience to consumers in all segments.

Questions

1. What does brand Maruti mean to you? Do you think Maruti can successfully customize its offerings to match consumer desires and preferences?
2. Are you willing to buy a MUL product priced at Rs. 25,00,000? Why and Why not? Discuss.
3. Should MUL try to be everything to everybody by offering on variants at almost all price points? Or should it consolidate and expand its market share in economy segment?

Career Appendix

One of the most important decisions in your life is choosing a career. Not only will your career choice affect your income and lifestyle, but it also will have a major impact on your happiness and self-fulfillment.

You can use many of the basic concepts of marketing introduced in this book to get the career you want by marketing yourself. The purpose of marketing is to create exchanges that satisfy individual as well as organizational objectives, and a career is certainly an exchange situation for both you and an organization. The purpose of this appendix is to help you market yourself to prospective employers by providing some helpful tools and information.

Available Careers

- *Sales:* There are more opportunities in sales than in any other area of marketing. Sales positions vary greatly among companies. Some selling positions focus more on providing information; others emphasize locating potential customers, making presentations to committees, and closing the sale. Because compensation is often in the form of salary plus commission, there are few limits on the amount of money a person can make and therefore great potential. Sales positions can be found in many organizations, including manufacturing, wholesaling, retailing, insurance, real estate, financial services, and many other service businesses.
- *Public relations:* Public relations firms help create an image or a message for an individual or organization and communicate it effectively to a desired audience. All types of firms, profit and nonprofit organizations, individuals, and even countries employ public relations specialists. Communication skills, both written and oral, are critical for success in public relations.
- *Retailing:* Retail careers require many skills. Retail personnel may manage a sales force or other personnel, select and order merchandise, and be responsible for promotional activities, inventory control, store security, and accounting. Large retail stores have a variety of positions, including store or department manager, buyer, display designer, and catalog manager.
- *Advertising:* Many organizations employ advertising specialists. Advertising agencies are the largest employers; however, manufacturers, retailers, banks, radio and television stations, hospitals, and insurance agencies all have advertising departments. Creativity, artistic talent, and communication skills are a few of the attributes needed for a successful career in advertising. Account executives serve as a liaison between the advertising agency and the client. Account executives must have a good knowledge of business practices and possess excellent sales skills.
- *Marketing management:* Marketing managers develop the firm's detailed marketing strategy. With the help of subordinates, including market research managers and product development managers, they determine the demand for products and services offered by the firm and its competitors. In addition, they identify potential markets—for example, business firms, wholesalers, retailers, government, or the general public. Marketing managers develop pricing strategy with an eye toward maximizing the firm's share of the market and its profits while ensuring that the firm's customers are satisfied. In collaboration with sales, product development, and other managers, they monitor trends that indicate the need for new products and services and oversee product development. Marketing managers work with advertising and promotion managers to promote the firm's products and services and to attract potential users.
- *Marketing research:* The most rapid growth in marketing careers is in marketing research.

Marketing research firms, advertising agencies, universities, private firms, nonprofit organizations, and governments provide growing opportunities in marketing research. Researchers conduct industry research, advertising research, pricing and packaging research, new-product testing, and test marketing. Researchers are involved in one or more stages of the research process, depending on the size of the organization conducting the research. Marketing research requires knowledge of statistics, data processing and analysis, psychology, and communication.

- ***Product management:*** Product managers coordinate all or most of the activities required to market a product. Thus, they need a general knowledge of all aspects of marketing. Product managers are responsible for the successes and failures of a product and are compensated well for this responsibility. Most product managers have previous sales experience and skills in communication. The position of product manager is a major step in the career path of top-level marketing executives.

Starting in a marketing job is also one of the best routes to the top of any organization. More CEOs come from sales and marketing backgrounds than from any other field. As examples, Lee Iacocca (Chrysler), Nitin Paranjpe (HUL), Vinita Bali (Britannia), and Sunil Duggal (Dabur India) came up through sales and marketing. Typically, a college graduate enters the marketing field in a sales position, then moves to sales supervisor, and next sales manager at the district, regional, and national levels. Individuals who prefer to advance through the ranks of marketing management can usually make a career move into product or brand management or another marketing headquarters job after serving for a couple of years in the initial sales position.

Probably the most difficult part of job hunting is deciding exactly what type of work you would like. Many students have had no working experience other than summer jobs, so they are not sure what career to pursue. Too often, college students and their parents rush toward occupational fields that seem to offer the highest monetary payoff or are currently "hot," instead of looking at the long run over a 40- to 50-year working life. One straightforward approach to deciding what type of job to undertake is to do a "self-analysis." This involves honestly asking yourself what your skills, abilities, and interests really are and then identifying occupational fields that match up well with your personality profile. Some students prefer to take various vocational aptitude tests to help identify their interests and abilities. Your college's placement office or psychology department can inform you about the availability of these tests. You may find it useful to develop a FAB (feature–advantage–benefit) matrix that shows what your skills are, why they offer an advantage, and how they would benefit an employer. Exhibit 1 shows an example.

EXHIBIT 1

The FAB Matrix

Need of Employer This job requires . . .	Feature of Job Applicant I have . . .	Advantage of Feature This feature means that . . .	Benefit to Employer You will . . .
• Frequent sales presentations to individuals and groups.	• Taken 10 classes that required presentations.	• I require limited or no training in making presentations.	• Save on the cost of training and have an employee with the ability and confidence to be productive early.
• Knowledge of personal computers, software, and applications.	• Taken a personal computer course and used Lotus in most upper-level classes.	• I can already use Word, Excel, dBase, SAS, SPSS, and other software.	• Save time and money on training.
• A person with management potential.	• Been president of a student marketing group and social fraternity president for two years.	• I have experience leading people.	• Save time because I am capable of stepping into a leadership position as needed.

Your First Marketing Assignment

Marketing yourself to a prospective employer will usually be your first big marketing assignment. With your services (as represented by your qualifications, education, training, and personal characteristics) as the product, you must convince prospective employers that they should buy your services over those of many other candidates for the job. All the steps of the marketing and sales process apply: identifying opportunities, developing yourself as a product, prospecting for potential employers, planning your approach to them, approaching with a résumé and cover letter, making your sales presentation and demonstrating your qualifications in a personal interview, dealing with objections or giving reasons why the employer should hire you over other candidates, attempting to close the sale by enthusiastically asking for the job and employing appropriate closing techniques, and following up by thanking the prospective employer for the interview and reinforcing a positive impression.

Prospecting for a Potential Employer

After you have determined what you are selling (your skills, interests, and so forth) ad identified the type of job you think you would like, you might begin your personal selling process by looking at the annual placement reports of your college. This would provide you a variety of information about prospective employers and lists the organizations according to the types of jobs they have available—for example, advertising, banking, marketing research, and sales. Another very important source is an online search on the Internet. Other sources of information about prospective employers include directories such as those published by Dun and Bradstreet, and Standard and Poor's ; the Yellow Pages of telephone books in cities where you would like to live and work; and classified sections of The Economic Times or city newspapers. Before contacting a particular company, look up its annual report and stock evaluation from different sources to learn as much as possible about the company and its prospects for the future.

College Placement Office

Use your college placement office to find out which companies are going to be interviewing on campus on what dates; then sign up for interviews with those companies that seem to best match your job skills and requirements. Usually, the college placement office has books, pamphlets, or files that will give you leads on other prospective employers that may not be interviewing on campus that term.

Job-Hunting Expenses

Although campus interviews are convenient, job hunting, nevertheless, can be expensive. Printing your resume, typing cover letters, and buying new clothing will require a sizeable outlay of money. One must be prepared for all such expenses and decide in advance the possible expense bearing items.

The Internet

The Internet is the fastest-growing medium for job searching today. Many companies are using the Internet to assist them in their recruiting efforts. Some companies are even conducting initial interviews online via videoconferencing. Just as some companies post jobs on a bulletin board, companies can list job opportunities on job posting Web sites. Some of the more popular job search Web sites are listed in Exhibit 2. These sites also contain information about résumé writing and interviewing, as well as tips that you can use to secure the job that you want.

EXHIBIT 2

Helpful Internet Addresses for Job Searches/Résumé Writing

Naukri	**http://www.naukri.com**
The Monster Board	**http://www.monsterindia.com**
Times Jobs	**http://www.timesjobs.com**
Shine	**http://www.shine.com**
Employment News	**http://www.employmentnews.gov.in**

Employment Agencies

Although many employment agencies receive fees from employers for providing good job candidates, others charge seekers a good amount of fees for helping them find jobs. Therefore, make sure you fully understand the fee arrangement before signing up with an employment agency. Some employment agencies may not be worth your time and/or money because they use a programmed approach to helping you write your résumé and cover letter and prospect for potential employers. Potential employers have seen these "canned" formats and approaches so many times that your personal advertisement (your résumé and cover letter) will be almost indistinguishable from others.

The Hidden Job Market

It has been estimated that nearly 90 percent of available jobs are never advertised and never reach employment agency files, so creative resourcefulness often pays off in finding the best jobs. Consider every reasonable source for leads. Sometimes your professors, deans, or college administrators can give you names and contact persons at companies that have hired recent graduates.

Do not be bashful about letting other people know that you are looking for work. Classmates, friends, and business associates of your family may be of help not only directly but also indirectly, acting as extra pairs of eyes and ears alert to job opportunities for you.

Planning Your Approach (The Preapproach)

After conducting your self-analysis and identifying potential employers looking for people with your abilities and interests, you need to prepare your résumé (or personal advertisement). Your résumé should focus on your achievements to date, your educational background, your work experience, and your special abilities and interests. Some students make the mistake of merely listing their assigned responsibilities on different jobs without indicating what they accomplished on the job. If you achieved something on the job, say it—for example, "Helped computerize office files," "Increased sales in my territory by 10 percent," "Received a 15 percent raise after three months on the job," or "Promoted to assistant store manager after four months." When looking for a job, remember that employers are looking for a track record of achievement, so you must distinguish yourself from those who may have had the same assigned job responsibilities as you did but performed poorly. If your work experience is minimal, consider a "skills" résumé, in which you emphasize your particular abilities, such as organizing, programming, or leadership skills, and give supporting evidence whenever you can. Examples of various types of resumes can be found from the college placement office and in various other job-hunting publications. Exhibit 2 lists some web sites where you can learn about resume formats.

Remember that there is no one correct format for your résumé. A little tasteful creativity can help differentiate your résumé from countless look-alike résumés. If you are a young college graduate, your résumé will usually be only one page long, but do not worry about going to a second page if you have something important to present. One student so blindly followed the one-page résumé rule that he left out having served in the military—service that is usually viewed very positively by prospective employers, especially if it involved significant leadership responsibilities or work experience.

If you know what job you want, you may want to put your job objective near the top of your résumé. If you are not sure what job you want or want to send out the same résumé for several different jobs, then you can describe your job objective in your cover letter. A key element in the cover letter is convincing the prospective employer to grant you an interview. Thus, you must talk in terms of the employer's interests, not just your own. You are answering the question: "Why should we hire you?" You may need to send a letter with your résumé enclosed to a hundred or more companies to obtain five to ten interviews, so do not be discouraged if you get replies from only a few companies or are told by many companies that they have no job opportunities at present. You will probably need only a few interviews and just one job offer to get your career started.

Review some of the publications and sources mentioned in the previous section on prospecting to learn as much as you can about your prospective employer so that you can tailor your cover letter. Remember, the employer is thinking in terms of the company's needs, not yours. For one example of a résumé, see Exhibit 3. A cover letter is illustrated in Exhibit 4.

Making Your Approach

Prospective employers can be approached by mail, telephone, the Internet, or personal contact. Personal contact is best, but this usually requires that you know someone with influence who can arrange an interview for you. Of course, a few enterprising students have devised elaborate and sometimes successful schemes to get job interviews. For example, we know of one young man who simply went to the headquarters of the company he wanted to work for and asked to see the president. Told that the president of the company could not see him, the student said that he was willing to wait until the president had time. This audacious individual went back three different days until the president finally agreed to see him, perhaps mainly out of curiosity about what sort of young man would be so outrageous in his job search.

Fortunately for this young man, he had a lot to offer and was able to communicate this to the presi-

EXHIBIT 3

Sample Résumé

RACHEL E. SANFORD
2935 Mountain View Road
Ellington, PA 19401
(216) 567-0000

JOB OBJECTIVE	Sales representative for a consumer-products company
EDUCATION	Graduated *cum laude* with BS in Marketing Management (June 2006), University of Southern Pennsylvania. Career-related courses included Selling and Sales Management, Public Speaking, Business Writing, Public Relations, Marketing Research, Computer Programming, and Multivariate Data Analysis.
ACTIVITIES AND HONORS	President, Student Marketing Association; Vice president, Chi Omega Sorority; Captain, women's varsity tennis team; sportswriter for the *Campus View* student newspaper. Named to Who's Who among American College Students, 2004–2005. On Dean's List all four years. Overall grade point average = 3.65.
WORK EXPERIENCE	
Summer 2005	*Sales representative*, Peabody Manufacturing Company. Sold women's blouses to boutiques and small department stores in southeastern Pennsylvania. Exceeded assigned sales quota by 20 percent; named "outstanding" summer employee for 2005.
Summer 2004	*Buyer*, Hamm's Department Stores, Inc., Midway, Pa. Developed purchase plan, initiated purchase orders, monitored and controlled expenditures for nearly $2 million (₹9 crore) worth of women's clothing. Made monthly progress reports (written and oral) to Hamm's Executive Committee. Received 15 percent bonus as #2 buyer in the six stores of the Hamm's chain in special "Back to School" purchasing competition.
Summer 2003	*Retail clerk*, Hamm's Department Stores, Inc., Midway, Pa. After 3 months, received 10 percent pay raise and promotion to evening salesclerk supervisor over seven part-time salesclerks. Devised new inventory control system for handbags and accessories that cut costs over $50,000 (₹22,50,000) annually.
Summer 2002	*Cosmetics salesperson*, Heavenly Charm, Inc., Midway, Pa. Sold $63,000 (₹28,35,000) worth of Heavenly Charm cosmetics door to door. Named #1 salesperson in the sales region. Offered full-time job as sales supervisor.
INTERESTS	Tennis, golf, public speaking, short story writing, and reading biographies.

dent, so he was hired. This unorthodox approach shows how far people have gone to impress potential employers, and if you feel comfortable doing it, then go ahead. A personal contact within the company certainly can win you some special attention and enable you to avoid competing head-on with the large number of other candidates looking for a job. Most students, however, start their approach in the traditional way by mailing their résumé and cover letter to the recruiting department of the company. More recently, students have begun to e-mail their résumés, and some companies are requiring this as a means of screening out applicants who are not computer literate. Unless your résumé matches a particular need at that time, it will probably be filed away for possible future reference or merely discarded. To try to get around the system, some students send their letter by express mail or mailgram or address it to a key executive, with "Personal" written on the envelope. These students believe that bypassing the company's personnel office will increase the likelihood that their cover letter and résumé will be read by someone with authority to hire. Using gimmicks, no matter how creative, to get a job interview will offend some executives and thus cause you to be rejected from consideration for a job. But you can probably also be sure that a few executives will admire your efforts and grant you an interview.

Only you know how comfortable you feel with different approaches to obtaining a job interview. We advise you not to use an approach that is out of character for you and thus will make you feel awkward and embarrassed.

EXHIBIT 4

Sample Cover Letter

Rachel E. Sanford
2935 Mountain View Road
Ellington, PA 19401

Mr. Samuel Abramson
District Sales Manager
Hixson Appliance Company
Philadelphia, PA 19103

Dear Mr. Abramson:

Hixson has been a familiar name to me ever since I was barely able to see over my mother's kitchen counter. Virtually every appliance we had was a Hixson, so I know firsthand what fine quality products you sell. My career interest is in sales, and there is no company that I would rather work with than Hixson Appliance.

I will be graduating this June from Southern Pennsylvania University with a BS in marketing management, and I would like you to consider me for a job as a sales representative with your company. As you can see in my enclosed résumé, I have successfully worked in sales jobs during three of the last four summers. My college course electives (e.g., public speaking, business writing, and public relations) have been carefully selected with my career objective in mind. Even my extracurricular activities in sports and campus organizations have helped prepare me for working with a variety of people and competitive challenges.

Will you please grant me an interview so that I can convince you that I'm someone you should hire for your sales team? I'll call you next Thursday afternoon to arrange an appointment at your convenience.

Look forward to meeting you soon.

Sincerely,

Rachel E. Sanford

Enclosure

Making Your Sales Presentation

Your personal sales presentation will come during the interview with the prospective employer's recruiters or interviewers. Like any presentation, it requires thorough preparation and an effective follow-up, as well as a solid performance during the interview itself.

Pre-Interview Considerations

Preparing for the interview is crucial. You will already have gathered information on the company, as suggested in the preceding sections; you should review it now. Exhibit 5 shows a pre-interview checklist that can help you prepare. In addition, the self-assessment test in Exhibit 6 can help you determine if you're ready for the interview.

Keep the following in mind in preparing for your interview:

- Find out the exact place and time of the interview.
- Be certain you know the interviewer's name and how to pronounce it if it looks difficult.
- Do some research on the company with which you are interviewing—talk to people and read the company literature to know what its products or services are, where its offices are located, what its growth has been, and how its prospects look for the future.
- Think of two or three good questions that you would like to ask during your interview.
- Plan to arrive at the designated place for your interview a little early so that you will not feel rushed and worried about being on time.
- Plan to dress in a manner appropriate to the job for which you are interviewing.

EXHIBIT 5

Before the Interview

- **Practice**
  - ✓ Questions you may be asked
  - ✓ Questions you want to ask about the position and organization
  - ✓ Role-playing an interview
- **Self-assessment**
  - ✓ Goals
  - ✓ Skills, abilities, accomplishments
  - ✓ Work values (important factors you look for in a job)
  - ✓ Experiences
  - ✓ Personality
- **Research**
  - ✓ Obtain company literature
  - ✓ Write or visit the organization
  - ✓ Talk to people familiar with the organization
- Obtain references
- **Plan ahead**
  - ✓ Attire to be worn to the interview
  - ✓ Directions to the interview site
  - ✓ Time of arrival (get there with at least 5–10 minutes to spare)

A guide for the interview conversation itself is to prepare nine positive thoughts before you go in for the interview:

- Three reasons why you selected the employer to interview
- Three reasons you particularly like the employer
- Three assets you have that should interest the employer

Try to make a positive impression on everyone you encounter in the company, even while waiting in the lobby for your interview. Sometimes managers will ask their receptionists and secretaries for an opinion of you, and your friendliness, courtesy, professional demeanor, personal habits, and the like will all be used to judge you. Even the magazines you choose to read while waiting can be a positive or negative factor. For instance, it will probably be less impressive if you leaf through a popular maga-

EXHIBIT 6

Self-Assessment Test

How assertive are you (or will you be) as you interview for a position? Listed below are questions that will help you to evaluate yourself: answer yes or no to the questions, being honest with yourself. If you have five or fewer yes answers, you still have some work to do. A good score is seven or more yes answers.

Yes	No	
--------	--------	Have you made an effort to research the company before the interview?
--------	--------	Have you prepared several questions that you want to ask?
--------	--------	If an interviewer asks a personal question unrelated to the job, will you be able to tactfully call this to his attention?
--------	--------	If an interviewer gives you a hypothetical job-related problem, do you have confidence in your ability to respond in a timely and succinct manner?
--------	--------	If the interviewer seems distracted or uninterested during your interview, will you be able to steer the interview back on track and gain her attention?
--------	--------	When you meet the interviewer, will you be the first to introduce yourself and begin the conversation?
--------	--------	If the interviewer continually interrupts when you are responding to questions or giving information about yourself, can you politely handle this?
--------	--------	If the interviewer never gives you the opportunity to talk about yourself and you have only five minutes remaining in the interview, have you thought about phrases or ways to redirect the interview and regain control of the process?
--------	--------	When the interviewer is beginning to close the interview, are you prepared to ask questions about how you stand, what the determining factors are for candidate selection, and by what date you will have an answer?

zine like *People* or *Sports Illustrated* than if you read something more professional such as *BusinessWeek* or *The Wall Street Journal*.

During the Interview

During the interview, do not be merely a passive respondent to the interviewer's questions. Being graciously assertive by asking reasonable questions of your own will indicate to the interviewer that you are alert, energetic, and sincerely interested in the job. The personal interview is your opportunity to persuade the prospective employer that you should be hired. To use a show business analogy, you will be onstage for only a short time (during the personal interview), so try to present an honest but positive image of yourself. Perhaps it will help you to be alert and enthusiastic if you imagine that you are being interviewed on television. Exhibit 7 lists a number of questions that are frequently asked during interviews.

Sometimes prospective employers will ask you to demonstrate certain abilities by having you write a timed essay about some part of your life, sell something (such as a desk calculator) to the interviewer, or respond to hostile questions. Be calm and confident during any such unorthodox interviewing approaches and you will make a good impression. Remember, most employers want you to perform well because they are looking for the best people they can find in a given time frame for the money they have to offer.

If you are given intelligence, aptitude, or psychological tests, you should try to be honest so that you do not create unrealistic expectations that you will not be able to fulfill. It is just as important that you do not create a false impression and begin with a company that is not right for you as it is to secure employment in the first place. Many experts say that it is not very difficult to "cheat" on aptitude or psychological tests if you are able to "play the role" and provide the answers that you know the company wants to read. Usually, the so-called safe approach in most personality and preference (interest) tests is to not take extreme positions on anything that is not clearly associated with the job you are applying for. For sales jobs, it is probably safe to come across as highly extroverted and interested in group activities, but it may not be safe to appear to be overly interested in literature, music, art, or any solitary activity. In addition, the "right" answers tend to indicate a conservative, goal-oriented, money-motivated, and gregarious personality.

Dealing with Objections. Sometimes interviewers will bluntly ask, "Why should we hire you?" This requires that you think in terms of the employer's needs and present in concise form all your major "selling points." Also, sometimes the interviewer may bring up reasons why you are not the ideal candidate. For example, he or she may say: (1) "We're really looking for someone with a little more experience"; (2) "We'd like to get someone with a more technical educational background"; or (3) "We need someone to start work within two weeks." These kinds of statements are similar to objections or requests for additional information. In other words, the interviewer is saying, "Convince me that I shouldn't rule you out for this reason." To overcome such objections, you might respond to each, respectively, along the following lines:

(1) "I've had over a year's experience working with two different companies during my summer vacations, and I've worked part-time with a third company all during college. I'm a fast learner, and I've adapted well to each of the three companies, so I feel that my working experience is equivalent to that of someone who has had three or four years' experience with the same company."

(2) "Although I didn't choose to earn a technical undergraduate degree, I've taken several technical courses in college, including basic engineering courses, chemistry, physics, and two years of math. I'm very confident that I can quickly learn whatever is necessary technically to do the job, and my real strength is that my education has been a blend of technical and managerial courses."

(3) "Well, I do have one more term of school, so I couldn't start full-time work in two weeks, but perhaps we could work out an arrangement in which I could work part-time—maybe Friday, Saturday, and Sunday or on weekends until I graduate."

Good "salespeople" do not allow an objection to block a sale. Providing reasonable solutions or alternative perspectives can often overcome objections or, at least, allow room for further negotiation toward a compromise solution.

How to Act during the Interview. The following can help you behave appropriately during the interview:

- Think positive. Be enthusiastic, interested, knowledgeable, and confident.
- Take few notes. It is acceptable to take notes during the interview, but limit them to things that are essential to remember. You want to focus more on listening and observing rather than writing.

EXHIBIT 7

Some Questions Frequently Asked During a Job Interview

- Of the jobs you've had to date, which one did you like best? Why?
- Why do you want to work for our company?
- Tell me what you know about our company.
- Do any of your relatives or friends work for our company? If so, in what jobs?
- Tell me about yourself, your strengths, weaknesses, career goals, and so forth.
- Is any member of your family a professional marketer? If so, what area of marketing?
- Why do you want to start your career in marketing?
- Persuade me that we should hire you.
- What extracurricular activities did you participate in at college? What leadership positions did you have in any of these activities?
- What benefits have you derived from participation in extracurricular activities that will help you in your career?
- Where do you see yourself within our company in five years? In ten years? Twenty years?
- What is your ultimate career goal?
- What do you consider your greatest achievement to date?
- What is your biggest failure to date?
- What is (was) your favorite subject in school? Why?
- Are you willing to travel and possibly relocate?
- How would the people who know you describe you?
- How would you describe yourself?
- What do you like most about marketing?
- What do you like least about marketing?
- If we hire you, how soon could you start work?
- What is the minimum we would have to offer you to come with us?
- What goals have you set for yourself? How are you planning to achieve them?
- Who or what has had the greatest influence on the development of your career interests?
- What factors did you consider in choosing your major?
- Why are you interested in our organization?
- What can you tell me about yourself?
- What two or three things are most important to you in a position?
- What kind of work do you want to do?
- What can you tell me about a project you initiated?
- What are your expectations of your future employer?
- What is your GPA? How do you feel about it? Does it reflect your ability?
- How do you resolve conflicts?
- What do you feel are your strengths? Your weaknesses? How do you evaluate yourself?
- What work experience has been the most valuable to you and why?
- What was the most useful criticism you ever received, and who was it from?
- Can you give an example of a problem you have solved and the process you used?
- Can you describe the project or situation that best demonstrates your analytical skills?

EXHIBIT 7

Some Questions Frequently Asked During a Job Interview (continued)

- What has been your greatest challenge?
- Can you describe a situation where you had a conflict with another individual and explain how you dealt with it?
- What are the biggest problems you encountered in college? How did you handle them? What did you learn from them?
- What are your team-player qualities? Give examples.
- Can you describe your leadership style?
- What interests or concerns you about the position or the company?
- In a particular leadership role you had, what was the greatest challenge?
- What idea have you developed and implemented that was particularly creative or innovative?
- What characteristics do you think are important for this position?
- How have your educational and work experiences prepared you for this position?
- Can you take me through a project where you demonstrated skills?
- How do you think you have changed personally since you started college?
- Can you tell me about a team project that you are particularly proud of and discuss your contribution?
- How do you motivate people?
- Why did you choose the extracurricular activities you did? What did you gain? What did you contribute?
- What types of situations put you under pressure, and how do you deal with the pressure?
- Can you tell me about a difficult decision you have made?
- Can you give an example of a situation in which you failed and explain how you handled it?
- Can you tell me about a situation when you had to persuade another person of your point of view?
- What frustrates you the most?
- Knowing what you know now about your college experience, would you make the same decisions?
- What can you contribute to this company?
- How would you react to having your credibility questioned?
- What characteristics are important in a good manager? How have you displayed one of these characteristics?
- What challenges are you looking for in a position?
- What two or three accomplishments have given you the most satisfaction?
- Can you describe a leadership role of yours and tell why you committed your time to it?
- How are you conducting your job search, and how will you make your decision?
- What is the most important lesson you have learned in or out of school?
- Can you describe a situation where you had to work with someone who was difficult? How was the person difficult,
- and how did you handle it?
- We are looking at a lot of great candidates; why are you the best person for this position?
- How would your friends describe you? Your professors?
- What else should I know about you?

- Relate to the interviewer. Build positive rapport with the interviewer. Listen and observe; relate yourself to the employer or position.
- Watch your body language. Be aware of nervousness (fidgeting, shaking leg, tapping, etc.). Project confidence (eye contact, firm handshake, upright posture).
- Be aware of the questions the employer asks. Answer with information relevant to the position. Provide a direct answer; avoid being long-winded.
- Think about the questions you ask. They should indicate that you know something about the job. Avoid questions that could easily be answered elsewhere (through research). Obtain information you need to know to be satisfied with the job (interviewing is a two-way process). Salary and benefit questions should be asked after the job is offered.
- Achieve effective closure. Ask when the employer expects to make a decision. Restate your interest and ability to perform the job. Show confidence and enthusiasm (smile, end with a firm handshake). Obtain the employer's business card, if possible (it may be useful when writing a thank-you letter).

Interview Questions. Too many employment applicants spend all their time preparing for the questions employers will ask them. Too often, they fail to ask vital questions that would help them learn if a job is right for them. Failing to ask important questions during the interview often leads to jobs that offer neither interest nor challenge. Too often, uninformed applicants accept positions hoping that they will develop into something more meaningful and rewarding later. Exhibit 8 suggests questions that you may want to ask.

EXHIBIT 8

Sample Interview Questions to Be Asked by Job Candidates

- Where is the organization going? What plans or projects are being developed to maintain or increase its market share? Have many new product lines been decided upon recently? Is the sales growth in the new product line sustainable?
- Who are the people with whom I will be working? May I speak with some of them?
- May I have a copy of the job description?
- What might be a typical first assignment?
- Do you have a performance appraisal system? How is it structured? How frequently will I be evaluated?
- What is the potential for promotion in the organization? In promotions, are employees ever transferred between functional fields? What is the average time to get to ------------------ level in the career path? Is your policy to promote from within, or are many senior jobs filled by experienced people from outside? Do you have a job posting system?
- What type of training will I receive? When does the training program begin? Is it possible to move through your program faster? About how many individuals go through your internship program?
- What is the normal routine of a (an) ------------------ like? Can I progress at my own pace, or is it structured? Do employees normally work overtime?
- How much travel is normally expected? Is a car provided to traveling personnel?
- How much freedom is given to new people? How much discipline is required? How much input does the new person have? How much decision-making authority is given to new personnel?
- How frequently do you relocate employees? Is it possible to transfer from one division to another?
- What is the housing market for a single person in ------------------ (city)? Is public transportation adequate?
- How much contact with and exposure to management is there?
- How soon should I expect to report to work?

Closing the Sale

Although it is not likely that a prospective employer will offer you a job immediately after the job interview, you should nevertheless let the interviewer know that you definitely want the job and are confident that you will do an excellent job for the employer. You will need to use your best judgment on how to best do this.

In each stage of the personal selling process, you should be looking for feedback from the interviewer's body language and voice inflections or tone.

Following Up the Interview

Within a few days after any job interview, whether you want the job or not, it is business courtesy to write thank-you letters to interviewers. In these letters you can reinforce the positive impression you made in the interview and again express your keen interest in working for the company. If you do not hear from the company within a few weeks, it may be appropriate to write another letter expressing your continuing interest in the job and asking for a decision so that you can consider other options if necessary. As a possible reason for this follow-up letter, you might mention an additional personal achievement since the interview, give a more detailed answer to one of the interviewer's questions, or perhaps send a newspaper or magazine article of interest. A neat, well-written, courteous follow-up letter gives you a chance not only to make a stronger impression on the interviewer but also to exhibit positive qualities such as initiative, energy, sensitivity to others' feelings, and awareness of business protocol.

Many applicants fail to write a thank-you letter after an interview, yet many employers say that the deciding factor between several similar job candidates is often the thank-you note. The thank-you letter should be typewritten. If the interviewer is a very technology-driven person, a thank-you e-mail may also be appropriate. However, the personal touch of a typewritten and hand-signed letter leaves a better impression.

Be sure to write a follow-up letter in all of the following situations:

- After two or three weeks of no reply.
- When a job has been refused. Express your regret that no job is available and ask if you might be considered in the future. Also, ask how you could improve yourself to better fit what the company is looking for.
- After an interview. Express your thanks for the interviewer's time and courtesy. Answer any unanswered questions and clarify any misconceptions.
- To accept a job (even if previously done in person or on the phone). State your acceptance. Reiterate the agreement, the time for beginning work, and the like. Do not start asking for favors.
- To refuse a job offer. Graciously decline the offer. Be warm and interested and indicate that you appreciate the offer.

Follow-up letters are also appropriate after you have received replies to both solicited and unsolicited letters of inquiry. Always make certain that your letters possess the attitude, quality, and skill of a professional.

On The Job

Working Conditions

Advertising, marketing, promotions, public relations, and sales managers work in offices close to those of top managers. Long hours, including evenings and weekends, are common. About 44 percent of advertising, marketing, and public relations managers work more than 40 hours per week. Substantial travel may also be involved. For example, attendance at meetings sponsored by associations or industries is often mandatory. Sales managers travel to local, regional, and national offices and to various dealers and distributors. Advertising and promotions managers may travel to meet with clients or representatives of communications media. At times, public relations managers travel to meet with special interest groups or government officials. Job transfers between headquarters and regional offices are common, particularly among sales managers.

Moving Up the Ladder

Most advertising, marketing, promotions, public relations, and sales management positions are filled by promoting experienced staff or related professional personnel. For example, many managers are former sales representatives, purchasing agents, buyers, or product, advertising, promotions, or public relations specialists. In small firms, where the number of positions is limited, advancement to a management position usually comes slowly. In large firms, promotion may occur more quickly.

Although experience, ability, and leadership are emphasized for promotion, advancement can be accelerated by participation in management training programs conducted by many large firms. Many firms also provide their employees with continuing education opportunities, either in-house or at local colleges and universities, and encourage employee participation in seminars and conferences, often provided by professional societies. In collaboration with colleges and universities, numerous marketing and related associations sponsor national or local management training programs. Staying abreast of what is happening in your industry and getting involved in related industry associations can be important for your career advancement.

Your Early Working Career

Even though you want to choose a company that you will stay with throughout your working life, it is realistic to recognize that you will probably work for three, four, or more companies during your career. If you are not fully satisfied with your job or company during the first few years of your full-time working life, remember that you are building experience and knowledge that will increase your marketability for future job opportunities. Keep a positive outlook and do the best you can in all job assignments—and your chance for new opportunities will come. Do not be too discouraged by mistakes that you may make in your career; nearly every successful person has made and continues to make many mistakes. View these mistakes largely as learning experiences, and they will not be too traumatic or damaging to your confidence.

Good luck in your marketing career!

CHAPTER REVIEW

1 An Overview of Marketing

KEY TERMS

LO 1

marketing the activity, set of institutions, and processes for creating, communicating, delivering, and exchanging offerings that have value for customers, clients, partners, and society at large

exchange people giving up something in order to receive something they would rather have

LO 2

production orientation a philosophy that focuses on the internal capabilities of the firm rather than on the desires and needs of the marketplace

sales orientation the ideas that people will buy more goods and services if aggressive sales techniques are used and that high sales result in high profits

marketing concept the idea that the social and economic justification for an organization's existence is the satisfaction of customer wants and needs while meeting organizational objectives

market orientation a philosophy that assumes that a sale does not depend on an aggressive sales force but rather on a customer's decision to purchase a product; it is synonymous with the marketing concept

societal marketing orientation the idea that an organization exists not only to satisfy customer wants and needs and to meet organizational objectives but also to preserve or enhance individuals' and society's long-term best interests

KEY CONCEPTS

LO 1 **Define the term *marketing*.** Marketing is the activity, set of institutions, and processes for creating, communicating, delivering, and exchanging offerings that have value for customers, clients, partners, and society at large. Marketing also requires all facets of a company to work together to pool ideas and resources. One major goal of marketing is to create an exchange. An exchange has five conditions, as listed below. Even if all five conditions are met, an exchange might not occur. People engage in marketing whether or not an exchange happens.

Five conditions of exchange

1. There must be at least two parties.
2. Each party has something that might be of value to the other party.
3. Each party is capable of communication and delivery.
4. Each party is free to accept or reject the exchange offer.
5. Each party believes it is appropriate or desirable to deal with the other party.

LO 2 **Describe four marketing management philosophies.** The role of marketing and the character of marketing activities within an organization are strongly influenced by its philosophy and orientation. A production-oriented organization focuses on the internal capabilities of the firm rather than on the desires and needs of the marketplace. A sales orientation is based on the beliefs that people will buy more products if aggressive sales techniques are used and that high sales volumes produce high profits. A market-oriented organization focuses on satisfying customer wants and needs while meeting organizational objectives. A societal marketing orientation goes beyond a market orientation to include the preservation or enhancement of individuals' and society's long-term best interests.

LO 3 **customer value** the relationship between benefits and the sacrifice necessary to obtain those benefits

customer satisfaction customers' evaluation of a good or service in terms of whether it has met their needs and expectations

relationship marketing a strategy that focuses on keeping and improving relationships with current customers

empowerment delegation of authority to solve customers' problems quickly—usually by the first person the customer notifies regarding a problem

teamwork collaborative efforts of people to accomplish common objectives

LO 3 **Discuss the differences between sales and market orientations.** First, sales-oriented firms focus on their own needs; market-oriented firms focus on customers' needs and preferences. Second, sales-oriented companies consider themselves to be deliverers of goods and services, whereas market-oriented companies view themselves as satisfiers of customers. Third, sales-oriented firms direct their products to everyone; market-oriented firms aim at specific segments of the population. Fourth, although the primary goal of both types of firms is profit, sales-oriented businesses pursue maximum sales volume through intensive promotion, whereas market-oriented businesses pursue customer satisfaction through coordinated activities.

	What is the organization's focus?	What business are you in?	To whom is the product directed?	What is your primary goal?	How do you seek to achieve your goal?
Sales Orientation	Inward, on the organization's needs	Selling goods and services	Everybody	Profit through maximum sales volume	Primarily through intensive promotion
Market Orientation	Outward on the wants and needs of customers	Satisfying customer wants and needs and delivering superior value	Specific groups of people	Profit through customer satisfaction	Through coordinated marketing and inter-functional activities

LO 4 **Describe several reasons for studying marketing.** First, marketing affects the allocation of goods and services that influence a nation's economy and standard of living. Second, an understanding of marketing is crucial to understanding most businesses. Third, career opportunities in marketing are diverse, profitable, and expected to increase significantly during the coming decade. Fourth, understanding marketing makes consumers more informed.

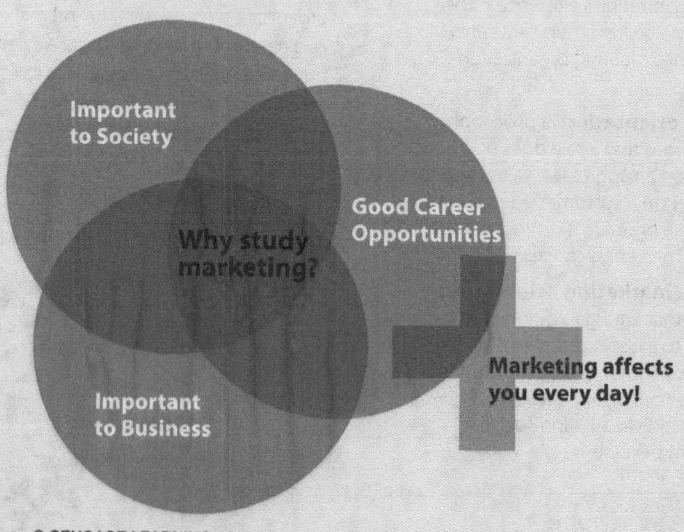

CHAPTER 2

Strategic Planning for Competitive Advantage

Learning Outcomes

LO 1 Understand the importance of strategic marketing and know a basic outline for a marketing plan

LO 2 Develop an appropriate business mission statement

LO 3 Describe the components of a situation analysis

LO 4 Explain the criteria for stating good marketing objectives

LO 5 Identify sources of competitive advantage

LO 6 Identify strategic alternatives

LO 7 Discuss target market strategies

LO 8 Describe the elements of the marketing mix

LO 9 Explain why implementation, evaluation, and control of the marketing plan are necessary

LO 10 Identify several techniques that help make strategic planning effective

A good strategic plan can help protect and grow the firm's resources.

LO1 The Nature of Strategic Planning

strategic planning the managerial process of creating and maintaining a fit between the organization's objectives and resources and the evolving market opportunities

Strategic planning is the managerial process of creating and maintaining a fit between the organization's objectives and resources and the evolving market opportunities. The goal of strategic planning is long-run profitability and growth. Thus, strategic decisions require long-term commitments of resources.

A strategic error can threaten a firm's survival. On the other hand, a good strategic plan can help protect and grow the firm's resources. For instance, if Bajaj had decided to focus only on manufacturing scooters, the organization would have faced difficulties in staying in the market. It survived by making the strategic decision to produce motorcycles as well. On the other hand, firms like LML struggled because they failed to adapt to changing market conditions and customer requirements.

Strategic marketing management addresses two questions: What is the organization's main activity at a particular time? How will it reach its goals? Here are some examples of strategic decisions:

- The potato chips market was dominated by Lays and a few regional players like Balaji. ITC identified this gap and launched its brand – Bingo. The brand offered some new and unique flavors and succeeded in garnering an impressive market share in quick time.

Note: All the figures in U.S. dollars are converted into rupee using the value $1 = ₹45.

planning the process of anticipating future events and determining strategies to achieve organizational objectives in the future

marketing planning designing activities relating to marketing objectives and the changing marketing environment

marketing plan a written document that acts as a guidebook of marketing activities for the marketing manager

▸▸ After being in the cosmetic industry, Tata Group decided to sell its flourishing brand Lakme to HLL (now HUL) to focus entirely on its retail activities.

All these decisions have affected or will affect each organization's long-run course, its allocation of resources, and ultimately its financial success. In contrast, an operating decision, such as changing the package design for Britannia's Bourbon biscuits or altering the menu to cater to national tastes like that of McDonald's, probably won't have a big impact on the long-run profitability of the company.

How do companies go about strategic marketing planning? How do employees know how to implement the long-term goals of the firm? The answer is a marketing plan.

What Is a Marketing Plan?

Planning is the process of anticipating future events and determining strategies to achieve organizational objectives in the future. **Marketing planning** involves designing activities relating to marketing objectives and the changing marketing environment. Marketing planning is the basis for all marketing strategies and decisions. Issues such as product lines, distribution channels, marketing communications, and pricing are all delineated in the **marketing plan**. The marketing plan is a written document that acts as a guidebook of marketing activities for the marketing manager. In this chapter, you will learn the importance of writing a marketing plan and the types of information contained in a marketing plan.

Why Write a Marketing Plan?

By specifying objectives and defining the actions required to attain them, you can provide in a marketing plan the basis by which actual and expected performance can be compared. Marketing can be one of the most expensive and complicated business activities, but it is also one of the most important. The written marketing plan provides clearly stated activities that help employees and managers understand and work toward common goals.

Writing a marketing plan allows you to examine the marketing environment in conjunction with the inner workings of the business. Once the marketing plan is written, it serves as a reference point for the success of future activities. Finally, the marketing plan allows the marketing manager to enter the marketplace with an awareness of possibilities and problems.

Marketing Plan Elements

Marketing plans can be presented in many different ways. Most businesses need a written marketing plan because a marketing plan is large and can be complex. Details about tasks and activity assignments may be lost if communicated orally. Regardless of the way a marketing plan is presented, some elements are common to all marketing plans. Exhibit 2.1 shows these elements, which include defining the business mission, performing a situation analysis, defining objectives, delineating a target market, and establishing

EXHIBIT 2.1

Elements of a Marketing Plan

components of the marketing mix. Other elements that may be included in a plan are budgets, implementation timetables, required marketing research efforts, or elements of advanced strategic planning.

Selecting which alternative to pursue depends on the overall company philosophy and culture. The choice also depends on the tool used to make the decision. Companies generally have one of two philosophies about when they expect profits. They either pursue profits right away or first seek to increase market share and then pursue profits. In the long run, market share and profitability are compatible goals. Many companies have long followed this credo: Build market share, and profits will surely follow. Spice Mobility Ltd. released the first dual-sim phone in India to gain market share before other domestic players such as Micromax and Karbonn mobiles and multinational companies like Nokia and Samsung entered the segment.

On the other hand, IBM stresses profitability and stock valuation over market share, quality, and customer service. As you can see, the same strategic alternative may be viewed entirely differently by different firms.

A number of tools exist to help managers select a strategic alternative. The most common of these tools are in matrix form. The portfolio matrix is described here in more detail.

Writing the Marketing Plan

The creation and implementation of a complete marketing plan will allow the organization to achieve marketing objectives and succeed. However, the marketing plan is only as good as the information it contains and the effort, creativity, and thought that went into its creation. Having a good marketing information system and a wealth of competitive intelligence (covered in Chapter 9) is critical to a thorough and accurate situation analysis. The role of managerial intuition is also important in the creation and selection of marketing strategies. Managers must weigh any information against its accuracy and their own judgment when making a marketing decision.

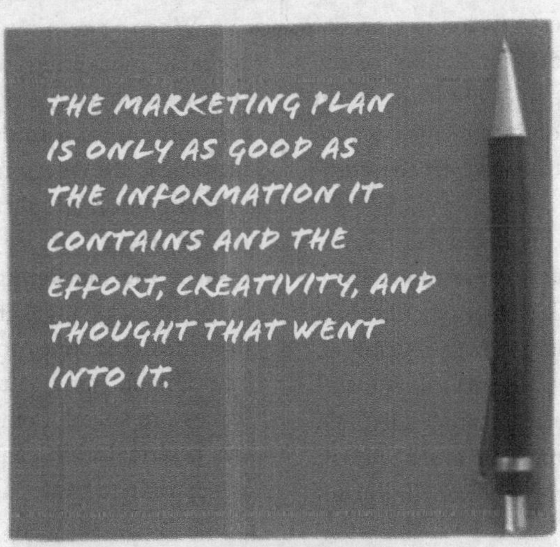

Note that the overall structure of the marketing plan (Exhibit 2.1) should not be viewed as a series of sequential planning steps. Many of the marketing plan elements are decided on simultaneously and in conjunction with one another. Further, every marketing plan has different content, depending on the organization, its mission, objectives, targets, and marketing mix components. There is not one single correct format for a marketing plan. Many organizations have their own distinctive format or terminology for creating a marketing plan. Every marketing plan should be unique to the firm for which it was created. Remember, however, that although the format and order of presentation should be flexible, the same types of questions and topic areas should be covered in any marketing plan.

mission statement a statement of the firm's business based on a careful analysis of benefits sought by present and potential customers and an analysis of existing and anticipated environmental conditions

LO 2 Defining the Business Mission

The foundation of any marketing plan is the firm's mission statement, which answers the question, "What business are we in?" The way a firm defines its business mission profoundly affects the firm's long-run resource allocation, profitability, and survival. The mission statement is based on a careful analysis of benefits sought by present and potential customers and an analysis of existing and anticipated environmental conditions. The firm's mission statement establishes boundaries for all subsequent decisions, objectives, and strategies.

A mission statement should focus on the market or markets the organization is attempting to serve rather than on the good or service offered. Otherwise, a new technology may quickly make the good or service obsolete and the mission statement irrelevant to

marketing myopia defining a business in terms of goods and services rather than in terms of the benefits customers seek

strategic business unit (SBU) a subgroup of a single business or collection of related businesses within the larger organization

SWOT analysis identifying internal strengths (S) and weaknesses (W) and also examining external opportunities (O) and threats (T)

environmental scanning collection and interpretation of information about forces, events, and relationships in the external environment that may affect the future of the organization or the implementation of the marketing plan

company functions. Business mission statements that are stated too narrowly suffer from **marketing myopia**—defining a business in terms of goods and services rather than in terms of the benefits customers seek. In this context, *myopia* means narrow, short-term thinking. For example, Frito-Lay defines its mission as being in the snack-food business rather than in the potato chip business.

Alternatively, business missions may be stated too broadly. "To provide products of superior quality and value that improve the lives of the world's consumers" is probably too broad a mission statement for any firm except Procter & Gamble. Care must be taken when stating what business a firm is in. For example, the mission of Royal Orchid Hotels Ltd. outlines three important aspects of its hospitality business:

- *To the guests:* "Royal Orchid Hotels is in the hospitality business to provide superior service with competitive pricing. We are committed to offer quality accommodation and services to our guests. We strive to achieve Excellence in Service and Standards."
- *To the employees:* "To provide all employees with a fair package of employment and a conducive working environment. This is done by recruiting and training employees who are keen to progress, willing to learn new skills and accept greater responsibilities."
- *To the community:* "To ensure each hotel recognizes its responsibilities and contribution to the community."[1]

By correctly stating the business mission in terms of the benefits that customers seek, the foundation for the marketing plan is set. Many companies are focusing on designing more appropriate mission statements because these statements are frequently displayed on the company's Web sites.

The organization may need to define a mission statement and objectives for a **strategic business unit (SBU)**, which is a subgroup of a single business or collection of related businesses within the larger organization. A properly defined SBU should have a distinct mission and specific target market, control over its resources, its own competitors, and plans independent of the other SBUs in the organization. Thus, a large firm such as Hindustan Unilever Ltd. may have marketing plans for each of its SBUs, which include food brands, personal care brands, and home care brands.

LO 3 Conducting a Situation Analysis

Marketers must understand the current and potential environment in which the product or service will be marketed. A situation analysis is sometimes referred to as a **SWOT analysis**—that is, the firm should identify its internal strengths (S) and weaknesses (W) and also examine external opportunities (O) and threats (T).

When examining internal strengths and weaknesses, the marketing manager should focus on organizational resources such as production costs, marketing skills, financial resources, company or brand image, employee capabilities, and available technology. For example, Dell's stock has fallen 42 percent since January 2007 in the American market, so management needs to examine strengths and weaknesses in the company and its competition. Dell has ₹27,000 crore server business (strength), but the shrinking PC market accounts for a significant 24 percent of sales (weakness). Competitors like IBM and Hewlett-Packard (HP) are moving heavily into software and consulting, so to avoid them, Dell might instead consider the ₹31,950 crore networking equipment market.[2] Another issue to consider in this section of the marketing plan is the historical background of the firm—its sales and profit history.

When examining external opportunities and threats, marketing managers must analyze aspects of the marketing environment. This process is called **environmental scanning**—the collection and interpretation of information about forces, events, and relationships in the external environment that may affect the future of the organization or the implementation of the marketing plan. Environmental scanning helps identify market opportunities and threats and provides guidelines for the design of marketing strategy. The six most often studied macroenvironmental forces are social, demographic, economic, technological, political and legal, and competitive. These forces are examined in detail in Chapter 4.

LO 4 Setting Marketing Plan Objectives

Before the details of a marketing plan can be developed, objectives for the plan must be stated. Without objectives, there is no basis for measuring the success of marketing plan activities.

A **marketing objective** is a statement of what is to be accomplished through marketing activities. To be useful, stated objectives should be:

- *Realistic:* Managers should develop objectives that have a chance of being met. For example, it may be unrealistic for start-up firms or new products to command dominant market share, given other competitors in the marketplace.
- *Measurable:* Managers need to be able to quantitatively measure whether or not an objective has been met. For example, it would be difficult to determine success for an objective that states, "To increase sales of toothpaste." If the company sells 1 percent more toothpaste, does that mean the objective was met? Instead, a specific number should be stated, "To increase sales of Babool brand toothpaste from ₹120 crore to ₹125 crore."
- *Time specific:* By what time should the objective be met? "To increase sales of Babool brand toothpaste between January 1, 2011 and December 31, 2011."
- *Compared to a benchmark:* If the objective is to increase sales by 15 percent, it is important to know the baseline against which the objective will be measured. Will it be current sales? Last year's sales? For example, "To increase sales of Babool brand toothpaste by 15 percent over 2010 sales of ₹120 crore."

Objectives must also be consistent with and indicate the priorities of the organization. Specifically, objectives flow from the business mission statement to the rest of the marketing plan.

Carefully specified objectives serve several functions. First, they communicate marketing management philosophies and provide direction for lower-level marketing managers so that marketing efforts are integrated and pointed in a consistent direction. Objectives also serve as motivators by creating something for employees to strive for. When objectives are attainable and challenging, they motivate those charged with achieving the objectives. Additionally, the process of writing specific objectives forces executives to clarify their thinking. Finally, objectives form a basis for control; the effectiveness of a plan can be gauged in light of the stated objectives.

LO 5 Competitive Advantage

Performing a SWOT analysis allows firms to identify their competitive advantage. A competitive advantage is a set of unique features of a company and its products that are perceived by the target market as significant and superior to the competition. It is the factor or factors that cause customers to patronize a firm and not the competition. There are three types of competitive advantage: cost, product/service differentiation, and niche.

Cost Competitive Advantage

Cost leadership can result from obtaining inexpensive raw materials, creating an efficient scale of plant operations, designing products for ease of manufacture, controlling overhead costs, and avoiding marginal customers. For example, many modern furniture design and production companies, like IKEA, consider creativity their unique competitive advantage. IKEA, however, also derives a significant cost competitive advantage by focusing on pricing. When developing a new product, the first decision IKEA designers make is how much the end product will cost in the store. Then they develop the design according to that number. The result is a fun, functional, high-quality product for much less than any of IKEA's competitors can match.[3] Having a **cost competitive advantage** means being the low-cost competitor in an industry while maintaining satisfactory profit margins.

A cost competitive advantage enables a firm to deliver superior customer value. Walmart, the world's leading low-cost general merchandise store, offers good value to customers because it focuses on providing a large selection of merchandise at low prices and good customer service. Walmart is able to keep its prices down because it has strong buying power in its relationships with suppliers. Costs can be reduced in a variety of ways:

marketing objective a statement of what is to be accomplished through marketing activities

competitive advantage a set of unique features of a company and its products that are perceived by the target market as significant and superior to the competition

cost competitive advantage being the low-cost competitor in an industry while maintaining satisfactory profit margins

experience curves curves that show costs declining at a predictable rate as experience with a product increases

product/service differentiation competitive advantage the provision of something that is unique and valuable to buyers beyond simply offering a lower price than that of the competition

- *Experience curves:* **Experience curves** tell us that costs decline at a predictable rate as experience with a product increases. The experience curve effect encompasses a broad range of manufacturing, marketing, and administrative costs. Experience curves reflect learning by doing, technological advances, and economies of scale. Firms like Boeing use historical experience curves as a basis for predicting and setting prices. Experience curves allow management to forecast costs and set prices based on anticipated costs as opposed to current costs.
- *Efficient labor:* Labor costs can be an important component of total costs in low-skill, labor-intensive industries such as product assembly and apparel manufacturing. Many U.S. publishers and software developers send data entry, design, and formatting tasks to India, where skilled engineers are available at lower overall cost.
- *No-frills goods and services:* Marketers can lower costs by removing frills and options from a product or service. U.S. based Southwest Airlines, for example, offers low fares but no seat assignments or meals. Low costs give Southwest a higher load factor and greater economies of scale, which, in turn, mean lower prices. Similar strategy is followed by IndiGo Airlines in India.
- *Government subsidies:* Governments can provide grants and interest-free loans to target industries. Such government assistance enabled Indian IT industry to become global leaders.
- *Product design:* Cutting-edge design technology can help offset high labor costs. BMW is a world leader in designing cars for ease of manufacture and assembly. Reverse engineering—the process of disassembling a product piece by piece to learn its components and obtain clues as to the manufacturing process—can also mean savings. Reverse engineering a low-cost competitor's product can save research and design costs. Japanese engineers have reversed many products, such as computer chips from Silicon Valley.
- *Reengineering:* Reengineering entails fundamental rethinking and redesign of business processes to achieve dramatic improvements in critical measures of performance. It often involves reorganizing functional departments such as sales, engineering, and production, into cross-disciplinary teams.
- *Production innovations:* Production innovations such as new technology and simplified production techniques help lower the average cost of production. Technologies such as computer-aided design (CAD) and computer-aided manufacturing (CAM) and increasingly sophisticated robots help companies such as Boeing, Ford, and General Electric reduce their manufacturing costs.
- *New methods of service delivery:* Medical expenses have been substantially lowered by the use of outpatient surgery and walk-in clinics. Online-only magazines deliver great savings, and even some print magazines are exploring ways to go online to save material and shipping costs.

© ISTOCKPHOTO.COM/HELDER ALMEIDA

Product/Service Differentiation Competitive Advantage

Because cost competitive advantages are subject to continual erosion, product/service differentiation tends to provide a longer lasting competitive advantage. The durability of this strategy tends to make it more attractive to many top managers. A **product/service differentiation competitive advantage** exists when a firm provides something that is unique and valuable to buyers beyond simply offering a lower price than that of the competition. Examples include brand names (Titan), a strong dealer network (HUL's FMCG products), product reliability (Nokia mobiles), or service (FedEx). Many bookshops and bookstores are very common, but there aren't many such businesses that deliver right to your house. Flipkart.com in India uses its distribution network to deliver books directly to homes. Instead of bringing customers to the books, Flipkart.com brings books to the customers.

© THOMAS NORTHCUT/GETTY IMAGES

Niche Competitive Advantage

A **niche competitive advantage** seeks to target and effectively serve a single segment of the market (see Chapter 8). For small companies with limited resources that potentially face giant competitors, niche targeting may be the only viable option. A market segment that has good growth potential but is not crucial to the success of major competitors is a good candidate for developing a niche strategy.

Many companies using a niche strategy serve only a limited geographic market. Indian Coffee House is a successful restaurant chain, found only in India, with major presence in state of Kerala. Jumbo King is another fast-food chain, largely based in India's Maharashtra state.

Building Sustainable Competitive Advantage

The key to having a competitive advantage is the ability to sustain that advantage. A **sustainable competitive advantage** is one that cannot be copied by the competition. For example, Activa, a gearless scooter from Honda, has held a steady share of the gearless scooter market over the years. Companies that tried to enter the market, for example, Kinetic Nova and Bajaj Saffire, failed to accomplish any sort of success. Reasons that defined the success of Honda Activa were top class engineering process of Honda and perception of smooth performance and fuel economy. In this case, low price was not a sustainable competitive advantage. Without a competitive advantage, target customers don't perceive any reason to patronize an organization instead of its competitors.

The notion of competitive advantage means that a successful firm will stake out a position unique in some manner from its rivals. Imitation by competitors

THE WHEEL THING

© DEVI/SHUTTERSTOCK.COM

Bicycle commuting in the United States has risen 35 percent in the last five years, but bike designs haven't kept pace. Most U.S. bikes are modeled on road or mountain bikes, which are made for racing speed or off-road durability, not everyday hauling. Rob Forbes wants to change all that with his new bike company Public. To design a commuter-friendly bike, he went straight to the commuter bike capital of the world—Utrecht, Holland, where rush hour is all bikes and no cars. Public's bikes look European. They're all colourfully appointed with fenders, racks, baskets, and kickstands, but models are light and durable enough for the hills and stairs common to the American commute. At many shops around the country, customers can test ride a Public bike before spending ₹38,250 to ₹54,000 on a new one. Adapting the European commuter bike for U.S. consumption may just be the key to bringing out the U.S. bikers.[1]

...an
...nnot be
...mpetition

...ation a ...g strategy that tries to ...e market share among ...ng customers

...arket development a marketing strategy that entails attracting new customers to existing products

indicates a lack of competitive advantage and almost ensures mediocre performance. Moreover, competitors rarely stand still, so it is not surprising that imitation causes managers to feel trapped in a seemingly endless game of catch-up. They are regularly surprised by the new accomplishments of their rivals.

Rather than copy competitors, companies need to build their own competitive advantages. The sources of tomorrow's competitive advantages are the skills and assets of the organization. Assets include patents, copyrights, locations, equipment, and technology that are superior to those of the competition. Skills are functions such as customer service and promotion that the firm performs better than its competitors. Marketing managers should continually focus the firm's skills and assets on sustaining and creating competitive advantages.

Remember, a sustainable competitive advantage is a function of the speed with which competitors can imitate a leading company's strategy and plans. Imitation requires a competitor to identify the leader's competitive advantage, determine how it is achieved, and then learn how to duplicate it.

LO 6 Strategic Directions

The end result of the SWOT analysis and identification of a competitive advantage is to evaluate the strategic direction of the firm. Selecting a strategic alternative is the next step in marketing planning.

Strategic Alternatives

To discover a marketing opportunity, management must know how to identify the alternatives. One method for developing alternatives is Ansoff's strategic opportunity matrix (see Exhibit 2.2), which matches products with markets. Firms can explore these four options:

- *Market penetration:* A firm using the **market penetration** alternative would try to increase market share among existing customers. If Hindustan Unilever started a major campaign for Fair & Lovely with aggressive advertising and price discounts to existing customers, it would be following a penetration strategy. Customer databases, discussed in Chapters 9 and 21, would help managers implement this strategy.
- *Market development:* **Market development** means attracting new customers to existing products. Ideally, new uses for old products stimulate additional sales among existing customers while also bringing in new buyers. McDonald's, for example, has opened restaurants in Russia, China, and Italy and is eagerly expanding into Eastern European countries. In the nonprofit area, the growing emphasis on continuing education and executive development by colleges and universities is a market development strategy.
- *Product development:* A **product development** strategy entails the creation of new products for present markets. McDonald's introduced vegetarian options in its Indian menu, keeping in mind the religious sentiments of the Indian population. Managers following the product development strategy can rely on their extensive knowledge of the target audience. They usually have a good feel for what customers like and dislike about current products and what existing needs are not being met. In addition, managers can rely on established distribution channels.
- *Diversification:* **Diversification** is a strategy of increasing sales by introducing new products into new markets. For example, ITC, that was originally a tobacco company,

EXHIBIT 2.2
Ansoff's Strategic Opportunity Matrix

	Present Product	New Product
Present Market	*Market Penetration* Amul selling milk to existing customer base.	*Product Development* Amul develops flavoured yogurt.
New Market	*Market Development* Amul enters markets such as Mauritius, UAE, Australia, and Singapore.	*Diversification* Amul enters pizza and quick service restaurant businesses.

diversified into several other businesses such as Wills Lifestyle (lifestyle retailing), Kitchens of India and Sunfeast (food business), and e-Choupal (agriculture business). Tata tea practiced a diversification strategy when it introduced flavored tea in the Indian market. Amul, originally a milk-selling company, has now diversified into multiple categories like ice-cream, flavored yogurt, and chocolates. A diversification strategy can be risky when a firm is entering unfamiliar markets. On the other hand, it can be very profitable when a firm is entering markets with little or no competition.

Selecting a Strategic Alternative

Recall that large organizations engaged in strategic planning may create strategic business units. Each SBU has its own rate of return on investment, growth potential, and associated risk. Management must find a balance among the SBUs that yields the overall organization's desired growth and profits with an acceptable level of risk. Some SBUs generate large amounts of cash, and others need cash to foster growth. The challenge is to balance the organization's "portfolio" of SBUs for the best long-term performance.

To determine the future cash contributions and cash requirements expected for each SBU, managers can use the Boston Consulting Group's portfolio matrix. The **portfolio matrix** classifies each SBU by its present or forecast growth and market share. The underlying assumption is that market share and profitability are strongly linked. The measure of market share used in the portfolio approach is *relative market share*, the ratio between the company's share and the share of the largest competitor. For example, if a firm has a 50 percent share and the competitor has 5 percent, the ratio is 10 to 1. If a firm has a 10 percent market share and the largest competitor has 20 percent, the ratio is 0.5 to 1.

Exhibit 2.3 is a hypothetical portfolio matrix for a computer manufacturer. The size of the circle in each cell of the matrix represents dollar sales of the SBU relative to dollar sales of the company's other SBUs. The portfolio matrix breaks SBUs into four categories:

- *Stars:* A **star** is a fast-growing market leader. For example, the iPad is Apple's current star. Star SBUs usually have large profits but need lots of cash to finance rapid growth. The best marketing tactic is to protect existing market share by reinvesting earnings in product improvement, better distribution, more promotion, and production efficiency. Management must capture new users as they enter the market.
- *Cash cows:* A **cash cow** is an SBU that generates more cash than it needs to maintain its market share. It is in a low-growth market, but the product has a dominant market share. Personal computers and laptops are categorized as cash cows in Exhibit 2.3. The basic strategy for a cash cow is to maintain market dominance by being the price leader and making technological improvements in the product. Managers should resist pressure to extend the basic line unless they can dramatically increase demand. Instead, they should allocate excess cash to the product categories where growth prospects are the greatest. Despite ending its "I'm a Mac" ad campaign, Apple sold more than 33.5 lakhs Macs in the first quarter of 2010 in the United States. (It sold 32.9 lakhs in all of 2004.) Another example is Nestle, which has two cash cows: Maggi Noodles and Cerelac.
- *Problem children:* A **problem child**, also called a **question mark**, shows rapid growth but poor profit margins. It has a low market share in a high-growth industry. Problem children need a great deal of cash. Without cash support, they eventually become dogs. The strategy options are to invest heavily to gain better market share, acquire competitors to get the necessary market share, or drop the SBU. Sometimes a firm can reposition the products of the SBU to move them into the star category. Videocon Mobile services is an example of question mark under Videocon umbrella's brand. The SBU has a small market share, though it has attracted heavy investments from the parent company.

product development a marketing strategy that entails the creation of new products for present markets

diversification a strategy of increasing sales by introducing new products into new markets

portfolio matrix a tool for allocating resources among products or strategic business units on the basis of relative market share and market growth rate

star in the portfolio matrix, a business unit that is a fast-growing market leader

cash cow in the portfolio matrix, a business unit that generates more cash than it needs to maintain its market share

EXHIBIT 2.3

Portfolio Matrix for a Large Computer Manufacturer

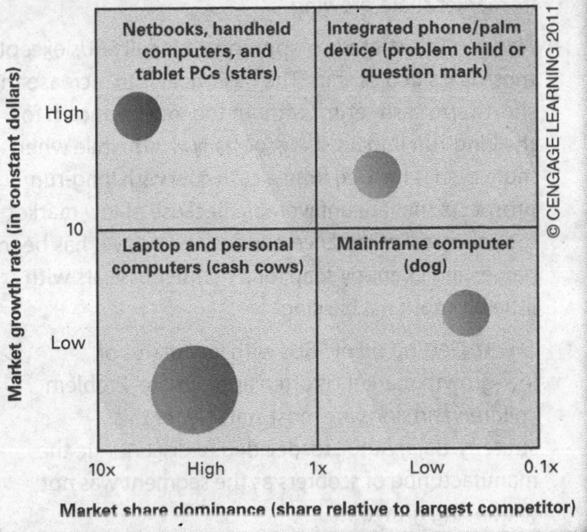

problem child (question mark) in the portfolio matrix, a business unit that shows rapid growth but poor profit margins

dog in the portfolio matrix, a business unit that has low growth potential and a small market share

marketing strategy the activities of selecting and describing one or more target markets and developing and maintaining a marketing mix that will produce mutually satisfying exchanges with target markets

market opportunity analysis (MOA) the description and estimation of the size and sales potential of market segments that are of interest to the firm and the assessment of key competitors in these market segments

- *Dogs:* A **dog** has low growth potential and a small market share. Most dogs eventually leave the marketplace. In the computer manufacturer example, the mainframe computer has become a dog. Other examples include Maruti's Baleno & Versa car models and Aquafresh toothpaste by Glaxo Smithkline. Coca Cola India removed Vanilla Coke from the market within one year of its launch. The strategy options for dogs are to harvest or divest.

After classifying the company's SBUs in the matrix, the next step is to allocate future resources for each. The four basic strategies are to:

- *Build:* If an organization has an SBU that it believes has the potential to be a star (probably a problem child at present), building would be an appropriate goal. The organization may decide to give up short-term profits and use its financial resources to achieve this goal. When ITC decided to enter biscuit industry, it knew it would face still competition from giants like Britannia and Parle. But it had faith in its offering and invested heavily in marketing activities to grab a share of the market.
- *Hold:* If an SBU is a very successful cash cow, a key goal would surely be to hold or preserve market share so that the organization can take advantage of the very positive cash flow. Apple plans to add some features, such as built-in projectors, to its Macintosh line to keep its market share growing.[5]
- *Harvest:* This strategy is appropriate for all SBUs except those classified as stars. The basic goal is to increase the short-term cash return without too much concern for the long-run impact. It is especially worthwhile when more cash is needed from a cash cow with long-run prospects that are unfavorable because of low market growth rate. For instance, Hindustan Unilever has been harvesting Lifebuoy soap for a number of years with little promotional backing.
- *Divest:* Getting rid of SBUs with low shares of low-growth markets is often appropriate. Problem children and dogs are most suitable for this strategy. Bajaj Auto Ltd. decided to discontinue the manufacturing of scooters as the segment was not witnessing growth.

LO7 Describing the Target Market

Marketing strategy involves the activities of selecting and describing one or more target markets and developing and maintaining a marketing mix that will produce mutually satisfying exchanges with target markets.

Target Market Strategy

A market segment is a group of individuals or organizations that share one or more characteristics. They therefore may have relatively similar product needs. For example, parents of newborn babies need formula, diapers, and special foods.

The target market strategy identifies the market segment or segments on which to focus. This process begins with a **market opportunity analysis (MOA)**—the description and estimation of the size and sales potential of market segments that are of interest to the firm and the assessment of key competitors in these market segments. After the firm describes the market segments, it may target one or more of them. There are three general strategies for selecting target markets.

Target market(s) can be selected by appealing to the entire market with one marketing mix, concentrating on one segment, or appealing to multiple market segments using multiple marketing mixes. The characteristics, advantages, and disadvantages of each strategic option are examined in Chapter 8. Target markets could be personal care products for new born babies (Johnson & Johnson Babycare), nutritional requirements of kids in the age group of 2–5 years (Junior Horlicks and Cadbury Bournvita Li'l Champs), premium casual wear for males in the age group 22–30 years (Parx by Raymond) or people who are either diabetic or health conscious (Sugar Free and Amul's Sugarfree Pro-Biotic Ice-Cream).

Any market segment that is targeted must be fully described. Demographics, psychographics, and buyer behavior should be assessed. Buyer behavior is covered in Chapters 6 and 7. If segments are differentiated by ethnicity, multicultural aspects of the marketing mix should be examined. If the target market is international, it is especially important to describe differences in culture, economic and technological development, and political structure that may affect the marketing plan. Global marketing is covered in more detail in Chapter 5.

LO 8 The Marketing Mix

The term marketing mix refers to a unique blend of product, place (distribution), promotion, and pricing strategies (often referred to as the four Ps) designed to produce mutually satisfying exchanges with a target market. The marketing manager can control each component of the marketing mix, but the strategies for all four components must be blended to achieve optimal results. Any marketing mix is only as good as its weakest component. For example, Tanishq's jewellery designs were considered too western during its initial years. The brand was able to win customers' satisfaction after it altered its designs to bring in the element of Indian ethnicity. The best promotion and the lowest price cannot save a poor product. Similarly, excellent products with poor placing, pricing, or promotion will likely fail.

Successful marketing mixes have been carefully designed to satisfy target markets. At first glance, Lux and Dove may appear to have roughly identical marketing mixes because they are both in the personal care soap business. However, Lux has always been portrayed as beauty soap, while Dove is showcased as a mild and moisturising soap. Lux has always used film celebrities to endorse the brand, whereas Dove uses ordinary women for signifying real beauty. Lux is priced as a value for money soap but Dove charges a premium price.

Variations in marketing mixes do not occur by chance. Astute marketing managers devise marketing strategies to gain advantages over competitors and best serve the needs and wants of a particular target market segment. By manipulating elements of the marketing mix, marketing managers can fine-tune the customer offering and achieve competitive success.

Product Strategies

Of the four Ps, the marketing mix typically starts with the product. The heart of the marketing mix, the starting point, is the product offering and product strategy. It is hard to design a place strategy, decide on a promotion campaign, or set a price without knowing the product to be marketed.

The product includes not only the physical unit but also its package, warranty, after-sale service, brand name, company image, value, and many other factors. A Titan watch has many product elements: the watch itself, shopping experience offered at the exclusive outlets, customer satisfaction guarantee, watches being a reflection of warmth, elegance and style, and the trust and prestige of the Titan brand name. We buy things not only for what they do (benefits) but also for what they mean to us (status, quality, or reputation).

Products can be tangible goods such as computers, ideas like those offered by a consultant, or services such as medical care. Products should also offer customer value. Product decisions are covered in Chapters 10 and 11, and services marketing is detailed in Chapter 12.

marketing mix a unique blend of product, place (distribution), promotion, and pricing strategies designed to produce mutually satisfying exchanges with a target market

four Ps product, place, promotion, and price, which together make up the marketing mix

Place (Distribution) Strategies

Place, or distribution, strategies are concerned with making products available when and where customers want them. Would you rather buy a kiwi fruit at the 24-hour grocery store within walking distance or fly to Australia to pick your own? A part of this P—place—is physical distribution, which involves all the business activities concerned with storing and transporting raw materials or finished products. The goal is to make sure products arrive in usable condition at designated places when needed. Place strategies are covered in Chapters 14 and 15.

Promotion Strategies

Promotion includes advertising, public relations, sales promotion, and personal selling. Promotion's role in the marketing mix is to bring about mutually satisfying exchanges with target markets by informing, educating, persuading, and reminding them of the benefits

©HEMERA/THINKSTOCK

implementation the process that turns a marketing plan into action assignments and ensures that these assignments are executed in a way that accomplishes the plan's objectives

of an organization or a product. A good promotion strategy, like using a popular public figure, such as Amitabh Bachchan, to endorse campaigns like Pulse Polio, can dramatically impact customer behavior. Each element of this P—promotion—is coordinated and managed with the others to create a promotional blend or mix. These integrated marketing communications activities are described in Chapters 16, 17, and 18. Technology-driven aspects of promotional marketing are covered in Chapter 21.

Pricing Strategies

Price is what a buyer must give up in order to obtain a product. It is often the most flexible of the four Ps—the quickest element to change. Marketers can raise or lower prices more frequently and easily than they can change other marketing mix variables. Price is an important competitive weapon and is very important to the organization because price multiplied by the number of units sold equals total revenue for the firm. Pricing decisions are covered in Chapters 19 and 20.

LO 9 Following Up on the Marketing Plan

Implementation

Implementation is the process that turns a marketing plan into action assignments and ensures that these assignments are executed in a way that accomplishes

PUTTING THE "STREET" IN STREET FIGHTER

The latest iteration of Capcom's *Street Fighter* is ultra-refined, with an updated shading style of graphics that makes gameplay even more artistic. Since its introduction into arcades in 1992, *Street Fighter* has developed a loyal following, but Capcom wanted to demonstrate the added features of *Super Street Fighter IV,* such as enhanced online experience and bonus rounds, and to emphasize the art of *Street Fighter.* To do so, game engineers teamed with five emerging urban and graphic artists to create print ads in their own signature style. The message illustrates the new sketch style of *Super Street fighter IV* with a notebook/doodle/graffiti look as well as driving the lower ₹1,799 price point in the United States. artists futura, 123klan, dalek, grotesk, and cody hudson showcase various graffiti styles and their own artistic histories in this unique and totally street ad campaign.[6]

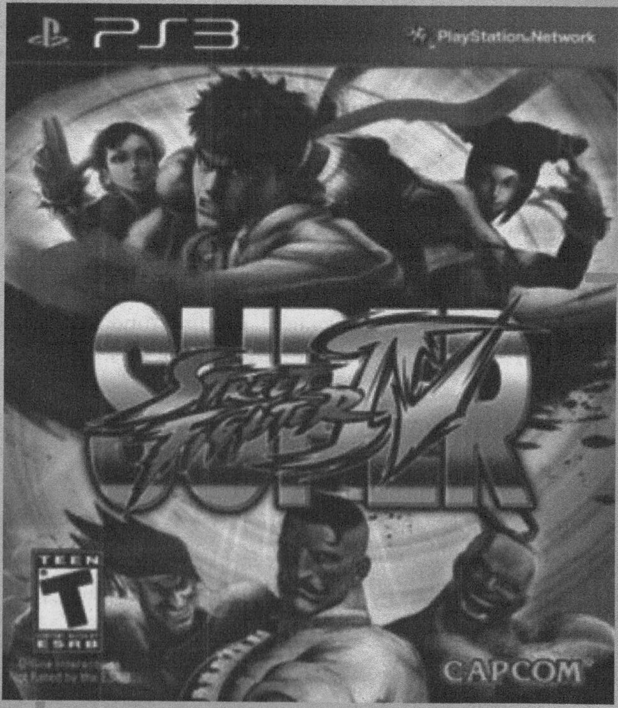

© SHNS PHOTO COURTESY CAPCOM/NEWSCOM

the plan's objectives. Implementation activities may involve detailed job assignments, activity descriptions, time lines, budgets, and lots of communication. Although implementation is essentially "doing what you said you were going to do," many organizations repeatedly experience failures in strategy implementation. Brilliant marketing plans are doomed to fail if they are not properly implemented. These detailed communications may or may not be part of the written marketing plan. If they are not part of the plan, they should be specified elsewhere as soon as the plan has been communicated.

Evaluation and Control

After a marketing plan is implemented, it should be evaluated. **Evaluation** entails gauging the extent to which marketing objectives have been achieved during the specified time period. Four common reasons for failing to achieve a marketing objective are unrealistic marketing objectives, inappropriate marketing strategies in the plan, poor implementation, and changes in the environment after the objective was specified and the strategy was implemented.

Once a plan is chosen and implemented, its effectiveness must be monitored. **Control** provides the mechanisms for evaluating marketing results in light of the plan's objectives and for correcting actions that do not help the organization reach those objectives within budget guidelines. Firms need to establish formal and informal control programs to make the entire operation more efficient.

Perhaps the broadest control device available to marketing managers is the **marketing audit**—a thorough, systematic, periodic evaluation of the objectives, strategies, structure, and performance of the marketing organization. A marketing audit helps management allocate marketing resources efficiently.

4 CHARACTERISTICS OF A MARKETING AUDIT:

- *Comprehensive:* The marketing audit covers all the major marketing issues facing an organization and not just trouble spots.
- *Systematic:* The marketing audit takes place in an orderly sequence and covers the organization's marketing environment, internal marketing system, and specific marketing activities. The diagnosis is followed by an action plan with both short-run and long-run proposals for improving overall marketing effectiveness.
- *Independent:* The marketing audit is normally conducted by an inside or outside party who is independent enough to have top management's confidence and has the ability to be objective.
- *Periodic:* The marketing audit should be carried out on a regular schedule instead of only in a crisis. Whether it seems successful or is in deep trouble, any organization can benefit greatly from such an audit.

Although the main purpose of the marketing audit is to develop a full profile of the organization's marketing effort and to provide a basis for developing and revising the marketing plan, it is also an excellent way to improve communication and raise the level of marketing consciousness within the organization. It is a useful vehicle for selling the philosophy and techniques of strategic marketing to other members of the organization.

LO 10 Effective Strategic Planning

Effective strategic planning requires continual attention, creativity, and management commitment. Strategic planning should not be an annual exercise in which managers go through the motions and forget about strategic planning until the next year. It should be an ongoing process because the environment is continually changing and the firm's resources and capabilities are continually evolving.

Sound strategic planning is based on creativity. Managers should challenge assumptions about the firm and the environment and establish new strategies. For example, several entrepreneurs in late 1990s realized the potential and reach of the Internet and started their business ventures on the online platform. With the dawn of the new millennium, as the popularity of the Internet started picking up, these online portal ventures struck gold and enjoyed the first mover advantage.

Perhaps the most critical element in successful strategic planning is top management's support and

evaluation gauging the extent to which the marketing objectives have been achieved during the specified time period

control provides the mechanisms for evaluating marketing results in light of the plan's objectives and for correcting actions that do not help the organization reach those objectives within budget guidelines

marketing audit a thorough, systematic, periodic evaluation of the objectives, strategies, structure, and performance of the marketing organization

participation. For example, Kishore Biyani, CEO of Future Group, personally visits people's homes, holds discussions with local community leaders and spends weeks walking streets of local markets to understand what products to stock in a new store.[7]

© ISTOCKPHOTO/THINKSTOCK

STRATEGIC PLANNING SHOULD BE AN ONGOING PROCESS, NOT AN ANNUAL EXERCISE.

Review and Applications

Understand the importance of strategic marketing and know a basic outline for a marketing plan. Strategic marketing planning is the basis for all marketing strategies and decisions. The marketing plan is a written document that acts as a guidebook of marketing activities for the marketing manager. A marketing plan provides the basis by which actual and expected performance can be compared.

Although there is no set formula or a single correct outline, a marketing plan should include basic elements such as stating the business mission, setting objectives, performing a situation analysis of internal and external environmental forces, selecting target market(s), delineating a marketing mix (product, place, promotion, and price), and establishing ways to implement, evaluate, and control the plan.

1.1 Your cousin wants to start his own business, but he has decided not to write a marketing plan because he thinks that preparing one would take too long. He says he doesn't need a formal proposal because he has already received funding from your uncle. Explain why it is important for him to write a plan anyway.

1.2 After graduation, you decide to take a position as the marketing manager for a small snack-food manufacturer. The company, Shur Snak, is growing, and this is the first time that the company has ever employed a marketing manager. Consequently, there is no marketing plan in place for you to follow. Outline a basic marketing plan for your boss to give her an idea of the direction you want to take the company.

1.3 How are Coke and Pepsi using their Web sites, **www.coca-cola.com** and **www.pepsi.com**, to promote their newest product offerings? Do you see hints of any future strategies the companies might implement? Where?

Develop an appropriate business mission statement. The mission statement is based on a careful analysis of benefits sought by present and potential customers and an analysis of existing and anticipated environmental conditions. The firm's mission statement establishes boundaries for all subsequent decisions, objectives, and strategies. A mission statement should focus on the market or markets the organization is attempting to serve rather than on the good or service offered.

2.1 Thinking back to question 1.2, write a business mission statement for Shur Snak. What elements should you include? Evaluate the mission statement you wrote against some of those you can find online.

Describe the components of a situation analysis. In the situation (or SWOT) analysis, the firm should identify its internal strengths (S) and weaknesses (W) and also examine external opportunities (O) and threats (T). When examining external opportunities and threats, marketing managers must analyze aspects of the marketing environment in a process called environmental scanning. The six most often studied macroenvironmental forces are social, demographic, economic, technological, political and legal, and competitive.

3.1 Competition in the insurance sector is fierce. Life Insurance Corporation of India (LIC India) dominates this sector, but private companies like Aviva India Met Life India, and ING Vysya are the top market players in the private sector. Perform a mini-situation analysis on one of the companies listed below by stating one strength , one weakness, one opportunity and one threat. You may want to consult the following websites as you build your grid.

LIC	**www.licindia.in**
Aviva	**www.avivaindia.com**
Met Life Insurance	**www.metlife.co.in**
ING Vysya	**www.inglife.co.in**

Explain the criteria for stating good marketing objectives. Objectives should be realistic, measurable, and time specific; and should be compared to a benchmark. They must also be consistent and indicate the priorities of the organization. Good marketing objectives communicate marketing management philosophies, provide management direction, motivate employees, force executives to think clearly, and form a basis for control.

4.1 Building on the Shur Snak example, imagine that your boss has stated that the marketing objective of the company is to do the best job of satisfying the needs and wants of the customer. Explain that although this objective is admirable, it does not meet the criteria for good objectives. What are these criteria? What is a specific example of a better objective for Shur Snak?

Identify sources of competitive advantage. A competitive advantage is a set of unique features of a company and its products that are perceived by the target market as significant and superior to the competition. There are three types of competitive advantages: cost, product/service differentiation, and niche strategies. Sources of cost competitive advantages include experience curves, efficient labor, no-frills goods and services, government subsidies, product design, reengineering, product innovations, and new methods of service delivery. A product/service differentiation competitive advantage exists when a firm provides something unique that is valuable to buyers beyond just low price. Niche competitive advantages come from targeting unique segments with specific needs and wants. The goal of all these sources of competitive advantage is to be sustainable.

5.1 Break into small groups and discuss examples (at least two per person) of the last few products you have purchased. What specific strategies were used to achieve competitive advantage? Is that competitive advantage sustainable against the competitors?

Identify strategic alternatives. The strategic opportunity matrix can be used to help management develop strategic alternatives. The four options are market penetration, product development, market development, and diversification. In selecting a strategic alternative, managers may use a portfolio matrix, which classifies strategic business units as stars, cash cows, problem children, or dogs, depending on their present or projected growth and market share.

6.1 Based on your SWOT analysis, decide what the strategic growth options are for the company you chose in question 3.1.

Discuss target market strategies. The target market strategy identifies which market segment or segments to focus on. This process begins with a market opportunity analysis (MOA), which describes and estimates the size and sales potential of market segments that are of interest to the firm. In addition, an assessment of key competitors in these market segments is performed. After the market segments are described, one or more may be targeted by the firm. The three strategies for selecting target markets are appealing to the entire market with one marketing mix, concentrating on one segment, or appealing to multiple market segments using multiple marketing mixes.

7.1 You are given the task of deciding the marketing strategy for a transportation company. How do the marketing mix elements change when the target market is (a) low-income workers without personal transportation, (b) corporate international business travelers, or (c) companies with urgent documents or perishable materials to be delivered to customers?

Describe the elements of the marketing mix. The marketing mix (or four Ps) is a blend of product, place, promotion, and pricing strategies designed to produce mutually satisfying exchanges with a target market. The starting point of the marketing mix is the product offering. Products can be tangible goods, ideas, or services. Place (distribution) strategies are concerned with making products available when and where customers want them. Promotion includes advertising, public relations, sales promotion, and personal selling. Price is what a buyer must give up to obtain a product and is often the easiest to change of the four marketing mix elements.

8.1 Choose three or four other students and make up a team. Create a marketing plan to increase enrollment in your school. Describe the four marketing mix elements that make up the plan.

Explain why implementation, evaluation, and control of the marketing plan are necessary. Before a marketing plan can work, it must be implemented; that is, people must perform the actions in the plan. The plan should also be evaluated to see if it has achieved its objectives. Poor implementation can be a major factor in a plan's failure. Control provides the mechanisms for evaluating marketing results in light of the plan's objectives and for correcting actions that do not help the organization reach those objectives within budget guidelines.

9.1 Have your school enrollment marketing plan team (from question 8.1) develop a plan to implement, evaluate, and control the marketing strategy.

Identify several techniques that help make strategic planning effective. First, management must realize that strategic planning is an ongoing process and not a once-a-year exercise. Second, good strategic planning involves a high level of creativity. The last requirement is top management's support and cooperation.

10.1 What techniques can make your school enrollment marketing plan more effective?

Exercises

APPLICATION EXERCISE

As you now know from reading the chapter, an important part of the strategy-making process involves scanning the environment for changes that affect your marketing efforts. This exercise is designed to introduce you to the business press and to help you make the connection between the concepts you learn in the classroom and real-world marketing activities.

Activities

1. Find a current article of substance in the business press (The Financial Times, Economic Times, Outlook Business, Business Today, etc.) that discusses topics you have covered in the course. Although this is only Chapter 2, you will be surprised by the amount of terminology you have already learned. If you are having trouble finding an article, read through the table of contents at the beginning of the book to familiarize yourself with the names of concepts that will be presented later in the course. Read your article carefully, making notes about relevant content.
2. Write a one-paragraph summary of the key points in your article; then write a list of the terms or concepts critical to understanding the article. Provide definitions of those terms. If you are unfamiliar with a term or concept that is central to the article, do some research in your textbook or see your professor during office hours. Relate these key points to the concepts in your text by citing page numbers.
3. Explain the environments that are relevant to the situation presented in the article. (Chapter 4 contains a full list of environmental factors.)

ETHICS EXERCISE

Axe deodorant is one of the leading deodorant brands in India. Axe advertisements have been known for its provocative and sexually oriented ads. Recently, an Axe advertisement on its new fragrance 'dark temptation' was banned by the Advertising Standards Council of India after it received several complaints. The ad shows that after applying the deodorant a man turns into a chocolate man with women wanting to get close to him. Similarly, other ads like lux Cozy and Amul Macho have also been banned for its provocative content.

Questions

1. Is marketing a product with adult content on TV ethical, where the younger audience is also exposed to it?
2. Would Axe do equally well, if it did not advertise itself with provocative ads?

MARKETING PLAN EXERCISE

Throughout the rest of this book, these end-of-chapter marketing plan exercises will help you build a strategic marketing plan for a company of your choosing. The company you choose should be one that interests you, such as the manufacturer of your favorite product, a local business where you would like to work, or even a business you would like to start yourself to satisfy an unmet need or want. Once you've completed the marketing plan exercise for each chapter in Part 1 of this textbook, you can complete the Part 1 Marketing Planning Worksheet on your companion Web site at **www.cengage.com/international.** Use the following exercises to guide you through the first part of your strategic marketing plan:

Questions

1. Describe your chosen company. How long has it been in business, or when will it start business? Who are the key players? Is the company small or large? Does it offer a good or service?
2. Write the mission statement of your company, keeping in mind the benefits offered to customers rather than the product or service sold. If you are starting the online arm of a traditional store, should you make any changes to the company's overall mission statement?
3. List at least three specific, measurable objectives for your company. Be sure these objectives relate to the mission statement and include a time frame.
4. Begin a SWOT analysis by determining the primary strength of your company by asking, "What is the key differential or competitive advantage of my firm?" What are other keys to the potential success of your company? What other strengths can your firm capitalize on?
5. Continue the SWOT analysis by taking an honest look at the weaknesses of your firm. How can you overcome them?

Short Case: TATA NANO

Prepared by
Dr. Dheeraj Sharma,
Indian Institute of Management, Ahmedabad

According to *Economic Times*, National Council for Applied Economic Research's (NCAER) Centre for Macro Consumer Research has predicted that by 2015, the middle class in India will be over 250 million (25 crore) from the current size of 160 million (16 crore).[8] These statistics demonstrate that there will continued growth in demand of automobiles in India for years to come. However, the price of typical two-wheeler was almost one-fourth the price of the cheapest car (Maruti 800) in the market. Hence, the automobile sector in India remained dominated by two wheelers. The four wheelers were considered somewhat of luxury item not within the reach of the common man. Examining and understanding the gap in the automobile market, Tata Motors Limited launched its new small car Tata Nano, at a price that was in the reach of the middle and lower middle class people. Tata Nano received significant publicity world-wide for building the cheapest car in the world with the lowest power consumption. Tata Nano also boasted of excellent fuel efficiency. Thus, Tata Nano provided an opportunity for the lower middle-class family to upgrade from two-wheeler to four wheeler market.[9] Thus, Tata Nano created a new segment within the economy segment of automobiles in India. This product provided a significant competitive advantage to Tata as it will be able to garner large market share in the automobile segment and also consolidate its position in the world of automobiles by building automobiles in most cost-efficient way.

However, Tata Motors was forced to raise the price of Nano on account of improvements in engine to meet the new emission standards. Further, Tata Motors was hit with production issues and unable to fulfill the advance order of the customers. Despite several hiccups in its journey from factory to the roads, Tata Motors billed Nano as somewhat successful launch. According to *Business Today*, the sales saw a substantial increase in 2011[10]. Furthermore, the introduction of Nano may have put some pressure on the two-wheeler market. Thus, it is expected that two-wheeler industry may come up with cheaper variants of motor-cycles at a very low introductory price. Introduction of cheaper introductory models of motor-cycles will make Nano's future even more competitive one.

Questions

1. Will Tata Nano provide Tata Motors with a sustainable competitive? Will increased gap between Tata Nano and two-wheelers blunt Tata Nano's competitive advantage?
2. What is the future of Tata Nano?
3. What are your suggestion for continued success of Tata Nano?

CHAPTER REVIEW

2 Strategic Planning for Competitive Advantage

KEY TERMS

LO 1

strategic planning the managerial process of creating and maintaining a fit between the organization's objectives and resources and the evolving market opportunities

planning the process of anticipating future events and determining strategies to achieve organizational objectives in the future

marketing planning designing activities relating to marketing objectives and the changing marketing environment

marketing plan a written document that acts as a guidebook of marketing activities for the marketing manager

LO 2

mission statement a statement of the firm's business based on a careful analysis of benefits sought by present and potential customers and an analysis of existing and anticipated environmental conditions

marketing myopia defining a business in terms of goods and services rather than in terms of the benefits customers seek

strategic business unit (SBU) a subgroup of a single business or collection of related businesses within the larger organization

LO 3

SWOT analysis identifying internal strengths (S) and weaknesses (W) and also examining external opportunities (O) and threats (T)

environmental scanning collection and interpretation of information about forces, events, and relationships in the external environment that may affect the future of the organization or the implementation of the marketing plan

LO 4

marketing objective a statement of what is to be accomplished through marketing activities

KEY CONCEPTS

LO 1

Understand the importance of strategic marketing and know a basic outline for a marketing plan. Strategic marketing planning is the basis for all marketing strategies and decisions. By specifying objectives and defining the actions required to attain them, a marketing plan provides the basis on which actual and expected performance can be compared.

Although there is no set formula or a single correct outline, a marketing plan should include elements such as defining the business mission, performing a situation analysis, defining objectives, delineating a target market, and establishing components of the marketing mix (product, place, promotion, and price). Other elements that may be included in a plan are budgets, implementation timetables, required marketing research efforts, or elements of advanced strategic planning.

LO 2

Develop an appropriate business mission statement. The firm's mission statement establishes boundaries for all subsequent decisions, objectives, and strategies. A mission statement should focus on the market(s) the organization is attempting to serve rather than on the good or service offered.

LO 3

Describe the components of a situation analysis. In the situation (or SWOT) analysis, the firm should identify its internal strengths (S) and weaknesses (W) and also examine external opportunities (O) and threats (T). When examining external opportunities and threats, marketing managers must analyze aspects of the marketing environment in a process called environmental scanning. The six macroenvironmental forces studied most often are social, demographic, economic, technological, political and legal, and competitive.

LO 4

Explain the criteria for stating good marketing objectives. Objectives should be realistic, measurable, and time specific; and should be compared to a benchmark. They must also be consistent and indicate the priorities of the organization. Good marketing objectives communicate marketing management philosophies, provide management direction, motivate employees, force executives to think clearly, and form a basis for control.

LO 5

Identify sources of competitive advantage. There are three types of competitive advantage: cost, product/service differentiation, and niche. Sources of cost competitive advantage include experience curves, efficient labor, no-frills goods and services, government subsidies, product design, reengineering, production innovations, and new methods of service delivery. A product/service differentiation competitive advantage exists when a firm provides something unique that is valuable to buyers beyond just low price. Niche competitive advantages come from targeting unique segments with specific needs and wants. The goal of all these sources of competitive advantage is to be sustainable.

LO 6

Identify strategic alternatives. The strategic opportunity matrix can be used to help management develop strategic alternatives. The four options are market penetration, market development, product development, and diversification. In selecting a strategic alternative, managers may use a portfolio matrix, which classifies strategic business units as stars, cash cows, problem children (or question marks), and dogs, depending on their present or projected growth and market share.

2 Strategic Planning for Competitive Advantage

LO 5

competitive advantage a set of unique features of a company and its products that are perceived by the target market as significant and superior to the competition

cost competitive advantage being the low-cost competitor in an industry while maintaining satisfactory profit margins

experience curves curves that show costs declining at a predictable rate as experience with a product increases

product/service differentiation competitive advantage the provision of something that is unique and valuable to buyers beyond simply offering a lower price than that of the competition

niche competitive advantage the advantage achieved when a firm seeks to target and effectively serve a small segment of the market

sustainable competitive advantage an advantage that cannot be copied by the competition

LO 6

market penetration a marketing strategy that tries to increase market share among existing customers

market development a marketing strategy that entails attracting new customers to existing products

product development a marketing strategy that entails the creation of new products for present markets

diversification a strategy of increasing sales by introducing new products into new markets

portfolio matrix a tool for allocating resources among products or strategic business units on the basis of relative market share and market growth rate

star in the portfolio matrix, a business unit that is a fast-growing market leader

cash cow in the portfolio matrix, a business unit that generates more cash than it needs to maintain its market share

problem child (question mark) in the portfolio matrix, a business unit that shows rapid growth but poor profit margins

dog in the portfolio matrix, a business unit that has low growth potential and a small market share

LO 7 **Discuss target market strategies.** Targeting markets begins with a market opportunity analysis (MOA), which describes and estimates the size and sales potential of market segments that are of interest to the firm. In addition, an assessment of key competitors in these market segments is performed. After the market segments are described, one or more may be targeted by the firm. The three strategies for selecting target markets are appealing to the entire market with one marketing mix, concentrating on one segment, and appealing to multiple market segments using multiple marketing mixes.

LO 8 **Describe the elements of the marketing mix.** The marketing mix is a blend of product, place, promotion, and pricing strategies (the four Ps) designed to produce mutually satisfying exchanges with a target market. The starting point of the marketing mix is the product offering—tangible goods, ideas, or services. Place (distribution) strategies are concerned with making products available when and where customers want them. Promotion includes advertising, public relations, sales promotion, and personal selling. Price is what a buyer must give up in order to obtain a product and is often the most flexible of the four marketing mix elements.

LO 9 **Explain why implementation, evaluation, and control of the marketing plan are necessary.** Before a marketing plan can work, it must be implemented—that is, people must perform the actions in the plan. The plan should also be evaluated to see if it has achieved its objectives. Poor implementation can be a major factor in a plan's failure. Control provides the mechanisms for evaluating marketing results in light of the plan's objectives and for correcting actions that do not help the organization reach those objectives within budget guidelines.

LO 10 **Identify several techniques that help make strategic planning effective.** First, management must realize that strategic planning is an ongoing process and not a once-a-year exercise. Second, good strategic planning involves a high level of creativity. The last requirement is top management's support and participation.

LO 7

marketing strategy the activities of selecting and describing one or more target markets and developing and maintaining a marketing mix that will produce mutually satisfying exchanges with target markets

market opportunity analysis (MOA) the description and estimation of the size and sales potential of market segments that are of interest to the firm and the assessment of key competitors in these market segments

LO 8

marketing mix a unique blend of product, place (distribution), promotion, and pricing strategies designed to produce mutually satisfying exchanges with a target market

four Ps product, place, promotion, and price, which together make up the marketing mix

LO 9

implementation the process that turns a marketing plan into action assignments and ensures that these assignments are executed in a way that accomplishes the plan's objectives

evaluation gauging the extent to which the marketing objectives have been achieved during the specified time period

control provides the mechanisms for evaluating marketing results in light of the plan's objectives and for correcting actions that do not help the organization reach those objectives within budget guidelines

marketing audit a thorough, systematic, periodic evaluation of the objectives, strategies, structure, and performance of the marketing organization

CHAPTER 3 Ethics and Social Responsibility

Learning Outcomes

LO 1 Explain the concept of ethical behavior

LO 2 Describe ethical behavior in business

LO 3 Discuss corporate social responsibility

If you have ever resented a line-cutter, then you understand ethics and have applied ethical standards in life.

LO 1 The Concept of Ethical Behavior

It has been said that ethics is something everyone likes to talk about but nobody can define. Others have noted that "defining ethics is like trying to nail Jello to the wall. You begin to think that you understand it, but that's when it starts squirting out between your fingers."

ethics the moral principles or values that generally govern the conduct of an individual or a group

Ethics refers to the moral principles or values that generally govern the conduct of an individual or a group. Ethics also can be viewed as the standard of behavior by which conduct is judged. Standards that are legal may not always be ethical, and vice versa. Laws are the values and standards enforceable by the courts. Ethics, then, consists of personal moral principles. For example, there is no legal statute that makes it a crime for someone to "cut in line." Yet, if someone doesn't want to wait in line and cuts to the front, it often makes others very angry.

If you have ever resented a line-cutter, then you understand ethics and have applied ethical standards in life. Waiting your turn in line is a social expectation that exists because lines ensure order and allocate the space and time needed to complete transactions. Waiting your turn is an expected but unwritten behavior that plays a critical role in an orderly society.[1]

So it is with ethics. Ethics consists of those unwritten rules we have developed for our interactions with one another. These unwritten rules govern us when we are sharing resources or honoring contracts. "Waiting your turn" is a higher standard than the laws that are passed to maintain order. Those laws

Note:* *All the figures in U.S. dollars are converted into rupee using the value $1 = ₹45.

HEALTH CLAIMS MADE BY FOOD PRODUCTS

Various companies have been advertising **health claims** on their food products to market to children and health-conscious shoppers. Complan, a health drink by Heinz India, claimed in its advertising that it helps in increasing children's height up to two inches. This claim was challenged by Maharashtra Food and Drug Administration (FDA) on the basis of "exaggerated claims in advertising," forbidden by Prevention of Food Adulteration Act 1954. Similarly, the Food Safety and Standards Authority of India (FSSAI) sent notices to Britannia (it claims that its NutriChoice biscuits are healthy), Nestle (it claims one of its Maggi variants is multigrain), and Cadbury (it claims that Bournvira Li'l Champs leads to brain development) seeking a justification for the claims made in their advertising. On the whole, agencies around the globe closely monitor the health claims made in food products to protect children and their parents from such misleading marketing messages that tout health benefits where there aren't any.[2]

apply when physical force or threats are used to push to the front of the line. Assault, battery, and threats are forms of criminal conduct for which the offender can be prosecuted. But the law does not apply to the stealthy line-cutter who simply sneaks to the front, perhaps using a friend and a conversation as a decoy for edging into the front. No laws are broken, but the notions of fairness and justice are offended by one individual putting himself above others and taking advantage of others' time and position.

Ethical questions range from practical, narrowly defined issues, such as a businessperson's obligation to be honest with his customers, to broader social and philosophical questions, such as whether a company is responsible for preserving the environment and protecting employee rights. Many ethical conflicts develop from conflicts between the differing interests of company owners and their workers, customers, and surrounding community. Managers must balance the ideal against the practical—that is, the need to produce a reasonable profit for the company's shareholders against honesty in business practices and concern for environmental and social issues.

morals the rules people develop as a result of cultural values and norms

LO 2 Ethical Behavior in Business

Morals are the rules people develop as a result of cultural values and norms. Culture is a socializing force that dictates what is right and wrong. Moral standards may also reflect the laws and regulations that affect social and economic behavior. Thus, morals can be considered a foundation of ethical behavior.

Morals are usually characterized as good or bad. "Good" and "bad" have different connotations, including "effective" and "ineffective." A good salesperson makes or exceeds the assigned quota. If the salesperson sells a new stereo or television set to a disadvantaged consumer—knowing full well that the person can't keep up the monthly payments—is the salesperson still a good one? What if the sale enables the salesperson to exceed his or her quota?

"Good" and "bad" can also refer to "conforming" and "deviant" behaviors. A doctor who runs large ads offering discounts on open-heart surgery would be considered bad, or unprofessional, in the sense of not conforming to the norms of the medical profession. "Bad" and "good" are also used to express the distinction between criminal and law-abiding behavior. And finally, different religions define "good" and "bad" in markedly different ways. A Muslim who eats pork would be considered bad, as would a fundamentalist Christian who drinks whiskey.

Morality and Business Ethics

Today's business ethics actually consist of a subset of major life values learned since birth. The values businesspeople use to make decisions have been acquired through family, educational, and religious institutions.

Ethical values are situation specific and time oriented. Everyone must have an ethical base that applies to conduct in the business world and in personal life. One approach to developing a personal set of ethics is to examine the consequences of a particular act. Who is helped or hurt? How long do the consequences last? What actions produce the greatest good for the greatest number of people? A second approach stresses the importance of rules. Rules come in the form of customs, laws, professional standards, and common sense. "Always treat others as you would like to be treated" is an example of a rule.

Another approach emphasizes the development of moral character within individuals. Ethical development can be thought of as having three levels:[3]

- *Preconventional morality,* the most basic level, is childlike. It is calculating, self-centered, and even selfish, based on what will be immediately punished or rewarded. Fortunately, most businesspeople have progressed beyond the self-centered and manipulative actions of preconventional morality.
- *Conventional morality* moves from an egocentric viewpoint toward the expectations of society. Loyalty and obedience to the organization (or society) become paramount. A marketing decision maker would be concerned only with whether the proposed action is legal and how it will be viewed by others.
- *Postconventional morality* represents the morality of the mature adult. At this level, people are less concerned about how others might see them and more concerned about how they see and judge themselves over the long run. A marketing decision maker who has attained a postconventional level of morality might ask, "Even though it is legal and will increase company profits, is it right in the long run? Might it do more harm than good in the end?"

Ethical Decision Making

There is rarely a cut-and-dried answer to ethical questions. Studies show that the following factors tend to influence ethical decision making and judgments:[4]

- *Extent of ethical problems within the organization:* Marketing professionals who perceive fewer ethical problems in their organizations tend to disapprove more strongly of "unethical" or questionable practices than those who perceive more ethical problems. Apparently, the healthier the ethical environment, the more likely it is that marketers will take a strong stand against questionable practices.
- *Top management's actions on ethics:* Top managers can influence the behavior of marketing professionals by encouraging ethical behavior and discouraging unethical behavior. Research found that when top managers develop a strong ethical culture, there is reduced pressure to perform unethical acts, fewer unethical acts are performed, and unethical behavior is reported more frequently.[5]
- *Potential magnitude of the consequences:* The greater the harm done to victims, the more likely it is that marketing professionals will recognize a problem as unethical.
- *Social consensus:* The greater the degree of agreement among managerial peers that an action is harmful, the more likely it is that marketers will recognize a problem as unethical. Research found that a strong ethical culture among co-workers decreases observations of ethical misconduct. In companies with strong ethical cultures, 8 percent of employees observed misconduct, compared with 31 percent in companies with weaker cultures.[6]
- *Probability of a harmful outcome:* The greater the likelihood that an action will result in a harmful outcome, the more likely it is that marketers will recognize a problem as unethical.
- *Length of time between the decision and the onset of consequences:* The shorter the length of time between the action and the onset of negative consequences, the more likely it is that marketers will perceive a problem as unethical.

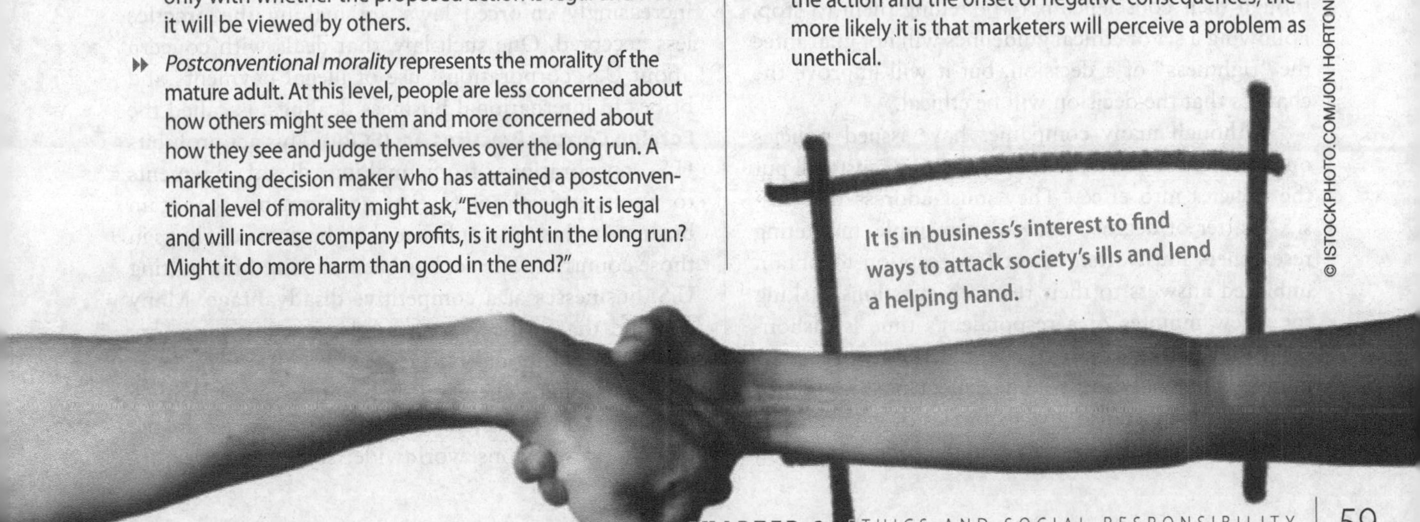

It is in business's interest to find ways to attack society's ills and lend a helping hand.

code of ethics a guideline to help marketing managers and other employees make better decisions

Foreign Corrupt Practices Act (FCPA) a law that prohibits U.S. corporations from making illegal payments to public officials of foreign governments to obtain business rights or to enhance their business dealings in those countries

- *Number of people to be affected:* The greater the number of persons affected by a negative outcome, the more likely it is that marketers will recognize a problem as unethical.

Ethical Guidelines

Many organizations have become more interested in ethical issues. One sign of this interest is the increase in the number of large companies that appoint ethics officers—from virtually none several years ago to almost 33 percent of large corporations today. In addition, many companies of various sizes have developed a **code of ethics** as a guideline to help marketing managers and other employees make better decisions. Creating ethics guidelines has several advantages:

- The guidelines help employees identify what their firm recognizes as acceptable business practices.
- A code of ethics can be an effective internal control on behavior, which is more desirable than external controls such as government regulation.
- A written code helps employees avoid confusion when determining whether their decisions are ethical.
- The process of formulating the code of ethics facilitates discussion among employees about what is right and wrong and ultimately leads to better decisions.

Businesses, however, must be careful not to make their code of ethics too vague or too detailed. Codes that are too vague give little or no guidance to employees in their day-to-day activities. Codes that are too detailed encourage employees to substitute rules for judgment. For instance, if employees are involved in questionable behavior, they may use the absence of a written rule as a reason to continue behaving that way, even though their conscience may be telling them to stop. Following a set of ethical guidelines will not guarantee the "rightness" of a decision, but it will improve the chances that the decision will be ethical.

Although many companies have issued policies on ethical behavior, marketing managers must still put the policies into effect. They must address the classic "matter of degree" issue. For example, marketing researchers must often resort to deception to obtain unbiased answers to their research questions. Asking for a few minutes of a respondent's time is dishonest if the researcher knows the interview will last 45 minutes. Not only must management post a code of ethics, but it must also give examples of what is ethical and unethical for each item in the code. Moreover,

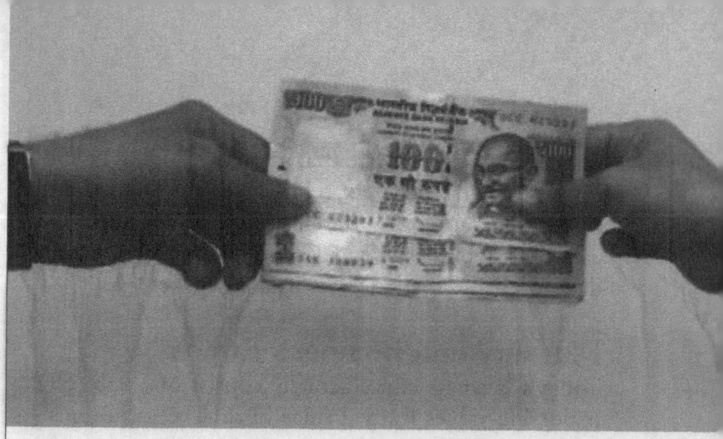

top management must stress to all employees the importance of adhering to the company's code of ethics. Without a detailed code of ethics and top management's support, creating ethical guidelines becomes an empty exercise.

The American Marketing Association's code of ethics highlights three general norms and six ethical values. Ethics training is an excellent way to help employees put good ethics into practice. In the 2008 National Business Ethics Survey (U.S.), the Ethics Resource Center, U.S. found that 75 percent of businesses have a physical, written code of ethics, but only 66 percent have ethics orientation or training in place. Businesses should remember that it is often mid- to lower-level employees who are best equipped to spot an ethical blindspot that managers miss when involved in keeping the company afloat. By encouraging and training employees to report unethical behaviors, businesses can keep out of ethical scandals and be well respected.[7]

Ethics in Other Countries

Studies suggest that ethical beliefs vary little from culture to culture. Certain practices, however, such as the use of illegal payments and bribes, are far more acceptable in some places than in others, though increasingly enforced laws are making the practice less accepted. One such law, that deals with concern about U.S. corporations' use of illegal payments and bribes in international business dealings, is called the **Foreign Corrupt Practices Act (FCPA)**. This act prohibits U.S. corporations from making illegal payments to public officials of foreign governments to obtain business rights or to enhance their business dealings in those countries. The act has been criticized for putting U.S. businesses at a competitive disadvantage. Many contend that bribery is an unpleasant but necessary part of international business, especially in countries such as China, where business gift giving is widely accepted and expected. But with an increase in the FCPA's prosecutions worldwide, some countries are implementing their own anti-bribery laws. For example, even though China is among the three countries with the most international corruption prosecutions by the FCPA, the country is working to develop its own anti-bribery laws. In 2010, Chinese courts imprisoned four employees of Rio Tinto, a mining company in London, for taking bribes.[8] In India too, we have the **Prevention of Corruption Act, 1988** that deals with matters of corruption and bribery. The penalties for such cases can range from imprisonment up to five years to an unlimited fine. Another agency that was set up to deal with such matters was the Central Vigilance Commission (CVC). However, the most effective measure for fighting bribery and corruption has been the **Right to Information (RTI) Act, 2005**. As per KPMG's Bribery and Corruption Survey 2011, 23 percent of the respondents voted RTI Act as the most effective measure to curb bribery and corruption, while 16 percent of the respondents felt it was CVC.[9]

LO 3 Corporate Social Responsibility

Corporate social responsibility (CSR) is a business's concern for society's welfare. This concern is demonstrated by managers who consider both the long-range best interests of the company and the company's relationship to the society within which it operates. The newest theory in social responsibility is called **sustainability.** This refers to the idea that socially responsible companies will outperform their peers by focusing on the world's social problems and viewing them as opportunities to build profits and help the world at the same time. It is also the notion that companies cannot thrive for long (i.e., lack sustainability) in a world where billions of people are suffering and are desperately poor. Thus, it is in business's interest to find ways to attack society's ills.

Another view is that business should focus on making a profit and leave social and environmental problems to nonprofit organizations and government. Economist Milton Friedman believed that the free market, and not companies, should decide what is best for the world.[10] Friedman argued that to the degree that business executives spend more money than necessary—to purchase delivery vehicles with hybrid engines, pay higher wages in developing countries, or even donate company funds to charity—they are

Prevention of Corruption Act an Indian act that deals with matters of corruption and bribery

Right to Information (RTI) Act an act of the Parliament of India that provides the citizens with a right to access to government information

corporate social responsibility (CSR) a business's concern for society's welfare

sustainability the idea that socially responsible companies will outperform their peers by focusing on the world's social problems and viewing them as opportunities to build profits and help the world at the same time

ENVIRONMENTAL ETHICS

© INDIATODAYIMAGES.COM

The Indian constitution identifies environmental protection as a fundamental duty of every citizen. Several laws and acts have been framed for safeguarding the natural environment. However, with rising industrial and corporate activities, the impact on environment has been quite hazardous. There has been gradual depletion of natural resources and pollution of all sorts—air, water, soil—has grown at an alarming rate. For example, alumina mining in Orissa in East India has been slammed for causing water and air pollution, thereby causing serious threat to health of local communities. Iron ore mining in Bellary district of Karnataka has also received flak for causing environmental degradation due to over-exploitation of the area. Coca-Cola too has been at the receiving end in Kerala for depleting water resources and polluting the area where their plant is located.[11]

pyramid of corporate social responsibility a model that suggests corporate social responsibility is composed of economic, legal, ethical, and philanthropic responsibilities and that the firm's economic performance supports the entire structure

spending shareholders' money to further their own agendas. Better to pay dividends and let the shareholders give the money away, if they choose.

Total CSR has four components: economic, legal, ethical, and philanthropic.[12] The **pyramid of corporate social responsibility,** as shown in Exhibit 3.1, portrays economic performance as the foundation for the other three responsibilities. At the same time that it pursues profits (economic responsibility), however, a business is expected to obey the law (legal responsibility); to do what is right, just, and fair (ethical responsibilities); and to be a good corporate citizen (philanthropic responsibility). These four components are distinct but together constitute the whole. Still, if the company doesn't make a profit, then the other three responsibilities are moot.

Growth of Social Responsibility

Social responsibility of businesses is growing around the world. A recent study of social responsibility in selected countries asked the following: "Does your company consider social responsibility factors when making business decisions?" The percentage of firms that said yes were Brazil, 62 percent; Canada, 54 percent; Australia, 52 percent; the United States, 47 percent; India, 38 percent; China, 35 percent; and Mexico, 26 percent.[13] Another survey pointed out that 47 percent of American firms was simply not adequate. Seventy-five percent felt that U.S. companies needed to do more in the area of social responsibility.[14]

United Nations Global Compact

One way that corporate firms can do more is by joining the United Nations Global Compact (UNGC). The UNGC, the world's largest global corporate citizenship initiative, has seen its ranks swell over the past few years. It was launched in India in 2000 and more than 100 companies have joined it till date, agreeing to abide by ten principles covering, among other things, human rights, labor practices, and the environment. In its tenth-anniversary Annual Review, the UNGC boasts more than 8,000 participants in 135 countries.

Firms are realizing that CSR isn't easy or quick. It doesn't work without long-term strategy, effort, and coordination throughout the enterprise. It doesn't always come cheap, either. And the payoff, both to society and the business itself, isn't always immediate. Businesses say they want to be responsible citizens, but that's often not their only reason for taking action. In a recent survey, the UNGC asked members why they had joined. "Networking opportunities" was the second most popular reason; "addressing humanitarian concerns" was third. The first was to "increase trust in company."[15]

EXHIBIT 3.1
Pyramid of Corporate Social Responsibility

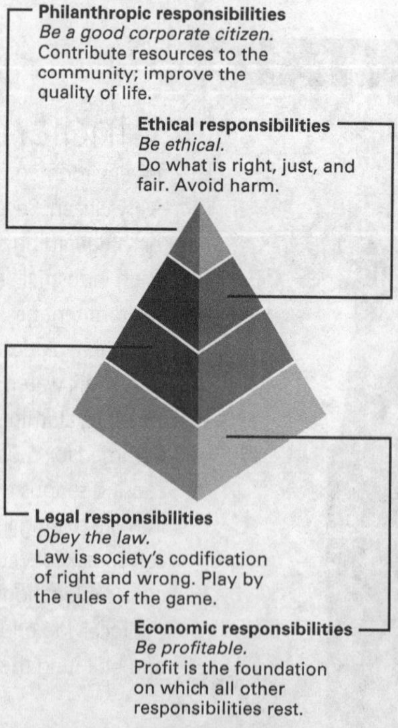

The Cost of Ignoring Social Responsibilities

Implementing a program for CSR can reap significant dividends, as a poll of 1,001 adults showed in 2010. Seventy percent of respondents said they would pay a premium price for goods from a socially responsible company, and 28 percent would pay as much as ₹450 more for a socially responsible company's product.

With that kind of potential payoff, it's not surprising that many companies are looking to increase awareness of their CSR. But making false claims about social responsibility can have huge costs.

Now BP's image is suffering because one of its oil rigs exploded in the Gulf of Mexico on April 20, 2010. At the time this was written, coastal economies were lagging without fishing or tourism, pressure from the White House was mounting, and BP was facing huge expenditures for the explosion. At a minimum, BP has had to dedicate a ₹90,000 crore fund to U.S. damage and wage claims, as mandated by the White House. In addition, BP has put aside a separate ₹450 crore fund to support the oil workers laid off by the ban on deepwater drilling. Some analysts estimate that the cleanup could cost nearly ₹4,50,000 crore, forcing BP into bankruptcy.[16]

Union Carbide had been in the midst of storm during the Bhopal Gas tragedy that struck in 1984. Around 20,000 people died and more than 5.5 lakh suffered bodily damage, when poisonous gases leaked from a faulty tank and spread into the houses situated near its plant. The company received heavy flak from all sections of the society and was asked to pay compensation, amounting to ₹713 crore to the victims.[17] The company was later purchased by Dow Chemical in 1999. Recently, there was a great furore over Dow Chemical being declared as one of the sponsors of London Olympics, 2012. Social groups, athletes, and Indian politicians demanded for shelving off the company's sponsorship due to its association with Union Carbide. However, the company views this sponsorship as a means of entering new markets like Russia and Brazil, and portraying itself as a solutions provider rather than a utilities company.[18]

© ISTOCKPHOTO/THINKSTOCK

Green Marketing

An outgrowth of the social responsibility movement is green marketing. **Green marketing** is the development and marketing of products designed to minimize negative effects on the physical environment or to improve the environment.[19] Not only can a company aid the environment through green marketing, but it often helps its bottom line as well. Environmentally aware consumers tend to earn more and are willing to pay more for green products. However, only a very small percentage of customers make their buying decisions based primarily on the environmentally friendly qualities of a product.[20] Also, marketers may have to educate the consumer about the green product if its environmental benefit is not readily apparent. To make the sale, the green marketer may even use a traditional non-green benefit. Toyota launched its international bestseller, Prius Hybrid, in 2010 in India. The launch signified the optimism that the carmakers have in the Indian market's desire for green vehicles. The car comes with an electric battery that supports the internal combustion engine and can be driven in three modes—power, eco, and electric. It gives a smooth driving experience, with almost zero noise level. Toyota managed in selling 150 units of the car since its launch. Recently, it launched a newer version of the car that comes with an additional solar ventilation system, along with the already present battery technology.[21]

green marketing
the development and marketing of products designed to minimize negative effects on the physical environment or to improve the environment

Some green products have practical consumer benefits that are readily apparent to consumers. A few examples are energy-efficient appliances (cut electric bills), heat-reflective windows (cut air-conditioning costs), and organic foods (no pesticides poisoning the food or planet).

Review and Applications

Explain the concept of ethical behavior. Ethics are the moral principles or values that generally govern the conduct of an individual or group. They are standards of behavior by which conduct is judged. Though many of these standards are considered legal, they are unethical. An ethics violation offends a person's sense of justice or fairness. Ethics basically constitute the unwritten rules developed to guide interactions. Many ethical questions arise from balancing the need to produce profit for shareholders and the expectation of a business to operate honestly and with respect to environmental and social issues.

1.1 It is sometimes said that ethics hold a person to higher standards than laws. Explain.

1.2 Moral relativists are basically time and place ethicists. Explain what this means.

Describe ethical behavior in business. Business ethics may be viewed as a subset of the values of society as a whole, with a foundation based on the cultural values and norms that constitute a culture's morals. The ethical conduct of businesspeople is shaped by societal elements, including family, education, and religious institutions. As members of society, businesspeople are morally obligated to consider the ethical implications of their decisions. Ethical decision making can be grouped into three basic approaches. The first approach examines the consequences of decisions. The second approach relies on rules and laws to guide decision making. The third approach is based on a theory of moral development that places individuals or groups in one of three developmental stages: preconventional morality, conventional morality, or postconventional morality.

In addition to personal influences, there are many business influences on ethical decision making. Some of the most influential include the extent of ethical problems within the organization, top management's actions on ethics, potential magnitude of the consequences, social consensus, probability of a harmful outcome, length of time between the decision and the onset of consequences, and the number of people affected.

Many companies develop a code of ethics to help their employees make ethical decisions. A code of ethics can help employees identify acceptable business practices, be an effective internal control on behavior, help employees avoid confusion when determining whether decisions are ethical, and facilitate discussion about what is right and wrong.

Studies show that ethical beliefs vary little from country to country. However, there are enough cultural differences, such as bribes or gift giving, that laws such as the *Foreign Corrupt Practices Act (FCPA)* have been put in place to discourage bribery and attempt to modify the current acceptance of such practices.

2.1 Explain the difference between ethics and morals and describe the relationship between the two.

2.2 What are the differences between pre-conventional morality, conventional morality, and post-conventional morality? Give an example of each.

2.3 Give several examples of how ethical practices can vary from one culture to the next.

Discuss corporate social responsibility. Responsibility in business refers to a firm's concern for the way its decisions affect society. Social responsibility has four components: economic, legal, ethical, and philanthropic. These are intertwined, yet the most fundamental is earning a profit. If a firm does not earn a profit, the other three responsibilities are moot. Most businesspeople believe they should do more than pursue profits. Although a company must consider its economic needs first, it must also operate within the law, do what is ethical and fair, and be a good corporate citizen. *Sustainability* is the concept that socially responsible companies will outperform their peers by focusing on the world's social problems and viewing them as an opportunity to earn profits and help the world at the same time. Social responsibility is growing, but it can be costly and the benefits are not always immediate. However, ignoring social responsibility can be even more expensive if customers perceive they are being taken advantage of. One branch of social responsibility is green marketing, which aids the environment and often the bottom line of a business.

3.1 Describe at least three situations in which you would not purchase the products of a firm even though it is very socially responsible.

3.2 A firm's only responsibility to society is to earn a fair profit. Comment.

3.3 Is sustainability a viable concept for India's Business?

3.4 Illustrate how there can be conflicts between the needs and desires of various stakeholders.

Exercises

APPLICATION EXERCISE

Many companies today are concerned with social responsibility. They may pursue philanthropic activities and/or strive to be ethical. Your goal for this assignment is to evaluate how firms are being socially responsible. Limit your answers to one page and provide a printout of the Web site you visited.

Activities

1. Choose a company and find that company's Web site on the Internet. Once you get to the Web site, look for information that tells you about the firm's efforts to be socially responsible. Look for things like news releases, company information, information about community programs, etc. Look in your textbook and your notes to help you define what might be considered socially responsible activities. Describe what you find and explain why you think the company is involved with the activities you describe.
2. Do the activities described on the Web site seem consistent with the company's products? Why or why not? (For example, a shoe company may sponsor a race that raises money to help prevent a disease. People who participate in the race may use that company's running shoes and therefore the race would be consistent with the company's products.)
3. Evaluate how effective you think the information you find is in terms of how it is presented, what impact it might have and whether it will help to sell the company's products. Be sure to support any claims you make.
4. Does the information you collected during this activity improve your evaluation of the company? Would it influence your decision to buy the company's product? Why or why not?

ETHICS EXERCISE

Kanika Mathur, a leading Bollywood actress is endorsing a skin rejuvenation cream. Advertisements in the form of TV ads and hoardings and posters are put up everywhere. The crème manufacturing company expects that the ads will pull in more consumers for the cream. However, in reality Kanika has undergone a couple of cosmetic surgeries to look the way she currently does. It is not the cream that Kanika is endorsing has made her look any better.

Questions

1. Should Kanika endorse a product she has not used herself for the prescribed purpose?
2. Is there any trade commission that will address this issue
3. What does Kanika risk in making false claims in her ads?

MARKETING PLAN EXERCISE

These end-of-chapter marketing plan exercises are designed to help you use what you learned in the chapter to build a strategic marketing plan for a company of your choosing. Once you've completed the marketing plan exercise for each chapter in Part 1 of this textbook, you can complete the Part 1 Marketing Planning Worksheet on your companion Web site at **www.cengage.com/international.**

In the first part of this exercise (Chapter 2) you described your chosen company, wrote its mission statement, and set its marketing objectives. Use the following exercises to guide you through the next part of your strategic marketing plan:

1. Identify any ethical issues that could impact your chosen firm. What steps should be taken to handle these issues?
2. How should your company integrate corporate social responsibility into its marketing plan?
3. In addition to suggestions for philanthropic responsibilities, write up a brief code of ethics for your firm. To see other codes of ethics, go to **www.iit.edu/libraries/csep/codes/coe.html.**

Short Case: ITC

Prepared by
Dr. Dheeraj Sharma,
Indian Institute of Management, Ahmedabad

Tobacco is one of the major health hazards prevailing in India and is one of the major causes of death. Globally, there is a significant debate on how tobacco adversely affects the social, economic, health and environmental factors of a country. The major cause of concern in its consumption lies in its increasing dependency, social acceptability, and aggressive marketing, targeting the youth. To an extent, the media is responsible in attracting the youth by associating such product with celebrities, glamour through both direct and indirect advertising.

Indian Tobacco Company (ITC) is the leading organization in the cigarette industry in India. The cigarette market is widely fragmented into several segments. ITC has an offering in almost all price ranges in cigarette industry. Its brands include Insignia, India Kings, Lucky Strike, Classic, Gold Flake, Navy Cut, Players, Scissors, Capstan, Berkeley, Bristol, Flake, Silk Cut, and Duke & Royal.[22]

India passed the Cigarettes and Other Tobacco Products Act in 2003 (COTPA). COTPA governs and regulates tobacco marketing, supply, production and distribution in India[23]. Before the enforcement of law, billboards with ads on Indian and International all forms of tobacco including cigarette brands could be seen. There were many companies that would sponsor various sports events promoting their brand name that was directly associated with cigarettes. To name among a few, Wills (brand of ITC) sponsored the cricket tournaments, Gold Flake (brand name of Geoffrey Philips India Ltd.) sponsored tennis tournaments, Four Square (brand of Geoffrey Philips India Ltd.) sponsored boat racing etc. Also, cultural events such as Filmfare awards were being sponsored by these companies like Manikchand, a manufacturer of gutka (chewing tobacco).[24]

Enforcement of Law:

Looking at the harmful effects of tobacco, Government enforced COTPA in many ways. This act banned smoking in public places, selling tobacco-based goods to minors, and any form of advertising of tobacco products. The act made it an obligation to mention the statutory warning on products like cigarettes, in English and in one Indian language: *"Chewing tobacco/cigarette smoking is injurious to health"* on the packaging of the product, etc.[25]

Reaction to Enforcement of Law:

COTPA came with a mixed reaction in the whole country. Those opposing the COTPA felt that Tobacco was one of the most profitable businesses and one of the main sources of providing employment not only in India but the world all over. The whole world economy has become somewhat dependent on the tobacco industry.[26] Also, many consumer groups were of the view that the law was interfering in the personal lives of people and that it is an individual decision. Lastly, tobacco companies further argued that that it was legal to manufacture and sell tobacco, then why was it not legal to advertise it?

However, many consumer groups countered the above. It was argued that the benefits of decrease in tobacco consumption would outweigh its negative effects on the economic interest. Illness of citizens of a country on account of tobacco usage resulted in economic burden on the country. Reduced tobacco consumption would lead to improvement of public health, reduction in diseases, and deaths leading to a more healthy and active work force. Healthy and active workforce would result in increased productivity and growth. In general, reduced tobacco consumption would also result in a better quality of life in terms of cleaner surroundings, fresh air, reduction in absenteeism, preservation of forest, healthier future citizens, etc.[27]

Questions

1. What are ethical dilemmas confronted by ITC as a rising concerns on tobacco marketing and distribution in India?
2. How should ITC respond to changes in consumer perspective on tobacco consumption in India?

3 Ethics and Social Responsibility

KEY TERMS

LO 1

ethics the moral principles or values that generally govern the conduct of an individual or a group

LO 2

morals the rules people develop as a result of cultural values and norms

code of ethics a guideline to help marketing managers and other employees make better decisions

Foreign Corrupt Practices Act (FCPA) a law that prohibits U.S. corporations from making illegal payments to public officials of foreign governments to obtain business rights or to enhance their business dealings in those countries

LO 3

corporate social responsibility (CSR) a business's concern for society's welfare

sustainability the idea that socially responsible companies will outperform their peers by focusing on the world's social problems and viewing them as opportunities to build profits and help the world at the same time

pyramid of corporate social responsibility a model that suggests corporate social responsibility is composed of economic, legal, ethical, and philanthropic responsibilities and that the firm's economic performance supports the entire structure

green marketing the development and marketing of products designed to minimize negative effects on the physical environment or to improve the environment

KEY CONCEPTS

LO 1

Explain the concept of ethical behavior. Ethics are the moral principles or values that generally govern the conduct of an individual or group. They are standards of behavior by which conduct is judged. Though many of these standards are considered legal, they are unethical. An ethics violation offends a person's sense of justice or fairness. Ethics basically constitute the unwritten rules developed to guide interactions. Many ethical questions arise from balancing the need to produce profit for shareholders and the expectation of a business to operate honestly and with respect to environmental and social issues.

LO 2

Describe ethical behavior in business. Business ethics may be viewed as a subset of the values of society as a whole, with a foundation based on the cultural values and norms that constitute a culture's morals. The ethical conduct of businesspeople is shaped by societal elements, including family, education, and religious institutions. As members of society, businesspeople are morally obligated to consider the ethical implications of their decisions. Ethical decision making can be grouped into three basic approaches. The first approach examines the consequences of decisions. The second approach relies on rules and laws to guide decision making. The third approach is based on a theory of moral development that places individuals or groups in one of three developmental stages: preconventional morality, conventional morality, or postconventional morality.

In addition to personal influences, there are many business influences on ethical decision making. Some of the most influential include the extent of ethical problems within the organization, top management's actions on ethics, potential magnitude of the consequences, social consensus, probability of a harmful outcome, length of time between the decision and the onset of consequences, and the number of people affected.

Many companies develop a code of ethics to help their employees make ethical decisions. A code of ethics can help employees identify acceptable business practices, be an effective internal control on behavior, help employees avoid confusion when determining whether decisions are ethical, and facilitate discussion about what is right and wrong.

Studies show that ethical beliefs vary little from country to country. However, there are enough cultural differences, such as bribes or gift giving, that laws such as the *Foreign Corrupt Practices Act (FCPA)* have been put in place to discourage bribery and attempt to modify the current acceptance of such practices.

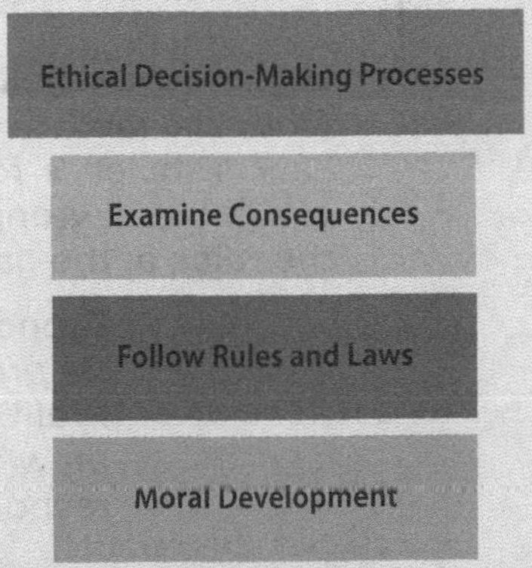

Some Factors Attributing to Ethical Conduct

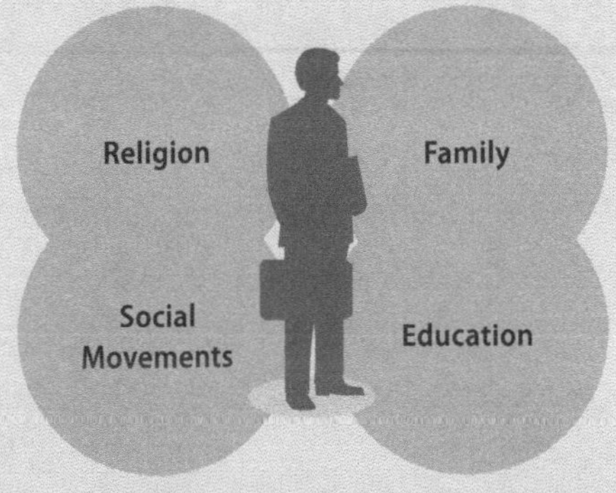

© CENGAGE LEARNING 2011

LO 3 **Discuss corporate social responsibility.** Responsibility in business refers to a firm's concern for the way its decisions affect society. Social responsibility has four components: economic, legal, ethical, and philanthropic. These are intertwined, yet the most fundamental is earning a profit. If a firm does not earn a profit, the other three responsibilities are moot. Most businesspeople believe they should do more than pursue profits. Although a company must consider its economic needs first, it must also operate within the law, do what is ethical and fair, and be a good corporate citizen. *Sustainability* is the concept that socially responsible companies will outperform their peers by focusing on the world's social problems and viewing them as an opportunity to earn profits and help the world at the same time. Social responsibility is growing, but it can be costly and the benefits are not always immediate. However, ignoring social responsibility can be even more expensive if customers perceive they are being taken advantage of. One branch of social responsibility is green marketing, which aids the environment and often the bottom line of a business.

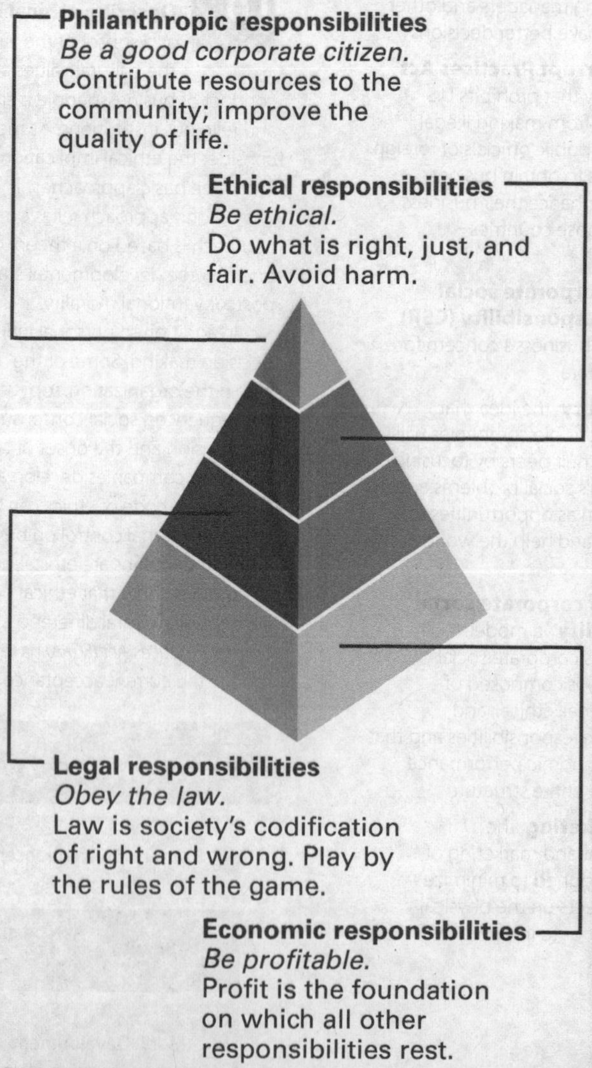

CHAPTER 4

The Marketing Environment

Learning Outcomes

LO 1 Discuss the external environment of marketing and explain how it affects a firm

LO 2 Describe the social factors that affect marketing

LO 3 Explain the importance to marketing managers of current demographic trends

LO 4 Identify consumer and marketer reactions to the state of the economy

LO 5 Identify the impact of technology on a firm

LO 6 Discuss the political and legal environment of marketing

LO 7 Explain the basics of foreign and domestic competition

Although managers can control the marketing mix, they cannot control elements in the external environment.

LO1 The External Marketing Environment

Perhaps the most important decisions a marketing manager must make relate to the creation of the marketing mix. Recall from Chapters 1 and 2 that a marketing mix is the unique combination of product, place (distribution), promotion, and price strategies. The marketing mix is, of course, under the firm's control and is designed to appeal to a specific group of potential buyers. A **target market** is a defined group that managers feel is most likely to buy a firm's product.

target market a defined group most likely to buy a firm's product

Managers must alter the marketing mix because of changes in the environment in which consumers live, work, and make purchasing decisions. Also, as markets mature, some new consumers become part of the target market; others drop out. Those who remain may have different tastes, needs, incomes, lifestyles, and buying habits than the original target consumers. Mattel's Barbie was the top-selling fashion doll in the United States for almost 50 years. Yet she fell victim to changing tastes and competition, most notably from Bratz, a line of edgier, more ethnically diverse dolls. Barbie's market share in 2000 was over 80 percent but now is less than 50 percent.[1] Mattel has launched a major marketing effort to regain market share. India too has witnessed a few innovations in Barbie that were made to customize the doll as per the Indian market. For instance, Barbie doll was crafted to look like the Bollywood star Katrina Kaif and was launched in India in 2011.[2]

***Note:** All the figures in U.S. dollars are converted into rupee using the value $1 = ₹45.*

environmental management when a company implements strategies that attempt to shape the external environment within which it operates

Although managers can control the marketing mix, they cannot control elements in the external environment that continually mold and reshape the target market. Controllable and uncontrollable variables affect the target market, whether it consists of consumers or business purchasers. The uncontrollable elements in the center of the environment continually evolve and create changes in the target market. In contrast, managers can shape and reshape the marketing mix to influence the target market. That is, managers react to changes in the external environment and attempt to create a more effective marketing mix.

Understanding the External Environment

Unless marketing managers understand the external environment, the firm cannot intelligently plan for the future. Thus, many organizations assemble a team of specialists to continually collect and evaluate environmental information, a process called environmental scanning. The goal in gathering the environmental data is to identify future market opportunities and threats.

Environmental Management

No single business is large or powerful enough to create major change in the external environment. Thus, marketing managers are basically adapters rather than agents of change. For example, despite the huge size of firms like General Electric, Walmart, Apple, and Caterpillar, they don't control social change, demographics, or other factors in the external environment.

However, just because a firm cannot fully control the external environment, it doesn't mean that it is helpless. Sometimes a firm can influence external events. For example, extensive lobbying by FedEx has enabled it to acquire virtually all the Japanese routes it has sought. When a company implements strategies that attempt to shape the external environment within which it operates, it is engaging in **environmental management.**

The factors within the external environment that are important to marketing managers can be classified as social, demographic, economic, technological, political and legal, and competitive.

LO 2 Social Factors

Social change is perhaps the most difficult external variable for marketing managers to forecast, influence, or integrate into marketing plans. Social factors include our attitudes, values, and lifestyles. Social

e-READER BONANZA BY BORDERS GROUP

As competing booksellers sell their own e-readers, Apple sells its iPad, and Sony broadens its line of devices, Borders Group is joining the fray—but with a strategy geared toward the middle-class customer who wants the status of new technology without paying a premium for it immediately. Borders research found that customers want to have several e-reader options value priced between ₹4,500 and ₹6,750. The group partnered with a series of technology teams to offer e-readers at lower price points. They've already launched two: the ₹6,705 Kobo eReader and the ₹5,355 Libre eBook reader pro. Borders group also plans to arrange sections in each store where customers can browse and purchase e-readers with the help of sales staff, offering a convenient one-stop shop for e-readers.

© GREGORY WRONA/ALAMY

factors influence the products people buy; the prices paid for products; the effectiveness of specific promotions; and how, where, and when people expect to purchase products.

A person's values are key determinants of what is important and not important, what actions to take or not to take, and how one behaves in social situations.

People typically form values through interaction with family, friends, and other influencers such as teachers, religious leaders, and politicians. The changing environment can also play a key role in shaping one's values.

Values influence our buying habits. Today's consumers are demanding, inquisitive, and discriminating. No longer willing to tolerate products that break down, they are insisting on high-quality goods that save time, energy, and often calories. Shoppers are also concerned about nutrition and want to know what's in their food, and many have environmental concerns.

The Growth of Component Lifestyles

A lifestyle is a mode of living; it is the way people decide to live their lives. In other words, they are choosing products and services that meet diverse needs and interests rather than conforming to traditional stereotypes.

In the past, a person's profession—for instance, banker—defined his or her lifestyle. Today, a person can be a banker and also a gourmet, fitness enthusiast, dedicated single parent, and Internet guru. Each of these lifestyles is associated with different goods and services and represents a target audience. **Component lifestyles** increase the complexity of consumers' buying habits. The unique lifestyles of every consumer can require a different marketing mix.

component lifestyles the practice of choosing goods and services that meet one's diverse needs and interests rather than conforming to a single, traditional lifestyle

The Changing Role of Families and Working Women

Component lifestyles have evolved because consumers can choose from a growing number of goods and services, and most have the money to exercise more options. The growth of dual-income families has resulted in increased purchasing power. Of the total employed Indian population in 2009, females constituted 27.3% of it.[3] The phenomenon of working women has probably had a greater effect on marketing than any other social change.

As women's earnings grow, so do their levels of expertise, experience, and authority. Working-age women are not the same group businesses targeted 30 years ago. They expect different things in life—from their jobs, from their spouses, and from the products and services they buy. With busy schedules, women are looking for solutions that are easy to understand and are less time consuming, thereby make their life easier. This has led to growth of

© ISTOCKPHOTO/THINKSTOCK
© PHOTODISC/THINKSTOCK

THE GROWTH OF DUAL-INCOME FAMILIES HAS RESULTED IN INCREASED PURCHASING POWER.

demography the study of people's vital statistics, such as age, race and ethnicity, and location

ready-to-cook food category, with brands like Kitchens of India, and MTR Foods operating well in the category.

There Is Never Enough Time

Research shows that the percentage of people who say they never have enough time to do all that they need to do keeps increasing.

A New York sociologist calls our emerging work-life culture "weisure time." There is no time to decompress. Also, new research has shown that being constantly tethered to e-mail, Smartphones, tablets, and other digital media can take a toll on a person's life and ability to focus. Such immersion in a digital life can cause multitaskers to have more fractured thinking and to have trouble shutting out irrelevant information—even when they are offline.[4]

LO 3 Demographic Factors

Another uncontrollable variable in the external environment—also extremely important to marketing managers—is demography, the study of people's vital statistics, such as age, race and ethnicity, and location. Demographics are significant because the basis for any market is people. Demographic characteristics are strongly related to consumer buyer behavior in the marketplace.

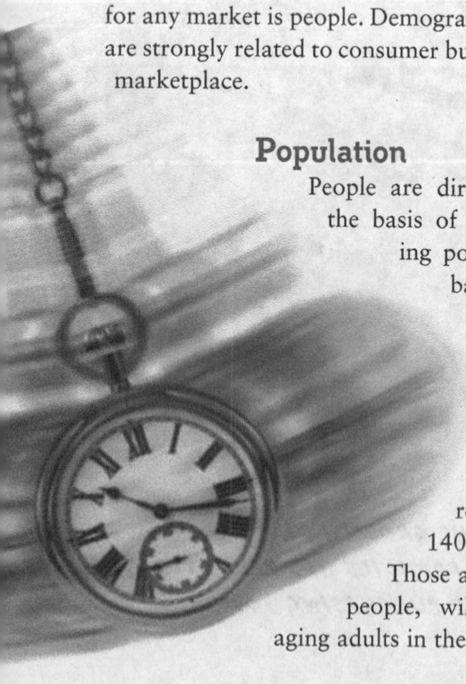

© ISTOCKPHOTO.COM/RTIMAGES

Population

People are directly or indirectly the basis of all markets, making population the most basic statistic in marketing. The Indian population is now slightly above 120 crore and is expected to reach more than 140 crore by 2025[5]. Those additional 20 crore people, will replace middle aging adults in the workforce, and in all likelihood, keep the economy vital and life interesting. But they also will further crowd cities and highways, put new strains on natural resources, and probably widen the gulf between society's haves and have-nots. India has about 399 people per square kilometre nationwide as of 2009[6], and is likely to increase to 426 people per square kilometre with the increase in population.[7] But the majority of the population increase is happening in just a dozen or so cities, such as Mumbai, New Delhi, Bengaluru, and Ahmedabad, while central and eastern states are growing slowly, if at all. Those who are able to move despite the difficult housing market and economic slowdown tend to downsize and relocate from the suburbs back to cities where there are more job openings.[8] This trend is likely to result in megacities of 2.5 crore or more as the population increases and jobs become available.

Population is a broad statistic that is particularly useful when broken into smaller increments. Age groups present opportunities to focus on a section of the population and offer opportunities for marketers. These groups are called babies and infants, kids, tweenagers, teens, twenty-somethings, thirty-somethings, middle-aged adults, and older population. You will find that each cohort group has its own needs, values, and consumption patterns.

Babies and Infants[9]

By 2009, number of babies and infants in India was 7.4 crore and they accounted for 6.3% of the entire population of India. With more number of parents in urban India becoming discerning and choosy customers with rising discretionary incomes, Indian market is slowly witnessing the entry of major players in baby care from all over the world. As of 2009, baby care sales in India were dominated by two categories—baby skin care and baby toiletries—contributing over 80% of all baby care value sales

Kids[10]

Children in the age group 3–8 years categorize as kids. In 2009, there were nearly 14.7 crore kids in India. Kids usually have no decision making power; it is the parents who decide on what clothes, shoes, and toys to buy for their kids.

Tweenagers[11]

These are the children falling in the age group 9–12 years. There were more than 9.6 crore tweenagers in

India in 2009. With a weekly allowance ranging from ₹50–100 in middle class families and ₹300–1,000 in rich families, the tweens have sufficient amount at their disposable to buy things like books, toys, and eatables. For purchasing big ticket items, the decision lies in the hands of the parents, though tweens use their "pestering power" to influence the buying decision. Their choices are mostly influenced by what they see in media or what their peers have.

Teens[12]

These are the children falling in the age group 13–19 years. They form a major part of Indian population and numbered to 16.5 crore in 2009. The teens like to consider themselves as fashion conscious. Over the past few years, several companies have launched products specifically for this segment such as Clean & Clear by Johnson & Johnson. The pocket money of teens ranges from ₹300–500 per week in middle class families to ₹1,000–3,000 per week in rich families. The teens mostly spend their pocket money on music, mobile phone bills, and fast food. They are also the most active group on social networking sites. This was highlighted in the survey carried out by the IT firm, Tata Consultancy Services, in the English medium schools in the age group 12–18 years. Social networking awareness was found in 93% of the respondents and 63% of urban students spent more than an hour online daily. 46% respondents used online resources for the purpose of accessing news. This segment is also highly comfortable with using electronic gadgets and new technologies available in the market.

Twenty-somethings[13]

Ever since 1995, this segment has been continuously increasing and is likely to be the second largest component (17.6%) of the total population by 2020. As of 2009, their number stood at 20.7 crore. This segment is technologically savvy and this has resulted in high consumption of electronics and computers. This group also spends significantly on personal care products. Urban Indian men are also becoming very conscious of their looks and men's grooming market is witnessing rapid growth. With more number of women entering employment, women's formal wear market too is growing at fast pace.

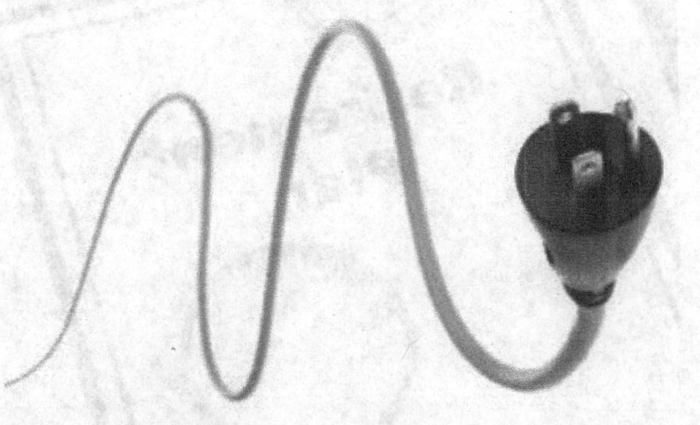

Thirty-somethings[14]

This segment is expected to form third largest constituent (15.4%) of total population by 2020. In 2009, this group numbered to 16.6 crore. In terms of urban India, this group generally consists of married couples with no kids or couples with one child. A major portion of the disposable income of this segment is spent on family activities such as eating out, travelling, and personal vehicles. Since most of them are double income couples, this group also spends its income on buying such electronic appliances that help them in completing household chores in less time.

Middle-aged Adults[15]

As of 2010, this segment, comprising of 40-64 years old, constituted largest proportion (21.9%) of Indian

© HEMERA/THINKSTOCK

population at a staggering 25.5 crore. Their major expenditure categories consist of health-related products, insurance products, children's education, retirement planning, vacations, and automobiles.

Older Population[16]

This group formed nearly 5% of India's total population in 2010 at 5.6 crore and is likely to rise to 6.3% in 2020. This segment mostly consists of retirees, who are dependent on their children for their day-to-day living. Majority of their expenditure happens on medication and health related products.

LO 4 Economic Factors

In addition to social and demographic factors, marketing managers must understand and react to the economic environment. The three economic areas of greatest concern to most marketers are consumers' incomes, inflation, and recession.

As disposable (or after-tax) incomes rise, more families and individuals can afford the "good life." In recent years, Indian incomes have risen at a significant pace and have shown quite a robust growth. Per capita disposable income in India stood at ₹39,857 in 2009 and was projected to rise to ₹43,016 in 2010. One and a half percent of the total Indian households qualified as well-off households i.e. those having a disposable income above ₹11,25,000 a year or more.

Education is the primary determinant of a person's earning potential. For example, the median income of a graduate/diploma holder was ₹85,215 as compared to ₹48,000 of a school pass-out.[17]

Along with "willingness to buy," or "ability to buy," income is a key determinant of target markets. A marketer who knows where the money is knows where the markets are. If you are seeking a new store location for Choupal Sagar, a retail chain that caters to lower-income rural consumers, especially farmers, you would probably concentrate on the states like Madhya Pradesh, Uttar Pradesh, and Maharashtra because these states are major contributors to agriculture in India and most households have annual incomes of less than ₹25,000.[18]

Purchasing Power

Rising incomes don't necessarily mean a higher standard of living. Increased standards of living are a function of purchasing power. **Purchasing power** is

purchasing power a comparison of income versus the relative cost of a set standard of goods and services in different geographic areas

© ISTOCKPHOTO/THINKSTOCK

measured by comparing income to the relative cost of a set standard of goods and services in different geographic areas, usually referred to as the cost of living. Another way to think of purchasing power is income minus the cost of living (i.e., expenses). In general, a cost of living index takes into account housing, food and groceries, transportation, utilities, health care, and miscellaneous expenses such as clothing, services, and entertainment.

When income is high relative to the cost of living, people have more discretionary income. That means they have more money to spend on nonessential items (in other words, on wants rather than needs). This information is important to marketers for obvious reasons. Consumers with high purchasing power can afford to spend more money without jeopardizing their budget for necessities like food, housing, and utilities. They also have the ability to purchase higher-priced necessities—for example, a more expensive car, a home in a more expensive neighborhood, or a designer handbag versus a purse from a discount store.

Inflation

Inflation is a measure of the decrease in the value of money, generally expressed as the percentage reduction in value since the previous year, which is the rate of inflation. Thus, in simple terms, an inflation rate of 5 percent means you will need 5 percent more units of money than you would have needed last year to buy the same basket of products. If inflation is 5 percent, you can expect that, on average, prices have risen by about 5 percent since the previous year. Of course, if pay raises are matching the rate of inflation, then employees will be no worse off in terms of the immediate purchasing power of their salaries.

inflation a measure of the decrease in the value of money, expressed as the percentage reduction in value since the previous year

recession a period of economic activity characterized by negative growth, which reduces demand for goods and services

In times of low inflation, businesses seeking to increase their profit margins can do so only by increasing their efficiency. If they significantly increase prices, no one will purchase their goods or services. The recent recession brought inflation rates to almost zero.

In creating marketing strategies to cope with inflation, managers must realize that, regardless of what happens to the seller's cost, the buyer is not going to pay more for a product than the subjective value he or she places on it. No matter how compelling the justification might be for a 10 percent price increase, marketers must always examine its impact on demand. Many marketers try to hold prices level for as long as is practical.

Recession

A **recession** is a period of economic activity characterized by negative growth. More precisely, a recession is defined as when the gross domestic product falls for two consecutive quarters. Gross domestic product is the total market value of all final goods and services produced during a period of time. The official beginning of the 2007–2009 recession was December 2007. While the causes of the recession are very complex, this one began with the collapse of inflated housing prices. Those high prices led people to take out mortgages they couldn't afford from banks that should have known the money would not be repaid. By 2008, the recession had spread around the globe. A very slow economic recovery began in July 2009.

The 2007–2009 recession, called "the Great Recession" by some, was the largest economic downturn since the Great Depression of 1929 to 1939 in the U.S. Unemployment rose from slightly over 4 percent to over 10 percent.[19] The unemployment rate has been slowly falling since mid-2010 due to job creation and people leaving the workforce entirely. Uncertain economic times have caused many consumers to shift to store brands that, on average, cost 46 percent less than manufacturers' brands.[20] Researchers found that during the recession, consumers were sticking very close to shopping lists and doing their best to completely empty their pantries before restocking. Also, consumers were going to fewer stores but selecting stores where they could get the widest array of products at the best value.

LO 5 Technological Factors

The recent economic downturn and slow recovery has had an impact on research and development (R&D) spending. In order to cut costs and boost short-term profits, many companies, particularly in the auto and drug industries, slashed R&D, product design, and laboratory spending. Other firms have taken a different tact and either increased or held R&D spending steady hoping that they can more effectively compete when the economy improves. Companies such as 3M, Microsoft, Google, Intel, and Cisco Systems have followed this strategy.

Research

Basic research (or *pure research*) attempts to expand the frontiers of knowledge but is not aimed at a specific, pragmatic problem. Basic research aims to confirm an existing theory or to learn more about a concept or phenomenon. For example, basic research might focus on high-energy physics. **Applied research**, in contrast, attempts to develop new or improved products. The United States has dramatically improved its track record in applied research. For example, the United States leads the world in applying basic research to aircraft design and propulsion systems. However, in 2009, non-Americans were granted more U.S. patents than resident inventors.[21] This is partially the result of U.S. companies sending R&D offshore. One reason R&D has moved offshore is that the United States once had the most generous tax credits for R&D. Now it ranks 17th among developed countries.

Stimulating Innovation

Companies attempting to innovate often limit their searches to areas they are already familiar with. This can help lead to incremental progress but rarely leads to a dramatic breakthrough. Companies are now using several approaches to keeping innovation strong. These include:

- *Build scenarios.* Some firms use teams of writers to imagine detailed opportunities and threats for their companies, partners, and collaborators in future markets.
- *Enlist the Web.* A few companies have created Web sites that act as literal marketplaces of ideas where they can go to look for help with scientific and business challenges.
- *Talk to early adopters.* Early adopters tend to be innovators themselves. They are risk takers and look for new things or wish for something better to help in daily tasks at home and work.
- *Use marketing research.* Find out what customers like and dislike about your products and competitors' products.
- *Create an innovative environment.* Let employees know that they have the "freedom to fail." Create intranets to encourage sharing ideas. Most importantly, top management must lead by example to create an atmosphere where innovation is encouraged and rewarded.
- *Cater to entrepreneurs.* Policies that reserve blocks of time for scientists or engineers to explore their own ideas have worked well at some companies. At 3M, scientists can spend 15 percent of their time on projects they dream up themselves, and the company has set procedures to take bright ideas forward, including grants and venture funding.[22]

basic research pure research that aims to confirm an existing theory or to learn more about a concept or phenomenon

applied research an attempt to develop new or improved products

Although developing new technology internally is a key to creating and maintaining a long-term competitive advantage, external technology is also important to managers for two reasons. First, by acquiring the technology, the firm may be able to operate more efficiently or create a better product. Second, a new technology may render existing products obsolete.

Innovation Carries to the Bottom Line Innovation pays off big for creative organizations. One study

TOP TEN MOST INNOVATIVE COMPANIES[23]

1. Apple (U.S.)
2. Google (U.S.)
3. Microsoft (U.S.)
4. IBM (U.S.)
5. Toyota Motor (Japan)
6. Amazon.com (U.S.)
7. LG Electronics (South Korea)
8. BYD (China)
9. General Electric (U.S.)
10. Sony (Japan)

found that the most innovative firms have an average profit margin growth that is 3 percent higher than that of the typical firm.[24] Other research found higher stock market returns among firms that spend heavily on R&D.[25]

LO 6 Political and Legal Factors

Business needs government regulation to protect innovators of new technology, the interests of society in general, one business from another, and consumers. In turn, government needs business because the marketplace generates taxes that support public efforts to educate our youth, pave our roads, protect our shores, and so on.

Every aspect of the marketing mix is subject to laws and restrictions. It is the duty of marketing managers or their legal assistants to understand these laws and conform to them, because failure to comply with regulations can have major consequences for a firm. Sometimes just sensing trends and taking corrective action before a government agency acts can help avoid regulation.

The challenge is not simply to keep the marketing department out of trouble, however, but to help it implement creative new programs to accomplish marketing objectives. It is all too easy for a marketing manager or sometimes a lawyer to say "no" to a marketing innovation that actually entails little risk. For example, an overly cautious lawyer could hold up sales of a desirable new product by warning that the package design could prompt a copyright infringement suit. Thus, it is important to have a thorough understanding of the laws established by the federal government, state governments, and regulatory agencies to govern marketing-related issues.

Federal Legislation

Federal laws that affect marketing fall into several categories of regulatory activity: competitive environment, pricing, advertising and promotion, and consumer privacy. The key pieces of legislation in these areas are summarized in Exhibit 4.1 given below.

Regulatory Agencies

Agencies such as Department of Consumer Affairs, Food Safety and Standards Authority of India, and Bureau of Indian Standards are directly and actively

EXHIBIT 4.1

Important laws governing business

Law	Functions performed
Arbitration and Reconciliation Act, 1996	Law relating to alternative redress of disputes among parties.
Companies Act, 1956	Governs all corporate bodies.
Competition Act, 2002	Law to ensure free and fair competition in the market.
Consumer Protection Act, 1986	Law relating to the protection of consumers from unscrupulous traders or manufacturers.
Environment Protection Act, 1986	Provides a framework for seeking environmental clearances.
Foreign Trade (Development and Regulation) Act, 1992	Empowers the central government to make provisions for the development and regulation of foreign trade by facilitating imports into, and augmenting exports from, India and for all matters connected therewith or incidental thereto.
Information Technology Act, 1999	Law governing e-commerce transactions.
Monopolies and Restrictive Trade Practices Act, 1969	The main objectives of the act are to provide for the establishment of a commission to prevent practices having an adverse effect on competition; to promote and sustain competition in markets in India; to protect the interests of consumers; and to ensure the freedom of trade carried out by the participants in the markets in India and for related matters.
Patents Act, Copyright Act, Trade Marks Act	Protects intellectual property rights.

Department of Consumer Affairs (DCA) an agency responsible for consumer welfare and protection and devises policies for consumer cooperatives; it also handles matters related to price monitoring and availability of essential commodities

Food Safety and Standards Authority of India (FSSAI) an agency that ensures availability of safe, healthy, and wholesome food for consumption by humans

Bureau of Indian Standards (BIS) an agency responsible for developing standardization and quality certifications for products and services in 14 distinct sectors

involved in marketing affairs. A brief introduction and the functions performed by these agencies are provided at this point.

Department of Consumer Affairs (DCA)[26] comes under Ministry of Consumer Affairs and Food & Public Distribution. The department is responsible for consumer welfare and protection and devises policies for consumer cooperatives and consumer movement across the country. It also takes care of matters related to monitoring of prices and availability of essential commodities. The Right to Information Act comes under the purview of DCA and it is also the controlling authority of other statutory bodies such as Bureau of Indian Standards and Weights and Measures.

Food Safety and Standards Authority of India (FSSAI)[27] was established under Food Safety and Standards Act, 2006. The main objective of the organization is to make certain the availability of safe, healthy, and wholesome food for consumption by humans. It is responsible for handling and regulating issues related to food such as their manufacturing, storage, distribution, sale, and import.

Some of the important functions performed by FSSAI are:

- Laying down standards and guidelines for articles of food and ensuring the enforcement of the standards thus notified
- Laying down guidelines for accreditation of such bodies that are engaged in the certification of food safety
- Laying down guidelines for accreditation of laboratories and notification of the laboratories that have been accredited
- Providing advice and support to Central and State Governments in matters related to framing of rules and policies with respect to food safety and nutrition
- Providing training program for such people involved or wanting to get involved in food business
- Promoting general awareness about safety and standards of food

Bureau of Indian Standards (BIS)[28] is responsible for developing standardization and quality certifications for products and services in 14 distinct sectors. Such certifications work as a third party guarantee to the customers regarding a product's quality, reliability and safety. More than 18,000 areas have been devised till date in different areas of technology. These standards can be in terms of product specifications, codes of practice, other guidelines, glossaries, and basic standards. The two most well known certification marks issued by BIS are ISI mark for industrial products and BIS Hallmark for gold jewellery.

LO 7 Competitive Factors

The competitive environment encompasses the number of competitors a firm must face, the relative size of the competitors, and the degree of interdependence within the industry. Management has little control over the competitive environment confronting a firm.

Competition for Market Share and Profits

Sometimes technology advances can usher in a whole new set of competitors that can change a firm's business model. American aircraft manufacturer Boeing still faces competition from European company Airbus, even though Airbus recently lost its edge in that ₹2,25,000 crore market. Airbus has been beset with problems, while Boeing's new 787 Dreamliner gave the company a much needed lift. By 2010, Boeing had sold over 866 Dreamliners, whereas the huge Airbus A350 lagged far behind. Both Boeing and Airbus have experienced delivery problems. Boeing's difficulties have been due to parts availability and a machinist strike. Airbus has experienced management and logistics problems.

Global Competition

With a fast growing economy and a burgeoning middle class population, many foreign competitors are considering India to be a ripe target market. Thus, an Indian marketing manager can no longer focus only on domestic competitors. In automobiles, textiles, watches, televisions, and many other areas, foreign competition has been strong. In the past, foreign firms penetrated Indian markets with a worldwide common product, but today the emphasis has switched to understand and adapt to the needs of Indian consumers. In automobiles, textiles, watches, televisions, steel, and many other areas, foreign competition has been

LOCATION, LOCATION, WE HAVE YOUR LOCATION

As Smartphones and mobile devices with Internet access have proliferated, so has the software available to consumers. Many apps provide information about your immediate area, restaurants, even traffic conditions. Some software can calculate your location to within 60 feet and then sell your location to nearby companies to advertise to you. Using consumer locations to sell advertisements has recently raised alarm bells, which spurred Rep. Rick Boucher (D-Virginia) to draft legislation. He, and most legislation-wary marketers, want consumers to know what kind of data is being collected about them, how long it is kept, and what it's used for. Developers may not be harmful, but hackers and accidents may be, depending on the information the developer has collected.[29]

© ISTOCKPHOTO.COM/JELENA POPIC

strong. Companies like Nestlé, Sony, Rolls-Royce, and Sandoz Pharmaceuticals are noted and regarded for their superior quality. Global competition is discussed in much more detail in Chapter 5.

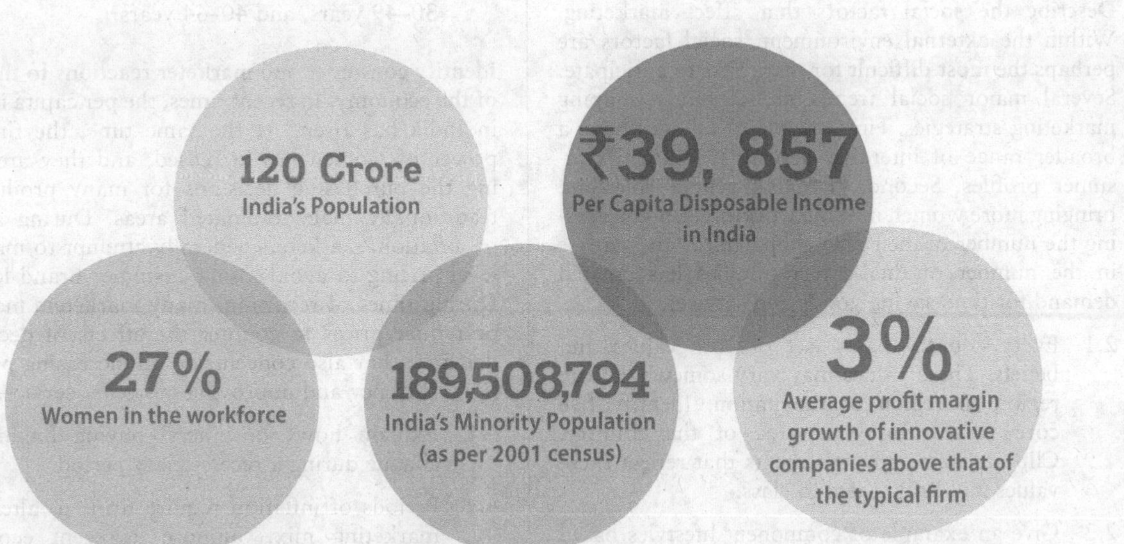

Review and Applications

Discuss the external environment of marketing and explain how it affects a firm. The external marketing environment consists of social, demographic, economic, technological, political and legal, and competitive variables. Marketers generally cannot control the elements of the external environment. Instead, they must understand how the external environment is changing and the impact of that change on the target market. Then marketing managers can create a marketing mix to effectively meet the needs of target customers.

1.1 What is the purpose of environmental scanning? Give an example.

1.2 Form six teams and make each one responsible for one of the uncontrollable elements in the marketing environment. Your boss, the company president, has asked each team to provide one-year and five-year forecasts of the major trends the firm will face. This firm is in the telecommunications equipment industry. It has no plans to become a telecommunications service provider like, for example, Airtel and RCom. Each team could use the library, the Internet, and other data sources to make its forecasts. Each team member should examine a minimum of one data source. The team members should then pool their data and prepare a recommendation. A spokesperson for each team should present the findings to the class.

Describe the social factors that affect marketing. Within the external environment, social factors are perhaps the most difficult for marketers to anticipate. Several major social trends are currently shaping marketing strategies. First, people of all ages have a broader range of interests, defying traditional consumer profiles. Second, changing gender roles are bringing more women into the workforce and increasing the number of men who shop. Third, an increase in the number of dual-career families has created demand for time-saving goods and services.

2.1 Every country has a set of core values and beliefs. These values may vary somewhat from region to region of the nation. Identify five core values for your area of the country. Clip magazine advertisements that reflect these values and bring them to class.

2.2 Give an example of component lifestyles based on someone you know.

Explain the importance to marketing managers of current demographic trends. Today, several basic demographic patterns are influencing marketing mixes. Because, the Indian population is increasing at a fast rate, marketers can rely on profits generated from the domestic markets. Contrarily, because the U.S. population is increasing at a slower rate, marketers can no longer rely on profits from generally expanding markets. Marketers are faced with increasingly experienced consumers among the younger generations such as tweens and teens. Also because the majority of the population is young, marketers are offering products that appeal more to the young consumers than to the middle-aged and older consumers.

3.1 Majority of the Indians are young. Describe how this affects the marketing mix for the following:

a. Talwalkars Fitness Clubs

b. McDonald's

c. Levi's Corporation

d. Walmart Stores

e. Goa Tourism

3.2 You have been asked to address a local Chamber of Commerce on the subject of "Twenty-somethings." Prepare an outline for your talk.

3.3 How should Ford Motor Company market differently to people in the age group 20–29, years, 30–49 years, and 40–64 years?

Identify consumer and marketer reactions to the state of the economy. In recent times, the per capita income in India has risen. At the same time, the financial power of women has increased, and they are making the purchasing decisions for many products in traditionally male-dominated areas. During a time of inflation, marketers generally attempt to maintain level pricing to avoid losing customer brand loyalty. During times of recession, many marketers maintain or reduce prices to counter the effects of decreased demand; they also concentrate on increasing production efficiency and improving customer service.

4.1 Explain how consumers' buying habits may change during a recessionary period.

4.2 Periods of inflation require firms to alter their marketing mix. Suppose a recent economic forecast predicts that inflation will be almost

10 percent during the next 18 months. Your company manufactures hand tools for the home gardener. Write a memo to the company president explaining how the firm may have to alter its marketing mix.

Identify the impact of technology on a firm. Monitoring new technology is essential to keeping up with competitors in today's marketing environment. India has improved in basic research in the recent years. However, a lot still needs to be done in this front. Without innovation, Indian companies cannot effectively compete in the global markets. Innovation is increasingly becoming a global process.

5.1 Give three examples of how technology has benefited marketers. Also, give several examples of firms that have been hurt because they did not keep up with technological changes.

Discuss the political and legal environment of marketing. All marketing activities are subject to state and federal laws and the rulings of regulatory agencies. Marketers are responsible for remaining aware of and abiding by such regulations. Some key federal laws that affect businesses and marketing are the Arbitration and Reconciliation Act, Companies Act, Competition Act, Consumer Protection Act, Environment Protection Act, Foreign Trade (Development and Regulation) Act, Information Technology Act, Monopolies and Restrictive Trade Practices Act, Patents Act, Copyright Act, and Trade Marks Act. Many laws, including privacy laws, have been passed to protect the consumer as well. The Department of Consumer Affairs, Food Safety and Standards Authority of India, and the Bureau of Indian Standards are the three regulatory agencies most involved in regulating marketing activities.

6.1 To what degree do you think the government should regulate marketing? Explain your position.

6.2 Can you think of any other areas where consumer protection laws are needed?

6.3 What topics are currently receiving attention in FDA News (www.fdanews.com)? What effect has the attention had on market share?

Explain the basics of foreign and domestic competition. The competitive environment encompasses the number of competitors a firm must face, the relative size of the competitors, and the degree of interdependence within the industry. Rising population growth, increase in disposable incomes, and changing lifestyles have heightened domestic competition.

7.1 Explain how the nature of competition is changing in India.

7.2 Might there be times when a company becomes too competitive? If so, what could be the consequences?

Exercises

APPLICATION EXERCISE

Demographic factors play a large role in shaping the external marketing environment. One of those demographic factors is culture. The importance of cultural understanding cannot be overstated, especially in today's global marketplace and our own multicultural country.

One way to be exposed to another culture is to examine the foods typical of that culture. In this exercise, you will need to work in a team to create a guide to ethnic dining in your city or area. The finished guide will be descriptive in nature; it is not meant to be a rating guide.

Activities

1. Identify ethnic dining categories for inclusion in your guide. Once you have identified categories for your area, make a list of restaurants for each category.
2. You will need to create a data collection form so that the same information is collected from each restaurant. For example, you will want to include the name, address, and phone number for each restaurant. Think of other information that would be helpful.
3. Divide up the restaurant list your team generated in activity 1 so that each team member is responsible for collecting information from a certain number of restaurants. Consider dividing the list geographically so that each team member can visit an assortment of ethnic restaurants. If your budget allows, eat at a few of the restaurants in addition to collecting the information. After you have all the information, meet to review and compare your findings.
4. Was there a meal or type of food that you particularly liked? Disliked? Which type of ethnic restaurant seemed most foreign to you? Why do you think that was?

ETHICS EXERCISE

Mr. Verma has developed a new "energy drink" designed to burn calories while sleeping, which he intends to market to target grossly overweight consumers. A study indicates that the 5% of the Indian population suffers from morbid obesity.[30] Mr Verma's mother, a doctor, argues that it's unethical to target the obese- that they are as vulnerable a target market as much as the elderly and children.

Questions

1. Is Mr. Verma targeting a "vulnerable" market?
2. Does the AMA Statement of Ethics address this issue? Go to **www.marketingpower.com** and review the statement. Then write a brief paragraph on what it contains that relates to Mr. Verma's marketing decision.

MARKETING PLAN EXERCISE

These end-of-chapter marketing plan exercises are designed to help you use what you learned in the chapter to build a strategic marketing plan for a company of your choosing. Once you've completed the marketing plan exercise for each chapter in Part 1 of this textbook, you can complete the Part 1 Marketing Planning Worksheet on your companion Web site at **www.cengage.com/international.** Now continue building your strategic marketing plan that you started in Chapter 2 by completing the following exercises:

1. Describe how your company will handle privacy concerns.
2. Scan the marketing environment. Identify opportunities and threats to your chosen company in areas such as technology, the economy, the political and legal environment, and competition. Is your competition foreign, domestic, or both? Also identify opportunities and threats based on possible market targets, including social factors, demographic factors, and multicultural issues.
3. Complete your company's SWOT analysis by identifying opportunities and threats in the external marketing environment by performing environmental scanning:
   a. List the demographic ethnic, and social trends that could impact your firm, by investigating data from the Indian Census of India at **www.censusindia.gov.in.**
   b. Determine which economic factors could influence the strategies of your firm by visiting the Department of Economic Affairs (DEA) website.
   c. Explore **www.lawguru.com** and report on at least three political and legal factors that could influence your marketing decisions.
   d. Investigate the websites of the government agencies that regulate your firm and industry and list at least six laws that regulate your business offering.
   e. Identify your key competitors. A simple "Yellow Pages" listing of all firms in the same business category can start your search.
   f. Competition often comes from companies that are working on the same exact market as yours. That is especially true on the Internet. After you search for your direct competition, look for and think about what other companies are positioned to execute a similar business strategy for your target market. Determine if there are any players who might be able to develop technology more quickly or reach your target customers more effectively than you.

Short Case

© AP PHOTO/ELIZABETH DALZIEL

The Indian marketing environment (both micro and macro) is dynamic and this necessitates all the companies operating in the market to keep designing its strategies according to the changes taking place in the environment from time to time.

Selling Coffee in the Land of Tea

Starbucks has been doing business in China since 1999 when they opened their first coffee shop in Beijing. Today, hundreds of Starbucks stores sell coffee in the land of tea, including one at the Great Wall. It has become one of the most popular brands among the country's 20-to-40-year-old upwardly mobile Chinese, or "Chuppies," as they're called, but so far China accounts for only about 10 percent of Starbucks' global sales. Nevertheless, Chairman Howard Schultz believes the country will someday be the company's largest market outside North America. "The market response," he says, "has exceeded our expectations."

This may seem surprising when you consider the fact that the majority of China's one billion-plus population are tea drinkers who didn't know what coffee was until Nestlé introduced a powdered version on store shelves in the 1980s. But Starbucks is betting that they can win the new generation over by marketing its signature product as an emblem of modern China's new sophistication.

"Coffee represents the change," says Wang Jinlong, president of Starbucks Greater China. "The disposable income is concentrated on the young people, and this is the place they want to come." Success in China could depend on how well Starbucks markets itself to what Wang calls the "little emperors." China's one-child law has spawned a generation that isn't interested in collective goals, he says. Instead, they embrace the Western belief in individuality that Starbucks embodies.

After surveying Chinese consumers, Starbucks compiled a list of the top reasons they go to cafés. Surprisingly, the number-one reason was "to gather with family and friends," while "to drink coffee" lagged behind at number six. Living spaces are generally small and cramped there, making places to congregate important to the Chinese.

Da Wei Sun, manager of outlets in Beijing, believes that Starbucks found success in China because they took this idea of a place to gather and gave people in the cities a "third space" beyond work and home, making it cool to have a latte and hang out. Starbucks offers more food on the Chinese menu, including duck sandwiches, moon pies, and green-tea cheesecake, than in other countries, and more seating as well. Only 20 percent of North American customers eat and drink inside the store after ordering, but the number is close to 90 percent in China.

China remains a communist country, so a change in its one-party dictatorship could potentially affect business overnight. Schultz says the key to establishing stores there is to first find local partners who understand the changing political and business landscapes. Starbucks initially entered China by authorizing local developers to use their brand and setting up joint ventures with partners.

Industry analyst Pei Liang advised that for long-term success in the country, Starbucks would need to acquire controlling stakes in its joint ventures. This, Pei explained, would strengthen management's control and put them in position to reap more of the profits as the market grew. "Licensing or holding a minority stake is an effective tool when first stepping into a new market because it involves a small investment," says Pei. "But Starbucks, the brand's owner, receives only royalty fees from the licensee."

In late 2006, Starbucks announced that it was buying out its partner in China and taking control of 60 stores. The market had changed after Beijing entered the World Trade Organization in 2001, making it easier for foreign companies to navigate alone. "Buying out one's partner is becoming more common," says industry consultant Kent D. Kedl. "Starbucks probably feels they know better how China works now so they can go it on their own."

Chairman Howard Schultz says that Starbucks will concentrate most of its future expansion efforts in China, and Kedl predicts they will see continued success there: "It's not just a drink in China. It's a destination. It's a place to be seen and a place to show how modern one is." And with China's economy continuing to grow in double digits, the number of Chuppies willing to pay $3.63 (₹163.35) for a Mocha Frappuccino Grande is likely to grow, too.

Source: "Starbucks Targets Growing China Market," *AsiaPulse News*, 6/13/2006; Janet Adamy, "Starbucks' Task China? Winning Over Tea Drinkers," *The Seattle Times*, 11/30/2006; Jeffrey S. Harrison, "Exporting a North American Concept to Asia", *Cornell Hotel & Restaurant Quarterly*, May 2005; Craig Harris, "Starbucks Sees China as Key to Its International Growth," *Seattle Post-Intelligencer*, 10/7/2006; Dexter Roberts, "Starbucks Caffeinates Its China Growth Plan," *Business Week Online*, 10/26/2006.

Questions

1. Many of the same environmental factors, such as cultural factors, that operate in the domestic market also exist internationally. Discuss the key cultural factors Starbucks had to consider as it expanded into China.
2. Discuss the key political and legal factors Starbucks had to consider in the Chinese marketplace. What are the risks of entering a country with these factors? What changes have occurred in China's political and legal structure to the advantage of foreign companies?
3. What demographic factors were important for Starbucks to understand in China? What were the demographics they decided to target?
4. What was the initial global-market strategy Starbucks employed to enter China? Discuss the advantages and disadvantages to this early strategy. How has their strategy changed since then and why?

4 The Marketing Environment

KEY TERMS

LO 1

target market a defined group most likely to buy a firm's product

environmental management when a company implements strategies that attempt to shape the external environment within which it operates

LO 2

component lifestyles the practice of choosing goods and services that meet one's diverse needs and interests rather than conforming to a single, traditional lifestyle

LO 3

demography the study of people's vital statistics, such as age, race and ethnicity, and location

LO 4

purchasing power a comparison of income versus the relative cost of a set standard of goods and services in different geographic areas

inflation a measure of the decrease in the value of money, expressed as the percentage reduction in value since the previous year

recession a period of economic activity characterized by negative growth, which reduces demand for goods and services

LO 5

basic research pure research that aims to confirm an existing theory or to learn more about a concept or phenomenon

applied research an attempt to develop new or improved products

KEY CONCEPTS

LO 1 **Discuss the external environment of marketing and explain how it affects a firm.** The external marketing environment consists of social, demographic, economic, technological, political and legal, and competitive variables. Marketers generally cannot control the elements of the external environment. Instead, they must understand how the external environment is changing and the impact of that change on the target market. Then marketing managers can create a marketing mix to effectively meet the needs of target customers.

LO 2 **Describe the social factors that affect marketing.** Within the external environment, social factors are perhaps the most difficult for marketers to anticipate. Several major social trends are currently shaping marketing strategies. First, people of all ages have a broader range of interests, defying traditional consumer profiles. Second, changing gender roles are bringing more women into the workforce and increasing the number of men who shop. Third, a greater number of dual-career families has created demand for time-saving goods and services.

LO 3 **Explain the importance to marketing managers of current demographic trends.** Today, several basic demographic patterns are influencing marketing mixes. Because, the Indian population is increasing at a fast rate, marketers can rely on profits generated from the domestic markets. Contrarily, because the U.S. population is increasing at a slower rate, marketers can no longer rely on profits from generally expanding markets. Marketers are also faced with increasingly experienced consumers among the younger generations such as teens and twenty-somethings. Also because the majority of the population is young, marketers are offering products that appeal more to the young consumers than to the middle-aged and older consumers.

LO 4 **Identify consumer and marketer reactions to the state of the economy.** In recent years, Indian incomes have risen at a significant pace. At the same time, the financial power of women has increased, and they are making the purchasing decisions for many products in traditionally male-dominated areas. During a time of inflation, marketers generally attempt to maintain level pricing to avoid losing customer brand loyalty. During times of recession, many marketers maintain or reduce prices to counter the effects of decreased demand; they also concentrate on increasing production efficiency and improving customer service.

LO 5 **Identify the impact of technology on a firm.** Monitoring new technology is essential to keeping up with competitors in today's marketing environment. India has improved in basic research in the recent years. However, a lot still needs to be done in this front. Without innovation, Indian companies cannot effectively compete in the global markets. Innovation is increasingly becoming a global process.

LO 6 **Department of Consumer Affairs (DCA)** an agency responsible for consumer welfare and protection and devises policies for consumer cooperatives; it also handles matters related to price monitoring and availability of essential commodities

Food Safety and Standards Authority of India (FSSAI) an agency that ensures availability of safe, healthy, and wholesome food for consumption by humans

Bureau of Indian Standards (BIS) an agency responsible for developing standardization and quality certifications for products and services in 14 distinct sectors

LO 6 **Discuss the political and legal environment of marketing.** All marketing activities are subject to state and federal laws and the rulings of regulatory agencies. Marketers are responsible for remaining aware of and abiding by such regulations. Some key federal laws that affect businesses and marketing are the Arbitration and Reconciliation Act, Companies Act, Competition Act, Consumer Protection Act, Environment Protection Act, Foreign Trade (Development and Regulation) Act, Information Technology Act, Monopolies and Restrictive Trade Practices Act, and Patents Act, Copyright Act, and Trade Marks Act. Many laws, including privacy laws, have been passed to protect the consumer as well. The Department of Consumer Affairs, Food Safety and Standards Authority of India, and the Bureau of Indian Standards are the three regulatory agencies most involved in regulating marketing activities.

LO 7 **Explain the basics of foreign and domestic competition.** The competitive environment encompasses the number of competitors a firm must face, the relative size of the competitors, and the degree of interdependence within the industry. Rising population growth, increase in disposable incomes, and changing lifestyles have heightened domestic competition.

CHAPTER 5
Developing a Global Vision

Learning Outcomes

LO 1 Discuss the importance of global marketing

LO 2 Discuss the impact of multinational firms on the world economy

LO 3 Describe the external environment facing global marketers

LO 4 Identify the various ways of entering the global marketplace

LO 5 List the basic elements involved in developing a global marketing mix

LO 6 Discover how the Internet is affecting global marketing

Over the past two decades, world trade has climbed from ₹9,00,000 crore a year to over ₹4,95,00,000 crore.

LO 1 Rewards of Global Marketing

Today, global revolutions are under way in many areas of our lives: management, politics, communications, and technology. The word *global* has assumed a new meaning, referring to a boundless mobility and competition in social, business, and intellectual arenas. **Global marketing**—marketing that targets markets throughout the world—has become an imperative for business.

global marketing marketing that targets markets throughout the world

global vision recognizing and reacting to international marketing opportunities, using effective global marketing strategies, and being aware of threats from foreign competitors in all markets

Indian managers must develop a global vision not only to recognize and react to international marketing opportunities but also to remain competitive at home. Often an Indian firm's toughest domestic competition comes from foreign companies. Moreover, a global vision enables a manager to understand that customer and distribution networks operate worldwide, blurring geographic and political barriers and making them increasingly irrelevant to business decisions. In summary, having a **global vision** means recognizing and reacting to international marketing opportunities, using effective global marketing strategies, and being aware of threats from foreign competitors in all markets.

Over the past two decades, world trade has climbed from ₹900,000 crore a year to over ₹495,00,000 crore. Countries and companies that were never considered major players in global marketing are now showing great skill and becoming important.

Today's marketers face many challenges to their customary practices. Product development costs are rising, the life of products is getting shorter, and new technology is spreading around the world faster than ever. But marketing winners relish the pace of change instead of fearing it.

***Note:** All the figures in U.S. dollars are converted into rupee using the value $1 = ₹45.*

job outsourcing
sending U.S. jobs abroad

Adopting a global vision can be very lucrative for a company. Gillette, for example, gets about two-thirds of its annual revenue from its international division. H.J. Heinz, the ketchup company, gets over half of its revenue from international sales. Although Cheetos and Ruffles haven't done very well in Japan, the potato chip has been quite successful. PepsiCo's (owner of Frito-Lay) overseas snack business brings in more than ₹14,625 crores annually. The William Wrigley Jr. Company, makers of Wrigley's Spearmint, Juicy Fruit, Double Mint, Orbit and other products, has global annual sales of over ₹21,150 crores.[1]

Global marketing is not a one-way street whereby only Indian companies sell their wares and services throughout the world. Foreign competition in the domestic market was relatively rare but now is found in almost every industry.

Importance of Global Marketing to India

Many countries, including India, depend more on international commerce than economies like United States. For example, France, Britain, and Germany all derive more than 19 percent of their gross domestic product (GDP) from world trade, compared to about 12 percent for the United States. India has witnessed remarkable growth in its trade to GDP ratio since the introduction of trade reforms. The ratio has increased from 15% in 1990 to 35% in 2005.[2] Nevertheless, the impact of international business on the Indian economy is still impressive:

INDIAN TRADE STATS

- Total exports from India in 2009-10 amounted to ₹ 8,45,534 crores[3]
- Export sector generated a direct employment of 90 lakhs jobs in 2004-05[4]
- In 2009, India attained a rank of 21 in the list of leading exporters in world merchandise[5]
- The micro, small and medium enterprise (MSME) sector in India accounts for about 40 percent of total exports of the country[6]

The Fear of Trade and Globalization The protests during meetings of the World Trade Organization, the World Bank, and the International Monetary Fund (the three organizations are discussed later in the chapter) show that many people fear world trade and globalization. What do they fear? The negatives of global trade are as follows:

- Lakhs of Americans have lost jobs due to imports, production shifts abroad, or outsourcing of tech jobs. Some find new jobs, but they often pay less.
- Lakhs of others fear losing their jobs, especially at those companies operating under competitive pressure.
- Employers often threaten to outsource jobs if workers do not accept pay cuts.
- Service and white-collar jobs are increasingly vulnerable to operations moving offshore.

Job Outsourcing The notion of **job outsourcing** (sending U.S. jobs abroad) has been highly controversial for the past several years. Many executives say that it is about corporate growth, efficiency, productivity, and revenue growth. Most companies see cost savings as a key driver in outsourcing. India, because of its educated, English-speaking population, has always been a popular country for receiving offshoring work, and other countries are gaining as well.

Benefits of Globalization Traditional economic theory says that globalization relies on competition to drive down prices and increase product and service quality. Business goes to the countries that operate most efficiently and/or have the technology to produce what is needed. In summary, globalization expands economic freedom, spurs competition, and raises the productivity and living standards of people in countries that open themselves to the global marketplace. For less developed countries, globalization also offers access to foreign capital, global export markets, and advanced technology while breaking the monopoly of inefficient and protected domestic producers. Faster growth, in turn, reduces poverty, encourages democratization, and promotes higher labor and environmental standards. Though government officials may face more difficult choices as a result of globalization, their citizens enjoy greater individual freedom. In this sense, globalization acts as a check on governmental power by making it more difficult for governments to abuse the freedom and property of their citizens.

Globalization deserves credit for helping lift many lakhs out of poverty and for improving standards of living of low-wage families. In developing countries around the world, globalization has created a vibrant middle class that has elevated the standards of living for hundreds of lakhs of people. In many developing countries around the world, life expectancies and health care have improved, as have educational opportunities.[7]

LO 2 Multinational Firms

India has a number of large companies that are global marketers. Many of them have been very successful. A company that is heavily engaged in international trade, beyond exporting and importing, is called a multinational corporation. A multinational corporation moves resources, goods, services, and skills across national boundaries without regard to the country in which its headquarters is located.

Many India-based multinationals earn a large percentage of their total revenue abroad. Exhibit 5.1 shows revenue abroad for some companies. Tata Group, India's largest corporate conglomerate, earns about three-fifths of its revenue overseas.[8] Bharat Forge, an auto ancillary major, earns about 66 percent of its revenues abroad, and about 70 percent of revenues of Hindalco Industries, an Aditya Birla Group company, come from outside India.[9]

Multinationals often develop their global business in stages. In the first stage, companies operate in one country and sell into others. Second-stage multinationals set up foreign subsidiaries to handle sales in one country. In the third stage, multinationals operate an entire line of business in another country. The fourth stage has evolved primarily due to the Internet and involves mostly high-tech companies. For these firms, the executive suite is virtual. Their top executives and core corporate functions are in different countries, wherever the firms can gain a competitive edge through the availability of talent or capital, low costs, or proximity to their most important customers.

multinational corporation a company that is heavily engaged in international trade, beyond exporting and importing

A multinational company may have several worldwide headquarters, depending on where certain markets or technologies are. Britain's APV, a maker of food-processing equipment, has a different headquarters for each of its worldwide businesses.

The role of multinational corporations in developing nations is a subject of controversy. The ability of multinationals to tap financial, physical, and human resources from all over the world and combine them economically and profitably can be of benefit to any country. They also often possess and can transfer the most up-to-date technology. Critics, however, claim that often the wrong kind of technology

EXHIBIT 5.1

Industrial Companies with the Largest Overseas Revenue

GROWTH STRATEGY

(Rs crore)

Companies	Total revenue	Revenues from overseas	% of total revenue from overseas
Tata Motors	92,519	54,758	59.2
Tata Steel	102,393	75,254	73.5
Hindalco	60,722	42,548	70.1
Bharti Airtel	73,718	19,156	26
Bharat Forge	3,327	2,182	65.6
M&M	33,692	3,610	10.7
Sun Pharma	4,076	2,142	52.6
Dr Reddy's	7,383	6,102	82.7
L&T	43,664	11,490	26.3
RComm	21,496	4,017	18.7

Source: Raj, R., "Foreign forays fuel ascent of Indian MNCs," *The Indian Express*, January 28, 2011, http://www.indianexpress.com/news/foreign-forays-fuel-ascent-of-indian-mncs/743031/0.

capital intensive
using more capital than labor in the production process

global marketing standardization
production of uniform products that can be sold the same way all over the world

is transferred to developing nations. Usually, it is **capital intensive** (requiring a greater expenditure for equipment than for labor) and thus does not substantially increase employment. A "modern sector" then emerges in the nation, employing a small proportion of the labor force at relatively high productivity and income levels and with increasingly capital-intensive technologies. In addition, multinationals sometimes support reactionary and oppressive regimes if it is in their best interests to do so. Other critics say that the firms take more wealth out of developing nations than they bring in, thus widening the gap between rich and poor nations. The petroleum industry in particular has been heavily criticized in the past for its actions in some developing countries.

To counter such criticism, more and more multinationals are taking a proactive role in being good global citizens. Sometimes companies are spurred to action by government regulation, and in other cases multinationals are attempting to protect their good brand name.

Blocking Foreign Investment

A new backlash against multinational corporations is that governments from China to Canada are placing restrictions on foreign purchases of factories, land, and companies in their countries. Even the United States can be seen as erecting barriers to foreign investment. U.S. Congress passed legislation to subject foreign investment in the United States to review by an interagency council that screens foreign purchases of U.S. assets with national-security implications or threatens U.S.-based companies' employment. For example, when Anshan Iron and Steel Group, a Chinese steel conglomerate, invested in the American Steel Development Company, lawmakers pushed for the Committee on Foreign Investment in the United States (CFIUS) to investigate. Investigations have historically caused the U.S. companies to withdraw from investment negotiations.[10]

Now China's new regulations let government officials block a local purchase by a multinational if it is a danger to "economic security." Russia has considered blocking foreign ownership in 39 "strategic sectors" of its economy. If more countries begin to block foreign investment by multinationals, it will definitely have a noticeable impact on global trade.

Global Marketing Standardization

Traditionally, marketing-oriented multinational corporations have operated somewhat differently in each country. They use a strategy of providing different product features, packaging, advertising, and so on. However, Ted Levitt, a former Harvard professor, described a trend toward what he referred to as "global marketing," with a slightly different meaning.[11] He contended that communication and technology have made the world smaller so that almost all consumers everywhere want all the things they have heard about, seen, or experienced. Thus, he saw the emergence of global markets for standardized consumer products on a huge scale, as opposed to segmented foreign markets with different products. In this book, global marketing is defined as individuals and organizations using a global vision to effectively market goods and services across national boundaries. To make the distinction, we can refer to Levitt's notion as **global marketing standardization**.

Global marketing standardization presumes that the markets throughout the world are becoming more alike. Firms practicing global marketing standardization produce "globally standardized products" to be sold the same way all over the world. Uniform production should enable companies to lower production and marketing costs and increase profits. Levitt cited Coca-Cola, Colgate-Palmolive, and McDonald's as successful global marketers. His critics point out, however, that the success of these three companies is really based on variation, not on offering the same product everywhere. McDonald's,

for example, changes its salad dressings and provides self-serve espresso for French tastes. It sells bulgogi burgers in South Korea and falafel burgers in Egypt. Further, the fact that Coca-Cola and Colgate-Palmolive sell some of their products in more than 160 countries does not signify that they have adopted a high degree of standardization for all their products globally. Only three Coca-Cola brands are standardized, and one of them, Sprite, has a different formulation in Japan.

Nevertheless, some multinational corporations are moving toward a degree of global marketing standardization. Alan Mulally, CEO of Ford, claims that his company is moving toward global marketing standardization with its new Focus. The new Focus is Ford's first truly global car—a single vehicle designed and engineered for customers in every region of the world and sold under one name. It is small, fuel efficient, and packed with technology and safety features that Mulally believes will appeal to consumers in Europe, Asia, and the Americas. "Why are we doing it this way?" he asked. "Because we believe the customer requirements are going to be more the same around the world than they are different."[12]

LO 3 External Environment Facing Global Marketers

A global marketer or a firm considering global marketing must consider the external environment. Many of the same environmental factors that operate in the domestic market also exist internationally. These factors include culture, economic and technological development, political structure and actions, demographic makeup, and natural resources.

Culture

Central to any society is the common set of values shared by its citizens that determines what is socially acceptable. Culture underlies the family, the educational system, religion, and the social class system. The network of social organizations generates overlapping roles and status positions. These values and roles have a tremendous effect on people's preferences and thus on marketers' options. A company that does not understand a country's culture is doomed to failure in that country. Cultural blunders lead to misunderstandings and often perceptions of rudeness or even incompetence. For example, when people in India shake hands, they sometimes do so rather limply. This isn't a sign of weakness or disinterest; instead, a soft handshake conveys respect. Avoiding eye contact is also a sign of deference in India.

The rights to reproduce Broadway plays are increasingly being sold overseas, but the plays encounter some difficulty in translating cultural idioms and humor into the native languages. Performers in Seoul, South Korea, are producing the first non-English performance of *Billy Elliot the Musical*, but they are experiencing some cultural roadblocks. There is no Korean wordplay to mimic Billy's misinterpretation of "Billy Elliot Esquire" for "Billy Elliot is queer," so the translation uses some Korean profanity that requires parental permission to say. Some of the characters are very straightforward and cannot be "translated" into Korean culture, but the company is hopeful that the overall similarities in the plot will resonate with the audiences.[13]

Language is another important aspect of culture that can create problems for marketers. Marketers must take care in translating product names, slogans, instructions, and promotional messages so as not to convey the wrong meaning. Free translation software, such as babelfish.

A billboard in Hamburg, Germany, for Walt Disney's and Phil Collins's new musical, *Tarzan*.

© T. LEHNE/LOTUSEATERS/ALAMY

© POOL/GETTY IMAGES

com or Google Translate, allows users to input text in one language and output in another language. But marketers must take care using the software, as it can have unintended results—the best being unintelligible, the worst being insulting.

Each country has its own customs and traditions that determine business practices and influence negotiations with foreign customers. In many countries, personal relationships are more important than financial considerations. For instance, skipping social engagements in Mexico may lead to lost sales. Negotiations in Japan often include long evenings of dining, drinking, and entertaining, and only after a close personal relationship has been formed do business negotiations begin.

Making successful sales presentations abroad requires a thorough understanding of the country's culture. Germans, for example, don't like risk and need strong reassurance. A successful presentation to a German client will emphasize three points: the bottom-line benefits of the product or service, that there will be strong service support, and that the product is guaranteed. In southern Europe, it is an insult to show a price list. Without negotiating, you will not close the sale. The English want plenty of documentation for product claims and are less likely to simply accept the word of the sales representative. Scandinavian and Dutch companies are more likely to approach business transactions as Americans do than are companies in any other country.

Economic and Technological Development

A second major factor in the external environment facing the global marketer is the level of economic development in the countries where it operates. In general, complex and sophisticated industries are found in developed countries, and more basic industries are found in less developed nations. Average family incomes are higher in the more developed countries compared to the less developed countries. Larger incomes mean greater purchasing power and demand not only for consumer goods and services but also for the machinery and workers required to produce consumer goods.

According to the World Bank, the combined gross national income (GNI) of the 210 nations for which data are available is approximately ₹2,59,20,000 crores. Divide that up among the world's 680 crores inhabitants, and you get just ₹3,81,150 for every man, woman, and child on Earth. The United States accounts for almost a third of the income earned worldwide, or ₹65,25,000 crores—more than any other single country. If America's GNI were divided equally among its 30.3 crore residents, each American would receive ₹21,13,650—5.5 times the world average. Even so, Americans are still not the richest people on the planet. That title goes to the residents of Luxembourg, where the per capita GNI is ₹28,94,400.[14]

Bloomberg Businessweek ranked the world's most expensive cities, adjusted against the dollar. New York City ranks 29th, and Tokyo, Japan, takes the top spot. A two-bedroom apartment costs more than ₹225,000 a month in Tokyo, and a store-bought steak is easily ₹2250. Oslo, Norway, takes the second spot, and Luanda, Angola, the third.[15]

Doing Business in China and India

The two countries of growing interest to many multinationals are India and China because of their huge economic potential. They have some of the highest growth rates in the world and are emerging as mega-markets. Cell phone users in China, for example, exceed 45 crores, and the estimated figure for India is 15 crores—a number that is growing by sixty lakhs new subscribers each month.

China and India also have the world's two largest populations, two of the world's largest geographical areas, greater linguistic and sociocultural diversity than any other country, and among the highest levels of income disparity in the world—some people are extremely poor whereas others are very rich. Given this scale and variety, there is no "average Chinese customer" or "average Indian customer." Because of this diversity, market success in China and India is rarely possible without finely segmenting the local market in each country and developing a strategy tailored to the needs of the targeted segments.[16]

However, relations between the United States and China have been strained. China restricts the exchange rate of the yuan, does not

© ISTOCKPHOTO.COM/ROYDEE

enforce U.S. patents, and maintains policies that encourage Chinese products over American products. The United States wants these things to change in order to maintain influence and heal from financial struggles caused by recession. China, protecting its businesses and asserting new global strength, is reluctant to change, however. China has the power and draw of a country with steadily increasing consumption and high growth potential, particularly for the United States. China is the fastest-growing importer of U.S. goods—up 330 percent since 2000. The rest of the world increased their imports from the United States only 29 percent. If trade fails, China loses significant U.S. imports, and the United States loses a rapid growth market.[17]

Political Structure and Actions

Political structure is a third important variable facing global marketers. Government policies run the gamut from no private ownership and minimal individual freedom to little central government and maximum personal freedom. As rights of private property increase, government-owned industries and centralized planning tend to decrease. But a political environment is rarely at one extreme or the other. India, for instance, is a republic with elements of socialism, monopoly capitalism, and competitive capitalism in its political ideology.

Some of the world's biggest corporations are facing intense pressure from China to allow state-approved unions to form in their Chinese facilities, though many companies fear that admitting the unions will give their Chinese employees the power to disrupt their operations and increase the cost of doing business.

A recent World Bank study found that the least amount of business regulation fosters the strongest economies.[18] The least regulated and most efficient economies are concentrated among countries with well established common-law traditions, including Australia, Canada, New Zealand, the United Kingdom, and the United States. On a par with the best performers are Singapore and Hong Kong. Not far behind are Denmark, Norway, and Sweden, social democracies that recently streamlined their business regulation. Vietnam has decentralized and begun eliminating red tape that had previously turned investors away. The country is also benefitting from political and labour strife in neighbouring countries. Intel is opening a ₹4500 crores plant in Vietnam, and the Vietnamese government hopes that others will follow.

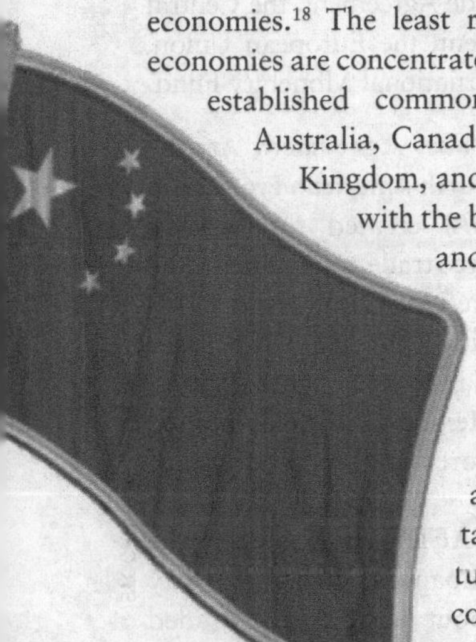

Mercosur the largest Latin American trade agreement; includes Argentina, Bolivia, Brazil, Chile, Colombia, Ecuador, Paraguay, Peru, and Uruguay

Legal Considerations Closely related to and often intertwined with the political environment are legal considerations. In France, nationalistic sentiments led to a law that requires pop music stations to play at least 40 percent of their songs in French (even though French teenagers love American and English rock and roll).

Many legal structures are designed to either encourage or limit trade.

- *Tariff: a tax levied on the goods entering a country.* Because a tariff is a tax, it will either reduce the profits of the firms paying the tariff or raise prices to buyers, or both. Normally, a tariff raises prices of the imported goods and makes it easier for domestic firms to compete. The United States maintains tariffs as high as 27 percent on Canadian softwood lumber because the Canadian government allegedly subsidizes the industry.
- *Quota: a limit on the amount of a specific product that can enter a country.* Several U.S. companies have sought quotas as a means of protection from foreign competition. For example, after Google stopped censoring its Chinese service, many Chinese companies boycotted the brand, including China Unicom, which had been using Google on its phones.[19]
- *Boycott: the exclusion of all products from certain countries or companies.* Governments use boycotts to exclude companies from countries with which they have a political dispute. Several Arab nations boycotted Coca-Cola because it maintained distributors in Israel.
- *Exchange control: a law compelling a company earning foreign exchange from its exports to sell it to a control agency, usually a central bank.* A company wishing to buy goods abroad must first obtain foreign currency exchange from the control agency. For instance, Avon Products drastically cut back new production lines and products in the Philippines because exchange controls prevented the company from converting pesos to dollars to ship back to the home office. The pesos had to be used in the Philippines.
- *Market grouping (also known as a common trade alliance): occurs when several countries agree to work together to form a common trade area that enhances trade opportunities.* The best-known market grouping is the European Union (EU).
- *Trade agreement: an agreement to stimulate international trade.* Not all government efforts are meant to stifle imports or investment by foreign corporations. The largest Latin American trade agreement is **Mercosur**, which includes Argentina, Bolivia, Brazil, Chile, Colombia, Ecuador, Paraguay, Peru, and Uruguay.

Uruguay Round an agreement to dramatically lower trade barriers worldwide; created the World Trade Organization

World Trade Organization (WTO) trade organization that replaced the old General Agreement on Tariffs and Trade (GATT)

General Agreement on Tariffs and Trade (GATT) a trade agreement that contained loopholes enabling countries to avoid trade-barrier reduction agreements

North American Free Trade Agreement (NAFTA) an agreement between Canada, the United States, and Mexico that created the world's largest free trade zone

The elimination of most tariffs among the trading partners has resulted in trade revenues of more than ₹72000 crores annually. The economic boom created by Mercosur will undoubtedly cause other nations to seek trade agreements on their own or to enter Mercosur.

The Uruguay Round, the Failed Doha Round, and Bilateral Agreements The **Uruguay Round** is an agreement that has dramatically lowered trade barriers worldwide. Adopted in 1994, the agreement has been signed by 151 nations. It is the most ambitious global trade agreement ever negotiated. The agreement has reduced tariffs by one-third worldwide—a move that has raised global income by ₹10,57,500 crores annually. Perhaps most notable is the recognition of new global realities. For the first time, an agreement covers services, intellectual property rights, and trade-related investment measures such as exchange controls.

The Uruguay Round made several major changes in world trading practices.

- *Entertainment, pharmaceuticals, integrated circuits, and software:* The rules protect patents, copyrights, and trademarks for 20 years. Computer programs receive 50 years of protection and semiconductor chips receive 10 years of protection. But many developing nations were given a decade to phase in patent protection for drugs. France, which limits the number of U.S. movies and television shows that can be shown, refused to liberalize market access for the U.S. entertainment industry.
- *Financial, legal, and accounting services:* Services came under international trading rules for the first time, creating a vast opportunity for these competitive U.S. industries. Now it is easier for managers and key personnel to be admitted to a country. Licensing standards for professionals, such as doctors, cannot discriminate against foreign applicants. That is, foreign applicants cannot be held to higher standards than domestic practitioners.
- *Agriculture:* Europe is gradually reducing farm subsidies, opening new opportunities for such U.S. farm exports as wheat and corn. Japan and Korea are beginning to import rice. But U.S. growers of sugar and citrus fruit have had their subsidies trimmed.
- *Textiles and apparel:* Strict quotas limiting imports from developing countries are being phased out, causing further job losses in the U.S. clothing trade. But retailers and consumers are the big winners, because past quotas have added ₹6,750 crores a year to clothing prices.
- *A new trade organization:* The **World Trade Organization (WTO)** replaced the old **General Agreement on Tariffs and Trade (GATT)**, which was created in 1948. WTO eliminated the extensive loopholes of which GATT members took advantage. Today, all WTO members must fully comply with all agreements under the Uruguay Round. The WTO also has an effective dispute settlement procedure with strict time limits to resolve disputes.

The latest round of WTO trade talks began in Doha, Qatar, in 2001. In the summer of 2008, after years of contentious meetings, the Doha Round collapsed. The demise of the Doha Round was the first multilateral (many nations) free trade act failure since World War II. The cost of the failure is estimated to be over ₹4,50,000 crores annually.

The failure of Doha has resulted in many countries seeking bilateral trade agreements. A bilateral agreement is simply a pact between two nations. America already has bilateral agreements with Australia, Bahrain, Chile, Israel, Jordan, Morocco, Peru, and Singapore. With recession troubles and suspicion toward the emerging Chinese market, pending bilateral trade agreements stalled in 2009. However, President Obama has been working to reopen a trade agreement with South Korea, a significant emerging market with the 14th largest economy in the world. President Obama also succeeded in bargaining with Russia to begin importing U.S. chicken again. Before banning U.S. chicken, Russia annually imported ₹3,375 crores worth of chicken parts.[20]

The trend toward globalization has resulted in the creation of additional agreements and organizations: the North American Free Trade Agreement, the Central America Free Trade Agreement, the European Union, the World Bank, and the International Monetary Fund.

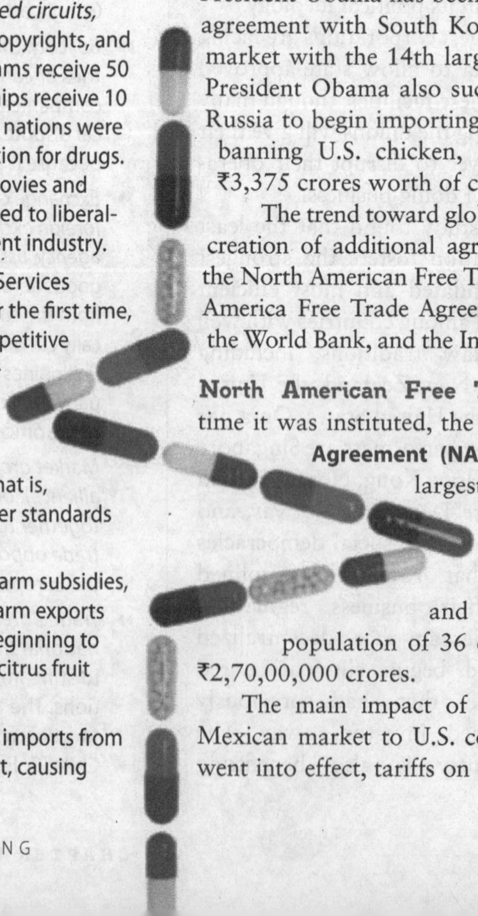

North American Free Trade Agreement At the time it was instituted, the **North American Free Trade Agreement (NAFTA)** created the world's largest free trade zone. Ratified by the U.S. Congress in 1993, the agreement includes Canada, the United States, and Mexico, with a combined population of 36 crores and an economy of ₹2,70,00,000 crores.

The main impact of NAFTA was to open the Mexican market to U.S. companies. When the treaty went into effect, tariffs on about half the items traded across the Rio Grande disappeared. The pact removed a web of Mexican licensing requirements, quotas, and tariffs that limited transactions in U.S. goods and services. For instance, the pact allowed U.S. and Canadian financial-services companies to own subsidiaries in Mexico.

In August 2007, the three member countries met in Canada to tweak NAFTA, but not make substantial changes. For example, the members agreed to further remove trade barriers on hogs, steel, consumer electronics, and chemicals. They also directed the North American Steel Trade Committee, which represents the three governments, to focus on subsidized steel from China.

The real question is whether NAFTA can continue to deliver rising prosperity in all three countries. America has certainly benefited from cheaper imports and more investment opportunities abroad. Exports to Mexico still only account for 1.1 percent of the economy, and imports from Mexico were less than 1.7 percent of the economy. Trade between Canada and the United States reached ₹33,30,000 crores in 2008, and U.S. capital invested in Canadian securities reached ₹1,87,650 crores in 2009— the largest annual American investment since 1977.[21]

President Obama has talked about renegotiating NAFTA because of the number of jobs lost to Mexico since NAFTA took effect. It is true that jobs in textile, auto parts, and electronics production have migrated to Mexico. Yet far more jobs have been lost to China than to Mexico. Investment in automation and information technology has led to massive reductions in factory workers everywhere—including China and Mexico. Moreover, the growth of the Mexican economy under NAFTA has created export opportunities and jobs (different jobs from pre-NAFTA) in America. For example, General Electric recently sold ₹1,575 crores in turbines built in Houston, more than 100 locomotives made in Erie, Pennsylvania, and numerous aircraft engines to Mexico.[22]

The U.S. Chamber of Commerce estimates that 54 lakhs U.S. jobs are directly related to trade agreements implemented through 2008 to eliminate or lower tariffs. Trade with the 14 countries in those agreements created 177 lakhs jobs, directly and indirectly.[23]

Central America Free Trade Agreement The **Central America Free Trade Agreement (CAFTA)** was instituted in 2005. Besides the United States, the agreement includes Costa Rica, the Dominican Republic, El Salvador, Guatemala, Honduras, and Nicaragua.

Between 2005 and 2007, trade between the United States and CAFTA countries grew 18 percent. The United States exported ₹1,03,500 crores of goods and services to CAFTA nations in 2007, up 33 percent since 2005. United States imported 85500 crores of goods and services from CAFTA nations, up 4 percent since 2005.[24] CAFTA has been an unqualified success. It has created new commercial opportunities for its members, has promoted regional stability, and is an impetus for economic development for an important group of U.S. neighbors.

Central America Free Trade Agreement (CAFTA) a trade agreement, instituted in 2005, that includes Costa Rica, the Dominican Republic, El Salvador, Guatemala, Honduras, Nicaragua, and the United States

European Union (EU) a free trade zone encompassing 27 European countries

European Union The **European Union (EU)** is one of the world's most important free trade zones and now encompasses most of Europe. More than a free trade zone, it is also a political and economic community. As a free trade zone, it guarantees the freedom of movement of people, goods, services, and capital between member states. It also maintains a common trade policy with outside nations and a regional development policy. The EU represents member nations in the WTO. Recently, the EU also began venturing into foreign policy as well, such as Iran's refining of uranium.

The European Union currently has 27 member states: Austria, Belgium, Bulgaria, Cyprus, the Czech Republic, Denmark, Estonia, Finland, France, Germany, Greece, Hungary, Ireland, Italy, Latvia, Lithuania, Luxembourg, Malta, the Netherlands, Poland, Portugal, Romania, Slovakia, Slovenia, Spain, Sweden, and the United Kingdom. There are currently four official candidate countries: Croatia, Iceland, the Republic of Macedonia, and Turkey. In addition, the western Balkan countries of Albania, Bosnia and Herzegovina, Montenegro, and Serbia are officially recognized as potential candidates.[25]

In early 2010, Greece entered a financial crisis that highlighted the challenges of a large currency union where member nations maintain responsibility for their own fiscal policies. Unable to devalue its currency to boost sales of products without injuring other member nations, Greece turned to member states for a bailout. The crisis has highlighted debt problems in other EU nations such as Hungary, Italy, Portugal, and Spain. After failing to meet strict budget-cutting measures imposed by EU and the International Monetary Fund, Hungary did not receive the next installment of financial aide, indicating how serious lenders are about implementing long-term fixes to irresponsible debt.[26]

The European Union Commission and the courts have not always been kind to U.S. multinationals. First, the EU court blocked a merger between two

World Bank an international bank that offers low-interest loans, advice, and information to developing nations

International Monetary Fund (IMF) an international organization that acts as a lender of last resort, providing loans to troubled nations, and also works to promote trade through financial cooperation

Group of Twenty (G-20) a forum for international economic development that promotes discussion between industrial and emerging-market countries on key issues related to global economic stability

U.S. companies—General Electric and Honeywell. In late 2007, it concluded that Microsoft used its dominance in desktop computer software to muscle into server software and media players. The EU courts said that Microsoft blocked competition and fined the company ₹2,758.5 crores.[27]

The EU is the largest economy in the world. The EU is also a huge market, with a population of nearly 50 crores. The United States and the EU have the largest bilateral trade and the investment relationship in world history. Together, they account for more than half of the global economy, while bilateral trade accounts for 7 percent of the world total. U.S. and EU companies have invested an estimated ₹90,00,000 crores in each other's economies, employing directly and indirectly as many as 1.4 crore workers. Nearly every U.S. state is involved with exporting to, importing from, or working for European firms.[28]

The EU is an attractive market, with purchasing power almost equal to that of the United States. But the EU presents marketing challenges because, even with standardized regulations, marketers will not be able to produce a single European product for a generic European consumer. With more than 15 different languages and individual national customs, Europe will always be far more diverse than the United States. Thus, product differences will continue to be necessary.

An entirely different type of problem facing global marketers is the possibility of a protectionist movement by the EU against outsiders. For example, European automakers have proposed holding Japanese imports at roughly their current 10 percent market share. The Irish, Danes, and Dutch don't make cars and have unrestricted home markets; they would be unhappy about limited imports of Toyotas and Nissans. But France has a strict quota on Japanese cars to protect Renault and Peugeot. These local carmakers could be hurt if the quota is raised at all.

The World Bank, the International Monetary Fund, and G-20 Two international financial organizations are instrumental in fostering global trade. The **World Bank** offers low-interest loans to developing nations. Originally, the purpose of the loans was to help these nations build infrastructure such as roads, power plants, schools, drainage projects, and hospitals. Now

© ISTOCKPHOTO.COM/AYZEK

the World Bank offers loans to help developing nations relieve their debt burdens. To receive the loans, countries must pledge to lower trade barriers and aid private enterprise. In addition to making loans, the World Bank is a major source of advice and information for developing nations. The **International Monetary Fund (IMF)** was founded in 1945, one year after the creation of the World Bank, to promote trade through financial cooperation and eliminate trade barriers in the process. The IMF makes short-term loans to member nations that are unable to meet their budgetary expenses. It operates as a lender of last resort for troubled nations. In exchange for these emergency loans, IMF lenders frequently extract significant commitments from the borrowing nations to address the problems that led to the crises. These steps may include curtailing imports or even devaluing the currency.

The **Group of Twenty (G-20)** Finance Ministers and Central Bank Governors was established in 1999 to bring together industrialized and developing economies to discuss key issues in the global economy. The G-20 is a forum for international economic development that promotes discussion between industrial and emerging-market countries on key issues related to global economic stability. By contributing to the strengthening of the international financial system and providing opportunities for discussion on national policies, international cooperation, and international financial institutions, the G-20 helps to support growth and development across the globe. The members of G-20 are shown in Exhibit 5.2.

In 2009, the G-20 met in Pittsburgh, Pennsylvania, where it adopted President Obama's proposed *Framework for Strong, Sustainable and Balanced Growth*. The document outlined a process to help avoid other financial crises such as those started in the financial markets in the United Sates in 2007. It also provided recommendations for long-term global growth.

EXHIBIT 5.2
Members of G-20

Argentina	European Union	Italy	South Africa
Australia	France	Japan	Republic of Korea
Brazil	Germany	Mexico	Turkey
Canada	India	Russia	United Kingdom
China	Indonesia	Saudi Arabia	United States

Demographic Makeup

The three most densely populated nations in the world arc China, India, and Indonesia. But that fact alone is not particularly useful to marketers. They also need to know whether the population is mostly urban or rural, because marketers may not have easy access to rural consumers. Belgium, with about 90 percent of the population living in urban settings, is an attractive market.

Another key demographic consideration is age. There is a wide gap between the older populations of the industrialized countries and the vast working-age populations of developing countries. This gap has enormous implications for economies, businesses, and the competitiveness of individual countries. It means that while Europe and Japan struggle with pension schemes and the rising cost of health care, countries like Brazil, China, and Mexico can reap the fruits of a demographic dividend: falling labor costs, a healthier and more educated population, and the entry of lakhs of women into the workforce. The demographic dividend is a gift of falling birthrates, and it causes a temporary bulge in the number of working-age people. Population experts have estimated that one-third of East Asia's economic miracle can be attributed to a beneficial age structure. But the miracle occurred only because the governments had policies in place to educate their people, create jobs, and improve health.

Natural Resources

A final factor in the external environment that has become more evident in the past decade is the shortage of natural resources. For example, petroleum shortages have created huge amounts of wealth for oil-producing countries such as Norway, Saudi Arabia, and the United Arab Emirates. Both consumer and industrial markets have blossomed in these countries. Other countries—such as Indonesia, Mexico, and Venezuela—were able to borrow heavily against oil reserves in order to develop more rapidly.

NATURAL RESOURCES STIFLED BY POLITICAL STRIFE

© FRCNTPAGE/SHUTTERSTOCK.COM

War-torn Afghanistan is struggling to rebuild. One way that it could build its economy is to mine its estimated ₹45,00,000 crore worth of mineral deposits. Exploration to find the deposits, however, relies on foreign companies braving the mine-littered countryside, reporting their findings, and then bidding on the rights to mine. Afghanistan lacks the equipment, capital, and stable firms to mine the deposits itself, but its government has encouraged exploration and bidding on its deposits. China's Metallurgical Group Corporation (MCC) won the mining right for a six hundred-crore-kilogram copper deposit in 2007. Mining has not yet begun—MCC had to build a road to the camp and clear land mines from three million square miles. Ore production has been deferred until 2014.[29]

exporting selling domestically produced products to buyers in other countries

buyer for export an intermediary in the global market who assumes all ownership risks and sells globally for its own account

export broker an intermediary who plays the traditional broker's role by bringing buyer and seller together

export agent an intermediary who acts like a manufacturer's agent for the exporter; the export agent lives in the foreign market

On the other hand, industrial countries such as Japan, the United States, and much of western Europe experienced an enormous transfer of wealth to the petroleum-rich nations. The high price of oil has created inflationary pressures in petroleum-importing nations. It also created major problems for airlines and other petroleum-dependent industries. Petroleum is not the only natural resource that affects international marketing. Warm climate and lack of water mean that many of Africa's countries will remain importers of foodstuffs. The United States, on the other hand, must rely on Africa for many precious metals. Vast differences in natural resources create international dependencies, huge shifts of wealth, inflation and recession, export opportunities for countries with abundant resources, and even a stimulus for military intervention.

LO 4 Global Marketing by the Individual Firm

A company should consider entering the global marketplace only after its management has a solid grasp of the global environment.

Companies decide to "go global" for a number of reasons. Perhaps the most important is to earn additional profits. Managers may feel that international sales will result in higher profit margins or more added-on profits. A second stimulus is that a firm may have a unique product or technological advantage not available to other international competitors. Such advantages should result in major business successes abroad. In other situations, management may have exclusive market information about foreign customers, marketplaces, or market situations not known to others. While exclusivity can provide an initial motivation for international marketing, managers must realize that competitors can be expected to catch up with the firm's information advantage. Finally, saturated domestic markets, excess capacity, and potential for economies of scale can also be motivators to "go global." Economies of scale mean that average per-unit production costs fall as output is increased.

Many firms form multinational partnerships—called strategic alliances—to assist them in penetrating global markets; strategic alliances are examined in Chapter 7. Five other methods of entering the global marketplace are, in order of risk, exporting, licensing and franchising, contract manufacturing, joint venture, and direct investment (see Exhibit 5.3).

Exporting

When a company decides to enter the global market, exporting is usually the least complicated and least risky alternative. **Exporting** is selling domestically produced products to buyers in other countries. A company can sell directly to foreign importers or buyers. The United States is the world's largest exporter.

Instead of selling directly to foreign buyers, a company may decide to sell to intermediaries located in its domestic market. The most common intermediary is the export merchant, also known as a **buyer for export**, which is usually treated like a domestic customer by the domestic manufacturer. The buyer for export assumes all risks and sells internationally for its own account. The domestic firm is involved only to the extent that its products are bought in foreign markets.

A second type of intermediary is the **export broker**, who plays the traditional broker's role by bringing buyer and seller together. The manufacturer still retains title and assumes all the risks. Export brokers operate primarily in agricultural products and raw materials.

Export agents, a third type of intermediary, are foreign sales agents-distributors who live in the

EXHIBIT 5.3

Risk Levels for Five Methods of Entering the Global Marketplace

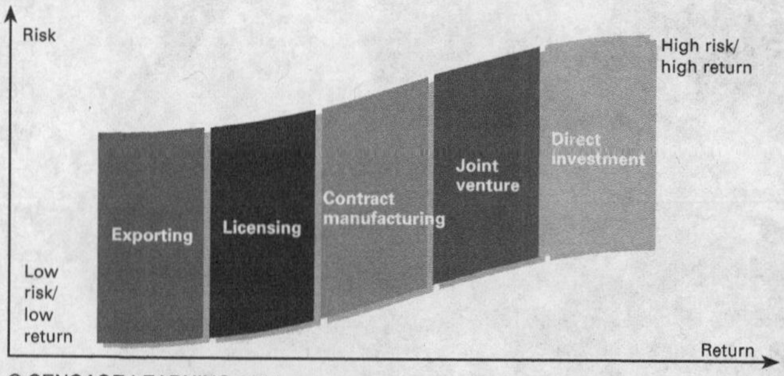

foreign country and perform the same functions as domestic manufacturers' agents, helping with international financing, shipping, and so on. The U.S. Department of Commerce has an agent-distributor service that helps about 5,000 U.S. companies each year find an agent or distributor in virtually any country of the world. A second category of agents resides in the manufacturer's country but represents foreign buyers. This type of agent acts as a hired purchasing agent for foreign customers operating in the exporter's home market.

Licensing and Franchising

Another effective way for a firm to move into the global arena with relatively little risk is to sell a license to manufacture its product to someone in a foreign country. **Licensing** is the legal process whereby a licensor allows another firm to use its manufacturing process, trademarks, patents, trade secrets, or other proprietary knowledge. The licensee, in turn, pays the licensor a royalty or fee agreed on by both parties.

For example, the owners of the rights to Broadway plays, such as Disney's The Lion King, have seen increasing revenue from foreign markets through licensing. The rights to produce the plays internationally have different price points, but foreign presenters begin by paying ₹90 lakhs in advance to stage a U.S. production. Replica shows, using licensed sets and costumes, cost the most; and non-replica shows, which pay for the rights to the play but not sets or costuming, cost less. Foreign revenue for licensing non-replica shows grew more than 10 percent in the last two years.[30]

A licensor must make sure it can exercise sufficient control over the licensee's activities to ensure proper quality, pricing, distribution, and so on. Licensing may also create a new competitor in the long run, if the licensee decides to void the license agreement. International law is often ineffective in stopping such actions. Two common ways of maintaining effective control over licensees are shipping one or more critical components from India or locally registering patents and trademarks to the Indian firm, not to the licensee. Garment companies maintain control by delivering only so many labels per day; they also supply their own fabric, collect the scraps, and do accurate unit counts.

licensing the legal process whereby a licensor allows another firm to use its manufacturing process, trademarks, patents, trade secrets, or other proprietary knowledge

contract manufacturing private-label manufacturing by a foreign company

joint venture when a domestic firm buys part of a foreign company or joins with a foreign company to create a new entity

Franchising is a form of licensing that has grown rapidly in recent years. The franchised businesses in India have been growing at a rate of 30-35 percent per annum, with the Indian franchise industry attaining a turnover of ₹45000 crores.[31] Over half of the international franchises are for fast-food restaurants and business services.

Contract Manufacturing Firms that do not want to become involved in licensing or to become heavily involved in global marketing may engage in **contract manufacturing**, which is private-label manufacturing by a foreign company. The foreign company produces a certain volume of products to specification, with the domestic firm's brand name on the goods. The domestic company usually handles the marketing. Thus, the domestic firm can broaden its global marketing base without investing in overseas plants and equipment. After establishing a solid base, the domestic firm may switch to a joint venture or direct investment.

Joint Venture

Joint ventures are somewhat similar to licensing agreements. In an international **joint venture**, the domestic firm buys part of a foreign company or joins with a foreign company to create a new entity. A joint venture is a quick and relatively inexpensive way to go global and to gain needed expertise. America's Walmart stores entered into a joint venture with the Indian group Bharti Enterprises, called Bharti Walmart Private Limited, to expand its presence in the highly attractive Indian retail market.

direct foreign investment active ownership of a foreign company or of overseas manufacturing or marketing facilities

Joint ventures can be very risky, however. Many fail; others fall victim to a takeover in which one partner buys out the other. Sometimes joint venture partners simply can't agree on management strategies and policies.

Direct Investment

Active ownership of a foreign company or of overseas manufacturing or marketing facilities is called **direct foreign investment.** Direct foreign investment by Indian firms during 2009-10 was about ₹46,350 crores.[32] Direct investors have either a controlling interest or a large minority interest in the firm. Thus, they have the greatest potential reward and the greatest potential risk. Because of the problems with contract manufacturing and joint ventures in China, multinationals are going it alone. Today, nearly five times as much foreign direct investment comes into China in the form of stand-alone efforts as comes in for joint ventures.

A firm may make a direct foreign investment by acquiring an interest in an existing company or by building new facilities. It might do so because it has trouble transferring some resource to a foreign operation or getting that resource locally. One important resource is personnel, especially managers. If the local labor market is tight, the firm may buy an entire foreign firm and retain all its employees instead of paying higher salaries than competitors.

India is a popular place for direct investment by foreign companies. In 2009-10, India had direct foreign investment inflows of ₹1,16,505 crores.[33] For example, in 2008, Japan based Daiichi-Sankyo bought Indian pharmaceutical Ranbaxy.

LO 5 The Global Marketing Mix

To succeed, firms seeking to enter into foreign trade must still adhere to the principles of the marketing mix. Information gathered on foreign markets through research is the basis for the four Ps of global marketing strategy: product, place (distribution), promotion, and price. Marketing managers who understand the advantages and disadvantages of different ways of entering the global market and the effect of the external environment on the firm's marketing mix have a better chance of reaching their goals.

The first step in creating a marketing mix is developing a thorough understanding of the global target market. Often this knowledge can be obtained through the same types of marketing research used in the domestic market (see Chapter 9). However, global marketing research is conducted in vastly different environments. Conducting a survey can be difficult in developing countries, where telephone ownership is growing but is not always common and mail delivery is slow or sporadic. Drawing samples based on known population parameters is often difficult because of the lack of data. In some cities in Africa, Asia, Mexico, and South America, street maps are unavailable, streets are unidentified, and houses are unnumbered. Moreover, the questions a marketer can ask may differ in other cultures. In some cultures, people tend to be more private than in the United States and will not respond to personal questions on surveys. For instance, in France, questions about one's age and income are considered especially rude.

© ISTOCKPHOTO/THINKSTOCK

Product and Promotion

With the proper information, a good marketing mix can be developed. One important decision is whether to alter the product or the promotion for the global marketplace. Other options are to radically change the product or to adjust either the promotional message or the product to suit local conditions.

One Product, One Message The strategy of global marketing standardization, which was discussed earlier, means developing a single product for all markets and promoting it the same way all over the world. For instance,

EXHIBIT 5.4

Emerging Markets Like American Brands

Top Brands in Various Countries

Argentina	
Car:	Ford
Fast food:	McDonald's
Makeup:	Avon
Mobile phone:	Sony
Motorcycle:	Honda
Television:	Philips
Cola:	Coca-Cola

China	
Beer:	Budweiser
Coffee (ready to drink):	Nestea
Fast food:	KFC
Mobile phone:	Panasonic
Soap:	Safeguard
Television:	Sony
Cola:	Coca-Cola

Egypt	
Designer clothing store:	Nike
Fuel:	Mobil
Hotel:	Hilton, Sheraton
Makeup:	Avon
Shampoo:	Pert Plus
Television:	Toshiba
Cola:	Pepsi

India	
Conditioner:	Garnier
Fast food:	McDonald's
Motor oil:	Castrol
MP3 player:	Sony
Coffee (ready to drink):	Nescafé
Television:	LG
Cola:	Pepsi

Romania	
Car:	Mercedes
Fast food:	McDonald's
Lipstick:	Avon
MP3 player:	Sony

Saudi Arabia	
Fast food:	McDonald's
Iced tea:	Lipton
Mobile phone:	Nokia
Packaged cheese:	Kraft
Salty snacks:	Lay's
Television:	Sony
Cola:	Pepsi

South Africa	
Car:	Toyota
Designer clothing store:	Levi's
Fast food:	KFC
Lipstick:	Revlon
Mobile phone:	Nokia
Television:	LG
Cola:	Coca-Cola

Thailand	
Beer:	Heineken
Car:	Toyota
Convenience store:	7-Eleven
Moisturizer:	Nivea
Whiskey/Scotch:	Johnnie Walker
Television:	Sony
Cola:	Pepsi

Turkey	
Car:	BMW
Cognac:	Rémy Martin
Designer clothing store:	DKNY, Gucci
Fast food:	McDonald's
Hotel:	Hilton
Iced tea:	Lipton
Cola:	Coca-Cola

Shampoo:	Head & Shoulders
Whiskey/Scotch:	Jack Daniels
Cola:	Coca-Cola

SOURCE: Synovate, Chicago (2007). Used by permission of Aegis Group, plc.

Procter & Gamble uses the same product and promotional themes for Head & Shoulders in China as it does in the United States. The advertising draws attention to a person's dandruff problem, which stands out in a nation of black-haired people. Head & Shoulders is now the best-selling shampoo in China despite costing over 300 percent more than local brands. In a recent survey, 13,000 consumers in 20 countries were asked about brand preferences across several product categories. In developing countries, local products were often viewed less favorably than global brands. Exhibit 5.4 reveals that Western brands sell quite well in the countries surveyed. The top cola brand in every country was either Pepsi or Coke.[34]

Global media—especially satellite and cable television networks such as CNN International, MTV Networks, and British Sky Broadcasting—make it possible to beam advertising to audiences unreachable a few years ago. Eighteen-year-olds in Paris often have more in common with 18-year-olds in New York than with their own parents. Almost all of MTV's advertisers run unified, English-language campaigns in the 28 nations the firm reaches. The audiences buy the same products, go to the same movies, listen to the same music, and sip the same colas. Global advertising merely works on that premise. Although teens throughout the world prefer movies above all other forms of television programming, they are closely followed by music videos, stand-up comedy, and then sports.

Global marketing standardization can sometimes backfire. Unchanged products may fail simply because of cultural factors. Any type of war game tends to do very poorly in Germany, even though Germany is by far the world's biggest game-playing nation. A successful game in Germany has plenty of details and thick rulebooks.

Sometimes the desire for absolute standardization must give way to practical considerations and local market dynamics. For example, because of the feminine connotations of the word *diet*, the European version of Diet Coke is Coca-Cola Light. Even if the brand name differs by market—as with Lay's potato chips, which are called Sabritas in Mexico—a strong visual relationship may be created by uniform application of the brandmark and graphic elements on packaging.

Product Invention In the context of global marketing, product invention can be taken to mean either creating a new product for a market or drastically changing an existing product. Nokia invented the Nokia 1100 handset especially for the Indian market and realized revenues well over ₹4,500 crores.[35]

McDonald's was once vilified for pushing its American-created fast food on the world. Now it is taking a different approach and selling more than ever in the global marketplace.

Product Adaptation Another alternative for global marketers is to slightly alter a basic product to meet local conditions. Unilever's Rexona brand deodorant sticks sell for ₹7 and up. They are big hits in Bolivia, India, Peru, and the Philippines—where Unilever has grabbed 60 percent of the deodorant market.

One of the world's best at product adaptation is the Korean firm LG Electronics. To meet the needs of Indian consumers, LG rolled out refrigerators with larger vegetable- and water-storage compartments, surge-resistant power supplies, and brightly colored finishes that reflect local preferences (red in the south, green in Kashmir). In Iran, LG offers a microwave oven with a preset button for reheating shish kebabs—a favorite dish. Saudi Arabians like LG's Primian refrigerator, which includes a special compartment for storing dates; the fruit, a Middle Eastern staple, spoils easily.

Promotion Adaptation

Another global marketing strategy is to maintain the same basic product but alter the promotional strategy. Bicycles are mainly pleasure vehicles in the United States. In many parts of the world, however, they are a family's main mode of transportation. Thus, promotion in these countries should stress durability and efficiency. In contrast, U.S. advertising may emphasize escaping and having fun.

Language barriers, translation problems, and cultural differences have generated numerous headaches for international marketing managers. Consider these examples:

- A toothpaste claiming to give users white teeth was especially inappropriate in many areas of Southeast Asia, where the well-to-do chew betel nuts and black teeth are a sign of higher social status.
- In Procter & Gamble's Japanese advertising for Camay soap, a man meeting a woman for the first time immediately compared her skin to that of a fine porcelain doll. The man came across as rude and disrespectful in Japan.
- A teenager careening down a store aisle on a grocery cart in a Coca-Cola ad was perceived as too rebellious in Singapore.

Place (Distribution)

Solving promotional and product problems does not guarantee global marketing success. The product still has to get adequate distribution. For example, Europeans don't play sports as much as Americans do, so they don't visit sporting-goods stores as often. Realizing this, Reebok started selling its shoes in about 800 traditional shoe stores in France. In one year, the company doubled its French sales.

To combat distribution problems, companies are using creative strategies. Colgate-Palmolive has introduced villagers in India to the concept of brushing teeth by rolling into villages with video vans that show half-hour infomercials on the benefits of toothpaste. The company received more than half of its revenue in the nation from rural areas until 2006. The rural market has been virtually invisible, due to a lack of distribution. Unilever's Indian subsidiary, Hindustan Lever, sells its cosmetics, toothpastes, and detergents door-to-door. It now has more than ten lakh direct-sales consultants.

In many developing nations, channels of distribution and the physical infrastructure are inadequate. In Africa, the continent's GDP is growing rapidly, and African businesses want to expand. Unfortunately, they face high tariffs, weak infrastructure, and severely impoverished populations. To expand into neighboring countries, Notore Chemicals Ltd., a Nigerian fertilizer company, appealed directly to the governments to develop a distribution chain across 20 African nations. Some East African countries are even developing a regional trade zone to encourage growth.[36]

American companies importing goods to the United States are facing other problems. Logistics has been a growing challenge for U.S. companies seeking to cut costs by shifting more production to countries where manufacturing is cheaper. Now, however, the rising costs for shipping goods are adding to their profit pressures. The surge in global trade in recent years has added to strains and charges for all forms of transport. As a result, some manufacturers are developing costly buffer stocks—which can mean setting up days' or weeks' worth of extra components—to avoid shutting down production lines and failing to make timely deliveries. Others are shifting to more expensive but more reliable modes of transport, such as air freight, which is faster and less prone to delays than ocean shipping.

Pricing

Once marketing managers have determined a global product and promotion strategy, they can select the remainder of the marketing mix. Pricing presents some unique problems in the global sphere. Exporters must not only cover their production costs but also consider transportation costs, insurance, taxes, and tariffs. When deciding on a final price, marketers must also determine how much customers are willing to spend on a particular product. Marketers also need to ensure that their foreign buyers will pay the price. Because developing nations lack mass purchasing power, selling to them often poses special pricing problems. Sometimes a product can be simplified in order to lower the price. The firm must not assume low-income countries are willing to accept lower quality, however, L'Oréal was unsuccessful in selling cheap shampoo in India, so the company targets the rising class. It now sells a ₹765 Paris face powder and a ₹1,125 Vichy sunscreen. Both products are very popular.

Exchange Rates The exchange rate is the price of one country's currency in terms of another country's

FLOATING SUPERMARKETS SERVICE RURAL INDIA

In Kerala, India, where multinationals struggle to distribute products to decentralized rural markets, the Triveni floating supermarket uses Kerala's criss-cross waterways to reach rural villages that don't have nearby markets. Carrying more than 2,000 products on waterways cuts time and costs: Triveni is able to aggregate small rural village distributions and hold its prices 10 percent lower than other land-based markets. By arriving at local jetties, customers spend less money for transportation and buy multinational brands, such as Colgate. Customers also have the option to special order large products, such as Samsung televisions, and have them delivered to the village.[37]

floating exchange rates a system in which prices of different currencies move up and down based on the demand for and the supply of each currency

dumping the sale of an exported product at a price lower than that charged for the same or a like product in the "home" market of the exporter

countertrade a form of trade in which all or part of the payment for goods or services is in the form of other goods or services

currency. If a country's currency *appreciates*, less of that country's currency is needed to buy another country's currency. If a country's currency *depreciates*, more of that currency will be needed to buy another country's currency.

How do appreciation and depreciation affect the prices of a country's goods? If the rupee depreciates relative to the American dollar, Indian residents will have to pay more rupees to buy American goods. To illustrate, suppose the rupee price of a dollar is ₹45 and that a Ford is priced at $14,000. At this exchange rate, an Indian resident pays ₹6,30,000 for a Ford (₹45 × $14,000 = ₹6,30,000). If the rupee depreciates to ₹50 to $1, then the Indian resident will have to pay ₹7,00,000 for the same Ford.

As the rupee depreciates, the prices of American goods rise for Indian residents, so they buy fewer American goods—thus, India's imports may decline. At the same time, as the rupee depreciates relative to the dollar, the dollar appreciates relative to the rupee. This means prices of Indian goods fall for the Americans, so they buy more Indian goods—and India's exports rise.

Currency markets operate under a system of **floating exchange rates**. Prices of different currencies "float" up and down based on the demand for and the supply of each currency. Global currency traders create the supply of and demand for a particular country's currency based on that country's investment, trade potential, and economic strength.

Dumping **Dumping** is the sale of an exported product at a price lower than that charged for the same or a like product in the "home" market of the exporter. This practice is regarded as a form of price discrimination that can potentially harm the importing nation's competing industries. Dumping may occur as a result of exporter business strategies that include (1) trying to increase an overseas market share, (2) temporarily distributing products in overseas markets to offset slack demand in the home market, (3) lowering unit costs by exploiting large-scale production, and (4) attempting to maintain stable prices during periods of exchange rate fluctuations.

© ISTOCKPHOTO.COM/CRAFTVISION

Historically, the dumping of goods has presented serious problems in international trade. As a result, dumping has led to significant disagreements among countries and diverse views about its harmfulness. Some trade economists view dumping as harmful only when it involves the use of "predatory" practices that intentionally try to eliminate competition and gain monopoly power in a market. They believe that predatory dumping rarely occurs and that antidumping rules are a protectionist tool whose cost to consumers and import-using industries exceeds the benefits to the industries receiving protection.

Countertrade Global trade does not always involve cash. Countertrade is a fast-growing way to conduct global business. In **countertrade**, all or part of the payment for goods or services is in the form of other goods or services. Countertrade is thus a form of barter (swapping goods for goods), an age-old practice whose origins have been traced back to cave dwellers. The U.S. Department of Commerce says that roughly 30 percent of all global trade is countertrade. In fact, both India and China have made billion-dollar government purchasing lists, with most of the goods to be paid for by countertrade.

One common type of countertrade is straight barter. For example, PepsiCo sends Pepsi syrup to Russian bottling plants and in payment gets Stolichnaya vodka, which is then marketed in the West. Another form of countertrade is the compensation agreement. Typically, a company provides technology and equipment for a plant in a developing nation and agrees to take full or partial payment in goods produced by that plant. For example, General Tire Company supplied equipment and know-how for a Romanian truck tire plant. In turn, General Tire sold the tires it received from the plant in the United States under the Victoria brand name. Both sides benefit even though they don't use cash.

LO 6 The Impact of the Internet

In many respects, "going global" is easier than it has ever been before. Opening an e-commerce site on the Internet immediately puts a company in the international marketplace. Sophisticated language translation software can make any site accessible to people around the world. Global shippers such as UPS, FedEx, and DHL help solve international e-commerce distribution complexities. E4X, Inc. offers software to ease currency conversions by allowing customers to pay in the currency of their choice. E4X collects the payment from the customer and then pays the site in U.S. dollars. Nevertheless, the promise of "borderless commerce" and the global "Internet economy" are still being restrained by the old brick-and-mortar rules, regulations, and habits. For example, Lands' End is not allowed to mention its unconditional refund policy on its e-commerce site in Germany because German retailers, which normally do not allow returns after 14 days, sued and won a court ruling blocking mention of it.

Opening an e-commerce site on the Internet . . .

. . . immediately puts a company in the international marketplace.

Review And Applications

Discuss the importance of global marketing. Businesspeople who adopt a global vision are better able to identify global marketing opportunities, understand the nature of global networks, create effective global marketing strategies, and compete against foreign competition in domestic markets.

1.1 What is meant by "having a global vision"? Why is it important?

1.2 Isolationists have suggested that U.S. would be much better off economically and politically if we just "built a wall" around the country and didn't deal with the outsiders. Do you think the same rationale can be applied to Indian Economy as well? Why or why not?

1.3 Discuss jobs outsourcing. Is it beneficial to Indian Firms?

Discuss the impact of multinational firms on the world economy. Multinational corporations are international traders that regularly operate across national borders. Because of their vast size and financial, technological, and material resources, multinational corporations have a great influence on the world economy. They have the ability to overcome trade problems, save on labor costs, and tap new technology. However, some countries are beginning to block foreign investment by multinationals.

2.1 Uttam kitchenware, a leading manufacturer of kitchen products and other household items is considering moving to global marketing standardization. What are the pros and cons of this strategy?

2.2 Do you believe that multinationals are beneficial or harmful to developing nations? Why? What could foreign governments do to make them more beneficial?

Describe the external environment facing global marketers. Global marketers face the same environmental factors as they do domestically: culture, economic, and technological development; political structure and actions; demography; and natural resources. Cultural considerations include societal values, attitudes, and beliefs; language; and customary business practices. A country's economic and technological status depends on its stage of industrial development, which, in turn, affects average family incomes. The political structure is shaped by political ideology and policies such as tariffs, quotas, boycotts, exchange controls, trade agreements, and market groupings. Demographic variables include the size of a population and its age and geographic distribution.

3.1 Many marketers now believe that teenagers in the developing countries are becoming "global consumers". That is, they all want any buy the same goods and services. Do you think this is true? If so, what has caused the phenomenon?

3.2 IKEA has withheld its entry in the Indian market, even after the new FDI policy permits 100% foreign ownership in the single-brand retail sector. Why do you think is the reason behind IKEA's reluctance?

3.3 Divide into six teams. Each team will be responsible for one of the following industries: entertainment; pharmaceuticals; computers and software; financial, legal, or accounting services; agriculture; and textiles and apparel. Interview one or more executives in each of these industries to determine how the WTO has affected and will affect their organizations. If a local firm cannot be contacted in your industry, use the library and the internet to prepare your report.

3.4 What are the major barriers to international trade? Explain how government policies may be used to either restrict or stimulate global marketing.

Identify the various ways of entering the global marketplace. Firms use the following strategies to enter global markets, in descending order of risk and profit: direct investment, joint venture, contract manufacturing, licensing and franchising, and exporting.

4.1 Indo-Dan, an upscale manufacturer of lamps and lampshades in India has decided to "go global". Top management is having trouble deciding how to develop the market. What are some market entry options for the firm?

4.2 What are some of the advantages and potential disadvantages of entering a joint venture?

4.3 Why is direct investment considered risky?

List the basic elements involved in developing a global marketing mix. A firm's major consideration is how much it will adjust the four Ps—product, promotion, place (distribution), and price—within each country.

One strategy is to use one product and one promotion message worldwide. A second strategy is to create new products for global markets. A third strategy is to keep the product basically the same but alter the promotional message. A fourth strategy is to slightly alter the product to meet local conditions.

5.1 The sale of cigarettes in developing countries has peaked. In this situation, should the Indian tobacco companies capitalize on this opportunity?

5.2 Describe the last three situations where an Indian company might want to keep the product the same, but alter the promotion. Also, give three examples where the product must be altered.

5.3 Explain how exchange rates can affect a firm's global sales.

Discover how the Internet is affecting global marketing. Simply opening a Web site can open the door for international sales. International carriers, like DHL, can help solve logistics problems. Language translation software can help an e-commerce business become multilingual. Yet cultural differences and old-line rules, regulations, and taxes hinder rapid development of e-commerce in many countries.

6.1 Describe how "going global" via the Internet presents opportunities and challenges.

6.2 Give several examples of how culture may hinder "going global" via the Internet.

Exercises

APPLICATION EXERCISE

To be effective as a marketer, it is important to know geography. How will you be able to decide whether to expand into a new territory (domestic or foreign) if you don't know where it is and something about its culture, currency, and economy? If you can't place the European countries on a blank map, or if you can't label the lower 48 states without a list to help you, you're not alone. In one study, students incorrectly located over 50 percent of European countries and over 25 percent of the states in the Unites States. To help you brush up on your geography, we've compiled some tools that you may find useful.

Activities

1. To review domestic geography, print a blank map of India and Asia. Label the maps. Name the states and the countries in the maps. For a challenge, add the state capitals to the map.
2. Once you have successfully labeled the India map, you may be ready to try labeling the world map. If so, go to www.clickandlearn.com and view the free, printable, blackline maps. Under the category of The World and Continents, choose the blackline detail map. This shows country outlines, whereas the basic blackline outline map shows only the continents. You will notice that there are also blackline maps for each continent, so if taking on the entire world is too daunting, start with more manageable blocks.
3. To be a global marketer, it is not enough to know where countries are located. You will need to know about the culture, the main exports, the currency, and even the main imports. Select a half-dozen or so countries with which you are unfamiliar, and research basic geographic information about them.

ETHICS EXERCISE

Ravi Electronics sells automated lighting for airport runways.. The government of an Eastern country had offered Ravi Electronics a contract to provide equipment for the major imports in the country. The official in charge of awarding the contract, however, is demanding a 5 percent kickback. He told Ravi Electronics to build this into a contract piece so that there would be no cost to Ravi Electronics. Without the kickback, Ravi Electronics loses the contract. Such kickbacks are considered a normal way of doing business in this country.

Questions

1. What should Ravi Electronics do?
2. Review the anti corruption acts implemented in India, and state whether it provides a solution to the case given above.

MARKETING PLAN EXERCISE

These end-of-chapter marketing plan exercises are designed to help you use what you learned in the chapter to build a strategic marketing plan for a company of your choosing. Once you've completed the marketing plan exercise for each chapter in Part 1 of this textbook, you can complete the Part 1 Marketing Planning Worksheet on your companion Web site at **www.cengage.com/international.** Now continue building your strategic marketing plan that you started in Chapter 2 by completing the following exercises:

1. Assume your company is or will be marketing globally. How should your company enter the global marketplace? How will international issues affect your firm?

2. If you choose an Internet presence, your product or service will be visible to a global community. Assess the international marketplace for your particular offering. A listing of international chambers of commerce is at **www.worldchambers.com** and the CIA World Factbook is at **www.cia.gov/cia/publications/factbook/index.html.**

Short Case: COCA-COLA CORPORATION

Prepared by
Dr. Dheeraj Sharma,
Indian Institute of Management, Ahmedabad

The opening up of the world economy and saturation in the domestic market is compelling the companies to expand their business across the borders. Along with this speedy communication, fast transportation facilities and new technology has all the more added to the reasons for the companies to go global. The entire world has now become one big market. This requires the companies not only to customize their product mix according to the individual countries but also to find out various similarities among them to build a competitive advantage.

Coca-Cola Corporation has its inception 100 years back in 1919 in U.S. Since then, it has expanded its business in more than 200 countries and is marketing its products in more than 500 brands and 3,500 beverage products.[39]

Coca-Cola system has about 300 bottling-partners, world over. The company sources the ingredients, makes and sells beverages bases and concentrates to their bottling partners, who in turn are responsible for owning the brand and marketing them. The global strategy used by Coca-Cola has made it one of the most valuable brands all over the world.

Global Strategies of Coca-Cola:

Blending of both standardized and adapted product:

With the technological advancements and globalization, the customers' needs and wants now have no boundaries and they now somewhat have become homogenous. But still there exists some cultural differences, which are specific to individual countries. Hence, Coca-Cola has a unique way to blend both standardized product and a product adapted according to the needs of local markets. To attain this, Coca-Cola produces the concentrated syrup mixture, and then sells it to many bottling companies across the world. These local bottlers in turn add sugar and water to the concentration to make the final drink. The sweetness of the drink is adjusted according to the preference of the local market.

Economies of Scale:

Coca-Cola operates in different countries through its bottling plants. This enables it to achieve economies of scale through bulk purchases, sharing of various marketing, production, and managerial resources, etc. across the countries.

Marketing Campaign:

With the availability of so many choices, one of the ways a company can differentiate itself is through providing them with a product above than its functional benefits. The company uses both a global advertising campaign, which it may customize as per the requirement of the country. For example, the global theme of Fanta "More Fanta, Less Serious" was adapted in India as "Zyada Fanta Zyada Fun". Also, looking at the success of the musical initiative "Coke Studio", the company is planning to take this concept to other countries globally. Coke has launched a global campaign "Open Happiness" in 2009, which it has adapted for India as well. However, it has been realized that the Coca-Cola ads have lost their charm in recent years because of its presence all over.[40] Coca-Cola has made a comeback with its new London 2012 Olympics advertisements, which features Mark Ronson.[41]

Product Packaging:

The company' packaging has been a great example of being global. The typical red color of the bottle with scripted letters and the curvy shape of the bottle is easily recognizable globally. Only a little change is made in the language mentioned on it, as per the national language of the individual country. Also the size of the bottles varies according the usage in different countries. For example, the largest available bottle size manufactured by Coca-Cola around the globe is of two liters, but looking at the trend in Mexico, where the whole family have their lunch together at home, it introduced a bottle size of two and half liters.

Pricing:

Coca-Cola faces a fierce competition with Pepsi in the Indian soft drink market. Hence, there has always been a price rivalry between the two. The price plays a prominent role in the consumer decision making, since the consumers would be willing to switch brands, if they find a difference in the pricing of the two brands. With the advent of summer, Coca-Cola has declared a drop in the price of its returnable glass bottles from ₹10 to ₹8 in 2012. The last time in 2003 also the company had reduced the price of its bottles to ₹5, but for all the products in its portfolio including Sprite, Thumps up, Limca, and Fanta.[42]

Hence, Coca-Cola can benefit a lot from its global strategy, but its decision to adapt its strategy according to the local markets can give it a more long lasting stability in the market.

Questions

1. It has been realized that the Coca-Cola ads have lost their charm in recent years. Would the company's global ad strategy be able to create the same magic again?
2. Will the reduction in price of Coca-Cola's returnable glass bottles lead to price wars?
3. Coca-Cola this time reduced the price for just its brand Coca-Cola and not for its other product portfolios. Will this lead to cannibalization of Thums-up?
4. Apart from the pricing methods and advertisements, what other methods of competition you think Coca-Cola can use to attract customers as well as dealers?

5 Developing a Global Vision

KEY TERMS

LO 1

global marketing marketing that targets markets throughout the world

global vision recognizing and reacting to international marketing opportunities, using effective global marketing strategies, and being aware of threats from foreign competitors in all markets

job outsourcing sending U.S. jobs abroad

LO 2

multinational corporation a company that is heavily engaged in international trade, beyond exporting and importing

capital intensive using more capital than labor in the production process

global marketing standardization production of uniform products that can be sold the same way all over the world

LO 3

Mercosur the largest Latin American trade agreement; includes Argentina, Bolivia, Brazil, Chile, Colombia, Ecuador, Paraguay, Peru, and Uruguay

Uruguay Round an agreement to dramatically lower trade barriers worldwide; created the World Trade Organization

World Trade Organization (WTO) a trade organization that replaced the old General Agreement on Tariffs and Trade (GATT)

General Agreement on Tariffs and Trade (GATT) a trade agreement that contained loopholes enabling countries to avoid trade-barrier reduction agreements

KEY CONCEPTS

LO 1 **Discuss the importance of global marketing.** Businesspeople who adopt a global vision are better able to identify global marketing opportunities, understand the nature of global networks, create effective global marketing strategies, and compete against foreign competition in domestic markets.

LO 2 **Discuss the impact of multinational firms on the world economy.** Multinational corporations are international traders that regularly operate across national borders. Because of their vast size and financial, technological, and material resources, multinational corporations have a great influence on the world economy. They have the ability to overcome trade problems, save on labor costs, and tap new technology. However, some countries are beginning to block foreign investment by multinationals.

LO 3 **Describe the external environment facing global marketers.** Global marketers face the same environmental factors as they do domestically: culture, economic, and technological development; political structure and actions; demography; and natural resources. Cultural considerations include societal values, attitudes, and beliefs; language; and customary business practices. A country's economic and technological status depends on its stage of industrial development, which, in turn, affects average family incomes. The political structure is shaped by political ideology and policies such as tariffs, quotas, boycotts, exchange controls, trade agreements, and market groupings. Demographic variables include the size of a population and its age and geographic distribution.

LO 4 **Identify the various ways of entering the global marketplace.** Firms use the following strategies to enter global markets, in descending order of risk and profit: direct investment, joint venture, contract manufacturing, licensing and franchising, and exporting.

LO 5 **List the basic elements involved in developing a global marketing mix.** A firm's major consideration is how much it will adjust the four Ps—product, promotion, place (distribution), and price—within each country. One

Risk Levels for Five Methods of Entering the Global Marketplace

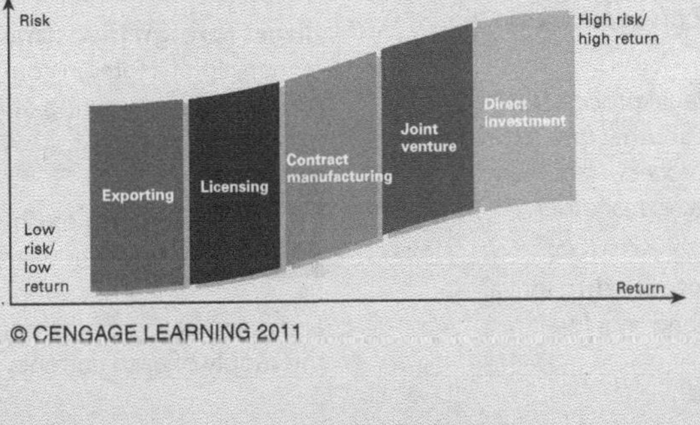

© CENGAGE LEARNING 2011

North American Free Trade Agreement (NAFTA) an agreement between Canada, the United States, and Mexico that created the world's largest free trade zone

Central America Free Trade Agreement (CAFTA) a trade agreement, instituted in 2005, that includes Costa Rica, the Dominican Republic, El Salvador, Guatemala, Honduras, Nicaragua, and the United States

European Union (EU) a free trade zone encompassing 27 European countries

World Bank an international bank that offers low-interest loans, advice, and information to developing nations

International Monetary Fund (IMF) an international organization that acts as a lender of last resort, providing loans to troubled nations, and also works to promote trade through financial cooperation

Group of Twenty (G-20) a forum for international economic development that promotes discussion between industrial and emerging-market countries on key issues related to global economic stability

LO 4 **exporting** selling domestically produced products to buyers in other countries

buyer for export an intermediary in the global market who assumes all ownership risks and sells globally for its own account

export broker an intermediary who plays the traditional broker's role by bringing buyer and seller together

export agent an intermediary who acts like a manufacturer's agent for the exporter; the export agent lives in the foreign market

licensing the legal process whereby a licensor allows another firm to use its manufacturing process, trademarks, patents, trade secrets, or other proprietary knowledge

contract manufacturing private-label manufacturing by a foreign company

strategy is to use one product and one promotion message worldwide. A second strategy is to create new products for global markets. A third strategy is to keep the product basically the same but alter the promotional message. A fourth strategy is to slightly alter the product to meet local conditions.

LO 6 **Discover how the Internet is affecting global marketing.** Simply opening a Web site can open the door for international sales. International carriers, like DHL, can help solve logistics problems. Language translation software can help an e-commerce business become multilingual. Yet cultural differences and old-line rules, regulations, and taxes hinder rapid development of e-commerce in many countries.

Opening an e-commerce site on the Internet . . .

. . . immediately puts a company in the international marketplace.

joint venture when a domestic firm buys part of a foreign company or joins with a foreign company to create a new entity

direct foreign investment active ownership of a foreign company or of overseas manufacturing or marketing facilities

LO 5 **floating exchange rates** a system in which prices of different currencies move up and down based on the demand for and the supply of each currency

dumping the sale of an exported product at a price lower than that charged for the same or a like product in the "home" market of the exporter

countertrade a form of trade in which all or part of the payment for goods or services is in the form of other goods or services

CASE 1

Aviva Life Insurance Company India Ltd.

Reducing Policy Turnaround Time to Build Customer Satisfaction

On an unusually warm day in late February 2008, Professor Arindam Banerjee (Arindam) of the Indian Institute of Management, Ahmedabad, was seated in the office of Abhay Johorey (Abhay), Director of Business Transformation at the head office of Aviva Life Insurance Ltd. in Gurgaon, near Delhi. Chirag Jain (Chirag), Director of Operations and a colleague of Abhay, was also present at this meeting with Arindam. Arindam had been invited by the two Aviva senior executives to understand the significant business transformation initiatives the organization had carried out in the last two years and identify opportunities to make such initiatives more pervasive in the organization. Even as they acknowledged with pride the excellent contribution their cross-functional team had made in improving certain business processes, Abhay and Chirag were unsure as to how the positive momentum created was to be sustained. They were particularly worried that while employee optimism had been created in the recent past, these significant transformations needed to be broad based in the organization and leveraged properly, lest it manifested itself into complacency.

They requested Arindam to study the recent process improvement initiatives that had been concluded in the underwriting process of Aviva's Life Insurance product and suggest approaches to take the learning across the organization. Specifically, they wanted a strategy to make process improvement for business excellence a part of the ongoing organization culture and not just a one-off initiative.

Arindam set about understanding the improvements undertaken in the medical underwriting process for life products. He hoped that this exercise would yield potential leads to develop a strategy for developing a culture for change in the organization.

C1.1 Introduction to the Problem

In January 2006, the annual sales meet at Jaipur was witness to some heated discussions between the top management and the sales team. The meeting was about discussing alternative ways to expand business in life products. The sales teams from different regions were adamant that unless large scale improvements were made in the *policy completion* process, there was little opportunity to significantly raise market share. They claimed that it took on an average, 30–45 days for Aviva to turnaround a policy from the time the prospective customer was "booked" on the company's accounts. In turn, its significant competitors were far more efficient and this was telling on the corporate image of the organization.

Motivation appeared low since sales staff from the Delhi office made a compelling argument that it was hard to convince prospects about the customer-orientation of the organization, unless the service levels were improved significantly. How could one convince the prospects that the organization was customer-friendly if the very first experience (policy issuance) with the organization for most of them was so tardy, they asked.

More serious problems were brimming when a recently acquired "Bancassurance" channel partner joined the chorus by expressing similar concerns. A significant amount of the life products were sold through partner banks (see Exhibit C1.1 for list of Banca partners), and many were not very happy getting their commissions late after completion of sales. Some questioned the need for Aviva to delay their payments to ensure the completion of a lengthy policy generation process.

Prepared by Professor Arindam Banerjee, Indian Institute of Management, Ahmedabad.

Research assistance provided by Mr. P Venkatesh, FPM student, Indian Institute of Management, Ahmedabad, and data and logistic support provided by the management of Aviva Life (India) Ltd. during this academic venture, are gratefully acknowledged.

Cases of the Indian Institute of Management, Ahmedabad, are prepared as a basis for classroom discussion. They are not designed to present illustrations of either correct or incorrect handling of administrative problems.

EXHIBIT C1.1
List of Banca partners[1]

1. ABN AMRO Bank
2. American Express Bank
3. The Lakshmi Vilas Bank Ltd.
4. Canara Bank
5. Punjab and Sind Bank
6. Centurion Bank of Punjab
7. IndusInd Bank

Evidently, the top management at Aviva was getting very concerned about the seriousness of the issue. While grumblings were being heard for some time, the vitriolic nature of the feedback at the Jaipur meet was something that could not be ignored any longer.

C1.2 Insurance Industry in India and Aviva Life

Aviva PLC was a 300-year old insurance company founded in the United Kingdom. It started as a general insurance company and added the life and pension products to its stable over the years. Currently, Aviva was known to be the market leader in pension products in Europe.

The insurance sector in India had been state controlled since 1956 when the government decided to merge the erstwhile life insurance companies (252 companies) and form the state-run Life Insurance Corporation of India (LIC). India was the 18th largest life insurance market in the world in the year 2008; although the penetration of the product had been abysmally low at 2.53% of GDP and, only 15% of the population had being insured so far.

In 1992, as a part of the economic reform measures undertaken, the government constituted the Malhotra Committee to look into the changes required in the insurance sector. The committee submitted its report in 1999 recommending a gradual opening up of the sector by allowing private participation to complement the role of the LIC. The report concluded that the penetration of the insurance products was not enough and more players were needed to provide opportunity to the Indian population to get insured. The Insurance Regulation and Development Act (IRDA) was thus enacted in 1999 purportedly to regulate the industry in its liberalized avatar. Till the year 2000, LIC monopolized the life products market. Until recently, it held about 48% of the market which was growing at 31% CAGR.

Aviva Life entered the Indian market as a collaborative venture between Aviva PLC and Dabur Ltd., a consumer non-durable company based in Delhi, in 2002. As the 12th private player in the Indian market, it was at least two years behind its nearest formidable competitor. As per the norms set by the IRDA, Aviva PLC had 26% stake in the operation with the rest controlled by Dabur. However, Aviva PLC had full control over the operations of the Indian venture. Unlike its predominant presence in pension products in Europe, the organization was primarily in the life insurance business in India. Currently, it had about 4% market share and ranked 9th among the 16 private players in India.

LIC with its forty five year head start in the life insurance sector, had a significant advantage in this industry. Besides its stature as a staple insurance provider in India, the organization was backed by the government which put private players at a disadvantage. LIC was way ahead of competition on claims handling, a critical area in the insurance business to create positive equity with the customers. Given Aviva's late entry into the market compared to some of its formidable competitors, it was under pressure to raise its stake in an already hard fought market.

The life insurance products were sold through two major channels—direct sales force (DSF) and banking partners (Bancassurance). The latter was a cross selling channel where the banking partner would provide access to its customer database for a commission. While traditional channels were dominated by established players like LIC, late entrants like Aviva attempted to temper such early advantages by investing significantly in the banking channel to secure a database of relatively "warm" leads. About half of Aviva's Life business had been secured through the Bancassurance channel and the rest had come from the DSF route.

An organization chart of Aviva Life Insurance is provided in Exhibit C1.2. About eighty percent of its employees were in the sales function, which highlights the nascent stage of its business in India.

[1] As of March 1, 2008. Source: www.avivaindia.com

EXHIBIT C1.2

Aviva India Management Team

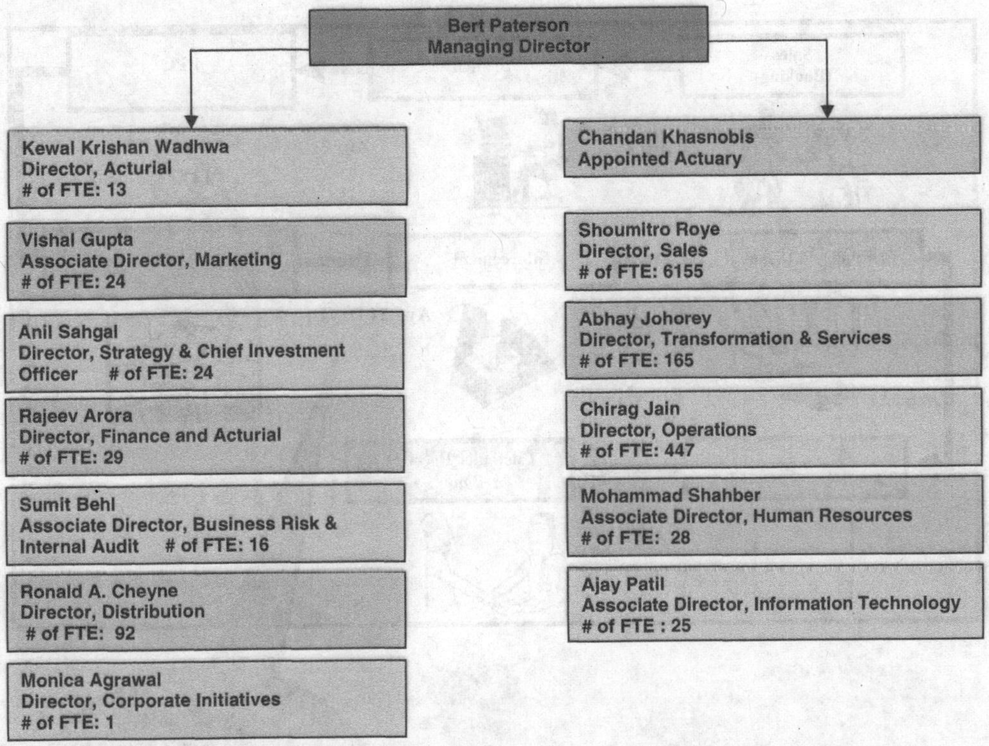

C1.3 The Life Insurance Product and the Selling Process

Among the insurance products that had a positive impact on the bottom line, the life product was the most significant. The product was designed to provide high risk coverage against death alongside a nominal investment rate of return that was paid out at the time of maturity. Given that the tenure of these products was relatively long, the investment value of the sum assured[2] collected from customers (through premiums) could be significant for many insurance companies. To manage the risk of early claims due to untimely death of the customer, most insurance companies administered a fairly evolved enquiry of the prospective customer which included family history and financials and health checks to assess the eligibility of the prospect for a certain risk cover. All policies were issued after a successful review of the documents supporting the above information. The nature of the medical examination was governed by the age of the prospect as well as the sum assured.

The erstwhile process of completing a prospective sale after booking was elaborate and is depicted in Exhibit C1.3. The "sales completion process" began with the sign-off on the insurance proposal by the prospect and the handing over of the cheque for an amount that covered the first premium (booking). The sales records were updated in the sale register (by branch operations) and transferred to the regional quality processing cell (RPC) that checked for form completion (financial details and address

[2] Amount of insurance bought by the customer.

EXHIBIT C1.3

Overall Sales completion Process

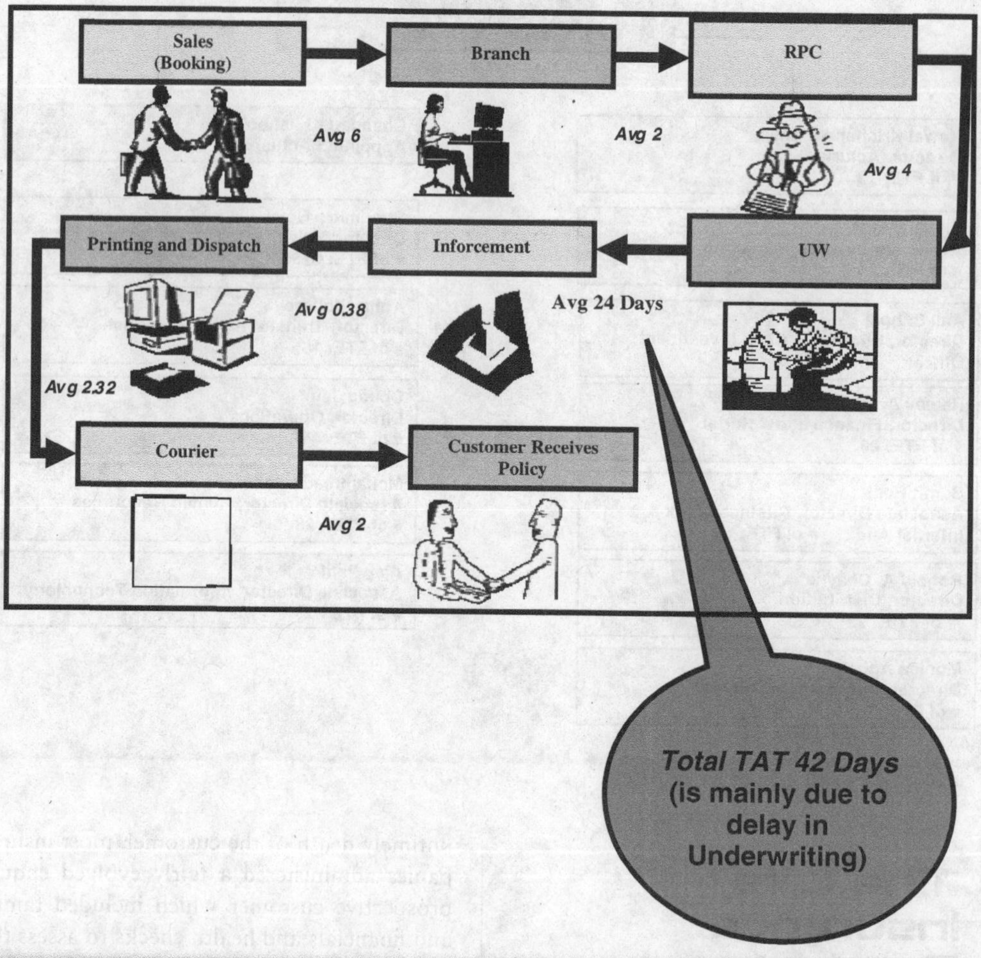

authentication) and logged the proposal into the operations bin. This event also initiated the SMNL (Star Medical Network Ltd), an outsourced operations service provider, to make medical appointments for the prospect's health check up at the nearest available certified (by Aviva) medical centres. SMNL would then collate all medical test reports for the prospects; and when the individual files were complete, they would send them to the Central Underwriting department at Head Office.

The underwriting process included checking the requirements for issuing the insurance policy and confirming that all specifications with regard to the sum assured were met (see Exhibit C1.4 for underwriting process). Should there be any discrepancy in the medical records, the underwriter had to decide whether the file should be sent back to the customer (through the SMNL and the branch network) for further details, or whether the case should be referred to the supervisor for assessment and sign-off.

There were limits for each underwriter on the insured amount that he/she could approve. If the amount was higher than the limit, approval had to be sought from the supervisor (Territory Manager). Supervisors also had limits to their authorization amounts and if the proposal amount was beyond their limit, it had to be referred to the "Head of Underwriting". For all non-standard proposals with completed records, the underwriting operation would take, on an average, 25 minutes to complete.

EXHIBIT C1.4
Underwriting Process

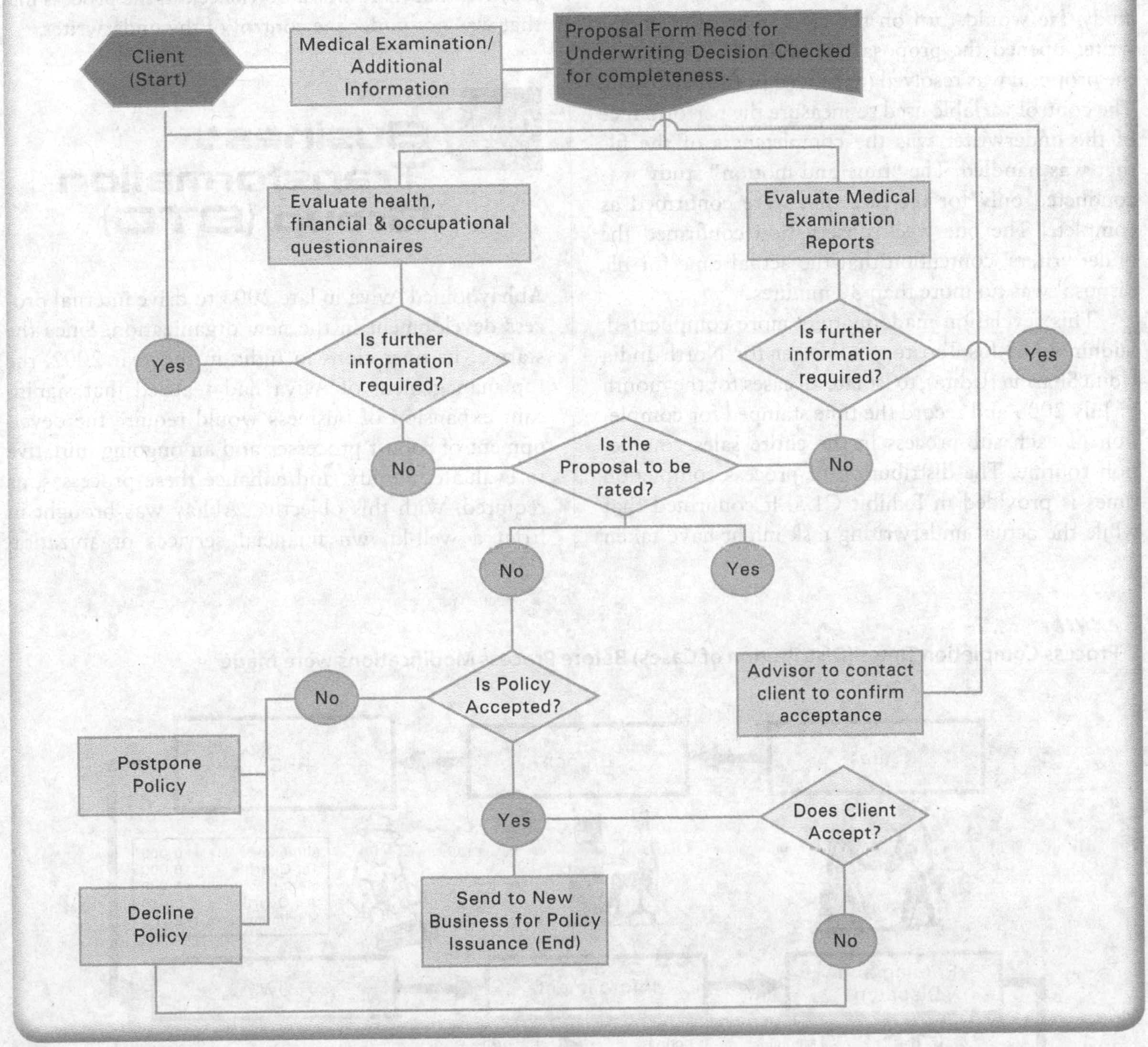

The Underwriting "Dilemma"

Chirag was visibly concerned about the strong negative feedback that he had received regarding underwriting delays, during the Jaipur meet. As he recalled later, "*....we were always perplexed as to how to get better control over customer dependent and vendor dependent processes, especially the turnaround times (TAT). Given the vast expanse of our operations and the large number of sales force, it was often deemed impossible. How the rest of the industry has operated and had no better ways to handle the problem added to our helplessness ...*".

Chirag brought up the matter before Sudhir Gupta (Sudhir), who was in charge of the entire underwriting operation.[3] They both agreed to refer the problem to the Quality Group to ascertain the actual time requirements for a typical underwriting task. While the regular internal dashboard metrics indicated that the underwriting task was on an average completed in a reasonable time, Chirag wanted an independent

[3] Reported to Vijaya Lakshmi, in charge of Underwriting and Claims Processing Operations. Vijaya reported to Chirag Jain.

validation of the same. A Quality Group representative was positioned next to the underwriter's desk for the following week to undertake a "time and motion" study. He would turn on the clock when the underwriter opened the proposal file and turn it off once the proposal was resolved (approved or turned down). The control variable used to measure the performance of the underwriter was the completeness of the file that was handled. The "time and motion" study was conducted only for the files that were confirmed as complete. The one week observation confirmed the underwriters' contention that the actual time for file disposal was no more than 30 minutes.

This revelation made matters more complicated. Sudhir asked his Territory Manager for North India Udita Sharma (Udita), to isolate all cases for the month of July 2006 and record the time stamped for completion of each sub-process in the entire sales completion routine. The distribution of process completion times is provided in Exhibit C1.5. It confirmed that while the actual underwriting task might have taken 30 minutes, the process was responsible for up to 24 days of delay in discharging its responsibility. Clearly, they felt that there was a bottleneck in the process line that was not under the control of the underwriter.

C1.4 Business Transformation Group (BTG)

Abhay joined Aviva in late 2005 to drive internal process development in the new organization. Since the start of its operations in India in the year 2002, the top management of Aviva had realized that significant expansion of business would require the development of robust processes and an ongoing initiative to evaluate, modify, and enhance these processes, as required. With this objective, Abhay was brought in from a well-known financial services organization

EXHIBIT C1.5
Process Completion Times (Distribution of Cases) Before Process Modifications were made

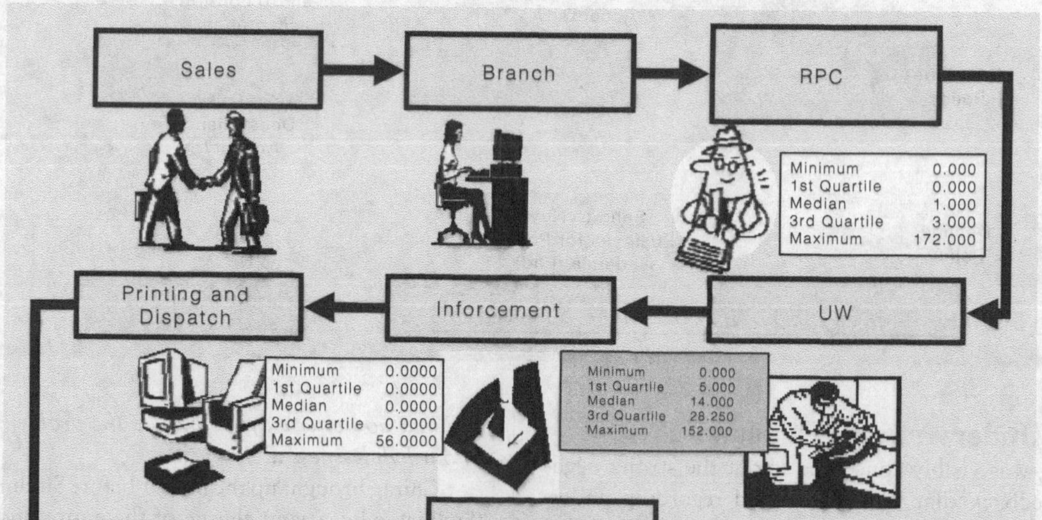

with a background in technology and internal process improvements. In the initial period of his tenure at Aviva, Abhay and Chirag, another senior executive brought in by the organization in early 2004 to provide the much needed leadership to the fledgling organization, together set up the processes of underwriting, customer service, policy issuance, premium handling, and claims processing. Eventually, Chirag was made in-charge of the entire internal operations and Abhay continued to work with a team of internal consultants to monitor and resolve process bottlenecks and suggest further enhancements.

Many of these improvement initiatives were focused on enhancing the customers' experience with the organization at all levels, mainly by ensuring that such interactions were managed in a coordinated manner. Given the manner in which the responsibility of customer management was transferred across functional teams (primarily between sales and operations), maintaining a high standard in customer relationship management required setting up performance metrics that incorporated cross-functional coordination issues. Additionally, Abhay's group was also charged with measuring these criteria continuously across various customer touch-points and providing regular feedback to the top management team on the soundness of the organization on these "health" parameters. Any adverse changes in the business health indicators would require a top level commitment to reverse the trend in a reasonable time frame. This was mandated by the Managing Director. The BTG led the organization's "health tracking" initiative (Balanced Scorecard initiative), and coordinated any process improvement and enhancement initiatives thereof. No wonder at times Abhay sardonically referred to his role as the "Mr. Fix-it" of the organization.

Underwriting "Delay" Diagnosis

Kunal Bhalla (Kunal) of the Quality Group[4] (part of the reconstituted BTG after Operations was hived off) was deputed to work with Sudhir to isolate the problem associated with the pile up of proposals in the underwriting section. A painstaking operation was carried out by Kunal, Sudhir and Udita (the joint solutions team) poring over the July 2006 proposals data.

Multiple cases were identified where the proposal was booked by the RPC and the cheque was encashed by the branch office operations staff member, who supported the sales. However, the actual completion of the medical tests, to be reviewed by the underwriter, was inordinately delayed. For instance, the medical examination was scheduled at times, over a week later from the time of the sign-off. Moreover, repeated iterations were required to ensure that the medical examination was completed appropriately. In many cases the case file was pending after the RPC had booked the case for over 15–20 days primarily because the follow up medical tests were not complete.

The joint solutions team undertook a review of data of the completion process and identified potential bottlenecks in the process. A detailed exposition of the completion process is given in Exhibit C1.6. They identified several potential reasons for a delay:

1. After the proposal was signed off (booked), sales staff would route the case to the SMNL for initiating the appointments for medical tests.
2. It was the responsibility of SMNL to make appointments with the medical centre(s) on behalf of the prospect and ensure that a completed medical file reached the Central Underwriting team in the head office at Gurgaon.
3. The quality of service provided by SMNL was not under constant scrutiny and hence the service provider may not have been motivated to provide the highest level of service.
4. Point # 3 was further substantiated by frequent incidences of prospects making multiple visits to the medical centre for the same test, which could have been accomplished in one visit if the coordination provided by SMNL was more effective.

Exhibit C1.7 shows the break up of the July 2006 underwriting cases into categories depicting the time taken at various steps in the medical enquiry process. The delay in the overall process due to the time taken for fixing medical appointments and subsequent medical report collations indicated a significant bottleneck that contributed to the lag. The actual underwriting time across cases which had delays in the medical enquiry process and the ones which did not, were comparable (see Underwriting Turnaround Time—UW TAT between Pre/Pre, Pre/Post, and Post/Post). From the data, it is possible to attribute about ten extra days, on an average, to waiting for the preliminary file completion.

Further, the team also identified that many cases (about 30–40% of the cases) required "follow up" medical enquiry or other additional details once the underwriting review was undertaken. These non-stan-

4. Headed by Ashit Saxena, who reported to Abhay Joharey.

EXHIBIT C1.6
Medical Enquiry Process

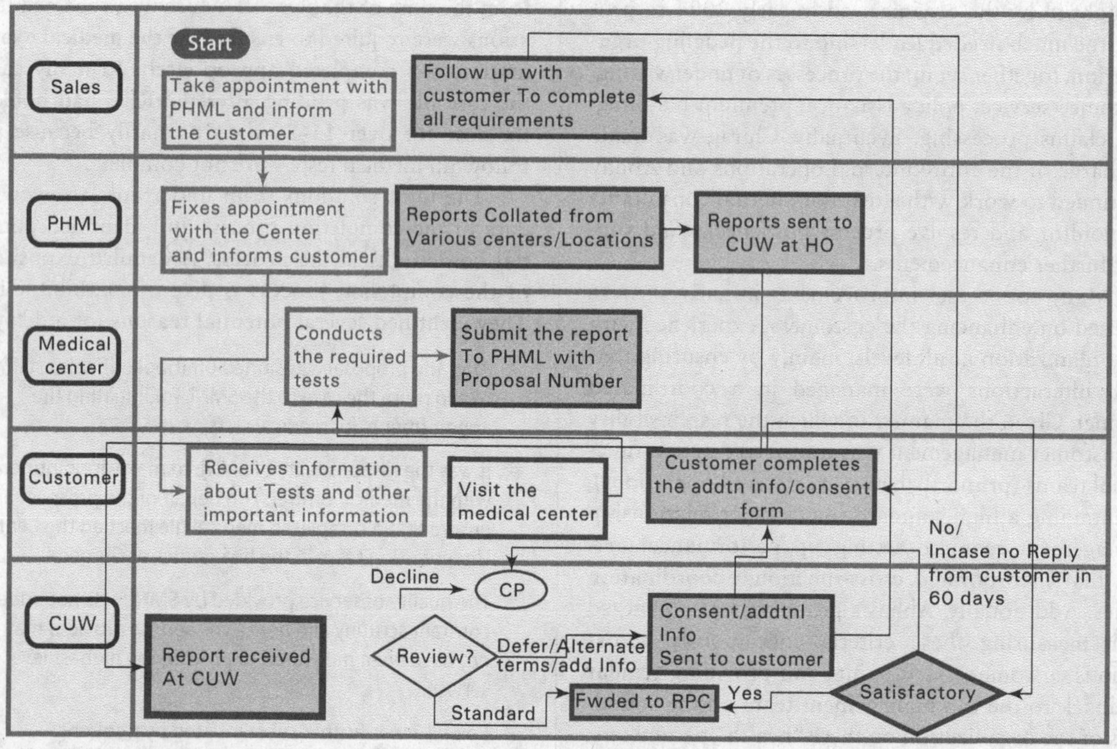

Highlighted processes (boxes) represent reasons for Delay.

EXHIBIT C1.7
Pre/Pre, Pre/Post, Post/Post Time Requirements

	# of Days			
July 06 Medical UW TAT[5] Break up	**Pre/Pre**	**Pre/Post**	**Post/Post**	**Overall**
Delay in Appointment Time	—	—	16.11	16.11
Delay in Report	—	3.84	5.36	4.71
UW TAT	15.28	11.61	11.93	12.93
Total TAT	***15.28***	***15.44***	***33.38***	***22.33***
# of Cases	**693**	600	817	2,110

** Pre/Pre : Medical Appointment and Report Pre RPC review*
** Pre/Post: Medical Appointment Pre RPC review and Report Post RPC review*
** Post/Post: Medical Appointment and Report Post RPC review*

[5] TAT-Turnaround Time

EXHIBIT C1.8

Breakup of Delays for Various Types of Cases

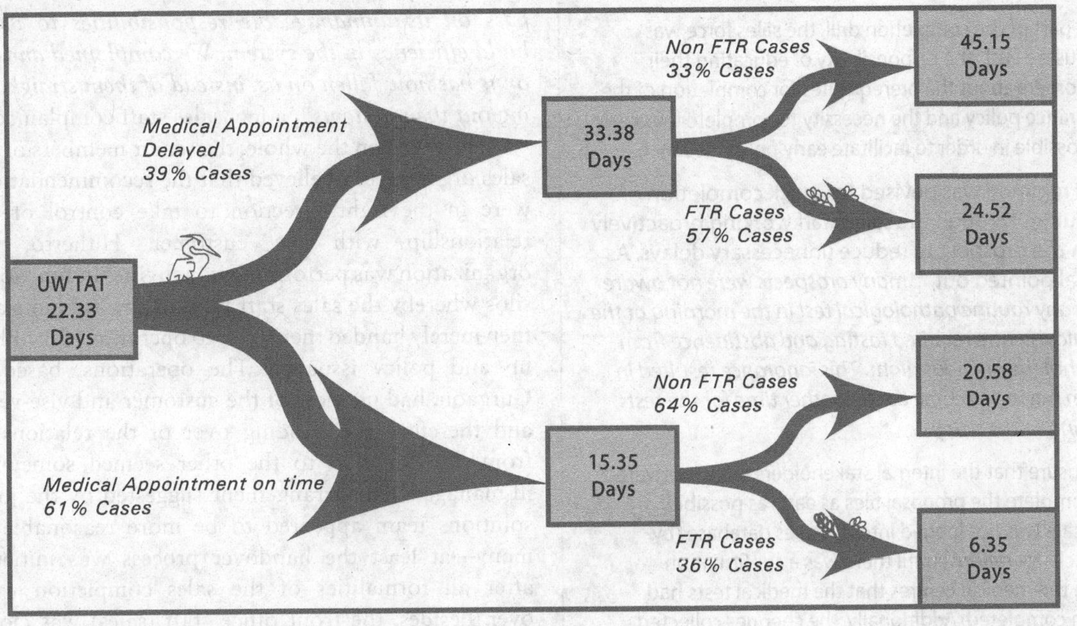

Note: Non-FTR cases require further medical tests

dard tests (non-FTR) delayed the process further by about 14–20 days on an average. Exhibit C1.8 shows the break up of the delays for various types of cases.

Sudhir and Kunal were somewhat relieved that the real bottleneck for the delay in completion of the underwriting operation had been isolated. Significantly, they inferred that the delay was occurring at the "hand over" point between sales and operations where the ownership of the case was not that well defined and the relationship management with the customer was inadvertently being done by an outsourced vendor (SMNL). Work was initiated to resolve the issues that were identified as quickly as possible.

C1.5 Taking Ownership of the Process

The joint solutions team determined that the core problem was the lack of ownership of the prospect, at least for some period of time. After the initial sign-off, contact with the prospect was handed over to an outsourced entity who really was not equipped to provide appropriate service levels expected by the organization. The outcome therefore was suboptimal and the perception formed by the prospect was that the organization cared little once the premium cheque had been collected by the sales staff.

It was felt necessary to divest SMNL of the responsibility of the logistics of medical appointments and reports. Sudhir was convinced that Aviva had to take complete control of the entire process of generating insurance policies until completion. Also, to maintain a single point of contact with the customer, the responsibility of completing the medical tests was transferred to the sales staff in the branches. The logic was that, given their proximity to the customer, the sales staff could manage the process better. A complete guide to managing the customer till policy issuance, was developed. The essence of the same is given below:

1. The responsibility of the salesperson did not end with the submission of the signed proposal and the cheque.
2. The salesperson was charged with initiating and managing the medical enquiry process and ensuring quick completion of the same. The contract with SMNL was thereby terminated.

3 The branch offices were equipped with informationals about the medical enquiry process for each type of proposal.

4 As a part of the completion drill, the sales force was entrusted with the responsibility of educating their customers about the prerequisites for completion of the insurance policy and the necessity to complete it as early as possible in order to facilitate early policy issuance.

5 This regimen was devised for quick completion of enquiries through the sales staff working proactively with the prospect to reduce unnecessary delays. As Kunal pointed out, "*...many prospects were not aware that any routine pathological test in the morning at the medical centre required fasting and abstinence from alcohol the previous night. This ignorance resulted in them having to come back another time for the tests, adding to the delays*".

6 To ensure that the internal stakeholders were motivated to complete the proposal files as early as possible, the sale was not logged into the sales database (by branch operations) until there was a confirmation from the medical centres that the medical tests had been completed. Additionally, the cheques collected from the customers for their first premium was kept at abeyance till all enquiry documentation was complete. This just added to the perception among customers that the organization was serious about completing all formalities towards policy issuance before the money was transferred from them.

7 Additionally, the team turned its attention to the non-standard cases (non-FTR) which amounted to about 33% of the cases. Such customized cases required additional medical tests which were the reason for protracted delays (14–20 days). Many such requirements were identified during the underwriter's review. The team decided to document most non-standard cases that required additional examination. The purpose was to equip the sales force to include these custom examinations as a part of the standard battery of tests in order to reduce the waiting period.

The joint solutions team presented its recommendations to the sales organization. There was some wariness in the audience while the initial proposals for changes were made. The reactions were predictably mixed. While many were positive about the need to take up the ownership of the customer to ensure speedy completion of the paperwork and provide better service, some sales managers viewed these measures as a means to transfer the responsibility of operations to the front office sales force with no added incentives. Surprisingly, a major Bancassurance channel partner was very enthusiastic that the organization transition to the new protocol at the earliest.

"*...it appears that Internal Operations wants to pass on its unmanageable responsibilities to us to build efficiency in the system. We complained and the onus has now fallen on us, instead of them straightening out their systems*", a few sales staff complained.

However, on the whole, the senior members of the sales organization believed that the recommendations were in the right direction to take control of the relationship with the customer. Hitherto, the organization was performing its activities in functional silos whereby the sales staff booked the accounts and then merely handed them over to operations for follow up and policy issuance. The operations, based at Gurgaon, had no view of the customer and vise-versa and therefore the handing over of the relationship from one function to the other seemed somewhat ill-managed. The arrangement suggested by the joint solutions team appeared to be more reasonable to many—at least the handover process was initiated after all formalities of the sales completion were over. Besides, the front office staff (sales) was closer to the prospect to facilitate faster completion of the formalities than a less motivated outsourced vendor or a back office staffer.

The Implementation Challenge

The challenges were significant. As Chirag recalled, "*...convincing the sales organization to take control was not easy. Besides the usual reluctance from some quarters to take up the responsibility, they needed serious training. It happened in a phased manner over a period of eight months*".

The training inputs were important both for retooling the sales force as well as for building their comfort level with the new protocol. Until now, the sales staff would normally assume that its responsibility was over with the proposal sign off. The account would be booked in the internal database and the motivation would shift to acquiring more accounts rather than completing the procedures for on-time policy issuance. The new process required initiating a training module for the sales force to educate them on the medical enquiry requirements. The proposal forms were redesigned to include details regarding the medical examinations to be conducted. This was done to ensure that these requirements were at the top-of-mind of both the sales team and the prospects at the time of sign-off. The BTG and the Underwriting team designed special informational posters that were hung prominently in the sales offices to promote awareness about these requirements. It was agreed that the change could be effected quickly if information could be disseminated to all parties as quickly as possible.

Mindset changes occurred slowly but surely. The North Zone was an important market for Aviva and the campaign to change was focused in this region first. The initial grumblings had largely died down over time.

"*The discontent that the sales organization was being made to clean up someone else's mess had largely dissipated, thankfully*", was the view expressed by one of the underwriting managers.

This had required sustained efforts from the underwriting group to provide full support to equip the front end staff with requisite tools to efficiently manage the medical enquiry process. "*Empowerment rather than passing the buck*" was the message that was emphasized during this exercise. Operationally, this meant frequent interactions with sales force to allay concerns, many rounds of data analysis to isolate problems and develop resolutions, numerous training and awareness campaigns within the organization to ensure proper calibration of all stakeholders.

In August 2007, the joint solutions team released the performance metrics based on the new operating protocol. By then, the team felt that enough time had elapsed since the new recommendations had been put in place to account for any change over "volatility". Udita of the Underwriting team compared the performance of the July 2007 proposals on dimensions of completion time with similar metrics for the proposals disposed a year ago (July 2006). The results of the July 2007 vintage are depicted in Exhibit C1.9. Clearly, the performance of majority of the cases had improved significantly. This was reflected in the average processing time coming down from 22 days in July 2006 (see Exhibit C1.7) to approximately 14 days in July 2007. A matter of concern was that the number of cases for which RPC had booked the proposals prior to the filing of the medical report was still substantial at about 20%. That appeared high given that specific measures were in place to ensure that RPC booked proposals only after the files were complete for underwriting review.

EXHIBIT C1.9

July 2007 (Pre/Pre. Pre/Post, Post/Post metric)

	# of Days			
July 07 Medical UW TAT[6] Break up	Pre/Pre	Pre/Post	Post/Post	Overall
Delay in Appointment Time	—	—	10.65	10.65
Delay in Report	—	2.44	1.60	1.64
UW TAT	6.12	8.84	18.37	8.83
Total TAT	***6.12***	***11.28***	***30.62***	***13.77***
# of Cases	**1,593**	226	452	2,271

** Pre/Pre : Medical Appointment and Report Pre RPC review*
** Pre/Post: Medical Appointment Pre RPC review and Report Post RPC review*
** Post/Post: Medical Appointment and Report Post RPC review*

C1.6 Joy of "Success"

Kunal and Sudhir felt really good about the results obtained from the process reengineering efforts. The operating parameters had improved considerably as was apparent from the statistics recorded. More importantly, this initiative was a hallmark of a cross-functional initiative that had worked out very successfully. As a benchmark in the organization which was primarily organized on functional silos, this effort was remarkable. They hoped that the camaraderie exhibited across functions would be pervasive across all similar cross-functional teams involved in improving organizational processes.

During the November 2007 regional sales meet in Delhi, several business partners expressed their satisfaction at the improvement in processing time. Some

6. TAT-Turnaround Time

lauded Aviva's alacrity in resolving a multi-functional bottleneck in such a short period of time. The Sales Director Soumitro Roye, was emphatic about the need to "take charge" of the customer. As he stated in his conversation with Arindam later, ".... *there was no alternative to providing a responsible in-house solution to the medical underwriting problem. And who else could do it better than the sales force who were in constant touch with the customers.*"

The Quality group assisted the Customer Satisfaction Measurement Team (CSM) to set up "listening posts" across various branch locations to review feedback from customers. Most customers who recorded their views stated that they had little to complain about the processing time of their insurance proposals. Some loyal customers expressed surprise at the recently improved efficiency of the processes. Many customers also felt that they would be comfortable recommending Aviva to their acquaintances, given the newly acquired enthusiasm in the organization as perceived by them. Customer satisfaction scores had improved tremendously. Exhibit C1.10 shows the volume growth between July 2006 and March 2007 and the simultaneous reduction in underwriting turnaround time and improvement in customer satisfaction scores measured by the CSM team.

"*No doubt I will recommend Aviva to my relatives*", said Gurmeet Kaur, a customer at the Ludhiana branch office.

"*No problem in this policy, medical test was also good*", said Nipendra Nath Chakraborty, a customer at the Kolkata branch.

"*Every activity was done on time. Its service was very good*", said Harjinder Singh, a long time customer in the Gurgaon branch.

It appeared that the tide had turned. However, senior executives like Chirag and Abhay knew that great results also posed a problem for the organization—sustaining these results required ensuring that the process improvements were continuously managed at the highest level to ensure that performance did not drop. That would be hard to attain given the level of organization commitment required. They wondered how such commitment could be sustained over a long period of time.

The Work that Remained Undone

The reactions from some other regions were more guarded. The original wariness about Operations "*cleaning up its act at the expense of sales*" was still very much alive in certain pockets. Perceptions at some of the branch offices were that the sales teams were not equipped to coordinate the medical enquiry process. Training on this new action item was inadequate and the newly added responsibility of coordinating the medical appointments and making sure that the prospect adhered to the prerequisites of the tests was an imposition. Earlier, the SMNL was responsible for the medical appointments. While their removal from service was indisputable, many felt that the branches required a competent internal coordinator instead to expedite the medical enquiry process. Sudhir was not entirely convinced about this argument. He claimed that most of the branches did no more than fifty medical cases in a month and therefore, the additional burden of coordinating the medical enquiry should not tax the sales force.

The market feedback in some regions was that the turnaround time had not reduced considerably in spite of CUW's claim. As someone in the branch operations explained, this was possible since the underwriting time was now better measured based on when the completed file with medical reports reached them; but the actual turnaround time as perceived by

EXHIBIT C1.10

Changes during July 2006–March 2007

	July'06		March'07	
Avg UW TAT (In Days)	**24.45**		**9.39**	
% Cases processed within 10 Days	42%		76%	
End to End TAT (In Days)	42.79		24.77	
Revenue (In Crores)	79.2		133.9	
	TTB	BTB	TTB	BTB
CSAT Top 2 Box *	26%	13%	76%	2%

* Customer Satisfaction Index

the customer had perhaps not changed much since the medical enquiry still took a long time compared to similar processes at competitor organizations.

Some others claimed that the turnaround time had indeed improved with the sales force directly coordinating the medical enquiry process. However, it was an added burden which took their attention away from booking incremental business. One branch manager mentioned that holding the sales force accountable for completing the enquiry meant that they would be somewhat careful about the "quality" of the prospect, i.e., they would now book only those cases where they felt that the prospect had a fair chance of successfully completing the medical examination. Others opined that they had become more selective about identifying their prospects by trying to restrict offering insurance to those with age below 45 years. These prospects did not have to undergo the medical examination and hence were easier to handle.

The Bancassurance channel support in a particular region stressed the need to decentralize some of the activities of underwriting in order to improve turnaround time. At the very least, some "underwriting expertise" could be deputed to the regions to help expedite the medical enquiry process. Additionally, they questioned the need to have all forms and documentation in English. According to them, customers were more comfortable with the vernacular language when filling up forms. They were also somewhat intrigued as to why Internal Operations was not open to the idea of printing forms and informationals in vernacular languages. A specific banking partner in the same region requested further reduction in turnaround time by streamlining operations to address competitive pressures. The current efficiency gained was not enough to effectively neutralize the aggressive response time of the competitors.

Overall, there was a feeling among the sales force that the initiative was focused more on reducing operational bottlenecks, but did not significantly serve the need for better "speed of delivery" to the customers. Some wondered why no one chose to ask for their suggestions when the process improvement initiatives were being discussed.

The Way Forward

Clearly, the senior management at Aviva had some work cut out to make its process improvement initiatives more acceptable to a broader set of employees within the organization. At the very least, there was a perception that operations had clipped an ineffective partner (SMNL) and loaded its responsibilities to the already busy sales force. A potential pitfall for the long run was that the spirit of "*taking ownership of the customer*" was still, by and large a distant dream. The organization was perhaps still working in functional silos and required more effective cross functional operations.

Arindam realized the concerns that were voiced by Chirag and Abhay during his first visit to the Aviva Office. What was still unclear to him was whether the key players, the front office players—the sales staff, bank partners and customers, were uniformly convinced about the improvements. Without their support, few improvement initiatives on customer satisfaction could be sustained in the long run.

CHAPTER 6 Consumer Decision Making

Consumers' product and service preferences are constantly changing.

Learning Outcomes

- **LO 1** Explain why marketing managers should understand consumer behavior
- **LO 2** Analyze the components of the consumer decision-making process
- **LO 3** Explain the consumer's postpurchase evaluation process
- **LO 4** Identify the types of consumer buying decisions and discuss the significance of consumer involvement
- **LO 5** Identify and understand the cultural factors that affect consumer buying decisions
- **LO 6** Identify and understand the social factors that affect consumer buying decisions
- **LO 7** Identify and understand the individual factors that affect consumer buying decisions
- **LO 8** Identify and understand the psychological factors that affect consumer buying decisions

LO 1 The Importance of Understanding Consumer Behavior

Consumers' product and service preferences are constantly changing. Marketing managers must understand these desires in order to create a proper marketing mix for a well-defined market. So it is critical that marketing managers have a thorough knowledge of consumer behavior. Consumer behavior describes how consumers make purchase decisions and how they use and dispose of the purchased goods or services. The study of consumer behavior also includes factors that influence purchase decisions and product use.

consumer behavior processes a consumer uses to make purchase decisions, as well as to use and dispose of purchased goods or services; also includes factors that influence purchase decisions and product use

Understanding how consumers make purchase decisions can help marketing managers in several ways. For example, if a manager knows through research that gas mileage is the most important attribute for a certain target market, the manufacturer can redesign a car to meet that criterion. If the firm cannot change the design in the short run, it can use promotion in an effort to change consumers' decision-making criteria, for example, by promoting style, durability, and cargo capacity.

Note:* *All the figures in U.S. dollars are converted into rupee using the value $1 = ₹45.

LO 2 The Consumer Decision-Making Process

When buying products, particularly new or expensive items, consumers generally follow the **consumer decision-making process** shown in Exhibit 6.1: (1) need recognition, (2) information search, (3) evaluation of alternatives, (4) purchase, and (5) postpurchase behavior. These five steps represent a general process that can be used as a guide for studying how consumers make decisions. It is important to note, though, that consumers' decisions do not always proceed in order through all of these steps. In fact, the consumer may end the process at any time or may not even make a purchase. The section on the types of consumer buying decisions later in the chapter discusses why a consumer's progression through these steps may vary. We begin, however, by examining the basic purchase process in greater detail.

consumer decision-making process a five-step process used by consumers when buying goods or services

need recognition result of an imbalance between actual and desired states

want recognition of an unfulfilled need and a product that will satisfy it

stimulus any unit of input affecting one or more of the five senses: sight, smell, taste, touch, hearing

Need Recognition

The first stage in the consumer decision-making process is need recognition. **Need recognition** occurs when consumers are faced with an imbalance between actual and desired states that arouses and activates the consumer decision-making process. A **want** is the new way that a consumer goes about addressing a need. For example, have you ever gotten blisters from an old running shoe? Or maybe you have seen a television commercial for a new sports car and wanted to buy it. Need recognition is triggered when a consumer is exposed to either an internal or an external **stimulus**. *Internal stimuli* are occurrences you experience, such as hunger or thirst. For example, you may hear your stomach growl and then realize you are hungry. *External stimuli* are influences from an outside source such as someone's recommendation of a new restaurant, the color of an automobile, the design of a package, a brand name mentioned by a friend, or an advertisement on television or radio.

A marketing manager's objective is to get consumers to recognize an imbalance between their present status and their preferred state. Advertising and sales promotion often provide this stimulus. Surveying buyer preferences provides marketers with information about consumer needs and wants that can be used to tailor products and services. Marketing managers can create wants on the part of the consumer. For example, when college students move into their own apartment or dorm room, they often need to furnish it and want new furniture rather than hand-me-downs from their parents. A want can be for a specific product, or it can be for a certain attribute or feature of a product. In this example, the college students not only need home furnishings but also want items that reflect their personal sense of style. Similarly, consumers may want ready-to-eat meals, drive-through dry-cleaning service, and Internet shopping to fill their need for convenience.

Another way marketers create new products and services to meet wants is by observing trends in the marketplace. IKEA, the home furnishing giant, watches the home decor trends and then creates affordable, trendy furniture. For example, marketers at IKEA realized that Generation Y consumers prefer furniture that is stylish, easy to clean, multifunctional, and portable. As a result, IKEA uses bold orange, pink, and green colors. The wood boasts a lacquered finish that can be wiped clean and doesn't need polish. IKEA also offers a space-saving, multifunction desk that can be converted into a dining table; it has wheels so that it can be easily moved.

EXHIBIT 6.1
Consumer Decision-Making Process

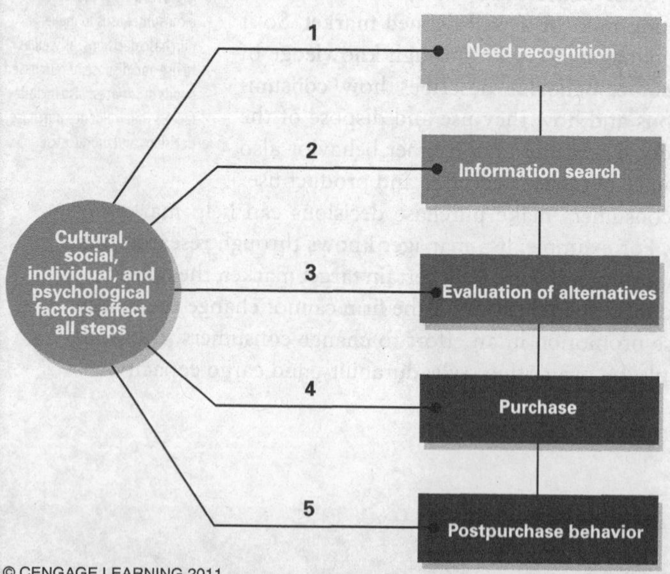

Consumers recognize unfulfilled wants in various ways. The two most common occur when a current product isn't performing properly and when the consumer is about to run out of something that is generally kept on hand. Consumers may also recognize unfulfilled wants if they become aware of a product that seems superior to the one currently used. Such wants are usually created by advertising and other promotional activities. For example, aware of the popularity of MP3s and consumers' desire to take their music with them, car stereo manufacturers such as Kenwood have added MP3 interfaces.

Marketers selling their products in global markets must carefully observe the needs and wants of consumers in various regions. LG Electronics, a Korean company, is anticipating rising demand for education among India's rural population. Increased levels of education often precede growth in purchasing power, so LG is targeting India's rural population by developing durable appliances for little cost. Brightly colored appliances are designed with surge stabilizers (to handle sporadic electric supply) and more durable plastic parts (to withstand harsher environments). Consumers in rural villages have responded well to the appliances—LG has seen a 30 percent growth in its rural sales.[1]

Information Search

After recognizing a need or want, consumers search for information about the various alternatives available to satisfy it. For example, you are new to a city and are looking for a rental accommodation, you go to www.justdial.com, give the details of the city and location to get the list of rental accommodations available. An information search can occur internally, externally, or both. In an **internal information search,** the person recalls information stored in the memory. This stored information stems largely from previous experience with a product. For example, while traveling with your family, you encounter a hotel where you stayed during spring break earlier that year. By searching your memory, you can probably remember whether the hotel had clean rooms and friendly service.

In contrast, an **external information search** seeks information in the outside environment. There are two basic types of external information sources: nonmarketing-controlled and marketing-controlled. A **nonmarketing-controlled information source** is not associated with marketers promoting a product. These information sources include personal experiences (trying or observing a new product), personal sources (family, friends, acquaintances, and co-workers who may recommend a product or service), and public sources (such as Underwriters Laboratories, *Consumer Reports*, and other rating organizations that comment on products and services). For example, if you are in the mood to go to the movies, you may search your memory for past experiences at various cinemas when determining which one to go to (personal experiences). To choose which movie you will see, you may rely on the recommendations of friends and family (personal sources). Alternatively, you may read the critical reviews in the newspaper or online (public sources). Marketers gather information on how these information sources work and use it to attract customers. For example, car manufacturers know that younger customers are likely to get information from friends and family, so they try to develop enthusiasm for their products via word of mouth.

Living in the digital age has changed the way consumers get nonmarketing-controlled information. It can be from blogs, social networking sites, Web sites, Web forums, consumer opinion sites such as www.mouthshut.com, www.tripadvisor.com, or www.epinions.com. Around 67 percent of the Web users in India use online reviews before making purchasing decisions.[2] Usage of social media sites has also increased, with more time being spent on such sites than on using personal email. In a study conducted by Nielsen on social media usage in India, 58 percent of the respondents cited "participating in discussions on issues/products/services" as one of the activities performed on social networking sites.[3] Many

internal information search the process of recalling past information stored in the memory

external information search the process of seeking information in the outside environment

nonmarketing-controlled information source a product information source that is not associated with advertising or promotion

© ISTOCKPHOTO/THINKSTOCK

marketing-controlled information source a product information source that originates with marketers promoting the product

consumers research products online before making an offline purchase, and then share the information and advice they gleaned online with other consumers.

The latest research has examined how consumers use information picked up on the Internet. For example, in Web forums, the information seeker has normally never met the information provider or ever interacted with the person before. Researchers found that an information provider's response speed, the extent to which the provider's previous responses within the forum had been positively evaluated by others, and the breadth of the provider's previous responses across different but related topics affected the information seeker's judgment about the value of the information. So, for example, if other information seekers had found the provider trustworthy, then the current seeker tended to believe the information.[4]

A **marketing-controlled information source** is biased toward a specific product because it originates with marketers promoting that product. Marketing-controlled information sources include mass media advertising (radio, newspaper, television, and magazine advertising), sales promotion (contests, displays, premiums, and so forth), salespeople, product labels and packaging, and the Internet. Many consumers, however, are wary of the information they receive from marketing-controlled sources, believing that most marketing campaigns stress the product's positive attributes and ignore its faults. These sentiments tend to be stronger among better-educated and higher-income consumers. Some marketing-controlled information sources can shift out of marketers' control, however, when there is bad news to report. When news media blanketed the airwaves with coverage of Cadbury's Dairy Milk being infected with worms, the chocolate-maker responded with a series of television ads featuring the famous bollywood actor, Mr. Amitabh Bachchan, and showed him visiting and inspecting a Cadbury plant and consuming a chocolate to signify that chocolate is safe. The bottom line of the Cadbury ads stressed the company's commitment to safety and continued investment in manufacturing and packaging of its chocolates.

The extent to which an individual conducts an external search depends on his or her perceived risk, knowledge, prior experience, and level of interest in the good or service. Generally, as the perceived risk of the purchase increases, the consumer enlarges the search and considers more alternative brands. For example, suppose that you want to purchase a surround sound system for your home stereo. The decision is relatively risky because of the expense and technical nature of the stereo system, so you are motivated to search for information about models, prices, options, compatibility with existing entertainment products, and capabilities. You may decide to compare attributes of many speaker systems because the value of the time expended finding the "right" stereo will be less than the cost of buying the wrong system.

A consumer's knowledge about the product or service will also affect the extent of an external information search. A consumer who is knowledgeable and well informed about a potential purchase is less likely to search for additional information. In addition, the more knowledgeable consumers are, the more efficiently they will conduct the search process, thereby requiring less time to search. For example, many consumers know that SpiceJet and other discount airlines have much lower fares, so they generally use the discounters and do not even check fares at other airlines.

The extent of a consumer's external search is also affected by confidence in one's decision-making

ability. A confident consumer not only has sufficient stored information about the product but also feels self-assured about making the right decision. People lacking this confidence will continue an information search even when they know a great deal about the product. Consumers with prior experience in buying a certain product will have less perceived risk than inexperienced consumers. Therefore, they will spend less time searching and limit the number of products they consider.

A third factor influencing the external information search is product experience. Consumers who have had a positive prior experience with a product are more likely to limit their search to items related to the positive experience. For example, when flying, consumers are likely to choose airlines with which they have had positive experiences, such as consistent on-time arrivals, and avoid airlines with which they had a negative experience, such as lost luggage.

Finally, the extent of the search is positively related to the amount of interest a consumer has in a product. A consumer who is more interested in a product will spend more time searching for information and alternatives. For example, suppose you are a dedicated runner who reads jogging and fitness magazines and catalogs. In searching for a new pair of running shoes, you may enjoy reading about the new brands available and spend more time and effort than other buyers in deciding on the right shoe.

The consumer's information search should yield a group of brands, sometimes called the buyer's **evoked set** (or **consideration set**), which are the consumer's most preferred alternatives. From this set, the buyer will further evaluate the alternatives and make a choice. Consumers do not consider all brands available in a product category, but they do seriously consider a much smaller set. For example, from the many brands of pizza available, consumers are likely to consider only the alternatives that fit their price range, location, take-out/delivery needs, and taste preferences. Having too many choices can, in fact, confuse consumers and cause them to delay the decision to buy or, in some instances, cause them not to buy at all.

Evaluation of Alternatives and Purchase

After getting information and constructing an evoked set of alternative products, the consumer is ready to make a decision. A consumer will use the information stored in memory and obtained from outside sources to develop a set of criteria. Recent research has shown that exposure to certain cues in your everyday environment can affect decision criteria and purchase.

The environment, internal information, and external information help consumers evaluate and compare alternatives. One way to begin narrowing the number of choices in the evoked set is to pick a product attribute and then exclude all products in the set that don't have that attribute. For example, assume Sam and Sid, both B-school graduates, are looking for their first apartment. They need a two-bedroom apartment, reasonably priced and located near their office. They want the apartment to be semi-furnished, have 24 hours water facility, and covered parking. Sam and Sid begin their search with all apartments in the given area and then systematically eliminate possibilities that lack the features they need. Hence, if there are 50 alternatives in the area, they may reduce their list to just ten apartments that possess all of the desired attributes. Another way to narrow the number of choices is to use cut-offs. Cut-offs are either minimum or maximum levels of an attribute that an alternative must pass to be considered. Suppose Sam and Sid set a maximum of ₹20,000 to spend on combined rent. Then all apartments with rent higher than ₹20,000 will be eliminated, further reducing the list of apartments from ten to eight. A final way to narrow the choices is to rank the attributes under consideration in order of importance and evaluate the products based on how well each performs on the most important attributes. To reach a final decision on one of the remaining eight apartments, Sam and Sid may decide proximity to office is the most important attribute. As a result, they will choose to rent the apartment closest to office.

If new brands are added to an evoked set, the consumer's evaluation of the existing brands in that set changes. As a result, certain brands in the original set may become more desirable. Suppose Sam and Sid find two apartments located equal distance from office, one priced at ₹15,000 and the other at ₹16,500. Faced with this choice, they may decide that the ₹16,500 apartment is too expensive given that a comparable apartment is cheaper. If they add another ₹18,000 apartment to the list, however, then they may perceive the ₹16,500 apartment as more reasonable and decide to rent it.

The purchase decision process described above is a piecemeal process. That is, the evaluation is made

evoked set (consideration set) a group of brands, resulting from an information search, from which a buyer can choose

cognitive dissonance inner tension that a consumer experiences after recognizing an inconsistency between behavior and values or opinions

by examining alternative advantages and disadvantages along important product attributes. A different way consumers can evaluate a product is according to a categorization process. The evaluation of an alternative depends upon the particular category to which it is assigned. Categories can be very general (motorized forms of transportation), or they can be very specific (Hero MotoCorp motorcycles). Typically, these categories are associated with some degree of liking or disliking. To the extent that the product can be assigned membership to a particular category, it will receive an evaluation similar to that attached to the category. If you go to the grocery store and see a new organic food on the shelf, you may evaluate it on your liking and opinions of organic food.

So, when consumers rely on a categorization process, a product's evaluation depends on the particular category to which it is perceived as belonging. Given this, companies need to understand whether consumers are using categories that evoke the desired evaluations. Indeed, how a product is categorized can strongly influence consumer demand. For example, what products come to mind when you think about the "morning beverages" category? To the soft drink industry's dismay, far too few consumers include sodas in this category. Several attempts have been made at getting soft drinks on the breakfast table, but with little success.

Brand extensions, in which a well-known and respected brand name from one product category is extended into other product categories, is one way companies employ categorization to their advantage. Brand extensions are a common business practice. Park Avenue, a men's wear brand from Raymond Group, has over the years extended its brand name in multiple categories like Park Avenue Woman, Park Avenue Soaps, Park Avenue Deodorants and Park Avenue Shaving Cream, among others. Sunfeast by ITC has extended its portfolio in the FMCG business from biscuit category to snacking category (Sunfeast Pasta) and instant noodles category (Sunfeast Yippee).

To Buy or Not to Buy Ultimately, the consumer has to decide whether to buy or not buy. Specifically, consumers must decide:

1. Whether to buy
2. When to buy
3. What to buy (product type and brand)
4. Where to buy (type of retailer, specific retailer, online or in store)
5. How to pay

When a person is buying an expensive or complex item, it is often a *fully planned purchase* based upon a lot of information. People rarely buy a new home simply on impulse. Often consumers will make a *partially planned purchase* when they know the product category they want to buy (shirts, pants, reading lamp, car floor mats) but wait until they get to the store to choose a specific style or brand. Finally, there is the *unplanned purchase*, which people buy on impulse. Research has found that up to 68 percent of the items bought during major shopping trips and 54 percent on smaller shopping trips are unplanned.[5]

LO 3 Postpurchase Behavior

When buying products, consumers expect certain outcomes from the purchase. How well these expectations are met determines whether the consumer is satisfied or dissatisfied with the purchase. For example, if a person bids on a used car stereo from eBay and wins, he may have fairly low expectations regarding performance. If the stereo's performance turns out to be of superior quality, then the person's satisfaction will be high because his expectations were exceeded. Conversely, if the person bid on a new car stereo expecting superior quality and performance, but the stereo broke within one month, he would be very dissatisfied because his expectations were not met. Price often influences the level of expectations for a product or service.

For the marketer, an important element of any postpurchase evaluation is reducing any lingering doubts that the decision was sound. When people recognize inconsistency between their values or opinions and their behavior, they tend to feel an inner tension called **cognitive dissonance**. For example, say someone is looking to upgrade her cell phone to a new Android Smart- phone. She can get a HTC Sensation for ₹32,000, with an 8 megapixel camera and all the up-to-date features. Or, for ₹7,500 she can buy the Samsung Galaxy Y, which has a 2 megapixel camera and competitive features. Prior to choosing the HTC Sensation, the shopper may experience inner tension

THE MILLION MEMBER FASHION IN-GROUP

High-end fashion isn't cheap and is often limited to those who have an "in" to the fashion industry. Fashionandyou.com offers that "in" - and a steep discount – to its 27 lakh members.[6] Fashionandyou.com is an exclusive online destination; featuring the best international and Indian designer brands in luxury, hi-fashion and lifestyle experiences for men, women, children and home. Authentic designer merchandise is offered with up to 80% off retail prices and is provided exclusively to the members through limited-time events. Normally, the sales begin at 11 am and on an average, continue for 3 days. The members are notified in advance though emails, SMS, and networking sites about the upcoming exclusive sale events. The site's access is restricted to registered members only, thereby making the customers feel they are part of an exclusive club.[7]

© INGRM PUBLISHING/THINKSTOCK

or anxiety because she is worried that the current top-of-the-line technology, which costs much more than the middle-of-the-line technology, will be obsolete in a couple of months. That feeling of dissonance arises as her worries over obsolescence battle her practical nature, which is focused on the lower cost of the Samsung Galaxy Y and its adequate—but not fancy—technology.

Consumers try to reduce dissonance by justifying their decision. They may seek new information that reinforces positive ideas about the purchase, avoid information that contradicts their decision, or revoke the original decision by returning the product. To ensure satisfaction, thereby reducing dissonance, the customer buying the HTC Sensation may talk to people who have the phone, read online reviews, and talk to her provider to obtain additional information. In some instances, people deliberately seek contrary information in order to refute it and reduce dissonance. Dissatisfied customers sometimes rely on word of mouth to reduce cognitive dissonance, by letting friends and family know they are displeased.

Marketing managers can help reduce dissonance through effective communication with purchasers. For example, a customer service manager may slip a note inside the package congratulating the buyer on making a wise decision. Postpurchase letters sent by manufacturers and dissonance-reducing statements in instruction booklets may help customers feel at ease with their purchase. Advertising that displays the product's superiority over competing brands or guarantees can also help relieve the possible dissonance of someone who has already bought the product.

LO 4 Types of Consumer Buying Decisions and Consumer Involvement

All consumer buying decisions generally fall along a continuum of three broad categories: routine response behavior, limited decision making, and

involvement the amount of time and effort a buyer invests in the search, evaluation, and decision processes of consumer behavior

routine response behavior the type of decision making exhibited by consumers buying frequently purchased, low-cost goods and services; requires little search and decision time

limited decision making the type of decision making that requires a moderate amount of time for gathering information and deliberating about an unfamiliar brand in a familiar product category

extensive decision making the most complex type of consumer decision making, used when buying an unfamiliar, expensive product or an infrequently bought item; requires use of several criteria for evaluating options and much time for seeking information

extensive decision making (see Exhibit 6.2). Goods and services in these three categories can best be described in terms of five factors: level of consumer involvement, length of time to make a decision, cost of the good or service, degree of information search, and the number of alternatives considered. The level of consumer involvement is perhaps the most significant determinant in classifying buying decisions. **Involvement** is the amount of time and effort a buyer invests in the search, evaluation, and decision processes of consumer behavior.

Frequently purchased, low-cost goods and services are generally associated with **routine response behavior.** These goods and services can also be called low-involvement products because consumers spend little time on search and decision before making the purchase. Usually, buyers are familiar with several different brands in the product category but stick with one brand. For example, a person may routinely buy Tropicana orange juice. Consumers engaged in routine response behavior normally don't experience need recognition until they are exposed to advertising or see the product displayed on a store shelf. Consumers buy first and evaluate later, whereas the reverse is true for extensive decision making. A consumer who has previously purchased a whitening toothpaste and was satisfied with it will probably walk to the toothpaste aisle and select that same brand without spending 20 minutes examining all other alternatives.

Limited decision making typically occurs when a consumer has previous product experience but is unfamiliar with the current brands available. Limited decision making is also associated with lower levels of involvement (although higher than routine decisions) because consumers expend only moderate effort in searching for information or in considering various alternatives. But what happens if the consumer's usual brand of whitening toothpaste is sold out? Assuming that toothpaste is needed, the consumer will be forced to choose another brand. Before making a final decision, the consumer will likely evaluate several other brands based on their active ingredients, their promotional claims, and the consumer's prior experiences.

Consumers practice **extensive decision making** when buying an unfamiliar, expensive product or an infrequently bought item. This process is the most complex type of consumer buying decision and is associated with high involvement on the part of the consumer. This process resembles the model outlined in Exhibit 6.1. These consumers want to make the right decision, so they want to know as much as they can about the product category and available brands. People usually experience the most cognitive dissonance when buying high-involvement products. Buyers use several criteria for evaluating their options and spend much time seeking information. Buying a home or a car, for example, requires extensive decision making.

The type of decision making that consumers use to purchase a product does not necessarily remain constant. For instance, if a routinely purchased product no longer satisfies, consumers may practice limited or extensive decision making to switch to another brand. And people who first use extensive decision making may then use limited or routine decision making for future purchases. For example, when a family gets a new puppy, they will spend a lot of time and energy trying out different toys to determine which one the dog prefers. Once the new owners learn that the dog prefers a bone to a ball, however, the purchase no longer requires extensive evaluation and will become routine.

EXHIBIT 6.2

Continuum of Consumer Buying Decisions

	Routine	Limited	Extensive
Involvement	Low	Low to moderate	High
Time	Short	Short to moderate	Long
Cost	Low	Low to moderate	High
Information Search	Internal only	Mostly internal	Internal and external
Number of Alternatives	One	Few	Many

Factors Determining the Level of Consumer Involvement

The level of involvement in the purchase depends on the five factors listed below.

- *Previous experience:* When consumers have had previous experience with a good or service, the level of involvement typically decreases. After repeated product trials, consumers learn to make quick choices. Because consumers are familiar with the product and know whether it will satisfy their needs, they become less involved in the purchase. For example, a consumer purchasing cereal has many brands to choose from—just think of any grocery store cereal aisle. If the consumer always buys the same brand because it satisfies his hunger, then he has a low level of involvement. When a consumer purchases cereal for the first time, however, it likely will be a much more involved purchase.
- *Interest:* Involvement is directly related to consumer interests, as in cars, music, movies, bicycling, or electronics. Naturally, these areas of interest vary from one individual to another. A person highly involved in bike racing will be more interested in the type of bike she owns and will spend quite a bit of time evaluating different bikes. If a person wants a bike only for recreation, however, he may be fairly uninvolved in the purchase and just look for a bike from the most convenient location.
- *Perceived risk of negative consequences:* As the perceived risk in purchasing a product increases, so does a consumer's level of involvement. The types of risks that concern consumers include financial risk, social risk, and psychological risk. First, financial risk is exposure to loss of wealth or purchasing power. Because high risk is associated with high-priced purchases, consumers tend to become extremely involved. Therefore, price and involvement are usually directly related: As price increases, so does the level of involvement. For example, someone who is purchasing a new car for the first time (higher perceived risk) will spend a lot of time and effort making this purchase. Second, consumers take social risks when they buy products that can affect people's social opinions of them (e.g., driving an old, beat-up car or wearing unstylish clothes). Third, buyers undergo psychological risk if they feel that making the wrong decision might cause some concern or anxiety. For example, some consumers feel guilty about eating foods that are not healthy, such as regular ice cream rather than fat-free frozen yogurt.
- *Situation:* The circumstances of a purchase may temporarily transform a low-involvement decision into a high-involvement one. High involvement comes into play when the consumer perceives risk in a specific situation. For example, an individual might routinely buy low-priced brands of liqor and wine. When the boss visits, however, the consumer might make a high-involvement decision and buy more prestigious brands.
- *Social visibility:* Involvement also increases as the social visibility of a product increases. Products often on social display include clothing (especially designer labels), jewelry, cars, and furniture. All these items make a statement about the purchaser and, therefore, carry a social risk.

Marketing Implications of Involvement

Marketing strategy varies according to the level of involvement associated with the product. For high-involvement product purchases, marketing managers have several responsibilities. First, promotion to the target market should be extensive and informative. A good ad gives consumers the information they

© FORD MOTOR COMPANY/PHOTOGRAPHY BY RON STRONG

culture the set of values, norms, attitudes, and other meaningful symbols that shape human behavior and the artifacts, or products, of that behavior as they are transmitted from one generation to the next

need for making the purchase decision and specifies the benefits and unique advantages of owning the product. For example, Tata advertised its new vehicle—Tata Ace—extensively to inform about the product and highlight its benefits. The product was targeted towards customers transporting goods through three wheelers. The product was positioned as a "mini-truck", offering convenient and speedily transportation at lower costs. It also made an emotional appeal to the customers by portraying the protagonist enjoying a good social status and creating self-employment opportunities for himself. This strategy helped the company in achieving tremendous success in the market.

For low-involvement product purchases, consumers may not recognize their wants until they are in the store. Therefore, in-store promotion is an important tool when promoting low-involvement products. Marketing managers focus on package design so the product will be eye-catching and easily recognized on the shelf. Examples of products that take this approach are Pears soap, Knorr soups, Tide detergent, and Heinz ketchup. In-store displays also stimulate sales of low-involvement products. A good display can explain the product's purpose and prompt recognition of a want. Displays of health and beauty aid items in supermarkets have been known to increase sales many times above normal. Coupons, rupee-off deals, and two-for-one offers also effectively promote low-involvement items.

Linking a product to a higher-involvement issue is another tactic that marketing managers can use to increase the sales or positive publicity of a low-involvement product. Proctor & Gamble channels a portion of its sales revenue each year towards its CSR initiative "Shiksha" (hindi term for education). The initiative was launched in 2004 with the aim of providing quality education to the uneducated, underprivileged children of India, in association with some of the leading NGOs of the country. The campaign is run for a stipulated time period annually, wherein each time customers buy any of the P&G products, a portion of the proceeds is contributed towards the education of underprivileged children. By 2010-11, the campaign had succeeded in impacting the lives of 1,50,000 children and planned to take the mark to 2,00,000. In 2010-11, Shiksha also started building over 20 schools across India and aimed to build at least 20 more next year.[8]

LO 5–LO 8 Factors Influencing Consumer Buying Decisions

The consumer decision-making process does not occur in a vacuum. On the contrary, underlying cultural, social, individual, and psychological factors strongly influence the decision process. These factors have an effect from the time a consumer perceives a stimulus through postpurchase behavior. Cultural factors, which include culture and values, subculture, and social class, exert a broad influence over consumer decision making. Social factors sum up the social interactions between a consumer and influential groups of people, such as reference groups, opinion leaders, and family members. Individual factors, which include gender, age, family life cycle stage, personality, self-concept, and lifestyle, are unique to each individual and play a major role in the type of products and services consumers want. Psychological factors determine how consumers perceive and interact with their environments and influence the ultimate decisions consumers make. They include perception, motivation, learning, beliefs, and attitudes. Exhibit 6.3 summarizes these influences.

LO 5 Cultural Influences on Consumer Buying Decisions

Of all the factors that affect consumer decision making, cultural factors exert the broadest and deepest influence. Marketers must understand the way people's culture and its accompanying values, as well as their subculture and social class, influence their buying behavior.

Culture and Values

Culture is the essential character of a society that distinguishes it from other cultural groups. The underly-

EXHIBIT 6.3
Factors that Affect the Consumer Decision-Making Process

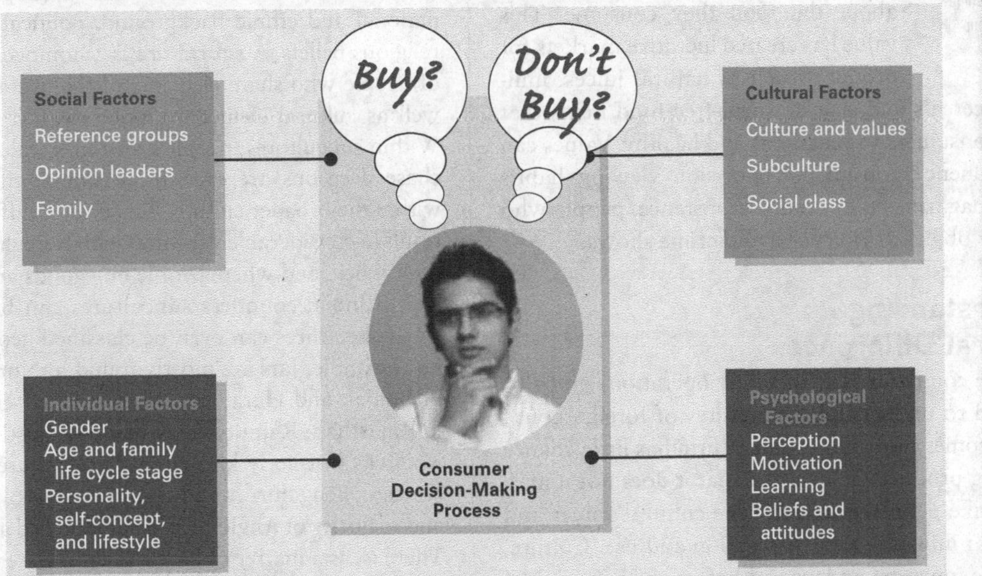

© ISTOCKPHOTO/THINKSTOCK

ing elements of every culture are the values, language, myths, customs, rituals, and laws that shape the behavior of the people, as well as the material artifacts, or products, of that behavior as they are transmitted from one generation to the next.

Culture is pervasive. Cultural values and influences are the ocean in which individuals swim, and yet most are completely unaware that it is there. What people eat, how they dress, what they think and feel, and what language they speak are all dimensions of culture. It encompasses all the things consumers do without conscious choice because their culture's values, customs, and rituals are ingrained in their daily habits.

Culture is functional. Human interaction creates values and prescribes acceptable behavior for each culture. By establishing common expectations, culture gives order to society. Sometimes these expectations are enacted into laws. For example, drivers in our culture must stop at a red light. Other times these expectations are taken for granted: Police stations and hospitals are open 24 hours, whereas banks are open only during bankers' hours.

Culture is learned. Consumers are not born knowing the values and norms of their society. Instead, they must learn what is acceptable from family and friends. Children learn the values that will govern their behaviour from parents, teachers, and peers. As members of our society, they learn to fold hands when they greet someone, to walk on the left-hand side of the road, and to eat their meal of dinner along with the rest of the family members.

Culture is dynamic. It adapts to changing needs and an evolving environment. The rapid growth of technology in today's world has accelerated the rate of cultural change. Television has changed entertainment patterns and family communication and has heightened public awareness of political and other news events. Automation has increased the amount of leisure time we have and, in some ways, has changed the traditional work ethic. Cultural norms will continue to evolve because of our need for social patterns that solve problems.

The most defining element of a culture is its **values**—the enduring beliefs shared by a society that a specific mode of conduct is personally or socially preferable to another mode of conduct. People's value systems have a great effect on their consumer behavior. Consumers with similar value systems tend to react alike to prices and other marketing-related inducements. Values also cor-

value the enduring belief that a specific mode of conduct is personally or socially preferable to another mode of conduct

subculture a homogeneous group of people who share elements of the overall culture as well as unique elements of their own group

respond to consumption patterns. For example, with a rise in health awareness levels, people are more concerned about the food they consume. This value has created lucrative markets for products such as natural juices, multigrain cereals and snacks, sugar-free food items that allow consumers to remain fit and healthy. Values can also influence consumers' television viewing habits or the magazines they read. For instance, people who strongly object to violence avoid crime shows.

Understanding Cultural Differences

As more companies expand their operations globally, the need to understand the cultures of foreign countries becomes more important. A firm has little chance of selling products in a culture that it does not understand. Like people, products have cultural values and rules that influence their perception and use. Culture, therefore, must be understood before the behavior of individuals within the cultural context can be understood. Colors, for example, may have different meanings in global markets than they do at home. In China, white is the color of mourning and brides wear red. In the United States, black is for mourning and brides wear white.

Language is another important aspect of culture that global marketers must consider. When translating product names, slogans, and promotional messages into foreign languages, they must be careful not to convey the wrong message. General Motors discovered too late that Nova (the name of an economical car) literally means "doesn't go" in Spanish; Pepsi faced a similar situation in Taiwan whereby its slogan of "Come Alive with Pepsi" translated to "Pepsi brings your ancestors back from the dead"; KFC slogan "finger lickin' good" translated as "eat your fingers off" in Chinese.

Although marketers expanding into global markets generally adapt their products and business formats to the local culture, some fear that increasing globalization, as well as the proliferation of the Internet, will result in a homogeneous world culture of the future. U.S. companies in particular, they fear, are Americanizing the world by exporting bastions of American culture, such as McDonald's fast-food restaurants, Microsoft software, Levis Jeans, and American movies and entertainment.

Subculture

A culture can be divided into subcultures on the basis of demographic characteristics, geographic regions, national and ethnic background, political beliefs, and religious beliefs. A **subculture** is a homogeneous group of people who share elements of the overall culture as well as cultural elements unique to their own group. Within subcultures, people's attitudes, values, and purchase decisions are even more similar than they are within the broader culture. Subcultural differences may result in considerable variation within a culture in what, how, when, and where people buy goods and services.

In India, countless subcultures can be identified. The subcultures can even be classified geographically. For example, Jats are mostly found in Northern states of Punjab and Harayana; Marwaris are concentrated in Rajasthan; Rajputs are found in Rajasthan and UP; Kodavas (formerly known as Coorgis) are situated in Kodagu, Bengaluru, and Mysore regions of Karnataka; and majority of Anglo Indians are located around Goa. There is, as a matter of fact, a great difference between the tastes and preferences across regions in India. For instance, when it comes to staple food preferences, the North Indians have a preference for wheat; the South Indians have a preference for rice; and East Indians have a preference for fish. Similarly, consumption of gold is the highest in the southern states. Well over 40 percent of total gold consumption in India is in the southern regions, while the eastern regions consume the least amount of gold.[9] The high consumption of gold in southern India can be attributed to the custom of buying gold and the metal being considered as a safe investment. There are several other products which have diverse consumption across different regions in India. For instance talcum powder is consumed heavily in Tamil Nadu; West Bengal is a big consumer of skin care products; and rural Punjab has a great fetish for luxury brands.[10] There are several other subcultures as well that can be identified throughout India. For instance, Enfield Bullet bikers, military families, old royal families, gays, lesbians, and transgenders are some of the other subcultures present in India. These subcultures have their own identifiable attitudes, values, and needs that distinguish them from the larger culture.

Once marketers identify subcultures, they can design special marketing campaigns to serve their needs. Some companies launch simultaneous campaigns to reach different subcultures. For the commercial of Pond's Dreamflower Talc, a bollywood movie song, "tera hone laga hoon," was used in Northern

India, while down south, specific songs were written for the states. Sunlight, a detergent brand from Unilever, sells in just two states—West Bengal and Kerala. Its ad campaign, therefore, is conceptualized and shot in Bengali and the same is dubbed in Malayalam for Kerala. Kaya Skin Clinic promotes different services in different regions, based on specific needs of each region. Therefore, while it focused on pigmentation solution in Tamil Nadu, in the North, it emphasized on skin beauty services.[11] Even the celebrities used in the advertising campaigns differ from region to region. Thums Up employed Bollywood actor Akshay Kumar as its brand ambassador in North India, but employed South Indian actor Mahesh Babu as its brand ambassador for Andhra Pradesh.[12]

Social Class

India, like other societies, has a social class system. A **social class** is a group of people who are considered nearly equal in status or community esteem, who regularly socialize among themselves both formally and informally, and who share behavioral norms.

A number of techniques have been used to measure social class, and a number of criteria have been used to define it. One view of contemporary India status structure is shown in Exhibit 6.4.

social class a group of people in a society who are considered nearly equal in status or community esteem, who regularly socialize among themselves both formally and informally, and who share behavioral norms

Since India is divided into two parts: urban and rural, there are separate socio economic classes for both. Occupation and education of the head of the household are key determinants of the Urban SEC system (classes A to E), while the rural SEC (R1 to R4) system is determined on the basis of education of the head of the household and the type of house lived in.[13] Exhibits 6.5 and 6.6 provide a detailed break-up of the urban and rural SECs.[14]

In terms of consumer buying patterns, the affluent are more likely to own their own home and purchase new cars and luxurious products. The very rich flex their financial muscles by spending more on vacations and cruises, and housekeeping and gardening services. The most affluent consumers are more likely to attend art auctions and galleries, dance performances,

EXHIBIT 6.4
India's Social Class

Upper Classes		
A1	1%	The chief wage earners of the upper class households either work in executive positions or work as businessmen or shop owners. They are mostly graduates or post-graduates.
A2	2.1%	
Middle Classes		
B1	2.5%	The chief wage earners are employed at clerical or supervisory levels, businessmen, shop owners, skilled workers, or petty traders. Most of them are educated till 10th or 12th grade and some might even have some college education.
B2	2.6%	
C	6.2%	
Lower Classes		
D	7.3%	The chief wage earners are majorly employed at unskilled workers, skilled workers, and petty traders. Their education is largely restricted to school education or else, they are illiterate.
E1	3.6%	
E2	5.8%	
Rural Socio-Economic Class		
R1	2.8%	The education of the chief wage earners can vary from being illiterate to having a graduate or post graduate or professional degree. The house types are classified as pucca, semi-pucca, or kutcha.
R2	8.1%	
R3	28%	
R4	29.9%	

SOURCE: The Marketing Whitebook 2009-2010, Business World

EXHIBIT 6.5

Urban SECs

Education	Illiterate	School: Upto 4 Years	School: 5-9 Years	SSC/ HSC	Some College but not Graduate	Graduate/ Post-Graduate General	Graduate/ Post-Graduate Professional
Unskilled Workers	E2	E2	E1	D	D	D	D
Skilled Workers	E2	E1	D	C	C	B2	B2
Petty Traders	E2	D	D	C	C	B2	B2
Shop Owners	D	D	C	B2	B1	A2	A2
Businessman/ Industrialists with No. of employees:	D	C	B2	B1	A2	A2	A1
None:	D	C	B2	B1	A2	A2	A1
1-9:	C	B2	B2	B1	A2	A1	A1
10+:	B1	B1	A2	A2	A1	A1	A1
Self Employed Professionals	D	D	D	B2	B1	A2	A1
Clerical/ Salesmen	D	D	D	C	B2	B1	B1
Supervisory Level	D	D	C	C	B2	B1	A2
Officers/ Executives - Junior	C	C	C	B2	B1	A2	A2
Officers/ Executives - Middle/ Senior	B1	B1	B1	B1	A2	A1	A1

EXHIBIT 6.6

Rural SECs

Education of Chief Wage Earner	Type of House		
	Pucca	**Semi-Pucca**	**Kutcha**
Illiterate	R4	R4	R4
(Self-Learning)/No School	R3	R4	R4
Up to Class 4	R3	R3	R4
Class 4-Class 9	R3	R3	R4
SSC/HSC	R2	R3	R3
College	R1	R2	R3
Graduation/PG – Gen	R1	R2	R3
Orifessuibak degree	R1	R2	R3

the theatre, museums, concerts, and sporting events. Marketers often pay attention to the superwealthy. The luxury book market is targeting superwealthy collectors with books sporting price tags that rival original artwork. For example, 10 limited edition copies of an autobiography by Indian cricket star Sachin Tendulkar feature a page with his blood mixed into the paper pulp. Even though a copy of the book cost ₹33,75,000, all 10 sold! The majority of Indians today define themselves as middle class, regardless of their actual income or educational attainment. This phenomenon most likely occurs because working-class Indians tend to aspire to the middle-class lifestyle, while some of those who do achieve affluence may downwardly aspire to respectable middle-class status as a matter of principle.

The working class is a distinct subset of the middle class. Interest in organized labor is one of the most common attributes among the working class. This group often rates job security as the most important reason for taking a job. The working-class person depends heavily on relatives and the community for economic and emotional support.

Lifestyle distinctions between the social classes are greater than the distinctions within a given class. The most significant difference between the classes occurs between the middle and lower classes, where there is a major shift in lifestyles. Members of the lower class have incomes at or below the poverty level.

Social class is typically measured as a combination of occupation, income, education, wealth, and other variables. For instance, affluent upper-class consumers are more likely to be salaried executives or self-employed professionals with at least an undergraduate degree. Working-class or middle-class consumers are more likely to be hourly service workers or blue-collar employees with only a high school education. Educational attainment, however, seems to be the most reliable indicator of a person's social and economic status. Those with college degrees or graduate degrees are more likely to fall into the upper classes, while those people with some college experience fall closest to traditional concepts of the middle class.

Marketers are interested in social class for two main reasons. First, social class often indicates which medium to use for advertising. Suppose an insurance company seeks to sell its policies to middle-class families. It might advertise during the local evening news because middle-class families tend to watch more television than other classes do. If the company wanted to sell more policies to upscale individuals, it might place a print ad in a business publication like the *Economic Times*. The Internet, long the domain of more educated and affluent families, is becoming an increasingly important advertising outlet for advertisers hoping to reach blue-collar workers and homemakers. As the middle class rapidly adopts the medium, marketers have to do more research to find out which Web sites will reach their audience.

reference group a group in society that influences an individual's purchasing behavior

Second, knowing what products appeal to which social classes can help marketers determine where to best distribute their products.

For the first time in a long while, however, industry analysts are seeing sales of supermarkets and hypermarkets picking up. Now the challenge has been courting consumers who fall in the middle-income level. The result is a fiercely competitive retail environment where focus is on offering price benefits and value for money products to the consumers. Overall, however, shares of discount chains are faring better during this particular penny-pinching economy than their full-priced and upscale counterparts, because discount retailers have focused on getting current customers to purchase a wider array of products in the store, rather than trying to attract new shoppers.[15]

LO 6 Social Influences on Consumer Buying Decisions

Many consumers seek out the opinions of others to reduce their search and evaluation effort or uncertainty, especially as the perceived risk of the decision increases. Consumers may also seek out others' opinions for guidance on new products or services, products with image-related attributes, or products for which attribute information is lacking or uninformative. Specifically, consumers interact socially with reference groups, opinion leaders, and family members to obtain product information and decision approval.

Reference Groups

All the formal and informal groups that influence the buying behavior of an individual are that person's **reference groups.** Consumers may use products or brands to identify with or become a member of a

primary membership group a reference group with which people interact regularly in an informal, face-to-face manner, such as family, friends, and co-workers

secondary membership group a reference group with which people associate less consistently and more formally than a primary membership group, such as a club, professional group, or religious group

aspirational reference group a group that someone would like to join

norm a value or attitude deemed acceptable by a group

EXHIBIT 6.7

Types of Reference Groups

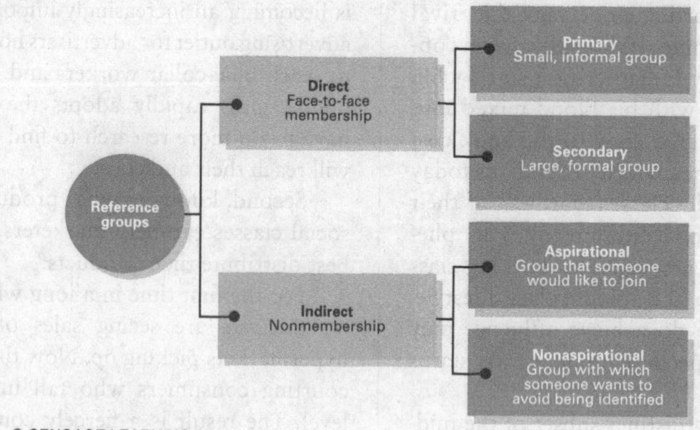

group. They learn from observing how members of their reference groups consume, and they use the same criteria to make their own consumer decisions.

Reference groups can be categorized very broadly as either direct or indirect (see Exhibit 6.7). Direct reference groups are face-to-face membership groups that touch people's lives directly. They can be either primary or secondary. **Primary membership groups** include all groups with which people interact regularly in an informal, face-to-face manner, such as family, friends, and co-workers. In contrast, people associate with **secondary membership groups** less consistently and more formally. These groups might include clubs, professional groups, and religious groups.

Consumers also are influenced by many indirect, nonmembership reference groups to which they do not belong. **Aspirational reference groups** are those a person would like to join. To join an aspirational group, a person must at least conform to the norms of that group. (**Norms** are the values and attitudes deemed acceptable by the group.) Thus, a person who wants to be elected to public office may begin to dress more conservatively, as other politicians do. He or she may go to many of the restaurants and social engagements that city and business leaders attend and try to play a role that is acceptable to voters and other influential people. Similarly, teenagers today may dye their hair and experiment with body piercing and tattoos. Athletes are an aspirational group for several market segments. To appeal to the younger market, Ranbaxy signed cricket star Yuvraj Singh to be the spokesperson for its Revital brand, and Reebok signed a deal with him for their cricket merchandise. Ranbaxy and Reebok assumed Singh would encourage consumers to purchase

Revital and Reebok equipments because they would like to identify with him.

Nonaspirational reference groups, or dissociative groups, influence our behavior when we try to maintain distance from them. A consumer may avoid buying some types of clothing or cars, going to certain restaurants or stores, or even buying a home in a certain neighborhood in order to avoid being associated with a particular group.

The activities, values, and goals of reference groups directly influence consumer behavior. For marketers, reference groups have three important implications: (1) They serve as information sources and influence perceptions; (2) they affect an individual's aspiration levels; and (3) their norms either constrain or stimulate consumer behavior. For example, research firms devoted to uncovering what's cool in the teen market have identified a couple of influential groups among today's teens based on their interests in clothes, music, and activities. Tracking these groups reveals how products become cool and how groups influence the adoption of cool products by other groups. A trend or fad often starts with teens who have the most innovative tastes. These teens are on the cutting edge of fashion and music, and they wear their attitude all over their bodies in the form of tattoos, body piercings, studded jewelry, or colored tresses. Certain fads embraced by these "Edgers" will spark an interest in the small group of teens researchers call "Influencers," who project the look other teens covet. Influencers also create their own trends in music and clothing choices. Once a fad is embraced and adopted by Influencers, the look becomes cool and desirable. The remaining groups that comprise the majority of the teen population will not embrace a fad until it gets its seal of approval from the Influencers.

opinion leader an individual who influences the opinions of others

nonaspirational reference group a group with which an individual does not want to associate

People with well-formed networks of somewhat overlapping reference groups and those with strong personal values are less susceptible to reference group influences.[16]

Opinion Leaders

Reference groups frequently include individuals known as group leaders, or **opinion leaders**—those who influence others. Obviously, it is important for marketing managers to persuade such people to purchase their goods or services.

Opinion leaders are often the first to try new products and services out of pure curiosity. They are typically

LG has developed a line of in-room "ArtCool" air conditioners that can display your favorite image under its clear front panel while cooling and purifying the air. Or consumers can enjoy classic art pieces by great artists on the front panel.

socialization process how cultural values and norms are passed down to children

self-indulgent and status seeking, making them more likely to explore unproven but intriguing products and services.[17] Technology companies have found that teenagers, because of their willingness to experiment, are key opinion leaders for the success of new technologies.

Opinion leadership is a casual phenomenon and is usually inconspicuous, so locating opinion leaders can be a challenge. Thus, marketers often try to create opinion leaders. On a national level, companies sometimes use movie stars, sports figures, and other celebrities to promote products, hoping they are appropriate opinion leaders. The effectiveness of celebrity endorsements varies, though, depending largely on how credible and attractive the spokesperson is and how familiar people are with him or her. Endorsements are most likely to succeed if a reasonable association between the spokesperson and the product can be established.

Increasingly, marketers are looking to social networking sites because these sites better identify the social trends that are shaping consumer behaviour. With their unprecedented ability to network and communicate with each other, young people rely on each others' opinions more than marketing messages when making purchase decisions. And blogs are becoming a key way that teens communicate their opinions. Consequently, today's marketers are reading teen blogs, developing products that meet the very specific needs that teens express there, and learning unique and creative ways to put key influencers in charge of marketing their brands for them. Marketers are also using other social networking and online media to determine and attract opinion leaders, which will be discussed in Chapter 22.

Family

The family is the most important social institution for many consumers, strongly influencing values, attitudes, self-concept, and buying behavior. For example, a family that strongly values good health will have a grocery list distinctly different from that of a family that views every dinner as a gourmet event. Moreover, the family is responsible for the **socialization process**, the passing down of cultural values and norms to children. Children learn by observing their parents' consumption patterns, so they tend to shop in a similar pattern.

Decision-making roles among family members tend to vary significantly, depending on the type of item purchased. Family members assume a variety of roles in the purchase process. *Initiators* suggest, initiate, or plant the seed for the purchase process. The initiator can be any member of the family. For example, Sister might initiate the product search by asking for a new bicycle as a birthday present. *Influencers* are those members of the family whose opinions are valued. In our example, Mom might function as a price-range watchdog, an influencer whose main role is to veto or approve price ranges. Brother may give his opinion on certain makes of bicycles. The *decision maker* is the family member who actually makes the decision to buy or not to buy. For example, Dad or Mom is likely to choose the final brand and model of bicycle to buy after seeking further information from Sister about cosmetic features such as color and then imposing additional criteria of his or her own, such as durability and safety. The *purchaser* (probably Dad or Mom) is the one who actually exchanges money for the product. Finally, the *consumer* is the actual user—Sister, in the case of the bicycle.

Marketers should consider family purchase situations along with the distribution of consumer and decision-maker roles among family members. Ordinary marketing views the individual as both decision maker and consumer. Family marketing adds several other possibilities: Sometimes more than one family member or all family members are involved in the decision, sometimes only children are involved in the decision, sometimes more than one consumer is involved, and sometimes the decision maker and the consumer are different people. In most households, when parental joint decisions are being made, spouses consider their partner's needs and perceptions to maintain decision fairness and harmony.This tends to minimize family conflict. Research also shows that in harmonious households, the spouse who has "won" a previous decision is less likely to use strong influence in a subsequent decision.[18] This balancing factor is key in maintaining long-term family harmony.

Children can have great influence over the purchase decisions of their parents. In many families, with both parents working and short on time, children are encouraged to participate. In addition, children in single-parent households become more involved in family decisions at an earlier age. Children are especially influential in decisions about food and eating out. Exactly how much of an influence kids have varies depending on factors such as age, race, socioeconomic status, and region. For example, *Restaurants & Institutions'* New American Diner Study shows that children age 5 or younger frequently influence restaurant visits, while children ages 6 to 18 have only occasional influence. Females, Generation Xers, Asian Americans, and Midwesterners are most likely to say children influence which restaurants they visit.[19] Children influence purchase decisions for many more products and services than food. Even though they are usually not the actual purchasers of such items, children often participate in decisions about toys, clothes, vacations, recreation, automobiles, and many other products. And if those children happen to be teenagers? There are 2 crore U.S. teens, and half of them receive as much as ₹1,755 a week. Teen spending power amounts to more than ₹9,00,000 crore, a significant amount of money for a group that is willing to spend.[20]

Traditionally, children learn about consumption from their parents. In today's technologically overloaded world, that trend is reversing. Teenagers and adult children often contribute information and influence the purchase of parents' technology products.[21] Often they even help with installation and show the parents how to use the product!

© STOCKBYTE/THINKSTOCK

LO 7 Individual Influences on Consumer Buying Decisions

A person's buying decisions are also influenced by personal characteristics that are unique to each individual, such as gender; age and life cycle stage; and personality, self-concept, and lifestyle. Individual characteristics are generally stable over the course of one's life. For instance, most people do not change their gender, and the act of changing personality or lifestyle requires a complete reorientation of one's life. In the case of age and life cycle stage, these changes occur gradually over time.

Gender

Physiological differences between men and women result in different needs, such as health and beauty products. Just as important are the distinct cultural, social, and economic roles played by men and women and the effects that these have on their decision-making processes. For example, the cosmetics industry is overwhelmingly focused on women and what they want. But with changing times and lifestyles, men have become equally aware about their appearance. This resulted in launch of specific products for men such as fairness creams, face washes, body lotion and sunscreen creams/lotions.

Trends in gender marketing are influenced by the changing roles of men and women in society. For example, men used to rely on the women in their lives to shop for them. Today, however, more men are shopping for themselves. Whether because of the advent of online shopping or retailers wising up to the way men like to shop, today more men are comfortable shopping for themselves.

Age and Family Life Cycle Stage

The age and family life cycle stage of a consumer can have a significant impact on consumer behavior. How old a consumer is generally indicates what products he or she may be interested in purchasing. Consumer tastes in food, clothing, cars, furniture, and recreation are often age related.

Related to a person's age is his or her place in the family life cycle. As Chapter 8 explains in more detail, the *family life cycle* is an orderly series of stages through which consumers' attitudes and behavioral tendencies evolve through maturity, experience, and changing income and status. Marketers often define their target markets in terms of family life cycle, such as "young singles," "young married couples with children," and "middle-aged married couples without children." For instance, young singles spend more than average on dining out, education, and entertainment. New parents typically increase their spending on health care, clothing, housing, and food and

LIFE STAGES VS. DEMOGRAPHICS

In a U.S. survey of 1,440 people ages 13 to 54, researchers asked questions based on life stages rather than demographics to see if there were clear differences between groups. The groups used were teens, college students, recent graduates, single no kids, new nesters, established families, married couples with no children, and empty nesters. By organizing the categories this way, researchers were able to identify clear differences between the life stage groups, some of which fall into the same demographic category. For example, new nesters and married couples with no children are two life stage groups that both fall into the Generation Y demographic group. Looking at those groups in terms of life stages, however, reveals different preferences. New nesters value and are satisfied with social networking to keep in touch with friends and family, whereas childless couples are less satisfied with social networking with family and friends and use the tools primarily to expand professional networks. Many differences such as these appeared between these two life stages and weren't as apparent when researchers looked at them as one demographic group. (We'll examine life stages in more detail in Chapter 8.)[22]

decrease their spending on alcohol, education, and transportation. Households with older children spend more on food, entertainment, personal care products, and education, as well as cars and gasoline. After their children leave home, spending by older couples on vehicles, women's clothing, health care, and long-distance calls typically increases. For instance, the presence of children in the home is the most significant determinant of the type of vehicle that's driven off the new car lot. Parents are the ultimate need-driven car consumers, requiring larger cars and trucks to haul their children and all their belongings. It comes as no surprise then that for all households with children, SUVs rank either first or second among new-vehicle purchases, followed by minivans.

Marketers should also be aware of the many nontraditional life cycle paths that are common today and provide insights into the needs and wants of such consumers as divorced parents, lifelong singles, and childless couples.

Life Events Another way to look at the life cycle is to look at major events in one's life over time. Life-changing events can occur at any time. A few examples are death of a spouse, moving, birth or adoption of a child, retirement, job loss, divorce, and marriage. Typically, such events are quite stressful, and consumers will often take steps to minimize that stress. Many times, such life-changing events will mean new consumption patterns.[23] A recent divorcee may try to improve his or her appearance by joining a health club and dieting. A person moving to a different city will need a new dentist, grocery store, auto service center, and doctor, to name a few shops and service providers. Marketers realize that life events often mean a chance to gain a new customer. And when you put your home on the market, very quickly you start getting flyers from moving companies promising a great price on moving your household goods.

Personality, Self-Concept, and Lifestyle

Each consumer has a unique personality. **Personality** is a broad concept that can be thought of as a way of organizing and grouping how an individual typically reacts to situations. Thus, personality combines psychological makeup and environmental forces. It includes people's underlying dispositions, especially their most dominant characteristics. Although personality is one of the least useful concepts in the study of consumer behavior, some marketers believe personality influences the types and brands of products purchased. For instance, the type of car, clothes, or jewelry a consumer buys may reflect one or more personality traits.

PHOTODISC/THINKSTOCK

Self-concept, or self-perception, is how consumers perceive themselves. Self-concept includes attitudes, perceptions, beliefs, and self-evaluations. Although self-concept may change, the change is often gradual. Through self-concept, people define their identity, which in turn provides for consistent and coherent behavior.

Self-concept combines the **ideal self-image** (the way an individual would like to be perceived) and the **real self-image** (how an individual actually perceives himself or herself). Generally, we try to raise our real self-image toward our ideal (or at least narrow the gap). Consumers seldom buy products that jeopardize their self-image. For example, someone who sees herself as a trendsetter wouldn't buy clothing that doesn't project a contemporary image.

Human behavior depends largely on self-concept. Because consumers want to protect their identity as individuals, the products they buy, the stores they patronize, and the credit cards they carry support their self-image. No other product quite reflects a person's self-image as much as the car he or she drives. For example, many young consumers do not like family sedans like the Honda Accord or Toyota Camry and say they would buy one for their parents but not for themselves.

By influencing the degree to which consumers perceive a good or service to be self-relevant, marketers can affect consumers' motivation to learn about, shop for, and buy a certain brand. Marketers also consider self-concept important because it helps explain the relationship between individuals' perceptions of themselves and their consumer behavior.

Many companies now use psychographics to better understand their market segments. For many years, marketers selling products to mothers conveniently assumed that all moms were fairly homogeneous and concerned about the same things—the health and well-being of their children—and that they could all be reached with a similar message. Psychographics is also effective with other market segments. Psychographics and lifestyle segmentation are discussed in more detail in Chapter 8.

personality a way of organizing and grouping the consistencies of an individual's reactions to situations

self-concept how consumers perceive themselves in terms of attitudes, perceptions, beliefs, and self-evaluations

ideal self-image the way an individual would like to be

real self-image the way an individual actually perceives himself or herself

LO 8 Psychological Influences on Consumer Buying Decisions

An individual's buying decisions are further influenced by psychological factors: perception, motivation, learning, and beliefs and attitudes. These factors are what consumers use to interact with their world. They are the tools consumers use to recognize their feelings, gather and analyze information, formulate thoughts and opinions, and take action. Unlike the other three influences on consumer behavior, psychological influences can be affected by a person's environment because they are applied on specific occasions. For example, you will perceive different stimuli and process these stimuli in different ways depending on whether you are sitting in class concentrating on the instructor, sitting outside of class talking to friends, or sitting in your dorm room watching television.

Perception

The world is full of stimuli. A stimulus is any unit of input affecting one or more of the five senses: sight, smell, taste, touch, and hearing. The process by which we select, organize, and interpret these stimuli into a meaningful and coherent picture is called **perception**. In essence, perception is how we see the world around us and how we recognize that we need some help in making a purchasing decision.

perception the process by which people select, organize, and interpret stimuli into a meaningful and coherent picture

selective exposure the process whereby a consumer notices certain stimuli and ignores others

selective distortion a process whereby a consumer changes or distorts information that conflicts with his or her feelings or beliefs

selective retention a process whereby a consumer remembers only that information that supports his or her personal beliefs

People cannot perceive every stimulus in their environment. Therefore, they use **selective exposure** to decide which stimuli to notice and which to ignore. A typical consumer is exposed to more than 2,500 advertising messages a day but notices only between 11 and 20.

The familiarity of an object, contrast, movement, intensity (such as increased volume), and smell are cues that influence perception. Consumers use these cues to identify and define products and brands. The shape of a product's packaging, such as Coca-Cola's signature contour bottle, can influence perception. Color is another cue, and it plays a key role in consumers' perceptions. Packaged foods manufacturers use color to trigger unconscious associations for grocery shoppers who typically make their shopping decisions in the blink of an eye. Ecological consequences and concerns have resulted in marketing initiatives such as "going green." Colors like natural greens, earthy browns, and strong yellows, as well as metallics such as steely silver, carbon black, gold, and copper, are popular for packaging. Color researchers speculate that technological overload has led to resurgence in the appreciation of simplistic luxury. Color names for fabrics and makeup reflect that trend with names such as Olay Natural White and Ponds Gold Radiance.[24]

What is perceived by consumers may also depend on the stimuli's vividness or shock value. Graphic warnings of the hazards associated with a product's use are perceived more readily and remembered more accurately than less vivid warnings or warnings that are written in text. Fragrance advertisements often make promises of the "outcome" of wearing their product, often the promise of a role transformation on the part of the wearer. David Rubin, brand development director for Axe deodorant, says Axe's theme from the very start has been "giving guys an edge in the mating game."[25]

Two other concepts closely related to selective exposure are selective distortion and selective retention. **Selective distortion** occurs when consumers change or distort information that conflicts with their feelings or beliefs. For example, suppose a college student buys a Philips MP3 player. After the purchase, if the student gets new information about an alternative brand, such as an Apple iPod, he or she may distort the information to make it more consistent with the prior view that the Philips player is just as good as the iPod, if not better. Business travelers who fly often may distort or discount information about airline crashes because they must use air travel constantly in their jobs.

Selective retention is remembering only information that supports personal feelings or beliefs. The consumer forgets all information that may be inconsistent. After reading a pamphlet that contradicts one's political beliefs, for instance, a person may forget many of the points outlined in it. Similarly, consumers may see a news report on suspected illegal practices by their favorite retail store but soon forget the reason the store was featured on the news.

Which stimuli will be perceived often depends on the individual. People can be exposed to the same stimuli under identical conditions but perceive them very differently. For example, two people viewing a television commercial may have different interpretations of the advertising message. One person may be thoroughly engrossed by the message and become highly motivated to buy the product. Thirty seconds after the ad ends, the second person may not be able to recall the content of the message or even the product advertised.

Marketing Implications of Perception Marketers must recognize the importance of cues, or signals, in consumers' perception of products. Marketing managers first identify the important attributes, such as price or quality, that the targeted consumers want in a product and then design signals to communicate these attributes. For example, consumers will pay more for candy in expensive-looking foil packages. But shiny labels on wine bottles signify less expensive wines; dull labels indicate more expensive wines. Marketers also often use price as a signal to consumers that the product is of higher quality than competing products. Of course, brand names send signals to consumers. The brand names of Close-Up toothpaste, Eveready batteries, and Vanish stain remover, for example, identify important product qualities. Names chosen for search engines and sites on the Internet, such as Yahoo!, Amazon.com, and Excite, are intended to convey excitement, intensity, and vastness. Companies may even change their names to send a message to consumers.

Consumers also associate quality and reliability with certain brand names. Companies watch their brand identity closely, in large part because a strong link has been established between perceived brand value and customer loyalty. Brand names that consistently enjoy high perceived value from consumers include Kodak, Disney, National Geographic, Mercedes-Benz, and Fisher-Price. Naming a product after a place can also add perceived value by association. Brand names using the words Santa Fe, Dakota, or Texas convey a sense of openness, freedom, and youth, but products named after other locations might conjure up images of pollution and crime. Marketing managers are also interested in the *threshold level of perception*, the minimum difference in a stimulus that the consumer will notice. This concept is sometimes referred to as the "just-noticeable difference." For

© LEIGH PRATHER/SHUTTERSTOCK.COM

ONE STUDY FOUND THAT THE JUST-NOTICEABLE DIFFERENCE IN A STIMULUS IS ABOUT A 20 PERCENT CHANGE. FOR EXAMPLE, CONSUMERS WILL LIKELY NOTICE A 20 PERCENT PRICE DECREASE MORE QUICKLY THAN ONE OF ONLY 15 PERCENT.

example, how much would Apple have to drop the price of its iPod Shuffle before consumers recognized it as a bargain—20%, 30%, 40% or more? One study found that the just-noticeable difference in a stimulus is about a 20 percent change. For example, consumers will likely notice a 20 percent price decrease more quickly than one of only 15 percent. This marketing principle can be applied to other marketing variables as well, such as package size or loudness of a broadcast advertisement.[26]

Besides changing such stimuli as price, package size, and volume, marketers can change the product or attempt to reposition its image. But marketers must be careful when adding features. How many new services will discounter Target need to add before consumers perceive it as a full-service department store? How many sporty features will General Motors have to add to a basic two-door sedan before consumers start perceiving it as a sports car?

Marketing managers who intend to do business in global markets should be aware of how foreign consumers perceive their products. For instance, in Japan, product labels are often written in English or French, even though they may not translate into anything meaningful. Many Japanese associate foreign words on product labels with the exotic, the expensive, and high quality.

Marketers have often been suspected of sending advertising messages subconsciously to consumers in what is known as *subliminal perception*. The

motive a driving force that causes a person to take action to satisfy specific needs

Maslow's hierarchy of needs a method of classifying human needs and motivations into five categories in ascending order of importance: physiological, safety, social, esteem, and self-actualization

controversy began when a researcher claimed to have increased popcorn and Coca-Cola sales at a movie theater after flashing "Eat popcorn" and "Drink Coca-Cola" on the screen every five seconds for 1/300th of a second, although the audience did not consciously recognize the messages. Almost immediately consumer protection groups became concerned that advertisers were brainwashing consumers, and this practice was pronounced illegal in California and Canada. Although the researcher later admitted to making up the data and scientists have been unable to replicate the study since, consumers are still wary of hidden messages that advertisers may be sending.

Motivation

By studying motivation, marketers can analyze the major forces influencing consumers to buy or not buy products. When you buy a product, you usually do so to fulfill some kind of need. These needs become motives when aroused sufficiently. For instance, suppose this morning you were so hungry before class that you needed to eat something. In response to that need, you stopped at Subway for a breakfast sandwich. In other words, you were motivated by hunger to stop at Subway. **Motives** are the driving forces that cause a person to take action to satisfy specific needs.

Why are people driven by particular needs at particular times? One popular theory is **Maslow's hierarchy of needs**, shown in Exhibit 6.8, which arranges needs in ascending order of importance: physiological, safety, social, esteem, and self-actualization. As a person fulfills one need, a higher-level need becomes more important.

The most basic human needs are *physiological*—that is, the needs for food, water, and shelter. Because they are essential to survival, these needs must be satisfied first. Ads showing a tempting pizza or an athlete gulping down Dabur Active fruit juice after a workout are examples of appeals to satisfy the physiological needs of hunger and thirst.

Safety needs include security and freedom from pain and discomfort. Marketers sometimes appeal to consumers' fears and anxieties about safety to sell their products. On the other hand, some companies or industries advertise to allay consumer fears. For example, customers are generally worried about recovery of insured amount from the insurance companies. Bharti AXA Life Insurance designed a campaign to allay this fear and promise the customers of paying the sum insured within 48 hours of claiming.

After physiological and safety needs have been fulfilled, *social needs*—especially love and a sense of belonging—become the focus. Love includes acceptance by one's peers, as well as sex and romantic love. Marketing managers probably appeal more to this need than to any other. Ads for clothes, cosmetics, and vacation packages suggest that buying the product can bring love. The need to belong is also a favourite of marketers, especially those marketing products to teens. Teens consider Apple's iPod to be not only their favourite branded product but also something that defines their generation. Other such brands include

© IMAGE SOURCE/JUPITERIMAGES

EXHIBIT 6.8

Maslow's Hierarchy of Needs

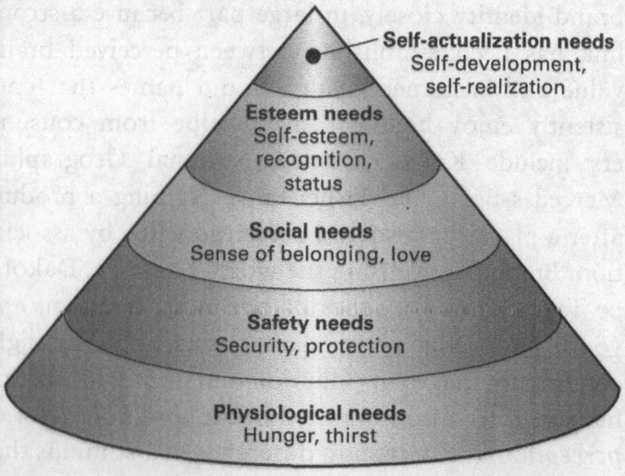

© CENGAGE LEARNING 2011

Axe, Face-book, Google, Cafe Coffee Day, Fastrack, MTV, and YouTube. The VP of Research at MTV says marketers need to understand a new dynamic in the "millennial generation" consumer. The relationship this generation has with their parents is completely different from previous generations. A parent can be a best friend. Brands that become too focused on "influential" teens can miss that parents can be the biggest influencer on this age group, especially when it comes to big-ticket items.[27]

Love is acceptance without regard to one's contribution. Esteem is acceptance based on one's contribution to the group. *Self-esteem needs* include self-respect and a sense of accomplishment. Esteem needs also include prestige, fame, and recognition of one's accomplishments. Montblanc pens, Mercedes-Benz automobiles, and Louis Vuitton stores all appeal to esteem needs.

The highest human need is *self-actualization*. It refers to finding self-fulfillment and self-expression, reaching the point in life at which "people are what they feel they should be." Maslow felt that very few people ever attain this level. Even so, advertisements may focus on this type of need. For example, American Express ads convey the message that acquiring its card is one of the highest attainments in life. Microsoft appealed to consumers' needs for self-actualization when it chose "I'm a PC and Windows 7 was my idea" as the slogan for Windows 7.

Learning

Almost all consumer behavior results from **learning**, which is the process that creates changes in behavior through experience and practice. It is not possible to observe learning directly, but we can infer when it has occurred by a person's actions. For example, suppose you see an advertisement for a new and improved cold medicine. If you go to the store that day and buy that remedy, we infer that you have learned something about the cold medicine.

There are two types of learning: experiential and conceptual. *Experiential learning* occurs when an experience changes your behavior. For example, if the new cold medicine does not relieve your symptoms, you may not buy that brand again. *Conceptual learning*, which is not acquired through direct experience, is the second type of learning. Assume, for example, that one of your friends went to a specific restaurant and tells you that their customer service is not good. The next time you would like to go out for dining, you will avoid going to that restaurant because your friend gave you a bad review. You have learned that you would not enjoy the overall experience there without even trying it.

learning a process that creates changes in behavior, immediate or expected, through experience and practice

stimulus generalization a form of learning that occurs when one response is extended to a second stimulus similar to the first

Reinforcement and repetition boost learning. Reinforcement can be positive or negative. If you see a vendor selling flavored yogurt (stimulus), buy it (response), and find the yogurt to be quite refreshing (reward), your behaviour has been positively reinforced. On the other hand, if you buy a new flavor of ice-cream and it does not taste good (negative reinforcement), you will not buy that flavor of ice-cream again (response). Without positive or negative reinforcement, a person will not be motivated to repeat the behavior pattern or to avoid it. Thus, if a new brand evokes neutral feelings, some marketing activity, such as a price change or an increase in promotion, may be required to induce further consumption. Learning theory is helpful in reminding marketers that concrete and timely actions are what reinforce desired consumer behavior.

Repetition is a key strategy in promotional campaigns because it can lead to increased learning. Most marketers use repetitious advertising so that consumers will learn what their unique advantage is over the competition. Generally, to heighten learning, advertising messages should be spread out over time rather than clustered together.

A related learning concept useful to marketing managers is **stimulus generalization**. In theory, stimulus generalization occurs when one response is extended to a second stimulus similar to the first. Marketers often use a successful, well-known brand name for a family of products because it gives consumers familiarity with and knowledge about each product in the family. Such brand name families spur the introduction of new products and facilitate the sale of existing items. Dettol relies on consumers' familiarity with its antiseptic to sell soaps, liquid hand washes and shaving creams; Sony's film division relies on name recognition from its home technology, such as the PlayStation. Maggi Soups and Maggi Pazzta rely on familiarity with Maggi noodles and Dove shampoo relies on familiarity with Dove soap. Branding is examined in more detail in Chapter 10.

Another form of stimulus generalization occurs when retailers or wholesalers design their packages to resemble well-known manufacturers' brands. Such imitation often confuses consumers, who buy the imitation thinking it's the original.

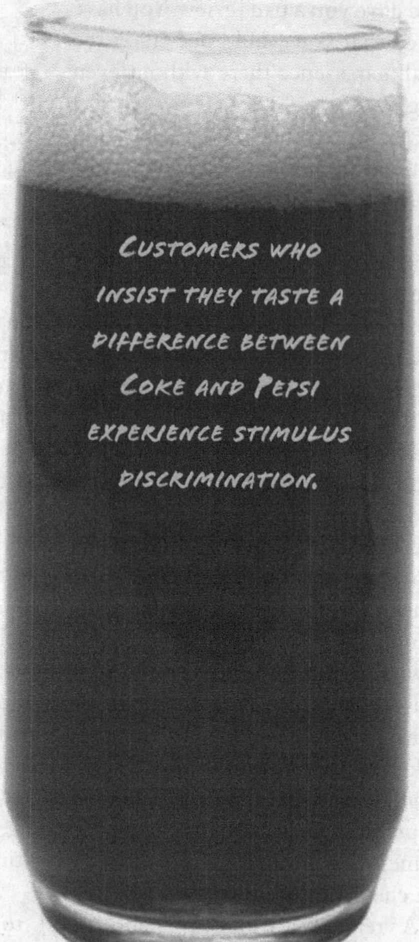

© ISTOCKPHOTO.COM/DONALD ERICKSON

The opposite of stimulus generalization is **stimulus discrimination**, which means learning to differentiate among similar products. Consumers may perceive one product as more rewarding or stimulating. For example, some consumers prefer Coca-Cola and others prefer Pepsi. Many insist they can taste a difference between the two brands.

With some types of products—such as aspirin, gasoline, bleach, and paper towels—marketers rely on promotion to point out brand differences that consumers would otherwise not recognize. This process, called product differentiation, is discussed in more detail in Chapter 8. Usually, product differentiation is based on superficial differences. For example, Oral-B tells consumers that it's the toothbrush "dentists use themselves worldwide."

stimulus discrimination a learned ability to differentiate among similar products

belief an organized pattern of knowledge that an individual holds as true about his or her world

attitude a learned tendency to respond consistently toward a given object

Beliefs and Attitudes

Beliefs and attitudes are closely linked to values. A **belief** is an organized pattern of knowledge that an individual holds as true about his or her world. A consumer may believe that Sony's Cyber-shot camera takes the best HD video, is easiest to use, and is the most reasonably priced. These beliefs may be based on knowledge, faith, or hearsay. Consumers tend to develop a set of beliefs about a product's attributes and then, through these beliefs, form a *brand image*—a set of beliefs about a particular brand. In turn, the brand image shapes consumers' attitudes toward the product.

An **attitude** is a learned tendency to respond consistently toward a given object, such as a brand. Attitudes rest on an individual's value system, which represents personal standards of good and bad, right and wrong, and so forth; therefore, attitudes tend to be more enduring and complex than beliefs.

For an example of the nature of attitudes, consider the differing attitudes of consumers around the world toward the practice of purchasing on credit. Americans have long been enthusiastic about charging goods and services and are willing to pay high interest rates for the privilege of postponing payment. To many European consumers, doing what amounts to taking out a loan—even a small one—to pay for anything seems absurd. Germans especially are reluctant to buy on credit. Italy has a sophisticated credit and banking system well suited to handling credit cards, but Italians prefer to carry cash, often huge wads of it. Although most Japanese consumers have credit cards, card purchases amount to less than 1 percent of all consumer transactions. The Japanese have long looked down on credit purchases but acquire cards to use while traveling abroad.

If a good or service is meeting its profit goals, positive attitudes toward the product merely need to be reinforced. If the brand is not succeeding, however, the marketing manager must strive to change target consumers' attitudes toward it. Changes in attitude tend to grow out of an individual's attempt to reconcile long-held values with a constant stream of new information. This change can be accomplished in three ways: changing beliefs about the brand's attributes, changing the relative importance of these beliefs, and adding new beliefs.

Changing Beliefs about Attributes The first approach is to turn neutral, negative, or incorrect beliefs about product attributes into positive ones. Hotmail, which debuted in 1996 and quickly garnered wide usage, is now perceived as less modern than other e-mail services, such as Gmail. To combat growing negative perceptions, Microsoft revamped the Hotmail site to make it more modern and to integrate it as part of its Windows Live program. The Windows Live program offers free, modern programs that allow users to manage multimedia, chatting, blogs, and e-mail. The new Windows Live Hotmail features include the ability to watch videos from YouTube and Hulu from within your e-mail, and even automatically track U.S.P.S. packages when an e-mail contains a tracking number. These features make Hotmail an updated, modern choice for personal e-mail. To change people's lingering beliefs about Hotmail, Microsoft launched a massive marketing campaign to demonstrate Hotmail's updated, modern features.[28]

Changing beliefs about a service can be more difficult because service attributes are intangible. Convincing consumers to switch hairstylists or lawyers or to go to a mall dental clinic can be much more difficult than getting them to change brands of razor blades. Image, which is also largely intangible, significantly determines service patronage. Service marketing is explored in detail in Chapter 12.

Changing the Importance of Beliefs The second approach to modifying attitudes is to change the relative importance of beliefs about an attribute. Marketers can also emphasize the importance of some beliefs over others. For example, when consumers thought of two-wheelers, it was mostly looked upon as a vehicle for males. However, when Hero Honda launched its 100cc scooter Pleasure, it positioned the scooter as a vehicle for females. The advertisements for the scooter carried the tagline "why should boys have all the fun?"

Adding New Beliefs The third approach to transforming attitudes is to add new beliefs. Although changes in consumption patterns often come slowly, cereal marketers are betting that consumers will eventually warm up to the idea of cereal as a snack. A television ad for Kelloggs Chocos features a tired boy returning home after his day at school and having Chocos as his "evening snack". Kellogg's India has cleverly positioned itself as a wholesome and nutritious snack for children after school. Knorr Soups has also positioned itself as "7 pm healthy snack". The commercials show hungry children wanting to eat something at 7 pm, with a worried mother that what will happen to their dinner if they eat snacks at 7 pm. Hence, she comes with the option of giving them Knorr Soups that are healthy and the best option to be had before dinner.

U.S. companies attempting to market their goods overseas may need to help consumers add new beliefs about a product in general. Coca-Cola and PepsiCo have both found it challenging to sell their diet cola brands to consumers in India partly because diet foods of any kind are a new concept in the country where malnutrition has been widespread until recently. Indians also have deep-rooted attitudes that anything labeled "diet" is meant for a sick person, such as a diabetic. As a general rule, most Indians are not diet conscious, preferring food prepared in the traditional manner that tastes good. Indians are also suspicious of the artificial sweeteners used in diet colas. India's Health Ministry has required warning labels on cans and bottles of Diet Coke and Diet Pepsi saying "Not Recommended for Children."[29]

Review and Applications

Explain why marketing managers should understand consumer behavior. Consumer behavior describes how consumers make purchase decisions and how they use and dispose of the products they buy. An understanding of consumer behavior reduces marketing managers' uncertainty when they are defining a target market and designing a marketing mix.

1.1 The type of decision making a consumer uses for a product does not necessarily remain constant. Why? Support your answer with an example from your own experience.

Analyze the components of the consumer decision-making process. The consumer decision-making process begins with need recognition, when stimuli trigger awareness of an unfulfilled want. If additional information is required to make a purchase decision, the consumer may engage in an internal or external information search. The consumer then evaluates the additional information and establishes purchase guidelines. Finally, a purchase decision is made.

2.1 Visit Carpoint's Web site at **http://autos.msn.com/**. How does the site assist consumers in the evaluation stage of choosing a new car? Develop your own hypothetical evoked set of three or four car models and present your comparisons. Which vehicle attributes would be most important in your purchase decision?

Explain the consumer's postpurchase evaluation process. Consumer postpurchase evaluation is influenced by prepurchase expectations, the prepurchase information search, and the consumer's general level of self-confidence. Cognitive dissonance is the inner tension that a consumer experiences after recognizing a purchased product's disadvantages. When a purchase creates cognitive dissonance, consumers tend to react by seeking positive reinforcement for the purchase decision, avoiding negative information about the purchase decision, or revoking the purchase decision by returning the product.

3.1 Recall an occasion when you experienced cognitive dissonance about a purchase. In a letter to a friend, describe the event and explain what you did about it.

Identify the types of consumer buying decisions and discuss the significance of consumer involvement. Consumer decision making falls into three broad categories. First, consumers exhibit routine response behavior for frequently purchased, low-cost items that require very little decision effort; routine response behavior is typically characterized by brand loyalty. Second, consumers engage in limited decision making for occasional purchases or for unfamiliar brands in familiar product categories. Third, consumers practice extensive decision making when making unfamiliar, expensive, or infrequent purchases. High-involvement decisions usually include an extensive information search and a thorough evaluation of alternatives. In contrast, low-involvement decisions are characterized by brand loyalty and a lack of personal identification with the product. The main factors affecting the level of consumer involvement are previous experience, interest, perceived risk of negative consequences (financial, social, and psychological), situation, and social visibility.

4.1 Describe the three categories of consumer decision-making behavior. Name typical products for which each type of consumer behavior is used.

4.2 Describe the level of involvement and the involvement factors likely to be associated with buying a new computer. Do you think Apple's Web site at **www.apple.com** simplifies or complicates the process for the average consumer? Explain.

Identify and understand the cultural factors that affect consumer buying decisions. Cultural influences on consumer buying decisions include culture and values, subculture, and social class. Culture is the essential character of a society that distinguishes it from other cultural groups. The underlying elements of every culture are the values, language, myths, customs, rituals, laws, and artifacts, or products, which are transmitted from one generation to the next. The most defining element of a culture is its values—the enduring beliefs shared by a society that a specific mode of conduct is personally or socially preferable to another mode of conduct. A culture can be divided into subcultures on the basis of demographic characteristics, geographic regions, national and ethnic background, political beliefs, and religious beliefs. Subcultures share elements of the overall culture as well as cultural elements unique to their own group. A social class is a group of people who are considered nearly equal in status or community esteem, who regularly socialize among themselves both formally and informally, and who share behavioral norms.

5.1 You are a new marketing manager for a firm that produces a line of athletic shoes to be targeted to the college student subculture. In a memo to your boss, list some product attributes that might appeal to this subculture and the steps in your customers' purchase processes, and recommend some marketing strategies that can influence their decision.

Identify and understand the social factors that affect consumer buying decisions. Social factors include such external influences as reference groups, opinion leaders, and family. Consumers seek out others' opinions for guidance on new products or services and products with image-related attributes or because attribute information is lacking or uninformative. Consumers may use products or brands to identify with or become a member of a reference group. Opinion leaders are members of reference groups who influence others' purchase decisions. Family members also influence purchase decisions; children tend to shop in similar patterns as their parents.

6.1 Family members play many different roles in the buying process: initiator, influencer, decision maker, purchaser, and consumer. Identify the person in your family who might play each of these roles in the purchase of a dinner at Pizza Hut, a summer vacation, Kellogg's breakfast cereal, a Levi's Jeans, cricket bat, an internet service provider, and a new car.

Identify and understand the individual factors that affect consumer buying decisions. Individual factors that affect consumer buying decisions include gender; age and family life-cycle stage; and personality, self-concept, and lifestyle. Beyond obvious physiological differences, men and women differ in their social and economic roles, and that affects consumer buying decisions. How old a consumer is generally indicates what products he or she may be interested in purchasing. Marketers often define their target markets in terms of consumers' life-cycle stage, following changes in consumers' attitudes and behavioral tendencies as they mature. Finally, certain products and brands reflect consumers' personality, self-concept, and lifestyle.

7.1 Assume you are involved in the following consumer decision situations: (a) renting a DVD to watch with your roommates, (b) choosing a fast-food restaurant to go to with a new friend, (c) buying a popular music compact disc, (d) buying jeans to wear to class. List the individual factors that would influence your decision in each situation and explain your responses.

Identify and understand the psychological factors that affect consumer buying decisions. Psychological factors include perception, motivation, learning, values, beliefs, and attitudes. These factors allow consumers to interact with the world around them, recognize their feelings, gather and analyze information, formulate thoughts and opinions, and take action. Perception allows consumers to recognize their consumption problems. Motivation is what drives consumers to take action to satisfy specific consumption needs. Almost all consumer behavior results from learning, which is the process that creates changes in behavior through experience. Consumers with similar beliefs and attitudes tend to react alike to marketing-related inducements.

8.1 How do beliefs and attitudes influence consumer behavior? How can negative attitudes toward a product be changed? How can marketers alter beliefs about a product? Give some examples of how marketers have changed negative attitudes about a product or added or altered beliefs about a product.

Exercises

APPLICATION EXERCISE

Principles of consumer behavior are evident in many areas of marketing. Perhaps the easiest place to see this critical foundation of marketing activity is in print ads.

Activities

1. Review the main concepts in this chapter and create a checklist that itemizes them. Then, comb through your favorite magazines and newspapers for advertisements that illustrate each concept. To get a wide variety of ads, you will need to look through several magazines. If you don't have many magazines at your disposal, go to the campus library periodical room. Photocopy the ads you select to support this chapter.
2. Because pictures can help reinforce understanding, consider doing this exercise for each chapter in the book. At the end of the semester,

you will have a portfolio of ads that illustrate the concepts in the entire book, which can help you study. Simply look through your portfolio and try to recall the concepts at work in each advertisement. This exercise can be a prelude to a longer study session for comprehensive exams.

ETHICS EXERCISE

Holy International is a nationally renowned school, with its students excelling in both studies and extra-curricular activities. The school has always believed that students should actively participate in extra-curricular activities as it helps in their overall development. With changing times, modelling and acting have also gained entry into the list of such activities and some of its students have earned both name and fame in this field. Not only this, the school has also been used as a shooting location by some of the advertising companies, owing to its serene surroundings. Apart from adding to school's popularity, this has also generated additional revenues for it. To take advantage of this, the school authorities are now planning to set up a separate team to visit and sell data about its students to companies and acting agencies so that they can be used as actors or models in advertisements and shows. It is also planning to come up with a marketing campaign, highlighting the school location and surroundings, to project itself as a suitable venue for shooting activities.

Questions

1. Is it correct on the school's part to sell its students' details to commercial agencies and portraying itself as an ideal shooting destination just for generating some additional revenue?
2. The Child Labour Prohibition and Regulation Act, 1986, does not allow employment of children below fourteen years of age in hazardous occupation. Some sections of the society have also protested against children shooting for long hours, at times in unfriendly conditions. In view of this, is it correct on the school's part to promote students' participation in advertisements, TV serials and reality shows?

MARKETING PLAN EXERCISE

The next step in preparing a marketing plan for the company you chose in Part 1 is to get a thorough understanding of the marketing opportunities in terms of marketing to customers. Once you've completed the marketing plan exercise for each chapter in Part 2 of this textbook, you can complete the Part 2 Marketing Planning Worksheet on your companion Web site at **www.cengage.com/international**. Complete the following exercises:

1. Describe the decision-making process that customers go through when purchasing your company's product or service. What are the critical factors that influence this purchase-behavior process? How will this decision-making affect your e-marketing focus and your market offering? If you have a brick-and-mortar presence, will you encourage any existing customers to shop on-line? Why or why not?
2. Nonmarketing periodicals can help you understand consumer behaviour and apply what you have learned to your marketing plan. Research articles from such publications as the *Journal of Applied Psychology, Journal of Business Ethics, Administrative Science Quarterly, Journal of Personality and Social Psychology*, and others. Select and read three articles that explore different topics (i.e., do not select three articles on psychology). Then, make a list of factors you think could affect consumer purchasing behavior. Include with each factor a way marketers could use this information to their benefit.

Short Case: VIDEOCON INDUSTRIES

Prepared by
Dr. Dheeraj Sharma,
Indian Institute of Management, Ahmedabad

Before the liberalization of the industry, Indian consumer durable industry was dominated by only Indian companies such as Godrej, Alwyn, Kelvinator, etc. However, post liberalization era saw the emergence of many foreign players like Sony, Samsung, LG, etc. entering into the market. The consumer durable market has seen a tremendous growth in the Indian market because of the rise in the income level and living standards of the Indian consumers, the ease of the availability of finance and the wide range of choices available to them. The industry is assumed to be at least at ₹350 billion (₹35,000 crore) in the year 2012[30] and grow at a CAGR of around 18% during 2011–2014.[31]

In this consumer durable market, Videocon is one of the giant players. Videocon group specializes in manufacturing consumer electronics and home appliances, D2H, mobile phones, mobile services, power plants, and display industry and its components. Videocon Industries Ltd. is a prominent player in the consumer electronics market (which includes refrigerator, television, air conditioner, washing machine, music systems, etc.). It has achieved a comfortable position for itself in terms of sales and customer satisfaction. It has the widest distribution network of about 10,000 dealers, sub-dealers and distributors across India. The multi brand strategy followed by Videocon, gives it a competitive advantage and an opportunity to cater to different needs of the consumers, which keeps on changing with time. Its multi brands include Electrolux, Hyundai, Sansui, Kenstar, Akai, Allwyn, Kelvinator. Videocon's focus on its customer's satisfaction is reflected in its mission that is obtained from their official website verbatim "*To delight and deliver beyond expectations through ingenious strategy, intrepid entrepreneurship, improved technology, innovative products, insightful marketing and inspired thinking about future.*"[32] The consumer electronics and home appliances division registered a growth of 20% over the last year in 2010.[33] The biggest contributor to the company's business has been the color TV and Flat Panel Display category. It aims to delight its customers with products, which go beyond fulfilling their basic needs and provide them with value for money proposition. All the more, providing extra service to its consumers like mobilized service engineers, service centers well stocked with spare parts, on time services and at the door step adds to its stars of delighting its customers both existing and new ones.

Videocon Industries has always been committed in providing its customers more than what it had promised. In line with providing customized products, according to the needs of the customers and the changing technological environment, Videocon industries launched various innovative products in 2010 such as world's first satellite LCD range in India, India's first tilt drum washing machine, India's first top load fully automatic washing machine with a direct drive motor, India's first touch-pad microwave, India's first four star and five star BEE rated washing machine, etc. This highly supports the company's mission statement in 2011, i.e., out of every ten product being sold in Indian market for any category of consumer durable; at least four should be from Videocon group.

Plans in 2012

Realizing that the company will have to lay continuous focus on its R&D activities, it is planning to invest ₹600 million in R&D in 2012. The main focus in the year 2012 would be on high-end products, which would give them high volume and will help in gaining market share in the high-end category. They are also planning to launch digital TV with bigger screen including 70 inch, 58 inch, 55 inch and 46 inch, and LEDs with Android platform in 2012. Further, they also plan to new range of washing machines, air conditioners, and other products in consumer durables and home appliances. As for the marketing activities in 2012, it would lay more emphasis on below the line activities. They are also planning to demonstrate their high-end products to the consumers, which would enable them to weigh the various alternatives before making any purchase decision.[34]

Questions

1. Is the multi brand strategy of Videocon apt or will it dilute its original brand name?
2. With an increase in competition from so many players in the market, how can Videocon assist the consumers in making consumer decisions?

6 Consumer Decision Making

KEY TERMS

LO 1

consumer behavior processes a consumer uses to make purchase decisions, as well as to use and dispose of purchased goods or services; also includes factors that influence purchase decisions and product use

LO 2

consumer decision-making process a five-step process used by consumers when buying goods or services

need recognition result of an imbalance between actual and desired states

want recognition of an unfulfilled need and a product that will satisfy it

stimulus any unit of input affecting one or more of the five senses: sight, smell, taste, touch, hearing

internal information search the process of recalling past information stored in the memory

external information search the process of seeking information in the outside environment

nonmarketing-controlled information source a product information source that is not associated with advertising or promotion

marketing-controlled information source a product information source that originates with marketers promoting the product

evoked set (consideration set) a group of brands, resulting from an information search, from which a buyer can choose

LO 3

cognitive dissonance inner tension that a consumer experiences after recognizing an inconsistency between behavior and values or opinions

LO 4

involvement the amount of time and effort a buyer invests in the search, evaluation, and decision processes of consumer behavior

KEY CONCEPTS

LO 1

Explain why marketing managers should understand consumer behavior. Consumer behavior describes how consumers make purchase decisions and how they use and dispose of the products they buy. An understanding of consumer behavior reduces marketing managers' uncertainty when they are defining a target market and designing a marketing mix.

LO 2

Analyze the components of the consumer decision-making process. The consumer decision-making process begins with need recognition, when stimuli trigger awareness of an unfulfilled want. If additional information is required to make a purchase decision, the consumer may engage in an internal or external information search. The consumer then evaluates the additional information and establishes purchase guidelines. Finally, a purchase decision is made.

LO 3

Explain the consumer's postpurchase evaluation process. Consumer postpurchase evaluation is influenced by prepurchase expectations, the prepurchase information search, and the consumer's general level of self-confidence. Cognitive dissonance is the inner tension that a consumer experiences after recognizing a purchased product's disadvantages. When a purchase creates cognitive dissonance, consumers tend to react by seeking positive reinforcement for the purchase decision, avoiding negative information about the purchase decision, or revoking the purchase decision by returning the product.

LO 4

Identify the types of consumer buying decisions and discuss the significance of consumer involvement. Consumer decision making falls into three broad categories. First, consumers exhibit routine response behavior for frequently purchased, low-cost items that require very little decision effort; routine response behavior is typically characterized by brand loyalty. Second, consumers engage in limited decision making for occasional purchases or for unfamiliar brands in familiar product categories. Third, consumers practice extensive decision making when making unfamiliar, expensive, or infrequent purchases. High-involvement decisions usually include an extensive information search and a thorough evaluation of alternatives. In contrast, low-involvement decisions are characterized by brand loyalty and a lack of personal identification with the product. The main factors affecting the level of consumer involvement are previous experience, interest, perceived risk of negative consequences (financial, social, and psychological), situation, and social visibility.

LO 5

Identify and understand the cultural factors that affect consumer buying decisions. Cultural influences on consumer buying decisions include culture and values, subculture, and social class. Culture is the essential character of a society that distinguishes it from other cultural groups. The underlying elements of every culture are the values, language, myths, customs, rituals, laws, and artifacts, or products, which are transmitted from one generation to the next. The most defining element of a culture is its values—the enduring beliefs shared by a society that a specific mode of conduct is personally or socially preferable to another mode of conduct. A culture can be divided into subcultures on the basis of demographic characteristics, geographic regions, national and ethnic background, political beliefs, and religious beliefs. Subcultures share elements of the overall culture as well as cultural elements unique to their own group. A social class is a group of people who are considered nearly equal in status or community esteem, who regularly socialize among themselves both formally and informally, and who share behavioral norms.

routine response behavior the type of decision making exhibited by consumers buying frequently purchased, low-cost goods and services; requires little search and decision time

limited decision making the type of decision making that requires a moderate amount of time for gathering information and deliberating about an unfamiliar brand in a familiar product category

extensive decision making the most complex type of consumer decision making, used when buying an unfamiliar, expensive product or an infrequently bought item; requires use of several criteria for evaluating options and much time for seeking information

LO 5

culture the set of values, norms, attitudes, and other meaningful symbols that shape human behavior and the artifacts, or products, of that behavior as they are transmitted from one generation to the next

value the enduring belief that a specific mode of conduct is personally or socially preferable to another mode of conduct

subculture a homogeneous group of people who share elements of the overall culture as well as unique elements of their own group

social class a group of people in a society who are considered nearly equal in status or community esteem, who regularly socialize among themselves both formally and informally, and who share behavioral norms

LO 6

reference group a group in society that influences an individual's purchasing behavior

primary membership group a reference group with which people interact regularly in an informal, face-to-face manner, such as family, friends, and co-workers

secondary membership group a reference group with which people associate less consistently and more formally than a primary membership group, such as a club, professional group, or religious group

aspirational reference group a group that someone would like to join

LO 7

norm a value or attitude deemed acceptable by a group

nonaspirational reference group a group with which an individual does not want to associate

opinion leader an individual who influences the opinions of others

socialization process how cultural values and norms are passed down to children

LO 8

personality a way of organizing and grouping the consistencies of an individual's reactions to situations

self-concept how consumers perceive themselves in terms of attitudes, perceptions, beliefs, and self-evaluations

ideal self-image the way an individual would like to be

real self-image the way an individual actually perceives himself or herself

perception the process by which people select, organize, and interpret stimuli into a meaningful and coherent picture

selective exposure the process whereby a consumer notices certain stimuli and ignores others

selective distortion a process whereby a consumer changes or distorts information that conflicts with his or her feelings or beliefs

selective retention a process whereby a consumer remembers only that information that supports his or her personal beliefs

motive a driving force that causes a person to take action to satisfy specific needs

---

LO 6 **Identify and understand the social factors that affect consumer buying decisions.** Social factors include such external influences as reference groups, opinion leaders, and family. Consumers seek out others' opinions for guidance on new products or services and products with image-related attributes or because attribute information is lacking or uninformative. Consumers may use products or brands to identify with or become a member of a reference group. Opinion leaders are members of reference groups who influence others' purchase decisions. Family members also influence purchase decisions; children tend to shop in similar patterns as their parents.

LO 7 **Identify and understand the individual factors that affect consumer buying decisions.** Individual factors that affect consumer buying decisions include gender; age and family life-cycle stage; and personality, self-concept, and lifestyle. Beyond obvious physiological differences, men and women differ in their social and economic roles, and that affects consumer buying decisions. How old a consumer is generally indicates what products he or she may be interested in purchasing. Marketers often define their target markets in terms of consumers' life-cycle stage, following changes in consumers' attitudes and behavioral tendencies as they mature. Finally, certain products and brands reflect consumers' personality, self-concept, and lifestyle.

LO 8 **Identify and understand the psychological factors that affect consumer buying decisions.** Psychological factors include perception, motivation, learning, values, beliefs, and attitudes. These factors allow consumers to interact with the world around them, recognize their feelings, gather and analyze information, formulate thoughts and opinions, and take action. Perception allows consumers to recognize their consumption problems. Motivation is what drives consumers to take action to satisfy specific consumption needs. Almost all consumer behavior results from learning, which is the process that creates changes in behavior through experience. Consumers with similar beliefs and attitudes tend to react alike to marketing-related inducements.

6 Consumer Decision Making

Maslow's hierarchy of needs a method of classifying human needs and motivations into five categories in ascending order of importance: physiological, safety, social, esteem, and self-actualization

learning a process that creates changes in behavior, immediate or expected, through experience and practice

stimulus generalization a form of learning that occurs when one response is extended to a second stimulus similar to the first

stimulus discrimination a learned ability to differentiate among similar products

belief an organized pattern of knowledge that an individual holds as true about his or her world

attitude a learned tendency to respond consistently toward a given object

CHAPTER 7 Business Marketing

Learning Outcomes

- **LO 1** Describe business marketing
- **LO 2** Describe the role of the Internet in business marketing
- **LO 3** Discuss the role of relationship marketing and strategic alliances in business marketing
- **LO 4** Identify the four major categories of business market customers
- **LO 5** Explain the National Industrial Classification
- **LO 6** Explain the major differences between business and consumer markets
- **LO 7** Describe the seven types of business goods and services
- **LO 8** Discuss the unique aspects of business buying behavior

The key characteristic distinguishing business products from consumer products is intended use, not physical form.

LO1 What Is Business Marketing?

business marketing the marketing of goods and services to individuals and organizations for purposes other than personal consumption

Business marketing is the marketing of goods and services to individuals and organizations for purposes other than personal consumption. The sale of a PC to your college or university is an example of business marketing. Business products include those that are used to manufacture other products, become part of another product, or aid the normal operations of an organization. The key characteristic distinguishing business products from consumer products is intended use, not physical characteristics.

How do you distinguish between a consumer and business product? A product that is purchased for personal or family consumption or as a gift is a consumer good. If that same product, such as a PC or a cell phone, is bought for use in a business, it is a business product. Some common items that are sold as both consumer goods and business products are office supplies (e.g., pens, paper, staple removers). Some items, such as forklifts, are more commonly sold as business products than as consumer goods.

The size of the business market in India and most other countries substantially exceeds that of the consumer market. In the business market, a single customer can account for a huge volume of purchases. For example, General Motors' purchasing department spends more than ₹5,62,500 crores per year on goods and services. General Electric, DuPont, and IBM spend over ₹270 crores per day on business purchases.[1] According to *BtoB Magazine*, some of the top business marketing brands in 2010 were Cisco Systems, Xerox, General Electric, Intel, Motorola, and Avaya.[2]

Note:* *All the figures in U.S. dollars are converted into rupee using the value $1 = ₹45.

LO 2 Business Marketing on the Internet

business-to-business electronic commerce the use of the Internet to facilitate the exchange of goods, services, and information between organizations

The use of the Internet to facilitate activities between organizations is called **business-to-business electronic commerce** (B-to-B or B2B e-commerce). This method of conducting business has evolved and grown rapidly throughout its short history. In 1995, the commercial Web sites that did exist were static. Only a few had data-retrieval capabilities. Frames, tables, and styles were not available. Security of any sort was rare, and streaming video did not exist. In 2005, there were more than hundred crore Internet users worldwide. In 2008, India was expected to account for about ₹67,500–90,000 crores of B2B e-commerce.[3] Before the Internet, customers had to call Dow Chemical and request a specification sheet for the products they were considering. The information would arrive a few days later by mail. After choosing a product, the customer could then place an order by calling Dow (during business hours, of course). Now, such information is available through MyAccount@Dow, which provides information tailored to the customer's requirements, such as secure internal monitoring of a customer's chemical tank levels. When tanks reach a predetermined level, reordering can be automatically triggered.[4]

Companies selling to business buyers face the same challenges as all marketers, including determining who, exactly, the market is and how best to reach them. This is particularly difficult in business marketing because business has rapidly moved online and overseas.[5]

Each year, BtoBonline.com identifies ten business marketing Web sites that are particularly good examples of how companies can use the Web to communicate with customers. Exhibit 7.1 identifies the ten great Web sites for 2010. Many of these companies have been recognized in past years for effectively communicating with their target markets.[6]

In addition to Web sites, what Web 2.0 technologies are companies using? Some of the other tools used in online marketing are blogs, videos, social networks, RSS feeds, and threaded discussion.[7]

EXHIBIT 7.1

Ten Great Web Sites

URL	Company	Target Audience
www.accenture.com	Accenture	C-level executives at large companies, government organizations and job seekers
www.airclic.com	Airclic	C-level supply chain and logistics decision makers across 13 industries, customers, current and prospective partners, media, investors, and influencers
www.dropbox.com	Dropbox	Businesses, consumers, mobile productivity users
www.freightcenter.com	FreightCenter, Inc.	Small to midsize shippers, with some focus on enterprise shippers
www.ixda.org	Interaction Design Association	Recruiters and members
www.istockphoto.com	iStockphoto	Businesses, designers, bloggers
www.macktrucks.com	Mack Trucks	Dealers and prospective Mack Truck buyers, including truckers, construction companies, refuse haulers, and other commerical companies
www.sas.com	SAS Institute, Inc.	Current and prospective customers, community members, employees, potential employees, media
www.shawfloors.com	Shaw Floors	Architects, interior designers, resellers, retailers, and consumers
www.tyco.com	Tyco International	Prospective and current employees, investment community, customers, community partners

SOURCE: Karen Bannan, "10 Great b2b Sites," *BtoB Magazine*, online, September 13, 2010, http://www.btobonline.com/article/20100913/FREE/309139988/10-great-b-to-b-sites.

Measuring Online Success

Three of the most important measurements of online success are recency, frequency, and monetary value. *Recency* relates to the fact that customers who have made a purchase recently are more likely to purchase again in the near future than customers who haven't purchased for a while. *Frequency* data help marketers identify frequent purchasers who are definitely more likely to repeat their purchasing behavior in the future. The *monetary value* of sales is important because big spenders can be the most profitable customers for a business.

NetGenesis has developed a number of equations that can help online marketers better understand their data. For example, combining frequency data with the length of time a visitor spent on the Web site (duration) and the number of site pages viewed during each visit (total site reach) can provide an analytical measure for your site's **stickiness** factor.

stickiness a measure of a Web site's effectiveness; calculated by multiplying the frequency of visits by the duration of a visit by the number of pages viewed during each visit (site reach)

$$\text{STICKINESS} = \text{FREQUENCY} \times \text{DURATION} \times \text{SITE REACH}$$

By measuring the stickiness factor of a Web site before and after a design or function change, the marketer can quickly determine whether visitors embraced the change. By adding purchase information to determine the level of stickiness needed to provide a desired purchase volume, the marketer gains an even more precise understanding of how a site change affected business. An almost endless number of factor combinations can be created to provide a quantitative method for determining buyer behavior online. First, though, the marketer must determine what measures are required and which factors can be combined to arrive at those measurements.[8]

Trends in B2B Internet Marketing

According to James Soto, president of the business marketing agency Industrial Strength Marketing, "the number one thing to keep in mind in terms of trends in B2B Internet marketing is the shift of sourcing to the Net." His firm has found that 90 percent of business buyers go to the Internet at some point during the buying process, and over 50 percent start the buying process online.[9]

An Internet marketing technique that hasn't yet lived up to its potential is RSS (Real Simple Syndication) feeds. RSS feeds are used to publish frequently updated materials such as blogs, news headlines, audio, and video in a standard format. RSS was originally touted as a replacement for e-mail, but companies are finding that RSS functions better as an e-mail supplement. If RSS feeds are not updated daily, customers will often unsubscribe. Company blogs provide a simple way to maintain a steady flow on the RSS feed and can also tie in nicely with e-mail newsletters.[10] For companies that don't already maintain an active Web presence, RSS usage may not be the most effective use of marketing time or money.

Over the past decade, marketers have become more and more sophisticated in the use of the Internet. Exhibit 7.2 compares three prominent Internet business marketing strategy initiatives from the late 1990s compared to five that are currently being pursued. Companies have had to transition from "We have a Web site because our customer does" to having a store that attracts, interests, satisfies, and retains customers. New applications that provide additional information about present and potential customers; increase efficiency; lower costs; increase supply chain efficiency; or enhance customer retention, loyalty, and trust are being developed each year. Chapter 21, Customer Relationship Management, describes several of these applications.

EXHIBIT 7.2
Evolution of E-Business Initiatives

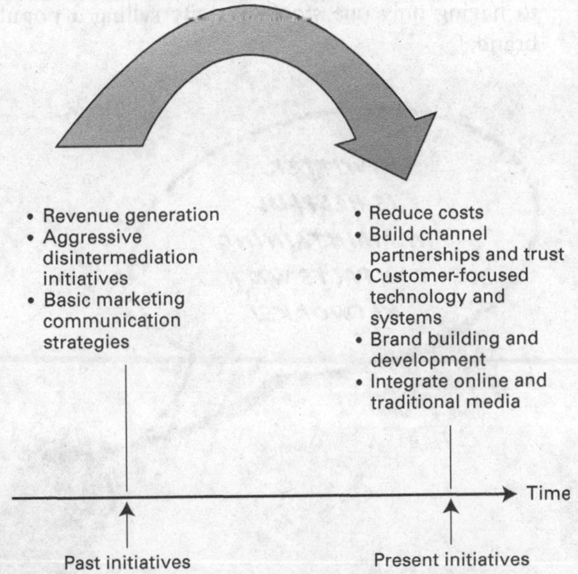

SOURCE: Andrew J. Rohm and Fareena Sultan, "The Evolution of E-Business," *Marketing Management*, January/February 2004, p. 35. Used by permission.

disintermediation the elimination of intermediaries such as wholesalers or distributors from a marketing channel

reintermediation the reintroduction of an intermediary between producers and users

strategic alliance (strategic partnership) a cooperative agreement between business firms

One term in Exhibit 7.2 that may be unfamiliar is **disintermediation**, which means eliminating intermediaries such as wholesalers or distributors from a marketing channel.[11] A prime example of disintermediation is Dell, which sells directly to business buyers and consumers. Large retailers such as Walmart use a disintermediation strategy to help reduce costs and prices.

A few years ago, many people thought the Internet would eliminate the need for distributors. Why would customers pay a distributor's markup when they could buy directly from the manufacturer with a few mouse clicks? Yet Internet disintermediation has occurred less frequently than many expected. The reason is that distributors often perform important functions such as providing credit, aggregation of supplies from multiple sources, delivery, and processing returns.

Many business customers, especially small firms, depend on knowledgeable distributors for information and advice that is not available to them online. You will notice in Exhibit 7.2 that building channel partnerships and trust has replaced aggressive disintermediation initiatives as a priority for most firms. Some firms have followed disintermediation with **reintermediation**, the reintroduction of an intermediary between producers and users. They realized that providing direct online purchasing only was similar to having only one store in a city selling a popular brand.

LO 3 Relationship Marketing and Strategic Alliances

As explained in Chapter 1, relationship marketing is a strategy that entails seeking and establishing ongoing partnerships with customers. Relationship marketing has become an important business marketing strategy as customers have become more demanding and competition has become more intense. Loyal customers are also more profitable than those who are price sensitive and perceive little or no difference among brands or suppliers.

Relationship marketing is increasingly important as business suppliers use platforms like Facebook, Twitter, and other social networking sites to advertise themselves to businesses. The social networking sites encourage businesses to shop around and research options for all their needs. This means that for many suppliers, retaining their current customers has become a primary focus, whereas acquiring new customers was the focus in the past. Maintaining a steady dialogue between the supplier and the customer is a proven way to gain repeat business.[12]

Building long-term relationships with customers offers companies a way to build competitive advantage that is hard for competitors to copy. For example, the FedEx PowerShip program includes a series of automated shipping, tracking, and invoicing systems that save customers time and money while solidifying their loyalty to FedEx. This produces a win-win situation.

Strategic Alliances

A **strategic alliance**, sometimes called a **strategic partnership**, is a cooperative agreement between business firms. Strategic alliances can take the form of licensing or distribution agreements, joint ventures, research and development consortia, and partnerships. They may be between manufacturers, manufacturers and customers, manufacturers and suppliers, and manufacturers and channel intermediaries.

Business marketers form strategic alliances to strengthen operations and better compete. Honest Tea,

© PHILIPPE WIDLING/DESIGN PICS/JUPITERIMAGES / © ISTOCKPHOTO.COM/GEOFFREY HOLMAN

SELLING BUSINESS TO BUSINESSES

Inc. Is a magazine and a supporting Web site (www.inc.com) aiming to help businesses from the ground up. With myriad how-to articles, *Inc.* helps people write their business plan and then offers reports about inspirational start-ups. Each installment of the magazine's series of how-to-sell-to interviews discusses how small businesses can get their foot in the door to become suppliers for large companies like Coca-Cola and UPS. *Inc.* sells inspiration and information to businesses through informed articles about small (and large) businesses that have experienced success.[13]

© ISTOCKPHOTO.COM/ROBYN MACKENZIE

a leader in the sustainable, organic beverage market in the United States, accepted a partnership with Coca-Cola in order to gain access to the beverage giant's larger, established distributors and get Honest Tea's healthier drinks into schools and supermarkets. Coca-Cola, now the largest shareholder of Honest Tea, encourages the brand to continue its pursuit of sustainable, organic, fair-trade beverages by providing new, top-of-the-line equipment set to Honest Tea's specifications.[14]

Starbucks, world's largest coffee chain, entered into a strategic alliance with India's Tata Coffee, Asia's largest coffee plantation company, in order to gain access to one of the fastest growing economies in the world, i.e., India for setting up cafes and sourcing and roasting coffee beans from Tata coffee estates. The two companies also plan to impart training on coffee growing and milling skills to local farmers, agronomists and technicians.[15]

Sometimes alliance partners are fierce competitors. For instance, in the face of rising fuel prices, the express-delivery service DHL has formed an alliance with rival company UPS. Under the agreement, UPS provides all airlift services for DHL in the United States. According to one DHL executive, "The customer doesn't actually see a difference at all . . . unless [he or she pays] attention to the color of the partner's planes."[16]

Other alliances are formed between companies that operate in completely different industries. As a part of its "Grameena Mobile Kranthi", meaning rural mobile revolution, Bharti Airtel, a mobile service provider in India, tied up with SKS Microfi nance, a non-banking fi nance company, and launched a bundled offering for the rural customers of India. The offer included a handset at affordable rates, with a free SIM and subsidized calling rates. While Airtel provided the SIMs and the network, SKS entered into a tie-up with Nokia for giving the handsets.[17]

For an alliance to succeed in the long term, it must be built on commitment and trust. **Relationship commitment** means that a firm believes an ongoing relationship with some other firm is so important that it warrants maximum efforts at maintaining it indefinitely.[18] A perceived breakdown in commitment by one of the parties often leads to a breakdown in the relationship.

Trust exists when one party has confidence in an exchange partner's reliability and integrity.[19] Some alliances fail when participants lack trust in their trading partners. For instance, General Motors, Ford, DaimlerChrysler, Nissan Motor Company, and Renault SA created an Internet automobile parts exchange, called Covisint, that they hoped would make ₹13,50,000 crores in sales per year. But the auto industry is characterized

relationship commitment a firm's belief that an ongoing relationship with another firm is so important that the relationship warrants maximum efforts at maintaining it indefinitely

trust the condition that exists when one party has confidence in an exchange partner's reliability and integrity

keiretsu a network of interlocking corporate affiliates

original equipment manufacturers (OEMs) individuals and organizations that buy business goods and incorporate them into the products they produce for eventual sale to other producers or to consumers

by mistrust between buyers and sellers. And, after being forced to accept price concessions for years, suppliers were reluctant to participate in the exchange.

Relationships in Other Cultures

Although the terms *relationship marketing* and *strategic alliances* are fairly new, and popularized mostly by American business executives and educators, the concepts have long been familiar in other cultures. Businesses in China, Japan, Korea, Mexico, and much of Europe rely heavily on personal relationships. Chapter 21 explores customer relationship management in detail.

In Japan, for example, exchange between firms is based on personal relationships that are developed through what is called *amae*, or indulgent dependency. *Amae* is the feeling of nurturing concern for, and dependence upon, another. Reciprocity and personal relationships contribute to *amae*. Relationships between companies can develop into a ***keiretsu***—a network of interlocking corporate affiliates. Within a *keiretsu,* executives may sit on the boards of their customers or their suppliers. Members of a *keiretsu* trade with each other whenever possible and often engage in joint product development, finance, and marketing activity. For example, the Toyota Group *keiretsu* includes 14 core companies and another 170 that receive preferential treatment. Toyota holds an equity position in many of these 170 member firms and is represented on many of their boards of directors.

Many firms have found that the best way to compete in Asian countries is to form relationships with Asian firms. For example, German automaker Volkswagen has an alliance with Suzuki Motor Corporation to work on developing new hybrid and electric vehicles under both brands.[20]

LO 4 Major Categories of Business Customers

The business market consists of four major categories of customers: producers, resellers, governments, and institutions.

Producers

The producer segment of the business market includes profit-oriented individuals and organizations that use purchased goods and services to produce other products, to incorporate into other products, or to facilitate the daily operations of the organization. Examples of producers include construction, manufacturing, transportation, finance, real estate, and food service firms. Some of these firms are small, and others are among the world's largest businesses.

Producers are often called **original equipment manufacturers** or **OEMs.** This term includes all individuals and organizations that buy business goods and incorporate them into the products they produce for eventual sale to other producers or to consumers. Companies such as General Motors that buy steel, paint, tires, and batteries are said to be OEMs.

Resellers

The reseller market includes retail and wholesale businesses that buy finished goods and resell them for a profit. A retailer sells mainly to final consumers; wholesalers sell mostly to retailers and other organizational customers. Consumer product firms like Procter & Gamble, Kraft Foods, and Coca-Cola sell directly to large retailers and retail chains and through wholesalers to smaller retail units. Retailing is explored in detail in Chapter 15.

Business product distributors are wholesalers that buy business products and resell them to business customers. They often carry thousands of items in stock and employ sales forces to call on business customers. Businesses that wish to buy a gross of pencils or a hundred pounds of fertilizer typically purchase these items from local distributors rather than directly from manufacturers such as Faber-Castell Pencil or Dow Chemical.

Governments

A third major segment of the business market is government. Government organizations include thousands of federal, state, and local buying units. They make up what may be the largest single market for goods and services in the world.

Contracts for government purchases are often put out for bid. Interested vendors submit bids (usually sealed) to provide specified products during a particular time. Sometimes the lowest bidder is awarded the contract. When the lowest bidder is not awarded the contract, strong evidence must be presented to justify the decision. Grounds for rejecting the lowest bid include lack of experience, inadequate financing, or poor past performance. Bidding allows all potential suppliers a fair chance at winning government contracts and helps ensure that public funds are spent wisely.

Federal Government Name just about any good or service and chances are that someone in the federal government uses it.

Although much of the federal government's buying is centralized, no single federal agency contracts for all the government's requirements, and no single buyer in any agency purchases all that the agency needs. We can view the federal government as a combination of several large companies with overlapping responsibilities and thousands of small independent units. One good source of information about government procurement is the website http://tenders.gov.in/index.htm.

State, County, and City Government Selling to states, counties, and cities can be less frustrating for both small and large vendors than selling to the federal government. Paperwork is typically simpler and more manageable than it is at the federal level. State and local buying agencies include school districts, highway departments, government-operated hospitals, and housing agencies.

Institutions

The fourth major segment of the business market consists of institutions that seek to achieve goals other than the standard business goals of profit, market share, and return on investment. This segment includes schools, hospitals, colleges and universities, churches, labor unions, fraternal organizations, civic clubs, foundations, and other so-called nonbusiness organizations. Xerox offers educational and medical institutions the same prices as government agencies (the lowest that Xerox offers) and has a separate sales force that calls on these customers.

National Industrial Classification (NIC) a division of Ministry of Statistics and Programme Implementation, Government of India

LO 5 National Industrial Classification

The **National Industrial Classification (NIC)** in India is entrusted in the hands of Central Statistical

GOOGLE GOING FOR GOVERNMENT

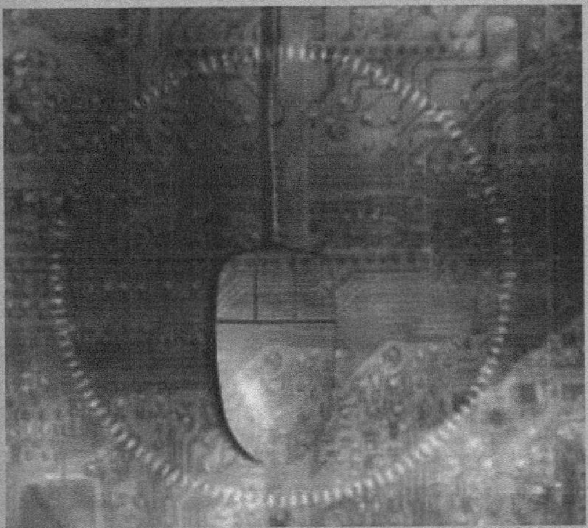

© FUSE/JUPITERIMAGES

Web-based Internet programs, such as Google Apps, offer the flexibility to access files and e-mails from any computer connected to the Internet. Despite the growing popularity of Google Apps among individuals, most businesses still use Microsoft's Outlook or other PC-bound e-mail applications. Microsoft currently serves 90 percent of US federal government e-mail. The federal government is looking to trim its annual budget by ₹3,42,000 crore, however, and it thinks it can do so by implementing Web-based programs. Google and Microsoft are now competing to win the job—Google Apps passed security certification (the first Web-based program to do so), and Microsoft's Exchange is undergoing review. The initial contract is for 15,000 federal e-mail accounts. Google is hoping to build on the success it has had in Los Angeles winning the bid for the local government's 34,000 employees to switch to Google Apps. The transition to Google's Web-based computing is anticipated to save the city an estimated ₹24.75 crore over the five-year contract period.[21]

derived demand
the demand for business products

Organisation (CSO), a division of Ministry of Statistics and Programme Implementation, Government of India. The first such classification was released in 1962. Since then, the classification has come a long way and undergone several modifications. The most up-to-date classification was published in 2008, on the lines of International Standard Industrial Classification (ISIC), Revision 4. Goods- or service-producing firms that use identical or similar production processes are grouped together.

How NIC Works

All the activities are first classified into "section", the coding being done alphabetically from A to U. The sections are further divided into "division" and allotted a 2-digit numeric code. The divisions are then categorized as "group" with 3-digit numeric code, which is further subdivided as "class" with 4-digit numeric code and then into "sub-class" with 5-digit numeric code.

Level	Description
Section C	Manufacturing
Division 13	Manufacture of textiles
Group 131	Spinning, weaving, and finishing of textiles
Class 1311	Preparation and spinning of textile fibres
Sub-Class 13111	Preparation and spinning of cotton fibre including blended cotton

NIC is an extremely valuable tool for business marketers engaged in analyzing, segmenting, and targeting markets. Each classification group is relatively homogeneous in terms of raw materials required, components used, manufacturing processes employed, and problems faced. The more digits in a code, the more homogeneous the group. Therefore, if a supplier understands the needs and requirements of a few firms within a classification, requirements can be projected for all firms in that category. The number, size, and geographic dispersion of firms can also be identified. This information can be converted to market potential estimates, market share estimates, and sales forecasts. It can also be used for identifying potential new customers. NIC codes can help identify firms that may be prospective users of a supplier's goods and services.[22]

LO 6 Business versus Consumer Markets

The basic philosophy and practice of marketing are the same whether the customer is a business organization or a consumer. Business markets do, however, have characteristics different from consumer markets.

Demand

Consumer demand for products is quite different from demand in the business market. Unlike consumer demand, business demand is derived, inelastic, joint, and fluctuating.

Derived Demand The demand for business products is called **derived demand** because organizations buy products to be used in producing their customers' products. For instance, the number of drills or lathes that a manufacturing firm needs is "derived from," or based upon the demand for, products that are produced using these machines. Because demand is derived, business marketers must carefully monitor demand patterns and changing preferences in final consumer markets, even though their customers are not in those markets. Moreover, business marketers must carefully monitor their customers' forecasts, because derived demand is based on expectations of future demand for those customers' products.

Some business marketers not only monitor final consumer demand and customer forecasts but also try to influence final consumer demand. Aluminum producers use television and magazine advertisements to point out the convenience and recycling opportunities that aluminum offers to consumers who can choose to purchase soft drinks in either aluminum or plastic containers.

Inelastic Demand The demand for many business products is inelastic with regard to price. *Inelastic demand* means that an increase or decrease in the price of the product will not significantly affect demand for the product. This will be discussed further in Chapter 19.

The price of a product used in the production of, or as part of, a final product is often a minor portion of the final product's total price. Therefore, demand for the final consumer product is not affected. If the price of automobile paint or spark plugs rises significantly, say, 200 percent in one year, do you think the number of new automobiles sold that year will be affected? Probably not.

Joint Demand **Joint demand** occurs when two or more items are used together in a final product. For example, a decline in the availability of memory chips will slow production of microcomputers, which will in turn reduce the demand for disk drives. Likewise, the demand for Apple operating systems exists as long as there is demand for Apple computers. Sales of the two products are directly linked.

Fluctuating Demand The demand for business products—particularly new plants and equipment—tends to be less stable than the demand for consumer products. A small increase or decrease in consumer demand can produce a much larger change in demand for the facilities and equipment needed to make the consumer product. Economists refer to this phenomenon as the **multiplier effect** (or **accelerator principle**).

Cummins Engine Company, a producer of heavy-duty diesel engines, uses sophisticated surface grinders to make parts. Suppose Cummins is using 20 surface grinders. Each machine lasts about ten years. Purchases have been timed so 2 machines will wear out and be replaced annually. If the demand for engine parts does not change, 2 grinders will be bought this year. If the demand for parts declines slightly, only 18 grinders may be needed and Cummins won't replace the worn ones. However, suppose that next year demand returns to previous levels plus a little more. To meet the new level of demand, Cummins will need to replace the two machines that wore out in the first year, the two that wore out in the second year, plus one or more additional machines. The multiplier effect works this way in many industries, producing highly fluctuating demand for business products.

Purchase Volume

Business customers buy in much larger quantities than consumers. Just think how large an order McDonald's typically places for potatoes for its French Fries and tomatoes used to produce Maggi Tomato Ketchup.

Number of Customers

Business marketers usually have far fewer customers than consumer marketers. The advantage is that it is a lot easier to identify prospective buyers, monitor current customers' needs and levels of satisfaction, and personally attend to existing customers. The main disadvantage is that each customer becomes crucial—especially for those manufacturers that have only one customer. In many cases, this customer is the U.S. government. The success or failure of one bid can make the difference between prosperity and bankruptcy. Boeing, trying to regain its position as the dominant tanker plane developer, has been vying for more than three years to win the U.S. Air Force's ₹1,57,500 crore bid to supply refuelling planes. Its main competition is European Aeronautic Defence and Space Company, currently the world's leading supplier of tanker planes.[23]

joint demand the demand for two or more items used together in a final product

multiplier effect (accelerator principle) phenomenon in which a small increase or decrease in consumer demand can produce a much larger change in demand for the facilities and equipment needed to make the consumer product

Location of Buyers

Business customers tend to be much more geographically concentrated than consumers. For instance, while the diamond processing and polishing industry is concentrated in Western India, the software companies are majorly located in Southern India, and the mining industry is situated in Eastern India.

Distribution Structure

Many consumer products pass through a distribution system that includes the producer, one or more wholesalers, and a retailer. In business marketing, however, because of many of the characteristics already mentioned, channels of distribution for business marketing are typically shorter. Direct channels, where manufacturers market directly to users, are much more common. The use of direct channels has increased dramatically in the past decade with the introduction

THE SUCCESS OR FAILURE OF ONE BID CAN MAKE THE DIFFERENCE BETWEEN PROSPERITY AND BANKRUPTCY.

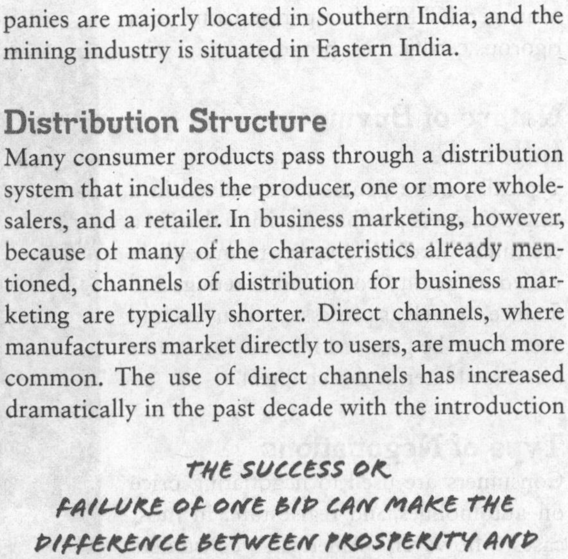

business-to-business online exchange an electronic trading floor that provides companies with integrated links to their customers and suppliers

reciprocity a practice where business purchasers choose to buy from their own customers

of various Internet buying and selling schemes. One such technique is called a **business-to-business online exchange**, which is an electronic trading floor that provides companies with integrated links to their customers and suppliers. The goal of B2B exchanges is to simplify business purchasing and to make them more efficient. For example, Indiamart claims to have more than 20 lakhs buyers and suppliers as its registered customers.[24] Exchanges such as Indiamart facilitate direct channel relationships between producers and their customers.

Nature of Buying

Unlike consumers, business buyers usually approach purchasing rather formally. Businesses use professionally trained purchasing agents or buyers who spend their entire career purchasing a limited number of items. They get to know the items and the sellers well. Some professional purchasers earn the designation of Certified Purchasing Manager (CPM) after participating in a rigorous certification program.

Nature of Buying Influence

Typically, more people are involved in a single business purchase decision than in a consumer purchase. Experts from fields as varied as quality control, marketing, and finance, as well as professional buyers and users, may be grouped in a buying center (discussed later in this chapter).

Type of Negotiations

Consumers are used to negotiating price on automobiles and real estate. In most cases, however, American consumers expect sellers to set the price and other conditions of sale, such as time of delivery and credit terms. In contrast, negotiating is common in business marketing. Buyers and sellers negotiate product specifications, delivery dates, payment terms, and other pricing matters. Sometimes these negotiations occur during many meetings over several months. Final contracts are often very long and detailed.

Use of Reciprocity

Business purchasers often choose to buy from their own customers, a practice known as **reciprocity**. This practice is neither unethical nor illegal unless one party coerces the other and the result is unfair competition. Reciprocity is generally considered a reasonable business practice. If all possible suppliers sell a similar product for about the same price, doesn't it make sense to buy from those firms that buy from you?

Use of Leasing

Consumers normally buy products rather than lease them. But businesses commonly lease expensive equipment such as computers, construction equipment and vehicles, and automobiles. Leasing allows firms to reduce capital outflow, acquire a seller's latest products, receive better services, and gain tax advantages.

The lessor, the firm providing the product, may be either the manufacturer or an independent firm. The benefits to the lessor include greater total revenue from

COURTESY OF MICHIGAN ECONOMIC DEVELOPMENT CORPORATION (MEDC)

leasing compared to selling and an opportunity to do business with customers who cannot afford to buy.

Primary Promotional Method

Business marketers tend to emphasize personal selling in their promotion efforts, especially for expensive items, custom-designed products, large-volume purchases, and situations requiring negotiations. The sale of many business products requires a great deal of personal contact. Personal selling is discussed in more detail in Chapter 18.

LO 7 Types of Business Products

Business products generally fall into one of the following seven categories, depending on their use: major equipment, accessory equipment, raw materials, component parts, processed materials, supplies, and business services.

Major Equipment

Major equipment includes capital goods such as large or expensive machines, mainframe computers, blast furnaces, generators, airplanes, and buildings. (These items are also commonly called **installations.**) Major equipment is depreciated over time rather than charged as an expense in the year it is purchased. In addition, major equipment is often custom designed for each customer. Personal selling is an important part of the marketing strategy for major equipment because distribution channels are almost always direct from the producer to the business user.

Accessory Equipment

Accessory equipment is generally less expensive and shorter-lived than major equipment. Examples include portable drills, power tools, microcomputers, and fax machines. Accessory equipment is often charged as an expense in the year it is bought rather than depreciated over its useful life. In contrast to major equipment, accessories are more often standardized and are usually bought by more customers. These customers tend to be widely dispersed. For example, all types of businesses buy microcomputers.

Local industrial distributors (wholesalers) play an important role in the marketing of accessory equipment because business buyers often purchase accessories from them. Regardless of where accessories are bought, advertising is a more vital promotional tool for accessory equipment than for major equipment.

Raw Materials

Raw materials are unprocessed extractive or agricultural products—for example, mineral ore, lumber, wheat, corn, fruits, vegetables, and fish. Raw materials become part of finished products. Extensive users, such as steel or lumber mills and food canners, generally buy huge quantities of raw materials. Because there is often a large number of relatively small sellers of raw materials, none can greatly influence price or supply. Thus, the market tends to set the price of raw materials, and individual producers have little pricing flexibility. Promotion is almost always via personal selling, and distribution channels are usually direct from producer to business user.

Component Parts

Component parts are either finished items ready for assembly or products that need very little processing before becoming part of some other product. Kirloskar diesel engines are component parts used in industrial and power generation applications. Other examples include spark plugs, tires, and electric motors for automobiles. A special feature of component parts is that they can retain their identity after becoming part of the final product. For example, automobile tires are clearly recognizable as part of a car. Moreover, because component parts often wear out, they may need to be replaced several times during the life of the final product. Thus, there are two important markets for many component parts: the original equipment manufacturer (OEM) market and the replacement market.

major equipment (installations) capital goods such as large or expensive machines, mainframe computers, blast furnaces, generators, airplanes, and buildings

accessory equipment goods, such as portable tools and office equipment, that are less expensive and shorter-lived than major equipment

raw materials unprocessed extractive or agricultural products, such as mineral ore, lumber, wheat, corn, fruits, vegetables, and fish

component parts either finished items ready for assembly or products that need very little processing before becoming part of some other product

processed materials products used directly in manufacturing other products

The availability of component parts is often a key factor in OEMs meeting their production deadlines. For example, Boeing has had to delay final assembly of Boeing 787 Dreamliners by more than three years because of slower than expected completion of components prior to their arrival at the final assembly line. In addition to delayed sales and customer disappointment and dissatisfaction, Boeing has already paid billions in penalties and has damaged credibility with customers. Despite the setbacks and the fact that there are only six Dreamliners currently flying, Boeing has 866 of the planes on back-order.[25]

The difference between unit costs and selling prices in the OEM market is often small, but profits can be substantial because of volume buying.

The replacement market is composed of organizations and individuals buying component parts to replace worn-out parts. Because components often retain their identity in final products, users may choose to replace a component part with the same brand used by the manufacturer—for example, the same brand of automobile tires or battery. The replacement market operates differently from the OEM market, however. Whether replacement buyers are organizations or individuals, they tend to demonstrate the characteristics of consumer markets that were shown in Learning Outcome 6. Consider, for example, an automobile replacement part. Purchase volume is usually small, and there are many customers, geographically dispersed, who typically buy from car dealers or parts stores. Negotiations do not occur, and neither reciprocity nor leasing is usually an issue.

Manufacturers of component parts often direct their advertising toward replacement buyers. General Motors and other carmakers compete with independent firms in the market for replacement automobile parts.

Processed Materials

Processed materials are products used directly in manufacturing other products. Unlike raw materials, they have had some processing. Examples include sheet metal, chemicals, specialty steel, treated lumber, corn syrup, and plastics. Unlike component parts, processed materials do not retain their identity in final products.

Most processed materials are marketed to OEMs or to distributors servicing the OEM market. Processed materials are generally bought according to

© STOCKBYTE

"BUSINESS BUYING BEHAVIOR HAS **FIVE IMPORTANT** ASPECTS: BUYING CENTERS, **EVALUATIVE CRITERIA**, BUYING SITUATIONS, BUSINESS **ETHICS**, AND CUSTOMER SERVICE."

customer specifications or to some industry standard, as is the case with steel and plywood. Price and service are important factors in choosing a vendor.

Supplies

Supplies are consumable items that do not become part of the final product—for example, lubricants, detergents, paper towels, pencils, and paper. Supplies are normally standardized items that purchasing agents routinely buy. Supplies typically have relatively short lives and are inexpensive compared to other business goods. Because supplies generally fall into one of three categories—maintenance, repair, or operating supplies—this category is often referred to as MRO items. Competition in the MRO market is intense. Bic and Paper Mate, for example, battle for business purchases of inexpensive ballpoint pens.

Business Services

Business services are expense items that do not become part of a final product. Businesses often retain outside providers to perform janitorial, advertising, legal, management consulting, marketing research, maintenance, and other services. Contracting an outside provider makes sense when it costs less than hiring or assigning an employee to perform the task and when an outside provider is needed for particular expertise.

LO 8 Business Buying Behavior

As you probably have already concluded, business buyers behave differently from consumers. Understanding how purchase decisions are made in organizations is a first step in developing a business selling strategy. Business buying behavior has five important aspects: buying centers, evaluative criteria, buying situations, business ethics, and customer service.

supplies consumable items that do not become part of the final product

business services expense items that do not become part of a final product

buying center all those people in an organization who become involved in the purchase decision

Buying Centers

In many cases, more than one person is involved in a purchase decision. Identifying who these people are and the roles they play greatly enhances the salesperson's chances for success.[26]

A **buying center** includes all those people in an organization who become involved in the purchase decision. Membership and influence vary from company to company. For instance, in engineering-dominated firms like Larsen & Toubro, the buying center may consist almost entirely of engineers. In marketing-oriented firms like Toyota and IBM, marketing and engineering have almost equal authority. In consumer goods firms like Procter & Gamble, product managers and other marketing decision makers may dominate the buying center. In a small manufacturing company, almost everyone may be a member.

The number of people involved in a buying center varies with the complexity and importance of a purchase decision. The composition of the buying group will usually change from one purchase to another and sometimes even during various stages of the buying process. To make matters more complicated, buying centers do not appear on formal organization charts.

For example, even though a formal committee may have been set up to choose a new plant site, it is only part of the buying center. Other people, like the company president, often play informal yet powerful roles. In a lengthy decision-making process, such as finding a new plant location, some members may drop out of the buying center when they can no longer play a useful role. Others whose talents are needed then become part of the center. No formal announcement of "who is in" and "who is out" is ever made.

Roles in the Buying Center As in family purchasing decisions, several people may play a role in the business purchase process.

BUSINESS PURCHASING ROLES

- *Initiator:* the person who first suggests making a purchase.
- *Influencers/Evaluators:* people who influence the buying decision. They often help define specifications and provide information for evaluating options. Technical personnel are especially important as influencers.
- *Gatekeepers:* group members who regulate the flow of information. Frequently, the purchasing agent views the gatekeeping role as a source of his or her power. A secretary may also act as a gatekeeper by determining which vendors get an appointment with a buyer.
- *Decider:* the person who has the formal or informal power to choose or approve the selection of the supplier or brand. In complex situations, it is often difficult to determine who makes the final decision.
- *Purchaser:* the person who actually negotiates the purchase. It could be anyone from the president of the company to the purchasing agent, depending on the importance of the decision.
- *Users:* members of the organization who will actually use the product. Users often initiate the buying process and help define product specifications.

Implications of Buying Centers for the Marketing Manager Successful vendors realize the importance of identifying who is in the decision-making unit, each member's relative influence in the buying decision, and each member's evaluative criteria. Successful selling strategies often focus on determining the most important buying influences and tailoring sales presentations to the evaluative criteria most important to these buying center members. For example, Ultra Tech Cement has used the proposition that engineers are the most important influencers and deciders in cement purchase decisions.

Evaluative Criteria

Business buyers evaluate products and suppliers against three important criteria: quality, service, and price—in that order.

Quality In this case, quality refers to technical suitability. A superior tool can do a better job in the production process, and superior packaging can increase dealer and consumer acceptance of a brand. Evaluation of quality also applies to the salesperson and the salesperson's firm. Business buyers want to deal with reputable salespeople and companies that are financially responsible. Quality improvement should be part of every organization's marketing strategy.

Service Almost as much as they want satisfactory products, business buyers want satisfactory service. A purchase offers several opportunities for service. Suppose a vendor is selling heavy equipment. Prepurchase service could include a survey of the buyer's needs. After thorough analysis of the survey findings, the vendor could prepare a report and recommendations in the form of a purchasing proposal. If a purchase results, postpurchase service might consist of installing the equipment and training those who will be using it. Postsale services may also include maintenance and repairs. Another service that business buyers seek is dependability of supply. They must be able to count on delivery of what was ordered when it is scheduled to be delivered. Buyers also welcome services that help them sell their finished products. Services of this sort are especially appropriate when the seller's product is an identifiable part of the buyer's end product.

Price Business buyers want to buy at low prices—at the lowest prices, under most circumstances. However, a buyer who pressures a supplier to cut prices to a point at which the supplier loses money on the sale almost forces shortcuts on quality. The buyer also may, in effect, force the supplier to quit selling to him or her. Then a new source of supply will have to be found.

Buying Situations

Often, business firms, especially manufacturers, must decide whether to make something or buy it from an outside supplier. The decision is essentially one of economics. Can an item of similar quality be bought at a lower price elsewhere? If not, is manufacturing it in-house the best use of limited company resources? If a firm does decide to buy a product instead of making it, the purchase will be a new buy, a modified rebuy, or a straight rebuy.

New Buy A **new buy** is a situation requiring the purchase of a product for the first time. For example, suppose a manufacturing company needs a better way to page its managers while they are working on the shop floor. Currently, each of the several managers has a distinct ring—for example, two short and one long—that sounds over the plant intercom whenever he or she is being paged by anyone in the factory. The company decides to replace its buzzer system of paging with handheld wireless radio technology that will allow managers to communicate immediately with the department initiating the page. This situation represents the greatest opportunity for new vendors. No long-term relationship has been established for this product, specifications may be somewhat fluid, and buyers are generally more open to new vendors.

If the new item is a raw material or a critical component part, the buyer cannot afford to run out of supply. The seller must be able to convince the buyer that the seller's firm can consistently deliver a high-quality product on time.

Modified Rebuy A **modified rebuy** is normally less critical and less time-consuming than a new buy. In a modified rebuy situation, the purchaser wants some change in the original good or service. It may be a new color, greater tensile strength in a component part, more respondents in a marketing research study, or additional services in a janitorial contract.

Because the two parties are familiar with each other and credibility has been established, the buyer and seller can concentrate on the specifics of the modification. But in some cases, modified rebuys are open to outside bidders. The purchaser uses this strategy to ensure that the new terms are competitive. An example would be the manufacturing company buying radios with a vibrating feature for managers who have trouble hearing the ring over the factory noise. The firm may open the bidding to examine the price/quality offerings of several suppliers.

new buy a situation requiring the purchase of a product for the first time

modified rebuy a situation in which the purchaser wants some change in the original good or service

straight rebuy a situation in which the purchaser reorders the same goods or services without looking for new information or investigating other suppliers

Straight Rebuy A **straight rebuy** is a situation vendors prefer. The purchaser is not looking for new information or other suppliers. An order is placed and the product is provided as in previous orders. Usually, a straight rebuy is routine because the terms of the purchase have been agreed to in earlier negotiations. An example would be the previously cited manufacturing company purchasing additional radios for new managers from the same supplier on a regular basis.

One common instrument used in straight rebuy situations is the purchasing contract. Purchasing con-

GETTING AHEAD WITH BIG BUSINESS

© ISTOCKPHOTO.COM/NIELS LAAN

When a small manufacturer or supplier lands a contract with a large corporation, it's a big deal. But getting the attention of the decision maker at places like Northrop Grumman, Coca-Cola, or Dell can be daunting and disheartening. The key to selling to large corporations requires spending time getting to know the company and how it operates. Most large corporations like smaller companies because of easy access to the small firm's CEO and the ability to modify production or delivery dates quickly. Dell is looking for companies with long-term plans and a willingness to marry their culture to Dell's. Coca-Cola is looking for companies that bring specific value Coke doesn't already have and for companies willing to work within the system and not try to bypass it.[27]

tracts are used with products that are bought often and in high volume. In essence, the purchasing contract makes the buyer's decision-making routine and promises the salesperson a sure sale. The advantage to the buyer is a quick, confident decision and, to the salesperson, reduced or eliminated competition. Suppliers must remember not to take straight rebuy relationships for granted. Retaining existing customers is much easier than attracting new ones.

Business Ethics

As we noted in Chapter 3, ethics refers to the moral principles or values that generally govern the conduct of an individual or a group. Ethics can also be viewed as the standard of behavior by which conduct is judged.

Although we have heard a lot about corporate misbehavior in recent years, most people, and most companies, follow ethical practices. To help achieve this, over half of all major corporations offer ethics training to employees. Many companies also have codes of ethics that help guide buyers and sellers. For example, Infosys has a clearly written code of conduct available on their corporate Web site that acts as an ethical guide for all its employees.

Customer Service

Business marketers are increasingly recognizing the benefits of developing a formal system to monitor customer opinions and perceptions of the quality of customer service. Companies such as McDonald's, Westside, and Lexus build their strategies not only around products but also around a few highly developed service skills. These companies understand that keeping current customers satisfied is just as important as attracting new ones, if not more so. Leading-edge firms are obsessed not only with delivering high-quality customer service but also with measuring satisfaction, loyalty, relationship quality, and other indicators of nonfinancial performance.

© AP IMAGES/PRNEWSFOTO/VIRGIN AMERICA

Most firms find it necessary to develop measures unique to their own strategies, value propositions, and target markets.

Some customers are more valuable than others. They may have greater value because they spend more, buy higher-margin products, have a well-known name, or have the potential of becoming a bigger customer in the future. Some companies selectively provide different levels of service to customers based on their value to the business. By giving the most valuable customers superior service, a firm is more likely to keep them happy, hopefully increasing retention of these high-value customers and maximizing the total business value they generate over time.

To achieve this goal, the firm must be able to divide customers into two or more groups based on their value. It must also create and apply policies that govern how service will be allocated among groups. Policies might establish which customers' phone calls get "fast tracked" and which customers are directed to use the Web and/or voice self-service, how specific e-mail questions are routed, and who is given access to online chat and who isn't.[28]

Providing different customers with different levels of service is a very sensitive matter. It must be handled very carefully and very discreetly to avoid offending lesser-value, but still important, customers.

Review and Applications

Describe business marketing. Business marketing provides goods and services that are bought for use in business rather than for personal consumption. Intended use, not physical characteristics, distinguishes a business product from a consumer product.

1.1 As the marketing manager for Huggies diapers made by Kimberly-Clark, you are constantly going head-to-head with Pampers, produced by rival Procter & Gamble. You are considering unlocking the potential of the business market to increase your share of the disposable diaper market, but how? Write an outline of several ways you could transform this quintessentially consumer product into a successful business product as well.

Describe the role of the Internet in business marketing. The rapid expansion and adoption of the Internet have made business markets more competitive than ever before. The number of business buyers and sellers using the Internet is rapidly increasing. Firms are seeking new and better ways to expand markets and sources of supply, increase sales and decrease costs, and better serve customers. Marketers are becoming more sophisticated in their use of the Internet and are developing quantitative methods that can be used to better measure online success.

2.1 How could you use the Web site **BtoBonline.com** to help define a target market and develop a marketing plan?

2.2 Reconsider question 1.1. How could you use the Internet in your business marketing of Huggies diapers?

Discuss the role of relationship marketing and strategic alliances in business marketing. Relationship marketing entails seeking and establishing long-term alliances or partnerships with customers. A strategic alliance is a cooperative agreement between business firms. Firms form alliances to leverage what they do well by partnering with others that have complementary skills.

3.1 Why is relationship or personal selling the best way to promote in business marketing?

Identify the four major categories of business market customers. Producer markets consist of for-profit organizations and individuals that buy products to use in producing other products, as components of other products, or in facilitating business operations. Reseller markets consist of wholesalers and retailers that buy finished products to resell for profit. Government markets include federal, state, county, and city governments that buy goods and services to support their own operations and serve the needs of citizens. Institutional markets consist of very diverse nonbusiness institutions whose main goals do not include profit.

4.1 Understanding businesses is key to business marketing. Publications like *CII publications and Economist* can give you insights into many business marketing concepts. Research the industrial publications to find an article on a business marketer that interests you. Write a description of the company using as many concepts from the chapter as possible. What major category or categories of business market customers does this firm serve?

4.2 What do you have to do to get a government contract? Check out the website **http://tenders.gov.in/index.htm** to find out. Does it seem worth the effort?

Explain the National Industrial Classification. The NIC provides a way to identify, analyze, segment, and target business and government markets. Organizations can be identified and compared by a numeric code indicating business sector, subsector, industry group, and industry. NIC is a valuable tool for analyzing, segmenting, and targeting business markets.

5.1 Pick a product and determine its NIC code. How easy was it to trace the groups and sectors?

Explain the major differences between business and consumer markets. In business markets, demand is derived, price-inelastic, joint, and fluctuating. Purchase volume is much larger than in consumer markets, customers are fewer in number and more geographically concentrated, and distribution channels are more direct. Buying is approached more formally using professional purchasing agents, more people are involved in the buying process, negotiation is more complex, and reciprocity and leasing are more common. And, finally, selling strategy in business markets normally focuses on personal contact rather than on advertising.

6.1 How might derived demand affect the manufacturing of an automobile?

6.2 Your boss has just asked you, the company purchasing manager, to buy new computers for an entire department. As you have just recently purchased a new home computer, you are well-educated about the various products available. How will your buying process for the company differ from your recent purchase for yourself?

Describe the seven types of business goods and services. Major equipment includes capital goods, such as heavy machinery. Accessory equipment is typically less expensive and shorter-lived than major equipment. Raw materials are extractive or agricultural products that have not been processed. Component parts are finished or near-finished items to be used as parts of other products. Processed materials are used to manufacture other products. Supplies are consumable and not used as part of a final product. Business services are intangible products that many companies use in their operations.

7.1 In small groups, brainstorm examples of companies that feature the products in different business categories. (Avoid examples already listed in the chapter.) Compile a list of ten specific business products including at least one in each category. Then match up with another group. Have each group take turns naming a product and have the other group identify its appropriate category. Try to resolve all discrepancies by discussion. Some identified products may appropriately fit into more than one category.

Discuss the unique aspects of business buying behavior. Business buying behavior is distinguished by five fundamental characteristics. First, buying is normally undertaken by a buying center consisting of many people who range widely in authority level. Second, business buyers typically evaluate alternative products and suppliers based on quality, service, and price—in that order. Third, business buying falls into three general categories: new buys, modified rebuys, and straight rebuys. Fourth, the ethics of business buyers and sellers are often scrutinized. Fifth, customer service before, during, and after the sale plays a big role in business purchase decisions.

8.1 A colleague of yours has sent you an e-mail seeking your advice as he attempts to sell a new voice-mail system to a local business. Send him a return e-mail describing the various people who might influence the customer's buying decision. Be sure to include suggestions for dealing with the needs of each of these individuals.

8.2 Intel Corporation supplies microprocessors to Hewlett-Packard for use in its computers. Describe the buying situation in this relationship, keeping in mind the rapid advance of technology in this industry.

Exercises

APPLICATION EXERCISE

Purchasing agents are often offered gifts and gratuities. Increasingly, though, companies are restricting the amount and value of gifts that their purchasing managers can accept from vendors. The idea is that purchasing managers should consider all qualified vendors during a buying decision instead of only those who pass out great event tickets. This exercise asks you to consider whether accepting various types of gifts is ethical.[29]

Activities

1. Review the following list of common types of gifts and favors. Put a check mark next to the items that you think it would be acceptable for a purchasing manager to receive from a vendor.

   Advertising souvenirs
   Clothing
   Discounts on personal purchases
   Golf outings
   Large appliances
   Lunches
   Tickets (sports, theater, amusement parks, etc.)
   Vacation trips
   Automobiles
   Dinners
   Food and liquor
   Holiday gifts
   Loans of money
   Small-value appliances
   Trips to vendor plants

2. Now look at your list of acceptable gifts through various lenses. Would your list change if the purchasing manager's buying decision involved a low-cost item (say, pens)? Why or why not? What if the decision involved a very expensive purchase (like a major installation)?

3. Form a team and compare your lists. Discuss (or debate) any discrepancies.

ETHICS EXERCISE

Ajit Sethi, purchasing manager for an automobile manufacturer, is responsible for buying INR 25 crore of supplies every year. He has a preferred list of certified suppliers who are awarded a large percentage of his business. Ajit has been offered a paid weekend for two in Kerala as a Diwali present from a supplier with whom he has done business for a decade and built a very good relationship.

Questions

1. Would it be legal and ethical for Ajit Sethi to accept this gift?
2. How is this addressed in the AMA Statement of Ethics? Go to the AMA Web site at **www.marketingpower.com/About AMA/** and reread the Statement of Ethics. Write a brief paragraph summarizing where the AMA stands on the issue of supplier gifts.

MARKETING PLAN EXERCISE

For continued general assistance in business plans and marketing plans, visit **www.bplans.com** or **www.businessplans.org.** You should also refer to the Marketing Plan Outline–Appendix I in Chapter 2 for additional checklist items. Complete the following exercises to continue the marketing plan you began in Chapter 2:

1. Identify the NIC code for your chosen company's industry (http://mospi.nic.in/Mospi_New/upload/nic_2008_17apr09.pdf) and perform a brief industry analysis of your firm's industry, based on the NIC code.
2. Make a list of consumer markets and business markets for your company's product or business offering. Which is the more important market for your company? Why?
3. How does the buying process differ for consumer markets and business markets for your chosen company's product or business offering?

Short Case: HEWLETT PACKARD INDIA

Prepared by
Dr. Dheeraj Sharma,
Indian Institute of Management, Ahmedabad

Hewlett Packard (HP), was jointly formed by William Hewlett and David Packard in 1938, is one of the leading brands in the computer industry which provide products for both business and personal use. It established itself in India in 1988. It provides a more personalized, better and even cheaper alternatives to the users than Apple and Dell. With its merging with Compaq in 2002, it has become one of the major players in notebooks, desktops, and business servers in large number of markets. HP's product portfolio caters to the household and business needs of government organizations, small or large enterprises, and graphic art and design industry. The main reason for its success has been the commitment of its team members towards providing solutions to the problems faced by its customers in a most effective manner and in lesser amount of time.

HP SOLUTIONS FOR BUSINESS USE

To ensure that the needs of the small and medium scale businessmen are catered to their fullest, HP offers a wide range of products such as printers, scanners, desktops, network storage solutions, monitors, notebook, scanners, faxes, etc.[30] HP attempts to meet the needs of small business and the needs of the large enterprises are catered too with its wide range of products like laptops, desktops, and workstations, printers, monitor and accessories, ink, toner and paper, etc.

HP believed in providing a complete solution to the users of its product. It also provides add-on benefits to the product to ensure the maximum satisfaction to the users of its product. It also provides solutions.

HP care pack services provide premium support to meet the needs of the business environment. It ensures that the call once logged in is responded the same business day and attended before the end of the next business day. HP also expands and extends standard warranties for their products. *HP Imaging Printing and Support* offer solutions related to printers right from its installation.[31] HP has also launched a free *HP Smart Chat*, facility, where live HP representatives provide a helping hand in providing answer to the queries regarding HP products, providing expert advice on right solutions, assisting in selecting the right technology for the business, etc.[32] HP also has an efficient *customer care*, devoted to provide customers' assistance, right from the purchase of the products till its end. Assistance is in the form of self help, e-mail HP, call HP and interact online with HP. The services, to mention a few include providing solutions to the pre purchase and post purchase queries, attending to the complains of the customers, giving them technical support after the purchase is made etc.[33] HP also provides some other facilities like *Creative Studio* for business, which enables discovering free templates for business use like letter heads business cards, etc.[34]

As per Punit Chadha, the Director of Graphic Solutions Business, Imaging & Printing Group, HP India, HP has always been committed in providing the best quality products at a competitive price and performance. This allows the business to grow profitably with increased efficiency, output of high quality and reliability.[35] Keeping this in mind the company launched 'Trade In Trade Out' program, which enabled the corporate to exchange and upgrade their used high-end printers with new HP Designjet printer at special rates. The used products were taken back and recycled to reduce the effect of this technological product on environment.

To capture the existing demands in the verticals like educational institutes, law firm, telecom companies, etc, HP adopted a micro-market strategy. It provided solutions based on cloud computing for many key verticals. For this it has already undergone partnership with many Indian software companies.[36] For small offices and businesses, HP has introduced printers that enable them to produce documents of a good quality at a reasonable cost. HP's new products are made environment friendly with its Auto-on and Auto-off technology.[37]

LOSING OF THE MARKET SHARE:

When HP entered the market and merged with Compaq in 2002, it was an unquestionable market leader for many years. However, with the passage of time, HP lost its share to its competitors Dell and Acer. In the second quarter of 2011, Acer overtook HP and secured second position with a market share of 12.1 per cent in the PC market. Dell held the first position with market share of 17 per cent. However, HP stood at the third position with a share of 11.2 per cent from 15 per cent two years ago in the PC market.[38] As a result, HP announced spinning off or even selling off its PC business. The decision was taken to increase the business in the service segment of HP. However, this came with a lot of retaliation from the customers and partners across the country. This was because the PC business (PCB) contributed one third of the total revenues of HP. It was a $40 billion business operating in more than 170 countries in the world.[39] Later on it was realized that the cost associated with the spinning off would overweigh the benefits of dropping the PC business. Hence, the idea of spinning off the PCB was dropped and it continued to be a part of the HP business.[40] Another recent breakthrough came when HP decided to merge its printer unit with its PC business in 2012. This was done looking at the falling profit of the HP printer market by 10 per cent last year. HPs printer market was a shining star few years back, but now the scene has changed. Ink sales fell by 6 per cent, office printers by 5 per cent and consumer printers by 15 per cent by the end of January 2012.[41]

FUTURE PLANS:

As for the future plans, the company is now planning to enter the small sector, in tier III and tier IV cities and is planning to invest a heavily in it. Also, the company has declared to spend a sum of $300 million in global marketing campaign.[42] They are planning on using multiple marketing channels to market their products.

Questions

1. What do you think was the reason for HP losing its market share to Dell and Acer in the second quarter of 2011?
2. Was the company right in taking back its spin-off decision? Give justifications.
3. Would the company's decision of merging its printer market with its PC business reaps the benefit it has expected?
4. Do you think the company will succeed in its plan to enter the tier-III and tier-IV cities in small towns? Discuss.
5. Apart from the branded segments there are also local players in the industry providing products at a lower cost. How can HP compete with it?

7 Business Marketing

KEY TERMS

LO 1

business marketing the marketing of goods and services to individuals and organizations for purposes other than personal consumption

LO 2

business-to-business electronic commerce the use of the Internet to facilitate the exchange of goods, services, and information between organizations

stickiness a measure of a Web site's effectiveness; calculated by multiplying the frequency of visits by the duration of a visit by the number of pages viewed during each visit (site reach)

disintermediation the elimination of intermediaries such as wholesalers or distributers from a marketing channel

reintermediation the reintroduction of an intermediary between producers and users

LO 3

strategic alliance (strategic partnership) a cooperative agreement between business firms

relationship commitment a firm's belief that an ongoing relationship with another firm is so important that the relationship warrants maximum efforts at maintaining it indefinitely

trust the condition that exists when one party has confidence in an exchange partner's reliability and integrity

keiretsu a network of interlocking corporate affiliates

LO 4

original equipment manufacturers (OEMs) individuals and organizations that buy business goods and incorporate them into the products they produce for eventual sale to other producers or to consumers

KEY CONCEPTS

LO 1 **Describe business marketing.** Business marketing provides goods and services that are bought for use in business rather than for personal consumption. Intended use, not physical characteristics, distinguishes a business product from a consumer product.

LO 2 **Describe the role of the Internet in business marketing.** The rapid expansion and adoption of the Internet have made business markets more competitive than ever before. The number of business buyers and sellers using the Internet is rapidly increasing. Firms are seeking new and better ways to expand markets and sources of supply, increase sales and decrease costs, and better serve customers. Marketers are becoming more sophisticated in their use of the Internet and are developing quantitative methods that can be used to better measure online success.

LO 3 **Discuss the role of relationship marketing and strategic alliances in business marketing.** Relationship marketing entails seeking and establishing long-term alliances or partnerships with customers. A strategic alliance is a cooperative agreement between business firms. Firms form alliances to leverage what they do well by partnering with others that have complementary skills.

LO 4 **Identify the four major categories of business market customers.** Producer markets consist of for-profit organizations and individuals that buy products to use in producing other products, as components of other products, or in facilitating business operations. Reseller markets consist of wholesalers and retailers that buy finished products to resell for profit. Government markets include federal, state, county, and city governments that buy goods and services to support their own operations and serve the needs of citizens. Institutional markets consist of very diverse nonbusiness institutions whose main goals do not include profit.

LO 5 **Explain the National Industrial Classification.** The NIC provides a way to identify, analyze, segment, and target business and government markets. Organizations can be identified and compared by a numeric code indicating business sector, subsector, industry group, and industry. NIC is a valuable tool for analyzing, segmenting, and targeting business markets.

LO 6 **Explain the major differences between business and consumer markets.** In business markets, demand is derived, price-inelastic, joint, and fluctuating. Purchase volume is much larger than in consumer markets, customers are fewer in number and more geographically concentrated, and distribution channels are more direct. Buying is approached more formally using professional purchasing agents, more people are involved in the buying process, negotiation is more complex, and reciprocity and leasing are more common. And, finally, selling strategy in business markets normally focuses on personal contact rather than on advertising.

LO 7 **Describe the seven types of business goods and services.** Major equipment includes capital goods, such as heavy machinery. Accessory equipment is typically less expensive and shorter-lived than major equipment. Raw materials are extractive or agricultural products that have not been processed. Component parts are finished or near-finished items to be used as parts of other products. Processed materials are used to manufacture other products. Supplies are consumable and

LO 5 **National Industrial Classification (NIC)** a division of Ministry of Statistics and Programme Implementation, Government of India

LO 6 **derived demand** the demand for business products

joint demand the demand for two or more items used together in a final product

multiplier effect (accelerator principle) phenomenon in which a small increase or decrease in consumer demand can produce a much larger change in demand for the facilities and equipment needed to make the consumer product

business-to-business online exchange an electronic trading floor that provides companies with integrated links to their customers and suppliers

reciprocity a practice where business purchasers choose to buy from their own customers

LO 7 **major equipment (installations)** capital goods such as large or expensive machines, mainframe computers, blast furnaces, generators, airplanes, and buildings

accessory equipment goods, such as portable tools and office equipment, that are less expensive and shorter-lived than major equipment

raw materials unprocessed extractive or agricultural products, such as mineral ore, lumber, wheat, corn, fruits, vegetables, and fish

component parts either finished items ready for assembly or products that need very little processing before becoming part of some other product

processed materials products used directly in manufacturing other products

supplies consumable items that do not become part of the final product

business services expense items that do not become part of a final product

LO 8 **buying center** all those people in an organization who become involved in the purchase decision

new buy a situation requiring the purchase of a product for the first time

modified rebuy a situation in which the purchaser wants some change in the original good or service

straight rebuy a situation in which the purchaser reorders the same goods or services without looking for new information or investigating other suppliers

Characteristic	Business Market	Consumer Market
Demand	Organizational	Individual
Purchase volume	Larger	Smaller
Number of customers	Fewer	Many
Location of buyers	Geographically concentrated	Dispersed
Distribution structure	More direct	More indirect
Nature of buying	More professional	More personal
Nature of buying influence	Multiple	Single
Type of negotiations	More complex	Simpler
Use of reciprocity	Yes	No
Use of leasing	Greater	Lesser
Primary promotional method	Personal selling	Advertising

and not used as part of a final product. Business services are intangible products that many companies use in their operations.

LO 8 **Discuss the unique aspects of business buying behavior.** Business buying behavior is distinguished by five fundamental characteristics. First, buying is normally undertaken by a buying center consisting of many people who range widely in authority level. Second, business buyers typically evaluate alternative products and suppliers based on quality, service, and price—in that order. Third, business buying falls into three general categories: new buys, modified rebuys, and straight rebuys. Fourth, the ethics of business buyers and sellers are often scrutinized. Fifth, customer service before, during, and after the sale plays a big role in business purchase decisions.

CHAPTER 8

Segmenting and Targeting Markets

Learning Outcomes

- **LO 1** Describe the characteristics of markets and market segments
- **LO 2** Explain the importance of market segmentation
- **LO 3** Discuss criteria for successful market segmentation
- **LO 4** Describe the bases commonly used to segment consumer markets
- **LO 5** Describe the bases for segmenting business markets
- **LO 6** List the steps involved in segmenting markets
- **LO 7** Discuss alternative strategies for selecting target markets
- **LO 8** Explain one-to-one marketing
- **LO 9** Explain how and why firms implement positioning strategies and how product differentiation plays a role

Market segmentation plays a key role in the marketing strategy of almost all successful organizations.

LO 1 Market Segmentation

The term *market* means different things to different people. We are all familiar with the supermarket, stock market, labor market, fish market, and flea market. All these types of markets share several characteristics. First, they are composed of people (consumer markets) or organizations (business markets). Second, these people or organizations have wants and needs that can be satisfied by particular product categories. Third, they have the ability to buy the products they seek. Fourth, they are willing to exchange their resources, usually money or credit, for desired products. In sum, a **market** is (1) people or organizations with (2) needs or wants and with (3) the ability and (4) the willingness to buy. A group of people or an organization that lacks any one of these characteristics is not a market.

market people or organizations with needs or wants and the ability and willingness to buy

market segment a subgroup of people or organizations sharing one or more characteristics that cause them to have similar product needs

Within a market, a **market segment** is a subgroup of people or organizations sharing one or more characteristics that cause them to have similar product needs. At one extreme, we can define every person and every organization in the world as a market segment because each is unique. At the other extreme, we can define the entire consumer market as one large market segment and the business market as another large segment. All people have some similar characteristics and needs, as do all organizations.

***Note:** All the figures in U.S. dollars are converted into rupee using the value $1 = ₹45.*

market segmentation the process of dividing a market into meaningful, relatively similar, and identifiable segments or groups

From a marketing perspective, market segments can be described as somewhere between the two extremes. The process of dividing a market into meaningful, relatively similar, and identifiable segments or groups is called **market segmentation**. The purpose of market segmentation is to enable the marketer to tailor marketing mixes to meet the needs of one or more specific segments.

LO 2 The Importance of Market Segmentation

Until the 1960s, few firms practiced market segmentation. When they did, it was more likely a haphazard effort than a formal marketing strategy. Before 1960, for example, the Coca-Cola Company produced only one beverage and aimed it at the entire soft drink market. Today, Coca-Cola offers more than a dozen different products to market segments based on diverse consumer preferences for flavors and calorie and caffeine content. Coca-Cola offers traditional soft drinks, energy drinks (Burn), flavoured teas (Nestea), fruit drinks (Minute Maid), and water (Kinley).

Market segmentation plays a key role in the marketing strategy of almost all successful organizations and is a powerful marketing tool for several reasons. Most important, nearly all markets include groups of people or organizations with different product needs and preferences. Market segmentation helps marketers define customer needs and wants more precisely. Because market segments differ in size and potential, segmentation helps decision makers to more accurately define marketing objectives and better allocate resources. In turn, performance can be better evaluated when objectives are more precise.

W, a successful women's fashion retailer, thrives by marketing to women aged 25 to 55 who like to wear comfortable, yet stylish, clothing. It sells private-label clothing that comes in six different sizes. Nestlé modifies its portfolio to increase its market share in emerging economies, such as China, India, Malaysia, and Thailand. It sells food goods enriched with vitamins and has seen sales of enhanced milk products increase.[1]

LO 3 Criteria for Successful Segmentation

Marketers segment markets for three important reasons. First, segmentation enables marketers to identify groups of customers with similar needs and to analyze the characteristics and buying behavior of these groups. Second, segmentation provides marketers with information to help them design marketing mixes specifically matched with the characteristics and desires of one or more segments. Third, segmentation is consistent with the marketing concept of satisfying customer wants and needs while meeting the organization's objectives.

To be useful, a segmentation scheme must produce segments that meet four basic criteria:

1. *Substantiality:* A segment must be large enough to warrant developing and maintaining a special marketing mix. This criterion does not necessarily mean that a segment must have many potential customers. Marketers of custom-designed homes and business buildings, commercial airplanes, and large computer systems typically develop marketing programs tailored to each potential customer's needs. In most cases, however, a market segment needs many potential customers to make commercial sense. In the 1980s, home banking would have failed because not enough people owned personal computers. Today, a larger number of people own computers, and home banking is a thriving industry.
2. *Identifiability and measurability:* Segments must be identifiable and their size measurable. Data about the population within geographic boundaries, the number of people in various age categories, and other social and demographic characteristics are often easy to get, and they provide fairly concrete measures of segment size. Suppose that a social service agency wants to identify segments by their readiness to participate in a drug and alcohol program or in prenatal care. Unless the agency can measure how many people are willing, indifferent, or unwilling to participate, it will have trouble gauging whether there are enough people to justify setting up the service.
3. *Accessibility:* The firm must be able to reach members of targeted segments with customized

marketing mixes. Some market segments are hard to reach—for example, senior citizens (especially those with reading or hearing disabilities), individuals who don't speak English, and the illiterate.

Responsiveness: Markets can be segmented using any criteria that seem logical. Unless one market segment responds to a marketing mix differently than other segments, however, that segment need not be treated separately. For instance, if all customers are equally price conscious about a product, there is no need to offer high-, medium-, and low-priced versions to different segments.

LO 4 Bases for Segmenting Consumer Markets

Marketers use **segmentation bases**, or **variables**, which are characteristics of individuals, groups, or organizations, to divide a total market into segments.

segmentation bases (variables) characteristics of individuals, groups, or organizations

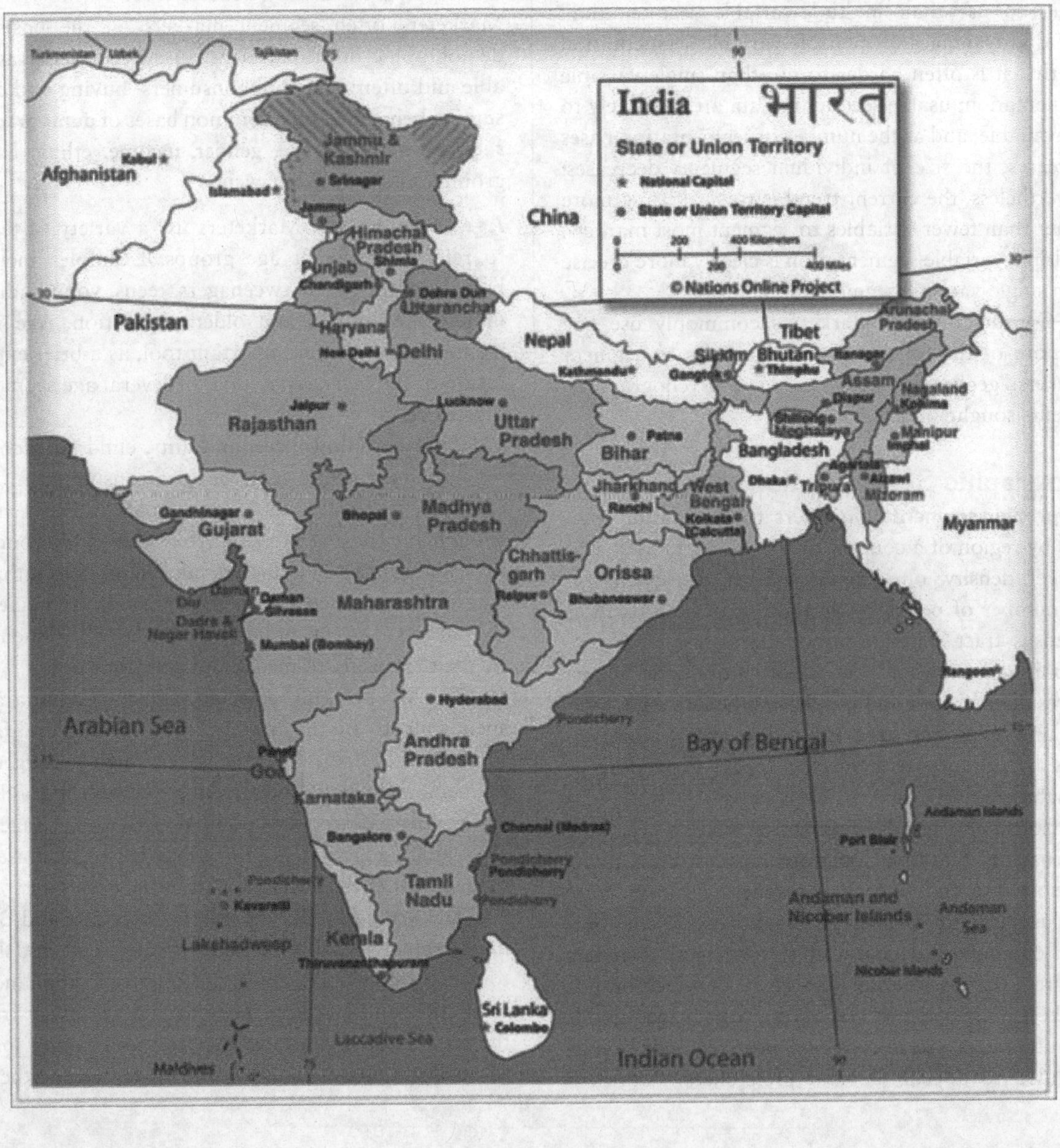

geographic segmentation
segmenting markets by region of a country or the world, market size, market density, or climate

demographic segmentation
segmenting markets by age, gender, income, ethnic background, and family life cycle

The choice of segmentation bases is crucial because an inappropriate segmentation strategy may lead to lost sales and missed profit opportunities. The key is to identify bases that will produce substantial, measurable, and accessible segments that exhibit different response patterns to marketing mixes.

Markets can be segmented using a single variable, such as age group, or several variables, such as age group, gender, and education. Although it is less precise, single-variable segmentation has the advantage of being simpler and easier to use than multiple-variable segmentation. The disadvantages of multiple-variable segmentation are that it is often harder to use than single-variable segmentation; usable secondary data are less likely to be available; and as the number of segmentation bases increases, the size of individual segments decreases. Nevertheless, the current trend is toward using more rather than fewer variables to segment most markets. Multiple-variable segmentation is clearly more precise than single-variable segmentation.

Consumer goods marketers commonly use one or more of the following characteristics to segment markets: geography, demographics, psychographics, benefits sought, and usage rate.

Geographic Segmentation

Geographic segmentation refers to segmenting markets by region of a country or the world, market size, market density, or climate. Market density means the number of people within a unit of land, such as a census tract. Climate is commonly used for geographic segmentation because of its dramatic impact on residents' needs and purchasing behaviour. Clothing, umbrellas, and air-conditioning and heating systems are products with varying appeal, depending on climate.

Consumer goods companies take a regional approach to marketing for four reasons. First, many firms need to find new ways to generate sales because of sluggish and intensely competitive markets. Second, computerized checkout stations with scanners give retailers an accurate assessment of which brands sell best in their region. Third, many packaged-goods manufacturers are introducing new regional brands intended to appeal to local preferences. Fourth, a more regional approach allows consumer goods companies to react more quickly to competition. Nokia has targeted rural India for years by manufacturing rugged, yet sleek, cell phones and sending an army of customer service vans all over the countryside to demonstrate the company's commitment to helping customers—wherever they live—with any technological difficulties. In urban areas, Nokia has more than 700 stationary care centers to assist its growing urban customer base as well. Because of Nokia's attention to customer service, Nokia holds 60 percent of India's handset market.[2]

Demographic Segmentation

Marketers often segment markets on the basis of demographic information because it is widely available and often related to consumers' buying and consuming behavior. Some common bases of **demographic segmentation** are age, gender, income, ethnic background, and family life cycle.

Age Segmentation Marketers use a variety of terms to refer to different age groups. Examples include babies, infants, kids, tweenagers, teens, young adults, middle-aged adults and older population. Age segmentation can be an important tool, as a brief exploration of the market potential of several age segments illustrates.

Through allowances, and gifts, children account for and influence a great deal of consumption. For example, tweens (9 to 12 years old) in India hold enough purchasing power to buy things like books, toys, and eatables. For higher value items like clothing, footwear, and video games, the decisions are made by the parents. Tweens' preferences are largely influenced by their exposure to media and peer choices.[3]

Teens is a highly growing segment of India and spends mostly on music, mobile phone bills, and fastfood. Usage of the Internet is very high among this segment, with social networking and viewing videos on. Youtube being very popular activities. Usage of electronic gadgets is high and has led to increase in demand for such products.[4]

The young adults (people in their 20s and 30s) have high disposable incomes at their end and like to spend on vehicles, consumer electronic appliances, cosmetics, and clothing. They do not shy away from the idea of buying goods on credit and taking loans for such requirements. They are also open to voicing their opinions on social networking sites about current trends and issues.[5]

The middle-aged adults (40 to 64 years old) are very aware of their family responsibilities and thus, they make purchasing decisions with thought for and input from their families. They are concerned about their own careers and health, and their children's education, careers, and marriage. Their spending habits are very cautious as they were born in the era of constrained resources.[6]

The older population generally consists of the retired population. However, many self-employed people, such as doctors, lawyers, farmers, and business owners continue working till late age. They spend considerably on health related products and medication.[7]

Gender Segmentation Women are an experienced purchasing group with the responsibility of purchasing the majority of household items. They also are increasingly part of what were once considered all-male markets, such as scooters. In 2011, women made 12–14 percent of all two-wheeler users in India and accounted for 30–35 percent of total sales.[8] The two-wheeler industry has been forced to respond by developing more vehicles for female segment and changing its advertising strategy. On the other hand, traditionally female markets are trying to entice men to purchase from them. With young urban men becoming increasingly concerned of their appearance, cosmetics companies realize the potential in male grooming and personal care products, particularly fairness products, shaving products, and deodorants. The value sales of men's grooming reached almost ₹2,500 crores in 2010, and showed a growth of 19 percent.[9] Gillette, Garnier and Vaseline are focusing on this growing market with a whole new range of products.

Marketers of products such as clothing, cosmetics, personal-care items, magazines, jewelry, and gifts still commonly segment markets by gender. For instance, the fortnightly magazine, *Femina*, targets women readers with a wide variety of articles that they would enjoy. Financial investment and savings product are mostly targeted towards men as they are the primary income earning member in the family.

Income Segmentation Income is a popular demographic variable for segmenting markets because income level influences consumers' wants and determines their buying power. Many markets are segmented by income, including the markets for personal care products, automobiles, and food. Hypermarkets like Hypercity and More appeal to many income segments. High-income customers looking for luxury want outstanding customer service. For example, fashion companies use computer technology to customize upscale products that are designed specifically for their wealthy customers' needs.[10] Other companies try to appeal to low-income customers. Tata Chemicals launched its low cost water purifier for the lower income groups of India who lacked access to safe drinking water. The product comes in three different variants, namely Tata Swach, Tata Swach Smart, and Tata Swach Smart Magic, with price points of ₹999, ₹749, and ₹499 respectively.[11]

family life cycle (FLC) a series of stages determined by a combination of age, marital status, and the presence or absence of children

Family Life Cycle Segmentation The demographic factors of gender, age, and income often do not sufficiently explain why consumer buying behavior varies. Frequently, consumption patterns among people of the same age and gender differ because they are in different stages of the family life cycle. The **family life cycle (FLC)** is a series of stages determined by a combination of age, marital status, and the presence or absence of children.

psychographic segmentation
market segmentation on the basis of personality, motives, lifestyles, and geodemographics

The life cycle stage consisting of the married-couple household is considered the traditional family in India. Today, however, with the slight increase in average marriage age, single adults are increasingly in the majority. As of 2009, 49.6 percent of total Indian population comprised of singles, while 45.6 percent were married people.[12] Depending on the stage in life cycle, consumption pattern of customers undergoes transformation. While singles generally spend their disposable income on branded apparel, footwear, eating out, and going to movies, married people spend their income on kitchen appliances, consumer electronic goods, and furniture. Similarly, the emphasis of young parents shifts to savings and investment schemes to provide for their children's education and plan for their own old age. These days, finance companies offer special products for retired people so that they can lead a smooth life even after retirement. For example, HDFC Standard Life Insurance offers special plans for the old aged, promoting the concept of self-respect.

Psychographic Segmentation

Age, gender, income, ethnicity, FLC stage, and other demographic variables are usually helpful in developing segmentation strategies, but often they don't paint the entire picture. Demographics provide the skeleton, but psychographics add meat to the bones. **Psychographic segmentation** is market segmentation on the basis of the variables in the box to the right.

Psychographic variables can be used individually to segment markets or be combined with other variables to provide more detailed descriptions of market segments. One approach is for marketers and advertisers to purchase information from a collector, such as Nielsen Homescan, in order to understand the audience and what they want. Homescan, the consumer panel of the research firm Nielsen, gathers information about buying habits of the consumers

BRINGING INDIA TO INDIAN AMERICANS

Indian Americans represent a small part of the ethnic makeup of the United States, but more than 20 lakh Indian Americans have seen their culture come to the mainstream with the success of *Slumdog Millionaire*. India and people from other South Asian countries, including Pakistan, Bangladesh, Sri Lanka, and Nepal, represent a relatively affluent and highly educated group in the United States, making them a desirable segment. State Farm recently ran a karaoke contest and sent the winner on a trip to India to sing in a Bollywood video. IFC even launched a miniseries called *Bollywood Hero* hoping to gain viewers from the Bollywood craze.[13]

© FOODPIX/JUPITERIMAGES/GETTY IMAGES

across grocery and fresh foods products. The information is collected from panels that are representative of household population; thus the consumption pattern of these panels can be grossed up to be representative of all the households. The panel households are given a handheld terminal that captures the purchasing details such as product name, quantity bought, price and purchase outlet. Such information is of significant importance to retailers as it helps them in developing their retail strategies; they can effectively plan their product mix, brand mix, stock replenishment and promotion campaigns.

An automaker can purchase that list and the list of people who visit car blogs and then target ads to the "young digerati" interested in cars.[14]

Benefit Segmentation

Benefit segmentation is the process of grouping customers into market segments according to the benefits they seek from the product. Most types of market segmentation are based on the assumption that this variable and customers' needs are related. Benefit segmentation is different because it groups potential customers on the basis of their needs or wants rather than some other characteristic, such as age or gender. The snack-food market, for example, can be divided into six benefit segments: nutritional snackers, weight watchers, guilty snackers, party snackers, indiscriminate snackers, and economical snackers.

Customer profiles can be developed by examining demographic information associated with people seeking certain benefits. This information can be used to match marketing strategies with selected target markets. The many different types of toothpastes are aimed at consumers looking for different benefits. For example, Colgate offers the proposition of strong teeth, while Close Up highlights the benefit of fresh breath and confidence in close situations. Pepsodent highlights the benefit of fighting germs; Sensodyne is designed for people with sensitive teeth; and Meswak is positioned as a herbal toothpaste.

Usage-Rate Segmentation

Usage-rate segmentation divides a market by the amount of product bought or consumed. Categories vary with the product, but they are likely to include some combination of the following: former users, potential users, first-time users, light or irregular users, medium users, and heavy users. Segmenting

PSYCHOGRAPHIC SEGMENTATION VARIABLES

- *Personality:* Personality reflects a person's traits, attitudes, and habits. Clothing is the ultimate personality descriptor. Fashionistas wear high-end, trendy clothes, and hipsters enjoy jeans and tee-shirts with tennis shoes. People buy clothes that they feel represent their personality and give others an idea of who they are.
- *Motives:* Marketers of baby products and life insurance appeal to consumers' emotional motives—namely, to care for their loved ones. Using appeals to economy, reliability, and dependability, carmakers like Subaru and Suzuki target customers with rational motives. Carmakers like Mercedes-Benz, Jaguar, and Cadillac appeal to customers with status-related motives.
- *Lifestyles:* Lifestyle segmentation divides people into groups according to the way they spend their time, the importance of the things around them, their beliefs, and socioeconomic characteristics such as income and education. For example, LEED-certified appliances appeal to environmentally conscious "green" consumers. Flavored and frozen yoghurt is promoted to consumers who are health conscious.
- *Geodemographics:* **Geodemographic segmentation** clusters potential customers into neighborhood lifestyle categories. It combines geographic, demographic, and lifestyle segmentations. Geodemographic segmentation helps marketers develop marketing programs tailored to prospective buyers who live in small geographic regions, such as neighborhoods, or who have very specific lifestyle and demographic characteristics. H-E-B Grocery Company, a 304-store, Texas-based supermarket chain, specializes in developing its own branded products designed to meet the needs and tastes of specific communities. In the Rio Grande Valley, where summers are hot and many residents don't have air-conditioning, H-E-B markets its own brand of rubbing oil that helps cool the skin while adding moisturizers. Along the southern border, the grocer stocks *discos*, large metal disks that Mexican Americans use to cook brisket. In Detroit, Home Depot has stores in some neighborhoods that have charcoal barbeque grills, while others offer gas grills.[15]

benefit segmentation the process of grouping customers into market segments according to the benefits they seek from the product

usage-rate segmentation dividing a market by the amount of product bought or consumed

geodemographic segmentation segmenting potential customers into neighborhood lifestyle categories

80/20 principle
a principle holding that 20 percent of all customers generate 80 percent of the demand

by usage rate enables marketers to focus their efforts on heavy users or to develop multiple marketing mixes aimed at different segments. Because heavy users often account for a sizable portion of all product sales, some marketers focus on the heavy-user segment.

The **80/20 principle** holds that 20 percent of all customers generate 80 percent of the demand. Although the percentages usually are not exact, the

EXHIBIT 8.1
Family Life Cycle

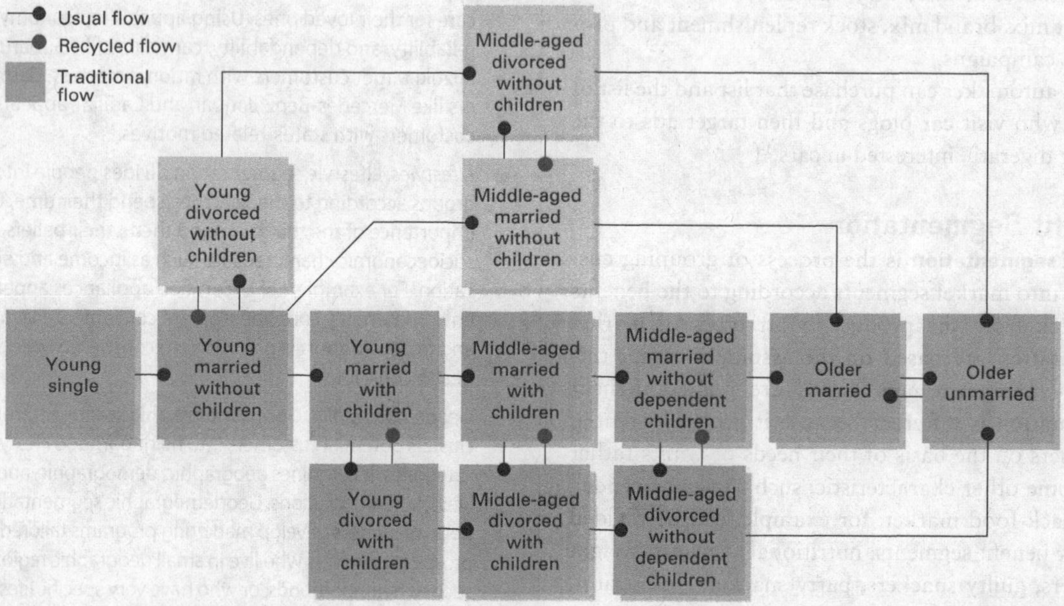

Young single	**Young married or divorced without children**	**Young married or divorced with children**	**Middle-aged married or divorced with or without children**	**Middle-aged married or divorced without dependent children**	**Older married**	**Older unmarried**
Few financial burdens Fashion opinion leaders Recreation oriented Buy: basic kitchen equipment, basic furniture, cars, equipment for mating game, vacations	Better off financially than they will be in near future Highest purchase rate and highest average purchase of durables Buy: cars, refrigerators, stoves, sensible and durable furniture, vacations	Home purchasing at peak Liquid assets low Dissatisfied with financial position and amount of money saved Interested in new products Like advertised products Buy: washers, dryers, televisions, baby food, chest rubs, cough medicine, vitamins, dolls, wagons, sleds, skates	Financial position still better More wives work Some children get jobs Hard to influence with advertising High average purchase of durables Buy: new and more tasteful furniture, auto travel, unnecessary appliances, boats, dental services, magazines	Home ownership at peak Most satisfied with financial position and money saved Interested in travel, recreation, self-education Make gifts and contributions Not interested in new products Buy: vacations, luxuries, home improvements	Drastic cut in income Keep home Buy: medical appliances; medical care; products that aid health, sleep, and digestion	Drastic cut in income Special need for attention, affection, and security Buy: same medical and product needs as other older group

general idea often holds true. For example, in case of cigarette industry, the chain smoker, i.e., the heavy user, accounts for only one of five cigarette patrons but makes about 50 to 60 percent of all cigarette purchases. The needs of heavy users differs from the needs of other usage-rate groups. They have intense needs for product and service selection and a variety of types of information, as well as an emotional attachment to the product category. Individuals in this group spend 4 to 14 times as much in their favored product category than do light users.[16]

Developing customers into heavy users is the goal behind many frequency/loyalty programs like the airlines' frequent flyer programs. Many supermarkets and other retailers have also designed loyalty programs that reward the heavy-user segment with deals available only to them, such as in-store coupon dispensing systems, loyalty card programs, and special price deals on selected merchandise.

LO 5 Bases for Segmenting Business Markets

The business market consists of four broad segments: producers, resellers, government, and institutions. (For a detailed discussion of the characteristics of these segments, see Chapter 7.) Whether marketers focus on only one or on all four of these segments, they are likely to find diversity among potential customers. Thus, further market segmentation offers just as many benefits to business marketers as it does to consumer product marketers.

Company Characteristics

Company characteristics, such as geographic location, type of company, company size, and product use, can be important segmentation variables. Some markets tend to be regional because buyers prefer to purchase from local suppliers, and distant suppliers may have difficulty competing in terms of price and service. Therefore, firms that sell to geographically concentrated industries benefit by locating close to their markets.

Segmenting by customer type allows business marketers to tailor their marketing mixes to the unique needs of particular types of organizations or industries. Many companies are finding this form of segmentation to be quite effective. Smartphone developers like Research In Motion (RIM) have identified hospitals as a viable segment in the United States. The goal is to push hospitals to integrate the developers' phones into a paperless care system. RIM's BlackBerry is developing care apps, and doctors can call one another rather than use a pager system. One app allows emergency medical services teams to send patient information directly to doctors' BlackBerrys, getting patients into surgery more quickly. Thirty-seven percent of U.S. doctors use RIM's BlackBerry, which is more than other Smartphones.[17] Volume of purchase (heavy, moderate, light) is a commonly used basis for business segmentation. Another is the buying organization's size, which may affect its purchasing procedures, the types and quantities of products it needs, and its responses to different marketing mixes.

© ISTOCKP-HOTO.COM/JOSE MANUEL GELPI DIAZ

satisficers business customers who place an order with the first familiar supplier to satisfy product and delivery requirements

optimizers business customers who consider numerous suppliers (both familiar and unfamiliar) solicit bids, and study all proposals carefully before selecting one

Banks frequently offer different services, lines of credit, and overall attention to commercial customers based on their size. Many products, especially raw materials like steel, wood, and petroleum, have diverse applications. How customers use a product may influence the amount they buy, their buying criteria, and their selection of vendors. For example, a producer of springs may have customers who use the product in applications as diverse as making machine tools, bicycles, surgical devices, office equipment, telephones, and missile systems.

Buying Processes

Many business marketers find it helpful to segment customers and prospective customers on the basis of how they buy. For example, companies can segment some business markets by ranking key purchasing criteria, such as price, quality, technical support, and service.

The purchasing strategies of buyers may provide useful segments. Two purchasing profiles that have been identified are satisficers and optimizers. **Satisficers** contact familiar suppliers and place the order with the first one to satisfy product and delivery requirements. **Optimizers** consider numerous suppliers (both familiar and unfamiliar), solicit bids, and study all proposals carefully before selecting one.

The personal characteristics of the buyers themselves (their demographic characteristics, decision style, tolerance for risk, confidence level, job responsibilities, and so on) influence their buying behavior and thus offer a viable basis for segmenting some business markets. IBM computer buyers, for example, are sometimes characterized as being more risk averse than buyers of less expensive computers that perform essentially the same functions. In advertising, therefore, IBM stresses its reputation for high quality and reliability.

LO 6 Steps in Segmenting a Market

The purpose of market segmentation, in both consumer and business markets, is to identify marketing opportunities.

1. *Select a market or product category for study:* Define the overall market or product category to be studied. It may be a market in which the firm already competes, a new but related market or product category, or a totally new market. For instance, with the rise in health awareness levels, various new products were introduced in the market offering the proposition of healthy eating. Parle Agro introduced its snack brand, *Hippo*, that was baked and not fried; Britannia came up with a whole new healthy biscuit range called Nutrichoice; and Dabur introduced a new juice line called Real Activ juices.
2. *Choose a basis or bases for segmenting the market:* This step requires managerial insight, creativity, and market knowledge. There are no scientific procedures for selecting segmentation variables. However, a successful segmentation scheme must produce segments that meet the four basic criteria discussed earlier in this chapter.
3. *Select segmentation descriptors:* After choosing one or more bases, the marketer must select the segmentation descriptors. Descriptors identify the specific segmentation variables to use. For example, if a company selects demographics as a basis of segmentation, it may use age, occupation, and income as descriptors. A company that selects usage segmentation needs to decide whether to go after heavy users, nonusers, or light users.
4. *Profile and analyze segments:* The profile should include the segments' size, expected growth, purchase frequency, current brand usage, brand loyalty, and long-term sales and profit potential. This information can then be used to rank potential market segments by profit opportunity, risk, consistency with organizational mission and objectives, and other factors important to the firm.
5. *Select target markets:* Selecting target markets is not a part of but a natural outcome of the segmentation process. It is a major decision that influences and often directly determines the firm's marketing mix. This topic is examined in greater detail later in this chapter.
6. *Design, implement, and maintain appropriate marketing mixes:* The marketing mix has been described as product, place (distribution), promotion, and pricing strategies intended to bring about mutually satisfying exchange relationships with target markets. These topics are explored in detail in Chapters 10 through 20.

Markets are dynamic, so it is important that companies proactively monitor their segmentation strategies over time. Often, once customers or prospects have been assigned to a segment, marketers think their task is done. Once customers are assigned to an age segment, for example, they stay there until they reach the next age bracket or category, which could be ten years in the future. Thus, the segmentation classifications are static, but the customers and prospects are changing. Dynamic segmentation approaches adjust to fit the changes that occur in customers' lives.

LO 7 Strategies for Selecting Target Markets

So far, this chapter has focused on the market segmentation process, which is only the first step in deciding whom to approach about buying a product. The next task is to choose one or more target markets. A **target market** is a group of people or organizations for which an organization designs, implements, and maintains a marketing mix intended to meet the needs of that group, resulting in mutually satisfying exchanges. Because most markets will include customers with different characteristics, lifestyles, backgrounds, and income levels, it is unlikely that a single marketing mix will attract all segments of the market. Thus, if a marketer wishes to appeal to more than one segment of the market, it must develop different marketing mixes. For example, Titan targets different customer segments with different brands—Titan Raga for women, Fastrack for youth segment, and Sonata for customers who want good looking but value-for-money watches. The three general strategies for selecting target markets—undifferentiated, concentrated, and multisegment targeting—are illustrated on the next page in Exhibit 8.2, which also illustrates the advantages and disadvantages of each targeting strategy.

target market a group of people or organizations for which an organization designs, implements, and maintains a marketing mix intended to meet the needs of that group, resulting in mutually satisfying exchanges

undifferentiated targeting strategy a marketing approach that views the market as one big market with no individual segments and thus uses a single marketing mix

Undifferentiated Targeting

A firm using an **undifferentiated targeting strategy** essentially adopts a mass-market philosophy, viewing the market as one big market with no individual segments. The firm uses one marketing mix for the entire market. A firm that adopts an undifferentiated targeting strategy assumes that individual customers have similar needs that can be met with a common marketing mix.

The first firm in an industry sometimes uses an undifferentiated targeting strategy. With no competition, the firm may not need to tailor marketing mixes to the preferences of market segments. Henry Ford's famous comment about the Model T is a classic example of an undifferentiated targeting strategy: "They can have their car in any color they want, as long as it's black." When Maruti Suzuki launched its best selling car, Maruti 800, way back in 1983, it was available in very limited colors, with extra price being charged for the white color model. At one time, Coca-Cola used this strategy with a single product and a single size of its familiar green bottle. Marketers of commodity products, such as flour and sugar, are also likely to use an undifferentiated targeting strategy.

One advantage of undifferentiated marketing is the potential for saving on production and marketing. Because only one item is produced, the firm should be able to achieve economies of mass production. Also, marketing costs may be lower when there is only one product to promote and a single channel of distribution. Too often, however, an undifferentiated strategy emerges by default rather than by design, reflecting a failure to consider the advantages of a segmented approach. The result is often sterile, unimaginative product offerings that have little appeal to anyone.

EXHIBIT 8.2

Advantages and Disadvantages of Target Marketing Strategies

Targeting Strategy	Advantages	Disadvantages
Undifferentiated Targeting	• Potential savings on production/marketing costs	• Unimaginative product offerings • Company more susceptible to competition
Concentrated Targeting	• Concentration of resources • Can better meet the needs of a narrowly defined segment • Allows some small firms to better compete with larger firms • Strong positioning	• Segments too small, or changing • Large competitors may more effectively market to niche segment
Multisegment Targeting	• Greater financial success • Economies of scale in producing/marketing	• High costs • Cannibalization

concentrated targeting strategy a strategy used to select one segment of a market for targeting marketing efforts

niche one segment of a market

Another problem associated with undifferentiated targeting is that it makes the company more susceptible to competitive inroads. Hindustan Unilever's Surf lost a big share of the detergent market to Nirma before it changed to a multi-segment targeting strategy. Despite entering India in 1990, Pepsi was unable to maintain its first mover advantage and was soon overtaken by Coca-Cola that entered three years later in 1993.

You might think a firm producing a standard product such as paints would adopt an undifferentiated strategy. However, this market has industrial segments and consumer segments. Industrial buyers want an economical, durable product in large quantities. The consumer market demands a more versatile product in smaller quantities. Within the consumer market, the product is differentiated with plethora of color options, exterior or interior walls, metal or wooden surfaces, and economy priced or luxury priced.

Undifferentiated marketing can succeed in certain situations, though. A small grocery store in a small, isolated town may define all of the people who live in the town as its target market. It may offer one marketing mix and generally satisfy everyone in town. This strategy is not likely to be as effective if there are three or four grocery stores in town.

Concentrated Targeting

With a **concentrated targeting strategy**, a firm selects a market **niche** (one segment of a market) for targeting its marketing efforts. Because the firm is appealing to a single segment, it can concentrate on understanding the needs, motives, and satisfactions of that segment's members and on developing and maintaining a highly specialized marketing mix. Some firms find that concentrating resources and meeting the needs of a narrowly defined market segment is more profitable than spreading resources over several different segments.

Mederma is a specialty brand that helps in treatment of scars. Though, on a general basis, it comes under the skincare market; but specialty wise, it is a dermatology product. Nycil is the market leader in the prickly heat powder category and Burnol is a burn specialist.

Small firms often adopt a concentrated targeting strategy to compete effectively with much larger firms. For example, naukri.com rose to number one in the online job portal industry by catering to people searching for a job opportunity. It then expanded into the matrimony and real estate online classifieds as well. Some other firms use a concentrated strategy to establish a strong position in a desirable market segment. Porsche, for instance, targets an upscale automobile market through "class appeal, not mass appeal."

Concentrated targeting violates the old adage "Don't put all your eggs in one basket." If the chosen segment is too small or if it shrinks because of environmental changes, the firm may suffer negative consequences. For instance, Lux had such a strong positioning in the minds of the consumers as a beauty soap that when it launched shampoos by the same name, it received a lukewarm response. The customers found it difficult to associate a skin care brand with hair care. The brand realized its mistake and instead expanded itself in the skin care category by launching Lux international range and body washes.

A concentrated strategy can also be disastrous for a firm that is not successful in its narrowly defined target market.

Multisegment Targeting

A firm that chooses to serve two or more well-defined market segments and develops a distinct marketing mix for each has a **multisegment targeting strategy**. Horlicks was historically available as a health food drink targeting children in the age group 8–14 years. However, over the years, the brand has segmented its customers into various core groups based on the type of value they seek from the food drink. Young toddlers in the age group 2–5 years

multisegment targeting strategy a strategy that chooses two or more well-defined market segments and develops a distinct marketing mix for each

NAUKRI.COM PORTAL

Naukri.com became successful by offering a large database of jobseekers as well as recruitment opportunities available, offering comprehensive services to both its corporate clients and job seekers, and designing an easy to use and hassle free website.

cannibalization a situation that occurs when sales of a new product cut into sales of a firm's existing products

one-to-one marketing an individualized marketing method that utilizes customer information to build long-term, personalized, and profitable relationships with each customer

require essential nutrients for mental and physical development and this led to the launch of Junior Horlicks. Similarly, since nutritional requirements of pregnant women are different from other women, there is Mother's Horlicks for pregnant women and Women's Horlicks for women between 19–50 years of age.[18]

Multisegment targeting offers many potential benefits to firms, including greater sales volume, higher profits, larger market share, and economies of scale in manufacturing and marketing. Yet it may also involve greater product design, production, promotion, inventory, marketing research, and management costs. Before deciding to use this strategy, firms should compare the benefits and costs of multisegment targeting to those of undifferentiated and concentrated targeting.

Another potential cost of multisegment targeting is **cannibalization**, which occurs when sales of a new product cut into sales of a firm's existing products. For example, Apple's iPhone and iPad may be causing sales of the iPod to drop, and there is some fear that the iPad will take away Mac sales, Apple's cash cow. The only evidence of those fears being realized is the 17 percent drop in sales of iPods since the release of the iPad.[19] In many cases, however, companies prefer to steal sales from their own brands rather than lose sales to a competitor. Also, in today's fast-paced world of Internet business, some companies are willing to cannibalize existing business to build new business.

LO 8 One-to-One Marketing

Most businesses today use a mass-marketing approach designed to increase *market share* by selling their products to the greatest number of people. For many businesses, however, it is more efficient and profitable to use one-to-one marketing to increase *share of customer*—in other words, to sell more products to each customer. **One-to-one marketing** is an individualized marketing method that utilizes customer information to build long-term, personalized, and profitable relationships with each customer. The goal is to reduce costs through customer retention and increase revenue through customer loyalty.

The difference between one-to-one marketing and the traditional mass-marketing approach can be compared to shooting a rifle and a shotgun. If you have good aim, a rifle is the more efficient weapon to use. A shotgun, on the other hand, increases your odds of hitting the target when it is more difficult to focus. Instead of scattering messages far and wide across the spectrum of mass media (the shotgun approach), one-to-one marketers look for opportunities to communicate with each individual customer (the rifle approach).

Customers who customize have been found to be more loyal. Several factors suggest that personalized communications and product customization will continue to expand as more companies understand why and how their customers make and execute purchase decisions.

At least four trends will lead to the continuing growth of one-to-one marketing: *personalization*, *time savings*, *loyalty*, and *technology*.

- *First*, one-size-fits-all marketing is no longer relevant. Consumers want to be treated as the individuals they are, with their own unique sets of needs and wants. By its personalized nature, one-to-one marketing can fulfill this desire.

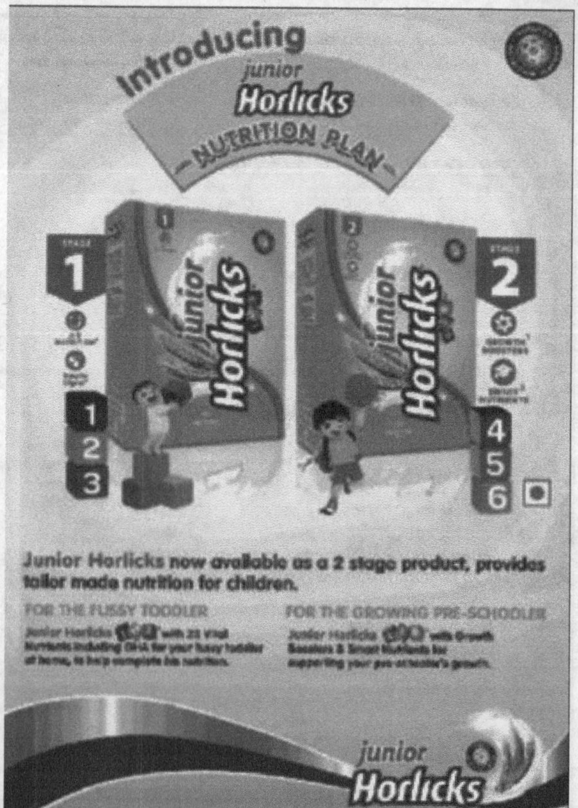

- *Second,* direct and personal marketing efforts will continue to grow to meet the needs of consumers who no longer have the time to spend shopping and making purchase decisions. With the personal and targeted nature of one-to-one marketing, consumers can spend less time making purchase decisions and more time doing the things that are important.
- *Third,* consumers will be loyal only to those companies and brands that have earned their loyalty and reinforced it at every purchase occasion. One-to-one marketing techniques focus on finding a firm's best customers, rewarding them for their loyalty, and thanking them for their business.
- *Fourth,* mass-media approaches will decline in importance as advances in market research and database technology allow marketers to collect detailed information on their customers. New technology offers one-to-one marketers a more cost-effective way to reach customers and enables businesses to personalize their messages. For example, MyYahoo.com greets each user by name and offers information in which the user has expressed interest. With the help of database technology, one-to-one marketers can track their customers as individuals, even if they number in the millions.

One-to-one marketing is a huge commitment and often requires a 180-degree turnaround for marketers who spent the last half of the 20th century developing and implementing mass-marketing efforts. Although mass marketing will probably continue to be used, especially to create brand awareness or to remind consumers of a product, the advantages of one-to-one marketing cannot be ignored.

LO 9 Positioning

The development of any marketing mix depends on positioning, a process that influences potential customers' overall perception of a brand, product line, or organization in general. Position is the place a product, brand, or group of products occupies in consumers' minds relative to competing offerings. Consumer goods marketers are particularly concerned with positioning. Hindustan Unilever Limited, for example, markets 8 different soaps, each with a unique position, such as pure and gentle, germ-free, or real beauty.

Positioning assumes that consumers compare products on the basis of important features. Marketing efforts that emphasize irrelevant features are therefore likely to misfire. For example, Pepsi Blue and Coke Vanilla failed because consumers did not perceive any major benefit in the new offering and viewed it as more of a marketing gimmick.

Effective positioning requires assessing the positions occupied by competing products, determining the important dimensions underlying these positions, and choosing a position in the market where the organization's marketing efforts will have the greatest impact. Himalaya Drug Company's positioning strategy focuses on herbal healthcare as its entire product range is made from ayurvedic ingredients, thereby promising good health and well being. As the previous example illustrates, **product differentiation** is a positioning strategy that many firms use to distinguish their products from those of competitors. The distinctions can be either real or perceived. IFB was the first company to introduce front loading washing machine in the Indian market. Similarly, Ezee has differentiated itself in the fabric care category by positioning itself as specialist detergent for woollens. The marketer attempts to convince consumers that a particular brand is distinctive

positioning developing a specific marketing mix to influence potential customers' overall perception of a brand, product line, or organization in general

position the place a product, brand, or group of products occupies in consumers' minds relative to competing offerings

product differentiation a positioning strategy that some firms use to distinguish their products from those of competitors

perceptual mapping a means of displaying or graphing, in two or more dimensions, the location of products, brands, or groups of products in customers' minds

and that they should demand it over competing brands.

However, many everyday products, such as aspirin, incense sticks, talcum powder, and some soaps, are differentiated by such trivial means as brand names, packaging, colour, smell, or "secret" additives. The marketer attempts to convince consumers that a particular brand is distinctive and that they should demand it over competing brands.

Some firms, instead of using product differentiation, position their products as being similar to competing products or brands. Two examples of this positioning include artificial sweeteners advertised as tasting like sugar or margarine tasting like butter.

Perceptual Mapping

Perceptual mapping is a means of displaying or graphing, in two or more dimensions, the location of products, brands, or groups of products in customers' minds.

Positioning Bases

Firms use a variety of bases for positioning, including the following:

- *Attribute:* A product is associated with an attribute, product feature, or customer benefit. The advertising campaign of Eno, an antacid from GlaxoSmithKline, highlights the benefit of "fast relief in 6 seconds"; and Maruti Suzuki highlights the benefit of "most fuel efficient cars".
- *Price and quality:* This positioning base may stress high price as a signal of quality or emphasize low price as an indication of value. The Indian aviation industry is a prime example of positioning on the basis of price. While Jet Airways has positioned itself as a premium, full-service airline; others such as SpiceJet and IndiGo have followed the strategy of low-cost, no-frills players.
- *Use or application:* Stressing uses or applications can be an effective means of positioning a product with buyers. Vicks Vaporub has distinctly positioned itself as a rub for a child's cold to be applied in night for all-day relief. Odomos Cream must be used for effective and safe protection from mosquito bites.
- *Product user:* This positioning base focuses on a personality or type of user. Madura Garments has several different brands: Louis Philippe is a premium, sophisticated formal wear for men with impeccable taste; Van Heusen offers formal executive wear for 25–45 years old professionals; Allen Solly introduced the concept of Friday

EXHIBIT 8.3

Perceptual Map and Positioning Strategy for Saks' Department Stores

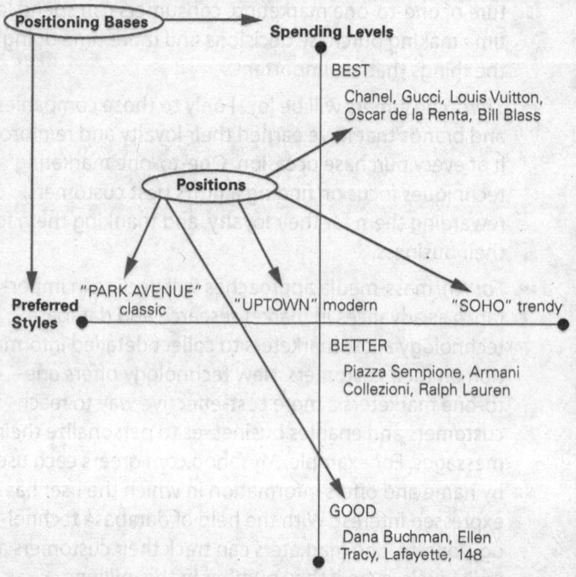

SOURCE: Vanessa O'Connell, "Park Avenue Classic or Soho Trendy?" *Wall Street Journal*, April 20, 2007, B1.

Dressing and offers premium casual wear; and Peter England is a mid-priced formal wear, offering value for money range for young men who have just started their career.[20]

- *Product class:* The objective here is to position the product as being associated with a particular category of products—for example, positioning a margarine brand with butter or showing the washing power of liquid dishwash as compared to dishwash bar. Alternatively, products can be disassociated with a category.
- *Competitor:* Positioning against competitors is part of any positioning strategy. Clinic All Clear and Head and Shoulders compete in the anti-dandruff shampoo segment. Their advertisement campaigns are always shown taking a dig at each other. Another famous example is HUL taking on P&G's advertising campaign "A Mystery Shampoo!! 80% women say is better than anything else" with its "There is no mystery. Dove is the No.1 shampoo" campaign.
- *Emotion:* Positioning using emotion focuses on how the product makes customers feel. A number of companies use this approach. For example, Tata Tea's "Jaago Re" campaign initiated social awakening among people on issues affecting the nation; Bajaj Scooters are fondly remembered for their illustrious campaign

"Hamara Bajaj" that captured the joyful emotions of a middle class family riding the scooter.

Repositioning

Sometimes products or companies are repositioned in order to sustain growth in slow markets or to correct positioning mistakes. **Repositioning** is changing consumers' perceptions of a brand in relation to competing brands. For example, Coca Cola launched a 200ml smaller version of its soft drink, priced at ₹5, only to make it more affordable and expand the market substantially. It even launched a campaign with the famous tagline "paanch matlab chhota coke".

An entire industry of firms that need to think about repositioning is the supermarket industry. For more than a decade, Walmart has been expanding in both rural and metro areas. The result has generally been devastating to competitors, especially independent grocers. Consulting firm Retail Forward predicts that two supermarkets will go out of business for every Walmart Supercenter that opens in the United States. The Strategic Resource Group adds 27 leading national and regional supermarket operators have either gone bankrupt or have liquidated since Walmart went national with Supercenters.[21] Because Walmart owns the low price position, competitors have to establish viable alternative positions.

repositioning
changing consumers' perceptions of a brand in relation to competing brands

Review and Applications

Describe the characteristics of markets and market segments. A market is composed of individuals or organizations with the ability and willingness to make purchases to fulfill their needs or wants. A market segment is a group of individuals or organizations with similar product needs as a result of one or more common characteristics.

1.1 Mercedes-Benz is thinking about advertising its cars to college students. Do you think that college students are a viable potential market for Mercedes? Why or why not?

1.2 Go to the Web site **www.careermag.com.** How are visitors to the site segmented when seeking relevant job openings? Report your results.

Explain the importance of market segmentation. Before the 1960s, few businesses targeted specific market segments. Today, segmentation is a crucial marketing strategy for nearly all successful organizations. Market segmentation enables marketers to tailor marketing mixes to meet the needs of particular population segments. Segmentation helps marketers identify consumer needs and preferences, areas of declining demand, and new marketing opportunities.

2.1 Describe market segmentation in terms of the historical evolution of marketing.

Discuss criteria for successful market segmentation. Successful market segmentation depends on four basic criteria: (1) a market segment must be substantial and have enough potential customers to be viable; (2) a market segment must be identifiable and measurable; (3) members of a market segment must be accessible to marketing efforts; and (4) a market segment must respond to particular marketing efforts in a way that distinguishes it from other segments.

3.1 As a marketing consultant for a chain of hair salons, you have been asked to evaluate the kids' market as a potential segment for the chain to target. Write a memo to your client discussing your evaluation of the kids' segment in terms of the four criteria for successful market segmentation.

Describe the bases commonly used to segment consumer markets. Five bases are commonly used for segmenting consumer markets. Geographic segmentation is based on region, size, density, and climate characteristics. Demographic segmentation is based on age, gender, income level, ethnicity, and family life-cycle characteristics. Psychographic segmentation includes personality, motives, and lifestyle characteristics. Benefits sought is a type of segmentation that identifies customers according to the benefits they seek in a product. Finally, usage segmentation divides a market by the amount of product purchased or consumed.

4.1 Choose magazine ads for five different consumer products. For each ad, write a description of what you think the demographic characteristics of the targeted market are.

4.2 Investigate how SpiceJet Airlines (www.spicejet.com) uses its Web site to cater to its market segments.

4.3 Is it possible to identify a single market for two distinctly different products? For example, how substantial is the market composed of consumers who use Blackberry and who drive Toyota Corollas? Can you think of other product combinations that would interest a single market? (Do not use products that are complementary, like a bike and a bike helmet. Think of products, like the iPod and the car, that are very different.) Complete the following sentences and describe the market for each set of products you pair together.

Consumers of:

Amul ProLife probiotic ice cream could also be a target market for ___________.

Proactiv Solution skin care products could also be a target market for ___________.

Sony Playstations could also be a target market for ___________.

Specialty luggage tags could also be a target market for ___________.

Describe the bases for segmenting business markets. Business markets can be segmented on two general bases: First, businesses segment markets based on company characteristics, such as customers' geographic location, type of company, company size, and product use. Second, companies may segment customers based on the buying processes those customers use.

5.1 Choose five ads from business publications such as *Business World, BusinessWeek, Business Today, and Business India*. For each ad, write a description of how you think the company has segmented its business market.

List the steps involved in segmenting markets. Six steps are involved when segmenting markets: (1) selecting a market or product category for study; (2) choosing a basis or bases for segmenting the market; (3) selecting segmentation descriptors; (4) profiling and evaluating segments; (5) selecting target markets; and (6) designing, implementing, and maintaining appropriate marketing mixes.

6.1 Write a letter to the president of your bank suggesting ideas for increasing profits and enhancing customer service by improving segmentation and targeting strategies.

Discuss alternative strategies for selecting target markets. Marketers select target markets using three different strategies: undifferentiated targeting, concentrated targeting, and multisegment targeting. An undifferentiated targeting strategy assumes that all members of a market have similar needs that can be met with a single marketing mix. A concentrated targeting strategy focuses all marketing efforts on a single market segment. Multisegment targeting is a strategy that uses two or more marketing mixes to target two or more market segments.

7.1 Form a team with two or three other students. Create an idea for a new product. Describe the segment (or segments) you are going to target with the product and explain why you chose the targeting strategy you did.

7.2 Go to the Web sites of Shoppers' Stop, **www.shoppersstop.com**, and MegaMart, **www.megamartstores.com** Compare the presentation of women's fashions at the Websites. What are the major differences? Which site is more designer focused, and which is more brand focused? Which company's approach do you think will appeal more to the target market of 25 to 35 year old urban, corporate working women?

Explain one-to-one marketing. One-to-one marketing is an individualized marketing method that utilizes customer information to build long-term, personalized, and profitable relationships with each customer. Successful one-to-one marketing comes from understanding customers and collaborating with them rather than using them as targets for generic messages. Database technology makes it possible for companies to interact with customers on a personal, one-to-one basis.

8.1 You are the marketing manager for a specialty retailer that sells customized handbags. Write a memo to your boss describing how the company could benefit from one-to-one marketing.

Explain how and why firms implement positioning strategies and how product differentiation plays a role. Positioning is used to influence consumer perceptions of a particular brand, product line, or organization in relation to competitors. The term *position* refers to the place that the offering occupies in consumers' minds. To establish a unique position, many firms use product differentiation, emphasizing the real or perceived differences between competing offerings. Products may be differentiated on the basis of attribute, price and quality, use or application, product user, product class, or competitor.

9.1 Choose a product category (e.g., motorcycles), and identify at least three different brands and their respective positioning strategies. How is each position communicated to the target audience?

Exercises

APPLICATION EXERCISE

How tightly do you fit into a particular market segment? Do you think you can be neatly classified? If you think your purchasing habits make you an enigma to marketers, you may need to think again.[22]

Activities

1. Identify four to five locations in your home town/current city on the basis of profile of the people residing in that particular location. Each location will represent a specific cluster of customers.
2. Now pick a product category, like automobiles, athletic shoes, beverages, or health and beauty products. Then think about which products in that category would appeal to each of the customer clusters. It may so happen that a particular product may appeal to one cluster but not to others.
3. Create a perceptual map for the product you chose. Write a short statement that describes the overall position of each product with an explanation of why you located it where you did on the perceptual map.

ETHICS EXERCISE

Tobacco companies are frequently criticized for targeting potential customers below the legal age to purchase and use their products. If these companies are actually following such a demographic targeting strategy, most would agree that it is unethical if not illegal.

Questions

1. Is marketing tobacco products to younger consumers unethical?
2. Many are beginning to argue that fast-food companies, such as McDonald's, are knowingly marketing unhealthy food to consumers. Is it unethical for fast-food companies to market kids' meals to children?
3. What does the AMA Statement of Ethics have to say about marketing unhealthy or harmful products to consumers, particularly children and young adults? Go to the AMA Web site at **www.marketingpower.com** to review the statement of ethics (**www.marketingpower.com/AboutAMA/Pages/Statement of Ethics.aspx**). Write a brief paragraph summarizing where the AMA stands on this important issue.

MARKETING PLAN EXERCISE

Once you've completed the marketing plan exercise for each chapter in Part 2 of this textbook, you can complete the Part 2 Marketing Planning Worksheet on your companion Web site at **www.cengage.com/international.** Complete the following exercises to continue the marketing plan you began in Chapter 2:

1. To whom does your company market (consumer, industrial, government, not-for-profit, or a combination of targets)? Within each market, are there specific segments or niches that your company can concentrate on? If so, which one(s) would you focus on and why? What are the factors used to create these segments? What are the Internet capabilities in those markets? If you try to encourage those segments to access your product or service via the Internet, will that change which segments are most important to your business? How? What are the factors used to create these segments? Which segments should your company focus on and why?
2. Describe your company's target market segment(s). use demographics, psychographics, geographics, economic factors, size, growth rates, trends, NIC codes, and any other appropriate descriptors. What role does the Internet play in your target market's life? How is the target market for your Internet business different from that of a traditional business in your market?
3. Using the list of key competitive advantages you described in Part 1 of your marketing plan, create a series of positioning grids, using two factors each as dimensions. (See grids in LO9 in your textbook, for an example.) Then plot the list of key competitors you identified earlier onto these positioning grids. Is your company too close to a key competitor? Are there spaces where the consumer needs and wants are unsatisfied? Consider how the Internet changes what factors are important to your success in your market space. Is technology the most important factor for your firm, or are there other ways for you to differentiate from and beat your competition?

Short Case: ZEE TELEFILMS LTD.

Prepared by
Dr. Dheeraj Sharma,
Indian Institute of Management, Ahmedabad

During the era, when the televisions were introduced in 1959, it was only Doordarshan (DD), which was used as a medium for spreading social causes. It produced programs focusing on national integration, agricultural development, education, health, family welfare, etc. The Indian consumers had no choice, but to agree to terms and conditions with regard to the types of programs being telecasted and the fare being charged. However, things changed during 1980s with the advent of Asian Games that DD introduced their new channel DD Metro, thus providing exclusive entertainment to the urban viewers. By that time there was no market segment and whole India was looked upon as "one big Indian family". Everybody watched the same programs Humlog, Chitrahaar, News, Ramayana, etc. DD was the only market player at that time and hence the concept of marker segmentation was not applicable.

However, the major revolution to the cable industry came when Star TV launched its four channels in 1991. However, these channels could not have a mass coverage since all the channels were in English and the majority of Indian consumers were Hindi speaking.

The major revolution in the television history came when Zee Telefilms Ltd., led by Subhash Chandra, came up with Zee TV–India's first Hindi satellite channel in October 1992. At first it introduced Hindi channel on an experimental basis with telecast for only 3 hours. This was the era of "Banegi Apni Baat", "Tara", "Zee Horror Show," and "Amaanat". This drove the whole country crazy. Subhash Chandra, along with the Star group of companies entered into a joint venture for television broadcasting in India.

Later on, with the increase in the willingness of the Indian consumers to pay more and their demand for more variety in the programs broadcasted, gave motivation to many new domestic and international channels to enter into the Indian television industry. Zee also segmented the market and launched many channels according to the needs and demand of the consumers from time to time. It introduced regional channels for specific regions like Zee Bangla, Zee Punjabi, Zee Gujarati, etc. Then it introduced Zee Cinema for movie lovers, Zee music for music lovers, Zee Sports for sport lovers, Zee News for those who wanted to get themselves updated of the current happenings in the country. It also introduced CNBC in English and CNBC Awaaz in Hindi for different linguistic people.[23]

Over the years Zee has been able to build a strong connection with its viewers through its diverse portfolio of programs, at least one for each. Zee is the pioneer in distributing its content through satellite, cable, and the Internet. In 2010, Zee launched a 24 hours food channel Zee Khana Khazana, Ten Cricket for exclusive cricket lovers, Ten Action+ for the football lovers. In 2012, it launched Ten Golf, a 24 hours channel for Golf lovers.

Apart from the various programs that Zee has launched, it has also not lagged behind in the technological aspect. With the DTH service gaining popularity in India, Zee also launched its DTH services for its customers, who want a better quality picture and sound, which the traditional cable TV cannot provide. It has added around 50 new channels to this platform. In February 2012, Zee has also launched Ditto TV for its tech savvy customers. It is India's first Over- the -Top TV (OTT) platform, which enables the consumers to view live TV channels and on demand video content on their mobiles, laptops, tablets, desktops, connected TV, and entertainment boxes.[24]

The television industry now seems to have no end with channels like Colors, Star TV, SAB TV, Sony TV, etc., in the market, all competing for the top position by offering variety of programs.

Question

1. Zee has a diverse portfolio of programs, at least one for each. Is Zee doing right in its strategy of segmenting, targeting, and positioning?

8 Segmenting and Targeting Markets

KEY TERMS

LO 1

market people or organizations with needs or wants and the ability and willingness to buy

market segment a subgroup of people or organizations sharing one or more characteristics that cause them to have similar product needs

market segmentation the process of dividing a market into meaningful, relatively similar, and identifiable segments or groups

LO 4

segmentation bases (variables) characteristics of individuals, groups, or organizations

geographic segmentation segmenting markets by region of a country or the world, market size, market density, or climate

demographic segmentation segmenting markets by age, gender, income, ethnic background, and family life cycle

family life cycle (FLC) a series of stages determined by a combination of age, marital status, and the presence or absence of children

psychographic segmentation market segmentation on the basis of personality, motives, lifestyles, and geodemographics

geodemographic segmentation segmenting potential customers into neighborhood lifestyle categories

benefit segmentation the process of grouping customers into market segments according to the benefits they seek from the product

usage-rate segmentation dividing a market by the amount of product bought or consumed

80/20 principle a principle holding that 20 percent of all customers generate 80 percent of the demand

KEY CONCEPTS

LO 1 **Describe the characteristics of markets and market segments.** A market is composed of individuals or organizations with the ability and willingness to make purchases to fulfill their needs or wants. A market segment is a group of individuals or organizations with similar product needs as a result of one or more common characteristics.

LO 2 **Explain the importance of market segmentation.** Before the 1960s, few businesses targeted specific market segments. Today, segmentation is a crucial marketing strategy for nearly all successful organizations. Market segmentation enables marketers to tailor marketing mixes to meet the needs of particular population segments. Segmentation helps marketers identify consumer needs and preferences, areas of declining demand, and new marketing opportunities.

LO 3 **Discuss criteria for successful market segmentation.** Successful market segmentation depends on four basic criteria: (1) a market segment must be substantial and have enough potential customers to be viable; (2) a market segment must be identifiable and measurable; (3) members of a market segment must be accessible to marketing efforts; and (4) a market segment must respond to particular marketing efforts in a way that distinguishes it from other segments.

LO 4 **Describe the bases commonly used to segment consumer markets.** Five bases are commonly used for segmenting consumer markets. Geographic segmentation is based on region, size, density, and climate characteristics. Demographic segmentation is based on age, gender, income level, ethnicity, and family life-cycle characteristics. Psychographic segmentation includes personality, motives, and lifestyle characteristics. Benefits sought is a type of segmentation that identifies customers according to the benefits they seek in a product. Finally, usage segmentation divides a market by the amount of product purchased or consumed.

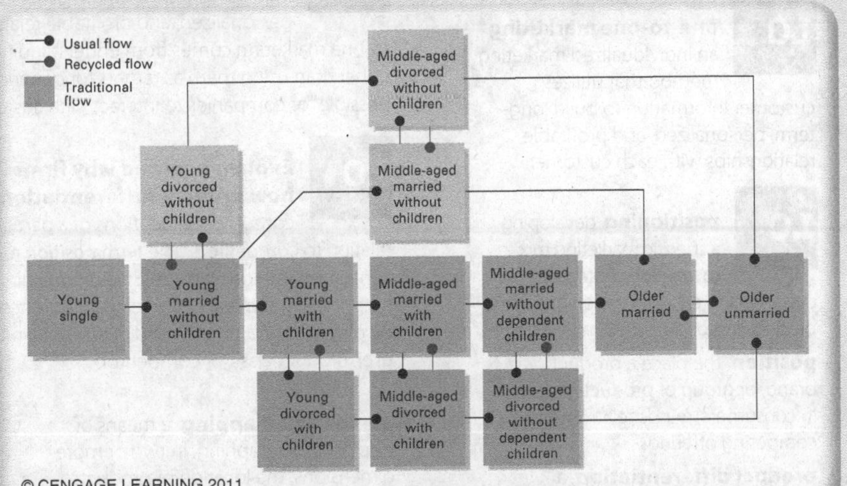

© CENGAGE LEARNING 2011

LO 5 **satisficers** business customers who place an order with the first familiar supplier to satisfy product and delivery requirements

optimizers business customers who consider numerous suppliers (both familiar and unfamiliar), solicit bids, and study all proposals carefully before selecting one

LO 7 **target market** a group of people or organizations for which an organization designs, implements, and maintains a marketing mix intended to meet the needs of that group, resulting in mutually satisfying exchanges

undifferentiated targeting strategy a marketing approach that views the market as one big market with no individual segments and thus uses a single marketing mix

concentrated targeting strategy a strategy used to select one segment of a market for targeting marketing efforts

niche one segment of a market

multisegment targeting strategy a strategy that chooses two or more well-defined market segments and develops a distinct marketing mix for each

cannibalization a situation that occurs when sales of a new product cut into sales of a firm's existing products

LO 8 **one-to-one marketing** an individualized marketing method that utilizes customer information to build long-term, personalized, and profitable relationships with each customer

LO 9 **positioning** developing a specific marketing mix to influence potential customers' overall perception of a brand, product line, or organization in general

position the place a product, brand, or group of products occupies in consumers' minds relative to competing offerings

product differentiation a positioning strategy that some firms use to distinguish their products from those of competitors

LO 5 **Describe the bases for segmenting business markets.** Business markets can be segmented on two general bases: First, businesses segment markets based on company characteristics, such as customers' geographic location, type of company, company size, and product use. Second, companies may segment customers based on the buying processes those customers use.

LO 6 **List the steps involved in segmenting markets.** Six steps are involved when segmenting markets: (1) selecting a market or product category for study; (2) choosing a basis or bases for segmenting the market; (3) selecting segmentation descriptors; (4) profiling and evaluating segments; (5) selecting target markets; and (6) designing, implementing, and maintaining appropriate marketing mixes.

LO 7 **Discuss alternative strategies for selecting target markets.** Marketers select target markets using three different strategies: undifferentiated targeting, concentrated targeting, and multisegment targeting. An undifferentiated targeting strategy assumes that all members of a market have similar needs that can be met with a single marketing mix. A concentrated targeting strategy focuses all marketing efforts on a single market segment. Multisegment targeting is a strategy that uses two or more marketing mixes to target two or more market segments.

Targeting Strategy	Advantages	Disadvantages
Undifferentiated Targeting	• Potential savings on production/marketing costs	• Unimaginative product offerings • Company more susceptible to competition
Concentrated Targeting	• Concentration of resources • Can better meet the needs of a narrowly defined segment • Allows some small firms to better compete with larger firms • Strong positioning	• Segments too small, or changing • Large competitors may more effectively market to niche segment
Multisegment Targeting	• Greater financial success • Economies of scale in producing/marketing	• High costs • Cannibalization

LO 8 **Explain one-to-one marketing.** One-to-one marketing is an individualized marketing method that utilizes customer information to build long-term, personalized, and profitable relationships with each customer. Successful one-to-one marketing comes from understanding customers and collaborating with them rather than using them as targets for generic messages. Database technology makes it possible for companies to interact with customers on a personal, one-to-one basis.

LO 9 **Explain how and why firms implement positioning strategies and how product differentiation plays a role.** Positioning is used to influence consumer perceptions of a particular brand, product line, or organization in relation to competitors. The term *position* refers to the place that the offering occupies in consumers' minds. To establish a unique position, many firms use product differentiation, emphasizing the real or perceived differences between competing offerings. Products may be differentiated on the basis of attribute, price and quality, use or application, product user, product class, or competitor.

perceptual mapping a means of displaying or graphing, in two or more dimensions, the location of products, brands, or groups of products in customers' minds

repositioning changing consumers' perceptions of a brand in relation to competing brands

CHAPTER 9

Decision Support Systems and Marketing Research

Learning Outcomes

LO 1 Explain the concept and purpose of a marketing decision support system

LO 2 Define marketing research and explain its importance to marketing decision making

LO 3 Describe the steps involved in conducting a marketing research project

LO 4 Discuss the profound impact of the Internet on marketing research

LO 5 Discuss the growing importance of scanner-based research

LO 6 Explain when marketing research should be conducted

LO 7 Explain the concept of competitive intelligence

Whether a research project costs ₹9,000 or ₹9 crore, the same general process should be followed.

LO1 Marketing Decision Support Systems

Accurate and timely information is the lifeblood of marketing decision making. Good information can help an organization maximize sales and efficiently use scarce company resources. To prepare and adjust marketing plans, managers need a system for gathering everyday information about developments in the marketing environment—that is, for gathering **marketing information.** The system most commonly used these days for gathering marketing information is called a *marketing decision support system.*

marketing information
everyday information about developments in the marketing environment that managers use to prepare and adjust marketing plans

decision support system (DSS)
an interactive, flexible, computerized information system that enables managers to obtain and manipulate information as they are making decisions

A marketing **decision support system (DSS)** is an interactive, flexible, computerized information system that enables managers to obtain and manipulate information as they are making decisions. A DSS bypasses the information-processing specialist and gives managers access to useful data from their own desks.

These are the characteristics of a true DSS:

- *Interactive:* Managers give simple instructions and see immediate results. The process is under their direct control. Managers don't have to wait for scheduled reports.
- *Flexible:* A DSS can sort, regroup, total, average, and manipulate the data in various ways. It will shift gears as the user changes topics, matching information to the problem at hand.

***Note:* All the figures in U.S. dollars are converted into rupee using the value $1 = ₹45.**

database marketing the creation of a large computerized file of customers' and potential customers' profiles and purchase patterns

marketing research the process of planning, collecting, and analyzing data relevant to a marketing decision

- *Discovery oriented:* Managers can probe for trends, isolate problems, and ask "what if" questions.
- *Accessible:* Managers who aren't skilled with computers can easily learn how to use a DSS. Novice users should be able to choose a standard, or default, method of using the system. They can bypass optional features so they can work with the basic system right away while gradually learning to apply its advanced features.

Perhaps the fastest-growing use of a DSS is for **database marketing**, which is the creation of a large computerized file of customers' and potential customers' profiles and purchase patterns. It is usually the key tool for successful one-to-one marketing, which relies on very specific information about a market.

LO 2 The Role of Marketing Research

Marketing research is the process of planning, collecting, and analyzing data relevant to a marketing decision. The results of this analysis are then communicated to management. Thus, marketing research is the function that links the consumer, customer, and public to the marketer through information. Marketing research plays a key role in the marketing system. It provides decision makers with data on the effectiveness of the current marketing mix and insights for necessary changes. Furthermore, marketing research is a main data source for both management information systems and DSS. In other words, the findings of a marketing research project become data in a DSS.

Marketing research has three roles: descriptive, diagnostic, and predictive. Its *descriptive* role includes gathering and presenting factual statements. For example, what is the historic sales trend in the industry? What are consumers' attitudes toward a product and its advertising? Its *diagnostic* role includes explaining data, such as determining the impact on sales of a change in the design of the package. Its *predictive* function is to address "what if" questions. For example, how can the researcher use the descriptive and diagnostic research to predict the results of a planned marketing decision?

LO 3 Steps in a Marketing Research Project

EXHIBIT 9.1

The Marketing Research Process

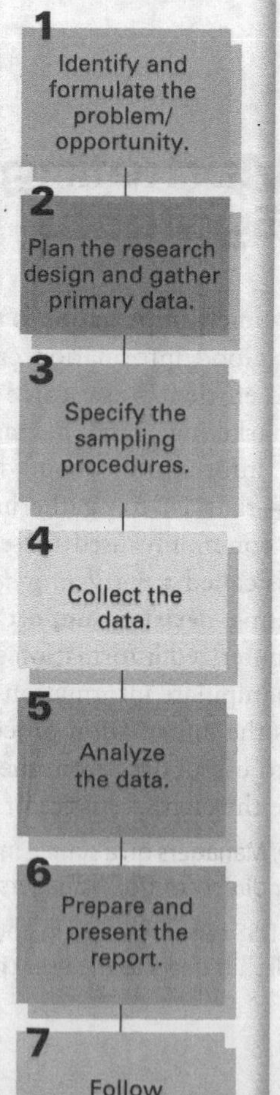

© CENGAGE LEARNING 2011

Virtually all firms that have adopted the marketing concept engage in some marketing research because it offers decision makers many benefits. Some companies spend millions on marketing research; others, particularly smaller firms, conduct informal, limited-scale research studies.

Whether a research project costs ₹9,000 or ₹9 crore, the same general process should be followed. The marketing research process is a scientific approach to decision making that maximizes the chance of getting accurate and meaningful results. Exhibit 9.1 traces the seven steps in the research process, which begins with the recognition of a marketing problem or opportunity. As changes occur in the firm's external environment, marketing managers are faced with the questions, "Should we change the existing marketing mix?" and, if so, "How?" Marketing research may be used to evaluate product, promotion, distribution, or pricing alternatives.

After years of research, Procter & Gamble (P&G) relaunched its ubiquitous hair-care line Pantene in 2010. In 2009, Pantene's U.S. sales dropped 9 percent, more than the 3 percent decline for the shampoo market as a whole. P&G had already been working on ways to differentiate Pantene from other hair-care lines but needed a specific place to focus its research.

Pantene researchers delved into women's reactions to "bad hair days," a challenging, subjective area that is lightly touched on by only a few other hair-care companies. But P&G faced the problem head on, surveying women about their feelings when using certain hair products. The ultimate goal for Pantene was to help women have a "good hair day." After one week of using Pantene products, women using the new formula reported more joy than the control group. The company is still collecting sales figures, but with brighter packaging and slimmer product lines to ease consumer confusion, managers remain optimistic that their hallmark line will bounce back from the recession stronger than before.[1]

The Pantene story illustrates an important point about problem/opportunity definition. The **marketing research problem** is information oriented. It involves determining what information is needed and how that information can be obtained efficiently and effectively. The **marketing research objective**, then, is to provide insightful decision-making information. This requires specific pieces of information needed to solve the marketing research problem. Managers must combine this information with their own experience and other information to make proper decisions. Procter & Gamble's marketing research problem was to gather specific information about how a woman's hair affects her feelings and mood. The marketing research objectives were to reformulate Pantene to affect women's hair more positively and reposition the brand as an antidote to bad hair days.

In contrast, the **management decision problem** is action oriented. Management problems tend to be much broader in scope and far more general than marketing research problems, which must be narrowly defined and specific if the research effort is to be successful. Sometimes several research studies must be conducted to solve a broad management problem. For Pantene, the management decision problem was deciding how to win women back after the recession.

Secondary Data

A valuable tool throughout the research process but particularly in the problem/opportunity identification stage is **secondary data**—data previously collected for any purpose other than the one at hand. Secondary information originating within the company includes documents such as annual reports, reports to stockholders, product testing results perhaps made available to the news media, and house periodicals composed by the company's personnel for communication to employees, customers, or others. Often this information is incorporated into a company's internal database.

Innumerable outside sources of secondary information also exist, principally in the forms of government departments and agencies (federal, state, and local) that compile and publish summaries of business data. Trade and industry associations also publish secondary data. Still more data are available in business periodicals and other news media that regularly publish studies and articles on the economy, specific industries, and even individual companies. The unpublished summarized secondary information from these sources corresponds to internal reports, memos, or special-purpose analyses with limited circulation. Economic considerations or priorities in the organization may preclude publication of these summaries. Most of the sources listed above can be found on the Internet.

Secondary data save time and money if they help solve the researcher's problem. Even if the problem is not solved, secondary data have other advantages. They can aid in formulating the problem statement and suggest research methods and other types of data needed for solving the problem. In addition, secondary data can pinpoint the kinds of people to approach and their locations and serve as a basis of comparison for other data. The disadvantages of secondary data stem mainly from a mismatch between the researcher's unique problem and the purpose for which the secondary data were originally gathered, which are typically different. For example, a company wanted to determine the market potential for a

Marketing research enabled Procter & Gamble to reevaluate its Pantene brand, resulting in new packaging, a new formula, and fewer products.

marketing research problem
determining what information is needed and how that information can be obtained efficiently and effectively

marketing research objective
the specific information needed to solve a marketing research problem; the objective should be to provide insightful decision-making information

management decision problem
a broad-based problem that uses marketing research in order for managers to take proper actions

secondary data
data previously collected for any purpose other than the one at hand

marketing research aggregator a company that acquires, catalogs, reformats, segments, and resells reports already published by marketing research firms

research design specifies which research questions must be answered, how and when the data will be gathered, and how the data will be analyzed

primary data information that is collected for the first time; used for solving the particular problem under investigation

fireplace log made of coal rather than compressed wood by-products. The researcher found plenty of secondary data about total wood consumed as fuel, quantities consumed in each state, and types of wood burned. Secondary data were also available about consumer attitudes and purchase patterns of wood by-product fireplace logs. The wealth of secondary data provided the researcher with many insights into the artificial log market. Yet nowhere was there any information that would tell the firm whether consumers would buy artificial logs made of coal.

The quality of secondary data may also pose a problem. Often secondary data sources do not give detailed information that would enable a researcher to assess their quality or relevance. Whenever possible, a researcher needs to address these important questions: Who gathered the data? Why were the data obtained? What methodology was used? How were classifications (such as heavy users vs. light users) developed and defined? When was the information gathered?

The New Age of Secondary Information: The Internet

Although necessary in almost any research project, gathering secondary data has traditionally been a tedious and boring job. The researcher often had to write to government agencies, trade associations, or other secondary data providers and then wait days or weeks for a reply that might never come. Often, one or more trips to the library were required and the researcher might have found that needed reports were checked out or missing. Now, however, the rapid development of the Internet has eliminated much of the drudgery associated with the collection of secondary data.

Marketing Research Aggregators

The **Marketing Research Aggregator** industry is an ₹540 crore business that is growing about 6 percent a year in the United States. Companies in this field acquire, catalog, reformat, segment, and resell reports already published by large and small marketing research firms. Even Amazon.com has added a marketing research aggregation area to its high-profile e-commerce site.

The role of aggregator firms is growing because their databases of research reports are getting bigger and more comprehensive—and more useful—as marketing research firms get more comfortable using resellers as a sales channel. Meanwhile, advances in Web technology are making the databases easier to search and deliveries speedier. By slicing and repackaging research reports into narrower, more specialized sections for resale to small- and medium-sized clients who often cannot afford to commission their own studies or buy full reports, the aggregators are essentially nurturing a new target market for the information. Some major aggregators are mindbranch.com, aarkstore.com, and usadata.com.

Planning the Research Design and Gathering Primary Data

Good secondary data can help researchers conduct a thorough situation analysis. With that information, researchers can list their unanswered questions and rank them. Researchers must then decide the exact information required to answer the questions. The **research design** specifies which research questions must be answered, how and when the data will be gathered, and how the data will be analyzed. Typically, the project budget is finalized after the research design has been approved.

Sometimes research questions can be answered by gathering more secondary data; otherwise, primary data may be needed. **Primary data**, or information collected for the first time, are used for solving the particular problem under investigation. The main advantage of primary data is that they will answer a specific research question that secondary data cannot answer. In Procter & Gamble's research for Pantene, managers used a psychological questionnaire to determine how hair products affected women's daily attitudes. For one week, one group of women used the old Pantene formula, and the other group used the new formula. This primary data revealed that women using the new Pantene felt more excited, proud, interested, and attentive than the other group—positive emotions that the

Pantene research group could not have discovered through secondary research.[2] Moreover, primary data are current and researchers know the source. Sometimes researchers gather the data themselves rather than assign projects to outside companies. Researchers also specify the methodology of the research. Secrecy can be maintained because the information is proprietary. In contrast, much secondary data is available to all interested parties for relatively small fees or free.

Gathering primary data is expensive; costs can range from a few thousand rupees for a limited survey to several million for a nationwide study. For instance, a nationwide, 15-minute telephone interview with 1,000 adult males can cost ₹22,50,000 for everything, including a data analysis and report. Because primary data gathering is so expensive, firms may cut back on the number of in-person interviews to save money and use an Internet study instead. Larger companies that conduct many research projects use another cost-saving technique. They *piggyback studies*, or gather data on two different projects using one questionnaire. Nevertheless, the disadvantages of primary data gathering are usually offset by the advantages. It is often the only way of solving a research problem. And with a variety of techniques available for research—including surveys, observations, and experiments—primary research can address almost any marketing question.

Survey Research The most popular technique for gathering primary data is **survey research**, in which a researcher interacts with people to obtain facts, opinions, and attitudes. Exhibit 9.2 on the next page summarizes the characteristics of traditional forms of survey research.

In-Home Personal Interviews Although in-home personal interviews often provide high-quality information, they tend to be very expensive because of the interviewers' travel time and mileage costs. Therefore, they are rapidly disappearing from the American and European researchers' survey toolbox. They are, however, still popular in many countries around the globe.

Mall Intercept Interviews The **mall intercept interview** is conducted in the common area of a shopping mall or in a market research office within the mall. To conduct this type of interview, the research firm rents office space in the mall or pays a significant daily fee. One drawback is that it is hard to get a representative sample of the population. One advantage is the ability of the interviewer to probe when necessary—a technique used to clarify a person's response and ask for more detailed information.

Mall intercept interviews must be brief. Only the shortest ones are conducted while respondents are standing. Usually, researchers invite respondents into the office for interviews, which are still generally less than 15 minutes long. The overall quality of mall intercept interviews is about the same as telephone interviews.

Marketing researchers are applying computer technology in mall interviewing. The first technique is **computer-assisted personal interviewing**. The researcher conducts in-person interviews, reads questions to the respondent off a computer screen, and directly keys the respondent's answers into the computer. A second approach is **computer-assisted self-interviewing.** A mall interviewer intercepts and directs willing respondents to nearby computers. Each respondent reads questions off a computer screen and directly keys his or her answers into a computer. The third use of technology is fully automated self-interviewing. Respondents are guided by interviewers or independently approach a centrally located computer station or kiosk, read questions off a screen, and directly key their answers into the station's computer.

Telephone Interviews Telephone interviews costs less than personal interviews, but cost is rapidly increasing due to respondent refusals to participate. Most telephone interviewing is conducted from a specially designed phone room called a **central-location telephone (CLT) facility.** A phone room has many phone lines, individual interviewing stations, sometimes monitoring equipment, and headsets. The research firm typically will interview people nationwide from a single location. The federal "Do Not Call" law does not apply to survey research.

Most CLT facilities offer computer-assisted interviewing. The interviewer reads the questions from a computer screen and enters the respondent's data directly into the computer, saving time. Hallmark Cards found that an interviewer administered a printed questionnaire for its Shoebox greeting cards in 28 minutes. The same questionnaire administered with computer assistance took only 18 minutes. The researcher can stop the survey at any point and immediately print out the survey results, allowing the research design to be refined as necessary.

survey research the most popular technique for gathering primary data, in which a researcher interacts with people to obtain facts, opinions, and attitudes

mall intercept interview a survey research method that involves interviewing people in the common areas of shopping malls

computer-assisted personal interviewing an interviewing method in which the interviewer reads questions from a computer screen and enters the respondent's data directly into the computer

computer-assisted self-interviewing an interviewing method in which a mall interviewer intercepts and directs willing respondents to nearby computers where each respondent reads questions off a computer screen and directly keys his or her answers into a computer

central-location telephone (CLT) facility a specially designed phone room used to conduct telephone interviewing

EXHIBIT 9.2

Characteristics of Traditional Forms of Survey Research

Characteristic	In-Home Personal Interviews	Mall Intercept Interviews	Central-Location Telephone Interviews	Self-Administered and One-Time Mail Surveys	Mail Panel Surveys	Executive Interviews	Focus Groups
Cost	High	Moderate	Moderate	Low	Moderate	High	Low
Time span	Moderate	Moderate	Fast	Slow	Relatively slow	Moderate	Fast
Use of interviewer probes	Yes	Yes	Yes	No	Yes	Yes	Yes
Ability to show concepts to respondent	Yes (also taste tests)	Yes (also taste tests)	No	Yes	Yes	Yes	No
Management control over interviewer	Low	Moderate	High	N/A	N/A	Moderate	High
General data quality	High	Moderate	High to moderate	Moderate to low	Moderate	High	Moderate
Ability to collect large amounts of data	High	Moderate	Moderate to low	Low to moderate	Moderate	Moderate	Moderate
Ability to handle complex questionnaires	High	Moderate	High, if computer aided	Low	Low	High	N/A

Mail Surveys Mail surveys have several benefits: relatively low cost, elimination of interviewers and field supervisors, centralized control, and actual or promised anonymity for respondents (which may draw more candid responses). A disadvantage is that mail questionnaires usually produce low response rates because certain elements of the population tend to respond more than others. The resulting sample may therefore not represent the surveyed population. Another serious problem with mail surveys is that no one probes respondents to clarify or elaborate on their answers.

Mail panels offer an alternative to the one-shot mail survey. A mail panel consists of a sample of households recruited to participate by mail for a given period. Panel members often receive gifts in return for their participation. Essentially, the panel is a sample used several times. In contrast to one-time mail surveys, the response rates from mail panels are high. Rates of 70 percent (of those who agree to participate) are not uncommon.

executive interview a type of survey that involves interviewing businesspeople at their offices concerning industrial products or services

focus group seven to ten people who participate in a group discussion led by a moderator

Executive Interviews An **executive interview** involves interviewing businesspeople at their offices concerning industrial products or services, a process that is very expensive. First, individuals involved in the purchase decision for the product in question must be identified and located, which can itself be expensive and time-consuming. Once a qualified person is located, the next step is to get that person to agree to be interviewed and to set a time for the interview.

Finally, an interviewer must go to the particular place at the appointed time. Long waits are frequently encountered; cancellations are not uncommon. This type of survey requires the very best interviewers because they are frequently interviewing on topics that they know very little about.

Focus Groups A **focus group** is a type of personal interviewing. Often recruited by random telephone screening, seven to ten people with certain desired characteristics form a focus group. These qualified consumers are usually offered an incentive (typically ₹1,350 to ₹2,250) to participate in a group discussion.

The meeting place (sometimes resembling a living room, sometimes featuring a conference table) has audiotaping and perhaps videotaping equipment. It also likely has a viewing room with a one-way mirror so that clients (manufacturers or retailers) may watch the session. During the session, a moderator, hired by the research company, leads the group discussion. Focus groups can be used to gauge consumer response to a product or promotion and are occasionally used to brainstorm new product ideas or to screen concepts for new products. Focus groups also represent an efficient way of learning how products are actually used in the home. Panelists' descriptions of how they perform tasks highlight need gaps, which can improve an existing product or demonstrate how a new product might be received. It is estimated that over 600,000 focus groups are conducted around the world each year.[3]

Questionnaire Design All forms of survey research require a questionnaire. Questionnaires ensure that all respondents will be asked the same series of questions. Questionnaires include three basic types of questions: open-ended, closed-ended, and scaled-response. An **open-ended question** encourages an answer phrased in the respondent's own words. Researchers get a rich array of information based on the respondent's frame of reference (What do you think about the new flavor?). In contrast, a **closed-ended question** asks the respondent to make a selection from a limited list of responses. Closed-ended questions can either be what marketing researchers call *dichotomous* (Do you like the new flavor? Yes or No.) or *multiple choice*. A **scaled-response question** is a closed-ended question designed to measure the intensity of a respondent's answer. The "What do you think?" question that opened the chapter is a scaled-response question.

Closed-ended and scaled-response questions are easier to tabulate than open-ended questions because response choices are fixed. On the other hand, unless the researcher designs the closed-ended question very carefully, an important choice may be omitted.

A good question must be clear and concise and avoid ambiguous language. The answer to the question "Do you live within ten minutes of here?" depends on the mode of transportation (maybe the person walks), driving speed, perceived time, and other factors. Language should also be clear. As such, jargon should be avoided, and wording should be geared to the target audience. A question such as "What is the level of efficacy of your preponderant detergent powder?" would probably be greeted by a lot of blank stares. It would be much simpler to say "Are you (1) very satisfied, (2) somewhat satisfied, or (3) not satisfied with your current brand of detergent powder?"

Stating the survey's purpose at the beginning of the interview may improve clarity, but it may also increase the chances of receiving biased responses. Many times,

open-ended question an interview question that encourages an answer phrased in the respondent's own words

closed-ended question an interview question that asks the respondent to make a selection from a limited list of responses

scaled-response question a closed-ended question designed to measure the intensity of a respondent's answer

MARKETING RESEARCH—UNPLUGGED

Approximately 18 percent of homes in the United States do not have a tethered landline phone and only have cell phones. This number is expected to continue to rise, posing some problems for telephone surveys. Federal law forbids automatic dialers for cell phone interviewing, so all calls must be dialed manually, which raises interviewing costs. However, because cell phone–only homes have a different demographic, those costs are normally viewed as a necessary expense. Cell phone–only households tend to be younger, have slightly lower incomes, and are more likely to rent than tethered-telephone households. Some research firms also reimburse respondents for the cost of the minutes used, which further raises interviewing costs.[4]

© ISTOCKPHOTO.COM/ZOLWIKS

observation research a research method that relies on four types of observation: people watching people, people watching an activity, machines watching people, and machines watching an activity

mystery shoppers researchers posing as customers who gather observational data about a store

behavioral targeting (BT) a form of observation marketing research that uses data mining coupled with identifying Web surfers by their IP addresses

respondents will try to provide answers that they believe are "correct" or that the interviewer wants to hear. To avoid bias at the question level, researchers should avoid leading questions and adjectives that cause respondents to think of the topic in a certain way.

Finally, to ensure clarity, the interviewer should avoid asking two questions in one—for example, "How did you like the taste and texture of the Domino's choco lava cake?" This should be divided into two questions, one concerning taste and the other texture.

Observation Research In contrast to survey research, **observation research** depends on watching what people do. Specifically, it can be defined as the systematic process of recording the behavioral patterns of people, objects, and occurrences without questioning them. A market researcher using the observation technique witnesses and records information as events occur or compiles evidence from records of past events. Carried a step further, observation may involve watching people or phenomena and may be conducted by human observers or machines. Examples of these various observational situations are shown in Exhibit 9.3.

Two common forms of people-watching-people research are one-way mirror observations and mystery shoppers.

At the Fisher-Price Play Laboratory in New York, children are invited to spend 12 sessions playing with toys. Toy designers watch through one-way mirrors to see how children react to Fisher-Price and other makers' toys. A one-way mirror allows the researchers to see the participants, but the participants cannot see the researchers. Fisher-Price, for example, had difficulty designing a toy lawn mower that children would play with. A designer, observing behind the mirror, noticed the children's fascination with soap bubbles. He then created a lawn mower that spewed soap bubbles. It sold over a lakh units in the first year.

Mystery Shoppers **Mystery shoppers** are researchers posing as customers who gather observational data about a store (e.g., are the shelves neatly stocked?) and collect data about customer/employee interactions. The interaction is not an interview, and communication occurs only so that the mystery shopper can observe the actions and comments of the employee. Mystery shopping is, therefore, classified as an observational marketing research method even though communication is often involved.

Behavioral Targeting **Behavioral targeting (BT)** began as a simple process by placing cookies on users' browsers to track which Web sites they visited and ultimately match the user with ads they would most likely investigate. Today, BT combines a consumer's online activity with psychographic and demographic profiles compiled in databases (discussed in Chapters 4 and 8). Because of the potential effectiveness of BT advertising, its popularity is skyrocketing.

Social networking, which is discussed in depth in Chapter 22, is the fastest-growing area of BT. The information that a member of MySpace or Facebook shares, in combination with his demographic and psychographic information, becomes a very powerful tool for ad placement. Critics call this form of BT *conversational eavesdropping analysis*, but advocates call it *user-declared information targeting*.[5] It is an apt description because the information is posted by members in their profiles. Say Rahul posts river rafting as an interest on his profile. Because he declared his interest, it is more concrete marketing knowledge. A note that someone from that computer's address visited a river rafting Web site is less concrete because anyone could have been using that computer. Both Facebook and MySpace allow marketers to target ads to members based upon profile information. Many large companies use BT. When PepsiCo wanted to promote Aquafina Alive on the Web in the U.S.

EXHIBIT 9.3
Observational Situations

Situation	Example
People watching people	Observers stationed in electronic stores watch consumers select hand blenders; the purpose is to see how much comparison shopping people do at the point of purchase.
People watching an activity	An observer stationed at an intersection counts traffic moving in various directions.
Machines watching people	Movie or videotape cameras record behavior as in the people-watching-people example above.
Machines watching an activity	Traffic-counting machines monitor traffic flow.

market, the company placed ads only on sites visited by people interested in healthy lifestyles.

Ethnographic Research Ethnographic research comes to marketing from the field of anthropology. The technique is becoming increasingly popular in commercial marketing research. **Ethnographic research**, or the study of human behavior in its natural context, involves observation of behavior and physical setting. Ethnographers directly observe the population they are studying. As "participant observers," ethnographers can use their intimacy with the people they are studying to gain richer, deeper insights into culture and behavior—in short, what makes people do what they do.

The at-home consumption market is one that eludes much research. Anthropologists and other observational researchers can't sit in people's homes and monitor which electronic devices they are using and how they use them. Questionnaires rely on one-time truthful responses and the respondent's memory.

Virtual Shopping Advances in computer technology have enabled researchers to simulate an actual retail store environment on a computer screen. Depending on the type of simulation, a shopper can "pick up" a package by touching its image on the monitor and rotate it to examine all sides. Like buying on most online retailers, the shopper touches the shopping cart to add an item to the basket. During the shopping process, the computer unobtrusively records the amount of time the consumer spends shopping in each product category, the time the consumer spends examining each side of a product, the quantity of product the consumer purchases, and the order in which items are purchased.

Computer-simulated environments like this one offer a number of advantages over older research methods. First, the virtual store duplicates the distracting clutter of an actual market. Consumers can shop in an environment with a realistic level of complexity and variety. Second, researchers can set up and alter the tests very quickly. Data collection is also fast and error free because the information generated by the purchase is automatically tabulated and stored by the computer. Third, production costs are low because displays are created electronically. Once the hardware and software are in place, the cost of a test is largely a function of the number of respondents, who generally are given a small incentive to participate. Fourth, the simulation has a high degree of flexibility. It can be used to test entirely new marketing concepts or to fine-tune existing programs.[6]

Virtual shopping research is growing rapidly as companies such as Frito-Lay, Goodyear, Procter & Gamble, General Mills, and Coca-Cola realize the benefits from this type of observation research. All are vying for very limited retail shelf space. Any process, such as virtual shopping, that can speed product development time and lower costs is always welcomed by manufacturers.

ethnographic research the study of human behavior in its natural context; involves observation of behavior and physical setting

experiment a method a researcher uses to gather primary data

sample a subset from a larger population

universe the population from which a sample will be drawn

probability sample a sample in which every element in the population has a known statistical likelihood of being selected

Experiments An **experiment** is a method a researcher can use to gather primary data. The researcher alters one or more variables—price, package design, shelf space, advertising theme, advertising expenditures—while observing the effects of those alterations on another variable (usually sales). The best experiments are those in which all factors are held constant except the ones being manipulated. The researcher can then observe what changes in sales, for example, result from changes in the amount of money spent on advertising.

Specifying the Sampling Procedures

Once the researchers decide how they will collect primary data, their next step is to select the sampling procedures they will use. A firm can seldom take a census of all possible users of a new product, nor can they all be interviewed. Therefore, a firm must select a sample of the group to be interviewed. A **sample** is a subset from a larger population.

Several questions must be answered before a sampling plan is chosen. First, the population, or **universe**, of interest must be defined. This is the group from which the sample will be drawn. It should include all the people whose opinions, behavior, preferences, attitudes, and so on, are of interest to the marketer. For example, in a study whose purpose is to determine the market for a new organic tea, the universe might be defined to include all current buyers of organic tea.

After the universe has been defined, the next question is whether the sample must be representative of the population. If the answer is yes, a probability sample is needed. Otherwise, a nonprobability sample might be considered.

Probability Samples A **probability sample** is a sample in which every element in the population has a known statistical likelihood of being selected. Its most

random sample a sample arranged in such a way that every element of the population has an equal chance of being selected as part of the sample

nonprobability sample any sample in which little or no attempt is made to get a representative cross section of the population

convenience sample a form of nonprobability sample using respondents who are convenient or readily accessible to the researcher—for example, employees, friends, or relatives

measurement error an error that occurs when there is a difference between the information desired by the researcher and the information provided by the measurement process

sampling error an error that occurs when a sample somehow does not represent the target population

frame error an error that occurs when a sample drawn from a population differs from the target population

random error an error that occurs when the selected sample is an imperfect representation of the overall population

field service firm a firm that specializes in interviewing respondents on a subcontracted basis

desirable feature is that scientific rules can be used to ensure that the sample represents the population.

One type of probability sample is a **random sample**—a sample arranged in such a way that every element of the population has an equal chance of being selected as part of the sample. For example, suppose a university is interested in getting a cross section of student opinions on a proposed sports complex to be built using student activity fees. If the university can acquire an up-to-date list of all the enrolled students, it can draw a random sample by using random numbers from a table (found in most statistics books) to select students from the list. Common forms of probability and nonprobability samples are shown in Exhibit 9.4.

Nonprobability Samples Any sample in which little or no attempt is made to get a representative cross section of the population can be considered a **nonprobability sample**. Therefore the probability of selection of each sampling unit is not known. A common form of a nonprobability sample is the **convenience sample**, which uses respondents who are convenient or readily accessible to the researcher—for instance, employees, friends, or relatives.

Nonprobability samples are acceptable as long as the researcher understands their nonrepresentative nature. Because of their lower cost, nonprobability samples are the basis of much marketing research.

Types of Errors Whenever a sample is used in marketing research, two major types of errors may occur: measurement error and sampling error. **Measurement error** occurs when there is a difference between the information desired by the researcher and the information provided by the measurement process. For example, people may tell an interviewer that they purchase Pepsodent toothpaste when they do not. Measurement error generally tends to be larger than sampling error.

Sampling error occurs when a sample somehow does not represent the target population. Sampling error can be one of several types. Nonresponse error occurs when the sample actually interviewed differs from the sample drawn. This error happens because the original people selected to be interviewed either refused to cooperate or were inaccessible.

Frame error, another type of sampling error, arises if the sample drawn from a population differs from the target population. For instance, suppose a telephone survey is conducted to find out Mumbai housewives' attitudes toward supermarkets. If a Mumbai telephone directory is used as the *frame* (the device or list from which the respondents are selected), the survey will contain a frame error. Not all Mumbai housewives have a phone, and many phone numbers are unlisted. An ideal sample (e.g., a sample with no frame error) matches all important characteristics of the target population to be surveyed. Could you find a perfect frame for Mumbai housewives?

Random error occurs when the selected sample is an imperfect representation of the overall population. Random error represents how accurately the chosen sample's true average (mean) value reflects the population's true average (mean) value. For example, we might take a random sample of housewives in Mumbai and find that 16 percent regularly visit supermarkets. The next day we might repeat the same sampling procedure and discover that 14 percent regularly visit supermarkets. The difference is due to random error. Error is common to all surveys, yet it is often not reported or is underreported. Typically, the only error mentioned in a written report is sampling error.

Collecting the Data

Marketing research field service firms collect most primary data. A **field service firm** specializes in interviewing respondents on a subcontracted basis. Many have offices, often in malls, throughout the country. A typical marketing research study involves data collection in several cities, which requires the marketer to work with a comparable number of field service firms. Besides conducting interviews, field service firms provide focus group facilities, mall intercept locations, test product storage, and kitchen facilities to prepare test food products.

Analyzing the Data

After collecting the data, the marketing researcher proceeds to the next step in the research process: data analysis. The purpose of this analysis is to interpret and draw conclusions from the mass of collected data. The marketing researcher tries to organize and

EXHIBIT 9.4
Types of Samples

	Probability Samples
Simple Random Sample	Every member of the population has a known and equal chance of selection.
Stratified Sample	The population is divided into mutually exclusive groups (such as gender or age), then random samples are drawn from each group.
Cluster Sample	The population is divided into mutually exclusive groups (such as geographic areas), then a random sample of clusters is selected. The researcher then collects data from all the elements in the selected clusters or from a probability sample of elements within each selected cluster.
Systematic Sample	A list of the population is obtained—e.g., all persons with a checking account at XYZ Bank—and a skip interval is obtained by dividing the sample size by the population size. If the sample size is 100 and the bank has 1,000 customers, then the skip interval is 10. The beginning number is randomly chosen within the skip interval. If the beginning number is 8, then the skip pattern would be 8, 18, 28, ...
	Nonprobability Samples
Convenience Sample	The researcher selects the easiest population members from which to obtain information.
Judgment Sample	The researcher's selection criteria are based on personal judgment that the elements (persons) chosen will likely give accurate information.
Quota Sample	The researcher finds a prescribed number of people in several categories—e.g., owners of large dogs versus owners of small dogs. Respondents are not selected on probability sampling criteria.
Snowball Sample	Additional respondents are selected on the basis of referrals from the initial respondents. This method is used when a desired type of respondent is hard to find—e.g., persons who have taken round-the-world tours in the last three years. This technique employs the old adage "Birds of a feather flock together."

analyze those data by using one or more techniques common to marketing research: one-way frequency counts, cross-tabulations, and more sophisticated statistical analysis. Of these three techniques, one-way frequency counts are the simplest. One-way frequency tables simply record the responses to a question. For example, the answers to the question "What brand of instant noodles do you buy most often?" would provide a one-way frequency distribution. One-way frequency tables are always done in data analysis, at least as a first step, because they provide the researcher with a general picture of the study's results. A **cross-tabulation** lets the analyst look at the responses to one question in relation to the responses to one or more other questions. For example, what is the association between gender and the brand of instant noodles bought most frequently?

Researchers can use many other more powerful and sophisticated statistical techniques, such as hypothesis testing, measures of association, and regression analysis. A description of these techniques goes beyond the scope of this book but can be found in any good marketing research textbook. The use of sophisticated statistical techniques depends on the researchers' objectives and the nature of the data gathered.

Preparing and Presenting the Report

After data analysis has been completed, the researcher must prepare the report and communicate the conclusions and recommendations to management. This is a key step in the process. If the marketing researcher wants managers to carry out the recommendations, he or she must convince them that the results are credible and justified by the data collected.

Researchers are usually required to present both written and oral reports on the project. Today, the written report is no more than a copy of the PowerPoint slides used in the oral presentation. Both reports should be tailored to the audience. They should begin with a clear, concise statement of the research objectives, followed by a complete, but brief and simple, explanation of the research design or methodology employed. A summary of major findings should come next. The

cross-tabulation a method of analyzing data that lets the analyst look at the responses to one question in relation to the responses to one or more other questions

conclusion of the report should also present recommendations to management.

Most people who enter marketing will become research users rather than research suppliers. Thus, they must know what to notice in a report. As with many other items we purchase, quality is not always readily apparent. Nor does a high price guarantee superior quality. The basis for measuring the quality of a marketing research report is the research proposal. Did the report meet the objectives established in the proposal? Was the methodology outlined in the proposal followed? Are the conclusions based on logical deductions from the data analysis? Do the recommendations seem prudent, given the conclusions?

Following Up

The final step in the marketing research process is to follow up. The researcher should determine why management did or did not carry out the recommendations in the report. Was sufficient decision-making information included? What could have been done to make the report more useful to management? A good rapport between the product manager, or whoever authorized the project, and the market researcher is essential. Often they must work together on many studies throughout the year.

Typically, the research process flows rather smoothly from one step to the next in the United States. However, in India, this process is largely restricted to metro cities. Market research is yet to take off in smaller cities and towns in India. In a diverse country like India, with 28 states and 9 union territories and different languages spoken in each state, conducting a national level research is a difficult task as translation of questions in different languages can be costly. Moreover, with differing buying behaviours across states, a common set of questions may not really work and different questions may have to be prepared for each location. Therefore, though research methods like ethnographic research, focus group discussions, and interviews may be useful in non-metros, yet they may be equally expensive and time consuming.

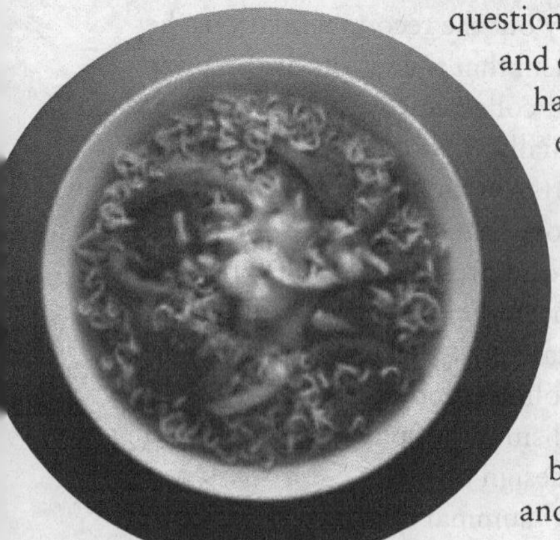

© COMSTOCK/THINKSTOCK

LO 4 The Profound Impact of the Internet on Marketing Research

Today, about one-fifth of the world's population is online. Internet data collection is also rated as having the greatest potential for further growth.

Advantages of Internet Surveys

The huge growth in the popularity of Internet surveys is the result of the many advantages offered by the Internet. The specific advantages of Internet surveys are related to many factors:

- *Rapid development, real-time reporting:* Internet surveys can be broadcast to thousands of potential respondents simultaneously. Respondents complete surveys simultaneously, then results are tabulated and posted for corporate clients to view as the returns arrive. The result: survey results can be in a client's hands in significantly less time than would be required for traditional surveys.
- *Dramatically reduced costs:* The Internet can cut costs by 25 to 40 percent and provide results in half the time it takes to do traditional telephone surveys. Traditional survey methods are labor-intensive efforts incurring training, telecommunications, and management costs. Electronic methods eliminate these completely. While costs for traditional survey techniques rise proportionally with the number of interviews desired, electronic solicitations can grow in volume with little increase in project costs.
- *Personalized questions and data:* Internet surveys can be highly personalized for greater relevance to each respondent's own situation, thus speeding the response process.
- *Improved respondent participation:* Internet surveys take half as much time to complete as phone interviews, can be accomplished at the respondent's convenience (after work hours), and are much more stimulating and engaging. As a result, Internet surveys enjoy much higher response rates.
- *Contact with the hard-to-reach:* Certain groups—doctors, high-income professionals, top management in Global 2000 firms—are among the most surveyed on the planet and the most difficult to reach. Many of these groups are well represented online. Internet surveys provide convenient anytime/anywhere access that makes it easy for busy professionals to participate.

SHOPPING PERSONALITIES—THE TRENDS[7]

© HEMERA/THINKSTOCK

In order to understand the shopping habits and personality traits of Indian mall shoppers, a study was conducted and published in *Journal of Retailing and Consumer Services* to ascertain the buying behaviour of different purchasers. The results of the study indicated that each customer group possesses very distinct characteristics and demonstrates a unique buying behavior pattern. The aforementioned study proposed the following seven different segments of customers frequenting the malls across the country:

- *Mall Enthusiast.* Has an active lifestyle and enjoys window-shopping. Does all his shopping at the mall and is satisfied with prices at the mall stores. Shopping is done with family as well as friends and enjoys the overall shopping experience at the mall. Falls in the age group 36–45, has a working wife and the total monthly household income is well above ₹60,000.
- *Price Conscious Shopper.* Is a price sensitive window shopper and is not happy with the prices of mall stores. Visits the mall frequently but buys occasionally. Overall, satisfied with the attributes and amenities of the mall. Comes in age group 46–55, belongs to a double income middle class family, with a monthly income of ₹30,000–₹60,000.
- *Traditionalist.* Enjoys window-shopping and buys clothes, accessories, or small value items at the mall. Not a tech savvy person and has a liking for homebound activities. Belongs to the age group 46–55 and monthly household income is around ₹10,000–₹30,000.
- *Disinterested Shopper.* Has no interest in malls and shopping. Visit to a mall, if it happens, is a family activity for the purpose of eating out or watching a movie or purchasing an occasional item. Is more homebound and does not get influenced by media. Lies in the age group 26–35, is married, and has a double income household with a monthly earning of ₹30,000–₹60,000.
- *Aspirational Shopper.* Visits the mall with family and purchases things on an impulse. Price sensitivity is moderate and gives importance to location and amenities of the mall. Falls in the age group 26–35, has a small family, and has a double income household with a monthly income of ₹10,000–₹30,000.
- *Student Shopper.* A young window-shopper, who visits the mall with family or friends quite frequently. Is satisfied with all the features of a mall, including prices of the stores. Belongs to the age group 18–25, is unmarried, has working parents, and the monthly household income is between ₹30,000–₹60,000.
- *Experience Shopper.* Is a price sensitive window-shopper and visits the mall with family or friends for eating out or watching movies. Is usually satisfied with the entire mall experience. Enjoys homebound as well as social activities. Lies in the age group 26–35, is an affluent bachelor, and has a monthly household income anywhere between ₹30,000–₹60,000.

Uses of the Internet by Marketing Researchers

Marketing researchers are using the Internet to administer surveys, conduct focus groups, and perform a variety of other types of marketing research.

Methods of Conducting Online Surveys There are several basic methods for conducting online surveys: Web survey systems, survey design and Web hosting sites, and online panel providers.

Web Survey Systems Web survey systems are software systems specifically designed for Web questionnaire construction and delivery. They consist of an integrated questionnaire designer, Web server, database, and data delivery program, designed for use by nonprogrammers. The Web server distributes the questionnaire and files responses in a database. The user can query the server at any time via the Web for completion statistics, descriptive statistics on responses, and graphical displays of data. Some popular online survey research software packages are SurveyMonkey, SurveyPro, and QuestionPro.

Survey Design and Web Hosting Sites Several Web sites allow the researcher to design a survey online without loading design software. The survey is then administered on the design site's server. Some offer tabulation and analysis packages as well. One popular site that offers Web hosting services is GoDaddy.

Online Panel Providers Often researchers use online panel providers for a ready-made sample population. Online panel providers such as Survey Sampling International and e-Rewards pre-recruit people who agree to participate in online market research surveys. In India, there are no major companies that provide such online panel services.

Some online panels are created for specific industries and may have a few thousand panel members, while the large commercial online panels have millions of people waiting to be surveyed. When people join online panels, they answer an extensive profiling questionnaire that enables the panel provider to target research efforts to panel members who meet specific criteria.

Online Focus Groups A relatively recent development in qualitative research is the online or cyber focus group. A number of organizations are currently offering this new means of conducting focus groups. The process is fairly simple. The research firm builds a database of respondents via a screening questionnaire on its Web site. When a client comes to a firm with a need for a particular focus group, the firm goes to its database and identifies individuals who appear to qualify. It sends an e-mail message to these individuals, asking them to log on to a particular site at a particular time scheduled for the group. The firm pays them an incentive for their participation.

The firm develops a discussion guide similar to the one used for a conventional focus group, and a moderator runs the group by typing in questions online for all to see. The group operates in an environment similar to that of a chat room so that all participants see all questions and all responses. The firm captures the complete text of the focus group and makes it available for review after the group has finished.

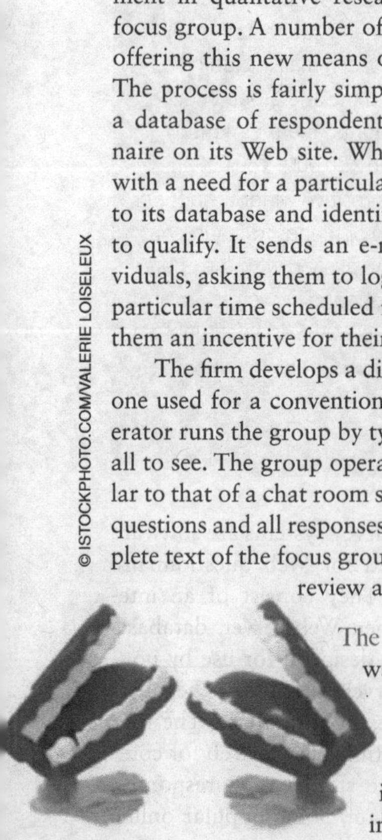

The Moderator's Role The basic way the moderator communicates with respondents in an online focus group is by typing all questions, instructions, and probes into the text-entry area of the chat room in real time (live, on-the-spot). An advantage of the freestyle method is that it forces the moderator to adapt to the group rather than use a series of canned questions. A disadvantage is that typing everything freestyle (or even copying and pasting from a separate document) takes time.

Online focus groups also allow respondents to view things such as a concept statement, a mockup of a print ad, or a short product demonstration video. The moderator simply provides a URL reference for the respondents to go to in another browser window. One of the risks of doing this, however, is that once respondents open another browser, they have "left the room" and the moderator may lose their attention; researchers must hope that respondents will return within the specified amount of time.

More advanced virtual focus group software reserves a frame (section) of the screen for stimuli to be shown. Here, the moderator has control over what is shown in the stimulus area. The advantage of this approach is that the respondent does not have to do any work to see the stimuli.

Advantages of Online Focus Groups Many advantages are claimed for cyber groups:

- *Better participation rates:* Typically, online focus groups can be conducted over the course of days; once participants are recruited, they are less likely to pull out due to time conflicts.
- *Cost-effectiveness:* Face-to-face focus groups incur costs for facility rental, airfare, hotel, and food. None of these costs is incurred with online focus groups.
- *Broad geographic scope:* Time is flexible online; respondents can be gathered from all over the world.
- *Accessibility:* Online focus groups give you access to individuals who otherwise might be difficult to recruit (e.g., business travelers, senior executives, mothers with infants).
- *Honesty:* From behind their screen names, respondents are anonymous to other respondents and tend to talk more freely about issues that might create inhibitions in a face-to-face group.

Web Community Research

A Web community is a carefully selected group of consumers who agree to participate in an ongoing dialogue with a particular corporation.[8] All community interaction takes place on a custom-designed Web site. During the life of the community—which may last anywhere from six months to a year or more—community members respond to questions posed by the corporation on a regular basis. In addition to responding to the corporation's questions, community members talk to one another about topics that are of interest to them.

The popularity and power of Web communities initially came from several key benefits. They:

- engage customers in a space where they are comfortable, allowing clients to interact with them on a deeper level,
- achieve customer-derived innovations,
- establish brand advocates who are emotionally invested in a company's success, and
- offer real-time results, enabling clients to explore ideas that normal time constraints prohibit.

Additionally, Web communities help companies create a customer-focused organization by putting employees into direct contact with consumers from the comfort of their own desks, as well as providing cost-effective, flexible research. Fastrack seeks feedback from its fans on online communities on issues like brand positioning and product pricing. It also offers a product preview to selected fans on its communities before officially launching the product in the market. This helps the company in gaining qualitative customer feedback.[9]

The Role of Consumer-Generated Media in Marketing Research

Consumer-generated media (CGM) is that media that consumers generate themselves and share among themselves. CGM comes from various sources, such as blogs, message boards, review sites, podcasts, etc. Because it is consumer based, CGM is trusted more than traditional forms of advertising and promotion. A popular CGM website in India is mouthshut.com.[10]

CGM can be influenced but not controlled by marketers. Nielsen BuzzMetrics is the leading marketing research firm tracking CGM. BrandPulse is BuzzMetrics' most popular product. BrandPulse can tell a company how much "buzz" exists, where online discussion is taking place, the tone of the discussion, and which issues are most important. BrandPulse provides timely understanding of the opinions and trends affecting a company or brand. Other BuzzMetrics products can go into further detail, depending on what information the customer needs, such as detecting who would be a good candidate for relationship marketing programs.[11]

LO 5 Scanner-Based Research

Scanner-based research has gained prominence in North America in last few years. It is yet to gain prominence in India, though. **Scanner-based research** is a system for gathering information from a single group of respondents by continuously monitoring the advertising, promotion, and pricing they are exposed to and the things they buy. The variables measured are advertising campaigns, coupons, displays, and product prices. The result is a huge database of marketing efforts and consumer behavior.

Using household panels is a common practice in almost all the services in the United States. The two major scanner-based suppliers are Information Resources, Inc. (IRI) and the A. C. Nielsen Company. Each has about half of the market. However, IRI is the founder of scanner-based research. IRI's first product is called **BehaviorScan**. A household panel (a group of 3,000 long-term participants in the research project) has been recruited and maintained in each BehaviorScan town. Each panel member shops with an ID card, which is presented at the checkout in scanner-equipped grocery stores and drugstores, allowing IRI to track electronically each household's purchases, item by item, over time. It uses microcomputers to measure television viewing in each panel household and can send special commercials to panel member television sets. With such a measure of household purchasing, it is possible to manipulate marketing variables, such as television advertising or consumer promotions, or to introduce a new product and analyze real changes in consumer buying behavior.

IRI's most successful product is **InfoScan**—a scanner-based sales-tracking service for the consumer packaged-goods industry. Retail sales, detailed consumer purchasing information (including measurement of store loyalty and total grocery basket expenditures), and promotional activity by manufacturers and retailers are monitored and evaluated for all bar-coded products. Data are collected weekly from more than 70,000 supermarkets, drugstores, and mass merchandisers.[12]

Some companies have begun studying microscopic changes in skin moisture, heart rate, brain waves, and other biometrics to see how consumers react to things such as package designs and ads. This **neuromarketing** approach is a fresh attempt to better understand consumers' responses to promotion and purchase motivations.

consumer-generated media (CGM) media that consumers generate and share among themselves

scanner-based research a system for gathering information from a single group of respondents by continuously monitoring the advertising, promotion, and pricing they are exposed to and the things they buy

BehaviorScan a scanner-based research program that tracks the purchases of 3,000 households through store scanners in each research market

InfoScan a scanner-based sales-tracking service for the consumer packaged-goods industry

neuromarketing a field of marketing that studies the body's responses to marketing stimuli

competitive intelligence (CI) an intelligence system that helps managers assess their competition and vendors in order to become more efficient and effective competitors

After the Pantene research group finalized its research on the shampoo's formula, it began testing the response to new Pantene commercials. Researchers hooked viewers to an electroencephalogram to measure brainwaves as they watched the commercials. In one ad, viewers were distracted by a frustrated model dealing with her hair. The commercial was edited to focus more on the model's hair and less on her expression.[13]

In India, such research has not yet picked up because organized retail is still a very small part of the overall retail market. Organized retailers have to face various challenges like retail not being recognized as an industry, high real estate costs, and poor infrastructure. The mom-n-pop shops still dominate the retail market and these shop owners know the retail baskets of their customers due to their frequent interactions and personal relations with the customers. However, recent studies conducted have used techniques like brain-scan to understand customer behaviour. One such study was conducted by a professor at Indian Institute of Management, Ahmedabad, that explored the gender differences in customer brand relationships, with regards to affect and cognition.[14]

LO 6 When Should Marketing Research Be Conducted?

When managers have several possible solutions to a problem, they should not instinctively call for marketing research. In fact, the first decision to make is whether to conduct marketing research at all.

© ISTOCKPHOTO.COM/ANNEDDE

Some companies have been conducting research in certain markets for many years. Such firms understand the characteristics of target customers and their likes and dislikes about existing products. Under these circumstances, further research would be repetitive and waste money. This tactic, however, can backfire. Marketers may think they understand a particular market thoroughly and so bypass market research for a product, only to have the product fail and be withdrawn from the market.

If information were available and free, managers would rarely refuse more, but because marketing information can require a great deal of time and expense to accumulate, they might decide to forego additional information. Ultimately, the willingness to acquire additional decision-making information depends on managers' perceptions of its quality, price, and timing. Research should be undertaken only when the expected value of the information is greater than the cost of obtaining it.

LO 7 Competitive Intelligence

Derived from military intelligence, competitive intelligence is an important tool for helping a firm overcome a competitor's advantage. Specifically, competitive intelligence can help identify the advantage and play a major role in determining how it was achieved.

Competitive intelligence (CI) helps managers assess their competitors and their vendors in order to become more efficient and effective competitors. Intelligence is analyzed information. It becomes decision-making intelligence when it has implications for the organization. For example, a primary competitor may have plans to introduce a product with performance standards equal to those of the company gathering the information but with a 15 percent cost advantage. The new product will reach the market in eight months. This intelligence has important decision-making and policy consequences for management. CI and environmental scanning (see Chapter 2) combine to create marketing intelligence. Marketing intelligence is then used as input into a marketing decision support system.

The Internet is an important resource for gathering CI, but noncomputer sources can be equally valuable. Some examples include company salespeople, industry experts, CI consultants, government agencies, Uniform Commercial Code filings, suppliers, periodicals, the Yellow Pages, and industry trade shows.

Review and Applications

Explain the concept and purpose of a marketing decision support system. A decision support system (DSS) makes data instantly available to marketing managers and allows them to manipulate the data themselves to make marketing decisions. Four characteristics make DSSs especially useful to marketing managers: They are interactive, flexible, discovery oriented, and accessible. That is, they give managers access to information immediately and without outside assistance; they allow users to manipulate data in a variety of ways and to answer "what if" questions; and they are accessible to novice computer users.

- *Interactive:* Managers give simple instructions and see immediate results. The process is under their direct control; no computer programmer is needed. Managers don't have to wait for scheduled reports.
- *Flexible:* A DSS can sort, regroup, total, average, and manipulate the data in various ways. It will shift gears as the user changes topics, matching information to the problem at hand. For example, the CEO can see highly aggregated figures, and the marketing analyst can view very detailed breakouts.
- *Discovery-oriented:* Managers can probe for trends, isolate problems, and ask "what if" questions.
- *Accessible:* Managers who aren't skilled with computers can easily learn how to use a DSS. Novice users should be able to choose a standard, or default, method of using the system. They can bypass optional features so they can work with the basic system right away while gradually learning to apply its advanced features.

1.1 In the absence of company problems, is there any reason to develop a marketing DSS?

1.2 Explain the difference between marketing research and a DSS.

Define marketing research and explain its importance to marketing decision making. Marketing research is a process of collecting and analyzing data for the purpose of solving specific marketing problems. Marketers use marketing research to explore the profitability of marketing strategies. They can examine why particular strategies failed and analyze characteristics of specific market segments. Managers can use research findings to help keep current customers. Moreover, marketing research allows management to behave proactively, rather than reactively, by identifying newly emerging patterns in society and the economy.

2.1 The task of marketing is to create exchanges. What role might marketing research play in the facilitation of the exchange process?

2.2 Marketing research has traditionally been associated with manufacturers of consumer goods. Today, however, an increasing number of organizations, both profit and nonprofit, are using marketing research. Why do you think this trend exists? Give some examples of specific reasons why organizations might use marketing research.

2.3 Write a reply to the following statement: "I own a restaurant in the downtown area. I see customers every day who I know on a first-name basis. I understand their likes and dislikes. If I put something on the menu and it doesn't sell, I know that they didn't like it. This is all of the marketing research I need to do."

2.4 Give an example of (a) the descriptive role of marketing research, (b) the diagnostic role, and (c) the predictive function of marketing research.

Describe the steps involved in conducting a marketing research project. The marketing research process involves several basic steps. First, the researcher and the decision maker must agree on a problem statement or set of research objectives. The researcher then creates an overall research design to specify how primary data will be gathered and analyzed. Before collecting data, the researcher decides whether the group to be interviewed will be a probability or nonprobability sample. Field service firms are often hired to carry out data collection. Once data have been collected, the researcher analyzes them using statistical analysis. The researcher then prepares and presents oral and written reports, with conclusions and recommendations, to management. As a final step, the researcher determines whether the recommendations were implemented and what could have been done to make the project more successful.

3.1 Critique the following methodologies and suggest more appropriate alternatives:

a. A supermarket was interested in determining its image. It dropped a short questionnaire into the grocery bag of each customer before putting in the groceries.

b. To assess the extent of its trade area, a shopping mall stationed interviewers in the parking lot every Monday and Friday evening.

Interviewers walked up to people after they had parked their cars and asked them for their house locations.

c. To assess the popularity of a new movie, a major studio invited people to send SMS and vote yes, they would see it again, or no, they would not. Each SMS cost ₹3 to the sender.

3.2 You have been charged with determining how to attract more business majors to your school. Write an outline of the steps you would take, including the sampling procedures, to accomplish the task.

3.3 Why are secondary data sometimes preferable to primary data?

3.4 What is a marketing research aggregator? What role do these aggregators play in marketing research?

3.5 Discuss when focus groups should and should not be used.

3.6 Divide the class into teams of eight persons. Each group will conduct a focus group on the quality and number of services that your college is providing to its students. One person from each group should be chosen to act as moderator. Remember, it is the moderator's job to facilitate discussion, not to lead the discussion. These groups should last approximately 45 minutes. If possible, the groups should be videotaped or recorded. Upon completion, each group should write a brief report of its results. Consider offering to meet with the dean of students to share the results of your research.

3.7 Why do companies hire mystery shoppers?

3.8 Ethnographic research is a new (and expensive) trend in marketing research. Find an article on ethnographic research. Read and summarize the article. What is your opinion of ethnographic research? Do you think it will be the wave of the future? Explain your reasoning.

Discuss the profound impact of the Internet on marketing research. The Internet has vastly simplified the secondary data search process, placing more sources of information in front of researchers than ever before. Internet survey research is surging in popularity. Internet surveys can be created rapidly and reported in real time. They are also relatively inexpensive and can easily be personalized. Often researchers can use the Internet to contact respondents who are difficult to reach by other means. The Internet can also be used to conduct focus groups, analyze consumer-generated media, engage in behavioral targeting, distribute research proposals and reports, and to facilitate collaboration between the client and the research supplier. Clients can access real-time data and analyze the information as the collection process continues.

4.1 Go to **www.SRIC-bi.com** and take the VALS Survey. Report on how marketing researchers are using this information.

4.2 Divide the class into teams. Each team should go to a different opt-in survey site on the Web and participate in an online survey. A spokesperson for each team should report the results to the class.

4.3 What are various ways to obtain respondents for online surveys?

4.4 Describe the advantages and disadvantages of online surveys.

Discuss the growing importance of scanner-based research. A scanner-based research system enables marketers to monitor a market panel's exposure and reaction to such variables as advertising, coupons, store displays, packaging, and price. By analyzing these variables in relation to the panel's subsequent buying behavior, marketers gain useful insight into sales and marketing strategies.

5.1 Why has scanner-based research been seen as "the ultimate answer" for marketing researchers? Do you see any disadvantages of this methodology?

5.2 Detractors claim that scanner-based research is like "driving a car down the road looking only in the rearview mirror." What does this mean? Do you agree?

Explain when marketing research should be conducted. Because acquiring marketing information can be time-consuming and costly, deciding to acquire additional decision-making information depends on managers' perceptions of its quality, price, and timing. Research, therefore, should be undertaken only when the expected value of the information is greater than the cost of obtaining it.

6.1 When should marketing research be conducted? What are the likely situations when primary marketing research and secondary marketing research is applicable?

6.2 You are the marketing manager of a FMCG company called Imperial Limited. Your company is planning to launch talcum powder and has selected three possible fragrance choices—sandalwood, jasmine, and lavender. You have been asked to conduct market research to find out customer preference for each of these fragrances.

However, a similar market research was conducted 2 years ago when the company wanted to launch a new soap in the market and had the three same fragrances. The research had shown that customers preferred lavender fragrance to the other two options. In your capacity as a decision maker, will you undertake the marketing research process all over again or use the results of the previous research?

Explain the concept of competitive intelligence. Competitive intelligence (CI) helps managers assess their competition and their vendors in order to become more efficient and effective competitors. Intelligence is analyzed information, and it becomes decision-making intelligence when it has implications for the organization. By helping managers assess their competition and vendors, CI leads to fewer surprises. The Internet and databases accessed via the Internet offer excellent sources of CI.

7.1 Why do you think that CI is so hot in today's environment?

7.2 Prepare a memo to your boss at Indigo Airlines and outline why the organization needs a CI unit.

7.3 Form a team with three other students. Each team must choose a firm in the PC manufacturing industry and then go to the Web site of the firm and acquire as much CI as possible. Each team will then prepare a five-minute oral presentation on its findings.

Exercises

APPLICATION EXERCISE

For its study, *Teens and Healthy Eating: Fad or Trend?*, Hyderabad based Matrix Market Research focused on snacking. Among its findings: teens eat an average of three snacks per day; breakfast is the meal they skip most often. Despite a variety of snacks on store shelves, when it comes to healthier eating, it is a bit of teenage wasteland. Matrix asked 520 teen respondents to conjure up new foods they had gobble up. The following are some of their ideas:

- "Travel fruit. Why can't fruit be packed in packets like chips or cookies?"—Female, age 17.
- "A drink that contains five servings of fruits and vegetable."—Male, age 16.
- "I would invent all natural and fat-free, vitamin enhanced-cookies and chips that has great flavour."—Female, age 16.
- "I would make fruit-based cookies."—Female, age 15.
- "I would create some sort of microwaveable pasta."—Male, age 18.
- "A juice where you could get all the nutrients you need, that tastes good, helps you stay in shape, and is good for you. Has vitamins A, B, C, Iron. Packaging would be bright."—Female, age 17.
- "A breakfast shake for teens. Something easy that tastes good, not necessarily for dieters. Something to balance you off in the morning."—Male, age 18.

Activities

1. You are a new product development specialist at Britannia. What guidance can you get from the Matrix study?
2. Choose one of the suggestions from the above list of healthy snack concepts. Imagine that your company is interested in turning the idea into a new product but wants to conduct market research before investing in product development. Design a marketing research plan that will give company managers the information they need before engaging in new-product development of the idea. (Hint: Use steps 1–3 in Exhibit 9.1 as a guide.)
3. Once you have finished your plan, collect the data. Depending on the data-collection methods you have outlined in your plan, you may need to make adjustments so that you can collect actual data to analyze.
4. Analyze the data you collected and create a report for your company either recommending that the company pursue the idea you chose or investigate another.

ETHICS EXERCISE

Sumit Verma owns a small marketing research firm in Vadodra, Gujarat, which employs 60 people. Most employees are the sole breadwinners in their families. Sumit's firm has not fared well for the past two years and is on the verge of bankruptcy. The company recently surveyed over 2500 people in Gujarat about new-car purchase plans for Gujarat Institute of Development Research (GIDR).

Because the study identified many hot prospects for new cars, a car dealer has offered Sumit ₹3 lakh for the names and phone numbers of people saying they are "likely" or "very likely" to buy a new car within the next 12 months. Sumit needs the money to avoid laying off a number of employees.

Questions

1. Should Sumit Verma sell the names?
2. Does the AMA Statement of Ethics address this issue? Go to [**www.marketingpower.com/AboutAMA/Pages/Statement of Ethics.aspx**]. Then write a brief paragraph on what the AMA Statement of Ethics contains that relates to Sumit Verma's dilemma.

MARKETING PLAN EXERCISE

For the marketing plan exercise in Chapter 6, you considered the consumer decision-making process as it applies to your marketing plan; in Chapter 7, you analyzed your potential business markets. In Chapter 8, you identified your company's target market and its various segments. Now complete the following exercises to find out more about your competitors and customers through marketing research—a key to any strategic marketing plan. Once completed, you can use your answers to complete the Marketing Plan Worksheet for Part 2, which you can find on your companion Web site at **www.cengage.com/international**.

1. Are there any critical issues that must be explored with primary marketing research before you can implement your marketing plan for your chosen company? These might include items such as customer demand, purchase intentions, customer perceptions of product quality, price perceptions, and reaction to critical promotion. List some critical research questions and decide which form of research you would use.
2. Design a brief Internet customer satisfaction survey that you could place on your company Web site. Use the "SurveyMonkey" to help you with your questionnaire at www.surveymonkey.com.
3. What type of competitive intelligence will you need to gather in order to monitor your market space? How can analyzing the job offerings, mission or "about us" statement, products and services descriptions, or other general information on your competitors' Web sites help you figure our their strategic direction? What areas of a Web site could you scan to gather competitive information?

Short Case: SANTOOR

Prepared by
Dr. Dheeraj Sharma,
Indian Institute of Management, Ahmedabad

The India soap market consists of more than 100 brands, however not all are successful and have their presence felt in the market. The soap category is divided into three segments, ie., economy (like Lifebuoy), popular (like Lux, Hamam, etc.) and premium (like Vivel, Lux international, Dove, etc.) segments. Soap marketers are one of the huge spenders on marketing research.

WIPRO'S NEW ENTRY: SANTOOR:

With the help of marketing research, Wipro found an opportunity to make an entry in the popular soap segment category and introduced a sandalwood-turmeric based soap called "Santoor".

Phase I:

Before introducing Santoor, the company tested seven different concepts in the market, of which the sandalwood-turmeric concept was liked by the majority. It gave the benefit of skin care and beauty together and saved the time of the consumers, who used to make the paste of sandalwood and turmeric to apply it on their face to look beautiful. The brand name Santoor was derived from the first three letters of both the ingredients "san"dalwood and "tur"meric. At that time Moti and Mysore Sandal were the only sandal based soaps available in the market but they were in the premium category. The company test marketed the product in Bangalore in 1985, and based on the feedback obtained, laid more emphasis on its ingredients and strengthened its perfume/fragrance. The product saw a good acceptance among consumers and trade people.

Phase II:

Santoor was doing very well for two to three years of its launching. But afterwards, the price of all the popular soaps had to be increased due to the increase in the prices of vegetable oils (used in determining the lathering ability), packaging costs and imposition of excise duties. Santoor was badly affected with this.

Also since Santoor was still new in the market, its brand loyalty was not too good and the consumers were ready to switch their brands. Looking at the huge potential that Santoor had, Wipro appointed Draftfcb-Ulka the responsibility to handle the situation. The agency carried out research to identify the response of the consumers towards Santoor and beauty soaps in general. It was found that the product had a very small user base of only those who wanted a sandalwood based soap. On other parameters like fragrance, good for skin, lathering effect, etc., Santoor was a successful product. However, Santoor was seen as a traditional middle class brand, whose woman was neither noticed nor looked up to.

Thus, Santoor had to retain its existing users and along with it go for new users. It had a tough challenge of offering the same value to its existing users and at the same time attract the non-users. Hence, it had to change its product image from a middle class woman to a "younger looking skin", on one hand and to keep its ingredients sandalwood and turmeric intact on the other.

The agency then planned its advertising strategy keeping the above fact in mind and then positioned it as "good for skin-younger looking skin". It also followed the idea of a "mistaken identity" in its ad to execute the younger looking skin promise saying *"meri twacha se meri umar ka pata hi nahin chalta"*. The product was a huge success and has not looked back since 1989, though it has undergone some changes in its products like packaging, fragrance, etc.[15]

Santoor now enjoys the position of third largest soap brand in India and is the largest selling brand in southern parts of the country.[16]

With the changing role of women in recent times, on the 25th anniversary of the brand Draftfcb Ulka has created a new milestone for Santoor while keeping the core value of the product, i.e., providing younger looking skin intact. It has modernized the brand by changing its logo, the old pack and developed new tagline—'skin that lies about you age' for the brand. Its ad shows a beautiful woman of today in all spheres of life—a photographer, musician, choreographer, etc. who come together to cover off the "sunhera" Santoor.[17]

Questions

1. In a highly competitive market with so many brands available, is it viable to look beyond the functional benefit of the product?
2. Wipro is targeting its brand Santoor towards women. Is its strategy correct, when most of the other companies in the market are targeting their products towards the whole family?

9 Decision Support Systems and Marketing Research

KEY TERMS

LO 1

marketing information everyday information about developments in the marketing environment that managers use to prepare and adjust marketing plans

decision support system (DSS) an interactive, flexible, computerized information system that enables managers to obtain and manipulate information as they are making decisions

database marketing the creation of a large computerized file of customers' and potential customers' profiles and purchase patterns

LO 2

marketing research the process of planning, collecting, and analyzing data relevant to a marketing decision

LO 3

marketing research problem determining what information is needed and how that information can be obtained efficiently and effectively

marketing research objective the specific information needed to solve a marketing research problem; the objective should be to provide insightful decision-making information

management decision problem a broad-based problem that uses marketing research in order for managers to take proper actions

secondary data data previously collected for any purpose other than the one at hand

marketing research aggregator a company that acquires, catalogs, reformats, segments, and resells reports already published by marketing research firms

research design specifies which research questions must be answered, how and when the data will be gathered, and how the data will be analyzed

KEY CONCEPTS

LO 1

Explain the concept and purpose of a marketing decision support system. A decision support system (DSS) makes data instantly available to marketing managers and allows them to manipulate the data themselves to make marketing decisions. Four characteristics make a DSS especially useful to marketing managers: They are interactive, flexible, discovery oriented, and accessible. Decision support systems give managers access to information immediately and without outside assistance. They allow users to manipulate data in a variety of ways and to answer "what if" questions. And, finally, they are accessible to novice computer users.

LO 2

Define marketing research and explain its importance to marketing decision making. Marketing research is a process of collecting and analyzing data for the purpose of solving specific marketing problems. Marketers use marketing research to explore the profitability of marketing strategies. They can examine why particular strategies failed and analyze characteristics of specific market segments. Managers can use research findings to help keep current customers. Moreover, marketing research allows management to behave proactively, rather than reactively, by identifying newly emerging patterns in society and the economy.

LO 3

Describe the steps involved in conducting a marketing research project. The marketing research process involves several basic steps. First, the researcher and the decision maker must agree on a problem statement or set of research objectives. The researcher then creates an overall research design to specify how primary data will be gathered and analyzed. Before collecting data, the researcher decides whether the group to be interviewed will be a probability or nonprobability sample. Field service firms are often hired to carry out data collection. Once data have been collected, the researcher analyzes them using statistical analysis. The researcher then prepares and presents oral and written reports, with conclusions and recommendations, to management. As a final step, the researcher determines whether the recommendations were implemented and what could have been done to make the project more successful.

LO 4

Discuss the profound impact of the Internet on marketing research. The Internet has vastly simplified the secondary data search process, placing more sources of information in front of researchers than ever before. Internet survey research is surging in popularity. Internet surveys can be created rapidly, are reported in real time, are relatively inexpensive, and are easily personalized. Often researchers use the Internet to contact respondents who are difficult to reach by other means. The Internet can also be used to conduct focus groups, analyze consumer-generated media, engage in behavioral targeting, distribute research proposals and reports, and to facilitate collaboration between the client and the research supplier. Clients can access real-time data and analyze the information as the collection process continues.

LO 5

Discuss the growing importance of scanner-based research. A scanner-based research system enables marketers to monitor a market panel's exposure and reaction to such variables as advertising, coupons, store displays, packaging, and price. By analyzing these variables in relation to the panel's subsequent buying behavior, marketers gain useful insight into sales and marketing strategies.

LO 6 **Explain when marketing research should be conducted.** Because acquiring marketing information can be time-consuming and costly, deciding to acquire additional decision-making information depends on managers' perceptions of its quality, price, and timing. Research, therefore, should be undertaken only when the expected value of the information is greater than the cost of obtaining it.

LO 7 **Explain the concept of competitive intelligence.** Competitive intelligence (CI) helps managers assess their competition and their vendors in order to become more efficient and effective competitors. Intelligence is analyzed information, and it becomes decision-making intelligence when it has implications for the organization. By helping managers assess their competition and vendors, CI leads to fewer surprises. CI is part of a sound marketing strategy, helps companies respond to competitive threats, and helps reduce unnecessary costs. The Internet and databases accessed via the Internet offer excellent sources of CI.

primary data information that is collected for the first time; used for solving the particular problem under investigation

survey research the most popular technique for gathering primary data, in which a researcher interacts with people to obtain facts, opinions, and attitudes

mall intercept interview a survey research method that involves interviewing people in the common areas of shopping malls

computer-assisted personal interviewing an interviewing method in which the interviewer reads questions from a computer screen and enters the respondent's data directly into the computer

computer-assisted self-interviewing an interviewing method in which a mall interviewer intercepts and directs willing respondents to nearby computers where each respondent reads questions off a computer screen and directly keys his or her answers into a computer

central-location telephone (CLT) facility a specially designed phone room used to conduct telephone interviewing

executive interview a type of survey that involves interviewing businesspeople at their offices concerning industrial products or services

focus group seven to ten people who participate in a group discussion led by a moderator

open-ended question an interview question that encourages an answer phrased in the respondent's own words

closed-ended question an interview question that asks the respondent to make a selection from a limited list of responses

scaled-response question a closed-ended question designed to measure the intensity of a respondent's answer

observation research a research method that relies on four types of observation: people watching people, people watching an activity, machines watching people, and machines watching an activity

mystery shoppers researchers posing as customers who gather observational data about a store

behavioral targeting (BT) a form of observation marketing research that uses data mining coupled with identifying Web surfers by their IP addresses

ethnographic research the study of human behavior in its natural context; involves observation of behavior and physical setting

experiment a method a researcher uses to gather primary data

sample a subset from a larger population

universe the population from which a sample will be drawn

probability sample a sample in which every element in the population has a known statistical likelihood of being selected

random sample a sample arranged in such a way that every element of the population has an equal chance of being selected as part of the sample

nonprobability sample any sample in which little or no attempt is made to get a representative cross section of the population

convenience sample a form of nonprobability sample using respondents who are convenient or readily accessible to the researcher—for example, employees, friends, or relatives

measurement error an error that occurs when there is a difference between the information desired by the researcher and the information provided by the measurement process

sampling error an error that occurs when a sample somehow does not represent the target population

frame error an error that occurs when a sample drawn from a population differs from the target population

random error an error that occurs when the selected sample is an imperfect representation of the overall population

field service firm a firm that specializes in interviewing respondents on a subcontracted basis

cross-tabulation a method of analyzing data that lets the analyst look at the responses to one question in relation to the responses to one or more other questions

LO 4 **consumer-generated media (CGM)** media that consumers generate and share among themselves

LO 5 **scanner-based research** a system for gathering information from a single group of respondents by continuously monitoring the advertising, promotion, and pricing they are exposed to and the things they buy

BehaviorScan a scanner-based research program that tracks the purchases of 3,000 households through store scanners in each research market

InfoScan a scanner-based sales-tracking service for the consumer packaged-goods industry

neuromarketing a field of marketing that studies the body's responses to marketing stimuli

LO 7 **competitive intelligence (CI)** an intelligence system that helps managers assess their competition and vendors in order to become more efficient and effective competitors

CASE 2

Makemytrip.com (A)

> I am amazed to see the way in which the Indian online travel market is taking off. The market for buying travel online is ripe and shift from offline to online booking is getting accelerated. We intend to seize this opportunity by launching our site well before the competition—this would enable us to take a sizable lead.
>
> Deep Kalra,
> Founder and Chief Executive Officer

On June 5, 2005, three months before the launch of Indian operations of Makemytrip.com (MMT), Deep Kalra, founder and Chief Executive Officer, held a meeting with key members of the company at the Delhi office to review the launch plan of MMT India. The core team comprised Keyur Joshi (co-founder and COO), Sachin Bhatia (co-founder and Chief Marketing Officer), Amit Saberwal (Vice President–Business Development), Venkatesh Bharadwaj (Head–Technology), Sanjeev Bhasin (Head–Operations), and Gayatri Buddha (Assistant Vice President–Marketing). The objective of the meeting was to evaluate and fine tune various components of the launch plan.

C2.1 MakeMyTrip.com

MMT was launched in US in 2000 to cater to the niche US-to-India travel market. The company survived the dotcom bust and the 9/11 tragedy and was able to break even in 2002. The website emerged as the foremost online travel service provider in the US-to-India market. By 2004, it had garnered 3.5 per cent share of this NRI market (₹4,500 crore/$1 billion) which was dominated by ethnic agents who were either consolidators (wholesalers) or sub-agents. With over 1,00,000 customers and 1,30,000 registered users in US, Makemytrip had a renewal rate of 30 per cent. NRIs could book tickets to India online or could call travel consultants who were available 24x7 on the US toll free 1800-India-10. The company had offices in New York and Sydney. According to Kalra, the factors which worked well for the company were an all-pervasive entrepreneurial spirit along with cohesive culture and homegrown HR practices. Employees were given opportunity to be owners of the company by holding stocks.

In 2004, big online travel agents like Expedia, Orbitz, and Travelocity commanded the lion's share of the $52.1 billion (₹2,292.4 billion) domestic and international market, which was estimated to touch $62.3 billion (₹2,741.2 billion). The online travel market was expected to account for 25 per cent of the overall US travel market in 2005.[1] The online travel market in US was getting popular as customer service was given higher preference. Online travel service providers were attracting customers by offering customer service and bundling products such as flight ticket booking with hotel booking, car rental, and even entertainment at destination.

C2.2 MMT India Operation

In the meeting with key members, a decision was taken to launch the India website in September 2005. Kalra believed that there was strong indication of a healthy growth for travel products/services in India. There was a compelling need to provide a platform for buying and selling travel products/services. MMT identified the gap between demand and supply and decided to offer a user friendly and convenient online interactive interface to the consumer. The company received an investment of $8 million (₹352 million) from SB Asia Infrastructure Fund (SAIF), a leading Asian private equity firm. Kalra justified his decision to start operations in India thus: "The launch of MMT India was not really a shift of focus; we wanted to launch the India business because the time was just right." Low cost carriers (LCCs) had made air travel cheaper, thus opening up the market for air travel and leisure holidaying beyond visiting friends and family. The young India had more disposable income and a greater desire to travel. The airlines' move to e-ticketing also paved

Written by Sanjay Kumar Kar, Academic Associate, under the supervision of Professor Abhinandan Kumar Jain, Indian Institute of Management, Ahmedabad.
The author is grateful to Mr. Deep Kalra and other executives of Makemytrip.com for their cooperation and support.

1. http://www.forbes.com/2006/02/17/travelocity-orbitz-tripadvisor-in_mr_bow0217_inl.html

the way for travel e-commerce. The travel market was ready to evolve to the next level (online) and MMT was preparing to launch at the most opportune time. As the first and only comprehensive online travel site with real time booking for flights, hotels, holidays, and cars, MMT was in the process of bringing a revolution in the way travel products were bought in India.

C2.3 Business Model

Gayatri Buddha termed MMT's business model as a simple B2C. Customer could use either MMT website or its call centre to book air tickets, hotel rooms, and travel packages. There were three enabling components: technology, people and process, and supplier relations. The earlier experience in US indicated that strong relationship with suppliers such as domestic airlines including LCCs, international airlines, and hotels would help the company run the business model. Technology was identified as a cornerstone. MMT had already developed proprietary technology which would help it link all supplier sites to check the inventory and compare prices. In fact, the search engine the company had developed would enable it to offer the lowest possible price to the customer. The booking engine would also enable customers to customize their flight booking and hotel packages to maximize savings. Being a travel commerce website, the company believed that its own products would generate adequate revenue to successfully run the business model without depending on revenue generated from selling advertisement space on the website. Advertisements on the website might distract or divert visitors from their main objective of searching or booking travel products on MMT's website. The other key component of the business model would be employees having domain specific skills in order to help MMT develop and offer suitable products and services for the travel consumer.

C2.4 Projections

Headquartered in New Delhi, MMT projected a turnover of ₹600 crore ($130 million) by FY 2007. The Indian operations were estimated to contribute over 50 per cent of MMT's projected turnover and MMT was expecting that in the initial years 90 per cent sales would be online and rest through its call centre and physical branch offices. The business model focused on generating revenue from travellers to and from within India. By the end of 2006, MMT was expecting to acquire a strong customer base of over 3,50,000 delighted customers and selling over 3000 flight tickets, 300 hotel room nights, and over 50 holiday packages every day.[2] MMT was planning to have a headcount of over 650 by 2007.

C2.5 Indian Travel and Tourism Industry Environment, Indian Customer, and Segmentation

Air traffic in India was expected to grow by 5 million passengers each year over the next 10 years. Domestic air traffic grew at 24.2 per cent from 32.09 million in April 2004 to 39.86 million in April 2005. During the same period international traffic grew from 16.63 million to 19.41 million passengers.[3] India's domestic air passenger market was expected to grow at over 30 per cent in 2005-6. The decision to allow private airlines to fly on international routes was expected to facilitate more flow of air passengers. Also the initiatives taken by the aviation ministry to modernize 80 airports would help the growth of India's international air traffic. According to one industry estimate, it would grow by 25 per cent for the next five years.

In the annual plan (of Govt of India) 2004/2005 ₹5,000 million was allocated to the Ministry of Tourism for tourism development. For the annual plan 2005/2006, the allocation was ₹7,860 million. During the period under consideration, tourism contributed 2.5 per cent to India's GDP. National tourism spending, comprising domestic tourism expenditure and incoming tourist receipts, was estimated to be approximately ₹880 billion in 2005, up by more than 15 per

2. Email communication from Gayatri Buddha.
3. http://www.capitaline.com/user/framepage.asp?id=1

cent in current value terms from the previous year. Travel within the country was expected to be about 66 per cent of the total expenditure and accommodation contributed about 22 per cent.

In spite of these encouraging figures, several factors inhibited the growth of tourism:

- high taxes on hotel tariffs (service tax: 8 per cent on specified services, luxury tax: 12.5 per cent on rooms on actual)
- service taxes on foreign exchange earnings of travel agents
- union and state governments were charging about 35–40 per cent road passenger, toll, luxury, and sales taxes on the proceeds of travel operators
- insufficient facilities and poor maintenance at many holiday destinations and tourist locations

Travel and Tourism Market in India

In 2004, foreign tourist arrival in India grew at 23.5 per cent to reach 3.46 million and was projected to reach 3.92 million[4] at the end of 2005. Visitors to India spent ₹222.5 billion (US $4.9 billion) during their stay in 2004, with an average spend of ₹65,460 ($1,451) per person.[5] According to industry sources 50 million airline seats were expected to be available for sale in India in 2006.

In 2005, around 98 per cent of the outbound travel from India was by air. Air travel grew at a rate of almost 17 per cent in current value terms, compared with 15 per cent in 2004.[6] Outbound trips were estimated to cross 6 million in 2006. Indians travelled abroad for three main reasons: business, leisure, and visiting friends and relatives. The 'other' category accounted for 34 per cent of total departures to international destinations, contributed by people who went for purposes like education, attending conventions, and religious and pilgrimage journeys. A large Indian diaspora was the key driver for people travelling abroad. This segment accounted for 21 per cent of departures. In 2005, the leisure traveller segment grew by 21 per cent over 2004 (Exhibit C2.1) and contributed 17 per cent of outbound departures.

EXHIBIT C2.1

Departures by Purpose of Visit: 2000–2005

(thousands)

	2000	2001	2002	2003	2004*	2005*
Business	1,154.80	1,179.40	1,340.00	1,355.20	1,495.40	1,731.20
Leisure	679.9	691.4	750.5	767.5	853.1	1,032.60
Visiting friends/relatives	807	823.4	959.1	1,019.80	1,082.10	1,310.80
Others	1,773.80	1,870.30	1,890.60	1,357.50	1,969.40	2,108.40
Total	4,415.50	4,564.50	4,940.20	4,500.00	5,400.00	6,183.00

* Estimated

Source: http://www.gmid.euromonitor.com/Reports.aspx

Indians made almost 391 million domestic trips in 2005; this was about 12.7 per cent higher than that in 2004. In 2005, domestic air travel contributed just about 2.85 million trips compared to 74 million trips by rail and 312 million by road. However, air travel was the growing mode with an impressive 37 per cent growth over the previous year.

Indian Consumer

Average household spending in India grew at 5.3 per cent annually between 1994 and 2004.[7] According to the KSA Technopak survey conducted in 2002, Indian consumers were spending 15.6 per cent of their annual earnings for vacation/eating out; this was the second largest spending category after grocery spending. Consumers aged 24–34 years were spending the maximum on eating out whereas consumers in the age group of 45–58 years were spending maximum on vacations. Indian consumers were moving towards the use of financial cards rather than using cash for their purchasing activities and the most popular mode of payment was the credit card (70 per cent). The number

4. http://timesfoundation.indiatimes.com/articleshow/1365895.cms
5. Recent trends in spending by visitors to India: An analysis of Visa card spending in India by international card holders, 2005.
6. *Euromonitor Report,* Travel and Tourism - India.
7. http://www.micm-asianow.com/issue1-2005/cycles.htm

of credit cards in use had increased from 26.9 million in December 31, 2003, to 43.3 million a year later. During 2003-4, 185.5 million credit card transactions were effected, amounting to ₹358,700 million.[8]

Segmenting Indian Travellers

The travel market in India could be broadly divided into two major segments: personal travel and tourism and business travel. In the first category, purposes of visit might be pilgrimage/religious and visiting families/friends. The second category included those who travelled for official purposes, corporate and governmental.

Personal Travel and Tourism The personal travel and tourism segment looked for the best deals. The estimated segment size was about ₹1,034 billion in 2005 and was projected to grow to ₹3,748.7 billion by 2015 (Exhibit C2.2).

EXHIBIT C2.2

Travel and Tourism Industry in India

(₹ billion)

Travel & Tourism Segments	2000	2001	2002	2003	2004E	2005E	2015P
Personal Travel and Tourism*	596.4	651.0	708.0	791.0	908.1	1,034.0	3,748.7
Business Travel and Tourism	101.6	94.2	86.8	96.0	114.0	134.0	402.2
— Corporate	90.0	83.6	76.8	84.8	101.1	118.9	361.3
— Government	11.7	10.7	10.0	11.2	12.8	15.1	40.9
Govt. Expenditures–Individual	7.4	8.0	8.7	9.9	10.7	12.2	37.6
Visitor Exports**	142.4	143.5	142.0	141.5	159.5	175.8	697.3
Total Travel and ourism Consumption	847.8	896.8	945.5	1,038.4	1,192.3	1,355.9	4,885.7

* Travel and Tourism personal consumption category includes all personal spending by an economy's residents on travel and tourism services (lodging, transportation, entertainment, meals, financial services, etc) and goods (durable and non-durable) used for travel and tourism activities. Spending may occur before, during, or after a trip. Spending covers all travel and tourism, outbound, and domestic.

** Expenditures by international visitors on goods and services within the resident economy.

SOURCE: *World Travel and Tourism Council (WTTC) Report on Travel and Tourism in India, 2005*

Business Travel The business travel segment declined at a compound annual growth rate (CAGR) of 7.6 per cent during 2001 and 2002. But the segment recovered well in 2003 and registered 10.6 per cent growth over the previous year. This segment was estimated at ₹134 billion in 2005 and would touch ₹402.2 billion by 2015 (Exhibit C2.2). The category included spending by government and industry on goods and services (transportation, accommodation, meals, entertainment, etc.) for business-related travel of their employees. The number of low cost carriers (LCCs) was increasing and the cost of air travel was expected to come down. Even though most of the business centers in India were connected by an excellent railway network, most of corporate travel in India was by air. One of the significant drivers of growing corporate travel was the strong growth of IT and IT enabled services. Technology companies in India allocated between 6 and 10 per cent of sales as travel expenses (in the first quarter of 2002 it was 7 per cent at Infosys, one of the leading IT Company), compared to 2 to 3 per cent which was the norm for most other businesses.[9] Online booking was expected to get a boost with the expansion of e-ticketing, credit card usage, increased air capacity, and other factors.

Online Travel and Tourism Market in India

Internet User Base One of the reasons for the growth in the travel market was the rate of Internet penetration (see Exhibit C2.3). Online consumer purchasing reached approximately $130 million (₹5,720 million) in 2004-2005, according to the Internet and Online Association of India (IOAI). This was expected to

8. http://www.hindu.com/2005/05/20/stories/2005052000441000.htm

9. http://www.travelweeklyweb.com/article.asp?id=15530

EXHIBIT C2.3

Internet Usage in India

	Users (million)	Population (million)	Penetration (%)
1998	1.4	977	0.14
1999	2.8	993	0.28
2000	5.5	1,010	0.54
2001	7.0	1,027	0.68
2002	16.5	1,047	1.58
2003	22.5	1,086	2.07
2004	39.2	1,106	3.54
2005	50.6	1,131	4.47

SOURCE: http://www.internetworldstats.com/asia/in.htm and www.sebi.gov.in/dp/infodraft.pdf

grow sharply over the next two years, to reach $550 million (₹ 24,200 million) by 2006-2007.[10]

Online Travel Market A recent report by PhoCusWright, "The Emerging Online Travel Marketplace in India," showed that online leisure/unmanaged business travel gross bookings in India totalled $295 million (₹12,980 million) in 2005. This would increase nearly sevenfold to US$ 2.0 billion (₹88 billion) by 2008. The report also found that, in 2005, 2.2 per cent of total travel was booked online. Further, the predictions for a strong growth in the Internet channel expected the percentage of online bookings to approach double digits by 2008. In the case of transportation, online sales through intermediaries were expected to reach ₹25,538 million by 2010, up from ₹1,576 million in 2005 (Exhibit C2.4(A)).

EXHIBIT C2.4(A)

Internet Sales by Sector: Internet Transaction Value 2005–2010

(₹ million)

	2005	2006	2007	2008	2009	2010
Internet	23,173.0	35,501.0	53,287.0	78,918.0	114,746.8	159,612.7
— Direct suppliers	21,597.2	32,660.9	48,491.1	70,237.0	98,682.2	134,074.7
— Intermediaries	1,575.8	2,840.1	4,795.8	8,681.0	16,064.5	25,538.0
Others	1,080,301.2	1,239,225.1	1,421,031.7	1,632,244.8	1,871,420.6	2,148,976.8
Total	1,103,474.2	1,274,726.1	1,474,318.7	1,711,162.8	1,986,167.4	2,308,589.6

SOURCE: http://www.gmid.euromonitor.com/Reports.aspx

Online Hotel Booking According to the Euromonitor report, online sales in travel accommodation were valued at ₹6 billion in 2005, up by 29 per cent in current value terms from 2004. However, the Internet contributed a mere 3 per cent of total sales in the travel accommodation sector.[11] That offered a great opportunity for OTS providers to grow the category and capture a higher market share. Travel accommodation through intermediaries grew over 55 per cent in 2005 (Exhibit C2.4(B)). A recent study conducted by IAMAI reported that the 26–45 years age group was the highest purchaser of hotel rooms online, accounting for 72 per cent of purchases with a lion's share of 53 per cent made by the 26–35 years age group.

[10] http:// www.etcnewmedia.com/ review/ default.asp?SectionID=11&CountryID=61

[11] http://www.gmid.euromonitor.com/Reports.aspx

EXHIBIT C2.4(B)

Travel Accommodation: Internet Sales by Direct Suppliers and Intermediaries: Internet Transaction Value 2000–2005

(₹ million)

	2000	2001	2002	2003	2004	2005
Internet	890.2	1,259.6	2,300	3,939.8	4,696.3	6,034.7
— Direct suppliers	761.7	1,056.5	1,712.6	2,711	3,123	3,590.7
— Intermediaries	128.5	203.1	587.4	1,228.9	1,573.3	2,444.1
Others	104,401	116,034.7	124,847	142,406.4	162,138.4	189,666.9
Total	105,291.1	117,294.3	127,147	146,346.2	166,834.7	195,701.6

SOURCE: http://www.gmid.euromonitor.com/Reports.aspx

Margin Structure The leading international online travel service provider Expedia's revenues were about 12–14 per cent of gross sales.[12] Informed sources in India estimated that the industry earned margins of about 4–8 per cent on air tickets, 8–12 per cent on hotel bookings, and over 12 per cent on both domestic and international holiday packages.

C2.6 Competitive Environment

MMT faced competition from other OTS providers and suppliers themselves. Kalra mentioned that when MMT started to think about its India operation it did not estimate more than four competitors. However, he expected competition to be fierce in the next couple of years as multiple well-funded online ventures were likely to be around. This would be a very positive development for the overall market growth, as many other companies would share the burden of educating the customer regarding the benefit of buying travel products online. He was confident enough to lead from the front with his experience, more importantly his customer base from the US market.

Yatra.com

Yatra.com was expected to be launched by August 2006 to help businesses and consumers by offering travel-related information, pricing, availability and reservations for airlines, hotels, railway, buses, and car rentals across 5,000 large cities and small rural areas throughout India.

Yatra.com was likely to be one of the strong competitors within a couple of years. The portal was planning to have relationship with over 1,000 hotels in India to provide a better choice to the consumer. The basic objective of Yatra.com was to empower the consumer by providing more information to make his travel decision easier and better. According industry sources Yatra.com was planning to work on flexi-search tools which would enable consumers to search and compare prices two days either side. Yatra.com was most likely to offer a wide variety of travel packages which included weekend trips, religious and honeymoon trips, bus services, domestic and international hotel bookings, and car rentals.

Travelguru.com

Travelguru.com was scheduled to be launched in December 2005. WestBridge Capital Partners, a venture capital fund, was expected to provide funding to Travelguru.com. Travelguru planned to offer services through the MICE (Meeting, Incentive, Conference, and Event) team to arrange conferences, meetings, and events for consumers or corporate clients. Services to be offered included the following:

- planning a cost-effective budget
- assistance with airline bookings
- assistance with hotel bookings
- assistance with transportation
- planning sightseeing trips

12. http://www.onlinetravelreview.com/online_travel_review/airlines_in_india/index.html

Cleartrip.com

Cleartrip.com, another online travel agent, was planning to enter the market by August 2006. This company was said to be funded by Ram Shriram's Sherpalo Ventures and Kleiner Perkins Caufield Sz Byers, two leading US based venture capital firms. Cleartrip.com was planning to allow customers to select from over 900 domestic hotels across India and a comprehensive selection of established network carriers and LCCs operating in the domestic market. To provide superior choice Cleartrip.com was in talks with Abacus, Asia's leading global distribution system, to provide access to airline inventory and fares. Cleartrip.com planned to spend about ₹30 crore[13] (₹300 million) in the first year on advertising.

Suppliers Web Sites

According to one estimate, 75 per cent of airlines tickets were sold from airlines' websites and 12 per cent of online air ticket sales were taking place through non-airline sites.[14] LCCs posed the biggest challenge to MMT as they started selling tickets both offline and online. Six new LCCs were launched in India in 2005, and there seemed to be room for more. SpiceJet was an outstanding performer during the year. It sold over 5,000 tickets online for the first flight on May 23, 2005, and sold 37,348 tickets on the first date of booking. Suppliers had the advantage of e-ticketing and travellers did not need to wait for delivery of ticket. To provide a wider range of products, LCCs were looking for alliances and tie-ups. So, MMT expected to see some hybrid models in the near future.

Travel Agents and Tour Operators

In 2004, there were 23,450 outlets of travel agents and 4,450 outlets of tour operators in India. According to one source, travel agents earned a margin of around 5 per cent on booking air tickets, about 10 per cent on hotel booking, and more than 10 per cent on holiday packages. One of the travel agents in Ahmedabad said that it booked 30–40 air tickets a day. Travel agents had started to realize that the Internet could be an important means to market their products and this medium provided 7 per cent of their business. However, this was not real time in terms of price comparison across all airlines at one go and travel agents might not pose serious challenges to MMT.

C2.7 Strategic View and Choices by MMT

MMT's View of the Consumer

According to Kalra, Indian travel consumers were distinct for the following reasons:

- short lead-time for booking holidays (3–6 weeks)
- preference for pre-planned travel
- attitude towards travel: status is important
- specific needs (e.g. dietary) because of their social/religious background
- no specific language problems: many Indians spoke English
- preference for familiar Indian food
- Indian consumers were largely going to travel agents or tour operators for buying travel products even though they offered limited choices

MMT realized that there was a need to offer a unique service that would help travellers to make their own decision regarding travel (and minimize the dependence on travel agents). MMT believed that there was a virtuous cycle (enduring benefits = strong entrenchment in the mind space = visits = satisfaction = repeat visits) working in the travel market. MMT was designed to close the loop between info search and actual execution, i.e. conversion/purchase.

Market Segmentation by MMT

MMT identified four potential segments (see Exhibit C2.5).

Choice of Target Customer

The major target customer for MMT was the metro male in the age group of 24–44 years, married with a monthly household income of over ₹30,000 in families which were Internet savvy with usage beyond email, transacted on the Internet before, deal hunters, and early adopters (those were inclined to try new things). In India most of the consumers were deal hunters and therefore MMT realized that offering the best possible price to the consumer would certainly help not only lure but also retain customers. For that purpose,

13. http://www.thehindubusinessline.com/ew/2006/09/25/stories/2006092500070100.htm
14. http://www.iamai.in/section.php3?secid=23Szpress_id=908Szmon=3

EXHIBIT C2.5
Potential Segments

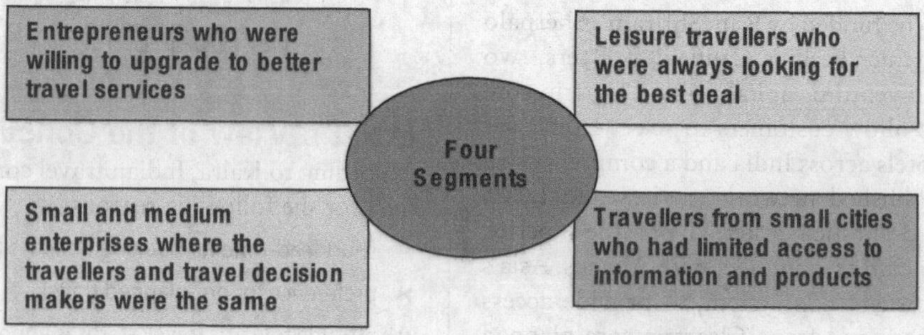

MMT had planned the unbeatable proposition of giving consumers the lowest possible price in the market.

Branding and Positioning

MMT was trying to position itself as a total travel solution provider with convenience as a key driver. The most important objective of the positioning strategy was to occupy space in the mind of the customer as the lowest air fare provider in the country. The MMT brand was really well placed to offer the modern convenience of an online, one-stop shop, and comprehensive travel solutions to travellers (see Exhibit C2.6).

Product Offerings

MMT planned to provide a comprehensive basket of products and services, starting with outbound and domestic travel services for leisure and small-business travellers. The following products/services were planned to be offered:

- *air tickets:* customers would get the opportunity to search, compare, and book tickets on any airline, including LCCs and full service airlines
- *hotel reservations:* customers would have the option of real-time booking of rooms in over 1,500 hotels at discounted tariffs

EXHIBIT C2.6
Value Propositions of Brand MMT

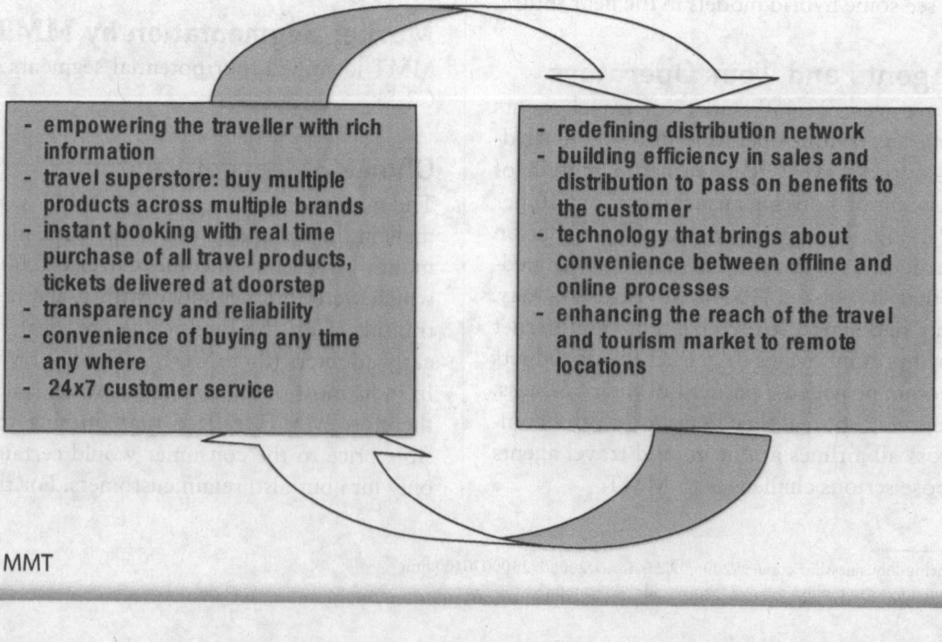

SOURCE: MMT

- *car/taxi bookings:* customers would be provided opportunity to book car at special prices for airport transfers and other trips
- *holiday packages:* facility to buy holiday packages within India or foreign holidays at great prices
- *road-trips:* myriad options would be available for motorable trips from all large cities in India with interactive maps
- *weekend breaks:* would offer great opportunity with thousands of options for short stay holidays at all price points
- MMT was planning to offer B2B services too. Local agents around the world would be able to access the above products through its extranet, IndiaAhoy.com

MMT planned to enrich its wide variety of products with unbeatable offerings like money back guarantee (MBG), Visa-Kingfisher offer, lowest airfare guarantee, and India's lowest prices. MMT wanted to be a one-stop shop to cater to all travel requirements when planning a trip. The money back guarantee would mean 20 per cent cash back on hotels and holidays bookings if MMT failed to deliver the promise. For example, if MMT promised that the hotel room would be sea facing, it would be genuinely sea facing. If that did not happen, MMT would offer 20 per cent cash back to the customer.[15] Through the Visa-Kingfisher offer, MMT was planning to provide 20 per cent cash back to all customers who would use their Visa credit card to book any ticket on Kingfisher Airlines. As Gayatri Buddha explained, "This was the first time in India that the cash back was to be offered on air tickets on a large scale." MMT was also in the process of getting into several partnerships with media channels such as the National Geographic and banks like HSBC and ICICI to reach out to a wider and new audience all the time.

According to MMT's internal revenue estimation, contribution of air tickets would be 85 per cent and hotels and holidays would contribute 15 per cent. Again, domestic booking was expected to dominate with a share of 90 per cent compared to international booking's 10 per cent. However, MMT was planning to reduce the overdependence on flight bookings by diversifying into other product offerings. As part of constant product innovation, MMT decided to offer suitable promotional offers from time to time. For higher customer retention MMT was planning to tie up with I-mint, the largest consumer reward programme that aided the consumer to mint more points on every purchase of travel products, shopping, fuel, and mobile phones. Consumer could buy products or services across different categories and accumulate points for redeeming later. A tie-up with I-mint meant that every registered user of MMT would receive an I-mint card.

MMT had planned to offer the Super Saver programme and Super Tripper offers as regular features. The objective of the Super Saver programme was to provide significant savings to the consumer while booking under this scheme. In the Super Tripper offer MMT planned to give cash discounts, special rewards like travel goodies, and invitations to special events. Some of the Super Tripper offers were ICICI Lombard free baggage insurance and free personal insurance with purchase of air tickets from MMT.

C2.8 Launch Plan

MMT wanted to achieve the following objectives through the launch campaign:

- to communicate that MMT offers online one-stop-shop solution to travel consumers
- to build excitement through every customer contact
- communicate a strong proposition and deliver consistently on the promise
- build empathy via relevance

Campaign Design

The underlying factors behind the advertising campaign were that customers were deal hunters and looked for the cheapest price with assurance. Therefore, the campaign focused on the lowest airfare guarantee to push trials. The tallest claim in the market—"If you find a lower fare we pay the difference"—was designed to serve the purpose of grabbing the attention. When customers bought travel products through an intermediary, the anxiety of being cheated was very real, and customer needed a guarantee that assured them the best deal.

Advertising Budget

The company planned to spend approximately ₹30 million on advertising and marketing activities during

15. Email communication from Gayatri Buddha.

the three months launch phase. It decided to spend about 40 per cent on TV, 30 per cent on the Internet, 5 per cent on outdoor, 5 per cent on print, 5 per cent on below the line (BTL) advertising, and 15 per cent on analytics, public relations (PR), and other marketing related activities.[16]

Media Selection and Advertisements

To build the brand, MMT planned to adopt aggressive frequency build-up to enhance usage and traction. The media objective was to create a 360 degree loop to reach the target customer through all feasible media options:

- *TV:* This medium was carefully chosen to build on "Nothing is more attractive than MMT offer." Simultaneously, other critical elements like smart "new kid on the block" personality was to be communicated
- *Print:* This medium was chosen to continue the excitement created through TV advertisements. The advertisement was deliberately placed by blocking the strip position at the bottom of the page to build on the rock bottom prices theme. City- relevant offers were to be used to gain traction on the website. Examples of print advertisements are given in Exhibit C2.7(A).
- *Internet:* Launch with high visibility properties like frame-spot at the bottom of the page, shoskele, and page-tear. In Exhibit C2.7(B) some Internet advertisements are given.
- *Outdoors:* Airports being the most important and critical place for promoting travel- related websites, live promotion themes were planned with the help of people with banners to carry on the Launch TVC. Some of outdoor advertisements are given in Exhibit C2.7(C).

Television Advertisement The TV channels were chosen to give high frequency at a base reach of 40 per cent in all markets. MMT did not want to go after the high reach mass channels because it wanted to target the Internet savvy, male audience living in metros and mini-metros. It chose two English news channels (NDTV, CNBC), four Infotainment channels (National Geographic, Discovery, Discovery Travel and Living, AXN), two English movie channels (Star Movies, HBO), one Hinglish entertainment (Star One), and one Hindi movie channel (Zee Cinema). Selecting these channels automatically reduced the amount of wastage while targeting the core audience, essentially male and between 24–44 years. Time slots were allocated with adequate care to ensure higher viewership. To reach the targeted audience 60 per cent of the total time was planned to be evening prime time (6 to 12 pm) and 40 per cent was RODP (run of the day programming). Of the 40 per cent of RODP spots, around 50 per cent were during weekends.[17] The commercials were planned to be shown for 20 seconds.

Beach TVC This commercial was shot on a beach and the creative execution of the advertisement read as follows:

> Makemytrip.com got India's hottest model for this beach shoot but the offer is so big that you might not be able see her. Sorry! For the lowest air fare guarantee log on to makemytrip.com.

The idea was to show that MMT would offer the lowest air fare and customers could book cheapest air tickets on makemytrip.com (see Exhibit C2.8).

Celebrity TVC The creativity of this commercial reinforced the key proposition of the lowest air fare guarantee offered by MMT. The commercial clearly showed that MMT would pay the difference if the customer could find a lower air fare than that on MMT. The advertisement made it appear that MMT hired India's biggest celebrity for the advertisement, but the offer was so big that the viewers would not be able to see him (see Exhibit C2.8).

Viral Campaign The primary goal of the viral campaigns was to promote the lowest airfares guarantee offered by MMT and generate excitement in the market. The emphasis was on the most competitive airfare offers in India and the assurance of paying back the difference to the customer if he found lower fare than that offered by MMT. Thus a strong message needed to be sent across to establish the credibility of the company that takes care of its promises. The campaign was aimed at creating a new breed of air travellers. A manifestation of this trend was conveyed through another message to the target audience, "Wish, Click, and Go". Two virals were created to build the MMT brand and to entice travellers to make use of the low airfares. According to Gayatri Buddha, all the viral campaigns were planned to be online with very low investment in either production or media since a good viral spread on its own merit. More precisely, each

16. Email communication from Deep Kalra and Gayatri Buddha.
17. ibid.

EXHIBIT C2.7(A)
Print Advertisement

SOURCE: MMT

EXHIBIT C2.7(B)

Print Advertisement for Trade

SOURCE: MMT

viral was estimated to cost around ₹2–3 lakh, which included production and initial media push.[18]

Creatives of Virals[19] A series of well thought out virals were planned. The first of the viral series, Sita Haran, was centered on the Ramayan where Sita, wife of Rama, was kidnapped by Ravana. Rama killed Ravana to rescue Sita and the day is celebrated as Dussera in India to mark the victory of good over evil. In the viral, however, Ravana, while on a mission to hoodwink and kidnap Sita, came across the exciting offer and, unable to resist it, rushed off to claim it. This creative was designed to capture the excitement in the market during Dussera.

18. Email communication from Gayatri Buddha.

19. http://www.marketingsherpa.com/vas2006/6.html

EXHIBIT C2.7(C)

Internet Advertisement

SOURCE: MMT

EXHIBIT C2.7(D)

Outdoor Advertisement

SOURCE: MMT

EXHIBIT C2.8
TVC Advertisements

MMT hired the biggest celebrity in India and hidden behind the biggest offer from MMT.

MMT would pay back the difference if any one finds a lower airfare than MMT.

Beach TVC Advertisement

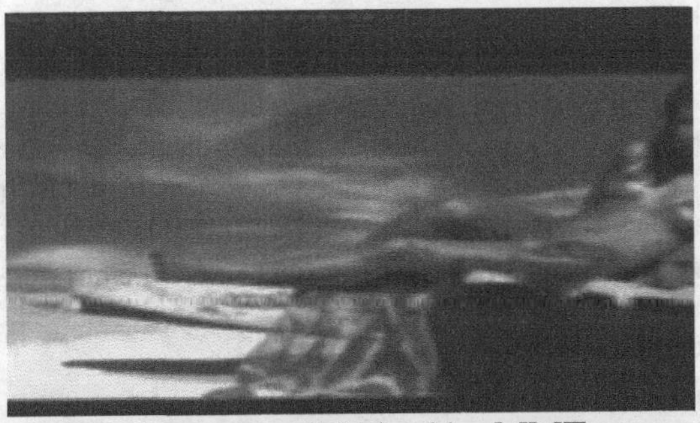

India's hottest model hired by MMT

Model is partially hidden by the MMT's offer

Two kids were disappointed as they could not see the hottest model

MMT would offer lowest air fare in India

The second was a continuation of sorts in which a humorous twist was added to the kidnapping incident. The two brothers, Ram and Lakshman, along with their faithful devotee Hanuman pick the affordable airfares offered by MMT to reach Sri Lanka to rescue Sita as quickly as possible but in the original epic the journey was treacherous.

One of the most interesting and exciting virals of the series was "The Moving Train." This was designed to convey the message that travel by airline was comparatively cheaper. This film bore allusions to the popular Bollywood blockbuster movie *Sholay*. The dacoits chase a train on horseback accompanied by the characteristic action movie soundtrack. After a long chase they finally manage to board the train and threaten the passengers to stay still. A sudden calm greets the announcement, and realization seems to dawn on one of the dacoits. His equally perplexed henchman moans, "There is no one in the train!" That very moment the hapless gang sees a plane flying by full of happy passengers. Even as the dacoits stare at the plane, one of them asks, "Kya ab hawai jahaj ko lootiyega ka?" (Will you now loot the airplane?)

The virals were to be emailed through the network of clients of Webchutney and registered users of MMT. The virals were also to be sent out to several forums such as viral monitor, online communities, and marketing based blogs. They were also to be placed in the MMT website so that that the films could reach a wider viewer base.

The viral campaigns were expected to generate tremendous amount of buzz in the market, specifically in the blogosphere. Such kind of interesting and innovative campaigns were expected to be covered by a number of leading national newspapers such as *Business Standard, Times of India,* and *Hindustan Times*. Similarly, online portals such as Agencyfaqs.com, Exchange4media.com, and rediff.com were likely to give maximum free publicity to MMT by covering the interesting campaign. The virals were also planned to be sent out to viral monitors like Chinwag and Lycos to get international traction as well.

C2.9 Challenges Ahead of MMT

Some reports estimated that MMT was expected to see very strong growth in constant value terms between 2005 and 2010 at a CAGR of 75 per cent in total transportation, and a substantial 82 per cent in air transportation. But intense competition from new entrants, suppliers, and online sites like indiatimes.com and rediff.com might make the journey a bit stiffer. Kalra felt that there were tough challenges:

- the online travel market in India was getting bigger and bigger. By the process the number of players was expected to increase and competition would be coming into its own
- low internet penetration in India was making the business more difficult for OTS to reach the mass market
- suppliers were selling their products online, hence they would be posing the biggest challenge to MMT and the intensity of competition would increase in the future
- hybrid OTS provider models might evolve in the future.

Questions for Preparation and Discussion

1. Review the strategy and launch plans of MMT for India.
2. If necessary, recommend suitable changes in the strategy and plans to achieve a leadership position in the Indian market.

CHAPTER 10 Product Concepts

Learning Outcomes

LO 1 Define the term *product*

LO 2 Classify consumer products

LO 3 Define the terms *product item*, *product line*, and *product mix*

LO 4 Describe marketing uses of branding

LO 5 Describe marketing uses of packaging and labeling

LO 6 Discuss global issues in branding and packaging

LO 7 Describe how and why product warranties are important marketing tools

The product is the starting point in creating a marketing mix.

LO 1 What Is a Product?

The product offering, the heart of an organization's marketing program, is usually the starting point in creating a marketing mix. A marketing manager cannot determine a price, design a promotion strategy, or create a distribution channel until the firm has a product to sell. Moreover, an excellent distribution channel, a persuasive promotion campaign, and a fair price have no value when the product offering is poor or inadequate.

product everything, both favorable and unfavorable, that a person receives in an exchange

A **product** may be defined as everything, both favorable and unfavorable, that a person receives in an exchange. A product may be a tangible good like a pair of shoes, a service like a haircut, an idea like "don't litter," or any combination of these three. Packaging, style, color, options, and size are some typical product features. Just as important are intangibles such as service, the seller's image, the manufacturer's reputation, and the way consumers believe others will view the product.

To most people, the term *product* means a tangible good. However, services and ideas are also products. (Chapter 12 focuses specifically on the unique aspects of marketing services.) The marketing process identified in Chapter 1 is the same whether the product marketed is a good, a service, an idea, or some combination of these.

***Note:** All the figures in U.S. dollars are converted into rupee using the value $1 = ₹45.*

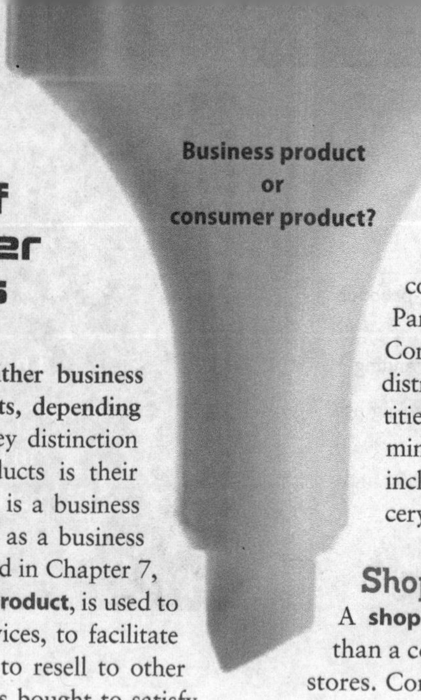

Business product
or
consumer product?

© ISTOCKPHOTO.COM/MILOS LUZANIN

LO 2 Types of Consumer Products

Products can be classified as either business (industrial) or consumer products, depending on the buyer's intentions. The key distinction between the two types of products is their intended use. If the intended use is a business purpose, the product is classified as a business or industrial product. As explained in Chapter 7, a **business product**, or **industrial product**, is used to manufacture other goods or services, to facilitate an organization's operations, or to resell to other customers. A **consumer product** is bought to satisfy an individual's personal wants. Sometimes the same item can be classified as either a business or a consumer product, depending on its intended use. Examples include lightbulbs, pencils and paper, and computers.

We need to know about product classifications because business and consumer products are marketed differently. They are marketed to different target markets and tend to use different distribution, promotion, and pricing strategies.

Chapter 7 examined seven categories of business products: major equipment, accessory equipment, component parts, processed materials, raw materials, supplies, and services. This chapter examines an effective way of categorizing consumer products. Although there are several ways to classify them, the most popular approach includes these four types: convenience products, shopping products, specialty products, and unsought products. This approach classifies products according to how much effort is normally used to shop for them.

business product (industrial product) a product used to manufacture other goods or services, to facilitate an organization's operations, or to resell to other customers

consumer product a product bought to satisfy an individual's personal wants

convenience product a relatively inexpensive item that merits little shopping effort

shopping product a product that requires comparison shopping because it is usually more expensive than a convenience product and is found in fewer stores

specialty product a particular item that consumers search extensively for and are very reluctant to accept substitutes

Convenience Products

A **convenience product** is a relatively inexpensive item that merits little shopping effort—that is, a consumer is unwilling to shop extensively for such an item. Bread, soft drinks, biscuits, soaps, and staples fall into the convenience product category.

Consumers buy convenience products regularly, usually without much planning. Nevertheless, consumers do know the brand names of popular convenience products, such as Coca-Cola, Parle-G biscuit, and Old Spice deodorant. Convenience products normally require wide distribution in order to sell sufficient quantities to meet profit goals. For example, the mint candy Chlormint is available everywhere, including Big Bazaar, Reliance Fresh, local grocery shops, corner paan shops, and tea stalls.

Shopping Products

A **shopping product** is usually more expensive than a convenience product and is found in fewer stores. Consumers usually buy a shopping product only after comparing several brands or stores on style, practicality, price, and lifestyle compatibility. They are willing to invest some effort into this process to get the desired benefits.

There are two types of shopping products: homogeneous and heterogeneous. Consumers perceive *homogenous shopping* products as basically similar—for example, microwave ovens, juicer mixers, refrigerators, and televisions. With homogenous shopping products, consumers typically look for the lowest-priced brand that has the desired features. For example, they might compare Godrej, Whirlpool, and LG refrigerators.

In contrast, consumers perceive *heterogeneous* shopping products as essentially different—for example, furniture, clothing, housing, and universities. Consumers often have trouble comparing heterogeneous shopping products because the prices, quality, and features vary so much. The benefit of comparing heterogeneous shopping products is "finding the best product or brand for me"; this decision is often highly individual. For example, it would be difficult to compare a small, private college with a large, public university.

Specialty Products

When consumers search extensively for a particular item and are very reluctant to accept substitutes, that item is a **speciality product**. Omega watches, Rolls-Royce automobiles, Bose speakers, Louis Vuitton bags, and highly specialized forms of medical care are generally considered speciality products.

Marketers of specialty products often use selective, status-conscious advertising to maintain a product's exclusive image. Distribution is often limited to one or a very few outlets in a geographic area. Brand names and quality of service are often very important.

Unsought Products

A product unknown to the potential buyer or a known product that the buyer does not actively seek is referred to as an **unsought product.** New products fall into this category until advertising and distribution increase consumer awareness of them.

Some goods are always marketed as unsought items, especially needed products we do not like to think about or care to spend money on. Insurance, mutual funds, and similar items require aggressive personal selling and highly persuasive advertising. Salespeople actively seek leads to potential buyers. Because consumers usually do not seek out this type of product, the company must go directly to them through a salesperson, direct mail, or direct response advertising.

LO 3 Product Items, Lines, and Mixes

Rarely does a company sell a single product. More often, it sells a variety of things. A **product item** is a specific version of a product that can be designated as a distinct offering among an organization's products. Maggi's Cream of Mushroom soup is an example of a product item (see Exhibit 10.1).

A group of closely related product items is called a **product line.** For example, the column in Exhibit 10.1 titled "Soups" represents one of Maggi's product lines. Different container sizes and shapes also distinguish items in a product line. Sprite, for example, is available in cans and various plastic containers. Each size and each container are separate product items.

An organization's **product mix** includes all the products it sells. All Maggi's products—2-minute noodles, sauces, soups, bhuna masala, and pazzta—constitute its product mix. Each product item in the product mix may require a separate marketing strategy. Organizations derive several benefits from organizing related items into product lines.

Product mix width (or breadth) refers to the number of product lines an organization offers. In Exhibit 10.1, for example, the width of Maggi's product mix is five product lines. **Product line depth** is the number of product items in a product line. As shown in Exhibit 10.1, the sauces product line consists of three product items; the pazzta product line includes four product items.

Firms increase the *width* of their product mix to diversify risk. To generate sales and boost profits,

unsought product a product unknown to the potential buyer or a known product that the buyer does not actively seek

product item a specific version of a product that can be designated as a distinct offering among an organization's products

product line a group of closely related product items

product mix all products that an organization sells

product mix width the number of product lines an organization offers

product line depth the number of product items in a product line

EXHIBIT 10.1
Maggi's Product Lines and Product Mix

Width of the Product Mix ⟵⟶

Depth of the Product Lines — DEPTH

2-Minute Noodles	Sauces	Soups	Bhuna Masala	Pazzta
Meri Masala	Rich Tomato	Rich Tomato	Gravy Dishes	Cheese Macaroni
Masala Dumdaar	Oriental Chilli Garlic	Mixed Vegetable	Vegetables and Dal	Masala Penne
Chicken	Hot & Sweet Tomato Chilli	Cream of Mushhroom		Tomato Twist
Tricky Tomato		Hot & Sour Vegetable		Mushroom Penne
Thrillin Curry		Sweet Corn Vegetable		
Vegetable Atta		Masala Noodles		
Vegetable Multigrainz		Creamy Chicken		

product modification changing one or more of a product's characteristics

planned obsolescence the practice of modifying products so those that have already been sold become obsolete before they actually need replacement

firms spread risk across many product lines rather than depend on only one or two. Firms also widen their product mix to capitalize on established reputations. The Amul milk brand extended its name to include butter, cheese, ice cream, traditional sweets, curd, and chocolates.

Firms increase the *depth* of their product lines to attract buyers with different preferences, to increase sales and profits by further segmenting the market, to capitalize on economies of scale in production and marketing, and to even out seasonal sales patterns. LG's line of Optimus Smartphones has ten different options, including the Optimus Chic, which is aimed at fashionistas who appreciate sleek curves on their phones.[1]

BENEFITS OF PRODUCT LINES

- *Advertising economies:* Product lines provide economies of scale in advertising. Several products can be advertised under the umbrella of the line. Maggi can talk about its sauce being "its different!" and promote the entire line.
- *Package uniformity:* A product line can benefit from package uniformity. All packages in the line may have a common look and still keep their individual identities. Maggi soup is a good example.
- *Standardized components:* Product lines allow firms to standardize components, thus reducing manufacturing and inventory costs. For example, General Motors uses the same parts on many automobile makes and models.
- *Efficient sales and distribution:* A product line enables sales personnel for companies like Procter & Gamble to provide a full range of choices to customers. Distributors and retailers are often more inclined to stock the company's products if it offers a full line. Transportation and warehousing costs are likely to be lower for a product line than for a collection of individual items.
- *Equivalent quality:* Purchasers usually expect and believe that all products in a line are about equal in quality. Consumers expect that all Maggi sauces and all Gillette razors will be of similar quality.

Adjustments to Product Items, Lines, and Mixes

Over time, firms change product items, lines, and mixes to take advantage of new technical or product developments or to respond to changes in the environment. They may adjust by modifying products, repositioning products, or extending or contracting product lines.

Product Modification Marketing managers must decide if and when to modify existing products. **Product modification** changes one or more of a product's characteristics:

- *Quality modification:* change in a product's dependability or durability. Reducing a product's quality may let the manufacturer lower the price and appeal to target markets unable to afford the original product. Karbonn Mobile does not have the same high-function capabilities as a Blackberry or HTC, but the lower price point makes it a viable mobile option. Conversely, increasing quality can help the firm compete with rival firms. Increasing quality can also result in increased brand loyalty, greater ability to raise prices, or new opportunities for market segmentation.
- *Functional modification:* change in a product's versatility, effectiveness, convenience, or safety. Before, each company had to hang a satellite for each unit, which could be unsightly and against apartment codes, but functional improvements in the technology now makes satellite service a viable apartment option.[2]
- *Style modification:* aesthetic product change rather than a quality or functional change. Clothing and auto manufacturers commonly use style modifications to motivate customers to replace products before they are worn out.

Planned obsolescence is a term commonly used to describe the practice of modifying products so that those that have already been sold become obsolete before they actually need replacement. For example, products such as printers and cell phones become obsolete because technology changes so quickly.

Some argue that planned obsolescence is wasteful; some claim it is unethical. Marketers respond that consumers favor style modifications because they like changes in the appearance of goods such as clothing and cars. Marketers also contend that consumers, not manufacturers and marketers, decide when styles are obsolete.

Repositioning Repositioning, as Chapter 8 explained, involves changing consumers' perceptions of a brand.

© TERRI MILLER/E-VISUAL COMMUNICATIONS, INC.

Tata Indica was launched in 1999 in the small car segment. But as time led by, the car was being used as a passenger car and customers were reluctant to buy it as a family car. The Tata team reworked on the car and reintroduced it as Tata Indica Vista in the Indian market. The new car promised to deliver a sedan like experience and boasted of new looks and powerful engine system. New features were added to offer quality experience to the customers and make their drive pleasurable.[3]

Product Line Extensions A **product line extension** occurs when a company's management decides to add products to an existing product line in order to compete more broadly in the industry. Hasbro/Mattel has added a series of games using the Scrabble name, some without boards or tiles, such as Scrabble Slam and a version with proper noun usage called Scrabble Trickster.[4]

A company can add too many products, or demand can change for the type of products that were introduced over time. When this happens, a product line is overextended. Product lines can be overextended when:

- Some products in the line do not contribute to profits because of low sales or cannibalize sales of other items in the line.
- Manufacturing or marketing resources are disproportionately allocated to slow-moving products.
- Some items in the line are obsolete because of new product entries in the line or new products offered by competitors.

Product Line Contraction Sometimes, marketers can get carried away with product extensions. (Does the world really need 31 varieties of Head & Shoulders shampoo?) Contracting product lines is a strategic way to deal with overextension. For example, when Procter & Gamble's Pantene brand lost 9 percent of sales in 2009, P&G marketing research showed that shoppers were overwhelmed by the wall of white. Pantene had 165 different products grouped into 14 collections. In an effort to regain the lost sales, P&G cut product offering to 120 items in four groups.[5]

Three major benefits are likely when a firm contracts overextended product lines. First, resources become concentrated on the most important products. Second, managers no longer waste resources trying to improve the sales and profits of poorly performing products. Third, new product items have a greater chance of being successful because more financial and human resources are available to manage them.

product line extension adding additional products to an existing product line in order to compete more broadly in the industry

brand a name, term, symbol, design, or combination thereof that identifies a seller's products and differentiates them from competitors' products

brand name that part of a brand that can be spoken, including letters, words, and numbers

brand mark the elements of a brand that cannot be spoken

brand equity the value of company and brand names

LO 4 Branding

The success of any business or consumer product depends in part on the target market's ability to distinguish one product from another. Branding is the main tool marketers use to distinguish their products from those of the competition.

A **brand** is a name, term, symbol, design, or combination thereof that identifies a seller's products and differentiates them from competitors' products. A **brand name** is that part of a brand that can be spoken, including letters (ITC, ICICI, NDTV, ESPN), words (Samsung, Bata), and numbers (Nokia 1100, Haywards 5000). The elements of a brand that cannot be spoken are called the **brand mark**—for example, the well-known Mercedes-Benz and Nike symbols.

Benefits of Branding

Branding has three main purposes: product identification, repeat sales, and new-product sales. The most important purpose is *product identification*. Branding allows marketers to distinguish their products from all others. Many brand names are familiar to consumers and indicate quality.

The term **brand equity** refers to the value of company and brand names. A brand that has high

global brand a brand that obtains at least a third of its earnings from outside its home country, is recognizable outside its home base of customers, and has publicly available marketing and financial data

brand loyalty consistent preference for one brand over all others

manufacturer's brand the brand name of a manufacturer

private brand a brand name owned by a wholesaler or a retailer

captive brand a brand manufactured by a third party for an exclusive retailer, without evidence of that retailer's affiliation

individual branding using different brand names for different products

awareness, perceived quality, and brand loyalty among customers has high brand equity. Starbucks, Apple, and Colgate are companies with high brand equity. A brand with strong brand equity is a valuable asset.

The term **global brand** refers to a brand that obtains at least a third of its earnings from outside its home country, is recognizable outside its home base of customers, and has publicly available marketing and financial data. Yum! Brands, which owns Pizza Hut, KFC, and Taco Bell, is a good example of a company that has developed strong global brands. Yum! believes that it has to adapt its restaurants to local tastes and different cultural and political climates. In Japan, for instance, KFC sells tempura crispy strips. In northern England, KFC focuses on gravy and potatoes, and in Thailand it offers rice with soy or sweet chilli sauce. Pizza Hut launched pizzas in chaat flavors in India to cater to the local tastes of the customers.

The best generator of *repeat sales* is satisfied customers. Branding helps consumers identify products they wish to buy again and avoid those they do not. **Brand loyalty**, a consistent preference for one brand over all others, is quite high in some product categories. More than half the consumers in product categories such as cigarettes, mayonnaise, toothpaste, coffee, headache remedies, bath soap, and ketchup are loyal to one brand. Many students go to college and purchase the same brands they used at home rather than choosing by price. Brand identity is essential to developing brand loyalty.

The third main purpose of branding is to *facilitate new-product sales*. Having a well-known and respected company and brand name is extremely useful when introducing new products.

Branding Strategies

Firms face complex branding decisions. Firms may choose to follow a policy of using manufacturers' brands, private (distributor) brands, or both. In either case, they must then decide among a policy of individual branding (different brands for different products), family branding (common names for different products), or a combination of individual branding and family branding.

Manufacturers' Brands versus Private Brands The brand name of a manufacturer—such as Kodak, Xerox, and IBM—is called a **manufacturer's brand.** Sometimes "national brand" is used as a synonym for "manufacturer's brand." This term is not always accurate, however, because many manufacturers serve only regional markets. Using "manufacturer's brand" precisely defines the brand's owner.

A **private brand**, also known as a private label or store brand, is a brand name owned by a wholesaler or a retailer. Future Group's Tasty Treat brand is a popular private label. Similarly, Westside sells mid-priced private label apparel under brand names such as Nuon, Gia, Richmond, and Ascot[6]. Part of the reason for the success of private brands is due to perceptions about quality. A survey conducted for the Private Label Manufacturers Association in New York found that 41 percent of shoppers identify themselves as frequent buyers of store brands, and seven out of ten feel the private label products they buy are as good as, if not better than, their national brand counterparts.[7]

Retailers love consumers' greater acceptance of private brands. Because overhead is low and there are no marketing costs, private label products bring 10 percent higher profit margins, on average, than manufacturers' brands. More than that, a trusted store brand can differentiate a chain from its competitors. Exhibit 10.2 illustrates key issues that wholesalers and retailers should consider in deciding whether to sell manufacturers' brands or private brands. Many firms offer a combination of both. Instead of marketing private brands as cheaper and inferior to manufacturers' brands, many retailers are creating and promoting their own **captive brands**. These brands carry no evidence of the store's affiliation, are manufactured by a third party, and are sold exclusively at the chains. This strategy allows the retailer to ask a price similar to manufacturer's brands, and they are typically displayed alongside mainstream products. For example, Feasters Noodles Family Pack, a line of instant noodles available only at Aditya Birla Retail, generates category revenues worth 40 percent.[8]

Walgreens, in the United States, has grown to become one of the top brands in the entire hair-care category.[9]

Individual Brands versus Family Brands Many companies use different brand names for different products, a practice referred to as **individual branding.**

EXHIBIT 10.2

Comparison of Manufacturers' and Private Brands from the Reseller's Perspective

Key Advantages of Carrying Manufacturers' Brands	Key Advantages of Carrying Private Brands
• Heavy advertising to the consumer by manufacturers such as Procter & Gamble helps develop strong consumer loyalties.	• A wholesaler or retailer can usually earn higher profits on its own brand. In addition, because the private brand is exclusive, there is less pressure to mark down the price to meet competition.
• Well-known manufacturers' brands, such as Kodak and Fisher-Price, can attract new customers and enhance the dealer's (wholesaler's or retailer's) prestige.	• A manufacturer can decide to drop a brand or a reseller at any time or even become a direct competitor to its dealers.
• Many manufacturers offer rapid delivery, enabling the dealer to carry less inventory.	• A private brand ties the customer to the wholesaler or retailer. A person who wants a DieHard battery must go to Sears.
• If a dealer happens to sell a manufacturer's brand of poor quality, the customer may simply switch brands and remain loyal to the dealer.	• Wholesalers and retailers have no control over the intensity of distribution of manufacturers' brands. Walmart store managers don't have to worry about competing with other sellers of Sam's American Choice products or Ol' Roy dog food. They know that these brands are sold only in Walmart and Sam's Club stores.

Companies use individual brands when their products vary greatly in use or performance. For instance, it would not make sense to use the same brand name for a pair of dress socks and a cricket bat. VIP targets different segments of the travel luggage market with Carlton, VIP, Skybags, Aristocrat, Alfa, and Footloose brands.

In contrast, a company that markets several different products under the same brand name is using a **family brand.** Tata's family brand includes insurance, teleservices, steel, motors, beverages, satellite television services, and IT services. The Heinz brand name is attached to products such as ketchup, mustard, and pickles.

Co-branding **Co-branding** entails placing two or more brand names on a product or its package. Three common types of co-branding are ingredient branding, cooperative branding, and complementary branding. *Ingredient branding* identifies the brand of a part that makes up the product— for example, majority of the computer and laptop makers attach a sticker on their machine that reads "Intel Inside", certifying that the machine is made from genuine Intel products. Likewise, Lycra is a fabric ingredient used in the manufacturing of a variety of garments. *Cooperative branding* occurs when two brands receiving equal treatment (in the context of an advertisement) borrow from each other's brand equity. ICICI launched a co-branded credit card with Big Bazaar to reward the loyal customers of the store chain. Finally, with *complementary branding*, products are advertised or marketed together to suggest usage, such as Luminous Power Technologies' inverter and battery.

family branding marketing several different products under the same brand name

co-branding placing two or more brand names on a product or its package

IMAGE COURTESY OF THE ADVERTISING ARCHIVES

trademark the exclusive right to use a brand or part of a brand

service mark a trademark for a service

generic product name identifies a product by class or type and cannot be trademarked

Co-branding is a useful strategy when a combination of brand names enhances the prestige or perceived value of a product or when it benefits brand owners and users. For example, HUL entered into a co-branding agreement with Disney's Tangled due to a direct connect between Rapunzel's story and Clinic Plus shmapoo's benefit of making hair long and strong.[10] Co-branding may be used to increase a company's presence in markets where it has little or no market share.

Trademarks

A **trademark** is the exclusive right to use a brand or part of a brand. Others are prohibited from using the brand without permission. A **service mark** performs the same function for services, such as SBI and Idea. Parts of a brand or other product identification may qualify for trademark protection. Some examples are:

- *Sounds*, such as the MGM lion's roar.
- *Shapes*, such as the Jeep front grille and the Coca-Cola bottle.
- *Ornamental color or design*, such as the decoration on Nike tennis shoes, the black-and-copper color combination of a Duracell battery, Levi's small tag on the left side of the rear pocket of its jeans, or the cutoff black cone on the top of Cross pens.
- *Catchy phrases*, such as Raymond's "The Complete Man," Mountain Dew's "Do the Dew," and Nike's "Just Do It!".
- *Abbreviations*, such as Bud, Coke, or The Met.

© ISTOCKPHOTO.COM/MUSTAFA DELIORMANLI

In November 1999, legislation went into effect in the United States that explicitly applies trademark law to the online world. This law includes financial penalties for those who violate trademarked products or register an otherwise trademarked term as a domain name.[11]

Companies that fail to protect their trademarks face the possibility that their product names will become generic. A **generic product name** identifies a product by class or type and cannot be trademarked. Former brand names that were not sufficiently protected by their owners and were subsequently declared to be generic product names by U.S. courts include aspirin, cellophane, linoleum, thermos, kerosene, monopoly, cola, and shredded wheat.

Companies such as Rolls-Royce, Cross, Xerox, Levi Strauss, Nike, and McDonald's aggressively enforce their trademarks. Rolls-Royce, Coca-Cola, and Xerox even run newspaper and magazine ads stating that their names are trademarks and should not be used as descriptive or generic terms.

NO BRAND, NO BUZZ

Commodity products like salt, sugar, wheat flour, pulses and rice are largely sold in unbranded forms. It is difficult to create any kind of differentiation in these products and price is the sole determining factor at the time of purchasing. With numerous fragmented players operating in the market, the customers cannot really tell one product from the other. Tata Salt pioneered the concept of branded salt in India in 1983. It was the first packaged iodised salt launched in the country, with the promise of purity and consistency. The launch also supported the cause of the then Indian government - that of promoting iodised salt to curb iodine deficiency diseases. The novel value proposition helped Tata Salt in building credibility and establishing a formidable position in the market. The trust that the consumers have in the brand can be gauged from the fact that Tata Salt has been ranked as the number one food brand for almost 10 years now in the survey of "most trusted brands" by The Economic Times Brand Equity.[14]

Despite severe penalties for trademark violations, trademark infringement lawsuits are not uncommon. Serious conflict can occur when brand names resemble one another too closely. Amul filed a similar case against two local shop owners in Gujarat, who operated shops under the name *Amul Chasmaghar* and *Amul Cut Piece Stores*. The court ruled that there was an infringement of trademark and ordered the two shop owners to stop using the name.[12]

Companies must also contend with fake or unauthorized brands. Knockoffs of trademarked clothing lines are easy to find in cheap shops all over the world, and loose imitations are found in some reputable department stores as well. Producers of the Hollywood movie, *Hitch*, planned to file a lawsuit against the producers of *Partners*, a Bollywood movie, on the account that *Partners* was an obvious copy of *Hitch*.[13]

In Europe, you can sue counterfeiters only if your brand, logo, or trademark is formally registered. Until recently, formal registration was required in each country in which a company sought protection. A company can now register its trademark in all European Union (EU) member countries with one application.

LO 5 Packaging

Packages have always served a practical function—that is, they hold contents together and protect goods as they move through the distribution channel. Today, however, packaging is also a container for promoting the product and making it easier and safer to use.

Packaging Functions

The three most important functions of packaging are to contain and protect products; promote products; and facilitate the storage, use, and convenience of products. A fourth function of packaging that is becoming increasingly important is to facilitate recycling and reduce environmental damage.

Containing and Protecting Products The most obvious function of packaging is to contain products that are liquid, granular, or otherwise divisible. Packaging also enables manufacturers, wholesalers, and retailers to market products in specific quantities, such as kilograms.

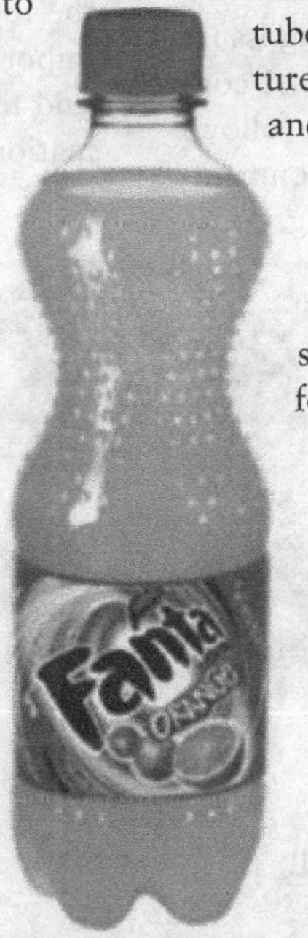

Physical protection is another obvious function of packaging. Most products are handled several times between the time they are manufactured, harvested, or otherwise produced and the time they are consumed or used. Many products are also shipped, stored, and inspected several times between production and consumption. Some, like milk, need to be refrigerated. Others, like beer, are sensitive to light. Still others, like medicines and bandages, need to be kept sterile. Packages protect products from breakage, evaporation, spillage, spoilage, light, heat, cold, infestation, and many other conditions.

Promoting Products Packaging does more than identify the brand, list the ingredients, specify features, and give directions. A package differentiates a product from competing products and may associate a new product with a family of other products from the same manufacturer. Fanta, the orange flavoured drink from Coca-Cola, redid its packaging with a more youthful style, and introduced the spin bottle in the year 2005 that reflected the fun element of the brand. The brand has always been targeting the youth and the new packaging, along with a change in the formulation, intended to symbolize the exuberance and excitement of the youth.[15] HUL partnered with Disney to design new packaging for its brand *Kissan Jam*. The product was launched in easy-to-squeeze tubes and was named *Kissan Jam Squeeze*. The tubes were launched in vibrant colours and featured famous Disney characters such as Mougli and Sher Khan.[16]

Packages use designs, colors, shapes, and materials to try to influence consumers' perceptions and buying behavior. For example, marketing research shows that health-conscious consumers are likely to think that any food is probably good for them as long as it comes in green packaging. Packaging can also influence consumer perceptions of quality and/or prestige. And packaging has a measurable effect on sales. Tropicana attempted to redesign its packaging with a more modern design, but the customer response was so negative that the company returned to its previous packaging—the iconic orange with a straw in it.[17]

persuasive labeling a type of package labeling that focuses on a promotional theme or logo, and consumer information is secondary

informational labeling a type of package labeling designed to help consumers make proper product selections and lower their cognitive dissonance after the purchase

Facilitating Storage, Use, and Convenience Wholesalers and retailers prefer packages that are easy to ship, store, and stock on shelves. They also like packages that protect products, prevent spoilage or breakage, and extend the product's shelf life.

Consumers' requirements for storage, use, and convenience cover many dimensions. Consumers are constantly seeking items that are easy to handle, open, and reclose, although some consumers want packages that are tamperproof or childproof. Research indicates that hard-to-open packages are among consumers' top complaints.[18] Surveys conducted in the United States by *Sales & Marketing Management* magazine revealed that consumers dislike—and avoid buying—leaky ice cream boxes, overly heavy or fat vinegar bottles, immovable pry-up lids on glass bottles, key-opener sardine cans, and hard-to-pour cereal boxes.

Some firms use packaging to segment markets. For example, Calcium Sandoz comes in different packaging for different segments – a distinct puppy pack for children and an exclusive woman's face shaped pack for women. Different-sized packages appeal to heavy, moderate, and light users. Maggi's Cuppa Mania instant noodles is packaged in a cup-shaped container and is targeted towards busy, time-crunched executives.[19] Packaging convenience can increase a product's utility and, therefore, its market share and profits.

Facilitating Recycling and Reducing Environmental Damage One of the most important packaging issues today is eco-consciousness. In a recent study of consumers, a majority said they would give up the following conveniences if it would benefit the environment: packaging designed for easy stacking or storing, packaging that can be used for cooking, and packaging designed for easy transport.[20] Some firms use their packaging to target environmentally concerned market segments. For example, Frito-Lay introduced 100 percent compostable bags in the United States for its product—SunChips with a label from Biodegradable Products Institute (BPI) to remind consumers to compost the chip bags. BPI has a labeling program that certifies that the products carrying the label will degrade completely in commercial compost facilities. Programs like these help educate manufacturers, legislators, and consumers about the benefits and how to compost.[21]

© ISTOCKPHOTO.COM/FILONMAR

Labeling

An integral part of any package is its label. Labeling generally takes one of two forms: persuasive or informational. **Persuasive labeling** focuses on a promotional theme or logo, and consumer information is secondary. Note that the standard promotional claims—such as "new," "improved," and "super"—are no longer very persuasive. Consumers have been saturated with "newness" and thus discount these claims.

Informational labeling, in contrast, is designed to help consumers make proper product selections and lower their cognitive dissonance after the purchase. Most major furniture manufacturers affix labels to their wares that explain the products' construction features, such as type of frame, number of coils, and fabric characteristics. The Nutritional Labeling and Education Act of 1990, United States, mandated detailed nutritional information on most food packages and standards for health claims on food packaging. An important outcome of this legislation has been guidelines from the Food and Drug Administration for using terms such as *low fat*, *light*, *reduced cholesterol*, *low sodium*, *low calorie*, *low carb*, and *fresh*. In India too, as per the Prevention of Food Adulteration Rules, 1955, that come under the purview of Prevention of Food Adulteration Act, 1954, it is mandatory for food manufacturers to disclose health and nutritional information on the food labels. Getting the right information is very important to consumers—so much so that 59 percent said they check and understand the nutritional information given on food packaging.[22]

Greenwashing There are numerous products in every product category that use *greenwashing* to try and sell products. Greenwashing is when a product or company attempts to give the impression of environmental friendliness whether or not it is environmentally friendly.

There are many ways a company can greenwash its products because environmental certification is not regulated by the government. Companies find their own certification, and whereas

SHOOTING FOR GLOBAL BRANDING

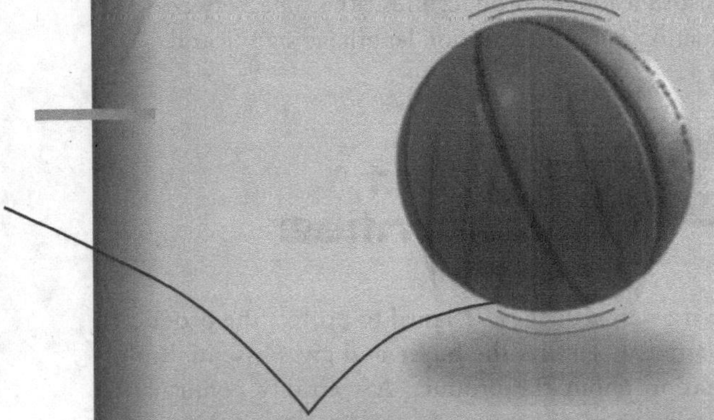

Nike Brand president Charlie Denson views endorsements from players like LeBron James (Miami Heat) and Stephen Strasburg (Washington Nationals) in terms of their potential for becoming assets to the brand. If LeBron wins championships, his endorsement carries greater weight for Nike. In addition to carrying weight in the United States, endorsements from basketball players puts Nike into the global market, which is increasingly important as the International Basketball Federation (FIBA) strives to make the World Championship a noteworthy event. Nike already has a strong presence at global sporting events such as the World Cup, which they entered as one of the largest soccer brands (including subsidiary Umbro). Denson has said that Nike is "dealing with a global game in terms of marketing." It is a game he has apparently embraced.[23]

some certification organizations, such as EcoLogo, work with third-party scientists to verify emissions or biodegradability, others rely on the company to verify that its product is green. Some companies do not provide any evidence to support their claims. Others lie. With more than 300 possible certification labels, ranging in price from free to thousands of dollars, the possibilities of false or misleading environmental claims are real.

The Energy Star program, which can earn consumers tax breaks and claims to save them money on their electric bills, relies on the appliance manufacturers to self-certify their products. As a result, LG had to pay for consumers' electric bills when one of its Energy Star refrigerator lines failed to meet U.S. Department of Energy testing standards.[24]

Universal Product Codes

The **universal product codes (UPCs)** that appear on most items in supermarkets and other high-volume outlets were first introduced in 1974. Because the numerical codes appear as a series of thick and thin vertical lines, they are often called *bar codes*. The lines are read by computerized optical scanners that match codes with brand names, package sizes, and prices. They also print information on cash register tapes and help retailers rapidly and accurately prepare records of customer purchases, control inventories, and track sales. The UPC system and scanners are also used in scanner-based research (see Chapter 9).

LO 6 Global Issues in Branding and Packaging

When planning to enter a foreign market with an existing product, a firm has three options for handling the brand name:

universal product codes (UPCs) a series of thick and thin vertical lines (bar codes), readable by computerized optical scanners, that represent numbers used to track products

- *One brand name everywhere:* This strategy is useful when the company markets mainly one product and the brand name does not have negative connotations in any local market. The Coca-Cola Company uses a one-brand-name strategy in more than 195 countries around the world. The advantages of a one-brand-name strategy are greater identification of the product from market to market and ease of coordinating promotion from market to market.
- *Adaptations and modifications:* A one-brand-name strategy is not possible when the name cannot be pronounced in the local language, when the brand name is owned by someone else, or when the brand name has a negative or vulgar connotation in the local language. The Iranian detergent "Barf," for example, might encounter some problems in the U.S. market.
- *Different brand names in different markets:* Local brand names are often used when translation or pronunciation problems occur, when the marketer wants the brand to appear to be a local brand, or when regulations

warranty a confirmation of the quality or performance of a good or service

express warranty a written guarantee

implied warranty an unwritten guarantee that the good or service is fit for the purpose for which it was sold

require localization. Gillette's Silkience hair conditioner is called Soyance in France and Sientel in Italy. Coca-Cola's Sprite brand had to be renamed Kin in Korea to satisfy a government prohibition on the unnecessary use of foreign words.

In addition to global branding decisions, companies must consider global packaging needs. Three aspects of packaging that are especially important in international marketing are labeling, aesthetics, and climate considerations. The major *labeling* concern is properly translating ingredient, promotional, and instructional information on labels. Care must also be employed in meeting all local labeling requirements. Several years ago, an Italian judge ordered that all bottles of Coca-Cola be removed from retail shelves because the ingredients were not properly labeled. Labeling is also harder in countries like Belgium and Finland, which require packaging to be bilingual.

Package *aesthetics* may also require some attention. Even though simple visual elements of the brand, such as a symbol or logo, can be a standardizing element across products and countries, marketers must stay attuned to cultural traits in host countries. For example, colors may have different connotations. Red is associated with witchcraft in some countries, green may be a sign of danger, and white may be symbolic of death. Such cultural differences could necessitate a packaging change if colors are chosen for another country's interpretation. In the United States, green typically symbolizes an eco-friendly product, but that packaging could keep customers away in a country where green indicates danger. Aesthetics also influence package size. Soft drinks are not sold in six-packs in countries that lack refrigeration. In some countries, products such as detergent may be bought only in small quantities because of a lack of storage space. Other products, such as cigarettes, may be bought in small quantities, and even single units, because of the low purchasing power of buyers.

Extreme climates and long-distance shipping necessitate sturdier and more durable packages for goods sold overseas. Spillage, spoilage, and breakage are all more important concerns when products are shipped long distances or frequently handled during shipping and storage. Packages may also have to ensure a longer product life if the time between production and consumption lengthens significantly.

LO 7 Product Warranties

Just as a package is designed to protect the product, a warranty protects the buyer and gives essential information about the product. A warranty confirms the quality or performance of a good or service. An **express warranty** is a written guarantee. Express warranties range from simple statements—such as "100-percent cotton" (a guarantee of quality) and "complete satisfaction guaranteed" (a statement of performance)—to extensive documents written in technical language. In contrast, an **implied warranty** is an unwritten guarantee that the good or service is fit for the purpose for which it was sold. All sales have an implied warranty under the Uniform Commercial Code.

United States' Congress passed the Magnuson-Moss Warranty–Federal Trade Commission Improvement Act in 1975 to help consumers understand warranties and get action from manufacturers and dealers. A manufacturer that promises a full warranty must meet certain minimum standards, including repair "within a reasonable time and without charge" of any defects and replacement of the merchandise or a full refund if the product does not work "after a reasonable number of attempts" at repair. Any warranty that does not live up to this tough prescription must be "conspicuously" promoted as a limited warranty.

Review and Applications

Define the term product. A product is anything, desired or not, that a person or organization receives in an exchange. The basic goal of purchasing decisions is to receive the tangible and intangible benefits associated with a product. Tangible aspects include packaging, style, color, size, and features. Intangible qualities include service, the retailer's image, the manufacturer's reputation, and the social status associated with a product. An organization's product offering is the crucial element in any marketing mix.

1.1 Form a team of four or five members. Have the team determine what the tangible and intangible benefits are for a computer, a tube of toothpaste, a beauty salon, and a dentist.

Classify consumer products. Consumer products are classified into four categories: convenience products, shopping products, specialty products, and unsought products. Convenience products are relatively inexpensive and require limited shopping effort. Shopping products are of two types: homogeneous and heterogeneous. Because of the similarity of homogeneous products, they are differentiated mainly by price and features. In contrast, heterogeneous products appeal to consumers because of their distinct characteristics. Specialty products possess unique benefits that are highly desirable to certain customers. Finally, unsought products are either new products or products that require aggressive selling because they are generally avoided or overlooked by consumers.

2.1 Break into groups of four or five. Have the members of the group classify each of the following products into the category (convenience, shopping, specialty, unsought) that they think fits best from their perspective as consumers (i.e., if they were buying the product): Coca-Cola (brand), car stereo, winter coat, pair of shoes, life insurance, blue jeans, fast-food hamburgers, shampoo, canned vegetables, curtains.

2.2 Although major appliances, like washers and dryers, are usually considered homogeneous shopping products, the high-efficiency front-loaders that boast many more features than standard machines are gaining in popularity. Do you think high-efficiency technology is enough to make washers and dryers heterogeneous shopping products? Explain.

Define the terms *product item*, *product line*, and *product mix*. A product item is a specific version of a product that can be designated as a distinct offering among an organization's products. A product line is a group of closely related products offered by an organization. An organization's product mix includes all the products it sells. Product mix width refers to the number of product lines an organization offers. Product line depth is the number of product items in a product line. Firms modify existing products by changing their quality, functional characteristics, or style. Product line extension occurs when a firm adds new products to existing product lines.

3.1 A local civic organization has asked you to give a luncheon presentation about planned obsolescence. Rather than pursuing a negative approach by talking about how businesses exploit customers through planned obsolescence, you have decided to talk about the benefits of producing products that do not last forever. Prepare a one-page outline of your presentation.

3.2 Go to Unilever's Web site at **www.unilever.com.** Can Unilever delete anything from its product lines? Visit the company's product category pages on its "Brands" Web page to see the number of existing products and new products planned. Write a proposal for contracting one of Unilever's product lines.

Describe marketing uses of branding. A brand is a name, term, or symbol that identifies and differentiates a firm's products. Established brands encourage customer loyalty and help new products succeed. Branding strategies require decisions about individual, family, manufacturers', and private brands.

4.1 A local supermarket would like to introduce its own brand of paper goods (e.g., paper towels, facial tissue, etc.) to sell alongside its current inventory. The company has hired you to generate a report outlining the advantages and disadvantages of doing so. Write the report.

Describe marketing uses of packaging and labeling. Packaging has four functions: containing and protecting products; promoting products; facilitating product storage, use, and convenience; and facilitating recycling and reducing environmental damage. As a tool for promotion, packaging identifies the brand and its features. It also serves the critical function of differentiating a product from competing products and linking it with related products from the same manufacturer. The label is an integral part of the package, with persuasive and informational functions. In essence, the package is the marketer's last chance to influence buyers before they make a purchase decision.

5.1 Find a product at home that has a distinctive package. Write a paragraph evaluating that package based on the four functions of packaging discussed in the chapter.

Discuss global issues in branding and packaging. In addition to brand piracy, international marketers must address a variety of concerns regarding branding and packaging, including choosing a brand-name policy, translating labels and meeting host-country labeling requirements, making packages aesthetically compatible with host-country cultures, and offering the sizes of packages preferred in host countries.

6.1 List the countries to which Levi Strauss & Co. markets through the Web site **www.levi.com.** How do the product offerings differ between the U.S. and European selections?

Describe how and why product warranties are important marketing tools. Product warranties are important tools because they offer consumers protection and help them gauge product quality.

7.1 Think of some product categories that offer product guarantees. Compare the terms and conditions of guarantee of one category with another. What differences do you find between the guarantee offered for two different product categories? What do you think may happen if these product categories stop offering guarantee?

Exercises

APPLICATION EXERCISE

What is your favourite brand of potato chips? Chances are it is Lay's. In fact, Lay's chips are so popular that they have dominated the category for a long time. But before Lay's chips were launched in India, we had another brand serving the Indian market – Uncle Chips. But with Lay's superior distribution and advertising, Uncle Chips was soon outmatched and the sales plummeted. Uncle Chips was finally taken over by PepsiCo, who is also the owner of Lay's chips. Now, the company is making an attempt to give Uncle Chips a facelift to offer more variety and choice to the customers, in the wake of new competition entering the market. You are part of PepsiCo team deciding what to do with the Uncle Chips brand.

Activities

1. Can you re-create Uncle Chips through a name change? What kind of brand name could supplement Lay's? Make a list of three to five possibilities.
2. How can you package your renewed chips to make it stand out on the shelf? What about package size? Draft a brief packaging plan for the new Uncle Chips (or whatever name you chose).
3. Can you modify the original formula to make something new and more competitive? Will a brand extension work here? Why or why not?

ETHICS EXERCISE

A product that a potential buyer knows about but is not actively seeking is called an unsought product. Is the marketing of unsought products unethical? Discuss your answer in terms of the AMA Statement of Ethics, found at **www.marketingpower.com.**

MARKETING PLAN EXERCISE

In the first part of your strategic marketing plan, you stated your business mission and objectives, and performed a detailed SWOT analysis. In the second part of the plan you identified and described target market segments and described their buying behaviors and decision-making processes. In addition, you identified sources of competitive intelligence and the need for any further marketing research before the marketing plan could be implemented. The next stages of the strategic planning process involve defining the elements of the marketing mix: (Part 3) product, (Part 4) place, (Part 5) promotion, and (Part 6) pricing strategies.

After reading Chapter 10, you can use the following exercises to guide you through the third part of your strategic marketing plan:

1. How would you classify the offering to your customers? Is it a consumer product? A business-to-business product? A good or a service? How does this classification change the focus of your e-marketing plan? Is your product unique

enough to be patented? Check with the U.S. Patent and Trademark Office at **www.uspto.gov**.

2. Place your company's offerings into a product portfolio. Consider the broader impact of marketing a product item within a line or mix. Factors to consider are those such as price, image, complementary products, distribution relationship, and so on. Are there any special product features that selling on the Internet would allow you to add or force you to take away?

3. Does your chosen company have a brand name and brand mark? If not, design both. If so, evaluate the ability of the brand name and mark to communicate effectively to the target market. Is strong branding more or less important in an Internet environment? Why? What makes branding so important?

4. What will your company Internet address be? To check and see what URLs are available, go to **www.companyname.com** and try some out. Should your URL be the same as your company name? Why or why not? What happens if a customer mistypes your name? Should you register under alternative spellings?

5. Is the product packaged and labeled? How should it be packaged and why? Does the package and label design match other communications tools? How is this an opportunity to communicate with your customers?

6. Evaluate warranties or guarantees offered by your firm, including product return policies. How will customers return products they purchased from the Web site? Design the parameters for warranties and return policies. Should your return policy be stricter on-line than offline? Why or why not?

Short Case: GARNIER FRUCTIS FORTIFYING SHAMPOO +OIL

Prepared by
Dr. Dheeraj Sharma,
Indian Institute of Management, Ahmedabad

Garnier is an old and trusted name in the Indian cosmetic industry. It is involved in selling various creams, face and body washes, haircolor, hair gels, deodorants, shampoos, etc.

Garnier Fructis shampoo is one of the leading shampoo brands in India. It has launched various types of shampoos in different ranges. It offers specialized shampoos and conditioners for long hair, curly hair, straight hair, damaged hair, dry hall, etc., and for hair problems like hall fall, dandruff, and damaged hair. Recently, Garnier came up with this really innovative product called Garnier Fructis Fortifying Shampoo +Oil. This product was created keeping in mind the Indian tradition of applying coconut oil, massaging the scalp and leaving it overnight. This was done to make hair healthy by providing it with nutrition and conditioning from the oil. Similarly, shampooing was a practice to clean the dirt and the accumulated natural oil in one's hair. Today, this tradition is not widely practiced by the people in the younger generation. People don't really have the time to oil, massage, and then leave their hair overnight, to wash it off the next morning. Garnier's Fructis Fortifying Shampoo +Oil, 2 in 1 shampoo was created to solve this problem. Garnier claims that this product will penetrate the oil to each layer of hair and will nourish them from within. The result of using this product would be smooth and shiny hair by just spending two minutes.[25]

The targets for this product are the people who do not have enough time oil their hair, and who did not like the practice of applying hair oil regularly. This product, if successful, could also lead to a shift from hair oil users to using the "Fructis shampoo +oil" shampoo.

Questions

1. Do you think by launching the Fructis Fortifying Shampoo +oil, Garnier is trying to compete with the hair-oil manufacturers? Do you think people will actually switch to using the shampoo as a substitute for hairoil?

2. Given that many people in India shampoo their hair to get rid of the oil in it. Do you think Garnier has the right positioning?

10 | Product Concepts

KEY TERMS

LO 1

product everything, both favorable and unfavorable, that a person receives in an exchange

LO 2

business product (industrial product) a product used to manufacture other goods or services, to facilitate an organization's operations, or to resell to other customers

consumer product a product bought to satisfy an individual's personal wants

convenience product a relatively inexpensive item that merits little shopping effort

shopping product a product that requires comparison shopping because it is usually more expensive than a convenience product and is found in fewer stores

specialty product a particular item that consumers search extensively for and are very reluctant to accept substitutes

unsought product a product unknown to the potential buyer or a known product that the buyer does not actively seek

LO 3

product item a specific version of a product that can be designated as a distinct offering among an organization's products

product line a group of closely related product items

product mix all products that an organization sells

product mix width the number of product lines an organization offers

product line depth the number of product items in a product line

product modification changing one or more of a product's characteristics

KEY CONCEPTS

LO 1 **Define the term *product*.** A product is anything, desired or not, that a person or organization receives in an exchange. The basic goal of purchasing decisions is to receive the tangible and intangible benefits associated with a product. Tangible aspects include packaging, style, color, size, and features. Intangible qualities include service, the retailer's image, the manufacturer's reputation, and the social status associated with a product. An organization's product offering is the crucial element in any marketing mix.

LO 2 **Classify consumer products.** Consumer products are classified into four categories: convenience products, shopping products, specialty products, and unsought products. Convenience products are relatively inexpensive and require limited shopping effort. Shopping products are of two types: homogeneous and heterogeneous. Because of the similarity of homogeneous products, they are differentiated mainly by price and features. In contrast, heterogeneous products appeal to consumers because of their distinct characteristics. Specialty products possess unique benefits that are highly desirable to certain customers. Finally, unsought products are either new products or products that require aggressive selling because they are generally avoided or overlooked by consumers.

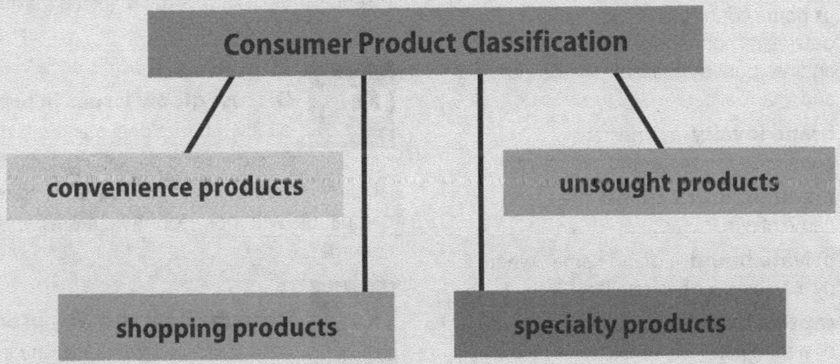

© CENGAGE LEARNING 2011

LO 3 **Define the terms *product item, product line,* and *product mix.*** A product item is a specific version of a product that can be designated as a distinct offering among an organization's products. A product line is a group of closely related products offered by an organization. An organization's product mix includes all the products it sells. Product mix width refers to the number of product lines an organization offers. Product line depth is the number of product items in a product line. Firms modify existing products by changing their quality, functional characteristics, or style. Product line extension occurs when a firm adds new products to existing product lines.

LO 4 **Describe marketing uses of branding.** A brand is a name, term, or symbol that identifies and differentiates a firm's products. Established brands encourage customer loyalty and help new products succeed. Branding strategies require decisions about individual, family, manufacturers', and private brands.

planned obsolescence the practice of modifying products so those that have already been sold become obsolete before they actually need replacement

product line extension adding additional products to an existing product line in order to compete more broadly in the industry

LO 4 **brand** a name, term, symbol, design, or combination thereof that identifies a seller's products and differentiates them from competitors' products

brand name that part of a brand that can be spoken, including letters, words, and numbers

brand mark the elements of a brand that cannot be spoken

brand equity the value of company and brand names

global brand a brand that obtains at least a third of its earnings from outside its home country, is recognizable outside its home base of customers, and has publicly available marketing and financial data

brand loyalty a consistent preference for one brand over all others

manufacturer's brand the brand name of a manufacturer

private brand a brand name owned by a wholesaler or a retailer

captive brand a brand manufactured by a third party for an exclusive retailer, without evidence of that retailer's affiliation

individual branding using different brand names for different products

family branding marketing several different products under the same brand name

co-branding placing two or more brand names on a product or its package

trademark the exclusive right to use a brand or part of a brand

service mark a trademark for a service

generic product name identifies a product by class or type and cannot be trademarked

Comparing Manufacturers' and Private Brands from the Reseller's Perspective

Key Advantages of Carrying Manufacturers' Brands	Key Advantages of Carrying Private Brands
• Heavy advertising to the consumer by manufacturers such as Procter & Gamble helps develop strong consumer loyalties.	• A wholesaler or retailer can usually earn higher profits on its own brand. In addition, because the private brand is exclusive, there is less pressure to mark down the price to meet competition.
• Well-known manufacturers' brands, such as Kodak and Fisher-Price, can attract new customers and enhance the dealer's (wholesaler's or retailer's) prestige.	• A manufacturer can decide to drop a brand or a reseller at any time or even become a direct competitor to its dealers.
• Many manufacturers offer rapid delivery, enabling the dealer to carry less inventory.	• A private brand ties the customer to the wholesaler or retailer. A person who wants a DieHard battery must go to Sears.
• If a dealer happens to sell a manufacturer's brand of poor quality, the customer may simply switch brands and remain loyal to the dealer.	• Wholesalers and retailers have no control over the intensity of distribution of manufacturers' brands. Walmart store managers don't have to worry about competing with other sellers of Sam's American Choice products or Ol' Roy dog food. They know that these brands are sold only in Walmart and Sam's Club stores.

LO 5 **Describe marketing uses of packaging and labeling.** Packaging has four functions: containing and protecting products; promoting products; facilitating product storage, use, and convenience; and facilitating recycling and reducing environmental damage. As a tool for promotion, packaging identifies the brand and its features. It also serves the critical function of differentiating a product from competing products and linking it with related products from the same manufacturer. The label is an integral part of the package, with persuasive and informational functions. In essence, the package is the marketer's last chance to influence buyers before they make a purchase decision.

LO 6 **Discuss global issues in branding and packaging.** In addition to brand piracy, international marketers must address a variety of concerns regarding branding and packaging, including choosing a brand-name policy, translating labels and meeting host-country labeling requirements, making packages aesthetically compatible with host-country cultures, and offering the sizes of packages preferred in host countries.

LO 7 **Describe how and why product warranties are important marketing tools.** Product warranties are important tools because they offer consumers protection and help them gauge product quality.

LO 5 **persuasive labeling** a type of package labeling that focuses on a promotional theme or logo, and consumer information is secondary

informational labeling a type of package labeling designed to help consumers make proper product selections and lower their cognitive dissonance after the purchase

universal product codes (UPCs) a series of thick and thin vertical lines (bar codes), readable by computerized optical scanners, that represent numbers used to track products

LO 7 **warranty** a confirmation of the quality or performance of a good or service

express warranty a written guarantee

implied warranty an unwritten guarantee that the good or service is fit for the purpose for which it was sold

CHAPTER 11

Developing and Managing Products

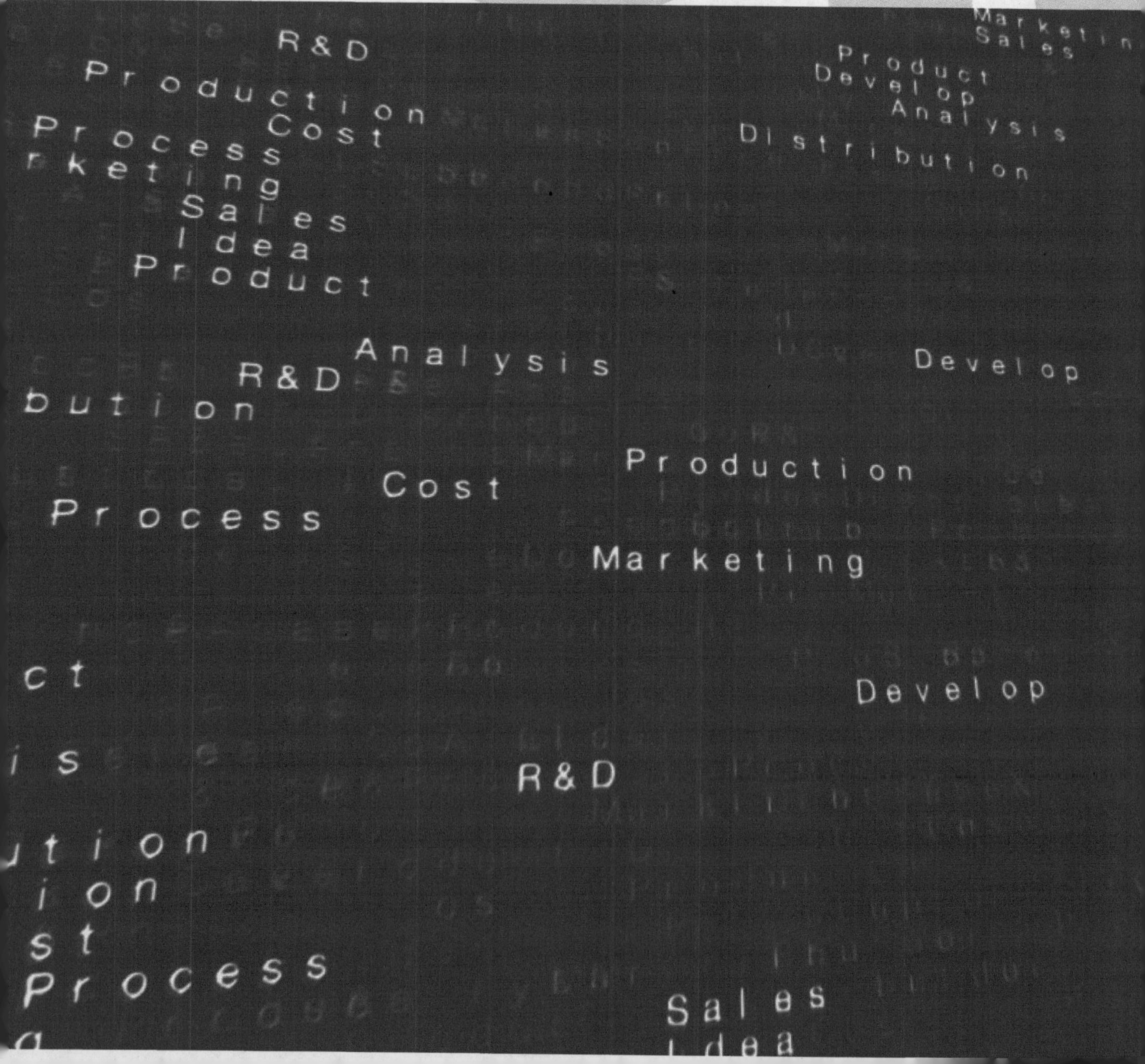

Learning Outcomes

LO 1 Explain the importance of developing new products and describe the six categories of new products

LO 2 Explain the steps in the new-product development process

LO 3 Discuss global issues in new-product development

LO 4 Explain the diffusion process through which new products are adopted

LO 5 Explain the concept of product life cycles

The average fast-moving consumer goods company introduces 70 to 80 new products per year.

LO 1 The Importance of New Products

New products are important to sustain growth, increase revenues and profits, and replace obsolete items. Research by *BusinessWeek* and the Boston Consulting Group revealed that the world's 25 most innovative companies have higher average stock returns and higher average revenue growth than companies that were not included in this group.[1] The *BusinessWeek*–Boston Consulting Group's list includes firms such as Apple, Google, Microsoft, IBM, and Toyota.[2] These firms are known for innovative products. Other firms on the list are known for innovative business models, innovative customer experience, and/or innovative processes.[3]

new product a product new to the world, the market, the producer, the seller, or some combination of these

Categories of New Products

The term **new product** is somewhat confusing because its meaning varies widely. Actually, the term has several "correct" definitions. A product can be new to the world, to the market, to the producer or seller, or some combination of these. There are six categories of new products:

- *New-to-the-world products (also called discontinuous innovations):* These products create an entirely new market. New-to-the-world products represent the smallest category of new products.

©ISTOCKPHOTO/THINKSTOCK

***Note:** All the figures in U.S. dollars are converted into rupee using the value $1 = ₹45.*

new-product strategy a plan that links the new-product development process with the objectives of the marketing department, the business unit, and the corporation

- *New product lines:* These products, which the firm has not previously offered, allow it to enter an established market. For example, ITC, a tobacco-to-hotels conglomerate, introduced a range of soaps and shampoos called Fiama Di Wills and Vivel for the premium and mid-market segment respectively to enter the personal care market.[4]
- *Additions to existing product lines:* This category includes new products that supplement a firm's established line. Brooke Bond's Red Label tea added to its tea line with the Red Label Natural Care, which enhances the health immunity and reduces the chances of falling ill.
- *Improvements or revisions of existing products:* The "new and improved" product may be significantly or only slightly changed. Surf Excel, a detergent brand from HUL, released a new version of its product, called Surf Excel Matic, that specialized in removing tough stains in the washing machine itself.[5]
- *Repositioned products:* These are existing products targeted at new markets or market segments, or ones repositioned to change the current market's perception of the product, which may be done to boost declining sales. Indian telecom service provider brand Airtel, hoping to reach out to global audience and promoting its 3G offerings, repositioned itself as a brand that delivers anything the consumers desire, anytime and anywhere.[6]
- *Lower-priced products:* This category refers to products that provide performance similar to competing brands at a lower price. HP LaserJet 3100 is a scanner, copier, printer, and fax machine combined. This new product is priced lower than many conventional color copiers and much lower than the combined price of the four items purchased separately.

LO 2 The New-Product Development Process

The management consulting firm Booz Allen Hamilton has studied the new-product development process for more than 30 years. Analyzing five major studies undertaken during this period, the firm has concluded that the companies most likely to succeed in developing and introducing new products are those that take the following actions:

- Make the long-term commitment needed to support innovation and new-product development.
- Use a company-specific approach, driven by corporate objectives and strategies, with a well-defined new-product strategy at its core.
- Capitalize on experience to achieve and maintain competitive advantage.
- Establish an environment—a management style, organizational structure, and degree of top management support—conducive to achieving company-specific new-product and corporate objectives.

Most companies follow a formal new-product development process, usually starting with a new-product strategy. Exhibit 11.1 traces the seven-step process, which is discussed in detail in this section. The exhibit is funnel shaped to highlight the fact that each stage acts as a screen. The purpose is to filter out unworkable ideas.

New-Product Strategy

A **new-product strategy** links the new-product development process with the objectives of the marketing department, the business unit, and the corporation. A new-product strategy must be compatible with these

EXHIBIT 11.1
New-Product Development Process

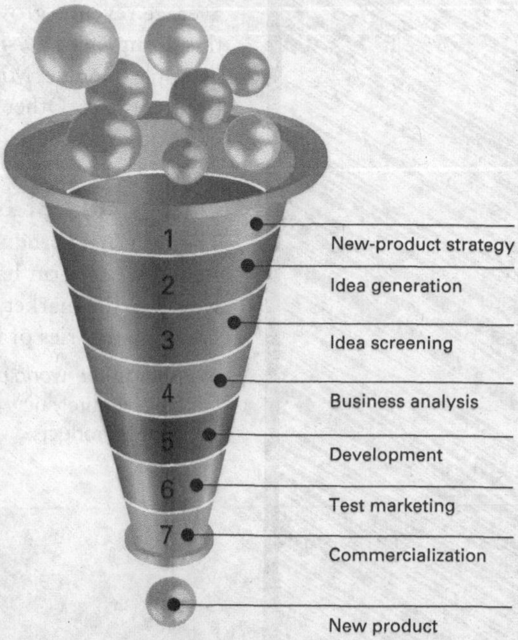

objectives, and in turn, all three of the objectives must be consistent with one another.

A new-product strategy is part of the organization's overall marketing strategy. It sharpens the focus and provides general guidelines for generating, screening, and evaluating new-product ideas. The new-product strategy specifics the roles that new products must play in the organization's overall plan and describes the characteristics of products the organization wants to offer and the markets it wants to serve.

In the traditional development process of new products, many versions of a core idea are discussed, tested, winnowed, and retested until a winning product emerges. Businesses should expect four out of five new products to fail under a strict traditional model.[7] However, companies continue to work to innovate. For example, Procter & Gamble has made a public commitment to introduce ₹90,000 crore worth of "sustainable, innovative products" between 2008 and 2013.[8]

Idea Generation

New-product ideas come from many sources, including customers, employees, distributors, competitors, vendors, research and development (R&D), and consultants.

- *Customers:* The marketing concept suggests that customers' wants and needs should be the springboard for developing new products. Companies can derive insight from listening to Internet chatter or reading blogs, which often indicate early trends or areas consumers are interested in seeing develop or change. Garnier came up with the Indian specific innovation of Fructis Shampoo + Oil from the consumer insight that girls know the importance of oiling their hair but could not do so due to lack of time.[9] Nestle launched a campaign called "Me & Meri Maggi" on the occasion of 25th anniversary of Maggi. The customers were asked to share their Maggi moments, stories, and receipes and this paved the way for launch of new flavours based on the experiences shared by the customers. This approach is far from an intuitive extension of previous new-product development and advertising practices.
- *Employees:* Marketing personnel—advertising and marketing research employees, as well as salespeople—often create new-product ideas because they analyze and are involved in the marketplace. Encouraging employees from different divisions to exchange ideas is also a useful strategy.

  Some firms reward employees for coming up with creative new ideas. In *Bloomberg Businessweek's* annual ranking of the Most Innovative Companies, 15 of the top 50 are Asian, up from only 5 in 2006. The increase isn't surprising when you look at the importance upper-level executives place on innovation. In China, 95 percent said that innovation was key to economic growth. Only 72 percent of U.S. upper-level executives agreed. There is a similar trend in spending on innovation—88 percent of Chinese executives plan to increase their innovation budgets, but only 48 percent said the same thing in the United States.[10]
- *Distributors:* A well-trained sales force routinely asks distributors about needs that are not being met. Because they are closer to end users, distributors are often more aware of customer needs than are manufacturers.

  In a survey by Prophet, results found that 75 percent of model innovators actively involve their vendors and suppliers in new product development.[11] Procter & Gamble has reported that its innovation productivity has increased 60 percent due to external collaborations.[12]
- *Vendors:* 7-Eleven, Inc., an international chain of convenience stores, regularly forges partnerships with vendors to create proprietary products. Coca-Cola invented the flavor blue vanilla for a 7-Eleven Slurpee drink, and the matching Laffy Taffy Blue Vanilla Rope candy was developed by Nestlé's Wonka division exclusively for 7-Eleven.
- *Competitors:* No firms rely solely on internally generated ideas for new products. A big part of any organization's marketing intelligence system should be monitoring the performance of competitors' products. One purpose of competitive monitoring is to determine which, if any, of the competitors' products should be copied. There is plenty of information about competitors on the Internet.
- *Research and development:* R&D is carried out in four distinct ways. You learned about basic research and applied research in Chapter 4. The other two ways are product development and product modification. **Product development** goes beyond applied research by converting applications into marketable products. *Product modification* makes cosmetic or functional changes in existing products. Many new-product breakthroughs come from R&D activities. Procter & Gamble, the world's largest household goods manufacturer, has 9,000 research and development employees.[13]

  IBM has research and innovation labs all over the world, and in 2010 the company announced plans

product development a marketing strategy that entails the creation of marketable new products; the process of converting applications for new technologies into marketable products

brainstorming the process of getting a group to think of unlimited ways to vary a product or solve a problem

screening the first filter in the product development process, which eliminates ideas that are inconsistent with the organization's new-product strategy or are obviously inappropriate for some other reason

to open a new one in São Paulo, Brazil. The goal is to increase sales in rapidly emerging markets like Brazil, and to help Brazil find ways to manage and encourage growth. IBM will help Brazil extract natural resources with new technology developed for the area. IBM then hopes to export those new advances to China and India. By having innovation centers located all over the world, IBM is able to increase its network and generate new ideas based on how different countries operate.[14]

- *Consultants:* Outside consultants are always available to examine a business and recommend product ideas. Examples include professors of premier business management institutes like IIMs, and companies like McKinsey, Boston Consulting Group, and Booz Allen Hamilton. Traditionally, consultants determine whether a company has a balanced portfolio of products and, if not, what new-product ideas are needed to offset the imbalance.

Creativity is the wellspring of new-product ideas, regardless of who comes up with them. A variety of approaches and techniques have been developed to stimulate creative thinking. The two considered most useful for generating new-product ideas are brainstorming and focus group exercises. The goal of **brainstorming** is to get a group to think of unlimited ways to vary a product or solve a problem. Group members avoid criticism of an idea, no matter how ridiculous it may seem. Objective evaluation is postponed. The sheer quantity of ideas is what matters. As noted in Chapter 9, an objective of focus group interviews is to stimulate insightful comments through group interaction. In the industrial market, machine tools, keyboard designs, aircraft interiors, and backhoe accessories have evolved from focus groups.

Idea Screening

After new ideas have been generated, they pass through the first filter in the product development process. This stage, called **screening**, eliminates ideas that are inconsistent with the organization's new-product strategy or are obviously inappropriate for

ROYALTY-FREE RESEARCH

Some companies feel that supporting up-and-coming engineers is important for the future, and those companies that do so tend to profit from their investment. The Massachusetts Institute of Technology (MIT) Media Lab is home to some of the top engineers in the world. The Media Lab is designed to allow engineers to creatively explore and create whatever ideas strike them as interesting or useful. The Media Lab is also funded by corporations. Sixty companies pay ₹90 lakh a year for the rights to any intellectual property developed in the lab, without having to pay royalties for use. Some companies, like Procter & Gamble, pay extra to have research scientists in the Media Lab work with students and monitor projects. However, the companies cannot direct avenues of study, so if a bright engineer wants to focus on motion-sensing gloves that can only be unlocked by the correct fist bump combination, she can.[15]

some other reason. The new-product committee, the new-product department, or some other formally appointed group performs the screening review. General Motors' Advanced Portfolio Exploration Group (APEx) knows that only one out of every twenty new car concepts developed by the group will ever become a reality. That's not a bad percentage. In the pharmaceutical business, the percentage is much lower. Most new-product ideas are rejected at the screening stage.

Concept tests are often used at the screening stage to rate concept (or product) alternatives. A **concept test** evaluates a new-product idea, usually before any prototype has been created. Typically, researchers get consumer reactions to descriptions and visual representations of a proposed product.

Concept tests are considered fairly good predictors of success for line extensions. However, concept tests are usually inaccurate in predicting the success of new products that create new consumption patterns and require major changes in consumer behavior—such as microwave ovens, VCRs, computers, and word processors.

Business Analysis

New-product ideas that survive the initial screening process move to the **business analysis** stage, where preliminary figures for demand, cost, sales, and profitability are calculated. For the first time, costs and revenues are estimated and compared. Depending on the nature of the product and the company, this process may be simple or complex.

The newness of the product, the size of the market, and the nature of the competition all affect the accuracy of revenue projections. In an established market like soft drinks, industry estimates of total market size are available. Forecasting market share for a new entry is a bigger challenge.

Analyzing overall economic trends and their impact on estimated sales is especially important in product categories that are sensitive to fluctuations in the business cycle. If consumers view the economy as uncertain and risky, they will put off buying durable goods such as major home appliances, automobiles, and homes. Likewise, business buyers postpone major equipment purchases if they expect a recession. Understanding the market potential is important because costs increase dramatically once a product idea enters the development stage.

COMMON QUESTIONS IN THE BUSINESS ANALYSIS STAGE

- What is the likely demand for the product?
- What impact would the new product probably have on total sales, profits, market share, and return on investment?
- How would the introduction of the product affect existing products? Would the new product cannibalize existing products?
- Would current customers benefit from the product?
- Would the product enhance the image of the company's overall product mix?
- Would the new product affect current employees in any way? Would it lead to increasing or reducing the size of the workforce?
- What new facilities, if any, would be needed?
- How might competitors respond?
- What is the risk of failure? Is the company willing to take the risk?

Development

In the early stage of **development**, the R&D or engineering department may develop a prototype of the product. During this stage, the firm should start sketching a marketing strategy. The marketing department should decide on the product's packaging, branding, labeling, and so forth. In addition, it should map out preliminary promotion, price, and distribution strategies. The feasibility of manufacturing the product at an acceptable cost should be thoroughly examined. The development stage can last a long time and thus be very expensive. It took 10 years for P&G to develop Crest toothpaste, 15 years to develop the Polaroid Colorpack camera and the Xerox copy machine, 18 years for General Foods to develop Minute Rice, and 51 years to develop the television. Gillette developed three shaving systems over a 27-year period (Trac II, Atra, and Sensor) before introducing the Mach3 in 1998 and Fusion in 2006.[16]

The development process works best when all the involved areas (R&D, marketing, engineering, production, and even suppliers) work together rather

concept test a test to evaluate a new-product idea, usually before any prototype has been created

business analysis the second stage of the screening process where preliminary figures for demand, cost, sales, and profitability are calculated

development the stage in the product development process in which a prototype is developed and a marketing strategy is outlined

simultaneous product development a team-oriented approach to new-product development

than sequentially, a process called **simultaneous product development.** This approach allows firms to shorten the development process and reduce costs. With simultaneous product development, all relevant functional areas and outside suppliers participate in all stages of the development process. Rather than proceeding through highly structured stages, the cross-functional team operates in unison. Involving key suppliers early in the process capitalizes on their knowledge and enables them to develop critical component parts.

The Internet is a useful tool for implementing simultaneous product development. On the Web, multiple partners from a variety of locations can meet regularly to assess new-product ideas, analyze markets and demographics, and review cost information. Ideas judged to be feasible can quickly be converted into new products. Without the Internet, it would be impossible to conduct simultaneous product development from different parts of the world. Global R&D is important for two reasons. First, large companies have become global and are no longer focused only on one market. Global R&D is necessary to connect with customers in different parts of the world. Second, companies want to tap into the world's best talent—which isn't always found in the United States.[17]

Some firms use online brain trusts to solve technical problems. InnoCentive, Inc. is a network of 80,000 self-selected science problem solvers in 173 countries. Its clients include Boeing, DuPont, and Procter & Gamble. Procter & Gamble has another program called Connect + Develop Model. When the company selects an idea for development, it no longer tries to develop it from the ground up with its own resources and time. Instead, it issues a brief to its network of thinkers, researchers, technology entrepreneurs, and inventors around the world, hoping to generate dialogue, suggestions, and solutions.[18]

Innovative firms are also gathering a variety of R&D input from customers online. Nokia, through its online lab, enables users worldwide to download beta applications and give their opinion to the product development teams for further modifications. Swarovski, an Austrian crystal and jewellery company, provides an opportunity to its customers to design and create their own jewellery using its software tool.[19]

Laboratory tests are often conducted on prototype models during the development stage. User safety is an important aspect of laboratory testing, which actually subjects products to much more severe treatment than is expected by end users. The ISI mark, issued by Bureau of Indian Standards (BIS), is a certification that ensures a given product is in conformation with the quality standards set by the government. There are 16 product categories for which such standards have been set by BIS.[20]

Many products that test well in the laboratory are also tried out in homes or businesses. Examples of product categories well suited for such use tests include human and pet food products, household cleaning products, and industrial chemicals and supplies. These

BREAKING THROUGH THE GLASS MARKET

© AP IMAGES/PRNEWSFOTO/VERIZON WIRELESS

Corning is familiar with the gap between invention and commercial application. (Its technology for optical fiber was invented in 1934 but wasn't used until the 1970s.) In 1962, Corning developed a promising ultra-strong glass. But, lacking commercial application, the innovation gathered proverbial dust waiting for people to need strong glass that was hard to break, scratch, or dent even when very thin. Today, touch screens on cell phones and frameless flat-screen televisions call for exactly that product. Motorola's Droid phone already has Gorilla Glass, which now pulls in ₹765 crore a year since finding its first customer in 2008. Corning knows that in the long run, innovation pays off, which is why it allocates 10 percent of revenue to research. Other Corning inventions waiting in the wings include spools of paper-thin flexible glass ready for an application.[21]

products are all relatively inexpensive, and their performance characteristics are apparent to users. For example, Procter & Gamble tests a variety of personal and home-care products in the community around its Cincinnati, Ohio, headquarters.

Test Marketing

After products and marketing programs have been developed, they are usually tested in the marketplace. **Test marketing** is the limited introduction of a product and a marketing program to determine the reactions of potential customers in a market situation. Test marketing allows management to evaluate alternative strategies and to assess how well the various aspects of the marketing mix fit together. Even established products are test marketed to assess new marketing strategies.

The cities chosen as test sites should reflect market conditions in the new product's projected market area. Yet no "magic city" exists that can universally represent market conditions, and a product's success in one city doesn't guarantee that it will be a nationwide hit. When selecting test market cities, researchers should therefore find locations where the demographics and purchasing habits mirror the overall market. The company should also have good distribution in test cities. When GSK wanted to test its new variant of Horlicks called Asha, meant for the rural consumers, it used Andhra Pradesh and Karnataka as its test market because these states were representative of the company's other markets across the country. Horlicks is also a dominating player in the south and gets 30–35% of its sales from rural areas.[22] Moreover, test locations should be isolated from the media. If the television stations in a particular market reach a very large area outside that market, the advertising used for the test product may pull in many consumers from outside the market. The product may then appear more successful than it really is.

© ISTOCKPHOTO.COM/SCOL22

test marketing the limited introduction of a product and a marketing program to determine the reactions of potential customers in a market situation

simulated (laboratory) market testing the presentation of advertising and other promotional materials for several products, including a test product, to members of the product's target market

The High Costs of Test Marketing Test marketing frequently takes one year or longer, and costs can exceed ₹4.5 crore. Some products remain in test markets even longer. Google plans to test-market an ultra-high-speed broadband network in one or more communities at a competitive price. The search giant plans to test its fiber-to-the-home concept by providing up to 5,00,000 homes with 1-gigabyte-per-second broadband access. Communities in every state except Delaware have requested to be one of the test markets. Topeka, Kansas, even renamed the town for a month to Google, Kansas, in an effort to be chosen.[23] Despite the cost, many firms believe it is better to fail in a test market than in a national introduction. Because test marketing is so expensive, some companies do not test line extensions of well-known brands.

The high cost of test marketing is not just financial. One unavoidable problem is that test marketing exposes the new product and its marketing mix to competitors before its introduction. Thus, the element of surprise is lost. Competitors can also sabotage or "jam" a testing program by introducing their own sales promotion, pricing, or advertising campaign. The purpose is to hide or distort the normal conditions that the testing firm might expect in the market.

Alternatives to Test Marketing Many firms are looking for cheaper, faster, safer alternatives to traditional test marketing. In the early 1980s, Information Resources, Inc. pioneered one alternative: scanner-based research (discussed in Chapter 8). A typical supermarket scanner test costs about ₹1,35,00,000. Another alternative to traditional test marketing is **simulated (laboratory) market testing**. Advertising and other promotional materials for several products, including the test product, are shown to members of the product's target market. These people are then

commercialization the decision to market a product

taken to shop at a mock or real store, where their purchases are recorded. Shopper behavior, including repeat purchasing, is monitored to assess the product's likely performance under true market conditions. Research firms offer simulated market tests for ₹11,25,000 to ₹45,00,000, compared to ₹4.5 crore or more for full-scale test marketing.

Government regulation can affect test marketing, particularly in the tobacco industry. With steadily declining U.S. cigarette sales, Reynolds American (maker of Camel cigarettes) hoped to diversify with smokeless, spitless tobacco in the form of dissolvable lozenges, sticks, and strips. Testing for Camel Orbs, a pressed tobacco lozenge that looks similar to a small breath mint, hit roadblocks from several protest groups, who say that the candy-like shape and the bright packaging encourage children to try—and get hooked on—the product. The FDA has requested that Reynolds provide research on the usage and perception of the product on people under 25 years of age. Tightened legislation on how tobacco products can be marketed also limits how aware a test market is of the product.[24]

The Internet offers a fast, cost-effective way to conduct test marketing. Procter & Gamble uses the Internet to assess customer demand for potential new products. Many products that are not available in grocery stores or drugstores can be sampled from P&G's corporate Web site (www.pg.com).[25]

Despite these alternatives, most firms still consider test marketing essential for most new products. The high price of failure simply prohibits the widespread introduction of most new products without testing.

Commercialization

The final stage in the new-product development process is **commercialization**, the decision to market a product. The decision to commercialize the product sets several tasks in motion: ordering production materials and equipment, starting production, building inventories, shipping the product to field distribution points, training the sales force, announcing the new product to the trade, and advertising to potential customers.

The time from the initial commercialization decision to the product's actual introduction varies. It can range from a few weeks for simple products that use existing equipment to several years for technical products that require custom manufacturing equipment. And the total cost of development and initial introduction can be staggering. Gillette spent ₹3,375 crore developing Mach 3, and the first-year marketing budget for the new three-bladed razor was ₹1,350 crore.

The most important factor in successful new-product introduction is a good match between the product and market needs—as the marketing concept would predict. Successful new products deliver a meaningful and perceivable benefit to a sizable number of people or organizations and are different in some meaningful way from their intended substitutes. Firms that routinely

FORWARD THINKING reverse engineering

Tata Technologies, looking to put the Indian population in cars, developed a ten-foot long, five-passenger car that retails in India between ₹1,00,000 and ₹1,12,500. Now, the Nano has visitors from around the world looking for ways to implement Tata's lean engineering into other vehicles and reduce manufacturing costs. Marrying simple design, few features, and inexpensive materials can clearly introduce cost savings. Because the Nano lacks most safety features (including airbags), significant cost savings won't mean much in markets with significant automobile regulations, like the United States and Europe.[26]

© PAUL PRESCOTT/SHUTTERSTOCK.COM

experience success in new-product introductions tend to share the following characteristics:

- A history of listening carefully to customers
- An obsession with producing the best product possible
- A vision of what the market will be like in the future
- Strong leadership
- A commitment to new-product development
- A project-based team approach to new-product development
- Getting every aspect of the product development process right

LO 3 Global Issues in New-Product Development

Increasing globalization of markets and competition provides a reason for multinational firms to consider new-product development from a worldwide perspective. A firm that starts with a global strategy is better able to develop products that are marketable worldwide. In many multinational corporations, every product is developed for potential worldwide distribution, and unique market requirements are built in whenever possible.

Some global marketers design their products to meet regulations in their major markets and then, if necessary, meet smaller markets' requirements country by country. Nissan develops lead-country car models that, with minor changes, can be sold in most markets. With this approach, Nissan has been able to reduce the number of its basic models from 48 to 18. Some products, however, have little potential for global market penetration without modification. In other cases, companies cannot sell their products at affordable prices and still make a profit in many countries.

LO 4 The Spread of New Products

Managers have a better chance of successfully marketing products if they understand how consumers learn about and adopt products.

Diffusion of Innovation

An **innovation** is a product perceived as new by a potential adopter. It really doesn't matter whether the product is "new to the world" or some other category of new product. If it is new to a potential adopter, it is an innovation in this context. **Diffusion** is the process by which the adoption of an innovation spreads.

innovation a product perceived as new by a potential adopter

diffusion the process by which the adoption of an innovation spreads

Five categories of adopters participate in the diffusion process:

- *Innovators:* the first 2.5 percent of all those who adopt the product. Innovators are eager to try new ideas and products, almost as an obsession. In addition to having higher incomes, they are more worldly and more active outside their community than noninnovators. They rely less on group norms and are more self-confident. Because they are well educated, they are more likely to get their information from scientific sources and experts. Innovators are characterized as being venturesome.
- *Early adopters:* the next 13.5 percent to adopt the product. Although early adopters are not the very first, they do adopt early in the product's life cycle. Compared to innovators, they rely much more on group norms and values. They are also more oriented to the local community, in contrast to the innovators' worldly outlook. Early adopters are more likely than innovators to be opinion leaders because of their closer affiliation with groups. Early adopters are a new product's best friends.[27] The respect of others is a dominant characteristic of early adopters.
- *Early majority:* the next 34 percent to adopt. The early majority weighs the pros and cons before adopting a new product. They are likely to collect more information

© ISTOCKPHOTO.COM/VASKO MIOKOVIC / © ISTOCKPHOTO.COM/GEOFFREY HOLMAN

and evaluate more brands than early adopters, therefore extending the adoption process. They rely on the group for information but are unlikely to be opinion leaders themselves. Instead, they tend to be opinion leaders' friends and neighbors. The early majority is an important link in the process of diffusing new ideas because they are positioned between earlier and later adopters. A dominant characteristic of the early majority is deliberateness.

- *Late majority:* the next 34 percent to adopt. The late majority adopts a new product because most of their friends have already adopted it. Because they also rely on group norms, their adoption stems from pressure to conform. This group tends to be older and below average in income and education. They depend mainly on word-of-mouth communication rather than on the mass media. The dominant characteristic of the late majority is skepticism.
- *Laggards:* the final 16 percent to adopt. Like innovators, laggards do not rely on group norms. Their independence is rooted in their ties to tradition. Thus, the past heavily influences their decisions. By the time laggards adopt an innovation, it has probably been outmoded and replaced by something else. For example, they may have bought their first black-and-white television set after color television was already widely diffused. Laggards have the longest adoption time and the lowest socioeconomic status. They tend to be suspicious of new products and alienated from a rapidly advancing society. The dominant value of laggards is tradition. Marketers typically ignore laggards, who do not seem to be motivated by advertising or personal selling and are virtually impossible to reach online.

Note that some product categories may never be adopted by 100 percent of the population. The adopter categories refer to all of those who will eventually adopt a product, not the entire population.

Product Characteristics and the Rate of Adoption

Five product characteristics can be used to predict and explain the rate of acceptance and diffusion of a new product:

- *Complexity:* the degree of difficulty involved in understanding and using a new product. The more complex the product, the slower is its diffusion.
- *Compatibility:* the degree to which the new product is consistent with existing values and product knowledge, past experiences, and current needs. Incompatible products diffuse more slowly than compatible products.
- *Relative advantage:* the degree to which a product is perceived as superior to existing substitutes. Because it can store and play back thousands of songs, the iPod has a clear relative advantage over the portable CD player.
- *Observability:* the degree to which the benefits or other results of using the product can be observed by others and communicated to target customers. For instance, fashion items and automobiles are highly visible and more observable than personal-care items.
- *"Trialability":* the degree to which a product can be tried on a limited basis. It is much easier to try a new toothpaste or breakfast cereal than a new automobile or microcomputer.

Marketing Implications of the Adoption Process

Two types of communication aid the diffusion process: *word-of-mouth communication* among consumers and communication from marketers to consumers. Word-of-mouth communication within and across groups speeds diffusion. Opinion leaders discuss new products with their followers and with other opinion leaders. Marketers must therefore ensure that opinion leaders have the types of information desired in the media that they use. Suppliers of some products, such as professional and health care services, rely almost solely on word-of-mouth communication for new business.

The second type of communication aiding the diffusion process is *communication directly from the marketer to potential adopters*. Messages directed toward early adopters should normally use different appeals than messages directed toward the early

© ISTOCKPHOTO.COM/RUDYANTO WIJAYA

majority, the late majority, or the laggards. Early adopters are more important than innovators because they make up a larger group, are more socially active, and are usually opinion leaders.

As the focus of a promotional campaign shifts from early adopters to the early majority and the late majority, marketers should study the dominant characteristics, buying behavior, and media characteristics of these target markets. Then they should revise messages and media strategy to fit. The diffusion model helps guide marketers in developing and implementing promotion strategy.

LO 5 Product Life Cycles

The product life cycle (PLC) is one of the most familiar concepts in marketing. Few other general concepts have been so widely discussed. Although some researchers and consultants have challenged the theoretical basis and managerial value of the PLC, many believe it is a useful marketing management diagnostic tool and a general guide for marketing planning in various life cycle stages.[28]

The PLC is a biological metaphor that traces the stages of a product's acceptance, from its introduction (birth) to its decline (death). As Exhibit 11.2 shows, a product progresses through four major stages: introduction, growth, maturity, and decline.

product life cycle (PLC) a concept that provides a way to trace the stages of a product's acceptance, from its introduction (birth) to its decline (death)

product category all brands that satisfy a particular type of need

The PLC concept can be used to analyze a brand, a product form, or a product category. The PLC for a product form is usually longer than the PLC for any one brand. The exception would be a brand that was the first and last competitor in a product form market. In that situation, the brand and product form life cycles would be equal in length. Product categories have the longest life cycles. A **product category** includes all brands that satisfy a particular type of need such as shaving products, passenger automobiles, or soft drinks.

The time a product spends in any one stage of the life cycle may vary dramatically. Some products, such as fad items, move through the entire cycle in weeks. Others, such as electric clothes washers and dryers, stay in the maturity stage for decades. Exhibit 11.2 illustrates the typical life cycle for a consumer durable good, such as a washer or dryer. In contrast, Exhibit 11.3 on the next page illustrates typical life

EXHIBIT 11.2
Four Stages of the Product Life Cycle

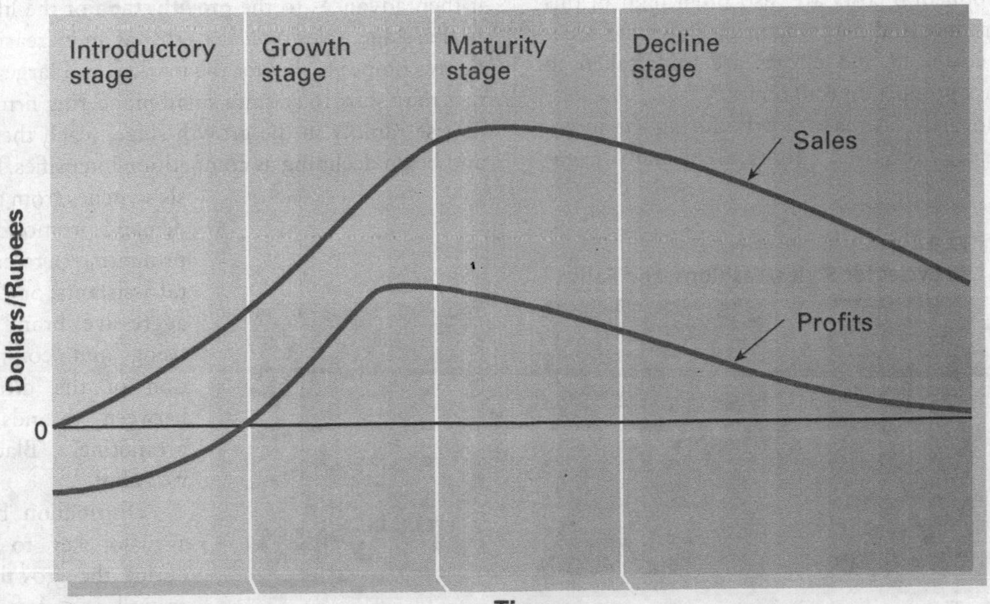

introductory stage the full-scale launch of a new product into the marketplace

growth stage the second stage of the product life cycle when sales typically grow at an increasing rate, many competitors enter the market, large companies may start to acquire small pioneering firms, and profits are healthy

cycles for styles (such as formal, business, or casual clothing), fashions (such as miniskirts or baggy jeans), and fads (such as leopard-print clothing). Changes in a product, its uses, its image, or its positioning can extend that product's life cycle.

The PLC concept does not tell managers the length of a product's life cycle or its duration in any stage. It does not dictate marketing strategy. It is simply a tool to help marketers forecast future events and suggest appropriate strategies.

Introductory Stage

The **introductory stage** of the PLC represents the full-scale launch of a new product into the marketplace. Computer databases for personal use, room-deodorizing air-conditioning filters, and wind-powered home electric generators are all product categories that have recently entered the PLC. A high failure rate, little competition, frequent product modification, and limited distribution typify the introductory stage of the PLC.

Marketing costs in the introductory stage are normally high for several reasons. High dealer margins are often needed to obtain adequate distribution, and incentives are needed to get consumers to try the new product. Advertising expenses are high because of the need to educate consumers about the new product's benefits. Production costs are also often high in this stage, as product and manufacturing flaws are identified and corrected and efforts are undertaken to develop mass production economies.

Sales normally increase slowly during the introductory stage. Moreover, profits are usually negative because of R&D costs, factory tooling, and high introduction costs. The length of the introductory phase is largely determined by product characteristics, such as the product's advantages over substitute products, the educational effort required to make the product known, and management's commitment of resources to the new item. A short introductory period is usually preferred to help reduce the impact of negative earnings and cash flows. As soon as the product gets off the ground, the financial burden should begin to diminish. Also, a short introduction helps dispel some of the uncertainty as to whether the new product will be successful.

Promotion strategy in the introductory stage focuses on developing product awareness and informing consumers about the product category's potential benefits. At this stage, the communication challenge is to stimulate primary demand—demand for the product in general rather than for a specific brand. Intensive personal selling is often required to gain acceptance for the product among wholesalers and retailers. Promotion of convenience products often requires heavy consumer sampling and couponing. Shopping and specialty products demand educational advertising and personal selling to the final consumer.

Growth Stage

If a product category survives the introductory stage, it then advances to the **growth stage** of the life cycle. In this stage, sales typically grow at an increasing rate, many competitors enter the market, and large companies may start to acquire small pioneering firms. Profits rise rapidly in the growth stage, reach their peak, and begin declining as competition intensifies. Emphasis switches from primary demand promotion (e.g., promoting personal digital assistants, or PDAs) to aggressive brand advertising and communication of the differences between brands (e.g., promoting BlackBerry vs. Palm).

Distribution becomes a major key to success during the growth stage, as well as in later stages. Manufacturers scramble to sign up dealers and

EXHIBIT 11.3

Product Life Cycles for Styles, Fashions, and Fads

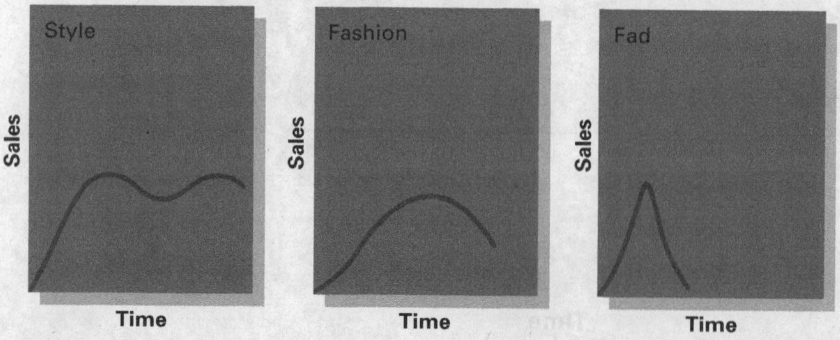

distributors and to build long-term relationships. Without adequate distribution, it is impossible to establish a strong market position.

XFit, a stretch denim material, has paired with denim labels in the U.S. to get its product to retailers. The stretch denim market has 35 percent of the market, and customers want a jean that holds its shape but fits comfortably. XFit relies on designers to label jeans with information about the benefits of XFit. If the label doesn't resonate with customers or differentiate the material from other stretch denims, XFit will lose its place in the stretch fiber market.[29]

Maturity Stage

A period during which sales increase at a decreasing rate signals the beginning of the **maturity stage** of the life cycle. New users cannot be added indefinitely, and sooner or later the market approaches saturation. Normally, this is the longest stage of the PLC. Many major household appliances are in the maturity stage of their life cycles.

For shopping products such as durable goods and electronics, and many specialty products, annual models begin to appear during the maturity stage. Product lines are lengthened to appeal to additional market segments. Service and repair assume more important roles as manufacturers strive to distinguish their products from others. Product design changes tend to become stylistic (How can the product be made different?) rather than functional (How can the product be made better?).

As prices and profits continue to fall, marginal competitors start dropping out of the market. Dealer margins also shrink, resulting in less shelf space for mature items, lower dealer inventories, and a general reluctance to promote the product. Thus, promotion to dealers often intensifies during this stage in order to retain loyalty.

Heavy consumer promotion by the manufacturer is also required to maintain market share. Cutthroat competition during this stage can lead to price wars. Another characteristic of the maturity stage is the emergence of "niche marketers" that target narrow, well-defined, underserved segments of a market.

Decline Stage

A long-run drop in sales signals the beginning of the **decline stage**. The rate of decline is governed by how rapidly consumer tastes change or substitute products are adopted. Many convenience products and fad items lose their market overnight, leaving large inventories of unsold items, such as designer jeans. Others die more slowly. Total revenue from physical formats of music sales in India was ₹320 crore in 2010. In 2006 that figure was ₹634 crore. Physical music's share in total revenues fell from nearly 81% in 2006 to just 38% in 2010. Revenue has fallen each year since then and shows little sign of stopping.[30] It appears that the popularity of digital download options are rapidly making audio cassettes and CDs obsolete.

maturity stage a period during which sales increase at a decreasing rate

decline stage a long-run drop in sales

Some firms have developed successful strategies for marketing products in the decline stage of the PLC. They eliminate all nonessential marketing expenses and let sales decline as more and more customers discontinue purchasing the products. Eventually, the product is withdrawn from the market.

Some firms practice what management sage Peter Drucker has called "organized abandonment," which is based upon a periodic audit of all goods and services that a firm markets. One key question is, if we weren't already marketing the product, would we be willing to introduce it now? If the answer is "no," the product should be carefully considered as a candidate for elimination from the product mix.[31]

Implications for Marketing Management

The PLC concept encourages marketing managers to plan so that they can take the initiative instead of reacting to past events. The PLC is especially useful as a predicting or forecasting tool. Because products pass through distinctive stages, it is often possible to estimate a product's location on the curve using historical data. Profits, like sales, tend to follow a predictable path over a product's life cycle.

Exhibit 11.4 shows the relationship between the adopter categories and stages of the PLC. Note that the various categories of adopters first buy products in different stages of the life cycle. Almost all sales in the maturity and decline stages represent repeat purchasing.

© ISTOCKPHOTO.COM/THOMAS FLÜGGE

EXHIBIT 11.4

Relationships between the Diffusion Process and the Product Life Cycle

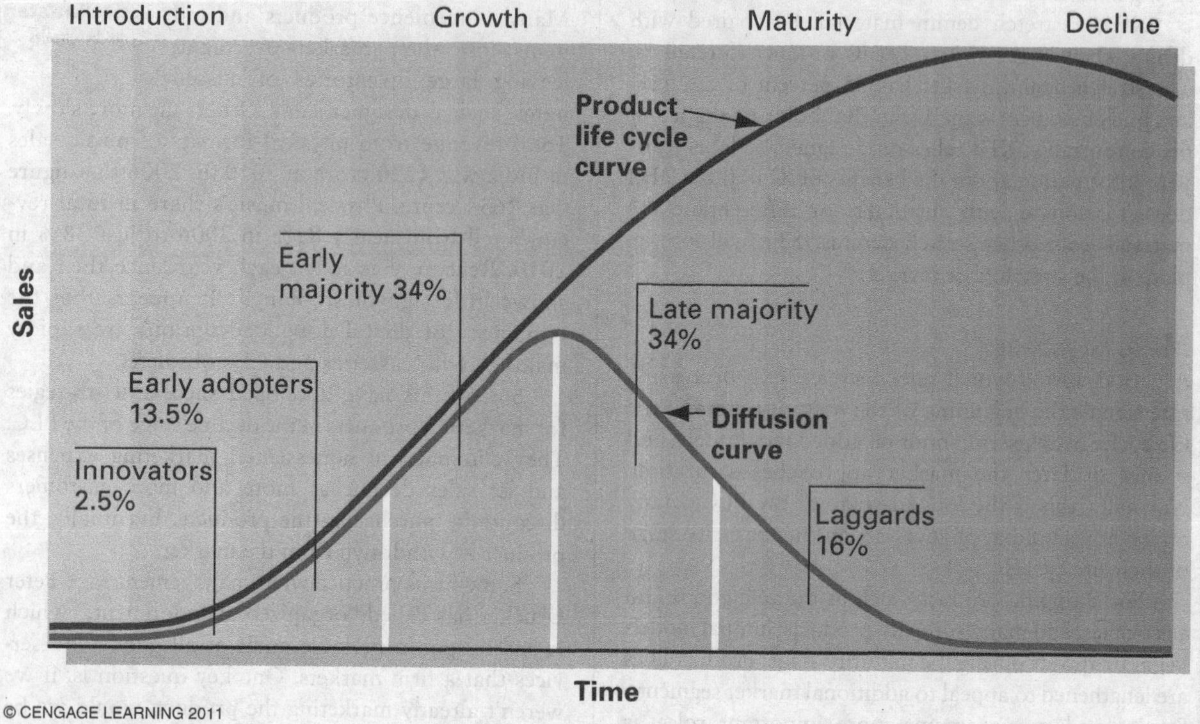

ANATOMY OF
A PRODUCT LIFE CYCLE: VCR

VCR sales dropped rapidly in the face of growing DVD competition.

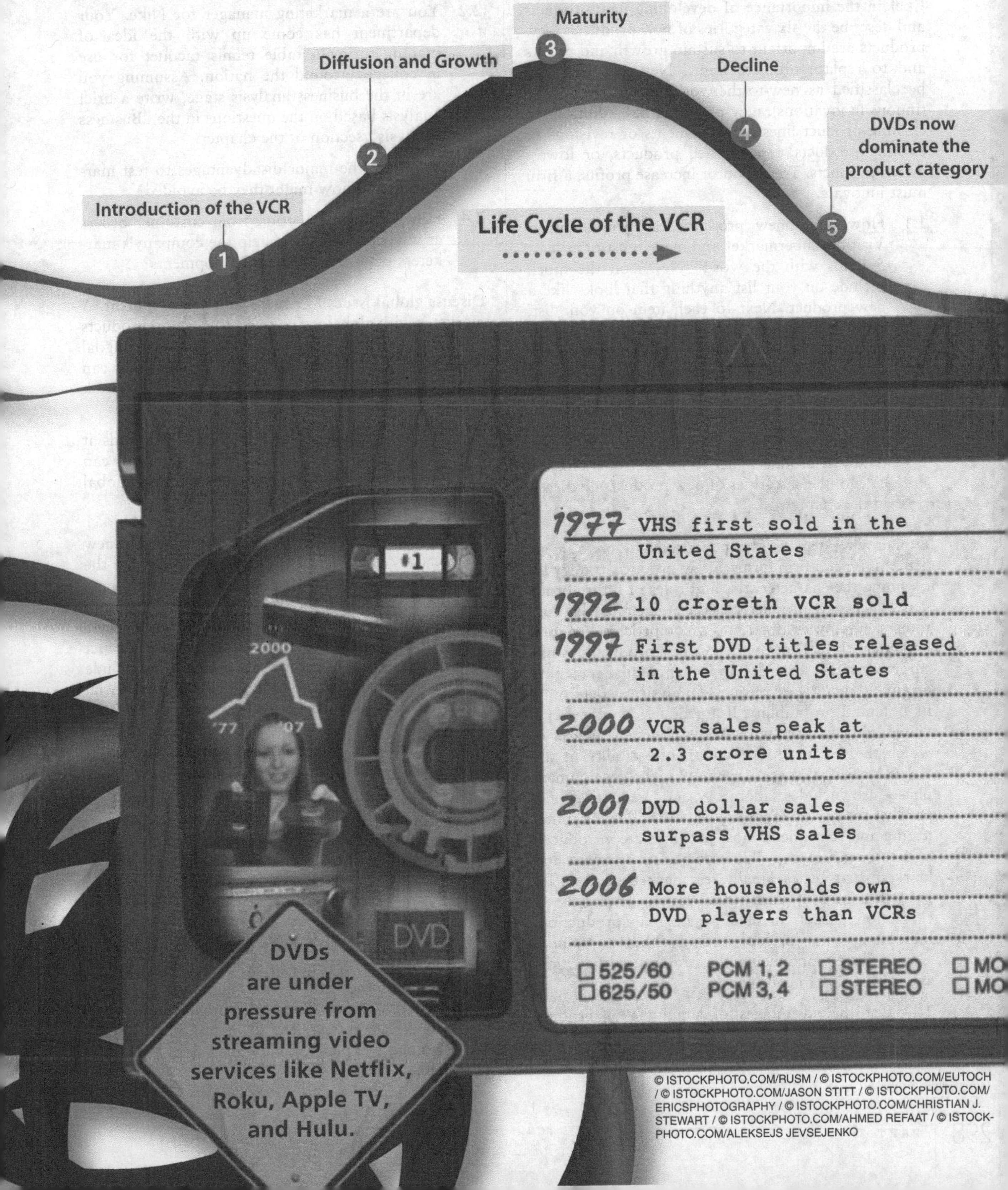

Review and Applications

Explain the importance of developing new products and describe the six categories of new products. New products are important to sustain growth and profits and to replace obsolete items. New products can be classified as new-to-the-world products (discontinuous innovations), new product lines, additions to existing product lines, improvements or revisions of existing products, repositioned products, or lower-priced products. To sustain or increase profits, a firm must innovate.

1.1 How many new products can you identify? Visit the supermarket and make a list of at least 5 items with the word "New" on the label. Include on your list anything that looks like a new product. Next to each item on your list, write the category of new product that best describes the item. Share your results with the class.

1.2 New entertainment products aren't necessarily media products. Form a team of three or four students and brainstorm new nonmedia entertainment products. Try to identify one item for each of the categories of new products discussed in the chapter.

Explain the steps in the new-product development process. First, a firm forms a new-product strategy by outlining the characteristics and roles of future products. Then new-product ideas are generated by customers, employees, distributors, competitors, vendors, and internal R&D personnel. Once a product idea has survived initial screening by an appointed screening group, it undergoes business analysis to determine its potential profitability. If a product concept seems viable, it progresses into the development phase, in which the technical and economic feasibility of the manufacturing process is evaluated. The development phase also includes laboratory and use testing of a product for performance and safety. Following initial testing and refinement, most products are introduced in a test market to evaluate consumer response and marketing strategies. Finally, test market successes are propelled into full commercialization. The commercialization process involves starting up production, building inventories, shipping to distributors, training a sales force, announcing the product to the trade, and advertising to consumers.

2.1 List the advantages of simultaneous product development.

2.2 You are a marketing manager for Nike. Your department has come up with the idea of manufacturing a table tennis racquet for use in colleges around the nation. Assuming you are in the business analysis stage, write a brief analysis based on the questions in the "Business Analysis" section of the chapter.

2.3 What are the major disadvantages to test marketing, and how might they be avoided?

2.4 How could information from customer orders at **www.pizzahut.com** help the company's marketers plan new-product developments?

Discuss global issues in new-product development. A marketer with global vision seeks to develop products that can easily be adapted to suit local needs. The goal is not simply to develop a standard product that can be sold worldwide. Smart global marketers also look for good product ideas worldwide.

3.1 Visit **www.pg.com** and look at the brands it offers around the world. What conclusions can you draw about Procter & Gamble's global new-product development strategy?

Explain the diffusion process through which new products are adopted. The diffusion process is the spread of a new product from its producer to ultimate adopters. Adopters in the diffusion process belong to five categories: innovators, early adopters, the early majority, the late majority, and laggards. Product characteristics that affect the rate of adoption include product complexity, compatibility with existing social values, relative advantage over existing substitutes, observability, and "trialability." The diffusion process is facilitated by word-of-mouth communication and communication from marketers to consumers.

4.1 Describe some products whose adoption rates have been affected by complexity, compatibility, relative advantage, observability, and/or "trialability."

4.2 What type of adopter behavior do you typically follow? Explain.

4.3 Review Exhibit 11.4. Analyze each product on the graph according to the characteristics that influence the rate of adoption. For example, what can you conclude from the data about the relative advantage of DVD audio? Write one to two pages explaining your analysis.

Explain the concept of product life cycles. All brands and product categories undergo a life cycle with four stages: introduction, growth, maturity, and decline. The rate at which products move through these stages varies dramatically. Marketing managers use the product life cycle concept as an analytical tool to forecast a product's future and devise effective marketing strategies.

5.1 What is Colgate doing to compete successfully in the maturity stage? Go to its web site to find out.

Exercises

APPLICATION EXERCISE

A simple statistical analysis will help you better understand the types of new products. As in the Application Exercise in Chapter 6, you will be using print advertisements, but you will also be adding information from other sources (TV ads, trips to the store, and the like).[32]

Activities

1. Compile a list of 30 new products. If you are building a portfolio of ads (see the Application Exercise in Chapter 6), you can generate part of this list as you collect print advertisements for the topics in this chapter. Consider tabulating television ads for new products that are aired during programs you normally watch. A trip to the grocery could probably yield your entire list, but then your list would be limited to consumer products.

2. Make a table with six columns labeled as follows: new-to-the-world products, new product line, addition to existing product line, improvement/revision of existing product line, repositioned product, and lower-priced product.

3. Place each of your 30 new products into one of the six categories. Tabulate your results at the bottom of each column. What conclusions can you draw from the distribution of your products? Consider adding your results together with the rest of the class to get a larger and more random sample.

ETHICS EXERCISE

One source of new product ideas is competitors. Puneet Modi recently joined A1 Speciality Products as a brand manager. His new boss told him, "We don't have a budget for new-product development. We just monitor our competitors' new-product introductions and offer knockoffs of any that look like they will be successful."

Questions

1. Is this practice ethical?
2. Does the AMA Statement of Ethics address this issue? Go to **www.marketingpower.com** and review the statement. Then, write a brief paragraph on what the AMA Statement of Ethics contains that relates to knockoff products.

MARKETING PLAN EXERCISE

Complete the following exercises to continue building your strategic marketing plan for Part 3—Product Decisions. (See Marketing Planning Worksheet, Part 3, on your companion Web site at **www.cengage.com/international.**) You should also refer to Appendix I of Chapter 2 for additional marketing plan checklist items (Marketing Mix—Product).

1. Place your company's product in the appropriate stage of the product life cycle. What are the implications of being in this stage? Would the PLC be lengthened, shortened, or not affected by selling your product or service online? Would selling your offering on the Internet make it seem earlier on the PLC to your customers? Why?

2. What categories of adopters are likely to buy your company's products? Is the product diffusing slowly or quickly throughout the marketplace? Why? What elements of the diffusion process can you control to make sure your offering diffuses more quickly throughout the adopter categories and marketplace in general? Will positive word-of-mouth be easier or harder to generate online?

Short Case: KELLOGG'S SPECIAL K

Prepared by
Dr. Dheeraj Sharma,
Indian Institute of Management, Ahmedabad

Kellogg's is the leading producer in the cereals and convenience food industry, globally. It was formed in the year 1906 in Battle Creek, Michigan. It has had a history of providing healthy breakfast for more than 100 years. Today, it sells its products in more than 180 countries and has its manufacturing base in 18 countries. It markets more than 1500 products worldwide, which includes more than 100 ready-to-eat cereals.[33]

Kellogg's entered the Indian market in 1995 and has invested over ₹150 crores. Currently, Kellogg's has earned a 60 percent share in the ₹400-crore cereal market in India.[34] It is famous for its flagship brand Kellogg's Corn Flakes, which come in flavors like chocolate, honey, muesli, oats, etc. It offers different products for requirements like digestive regularity, weight control, and heart health.[35]

The traditional Indian breakfast in India consists of *roti*, *paratha*, *poori*, *dal*, *upma*, *dosa*, *idli*, fish, etc, depending on which region people come from. Kellogg's products were alien to the Indian market. Kellogg's to establish itself in the Indian market had to face many challenges like non-acceptability of goods, lack of adaptability, unchanged traditional eating habits, skepticism for processed food, and price sensitive customers. Kellogg's fought through these hurdles and successfully penetrated in the Indian markets using various marketing strategies. It created awareness of its product by educating people about the benefits of eating cereals for breakfast. It advertised its products on TV, and also manufactured tailored goods suitable to the Indian market. Innovative marketing along with efficient brand-building activities and an efficient supply chain network, enabled Kellogg's to create its market in the breakfast segment in India.

Gradually, with increase in the acceptability of Kellogg's products in the Indian market, Kellogg's expanded its range of products. Recently, it launched a new brand called *Kellogg's Special K,* which consisted of cereals, bars, and snacks.[36] This brand was offered as a low-fat breakfast option. The target consumers were the working, and health-conscious women. However, this product was not very successful in the beginning. Kellogg's then made a comeback with a better advertising strategy. It then appointed the actress Lara Dutta as its brand ambassador. In the TV commercial she promoted the product by stating that the secret behind her maintained physic is eating *Kellogg's Special K* everyday for breakfast. The USP of this product was that it was 98% fat free, full of fiber, Vitamin A, B, and C. It is made from wheat and is coated with honey for taste.[37]

The product got good reviews but Kellogg's limited its market to a niche customer base. Anupam Dutta, MD, Kellogg's India said to *Business Standard*, "the brand meets a specific consumer need, has been growing at a terrific pace across the globe. It took nearly 50 years to deliver annual sales of $1 billion (₹4,500 crore), but took only two more years to grow its annual sales to $1.5 billion (₹6,750 crore). Plus it targets Indian customers who are getting increasingly health conscious."[38]

Questions

1. Kellogg's Special K products are only meant to target weight and health conscious women. Is this positioning right?
2. What are the advantages and the disadvantages of this positioning? Is Kellogg's restricting its market?

11 Developing and Managing Products

KEY TERMS

LO 1

new product a product new to the world, the market, the producer, the seller, or some combination of these

LO 2

new-product strategy a plan that links the new-product development process with the objectives of the marketing department, the business unit, and the corporation

product development a marketing strategy that entails the creation of marketable new products; the process of converting applications for new technologies into marketable products

brainstorming the process of getting a group to think of unlimited ways to vary a product or solve a problem

screening the first filter in the product development process, which eliminates ideas that are inconsistent with the organization's new-product strategy or are obviously inappropriate for some other reason

concept test a test to evaluate a new-product idea, usually before any prototype has been created

business analysis the second stage of the screening process where preliminary figures for demand, cost, sales, and profitability are calculated

development the stage in the product development process in which a prototype is developed and a marketing strategy is outlined

simultaneous product development a team-oriented approach to new-product development

test marketing the limited introduction of a product and a marketing program to determine the reactions of potential customers in a market situation

KEY CONCEPTS

LO 1 **Explain the importance of developing new products and describe the six categories of new products.** New products are important to sustain growth and profits and to replace obsolete items. New products can be classified as new-to-the-world products (discontinuous innovations), new product lines, additions to existing product lines, improvements or revisions of existing products, repositioned products, or lower-priced products. To sustain or increase profits, a firm must innovate.

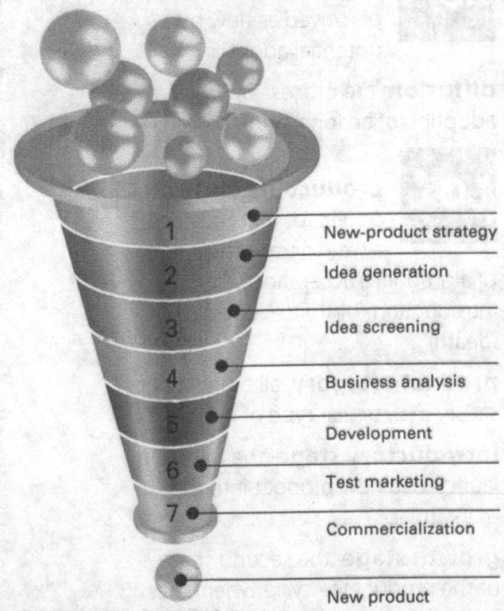

© CENGAGE LEARNING 2011

LO 2 **Explain the steps in the new-product development process.** First, a firm forms a new-product strategy by outlining the characteristics and roles of future products. Then new-product ideas are generated by customers, employees, distributors, competitors, vendors, and internal R&D personnel. Once a product idea has survived initial screening by an appointed screening group, it undergoes business analysis to determine its potential profitability. If a product concept seems viable, it progresses into the development phase, in which the technical and economic feasibility of the manufacturing process is evaluated. The development phase also includes laboratory and use testing of a product for performance and safety. Following initial testing and refinement, most products are introduced in a test market to evaluate consumer response and marketing strategies. Finally, test market successes are propelled into full commercialization. The commercialization process involves starting up production, building inventories, shipping to distributors, training a sales force, announcing the product to the trade, and advertising to consumers.

LO 3 **Discuss global issues in new-product development.** A marketer with global vision seeks to develop products that can easily be adapted to suit local needs. The goal is not simply to develop a standard product that can be sold worldwide. Smart global marketers also look for good product ideas worldwide.

LO 4 **Explain the diffusion process through which new products are adopted.** The diffusion process is the spread of a new product from its producer to ultimate adopters. Adopters in the diffusion process belong to five categories: innovators, early adopters, the early majority, the late majority, and laggards

simulated (laboratory) market testing the presentation of advertising and other promotional materials for several products, including a test product, to members of the product's target market

commercialization the decision to market a product

LO 4

innovation a product perceived as new by a potential adopter

diffusion the process by which the adoption of an innovation spreads

LO 5

product life cycle (PLC) a concept that provides a way to trace the stages of a product's acceptance, from its introduction (birth) to its decline (death)

product category all brands that satisfy a particular type of need

introductory stage the full-scale launch of a new product into the marketplace

growth stage the second stage of the product life cycle when sales typically grow at an increasing rate, many competitors enter the market, large companies may start to acquire small pioneering firms, and profits are healthy

maturity stage a period during which sales increase at a decreasing rate

decline stage a long-run drop in sales

Product characteristics that affect the rate of adoption include product complexity, compatibility with existing social values, relative advantage over existing substitutes, observability, and "trialability." The diffusion process is facilitated by word-of-mouth communication and communication from marketers to consumers.

LO 5 **Explain the concept of product life cycles.** All brands and product categories undergo a life cycle with four stages: introduction, growth, maturity, and decline. The rate at which products move through these stages varies dramatically. Marketing managers use the product life cycle concept as an analytical tool to forecast a product's future and devise effective marketing strategies.

What is Colgate doing to compete successfully in the maturity stage? Go to its web site to find out.

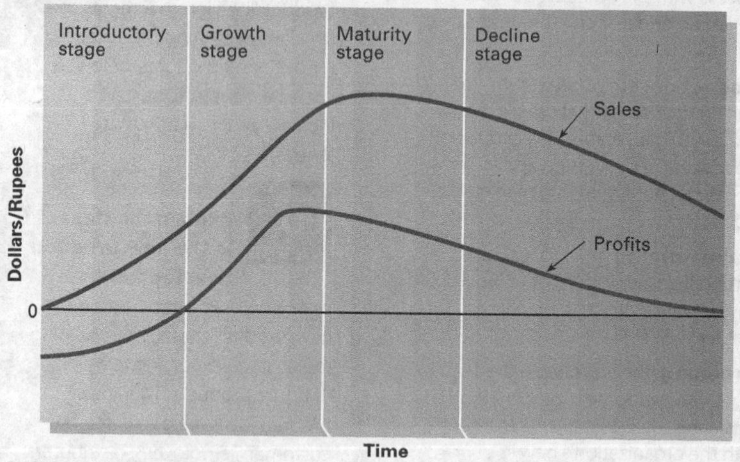

© CENGAGE LEARNING 2011

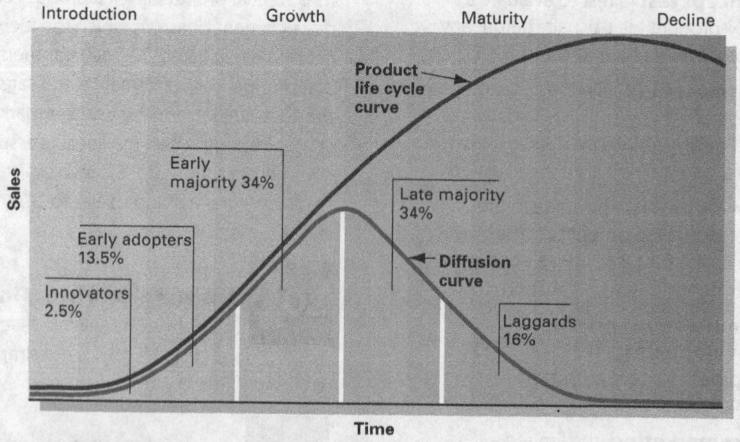

© CENGAGE LEARNING 2011

CHAPTER 12

Services and Nonprofit Organization Marketing

Learning Outcomes

LO 1 Discuss the importance of services to the economy

LO 2 Discuss the differences between services and goods

LO 3 Describe the components of service quality and the gap model of service quality

LO 4 Develop marketing mixes for services

LO 5 Discuss relationship marketing in services

LO 6 Explain internal marketing in services

LO 7 Discuss global issues in services marketing

LO 8 Describe nonprofit organization marketing

"Around 55 percent of Indian GDP contribution comes from the service sector."

LO1 The Importance of Services

service the result of applying human or mechanical efforts to people or objects

A service is the result of applying human or mechanical efforts to people or objects. Services involve a deed, a performance, or an effort that cannot be physically possessed. Today, the service sector substantially influences the Indian economy. It contributes around 55 percent to gross domestic product of India and employs around 25 percent of total employed people in the country. It also accounts for more than 33 percent of total exports from India.[1] The demand for services is expected to continue. Much of this demand results from demographics. An aging population will need nurses, home health care workers, physical therapists, and social workers. Demand for information managers, such as computer engineers and systems analysts, will also increase. There is also a growing market for service companies worldwide.

The marketing process described in Chapter 1 is the same for all types of products, whether they are goods or services. In addition, although a comparison of goods and services marketing can be beneficial, in reality it is hard to distinguish clearly between manufacturing and service firms. Indeed, many manufacturing firms can point to service as a major factor in their success. For example, maintenance and repair services offered by the manufacturer are important to buyers of copy machines. Nevertheless, services have some unique characteristics that distinguish them from goods, and marketing strategies need to be adjusted for these characteristics.

***Note:** All the figures in U.S. dollars are converted into rupee using the value $1 = ₹45.*

LO 2 How Services Differ from Goods

Services have four unique characteristics that distinguish them from goods. Services are intangible, inseparable, heterogeneous, and perishable.

Intangibility

The basic difference between services and goods is that services are intangible performances. Because of their **intangibility**, they cannot be touched, seen, tasted, heard, or felt in the same manner that goods can be sensed.

Evaluating the quality of services before or even after making a purchase is harder than evaluating the quality of goods because, compared to goods, services tend to exhibit fewer search qualities. A **search quality** is a characteristic that can be easily assessed before purchase—for instance, the color of an appliance or automobile. At the same time, services tend to exhibit more experience and credence qualities. An **experience quality** is a characteristic that can be assessed only after use, such as the quality of a meal in a restaurant. A **credence quality** is a characteristic that consumers may have difficulty assessing even after purchase because they do not have the necessary knowledge or experience. Medical and consulting services are examples of services that exhibit credence qualities.

These characteristics also make it harder for marketers to communicate the benefits of an intangible service than to communicate the benefits of tangible goods. Thus, marketers often rely on tangible cues to communicate a service's nature and quality. For example, Life Insurance Corporation of India uses a symbol of two hands safeguarding a lamp as a tangible reminder of the protection that insurance provides.

The facilities that customers visit, or from which services are delivered, are a critical tangible part of the total service offering. Messages about the organization are communicated to customers through such elements as the decor, the clutter or neatness of service areas, and the staff's manners and dress. In order to make a hotel stay a defined all-sensory experience, many hotels are using ambient scenting to create a unique experience. And because scent triggers specific emotions and brain function, some hotels, like the Mandarin Oriental Miami, use different scents in different areas to create an ideal environment. Its conference rooms are perfumed with a blend called Meeting Sense that claims to enhance productivity.[2]

intangibility the inability of services to be touched, seen, tasted, heard, or felt in the same manner that goods can be sensed

search quality a characteristic that can be easily assessed before purchase

experience quality a characteristic that can be assessed only after use

credence quality a characteristic that consumers may have difficulty assessing even after purchase because they do not have the necessary knowledge or experience

inseparability the inability of the production and consumption of a service to be separated; consumers must be present during the production

heterogeneity the variability of the inputs and outputs of services, which causes services to tend to be less standardized and uniform than goods

Inseparability

Goods are produced, sold, and then consumed. In contrast, services are often sold, produced, and consumed at the same time. In other words, their production and consumption are inseparable activities. This **inseparability** means that, because consumers must be present during the production of services like haircuts or surgery, they are actually involved in the production of the services they buy. That type of consumer involvement is rare in goods manufacturing.

Simultaneous production and consumption also means that services normally cannot be produced in a centralized location and consumed in decentralized locations, as goods typically are. Services are also inseparable from the perspective of the service provider. Thus, the quality of service that firms are able to deliver depends on the quality of their employees.

Heterogeneity

One great strength of McDonald's is consistency. Whether customers order a McVeggie in New Delhi or Hyderabad, they know exactly what they are going to get. This is not the case with many service providers. Because services have greater **heterogeneity** or variability of inputs and outputs, they tend to be less standardized and uniform than goods. For example,

© INDIATODAYIMAGES.COM

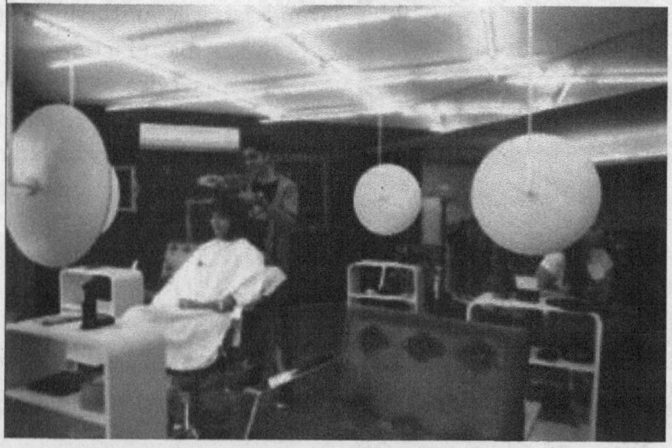

physicians in a group practice or barbers in a barber shop differ within each group in their technical and interpersonal skills. Because services tend to be labor intensive and production and consumption are inseparable, consistency and quality control can be hard to achieve.

Standardization and training help increase consistency and reliability. Marriot is known for standardizing its hotels down to the smallest detail—from how much bleach is used to clean the floor and which flushers are on bathroom toilets. These standards for high-quality service across the company's different hotel chains allow travelers to have confidence that their hotel will match expectations.[3]

Perishability

The fourth characteristic of services is their **perishability**, which means that they cannot be stored, warehoused, or inventoried. An empty hotel room or airplane seat produces no revenue that day. The revenue is lost. Yet service organizations are often forced to turn away full-price customers during peak periods.

One of the most important challenges in many service industries is finding ways to synchronize supply and demand. The philosophy that some revenue is better than none has prompted many hotels to offer deep discounts on weekends and during the off-season.

LO 3 Service Quality

Because of the four unique characteristics of services, service quality is more difficult to define and measure than is the quality of tangible goods. Business executives rank the improvement of service quality as one of the most critical challenges facing them today.

Research has shown that customers evaluate service quality by the following five components:[4]

- ***Reliability:*** the ability to perform the service dependably, accurately, and consistently. Reliability is performing the service right the first time. This component has been found to be the one most important to consumers.
- ***Responsiveness:*** the ability to provide prompt service. Examples of responsiveness include calling the customer back quickly, serving lunch fast to someone who is in a hurry, or mailing a transaction slip immediately. The ultimate in responsiveness is offering service 24 hours a day, seven days a week.
- ***Assurance:*** the knowledge and courtesy of employees and their ability to convey trust. Skilled employees who treat customers with respect and make customers feel that they can trust the firm exemplify assurance.
- ***Empathy:*** caring, individualized attention to customers. Firms whose employees recognize customers and learn their specific requirements are providing empathy.
- ***Tangibles:*** the physical evidence of the service. The tangible parts of a service include the physical facilities, tools, and equipment used to provide the service, as well as the appearance of personnel.

Overall service quality is measured by combining customers' evaluations for all five components.

The Gap Model of Service Quality

A model of service quality called the **gap model** identifies five gaps that can cause problems in service delivery and influence customer evaluations of service quality.[5] These gaps are illustrated in Exhibit 12.1:

- *Gap 1:* the gap between what customers want and what management thinks customers want. This gap results from a lack of understanding or a misinterpretation of the customers' needs, wants, or desires. A firm that does little or no customer satisfaction research is likely to experience this gap. To close gap 1, firms must stay

perishability the inability of services to be stored, warehoused, or inventoried

reliability the ability to perform a service dependably, accurately, and consistently

responsiveness the ability to provide prompt service

assurance the knowledge and courtesy of employees and their ability to convey trust

empathy caring, individualized attention to customers

tangibles the physical evidence of a service, including the physical facilities, tools, and equipment used to provide the service

gap model a model identifying five gaps that can cause problems in service delivery and influence customer evaluations of service quality

EXHIBIT 12.1

Gap Model of Service Quality

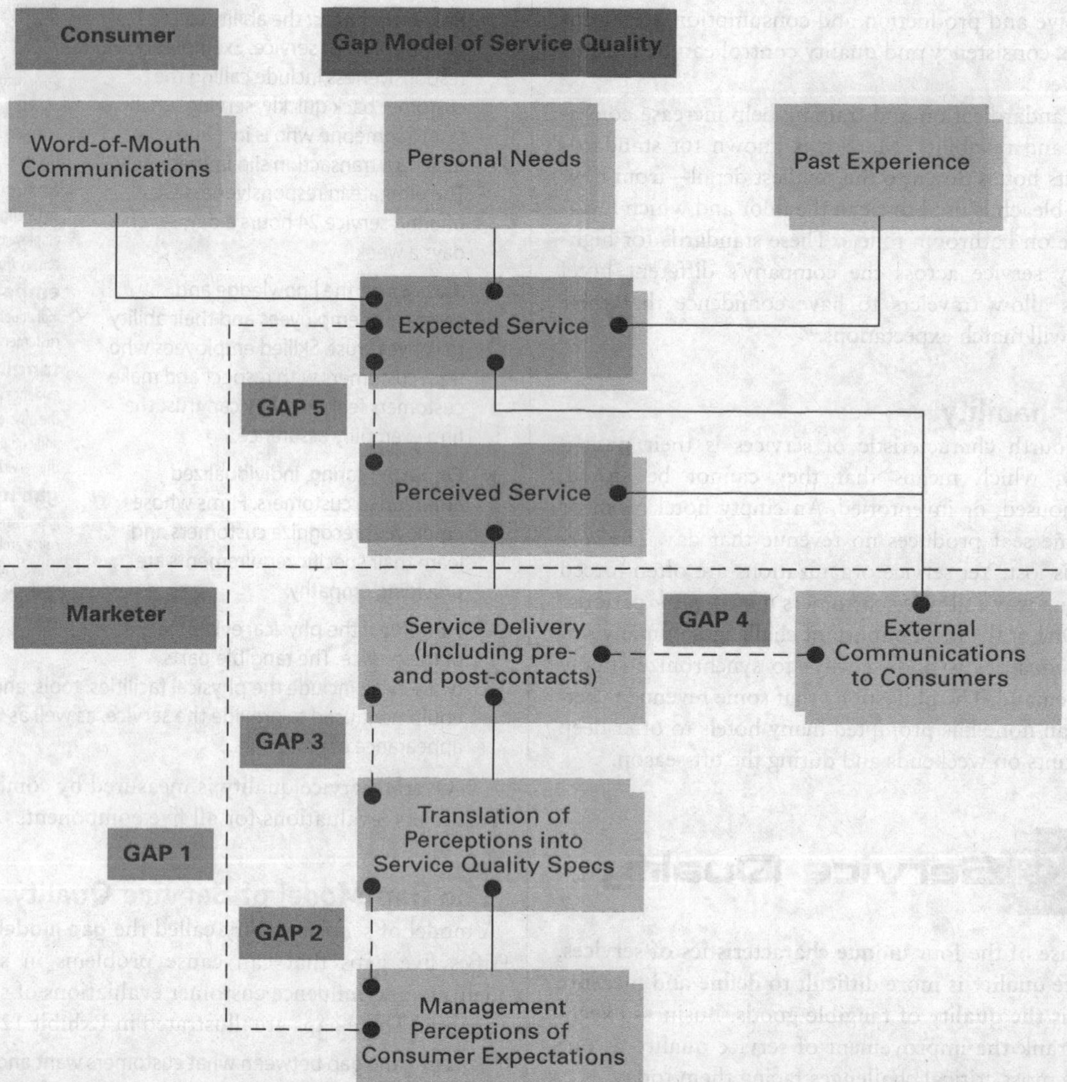

The gap analysis model measures consumer perceptions of service quality. Managers use the model to analyze sources of quality problems and to understand how service quality can be improved.

attuned to customer wishes by doing research on customer needs and satisfaction.

- *Gap 2:* the gap between what management thinks customers want and the quality specifications that management develops to provide the service. Essentially, this gap is the result of management's inability to translate customers' needs into delivery systems within the firm. For example, when KFC once rated its managers' success according to "chicken efficiency," or how much chicken they threw away at closing, consumers who came in late would either have to wait for chicken to be cooked or settle for chicken several hours old.
- *Gap 3:* the gap between the service quality specifications and the service that is actually provided. If both gaps 1 and 2 have been closed, then gap 3 is

due to the inability of management and employees to do what should be done. Management needs to ensure that employees have the skills and the proper tools to perform their jobs. Other techniques that help to close gap 3 are training employees so they know what management expects and encouraging teamwork.

- *Gap 4:* the gap between what the company provides and what the customer is told it provides. This is clearly a communication gap. It may include misleading or deceptive advertising campaigns promising more than the firm can deliver or doing "whatever it takes" to get the business. To close this gap, companies need to create realistic customer expectations through honest, accurate communication about what the firms can provide.
- *Gap 5:* the gap between the service that customers receive and the service they want. This gap can be positive or negative. For example, if a patient expects to wait 20 minutes in the physician's office before seeing the physician but actually waits only 10 minutes, the patient's evaluation of service quality will be high. However, a 40-minute wait would result in a lower evaluation.

When one or more of these gaps is large, service quality is perceived as low. As the gaps shrink, service quality perception improves.

LO 4 Marketing Mixes for Services

Services' unique characteristics—intangibility, inseparability of production and consumption, heterogeneity, and perishability—make marketing more challenging. Elements of the marketing mix (product, place, promotion, and pricing) need to be adjusted to meet the special needs created by these characteristics.

Product (Service) Strategy

A product, as defined in Chapter 10, is everything a person receives in an exchange. In the case of a service organization, the product offering is intangible and consists in large part of a process or a series of processes. Product strategies for service offerings include decisions on the type of process involved, core and supplementary services, standardization or customization of the service product, and the service mix.

Service as a Process Two broad categories of things get processed in service organizations: people and objects. In some cases, the process is physical, or tangible, while in others the process is intangible. Based on these characteristics, service processes can be placed into one of four categories:[6]

- *People processing* takes place when the service is directed at a customer. Examples are transportation services and health care.
- *Possession processing* occurs when the service is directed at customers' physical possessions. Examples are lawn care, dry-cleaning, and veterinary services.
- *Mental stimulus processing* refers to services directed at people's minds. Examples are theater performances and education.
- *Information processing* describes services that use technology or brainpower directed at a customer's assets. Examples are insurance and consulting.

core service the most basic benefit the consumer is buying

supplementary services a group of services that support or enhance the core service

Because customers' experiences and involvement differ for each of these types of services, marketing strategies may also differ. For example, people-processing services require customers to enter the *service factory*, which is a physical location, such as an aircraft, a physician's office, or a hair salon. In contrast, possession-processing services typically do not require the presence of the customer in the service factory. Marketing strategies for the former would therefore focus more on an attractive, comfortable physical environment and employee training on employee–customer interaction issues than would strategies for the latter.

Core and Supplementary Service Products The service offering can be viewed as a bundle of activities that includes the **core service**, which is the most basic benefit the customer is buying, and a group of **supplementary services** that support or enhance the core service. Exhibit 12.2 on the next page illustrates these concepts for an overnight stay at a luxury hotel. The core service is overnight rental of a bedroom, which involves people processing. The supplementary services, some of which involve information processing, include reservations, check-ins and check-outs, room service, and meals.

In many service industries, the core service becomes a commodity as competition increases. Thus, firms usually emphasize supplementary services to create a competitive advantage. On the other hand, some firms are positioning themselves in the marketplace by greatly reducing supplementary services.

Customization/Standardization An important issue in developing the service offering is whether to customize or standardize it. Customized services are more flexible

EXHIBIT 12.2

Core and Supplementary Services for a Luxury Hotel

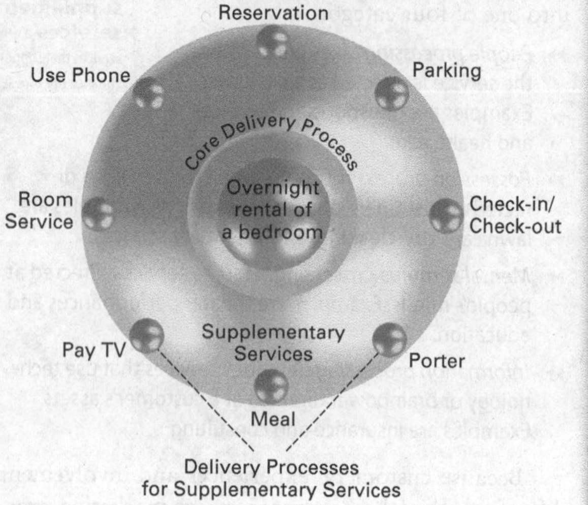

SOURCE: Lovelock, Christopher H.; Wirtz, Jochen, *Services Marketing*, 6th, ©2007. Electronically reproduced by permission of Pearson Education, Inc., Upper Saddle River, New Jersey.

and respond to individual customers' needs. They also usually command a higher price. Standardized services are more efficient and cost less.

Instead of choosing to either standardize or customize a service, a firm may incorporate elements of both by adopting an emerging strategy called **mass customization**. Mass customization uses technology to deliver customized services on a mass basis, which results in giving each customer whatever she or he asks for. Mass customization uses technology to deliver customized services on a mass basis, which results in giving each customer whatever she or he asks for. For example, Dell offers an opportunity to its customers to assemble their own computers or laptops themselves on its website and the company then builds the machine as requested by the customers before delivery.[7]

Personalization services can generate privacy questions and be controversial when implemented without customer approval. Facebook's Instant Personalization (IP) service is automatically checked on user profiles and imports profile data onto certain Web sites upon the user's next visit. For example, when a user visits Pandora, the online streaming radio service available in the United States, it will immediately begin playing music by bands that she has "liked" on her Facebook profile. IP also links real names and other public Facebook information to partner Web sites and other Facebook users. Unless a user turns off Web site–specific settings, she will automatically be publicizing information on her profile (location, name, phone number, etc.) when she uses sites like Pandora, Microsoft docs, and Yelp.[8]

mass customization a strategy that uses technology to deliver customized services on a mass basis

The Service Mix Most service organizations market more than one service. For example, ICICI group offers banking, life insurance, general insurance, securities, and home finance services. Each organization's service mix represents a set of opportunities, risks, and challenges. Each organization's service mix represents a set of opportunities, risks, and challenges. Each part of the service mix should make a different contribution to achieving the firm's goals. To succeed, each service may also need a different level of financial support. Designing a service strategy therefore means deciding what new services to introduce to which target market, what existing services to maintain, and what services to eliminate.

Place (Distribution) Strategy

Distribution strategies for service organizations must focus on such issues as convenience, number of outlets, direct versus indirect distribution, location, and scheduling. A key factor influencing the selection of a service provider is *convenience*. For example, infirm or elderly patients would probably prefer to use a doctor who makes house calls.

An important distribution objective for many service firms is the number of outlets to use or the number of outlets to open during a certain time. Generally, the intensity of distribution should meet, but not exceed, the target market's needs and preferences. Having too few outlets may inconvenience customers; having too many outlets may boost costs unnecessarily. Intensity of distribution may also depend on the image desired. Having only a few outlets may make the service seem more exclusive or selective.

The next service distribution decision is whether to distribute services to end users *directly* or *indirectly* through other firms. Because of the intangible nature of services, many service firms have to use direct distribution or franchising. Examples include legal, medical, accounting, and personal-care services. The newest form of direct distribution is the Internet. Most major airlines are now using online services to sell tickets directly to consumers, which results in lower distribution costs for the airlines. Other firms with standardized service packages have developed

IT'S OVER, LOVE MOOSEJAW

Some retailers are beginning to offer supplementary services as a way to continually engage customers outside of the store and develop customer loyalty. Outdoor equipment retailer Moosejaw in the United States offers an online break up service, where employees phone the unsuspecting other party at the customer's request—making breaking up easier for its customers. Less traumatically, Sears offers a mobile app called ManageMyLife that allows customers to plan projects, get advice, and even order merchandise and groceries for delivery.[9] In India, the mom-n-pop grocery stores offer services like home delivery of goods on the basis of a phone call, selling goods on credit, and providing a personalized treatment to the customers (example, addressing them by their first name) to build customer loyalty.[10]

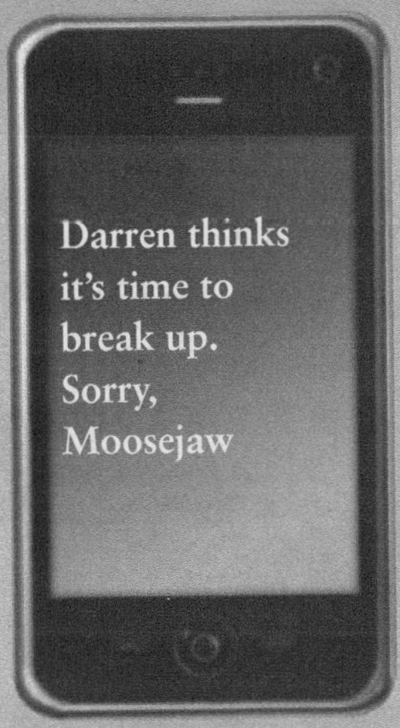

© ISTOCKPHOTO.COM/LAURENT DAVOUST

indirect channels using independent intermediaries. For example, Future Generali offers life and non-life insurance products to customers in the malls owned by Future Group. This distribution channel is termed as "mallassurance".[11]

The *location* of a service most clearly reveals the relationship between its target market strategy and distribution strategy. For time-dependent service providers such as airlines, physicians, and dentists, *scheduling* is often a more important factor.

Promotion Strategy

Consumers and business users have more trouble evaluating services than goods because services are less tangible. In turn, marketers have more trouble promoting intangible services than tangible goods. Here are four promotion strategies they can try:

- *Stressing tangible cues:* A tangible cue is a concrete symbol of the service offering.
- *Using personal information sources:* A personal information source is someone consumers are familiar with (such as a celebrity) or someone they admire or can relate to personally. Service firms may seek to simulate positive word-of-mouth communication among present and pro spective customers by using real customers in their ads.
- *Creating a strong organizational image:* One way to create an image is to manage the evidence, including the physical environment of the service facility, the appearance of the service employees, and the tangible items associated with a service (such as stationery, bills, and business cards). For example, McDonald's Golden Arches are instantly recognizable. Another way to create an image is through branding.
- *Engaging in postpurchase communication:* Postpurchase communication refers to the follow-up activities that a service firm might engage in after a customer transaction. Postcard surveys, telephone calls, and other types of follow-up show customers that their feedback matters.

Price Strategy

Considerations in pricing a service are similar to the pricing considerations to be discussed in Chapters 19 and 20. However, the unique characteristics of services present two special pricing challenges.

First, in order to price a service, it is important to define the unit of service consumption. For example, should pricing be based on completing a specific service task (cutting a customer's hair), or should it be time based (how long it takes to cut a customer's hair)? Some services include the consumption of goods, such as food

© FOODPIX/JUPITERIMAGES/GETTY IMAGES

and beverages. Restaurants charge customers for food and drink rather than the use of a table and chairs.

Second, for services that are composed of multiple elements, the issue is whether pricing should be based on a "bundle" of elements or whether each element should be priced separately. A bundled price may be preferable when consumers dislike having to pay "extra" for every part of the service (e.g., paying extra for baggage or food on an airplane), and it is simpler for the firm to administer. Alternatively, customers may not want to pay for service elements they do not use. Many furniture stores now have "unbundled" delivery charges from the price of the furniture. Customers who wish to can pick up the furniture at the store, saving on the delivery fee.

Marketers should set performance objectives when pricing each service. Three categories of pricing objectives have been suggested:[12]

- *Revenue-oriented pricing* focuses on maximizing the surplus of income over costs. A limitation of this approach is that determining costs can be difficult for many services.
- *Operations-oriented pricing* seeks to match supply and demand by varying prices. For example, matching hotel demand to the number of available rooms can be achieved by raising prices at peak times and decreasing them during slow times.
- *Patronage-oriented pricing* tries to maximize the number of customers using the service. Thus, prices vary with different market segments' ability to pay, and methods of payment (such as credit) are offered that increase the likelihood of a purchase.

A firm may need to use more than one type of pricing objective. In fact, all three objectives probably need to be included to some degree in a pricing strategy, although the importance of each type may vary depending on the type of service provided, the prices that competitors are charging, the differing ability of various customer segments to pay, or the opportunity to negotiate price. For customized services (such as construction services), customers may also have the ability to negotiate a price.

LO 5 Relationship Marketing in Services

Many services involve ongoing interaction between the service organization and the customer. Thus, they can benefit from relationship marketing, the strategy described in Chapter 1, as a means of attracting, developing, and retaining customer relationships. The idea is to develop strong loyalty by creating satisfied customers who will buy additional services from the firm and are unlikely to switch to a competitor. Satisfied customers are also likely to engage in positive word-of-mouth communication, thereby helping to bring in new customers.

Many businesses have found that it is more cost-effective to hang on to the customers they have than to focus only on attracting new ones. A bank executive, for example, found that increasing customer retention by 2 percent can have the same effect on profits as reducing costs by 10 percent.

Services that purchasers receive on a continuing basis (e.g., cable television, banking, insurance) can be considered membership services. This type of service naturally lends itself to relationship marketing. When services involve discrete transactions (e.g., in a movie theater, at a restaurant, or on public transportation), it may be more difficult to build membership-type relationships with customers. Nevertheless, services involving discrete transactions may be transformed into membership relationships using marketing tools. For example, the service could be sold in bulk (e.g., a theater series subscription or a commuter pass on public transportation). Or a service firm could offer special benefits to customers who choose to register with the firm (e.g., loyalty programs for hotels and airlines). The service firm that has a more formalized relationship with its customers has an advantage because it knows who its customers are and how and when they use the services offered.[13]

Relationship marketing can be practiced at three levels:[14]

- *Level 1:* The firm uses pricing incentives to encourage customers to continue doing business with it. Frequent flyer programs are an example of level 1 relationship marketing. This level of relationship marketing is the least effective in the long term because its price-based advantage is easily imitated by other firms.
- *Level 2:* This level of relationship marketing also uses pricing incentives but seeks to build social bonds with customers. The firm stays in touch with customers, learns about their needs, and designs services to meet those needs. Level 2 relationship marketing is often more effective than level 1 relationship marketing.
- *Level 3:* At this level, the firm again uses financial and social bonds but adds structural bonds to the formula. Structural bonds are developed by offering value-added services that are not readily available from other firms. Neo Cricket has developed many fans in a cricket crazy nation like India and secured the top spot in 2010 in the ratings for most watched sports channel.[15] In order to further engage its fans during Asia Cup 2010, the channel launched an online and offline contest called "Bano India ka lucky Charm" (become India's lucky charm). People were asked to give a witty and humorous reason as to why they thought they were Team India's lucky charm. The contest was promoted on social networking sites like Facebook and Twitter and advertisements were uploaded on Youtube. The objective of the whole campaign was to restore the faith of Indian fans and bring luck to their cricket team as India had not won the Asia Cup for 15 years.[16]

internal marketing treating employees as customers and developing systems and benefits that satisfy their needs

LO 6 Internal Marketing in Service Firms

Services are performances, so the quality of a firm's employees is an important part of building long-term relationships with customers. Employees who like their jobs and are satisfied with the firm they work for are more likely to deliver superior service to customers. In other words, a firm that makes its employees happy has a better chance of retaining customers. Thus, it is critical that service firms practice **internal marketing,** which means treating employees as customers and developing systems and benefits that satisfy their needs. To satisfy employees, companies have designed and instituted a wide variety of programs such as flextime, on-site day care, and concierge services. Leap Wireless, a telecommunications company in America, is committed to serving lower-income households and makes sure that its employees understand the importance of this demographic. The company donated employee time to renovate 90 local homes and provided a year of free phone and broadband service for each of those households. Likewise, Intel challenged employees to donate ten lakh hours of their time to charity and promised to provide matching grants. Besides increasing business value, employees returned energized to work for such an altruistic company.[17]

LO 7 Global Issues in Services Marketing

The international marketing of services is a major part of global business, and the United States has become the world's largest exporter of services. India also exports services in which it has a competitive advantage. Competition in international services is increasing rapidly, however. To be successful in the global marketplace, service firms must first determine the nature of their core product. Then the

TAXES HAVE BECOME THE BIGGEST SINGLE ITEM IN THE AMERICAN FAMILY BUDGET.

nonprofit organization an organization that exists to achieve some goal other than the usual business goals of profit, market share, or return on investment

nonprofit organization marketing the effort by nonprofit organizations to bring about mutually satisfying exchanges with target markets

marketing mix elements (additional services, place, promotion, pricing, distribution) should be designed to take into account each country's cultural, technological, and political environment.

Because of their competitive advantages, many U.S. service industries have been able to enter the global marketplace. U.S. banks, for example, have advantages in customer service and collections management.

LO 8 Nonprofit Organization Marketing

A **nonprofit organization** is an organization that exists to achieve some goal other than the usual business goals of profit, market share, or return on investment. Both nonprofit organizations and private-sector service firms market intangible products, and both often require the customer to be present during the production process. Both for-profit and nonprofit services vary greatly from producer to producer and from day to day, even from the same producer.

What Is Nonprofit Organization Marketing?

Nonprofit organization marketing is the effort by nonprofit organizations to bring about mutually satisfying exchanges with target markets. Although these organizations vary substantially in size and purpose and operate in different environments, most perform the following marketing activities:

- Identify the customers they wish to serve or attract (although they usually use other terms, such as *clients, patients, members,* or *sponsors*)
- Explicitly or implicitly specify objectives
- Develop, manage, and eliminate programs and services
- Decide on prices to charge (although they use other terms, such as *fees, donations, tuition, fares, fines,* or *rates*)
- Schedule events or programs, and determine where they will be held or where services will be offered
- Communicate their availability through brochures, signs, public service announcements, or advertisements

Often, the nonprofit organizations that carry out these functions do not realize they are engaged in marketing.

Unique Aspects of Nonprofit Organization Marketing Strategies

Like their counterparts in business organizations, nonprofit managers develop marketing strategies to bring about mutually satisfying exchanges with target markets. However, marketing in nonprofit organizations is unique in many ways—including the setting of marketing objectives, the selection of target markets, and the development of appropriate marketing mixes.

Objectives In the private sector, the profit motive is both an objective for guiding decisions and a criterion for evaluating results. Nonprofit organizations do not seek to make a profit for redistribution to owners or shareholders. Rather, their focus is often on generating enough funds to cover expenses.

Most nonprofit organizations are expected to provide equitable, effective, and efficient services that respond to the wants and preferences of multiple constituencies. These include users, payers, donors, politicians, appointed officials, the media, and the general public. Nonprofit organizations cannot measure their success or failure in strictly financial terms.

The lack of a financial "bottom line" and the existence of multiple, diverse, intangible, and sometimes vague or conflicting objectives make prioritizing objectives, making decisions, and evaluating performance hard for nonprofit managers. They must often use approaches different from the ones commonly used in the private sector.

Target Markets Three issues relating to target markets are unique to nonprofit organizations:

- *Apathetic or strongly opposed targets:* Private-sector organizations usually give priority to developing those market segments that are most likely to respond to particular offerings. In contrast, nonprofit organizations must often target those who are apathetic about or strongly opposed to receiving their services, such as vaccinations and psychological counseling.
- *Pressure to adopt undifferentiated segmentation strategies:* Nonprofit organizations often adopt undifferentiated strategies (see Chapter 8) by default. Sometimes they fail to recognize the advantages of targeting, or an undifferentiated approach may appear to offer economies of scale and low per-capita costs. In other instances, nonprofit organizations are pressured or required to serve the maximum number of people by targeting the average user.
- *Complementary positioning:* The main role of many nonprofit organizations is to provide services, with available resources, to those who are not adequately served by private-sector organizations. As a result, the nonprofit organization must often complement, rather than compete with, the efforts of others. The positioning task is to identify underserved market segments and to develop marketing programs that match their needs rather than target the niches that may be most profitable. For example, a university library may see itself as complementing the services of the public library rather than as competing with it.

Product Decisions There are three product-related distinctions between business and nonprofit organizations:

- *Benefit complexity:* Nonprofit organizations often market complex behaviors or ideas. Examples include the need to exercise or eat right and the need to quit smoking. The benefits that a person receives are complex, long term, and intangible, and therefore are more difficult to communicate to consumers.
- *Benefit strength:* The benefit strength of many nonprofit offerings is quite weak or indirect. What are the direct, personal benefits to you of teaching underprivileged children or donating blood? In contrast, most private-sector service organizations can offer customers direct, personal benefits in an exchange relationship.

NONPROFIT MIX AT A GLANCE

Product
- Benefit complexity
- Benefit strength
- Involvement

Promotion
- Professional volunteers
- Sales promotion activities
- Public service advertisements

Place
- Special facilities

Price
- Pricing objectives
- Nonfinancial pricing
- Indirect payment
- Separation between payers and users
- Below-cost pricing

- *Involvement:* Many nonprofit organizations market products that elicit very low involvement ("Prevent forest fires") or very high involvement ("Stop smoking"). The typical range for private-sector goods is much narrower. Traditional promotional tools may be inadequate to motivate adoption of either low- or high-involvement products.

Place (Distribution) Decisions A nonprofit organization's capacity for distributing its service offerings to potential customer groups when and where they want them is typically a key variable in determining the success of those service offerings. For example, many large universities have one or more satellite campus locations to provide easier access for students in other areas. Some educational institutions also offer classes to students at off-campus locations via interactive video technology or at home via the Internet.

The extent to which a service depends on fixed facilities has important implications for distribution decisions. Services like rail transit and lake fishing can be delivered only at specific points. Many nonprofit services, however, do not depend on special facilities.

Promotion Decisions Many nonprofit organizations are explicitly or implicitly prohibited from advertising, thus limiting their promotion options. Most federal

public service advertisement (PSA) an announcement that promotes a program of a federal, state, or local government or of a nonprofit organization

agencies fall into this category. Other nonprofit organizations simply do not have the resources to retain advertising agencies, promotion consultants, or marketing staff. However, nonprofit organizations have a few special promotion resources to call on:

- *Professional volunteers:* Nonprofit organizations often seek out marketing, sales, and advertising professionals to help them develop and implement promotion strategies. In some instances, an advertising agency donates its services in exchange for potential long-term benefits. Donated services create goodwill; personal contacts; and general awareness of the donor's organization, reputation, and competency.
- *Sales promotion activities:* Sales promotion activities that make use of existing services or other resources are increasingly being used to draw attention to the offerings of nonprofit organizations. Sometimes nonprofit charities even team up with other companies for promotional activities.
- *Public service advertising:* A **public service advertisement (PSA)** is an announcement that promotes a program of a federal, state, or local government or of a nonprofit organization. Unlike a commercial advertiser, the sponsor of the PSA does not pay for the time or space. Instead, it is donated by the medium. The PSAs run by Indian government are some of the most memorable advertisements of all time. For example, the "Mile Sur Mera Tumhara" campaign promoted national unity, integration, and harmony among diverse groups in India.

Pricing Decisions Five key characteristics distinguish the pricing decisions of nonprofit organizations from those of the profit sector:

- *Pricing objectives:* The main pricing objective in the profit sector is revenue or, more specifically, profit maximization, sales maximization, or target return on sales or investment. Many nonprofit organizations must also be concerned about revenue. Often, however, nonprofit organizations seek to either partially or fully defray costs rather than to achieve a profit for distribution to stockholders. Nonprofit organizations also seek to redistribute income—for instance, through taxation and sliding-scale fees. Moreover, they strive to allocate resources fairly among individuals or households or across geographic or political boundaries.
- *Nonfinancial prices:* In many nonprofit situations, consumers are not charged a monetary price but instead

© WWW.CRY.ORG

must absorb nonmonetary costs. The importance of those costs is illustrated by the large number of eligible citizens who do not take advantage of so-called "free" services for the poor. In many public assistance programs, about half the people who are eligible don't participate. Nonmonetary costs include time, embarrassment, and effort.

- *Indirect payment:* Indirect payment through taxes is common to marketers of "free" services, such as libraries, fire protection, and police protection. Indirect payment is not a common practice in the profit sector.
- *Separation between payers and users:* By design, the services of many charitable organizations are provided for those who are relatively poor and largely paid for by those who are better off financially. Although examples of separation between payers and users can be found in the profit sector (such as insurance claims), the practice is much less prevalent.
- *Below-cost pricing:* An example of below-cost pricing is university tuition. Virtually all private and public colleges and universities price their services below full cost.

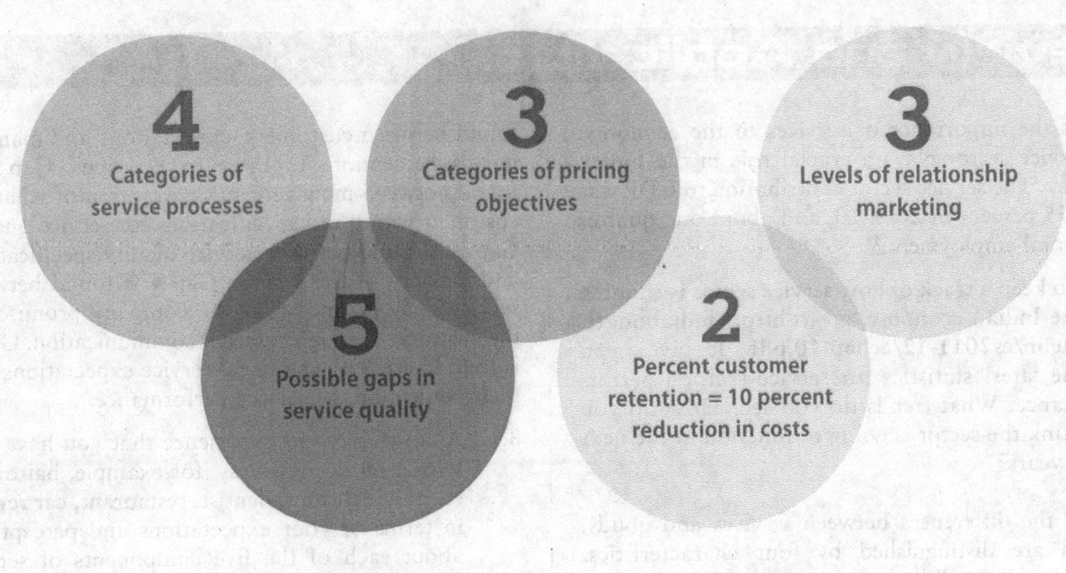
4
Categories of service processes
3
Categories of pricing objectives
3
Levels of relationship marketing
5
Possible gaps in service quality
2
Percent customer retention = 10 percent reduction in costs

Review and Applications

Discuss the importance of services to the economy. The service sector plays a crucial role in the Indian economy. The service sector contribution to GDP was about 55 percent in 2009-10, and about one quarter of the total employment.[18]

1.1 To keep a track of how service sector is shaping the Indian economy, go to **http://indiabudget.nic.in/es2011-12/echap-10.pdf.** It gives you the latest statistics for service sector's performance. What trends do you see? How do you think the sector is going to function in the next 5 years?

Discuss the differences between services and goods. Services are distinguished by four characteristics. Services are intangible performances in that they lack clearly identifiable physical characteristics, making it difficult for marketers to communicate their specific benefits to potential customers. The production and consumption of services occur simultaneously. Services are heterogeneous because their quality depends on such elements as the service provider, individual consumer, location, and so on. Finally, services are perishable in the sense that they cannot be stored or saved. As a result, synchronizing supply with demand is particularly challenging in the service industry.

2.1 Assume that you are a manager of a bank branch. Write a list of the implications of intangibility for your firm.

2.2 Burrp.com is a website that gives you reviews of restaurants, movies, shopping, etc. It also gives you updates and ratings night life, music and various events taking place in different cities. Go to **www.burrp.com.** In your opinion, are *Burrp* surveys goods or services?

Describe the components of service quality and the gap model of service quality. Service quality has five components: reliability (ability to perform the service dependably, accurately, and consistently), responsiveness (providing prompt service), assurance (knowledge and courtesy of employees and their ability to convey trust), empathy (caring, individualized attention), and tangibles (physical evidence of the service).

The gap model identifies five key discrepancies that can influence customer evaluations of service quality. When the gaps are large, service quality is low. As the gaps shrink, service quality improves. Gap 1 is found between customers' expectations and management's perceptions of those expectations. Gap 2 is found between management's perception of what the customer wants and specifications for service quality. Gap 3 is found between service quality specifications and delivery of the service. Gap 4 is found between service delivery and what the company promises to the customer through external communication. Gap 5 is found between customers' service expectations and their perceptions of service performance.

3.1 Analyze a recent experience that you have had with a service business (for example, hairdresser, movie theater, dentist, restaurant, car repair) in terms of your expectations and perceptions about each of the five components of service quality.

Develop marketing mixes for services. "Product" (service) strategy issues include what is being processed (people, possessions, mental stimulus, information), core and supplementary services, customization versus standardization, and the service mix. Distribution decisions involve convenience, number of outlets, direct versus indirect distribution, and scheduling. Stressing tangible cues, using personal sources of information, creating strong organizational images, and engaging in postpurchase communication are effective promotion strategies. Pricing objectives for services can be revenue oriented, operations oriented, patronage oriented, or any combination of the three.

4.1 Form a team with at least two other classmates, and come up with an idea for a new service. Develop a marketing mix strategy for the new service.

Discuss relationship marketing in services. Relationship marketing in services involves attracting, developing, and retaining customer relationships. There are three levels of relationship marketing: level 1 focuses on pricing incentives; level 2 uses pricing incentives and social bonds with customers; and level 3 uses pricing, social bonds, and structural bonds to build long-term relationships.

5.1 For the new service developed for question 4.1, have the members of the team discuss how they would implement a relationship marketing strategy.

Explain internal marketing in services. Internal marketing means treating employees as customers and developing systems and benefits that satisfy their needs. Employees who like their jobs and are happy with the firm they work for are more likely to deliver good service.

6.1 Choose a service firm with which you do a lot of business. Write a memo to the manager explaining the importance of internal marketing and outlining the factors internal marketing includes.

6.2 Go to **www.zagat.com** and investigate what the site offers. How does *Zagat* propose to help companies with internal services marketing?

Discuss global issues in services marketing. U.S. is world's largest exporter of services. India exports services in which it has a competitive advantage. To be successful globally, service firms must adjust their marketing mix for the environment of each target country.

7.1 What issues would you have to think about in going global with the new service that you developed in the questions above? How would you change your marketing mix to address those issues?

Describe nonprofit organization marketing. Nonprofit organizations pursue goals other than profit, market share, and return on investment. Nonprofit organization marketing facilitates mutually satisfying exchanges between nonprofit organizations and their target markets. Several unique characteristics distinguish nonbusiness marketing strategy, including: a concern with services and social behaviors rather than manufactured goods and profit; a difficult, undifferentiated, and in some ways marginal target market; a complex product that may have only indirect benefits and elicit very low involvement; distribution that may or may not require special facilities depending on the service provided; a relative lack of resources for promotion; and prices only indirectly related to the exchange between the producer and the consumer of services.

8.1 Form a team with two or three classmates. Using the promotion strategies discussed in the nonprofit section of this chapter, develop a promotion strategy for your college or university.

Exercises

APPLICATION EXERCISE

All people know quality when they see it—or do they? Let's take a look at some goods and services and then think about assessing their quality. For this exercise, work in teams of two to three and discuss each item before determining its final placement.[19]

Activities

1. Using the abbreviations in parentheses, place each of the following products and services along the continuum below: a new car (C), designer jeans (J), car oil change (O), dress dry cleaning (D), haircut (H), tax preparation software (T), college education (E).

   100 percent physical good ________________ 100 percent service

2. Once you have placed the items along the continuum, consider how easy it is to assess the quality of each item.

   Easy to assess quality ________________ Difficult to assess quality

3. What assumptions can you make about the ability to assess the quality of goods compared to services? Is it easier to assess the quality of some goods than others? What about for services?

ETHICS EXERCISE

Web sites such as **www.cancerpage.com** offer cancer patients sophisticated medical data and advice in exchange for personal information that is then sold to advertisers and business partners and used by the Web sites to create products to sell back to patients. Some argue that cancer patients visiting these sites are willingly exchanging their personal information for the sites' medical information. Others contend that this kind of exchange is unethical.

Questions

1. Is this practice ethical?
2. Does the AMA Statement of Ethics have anything to say about this issue? Go to **www.marketingpower.com** and review the statement. Then, write a brief paragraph on what the AMA Statement of Ethics contains that relates to this situation.

MARKETING PLAN EXERCISE

Continue your strategic marketing plan (and complete your Part 3 Marketing Plan Worksheet on your companion Web site at **www.cengage.com/international** by answering the following questions about your chosen company:

1. What service aspects are provided with the product? List specific examples of how you can incorporate all five elements of service quality into your offering. What tactics can you define that would minimize any potential service quality gaps? How is customer service handled? What elements of service quality can your firm focus on? What impact would selling on the Internet have on your customer service operation?
2. With whom should your chosen company practice relationship marketing? E-marketing is particularly vulnerable to breakdowns in client relationships. Which sorts of bonds should be stressed in the relationship marketing strategy? How can your company "touch" its customers differently online than offline? Are there advantages to online customer service? Disadvantages?

Short Case: TAJ HOTELS, RESORTS, AND PALACES

Prepared by
Dr. Dheeraj Sharma,
Indian Institute of Management, Ahmedabad

The Indian Hotel Company Limited (IHCL) is the parent company of Taj hotel, resorts, and palaces. It was founded by Jamshed ji Tata in 1903 with its first property in Mumbai. It is popular as the finest and largest luxury hotel chains in Asia. IHCL has 93 hotels in 55 prime locations across India.[20]

Service marketing mix of Taj hotels, resorts, and palaces:

Product: The hotels are categorized into three groups, luxury, business, and leisure. Taj believes their core product to be space. The *rooms* are skillfully decorated with different categories like luxury, superior, deluxe, or grand luxury. Every room is accompanied by amenities like color TV, speaker phones, Internet access, mini bar, personal safe, etc. The *dining facilities* include cuisines, drinks, snacks, pastries, Indian and international dishes, etc. The *recreational facilities* include the Jiva spa, health club, fitness centre swimming pool, gift shop, shopping arcade, bookshop, yacht, sports facilities, etc. It also provides facilities for conducting *business meetings* like workstations with computers, printers, laptops, mobile, color copier, secretarial services, etc.[21] The other *supplementary services* include travel arrangements, flight pick-ups, sight-seeing, ticketing, wake up call, laundry, baby sitting, currency exchange, car hire, doctor on call, etc.

Price: The price charged by Taj is higher than its counterparts and not affordable by all. This is due to its high overhead expenses and expenses incurred in maintaining its quality standards.

Place: Taj group of hotels have 93 hotels spread over 55 locations all over India. It is also present in 18 other countries like San Francisco, New York, London, Boston, etc. The main USP of Taj group is their unique concept of converting ancient buildings into hotels. It is present in all major cities in India.

Promotion: Hotel Taj keeps on providing various season and off-season promotional offers to its customers like honeymoon offer, Taj holidays, etc. to increase occupancy in their hotels. It also makes use of various promotional tools like brochures, leaflets, merchandising, display materials in the offices of tour operators, travel agents, tourist stops like airports, etc. Word of mouth publicity also plays a major role in its promotion. It also makes use of advertisements in business magazines, business newspapers, and TV channels to promote its services and facilities.

Physical evidence: The physical evidence of Taj hotels includes the lobby design, reception desk which is very attractive and skillfully decorated. The rooms are comfortable and have a very delightful ambience with all facilities. The employees are dressed in a very formal and elegant way. All equipments used are of high quality.

People: The hotel industry is a pure game of people. People aspect in Taj hotel is very well taken care of. It includes all front line representatives working in the hotel like the front desk representatives, housekeepers, waiters, waitresses, doormen, etc. and hotel sales executives, managers, senior executives, who are also responsible to provide training to the front line representatives because these front line employees are the one who create first impression in the mind of the customers. The training is provided to ensure that the service is delivered efficiently and on time as was promised.

Process: The process aspect provides a major reason for a customer delight or disappointment. Hotel Taj ensures systematic and timely flow of process, which is reflected in its quick check in, luggage at the doorstep, the serving of food with minimum time lag between the order time and its arrival, giving timely wake up call, easy check out, etc.

Thus hotel Taj has been able to provide high class service and able to justify its five star ratings. But it has to be very vigilant and dynamic to outweigh its competitors like Le-meridian, Hotel Trident, Centaur, Hyatt, etc. if it wants to gain an edge over them.

Questions

1. What type of clientele does Hotel Taj enjoy? With such intense competition in hospitality industry, do you think that Taj hotel will be able to continue to attract similar type of clientele?
2. Do you think Taj should also target other clientele group?

12 Services and Nonprofit Organization Marketing

KEY TERMS

LO 1

service the result of applying human or mechanical efforts to people or objects

LO 2

intangibility the inability of services to be touched, seen, tasted, heard, or felt in the same manner that goods can be sensed

search quality a characteristic that can be easily assessed before purchase

experience quality a characteristic that can be assessed only after use

credence quality a characteristic that consumers may have difficulty assessing even after purchase because they do not have the necessary knowledge or experience

inseparability the inability of the production and consumption of a service to be separated; consumers must be present during the production

heterogeneity the variability of the inputs and outputs of services, which causes services to tend to be less standardized and uniform than goods

perishability the inability of services to be stored, warehoused, or inventoried

LO 3

reliability the ability to perform a service dependably, accurately, and consistently

responsiveness the ability to provide prompt service

assurance the knowledge and courtesy of employees and their ability to convey trust

empathy caring, individualized attention to customers

tangibles the physical evidence of a service, including the physical facilities, tools, and equipment used to provide the service

KEY CONCEPTS

LO 1 **Discuss the importance of services to the economy.** The service sector plays a crucial role in the Indian economy. The service sector contribution to GDP was about 55 percent in 2009-10, and about one quarter of the total employment.

LO 2 **Discuss the differences between services and goods.** Services are distinguished by four characteristics. Services are intangible performances in that they lack clearly identifiable physical characteristics, making it difficult for marketers to communicate their specific benefits to potential customers. The production and consumption of services occur simultaneously. Services are heterogeneous because their quality depends on such elements as the service provider, individual consumer, location, and so on. Finally, services are perishable in the sense that they cannot be stored or saved. As a result, synchronizing supply with demand is particularly challenging in the service industry.

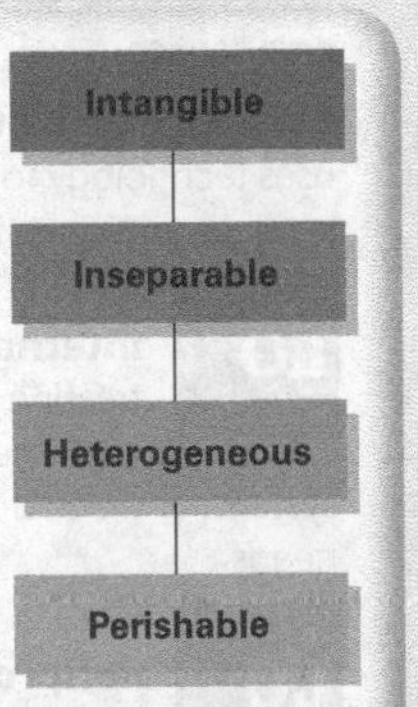

© CENGAGE LEARNING 2011

LO 3 **Describe the components of service quality and the gap model of service quality.** Service quality has five components: reliability (ability to perform the service dependably, accurately, and consistently), responsiveness (providing prompt service), assurance (knowledge and courtesy of employees and their ability to convey trust), empathy (caring, individualized attention), and tangibles (physical evidence of the service).

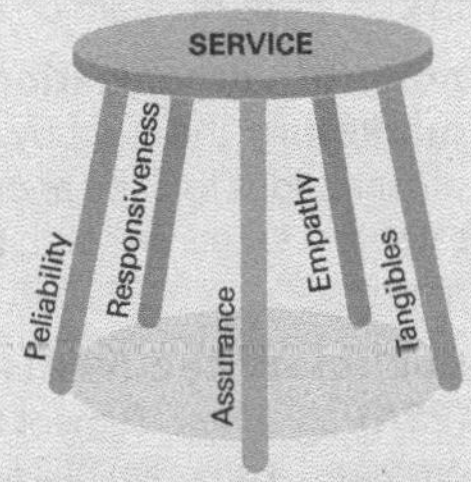

© CENGAGE LEARNING 2011

The gap model identifies five key discrepancies that can influence customer evaluations of service quality. When the gaps are large, service quality is low. As the gaps shrink, service quality improves. Gap 1 is found between customers' expectations and management's perceptions of those expectations. Gap 2 is found between management's perception of what the customer wants and specifications for service quality. Gap 3 is found between service quality specifications and delivery of the service. Gap 4 is found between service delivery and what the company promises to the customer through external communication. Gap 5 is found between customers' service expectations and their perceptions of service performance.

LO 4 **Develop marketing mixes for services.** "Product" (service) strategy issues include what is being processed (people, possessions, mental stimulus, information), core and supplementary services, customization versus standardization, and the service mix. Distribution decisions involve convenience, number of outlets, direct versus indirect distribution, and scheduling. Stressing tangible cues, using personal sources of information, creating strong organizational images, and engaging in postpurchase communication are effective promotion strategies. Pricing objectives for services can be revenue oriented, operations oriented, patronage oriented, or any combination of the three.

gap model a model identifying five gaps that can cause problems in service delivery and influence customer evaluations of service quality

LO 4

core service the most basic benefit the consumer is buying

supplementary services a group of services that support or enhance the core service

mass customization a strategy that uses technology to deliver customized services on a mass basis

LO 6

internal marketing treating employees as customers and developing systems and benefits that satisfy their needs

LO 8

nonprofit organization an organization that exists to achieve some goal other than the usual business goals of profit, market share, or return on investment

nonprofit organization marketing the effort by nonprofit organizations to bring about mutually satisfying exchanges with target markets

public service advertisement (PSA) an announcement that promotes a program of a federal, state, or local government or of a nonprofit organization

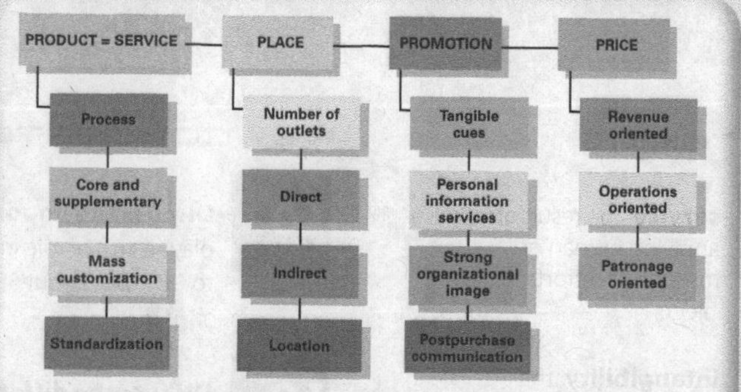

LO 5 **Discuss relationship marketing in services.** Relationship marketing in services involves attracting, developing, and retaining customer relationships. There are three levels of relationship marketing: level 1 focuses on pricing incentives; level 2 uses pricing incentives and social bonds with customers; and level 3 uses pricing, social bonds, and structural bonds to build long-term relationships.

LO 6 **Explain internal marketing in services.** Internal marketing means treating employees as customers and developing systems and benefits that satisfy their needs. Employees who like their jobs and are happy with the firm they work for are more likely to deliver good service.

LO 7 **Discuss global issues in services marketing.** U.S. is world's largest exporter of services. India exports services in which it has a competitive advantage. To be successful globally, service firms must adjust their marketing mix for the environment of each target country.

LO 8 **Describe nonprofit organization marketing.** Nonprofit organizations pursue goals other than profit, market share, and return on investment. Nonprofit organization marketing facilitates mutually satisfying exchanges between nonprofit organizations and their target markets. Several unique characteristics distinguish nonbusiness marketing strategy, including: a concern with services and social behaviors rather than manufactured goods and profit; a difficult, undifferentiated, and in some ways marginal target market; a complex product that may have only indirect benefits and elicit very low involvement; distribution that may or may not require special facilities depending on the service provided; a relative lack of resources for promotion; and prices only indirectly related to the exchange between the producer and the consumer of services.

CASE 3 A-One Starch Products Limited (A)

In July 1996, the Chief Executive of A-One Products Ltd. was considering what strategic options the company had for the future and how to decide on the best option. The objective was to adopt a strategy for A-One, which would lead the company to a path of growth and prosperity.

C3.1 Company Background

A-One Products Limited was established in the late thirties in Western India. A-One was a member of a large business group. Initially, A-One was set up for manufacturing starch used in the textile industry. However, over time, the company had added facilities to manufacture starch and its derivatives to meet the needs of the textile, paper, confectionery, chemical and other industries.

The company was started with one metric tonne of maize grinding capacity (corn wet milling capacity) per day. In 1996, its wet milling capacity was more than 100,000 tonnes per year. Over the years, several products were added to the company's product line. In 1996, it included, besides different types of starches, Corn Syrup, Dextrose, Anhydrous Dextrose, and Sorbitol. The manufacturing capacities of these products are given in Exhibit C3.1.

EXHIBIT C3.1
Manufacturing Facilities at A-One

Manufacturing facility	Current Capacity tonnes/year
Corn Wet Milling	100,000
Corn Syrup	16,000
Dextrose	16,000
Anhydrous Dextrose	6,000
Sorbitol	3,000

SOURCE : Company Records

The company increased its sales from 437 million in 1992-93 to 654 million in 1994-95. Its profit after tax was 2.66 million and 7.45 million in 1993 and 1995 respectively. (See Exhibit C3.2 for brief details of balance sheet and profit and loss statement.) Although A-One did not have a high market share, according to a widely respected industry source in 1993, A-One was "more or less leader in the industry for their technology and product quality".

C3.2 Starch and Its Derivatives

Starch is a natural polymer. Chemically, it is a complex carbohydrate with the formula $(C_6H_{12}O_6)_n$ where n was a number between 1000 and 10,000. Starch was a mixture of two polymers, one linear called *amylase,* which was soluble, and the other, a branched polymer called *amylopectin*, which was less soluble. Usually, starches contained about 25 percent amylase and 75 percent amylopectin. However, depending on the raw material from which the starch was produced, the composition of amylase and amylopectin might vary. Starch was commercially produced from maize, potatoes, wheat, tapioca etc. In India, starch was normally produced from maize and tapioca. Liquid starch could be used for producing dry starch, specialised starches, and several downstream products. Besides, depending on the raw material, several by-products were also produced.

Corn was used to produce starch through a process called the 'wet-milling' process. In this process, corn was steeped into water and a series of chemical and mechanical steps were used to produce *liquid starch* as the main intermediate product. The by-products of the process were (fibre) wet husk, oil cake, raw corn oil, and corn-gluten. Wet husk was a voluminous item, and needed to be disposed off as is (or after drying) as cattle feed. Corn-gluten was used as cattle/poultry feed. Liquid starch could be used to produce dry starch, liquid glucose, modified starches, and wet-dextrose. Wet-dextrose was further processed to produce glucose-D, dextrose mono-

---

Prepared by Professors Abhinandan K. Jain and Jahar Saha.

Cases of the Indian Institute of Management, Ahmedabad, are prepared as a basis for classroom discussion. They are not designed to present illustrations of either correct or incorrect handling of administrative problems.

EXHIBIT C3.2

A-One Starch Products Ltd. (A)

Balance Sheet as at 31 March			(₹ Million)
		Year	
	1993	1994	1995
Source of Funds			
Capital	15.50	15.50	15.50
Reserves and Surplus	78.73	79.09	85.39
Loans	143.99	156.70	153.82
Total	238.16	251.33	254.71
Application of Funds			
Fixed Asset	100.56	93.28	113.58
Investments	1.94	2.23	2.47
Total Fixed Assets and Investments	102.50	95.51	116.05
Current Assets, Loans and Advances	253.09	230.72	260.97
Current Liabilities & Provisions	118.43	75.71	122.89
Net Current Assets	134.66	155.00	138.10
Machinery Repairs	1.00	0.75	0.50
Total	238.16	251.33	254.71
Profit and Loss Account for the Year Ended 31 March			
Income			
Sales	436.88	553.39	653.87
Other Income	20.27	5.71	3.62
	457.17	559.10	657.49
Expenditure			
Material	195.19	262.84	295.76
Stores, Power, Fuel, Repairs, etc	145.21	176.35	188.77
Salaries and Wages	41.34	41.13	43.87
Others	62.00	64.16	69.75
Depreciation	10.70	10.03	9.21
	454.44	554.51	607.37
Profit before tax	2.70	4.60	7.76
Provision for tax	0.04	2.12	0.31
Profit for the year	2.66	2.48	7.45

SOURCE: Company Records

hydrate, anhydrous-dextrose, and sorbitol. The process of producing wet-dextrose produced an effluent by-product, hydrol, which was sweet, and its disposal was a difficult task. Exhibit C3.3 shows how corn is converted into different by-products, starch, and its derivatives.

Unmodified and modified starches were used primarily in the paper, textile, food, and pharmaceutical industries. Liquid glucose was used as a doctoring agent in food industry, as a base and anti-crystalliser in the pharma industry and in ice-creams to give shape

EXHIBIT C3.3

Flow Chart of Conversion of Corn to Starch and Other Products

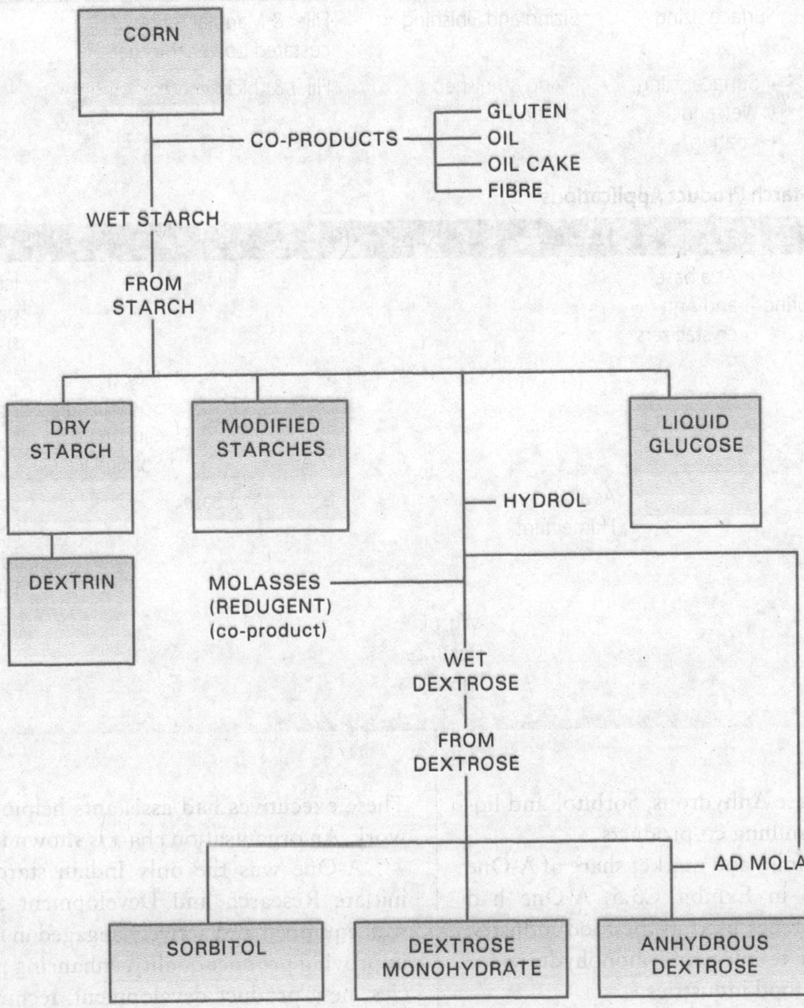

SOURCE: Company Records

and body. Dextrose-D was used as an energy drink in the food industry and as a feed for microorganisms in fermentation. Anhydrous Dextrose IP was used in the manufacture of dextrose intravenous fluids and in oral-rehydration products in the pharma industry. Sorbitol was used mainly in tooth-paste and for making vitamins in the pharmaceutical industry. Besides, starch could be further processed to meet specific needs of different industries. Exhibit C3.4 shows the usage of different products in different industries.

C3.3 A-One's Product Range

A-One had a diverse product range which included starches (starch powder, thin boiling starch, cationic starch, oxidised starch, cross linked starch, low microbial count starch), dextrins (yellow and white) and other speciality starches, downstream products (Dextrose

EXHIBIT C3.4

Segmentwise Starch Product Applications

Product	Paper	Textile	Food	Pharma
Unmodified starch	Surface sizing	Sizing and Finishing	Filler & Manufacturing of custared power, thickner	Tableting
Modified starch	• Surface sizing • Wet, and • Coating	Sizing & finished printing	Filler & thickner etc.	- do -

Segmentwise Non-Starch Product Applications

Product	Food	Pharma	Hygiene	IV Fluids	Inject	Syrups	Tablets	Others
Liquid Glucose	As a Doctoring Agent	As a base and Anti-crystallizers						Ice-Creams to give body and shape
DHH & Glucose - D	As a Energy Drink						Mfg. of Sorbitol Cal Gluconate Sorbitol Vit. C	
Sorbitol			As a Humectant			As a Base		Softner and Flavour in Tobacco Leather Tanning etc.
Anhydrous Dextrose I P				Mfg. of Dextrose Injections				

Monohydrate, Dextrose Anhydrous, Sorbitol and liquid glucose) and wet milling co-products.

The product portfolio and market share of A-One have been presented in Exhibit C3.5. A-One had been the leader in starches used in the food industry, speciality starches for textiles, and monohydrate for pharma, hygiene and food industries.

C3.4 A-One's Organisation

A-One was headed by the Managing Director. Two Vice Presidents (Manufacturing and Corporate Finance) and five senior managers in charge of Projects and Services, Technical Support, Marketing (Starch and Co-products), Marketing (Starch downstream products) and Human Resources, directly reported to him. In addition, two Managers (Materials and Information Technology Services) worked directly under him. These executives had assistants helping them in their work. An organisation chart is shown in Exhibit C3.6.

A-One was the only Indian starch company to initiate Research and Development activity. It was well equipped and actively engaged in monitoring and improving product quality, enhancing process efficiencies, new product development, technical services to customers and some basic research. A-One had developed speciality starches in its R & D lab.

A-One distributed its products through three different channels, namely, directly to customers (through head office or regional offices), through agents (against 'C' form or as consignment depots), and through retail agents. The retail agents bought in bulk and distributed to the smaller customers. They paid within seven days. They fixed their own price. Other agents were paid commission on sales. They were also paid cash discounts and additional commission for special services. The agents guaranteed collection of cash and they were also responsible for the settlement of complaints. There was concern in the company about whether or not, in certain products,

EXHIBIT C3.5

Equivalent Starch Consumption By Endusers in India

(In MT)

Product/ Industry	Unmodified Starch	Modified Starchs	Liquid Glucose	Dextrose & Glucose-D	Anhy. Dextrose	Sorbitol	Total
Paper	**1740**	**1390**					**3130**
	8800	11110					19910
Textiles	**13920**	**5560**					**19480**
	82500	17780					100280
Food	**870**	**330**	**12250**	**3050**			**16500**
	11000	6670	91630	21770			131070
Hygiene						**520**	**520**
						20720	20720
Pharma	**350**	**110**					**460**
Tablets	**5500**	**2000**					**7500**
Pharma				**1220**			**1220**
Ferment				22260			22260
Pharma			**785**			**350**	**1135**
Syrup			10780			16050	26830
IV Fluids/					**5480**		**5480**
Injection					12170		12170
ORS					**810**		**810**
					4060		4060
Others	**520**	**1670**	**100**	**490**		**90**	**2870**
	12100	9890	5390	1950		7000	36330
Total	**17400**	**9060**	**13135**	**4760**	**6290**	**960**	**51605**
	119900	47450	107800	45980	16230	43770	381030

Note: The figures are in metric tonnes and A-One's share in bold face.

SOURCE: Company Records

A-One was catering to too many smaller customers directly and thus too much time was spent in sales administration.

C3.5 Indian Starch Industry—Structure

In India, starch was produced from corn and tapioca. There were about 700 tapioca starch companies, mostly in the small scale sector. The Indian corn starch industry consisted of 12 firms. Of these, three were major, namely, Anil Starch, Sukhjit Starch and Maize Products Limited. These four firms, including A-One, produced 60 percent of the total starch and down stream products produced in India. Eleven firms were wet millers and one firm made speciality starches from bought out starches. The number of plants was 15 and these had different grind capacities and were located at different parts of the country.

The distribution of corn wet milling plants in terms of grind per day is shown in Exhibit C3.7.

Two firms, Anil Starch and Maize Products produced starch, speciality starches, and all downstream products. Two other manufacturers, who were not pro-

EXHIBIT C3.6
A-One Starch

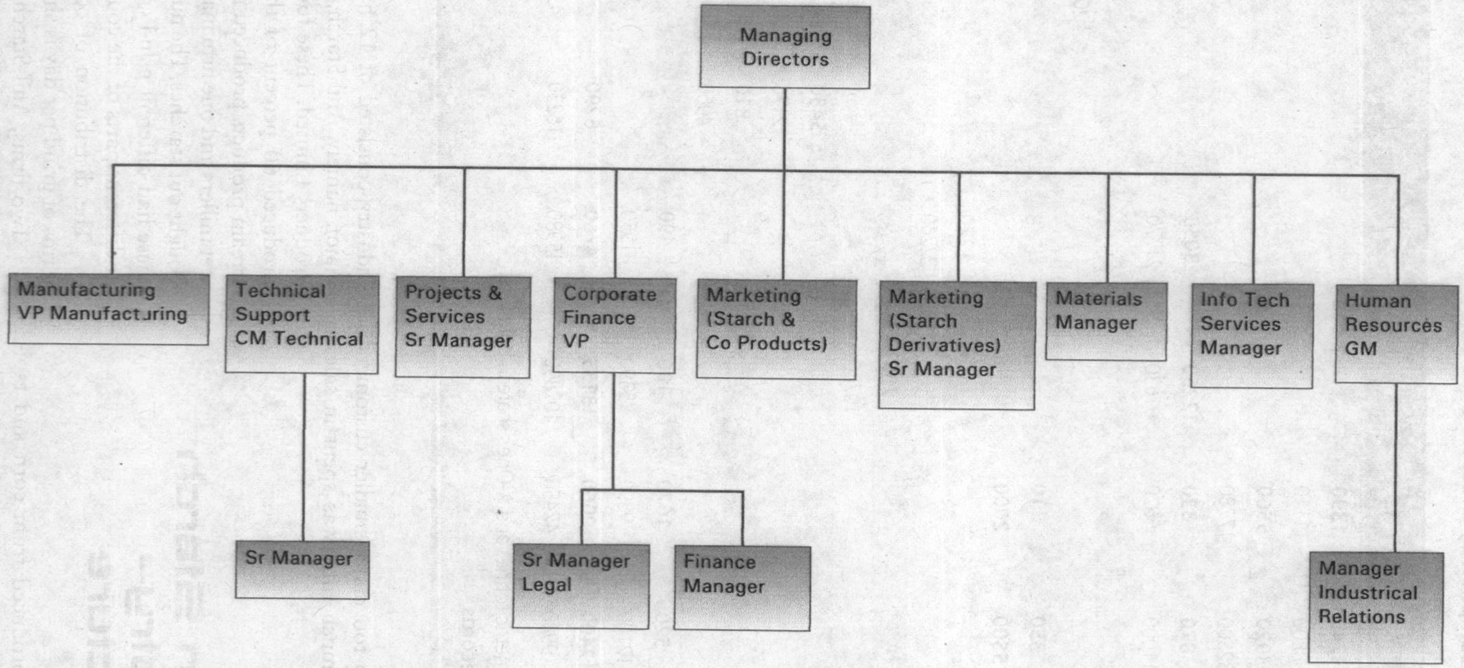

EXHIBIT C3.7

Capacity in Grind per day and the Number of Plants

Grind/day (MT)	No. of Plants
Greater than 250	2
100–150	5
40–60	8
Total	15

SOURCE: A-One's internal document

ducing all the downstream products, had announced plans for doing so.

There were producers who were not producing starch but were producing derivatives, liquid glucose, dextrose monohydrate, sorbitol.'

In volume terms, starch, speciality starch and downstream products constituted 41%, 15%, and 44% of the corn starch industry in India. Exhibit C3.8 presents a summary of competition in the three broad product categories in terms of nature of competition, number of competing firms and basis of competition. In Exhibit C3.5, product-wise total consumption of starch in different industries and the corresponding share of A-One have been presented.

In India 60 percent of dry starches were produced from maize and the remaining from tapioca. The production of maize had been increasing at the rate of 2.7 percent during 1981–91. However, prices of corn were fluctuating because the production was monsoon dependent and yields were also very low. For the year 1991–92, the yield was 1.3 tonnes per hectare as compared to a yield of 8.5 tonnes in the USA. In the manufacturing of starch, corn constituted about 42–47 percent of the ex-factory price of starch. The next highest element of cost was energy and this was 13 percent of the ex-factory price of starch.

EXHIBIT C3.8

Competition in Indian Corn Starch Industry

Products	Percent of Total market (Physical terms)	Characteristic of market	No. of competing firms	Basis of competition
Starch	41	Highly Competitive	11 Corn starch producers and large number of small tapioca starch producers	Price
Speciality starch	15	Oligopolistic	4	Quality
Down stream products	44	Oligopolistic	4	Quality

SOURCE: A-One's internal document

C3.6 Indian Starch Market

The total market size of starch industry in India was about 2500 crores. The customers constituted both the organised as well as unorganised sectors of Indian industry. The needs were also diverse. The major industry sectors needing starch or starch derivatives and their share in total consumption are shown in Exhibit C3.9.

Exhibit C3.10 shows the share of each product group in terms of equivalent starch consumption.

C3.7 User Industries

The uses of starch were diverse. They constituted units from the organized as well as unorganized sectors, in industries such as food and confectionery, textile, paper and pharmaceuticals.

The food and confectionery industry constituted about one third of the total starch consumption in

EXHIBIT C3.9
Industrywise Share in Total Consumption of Equivalent Starch Products

Sr. No.	Industry	Share in total equivalent starch (%)
1.	Paper	5.2
2.	Textiles	26.1
3.	Food	34.1
4.	Hygiene	5.4
5.	Pharma Tablets	2.1
6.	Pharma Fermentation	5.8
7.	Phara Syrups	7.0
8.	IV Fluids	3.6
9.	ORS	1.1
10.	Others	9.6
	Total	100.0

EXHIBIT C3.10
Products and Share in Total Equivalent Starch Consumption

Sr. No.	Product	Share in total consumption (%)
1.	Unmodified starch	31.2
2.	Modified starches	12.3
3.	Liquid Glucose	28.1
4.	Dextrose and Glucose D	12.0
5.	Anhydren dextrose	4.2
6.	Sorbitol	12.2
	Total	100.0

India. The users of liquid glucose, which was a major product going to confectioneries, were mostly in the unorganised sector. Among these customers, price was the major determinant of purchase. However, in pharmaceutical companies, as well as in confectionery companies producing branded products, quality was likely to play a significant role in purchase decisions. The quality would include product quality, as well as, packaging, service, delivery schedule and even aesthetics.

The food industry in India was at the developing stage. In recent years, the Government of India had emphasised agroprocessing and had extended fiscal incentives for the development of this sector. Pepsico, and several other companies were investing in this sector. The prospects of starch in the food industry could be assessed from the production and projected demand for some processed foods as given in Exhibit C3.11.

EXHIBIT C3.11
Production and Projected Demand for Some Processed Foods

('000 tonnes)

	Year		
	1988	1995	2000
Processed Food			
Bakery Products	620	1360	1736
Breads	178	637	1580
Dairy Products			
Baby Foods	54	95	190
Ice-cream (Million litres)	12	30	60
Instant Foods			
Macaroni/Noodles	12	39	96
Snack Foods	0.3	1	2
Expanded Snack Pellets	8	20	50
Corn Flakes	0.5	2	4

SOURCE: A-One's internal document

In textiles, starches were used in sizing to give strength to the yarn and also in the finishing of fabrics. Till recent years, Indian textile manufacturers had not demanded quality products. However, this changed during the last few years as the industry moved to quality products for the domestic market and as textile exports (both fabrics and apparels) were increasing. It was estimated that the consumption of starch in textile industry would increase at a compound rate of about five percent per year. In 1995, the consumption of starch in the textile industry was about 114,000 tonnes. It was estimated that the quality requirement in terms of specialised starch would increase.

In the paper industry, starches were used to increase the strength of the paper and for the retention of fines and fillers. In addition, starches were used to improve the smoothness, brightness and printability of paper. The broad categories of starches used in the paper industry were cationic starches, amphoteric starches, modified starches, oxidised starches and unmodified starches. It was estimated that the consumption of starches in paper making in India would increase at a compound rate of about 6.3 percent per year. In 1995, the consumption of starch in the Indian paper industry was 25,000 tonnes.

Although the consumption of starch in the Indian paper industry was low, it had the potential to increase at a faster rate with the increase in demand for better quality papers. In 1990, the demand for paper in India was 2.5 million tonnes with 0.3 million tonnes of newsprint. It was expected that by the year 2000, the demand for paper would be about 4.1 million tonnes and demand for newsprint was expected to triple. The starch required for paper was about 1% of the finished paper weight.

The major problem faced by the paper industry was the availability of raw materials. Due to various constraints on the price of paper (imposed by the Government of India) in the past, quality was never considered important. But this would change. As the constraints were removed, quality would play a major role in the choice of mills' product mix and hence the requirement of starch consumption. As a result, it was expected that more paper of better quality would be produced from recycled paper, which would necessitate better quality of starch in order to produce superior quality paper.

In the hygiene and pharmaceutical industry in India, starch and its derivatives had significant uses. Sorbitol was used in tooth-paste. Of the total Indian consumption of toothpaste, about 30 percent was consumed by the rural population which constituted 75 percent of the Indian population. With changing lifestyles, the rural consumption of toothpaste was likely to increase at a faster rate than consumption in urban India. The growth rate of consumption of toothpaste had been 12 percent per year in the recent past and it was estimated that the consumption of toothpaste would grow at a compound rate of 20 percent in the next five years. The total consumption of toothpaste in India was 44 million pounds and it was expected to increase two and a half times in five years. Toothpaste required 30 percent sorbitol (by weight).

In the pharmaceutical industry, liquid glucose was used in syrups, and starches were used as binding materials.

C3.8 Technology Prospects

The main technology of wet milling of corn was not likely to undergo a major change. However, it was not clear whether or not wheat would be used as a source of starch in India when the demand for starch increased in future. In Europe, wheat was also used for producing starch. Wheat starch could be used in most of the major industries, namely, textiles, paper, food, and pharmaceuticals.

C3.9 New Entrants in Starch Industry

The wet milling process with a small capacity would not be difficult to start. However, producers wanting to produce starch, its derivatives and downstream products in large volumes would require large capacities and access to sophisticated technology. As the Government of India was opening up the economy to foreign investors, it was likely that multinationals, on their own, or in collaboration with Indian Companies, would enter the Indian market. The signals were there that companies like Staley, Cerester, Cargill and National Starch were considering such moves.

C3.10 Government Policies

In India, the central government fixed the procurement prices of corn and this was likely to increase over time. The excise duty levied by Government of India on starch acetate and downstream products was 40 percent and 17 percent ad valorem respectively. These would be reduced over time and were unlikely to become an impediment to the use of starches and related products.

C3.11 Export Prospects

The prospect of exporting starch and related products could be assessed from Exhibits C3.12–C3.19. The data related to the estimated regional consumption for starch in the textile and paper industries in Asia and Africa, import of starch and allied products in Asia and the Middle East and Africa, estimated world production of cotton fabrics and estimated world production of paper have been presented in these exhibits.

C3.12 Challenges Facing Chief Executive

Chief Executive of A-One Products Ltd. was trying to decide the strategic options available to A-One and select the best option. The objective was to adopt a strategy for A-One, which would lead the company to a path of prosperity and growth.

EXHIBIT C3.12

Estimated Consumption of Starch in Textile & Paper Industry in Asia and Africa (including India)

('000 MT)

Industry	Year		
	1992	1995	2000
Textile	407	471	607
Paper	555	720	1062
Total	962	1191	1669

Note: Projections for the year 1995 and 2000 are based on historical data, however, in light of changing lifestyles we expect the figures to be higher.

SOURCE: A-One's internal document

EXHIBIT C3.13

Net Import of Starch and Allied Products

(million US $)

	Asia and Middle East	Africa	Total
1985	281	82	363
1986	365	102	467
1987	440	108	548
1988	334	118	452
1989	396	102	498

SOURCE: A-One's internal document

EXHIBIT C3.14

Estimated World Production of Cotton Fabrics

('000 MT)

	1995	Percentage	2000	Percentage
Africa	297	2.7%	332	2.7%
Americas	1459	13.5%	1802	14.6%
Europe/Russia	1601	14.8%	1152	9.3%
Asia/Oceania	7480	69.0%	9095	73.4%
Total	10837	100.0%	12381	100.0%

SOURCE: A-One's internal document

EXHIBIT C3.15

Estimated Production of Cotton Fabrics

('000 MT)

	1995	2000
India	1683	2148
Asia	5929	7697
Africa	284	305

Note: Projections for the year 1995 and 2000 are based on historical data, however, in light of changing lifestyles we expect the figures to be higher. Data for Asia excludes India.

Source: A-One's internal document

EXHIBIT C3.16

Estimated Consumption of Starch in Cotton Textile Industry

('000 MT)

	1995	2000
India	114	146
Asia	341	443
Africa	16	18

Note: Projections for the year 1995 and 2000 are based on historical data, however, in light of changing lifestyles we expect the figures to be higher. Data for Asia excludes India.

SOURCE: A-One's internal document

EXHIBIT C3.17

Estimated World Production of Paper

('000 MT)

	1995	Percentage	2000	Percentage
Africa	3237	1.2%	4369	1.3%
Americas	108382	40.2%	133072	38.2%
Europe/Russia	82755	30.7%	100014	28.7%
Asia/Oceania	75405	28.0%	110871	31.8%
Total	269779	100.0%	348326	100.0%

SOURCE: A-One's internal document

EXHIBIT C3.18

Estimated Production of Paper

('000 MT)

	1995	2000
India	2639	3592
Asia	70731	105014
Africa	3237	4372

Note: Projections for the year 1995 and 2000 are based on historical data, however, in light of changing lifestyles we expect the figures to be higher. Data for Asia excludes India.

SOURCE: A-One's internal document

EXHIBIT C3.19

Estimated Consumption of Starch in Paper Industry

('000 MT)

	1995	2000
India	25	34
Asia	665	987
Africa	31	41

Source: A-One's internal document

CHAPTER 13

Marketing Channels

Learning Outcomes

LO 1 Explain what a marketing channel is and why intermediaries are needed

LO 2 Define the types of channel intermediaries and describe their functions and activities

LO 3 Describe the channel structures for consumer and business products and discuss alternative channel arrangements

LO 4 Discuss the issues that influence channel strategy

LO 5 Describe the different channel relationship types and their unique costs and benefits

LO 6 Explain channel leadership, conflict, and partnering

LO 7 Discuss channels and distribution decisions in global markets

LO 8 Identify the special problems and opportunities associated with distribution in service organizations

The term *channel* is derived from the Latin word *canalis*, which means canal.

LO 1 Marketing Channels

A marketing channel can be viewed as a large canal or pipeline through which products, their ownership, communication, financing and payment, and accompanying risk flow to the consumer. Formally, a **marketing channel** (also called a **channel of distribution**) is a business structure of interdependent organizations that reach from the point of product origin to the consumer with the purpose of moving products to their final consumption destination. Marketing channels facilitate the physical movement of goods through the supply chain, representing "place" or "distribution" in the marketing mix (product, price, promotion, and place) and encompassing the processes involved in getting the right product to the right place at the right time.

Many different types of organizations participate in marketing channels. **Channel members** (also called *intermediaries*, *resellers*, and *middlemen*) negotiate with one another, buy and sell products, and facilitate the change of ownership between buyer and seller in the course of moving the product from the manufacturer into the hands of the final consumer. As products move to the final consumer, channel members facilitate the

marketing channel (channel of distribution)
a set of interdependent organizations that eases the transfer of ownership as products move from producer to business user or consumer

channel members
all parties in the marketing channel who negotiate with one another, buy and sell products, and facilitate the change of ownership between buyer and seller in the course of moving the product from the manufacturer into the hands of the final consumer

***Note:** All the figures in U.S. dollars are converted into rupee using the value $1 = ₹45.*

discrepancy of quantity the difference between the amount of product produced and the amount an end user wants to buy

discrepancy of assortment the lack of all the items a customer needs to receive full satisfaction from a product or products

distribution process by providing specialization and division of labor, overcoming discrepancies, and providing contact efficiency.

Providing Specialization and Division of Labor

According to the concept of *specialization and division of labor*, breaking down a complex task into smaller, simpler ones and allocating them to specialists will create greater efficiency and lower average production costs. Manufacturers achieve economies of scale through the use of efficient equipment capable of producing large quantities of a single product.

Marketing channels can also attain economies of scale through specialization and division of labor by aiding producers who lack the motivation, financing, or expertise to market directly to end users or consumers. In some cases, as with most consumer convenience goods, such as soft drinks, the cost of marketing directly to millions of consumers—taking and shipping individual orders—is prohibitive. For this reason, producers hire channel members, such as wholesalers and retailers, to do what the producers are not equipped to do or what channel members are better prepared to do. Channel members can do some things more efficiently than producers because they have built good relationships with their customers. Therefore, their specialized expertise enhances the overall performance of the channel.

Overcoming Discrepancies

Marketing channels also aid in overcoming discrepancies of quantity, assortment, time, and space created by economies of scale in production. For example, assume that MTR Foods can efficiently produce its Rice Idli instant mix only at a rate of 5,000 units in a typical day. Not even the most ardent idli fan could consume that amount in a year, much less in a day. The quantity produced to achieve low unit costs has created a **discrepancy of quantity**, which is the difference between the amount of product produced and the amount an end user wants to buy. By storing the product and distributing it in the appropriate amounts, marketing channels overcome quantity discrepancies by making products available in the quantities that consumers desire.

Mass production creates not only discrepancies of quantity but also discrepancies of assortment. A **discrepancy of assortment** occurs when a consumer does not have all of the items needed to receive full satisfaction from a product. For idlis to provide maximum satisfaction, several other products are required

LEAN, MEAN, RECESSION-SAVVY BURBERRY

Burberry showed strong profit in 2010 because of smart channel management. Once the recession hit, Burberry made necessary cuts and ensured that stock was under strict control. It then cut unprofitable lines and set prices for its traditional rainwear and scarves at levels to prevent markdown. To draw in new customers and expand its base, Burberry created a cheerful spring line and expanded its accessory line. Most importantly, Burberry kept its brand youthful by focusing on new ways to incorporate digital marketing into fashion shows and using social media to promote new lines. Its Art of the Trench Web site features photos of people wearing various styles of the iconic trench coat. Wearers are encouraged to submit photos, from which Burberry pulls favorites and creates a collage of trench coat looks from all over the world—and imbuing the trench coat with a youthful cool. Burberry also produced a live 3D broadcast of its runway show at London Fashion Week where users could change the camera angle on their computers to see the runway from different positions.[1]

© ALEX SEGRE/ALAMY

to complete the assortment. At the very least, most people want a knife, fork, plate, sambar[2], and coconut chutney[3]. Even though MTR Foods is a large consumer product company, it does not come close to providing the optimal assortment to go with its Rice Idli instant mix. To overcome discrepancies of assortment, marketing channels assemble in one place many of the products necessary to complete a consumer's needed assortment.

A **temporal discrepancy** is created when a product is produced but a consumer is not ready to buy it. Marketing channels overcome temporal discrepancies by maintaining inventories in anticipation of demand. For example, manufacturers of seasonal merchandise, such as winter wear or Christmas decorations, are in operation all year even though consumer demand is concentrated during certain months of the year.

Furthermore, because mass production requires many potential buyers, markets are usually scattered over large geographic regions, creating a **spatial discrepancy.** Often global, or at least nationwide, markets are needed to absorb the outputs of mass producers. Marketing channels overcome spatial discrepancies by making products available in locations convenient to consumers. For example, if all the MTR Foods Rice Idli instant mix is produced in Bengaluru in South India, then MTR Foods must use an intermediary to distribute the product to other regions of India.

temporal discrepancy a situation that occurs when a product is produced but a customer is not ready to buy it

spatial discrepancy the difference between the location of a producer and the location of widely scattered markets

Providing Contact Efficiency

The third need fulfilled by marketing channels is that they provide contact efficiency by reducing the number of stores customers must shop in to complete their purchases. Suppose you had to buy your milk at a dairy and your meat at a stockyard. You would spend a great deal of time, money, and energy just shopping for a few groceries. Marketing channels simplify distribution by cutting the number of transactions required to get products from manufacturers to consumers and making an assortment of goods available in one location.

Consider the example illustrated in Exhibit 13.1. Four consumers each want to buy a television set.

EXHIBIT 13.1

How marketing channels reduce the number of required transactions

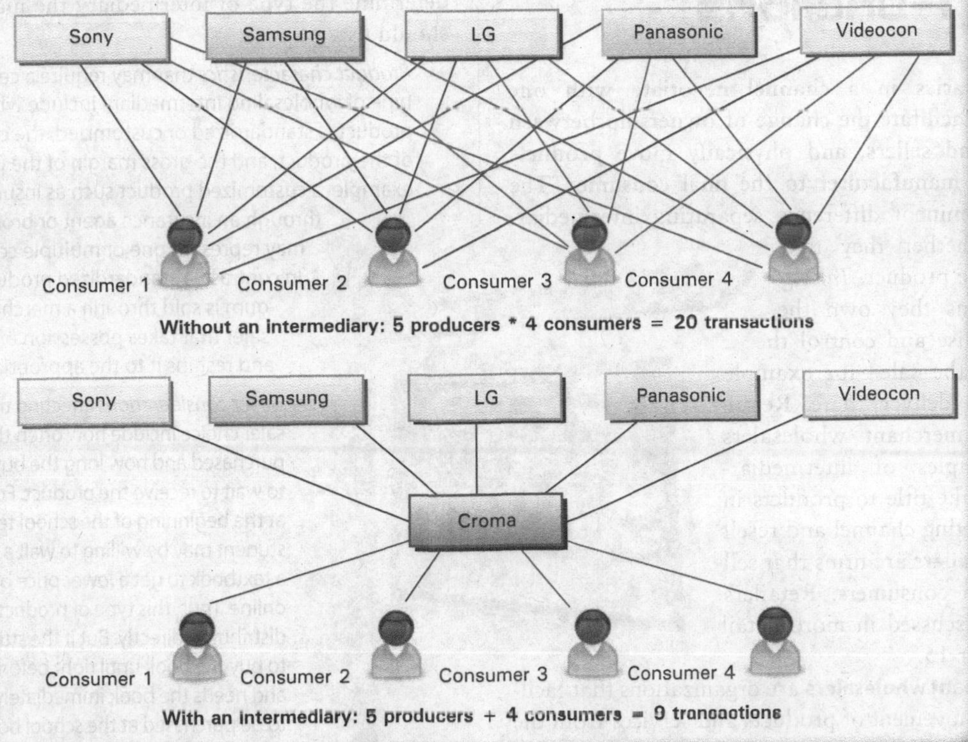

retailer a channel intermediary that sells mainly to consumers

merchant wholesaler an institution that buys goods from manufacturers and resells them to businesses, government agencies, and other wholesalers or retailers and that receives and takes title to goods, stores them in its own warehouses, and later ships them

agents and brokers wholesaling intermediaries who do not take title to a product but facilitate its sale from producer to end user by representing retailers, wholesalers, or manufacturers

Without a retail intermediary like Croma, television manufacturers Sony, Samsung, LG, Panasonic, and Videocon would each have to reach the four buyers who are in the target market, for a total of 20 transactions. However, when Croma acts as an intermediary between the producer and consumers, each producer has to make only one contact, reducing the number to 9 transactions. Each producer sells to one retailer rather than to four consumers. In turn, consumers buy from one retailer instead of five producers. Information technology has enhanced contact efficiency by making information on products and services easily available over the Internet. Shoppers can find the best bargains without physically searching for them.

LO 2 Channel Intermediaries and Their Functions

Intermediaries in a channel negotiate with one another, facilitate the change of ownership between buyers and sellers, and physically move products from the manufacturer to the final consumer. The most prominent difference separating intermediaries is whether they take title to the product. *Taking title* means they own the merchandise and control the terms of the sale—for example, price and delivery date. Retailers and merchant wholesalers are examples of intermediaries that take title to products in the marketing channel and resell them. **Retailers** are firms that sell mainly to consumers. Retailers will be discussed in more detail in Chapter 15.

Merchant wholesalers are organizations that facilitate the movement of products and services from the manufacturer to producers, resellers, governments, institutions, and retailers. All merchant wholesalers take title to the goods they sell, and most of them operate one or more warehouses where they receive goods, store them, and later reship them. Customers are mostly small- or medium-sized retailers, but merchant wholesalers also market to manufacturers and institutional clients.

Other intermediaries do not take title to goods and services they market but do facilitate the exchange of ownership between sellers and buyers. **Agents and brokers** simply facilitate the sale of a product from producer to end user by representing retailers, wholesalers, or manufacturers. Title reflects ownership, and ownership usually implies control. Unlike wholesalers, agents or brokers only facilitate sales and generally have little input into the terms of the sale. They do, however, get a fee or commission based on sales volume. For example, when selling a home, the owner usually hires a real estate agent who then brings potential buyers to see the house. The agent facilitates the sale by bringing the buyer and owner together but never actually takes ownership of the home.

Variations in channel structures are due in large part to variations in the numbers and types of wholesaling intermediaries. Generally, product characteristics, buyer considerations, and market conditions determine the type of intermediary the manufacturer should use.

- *Product characteristics* that may require a certain type of wholesaling intermediary include whether the product is standardized or customized, the complexity of the product, and the gross margin of the product. For example, a customized product such as insurance is sold through an insurance agent or broker who may represent one or multiple companies. In contrast, a standardized product such as gum is sold through a merchant wholesaler that takes possession of the gum and reships it to the appropriate retailers.
- *Buyer considerations* affecting the wholesaler choice include how often the product is purchased and how long the buyer is willing to wait to receive the product. For example, at the beginning of the school term, a student may be willing to wait a few days for a textbook to get a lower price by ordering online. Thus, this type of product can be distributed directly. But if the student waits to buy the book until right before an exam and needs the book immediately, it will have to be purchased at the school bookstore.

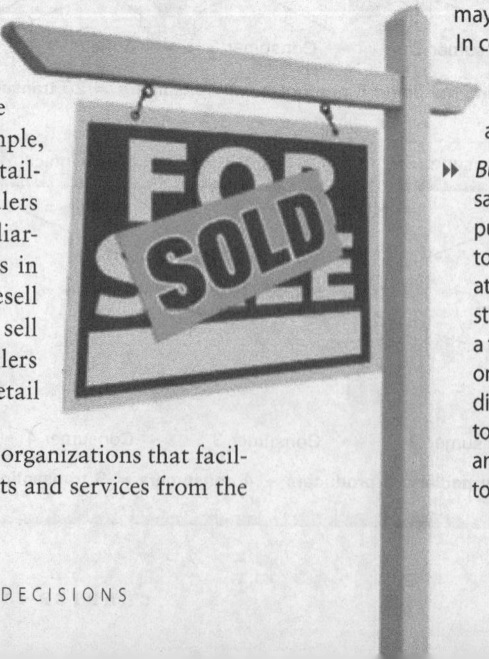

- *Market characteristics* determining the wholesaler type include how many buyers are in the market and whether they are concentrated in a general location or are widely dispersed. Gum and textbooks, for example, are produced in one location and consumed in many other locations. Therefore, a merchant wholesaler is needed to distribute the products. In contrast, in a home sale, the buyer and seller are localized in one area, which facilitates the use of an agent/broker relationship.

Channel Functions Performed by Intermediaries

Retailing and wholesaling intermediaries in marketing channels perform several essential functions that make the flow of goods between producer and buyer possible. The three basic functions that intermediaries perform are summarized in Exhibit 13.2.

Transactional functions involve contacting and communicating with prospective buyers to make them aware of existing products and explain their features, advantages, and benefits. Intermediaries in the channel also provide *logistical* functions. **Logistics** is the efficient and cost-effective forward and reverse flow and storage of goods, services, and related information into, through, and out of channel member companies. Logistics functions typically include transportation and storage of assets, as well as their sorting, accumulation, consolidation, and/or allocation for the purpose of conforming to customer requirements. For example, grading agricultural products typifies the sorting-out process, while consolidation of many lots of grade A eggs from different sources into one lot illustrates the accumulation process. Supermarkets or other retailers perform the assorting function by assembling thousands of different items that match their customers' desires. Similarly, while large companies typically have direct channels, many small companies depend on wholesalers to promote and distribute their products.

logistics the efficient and cost-effective forward and reverse flow and storage of goods, services, and related information into, through, and out of channel member companies

The third basic channel function, *facilitating*, includes research and financing. Research provides information about channel members and consumers by getting answers to key questions: Who are the buyers? Where are they located? Why do they buy? Financing ensures that channel members have the money to keep products moving through the channel to the ultimate consumer.

EXHIBIT 13.2

Marketing Channel Functions Performed by Intermediaries

Type of Function	Description
Transactional Functions	**Contacting and promoting:** Contacting potential customers, promoting products, and soliciting orders
	Negotiating: Determining how many goods or services to buy and sell, type of transportation to use, when to deliver, and method and timing of payment
	Risk taking: Assuming the risk of owning inventory
Logistical Functions	**Physically distributing:** Transporting and sorting goods to overcome temporal and spatial discrepancies
	Storing: Maintaining inventories and protecting goods
	Sorting: Overcoming discrepancies of quantity and assortment by
	Sorting out: Breaking down a heterogeneous supply into separate homogeneous stocks
	Accumulating: Combining similar stocks into a larger homogeneous supply
	Allocating: Breaking a homogeneous supply into smaller and smaller lots ("breaking bulk")
	Assorting: Combining products into collections or assortments that buyers want available at one place
Facilitating Functions	**Researching:** Gathering information about other channel members and consumers
	Financing: Extending credit and other financial services to facilitate the flow of goods through the channel to the final consumer

direct channel a distribution channel in which producers sell directly to consumers

Although individual members can be added to or deleted from a channel, someone must still perform these essential functions. They can be performed by producers, end users, or consumers; channel intermediaries such as wholesalers and retailers; and sometimes nonmember channel participants. For example, if a manufacturer decides to eliminate its private fleet of trucks, it must still have a way to move the goods to the wholesaler. This task may be accomplished by the wholesaler, which may have its own fleet of trucks, or by a nonmember channel participant, such as an independent trucking firm. Nonmembers also provide many other essential functions that may at one time have been provided by a channel member. For example, research firms may perform the research function, advertising agencies may provide the promotion function, transportation and storage firms may provide the physical distribution function, and banks may perform the financing function.

LO 3 Channel Structures

A product can take many routes to reach its final consumer. Marketers search for the most efficient channel from the many alternatives available. Marketing a consumer convenience good such as gum or candy differs from marketing a specialty good like a Giorgio Armani fragrance. The next sections discuss the structures of typical and alternative marketing channels for consumer and business-to-business products.

© INDIATODAYIMAGES.COM

A retailer channel is most common when the retailer is large, such as Shoppers' Stop, and can buy in large quantities directly from the manufacturer. Large retailers often bypass a wholesaler.

Channels for Consumer Products

Exhibit 13.3 illustrates the four ways manufacturers can route products to consumers. Producers use the **direct channel** to sell directly to consumers. Direct marketing activities—including telemarketing, mail-order and catalog shopping, and forms of electronic retailing such as online shopping and shop-at-home television networks—are a good example of this type of channel structure. There are no intermediaries. Producer-owned stores and factory outlet stores—Fabindia, Westside, and Bata—are examples of direct channels.

By contrast, an *agent/broker channel* is fairly complicated and typically used in markets with many small manufacturers and many retailers that lack the resources to find each other. Agents or brokers bring manufacturers and wholesalers together for negotiations, but they do not take

EXHIBIT 13.3
Marketing Channels for Consumer Products

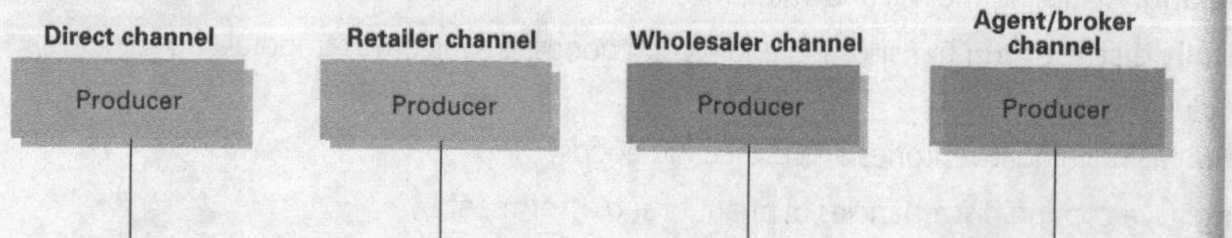

title to merchandise. Ownership passes directly to one or more wholesalers and then to retailers. Finally, retailers sell to the ultimate consumer of the product. For example, a food broker represents buyers and sellers of grocery products. The broker acts on behalf of many different producers and negotiates the sale of their products to wholesalers that specialize in foodstuffs. These wholesalers in turn sell to grocers and convenience stores.

Most consumer products are sold through distribution channels similar to the other two alternatives: the retailer channel and the wholesaler channel. A *retailer channel* is most common when the retailer is large and can buy in large quantities directly from the manufacturer. Walmart, Sears, and car dealers are examples of retailers that often bypass a wholesaler. A *wholesaler channel* is commonly used for low-cost items that are frequently purchased, such as candy, cigarettes, and magazines.

Channels for Business and Industrial Products

As Exhibit 13.4 illustrates, five channel structures are common in business and industrial markets. First, *direct channels* are typical in business and industrial markets. For example, manufacturers buy large quantities of raw materials, major equipment, processed materials, and supplies directly from other manufacturers. Manufacturers that require suppliers to meet detailed technical specifications often prefer direct channels. Apple used a direct channel to purchase chips for its iPad. To ensure that Toshiba would deliver flash memory chips for iPad construction, Apple paid the chip maker ₹2250 crore in July 2009, well in advance of the April 2010 release. Such guarantees happen most efficiently through the direct communication made possible by using a direct channel.[4] The channel from producer to government buyers is also a direct channel. Since much government buying is done through bidding, a direct channel is attractive.

Companies selling standardized items of moderate or low value often rely on *industrial distributors*. In many ways, an industrial distributor is like a supermarket for organizations. Industrial distributors are wholesalers and channel members that buy and take title to products. Moreover, they usually keep inventories of their products and sell and service them. Often small manufacturers cannot afford to employ their own sales force. Instead, they rely on manufacturers' representatives or selling agents to sell to either industrial distributors or users.

The Internet has enabled virtual distributors to emerge and has forced traditional industrial distributors to expand their business model. Many manufacturers and consumers are bypassing distributors and going direct, often via the Internet. Companies looking to drop the intermediary from the supply chain have created exchanges. International retailers use the Worldwide Retail Exchange to make purchases that in the past would have required telephone, fax, or face-to-face sales calls, and in so doing save approximately

EXHIBIT 13.4

Channels for Business and Industrial Products

dual distribution (multiple distribution) the use of two or more channels to distribute the same product to target markets

strategic channel alliance a cooperative agreement between business firms to use the other's already established distribution channel

15 percent in their purchasing costs. Finally, a third type of Internet marketplace is a private exchange. A *private exchange* is when a company creates a network so it can connect its business with that of its suppliers. Some large companies prefer private exchanges because they provide tighter security over transactions, especially when negotiating complex contracts.

Alternative Channel Arrangements

Rarely does a producer use just one type of channel to move its product. It usually employs several different or alternative channels, which include multiple channels, nontraditional channels, and strategic channel alliances.

Multiple Channels When a producer selects two or more channels to distribute the same product to target markets, this arrangement is called **dual distribution** (or **multiple distribution**). As more people embrace online shopping, an increasing number of retailers are using multiple distribution channels. For example, companies such as Dominos, Oriflame cosmetics, and PVR cinemas sell in-store, online, and through telephone orders.

Nontraditional Channels

Often nontraditional channel arrangements help differentiate a firm's product from the competition. Nontraditional channels include the Internet, mail-order channels, or infomercials. Although nontraditional channels may limit a brand's coverage, they can give a producer serving a niche market a way to gain market access and customer attention without having to establish channel intermediaries. Nontraditional channels can also provide another avenue of sales for larger firms. In order to increase and develop awareness in the market segment of adult women, Sony Pictures teamed up with the Home Shopping Network in the United States to stage a three-day shopping event featuring merchandise inspired by *Eat Pray Love*, a film adaptation of the best-selling autobiography of the same name.[5] The movie also helped in promoting tourism to India, with international tour operators and travelling websites offering travel packages to India.[6]

Strategic Channel Alliances

Companies often form **strategic channel alliances**, which enable them to use another manufacturer's already-established channel. Alliances are used most often when the creation of marketing channel relationships may be too expensive and time-consuming. Youtube and the Indian Premier League (IPL) signed a contract in 2010 allowing Youtube to broadcast IPL cricket matches live across the globe, except for United States. The matches could be viewed online on a dedicated channel called youtube.com/ipl. This was the first time a major sporting event was broadcasted on Youtube worldwide.[7]

Alliances can also prove more efficient when a company wants to run promotions. PepsiCo purchased its two major bottlers and has since been able to work directly with retailers abroad to create store-specific bundles for grocery stores (12-packs of Pepsi and large bags of chips) and for convenience stores (single bottles of Pepsi and small bags of chips). The purchase of its bottlers has also made it easier for Pepsi to work directly with stores to provide store-specific merchandise, like bringing Mexican brands to stores in San Antonio, Texas, that cater to Hispanics.[8]

Strategic channel alliances are proving to be more successful for growing businesses than mergers and acquisitions. This is especially true in global markets where cultural differences, distance, and other barriers can prove challenging.

LO 4 Making Channel Strategy Decisions

Devising a marketing channel strategy requires several critical decisions. Managers must decide what role distribution will play in the overall marketing strategy. In addition, they must be sure that the channel strategy chosen is consistent with product, promotion, and pricing strategies. In making these decisions, marketing managers must determine what factors will influence the choice of channel and what level of distribution intensity will be appropriate.

Factors Affecting Channel Choice

Managers must answer many questions before choosing a marketing channel. The final choice depends on the analysis of several factors, which often interact. These factors can be grouped as market factors, product factors, and producer factors.

Market Factors Among the most important market factors affecting the choice of distribution channel are target customer considerations. Specifically, managers should answer the following questions: Who are the potential customers? What do they buy? Where do they buy? When do they buy? How do they buy? Additionally, the choice of channel depends on whether the producer is selling to consumers or to industrial customers. Industrial customers' buying habits are very different from those of consumers. Industrial customers tend to buy in larger quantities and require more customer service.

The geographic location and size of the market are also important to channel selection. As a rule, if the target market is concentrated in one or more specific areas, then direct selling through a sales force is appropriate. When markets are more widely dispersed, intermediaries would be less expensive. The size of the market also influences channel choice. Generally, larger markets require more intermediaries.

Product Factors Products that are more complex, customized, and expensive tend to benefit from shorter and more direct marketing channels. These types of products sell better through a direct sales force. Examples include pharmaceuticals, scientific instruments, airplanes, and mainframe computer systems. On the other hand, the more standardized a product is, the longer its distribution channel can be and the greater the number of intermediaries that can be involved. For example, with the exception of flavor and shape, the formula for chewing gum is about the same from producer to producer. Chewing gum is also very inexpensive. As a result, the distribution channel for gum tends to involve many wholesalers and retailers.

The product's life cycle is also an important factor in choosing a marketing channel. In fact, the choice of channel may change over the life of the product. As products become more common and less intimidating to potential users, producers tend to look for alternative channels.

Another factor is the delicacy of the product. Perishable products such as vegetables and milk have a relatively short life span. Fragile products like bone china and crystal require a minimum amount of handling. Therefore, both require fairly short marketing channels. Online retailers such as eBay facilitate the sale of unusual or difficult-to-find products that benefit from a direct channel.

Producer Factors Several factors pertaining to the producer itself are important to the selection of a marketing channel. In general, producers with large financial, managerial, and marketing resources are better able to use more direct channels. These producers have the ability to hire and train their own sales forces, warehouse their own goods, and extend credit to their customers. Smaller or weaker firms, on the other hand, must rely on intermediaries to provide these services for them. Compared to producers with only one or two product lines, producers that sell several products in a related area are able to choose channels that are more direct.

STRATEGIC LOCATION ALLIANCE

Fast food joints love high traffic locations. With a rapid rise in the number of on-the-move customers, fast food chains have identified a new channel to tap these customers: transit locations like airports and stations—both railway and metro/local. The retail food chains are fast utilizing this new channel to reach their customers and increase their sales volumes. Cafe Coffee Day, a leading coffee chain, has presence across all big airports in the country. Similarly, McDonalds too has outlets at airports and stations in key Indian cities like Mumbai and Delhi.[9] In fact, it has strategically opened some of its outlets in Mumbai, close to major local stations like Andheri and Vile Parle, to cater to the local travelling population of the city.

A McDonalds outlet inside Delhi airport

intensive distribution a form of distribution aimed at having a product available in every outlet where target customers might want to buy it

selective distribution a form of distribution achieved by screening dealers to eliminate all but a few in any single area

Sales expenses then can be spread over more products.

A producer's desire to control pricing, positioning, brand image, and customer support also tends to influence channel selection. For instance, firms that sell products with exclusive brand images, such as designer perfumes and clothing, usually avoid channels in which discount retailers are present. Manufacturers of upscale products, such as Gucci (handbags) and Godiva (chocolates), may sell their wares only in expensive stores in order to maintain an image of exclusivity. Many producers have opted to risk their image, however, and test sales in discount channels. Louis Philippe expanded its distribution to include Lifestyle stores, Future Group's Central Malls, and Brand Factory outlets.

Levels of Distribution Intensity

Organizations have three options for intensity of distribution: intensive distribution, selective distribution, or exclusive distribution.

Intensive Distribution **Intensive distribution** is a form of distribution aimed at maximum market coverage. The manufacturer tries to have the product available in every outlet where potential customers might want to buy it. If buyers are unwilling to search for a product (as is true of convenience goods and operating supplies), the product must be very accessible to buyers. A low-value product that is purchased frequently may require a lengthy channel. For example, candy, chips, and other snack foods, which are found in almost every type of retail store, are typically sold to retailers in small quantities by food or candy wholesalers.

Most manufacturers pursuing an intensive distribution strategy sell to a large percentage of the wholesalers willing to stock their products. Retailers' willingness (or unwillingness) to handle items tends to control the manufacturer's ability to achieve intensive distribution. For example, a retailer already carrying ten brands of gum may show little enthusiasm for one more brand.

Selective Distribution **Selective distribution** is achieved by screening dealers and retailers to eliminate all but a few in any single area. Because only a few are chosen, the consumer must seek out the product. For example, Dr. Scholl's range of foot care products are available at selected retail outlets in India since it is a premium product and is targeted towards a specific customer segment. Selective distribution strategies often hinge on a manufacturer's desire to maintain a superior product image so as to be able to charge a premium price. DKNY clothing, for instance, is sold only in select retail outlets, mainly full-price department stores. Manufacturers sometimes expand selective distribution strategies, believing that doing so will enhance revenues without diminishing their product's image. For example, Burn, a new energy drink manufactured and bottled by Coca Cola, used selective distribution to position itself as a higher-end option to its target audience of youngsters and socially active adults. The drink was introduced at premium outlets such as pubs, discos, and resto-bars only in Mumbai, Delhi and NCR, and Bengaluru in order to draw the attention of "elite" customers.[10]

Recently, a high-tech form of selective distribution has emerged whereby products are pushed through to the membership of virtual social networks. Max New York Life Insurance promoted its *igenius programme* by creating a community for parents on the networking sites Facebook and Twitter. While the programme was aimed at wholesome development of children and awarding of scholarships worth ₹10 lakh, the community offered a chance to the parents to openly discuss issues about parenting as well as participate in the program.[11]

Next, an electronics retail chain, stocks a wide variety of irons, including Philips and Bajaj, to offer customers the most comprehensive hands-on iron selection for one-stop shopping.

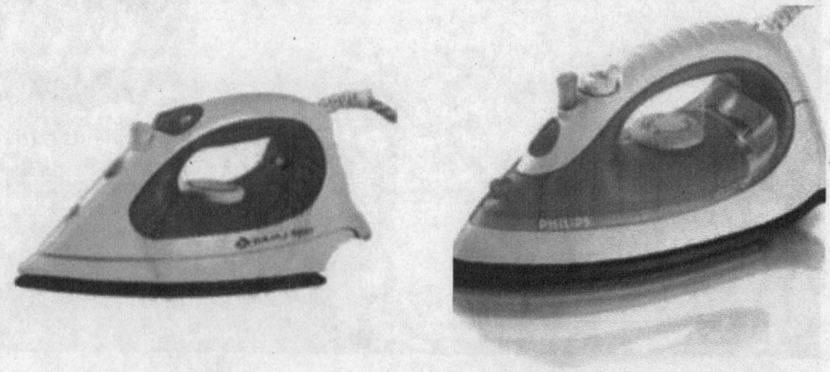

Exclusive Distribution The most restrictive form of market coverage is **exclusive distribution,** which entails only one or a few dealers within a given area. Because buyers may have to search or travel extensively to buy the product, exclusive distribution is usually confined to consumer specialty goods, a few shopping goods, and major industrial equipment. Products such as Rolls-Royce automobiles are distributed under exclusive arrangements.

Retailers and wholesalers may be unwilling to commit the time and money necessary to promote and service a product unless the manufacturer guarantees them an exclusive territory. This arrangement shields the dealer from direct competition and enables it to be the main beneficiary of the manufacturer's promotion efforts in that geographic area. With exclusive distribution, channels of communication are usually well established because the manufacturer works with a limited number of dealers rather than many accounts.

Exclusive distribution also takes place within a retailer's store rather than a geographic area—for example, when a retailer agrees not to sell a manufacturer's competing brands. Apple has had an exclusivity contract with AT&T in the United States since the release of the iPhone.

LO 5 Types of Channel Relationships

A marketing channel is more than a set of institutions linked by economic ties. Social relationships play an important role in building unity among channel members. Marketing managers should carefully consider the types of relationships they choose to foster between their company and other companies and in doing so pay close attention to the benefits and hazards associated with each relationship type. Relationships among channel members range from "loose" to "tight," taking the form of a continuum stretching from single transactions to complex interdependent relationships such as partnerships or alliances. The choice of relationship type is important for channel management because each relationship type carries with it different levels of time, financial, and resource investment. There are three basic types of relationships, organized here by degree of closeness:

- **Arm's-length relationships** are considered by channel members to be temporary or one-time-only and often arise from a sudden or unique need. These relationships are characterized by the companies' unwillingness or lack of ability to develop a closer type of relationship. Both parties typically retain their independence and pursue only their own interests while attempting to benefit from the goods or services provided by the other.
- **Cooperative relationships,** generally administered using some kind of formal contract, are used when a company wants less ambiguity but doesn't want the long-term and/or capital investment necessary in an integrated relationship. Cooperative relationships tend to be more flexible than integrated relationships but are more structured than arm's-length relationships, and they include nonequity agreements such as franchising and licensing as well as joint ventures and strategic alliances.
- **Integrated relationships** are closely bonded relationships characterized by formal arrangements that explicitly define the relationships to the involved channel members. There is vertical integration, where all the related channel members are owned by a single legal entity, and supply chains, which are several companies acting as one. Supply chains are discussed in detail in Chapter 14.

Based on these descriptions, it seems that integrated relationships would be the preferred relationship type in almost all company-to-company channel settings. However, highly integrated relationships also come with some significant costs and hazards. For example, the single-owner model is somewhat risky because a large amount of capital assets must be purchased or leased (requiring a potentially huge initial cash outlay), and the failure of any portion of the business may result in not only the economic loss of that portion but may

© ISTOCKPHOTO.COM/SIMONMCCONICO

exclusive distribution a form of distribution that establishes one or a few dealers within a given area

arm's-length relationship a relationship between companies that is loose, characterized by low relational investment and trust, and usually taking the form of a series of discrete transactions with no or low expectation of future interaction or service

cooperative relationship a relationship between companies that takes the form of informal partnership with moderate levels of trust and information sharing as needed to further each company's goals

integrated relationship a relationship between companies that is tightly connected, with linked processes across and between firm boundaries and high levels of trust and interfirm commitment

also reduce the value of the other business units (or render them totally worthless). Because these trade-offs are sometimes hard to justify, companies often look for the sort of "happy medium" of cooperative relationships.

LO 6 Managing Channel Relationships

In addition to considering the multiple different types of channel relationships and their costs and benefits, managers must also be aware of the social dimensions that are constantly impacting their relationships. The basic social dimensions of channels are power, control, leadership, conflict, and partnering.

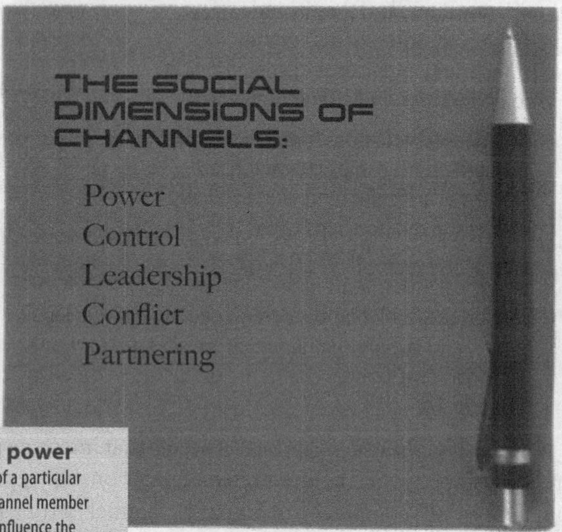

© ISTOCKPHOTO.COM/TRAVELLINGLIGHT

channel power the capacity of a particular marketing channel member to control or influence the behavior of other channel members

channel control a situation that occurs when one marketing channel member intentionally affects another member's behavior

channel leader (channel captain) a member of a marketing channel that exercises authority and power over the activities of other channel members

channel conflict a clash of goals and methods between distribution channel members

horizontal conflict a channel conflict that occurs among channel members on the same level

Channel Power, Control, and Leadership

Channel power is a channel member's ability to control or influence the behavior of other channel members. **Channel control** occurs when one channel member's power affects another member's behavior. To achieve control, a channel member assumes channel leadership and exercises authority and power. This member is termed the **channel leader**, or **channel captain**. In one marketing channel, a manufacturer may be the leader because it controls new-product designs and product availability. In another, a retailer may be the channel leader because it wields power and control over the retail price, inventory levels, and postsale service.

Channel Conflict

Inequitable channel relationships often lead to **channel conflict**, which is a clash of goals and methods among the members of a distribution channel. In a broad context, conflict may not be bad. Often it arises because staid, traditional channel members refuse to keep pace with the times. Removing an outdated intermediary may result in reduced costs for the entire channel. The Internet has forced many intermediaries to offer services such as merchandise tracking and inventory availability online.

Conflicts among channel members can be due to many different situations and factors. Oftentimes, conflict arises because channel members have conflicting goals. For instance, athletic footwear retailers want to sell as many shoes as possible in order to maximize profits, regardless of whether the shoe is manufactured by Nike, Adidas, or Puma, but the Nike manufacturer wants a certain sales volume and market share in each market.

Conflict can also arise when channel members fail to fulfill expectations of other channel members—for example, when a franchisee does not follow the rules set down by the franchisor, or when communications channels break down between channel members. Further, ideological differences and different perceptions of reality can also cause conflict among channel members. For instance, when it comes to return policies, a retailer's "the customer is always right" perspective will likely conflict with a wholesaler or manufacturer's perspective that people try to get something for nothing.

Conflict within a channel can be either horizontal or vertical. **Horizontal conflict** occurs among channel members on the same level, such as two or more different wholesalers or two or more different retailers that handle the same manufacturer's brands. This type of channel conflict is found most often when manufacturers practice dual or multiple distribution strategies. When Apple changed its distribution strategy and began opening its own stores, it angered Apple's traditional retail partners, some of whom ultimately filed lawsuits against the company. Horizontal conflict can also occur when some channel members feel that other members on the same level are being treated differently by the manufacturer.

Many marketers and customers regard horizontal conflict as healthy competition. Much more serious is

© ISTOCKPHOTO.COM/KONSTANTIN32

vertical conflict, which occurs between different levels in a marketing channel, most typically between the manufacturer and wholesaler or the manufacturer and retailer. Producer-versus-wholesaler conflict occurs when the producer chooses to bypass the wholesaler and deal directly with the consumer or retailer.

Dual distribution strategies can also cause vertical conflict in the channel. L'Oreal India has been following the dual distribution strategy quite successfully in India. Its products are retailed through multiple channels such as its own hair salons, pharmacies, department stores, and local beauty outlets. The cosmetic giant has, however, been careful not to cannabalize its product sales. Thus, the hair salons and pharmacies retail professional products, targeted toward beauty professionals and experts. L'Oreal has tried to avoid any vertical conflict by differentiating its brands for each of its store formats.[12]

Channel Partnering

Regardless of the locus of power, channel members rely heavily on one another. **Channel partnering**, or **channel cooperation**, is the joint effort of all channel members to create a channel that serves customers and creates a competitive advantage. Channel partnering is vital if each member is to gain something from other members. By cooperating, retailers, wholesalers, manufacturers, and suppliers can speed up inventory replenishment, improve customer service, and reduce the total costs of the marketing channel.

Channel alliances and partnerships help managers create the parallel flow of materials and information required to leverage the channel's intellectual, material, and marketing resources. The rapid growth in channel partnering is due to new enabling technology and the need to lower costs.

LO 7 Channels and Distribution Decisions for Global Markets

With the spread of free trade agreements and treaties in recent decades, such as the European Union and the North American Free Trade Agreement (NAFTA), global marketing channels and management of the channels have become increasingly important to Indian companies that export their products or manufacture abroad.

Developing Global Marketing Channels

Executives should recognize the unique cultural, economic, institutional, and legal aspects of each market before trying to design marketing channels in foreign countries. Manufacturers introducing products in global markets have to decide whether the product will be marketed directly, mostly by company salespeople, or through independent foreign intermediaries, such as agents and distributors. Using company salespeople generally provides more control and is less risky than using foreign intermediaries. However, setting up a sales force in a foreign country also entails a greater commitment, both financially and organizationally.

Marketers should be aware that channel structures and types abroad may differ from those in the United States. For instance, the more highly developed a nation is economically, the more specialized are its channel types. Therefore, a marketer wishing to sell in Germany or Japan will have several channel types to choose from. Conversely, developing countries such as Ethiopia, India, and Venezuela have limited channel types available, and they tend to shun the large-scale formats popular in the United States and Western Europe.

Marketers must also be aware that many countries have "gray" marketing channels in which products are distributed through unauthorized channel intermediaries. It is estimated that sales of counterfeit luxury items like Prada handbags and Big Bertha golf clubs have reached almost ₹9000 crore a year. The Internet has also

vertical conflict a channel conflict that occurs between different levels in a marketing channel, most typically between the manufacturer and wholesaler or between the manufacturer and retailer

channel partnering (channel cooperation) the joint effort of all channel members to create a channel that serves customers and creates a competitive advantage

proved to be a way for pirates to circumvent authorized distribution channels, especially in the case of popular prescription drugs.

LO 8 Channels and Distribution Decisions for Services

The fastest-growing part of our economy is the service sector. Although distribution in the service sector is difficult to visualize, the same skills, techniques, and strategies used to manage inventory can also be used to manage service inventory—for instance, hospital beds, bank accounts, or airline seats. The quality of the planning and execution of distribution can have a major impact on costs and customer satisfaction.

One thing that sets service distribution apart from traditional manufacturing distribution is that in a service environment, production and consumption are simultaneous. In manufacturing, a production setback can often be remedied by using safety stock or a faster mode of transportation. Such substitution is not possible with a service. The benefits of a service are also relatively intangible—that is, a consumer normally can't see the benefits of a service, such as a doctor's physical exam, but normally can see the benefits provided by a product, such as cold medicine relieving a stuffy nose.

Because service industries are so customer oriented, customer service is a priority. To manage customer relationships, many service providers, such as insurance carriers, physicians, hair salons, and financial services, use technology to schedule appointments, manage accounts, and disburse information. Service distribution focuses on three main areas:

- *Minimizing wait times:* Minimizing the amount of time customers wait in line is a key factor in maintaining the quality of service. Researchers report that people tend to overestimate the amount of time they spend waiting in line and that unexplained waits seem longer than explained waits.
- *Managing service capacity:* If service firms don't have the capacity to meet demand, they must either turn down some prospective customers, let service levels slip, or expand capacity. For instance, at tax time a tax preparation firm may have so many customers desiring its services that it has to either turn business away or add temporary offices or preparers.
- *Improving service delivery:* Service firms are now experimenting with different distribution channels for their services. Choosing the right distribution channel can increase the times that services are available or add to customer convenience. The Internet is fast becoming an alternative channel for delivering services. Consumers can now purchase plane tickets, plan a vacation cruise, reserve a hotel room, pay bills, purchase mutual funds, and receive electronic newspapers in cyberspace.

Review and Applications

Explain what a marketing channel is and why intermediaries are needed. A marketing channel is a business structure of interdependent organizations that reach from the point of product origin to the consumer with the purpose of physically moving products to their final consumption destination, representing "place" or "distribution" in the marketing mix, and encompassing the processes involved in getting the right product to the right place at the right time. Members of a marketing channel create a continuous and seamless system that performs or supports the marketing channel functions. Channel members provide economies to the distribution process in the form of specialization and division of labor; overcoming discrepancies in quantity, assortment, time, and space; and providing contact efficiency.

1.1 Your family runs a specialty ice cream parlor called Scoops. It manufactures its own ice cream in small batches and sells it only in small-sized containers. After someone not affiliated with the company sent six containers of its ice cream to a popular talk-show host, she proclaimed on her national TV show that it was the best ice cream she had ever eaten. Immediately after the broadcast, orders came flooding in, overwhelming your small-batch production schedule and your limited distribution system. The company's shipping manager thinks she can handle it, but you disagree. List the reasons why you need to restructure your channel of distribution.

Define the types of channel intermediaries and describe their functions and activities. The most prominent difference separating intermediaries is whether they take title to the product. Retailers and merchant wholesalers take title, but agents and brokers do not. Retailers are firms that sell mainly to consumers. Merchant wholesalers are organizations that facilitate the movement of products and services from the manufacturer to producers, resellers, governments, institutions, and retailers. Agents and brokers do not take title to the goods and services they market, but they do facilitate the exchange of ownership between sellers and buyers. Channel intermediaries perform three basic types of functions. Transactional functions include contacting and promoting, negotiating, and risk taking. Logistical functions performed by channel members include physical distribution, storing, and sorting functions. Finally, channel members may perform facilitating functions, such as researching and financing.

2.1 What kind of marketing channel functions can be performed over the Internet? Why do you think so?

Describe the channel structures for consumer and business products and discuss alternative channel arrangements. Marketing channels for consumer and business products vary in degree of complexity. The simplest consumer-product channel involves direct selling from producers to consumers. Businesses may sell directly to business or government buyers. Marketing channels grow more complex as intermediaries become involved. Consumer-product channel intermediaries include agents, brokers, wholesalers, and retailers. Business-product channel intermediaries include agents, brokers, and industrial distributors. Marketers often use alternative channel arrangements to move their products to the consumer. With dual distribution or multiple distribution, they choose two or more different channels to distribute the same product. Nontraditional channels help differentiate a firm's product from the competitor's or provide a manufacturer with another avenue for sales. Finally, strategic channel alliances are arrangements that use another manufacturer's already established channel.

3.1 Describe the most likely marketing channel structure for each of these consumer products: candy bars, Tupperware products, nonfiction books, new automobiles, farmers' market produce, and stereo equipment. Now, construct alternative channels for these same products.

3.2 You have been hired to design an alternative marketing channel for a firm specializing in the manufacturing and marketing of novelties for college student organizations. In a memo to the president of the firm, describe how the channel operates.

3.3 Building on question 1.1 determine a new channel structure for Scoops. Write a proposal to present to your key managers.

Discuss the issues that influence channel strategy. When determining marketing channel strategy, the channel manager must determine what market, product, and producer factors will influence the choice of channel. The manager must also determine the appropriate level of distribution intensity. Intensive distribution is distribution aimed at maximum market coverage. Selective distribution is achieved by screening dealers to eliminate all but a few in any single area. The most restrictive form of market coverage is exclusive distribution, which entails only one or a few dealers within a given area.

4.1 Decide which distribution intensity level—intensive, selective, or exclusive—is used for each of the following products, and explain why: Rado watches, Land Rover sport-utility vehicles, Cadbury Gems, special edition Barbie dolls, Close-Up toothpaste.

4.2 Now that you have a basic channel structure for Scoops (from question 3.3), form a team of three to four students and list the market, product, and producer factors that will affect your final channel structure.

Describe the different channel relationship types and their unique costs and benefits. Channel relationships can be plotted on a continuum ranging from Arm's-Length to integrated, with cooperative relationships somewhere in between. Arm's-Length relationships generally consist of unique transactions that are intended to occur once or very infrequently, and are pursued when closer relationships are undesirable or impractical. Although Arm's-Length relationships are low risk, they also provide few benefits in terms of favorable conditions for the agreement, and disputes are often resolved in court. Integrated relationships, on the opposite end of the spectrum, are very close relationships that are backed by formal agreements and can result in great efficiency and effectiveness. However, given that integrated relationships tend either to involve high levels of expense (in the case of vertical integration) or require enormous amounts of trust in the partner company (as in the case of supply chains), many companies prefer cooperative relationships in some settings. Cooperative relationships are a hybrid form of relationship that is governed by formal contract, are temporary, and are enforced by the agreement itself.

5.1 Working with another student in the class, decide when it would be most advantageous for large companies like Procter & Gamble, IBM, and/or Ford Motor Company to develop integrated relationships with smaller suppliers. Would the same rules for integrated relationship development also apply to customers? Why or why not?

Explain channel leadership, conflict, power, and partnering. Power, control, leadership, conflict, and partnering are the main social dimensions of marketing channel relationships. Channel power refers to the capacity of one channel member to control or influence other channel members. Channel control occurs when one channel member intentionally affects another member's behavior. Channel leadership is the exercise of authority and power. Channel conflict occurs when there is a clash of goals and methods among the members of a distribution channel. Channel conflict can be either horizontal, between channel members at the same level, or vertical, between channel members at different levels of the channel. Channel partnering is the joint effort of all channel members to create an integrated system that serves customers and creates a competitive advantage. Collaborating channel partners meet the needs of consumers more effectively by ensuring that the right products reach shelves at the right time and at a lower cost, boosting sales and profits.

6.1 Procter & Gamble and Wal-Mart are key partners in a shared channel. P&G is one of Wal-Mart's biggest suppliers, and Wal-Mart provides extremely detailed scanner data about customer purchases of P&G products. Wal-Mart has begun selling its own brand of Sam's Choice laundry detergent in bright orange bottles alongside P&G's Tide, but for a greatly reduced price. What do you think will be the impact of this new product on what has been a stable channel relationship?

Discuss channels and distribution decisions in global markets. Global marketing channels are becoming more important to the Indian economy seeking domestic and international growth. Manufacturers introducing products in foreign countries must decide what type of channel structure to use- in particular, whether the product should be marketed through direct channels or foreign intermediaries. Marketers should be aware that channel structures in foreign markets may be very different from those accustomed to in India. Global distribution expertise is also emerging as an important skill for channel managers as many countries are removing trade barriers.

7.1 Go to the World Trade Organization's Web site at **www.wto.org.** What can you learn at the site about how globalization affects channel management and other aspects of business?

Identify the special problems and opportunities associated with distribution in service organizations. Managers in service industries use the same skills, techniques, and strategies to manage logistics functions as managers in goods-producing industries. The distribution of services focuses on three main areas: minimizing wait times, managing service capacity, and improving service delivery.

8.1 Assume that you are the marketing manager of a hospital. Write a report indicating the distribution functions that concern you. Discuss the similarities and dissimilarities of distribution for services and for goods.

Exercises

APPLICATION EXERCISE

It may be easy to understand how distribution channels work just from reading, but you may still not appreciate their broad scope. This exercise will help you see for yourself how complex a single distribution channel is. Then, when you think of the number of products and services available on the market at any one time, you will understand how tremendous the national (and international) distribution network actually is.[13]

Activities

1. Create a list of approximately 20 products that you often purchase for personal use and/or that are present in your home.
2. For each of the products you listed, speculate whether the product was routed through the marketing channel using (a) exclusive, (b) selective, or (c) intensive distribution.
3. Now, for each product/distribution strategy combination, speculate as to the product, market, or producer factors that lead to this distribution strategy.
4. Finally, identify any potential alternative distribution channel options through which you might have purchased this product. Would the alternative channel choice have changed the way (location, timing, price) you purchased this good? Why or why not?

ETHICS EXERCISE

Wholesome Snacks, Inc., the maker of a variety of cookies and crackers, has just created a new vitamin-packed cookie. The new cookie has the potential to combat many of the health problems caused by malnutrition in children throughout poverty-stricken areas of the world. To date, however, many of the larger developing markets have resisted opening distribution channels to Wholesome's products. Wholesome realizes that its new cookie could also help open the door for the company to sell its less nutritious products in these markets. Therefore, the company is offering the new cookie at a low cost to government relief programs in exchange for the long-sought distribution channels. The company feels the deal is good for business, but the countries feel it is corporate bullying.

Questions

1. What do you think about Wholesome's idea for opening a new distribution channel?
2. Does the AMA Statement of Ethics address this issue? Go to **www.marketingpower.com** and review the code. Then, write a brief paragraph stating what the AMA Statement of Ethics contains that relates to distribution channels in developing nations.

MARKETING PLAN EXERCISE

In Part 1 of your strategic marketing plan, you stated your business mission and objectives and performed a detailed SWOT analysis. In Part 2 of the plan you identified and described target market segments, identified sources of competitive intelligence and the need for further marketing research. In Part 3, you began the process of defining the marketing mix, starting with the first component: product. The next stage of the strategic planning process continues defining the elements of the marketing mix, and this section focuses on place, or distribution. Use the following exercises to guide you through the distribution part of your strategic marketing plan:

1. Discuss the implications of dual/multiple distribution. If your chosen company sells through a major department store and its own catalog and then decides to have an online site or open its own store in a factory outlet, what will happen to channel relationships? To the final price offered to consumers? To promotional vehicles? Most e-marketers assume that a direct distribution channel, with no intermediaries, is the most efficient and least costly method for getting product offerings to customers. However, if you decide on a different distribution channel, you will also have to identify warehouses, fulfillment services, transportation firms, packing companies, and many other facilitating agencies. Does your company have the capabilities to handle this, or should your company invest in channel members to take over these tasks and functions?

2. Decide what channel(s) your company should be using. Describe the intermediaries involved and their likely behavior. What are the implications of these channels? Describe the conflict that might arise from having both an e-marketing offering as well as a brick-and-mortar offering. If distribution costs are different, will your company set the same or different prices for end customers?
3. Which distribution intensity level would be best for your company's product? Justify your decision.

Short Case: GO INDIGO

Prepared by
Dr. Dheeraj Sharma,
Indian Institute of Management, Ahmedabad

IndiGo Airlines was formed in the year 2006. In just about 6 years, it attained the second largest market share in the domestic airline industry.[14] It is known for its "Single class" and "low-cost airline" strategy. In 2008, it bagged the award for the "Best Domestic Low Cost Carrier". After five years of its success as a domestic airline, IndiGo got the license to launch international airlines. It has grown to operate nearly 272 flights each day.[15] IndiGo's success can be attributed to its low fares and no delays in the flight schedules.

The airline industry has a few players. Currently India is the 9th largest civil aviation market in the world, and it is anticipated to become the third largest aviation market in the world by 2020.[16] India is endowed with 4200 airports, 27,000 aircrafts, which provide to 2.5 billion passengers with connectivity to 40 countries. In terms of passenger traffic, this sector is growing at 16% and has a great potential to grow further.[17]

In India, taking a flight to travel was considered as a luxury before. However, with the entry of several players, flight rates have lowered and have made it affordable for everyone. This has increased the competition in this sector and each service provider is striving to woo its customers by enhancing their experience. The first step to attain this would be by making tickets, schemes, offers, etc., available to the customers in the easiest way possible. Go IndiGo uses various marketing channels to reach out to people/its customers.

It sells tickets via their call centers, IndiGo Website, via travel portals such as, Makemytrip, Yatra, cleartrip, expedia, etc., through its authorized IndiGo travel consultants, other travel agents, IndiGo ticket booking counters, and directly from the airport. Out of these options, the most popular option among the customers is online via booking via travel portals. Travel portals make ticket booking simple by giving the customers a host of price and airline options. Customers can pick the cheap and convenient deals without having to browse Websites of all the airlines. Similarly, ticket booking via travel agents is also quite popular, as the services provided here are more personalized. These marketing channels are being used by all airline companies. IndiGo recently launched "IndoGo Mobile Application". The application enables IndiGo customers to book tickets and receive details on their mobile. It also enables them to check-in, check flight status and schedules, and access the F&B menu on their mobile phones.

With the growth of the ICT sector, newer ways of marketing are emerging. A recent survey by Specialists in Air Transport and IT Solutions (SITA) reported that airlines are planning on using kiosks and social networking websites, to sell their services by 2014.[18] Airline companies are adapting these new marketing channels to improve their customer services by making services easily accessible, to explore new markets and revenue opportunities, to reduce the cost of business operations, and to increase business productivity. It has been proved that Web based marketing reduces the cost of marketing.[19]

Questions

1. What are the key trends in Marketing Channels for the Airline Industry in India?
2. What are the advantage and disadvantages of these new channels? Should IndiGo follow these trends?

13 Marketing Channels

KEY TERMS

LO 1

marketing channel (channel of distribution) a set of interdependent organizations that eases the transfer of ownership as products move from producer to business user or consumer

channel members all parties in the marketing channel who negotiate with one another, buy and sell products, and facilitate the change of ownership between buyer and seller in the course of moving the product from the manufacturer into the hands of the final consumer

discrepancy of quantity the difference between the amount of product produced and the amount an end user wants to buy

discrepancy of assortment the lack of all the items a customer needs to receive full satisfaction from a product or products

temporal discrepancy a situation that occurs when a product is produced but a customer is not ready to buy it

spatial discrepancy the difference between the location of a producer and the location of widely scattered markets

LO 2

retailer a channel intermediary that sells mainly to consumers

merchant wholesaler an institution that buys goods from manufacturers and resells them to businesses, government agencies, and other wholesalers or retailers and that receives and takes title to goods, stores them in its own warehouses, and later ships them

agents and brokers wholesaling intermediaries who do not take title to a product but facilitate its sale from producer to end user by representing retailers, wholesalers, or manufacturers

KEY CONCEPTS

LO 1 **Explain what a marketing channel is and why intermediaries are needed.** A marketing channel is a business structure of interdependent organizations that reach from the point of product origin to the consumer. Its purpose is to physically move products to their final consumption destination, representing "place" or "distribution" in the marketing mix. A marketing channel gets the right product to the right place at the right time. Members of a marketing channel create a continuous and seamless supply chain that performs or supports the marketing channel functions. Channel members provide economies to the distribution process in the form of specialization and division of labor; overcoming discrepancies in quantity, assortment, time, and space; and providing contact efficiency.

LO 2 **Define the types of channel intermediaries and describe their functions and activities.** The most prominent difference separating intermediaries is whether they take title to the product. Retailers and merchant wholesalers take title, but agents and brokers do not. Retailers are firms that sell mainly to consumers. Merchant wholesalers are those organizations that facilitate the movement of products and services from the manufacturer to producers, resellers, governments, institutions, and retailers. Agents and brokers facilitate the exchange of ownership between sellers and buyers. Channel intermediaries perform three basic types of functions. Transactional functions include contacting and promoting, negotiating, and risk taking. Logistical functions performed by channel members include physical distribution, storing, and sorting functions. Finally, channel members may perform facilitating functions, such as researching and financing.

LO 3 **Describe the channel structures for consumer and business products and discuss alternative channel arrangements.** Marketing channels for consumer and business products vary in degree of complexity. The simplest consumer-product channel involves direct selling from producers to consumers. Businesses may sell directly to business or government buyers. Marketing channels grow more complex as intermediaries become involved. Consumer-product channel intermediaries include agents, brokers, wholesalers, and retailers. Business-product channel intermediaries include agents, brokers, and industrial distributors. Marketers often use alternative channel arrangements to move their products to the consumer. With dual distribution or multiple distribution, they choose two or more different channels to distribute the same product. Nontraditional channels help differentiate a firm's product from the competitor's or provide a manufacturer with another avenue for sales. Finally, strategic channel alliances are arrangements that use another manufacturer's already established channel.

LO 4 **Discuss the issues that influence channel strategy.** When determining marketing channel strategy, the supply chain manager must determine what market, product, and producer factors will influence the choice of channel. The manager must also determine the appropriate level of distribution intensity. Intensive distribution is distribution aimed at maximum market coverage. Selective distribution is achieved by screening dealers to eliminate all but a few in any single area. The most restrictive form of market coverage is exclusive distribution, which entails only one or a few dealers within a given area.

LO 5 **Describe the different channel relationship types and their unique costs and benefits.** Channel relationships can be plotted on a continuum ranging from arm's length to integrated, with cooperative relationships somewhere in between. Arm's-length relationships generally consist of unique transactions that

logistics the efficient and cost-effective forward and reverse flow and storage of goods, services, and related information into, through, and out of channel member companies

LO 3 **direct channel** a distribution channel in which producers sell directly to consumers

dual distribution (multiple distribution) the use of two or more channels to distribute the same product to target markets

strategic channel alliance a cooperative agreement between business firms to use the other's already established distribution channel

LO 4 **intensive distribution** a form of distribution aimed at having a product available in every outlet where target customers might want to buy it

selective distribution a form of distribution achieved by screening dealers to eliminate all but a few in any single area

exclusive distribution a form of distribution that establishes one or a few dealers within a given area

LO 5 **arm's-length relationship** a relationship between companies that is loose, characterized by low relational investment and trust, and usually taking the form of a series of discrete transactions with no or low expectation of future interaction or service

cooperative relationship a relationship between companies that takes the form of informal partnership with moderate levels of trust and information sharing as needed to further each company's goals

integrated relationship a relationship between companies that is tightly connected, with linked processes across and between firm boundaries and high levels of trust and interfirm commitment

LO 6 **channel power** the capacity of a particular marketing channel member to control or influence the behavior of other channel members

channel control a situation that occurs when one marketing channel member intentionally affects another member's behavior

channel leader (channel captain) a member of a marketing channel that exercises authority and power over the activities of other channel members

channel conflict a clash of goals and methods between distribution channel members

horizontal conflict a channel conflict that occurs among channel members on the same level

vertical conflict a channel conflict that occurs between different levels in a marketing channel, most typically between the manufacturer and wholesaler or between the manufacturer and retailer

channel partnering (channel cooperation) the joint effort of all channel members to create a channel that serves customers and creates a competitive advantage

are intended to occur once or very infrequently and are pursued when closer relationships are undesirable or impractical. Though arm's-length relationships are low risk, they also provide few benefits in terms of favorable conditions for the agreement, and disputes are often resolved in court. Integrated relationships, on the opposite end of the spectrum, are very close relationships that are backed by formal agreements and can result in great efficiency and effectiveness. However, given that integrated relationships tend either to involve high levels of expense (in the case of vertical integration) or require enormous amounts of trust in the partner company (as in the case of supply chains), many companies prefer cooperative relationships in some settings. Cooperative relationships are a hybrid form of relationship that are governed by formal contract, are temporary, and are enforced by the agreement itself.

LO 6 **Explain channel leadership, conflict, and partnering.** Power, control, leadership, conflict, and partnering are the main social dimensions of marketing channel relationships. Channel power refers to the capacity of one channel member to control or influence other channel members. Channel control occurs when one channel member intentionally affects another member's behavior. Channel leadership is the exercise of authority and power. Channel conflict occurs when there is a clash of goals and methods among the members of a distribution channel. Channel conflict can be either horizontal, between channel members at the same level, or vertical, between channel members at different levels of the channel. Channel partnering is the joint effort of all channel members to create a supply chain that serves customers and creates a competitive advantage. Collaborating channel partners meet the needs of consumers more effectively by ensuring that the right products reach shelves at the right time and at a lower cost, boosting sales and profits.

LO 7 **Discuss channels and distribution decisions in global markets.** Global marketing channels are becoming more important to Indian companies seeking growth abroad. Manufacturers introducing products in foreign countries must decide what type of channel structure to use—in particular, whether the product should be marketed through direct channels or through foreign intermediaries. Marketers should be aware that channel structures in foreign markets may be very different from those they are accustomed to in India. Global distribution expertise is also emerging as an important skill for channel managers, as many countries are removing trade barriers.

LO 8 **Identify the special problems and opportunities associated with distribution in service organizations.** Managers in service industries use the same skills, techniques, and strategies to manage logistics functions as managers in goods-producing industries. The distribution of services focuses on three main areas: minimizing wait times, managing service capacity, and improving service delivery.

CHAPTER 14 Supply Chain Management

Learning Outcomes

LO 1 Define the terms *supply chain* and *supply chain management*, and discuss the benefits of supply chain management

LO 2 Discuss the concept of supply chain integration, and explain why each of the six types of integration is important

LO 3 Identify the eight key processes of excellent supply chain management, and discuss how each of these processes impacts the end customer

LO 4 Discuss the key strategic decisions supply chain managers must make when designing their companies' supply chains

LO 5 Describe the logistical components of the supply chain

LO 6 Explain why supply chain performance measurement is necessary and important

LO 7 Discuss new technology and emerging trends in supply chain management

In today's marketplace, products are being driven by customers.

LO 1 Supply Chains and Supply Chain Management

Many modern companies are turning to supply chain management for competitive advantage. A company's **supply chain** includes all of the companies involved in all of the upstream and downstream flows of products, services, finances, and information, from initial suppliers (the point of origin) to the ultimate customer (the point of consumption). The goal of **supply chain management** is to coordinate and integrate all of the activities performed by supply chain members into a seamless process, from the source to the point of consumption, ultimately giving supply chain managers "total visibility" of the supply chain both inside and outside the firm. The philosophy behind supply chain management is that by visualizing the entire supply chain, supply chain managers can maximize strengths and efficiencies at each level of the process to create a highly competitive, customer-driven supply system that is able to respond immediately to changes in supply and demand.

supply chain the connected chain of all of the business entities, both internal and external to the company, that perform or support the logistics function

supply chain management a management system that coordinates and integrates all of the activities performed by supply chain members into a seamless process, from the source to the point of consumption, resulting in enhanced customer and economic value

Supply chain management is completely customer driven. In the mass production era, manufacturers produced standardized products that were "pushed"

Note: All the figures in U.S. dollars are converted into rupee using the value $1 = ₹45.

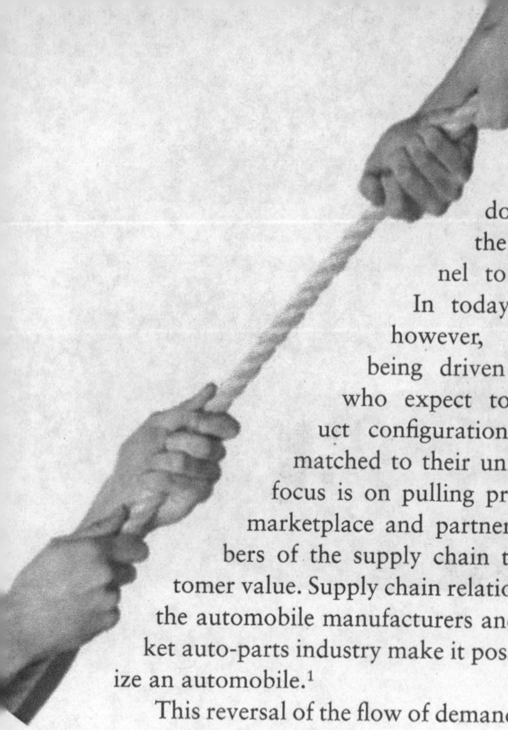

down through the supply channel to the consumer. In today's marketplace, however, products are being driven by customers, who expect to receive product configurations and services matched to their unique needs. The focus is on pulling products into the marketplace and partnering with members of the supply chain to enhance customer value. Supply chain relationships between the automobile manufacturers and the after-market auto-parts industry make it possible to customize an automobile.[1]

This reversal of the flow of demand from a "push" to a "pull" has resulted in a radical reformulation of market expectations and traditional marketing, production, and distribution functions. Integrated channel partnerships allow companies to respond with the unique product configuration and mix of services demanded by the customer. Today, supply chain management is both a *communicator* of customer demand that extends from the point of sale all the way back to the supplier, and a *physical flow* process that engineers the timely and cost-effective movement of goods through the entire supply pipeline.

Benefits of Supply Chain Management

Supply chain management is a key means of differentiation for a firm and a critical component in marketing and corporate strategy. Companies that focus on supply chain management commonly report lower inventory, transportation, warehousing, and packaging costs; greater supply chain flexibility; improved customer service; and higher revenues. Research has shown a clear relationship between supply chain performance and profitability.

For example, Sysco, a food distribution company based in Houston in the United States, uses a number of technical software and systems that have enabled it to reduce costs and speed delivery times. With the help of a software called *Roadnet*, the company was able to ascertain the most efficient truck routes. This helped the company in cutting down its diesel usage by as much as 8 percent in one year.[2]

supply chain integration when multiple firms in a supply chain coordinate their activities and processes so that they are seamlessly linked to one another in an effort to satisfy the customer

LO 2 Supply Chain Integration

A key principle of supply chain management is that multiple firms work together to perform tasks as a single, unified system rather than as several individual companies acting in isolation. Companies in a world-class supply chain combine their resources, capabilities, and innovations such that they are used for the best interest of the entire chain as a whole, with the goal being that overall performance of the supply chain will be greater than the sum of its parts. As firms become increasingly supply chain oriented, they develop management practices that are consistent with this systems approach.

Management practices that are reflective of a highly coordinated effort between supply chain partners are said to be "integrated." In other words, **supply chain integration** occurs when multiple firms in a supply chain coordinate their activities and processes so that they are seamlessly linked to one another in an effort to satisfy the customer. In a world-class supply chain, the customer may not know where the business activities of one firm or business unit end and where those of another begin—all the participating firms and business units appear to be reading from the same script.

In the practice of world-class supply chain management, six types of integration are sought by firms interested in providing top-level service to customers:[3]

- *Relationship integration* is the ability of two or more companies to develop social connections that serve to guide their interactions when working together. More specifically, relationship integration is the capability to develop and maintain a shared mental framework across companies that describes how they will depend on one another when working together. This includes the ways in which they will collaborate on activities or projects so that the customer gains the maximum amount of total value possible from the supply chain.
- *Measurement integration* reflects the idea that performance assessments should be transparent and measurable across the borders of different business units and firms, and also assess the performance of the supply chain as a whole while holding each individual firm or business unit accountable for meeting its own goals.

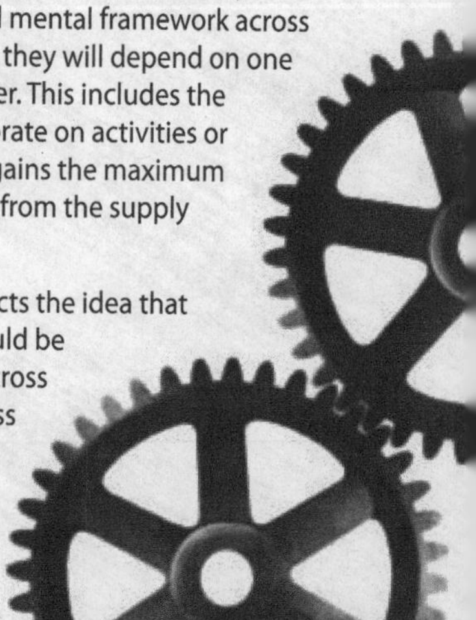

- *Technology and planning integration* refers to the creation and maintenance of information technology systems that connect managers across and through the firms in the supply chain; it requires information hardware and software systems that can exchange information when needed between customers, suppliers, and internal operational areas of each of the supply chain partners.
- *Material and service supplier integration* requires firms to link seamlessly to those outsiders that provide goods and services to them so that they can streamline work processes and thereby provide smooth, high-quality customer experiences. Both sides need to have a common vision of the total value creation process and be willing to share the responsibility for satisfying customer requirements to make supplier integration successful.
- *Internal operations integration* is the result of capabilities development toward the goal of linking internally performed work into a seamless process that stretches across departmental and/or functional boundaries with the goal of satisfying customer requirements.
- *Customer integration* is a competency that enables firms to offer long-lasting, distinctive, value-added offerings to those customers who represent the greatest value to the firm or supply chain. Highly customer-integrated firms assess their own capabilities and then match them to customers whose desires they can meet and who offer large enough sales potential for the linkage to be profitable over the long term.

Firms' success in achieving each of these types of integration is very important. Highly integrated supply chains (those that are successful in achieving many or all of these types of integration) have been shown to be better at satisfying customers, managing costs, delivering high-quality products, enhancing productivity, and utilizing company or business unit assets, all of which translate into greater profitability for the firms and their partners working together in the supply chain.

LO 3 The Key Processes of Supply Chain Management

When firms practice good supply chain management, their functional departments or areas, such as marketing, research and development, and/or production, are integrated both within and across the linked firms. Integration, then, is "how" excellent supply chain management works. The business processes on which the linked firms work together represent the "what" of supply chain management—they are the objects of focus on which firms, departments, areas, and people work together when seeking to reduce supply chain costs or generate additional revenues. **Business processes** are composed of bundles of interconnected activities that stretch across firms in the supply chain; they represent key areas that some or all of the involved firms are constantly working on in order to reduce costs and/or generate revenues for everyone throughout supply chain management. There are eight critical business processes on which supply chain managers must focus:

1. Customer relationship management
2. Customer service management
3. Demand management
4. Order fulfillment
5. Manufacturing flow management
6. Supplier relationship management
7. Product development and commercialization
8. Returns management[4]

Customer Relationship Management

The **customer relationship management (CRM) process** (discussed further in Chapter 21) allows companies to prioritize their marketing focus on different customer groups according to each group's long-term value to the company or supply chain. Once higher-value customers are identified, firms should focus on providing customized products and better service to this group than to others. The

business processes bundles of interconnected activities that stretch across firms in the supply chain

customer relationship management (CRM) process allows companies to prioritize their marketing focus on different customer groups according to each group's long-term value to the company or supply chain

customer service management process presents a multi-company, unified response system to the customer whenever complaints, concerns, questions, or comments are voiced

demand management process seeks to align supply and demand throughout the supply chain by anticipating customer requirements at each level and creating demand-related plans of action prior to actual customer purchasing behavior

customer relationship management process includes both segmentation of customers by value and the generation of customer loyalty for the most attractive segments—key activities that are enabled through customer integration. This process provides a set of comprehensive principles for the initiation and maintenance of customer relationships and is often carried out with the assistance of specialized CRM computer software.

Customer Service Management

Whereas the customer relationship management process is designed to identify and build relationships with good customers, the customer service management process is designed to ensure that those customer relationships remain strong. The **customer service management process** presents a multi-company, unified response system to the customer whenever complaints, concerns, questions, or comments are voiced. When the process is well executed, it can have a strong positive impact on revenues, often as a result of quick positive response to negative customer feedback, and sometimes even in the form of additional sales gained through the additional customer contact. Customers expect service from the moment a product is purchased until it is disposed of, and the customer service management process allows for touch points between the buyer and seller throughout this life cycle. The use of customer care software enables companies to enhance their customer service management process.

Demand Management

The **demand management process** seeks to align supply and demand throughout the supply chain by anticipating customer requirements at each level and creating demand-related plans of action prior to actual customer purchasing behavior. At the same time, demand management seeks to minimize the costs of serving multiple types of customers who have variable wants and needs. In other words, the demand management process allows companies in the supply chain to satisfy customers in the most efficient and effective ways possible. The activities such as customer data collection, forecasting of future demand, and the development of activities that serve to "smooth out" demand help bring available inventory into alignment with customer desires. Though it is very difficult to predict exactly what items and quantities customers will buy prior to purchase, demand management can ease the pressure on the production process and allow companies to satisfy most of their customers through greater flexibility in manufacturing, marketing, and sales programs. However, much of the uncertainty in demand plan-

DOLLAR DRINK? NOT TODAY

McDonald's worked to develop a large-scale marketing campaign in the American market to promote its new fruit smoothies in strawberry banana and wild berry flavors. But stores received their stock and promotional tools before the release day, and many began selling the smoothies at a quick pace—and in advance of the predetermined launch date. When managers reviewed the distribution schedule, they realized that the promotional price of $1(₹45)—and smoothie posters that called attention to the new product—would cause many locations to run out of the smoothie mix sooner than anticipated. McDonald's supply chain alerted the management, which then ordered franchisees to hold smoothie sales until the marketing campaign actually began.[5]

© RUBBERBALL/JUPITERIMAGES

ning can be mitigated by conducting collaborative planning, forecasting, and replenishment (CPFR) activities with the company's customers and suppliers. General Mills, one of the largest food companies in the world, is an American Fortune 500 Corporation with more than 100 leading food brands. Because of inefficiencies in the manufacturing and ordering processes, General Mills had an abundance of inventory of its Fruit Roll-Ups and Gushers fruit snacks. By combining the overstock into "mystery" fruit snacks pouches, General Mills created the sixth-fastest selling fruit snack in the market![6]

Order Fulfillment

One of the most fundamental processes in supply chain management is the order fulfillment process, which involves generating, filling, delivering, and providing on-the-spot service for customer orders. The **order fulfillment process** is a highly integrated process, often requiring persons from multiple companies and multiple functions to come together and coordinate to create customer satisfaction at a given place and time. The best order fulfillment processes reduce the time between order and customer receipt as much as possible while ensuring that the customer receives exactly what he or she wants. The shorter lead times are beneficial in that they allow firms to carry reduced inventory levels and free up cash that can be used on other projects. Overall, the order fulfillment process involves understanding both internal capabilities and external customer needs, and matching these together so that the supply chain maximizes profits while minimizing costs and waste.

When the order fulfillment process is managed diligently, the amount of time between order placement and receipt of the customer's payment following order shipment (known as the order-to-cash cycle) is minimized as much as possible. Since many firms do not view order fulfillment as a core competency (versus, for example, product development or marketing), they often outsource this function to a third-party logistics firm (3PL) that specializes in the order fulfillment process. The 3PL becomes a semi-permanent part of the firm's supply chain assigned to manage one or more specialized functions. When employed for the purposes of order fulfillment, the 3PL is contracted to manage the firm's order fulfillment process from beginning to end, thereby freeing up the firm's time and resources so that they can be expended on core business activities.

Manufacturing Flow Management

The **manufacturing flow management process** is concerned with ensuring that firms in the supply chain have the needed resources to manufacture with flexibility and to move products through a multi-stage production process. Firms with flexible manufacturing have the ability to create a wide variety of goods and/or services with minimized costs associated with changing production techniques. The manufacturing flow process includes much more than simple production of goods and services—it means creating flexible agreements with suppliers and shippers so that unexpected demand bursts can be accommodated.

The goals of the manufacturing flow management process are centered on leveraging the capabilities held by multiple members of the supply chain to improve overall manufacturing output in terms of quality, delivery speed, and flexibility, all of which tie to profitability.

order fulfillment process a highly integrated process, often requiring persons from multiple companies and multiple functions to come together and coordinate to create customer satisfaction at a given place and time

manufacturing flow management process concerned with ensuring that firms in the supply chain have the needed resources to manufacture with flexibility and to move products through a multi-stage production process

supplier relationship management process closely related to the manufacturing flow management process and contains several characteristics that parallel the customer relationship management process

Supplier Relationship Management

The **supplier relationship management process** is closely related to the manufacturing flow management process and contains several characteristics that parallel the customer relationship management process. The manufacturing flow management process is highly dependent on supplier relationships for flexibility. Furthermore, in a way similar to that found in the customer relationship management process, supplier relationship management provides structural support for developing and maintaining relationships with suppliers. Thus, integrating these two ideas, supplier relationship management supports manufacturing flow by identifying and maintaining relationships with highly valued suppliers. Just as firms benefit from developing close-knit and integrated relationships with customers, close-knit and integrated relationships with suppliers provide a means through which performance advantages can be gained.

The management of supplier relationships is a key step toward ensuring that firms' manufacturing resources are available, and thereby the supplier relationship management process has a direct impact on each supply chain member's bottom-line financial performance.

PepsiCo decided it needed more control over major parts of its supply chain and purchased two of its major bottlers. As a result, Pepsi is able to work more closely with its retailers.[7]

© ISTOCKPHOTO.COM/DONALD ERICKSON

Product Development and Commercialization

The **product development and commercialization process** (discussed in detail in Chapter 11) includes the group of activities that facilitates the joint development and marketing of new offerings among a group of supply chain partner firms. In many cases, new products and services are not the sole responsibility of a single firm that serves as inventor, engineer, builder, marketer, and sales agent; rather, they are often the product of a multi-company collaboration with multiple firms and business units playing unique roles in new product development, testing, and launch activities, among others. The capability for developing and introducing new offerings quickly is key for competitive success versus rival firms, so it is often advantageous to involve many supply chain partners in the effort. The process requires the close cooperation of suppliers and customers who provide input throughout the process and serve as advisors and co-producers for the new offering(s).

product development and commercialization process includes the group of activities that facilitates the joint development and marketing of new offerings among a group of supply chain partner firms

returns management process enables firms to manage volumes of returned product efficiently while minimizing returns-related costs and maximizing the value of the returned assets to the firms in the supply chain

Returns Management

The final supply chain management process deals with incidents where customers choose to return a product to the retailer or supplier, thus creating a reversed flow of goods within the supply chain. The **returns management process** enables firms to manage volumes of returned product efficiently while minimizing returns-related costs and maximizing the value of the returned assets to the firms in the supply chain. Returns have the potential to impact a firm's financial position in a major and negative way if mishandled. Certain industries, such as apparel e-retailing, can reach up to 40 percent of sales volume in returns.

In addition to the value of managing returns from a pure asset-recovery perspective, many firms are discovering that returns management also creates additional marketing and customer service touch points that can be leveraged for added customer value above and beyond normal sales and promotion-driven encounters. Handling returns gives the company an additional opportunity to please the customer, and customers who have positive experiences with the returns management process can become very confident buyers who are willing to reorder, since they know any problems they encounter with purchases will be quickly and fairly rectified. In addition, the returns management process allows the firm to recognize weaknesses in product design and/or areas for potential improvement through the direct customer feedback that initiates the process.

LO 4 Strategic Supply Chain Management Decisions

The establishment of supply chain integration and identification of key business processes make world-class supply chain management possible for businesses. However, to take advantage of these principles, supply chain managers must implement them in practice. Supply chain management strategies guide the implementation of key supply chain management principles. When implementing supply chain management, a number of strategic questions are relevant, and these must be answered by managers who are seeking to gain the benefits of the integrated, process-oriented supply chain. Some of the most important questions are:

- Based on the markets we compete in, the suppliers available, and the products we sell, what overarching supply chain strategy is most appropriate for my firm or business unit?
- What does the overall "map" of all of the firm's key supply chain members look like?

These strategic questions are among the most major that supply chain managers will answer as they steer the firm toward operational and financial successes.

CUSTOMER EXPERIENCE

Response to Customer Unpredictability in the Automotive Industry: Get Lean

In the ultra-competitive U.S. automobile industry, delivering the right car to the customer, in the right color, with the right features, at the right price, and in the shortest amount of time possible, is a critical determinant of customer satisfaction. Automobile makers both foreign and domestic know this, but are faced with a competing goal as well—minimizing inventory costs. Automakers need to sell as many cars as possible, but they also need to be sure to make only as many cars as customers will demand in order to be profitable. Thus, the Big 3 American companies, as well as foreign competitors such as Honda, Toyota, and Mercedes, are turning to lean supply chain management principles in order to get the job done. A lean supply chain is one that has been streamlined to reduce waste and/or other non-value–added activities, minimizing unnecessary inventory, time delays, and production costs.

Automakers have adopted lean supply chain principles as a method for improving customer outcomes. For example, Land Rover is using technologies such as **radio-frequency identification (RFID)** to track parts and finished automobiles' locations. Using RFID, managers can view the locations of components or finished goods on a virtual color-coded map in real time, so the company has constant, complete visibility of inventories and avoids unnecessary ordering of parts and/or manufacturing of models that are already represented within a shipment or geographic area. The company can then reinvest these savings into parts and finished cars that are actually needed at dealerships and/or manufacturing and service facilities.

Executives at Toyota also point out another key benefit of lean supply chain management: Nothing is manufactured until the customer places an order. Then and only then does the company place a replacement unit into production. As one manager at Toyota states, "most production schedules are based on (sales forecasts)…production should be based on sold end-customer orders, not forecasts… (this allows us to) eliminate just-in-case ordering and the 'noise' in the supply chain." By ordering and manufacturing on a lean, just-in-time basis, everyone in the supply chain holds less unwanted inventory and the customer gets the car they wanted quickly and at the lowest possible price. In other words, a lean supply chain enables the customer to buy exactly what they wanted, and the automobile company saves money at the same time by making only what they sell. Isn't that what is best for everyone?[8]

Supply Chain Strategies

Because products and marketplaces may differ substantially in their core characteristics from place to place and product to product, supply chain management strategies should be selected according to the situation at hand. In addition, because in many cases supply chains operate on a global scale, with far-away suppliers and customers communicating with, serving, or depending on local firms, companies must take care to adopt supply chain management strategies that strike a balance between the lower costs offered through global supply chain management and the assuredness of top-quality service that more localized solutions may provide.

One of the most interesting issues supply chain managers face in this regard is the mind-set of the firm. Most firms must choose between two strategic philosophies: high responsiveness to customers at any cost, or profitability through waste reduction (and therefore cost reduction) even if it means sometimes disappointing customers. These strategic philosophies are often referred to collectively in what has come to be known as the "lean" versus "agile" debate. The **lean supply chain management** strategy

radio-frequency identification (RFID) An automatic identification method that uses radio signals that work with scanned bar codes to identify products; data is stored in and retrieved from the RFID tag, which is attached to a product.

lean supply chain management The strategy that focuses primarily on the removal of waste from the supply chain to achieve the lowest total cost to the members of the supply chain system.

© AP PHOTO/KOJI SASAHARA

The lean supply chain management strategy—basically, removing excess of any kind—was made famous by Toyota. When properly implemented in the supply chain, going lean can prove to be a major strategic weapon.

agile supply chain management The supply chain strategy that focuses primarily on the ability of the firm to fulfill customer demand, even if this means somewhat higher costs.

Leagile supply chain strategy A supply chain management strategy that combines the best elements of the lean and agile strategies for a particular product/market combination.

embraces removal of waste from the supply chain system in whatever form it is found. Made famous by Toyota production engineer Taiichi Ohno, the lean strategy seeks to remove any excesses from the supply chain, including overproduction, product defects, excess inventories, unneeded processing, movement of people, transport of goods, or employee idling. In lean companies, these principles are sometimes adhered to even if it means disappointing a small customer segment that wants more customized services. The implementation of lean supply chain principles launched Toyota into the upper echelon of automakers in terms of performance and profitability, and has caused this strategy, when properly implemented, to become viewed as a major strategic weapon. Benetton, the Italian clothing company, has also used lean principles when reviving its brand in recent years. By narrowing its product lines through the removal of the sportswear category, outsourcing the production of high-margin accessories to China, building an extensive worldwide distribution network, and breaking up inventory into smaller, quickly dispatched shipments, the company posted its highest levels of profitability in several years.[9]

Lean supply chain management does have weaknesses as a competitive strategy. Though "going lean" works well in situations where the advantages generated by mass manufacturing are present, such as cases where relatively stable and predictable market demand and low variety of customer preferences exist, the lean strategy does not work as well when customers prefer more customized products and when demand is more unpredictable. Thus, in contrast to lean supply chain management, other companies sometimes choose to adopt **agile supply chain management** strategies. Whereas the lean strategy is mostly concerned with waste reduction, the agile strategy is concerned primarily with customer responsiveness, and focuses primarily on the ability of the firm to fulfill demand in situations where consumer wants and needs are less obvious. A key concept for the implementation of agile SCM is the notion of flexibility. Instead of relying on forecasts that drive production ahead of demand, agile supply chains adopt a wait-and-see approach where commitment to supply chain processes is unknown until the order is placed. They then make products customized to order specifications. With the agile strategy, the customer is always right, and is to be served to the utmost even if this means somewhat higher costs.

Although the lean and agile supply chain strategies may at first seem to include opposing perspectives and actions, this is not necessarily always the case. First, the two strategies do, in fact, share a common objective: to fulfill customer requirements at the lowest total cost to the members of the supply chain system. (The difference is at what point the firm determines that cost control becomes more important than customer demands. With the lean strategy, cost control becomes a priority much sooner, and with the agile strategy, customer focus remains the key much longer.) Because of this common goal, some of the elements of each strategy can be combined in a hybrid strategy. The bringing together of principles from each of the main strategic viewpoints has been termed a **Leagile supply chain strategy.** With the Leagile strategy, the best elements of each strategy for the particular product/market combination describing the firm are selected. For example, customers wishing to purchase a Toyota Scion can log onto the company Web site and build their car to a highly customized degree, including the selection of leather versus cloth seats, many different wheel types, and a wide variety of sound and video equipment. However, the base automobile is manufactured and shipped from within Japan using lean principles; only later are the "agile" components selected by the customer installed, with the final customization often occurring at the local dealership location. This delay in final production is called **postponement.** Through postponement, the Leagile supply chain management strategy allows the company to take advantage of many of the benefits of lean supply chain management while still providing the agility that makes many customer experiences more desirable.

The big question then is under what conditions should companies use lean, agile, and/or Leagile supply chain management strategies? The answer to this question depends largely on the characteristics of the supply market and customer demand for the product. In situations where aggregate customer demand is predictable, it is generally accepted that lean supply chain management offers the greatest benefits in terms of waste reduction associated with repetitive manufacturing flow and order fulfillment processes. However, when customer demand is less certain, the best supply chain management strategy to choose depends on supply market characteristics. Specifically, when there is an abundance of suppliers, and the supply market as a whole is quick and responsive, an agile strategy is usually best because it maximizes customer responsiveness at the lowest levels of risk. On the other hand, when the supply market is less certain, the firm may be better off implementing a Leagile strategy, with some generic inventory being held at strategic locations ready for quick customer adaptation and sale. These situations are depicted in Exhibit 14.1.

postponement
The delay in final production in the Leagile supply chain management strategy that enables the company to take advantage of many of the benefits of lean supply chain management while still providing the agility that improves customer experiences.

Mapping the Supply Chain

In addition to the selection and implementation of an overarching supply chain management strategy, firms must also understand the structure of their supply chain and the many relationships existing between members. In terms of their structure, all supply chains may be viewed as groupings of nodes and linkages, with the nodes being firms or business units/functions, and the links being the processes that connect them. A typical supply chain network looks like an uprooted tree laid upon its side, as shown in Exhibit 14.2. Viewing this exhibit, decisions related to supply chain structure are centered on which nodes should be included in the network and what level or degree of linkage should be used to connect any two nodes. With respect to the first question, firms consider issues such as how long the supply chain for a product should be and what number of suppliers or customers should be included in each level of the network. For example, many firms seek to "optimize" their collection of suppliers (supply base) by including only the certain number of suppliers that can be adequately managed through personal relationships,

EXHIBIT 14.1
Lean versus Agile Supply Chain Management

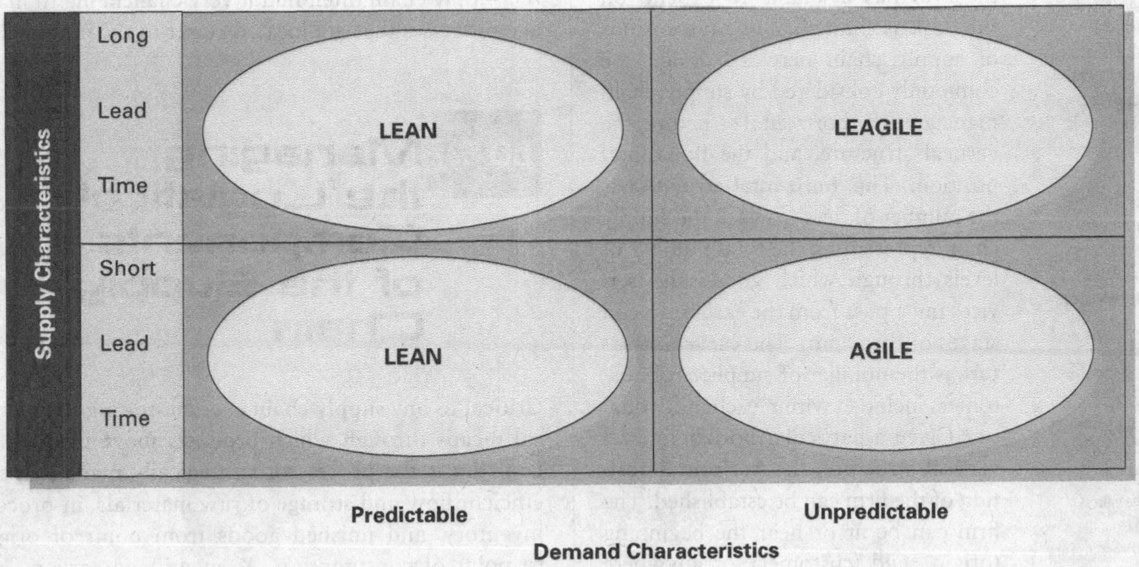

SOURCE: Martin Christopher, Helen Peck, and Denis Towill, "A Taxonomy for Selecting Global Supply Chain Stategies" (2007), *International Journal of Logistics Management*, Vol. 17, No. 2, pp. 277–287.

EXHIBIT 14.2

A Supply Chain Network Map

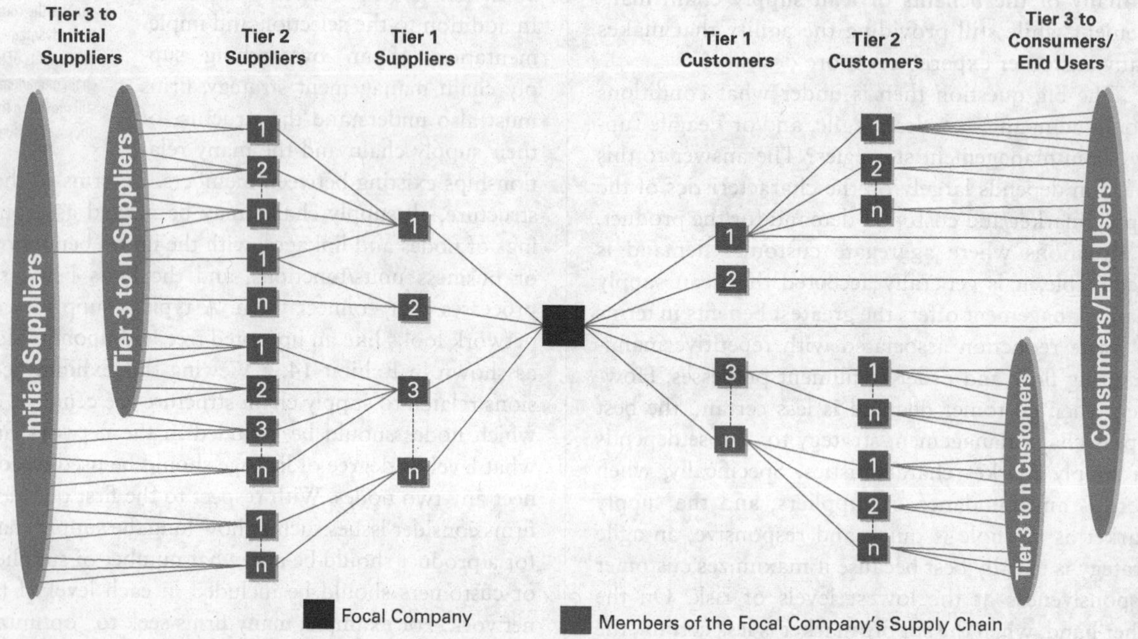

SOURCE: Douglas M. Lambert, Editor, *Supply Chain Management: Processes, Partnerships, Performance*, Third Edition, Sarasota, FL: Supply Chain Management Institute, 2008, p. 6 adapted from Douglas M. Lambert, Martha C.Cooper, and Janus D. Pagh, "Supply Chain Management Implementation Issues and Research Opportunities," *The International Journal of Logistics Management*, Vol. 9, No. 2, 1998, p. 3. Copyright 2008, Supply Chain Management Institute. For more information see: www.scm-institute.org.

horizontal structure One of three dimensions of supply chain network design; the number of tiers (columns) in the supply chain, representing the total number of levels through which goods and services must pass from the earliest to end stages of the chain.

vertical structure One of three dimensions of supply chain network design; the number of suppliers or customers included within each individual tier.

horizontal position One of three dimensions of supply chain network design; the position of a firm, relative to other firms, along the supply chain.

logistics the process of strategically managing the efficient flow and storage of raw materials, in-process inventory, and finished goods from point of origin to point of consumption

given that the amount of resources the firm has available to expend on this task is limited. Three dimensions of supply chain network design are commonly considered by supply chain managers: the horizontal structure, the vertical structure, and the horizontal position. The **horizontal structure** is the number of tiers (rows in the supply chain representing the total number of levels through which goods and services must pass from the earliest to end stages of the chain). The **vertical structure** is the number of suppliers or customers included within each individual tier. Given a particular horizontal and vertical structure, the **horizontal position** of the firm can be established. The firm can be at or near the beginning (origin), end (customer), or anywhere between in the supply chain. The horizontal position of the firm is important to establish, as firms that are located near one end of the supply chain often find it very challenging to manage processes that are located closer to the other end.

LO 5 Managing the Logistical Components of the Supply Chain

Critical to any supply chain is orchestrating the physical means through which products move through it. **Logistics** is the process of strategically managing the efficient flow and storage of raw materials, in-process inventory, and finished goods from point of origin to point of consumption. As mentioned earlier, supply chain management coordinates and integrates all of the activities performed by supply chain members into a seamless process. The supply chain consists of several interrelated and integrated logistical components: (1) sourcing and procurement of raw materials and supplies, (2) production scheduling, (3) order processing, (4) inventory control, (5) warehousing and materials handling, and (6) transportation.

The **logistics information system** is the link connecting all of the logistics components of the supply chain. The components of the system include, for example, software for materials acquisition and handling, warehouse-management and enterprise-wide solutions, data storage and integration in data warehouses, mobile communications, electronic data interchange, radio frequency identification (RFID) chips, and the Internet. Working together, the components of the logistics information system are the fundamental enablers of successful supply chain management.

The **supply chain team**, in concert with the logistics information system, orchestrates the movement of goods, services, and information from the source to the consumer. Supply chain teams typically cut across organizational boundaries, embracing all parties who participate in moving the product to market. The best supply chain teams also move beyond the organization to include the external participants in the chain, such as suppliers, transportation carriers, and third-party logistics suppliers. Members of the supply chain communicate, coordinate, and cooperate extensively.

Sourcing and Procurement

One of the most important links in the supply chain is that between the manufacturer and the supplier. Purchasing professionals are on the front lines of supply chain management. Purchasing departments plan purchasing strategies, develop specifications, select suppliers, and negotiate price and service levels.

The goal of most sourcing and procurement activities is to reduce the costs of raw materials and supplies. Purchasing professionals have traditionally relied on tough negotiations to get the lowest price possible from suppliers of raw materials, supplies, and components. Perhaps the biggest contribution purchasing can make to supply chain management, however, is in the area of vendor relations. Companies can use the purchasing function to strategically manage suppliers in order to reduce the total cost of materials and services. Through enhanced vendor relations, buyers and sellers can develop cooperative relationships that reduce costs and improve efficiency with the aim of lowering prices and enhancing profits. By integrating suppliers into their companies' businesses, purchasing managers have become better able to streamline purchasing processes, manage inventory levels, and reduce overall costs of the sourcing and procurement operations.

logistics information system the link that connects all the logistics functions of the supply chain

supply chain team an entire group of individuals who orchestrate the movement of goods, services, and information from the source to the consumer

mass customization (build-to-order) a production method whereby products are not made until an order is placed by the customer; products are made according to customer specifications

Production Scheduling

In traditional mass-market manufacturing, production begins when forecasts call for additional products to be made or when inventory control systems signal low inventory levels. The firm then makes a product and transports the finished goods to its own warehouses or those of intermediaries, where the goods wait to be ordered by retailers or customers. For example, many types of convenience goods, such as toothpaste, deodorant, and detergent, are manufactured based on past sales and demand and then sent to retailers to resell. Production scheduling based on pushing a product down to the consumer obviously has its disadvantages, the most notable being that companies risk making products that may become obsolete or that consumers don't want in the first place.

In a customer "pull" manufacturing environment, which is growing in popularity, production of goods or services is not scheduled until an order is placed by the customer specifying the desired configuration. This process, known as **mass customization**, or **build-to-order**, uniquely tailors mass-market goods and services to the needs of the individuals who buy them. Companies as diverse as

Certain industries, such as apparel e-retailing, can reach up to 40 percent of sales volume in returns.

just-in-time production (JIT) a process that redefines and simplifies manufacturing by reducing inventory levels and delivering raw materials at the precise time they are needed on the production line

order processing system a system whereby orders are entered into the supply chain and filled

BMW, Dell, Levi Strauss, Mattel, and a host of Web-based businesses are adopting mass customization to maintain or obtain a competitive edge.

As more companies move toward mass customization of goods—and away from mass marketing of them—the need to stay on top of consumer demand is forcing manufacturers to make their supply chains more flexible. Flexibility is critical to a manufacturer's success when dramatic swings in demand occur. To meet consumers' demand for customized products, companies are forced to adapt their manufacturing approach or even create a completely new process. Despite the fact that most car companies have a section on their Web site where customers can "build and price" their own car, build-to-order vehicles in the United States comprise less than 5 percent of total car sales. BMW is hoping that customization will help it surpass Lexus as the leading luxury car brand in the United States. Encouraging buyers to customize their BMWs is more challenging in the United States than in Germany. Whereas build-to-order cars are common in Europe, U.S. consumers are accustomed to driving away in their new cars, so BMW is working with its dealerships to promote the build-to-order models.[10]

Just-in-Time Manufacturing An important manufacturing process common today among manufacturers is just-in-time manufacturing. Borrowed from the Japanese, **just-in-time production (JIT)**, sometimes called *lean production*, requires manufacturers to work closely with suppliers and transportation providers to get necessary items to the assembly line or factory floor at the precise time they are needed for production. For the manufacturer, JIT means that raw materials arrive at the assembly line in guaranteed working order "just in time" to be installed, and finished products are generally shipped to the customer immediately after completion. For the supplier, JIT means supplying customers with products in just a few days, or even a few hours, rather than weeks. For the ultimate consumer, JIT means lower costs, shorter lead times, and products that more closely meet the consumer's needs. Many clothing retailers are working to shorten lead times because they were left with large amounts of unsold stock after the recession, and many are now trying to shorten their supply chain even further using a method called *chasing*. Chasing happens when a buyer orders a small amount of product to test in stores, and if the product sells well, the buyer quickly places a larger

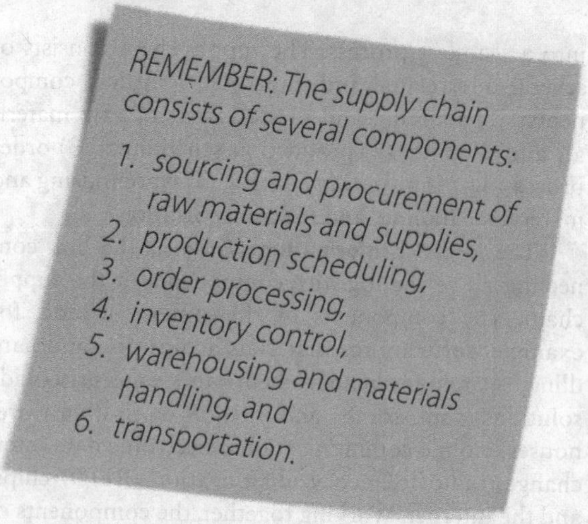

© ISTOCKPHOTO.COM/SUBJUG

order with the supplier and requires the new order to be delivered even faster. Aéropostale is a United States based specialty retailer of casual apparel, with its stores located in malls. The company uses this method to ensure that product moves through its stores quickly and with minimum discounting. However, rising cotton prices, shipping restrictions, and factories wary of small orders cause prices to rise and make chasing difficult. Aéropostale combats these challenges by working directly with cotton mills and ensuring that factories have a steady stream of orders, even if they are small.[11]

Order Processing

The order is often the catalyst that sets the supply chain in motion, especially in build-to-order environments. The **order processing system** processes the requirements of the customer and sends the information into the supply chain via the logistics information system. The order goes to the manufacturer's warehouse. If the product is in stock, the order is filled and arrangements are made to ship it. If the product is not in stock, it triggers a replenishment request that finds its way to the factory floor.

Proper order processing is critical to good service. As an order enters the system, management must monitor two flows: the flow of goods and the flow of information. Good communication among sales representatives, office personnel, and warehouse and shipping personnel is essential to correct order processing. Shipping incorrect merchandise or partially filled orders can create just as much dissatisfaction as stockouts or slow deliveries. The flow of goods and information must be continually monitored so that mistakes can be corrected before an invoice is prepared and the merchandise shipped.

Order processing is becoming more automated through the use of computer technology known as

electronic data interchange (EDI). The basic idea of EDI is to replace the paper documents that usually accompany business transactions, such as purchase orders and invoices, with electronic transmission of the needed information. A typical EDI message includes all the information that would traditionally be included on a paper invoice, such as product code, quantity, and transportation details. The information is usually sent via private networks, which are more secure and reliable than the networks used for standard e-mail messages. Most important, the information can be read and processed by computers, significantly reducing costs and increasing efficiency. Companies that use EDI can reduce inventory levels, improve cash flow, streamline operations, and increase the speed and accuracy of information transmission. EDI also creates a closer relationship between buyers and sellers.

Inventory Control

The **inventory control system** develops and maintains an adequate assortment of materials or products to meet a manufacturer's or a customer's demands. Inventory decisions, for both raw materials and finished goods, have a big impact on supply chain costs and the level of service provided. If too many products are kept in inventory, costs increase—as do risks of obsolescence, theft, and damage. If too few products are kept on hand, then the company risks product shortages and angry customers, and ultimately lost sales. The goal of inventory management, therefore, is to keep inventory levels as low as possible while maintaining an adequate supply of goods to meet customer demand. Nordstrom, a department store chain in the United States renowned for its superior customer service, has implemented new inventory management that fills online orders from distribution hubs or stores near the customer. By sending product to the customer from the nearest possible point, Nordstrom increases its shipping efficiency and better manages its inventory.[12]

Managing inventory from the supplier to the manufacturer is called **materials requirement planning (MRP)**, or **materials management.** This system

electronic data interchange (EDI) information technology that replaces the paper documents that usually accompany business transactions, such as purchase orders and invoices, with electronic transmission of the needed information to reduce inventory levels, improve cash flow, streamline operations, and increase the speed and accuracy of information transmission

inventory control system a method of developing and maintaining an adequate assortment of materials or products to meet a manufacturer's or a customer's demand

materials requirement planning (MRP) (materials management) an inventory control system that manages the replenishment of raw materials, supplies, and components from the supplier to the manufacturer

distribution resource planning (DRP) an inventory control system that manages the replenishment of goods from the manufacturer to the final consumer

automatic replenishment program a real-time inventory system that triggers shipments only when a good is sold to the end user

materials-handling system a method of moving inventory into, within, and out of the warehouse

also encompasses the sourcing and procurement operations, signaling when raw materials, supplies, or components will need to be replenished for the production of more goods. The system that manages the finished goods inventory from manufacturer to end user is commonly referred to as **distribution resource planning (DRP)**.

Both inventory systems use various inputs, such as sales forecasts, available inventory, outstanding orders, lead times, and mode of transportation to be used, to determine what needs to be done to replenish goods at all points in the supply chain. Marketers identify demand at each level in the supply chain, from the retailer back up the chain to the manufacturer, and use EDI to transmit important information throughout the channel.

Some inventory replenishment systems use little or no forecasting. These **automatic replenishment programs** trigger shipments only when a good is sold to the end user and use an EDI link connected with bar-code scanners so the supplier can view inventory in real time. When stock at the customer's location drops below predetermined levels, the supplier takes responsibility for restocking the shelves or the warehouse. This process often results in lower inventory levels.

Warehousing and Materials Handling

Although JIT manufacturing processes may eliminate the need to warehouse many raw materials, manufacturers may often keep some safety stock on hand in the event of an emergency, such as a strike at a supplier's plant or a catastrophic event that temporarily stops the flow of raw materials to the production line. Likewise, the final user may not need or want the goods at the same time the manufacturer produces and wants to sell them. Products such as grain and corn are produced seasonally, but consumers demand them year-round. Other products such as school uniforms and shoes are produced year-round, but consumers mostly buy them at the beginning of new session, usually around April or July.

Storage helps manufacturers manage supply and demand, or production and consumption. It provides time utility to buyers and sellers, which means that the seller stores the product until the buyer wants or needs it. But storing additional product does have disadvantages, including the costs of insurance on the stored product, taxes, obsolescence or spoilage, theft, and warehouse operating costs. Another drawback is opportunity costs—that is, the opportunities lost because money is tied up in stored product instead of being used for something else.

Because businesses are focusing on cutting supply chain costs, the warehousing industry is investing in services using sophisticated tracking technology such as materials-handling systems. An effective **materials-handling system** moves inventory into, within, and out of the warehouse quickly with minimal handling. With a manual, nonautomated materials-handling system, a product may be handled more than a dozen times. Each time it is handled, the cost and risk of damage increase; each lifting of a product stresses its package. Consequently, most manufacturers today have moved to automated systems. Scanners quickly identify goods entering and leaving a warehouse through bar codes affixed to the packaging. Automatic storage and retrieval systems store and pick goods in the warehouse or distribution center. Automated materials-handling systems decrease product handling, ensure accurate placement of product, and improve the accuracy of order picking and the rates of on-time shipment. For example, Dell uses a computer system called OptiPlex to run its factories. The computer software receives orders, sends requests for parts to suppliers, orders components, organizes assembly of the product, and even arranges for the product to be shipped. Instead of hundreds of workers, often fewer than six are working at a Dell factory at one time. An order for a few hundred computers can be filled in less than eight hours using the automated system. With the OptiPlex system, productivity has increased dramatically.

Transportation

Transportation typically accounts for 5 to 10 percent of the price of goods. Supply chain logisticians must

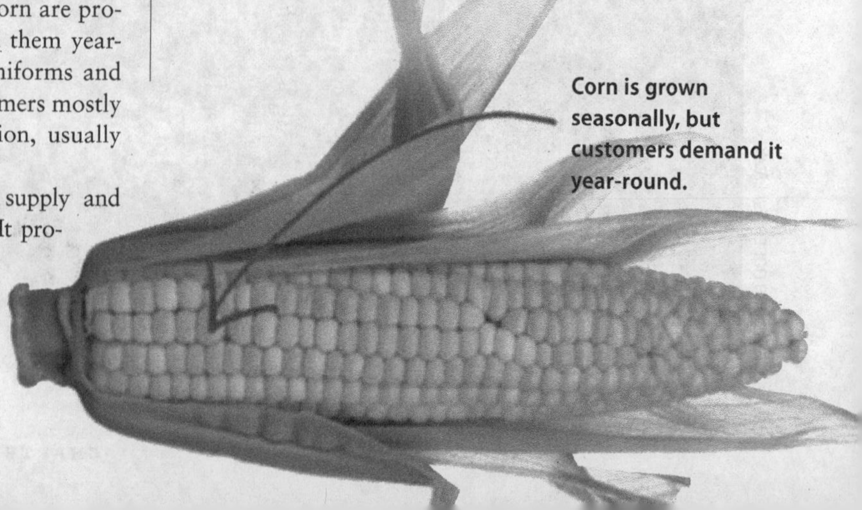

Corn is grown seasonally, but customers demand it year-round.

decide which mode of transportation to use to move products from supplier to producer and from producer to buyer. These decisions are, of course, related to all other logistics decisions. The five major modes of transportation are railroads, motor carriers, pipelines, water transportation, and airways. Supply chain managers generally choose a mode of transportation on the basis of several criteria:

- *Cost:* The total amount a specific carrier charges to move the product from the point of origin to the destination.
- *Transit time:* The total time a carrier has possession of goods, including the time required for pickup and delivery, handling, and movement between the point of origin and the destination.
- *Reliability:* The consistency with which the carrier delivers goods on time and in acceptable condition.
- *Capability:* The ability of the carrier to provide the appropriate equipment and conditions for moving specific kinds of goods, such as those that must be transported in a controlled environment (e.g., under refrigeration).
- *Accessibility:* A carrier's ability to move goods over a specific route or network.
- *Traceability:* The relative ease with which a shipment can be located and transferred.

The mode of transportation used depends on the needs of the shipper as they relate to these six criteria. Exhibit 14.3 compares the basic modes of transportation based on these criteria.

In many cases, especially in a JIT manufacturing environment, the transportation network replaces the warehouse or eliminates the expense of storing inventories as goods are timed to arrive the moment they're needed on the assembly line or for shipment to customers.

EXHIBIT 14.3

Criteria for Ranking Modes of Transportation

	Highest				Lowest
Relative Cost	Air	Truck	Rail	Pipe	Water
Transit Time	Water	Rail	Pipe	Truck	Air
Reliability	Pipe	Truck	Rail	Air	Water
Capability	Water	Rail	Truck	Air	Pipe
Accessibility	Truck	Rail	Air	Water	Pipe
Traceability	Air	Truck	Rail	Water	Pipe

LO 6 Supply Chain Performance Measurement

metrics Standard measures that can be used repeatedly to assess performance on a supply chain-related process.

A commonly repeated saying in business is, "That which cannot be measured, cannot be managed." This adage is especially true in the case of supply chain management, where multiple processes, each composed of different types of activities, are operated simultaneously with the goal of enhancing the performance of the business. Firms that are able to develop a well-thought-out system of supply chain measurement procedures are able to constantly monitor their processes, can see where they are doing well in addition to where they are failing, and are best able to gain a competitive advantage through better service and lower costs.

Because supply chains can be very complex and information is not always visible across firms operating in the same supply chain, many of the ways that managers try to measure their success or failure are not always reflective of the chain as a whole; many firms use measures of logistics performance for their own firm (such as on-time delivery rates, order cycle time, or inventory turnover) as proxies for the performance of the whole chain. However, recalling that a primary goal of supply chain management is the optimization of the entire system rather than any single firm within it, many companies are seeking to develop new metrics that will allow them a broader and more comprehensive viewpoint from which to study their supply chain's efficiency and effectiveness. **Metrics** are standard measures that can be used repeatedly to assess performance on a supply chain-related process. Common examples of metrics might include customer satisfaction ratings, orders picked from the warehouse per hour, or the ratio of operating assets to income. From the perspective of the supply chain manager, a good metric is characterized by five qualities:

- It creates understanding of strategic objectives and tactical plans.
- It promotes behaviors that are consistent with achieving these objectives.
- It allows for recording of actual results/outcomes, and therefore the firm can monitor progress toward objectives.

Balanced Scorecard Approach A measurement system used to evaluate overall supply chain performance.

- It allows companies to compare themselves to competitors (or benchmarks) and customer expectations.
- It motivates continuous improvement.

For firms using the logistics-proxy approach to supply chain measurement, several measures are often used across four unique categories of performance. The performance categories are customer satisfaction, time, cost, and asset utilization. Customer satisfaction measures often include metrics such as order fulfillment, satisfaction ratings taken from questionnaires, on-time deliveries, number of returned products, or length of delay in executing customer service activities. Time measures often employ metrics such as order-to-receipt time or source-to-make cycle time. Cost measures are often calculated as the total aggregate costs of the supply chain (on an activity basis) for a good or service, from creation through delivery. Asset utilization metrics frequently include days of inventory supply, asset performance ratios, or forecast accuracy, to name a few.

The Balanced Scorecard Approach

Because supply chain management is concerned with the performance of all firms in the system simultaneously, any performance measurement system used to evaluate a supply chain must address both the chain itself and all of the processes and firms that compose it. One method developed for this purpose is known as the **Balanced Scorecard Approach.** This approach, invented by Robert S. Kaplan and David P. Norton of Harvard Business School, combines multiple different categories of measurements that can be used at all levels of the supply chain. The Balanced Scorecard Approach is shown pictorially in Exhibit 14.4.

The Balanced Scorecard Approach is an effective method for assessing overall supply chain performance because it implicitly includes the linkage between the supply chain strategy adopted by the firm in conjunction with the processes undertaken to fulfill it. By using the Balanced Scorecard, firms gain different types of feedback related to their supply chain operations, including strategic data for high-level decision makers, diagnostic feedback to guide pro-

EXHIBIT 14.4

Balanced Scorecard Approach to Performance Measurement

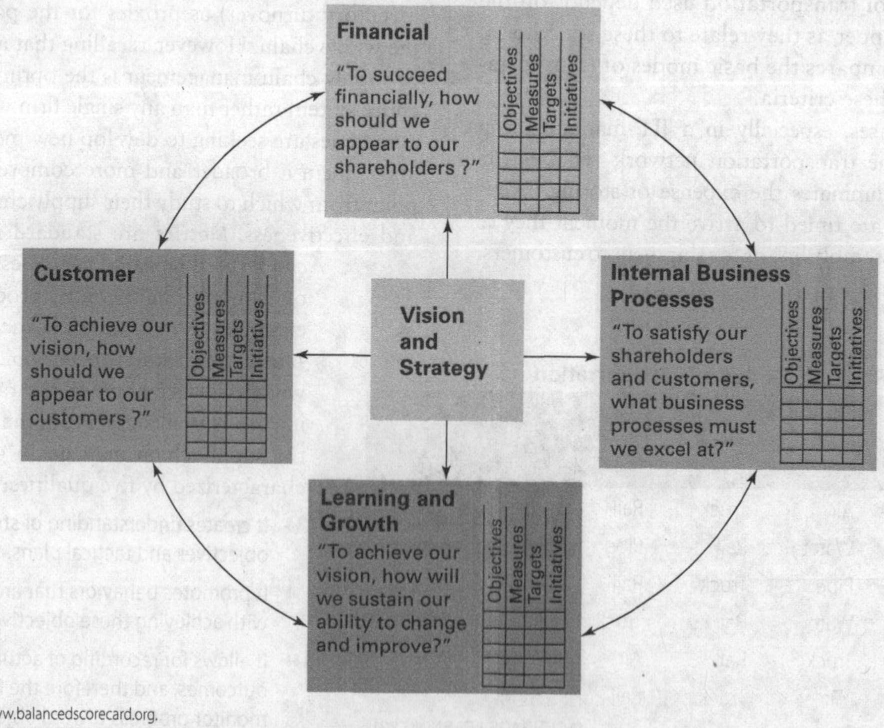

SOURCE: From www.balancedscorecard.org.

cess improvement, knowledge of trends in important metrics over time, feedback on the effectiveness of the performance measurements themselves, and data that can be used for forecasting future business activities.[13]

At each tier of the supply chain, the Balanced Scorecard addresses four areas of performance that are reflective of supply chain operations: customer-related performance metrics, financial metrics, learning and growth metrics, and of course, business process metrics. Firms take repeated measurements in each of these categories, and then alternate through a system whereby they do things to improve lagging performance in weak areas, check the results following implementation of changes, and act again based on new measurements.

LO 7 Trends in Supply Chain Management

Several technological advances and business trends are affecting the job of the supply chain manager today. Three of the most important trends are advanced computer technology, outsourcing of logistics functions, and electronic distribution.

Advanced Computer Technology

Advanced computer technology has boosted the efficiency of logistics dramatically with tools such as automatic identification systems (auto ID) using bar coding and radio frequency technology, communications technology, and supply chain software systems that help synchronize the flow of goods and information with customer demand. At Amazon.com's state-of-the-art fulfillment centers, technology is used to maximize efficiency. Incoming product is immediately sent to the first available empty shelf space. That means a shipment of golf balls could end up next to *Best American Short Stories 2011*. With its entry into the Indian market, Amazon is in the process of setting up a fulfilment center in Mumbai.[14] The usual process followed by the company is as and when the online orders come in, pickers, the employees who gather items from the warehouse, are given a list of items, a cart, and a route to follow, calculated by a computer gun to exactly fill the cart and to take the picker on the most efficient route through the warehouse. Once the cart is filled, the pickers drop items into bins that route to packaging. Packaging is also computer regulated—as a product comes up for packing, computers instruct which of the company's 15 different standard package sizes is the best fit for the order.[15]

outsourcing (contract logistics) a manufacturer's or supplier's use of an independent third party to manage an entire function of the logistics system, such as transportation, warehousing, or order processing

Smart tags are another type of advanced computer technology that is helping companies manage their supply chains. Walmart is beginning to require its clothing suppliers to put smart tags on the hang tags found on most items of clothing to be able to see if any pieces are missing in stores or in shipments. Previously, Walmart tracked palettes or boxes, allowing them to track shipments on large levels, but not to track individual items. The individual tags also allow Walmart to track individual pieces back to the manufacturer. Walmart hopes to use this itemized technology to reduce shoplifting and employee theft and to increase sales. American Apparel, a clothing manufacturer and retailer in the United States, tested similar technology and saw individual store sales rise as much as 14.3 percent compared to stores without the smart tags. Reducing theft allows types of merchandise that shoplifters tend to target to remain on the shelves and be sold, helping to increase the stores' likelihood to have better sales figures.[16]

Outsourcing Logistics Functions

External partners are becoming increasingly important in the efficient deployment of supply chain management. **Outsourcing**, or **contract logistics**, is a rapidly growing segment of the distribution industry in which a manufacturer or supplier turns over the entire function of buying and managing transportation or another function of the supply chain, such as warehousing, to an independent third party. To focus on their core competencies, companies turn their logistics functions over to firms with expertise in that area. Partners create and manage entire solutions for getting products where they need to be, when they need to be there. Because a logistics provider is focused, clients receive service in a timely, efficient manner, thereby increasing customers' level of satisfaction and boosting their perception of added value to a company's offerings. For example, Amazon received more than 1,84,000 advance orders on its website for the fourth book in the Harry Potter series. Seeing such a massive response from the customers, Amazon decided

© JOSHUA LOTT/BLOOMBERG VIA GETTY IMAGES

electronic distribution a distribution technique that includes any kind of product or service that can be distributed electronically, whether over traditional forms such as fiber-optic cable or through satellite transmission of electronic signals

to team up with Federal Express, the overnight courier service, to offer an overnight shipping deal to the first 2,50,000 customers ordering Harry Potter IV through its website. The deal enabled the company to get the novel at the customers' doorsteps right on the first day the book went on sale.[17] However, the offer was available only in the United States.

Third-party contract logistics allow companies to cut inventories, locate stock at fewer plants and distribution centers, and still provide the same service level or even better service. The companies then can refocus investment on their core business. In the fast food industry, McDonald's India has outsourced the entire back-end operation to a supply chain company called Radhakrishna Foodland Private Limited (RFPL). RFPL is totally responsible for logistic functions like warehousing, transportation, storage, and vending.[18] The cold chain system is used for transporting food ingredients from manufacturers' place to RFPL's distribution centres in order to maintain the freshness of the products.[19] From the distribution centres, the ingredients are further delivered at different McDonald's outlets as per their requirement. Outsourcing of logistics functions has helped Mcdonald's to focus on its core function—providing quick and quality service. Many firms are taking outsourcing one step further by allowing business partners to take over the final assembly of their product or its packaging in an effort to reduce inventory costs, speed up delivery, or better meet customer requirements.

Electronic Distribution

Electronic distribution is the most recent development in the logistics arena. Broadly defined, **electronic distribution** includes any kind of product or service that can be distributed electronically, whether over traditional forms such as fiber-optic cable or through satellite transmission of electronic signals. Most of the banks have started developing an additional business model around electronic distribution by offering net banking facilities to their customers.

Green Supply Chain Management

In response to the need for firms to both gain cost savings and act as leaders in protecting the natural environment, many are adopting green supply chain management principles as a key part of their supply chain strategy. Green supply chain management involves the integration of environmentally conscious thinking into all phases of key supply chain management processes. Such activities include green materials sourcing, the design of products with consideration given to their environmental impact based on packaging, shipment, and use, as well as end-of-life management for products including easy recycling and/or clean disposal. By enacting green supply chain management principles, firms hope to simultaneously generate cost savings and protect our natural resources from excess pollution, damage, and/or wastefulness.

A wire manufacturer in Georgia, a state in Southeastern United States, called Southwire converted one-third of its delivery fleet to hybrid vehicles, eliminated nearly all lead additives from its products, and reduced its landfill waste by 27 percent. Southwire supplies Pacific Gas & Electric, a company headquartered in San Francisco, who is taking part in an industry alliance to further green its supply chain.[20]

Global Logistics and Supply Chain Management

Global markets present their own sets of logistical challenges. It is critical for importers of any size to understand and cope with the legalities of trade in other countries. Shippers and distributors must be aware of the permits, licenses, and registrations they may need to acquire and, depending on the type of product they are importing, the tariffs, quotas, and other regulations that apply in each country. This multitude of different rules is why multinational companies are so committed to working through the World Trade Organization to develop a global set of rules and to encourage countries to participate.

Transportation can also be a major issue for companies dealing with global supply chains. Uncertainty regarding shipping usually tops the list of reasons companies, especially smaller ones, resist international markets. In some instances, poor infrastructure makes transportation dangerous and unreliable. And the process of moving goods across the borders of even the most industrialized nations can still be complicated by government regulations.

Review and Applications

Define the terms *supply chain* and *supply chain management*, and discuss the benefits of supply chain management. Supply chain management coordinates and integrates all of the activities performed by supply chain members into a seamless process from the source to the point of consumption. The responsibilities of a supply chain manager include developing channel design strategies, managing the relationships of supply chain members, sourcing and procurement of raw materials, scheduling production, processing orders, managing inventory and storing product, and selecting transportation modes. The supply chain manager is also responsible for managing customer service and the information that flows through the supply chain. The benefits of supply chain management include reduced costs in inventory management, transportation, warehousing, and packaging; improved service through techniques like time-based delivery and make-to-order; and enhanced revenues, which result from such supply chain-related achievements as higher product availability and more customized products.

1.1 Discuss the benefits of supply chain management. How does the implementation of supply chain management result in enhanced customer value?

Discuss the concept of supply chain integration and explain why each of the six types of integration is important. Supply chain integration occurs when multiple firms in a supply chain coordinate their activities and processes so that they are seamlessly linked to one another in the attempt to satisfy customers. The six types of integration are as follows: (1) Relationship integration is the ability of two or more firms to develop tight social connections among their employees, resulting in smoother personal interactions. (2) Measurement integration is the idea that performance assessments should be transparent and similar across all of the supply chain members. (3) Technology and planning integration refers to the creation and maintenance of supply chain technology systems that connect managers throughout the supply chain. (4) Material and service supplier integration reflects a focus on integrating processes and functions with those who provide the company with the things they need in order to execute their core functions. (5) Internal operations integration is the development of capabilities for the firm's internal functional areas to communicate and work together on processes and projects. (6) Customer integration implies that firms evaluate their own capabilities and use them to offer long-lasting, distinctive, value-added offerings in ways that best serve their customers.

2.1 Discuss the concept of supply chain integration. How does it result in better customer-related outcomes?

2.2 What are some of the likely outcomes of a firm's failure to embrace one or more supply chain integration types?

Identify the eight key processes of excellent supply chain management and discuss how each of these processes impacts the end customer. The key processes that leading supply chain companies focus on are (1) customer relationship management, (2) customer service management, (3) order fulfillment, (4) manufacturing flow management, (5) supplier relationship management, (6) product development and commercialization, (7) returns management, and (8) demand management. When firms practice excellent supply chain management, each of these processes is integrated from end to end in the supply chain. These processes are made up of bundles of interconnected activities that supply chain partners are constantly focused on when delivering value to the customer.

3.1 What are the key processes in supply chain management, and who performs them? How does each process lead to increased satisfaction on the part of the customer?

Discuss the key strategic decisions supply chain managers must make when designing their companies' supply chains. Based on the firm's goals, the markets it competes in, and the availability of supply, firms will adopt a lean, agile, or combination (Leagile) strategy for supply chain management. Lean firms focus on improving profitability through the removal of waste from the supply chain system. Alternatively, agile firms are concerned primarily with customer responsiveness and service, and seek to provide the highest levels of responsiveness possible, even if the costs of doing so are higher. Leagile firms adopt a position somewhere between lean and agile, with main components made and shipped using lean principles, but with agility gained late in the process through the postponement of final production. Firms should also learn to map their supply chains so that they can understand the linkages between firms in the network that are all seeking to achieve the common goal of customer satisfaction.

4.1 When should firms pursue lean, agile, and/or Leagile supply chain strategies?

4.2 What are the expected benefits that may come from supply chain mapping?

Describe the logistical components of the supply chain. The logistics supply chain consists of several interrelated and integrated logistical components: (1) sourcing and procurement of raw materials and supplies, (2) production scheduling, (3) order processing, (4) inventory control, (5) warehousing and materials-handling, and (6) transportation. The logistics information system is the link connecting all of the logistics components of the supply chain. Information technology connects the various components and partners of the supply chain into an integrated whole. The supply chain team, in concert with the logistics information system, orchestrates the movement of goods, services, and information from the source to the consumer. Supply chain teams typically cut across organizational boundaries, embracing all parties who participate in moving product to market. Procurement deals with the purchase of raw materials, supplies, and components according to production scheduling. Order processing monitors the flow of goods and information (order entry and order handling). Inventory control systems regulate when and how much to buy (order timing and order quantity). Warehousing provides storage of goods until needed by the customer while the materials-handling system moves inventory into, within, and out of the warehouse. Finally, the major modes of transportation are railroads, motor carriers, pipelines, waterways, and airways.

5.1 Assume that you are the supply chain manager for a producer of expensive, high-tech computer components. Identify the most suitable method(s) of transporting your product in terms of cost, transit time, reliability, capability, accessibility, and traceability. Now, assume you are the supply chain manager for a producer of milk. How does this change your choice of transportation?

Explain why supply chain performance measurement is necessary and important. Because supply chains are often very complex, with each firm in the chain seeking to fulfill its own goals, it is sometimes difficult to determine whether the supply chain as a whole is functioning well. Firms in the best supply chains develop and use common metrics to assess whether customers are satisfied and whether operations are completed in a timely fashion, at an acceptable level of cost, and with good asset utilization. Often, this includes the use of the Balanced Scorecard methodology, which ensures that not only will customers be satisfied, but also that the firm will execute its tasks with process efficiency, with financially acceptable returns, and in a way that allows for learning and growth for the company.

6.1 Why is supply chain performance measurement necessary and important?

6.2 How does the **Balanced Scorecard** Approach help firms within the supply chain to establish and meet common goals?

Discuss new technology and emerging trends in supply chain management. Several emerging trends are changing the job of today's supply chain manager. Technology and automation are bringing up-to-date distribution information to the decision maker's desk. Technology is also linking suppliers, buyers, and carriers for joint decision making, and it has created a new electronic distribution channel. Many companies are saving money and time by outsourcing third-party carriers to handle some or all aspects of the distribution process. Firms are taking major steps toward the goal of securing their supply chains from external threats.

7.1 Visit the Web site of Menlo Logistics at **www.menlolog.com.** What logistics functions can this third-party logistics supplier provide? How does its mission fit in with the supply chain management philosophy?

Exercises

APPLICATION EXERCISE

From your readings, you might feel that you have a general idea as to how supply chain management works. However, in reality, the practice of supply chain management can be very complicated. This exercise will help you to identify the complexities of managing a global supply chain in a real world setting. By following one of your favorite products as its many components migrate through the supply chain on their long road to your home or office, you may gain additional appreciation for the difficult tasks supply chain managers face daily.

Activities

1. Pick a product with which you are very familiar or that you anticipate being able to research

easily. You may want to consult family members, relatives, or even a former or current employer who can give you details of the business.

2. Map the supply chain of your product as far back as is feasible. A simple example is a diamond sold by a local jewelry store, purchased direct from diamond wholesalers in the Netherlands, bought by wholesalers from diamond centers in South Africa, brought out of mines owned by a company in South Africa. Identify as many participants in the channel as possible by company name and location.
3. Identify the mode of transportation used between each stage in the channel.
4. Identify by name and location the component parts of the product, if any. For example, let's expand the diamond example from a single diamond to a diamond necklace. You would need to trace the history of both the metal chain and the diamond back to their origins and forward until the point at which the diamond and chain are combined to form the diamond necklace.

ETHICS EXERCISE

For years, labor and environmental groups have criticized and pressured companies whose suppliers pay low wages, run sweatshops, use child labor, or use other similarly illicit labor practices. However, recently have U.S. companies begun to come under fire for sourcing materials from foreign companies who are using child labor to manufacture goods. When it was discovered that child workers were employed in making GAP clothes outsourced to India, GAP withdrew the garments. GAP stated that "We firmly believe that under no circumstances is it acceptable for children to produce or work on garments. These allegations are deeply upsetting and we take this situation very seriously. All of our suppliers and their subcontractors are required to guarantee that they will not use child labor to produce garments. In this situation, it's clear one of our vendors violated this agreement and a full investigation is under way."[21]

Questions

1. Should companies such as GAP avoid outsourcing manufacturing contracts in the developing world?
2. What are the pros and cons associated with using supplies or labor outsourced from supply chain partners (direct and indirect) based in countries where child labor, despite the implementation of Child Labor Act, contributes to 20% of the total employment?
3. Does AMA Statement of Ethics address the issue of use child labor in the supply chain management? Write a memo that describes how the AMA Statement of Ethics addresses the dilemma faced by the company.

MARKETING PLAN EXERCISE

As discussed in Chapter 13, Part 4 of the strategic planning process continues defining the elements of the marketing mix, and this section focuses on place (i.e., distribution). The following exercise is designed to continue leading you through the distribution decisions for your strategic marketing plan:

1. What physical distribution facilities will be needed to complete delivery of your chosen company's products and services to the buyer? Where should these facilities be located?
2. How should your company's product be distributed? Justify your selection of transportation mode(s). What other types of channel facilitators will you require for getting your product offering to your customers?

Short Case

CAN THE ICON OF THE LOGISTICS INDUSTRY SUCCEED IN INDIA?

Michael Dell had the idea of selling computer systems directly to customers when he was a student at the University of Texas. In 1985 his new company designed its first computer system and soon began offering next-day, on-site product service. By 1996 Dell was selling computers on the Internet, and by 2000 the company's Web site was pulling in $50 million (₹225 crore) a day in direct sales.

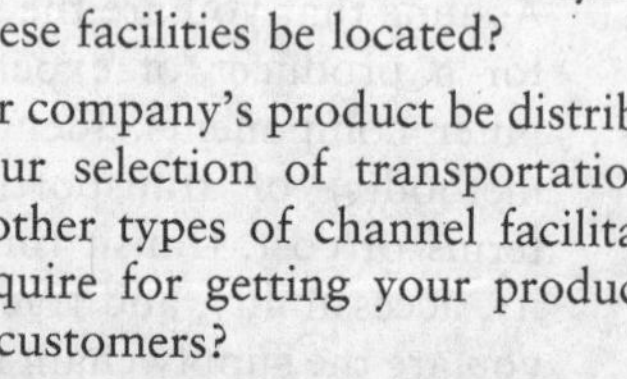
AP PHOTO/GAUTAM SINGH

Today Dell is well established as an icon of the logistics industry. Its lean business model has influenced countless other companies to follow its lead. Dell's 300,000-square-foot Morton L. Topfer Manufacturing Center (known as TMC) in Texas serves as ground zero for the build-to-order (or "just-in-time") manufacturing processes it's famous for. The TMC makes it possible for Dell to assemble hundreds of computers an hour, taking orders as they come in and making them to the customers' specifications. In the computer industry, technological equipment quickly becomes outdated, so Dell wants everything that goes out the door to be fresh off the assembly line—not losing value in a warehouse.

Dell's revolutionary supply chain is characterized by its minimum levels of inventory, a policy of paying suppliers only after the customers have paid Dell, and direct sales. Industry analysts say that these strategies have changed high-tech manufacturing the way Wal-Mart changed retail.

The question for Dell now is how to plan for future growth in emerging global markets such as China and India. Can Dell's business model, which is based on information, efficiency, and speed, work as well in parts of the world where the economic and social contexts are so different from how they are in the United States?

Dell has planned a major capital investment and expansion in its Indian operations, which would employ 20,000 people in a new manufacturing facility similar to TMC. Analysts predict that if Dell is successful in bringing its build-to-order implementation to India, it could spur a movement of manufacturing-focused foreign investment in the country.

A 2005 report by KPMG International concluded that China and India will be the world's two biggest economies by mid-century, and, "although India has underperformed in the last lap of the growth race, there is a strong possibility that India may well move ahead." Dell appears to agree. CEO Kevin Rollins explained: "India currently sells 4 million (40 lakh) computers per year and this is projected to rise to 10 million (1 crore) units annually in the next three to five years. Our workforce here is capable and the time is right for the second phase of expansion in contact center activities, research and development and…a manufacturing site."

Critics are skeptical that India will be as profitable as Dell hopes, however, citing the country's lack of reliable roads, power, and telecommunications. Although telecommunications have improved with a 53,000-mile fiber-optic network, India maintains only 2,000 miles of highways (the United States has 23 times that). Delivery chains rely almost exclusively on small vehicles with only three wheels that navigate on dirt roads. As for India's power supply, business owners experience nearly 20 significant outages every month (compared to 5 in China). Add to this the hassle of endless red tape required of businesses in India, labor regulations that force businesses to get government permission to lay off workers, and laws that require unanimous worker approval before companies can reorganize, and it becomes clear why critics wonder whether Dell can succeed there.

Dell counters that their computers are lightweight enough to be transported in the three-wheeled trucks that are the backbone of the Indian supply chain. And industry observer Clay Risen adds, "Dell's requirement that suppliers locate warehouses nearby suddenly seems an advantage—after all, the less the supply chain has to deal with the Indian transportation system, the better." Dell can concentrate on the urban middle class with the money to buy computers in major cities like New Delhi, where the country's infrastructure, power, and telecommunications systems are more reliable.

Even with the risks involved with doing business there, Dell has decided that India is too large and full of possibilities to ignore. The industry is watching and waiting to see how the computer giant fares. Dell's success—or failure—could determine whether more manufacturing companies follow its example in the future.[22]

Source: William Hoffman, "Dell Chief Targets Supply-Chain Gaps," *Shipping Digest*, 3/12/07; Clay Risen, "Dell Takes on India," *World Trade Magazine*, September 2006; David Hannon, "Dell Flies in the Right Direction," *Purchasing*, 11/17/05.

Questions

1. Describe how Dell's manufacturing processes represent a change in chain management from how things were done during the mass-production era. What does it mean that there has been a reversal of the flow of demand from a "push" to a "pull" system?
2. Describe the order processing system. How does it work in a company like Dell? As an order enters the system, what must management monitor? Why is it so important that the order processing system be executed well?
3. Describe the role that a supply chain manager at Dell might play. What would his or her responsibilities be? Why is there such high demand for supply chain managers in companies like Dell today?
4. Describe the benefits that Dell and other companies receive from supply chain management. What benefits do supply-chain–oriented companies commonly report? What has research shown?

14 Supply Chain Management

KEY TERMS

LO 1

supply chain the connected chain of all of the business entities, both internal and external to the company, that perform or support the logistics function

supply chain management a management system that coordinates and integrates all of the activities performed by supply chain members into a seamless process, from the source to the point of consumption, resulting in enhanced customer and economic value

LO 2

supply chain integration when multiple firms in a supply chain coordinate their activities and processes so that they are seamlessly linked to one another in an effort to satisfy the customer

LO 3

business processes bundles of interconnected activities that stretch across firms in the supply chain

customer relationship management (CRM) process allows companies to prioritize their marketing focus on different customer groups according to each group's long-term value to the company or supply chain

customer service management process presents a multi-company, unified response system to the customer whenever complaints, concerns, questions, or comments are voiced

demand management process seeks to align supply and demand throughout the supply chain by anticipating customer requirements at each level and creating demand-related plans of action prior to actual customer purchasing behavior

order fulfillment process a highly integrated process, often requiring persons from multiple companies and multiple functions to come together and coordinate to create customer satisfaction at a given place and time

KEY CONCEPTS

LO 1

Define the terms *supply chain* and *supply chain management*, and discuss the benefits of supply chain management. Management coordinates and integrates all of the activities performed by supply chain members into a seamless process from the source to the point of consumption. The responsibilities of a supply chain manager include developing channel design strategies, managing the relationships of supply chain members, sourcing and procurement of raw materials, scheduling production, processing orders, managing inventory and storing product, and selecting transportation modes. The supply chain manager is also responsible for managing customer service and the information that flows through the supply chain. The benefits of supply chain management include reduced costs in inventory management, transportation, warehousing, and packaging; improved service through techniques like time-based delivery and make-to-order; and enhanced revenues, which result from supply chain–related achievements such as higher product availability and more customized products.

LO 2

Discuss the concept of supply chain integration, and explain why each of the six types of integration is important. The six types of integration are as follows: (1) Relationship integration is the ability of two or more firms to develop tight social connections among their employees, resulting in smoother personal interactions. (2) Measurement integration is the idea that performance assessments should be transparent and similar across all the supply chain members. (3) Technology and planning integration refers to the creation and maintenance of supply chain technology systems that connect managers throughout the supply chain. (4) Material and service supplier integration reflects a focus on integrating processes and functions with those who provide the company with the things they need in order to execute their core functions. (5) Internal operations integration is the development of capabilities for the firm's internal functional areas to communicate and work together on processes and projects. (6) Customer integration implies that firms evaluate their own capabilities and use them to offer long-lasting, distinctive, value-added offerings in ways that best serve their customers.

LO 3

Identify the eight key processes of excellent supply chain management, and discuss how each of these processes impacts the end customer. The key processes that leading supply chain companies focus on are (1) customer relationship management, (2) customer service management, (3) demand management, (4) order fulfillment, (5) manufacturing flow management, (6) supplier relationship management, (7) product development and commercialization, and (8) returns management. When firms practice excellent supply chain management, each of these processes is integrated from end to end in the supply chain. These processes are made up of bundles of interconnected activities that supply chain partners are constantly focused on when delivering value to the customer.

LO 4

Discuss the key strategic decisions supply chain managers must make when designing their companies' supply chains. Based on the firm's goals, the markets it competes in, and the availability of supply, firms will adopt a lean, agile, or combination (Leagile) strategy for supply chain management. Lean firms focus on improving profitability through the removal of waste from the supply chain system. Alternatively, agile firms are concerned primarily with customer responsiveness and service, and seek to provide the highest levels of responsiveness possible, even if the costs of doing so are higher. Leagile firms adopt a position somewhere between lean and agile, with main components made and shipped using lean principles, but with agility gained

manufacturing flow management process concerned with ensuring that firms in the supply chain have the needed resources to manufacture with flexibility and to move products through a multi-stage production process

supplier relationship management process closely related to the manufacturing flow management process and contains several characteristics that parallel the customer relationship management process

product development and commercialization process includes the group of activities that facilitates the joint development and marketing of new offerings among a group of supply chain partner firms

returns management process enables firms to manage volumes of returned product efficiently while minimizing returns-related costs and maximizing the value of the returned assets to the firms in the supply chain

LO 4 **radio-frequency identification (RFID)** An automatic identification method that uses radio signals that work with scanned bar codes to identify products; data is stored in and retrieved from the RFID tag, which is attached to a product.

lean supply chain management The strategy that focuses primarily on the removal of waste from the supply chain to achieve the lowest total cost to the members of the supply chain system.

agile supply chain management The supply chain strategy that focuses primarily on the ability of the firm to fulfill customer demand, even if this means somewhat higher costs.

Leagile supply chain strategy A supply chain management strategy that combines the best elements of the lean and agile strategies for a particular product/market combination.

postponement The delay in final production in the Leagile supply chain management strategy that enables the company to take advantage of many of the benefits of lean supply chain management while still providing the agility that improves customer experiences.

horizontal structure One of three dimensions of supply chain network design; the number of tiers (columns) in the supply chain, representing the total number of levels through which goods and services must pass from the earliest to end stages of the chain.

vertical structure One of three dimensions of supply chain network design; the number of suppliers or customers included within each individual tier.

horizontal position One of three dimensions of supply chain network design; the position of a firm, relative to other firms, along the supply chain.

LO 5 **logistics** the process of strategically managing the efficient flow and storage of raw materials, in-process inventory, and

late in the process through the postponement of final production. Firms should also learn to map their supply chains so that they can understand the linkages between firms in the network that are all seeking to achieve the common goal of customer satisfaction.

LO 5 **Describe the logistical components of the supply chain.** The logistics supply chain consists of several interrelated and integrated logistical components: (1) sourcing and procurement of raw materials and supplies, (2) production scheduling, (3) order processing, (4) inventory control, (5) warehousing and materialshandling, and (6) transportation. The logistics information system is the link connecting all of the logistics components of the supply chain. Information technology connects the various components and partners of the supply chain into an integrated whole. The supply chain team, in concert with the logistics information system, orchestrates the movement of goods, services, and information from the source to the consumer. Supply chain teams typically cut across organizational boundaries, embracing all parties who participate in moving product to market. Procurement deals with the purchase of raw materials, supplies, and components according to production scheduling. Order processing monitors the flow of goods and information (order entry and order handling). Inventory control systems regulate when and how much to buy (order timing and order quantity). Warehousing provides storage of goods until needed by the customer while the materials-handling system moves inventory into, within, and out of the warehouse. Finally, the major modes of transportation are railroads, motor carriers, pipelines, waterways, and airways.

LO 6 **Explain why supply chain performance measurement is necessary and important.** Because supply chains are often very complex, with each firm in the chain seeking to fulfill its own goals, it is sometimes difficult to determine whether the supply chain as a whole is functioning well. Firms in the best supply chains develop and use common metrics to assess whether customers are satisfied and whether operations are completed in a timely fashion, at an acceptable level of cost, and with good asset utilization. Often, this includes the use of the Balanced Scorecard methodology, which ensures that not only will customers be satisfied, but also that the firm will execute its tasks with process efficiency, with financially acceptable returns, and in a way that allows for learning and growth for the company.

LO 7 **Discuss new technology and emerging trends in supply chain management.** Several emerging trends are changing the job of today's supply chain manager. Technology and automation are bringing up-to-date distribution information to the decision-maker's desk. Technology is also linking suppliers, buyers, and carriers for joint decision making, and it has created a new electronic distribution channel. Many companies are saving money and time by outsourcing to third-party carriers to handle some or all aspects of the distribution process. Firms are taking major steps toward the goal of securing their supply chains from external threats.

finished goods from point of origin to point of consumption

logistics information system the link that connects all the logistics functions of the supply chain

supply chain team an entire group of individuals who orchestrate the movement of goods, services, and information from the source to the consumer

mass customization (build-to-order) a production method whereby products are not made until an order is placed by the customer; products are made according to customer specifications

just-in-time production (JIT) a process that redefines and simplifies manufacturing by reducing inventory levels and delivering raw materials at the precise time they are needed on the production line

order processing system a system whereby orders are entered into the supply chain and filled

electronic data interchange (EDI) information technology that replaces the paper documents that usually accompany business transactions, such as purchase orders and invoices, with electronic transmission of the needed information to reduce inventory levels, improve cash flow, streamline operations, and increase the speed and accuracy of information transmission

inventory control system a method of developing and maintaining an adequate assortment of materials or products to meet a manufacturer's or a customer's demand

materials requirement planning (MRP) (materials management) an inventory control system that manages the replenishment of raw materials, supplies, and components from the supplier to the manufacturer

distribution resource planning (DRP) an inventory control system that manages the replenishment of goods from the manufacturer to the final consumer

automatic replenishment program a real-time inventory system that triggers shipments only when a good is sold to the end user

materials-handling system a method of moving inventory into, within, and out of the warehouse

LO 6

metrics Standard measures that can be used repeatedly to assess performance on a supply chain-related process.

Balanced Scorecard Approach A measurement system used to evaluate overall supply chain performance.

LO 7

outsourcing (contract logistics) a manufacturer's or supplier's use of an independent third party to manage an entire function of the logistics system, such as transportation, warehousing, or order processing

electronic distribution a distribution technique that includes any kind of product or service that can be distributed electronically, whether over traditional forms such as fiber-optic cable or through satellite transmission of electronic signals

CHAPTER 15 Retailing

Learning Outcomes

LO 1 Discuss the importance of retailing in the Indian economy

LO 2 Explain the dimensions by which retailers can be classified

LO 3 Describe the major types of retail operations

LO 4 Discuss nonstore retailing techniques

LO 5 Define *franchising* and describe its two basic forms

LO 6 List the major tasks involved in developing a retail marketing strategy

LO 7 Describe new developments in retailing

Retailers ring up over ₹19,00,000 crore in sales annually, about 30 percent of the gross domestic product.

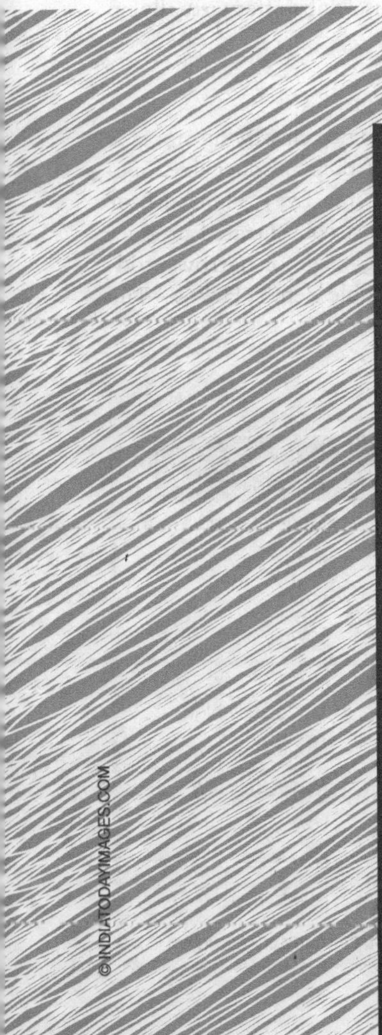

©INDIATODAYIMAGES.COM

LO 1 The Role of Retailing

retailing all the activities directly related to the sale of goods and services to the ultimate consumer for personal, nonbusiness use

Retailing—all the activities directly related to the sale of goods and services to the ultimate consumer for personal, non-business use—has enhanced the quality of our daily lives. When we shop for groceries, hair styling, clothes, books, and many other products and services, we are involved in retailing. The thousands of goods and services provided by retailers mirror the needs and styles of Indian society.

Retailing affects all of us directly or indirectly. The retailing industry is one of the largest employers in India; Indian retailers employed about 4 crore people in 2010, accounting for 9.4 percent of all Indian employment.[1] At the store level, retailing is still largely a mom-and-pop business. The organized retail holds a share of just 6.5 percent of the total retail market.[2] However, the Indian retail market has been growing rapidly over the last few years and has been ranked as the third most attractive retail market in the world in the AT Kearney Global Retail Development Index 2010.[3]

The Indian economy is heavily dependent on retailing. Retailers ringed up over ₹19,00,000 crore in sales in 2009-10, which is about 30 percent of gross domestic product.[4] Although most retailers are quite small, a few organizations like Future Group, Reliance Retail Ltd., and Aditya Birla Retail Ltd. have been operating at a massive scale.

***Note:* All the figures in U.S. dollars are converted into rupee using the value $1 = ₹45.**

LO 2 Classification of Retail Operations

independent retailers retailers owned by a single person or partnership and not operated as part of a larger retail institution

chain stores stores owned and operated as a group by a single organization

franchise the right to operate a business or to sell a product

A retail establishment can be classified according to its ownership, level of service, product, assortment, and price. Specifically, retailers use the latter three variables to position themselves in the competitive marketplace. (As noted in Chapter 8, positioning is the strategy used to influence how consumers perceive one product in relation to all competing products.) These three variables can be combined in several ways to create distinctly different retail operations. Exhibit 15.1 lists the major types of retail stores discussed in this chapter and classifies them by level of service, product assortment, price, and gross margin.

Ownership

Retailers can be broadly classified by form of ownership: independent, part of a chain, or franchise outlet. Retailers owned by a single person or partnership and not operated as part of a larger retail institution are **independent retailers**. Around the world, most retailers are independent, operating one or a few stores in their community. Local florists and ethnic food markets typically fit this classification.

Chain stores are owned and operated as a group by a single organization. Under this form of ownership, many administrative tasks are handled by the home office for the entire chain. The home office also buys most of the merchandise sold in the stores. The Mobile Store and Vijay Sales are examples of chains.

Franchises are owned and operated by individuals but are licensed by a larger supporting organization, such as Subway, Archies, and Baskin Robbins. The franchising approach combines the advantages of independent ownership with those of the chain store organization.

Level of Service

The level of service that retailers provide can be classified along a continuum, from full-service to self-service. Some retailers, such as exclusive clothing stores, offer high levels of service. They provide alterations, credit, delivery, consulting, liberal return policies, gift wrapping, and personal shopping. Retailers like factory outlets and warehouse clubs offer virtually no services.

Product Assortment

The third basis for positioning or classifying stores is by the breadth and depth of their product line. Specialty stores—for example, Titan Eye+, Planet M, or Godrej Interio—have the most concentrated product assortments, usually carrying single or narrow product lines, but with considerable depth. Helios—The

EXHIBIT 15.1

Types of Stores and Their Characteristics

Type of Retailer	Level of Service	Product Assortment	Price	Gross Margin
Department store	Moderately high to high	Broad	Moderate to high	Moderately high
Specialty store	High	Narrow	Moderate to high	High
Supermarket	Low	Broad	Moderate	Low
Hypermarket	Low	Broad	Low	Low
Drugstore	Low to moderate	Medium	Moderate	Low
Convenience store	Low	Medium to narrow	Moderately high	Moderately high
Full-line discount store	Moderate to low	Medium to broad	Moderately low	Moderately low
Specialty discount store	Moderate to low	Medium to broad	Moderately low to low	Moderately low
Warehouse club	Low	Broad	Low to very low	Low
Off-price retailer	Low	Medium to narrow	Low	Low
Restaurant	Low to high	Narrow	Low to high	Low to high

Watch Store, a part of Titan Industries Ltd., offers wide assortment of different brands in the time-wear category, such as Tag Heuer, Emporio Armani, Pierre Cardin, Fossil, and Diesel. On the other end of the spectrum, full-line discounters typically carry broad assortments of merchandise with limited depth. For example, Star Bazaar carries staple foods, personal care products, and household items. Typically, though, it carries a very limited range of household items, such as bed sheets. In contrast, a specialty home store, like Welhome, carries an extensive range of home decor products in a wide variety of designs and colors.

Other retailers, such as factory outlet stores, may carry only part of a single line. Nike stores sell only certain items of its own brand. Discount specialty stores like E-Zone carry a broad assortment in concentrated product lines, such as consumer durables.

Price

Price is the fourth way to position retail stores. Traditional department stores and specialty stores typically charge the full "suggested retail price." In contrast, discounters, factory outlets, and off-price retailers use low prices to lure shoppers.

₹19,125, ₹15,300, ₹10,125—with prices like these for a handbag, you might expect to be shopping at a designer boutique. But mid-level mall stores in U.S.A like Talbots, Abercrombie & Fitch, and Ann Taylor are taking advantage of the accessory shopper by selling handbags at near-designer prices. Clothing and other accessories vary in price for these retailers, but when the average price of an item sold is ₹4,275 at Talbots, ₹2,925 at Abercrombie & Fitch, and ₹1,800 at Ann Taylor, retailing a handbag for ₹19,125, ₹15,300, ₹10,125, respectively, may push these mid-level retailers' price position and they may lose their core customers. Hidesign, an Indian leather good company, has a strong presence in the premium segment in the market. Its product range has a starting price point lying anywhere between ₹3,000 to ₹12,000. In order to enter into luxury segment, the company planned to launch a new collection by Italian designer Alberto Ciaschini and bring the Italian brand, *Braccialini*, into the Indian market. Other brands operating in luxury segment are *Louis Vuitton* and *Gucci*, having their starting price points anywhere between ₹40,000 to ₹50,000.[5]

The different factors influencing the pricing strategy of a retailer are image of the store, its positioning, target audience, overall retail mix, and pricing policy.[6]

The last column in Exhibit 15.1 shows the typical **gross margin**—how much the retailer makes as a percentage of sales after the cost of goods sold is subtracted. The level of gross margin and the price level generally match. For example, a traditional jewelry store has high prices and high gross margins. A factory outlet has low prices and low gross margins. Markdowns on merchandise during sale periods and price wars among competitors, in which stores lower prices on certain items in an effort to win customers, cause gross margins to decline.

gross margin the amount of money the retailer makes as a percentage of sales after the cost of goods sold is subtracted

department store a store housing several departments under one roof

buyer a department head who selects the merchandise for his or her department and may also be responsible for promotion and personnel

LO 3 Major Types of Retail Operations

Traditionally, there have been several distinct types of retail stores, with each offering a different product assortment, type of service, and price level according to its customers' shopping preferences. Since modern retail is relatively a new phenomenon in India, retailers have been constantly experimenting with alternative formats. The last couple of years have witnessed opening and shutting down of stores in quick time as retailers are trying to understand what the consumers want and what are the best formats to reach them.

Department Stores

A **department store** carries a wide variety of shopping and specialty goods, including apparel, cosmetics, footwear, accessories, housewares, and sometimes furniture. A department store is quite large in size, with average area varying from 25,000 to 40,000 sq. ft. and between 50,000 to 1,00,000 Stock Keeping units (SKUs).[7] SKU refers to each and every item of inventory that is uniquely identifiable. Purchases are generally made within each department rather than at one central checkout area. Each department is treated as a separate buying center to achieve economies in promotion, buying, service, and control. Each department is usually headed by a **buyer**, a department head who not only selects the merchandise for his or her department but may also be responsible for promotion and for personnel. In order to have a consistent, uniform store image, central management sets broad policies about the types of merchandise carried and price ranges. Central management is also responsible for the overall advertising

AAFES MAKES MILITARY MONEY

AAFES, an agency of the U.S. Defense Department, sells everything from undershirts to electronics—877,000 different items in all—to military men, women, and their families. Nearly every U.S. military base has

AAFES exchanges, and AAFES is experimenting with larger centers that are basically shopping malls with various stores in one location. AAFES offers goods at about a 20 percent discount and does not charge sales tax, and two-thirds of direct sales revenue go to programs that support morale programs for soldiers and their families (₹1177.2 crore in 2009).[8]

© ISTOCKPHOTO.COM/SASCHA HAHN

specialty store a retail store specializing in a given type of merchandise

program, credit policies, store expansion, customer service, and so on. Most of the department stores are owned by national chains. Shoppers' Stop, Westside, Lifestyle, Globus, and Pantaloons are some of the largest department store chains in India.

Specialty Stores

Specialty store formats allow retailers to refine their segmentation strategies and tailor their merchandise to specific target markets. A **specialty store** is not only a type of store but also a method of retail operations—namely, specializing in a given type of merchandise. Examples include children's clothing, jewelry, books, medicine, toys, and home and interiors products. A typical specialty store carries a deeper but narrower assortment of specialty merchandise than a department store. Generally, specialty stores' knowledgeable sales clerks offer more attentive customer service. Lilliput Kidswear, Tanishq, Apollo Pharmacy, Home Stop, and Mom & Me are examples of chain specialty retailers. Consumers usually consider price to be secondary in specialty outlets. Instead, the distinctive merchandise, the store's physical appearance, and the caliber of the staff determine their popularity. The key characteristic of this format is attentive customer service.

Because of their attention to customers and limited product line, manufacturers often favor introducing new products in small specialty stores before moving on to larger retail and department stores.

Housing Works Thrift Shops, a chain based in New York in the United States, views itself as a specialty retailer because its stores take in and sell apparel and accessories from high-end designers like Gucci, Ralph Lauren, Diane Von Furstenberg, and DKNY. Because Housing Works offers low prices on such designer brand names, most of the chain's sales come from people entering the workforce who are looking for interviewing clothes at discounted prices. In India as well, there are store chains like Brand Factory, Megamart, and Loot that sell branded apparel and accessories at discounted prices to attract price-conscious customers. Their success is evident from the number of stores they are operating in the country—Megamart has 175 outlets while Loot has 160 stores in different cities in India.[9] These stores purchase stock surplus in bulk from major retailers and producers at 60-70% discount and operate at nearly 10% profitability, thus, allowing these discount retailers of branded *merchandize* ability to offer between 25-50% discounts to consumers.[10]

Supermarkets

In India, the retail sector is dominated by small independent shops often called *kirana* stores. However, increasing disposable income and changing lifestyle is resulting in consumers shifting slowly to organized retailers.[11] **Supermarkets** are large, departmentalized, self-service retailers that specialize in food and some non-food items. A conventional supermarket carries 5,000 to 10,000 SKUs.[12] A supermarket not only carries national and local brands but also keeps its own private labels. This helps in offering choice to the customers at reasonable prices. With major concentration on food-related products, supermarkets derive just about 22 percent of total sales from non-food items.[13] The value proposition offered by supermarkets is convenience, affordability, and variety. While supermarkets have experienced declining sales in developed economies in recent years, this format is witnessing a fast growth in India.[14]

To stand out in an increasingly competitive marketplace, many supermarket chains are tailoring marketing strategies to appeal to specific consumer segments. Most notable is the shift toward loyalty marketing programs that reward loyal customers carrying frequent shopper cards with discounts or gifts. Once scanned at the checkout, frequent shopper cards help supermarket retailers electronically track shoppers' buying habits. Examples of loyalty programs run by supermarkets are *Club More* by More supermarket chain and *Reliance One* by Reliance Fresh supermarkets.

Hypermarkets

Hypermarkets are combination stores of a supermarket and a department store. The stores carry a vast merchandise mix, with product categories like apparel, house wares, consumer durables, sports equipment, cosmetics, FMCG products, and fresh fruits and vegetables. The area of such stores ranges from anywhere between 50,000 to 1,00,000 sq. ft., with food and grocery being the anchor product categories and accounting for 60–70 percent of sales. The stores offer the benefits of shop-under-one-roof and discounted prices. Some major players in this format are Spencer's Hyper, More Megastore, Easy Day, Hypercity, and Reliance Mart.

Superstores

In the developed markets like the United States, conventional supermarkets are being replaced by bigger *superstores*, which are usually twice the size of supermarkets. Superstores meet the needs of today's customers for convenience, variety, and service by offering one-stop shopping for many food and non-food needs, as well as many services—including pharmacies, flower shops, salad bars, in-store bakeries, take-out food sections, sit-down restaurants, health food sections, video rentals, dry cleaning services, shoe repair, photo processing, and banking. Some even offer family dentistry or optical shops, and many now have gas stations. This tendency to offer a wide variety of nontraditional goods and services under one roof is called **scrambled merchandising**.

supermarket a large, departmentalized, self-service retailer that specializes in food and some nonfood items

hypermarket combination stores of a supermarket and a department store

scrambled merchandising the tendency to offer a wide variety of nontraditional goods and services under one roof

drugstore a retail store that stocks pharmacy-related products and services as its main draw

Drugstores

Drugstores stock pharmacy-related products and services as their main draw, but they also carry a substantial selection of over-the-counter (OTC) medicines, cosmetics, health and beauty aids, seasonal merchandise, speciality items such as greeting cards and a limited selection of toys, and some non-refrigerated convenience foods. In order to remain competitive, they have also added services such as 24-hour drive through pharmacies and low-cost health clinics staffed by nurse practitioners. This format is largely popular in western countries.

In India, the organized retail market of pharmacy chains has started to take off. Some of the national level pharmacy chains are Apollo Pharmacy, MedPlus, and Guardian Lifecare. There are certain regional players as well like 98.4 in Delhi and NCR and Planet Health in Gujarat. However, these chains carry a limited product mix, largely restricted to pharmacy and health care products, baby care products, and personal care products.

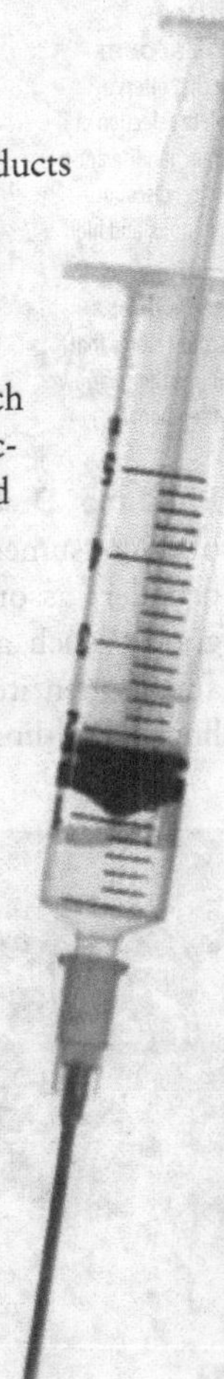

© ISTOCKPHOTO.COM/ANNA YU

convenience store a miniature supermarket, carrying only a limited line of high-turnover convenience goods

discount store a retailer that competes on the basis of low prices, high turnover, and high volume

full-line discount store a retailer that offers consumers very limited service and carries a broad assortment of well-known, nationally branded "hard goods"

mass merchandising a retailing strategy using moderate to low prices on large quantities of merchandise and lower levels of service to stimulate high turnover of products

speciality discount stores a retail store that offers a nearly complete selection of single-line merchandise and uses self-service, discount prices, high volume, and high turnover

category killers specialty discount stores that heavily dominate their narrow merchandise segment

Convenience Stores

A **convenience store** can be defined as a miniature supermarket, carrying only a limited line of high turnover convenience goods. These self-service stores are typically located near residential areas and are open for long hours, seven days a week. Such stores offer exactly what their name implies: convenient location, longer operating hours, and fast service. The customer pays a surcharge for convenience, so prices are almost always higher at a convenience store than at a supermarket. In India, these stores are referred to as *kirana* or mom-and-pop stores. Such stores have also started to come up at some of the petrol pump outlets in major Indian cities.

Discount Stores

A **discount store** is a retailer that competes on the basis of low prices, high turnover, and high volume. Discounters can be classified into four major categories: full-line discount stores, speciality discount stores, warehouse membership clubs, and off-price retailers.

Full-Line Discount Stores **Full-line discount stores** offer consumers very limited service, but carry a much broader assortment of nationally branded "hard goods" such as housewares, toys, automotive parts, and garden items, as well as clothing, bedding, and linens. Full-line discounters are often called mass merchandisers. **Mass merchandising** is the retailing strategy whereby retailers use moderate to low prices on large quantities of merchandise and lower levels of service to stimulate high turnover of products.

Wal-Mart is the largest full-line discount store in terms of sales and has more than 7,200 stores in four continents. It has also become a formidable retailing giant in online shopping.

Speciality Discount Stores **Speciality discount stores** are single-line stores, for example stores selling sporting goods, electronics, office supplies, housewares, or toys. They offer a nearly complete selection of single-line merchandise and use self-service, discount prices, high volume, and high turnover to their advantage. They are often termed as **category killers** because of their heavy dominance on a narrow merchandise segment. Some prominent global examples include Best Buy in electronics, IKEA in home furnishings, and Staples in office supplies. Category-dominant retailers like these serve their customers by offering a large selection of merchandise, stores that make shopping easy, and low prices every day, which eliminates the need for time-consuming comparison shopping.

Category killers have emerged in other specialty segments as wellin the developed markets, creating retailing empires in highly fragmented mom-and-pop markets. For instance, the home improvement industry, which for years was served by professional builders and small hardware stores, is now dominated by Home Depot and Lowe's in the U.S. markets.

Warehouse Membership Clubs **Warehouse membership clubs** sell a limited selection of brand name appliances, household items, and groceries. Selling

© INDIATODAYIMAGES.COM

Food drives the majority of the sales at hypermarkets.

© ISTOCKPHOTO.COM/DENIS GLADKIY / © ISTOCKPHOTO.COM/A-DIGIT

is done in bulk from warehouse outlets on a cash-and-carry basis to members only. Individual members of warehouse clubs are charged low or no membership fees. Such members are either small shop owners or larger, affluent households. Some stores operating in this format are Metro cash-and carry and Bharti Wal-Mart's Best Price Modern Wholesale.

Off-Price Retailers An **off-price retailer** sells at prices 25 percent or more below traditional department store prices. The merchandise offered is one of these: overruns, unsold end-of-season output, or seconds. Nevertheless, much off-price retailer merchandise is first-quality, current goods. An interesting variation of off-price concept is the **factory outlets**—off-price retail owned and operated by a manufacturer. Thus, it carries its own line of merchandise. Each season, from 5 to 10 percent of a manufacturer's output does not sell through regular distribution channels. Factory outlets help the manufacturers in regulating the sale of their surplus. Such outlets are usually located at out-of-the-way destinations, away from urban or suburban shopping areas to avoid sales cannibalization with manufacturer's own stores or department stores. Some popular factory outlets in India are those of Pantaloons and Levi's.

Restaurants

Restaurants straddle the line between retailing establishments and service establishments. Restaurants do sell tangible products food and drink—but they also provide a valuable service for consumers in the form of food preparation and food service. Some restaurants could even fall into the definition of a specialty retailer since they concentrate their menu offerings on a distinctive type of cuisine—for example, Mainland China restaurants and Barista coffee outlets.

Eating out has become an important part of Indians' daily activities and is growing in strength. The catering and food services market was worth ₹90,825 crore in 2009-10, with organized retail having a share of 10.7 percent.[15] The trend toward eating out has been fueled by the increase in working women and dual-income families.

The restaurant industry is one of the most entrepreneurial of businesses and one of the most competitive. Because barriers to entry are low, the opportunity appeals to many people. The risks, however, are great. About 50 percent of all new restaurants fail within the first year of operation. Restaurants face competition not only from other restaurants but also from the consumer who can easily choose to cook at home and the mushrooming tiffin services. Competition has fostered innovation and regular changes in menus in the restaurant industry.

warehouse membership clubs limited-service merchant wholesalers that sell a limited selection of brand name appliances, household items, and groceries on a cash-and-carry basis to members, usually small businesses and groups

off-price retailer a retailer that sells at prices 25 percent or more below traditional department store prices because it pays cash for its stock and usually doesn't ask for return privileges

factory outlet an off-price retailer that is owned and operated by a manufacturer

nonstore retailing shopping without visiting a store

kiosks small, freestanding pavilion, used for the purpose of sales, promotion activities, or giving information

automatic vending the use of machines to offer goods for sale

LO 4 Nonstore Retailing

The retailing methods discussed so far have been in-store methods, in which customers must physically shop at stores. In contrast, non-store retailing is the format where selling is done without using physical stores. The major forms of non-store retailing are kiosks, automatic vending, direct retailing, direct marketing, and electronic retailing.

Kiosks

Kiosks are small, freestanding pavilion, usually placed in a mall, within stores, stations, and airports. They are essentially used for the purpose of sales, promotion activities, or giving information.

Automatic Vending

Vending is the most pervasive retail business in the United States, with about 1.15 crore vending machines, selling a variety of merchandise like soft drinks, candy, ice cream, DVDs, and perfumes. The sales are done through vending machines, which are either coin or card operated, to dispense goods to customers round the clock. No sales personnel are required for operating these machines. The machines are mostly located at convenient locations such as stations, airports, or hotel lobbies. The format is yet to take off full-fledged manner in India, with its presence largely restricted to high traffic locations like airports, in the form of tea and coffee vending machines.

© ISTOCKPHOTO/THINKSTOCK

Direct Retailing

In **direct retailing**, representatives sell products door-to-door, office-to-office, or at home sales parties. Companies like Avon, Amway, and Eureka Forbes have used this approach for years.

Direct Marketing

Direct marketing, sometimes called **direct response marketing**, refers to the techniques used to get consumers to make a purchase from their home, office, or other nonretail setting. Its techniques include telemarketing, direct mail, catalogs and mail order, and electronic retailing. Shoppers using these methods are less bound by traditional shopping situations. Time-strapped consumers and those who live in rural or suburban areas are most likely to be direct response shoppers because they value the convenience and flexibility that direct marketing provides.

direct retailing the selling of products by representatives who work door-to-door, office-to-office, or at home sales parties

direct marketing (direct response marketing) techniques used to get consumers to make a purchase from their home, office, or other nonretail setting

telemarketing the use of the telephone to sell directly to consumers

online retailing a type of shopping available to consumers with personal computers and access to the Internet

Telemarketing **Telemarketing** is the use of the telephone to sell directly to consumers. It consists of outbound sales calls, usually unsolicited, and inbound calls—that is, orders through toll-free numbers. The technique has been used highly by financial products companies for selling products like credit cards and investment plans. However, with consumers complaining about outbound telemarketing, a "do-not-disturb" legislation was passed by government, benefitting such consumers who did not want to receive unsolicited telephone calls.

Direct Mail With direct mail, marketers can precisely target their customers and their demographics, geographics, and even psychographics. Mailing lists are either prepared from internal database or bought from external sources, after which postcards or e-mails are sent to prospective customers.

Catalog Retailing Catalogues are created and designed for highly segmented markets, giving a brief description of products available for selling. The format offers great convenience to customers as they can simply place the orders from their homes.

Electronic Retailing

Electronic retailing includes online retailing and the 24-hour, shop-at-home television networks.

Online Retailing **Online retailing**, or e-tailing, is a type of shopping available to consumers with personal computers and access to the Internet. It just requires turning on a computer, surfing retail websites, and selecting and ordering products online with the click of a mouse. This type of shopping is not only convenient but also less costly. It offers multiple benefits to customers, for example, shopping without leaving home, choosing from a wide selection of merchandise, comparing prices across Web sites, and getting the products delivered at the doorsteps. The element of time saving is very crucial as customers save time on travelling and standing in queues.

Despite so many advantages, online retailing has seen little growth in the Indian retail market. While total retail market in India was worth ₹19,48,916 crore in 2009–10, online retail constituted a petty .06 percent i.e. ₹1169 crore only. Some of the reasons identified for this apathy toward online retailing include inability to touch and feel products before purchasing, uncertainty about product quality that would be delivered, lack of trust on safety and security of online transactions, shopping still considered as a family outing, and the desire to bargain for better prices.[17]

There is, however, optimism about the future growth of this industry, with the rise in internet penetration levels and the burgeoning, highly tech-savvy youth segment. Examples of some of the e-tailing ventures in India include MakeMyTrip.com, Fnp.com (Ferns N Petals), Myntra.com, and Naaptol.com. Some of the established retailing empires too have

CATALOGS IN THE DIGITAL AGE

With e-commerce booming and environmentalists cracking down on waste, it would seem printed catalogs face certain doom. However, this might not be the case. Marketers mailed 1,700 crore catalogs last year, which amounts to 56 catalogs per person in the United States. A recent study concluded that customers who received a catalog spent 28 percent more money on that retailer's Web site. Though some companies are moving to an "iCatalog," the 12,524 catalogs available in print vastly outnumber the digital. Apparently, receiving a physical, visual reminder to visit a company's Web site makes catalogs more important than ever, and there is no substitute for the enticement of those glossy images.[16]

their presence in the online format like FutureBazaar.com and ShoppersStop.com.

Television Shopping It is a form of retailing wherein merchandise, along with the retail price, is displayed on television for home viewers. The viewers can place their orders directly on phone numbers provided and get the products delivered at home. Asian Sky Shop popularized this format in India.

LO 5 Franchising

A *franchise* is a continuing relationship in which a franchiser grants to a franchisee the business rights to operate or sell a product. The **franchisor** originates the trade name, product, methods of operation, and so on. The **franchisee**, in return, pays the franchisor for the right to use its name, product, or business methods. A franchise agreement between the two parties usually lasts for 10 to 20 years, at which time the agreement can be renewed if both parties are agreeable.

To be granted the rights to a franchise, a franchisee usually pays an initial, one-time franchise fee. The amount of this fee depends solely on the individual franchisor, but it generally ranges from ₹2 lakh to ₹20 lakh or higher. In addition to this initial franchise fee, the franchisee is expected to pay royalty fees, usually in the range of 2 to 10 percent of gross revenues. The franchisee may also be expected to pay advertising fees, which usually cover the cost of promotional materials and, if the franchise organization is large enough, regional or national advertising. A McDonald's franchise, for example, costs an initial fee per store plus a monthly fee based upon the restaurant's sales performance and base rent. In addition, a new McDonald's franchisee can also expect start-up costs to meet the equipment and pre-opening expenses. The size of the restaurant facility, area of the country, inventory, selection of kitchen equipment, signage, and style of decor and landscaping affect new restaurant costs.[18] Fees such as these are typical for all major franchisers, including KFC and Subway.

franchisor the originator of a trade name, product, methods of operation, and so on that grants operating rights to another party to sell its product

franchisee an individual or business that is granted the right to sell another party's product

Two basic forms of franchises are used today: product and trade name franchising and business format franchising. In *product and trade name franchising*, a dealer agrees to sell certain products provided by a manufacturer or a wholesaler. This approach has been used most widely in the auto and truck, soft-drink bottling, tire, and gasoline service industries. For example, a local tire retailer may hold a franchise to sell MRF tyres.

COMPANIES WITH HIGH FOCUS OF FRANCHISEE STORES

Companies	Total No. of Stores	Company-owned Stores	Franchised Stores	%age of Stores Franchised
KidZee	697	—	697	100%
Adidas	500	—	500	100%
Raymond's	453	—	453	100%
Domino's Pizza	270	—	270	100%
McDonald's	160	—	160	100%
Baskin Robbins	300	10	290	97%
World of Titan	274	10	264	96%
Koutons Retail	1400	59	1341	96%
Liberty	570	70	500	88%
Reebok	850	150	700	82%
Archies	550	100	450	82%
Khadim's	481	150	331	69%
Numero Uno	120	55	65	54
Subway	145	69	76	52%

Source: "Franchising: The New Engine for Retail Expansion," *Technopak perspective*, Volume 3/2010, http://www.technopak.com/Images/TPK-perspective-vol3.pdf.

retailing mix a combination of the six Ps—product, place, promotion, price, presentation, and personnel—to sell goods and services to the ultimate consumer

product offering the mix of products offered to the consumer by the retailer; also called the *product assortment* or *merchandise mix*

Business format franchising is an ongoing business relationship between a franchisor and a franchisee. Typically, a franchiser "sells" a franchisee the rights to use the franchisor's format or approach to doing business. This form of franchising has rapidly expanded through retailing, restaurant, food-service, hotel and motel, printing, and real estate franchises.

LO 6 Retail Marketing Strategy

Retailers must develop marketing strategies based on overall goals and strategic plans. Retailing goals might include more traffic, higher sales of a specific item, a more upscale image, or heightened public awareness of the retail operation. The strategies that retailers use to obtain their goals might include a sale, an updated decor, or a new advertisement. The key tasks in strategic retailing are defining and selecting a target market and developing the retailing mix to successfully meet the needs of the chosen target market.

Defining a Target Market

The first and foremost task in developing a retail strategy is to define the target market. This process begins with market segmentation, the topic of Chapter 8. Successful retailing has always been based on knowing the customer. Sometimes retailing chains flounder when management loses sight of the customers the stores should be serving. For example, Gap built a retail empire by offering updated, casual classics like white shirts and khaki pants that appealed to everyone from high school through middle age but began losing customers when it shifted toward trendier fashions with a limited appeal.

Target markets in retailing are often defined by demographics, geographics, and psychographics. Nature's Basket, a gourmet retail initiative of Godrej group, is targeted toward urban markets to target customers who want high-quality premium food. The company offers an exotic range of international food products like cheese, seafood, sauces, premium wines, organic food, and spices to cater to the tastes of its high-end customers. A lot of in-store activities are also planned, such as cooking classes and wine-and-cheese evenings, to create a buzz around the store. Despite operating in a niche segment, the business model has turned out to be a profitable one.[19]

Choosing the Retailing Mix

Retailers combine the elements of the retailing mix to come up with a single retailing method to attract the target market. The **retailing mix** consists of six Ps: the four Ps of the marketing mix (product, place, promotion, and price) plus presentation and personnel (see Exhibit 15.2).

The combination of the six Ps projects a store's image, which influences consumers' perceptions. Using these impressions of stores, shoppers position one store against another. A retail marketing manager must make sure that the store's positioning is compatible with the target customers' expectations. As discussed at the beginning of the chapter, retail stores can be positioned on three broad dimensions: service provided by store personnel, product assortment, and price. Management should use everything else—place, presentation, and promotion—to fine-tune the basic positioning of the store.

The Product Offering The first element in the retailing mix is the **product offering**, also called the *product assortment* or *merchandise mix*. Retailers decide what to sell on the basis of what their target market wants to buy. They can base their decision on market

EXHIBIT 15.2
The Retailing Mix

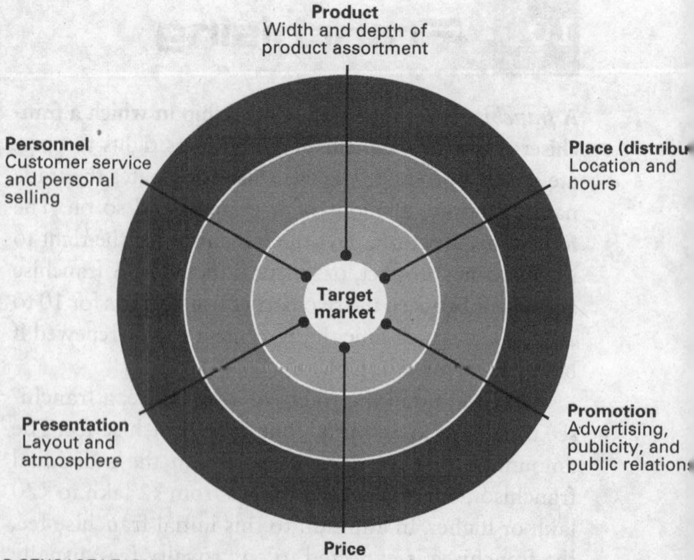

research, past sales, fashion trends, customer requests, and other sources. A recent approach, called *data mining*, uses complex mathematical models to help retailers make better product mix decisions. Retailers like Target and Wal-Mart use data mining to determine which products to stock at what price, how to manage markdowns, and how to advertise to draw target customers.

Developing a product offering is essentially a question of the width and depth of the product assortment. *Width* refers to the assortment of products offered; *depth* refers to the number of different brands offered within each assortment. Price, store design, displays, and service are important to consumers in determining where to shop, but the most critical factor is merchandise selection. This reasoning also holds true for online retailers. Amazon.com, for instance, is building the world's biggest online department store so that shoppers can get whatever they want with one click on their Web browsers. Like a traditional department store or mass merchandiser, Amazon offers considerable width in its product assortment with crores of different items, including books, music, toys, videos, tools and hardware, health and beauty aids, electronics, and software. Amazon has recently started a website called *Junglee.com* to test waters in the Indian market before making a full fledged entry into the e-commerce market of the country. Over 1.2 crore products are offered from both Indian and global brands.[20] Conversely, online specialty retailers, such as Babyoye.com and Lenskart.com, focus on a single category of merchandise, hoping to attract loyal customers with a larger depth of products at lower prices and better customer service. Many online retailers purposely focus on single product line niches that could never garner enough foot traffic to support a traditional brick-and-mortar store. For instance, Web sites such as bugbitingplants.com and petflytrap.com sell and ship live carnivorous plants in the United States.

After determining what products will satisfy target customers' desires, retailers must find sources of supply and evaluate the products. When the right products are found, the retail buyer negotiates a purchase contract. The buying function can either be performed in-house or be delegated to an outside firm. The goods must then be moved from the seller to the retailer, which means shipping, storing, and stocking the inventory. The trick is to manage the inventory by cutting prices to move slow goods and by keeping adequate supplies of hot-selling items in stock. As in all good systems, the final step is to evaluate the entire process to seek more efficient methods and eliminate problems and bottlenecks.

Promotion Strategy Retail promotion strategy includes advertising, public relations and publicity, and sales promotion. The goal is to help position the store in consumers' minds. Retailers design intriguing ads, stage special events, and develop promotions aimed at their target markets. Today's grand openings are a carefully orchestrated blend of advertising, merchandising, goodwill, and glitter. All the elements of an opening—press coverage, special events, media advertising, and store displays—are carefully planned.

Retailers' advertising is carried out mostly at the local level. Local advertising by retailers usually provides specific information about their stores, such as location, merchandise, hours, prices, and special sales. In contrast, national retail advertising generally focuses on image. For example, Target, a discounter retailer in the U.S., uses advertisements similar to designer fashion advertisements to depict high-quality goods. Paired with the ubiquitous red target and tag line "Expect more. Pay less," Target is demonstrating that it sells products that consumers normally aspire to own at prices they can afford.

Target's advertising campaign also takes advantage of cooperative advertising, another popular retail advertising practice. Traditionally, marketers would pay retailers to feature their products in store mailers, or a marketer would develop a television campaign for the product and simply tack on several retailers' names at the end. But Target's advertising makes use of a more collaborative trend by integrating products such as Tide laundry detergent or Coca-Cola into the actual campaign. Another common form of cooperative advertising involves promotion of exclusive products. For example, Target hires famous young designers for temporary partnerships, during which they develop reasonably priced product lines available exclusively at Target stores.

The Proper Location The retailing axiom "location, location, location" has long emphasized the importance of place to the retail mix. The location decision is important first because the retailer is making a large, semi-permanent commitment of resources that can reduce its future flexibility. Second, the location will affect the store's future growth and profitability.

Site location begins by choosing a community. Important factors to consider are the area's economic growth potential, the amount of competition, and geography.

destination stores
stores that consumers purposely plan to visit

After settling on a geographic region or community, retailers must choose a specific site. In addition to growth potential, the important factors to consider are neighborhood socioeconomic characteristics, traffic flows, land costs, zoning regulations, and public transportation. A particular site's visibility, parking, entrance and exit locations, accessibility, and safety and security issues are also important considerations. Additionally, a retailer should consider how its store will fit into the surrounding environment. Retail decision makers probably would not locate a The Loot store next door to a United Colours of Benetton store.

Retailers face one final decision about location: whether to have a freestanding unit or to become a tenant in a shopping center or mall.

Freestanding Stores An isolated, freestanding location is usually used by large retailers like Wal-Mart and sellers of shopping goods like furniture and cars because they are "destination" stores. **Destination stores** are stores consumers seek out and purposely plan to visit. An isolated store location may have the advantages of low site cost or rent and no nearby competitors. On the other hand, it may be hard to attract customers to a freestanding location, and no other retailers are around to share costs.

Perhaps the greatest reason for developing a freestanding site is greater visibility. Retailers often feel they get lost in huge centers and malls, but freestanding units can help stores develop an identity with shoppers. Also, an aggressive expansion plan may not allow time to wait for shopping centers to be built.

Shopping Centers The evolution of shopping centers can be traced back in the 1950s when the U.S. population started migrating to the suburbs. The first shopping centers were *strip centers*, typically located along busy streets, with parking space in front of the stores. They usually included a supermarket, a variety store, and perhaps a few specialty stores. Then *community shopping centers* emerged, with one or two small department stores, more specialty stores, a couple of restaurants, and several apparel stores. These community shopping centers provided off-street parking and a broader variety of merchandise.

Malls offering a much wider variety of merchandise first appeared in the mid-1970s. Malls are either entirely enclosed or roofed to allow shopping in any weather. They have acres of free parking. The *anchor stores* or *generator stores* (often major department stores) are usually located at opposite ends of the mall to create heavy foot traffic. The rest of the store mix consists of exclusive brand stores, speciality stores, hypermarkets, kiosks, and other retail formats. They also include movie cinemas and food joints to offer a complete shopping experience to the customers.

Store within a Store Store within a store is the concept of opening shops inside larger stores to expand retailing opportunities without risking investment in a separate store. Shoppers Stop entered into a tie-up with Cafe Coffee Day (CCD) to set up CCD coffee outlets in Shoppers' Stop stores.[21]

Pop-Up Shops Pop-up shops—tiny, temporary stores that stay in one location only for a few months—are a growing trend. They help retailers reach a wide market while avoiding high rent at retail locations. Matcha Source, an online retailer of Japanese green tea, opened a pop-up shop in Manhattan called Matcha Box. The store was so successful using social media tools to drive traffic that the retailer kept the temporary shop open an extra month.[22]

Retail Prices Another important element in the retailing mix is price. Retailing's ultimate goal is to sell products to consumers, and the right price is critical in ensuring sales. Because retail prices are usually based on the cost of the merchandise, an essential part of pricing is efficient and timely buying.

Price is also a key element in a retail store's positioning strategy. Higher prices often indicate a level of quality and help reinforce the prestigious image of retailers, as they do for FCUK and Wills Lifestyle. On the other hand, discounters and off-price retailers, such as Megamart and Brand Factory, offer a good value for money. There are even stores, such as My Dollar Store, where everything costs ₹99. My Dollar Store's single-price-point strategy is aimed at getting customers to make impulse purchases through what analysts call the "wow factor"—the excitement of discovering that an item costs less than ₹100.

Presentation of the Retail Store The presentation of a retail store helps determine the store's image and positions the retail store in consumers' minds. For instance, a retailer that wants to position itself as an upscale store would use a lavish or sophisticated presentation.

The main element of a store's presentation is its **atmosphere,** the overall impression conveyed by a store's physical layout, decor, and surroundings. The atmosphere might create a relaxed or busy feeling, a sense of luxury or efficiency, a friendly or cold attitude, a sense of organization or clutter, or a fun or serious mood. Crossword bookstores, targeted toward book lovers, offer seating facility, use bright lighting, and play soothing music to give a relaxed atmosphere to the customers so that they are comfortable and can read books leisurely.

The layout of retail stores is a key factor in their success. The goal is to use all of the store's space effectively, including aisles, fixtures, merchandise displays, and nonselling areas. In addition to making shopping easy and convenient for the customer, an effective layout has a powerful influence on traffic patterns and purchasing behavior.

Layout also includes where products are placed in the store. Many technologically advanced retailers are using a technique called *market-basket analysis* to sift through the data collected by their point-of-purchase scanning equipment. The analysis looks for products that are commonly purchased together to help retailers find ideal locations for each product. Wal-Mart uses market-basket analysis to determine where in the store to stock products for customer convenience. Kleenex tissues, for example, are in the paper-goods aisle and beside the cold medicines.

These are the most influential factors in creating a store's atmosphere:

- *Employee type and density:* Employee type refers to an employee's general characteristics—for instance, neat, friendly, knowledgeable, or service oriented. Density is the number of employees per thousand square feet of selling space. Whereas low employee density creates a "do-it-yourself," casual atmosphere, high employee density denotes readiness to serve the customer's every whim.
- *Merchandise type and density:* A prestigious retailer like Shoppers Stop carries the best brand names and displays them in a neat, uncluttered arrangement. Discounters and off-price retailers often carry seconds or out-of-season goods crowded into small spaces and hung on long racks by category—tops, pants, skirts, etc.—creating the impression that "We've got so much stuff, we're practically giving it away."
- *Fixture type and density:* Fixtures can be elegant (rich woods), trendy (chrome and smoked glass), or consist of old, beat-up tables, as in an antiques store. The fixtures should be consistent with the general atmosphere the store is trying to create.
- *Sound:* Sound can be pleasant or unpleasant for a customer. Music can entice customers to stay in the store longer and buy more or eat quickly and leave a table for others. It can also control the pace of the store traffic, create an image, and attract or direct the shopper's attention.
- *Odors:* Smell can either stimulate or detract from sales. Research suggests that people evaluate merchandise more positively, spend more time shopping, and are generally in a better mood when an agreeable odor is present. Retailers use fragrances as an extension of their retail strategy.

atmosphere the overall impression conveyed by a store's physical layout, decor, and surroundings

© ISTOCKPHOTO/THINKSTOCK

Well-lit stores, neatly stacked merchandise, and spacious aisles enhance the overall shopping experience of the customers and build a positive impression of the store.

- *Visual factors:* Colors can create a mood or focus attention and therefore are an important factor in atmosphere. Red, yellow, and orange are considered warm colors and are used when a feeling of warmth and closeness is desired. Cool colors like blue, green, and violet are used to open up closed-in places and create an air of elegance and cleanliness. Many retailers have found that natural lighting, either from windows or skylights, can lead to increased sales. Outdoor lighting can also affect consumer patronage.

Personnel and Customer Service People are a unique aspect of retailing. Most retail sales involve a customer–salesperson relationship, if only briefly. When customers shop at a grocery store, the cashiers check and bag their groceries. When customers shop at a prestigious clothier, the salesclerks may assist in the fitting process, offer alteration services, wrap purchases, and even serve champagne. Sales personnel provide their customers with the amount of service prescribed by the retail strategy of the store.

Retail salespeople serve another important selling function: They persuade shoppers to buy. They must therefore be able to persuade customers that what they are selling is what the customer needs. Salespeople are trained in two common selling techniques: trading up and suggestion selling. *Trading up* means persuading customers to buy a higher-priced item than they originally intended to purchase. To avoid selling customers something they do not need or want, however, salespeople should take care when practicing trading-up techniques. *Suggestion selling*, a common practice among most retailers, seeks to broaden customers' original purchases with related items. For example, if you go to any McDonald's outlet and order a wrap, the representative at the cash counter will ask if you would like to purchase a soft drink, or take a combo meal. Suggestion selling and trading up should always help shoppers recognize true needs rather than sell them unwanted merchandise.

Providing great customer service is one of the most challenging elements in the retail mix because customer expectations for service vary greatly. What customers expect in a department store is very different from what they expect in a discount store. Customer expectations also change. Ten years ago, shoppers wanted personal one-on-one attention. Today, most customers are happy to help themselves as long as they can easily find what they need.

Customer service is also critical for online retailers. Online shoppers expect a retailer's Web site to be user friendly, with readily available products and easy return process. Therefore, customer-friendly retailers must design their sites to give their customers the information they need regarding new products and sales. Companies like Amazon.com even offer products recommendations and personal shoppers. Some retailers have also started offering a cash-on-delivery service as Indian customers are apprehensive about online transactions, and many may not even possess a credit or debit card to conduct a transaction.

LO 7 New Developments in Retailing

In an effort to better serve their customers and attract new ones, retailers are constantly adopting new strategies. Two recent developments are interactivity and m-commerce.

Interactivity

Adding interactivity to the retail environment is one of the most popular strategies in retailing in the past few years. Small retailer as well as national chains are using interactivity in stores to differentiate themselves from the competition. The new interactive trend gets customers involved rather than just catching their eye. For example, Build-a-Bear in the United States enables customers to make their own stuffed animals by choosing which animals to stuff and then dressing and naming them. The company had entered India in 2007 and opened three stores—two in Mumbai and one in New Delhi. However, the stores were closed down one year later in 2008 due to certain strategy conflicts.[23]

M-Commerce

M-commerce (mobile e-commerce) enables consumers using wireless mobile devices to connect to the Internet and shop. M-commerce enjoyed early success overseas and has been gaining acceptance and popularity in the United States. Essentially, m-commerce goes beyond text message advertisements to allow consumers to purchase goods and services using wireless mobile devices, such as mobile telephones, pagers, personal digital assistants (PDAs), and handheld computers. M-commerce users adopt the new technology because it saves time and offers more convenience in a greater number of locations. Vending machines are an important venue for m-commerce. Both PepsiCo and Coca-Cola have developed smart vending technologies in the United States. Coca-Cola's Intelligent Vending, a "cashless" payment system, accepts credit cards, RFID devices, and hotel room keys and can be accessed via cell phone.[24]

M-Commerce Growth Potential There has been a veritable explosion in the number of consumers using mobile technology to do their shopping. This is a part of a bigger trend in which mobile technology allows people to do tasks on the go that they used to do at a desktop computer. Many major companies, ranging from Polo Ralph Lauren to Sears, already offer shopping on mobile phones, and the growth potential is huge. Currently, 3.5 percent of North American mobile phone users have purchased something directly with their phones.[25] There are nearly 26 crore data-capable mobile devices, 6.2 crore of which are fully Web-enabled smartphones or 3G-enabled laptops.[26] The gap between the number of smartphone shoppers and owners is expected to close. For this reason, Nick Taylor, the president of Usablenet, a firm that guides retailers in providing mobile Web content, argues that mobile shopping is not a passing trend. "Anyone in the *Fortune* 1000 or Internet Retail 500, to the extent that you believe your company needs a Web site, should have a mobile site." Airtel recently launched a mobile wallet service called *Airtel Money* that facilitates financial transactions through mobile phones. The users can store virtual money up to ₹5,000 on their mobiles in the form of prepaid account by exchanging cash for the same. They can use this money for several purposes, including shopping at over 7,000 merchant outlets. Bharti Retail is one such company that allows its customers to make payments using this facility.[27]

Suggestion selling seeks to broaden customers' original purchases with related items, such as USB cords, paper, or extra ink when buying a printer.

© ISTOCKPHOTO.COM/4X6

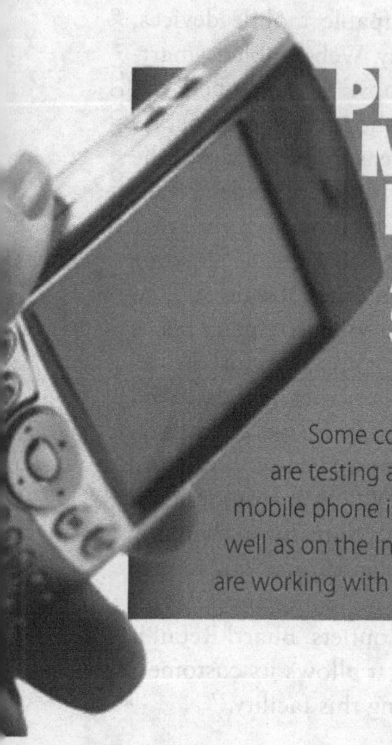

PICK UP THE MOBILE PHONE AND SHOP!

Some companies in the western countries are testing a process that would turn your mobile phone into a payment option in stores, as well as on the Internet. AT&T, Verizon, and T-Mobile are working with Discover Financial Services to allow customers to pay at a register by **waving their phones** in front of a scanner. The technology would reduce retailers' cost by removing credit card transaction fees and make payment a breeze for consumers. Other independent companies have developed software that makes paying via a mobile phone simpler. Zong allows users to enter their phone number to make Internet purchases, and Bling Nation works with establishments to allow customers to "tap and pay" with their mobile phones. But with 80 percent of consumers between the ages of 18 and 34 projected to use mobile financial services in the next five years, the technology could make or break companies that adopt it.[28]

© ISTOCKPHOTO.COM/DAVID MEHAREY

Review and Applications

Discuss the importance of retailing in the Indian economy. Retailing plays a vital role in the Indian economy for two main reasons. First, retailing industry is one of the largest employers in the country, employing about 4 crore people. Second, the contribution of retail industry to the country's GDP is quite significant at around 30 percent. However, Indian retail industry is largely unorganized, with organized retail having a share of just 6.5 percent of the total retail market.

1.1 To fully appreciate the role retailing plays in the Indian economy, it may be helpful to review a selection of press articles related to the retailing industry. Search for articles pertaining to retailing. Read a selection of articles, and report your findings to the class.

1.2 Keep a shopping journal that details all the retail establishments you visit in a week: how long you spent in each store, how much money you spent, and the reason for your visit. At the end of the week, review your journal and analyze your relationship to retail. As a class, compile your results to get a picture of shopping habits and consumer behavior.

Explain the dimensions by which retailers can be classified. Many different kinds of retailers exist. A retail establishment can be classified according to its ownership, level of service, product assortment, and price. On the basis of ownership, retailers can be broadly differentiated as independent retailers, chain stores, or franchise outlets. The level of service retailers provide can be classified along a continuum of high to low. Retailers also classify themselves by the breadth and depth of their product assortments; some retailers have concentrated product assortments, whereas others have extensive product assortments. Last, general price levels also classify a store, from discounters offering low prices to exclusive specialty stores where high prices are the norm. Retailers use these latter three variables to position themselves in the marketplace.

2.1 Form a team of three classmates to identify different retail stores in your city where pet supplies are sold. Include nonstore forms of retailing, such as catalogs, the Internet, or the local veterinarian. Team members should divide up and visit all the different retailing outlets for pet supplies. Prepare a report describing the differences in brands and products sold at each of the retailing formats and the differences in store characteristics and service levels. For example, which brands are sold via mass merchandiser, independent specialty store, or other venue? Suggest why different products and brands are distributed through different types of stores.

Describe the major types of retail operations. The major types of retail stores are department stores, specialty retailers, supermarkets, hypermarkets, drugstores, convenience stores, discount stores, and restaurants. Department stores carry a wide assortment of shopping and specialty goods, are organized into relatively independent departments, and offset higher prices by emphasizing customer service and décor. Specialty retailers typically carry a narrower but deeper assortment of merchandise, emphasizing distinctive products and a high level of customer service. *Supermarkets* are large self-service retailers that offer a wide variety of food products and some nonfood items. Hypermarkets are combination stores of a supermarket and a department store. Drugstores are retail formats that sell mostly prescription and over-the-counter medications, health and beauty aids, cosmetics, and specialty items. Convenience stores carry a limited line of high-turnover convenience goods. Discount stores offer low-priced general merchandise and consist of four types: full-line discounters, specialty discount retailers, warehouse clubs, and off-price retailers. Finally, restaurants straddle the line between the retailing and services industries; although restaurants sell a product, food and drink, to final consumers, they can also be considered service marketers because they provide consumers with the service of preparing food and sometimes table service.

3.1 Discuss the possible marketing implications of the recent trend toward hypermarkets, which combine a supermarket and a department store.

3.2 Would you be interested in buying luxury items, like expensive jewelry, at a warehouse club? Wal-Mart offered a ₹1.75 crores worth diamond solitaire ring during a recent Christmas shopping season. If you could afford such a ring, would you consider buying it at Wal-Mart? Why or Why not?

Discuss nonstore retailing techniques. Nonstore retailing, which is shopping outside a store setting, has four major categories. Kiosks are small, freestanding pavilion, used for the purpose of sales, promotion activities, or giving information. Automatic vending uses machines to offer products for sale. In direct retailing, the sales transaction occurs in a home setting, typically through door-to-door sales or party plan selling. Direct marketing refers to the techniques used to get consumers to buy from their homes or place of business. Those techniques include direct mail, catalog retailing, telemarketing, and electronic retailing, such as television shopping and online retailing.

4.1 How much does the most powerful computer with the fastest modem, most memory, largest monitor, biggest hard drive, and all the available peripherals cost at **www.dell.com**? Then visit a store like Croma or E-Zone and price a comparable computer. How can you explain any price differences between the two retail operations? Explain any differences in features that you encountered. What conclusions can you draw from your research?

4.2 Most catalog companies also offer online shopping. Identify such companies that offer both catalog and online retailing. Then compare the two retailing methods (paper and Internet) for prices, products, and so forth. Which do you prefer—the paper catalog or online shopping? Why?

Define *franchising* and describe its two basic forms. Franchising is a continuing relationship in which a franchisor grants to a franchisee the business rights to operate or to sell a product. Modern franchising takes two basic forms. In product and trade name franchising, a dealer agrees to buy or sell certain products or product lines from a particular manufacturer or wholesaler. Business format franchising is an ongoing business relationship in which a franchisee uses a franchisor's name, format, or method of business in return for several types of fees.

5.1 What advantages does franchising provide to franchisors as well as franchisees?

5.2 What do you need to do to become a franchisee of a store like Archies or Koutons Retail? Try to interact with the franchisees of such stores in your city to find out the process.

List the major tasks involved in developing a retail marketing strategy. Retail management begins with defining the target market, typically on the basis of demographic, geographic, or psychographic characteristics. After determining the target market, retail managers must develop the six variables of the retailing mix: product, promotion, place, price, presentation, and personnel.

6.1 Identify a successful retail business in your community. What marketing strategies have led to its success?

6.2 How can a company create an atmosphere on its Web site? Visit the pages of some of your favorite retailers to see if they have been able to re-create the store atmosphere on the Internet.

Describe new developments in retailing. Three major trends are evident in retailing today. First, adding interactivity to the retail environment is one of the most popular strategies in retailing in recent years. Small retailers as well as national chains are using interactivity to involve customers and set themselves apart from the competition. Second, m-commerce (mobile e-commerce) is gaining in popularity. M-commerce enables consumers to purchase goods and services using wireless mobile devices, such as mobile telephones, pagers, PDAs, and handheld computers.

7.1 Make a list of stores that actively incorporate some kind of interactivity or entertainment into their retailing strategy. Now, make a list of stores that do not, such as office supply stores. Compare your two lists. Select a company from your second list and draft a strategy to help it become more interactive.

Exercises

APPLICATION EXERCISE

After reading the chapter, you can see that differences in retailing are the result of strategy. To better understand the relationship between strategic retailing factors and consumer perceptions, you can conduct a simple observation exercise. First, pick a product to shop for, and then identify two stores where you have *never* shopped as places to look for your product. The two stores must be different types of retailers. For example, you can shop for a Microwave Oven at E-Zone (discount speciality store) and at company's exclusive outlet (example, LG or Samsung). Once you have identified what you are looking for and where you're going to look, visit each store and record your observations of specific strategic retailing factors.[29]

Activities

1. Go through each store and make careful observations of the following:
   - *Location:* Where is each store? How congested is the area of town where each store is located? What influence does the neighborhood have on your impression of the store? Would you travel to this store under normal circumstances? Write a detailed paragraph on the location of each store.
   - *Exterior atmosphere:* Is there parking? If so, is it convenient? Is it adequate? Observe other parking issues (cleanliness and size of the lot, size of spaces, well-lit, etc.). What kinds of stores are around the store you are visiting? Do you think being located next to them increases traffic at your store? Are direct competitors nearby? Is the building modern or historic? Is it attractive, clean, and appealing? Is the entrance inviting to shoppers?
   - *Interior atmosphere:* Compare the following attributes at each store: aisle width; lighting; number of customers; noise (background music, loudspeakers, etc.); store layout; signage; accessibility of the cashier; number of products available (depth and width of assortment); ability to inspect the product before purchase; quality of the fixtures (shelves, lights, etc.); availability of salespeople and their knowledge about the product; willingness of salespeople to help.
   - *Product:* Is your product available? If not, is there a satisfactory substitute? What is your perception of the quality of goods offered? Why do you think as you do?
   - *Price:* What is the price of the product/brand at this store? Is the price prominently marked? How do the prices at the two stores compare? How does the price compare to your expectations?
2. From which of these two stores would you actually purchase the item? Why, specifically? List the factors that played a role in your decision. Which factor is most important to you? If you would not purchase the item at either store, why not?
3. What are the three most important differences you observed between the stores?
4. Using the results of your research, write a short paper that outlines your observations. Conclude your paper with your answers to questions 2 and 3.

ETHICS EXERCISE

A–Z Grocery Company is well known for offering quality grocery products at the lowest prices in the market. When the company applied for a zoning change to build a new store in a middle-class neighborhood, several members of the city council objected because the company has no stores in low-income neighborhoods, where they argue the low prices are needed most. The company contends that it cannot operate profitably in these neighborhoods because of higher security and operating costs.

Questions

1. Should low-cost retailers be required to locate near low-income customers? Why or why not?
2. Does the AMA Statement of Ethics address this issue? Go to **www.marketingpower.com** and review the code. Then, write a brief paragraph on how the AMA Statement of Ethics relates to retailing locations.

MARKETING PLAN EXERCISE

Chapter 15 is the third and final chapter in Part 4, Distribution Decisions. Once you've completed this exercise, you can complete the Marketing Plan Worksheet for Part 4 on your companion Web site at **www.cengage.com/international**. Distribution is a key component of any business. For the e-business, distribution seems "invisible" to the consumer, because the consumer may not care where your firm is located but wants product delivery quickly and inexpensively. Creating a worldwide distribution system is an additional challenge to the marketer. Use the following exercises to guide you through the retail distribution part of your strategic marketing plan:

1. What types of retail establishments might be used for your firm's product? Are they in locations convenient to the target customers? What is the atmosphere of the facility for each type? How can you get the atmosphere of the brick-and-mortar offering to match the offering of your Web site?
2. If you have developed a service, to what other Web sites might you "distribute" your Internet-based service? How will working with these other Web sites help you reach your target audience? Are there other Web sites from which you might accept distribution deals in order to make your product or service offering stronger? Explain how strategic distribution with other Web sites or services can give you a competitive advantage.

Short Case: TANISHQ

Prepared by
Dr. Dheeraj Sharma,
Indian Institute of Management, Ahmedabad

Tanishq, a Tata product, launched itself in the jewelry market in 1995 under the brand Titan. It was initially involved in manufacturing, and in 2000 it entered the market as a jewelry retailer. Setting up a jewelry retail store in a country like India was indeed a challenge. Traditionally, India has had a very large unorganized jewelry market. Most of the Indian customers visit the local jewelers for making gold purchases. There was no concept of branded jewelry and gold was sold on the basis of trust. There were a lot of malpractices involved in selling gold to the consumers in this process. For example, gold could not be sold by the customer at the same price at which he/she was buying it.[30]

The current value of India's gold jewelry is estimated to be around ₹70,000 crore and is dominated by the local jewelers. Tata realized the potential of a trusted jewelry brand in India and decided to open Tanishq stores across the country. Tanishq competed with the unorganized gold jewelers by providing the customers with pure gold jewelry and by charging accurate prices. It did not apply a gold rate to the stones embedded in the jewelry, and it charged the same rate for selling or buying gold. Tanishq charged about 20–30 percent of the price of the gold purchased as its making charges, and the local jewelers did not have any fixed rate. Tanishq sold not only traditional Indian jewelry but also created designs for the modern working class. Also, it not only catered to the niche customers, but with its varied ranges of jewelry, it catered to customers of all sorts. Besides providing authentic jewelry, Tanishq also provided its customers with various discounts and offers during festivals. Its customer loyalty program called *Annutara* had been successful in maintaining its customer footfall. Until December 2011, Tanishq had 133 stores across 76 cities in India.[31] Fair practices and innovative marketing strategies helped Tanishq in building its customer base. Tanishq is an example in the retail market that shows how a firm could change/alter consumer's attitude and practices in making purchases.

It was realized that the elite feel of the Tanishq stores created a resistance from the rural customers in making purchases from it. The rural consumers contribute to about 60% of the total gold purchased in the country, and the value of the jewelry market in the rural and semi-rural areas is about ₹42,000 crores.[32] To capitalize the business opportunities in the rural areas, Tata came up with another gold jewelry store called "Gold Plus." These stores sold only 22 carat, and 18 carat traditional Indian jewelry, tailored for the rural demands. Today, Gold Plus is spread across 29 stores across six states, and it is the largest gold jewelry chain in Tamilnadu.[33] Tata is expanding its business in the domestic and the international markets.

Questions

1. Given the presence of small and independent jewelry shops in every corner of India, how can Tanishq compete with them?
2. Small and independent jewelers offer significantly more customization of jewelry, how can Tanishq increase its ability to customize?
3. Lastly, compared to small and independent jewelers, jewelry-making charges of Tanishq are significantly high. How can Tanishq overcome this price disadvantage?
4. Given that people of varied incomes and backgrounds live in cities, should Tata open Gold Plus chains in cities as well?

15 Retailing

KEY TERMS

LO 1

retailing all the activities directly related to the sale of goods and services to the ultimate consumer for personal, nonbusiness use

LO 2

independent retailers retailers owned by a single person or partnership and not operated as part of a larger retail institution

chain stores stores owned and operated as a group by a single organization

franchise the right to operate a business or to sell a product

gross margin the amount of money the retailer makes as a percentage of sales after the cost of goods sold is subtracted

LO 3

department store a store housing several departments under one roof

buyer a department head who selects the merchandise for his or her department and may also be responsible for promotion and personnel

specialty store a retail store specializing in a given type of merchandise

supermarket a large, departmentalized, self-service retailer that specializes in food and some nonfood items

hypermarket combination stores of a supermarket and a department store

scrambled merchandising the tendency to offer a wide variety of nontraditional goods and services under one roof

drugstore a retail store that stocks pharmacy-related products and services as its main draw

convenience store a miniature supermarket, carrying only a limited line of high-turnover convenience goods

KEY CONCEPTS

LO 1

Discuss the importance of retailing in the Indian economy. Retailing plays a vital role in the Indian economy for two main reasons. First, retailing industry is one of the largest employers in the country, employing about 4 crore people. Second, the contribution of retail industry to the country's GDP is quite significant at around 30 percent. However, Indian retail industry is largely unorganized, with organized retail having a share of just 6.5 percent of the total retail market.

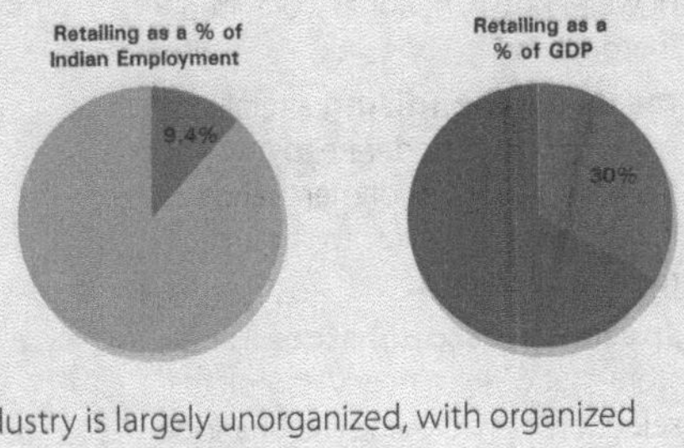

© CENGAGE LEARNING 2011

LO 2

Explain the dimensions by which retailers can be classified. Many different kinds of retailers exist. A retail establishment can be classified according to its ownership, level of service, product assortment, and price. On the basis of ownership, retailers can be broadly differentiated as independent retailers, chain stores, or franchise outlets. The level of service retailers provide can be classified along a continuum of high to low. Retailers also classify themselves by the breadth and depth of their product assortments; some retailers have concentrated product assortments, whereas others have extensive product assortments. Last, general price levels also classify a store, from discounters offering low prices to exclusive specialty stores where high prices are the norm. Retailers use these latter three variables to position themselves in the marketplace.

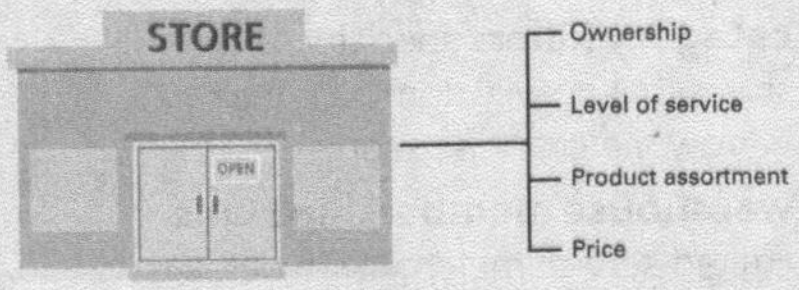

© CENGAGE LEARNING 2011

LO 3

Describe the major types of retail operations. The major types of retail stores are department stores, specialty retailers, supermarkets, hypermarkets, drugstores, convenience stores, discount stores, and restaurants. Department stores carry a wide assortment of shopping and specialty goods, are organized into relatively independent departments, and offset higher prices by emphasizing customer service and décor. Specialty retailers typically carry a narrower but deeper assortment of merchandise, emphasizing distinctive products and a high level of customer service. *Supermarkets* are large self-service retailers that offer a wide variety of food products and some nonfood items. Hypermarkets are combination stores of a supermarket and a department store. Drugstores are retail formats that sell mostly prescription and over-the-counter medications, health and beauty aids, cosmetics, and specialty items. Convenience stores carry a limited line of high-turnover convenience goods. Discount stores offer low-priced general merchandise and consist of four types: full-line discounters, specialty discount retailers, warehouse clubs, and off-price retailers. Finally, restaurants straddle the line between the retailing and services industries; although restaurants sell a product, food and drink, to final consumers, they can also be considered service marketers because they provide consumers with the service of preparing food and sometimes table service.

LO 4

Discuss nonstore retailing techniques. Nonstore retailing, which is shopping outside a store setting, has four major categories. Kiosks are small, freestanding pavilion, used for the purpose of sales, promotion activities, or giving information. Automatic vending uses machines to offer products for sale. In direct retailing, the sales transaction occurs in a home setting, typically through door to door sales or party plan selling. Direct marketing refers to the techniques used to get consumers

discount store a retailer that competes on the basis of low prices, high turnover, and high volume

full-line discount store a retailer that offers consumers very limited service and carries a broad assortment of well-known, nationally branded "hard goods"

mass merchandising a retailing strategy using moderate to low prices on large quantities of merchandise and lower levels of service to stimulate high turnover of products

specialty discount store a retail store that offers a nearly complete selection of single-line merchandise and uses self-service, discount prices, high volume, and high turnover

category killers specialty discount stores that heavily dominate their narrow merchandise segment

warehouse membership clubs limited-service merchant wholesalers that sell a limited selection of brand name appliances, household items, and groceries on a cash-and-carry basis to members, usually small businesses and groups

off-price retailer a retailer that sells at prices 25 percent or more below traditional department store prices because it pays cash for its stock and usually doesn't ask for return privileges

factory outlet an off-price retailer that is owned and operated by a manufacturer

to buy from their homes or place of business. Those techniques include direct mail, catalog retailing, telemarketing, and electronic retailing, such as television shopping and online retailing.

LO 5 **Define *franchising* and describe its two basic forms.** Franchising is a continuing relationship in which a franchisor grants to a franchisee the business rights to operate or to sell a product. Modern franchising takes two basic forms. In product and trade name franchising, a dealer agrees to buy or sell certain products or product lines from a particular manufacturer or wholesaler. Business format franchising is an ongoing business relationship in which a franchisee uses a franchisor's name, format, or method of business in return for several types of fees.

LO 6 **List the major tasks involved in developing a retail marketing strategy.** Retail management begins with defining the target market, typically on the basis of demographic, geographic, or psychographic characteristics. After determining the target market, retail managers must develop the six variables of the retailing mix: product, promotion, place, price, presentation, and personnel.

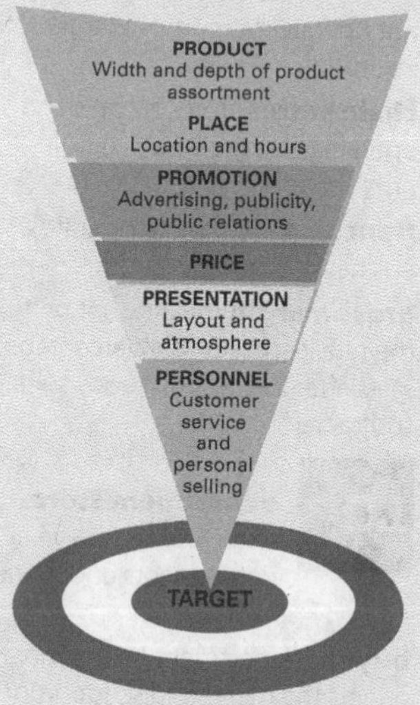

LO 7 **Describe new developments in retailing.** Three major trends are evident in retailing today. First, adding interactivity to the retail environment is one of the most popular strategies in retailing in recent years. Small retailers as well as national chains are using interactivity to involve customers and set themselves apart from the competition. Second, m-commerce (mobile e-commerce) is gaining in popularity. M-commerce enables consumers to purchase goods and services using wireless mobile devices, such as mobile telephones, pagers, PDAs, and handheld computers.

LO 4 **nonstore retailing** shopping without visiting a store

kiosks small, freestanding pavilion, used for the purpose of sales, promotion activities, or giving information

automatic vending the use of machines to offer goods for sale

direct retailing the selling of products by representatives who work door-to-door, office-to-office, or at home sales parties

direct marketing (direct response marketing) techniques used to get consumers to make a purchase from their home, office, or other nonretail setting

telemarketing the use of the telephone to sell directly to consumers

online retailing a type of shopping available to consumers with personal computers and access to the Internet

LO 5 **franchisor** the originator of a trade name, product, methods of operation, and so on that grants operating rights to another party to sell its product

franchisee an individual or business that is granted the right to sell another party's product

LO 6 **retailing mix** a combination of the six Ps—product, place, promotion, price, presentation, and personnel—to sell goods and services to the ultimate consumer

product offering the mix of products offered to the consumer by the retailer; also called the *product assortment* or *merchandise mix*

destination stores stores that consumers purposely plan to visit

atmosphere the overall impression conveyed by a store's physical layout, decor, and surroundings

CASE 4

Crossword–Customer Relationship Management*

In the morning of January 15, 2005, Sriram sat in his office in Mumbai awaiting Aniyan and Balaji. Aniyan had joined Crossword about nine months ago. Balaji looked after the Book Reward Programme (BRP), the customer loyalty programme of the store chain. Sriram had received the Customer Relationship Assessment Survey Report that was conducted three months ago. While waiting for the report his thoughts started drifting and his face broke into a smile as he reflected back. It seemed like yesterday, when he and his wife Anita founded Crossword along with a young team for India Book House limited with the vision of revolutionizing the concept of book retailing in India. The first Crossword store had opened in October 1992 at Mahalaxmi[2], Mumbai. The chain was later bought by K Raheja Corporation that also owned Shopper's Stop, India's leading lifestyle department store chain. Within two years of starting, Crossword had featured in Advertising Age International, USA, as one of the marketing superstars, whereas the Bookseller, UK, had described it as being on the cutting edge of retailing in India. He was happy with the report that Crossword was perceived as the country's leading bookstore with an image higher than all other book retailers on all parameters. However, the BRP was an area of concern. The programme had more than 60,000 members, but number of active BRP members was only 25,000. A re-activation was urgently required for the survival of the BRP programme. He had asked Aniyan and Balaji to assess the factors causing this phenomenon and to suggest measures for improving the BRP programme. His reverie was interrupted with a knock on the door. Aniyan and Balaji entered the office with the much awaited plan.

C4.1 Company

In 2005, Crossword had a turnover of about ₹59 crore[3]. Its nearest rival was a Chennai-based retailer with stores in Chennai, Kolkata and Bangalore. It projected a sale of ₹75 crore in 2004–05[4]. The other competitor, by contrast, had about ₹1.0 crore of business annually.[5] Crossword was one of India's fastest growing bookstores. It had twenty stores in Mumbai, Bangalore, Ahmedabad, Gurgaon, Pune, Vadodara, Kolkata, Chennai, and Hyderabad. (Exhibit C4.1). Twelve of these stores were franchised. Crossword had been able to change the way customers bought book by designing large, spacious, well laid out stores, with bright cheerful interiors that encouraged people to stay and browse. The stores were located centrally for the customers to reach easily. They were part of a shopping centres or malls, mostly on the high streets. Besides these large stores (5,000–10,000 sq. ft.), Crossword also used a smaller format stores(750–1000 sq. ft.) called Crossword Corner (CC) that were located to provide higher accessibility to customers. They were situated mostly as a part of larger stores that were proximous and attracted large number of shoppers from the vicinity. It was trying to tie up with large lifestyle stores such as Westside and Pantaloon which also offered multiple shopping choices. (A few of the CCs were already operating at some Shoppers' Stop and Piramyd outlets.) It was planning to set up CCs at railway stations and airports. CCs had been a successful concept that achieved 100 per cent return on capital employed in the first year of its operation.

Crossword was planned to be as a centre for the community. It aimed to be a place of cultural and social interaction where shoppers gravitated to be informed, entertained and enlightened. This was the core philosophy that would determine the way business would be carried out at the store. This reflected in its vision, mission and pledge (Exhibit C4.2). It organised book reading sessions, discussions and debates on varied subjects from literature and art and other general interest topics like child sexual abuse, war and peace, business and management, travel, parenting and health. Among the numerous writers who had visited the store were Arundhati Roy, Vikram Chandra, Vikram Seth, Tara Deshpande, Kiran Nagarkar, Andrew Motion, Michele Roberts, Sashi Tharoor, Shobha De, Charles Handy, Tarla Dalal and Jack Canfield. Promotional events included pictionary contests, quizzes, slide shows and the annual affair with Santa and his elves. Ian Anderson of Jethro Tull had also

* Case prepared by Prof. Piyush Kumar Sinha and Ms. Vandana Sood, Indian Institute of Management, Ahmedabad. The case is prepared as a basis for class discussion rather than to illustrate either effective or ineffective handling of an administrative situation.

[2] An upper strata locality
[3] 1 crore = 10 million
[4] The Chennai based store dealt in many other product categories besides the categories dealt by Crossword.
[5] The Hindu Business Line, "Book Store Boom", Aditi De, Internet Edition, March 29,2004

EXHIBIT C4.1

Crossword Situated in Cities of India

performed at Crossword. "While we do crossword puzzles for fun, they are also a learning experience. The name Crossword was chosen to reflect the fun and learning experience of a visit to the store. The name embodies our vision as a place and space for people who seek information, knowledge or just the pleasure of reading", replied Sriram on asking for the choice of the store name. Many families who normally would not think of visiting bookstores had started visiting Crossword on a regular basis.

Merchandise and Store Layout

Over the years, Crossword had become a destination store for books, magazines, music, CD-ROMS, toys and stationery. It not only offered a wide range of products, but created an ambience that would get the customer to spend more time, and money at the store. It believed in the WW (wallet and watch) concept that when the store made customers spend more time, likelihood of a sale increased. It encouraged the customers to enjoy a relaxing atmosphere, or to simply unwind during a break from work or just browse through its collection. The store created value through a model in which the customer was the focal point. (Exhibit C4.3).

The merchandise mix was standardised across all stores which was decided by the corporate team in Mumbai. Every outlet had five mandatory categories—

EXHIBIT C4.2

Vision, Mission and Pledge of Crossword

CROSSWORD

Our Vision

To be a dominant network of profitable community centers,
where people gravitate,
to be informed, to be entertained, and to be enlightened,
led by books and related products.

CROSSWORD

Our Mission

- To fulfill the information, knowledge and leisure needs of the community profitably through the retailing of books and related products. To be the dominant retailer in our category with at least 30% market share in the markets we operate in.
- To be customer focused in every aspect of the business. To build life-long relationships with customers.
- To build the reading habit, and to promote books. To nurture and reward the best of Indian writing.
- To create retail environments that are oases in the urban jungle - friendly, fun, relaxing and rewarding.
- To provide a platform for the cultural and social interaction of the community - to be a community center.

CROSSWORD

Our Pledge

Today and every day
I'll help make at least
One person's day,
For them to say
Thank God for Crossword

CROSSWORD

Our Values

1. Fun: We will build stores that are fun, enjoyable spaces to be in. We will build an organisation that people enjoy being with and working in.
2. Learning: We will create stores and an organisation that enable continuous learning.
3. Excellence: We will constantly strive for excellence in everything we do.
4. Fairness: We will always act fairly, with respect for all people, and with a win-win attitude.
5. Integrity: We will always conduct ourselves and act with integrity.
6. Social Responsibility: We will be socially responsible.
7. Make a Difference: We will work to make a difference to our customers, our stakeholders, our community and ourselves.

books, music, CDs, toys, and magazines. The other categories common to all stores were toys, stationery, gifts, magazines and CDs. The mix with respect to the titles and albums were ascertained based on sales and demand. The floor plan was decided in consultation with the in-house interior decorator. Books were allocated 60% of the floor space. The rest 40% of the space was occupied by other categories that were city specific. For instance, in Ahmedabad, the music section occupied 50% of the non book space. Each store had a store manager, department owner and customer service executive. The department owners took care of the departments and reported to the store manager. They were assisted by respective buyers and merchandisers. While the buyers were product specialists, the merchandisers were responsible for the sales targets.

For a target of ₹10 lakh[6] per year for a particular category, the category managers at any given time had to stock merchandise worth ₹2.5 lakh.[7]

Crossword stores had been laid out to encourage free and leisurely shopping. On arrival, the shopper was exposed to the displays of the latest offerings on the bestsellers/new releases of books and music. Following this, in the same aisle continued the other popular fare that included novels by Indian authors, crime thrillers, romance novels along with non-fiction like self-improvement books, management books and CD ROMs. This section was followed by the more serious and discerning palate such as philosophy, history, politics and books in local language. The third section featured specialty books on culinary, gardening beauty and fitness. The Gifts section with its wide array of stationery and greeting cards among other trinkets was kept in between the two sections. The arrangement of merchandise in one of the stores is shown in Exhibit C4.4. More than 90 percent of the shoppers were aware that Crossword was more than a bookstore and sold other merchandise as well.

The children's section was at the end of the store. It ensured that the shoppers traversed the entire length of the store and had a good look browsing at whatever the store had to offer. The books were juxtaposed to the toy and puzzles that were displayed to attract the child. The music section ran along the book section. The cash counter near the entrance signified the end of purchase. Impulse purchase merchandise like chocolates, magazines, newspapers and teabags were displayed prominently near the counter. The traffic flow could take three directions. One that led from books to the stationery and then to the children's books/

[6] 1 lakh – 0.10 million

[7] http://www.etstrategicmarketing.com/smjuly-aug3/art9.html

EXHIBIT C4.3

The Crossword Value Delivery Model

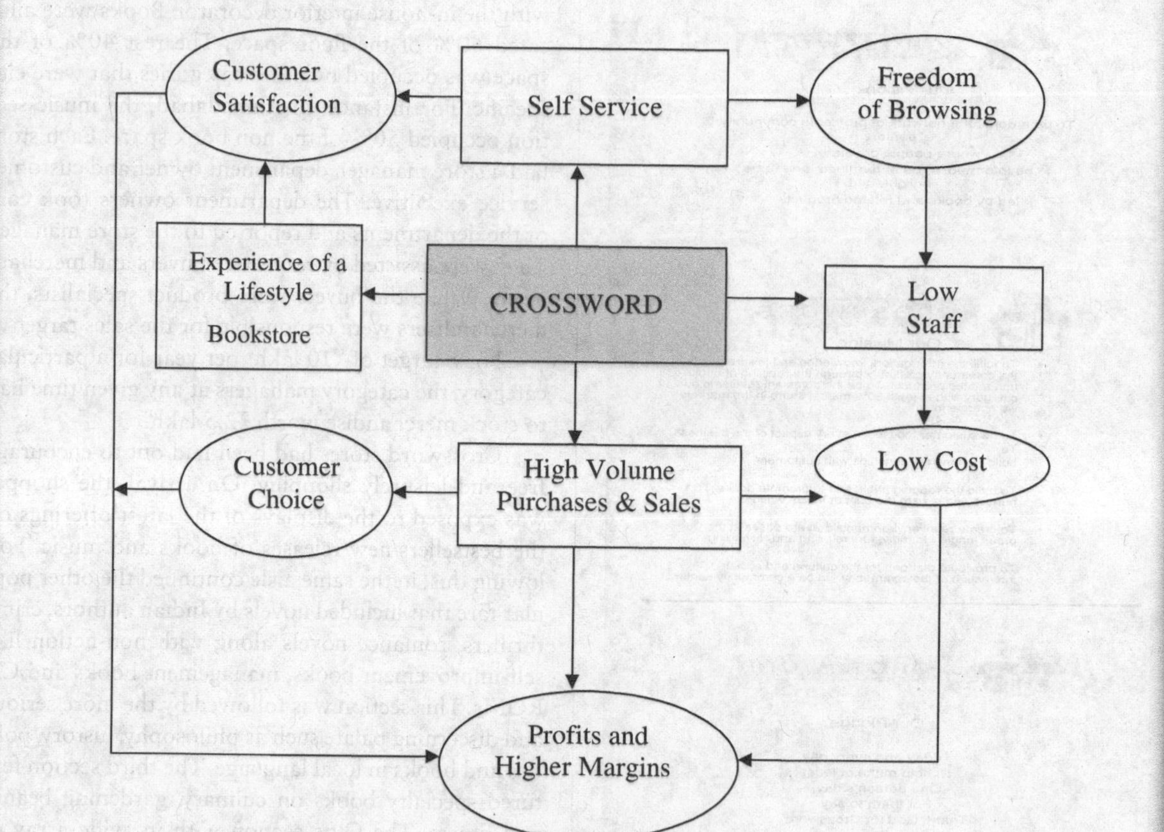

toys' section. The other followed the path from the entry to the music section towards the stationery and then to the children's' books/toys section. The third less frequented flow of traffic went into the Magazine and CD-ROM section. All routes ended into the children section and made the customer walk through the entire length of the store. At the same time, this section was away from the place of serious reader.

Store Ambience

Crossword provided a comfortable and pleasant ambience to its shoppers. The stores were brightly lit and clear signs defined the racks. Tables and chairs were provided to encourage browsing. The shelves in the middle of the store were not more than three to four feet in height. This made it convenient for all customers to access the merchandise as also a shopper could see across the store from the entrance. This gave a feeling of spaciousness to the store. The colours within the store were an extension of the basic Crossword theme colours. In the beginning the store followed a combination of yellow and black. The new stores had a softer colour combination. The spacing and utilisation of colours was well balanced that merged unobtrusively into the fixtures and the other elements of the interiors (Exhibit C4.5). The lighting of the store was mild and unobtrusive. It allowed for no hidden dark spaces and was conducive for reading and browsing the merchandise. Separate lights on the aisles gave the impact of a larger space. There were also adjustable reading lights above the racks that could be tilted to allow the reader to focus the light better. Light instrumental music played at the store. There was no apparent attempt at creating a deliberate olfactory experience for the visitor in terms of fragrances and scents. The only scent that sometimes pervaded

EXHIBIT C4.4
Merchandise Display

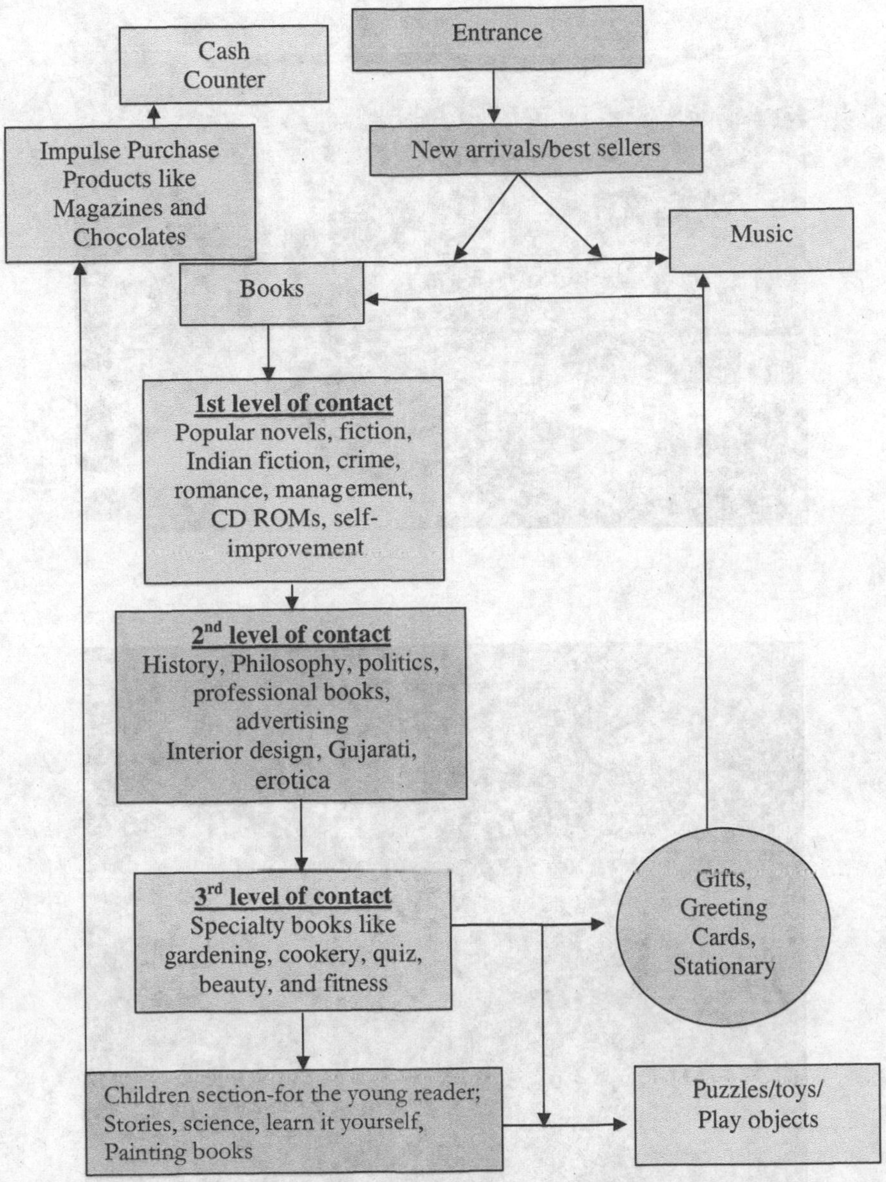

into the surroundings was the fragrance of the brews being prepared at the coffee shop in the store. The fixtures were aimed at enhancing the interactive experience of the shopper at the store. These interaction points included listening posts, TVs and pay phones. The wall had white texture that did not have a differentiating finish. The flooring in older store was a pleasant cream and brown. The floor tiles were shiny and polished well. Some shoppers found it uncomfortable in walking and standing for long. In the new stores the floor was carpeted. The spacing between the bookstands and the wall shelves was adequate for two shoppers to stand back to back without contact. The spacing between aisles was also adequate for walking

EXHIBIT C4.5

Photographs of Old and New Stores

unhindered by any fixtures unless the crowd was particularly heavy. Several books were kept at lower levels. The staff was alert to assist those browsing and picking books from these shelves.

Crossword had uniquely designed carry bags and pushcarts. These were placed strategically throughout the store for easy accessibility when the shoppers decided to take them for carrying their purchases. The visibility of all the signs and displays was ensured through careful placement based on space height and lighting considerations. There were various posters and portraits placed at strategic locations all over store. The posters guided the customers. They were witty ("SHOUT for help. This isn't a library"). The portraits of legends from across the fields of art, literature and politics were placed on the walls. Signs informing the latest sales figures of popular books were kept near the particular rack throughout the store. These were changed frequently depending upon the sales trend during that particular period. On many shelves the customers could find books recommended by Sriram. They carried a strip with his signature and promise of return of the book when the reader did not find it worthy. (Exhibit C4.6).

EXHIBIT C4.6
A Strip with Sriram's Signature Carried in the Book Recommended by Him With The Promise of Return if Not Found Readworthy

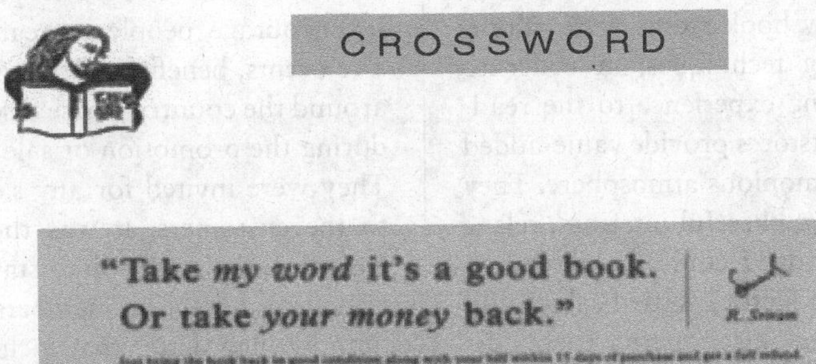

Sales Strategy

The sales strategy was designed to enable the shoppers in enjoying buying at the store. It strongly believed that sales were a definite output when the support to the shoppers was provided correctly. The key result areas for the store personnel, called Customer Support Executives, included 5 "S": Service, Sales, Stock, Section, and Support to the team. The team leaders and the store in-charge were also evaluated for the 6th 'S', Statutories. The shopping process was not to be interfered- by store personnel unless they were approached. They were responsible for the sections allocated to them for maintenance as well as for a pleasant shopping experience. Help desks were kept at several places. These personnel at the desks were staffed who could access the information on the availability and location of the merchandise through the computer. Every desk had a 'computer' that was connected to the main database. They could also register the request when the desired merchandise was not available. Customers were later informed when the merchandise arrived at the store.

Services

Crossword offered several services to the customers. Services like Dial-a-book, Fax-a-book and Email-a-book enabled customers to shop from their homes. The unobtrusively helpful staffs assisted them in finding the right book, the right CD or the right gift for the right occasion. The Crossword Gift Vouchers were popular. The store had a 'return, exchange and refunds' policy. The customer could return merchandise within fifteen days, although conditions applied. In most cases the replacements were made unconditionally. The store offered to exchange even those products that were bought and then gifted. The receiver of the gift could also ask for an exchange. The Cafe within the stores and the unique store experience made it easy and enjoyable for customers to shop at Crossword. The study had brought out that despite communicating the awareness of the additional services provided by Crossword was low. On an average only about one fourth of the customers are aware of the additional services provided.

C4.2 Book Retailing: The Indian Scenario

In India, the book retailing business was going through a major revolution. While the current market size of the industry was estimated to be around

₹3,000–6,000 crore. It was expected to grow by 15 per cent per annum. The store operated on a 40 percent gross margin. Consumers had started favouring stores that delivered experiences that appealed to their senses, hearts, and minds. Three trends that supported this belief were individualism, globalization and the symbolic experience.[8] From a tiny bookstore around the corner, the industry was witnessing stores with enticing layouts and service. Traditionally shopping for books was restricted only to book-lovers. Thus, browsing through these bookstores was seen as a book-lover's hobby. New book stores were adopting experiential marketing techniques, in order to offer a holistic book-buying experience to the readers. Besides books the bookstores provide value-added services that created a harmonious atmosphere. They offered comfortable seating, cheerful interiors, relaxing atmosphere, air-conditioned comfort, better layout, more space, nil "brush factor", little baskets and trolleys to hold books They also offered their customers a café, reading tables and chairs, comfortable corners and even toilet facilities. All of these ensured that the customers were able to browse in comfort for hours. Thus, positioned as lifestyle bookstores, they aimed to give their consumers a complete 'experience' encouraging them to stay and browse. The share of the new format stores was estimated to be no more than 15 percent. They operated with a net income of less than 5 percent.

Although mom and pop stores dealing in merchandise other than book did provide high level of personalised service, book retailers had done very little in terms of customising products or value-adding to their offering. Customer Relationship Management was at a nascent stage. Most of the retailers who had CRM initiatives did not collect or analysed customer data on a regular basis. In many cases the data was either just the addresses of the customers which were not updated or purchase data that was seldom used for developing strategies. They were aware that customer information capture and intelligent and rigorous warehousing and mining of transaction behaviour was a critical success factor in retailing. They had launched several programmes, based on the concept of rewarding customers for continuing patronage through a combination of priority services, price-offs or discounts, product previews and so on. Most such schemes involved both an entry fee and points system, with a number of points earned depending on the value of the purchase. Shoppers' Stop's First Citizen Club, Ebony's Ebony program, Vivek's Akshya, Bharat Petroleum's Petro card and Fleet Card, were some of the successful loyalty programs. However, most loyalty programme did not go beyond offering discounts on purchases. They seldom used them to build long lasting relationships with customers.

The Book Rewards Programme

Book Rewards Programme (BRP) was started by Crossword in 1999. The program offered rewards to encourage people to read more—through exclusive events, benefits, offers and discounts at all stores around the country. These discounts were offered only during the promotion or sale and not the year round. They were invited for any sale before it was opened to the customers. It was the only programme that gave accumulated points statement on the bill with every purchase. The members were sent "eWords", a monthly newsletter that included over 50 reviews of new books, events and best-seller lists. The marketing team had the task of coming up with a certain number of events at every store for the year. Innovative initiatives encouraged customers to frequent the store more and even take part in activities. The continuous collected feedback from the customer resulting in return, "the customers voting with their feet". Information from the Book Rewards Programme was shared with franchisees. The benefits and terms and conditions of BRP are given in Exhibit C4.7.

The basic qualifications for becoming a Book Rewards Member were "Knowing the Alphabet" and a payment of an enrolment fee of ₹150. The customer was required to fill up a Book Rewards Customer Profile and hand it over at the cash counter. A temporary card was issued immediately. The form was then processed within a minimum time period of two weeks. The customer was sent a Book Rewards Kit which includes a welcome letter, a membership booklet and the Book Rewards Card. The card operated on the principle of "The More You Read, The More You Gain". For every ₹40 spent at any Crossword outlet, a Book Rewards Member earned one point. So, for example, when a customer spent ₹100 at the store, two points were added. The extra sum of ₹20 was carried forward and added to reflect in the total points tally. The card could be used only after the customer had accumulated a minimum of 100 points. The card could be presented at any Crossword outlet to get

[8] http://www.etretailbiz.com/sept04/booksmart.htm

EXHIBIT C4.7

The Book Rewards Programme

Benefits

- Reward points on purchases - 1 point for every ₹40 spent
- Information on in-store offers and promotions
- Online checking of Points Balance
- Priority in buying/ordering new releases as well as events at the store
- Free subscription to "eWords"
- Exclusive offers
- Associate Membership Cards
- Gift-A-Membership

Terms and Conditions

- Benefits and offers available through program partners may change or be withdrawn without prior intimation. Crossword will not be responsible for any liability arising from such situations or from the use of such offers.
- No two offers or discounts can be clubbed unless specified otherwise.
- A BRP membership number can be entered against an institutional sale transaction only if full rates are paid against merchandise purchased. In other words, if any discount is afforded on an institutional sales order, you will not get Book Rewards points against it.
- The Book Rewards Membership is for individuals only—it is not a corporate card.
- A membership can be revoked or refused if a member/customer is involved in any act of fraud, shoplifting or cheating.
- Crossword reserves the right to revise terms and conditions governing the Book Rewards Membership without prior notice.
- Crossword reserves the right to modify or terminate the Book Rewards Programme at any given time. It may also decide to terminate membership for a period of time as decided by the management.
- Any dispute arising would fall under the Mumbai jurisdiction.

Source: http://www.crosswordbookstores.com/html/brp- how%20brp%20operates%20page1 .asp\

an update on points accumulated. Each point had a redemption value of ₹1. Customer started collecting points the moment they had enrolled. The points could be redeemed against Crossword gift vouchers and could be used to buy books, CD-ROMs, music or any other item available at the stores. These vouchers could also be gifted. The members also received exclusive offers, discounts and benefits like special tie-ups with various companies and their brands for better deals. As an original member, the customer became a Principal card holder. But the benefits of this program could be passed on to others as well. This could be done by enrolling the immediate family as Associate Members. A processing fee of ₹100 for each additional member was charged. The membership could also be gifted to friends. For this, Book Rewards Customer Profile of the nominee had to be filled up along with the enrolment fee of ₹150. The nominee received a separate Book Rewards Card and became a Principal card holder. The Associate Members was entitled to the same offers and privileges as Principal card holders. However, all points earned accrued to the Principal card holder and could be redeemed by the member. The members could also check their points tally by visiting the company website by entering their 16 digit card number and the date of birth. The cash memo issued on each purchase stated the current points accrued so far. The membership was valued for two-years. It was extended automatically when the member made a purchase at least once every two years. The programme was operational at all Crossword outlets. Purchases made at any Crossword outlets were added to the Book Rewards balance of the customers.

C4.3 BRP Member Profile

The BRP consisted of 60,000 members. A large number of the members were well-educated. Postgraduates and MBAs constituted the largest segment. There were more males than female members (1000:555). This was largely because the primary membership would be in the name of male members of the family. Number of members married were same as unmarried (999:1000). The store attracted a wide variety of customers. The top ten occupations of BRP members were executives (11.80%), top and middle level management (8.87%), IT professionals (8.54%), students (8.16%), home-maker (7.42%), self employed (7.39%), engineers (6.84%), doctors (6.62%), consultants (5.47%) and academicians (4.25%). A large number (22%–40%) of members came from outside the cities where the stores were located. About 65% of the members bought on Friday, Saturday and Sunday. November (20%) and August (12%) witnessed higher sales. February and March were lean months contributing just about 2% of the total sales. It was noticed that these months were generally lean months in book retail. Other months showed equal proportion (9%) of sales. Although there was no established rationale, it was thought that the visiting NRIs contributed to higher sales in November.

The BRP members contributed 32 percent to the total sales of Crossword. It ranged from 28% to 55% at different stores. Franchised stores contributed 40% of the total BRP sales. Among them the two leading stores were Ahmedabad (15%) and Bangalore (11%). The largest contribution (35%) came from one its own stores in Mumbai. Of the total BRP sales in 2004, 74% came from products priced within ₹500. Products priced between ₹225 and ₹350 contributed 25% of the total BRP sales. About 10% of the members bought products valued more than ₹1000, some of them (1% of total) spending as much as ₹4000 in the year.

Books contributed 68% of the total BRP sales. Children and Education (18%), fiction (15%), audio-visual (13%), management/business (10%) and CD-ROM (7%) and family, home and practical interest (7%) were leading categories of books. It was observed that 60% of the sales came from books priced upto ₹350 or lower. The fiction books priced at ₹350 and below accounted for 75% of the total fiction book sales to BRP members.

The average purchase value of the BRP members was ₹2500. This value was 2.6 times more than the average bill value of other customers. (Exhibit C4.8)

Based on the bill value BRP members belonged to five segments:

Crossword Tribes (10%): They represented customers who made large number of purchase visits. They had high cumulative annual bills as well as high average bill amount of ₹400 per visit or ₹1000 in case of 2 visits to the store. They contributed 48 percent of the total BRP sales.

Crossword Core (12%): These customers made frequent visits to the store. They also purchased a lot. Their average bill value ranged between ₹200 and ₹400 per visit. They contributed 17 percent of the total BRP sales.

Crossword Wannabes (19%): They represented customers with less than ₹4000 cumulative bill for the year, with an average bill value ranging between ₹100 and ₹200. They contributed 4 percent of the total BRP sales.

Crossword Eager Beavers (14%): They represented customers who purchased less than 10 items with a cumulative bill of ₹500–1000 for the year. They contributed 5 percent of the total BRP sales.

Crossword Climbers (45%): These customers had a cumulative bill value of less than ₹500

EXHIBIT C4.8
Average Bill Size

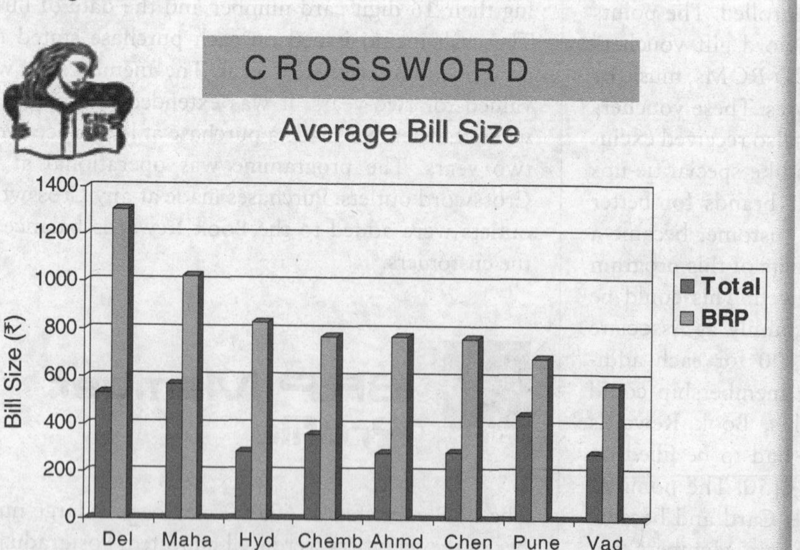

for the year. They purchased less than 5 items and contributed 26 percent of the total BRP sales.

Customer perception of Crossword and BRP Customers visited many stores to buy their books. Different stores posed as competition in different cities. Oxford was the only major chain stores present in city where Crossword operated. The major competitors in each of the cities are given in (Exhibit C4.9). Almost 70% of the customers bought from other stores, whereas 5% of the customers had also bought from international stores, mainly Borders and Barnes and Nobles. Crossword was perceived as a leading store well ahead of the local competitors, though it scored lower than international competitors. Customers found the store wanting in terms of prices and the arrangement of merchandise. Although on the overall experience it scored very high, even those who had rated the store as excellent expressed concern about value for money and price (**Exhibit C4.10**). BRP members rated the store higher than the walk-in customers on all parameters. In terms of loyalty measures, Crossword scored higher than even the international retailers in all aspects. These measures indicated that 26% of the customers were committed, 56% would recommend, 60% would continue to buy and 41% intended to increase the purchase from the store. About 80% of the customers indicated that they were truly loyal (high commitment and strong urge to continue). Only 17% felt trapped (low commitment but strong urge to continue).

Where are the Worms in Our Books?

Sriram was puzzled. "We have one of the largest loyalty programmes in the industry. The members yield much higher return than the walk-in customers. They also rate the store higher. We score well in terms of loyalty measure. Still we have just 40 percent of members who are active (purchased in one year) and contributing. Where is the worm?" he asked Aniyan and Balaji. I can see two reasons for this", replied Aniyan, "One, if you look at the overall importance attached to factors that lead to store loyalty, BRP plays a marginal role. Customers seem to come to us and even register for the programme because we do not seem to have any competition. The store, its overall quality, is the most important driver. Communication seems to be the next factor. BRP is not found to be a significant driver". At this point of time he showed one of the slides of the presentation of the findings of the survey (Exhibit C4.11). Balaji was not convinced. "I am not sure if this is due to lack of competition", he argued, "because when you look at the distribution of scores on the scale, while only 11% customers have found it excellent, about 75% of them have found it good (Exhibit C4.12). It could also be because many of them did not have enough experience of the store. We must remember that only 22% of our customers are frequent buyers".

"Let's look at the rating scores on the BRP in more detail. I am sure we would find some clues there. Balaji, could you show those slides that talk specifically of the BRP programme?", requested Sriram. The study had brought out that BRP members among all processes had rated two processes, billing and cashiering and communication, lower than walk-in customers (Exhibit C4.13). They also rated the store lower in almost all aspects of merchandise range and quality. They found the sales personnel very helpful, except in case of their ability to respond to queries. The aspect of display of book was

EXHIBIT C4.9

Customers Visiting Competition Book Stores

% of Crossword customers visited Competition Book Stores

MUMBAI	
A	33%
B	20%
C	8%
D	5%
E	3%

PUNE	
A	25%
B	13%
C	12%
D	11%
E	6%

AHMEDABAD	
A	22%
B	14%
C	9%
D	3%

BARODA	
A	30%
B	14%
C	6%

Only 5 % across the locations had visited the International; stores- BARNES & NOBLE & BORDERS

EXHIBIT C4.10(A)
Image Perceptions

Walk in Vs Loyalty

Top Box% (Excellent rating)	All total	Walk-in	Loyalty
Is a leading bookstore	51	47	69 ↑
Is run by professionals	35	32	52 ↑
Cares about its customers	34	31	50 ↑
Is a store I can trust	34	30	52 ↑
Provides an enjoyable shopping experience	39	37	54 ↑
Is the center of social Et culture interaction	30	30	33
Has a good variety of different types of books	37	35	51 ↑
Is a comfortable place to browse	36	32	60 ↑
Is Hassle free and time efficient	34	32	48 ↑
Prices recently released books competitively	30	29	35
Is uncluttered and well laid out	29	28	32
Has a welcoming and pleasing atmosphere	35	34	36
Provides responsive and personalized service	30	28	36
Understands interests of people and stocks books accordingly	31	30	37

↓↑ *Loyalty significantly lower/ahead than Walk-in*

EXHIBIT C4.10(B)
Image Perceptions

Top Box% (Strongly Agree)	Cross Word	National Benchmark	Benchmark
Is a leading bookstore	51	27 ↓	63
Is run by professionals	35	25 ↓	53 ↑
Cares about its customers	34	20 ↓	55 ↑
Is a store I can trust	34	21 ↓	59 ↑
Provides an enjoyable shopping experience	39	20 ↓	53
Is the center of social & culture interaction	30	15 ↓	28
Has a good variety of different types of books	37	19 ↓	59 ↑
Is a comfortable place to browse	36	19 ↓	44
Is Hassle free and time efficient	34	19 ↓	37
Prices recently released books competitively	30	22 ↓	41
Is uncluttered and well laid out	29	16 ↓	50 ↑
Has a welcoming and pleasing atmosphere	35	19 ↓	38
Provides responsive and personalized service	30	15 ↓	47 ↑
Understands interests and stocks books accordingly	31	17 ↓	50 ↑

↓↑ *Loyalty significantly lower/ahead than Walk-in*

Benchmark significantly lower/ahead than Crossword

not a major concern, though the members had indicated a desire for a better visibility of bestseller and new arrivals. The store feature appealed to them. "I think the major area for concern is the communication with BRP members within the store as well as away from it.," opined Balaji. "We have a low score on the communication on the whole as well as on its adequacy. More importantly, the members have rated

EXHIBIT C4.11

What Drives Loyalty At Crossword

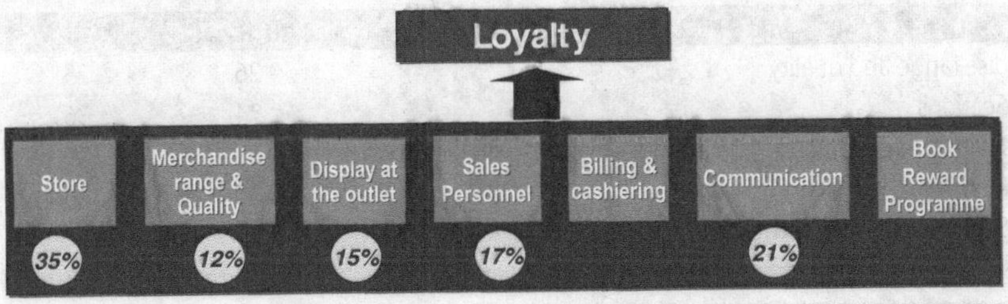

EXHIBIT C4.12

Overall Processes

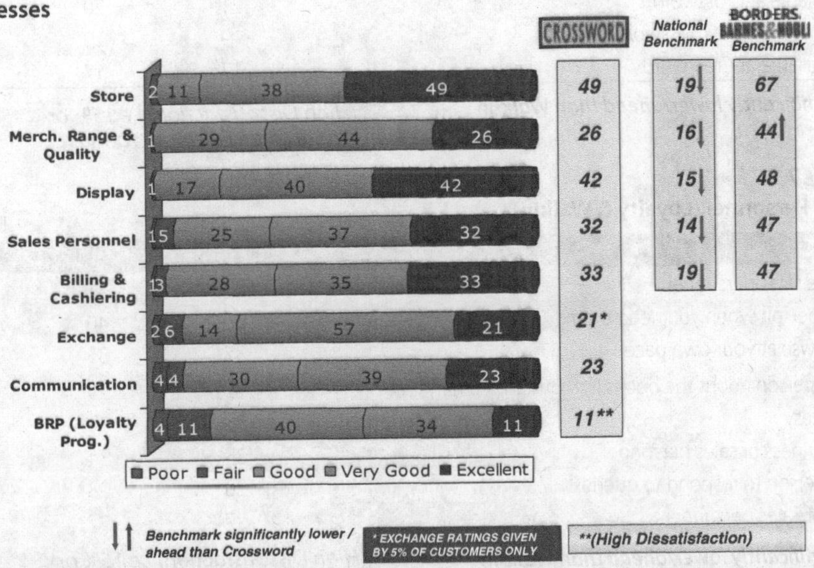

us lower than the walk-ins in terms of the relevance of it. They are not finding value in our communication. You may be right there. But I would say that we need to have a much more strategic view of our BRP programme. It has been five years since the programme began. This is the first real review that we had. In the mean time customer expectations have undergone a sea change", said Aniyan.

Sriram felt as if Aniyan was reading his mind. He said, "I would go by what you are saying Aniyan. We have so far focussed on growth opening new stores. While we may be doing pretty well as a chain, time may have come to also look at consolidating each of our stores. In my opinion, BRP should become the engine of our next phase of growth and cementing our leadership. We have the annual planning meeting scheduled in February. Let's present our strategy and plan for BRP to the Board. I would like to review the report by the end of this month and Balaji, you would have to take the lead in this."

EXHIBIT C4.13(A)

Attributes—Merchandise Range & Quality (Walk In Loyalty)

Top Box Score

	All Total	Walkin	Loyalty
Overall Merchandise range and quality	26	25	32
Range of Topics/Sections	34	36	22*
Selection of titles within each Topic/section in books in the Adult Section	29	29	25
Selection of authors	24	26	13*
Range of Topics/Sections in books in the Children's Section	31	32	24
Selection of titles within each Topic/section in the Childrens Section	29	28	29
Selection of authors in the Children's Section	20	21	15
Availability of new arrivals in books	22	23	20
Availability of best sellers	23	24	21
Range of Toys available at Crossword	24	26	16*
Range of Music available at Crossword	21	20	22
Range of Stationary available at Crossword	19	19	21
Range of Movies available at Crossword	17	17	19

↓↑ ***Loyalty significantly lower/ahead than Walk-in***

***(High Dissatisfaction) i.e 15% or more given Fair/poor ratings**

EXHIBIT C4.13(B)

Attributes—Sales Personnel (Loyalty & Walkin)

Top Box Score

	All Total	Walkin	Loyalty
Overall quality of the sales personnel	32	31	37
Availability of sales person when you need them	40	40	39
Allowing you to browse at your own pace	37	35	48 ↑
Knowledge of sales person about the books and other merchandise	29	29	30*
Politeness and courtesy	35	34	40
Friendliness & helpfulness of sales personnel	35	34	41
Ability of the sales person to respond to queries	28	28	27
Speed of response of Sales personnel	27	27	28

↓↑ ***Loyalty significantly lower/ahead than Walk-in***

***(High Dissatisfaction) i.e 15% or more given Fair/poor ratings**

EXHIBIT C4.13(C)

Attributes- Store—Loyalty & Walkin

Top Box Score

	All Total	Walkin	Loyalty
Overall Quality of Store	49	47	61 ↑
Adequacy of space in the store to allow browsing amongst various sections	45	44	53
Comfort of air conditioning/temperature in the store	35	35	38
Ability to provide adequate lighting in the store to allow for comfortable reading/browsing	32	31	37 ↑
Seating/book reading space inside the store	27*	26*	37* ↑
Seating arrangements to sit and browse through books.	29*	28*	36*
Ability to provide cheerful and warm ambience of the store	32	31	37
Parking arrangements outside the store	18*	18*	18* ↑
Location of the store	28	27	37

↓↑ ***Loyalty significantly lower/ahead than Walk-in***

EXHIBIT C4.13(D)

Attributes—Display Of Books (Store Wise)

Top Box Score

	All Total	Walkin	Loyalty
Overall quality of display of books	42	40	58 ↑
Convenience of arrangement/display of books	43	42	53 ↑
Neatness of arrangement of books	37	35	47 ↑
Shelf planning and layout	26	26	27
Visibility of new arrivals/best sellers	27	28	21
Visibility of recommendations	25	25	26
Attractiveness of display in the store	28	28	29
Overall quality of display of Music & Movies CDs/Cassettes	28	28	30
Overall quality of display of Toys Stationary & Stationary	26	26	26

↓↑ ***Loyalty significantly lower/ahead than Walk-in***

EXHIBIT C4.13(E)

Attributes—Billing and Cashiering (Loyalty and Walkin)

Top Box Score

	All Total	Walkin	Loyalty
Billing and cashiering	33	34	29
Efficiency & helpfulness of the cashier	39	38	45
Accuracy of billing	35	34	43 ↑
Adequacy of billing counters	32	32	32
Ability of cashier to deal with your queries on LBR Programme etc	28	28	29

↓↑ ***Loyalty significantly lower/ahead than Walk-in***

EXHIBIT C4.13(F)

Attributes—Communication (Loyalty/Walkin)

Top Box Score

	All Total	Walkin	Loyalty
Adequacy of communication	20	14	23
Relevance of communication	14	16	13

↓↑ ***Loyalty significantly lower/ahead than Walk-in***

CHAPTER 16 Integrated Marketing Communications

Learning Outcomes

LO 1 Discuss the role of promotion in the marketing mix

LO 2 Discuss the elements of the promotional mix

LO 3 Describe the communication process

LO 4 Explain the goals and tasks of promotion

LO 5 Discuss the AIDA concept and its relationship to the promotional mix

LO 6 Describe the factors that affect the promotional mix

LO 7 Discuss the concept of integrated marketing communications

Few goods or services can survive in the marketplace without effective promotion.

LO 1 The Role of Promotion in the Marketing Mix

Few goods or services, no matter how well developed, priced, or distributed, can survive in the marketplace without effective **promotion**—communication by marketers that informs, persuades, and reminds potential buyers of a product in order to influence an opinion or elicit a response.

promotion communication by marketers that informs, persuades, and reminds potential buyers of a product in order to influence an opinion or elicit a response

promotional strategy a plan for the optimal use of the elements of promotion: advertising, public relations, personal selling, and sales promotion

competitive advantage the unique set of features of a company and its products that are perceived by the target market as significant and superior to the competition

Promotional strategy is a plan for the optimal use of the elements of promotion: advertising, public relations, personal selling, and sales promotion. As Exhibit 16.1 on the next page shows, the marketing manager determines the goals of the company's promotional strategy in light of the firm's overall goals for the marketing mix—product, place (distribution), promotion, and price. Using these overall goals, marketers combine the elements of the promotional strategy (the promotional mix) into a coordinated plan. The promotion plan then becomes an integral part of the marketing strategy for reaching the target market.

The main function of a marketer's promotional strategy is to convince target customers that the goods and services offered provide a competitive advantage over the competition. A **competitive advantage** is the set of unique features of a company and its products that are perceived by the target market as significant and superior to the competition. Such features can include

Note: All the figures in U.S. dollars are converted into rupee using the value $1 = ₹45.

high product quality, rapid delivery, low prices, excellent service, or a feature not offered by the competition. For example, Toyota's Lexus line resonates with customers because it offers Mercedes-quality cars at a lower price. The luxury line implies that the driver is successful enough to buy what she wants and sensible enough to get a great price on it. The savvy, affluent customer position has given Lexus a competitive advantage in the luxury car market in the U.S.[1] With the growing demand for luxury cars in the Indian market, the company plans to launch its Lexus cars in India by 2013.

EXHIBIT 16.1
Role of Promotion in the Marketing Mix

© CENGAGE LEARNING 2011

LO 2 The Promotional Mix

Most promotional strategies use several ingredients—which may include advertising, public relations, sales promotion, and personal selling—to reach a target market. That combination is called the **promotional mix.** The proper promotional mix is the one that management believes will meet the needs of the target market and fulfill the organization's overall goals. The more funds allocated to each promotional ingredient and the more managerial emphasis placed on each technique, the more important that element is thought to be in the overall mix.

Advertising

Almost all companies selling a good or a service use advertising, whether in the form of a multi-million-dollar campaign or a simple classified ad in a newspaper. **Advertising** is any form of impersonal paid communication in which the sponsor or company is identified. Traditional media—such as television, radio, newspapers, magazines, books, direct mail, billboards, and transit cards (advertisements on buses and taxis and at bus stops)—are most commonly used to transmit advertisements to consumers. With the increasing fragmentation of traditional media choices, marketers are using new methods, such as Web sites, e-mail, blogs, and interactive video kiosks located in department stores and supermarkets, to send their advertisements to consumers. However, as the Internet becomes a more vital component of many companies' promotion and marketing mixes, consumers and lawmakers are increasingly concerned about possible violations of consumers' privacy. Social networking sites like Facebook are having to re-examine their privacy policies.

One of the primary benefits of advertising is its ability to communicate to a large number of people at one time. Cost per contact, therefore, is typically very low. Advertising has the advantage of being able to reach the masses (e.g., through national television networks), but it can also be microtargeted to small groups of potential customers, such as television ads on a targeted cable network. Although the *cost per contact* in advertising is very low, the *total cost* to advertise is typically very high. This hurdle tends to restrict advertising on a national basis. Chapter 17 examines advertising in greater detail.

Public Relations

Concerned about how they are perceived by their target markets, organizations often spend large sums to build a positive public image. **Public relations** is the marketing function that evaluates public attitudes, identifies areas within the organization the public may be interested in, and executes a program of action to earn public understanding and acceptance. Public relations helps an organization communicate with its customers, suppliers, stockholders, government officials, employees, and the community in which it operates. Marketers use public relations not only to maintain a positive image but also to educate the public about the

promotional mix the combination of promotional tools—including advertising, public relations, personal selling, and sales promotion—used to reach the target market and fulfill the organization's overall goals

advertising impersonal, one-way mass communication about a product or organization that is paid for by a marketer

public relations the marketing function that evaluates public attitudes, identifies areas within the organization the public may be interested in, and executes a program of action to earn public understanding and acceptance company's goals and objectives, introduce new products, and help support the sales effort.

Times of India's (TOI) "Teach India" program invites volunteers to spend two hours a week to teach the underprivileged children of the society. Based on the skills and availability of the volunteers, they are connected with a non-government organization (NGO), whose primary mission is education. The social initiative helps in bridging the gap between children who are deprived of education and people who have a desire and can contribute some time towards teaching such children. The initiative was launched in 2008 and in its first year itself, the program managed to garner huge response from various sections of the society. Besides 60 NGOs signing up for the cause, corporate organizations, schools, social organizations, and individuals too came forward to support the movement.[2] The initiative has helped TOI in presenting a community-minded and socially responsible image to its readers.

A public relations program can generate favorable **publicity**—public information about a company, product, service, or issue appearing in the mass media as a news item. Organizations generally do not pay for the publicity and are not identified as the source of the information, but they can benefit tremendously from it. Social media sites like Twitter provide publicity, especially for movies, and the amount of tweet publicity surrounding a movie may directly affect ticket sales. A recent study at the University of Texas at Austin discovered that the number of tweets about a certain movie correlated directly with box-office sales. *Zindagi Na Milegi Dobara* generated tremendous buzz on Twitter and attained an average rating of 4.5/5 from the tweeters[3], with box-office sales remaining steadily high for the weeks following release. In contrast, *Agent Vinod* got a lukewarm response on Twitter and managed a poor rating of 1.9/5 from the Tweeters.[4] Twitter is also a good platform to create buzz about an upcoming movie. *Ishaqzaade*, a soon to be released bollywood movie, garnered a good response on Twitter after the launch of its first official trailer.[5]

Although organizations do not directly pay for publicity, it should not be viewed as free. Preparing news releases, staging special events, and persuading media personnel to broadcast or print publicity messages costs money. Public relations and publicity are examined further in Chapter 17.

© ISTOCKPHOTO/THINKSTOCK

publicity public information about a company, product, service, or issue appearing in the mass media as a news item

sales promotion marketing activities—other than personal selling, advertising, and public relations—that stimulate consumer buying and dealer effectiveness

personal selling a purchase situation involving a personal, paid-for communication between two people in an attempt to influence each other

Sales Promotion

Sales promotion consists of all marketing activities—other than personal selling, advertising, and public relations—that stimulate consumer purchasing and dealer effectiveness. Sales promotion is generally a short-run tool used to stimulate immediate increases in demand. Sales promotion can be aimed at end consumers, trade customers, or a company's employees. Sales promotions include free samples, contests, premiums, trade shows, vacation giveaways, and coupons. A popular promotion for restaurants is clubbed offers. Pizza Hut offers fun meals for family like meal for 2 and meal for 4. Such offers allow customers to get an assorted mix of food items at much less value than original prices. They also have promotions in the form of coupons that entitle customers to get a free soft drink with a pizza or get a discount on ordering a second pizza. Many companies, like KFC, find that customers continue to eat at the restaurants even after the winning term of their prize expires.[6]

Marketers often use sales promotion to improve the effectiveness of other ingredients in the promotional mix, especially advertising and personal selling. Research shows that sales promotion complements advertising by yielding faster sales responses.[7]

Personal Selling

Personal selling is a purchase situation involving a personal, paid-for communication between two people in an attempt to influence each other. In this dyad, both the buyer and the seller have specific objectives they wish to accomplish. The buyer may need to minimize cost or assure a quality product, for instance, while the salesperson may need to maximize revenue and profits.

Traditional methods of personal selling include a planned presentation to one or more prospective

communication the process by which meanings are exchanged or shared through a common set of symbols

interpersonal communication direct, face-to-face communication between two or more people

mass communication the communication of a concept or message to large audiences

buyers for the purpose of making a sale. Whether it takes place face-to-face or over the phone, personal selling attempts to persuade the buyer to accept a point of view. For example, a car salesperson may try to persuade a car buyer that a particular model is superior to a competing model in certain features, such as gas mileage. Once the buyer is somewhat convinced, the salesperson may attempt to elicit some action from the buyer, such as a test-drive or a purchase. Frequently, in this traditional view of personal selling, the objectives of the salesperson are at the expense of the buyer, creating a win–lose outcome.

More current notions on personal selling emphasize the relationship that develops between a salesperson and a buyer. Initially, this concept was more typical in business-to-business selling situations, involving the sale of products like heavy machinery or computer systems. More recently, both business-to-business and business-to-consumer selling focus on building long-term relationships rather than on making a one-time sale.

Relationship selling emphasizes a win–win outcome and the accomplishment of mutual objectives that benefit both buyer and salesperson in the long term. Rather than focusing on a quick sale, relationship selling attempts to create a long-term, committed relationship based on trust, increased customer loyalty, and a continuation of the relationship between the salesperson and the customer. Personal selling, like other promotional mix elements, is increasingly dependent on the Internet. Most companies use their Web sites to attract potential buyers seeking information on products and services and to drive customers to their physical locations where personal selling can close the sale. Personal selling is discussed further in Chapter 18.

© GOODSHOOT/THINKSTOCK

LO 3 Marketing Communication

Promotional strategy is closely related to the process of communication. As humans, we assign meaning to feelings, ideas, facts, attitudes, and emotions. **Communication** is the process by which meanings are exchanged or shared through a common set of symbols. When a company develops a new product, changes an old one, or simply tries to increase sales of an existing good or service, it must communicate its selling message to potential customers. Marketers communicate information about the firm and its products to the target market and various publics through its promotion programs.

Communication can be divided into two major categories: interpersonal communication and mass communication. **Interpersonal communication** is direct, face-to-face communication between two or more people. When communicating face-to-face, people see the other person's reaction and can respond almost immediately. A salesperson speaking directly with a client is an example of an interpersonal marketing communication.

Mass communication involves communicating a concept or message to large audiences. A great deal of marketing communication is directed to consumers as a whole, usually through a mass medium such as television or newspapers. When a company advertises, it generally does not personally know the people with whom it is trying to communicate. Furthermore, the company is unable to respond immediately to consumers' reactions to its message. Instead, the marketing manager must wait to see whether people are reacting positively or negatively to the mass-communicated promotion. Any clutter from competitors' messages or other distractions in the environment can reduce the effectiveness of the mass-communication effort.

The Communication Process

Marketers are both senders and receivers of messages. As *senders*, marketers attempt to inform, persuade, and remind the target market to adopt courses of action compatible with the need to promote the purchase of goods and services. As *receivers*, marketers attune themselves to the target market in order to develop the appropriate messages, adapt existing messages, and spot new communication opportunities. In this way, marketing communication is a two-way, rather than one-way, process. The two-way nature of the communication process is shown in Exhibit 16.2.

The Sender and Encoding The **sender** is the originator of the message in the communication process. In an interpersonal conversation, the sender may be a parent, a friend, or a salesperson. For an advertisement or press release, the sender is the company or organization itself. For example, to take advantage of the Cricket World Cup (CWC) in 1999 and increase its biscuit sales, Britannia launched a huge marketing campaign called "Britannia Khao, World Cup Jao" in association with British Tourist Authority. The Britannia products came marked with the message "World Cup 99 Contest", with a certain number of "runs" printed on them. Once a customer managed to collect 100 runs by buying these offer packs, he/she was entitled to receive a free CWC 99 booklet by submitting the product wrappers. The wrappers could either be submitted to retail outlets (termed Prize Centres) participating in the offer or could be mailed to an address given by the company. The CWC 99 booklet contained a cut-out coupon and its counterfoil, which were to be sctrached by the customer to know what prize he/she has won. There were total 6 catogories of prizes—3-day trip to UK to watch a match for 100 winners, 100 21 inch colour TVs, 1000 cricket bats, 10,000 wrist watches, 1,00,000 Tiger Cashew Badam biscuit packs of 75 gram each, and 4,00,000 chekkers biscuit pack of 14 gram each. If a customer won any of the prizes in the first four categories, he/she was required to fill up his/her contact details in the coupon and either submit to the authorized wholesaler of Britannia or mail to the given company address. For customers who won either of the two biscuits, they could collect their prize from the Prize Centres on submission of the coupon.[8]

sender the originator of the message in the communication process

encoding the conversion of a sender's ideas and thoughts into a message, usually in the form of words or signs

channel a medium of communication—such as a voice, radio, or newspaper—for transmitting a message

Encoding is the conversion of the sender's ideas and thoughts into a message, usually in the form of words or signs. Britannia encoded the "Britannia Khao, World Cup Jao", Campaign message into ads showing how cricket was a central part of daily activities of customers. The ads carried an element of humor too—for example, a laundry man using a cricket pitch for ironing clothes. A basic principle of encoding is that what matters is not what the source says but what the receiver hears. One way of conveying a message that the receiver will hear properly is to use concrete words and pictures.

EXHIBIT 16.2
Communication Process

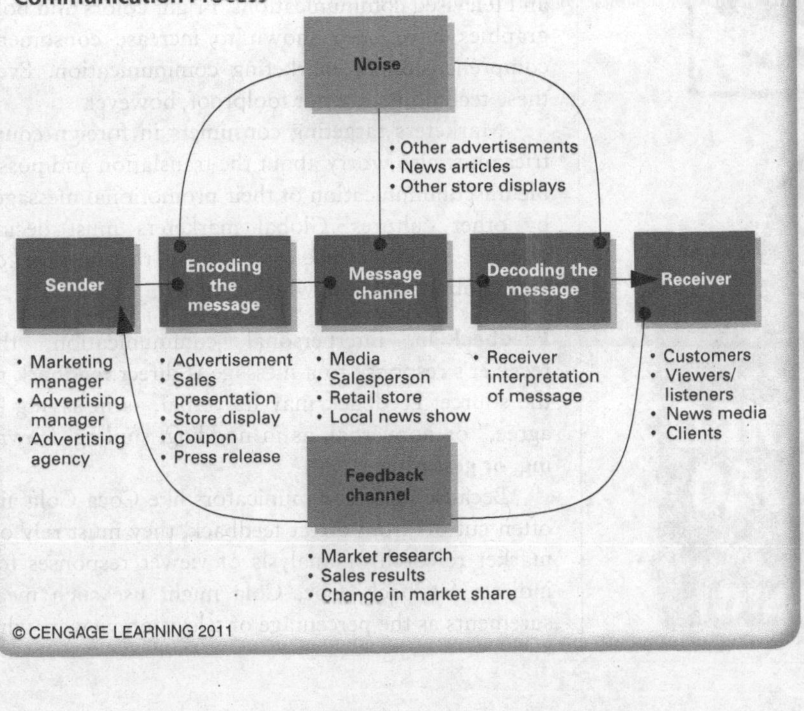

Message Transmission Transmission of a message requires a **channel**—a voice, radio, newspaper, computer, or other communication medium. A facial expression or gesture can also serve as a channel. The advertisements were promoted both on television and

noise anything that interferes with, distorts, or slows down the transmission of information

receiver the person who decodes a message

decoding interpretation of the language and symbols sent by the source through a channel

feedback the receiver's response to a message

in print to inform customers, generate excitement, and induce sales.

Reception occurs when the message is detected by the receiver and enters his or her frame of reference. In a two-way conversation such as a sales pitch given by a sales representative to a potential client, reception is normally high. In contrast, the desired receivers may or may not detect the message when it is mass communicated because most media are cluttered by **noise**—anything that interferes with, distorts, or slows down the transmission of information. In some media overcrowded with advertisers, such as newspapers and television, the noise level is high and the reception level is low. For example, competing network advertisements, other entertainment option advertisements, or other programming on the network itself might have hampered reception of Britannia's advertising campaign message. Transmission can also be hindered by situational factors such as physical surroundings like light, sound, location, and weather; the presence of other people; or the temporary moods consumers might bring to the situation. Mass communication may not even reach all the right consumers. Because Britannia was targeting an event with a dedicated audience of cricket fans, it was more likely that the target audience experienced the "Britannia Khao World Cup Jao" campaign, particularly the enthusiasm of collecting the CWC 99 booklet. However, other Britannia ads might have run when the target audience of cricket viewers was not watching.

The Receiver and Decoding Marketers communicate their message through a channel to customers, or **receivers**, who will decode the message. **Decoding** is the interpretation of the language and symbols sent by the source through a channel. Common understanding between two communicators, or a common frame of reference, is required for effective communication. Therefore, marketing managers must ensure a proper match between the message to be conveyed and the target market's attitudes and ideas.

Even though a message has been received, it will not necessarily be properly decoded—or even seen, viewed, or heard—because of selective exposure, distortion, and retention. Even when people receive a message, they tend to manipulate, alter, and modify it to reflect their own biases, needs, knowledge, and culture. Differences in age, social class, education, culture, and ethnicity can lead to miscommunication. Further, because people don't always listen or read carefully, they can easily misinterpret what is said or written. In fact, researchers have found that consumers misunderstand a large proportion of both printed and televised communications. Bright colors and bold graphics have been shown to increase consumers' comprehension of marketing communication. Even these techniques are not foolproof, however.

Marketers targeting consumers in foreign countries must also worry about the translation and possible miscommunication of their promotional messages by other cultures. Global marketers must decide whether to standardize or customize the message for each global market in which they sell.

Feedback In interpersonal communication, the receiver's response to a message is direct **feedback** to the source. Feedback may be verbal, as in saying "I agree," or nonverbal, as in nodding, smiling, frowning, or gesturing.

Because mass communicators like Coca-Cola are often cut off from direct feedback, they must rely on market research or analysis of viewer responses for indirect feedback. Coca-Cola might use such measurements as the percentage of television viewers who

EXHIBIT 16.3

Characteristics of the Elements in the Promotional Mix

	Advertising	Public Relations	Sales Promotion	Personal Selling
Mode of Communication	Indirect and impersonal	Usually indirect and impersonal	Usually indirect and impersonal	Direct and face-to-face
Communicator Control over Situation	Low	Moderate to low	Moderate to low	High
Amount of Feedback	Little	Little	Little to moderate	Much
Speed of Feedback	Delayed	Delayed	Varies	Immediate
Direction of Message	One-way	One-way	Mostly one-way	Two-way
Control over Message Content	Yes	No	Yes	Yes
Identification of Sponsor	Yes	No	Yes	Yes
Speed in Reaching Large Audience	Fast	Usually fast	Fast	Slow
Message Flexibility	Same message to all audiences	Usually no direct control over message audiences	Same message to varied targets	Tailored to prospective buyer

recognized, recalled, or stated that they were exposed to the company's messages. Indirect feedback enables mass communicators to decide whether to continue, modify, or drop a message. Web sites also facilitate feedback.

The Communication Process and the Promotional Mix

The four elements of the promotional mix differ in their ability to affect the target audience. For instance, promotional mix elements may communicate with the consumer directly or indirectly. The message may flow one way or two ways. Feedback may be fast or slow, a little or a lot. Likewise, the communicator may have varying degrees of control over message delivery, content, and flexibility. Exhibit 16.3 outlines characteristics among the promotional mix elements with respect to mode of communication, marketer's control over the communication process, amount and speed of feedback, direction of message flow, marketer's control over the message, identification of the sender, speed in reaching large audiences, and message flexibility.

From Exhibit 16.3, you can see that most elements of the promotional mix are indirect and impersonal when used to communicate with a target market, pro-

© PHOTODISC/ THINKSTOCK

viding only one direction of message flow. For example, advertising, public relations, and sales promotion are generally impersonal, one-way means of mass communication. Because they provide no opportunity for direct feedback, it is more difficult to adapt these promotional elements to changing consumer preferences, individual differences, and personal goals.

Personal selling, on the other hand, is personal, two-way communication. The salesperson receives immediate feedback from the consumer and can adjust the message in response. Personal selling, however, is very slow in dispersing the marketer's message to large audiences. A salesperson can only communicate to one person or a small group of people at one time.

The Impact of Web 2.0 on Marketing Communication

The Internet and related technologies are having a profound impact on marketing communication, including the promotional mix. Web 2.0 tools include blogs (online journals), podcasting (online radio shows), vodcasts (online videos and newscasts), and social networks such as MySpace and Facebook. In the beginning, these tools were primarily used by individuals to express themselves. But businesses began to see that these tools could be used to engage with consumers as well. The rise of blogging, for example, has created a completely new way for marketers to manage their image, connect with consumers, and generate interest in and desire for their companies' products.

Blogging alters the marketing communication process for the promotional elements that rely on mass communication—advertising, public relations, and sales promotion—by moving them away from impersonal, indirect communication toward a personalized, direct communication model. Blogs generated by companies (*corporate blogs*) allow marketers to have a direct, personalized feedback channel with customers, which is strikingly different from the communication model in Exhibit 16.2. Consumer-generated blogs are an indirect, personalized feedback channel. Blogs are discussed in more detail in Chapter 22.

LO 4 The Goals and Tasks of Promotion

People communicate with one another for many reasons. They seek amusement, ask for help, give assistance or instructions, provide information, and express ideas and thoughts. Promotion, on the other hand, seeks to modify behavior and thoughts in some way. For example, promoters may try to persuade consumers to have coffee at Cafe Coffee Day rather than at Barista. Promotion also strives to reinforce existing behaviour—for instance, getting consumers to continue visiting Cafe Coffee Day once they have switched.

© AP IMAGES/PRNEWSFOTO/APPLE

Promotion can perform one or more of three tasks: *inform* the target audience, *persuade* the target audience, or *remind* the target audience. Often a marketer will try to accomplish two or more of these tasks at the same time.

Informing

Informative promotion seeks to convert an existing need into a want or to stimulate interest in a new product. It is generally more prevalent during the early stages of the product life cycle. People typically will not buy a product or service or support a nonprofit organization until they know its purpose and its benefits to them. Informative messages are important for promoting complex and technical products such as automobiles, computers, and investment services. For example, when Apple released the iPhone in the U.S., its touch screen functions were new to the Smartphone category. To inform consumers of the phone's features and how it worked, Apple ran a series of commercials showing a hand manipulating the phone. The voiceover provided information about the benefits of the phone by telling a story around how the iPhone makes life easier. Similar commercials have run for the iPad to inform consumers about the benefits of a larger touch screen. Informative promotion is also important for a "new" brand being introduced into an "old" product class. The new product cannot establish itself against more mature products unless potential buyers are aware of it, value its benefits, and understand its positioning in the marketplace.

Persuading

Persuasive promotion is designed to stimulate a purchase or an action. Persuasion normally becomes the main promotion goal when the product enters the growth stage of its life cycle. By this time, the target market should have general product awareness and some knowledge of how the product can fulfill its wants. Therefore, the promotional task switches from informing consumers about the product category to persuading them to buy the company's brand rather than that of the competitor. At this time, the promotional message emphasizes the product's real and perceived competitive advantages, often appealing to emotional needs such as love, belonging, self-esteem, and ego satisfaction. For example, advertisers of phones using the Android operating system are trying to persuade users to purchase their phone instead of an iPhone (or even instead of another brand of Android phone). Advertising messages, therefore, are highlighting the unique technological benefits of Android phones, such as a faster processor or larger screen.

Persuasion can also be an important goal for very competitive mature product categories such as many household items and soft drinks. In a marketplace characterized by many competitors, the promotional message often encourages brand switching and aims to convert some buyers into loyal users. Critics believe that some promotional messages and techniques can be too persuasive, causing consumers to buy products and services they really don't need.

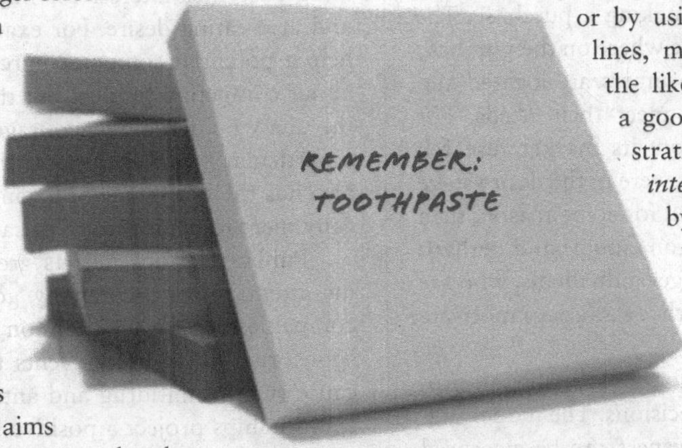

© ISTOCKPHOTO.COM/OLGA BOGATYRENKO

Reminding

Reminder promotion is used to keep the product and brand name in the public's mind. This type of promotion prevails during the maturity stage of the life cycle. It assumes that the target market has already been persuaded of the merits of the good or service. Its purpose is simply to trigger a memory. Colgate toothpaste and other consumer products often use reminder promotion.

LO 5 Promotional Goals and the AIDA Concept

The ultimate goal of any promotion is to get someone to buy a good or service or, in the case of nonprofit organizations, to take some action (e.g., donate blood). A classic model for reaching promotional goals is called the **AIDA concept.**[9] The acronym stands for *attention*, *interest*, *desire*, and *action*—the stages of consumer involvement with a promotional message.

AIDA concept a model that outlines the process for achieving promotional goals in terms of stages of consumer involvement with the message; the acronym stands for *attention, interest, desire,* and *action*

This model proposes that consumers respond to marketing messages in a cognitive (thinking), affective (feeling), and conative (doing) sequence. First, a promotion manager may focus on attracting a consumer's *attention* by training a salesperson to use a friendly greeting and approach, or by using loud volume, bold headlines, movement, bright colors, and the like in an advertisement. Next, a good sales presentation, demonstration, or advertisement creates *interest* in the product and then, by illustrating how the product's features will satisfy the consumer's needs, arouses *desire*. Finally, a special offer or a strong closing sales pitch may be used to obtain purchase *action*.

The AIDA concept assumes that promotion propels consumers along the following four steps in the purchase-decision process:

1. *Attention:* The advertiser must first gain the attention of the target market. A firm cannot sell something if the market does not know that the good or service exists. When Apple introduced the iPod for the first time in the U.S., the company needed to create awareness and gain attention for the new product, so Apple advertised and promoted it extensively through ads on television, in magazines, and on the Internet. Because the iPod was a brand extension of the Apple computer, it required less effort than an entirely new brand would have. At the same time, because the iPod was an innovative new product line, the promotion had to get customers' attention and create awareness of a new idea from an established company.
2. *Interest:* Simple awareness of a brand seldom leads to a sale. The next step is to create interest in the product. A print ad cannot tell potential customers all the features of the iPod. Thus, Apple had to arrange iPod demonstrations and target messages to innovators and early adopters to create interest in the new portable music players.
3. *Desire:* Potential customers for the Apple iPod may like the concept of a portable music player, but they may not feel it is necessarily better than a portable music player with fewer features. Therefore, Apple had to create brand preference with its iTunes Music Store, extended-life battery, clock and alarm, calendar and to-do list, photo storage, and other features. Specifically, Apple had to convince potential customers that the iPod was the best solution to meet their desire for a portable digital music player.

4 *Action:* Some potential target market customers may have been convinced to buy an iPod but had not yet made the actual purchase. To motivate them to take action, Apple continued advertising to more effectively communicate the features and benefits and also used promotions and price discounts.

Most buyers involved in high-involvement purchase situations pass through the four stages of the AIDA model on the way to making a purchase. The promoter's task is to determine where on the purchase ladder most of the target consumers are located and design a promotion plan to meet their needs. For example, if Apple learned from its market research that many potential customers were in the desire stage but had not yet bought an iPod for some reason, then Apple could place advertising on Google and perhaps in video games, to target younger individuals, who are the primary target market, with messages to motivate them to buy an iPod.

The AIDA concept does not explain how all promotions influence purchase decisions. The model suggests that promotional effectiveness can be measured in terms of consumers progressing from one stage to the next. However, the order of stages in the model, as well as whether consumers go through all steps, has been much debated. A purchase can occur without interest or desire, perhaps when a low-involvement product is bought on impulse. Regardless of the order of the stages or consumers' progression through these stages, the AIDA concept helps marketers by suggesting which promotional strategy will be most effective.[10] Strategy is often a matter of timing. Marketing managers for the film *Eat Pray Love*, based on the bestselling memoir by Elizabeth Gilbert, used the book's popularity and momentum to keep attention on the story as their colleagues at Sony Pictures created the movie. As the release date approached, Sony and Home Shopping Network (HSN) in the United States developed a direct mail campaign featuring products based on *Eat Pray Love* destinations (Italy, India, and Bali) and promoting the *Eat Pray Love* three-day sales event on HSN the week before the movie released. Using HSN's customer database allowed Sony to generate additional interest and desire to see the movie in HSN's target 35- to 45-year-old audience. Finally, several products, including perfume, used the *Eat Pray Love* title to keep the brand in people's minds.[11] With the movie shot at Indian locations as well, the movie helped in showcasing Brand India to the world audience and created an upsurge in number of tourists visiting India.

AIDA and the Promotional Mix

Exhibit 16.4 depicts the relationship between the promotional mix and the AIDA model. It shows that although advertising does have an impact in the later stages, it is most useful in gaining attention for goods or services. In contrast, personal selling reaches fewer people at first. Salespeople are more effective at creating customer interest for merchandise or a service and at creating desire. For example, advertising may help a potential computer purchaser gain knowledge about competing brands, but the salesperson may be the one who actually encourages the buyer to decide a particular brand is the best choice. The salesperson also has the advantage of having the computer physically there to demonstrate its capabilities to the buyer.

Public relations has its greatest impact in gaining attention for a company, good, or service. Many companies can attract attention and build goodwill by sponsoring community events that benefit a worthy cause such as antidrug and antigang programs. Such sponsorships project a positive image of the firm and its products into the minds of consumers and potential consumers. Book publishers push to get their titles on the best seller lists of major publications, such as *India Today* or *Outlook*. Book authors also make appearances on talk shows and at bookstores to personally sign books and speak to fans.

Sales promotion's greatest strength is in creating strong desire and purchase intent. Coupons and other

© F78/ZUMA PRESS/NEWSCOM

EXHIBIT 16.4

	Attention	Interest	Desire	Action
Advertising	Very effective	Very effective	Somewhat effective	Not effective
Public Relations	Very effective	Very effective	Somewhat effective	Not effective
Sales Promotion	Somewhat effective	Somewhat effective	Very effective	Somewhat effective
Personal Selling	Somewhat effective	Very effective	Very effective	Very effective

● Very effective ○ Somewhat effective ● Not effective

price-off promotions are techniques used to persuade customers to buy new products. Frequent buyer sales promotion programs, popular among retailers, allow consumers to accumulate points or rupees that can later be redeemed for goods. Frequent buyer programs tend to increase purchase intent and loyalty and encourage repeat purchases.

LO 6 Factors Affecting the Promotional Mix

Promotional mixes vary a great deal from one product and one industry to the next. Normally, advertising and personal selling are used to promote goods and services, supported and supplemented by sales promotion. Public relations helps develop a positive image for the organization and the product line. However, a firm may choose not to use all four promotional elements in its promotional mix, or it may choose to use them in varying degrees. The particular promotional mix chosen by a firm for a product or service depends on several factors: the nature of the product, the stage in the product life cycle, target market characteristics, the type of buying decision, funds available for promotion, and whether a push or a pull strategy will be used.

Nature of the Product

Characteristics of the product itself can influence the promotional mix. For instance, a product can be classified as either a business product or a consumer product. (Refer to Chapters 7 and 10.) As business products are often custom-tailored to the buyer's exact specifications, they are often not well suited to mass promotion. Therefore, producers of most business goods, such as computer systems or industrial machinery, rely more heavily on personal selling than on advertising. Advertising, however, still serves a purpose in promoting business goods. Advertising in trade media can help locate potential customers for the sales force. For example, print media advertising often includes coupons soliciting the potential customer to "fill this out for more detailed information."

In contrast, because consumer products generally are not custom-made, they do not require the selling efforts of a company representative who can tailor them to the user's needs. Thus, consumer goods are promoted mainly through advertising to create brand familiarity. Television and radio advertising, consumer-oriented magazines, and increasingly the Internet and other highly targeted media are used to promote consumer goods, especially nondurables. Sales promotion, the brand name, and the product's packaging are about twice as important for consumer goods as for business products. Persuasive personal selling is important at the retail level for goods such as automobiles and appliances.

The costs and risks associated with a product also influence the promotional mix. As a general rule, when the costs or risks of buying and using a product increase, personal selling becomes more important. In fact, inexpensive items cannot support the cost of a salesperson's time and effort unless the potential volume is high. On the other hand, expensive and complex machinery, cars, and new homes represent a considerable investment. A salesperson must assure buyers that they are spending their money wisely and not taking an undue financial risk.

Social risk is an issue as well. Many consumer goods are not products of great social importance because they do not reflect social position. People do not experience much social risk in buying a loaf of bread. However, buying many specialty products such as jewelry and clothing involves a social risk. Many consumers depend on sales personnel for guidance in making the "proper" choice.

Stage in the Product Life Cycle

The product's stage in its life cycle is a big factor in designing a promotional mix (see Exhibit 16.5 on the next page). During the *introduction stage*, the basic goal of promotion is to inform the target audience that the product is available. Initially, the emphasis is on the general product class—for example, mobile phones. This emphasis gradually changes to gaining attention for a particular brand, such as Nokia, Samsung, Sony Ericsson, or Motorola. Typically, both extensive advertising and public relations inform the target audience of the product class or brand and heighten awareness levels. Sales promotion encourages early trial of the product, and personal selling gets retailers to carry the product.

When the product reaches the *growth stage* of the life cycle, the promotion blend may shift. Often a change is necessary because different types of potential buyers are targeted. Although advertising and public relations continue to be major elements of the promotional mix, sales promotion can be reduced because consumers need fewer incentives to purchase. The promotional strategy is to emphasize the product's differential advantage over the competition. Persuasive promotion is used to build and maintain brand loyalty during the growth stage. By this stage, personal selling has usually succeeded in getting adequate distribution for the product.

As the product reaches the *maturity stage* of its life cycle, competition becomes fiercer, and thus persuasive and reminder advertising are more strongly emphasized. Sales promotion comes back into focus as product sellers try to increase their market share.

All promotion, especially advertising, is reduced as the product enters the *decline stage*. Nevertheless, personal selling and sales promotion efforts may be maintained, particularly at the retail level.

EXHIBIT 16.5

Product Life Cycle and the Promotional Mix

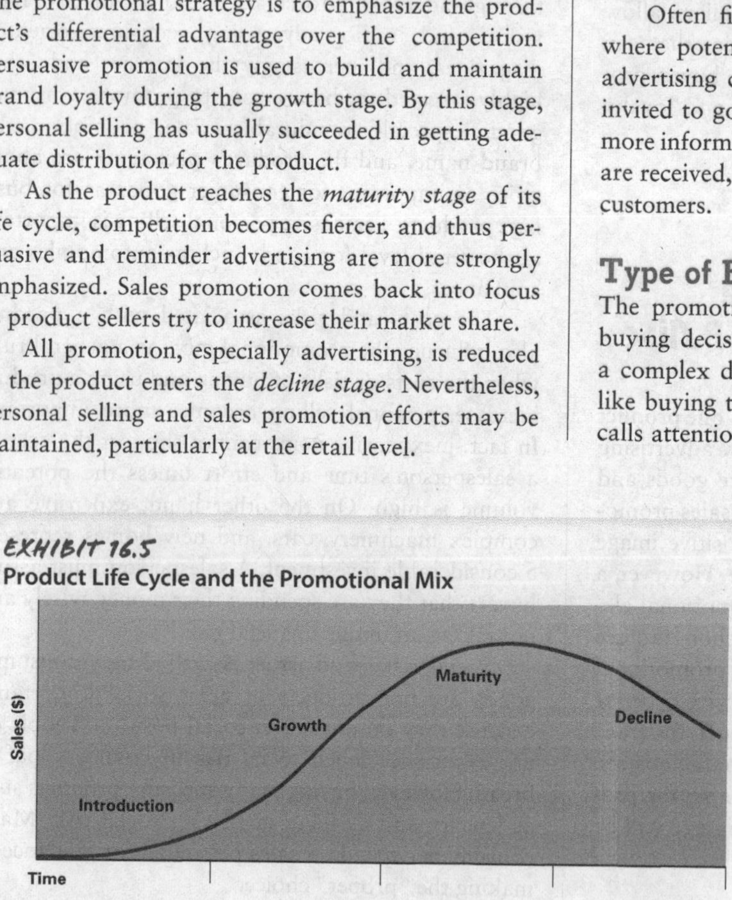

Preintroduction publicity; small amounts of advertising near introduction	Heavy advertising and public relations to build awareness; sales promotion to induce trial; personal selling to obtain distribution	Heavy advertising and public relations to build brand loyalty; decreasing use of sales promotion; personal selling to maintain distribution	Advertising slightly decreased—more persuasive and reminder in nature; increased use of sales promotion to build market share; personal selling to maintain distribution	Advertising and public relations drastically decreased; sales promotion and personal selling maintained at low levels

Target Market Characteristics

A target market characterized by widely scattered potential customers, highly informed buyers, and brand-loyal repeat purchasers generally requires a promotional mix with more advertising and sales promotion and less personal selling. Sometimes, however, personal selling is required even when buyers are well informed and geographically dispersed. Although industrial installations may be sold to well-educated people with extensive work experience, salespeople must be present to explain the product and work out the details of the purchase agreement.

Often firms sell goods and services in markets where potential customers are hard to locate. Print advertising can be used to find them. The reader is invited to go online, call, or mail in a reply card for more information. As the online queries, calls, or cards are received, salespeople are sent to visit the potential customers.

Type of Buying Decision

The promotional mix also depends on the type of buying decision—for example, a routine decision or a complex decision. For routine consumer decisions like buying toothpaste, the most effective promotion calls attention to the brand or reminds the consumer about the brand. Advertising and, especially, sales promotion are the most productive promotion tools to use for routine decisions.

If the decision is neither routine nor complex, advertising and public relations help establish awareness for the good or service. Suppose a man is looking for paint for redesigning his house. As a common man, he is not familiar with paints, yet he has seen a billboard on a traffic junction about Asian Paints and has seen an advertisement for the paint on television. He may be more likely to buy this brand because he is already aware of it. Online reviews are often important in this type of buying decision as well because the consumer has any number of other consumers' reviews easily accessible.

In contrast, consumers making complex buying decisions are

more extensively involved. They rely on large amounts of information to help them reach a purchase decision. Personal selling is most effective in helping these consumers decide. For example, consumers thinking about buying a car typically research the car online using corporate and third-party Web sites. However, few people buy a car without visiting the dealership. They depend on a salesperson to provide the information they need to reach a decision. In addition to online resources, print advertising may also be used for high-involvement purchase decisions because it can often provide a large amount of information to the consumer.

Available Funds

Money, or the lack of it, may easily be the most important factor in determining the promotional mix. A small, undercapitalized manufacturer may rely heavily on free publicity if its product is unique. If the situation warrants a sales force, a financially strained firm may turn to manufacturers' agents, who work on a commission basis with no advances or expense accounts. Even well-capitalized organizations may not be able to afford the advertising rates of publications like *Time Magazine*, *Reader's Digest*, and the *Wall Street Journal*, or the cost of running television commercials during *Bigg Boss*, *Indian Idol*, or the Cricket World Cup. The price of a high-profile advertisement in these media could support several salespeople for an entire year.

push strategy a marketing strategy that uses aggressive personal selling and trade advertising to convince a wholesaler or a retailer to carry and sell particular merchandise

When funds are available to permit a mix of promotional elements, a firm will generally try to optimize its return on promotion while minimizing the *cost per contact*, or the cost of reaching one member of the target market. In general, the cost per contact is very high for personal selling, public relations, and sales promotions like sampling and demonstrations. On the other hand, given the number of people national advertising reaches, it has a very low cost per contact. Usually, there is a trade-off among the funds available, the number of people in the target market, the quality of communication needed, and the relative costs of the promotional elements. There are plenty of low-cost options available to companies without a huge budget. Many of these include online strategies and public relations efforts, where the company relies on free publicity.

Push and Pull Strategies

The last factor that affects the promotional mix is whether a push or a pull promotional strategy will be used. Manufacturers may use aggressive personal selling and trade advertising to convince a wholesaler or a retailer to carry and sell their merchandise. This approach is known as a **push strategy** (see Exhibit 16.6

Though new cars can be researched online, consumers depend on a salesperson to help them reach a decision.

pull strategy a marketing strategy that stimulates consumer demand to obtain product distribution

below). The wholesaler, in turn, must often push the merchandise forward by persuading the retailer to handle the goods. The retailer then uses advertising, displays, and other forms of promotion to convince the consumer to buy the "pushed" products. Walmart uses aggressive discounts to consumers to push product out of its stores, such as selling 1.2 kg bottles of Heinz Ketchup for ₹45[12], or Big Bazaar offering special discounts on holidays, like discounting television or wooden sofa sets during its annual Republic Day discount sale.[13] This concept also applies to services.

At the other extreme is a **pull strategy**, which stimulates consumer demand to obtain product distribution. Rather than trying to sell to the wholesaler, the manufacturer using a pull strategy focuses its promotional efforts on end consumers or opinion leaders. A classic example of a pull strategy is the heavy advertising and promotion of toys on children's television programs. The demand created from such major advertising campaigns is likely to "pull" demand from children (and then their parents) and encourage retailers to stock those toys in their stores. As consumers begin demanding the product, the retailer orders the merchandise from the wholesaler. As consumers begin demanding the product, the retailer orders the merchandise from the wholesaler. The wholesaler, confronted with rising demand, then places an order for the "pulled" merchandise from the manufacturer. Consumer demand pulls the product through the channel of distribution (see Exhibit 16.6). Heavy sampling, introductory consumer advertising, rupee-off campaigns, and couponing are part of a pull strategy.

Rarely does a company use a pull or a push strategy exclusively. Instead, the mix will emphasize one of these strategies. For example, pharmaceutical companies generally use a push strategy, through personal selling and trade advertising, to promote their drugs and therapies to physicians. Sales presentations and advertisements in medical journals give physicians the detailed information they need to prescribe medication to their patients. Most pharmaceutical companies supplement their push promotional strategy with a pull strategy targeted directly to potential patients through advertisements in consumer magazines and on television.

LO7 Integrated Marketing Communications

Ideally, marketing communications from each promotional mix element (personal selling, advertising, sales promotion, and public relations) should be integrated—that is, the message reaching the consumer should be the same regardless of whether it is from an advertisement, a salesperson in the field, a magazine article, or a coupon in a newspaper insert.

From the consumer's standpoint, a company's communications are already integrated. Consumers do not think in terms of the four elements of promotion: personal selling, advertising, sales promotion, and public relations. Instead, everything is an "ad." The only people who recognize the distinctions among these communications elements are the marketers themselves. Unfortunately, many marketers neglect this fact when planning promotional messages and fail to integrate their communication efforts from one element to the next. The most common rift typically

EXHIBIT 16.6
Push Strategy versus Pull Strategy

occurs between personal selling and the other elements of the promotional mix.

This unintegrated, disjointed approach to promotion has propelled many companies to adopt the concept of **integrated marketing communications (IMC)**. IMC is the careful coordination of all promotional messages—traditional advertising, direct marketing, interactive, public relations, sales promotion, personal selling, event marketing, and other communications—for a product or service to assure the consistency of messages at every contact point where a company meets the consumer. Following the concept of IMC, marketing managers carefully work out the roles that various promotional elements will play in the marketing mix. Timing of promotional activities is coordinated, and the results of each campaign are carefully monitored to improve future use of the promotional mix tools. Typically, a marketing communications director is appointed who has overall responsibility for integrating the company's marketing communications.

Movie marketing campaigns benefit greatly from an IMC approach. *BbuddahHoga Tera Baap*, a 2011movie by Viacom 18 and AB Corp, marketed the movie by promising to bring back Amitabh Bachchan in his angry young man avatar that was immensely popular in 1970s and 1980s. The movie teaser portrayed the actor in his angry man image, and this was followed by the actor singing the title track of the movie. The print advertisements used Bachchan's dialogues, images, and style from some of his previous hits like *Deewar, Shahenshah, and Agneepath* before unveiling his new look in the movie.[14] *Don 2* also made use of technology for an innovative marketing of the movie. Tie ups were done with Google and Youtube to enable the viewers to watch the movie songs on their computers in 3D using 3D glasses. A game called "Don—The Social Mobsters Game" was also launched on Facebook to generate curiosity and excitement for the movie.[15]

integrated marketing communications (IMC) the careful coordination of all promotional messages for a product or a service to assure the consistency of messages at every contact point where a company meets the consumer

The IMC concept has been growing in popularity for several reasons. First, the proliferation of thousands of media choices beyond traditional television has made promotion a more complicated task. Instead of promoting a product just through mass media options, like television and magazines, promotional messages today can appear in many varied sources. Further, the mass market has also fragmented—more selectively segmented markets and an increase in niche marketing have replaced the traditional broad market groups that marketers promoted to in years past. Finally, marketers have slashed their advertising spending in favor of promotional techniques that generate immediate sales responses and those that are more easily measured, such as direct marketing. Thus, the interest in IMC is largely a reaction to the scrutiny that marketing communications has come under and, particularly, to suggestions that uncoordinated promotional activity leads to a strategy that is wasteful and inefficient.

Review And Applications

Discuss the role of promotion in the marketing mix. Promotion is communication by marketers that informs, persuades, and reminds potential buyers of a product in order to influence an opinion or elicit a response. Promotional strategy is the plan for using the elements of promotion—advertising, public relations, sales promotion, and personal selling—to meet the firm's overall objectives and marketing goals. Based on these objectives, the elements of the promotional strategy become a coordinated promotion plan. The promotion plan then becomes an integral part of the total marketing strategy for reaching the target market along with product, distribution, and price.

1.1 What is a promotional strategy? Explain the concept of a competitive advantage in relation to promotional strategy.

Discuss the elements of the promotional mix. The elements of the promotional mix include advertising, public relations, sales promotion, and personal selling. Advertising is a form of impersonal, one-way mass communication paid for by the source. Public relations is the function of promotion concerned with a firm's public image. Sales promotion is typically used to back up other components of the promotional mix by stimulating immediate demand. Finally, personal selling typically involves direct communication, in person or by telephone; the seller tries to initiate a purchase by informing and persuading one or more potential buyers.

2.1 As the promotional manager for a new line of cosmetics targeted to preteen girls, you have been assigned the task of deciding which promotional mix elements—advertising, public relations, sales promotion, and personal selling—should be used in promoting it. Your budget for promoting the preteen cosmetics line is limited. Write a promotional plan explaining your choice of promotional mix elements given the nature of the product, the stage in the product life cycle, the target market characteristics, the type of buying decision, available funds, and the use of a pull or push strategy.

Describe the communication process. The communication process has several steps. When an individual or organization has a message it wishes to convey to a target audience, it encodes that message using language and symbols familiar to the intended receiver and sends the message through a channel of communication. Noise in the transmission channel distorts the source's intended message. Reception occurs if the message falls within the receiver's frame of reference. The receiver decodes the message and usually provides feedback to the source. Normally, feedback is direct for interpersonal communication and indirect for mass communication.

3.1 Why is understanding the target market a crucial aspect of the communication process?

Explain the goals and tasks of promotion. The fundamental goals of promotion are to induce, modify, or reinforce behavior by informing, persuading, and reminding. Informative promotion explains a good's or service's purpose and benefits. Promotion that informs the consumer is typically used to increase demand for a general product category or to introduce a new good or service. Persuasive promotion is designed to stimulate a purchase or an action. Promotion that persuades the consumer to buy is essential during the growth stage of the product life cycle, when competition becomes fierce. Reminder promotion is used to keep the product and brand name in the public's mind. Promotions that remind are generally used during the maturity stage of the product life cycle.

4.1 Why might a marketing manager choose to promote his or her product using persuasion? Give some current examples of persuasive promotion.

4.2 Choose a partner from class and go together to interview the owners or managers of several small businesses in your city. Ask them what their promotional objectives are and why. Are they trying to inform, persuade, or remind customers to do business with them? Also determine whether they believe they have an awareness problem or whether they need to persuade customers to come to them instead of to competitors. Ask them to list the characteristics of their primary market, the strengths and weaknesses of their direct competitors, and how they are positioning their store to compete. Prepare a report to present in class summarizing your findings.

Discuss the AIDA concept and its relationship to the promotional mix. The AIDA model outlines the four basic stages in the purchase decision-making process, which are initiated and propelled by promotional activities: (1) attention, (2) interest, (3) desire, and (4) action. The components of the promotional mix have varying levels of influence at each stage of the

AIDA model. Advertising is a good tool for increasing awareness and knowledge of a good or service. Sales promotion is effective when consumers are at the purchase stage of the decision-making process. Personal selling is most effective in developing customer interest and desire.

5.1 Discuss the AIDA concept. How do these different stages of consumer involvement affect the promotional mix?

5.2 How does a Web site's ease of use affect its ability to create attention, interest, desire, and action? Visit the kitchen and bath pages of Kohler's Web site (**www.kohler.co.in**) and determine how successful the company is at moving consumers through the AIDA process.

Describe the factors that affect the promotional mix. Promotion managers consider many factors when creating promotional mixes. These factors include the nature of the product, product life-cycle stage, target market characteristics, the type of buying decision involved, availability of funds, and feasibility of push or pull strategies. Because most business products tend to be custom-tailored to the buyer's exact specifications, the marketing manager may choose a promotional mix that relies more heavily on personal selling. On the other hand, consumer products are generally mass produced and lend themselves more to mass promotional efforts such as advertising and sales promotion. As products move through different stages of the product life cycle, marketers will choose to use different promotional elements. For example, advertising is emphasized more in the introductory stage of the product life cycle than in the decline stage. Characteristics of the target market, such as geographic location of potential buyers and brand loyalty, influence the promotional mix as does whether the buying decision is complex or routine. The amount of funds a firm has to allocate to promotion may also help determine the promotional mix. Small firms with limited funds may rely more heavily on public relations, whereas larger firms may be able to afford broadcast or print advertising. Last, if a firm uses a push strategy to promote the product or service, the marketing manager may choose to use aggressive advertising and personal selling to wholesalers and retailers. If a pull strategy is chosen, then the manager often relies on aggressive mass promotion, such as advertising and sales promotion, to stimulate consumer demand.

6.1 Explain the difference between a "pull" and a "push" promotional strategy. Under what conditions should each strategy be used?

6.2 View the websites of the radio stations in your city and compare the promotions featured. What conclusions can you draw about the target market of each station based on the types of promotions they are currently running? Would any of the promotions entice you to tune to a station that you normally don't listen to?

Discuss the concept of integrated marketing communications. Integrated marketing communications is the careful coordination of all promotional messages for a product or service to ensure the consistency of messages at every contact point where a company meets the consumer—advertising, sales promotion, personal selling, public relations, as well as direct marketing, packaging, and other forms of communication. Marketing managers carefully coordinate all promotional activities to ensure that consumers see and hear one message. Integrated marketing communications has received more attention in recent years due to the proliferation of media choices, the fragmentation of mass markets into more segmented niches, and the decrease in advertising spending in favor of promotional techniques that generate an immediate sales response.

7.1 Discuss the importance of integrated marketing communications. Give some current examples of companies that are and are not practicing IMC.

7.2 What do you think is the role of Hallmark's Web site (**www.hallmark.com**) in the company's integrated marketing communications plan? What seems to be the marketing function of the site? Do you think the site is effective?

Exercises

APPLICATION EXERCISE 1

An important concept in promotion is semiotics, or the study of meaning and meaning-producing events. An understanding of semiotics can help you not only to identify objects (denotation) but also to grasp the utility of images and associations (connotation). By manipulating connotations of objects in advertising, you can create, change, or reinforce images for products. Thus, semiotics is a powerful tool for brand management and promotion.[17]

Activities

1. Make a list of ten images and associations that come to mind for each of the following items: cricket ball, DVD, spoon, rubber band.
2. Look through magazines and see if you can find print advertisements that include each of the items (cricket ball, DVD, spoon, rubber band) in a supporting role. What seems to be the message of each ad? How does the item help create or reinforce an image for the product being sold in the ad?
3. Think of an everyday object of your own. What are its likely connotations? For example, a dog in a car might signal a family vehicle, but a dog also connotes loyalty, "man's best friend," and dependability. What images and associations are likely with your item? Make a list of as many as you can.
4. Now use your object and list of associations to create an image for another product. Think of the likely connotations your object will have for a certain target market and how such connotations can support a brand image. For example, if your everyday object is a candle, you might choose lingerie for your product, based on a candle's romantic connotations.

ETHICS EXERCISE

Integrated Marketing Solutions is a consumer-products marketing services firm. Currently, the firm is handling the launch of a new book for one of its publishing clients. The campaign includes advance review copies for key book reviewers, "Coming Soon" posters for booksellers, an author book-signing tour, and several television interviews. Everything has been produced and scheduled for release next week. Today, Rohit Sethi, the accountant executive, has learned that although the book received numerous favorable reviews, the review quoted on all of the promotional materials is fabricated.

Questions

1. What should Rohit do?

MARKETING PLAN EXERCISE

In Part 4, you began the process of defining the marketing mix, starting with the components of product and distribution. The next stage of the strategic planning process continues defining the elements of the marketing mix, and this section—Part 5—focuses on promotion and communication decisions for the promotion mix, including advertising, public relations, sales promotion, and personal selling. Use the following exercises to guide you through the promotions part of your strategic marketing plan:

1. Define your promotional objectives. What specific results do you hope to accomplish, and which promotional tools will be responsible? How will you use promotions to differentiate yourself from your competition? Remember that promotions cannot be directly tied with sales because there are too many other factors (competition, environment, price, distribution, product, customer service, company reputation, and so on) that affect sales. State specific objectives that can be tied directly to the result of promotional activities—for example, number of people redeeming a coupon, share of audience during a commercial, percent attitude change before and after a telemarketing campaign, or number of people calling a toll-free information hotline. Remember to have offline promotions drive online traffic.
2. Design a promotional message or theme. Does this message inform, remind, persuade, or educate the target market? Make sure this message will work across both traditional and electronic media. How is your promotional message consistent with your branding? Is this message or slogan unique and important enough to be copyrighted?
3. Will you be designing and producing all your promotion tools in-house, or do you need to find an agency? What are the advantages of designing promotional tools in-house? Disadvantages?

Short Case: HERO MOTOCORP

Prepared by
Dr. Dheeraj Sharma,
Indian Institute of Management, Ahmedabad

Hero MotoCorp was formed after the joint venture between Hero Group and Honda called Hero-Honda was broken on December 16, 2010. After the automobile giant, Honda walked out of the venture, Hero made a strong comeback in the market as Hero MotoCorp (formally known as Hero Honda Motor Ltd).[18]

When Hero India Ltd and Honda were in a partnership, Hero was not allowed to export (except for Sri Lanka) its products and was also not allowed to use parts of the bike from any other country. However, with the Hero-Honda split, Hero could now export its products in foreign markets and could also avail parts of the bike from any company.[19] On

August 15, 2011, Hero MotoCorp revealed its new logo and new brand name "Hero MotoCorp" on August 9, 2011 in London. It launched its first model called 'Impulse' under the brand name Hero. It also advertised models Hunk and Passion Pro with its new song/anthem called "*Hum Mai Hai Hero*" composed by A R Rahman on TV and radio. This song soon became viral and became known to everyone.

On January 4, 2012, a day before 11th Auto Expo, Hero MotoCorp launched 3 new models, *Passion X pro*, *Maestro*, and *Ignitor*. Also, in continuation with Hero-Honda's partnership with International Hockey Federation (FIH) in 2010, Hero MotoCorp sponsored men's and women's hockey qualifying events in London Olympics 2012. The tournaments were named to "*Hero FIH Road to London*".[20]

Hero MotoCorp, to market itself used all platforms of communication. It had its advertisements in Newspapers, TV, Radio, and other sources of digital media. Today, Hero MotoCorp is the largest two-wheeler manufacturing company in the world and has 46% share in the two-wheeler market in India.[21] Its success after parting with Honda can be attributed to its innovation, business expansion, and integrated marketing communications. Its marketing strategies helped Hero make its name in the domestic and international market.

Questions

1. Has there been a drop in the consumer intent to purchase Hero-Honda models after their split?
2. Can Hero MotoCorp generate interest in new products?
3. Will HMCL retain patronage? How will you evaluate the success of this IMC campaign?

16 Integrated Marketing Communications

KEY TERMS

LO 1

promotion communication by marketers that informs, persuades, and reminds potential buyers of a product in order to influence an opinion or elicit a response

promotional strategy a plan for the optimal use of the elements of promotion: advertising, public relations, personal selling, and sales promotion

competitive advantage the unique set of features of a company and its products that are perceived by the target market as significant and superior to the competition

LO 2

promotional mix the combination of promotional tools—including advertising, public relations, personal selling, and sales promotion—used to reach the target market and fulfill the organization's overall goals

advertising impersonal, one-way mass communication about a product or organization that is paid for by a marketer

public relations the marketing function that evaluates public attitudes, identifies areas within the organization the public may be interested in, and executes a program of action to earn public understanding and acceptance

publicity public information about a company, product, service, or issue appearing in the mass media as a news item

sales promotion marketing activities—other than personal selling, advertising, and public relations—that stimulate consumer buying and dealer effectiveness

personal selling a purchase situation involving a personal, paid-for communication between two people in an attempt to influence each other

KEY CONCEPTS

LO 1 **Discuss the role of promotion in the marketing mix.** Promotion is communication by marketers that informs, persuades, and reminds potential buyers of a product in order to influence an opinion or elicit a response. Promotional strategy is the plan for using the elements of promotion—advertising, public relations, sales promotion, and personal selling—to meet the firm's overall objectives and marketing goals. Based on these objectives, the elements of the promotional strategy become a coordinated promotion plan. The promotion plan then becomes an integral part of the total marketing strategy for reaching the target market along with product, distribution, and price.

LO 2 **Discuss the elements of the promotional mix.** The elements of the promotional mix include advertising, public relations, sales promotion, and personal selling. Advertising is a form of impersonal, one-way mass communication paid for by the source. Public relations is the function of promotion concerned with a firm's public image. Sales promotion is typically used to back up other components of the promotional mix by stimulating immediate demand. Finally, personal selling typically involves direct communication, in person or by telephone; the seller tries to initiate a purchase by informing and persuading one or more potential buyers.

LO 3 **Describe the communication process.** The communication process has several steps. When an individual or organization has a message it wishes to convey to a target audience, it encodes that message using language and symbols familiar to the intended receiver and sends the message through a channel of communication. Noise in the transmission channel distorts the source's intended message. Reception occurs if the message falls within the receiver's frame of reference. The receiver decodes the message and usually provides feedback to the source. Normally, feedback is direct for interpersonal communication and indirect for mass communication.

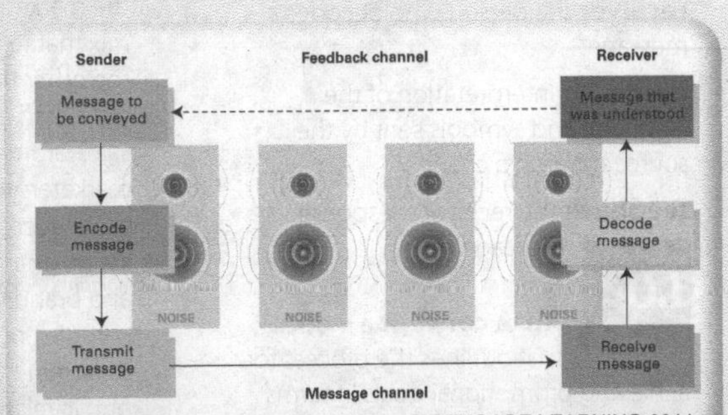

© CENGAGE LEARNING 2011

LO 4 **Explain the goals and tasks of promotion.** The fundamental goals of promotion are to induce, modify, or reinforce behavior by informing, persuading, and reminding. Informative promotion explains a good's or service's purpose and benefits. Promotion that informs the consumer is typically used to increase demand for a general product category or to introduce a new good or service. Persuasive promotion is designed to stimulate a purchase or an action. Promotion that persuades the consumer to buy is essential during the growth stage of the product life cycle, when competition becomes fierce. Reminder promotion is used to keep the product and brand name in the public's mind. Promotions that remind are generally used during the maturity stage of the product life cycle.

LO 5 **Discuss the AIDA concept and its relationship to the promotional mix.** The AIDA model outlines the four basic stages in the purchase decision-making process, which are initiated and propelled by promotional activities:

LO 3 **communication** the process by which meanings are exchanged or shared through a common set of symbols

interpersonal communication direct, face-to-face communication between two or more people

mass communication the communication of a concept or message to large audiences

sender the originator of the message in the communication process

encoding the conversion of a sender's ideas and thoughts into a message, usually in the form of words or signs

channel a medium of communication—such as a voice, radio, or newspaper—for transmitting a message

noise anything that interferes with, distorts, or slows down the transmission of information

receiver the person who decodes a message

decoding interpretation of the language and symbols sent by the source through a channel

feedback the receiver's response to a message

LO 5 **AIDA concept** a model that outlines the process for achieving promotional goals in terms of stages of consumer involvement with the message; the acronym stands for *attention*, *interest*, *desire*, and *action*

LO 6 **push strategy** a marketing strategy that uses aggressive personal selling and trade advertising to convince a wholesaler or a retailer to carry and sell particular merchandise

pull strategy a marketing strategy that stimulates consumer demand to obtain product distribution

LO 7 **integrated marketing communications (IMC)** the careful coordination of all promotional messages for a product or a service to assure the consistency of messages at every contact point where a company meets the consumer

(1) attention, (2) interest, (3) desire, and (4) action. The components of the promotional mix have varying levels of influence at each stage of the AIDA model. Advertising is a good tool for increasing awareness and knowledge of a good or service. Sales promotion is effective when consumers are at the purchase stage of the decision-making process. Personal selling is most effective in developing customer interest and desire.

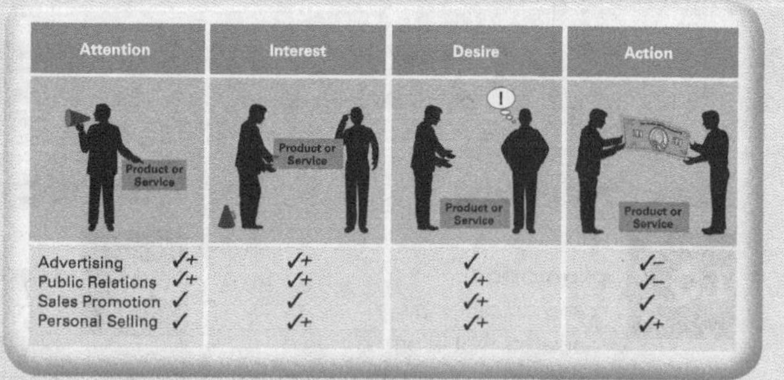

LO 6 **Describe the factors that affect the promotional mix.** Promotion managers consider many factors when creating promotional mixes. These factors include the nature of the product, product life-cycle stage, target market characteristics, the type of buying decision involved, availability of funds, and feasibility of push or pull strategies. Because most business products tend to be custom-tailored to the buyer's exact specifications, the marketing manager may choose a promotional mix that relies more heavily on personal selling. On the other hand, consumer products are generally mass produced and lend themselves more to mass promotional efforts such as advertising and sales promotion. As products move through different stages of the product life cycle, marketers will choose to use different promotional elements. For example, advertising is emphasized more in the introductory stage of the product life cycle than in the decline stage. Characteristics of the target market, such as geographic location of potential buyers and brand loyalty, influence the promotional mix as does whether the buying decision is complex or routine. The amount of funds a firm has to allocate to promotion may also help determine the promotional mix. Small firms with limited funds may rely more heavily on public relations, whereas larger firms may be able to afford broadcast or print advertising. Last, if a firm uses a push strategy to promote the product or service, the marketing manager may choose to use aggressive advertising and personal selling to wholesalers and retailers. If a pull strategy is chosen, then the manager often relies on aggressive mass promotion, such as advertising and sales promotion, to stimulate consumer demand.

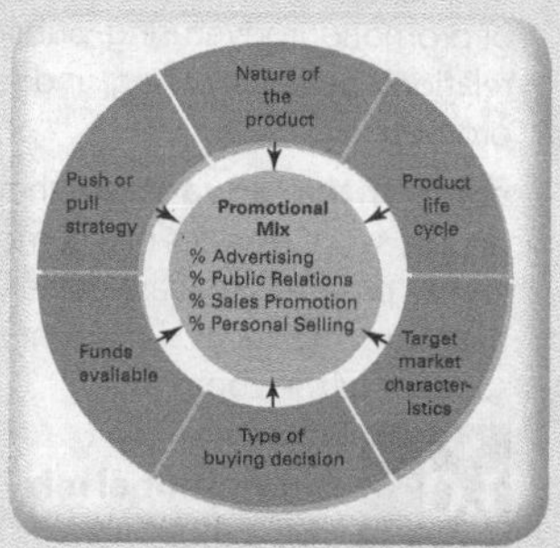

LO 7 **Discuss the concept of integrated marketing communications.** Integrated marketing communications is the careful coordination of all promotional messages for a product or service to ensure the consistency of messages at every contact point where a company meets the consumer—advertising, sales promotion, personal selling, public relations, as well as direct marketing, packaging, and other forms of communication. Marketing managers carefully coordinate all promotional activities to ensure that consumers see and hear one message. Integrated marketing communications has received more attention in recent years due to the proliferation of media choices, the fragmentation of mass markets into more segmented niches, and the decrease in advertising spending in favor of promotional techniques that generate an immediate sales response.

CHAPTER 17 Advertising and Public Relations

Learning Outcomes

LO 1 Discuss the effects of advertising on market share and consumers

LO 2 Identify the major types of advertising

LO 3 Discuss the creative decisions in developing an advertising campaign

LO 4 Describe media evaluation and selection techniques

LO 5 Discuss the role of public relations in the promotional mix

AT&T, General Motors, Procter & Gamble, and Time Warner each spend almost ₹45 crore a day on national advertising in the United States alone.

LO 1 The Effects of Advertising

Advertising is defined in Chapter 16 as impersonal, one-way mass communication about a product or organization that is paid for by a marketer. It is a popular form of promotion, especially for consumer packaged goods and services. Advertising expenditures typically increase annually but declined in 2009 due to economic conditions. In 2008, in United States alone, 37 companies each spent more than ₹4,500 crore on advertising, and the top 100 global advertisers accounted for ₹5,30,550 crore in ad spending. The top five spenders? Procter & Gamble (₹43,785 crore), Unilever (₹25,740 crore), L'Oreal (₹18,180 crore), General Motors (₹16,515 crore), and Toyota (₹14,400 crore). In 2009, however, total ad spending dropped lower than the amount spent by just the top 100 global advertisers the previous year to ₹5,26,500 crore.

Ad spends in India accounted for ₹26,600 crore in 2010, recording a growth of 17 percent over previous year. Print media accounted for 47 percent of total ad revenues, with major contribution coming from categories like education, services, and banking and financial services. Other categories like FMCG and Auto spent dominantly on television.[1] During the period of July 09 to June 2010, India posted the highest growth rate in ad spends in the entire Asia Pacific region at 28 percent.[2]

The amount of money budgeted for advertising by some firms is staggering. AT&T, General Motors, Procter & Gamble, and Time Warner each spend almost ₹ 45 crore a day on national advertising in the United States alone. If local advertising, sales promotion, and public relations are included, this figure rises much higher. HUL, Reckitt Benckiser, and Cadbury India Ltd. were the three biggest advertisers in India in 2010[3], with HUL being the largest advertiser and having an annual advertising budget of more than ₹2,000 crore.[4] Spending on advertising varies by industry.

***Note:** All the figures in U.S. dollars are converted into rupee using the value $1 = ₹45.*

advertising response function
a phenomenon in which spending for advertising and sales promotion increases sales or market share up to a certain level but then produces diminishing returns

Advertising and Market Share

Today's most successful brands of consumer goods, like Lux soap and Coca-Cola, were built by heavy adver-tising and marketing investments long ago. Today's advertising rupees for successful consumer brands are spent on maintaining brand awareness and market share.

New brands with a small market share tend to spend proportionately more for advertising and sales promotion than those with a large market share, typically for two reasons. First, beyond a certain level of spending for advertising and sales promotion, diminishing returns set in. That is, sales or market share begins to decrease no matter how much is spent on advertising and sales promotion. This phenomenon is called the **advertising response function**. Understanding the advertising response function helps marketers use budgets wisely. A market leader like Hindustan Unilever's Vaseline typically spends proportionately less on advertising than a newer line such as Proctor & Gamble's Olay brand. Vaseline has already captured the attention of the majority of its target market. It only needs to remind customers of its product.

The second reason new brands tend to require higher spending for advertising and sales promotion is that a certain minimum level of exposure is needed to measurably affect purchase habits. If P&G advertised its Olay brand in only one or two publications and bought only one or two television spots, it would not achieve the exposure needed to penetrate consumers' perceptual defenses and affect purchase intentions.

The Effects of Advertising on Consumers

Advertising affects consumers' daily lives, informing them about products and services and influencing their attitudes, beliefs, and ultimately their purchases. Advertising affects the television programs people watch, the content of the newspapers they read, the politicians they elect, the medicines they take, and the toys their children play with.

Though advertising cannot change consumers' deeply rooted values and attitudes, advertising may succeed in transforming a person's negative attitude toward a product into a positive one. For instance, serious or dramatic advertisements are more effective at changing consumers' negative attitudes. Humorous ads, on the other hand, have been shown to be more effective at shaping attitudes when consumers already have a positive image of the advertised brand.[5]

Advertising also reinforces positive attitudes toward brands. When consumers have a neutral or favourable frame of reference toward a product or brand, advertising often positively influences them. When consumers are already highly loyal to a brand, they may buy more of it when advertising and promotion for that brand increase.[6] This is why market leaders spend crore of rupees annually to reinforce and remind their loyal customers about the benefits of their products. For example, Parle spent around 20 crore advertising its Frooti brand in the summers of 2010.[7]

Advertising can also affect the way consumers rank a brand's attributes. For example, in years past, car ads emphasized such brand attributes as roominess, speed, and low maintenance. Today, however, car marketers have added safety, versatility, customization, and fuel efficiency to the list.

© INGRAMPUBLISHING/THINKSTOCK

ADVERTISING AFFECTS THE CONTENT OF THE NEWSPAPERS CONSUMERS READ.

LO 2 Major Types of Advertising

A firm's promotional objectives determine the type of advertising it uses. If the goal of the promotion plan is to build up the image of the company or the industry, **institutional advertising** may be used. In contrast, if the advertiser wants to enhance the sales of a specific good or service, **product advertising** is used.

Institutional Advertising

Historically, advertising in India has been product oriented. Today, however, companies market multiple products and need a different type of advertising. Institutional advertising, or corporate advertising, promotes the corporation as a whole and is designed to establish, change, or maintain the corporation's identity. It usually does not ask the audience to do anything but maintain a favorable attitude toward the advertiser and its goods and services.

© AP IMAGES/PRNEWSFOTO/PEABODY ENERGY

Institutional advertising is designed to promote, establish, change, or maintain a corporation's positive identity. Usually the audience isn't asked to do anything except maintain a favorable attitude toward the institution.

A form of institutional advertising called **advocacy advertising** is typically used to safeguard against negative consumer attitudes and to enhance the company's credibility among consumers who already favor its position. Corporations often use advocacy advertising to express their views on controversial issues. At other times, firms' advocacy campaigns react to criticism or blame, some in direct response to criticism by the media. Other advocacy campaigns may try to ward off increased regulation, damaging legislation, or an unfavorable outcome in a lawsuit.

As BP worked to stop the oil leak in the Gulf of Mexico, the company was also spending ₹225 crore on television advertising. One advertisement featured then CEO Tony Hayward apologizing for the spill and promising that BP would pay for the cleanup. BP hoped to quell some of the anger against the company by positioning itself as a group that made a terrible mistake, but one that was working very hard to correct that mistake. On the other hand, Union Carbide made little efforts to rectify its image in the aftermath of Bhopal gas tragedy.

institutional advertising a form of advertising designed to enhance a company's image rather than promote a particular product

product advertising a form of advertising that touts the benefits of a specific good or service

advocacy advertising a form of advertising in which an organization expresses its views on controversial issues or responds to media attacks

pioneering advertising a form of advertising designed to stimulate primary demand for a new product or product category

Product Advertising

Unlike institutional advertising, product advertising promotes the benefits of a specific good or service. The product's stage in its life cycle often determines which type of product advertising is used: pioneering advertising, competitive advertising, or comparative advertising.

Pioneering Advertising **Pioneering advertising** is intended to stimulate primary demand for a new product or product category. Heavily used during the introductory stage of the product life cycle, pioneering advertising offers consumers in-depth information about the benefits of the product class. Pioneering advertising also seeks to create interest. Manufacturers and sellers of sensitive toothpastes have been increasing their advertising volume to create a market for the new category. For instance, GlaxoSmithKline launched print and television ad campaigns and opted for endorsements by dentists to promote and inform readers about tooth sensitivity and its Sensodyne toothpaste.[8] The company spent close to ₹25 crore in marketing of the brand.[9] Similarly, Colgate–Palmolive

competitive advertising a form of advertising designed to influence demand for a specific brand

comparative advertising a form of advertising that compares two or more specifically named or shown competing brands on one or more specific attributes

advertising campaign a series of related advertisements focusing on a common theme, slogan, and set of advertising appeals

advertising objective a specific communication task that a campaign should accomplish for a specified target audience during a specified period

launched an aggressive campaign to promote its new offering—Colgate Sensitive Pro-Relief. The company promoted its product through different communication channels like television, print, online, radio, and in-store activation.[10]

Competitive Advertising Firms use competitive or brand advertising when a product enters the growth phase of the product life cycle and other companies begin to enter the marketplace. Instead of building demand for the product category, the goal of **competitive advertising** is to influence demand for a specific brand. Often, promotion becomes less informative and appeals more to emotions during this phase. Advertisements may begin to stress subtle differences between brands, with heavy emphasis on building recall of a brand name and creating a favorable attitude toward the brand. Automobile advertising has long used very competitive messages, drawing distinctions based on such factors as quality, performance, and image.

Comparative Advertising **Comparative advertising** directly or indirectly compares two or more competing brands on one or more specific attributes. Some advertisers even use comparative advertising against their own brands. Products experiencing slow growth or those entering the marketplace against strong competitors are more likely to employ comparative claims in their advertising.

In India, the comparative representation of products and services is regulated through Monopolies and Restrictive Trade Practices Act (MRTP Act), 1969. The practice of comparative representation is regarded as an "unfair trade practice" and is covered under Sec 36 A of the MRTP Act. The provision for such representation states that it is an unfair practice if it disparages the goods, services or trade of another person by giving false or misleading facts, whether orally or in writing or by visible representation.[11]

In 1997, Colgate-Palmolive sued Hindustan Lever Ltd. (now Hindustan Unilever Ltd.) for making false claims and misleading consumers and disparaging the Colgate brand in advertisement for HLL's New Pepsodent toothpaste. The ad claimed that "New Pepsodent is 102 percent better than the leading toothpaste." Colgate said that there is no sufficient evidence to support such claims that Pepsodent is 102 percent better and that is better than Colgate. The case was presented before Monopolies and Restrictive Trade Practices Commission, which pronounced that it was a case of comparative advertising and disparagement of Colgate's products and ordered HLL to discontinue the usage of the claim of being 102 percent better and comparison with the leading toothpaste.[12]

LO 3 Creative Decisions in Advertising

Advertising strategies are typically organized around an advertising campaign. An **advertising campaign** is a series of related advertisements focusing on a common theme, slogan, and set of advertising appeals. It is a specific advertising effort for a particular product that extends for a defined period of time.

Before any creative work can begin on an advertising campaign, it is important to determine what goals or objectives the advertising should achieve. An **advertising objective** identifies the specific communication task that a campaign should accomplish for a specified target audience during a specified period. The objectives of a specific advertising campaign often depend on the overall corporate objectives and the product being advertised.

The DAGMAR approach (Defining Advertising Goals for Measured Advertising Results) is one method of setting objectives. According to this method, all advertising objectives should precisely define the target audience, the desired percentage change in some specified measure of effectiveness, and the time frame in which that change is to occur.

Once objectives are defined, creative work can begin on the advertising campaign. Advertising campaigns often follow the AIDA model, which was discussed in Chapter 16. Depending on where consumers are in the AIDA process, the creative development

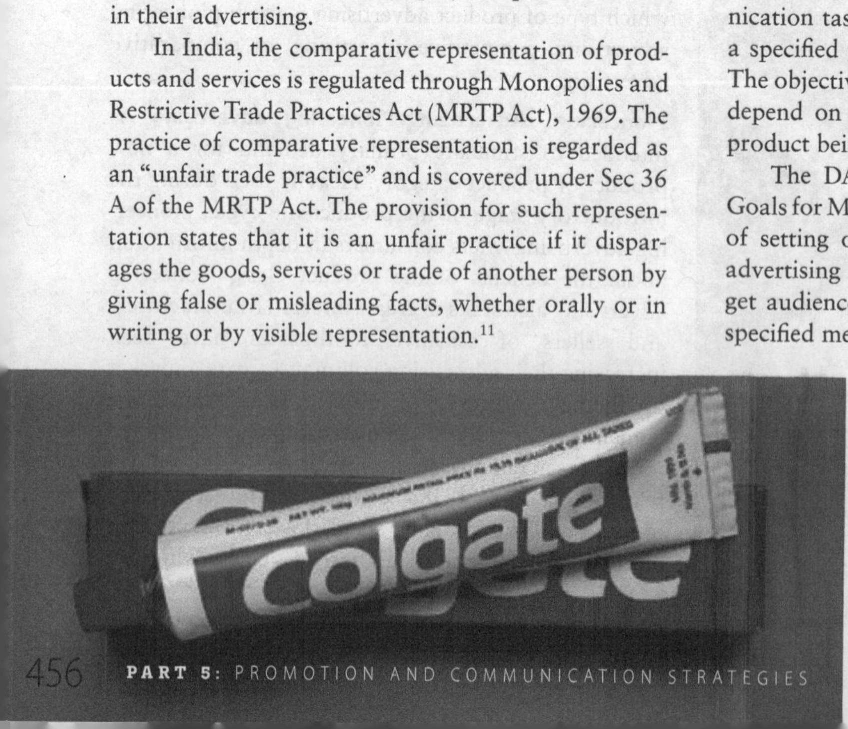

© INDIATODAYIMAGES.COM

of an advertising campaign might focus on creating attention, arousing interest, stimulating desire, or ultimately leading to the action of buying the product. Specifically, creative decisions include identifying product benefits, developing and evaluating advertising appeals, executing the message, and evaluating the effectiveness of the campaign.

Identifying Product Benefits

A well-known rule of thumb in the advertising industry is "Sell the sizzle, not the steak"—that is, in advertising, the goal is to sell the benefits of the product, not its attributes. An attribute is simply a feature of the product such as its easy-open package or special formulation. A benefit is what consumers will receive or achieve by using the product. A benefit should answer the consumer's question "What's in it for me?" Benefits might be such things as convenience or savings. A quick test to determine whether you are offering attributes or benefits in your advertising is to ask "So?" Consider this example:

- *Attribute:* "enriched with 8 essential nutrients, Kellogg's Special K is a low-fat breakfast option that is 98% fat free, and is made from wheat.[13] So . . . ?"
- *Benefit:* "So . . . Special K, a 'shape management' cereal, is a healthier way of losing weight—up to 2.5 kg in just 2 weeks. It is for the health conscious women who are concerned about losing weight."[14]

Developing and Evaluating Advertising Appeals

An **advertising appeal** identifies a reason for a person to buy a product. Developing advertising appeals, a challenging task, is typically the responsibility of the creative people in the advertising agency. Advertising appeals typically play off consumers' emotions or address some need or want the consumer has.

Advertising campaigns can focus on one or more advertising appeals. Often the appeals are quite general, thus allowing the firm to develop a number of subthemes or mini campaigns using both advertising and sales promotion. Several possible advertising appeals are listed in Exhibit 17.1.

Choosing the best appeal from those developed normally requires market research. Criteria for evaluation include desirability, exclusiveness, and believability. The appeal first must make a positive impression on and be desirable to the target market. It must also be exclusive or unique; consumers must be able to distinguish the advertiser's message from competitors' messages. Most important, the appeal should be believable. An appeal that makes extravagant claims not only wastes promotional dollars but also creates ill will for the advertiser.

advertising appeal a reason for a person to buy a product

unique selling proposition a desirable, exclusive, and believable advertising appeal selected as the theme for a campaign

The advertising appeal selected for the campaign becomes what advertisers call its **unique selling proposition.** The unique selling proposition usually becomes the campaign's slogan. Red Bull's "Red Bull gives you wings" touts its benefits, including improved concentration and reaction time, improved performance, and increased endurance (www.redbull.com). Effective slogans often become so ingrained that consumers hearing the slogan can immediately conjure up images of the product.

Executing the Message

Message execution is the way an advertisement portrays its information. In general, the AIDA plan (see

EXHIBIT 17.1
Common Advertising Appeals

Profit	Lets consumers know whether the product will save them money, make them money, or keep them from losing money.
Health	Appeals to those who are body conscious or who want to be healthy; love or romance is used often in selling cosmetics and perfumes.
Fear	Can center around social embarrassment, growing old, or losing one's health; because of its power, requires advertiser to exercise care in execution.
Admiration	Frequently highlights celebrity spokespeople.
Convenience	Is often used for fast-food restaurants and microwave foods.
Fun and Pleasure	Are the keys to advertising vacations, beer, amusement parks, and more.
Vanity and Egotism	Are used most often for expensive or conspicuous items such as cars and clothing.
Environmental Consciousness	Centers around protecting the environment and being considerate of others in the community.

EXHIBIT 17.2

Eleven Common Executional Styles for Advertising

Slice-of-Life	Depicts people in normal settings, such as at the dinner table or in their car. McDonald's often uses slice-of-life styles showing youngsters munching on french fries from Happy Meals on family outings.
Lifestyle	Shows how well the product will fit in with the consumer's lifestyle. With access to the BBM service on their Blackberry smartphones, youngsters were able to share music files, videos, pictures, and jokes with their friends in quick time.
Spokesperson/ Testimonial	Can feature a celebrity, company official, or typical consumer making a testimonial or endorsing a product. Aishwarya Rai Bachchan represents L'Oreal Total Repair 5 shampoo, while Katrina Kaif is the face of Yardley London fragrance.
Fantasy	Creates a fantasy for the viewer built around use of the product. Carmakers often use this style to let viewers fantasize about how they would feel speeding around tight corners or down long country roads in their cars.
Humorous	Advertisers often use humor in their ads, such as Mentos' "Dimag ki Batti Jala De" campaign, Flipkart.com's "No Kidding. No Worries" advertisement series, or Amul butter's advertisements with a pun on current affairs.
Real/Animated Product	Creates a character that represents the product in advertisements, such as Vodafone's ZooZoos, Amul butter girl dressed in a polka-dotted frock, or 7-Up's iconic Fido Dido.
Symbols	Air India's Maharaja was symbolic of Indian heritage and became a cult classic for the airline service provider.
Mood or Image	Builds a mood or image around the product, such as peace, love, or beauty. De Beers ads depicting shadowy silhouettes wearing diamond engagement rings and diamond necklaces portrayed passion and intimacy while extolling that "a diamond is forever."
Demonstration	Shows consumers the expected benefit. Many consumer products use this technique. Laundry detergent spots are famous for demonstrating how their product will clean clothes whiter and brighter. Castrol GTX demonstrated in television commercials how the sludge busters present in the product help in protecting the car engine from dirt.
Musical	Conveys the message of the advertisement through song. For example, Californida Almonds' ad depicted a mother's care in all little things in life, such as making her child eat almonds in the morning, with the song "Tumse Hi" from the movie Jab We Met being played at the start of the commercial.
Scientific	Uses research or scientific evidence to give a brand superiority over competitors. Pain relievers like Crocin advance and Moov neck and shoulder use scientific evidence in their ads.

Chapter 16) is a good blueprint for executing an advertising message. Any ad should immediately draw the reader's, viewer's, or listener's attention. The advertiser must then use the message to hold interest, create desire for the good or service, and ultimately motivate a purchase.

The style in which the message is executed is one of the most creative elements of an advertisement. Exhibit 17.2 lists some examples of executional styles used by advertisers. Executional styles often dictate what type of media is to be employed to convey the message. Scientific executional styles lend themselves well to print advertising where more information can be conveyed. Testimonials by athletes are one of the more popular executional styles.

Injecting humor into an advertisement is a popular and effective executional style. Humorous executional styles are more often used in radio and television advertising than in print or magazine advertising where humor is less easily communicated. Humorous ads are typically used for lower-risk, low-involvement, routine purchases such as candy, cigarettes, and casual jeans than for higher-risk purchases or those that are expensive, durable, or flamboyant.[15]

Sometimes a company will modify its executional styles to make its advertising more effective. For decades, Procter & Gamble has advertised shampoo in China using a demonstrational executional style. Television ads demonstrated how the science of shampoo worked and then showed a woman with nice, shiny hair. Because today's urban Chinese no longer make solely utilitarian purchases, P&G now uses emotional appeals in its advertisements. One shows a woman emerging from an animated cocoon as a sophisticated butterfly while a voice purrs, "Head & Shoulders metamorphosis—new life for hair."[16]

Postcampaign Evaluation

Evaluating an advertising campaign can be the most demanding task facing advertisers. How can an advertiser assess if the campaign led to an increase in sales or market share or elevated awareness of the product? Most advertising campaigns aim to create an image for the good or service instead of asking for action, so their real effect is unknown. So many variables shape the effectiveness of an ad that advertisers often must guess whether their money has been well spent. Nonetheless, marketers spend considerable time studying advertising effectiveness and its probable impact on sales, market share, or awareness.

Testing ad effectiveness can be done either before or after the campaign. Before a campaign is released, marketing managers use pretests to determine the best advertising appeal, layout, and media vehicle. After advertisers implement a campaign, they use several monitoring techniques to determine whether the campaign has met its original goals. Even if a campaign has been highly successful, advertisers still typically do a postcampaign analysis to identify how the campaign might have been more efficient and what factors contributed to its success.

GETTING TOURISTS TO TRAVEL TO THE COUNTRY OF DIVERSITY

Brand India has always been strong to reckon with on the world map. The beautiful landscape and the glorious heritage of the country have always been successful in attracting global tourists. To further boost the tourism industry and increase the inflow of tourists, ministry of tourism in India launched the *Incredible India* campaign in 2002. The campaign showcased the unique offerings of India such as historical monuments, wellness tourism, and spirituality. The campaign proved to be a winner in catching the attention of the international audience and drawing them to visit the country. While a total of 34.67 lakh foreign tourists travelled to India during January–August 2010, the number grew by 10.2 percent to reach 38.19 lakh during January–August 2011. In fact, the month of August 2011 recorded 4.02 lakh foreign tourist arrivals as compared to 3.82 lakh in August 2010 and 3.70 lakh in August 2009.[17] Individual states have also been promoting tourism quite profoundly and reaping the benefits. Kerala Tourism's "God's Own Country" campaign highlights the scenic landscape of the state and has been instrumental in raising Kerala's share from 9 percent in 2009 to 11 percent in 2011 in the country's tourism. Gujarat Tourism roped in Bollywood celebrity Amitabh Bachchan for its "Khushboo Gujarat Ki" campaign and has been advertising its rich heritage extensively. The campaign has resulted in increasing the tourist inflow to the state by 40 percent.[18]

LO 4 Media Decisions in Advertising

medium the channel used to convey a message to a target market

media planning the series of decisions advertisers make regarding the selection and use of media, allowing the marketer to optimally and cost-effectively communicate the message to the target audience

cooperative advertising an arrangement in which the manufacturer and the retailer split the costs of advertising the manufacturer's brand

A major decision for advertisers is the choice of **medium**—the channel used to convey a message to a target market. **Media planning**, therefore, is the series of decisions advertisers make regarding the selection and use of media, allowing the marketer to optimally and cost-effectively communicate the message to the target audience. Specifically, advertisers must determine which types of media will best communicate the benefits of their product or service to the target audience and when and for how long the advertisement will run.

Promotional objectives and the appeal and executional style of the advertising strongly affect the selection of media. Both creative and media decisions are made at the same time: Creative work cannot be completed without knowing which medium will be used to convey the message to the target market. In many cases, the advertising objectives dictate the medium and the creative approach to be used. For example, if the objective is to demonstrate how fast a product operates, a television commercial that shows this action may be the best choice.

Indian advertisers spend roughly ₹22,500 crore annually on media monitored by national reporting services—newspapers, magazines, radio, television, the Internet, and outdoor. The remainder is spent on unmonitored media, such as direct mail, trade exhibits, cooperative advertising, brochures, coupons, catalogs, and special events. Roughly 40 percent of all media spend goes toward television ads, and about 45 percent for print ads. But these traditional mass-market mediums may decline in usage as more targeted mediums grow.

Media Types

Advertising media are channels that advertisers use in mass communication. The six major advertising media are newspapers, magazines, radio, television, outdoor media, and the Internet. Exhibit 17.3 summarizes the advantages and disadvantages of some of these major channels. In recent years, however, alternative media channels have emerged that give advertisers innovative ways to reach their target audience and avoid advertising clutter.

Newspapers The advantages of newspaper advertising include geographic flexibility and timeliness. Because copywriters can usually prepare newspaper ads quickly and at a reasonable cost, local merchants can reach their target market almost daily. Because newspapers are generally a mass-market medium, however, they may not be the best vehicle for marketers trying to reach a very narrow market. Newspaper advertising also encounters a lot of distractions from competing ads and news stories; thus, one company's ad may not be particularly visible.

The main sources of newspaper ad revenue are local retailers, classified ads, and cooperative advertising. In **cooperative advertising**, the manufacturer and the retailer split the costs of advertising the manufacturer's brand. One reason manufacturers use cooperative advertising is the impracticality of listing all their dealers in national advertising. Also, cooperative advertising encourages retailers to devote more effort to the manufacturer's lines.

Magazines Compared to the cost of other media, the cost per contact in magazine advertising is usually high. The cost per potential customer may be much lower, however, because magazines are often targeted to specialized audiences and thus reach more potential customers.

One of the main advantages of magazine advertising is its market selectivity. Magazines are published for virtually every market segment. For instance, *Vogue* is a leading fashion magazine; *Business World* is a business magazine for executives; *National Geographic* is a magazine for environment lovers; *Filmfare* is targeted towards movie buffs; and *Competition Success Review* is a general knowledge magazine geared towards students appearing in competitive exams.

Radio Radio has several strengths as an advertising medium: selectivity and audience segmentation, a large out-of-home audience, low unit and production costs, timeliness, and geographic flexibility. Local advertisers are the most frequent users of radio advertising, contributing over three-quarters of all radio ad revenues. Like newspapers, radio also lends itself well to cooperative advertising.

EXHIBIT 17.3

Advantages and Disadvantages of Major Advertising Media

Medium	Advantages	Disadvantages
Newspapers	Geographic selectivity and flexibility; short-term advertiser commitments; news value and immediacy; year-round readership; high individual market coverage; co-op and local tie-in availability; short lead time	Little demographic selectivity; limited color capabilities; low pass-along rate; may be expensive
Magazines	Good reproduction, especially for color; demographic selectivity; regional selectivity; local market selectivity; relatively long advertising life; high pass-along rate	Long-term advertiser commitments; slow audience buildup; limited demonstration capabilities; lack of urgency; long lead time
Radio	Low cost; immediacy of message; can be scheduled on short notice; relatively no seasonal change in audience; highly portable; short-term advertiser commitments; entertainment carryover	No visual treatment; short advertising life of message; high frequency required to generate comprehension and retention; distractions from background sound; commercial clutter
Television	Ability to reach a wide, diverse audience; low cost per thousand; creative opportunities for demonstration; immediacy of messages; entertainment carryover; demographic selectivity with cable stations	Short life of message; some consumer skepticism about claims; high campaign cost; little demographic selectivity with network stations; long-term advertiser commitments; long lead times required for production; commercial clutter
Internet	Fastest-growing medium; ability to reach a narrow target audience; relatively short lead time required for creating Web-based advertising; moderate cost	Difficult to measure ad effectiveness and return on investment; ad exposure relies on "click-through" from banner ads; not all consumers have access to the Internet
Outdoor Media	Repetition; moderate cost; flexibility; geographic selectivity	Short message; lack of demographic selectivity; high "noise" level distracting audience

As Indians become more mobile and pressed for time, network television and newspapers have lost viewers and readers, particularly in the youth market, but radio is experiencing a resurgence in popularity because its immediate, portable nature meshes so well with a fast-paced lifestyle. The ability to target specific demographic groups is a major selling point for radio stations, attracting advertisers pursuing narrowly defined audiences that are more likely to respond to certain kinds of ads and products. Radio listeners tend to listen habitually and at predictable times, with the most popular being "drive time," when commuters form a vast captive audience. Finally, satellite radio has attracted new audiences that are exposed to ads, which were not previously allowed on that format.

Television Television broadcasters include network television, independent stations, cable television, and a relative newcomer, direct broadcast satellite television. Network television reaches a wide and diverse market, and cable television and direct broadcast satellite systems, such as Tata Sky and DishTV, broadcast a multitude of channels devoted to highly segmented markets. Because of its targeted channels, cable television is often characterized as "narrowcasting" by media buyers.

infomercial a 30-minute or longer advertisement that looks more like a television talk show than a sales pitch

advergaming placing advertising messages in Web-based or video games to advertise or promote a product, service, organization, or issue

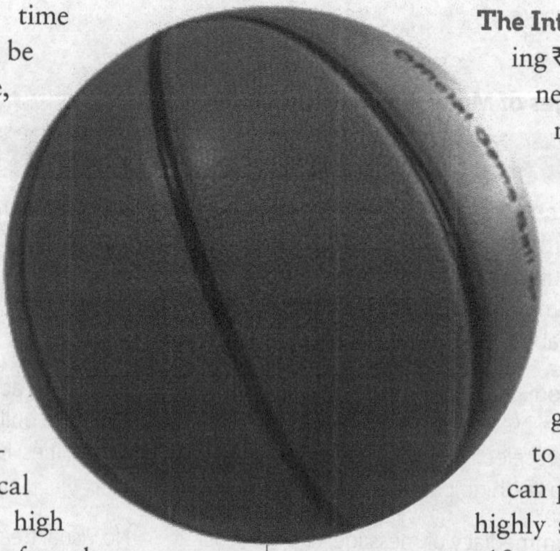

© ISTOCKPHOTO.COM/BENJAMIN GOODE

Advertising time on television can be very expensive, especially for network and popular cable channels. Special events and first-run prime-time shows for top-ranked television programs generate around 50 percent of revenues and command the highest rates for a typical 10-second spot, going up to as high as ₹2 lakh.[20] A 10-second spot before the start of Cricket World Cup 2011 cost ₹4-5 lakh. The same cost went up to ₹25 lakh during the final match.[21]

One of the more successful recent television formats to emerge is the **infomercial**, a 30-minute or longer advertisement, which is relatively inexpensive to produce and air. Advertisers say the infomercial is an ideal way to present complicated information to potential customers, which other advertising vehicles typically don't allow time to do. Some companies are now producing infomercials with a more polished look, which is being embraced by mainstream marketers.

Probably the most significant trend to affect television advertising is the rise in popularity of digital TV networks like Dish TV and Tata Sky. These networks offer the viewers the option of watching programs with no ad breaks in between. Like marketers and advertisers, networks are also highly concerned about ad skipping. If consumers are not watching advertisements, then marketers will spend a greater proportion of their advertising budgets on alternative media, and a critical revenue stream for networks will disappear. Nielsen, a research company, is also working to monitor home-media usage through in-home measurement tools. By understanding where consumer attention lies, companies will be able to target audiences in an increasingly fragmented media market.[22] Nielsen suggests that products featured in these 30-second dramas are remembered better than if they had been featured in a traditional advertisement, but the most effective method is to follow the hybrid, dramatic ad with a traditional ad for the same product.[23]

The Internet With ad revenues exceeding ₹99,000 crore annually, the Internet has become a solid advertising medium. In 2009, marketers spent more to advertise online than in magazines—12.6 percent of global ad spending was online, and 10.3 percent was in magazines.[24] Internet advertising is becoming more versatile and able to target specific groups. Google offers the ability to *audience buy*, where advertisers can purchase ad space targeted to a highly specific group, such as women ages 18 to 34 who like basketball.[25]

Popular Internet sites and search engines generally sell advertising space to marketers to promote their goods and services. Internet surfers click on these ads to be linked to more information about the advertised product or service. Leading advertisers, as well as companies whose ad budgets are not as large, have also become big Internet advertisers.

One of the most popular approaches for Internet advertising is search engine ads. Marketers' primary objective in using search engine ads is to enhance brand awareness. They do this through paid placement of ads tied to key words used in search engines—when someone clicks on the ad, the advertiser pays the search engine a fee. Search engine advertising accounts for half of all money spent on Internet advertising. Search engines also generate nearly half of all Internet ad revenue. The next largest source of Internet revenue is through display and banner ads.[26]

Advergaming **Advergaming** is another popular Internet advertising format in which companies put ad messages in Web-based or video games to advertise or promote a product, service, organization, or issue. Sometimes the entire game amounts to a virtual commercial; other times advertisers sponsor games or buy ad space for a product placement in them. Microsoft and Chevrolet teamed up in U.S. to allow players to "test-drive" a Chevy Volt in "Kinect Joy Ride," a racing game that uses Microsoft's motion-control hardware called Kinect. The hands-free controller is one of the newest innovations in the game market, and the Chevy Volt is an innovative electric car. Players can test-drive the Volt by watching an advertisement before playing the game.[27]

Outdoor Media Outdoor or out-of-home advertising is a flexible, low-cost medium that may take a variety of forms. Examples include billboards, skywriting, giant inflatables, mini billboards in malls and on bus stop shelters, signs in sports arenas, and lighted moving signs in bus terminals and airports, as well as ads painted on cars, trucks, buses, water towers, manhole covers, drinking glass coasters, and even people, called "living advertising." The plywood scaffolding surrounding downtown construction sites often holds ads, which in places like Manhattan's Times Square, can reach over ten lakh viewers a day.

Outdoor advertising reaches a broad and diverse market and is therefore ideal for promoting convenience products and services as well as directing consumers to local businesses. One of outdoor advertising's main advantages over other media is that its exposure frequency is very high, yet the amount of clutter from competing ads is very low. Outdoor advertising also can be customized to local marketing needs, which is why local businesses are the leading outdoor advertisers in any given region.

Alternative Media To cut through the clutter of traditional advertising media, advertisers are developing new media vehicles, like shopping carts in grocery stores, computer screen savers, DVDs, CDs, interactive kiosks in department stores, advertisements run before movies at the cinema, posters on bathroom stalls, and "advertainments"—mini movies that promote a product and are shown via the Internet.

Marketers are looking for more innovative ways to reach captive and often bored commuters. For instance, subway systems are now showing ads via lighted boxes installed along tunnel walls. Other advertisers seek consumers at home. Some marketers have begun replacing hold music on customer service lines with advertisements and movie trailers. This strategy generates revenue for the company being called and catches undistracted consumers for advertisers. The trick is to amuse and interest this captive audience without annoying them during their 10- to 15-minute wait.[28]

© ISTOCKPHOTO.COM/ALEX SLOBODKIN

Video games are emerging as an excellent medium for reaching males ages 18 to 34. Massive, Inc. a New York based company and a subsidiary of Microsoft started a video game advertising network and established a partnership with Nielsen Entertainment, Inc. to provide ad ratings. Massive can insert ads with full motion and sound into games played on Internet-connected computers. Massive has also developed a way to measure the effectiveness of their video game advertisements called AdEffx Action Lift for Gaming. In a recent partnership, after gamers saw Microsoft Bing ads in games, 71 percent recalled that they saw the ad and 60 percent had a more favorable opinion of Bing.[29]

Cell phones are particularly useful for reaching the youth market. Mobile advertising has substantial upside potential when you consider there are more than four billion cell phone users in the world. Today's GPS capability allows you to receive "location-based" advertising on your cell phone. For example, a nearby restaurant can alert you about specials when you're in the neighborhood. Cell phone advertising is less popular in the United States than in Europe and Asia, where cell phone owners utilize text messaging more often.[30]

Companies perceive large growth potential in mobile advertising, particularly through text-messaging ads or coupons. India has witnessed huge growth in the mobile advertising market in recent times. According to a research report by InMobi, world's largest independent mobile advertising network, India became the largest mobile advertising market in the entire Asia-Pacific region in 2010 after registering a growth of 22 percent in mobile ad impressions.[31] In another research conducted by InMobi in 2010 in partnership with comScore, it found that mobile advertising was highly accepted by Indian consumers, with 72 percent of them comfortable with this form of advertising, and over 50 percent showing their willingness to receive personalized advertisements.[32]

media mix the combination of media to be used for a promotional campaign

cost per contact the cost of reaching one member of the target market

reach the number of target consumers exposed to a commercial at least once during a specific period, usually four weeks

frequency the number of times an individual is exposed to a given message during a specific period

audience selectivity the ability of an advertising medium to reach a precisely defined market

Media Selection Considerations

An important element in any advertising campaign is the **media mix**, the combination of media to be used. Media mix decisions are typically based on several factors: cost per contact, reach, frequency, target audience considerations, flexibility of the medium, noise level, and the life span of the medium.

Cost per contact is the cost of reaching one member of the target market. Naturally, as the size of the audience increases, so does the total cost. Cost per contact enables an advertiser to compare media vehicles, such as television versus radio or magazine versus newspaper, or more specifically *India Today* versus *Times of India*. An advertiser debating whether to spend local advertising rupees for television spots or radio spots could consider the cost per contact of each. The advertiser might then pick the vehicle with the lowest cost per contact to maximize advertising punch for the money spent.

Reach is the number of target consumers who are exposed to a commercial at least once during a specific period, usually four weeks. Media plans for product introductions and attempts at increasing brand awareness usually emphasize reach. For example, an advertiser might try to reach 70 percent of the target audience during the first three months of the campaign. Reach is related to a medium's ratings, generally referred to in the industry as *gross ratings points*, or GRP. A television program with a higher GRP (or TRP) means that more people are tuning in to the show and the reach is higher. Accordingly, as GRP increases for a particular medium, so does cost per contact.

Because the typical ad is short-lived and because often only a small portion of an ad may be perceived at one time, advertisers repeat their ads so that consumers will remember the message. **Frequency** is the number of times an individual is exposed to a given message during a specific period. Advertisers use average frequency to measure the intensity of a specific medium's coverage. For example, Coca-Cola might want an average exposure frequency of five for its Minute Maid television ads. That means that each of the television viewers who saw the ad saw it an average of five times.

Media selection is also a matter of matching the advertising medium with the product's target market. If marketers are trying to reach ardent travel enthusiasts, they might select *Outlook Traveller* magazine. A medium's ability to reach a precisely defined market is its **audience selectivity**. Some media vehicles, like general newspapers and network television, appeal to a wide cross section of the population. Others—such as *Verve, Autocar India, Chip,* Cartoon Network, MTV, ESPN, and Food Food—appeal to very specific groups.

The *flexibility* of a medium can be extremely important to an advertiser. For example, because of layouts and design, the lead time for magazine advertising is considerably longer than for other media types and so is less flexible. By contrast, radio and Internet advertising provide maximum flexibility. If necessary, an advertiser can change a radio ad on the day it is aired.

Noise level is the level of distraction to the target audience in a medium. Noise can be created by competing ads, as when a street is lined with billboards or when a television program is cluttered with competing ads. Whereas newspapers and magazines have a high noise level, direct mail is a private medium with a low noise level. Typically, no other advertising media or news stories compete for direct mail readers' attention.

Media have either a short or a long *life span*, which means that messages can either quickly fade or persist as tangible copy to be carefully studied. A radio commercial may last less than a minute, but advertisers can overcome this short life span by repeating radio ads often. In contrast, a magazine has a relatively long life span, which is further increased by a high pass-along rate.

Media planners have traditionally relied on the above factors in selecting an effective media mix, with reach, frequency, and cost often the overriding criteria. Well-established brands with familiar messages, however, probably need fewer exposures to be effective, while newer or unfamiliar brands likely need more exposures to become familiar. In addition, today's media planners have more media options than ever before. (There were over 570 television stations across the country in 2010[33] compared to 30 years ago, when there was just one.)

The proliferation of media channels is causing *media fragmentation* and forcing media planners to pay as much attention to where they place their advertising as to how often the advertisement is repeated. That is, marketers should evaluate reach *and* frequency in assessing the effectiveness of advertising. In certain situations, it may be important to reach potential consumers through as many media vehicles as possible. When this approach is considered, however, the budget must be large enough to achieve sufficient levels of frequency to have an impact. In evaluating reach versus frequency, therefore, the media planner ultimately must select an approach that is most likely to result in the ad being understood and remembered when a purchase decision is being made.

Advertisers also evaluate the qualitative factors involved in media selection. These include such things as attention to the commercial and the program, involvement, program liking, lack of distractions, and other audience behaviors that affect the likelihood that a commercial message is being seen and, hopefully, absorbed. While advertisers can advertise their product in as many media as possible and repeat the ad as many times as they like, the ad still may not be effective if the audience is not paying attention. Research on audience attentiveness for television, for example, shows that the longer viewers stay tuned to a particular program, the more memorable they find the commercials. Contrary to long-held assumptions, "holding power" can be more important than ratings (the number of people tuning in to any part of the program) when selecting media vehicles. Top-ranked shows like *Kaun Banega Crorepati*, *Jhalak Dikhhla Jaa*, and *Bigg Boss* draw many viewers, but those viewers may be unlikely to remember the commercials they watch, perhaps because they are so intensely focused on the shows themselves. Advertising spots during less popular shows, which reach fewer viewers and cost less, may be more likely to make a memorable impression with a limited audience.

media schedule
designation of the media, the specific publications or programs, and the insertion dates of advertising

Additional research highlights the benefits of cross-media advertising campaigns. Viewers who encounter ads both on traditional television and online are most likely to remember and respond to them. Listerine ran a recent campaign in the United States on ABC and ABC.com and found that its mouthwash sales increased 33 percent more among viewers who saw the ad in both places.[34]

Media Scheduling

After choosing the media for the advertising campaign, advertisers must schedule the ads. A **media schedule** designates the medium or media to be used (such as magazines, television, or radio), the specific vehicles (such as *India Today* magazine, the show *Kaun Banega Crorepati* on television, or the *Mirchi Top 20* national radio program), and the insertion dates of the advertising.

ADVERTISING ON TV NOT ALWAYS "LOST"

© COLIN ANDERSON/BLEND IMAGES/JUPITERIMAGES

ABC is a leading television network in the United States. The viewers of its successful drama series, *Lost*, have typically exhibited stronger engagement with advertisements during the show than most other shows—on average, they exhibit 27 percent better brand recall than viewers of other prime-time programs. In addition, series finales tend to have stronger advertising engagement numbers. These two factors encouraged advertisers to pay the whopping ₹4 crore price tag for 30-second spots during the final *Lost* episode. The investment seems to have paid off. The ads had 51 percent better brand recall, 92 percent higher message recall, and 66 percent better likeability against other prime-time shows. The particular favorite was an advertisement by the Target retail chain where the *Lost* Smoke Monster was used to advertise First-Alert smoke detectors.[35]

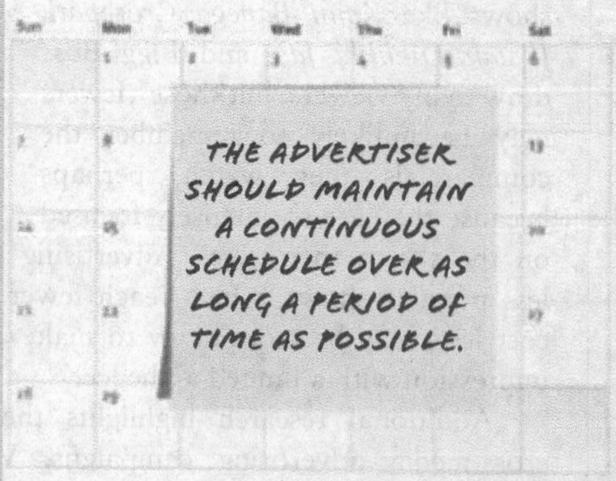

© ISTOCKPHOTO.COM/THORSTEN RUST

continuous media schedule a media scheduling strategy in which advertising is run steadily throughout the advertising period; used for products in the later stages of the product life cycle

flighted media schedule a media scheduling strategy in which ads are run heavily every other month or every two weeks, to achieve a greater impact with an increased frequency and reach at those times

pulsing media schedule a media scheduling strategy that uses continuous scheduling throughout the year coupled with a flighted schedule during the best sales periods

seasonal media schedule a media scheduling strategy that runs advertising only during times of the year when the product is most likely to be used

There are four basic types of media schedules:

- Products in the later stages of the product life cycle, which are advertised on a reminder basis, use a **continuous media schedule.** A continuous schedule allows the advertising to run steadily throughout the advertising period. Examples include Pears soap and Parachute hair oil, which may have an ad in the newspaper every Sunday and a television commercial on Star Plus every Wednesday at 8:00 P.M. over a three-month time period.
- With a **flighted media schedule**, the advertiser may schedule the ads heavily every other month or every two weeks to achieve a greater impact with an increased frequency and reach at those times. Cadbury Celebrations schedules heavy television advertising during months of August and October, when two of the major Indian festivals are celebrated—Raksha Bandhan and Diwali respectively.
- A **pulsing media schedule** combines continuous scheduling with flighting. Continuous advertising is simply heavier during the best sale periods. A retail department store may advertise on a year-round basis but place more advertising during certain sale periods such as Republic Day, Independence Day, and Diwali.
- Certain times of the year call for a **seasonal media schedule**. Products like cough syrup and sunscreen, which are used more during certain times of the year, tend to follow a seasonal strategy.

New research comparing continuous media schedules versus flighted ones finds that continuous schedules for television advertisements are more effective than flighting in driving sales. The research suggests that it may be more important to get exposure as close as possible to the time when someone is going to make a purchase. Therefore, the advertiser should maintain a continuous schedule over as long a period of time as possible. Often called *recency planning*, this theory of scheduling is now commonly used for scheduling television advertising for frequently purchased products, such as Coca-Cola or Tide detergent. Recency planning's main premise is that advertising works by influencing the brand choice of people who are ready to buy.

LO 5 Public Relations

***Public relations* is the element in the promotional mix that evaluates public attitudes, identifies issues that may elicit public concern, and executes programs to gain public understanding and acceptance.** Public relations is a vital link in a progressive company's marketing communication mix. Marketing managers plan solid public relations campaigns that fit into overall marketing plans and focus on targeted audiences. These campaigns strive to maintain a positive image of the corporation in the eyes of the public. As such, they should capitalize on the factors that enhance the firm's image and minimize the factors that could generate a negative image.

Publicity is the effort to capture media attention—for example, through articles or editorials in publications or through human-interest stories on radio or television programs. Corporations usually initiate publicity through a press release that furthers their public relations plans. A company about to introduce a new product or open a new store may send press releases to the media in the hope that the story will be published or broadcast. Savvy publicity can often create overnight sensations or build up a reserve of goodwill with consumers. Corporate donations and sponsorships can also create favorable publicity.

Public relations departments may perform any or all of the following functions:

- *Press relations:* Placing positive, newsworthy information in the news media to attract attention to a product, a service, or a person associated with the firm or institution
- *Product publicity:* Publicizing specific products or services
- *Corporate communication:* Creating internal and external messages to promote a positive image of the firm or institution
- *Public affairs:* Building and maintaining national or local community relations

- *Lobbying:* Influencing legislators and government officials to promote or defeat legislation and regulation
- *Employee and investor relations:* Maintaining positive relationships with employees, shareholders, and others in the financial community
- *Crisis management:* Responding to unfavorable publicity or a negative event

Major Public Relations Tools

Public relations professionals commonly use several tools, many of which require an active role on the part of the public relations professional, such as writing press releases and engaging in proactive media relations. Sometimes, however, these techniques create their own publicity.

New-Product Publicity Publicity is instrumental in introducing new products and services. Publicity can help advertisers explain what's different about their new product by prompting free news stories or positive word of mouth about it. During the introductory period, an especially innovative new product often needs more exposure than conventional, paid advertising affords. Public relations professionals write press releases or develop videos in an effort to generate news about their new product. They also jockey for exposure of their product or service at major events, on popular television and news shows, or in the hands of influential people. The Internet now helps marketers create their own events and spread excitement through consumer groups. Vodafone hit the publicity jackpot with the "Zoozoos". What began as a television spot turned into an Internet storm as people began following these adorable characters in the online space. The Zoozoo brand page on Facebook had more than 65,000 fans and received more than 25 lakh page views. Vodafone jumped on the opportunity and arranged for uploading the Zoozoo commercials exclusively for its Facebook members, even before they were aired on television. Apart from this, a video on making of the commercials was also added, along with downloadable sound files of the ads. The commercials received more than 3,700 comments while the brand page wall attracted 2,400 messages from the fans. The fan following of Zoozoos was not restricted to Facebook only. Its Youtube channel, VodafoneIPL, was the second most subscribed channel in India and Zoozoo was the third highest searched word on Google.[36]

Product Placement Marketers are increasingly using product placement to reinforce brand awareness and create favorable attitudes. **Product placement** is a strategy that involves getting one's product, service, or name to appear in a movie, television show, radio program, magazine, newspaper, video game, video or audio clip, book, or commercial for another product; on the Internet; or at special events. Including an actual product, such as a can of Pepsi, adds a sense of realism to a movie, television show, video game, book, or similar vehicle that cannot be created by a can simply marked "soda." Product placements are arranged through barter (trade of product for placement), through paid placements, or at no charge when the product is viewed as enhancing the vehicle it is placed in.

product placement a public relations strategy that involves getting a product, service, or company name to appear in a movie, television show, radio program, magazine, newspaper, video game, video or audio clip, book, or commercial for another product; on the Internet; or at special events

Paid product placement expenditures were about ₹13,500 crore globally in 2006, though unpaid product placements were valued around ₹33,500 crore. United States, at ₹16,650 crore in 2008, is the largest and fastest growing market for paid product placement.[37] More than two-thirds of product placements are in movies and television shows, with product placements in movies valued at around ₹8,100 crore globally in 2010. The product placement market in movies in India is estimated to be ₹1,000 crore.[38] However, placements in other alternative media are growing, particularly on the Internet and in video games. Digital technology now enables companies to "virtually" place

© ISTOCKPHOTO.COM/ANDREW RICH

sponsorship a public relations strategy in which a company spends money to support an issue, cause, or event that is consistent with corporate objectives, such as improving brand awareness or enhancing corporate image

cause-related marketing a type of sponsorship involving the association of a for-profit company and a nonprofit organization; through the sponsorship, the company's product or service is promoted, and money is raised for the nonprofit

their products in any audio or video production. More than two-thirds of product placements are in movies and television shows, but placements in other alternative media are growing, particularly on the Internet and in video games. Digital technology now enables companies to "virtually" place their products in any audio or video production. Virtual placement not only reduces the cost of product placement for new productions but also enables companies to place their products in previously produced programs, such as reruns of television shows. Overall, companies obtain valuable product exposure, brand reinforcement, and increased sales through product placement, often at a much lower cost than in mass media like television ads.

Consumer Education Some major firms believe that educated consumers are better, more loyal customers. Financial planning firms often sponsor free educational seminars on money management, retirement planning, and investing in the hope that the seminar participants will choose the sponsoring organization for their future financial needs.

Sponsorship Sponsorships are increasing both in number and as a proportion of companies' marketing budgets, with global spending reaching ₹2,08,350 crore in 2010.[39] United States alone accounted for ₹77,400 crore worth of sponsorship.[40] Probably the biggest reason for the increasing use of sponsorships is the difficulty of reaching audiences and differentiating a product from competing brands through the mass media.

With **sponsorship**, a company spends money to support an issue, cause, or event that is consistent with corporate objectives, such as improving brand awareness or enhancing corporate image. The biggest category is sports, which accounts for almost 70 percent of spending in sponsorships. Non-sports categories include entertainment tours and attractions, causes, arts, festivals, fairs and annual events, and association and membership organizations.[41]

Although the most popular sponsorship events are still those involving sports, music, or the arts, companies have recently been turning to more specialized events such as tie-ins with schools, charities, and other community service organizations. Marketers sometimes even create their own events tied around their products.

Corporations sponsor issues as well as events. Sponsorship issues are quite diverse, but the three most popular are education, health care, and social programs. Firms often donate a percentage of sales or profits to a worthy cause favored by their target market.

A special type of sponsorship, **cause-related marketing**, involves the association of a for-profit company with a nonprofit organization. Through the sponsorship, the company's product or service is promoted, and money is raised for the nonprofit. In a common type of cause-related sponsorship, a company agrees to donate a percentage of the purchase price for a particular item to a charity, but some arrangements are more complex. For example, schools around the United States collect Campbell's soup labels and General Mills cereal box tops because those companies will donate to the school a certain amount for every label or top submitted. Several studies indicate that some consumers consider a company's reputation when making purchasing decisions and that a company's community involvement boosts employee morale and loyalty.[42]

TOMS shoes in California was founded on the premise that one pair of shoes would be given to a child in need for every pair of shoes purchased. TOMS gave away its millionth pair in 2010.

© AP IMAGES/PRNEWSFOTO/TOMS SHOES

Company Web Sites Companies increasingly are using the Internet in their public relations strategies. Company Web sites are used to introduce new products, promote existing products, obtain consumer feedback, post news releases, communicate legislative and regulatory information, showcase upcoming events, provide links to related sites, release financial information, interact with customers and potential customers, and perform many more marketing activities. Online reviews from opinion leaders and other consumers help marketers sway purchasing decisions in their favor. On Playstation.com, Sony has online support, events and promotions, game trailers, and new and updated product releases. The site also includes message boards where the gaming community exchanges tips on games, votes on lifestyle issues like music and videos, and learns about promotional events.[43]

Web sites are also key elements of integrated marketing communications strategies. Kraft Foods, an American multinational giant in confectionery, food, and beverage categories, worked with Meredith Integrated Marketing to develop a print magazine with family-friendly recipes. Kraft's Web site aggregates user and magazine recipes in an easily searchable format. Users can even make their own recipe box. Kraft also developed a recipe iPhone app with how-to videos and built-in shopping lists.[44]

More and more often, companies are also using blogs—both corporate and noncorporate—as a tool to manage their public images. Noncorporate blogs cannot be controlled, but marketers must monitor them to be aware of and respond to negative information and encourage positive content. In addition to "getting the message out," companies are using blogs to create communities of consumers who feel positively about the brand. The hope is that positive attitude toward the brand will build into strong word-of-mouth marketing. Companies must exercise caution when diving into corporate blogging, however. Coca-Cola launched a blog authored by a fictional character that did little except parrot the company line. Consumers immediately saw the blog for what it was (a transparent public relations platform) and lambasted Coca-Cola for its insincerity.[45]

crisis management a coordinated effort to handle all the effects of unfavorable publicity or another unexpected unfavorable event

Managing Unfavorable Publicity

Although marketers try to avoid unpleasant situations, crises do happen. In our free-press environment, publicity is not easily controlled, especially in a crisis. **Crisis management** is the coordinated effort to handle the effects of unfavorable publicity, ensuring fast and accurate communication in times of emergency.

When users found that holding their iPhone 4 a certain way caused poor reception and dropped calls, the media ran a slew of negative stories questioning the iPhone 4's design and useability. In his intial response to negative publicity, Steve Jobs tried to deflect attacks on the design of the iPhone's antenna by attacking phones by Apple's competitors. Ultimately, however, Jobs and the Apple team offered full refunds on the iPhone 4 for unsatisfied customers or a free cover that helped alleviate the problems caused by the poorly designed antenna. The offers deflated the negative press, and by showing good faith to customers who purchased the phone, Apple may have increased loyalty for its products and its brand.[46]

Review And Applications

Discuss the effects of advertising on market share and consumers. Advertising helps marketers increase or maintain brand awareness as well as market share. Typically, more is spent to advertise new brands with a small market share than to advertise older brands. Brands with a large market share use advertising mainly to maintain their share of the market. Advertising affects consumers' daily lives as well as their purchases. Although advertising can seldom change strongly held consumer attitudes and values, it may transform a consumer's negative attitude toward a product into a positive one. Additionally, when consumers are highly loyal to a brand, they may buy more of that brand when advertising is increased. Lastly, advertising can also change the importance of a brand's attributes to consumers. By emphasizing different brand attributes, advertisers can change their appeal in response to consumers' changing needs or try to achieve an advantage over competing brands.

1.1 Discuss the reasons why new brands with a smaller market share spend proportionately more on advertising than brands with a larger market share.

1.2 Form a three-person team. Divide the responsibility for getting newspaper advertisements and menus for several local restaurants. While you are at the restaurants to obtain copies of their menus, observe the atmosphere and interview the manager to determine what he or she believes are the primary reasons people choose to dine there. Pool your information and develop a table comparing the restaurants in terms of convenience of location, value for the money, food variety and quality, atmosphere, and so on. Rank the restaurants in terms of their appeal to college students. Explain the basis of your rankings. What other market segment would be attracted to the restaurants and why? Do the newspaper advertisements emphasize the most effective appeal for a particular restaurant? Explain.

Identify the major types of advertising. Advertising is any form of impersonal, paid communication in which the sponsor or company is identified. The two major types of advertising are institutional advertising and product advertising. Institutional advertising is not product oriented; rather, its purpose is to foster a positive company image among the general public, investment community, customers, and employees. Product advertising is designed mainly to promote goods and services, and it is classified into three main categories: pioneering, competitive, and comparative. A product's place in the product life cycle is a major determinant of the type of advertising used to promote it.

2.1 At what stage in a product's life cycle are pioneering, competitive, and comparative advertising most likely to occur? Give a current example of each type of advertising.

Discuss the creative decisions in developing an advertising campaign. Before any creative work can begin on an advertising campaign, it is important to determine what goals or objectives the advertising should achieve. The objectives of a specific advertising campaign often depend on the overall corporate objectives and the product being advertised. Once objectives have been defined, creative work can begin on the advertising campaign. Creative decisions include identifying the product's benefits, developing possible advertising appeals, evaluating and selecting the advertising appeals, executing the advertising message, and evaluating the effectiveness of the campaign.

3.1 What is an advertising appeal? Give some examples of advertising appeals you have observed recently in the media.

3.2 Design a full-page magazine advertisement for a new brand of soft drink. The name of the new drink and its package design are at your discretion. On a separate sheet, specify the benefits stressed or appeals made in the advertisement.

Describe media evaluation and selection techniques. Media evaluation and selection make up a crucial step in the advertising campaign process. Major types of advertising media include newspapers, magazines, radio, television, outdoor advertising such as billboards and bus panels, and the Internet. Recent trends in advertising media include video shopping carts, computer screen savers, cinema and DVD advertising, cell phones, and videogames. Promotion managers choose the advertising campaign's media mix on the basis of the following variables: cost per contact, reach, frequency, characteristics of the target audience, flexibility of the medium, noise level, and the life span of the medium. After choosing the media mix, a media schedule designates when the advertisement will appear and the specific vehicles it will appear in.

4.1 What are the advantages of radio advertising? Why is radio expanding as an advertising medium?

4.2 You are the advertising manager of a sailing magazine, and one of your biggest potential advertisers has questioned your rates. Write the firm a letter explaining why you believe your audience selectivity is worth the extra expense for advertisers.

4.3 Identify an appropriate media mix for the following products:
   a. Chewing tobacco
   b. *Vogue* magazine
   c. Mosquito repellent
   d. Car fragrance
   e. "Don't Drink and Drive" campaign by state government

4.4 How easy is it to find out about advertising options on the Internet? Go to Yahoo!'s advertiser page (**www.yahoo.com/info/advertising**). What kind of information do they require from you?

Discuss the role of public relations in the promotional mix. Public relations is a vital part of a firm's promotional mix. A company fosters good publicity to enhance its image and promote its products. Popular public relations tools include new-product publicity, product placements, consumer education, sponsorships, and Internet Web sites. An equally important aspect of public relations is managing unfavorable publicity to minimize damage to a firm's image.

5.1 How can advertising and publicity work together? Give an example.

5.2 As the new public relations director for a sportswear company, you have been asked to set public relations objectives for a new line of athletic shoes to be introduced to the teen market. Draft a memo outlining the objectives you propose for the shoe's introduction and your reasons for them.

5.3 Review the newspapers in your area for one week. Try to review several and varied newspapers (local, campus, cultural, countercultural, etc.) During this period, cut out all the event advertisements that list sponsors. Once you have your collection, spread them out so you can see them all at once. Identify any patterns or connections between the type of event and its sponsors. Identify companies that sponsor more than one event. What do sponsors tell you about target markets? After analyzing the ads, write a brief paragraph summarizing your discoveries.

Exercises

APPLICATION EXERCISE 1

You may think that creating advertising is easy. After all, you have a lot of experience with advertising, having been bombarded with advertisements since you were a child. But creating advertising presents real challenges. In this exercise, you will be challenged to create an ad for a new product for animal use that is based on a product used by humans. Some examples include socks for dogs, claw polish for tigers, and "Minute Mice" for cats. You can pick any product and any animal, but the combination must make sense.[47]

Activities

1. You have been hired by the purveyor of your chosen product to create a print advertisement. Lay out your ad on a piece of paper that is no smaller than 8.5 by 11 inches and no larger than 11 by 14 inches. Include a headline, illustration, logo, and body copy. Your illustration may be either hand-drawn or clipped from a magazine.
2. Include the copy for your ad directly on the front of the ad unless your copy blocks are too large for you to be legible or neat. If that is the case, then label your copy blocks with letters, put them on the back of your ad, and write the corresponding letter in the appropriate place on the front of the ad.
3. Don't forget to pick your own brand name for the product or service (like "Minute Mice").

APPLICATION EXERCISE 2

In this age of 24-hour cable news channels, tabloid news shows, and aggressive local and national news reporters intent on exposing corporate wrongdoing, one of the most important skills for a manager to learn is how to deal effectively with the press. Test your ability to deal effectively with the press by putting yourself in the following situation. To make the situation more realistic read the scenario and then give yourself two minutes to write a response to each question.[48]

Activity

Soft drink companies have time and again faced controversies about their product content. Few years back, they found themselves surrounded by the controversy of pesticide content in their product and there was hue and cry to withdraw the supplies of soft drink majors.

You are the vice president, marketing of Coca Cola India and a TV reporter from CNBC called you to get your response to this controversy. When he and the camera crew arrived, he asked you the following questions:

1. "It has been found that soft drinks manufactured by your company contain a good amount of pesticide residue. What do you have to say to this claim?"
2. "With the presence of such toxic pesticides in your product, don't you think you are playing with the health and lives of naive customers?"

ETHICS EXERCISE

Creative Advertising Agency has been asked to help its largest client improve its corporate image after a highly publicized product recall. The client requests a television advertisement highlighting the company's generous donation of products to low-income families. The only such donation the company has made, however, is a donation of the recalled products. The account executive fears promoting the donation could cause further consumer backlash, but the client continues to press for the spot.

Questions

1. Should Creative Advertising meet the client's expectations (i.e., create the promotional spot) or risk losing the account? Explain your reasoning.
2. What does the AMA Statement of Ethics say about truth in advertising? Go to **www.marketingpower.com** and review the code. Then, write a brief paragraph describing how the AMA Statement of Ethics relates to this issue.

MARKETING PLAN EXERCISE

In Part 5 of your strategic marketing plan you'll continue defining the elements of the marketing mix, focusing on promotion and communication decisions. Use the following exercises to guide you through the advertising and public relations decisions you'll make for your chosen company:

1. Investigate different media placement rates (such as for a school newspaper, local newspaper, national newspaper, local radio station, local TV station, general or specialty interest magazine, local billboard, transit advertising, or the Internet). You can call local media to find out these rates. Which media should your firm use? Which media can your firm afford? When should media be used?
2. Are there different advertising concerns for the Internet-only firm than for the firm with an established brick-and-mortar presence? If so, what are they? Design the advertising for each medium selected in question 1. Do all advertising pieces carry a uniform theme and style? Is there sufficient information about benefits offered to consumers? Do customers have an option for obtaining further information?
3. List the public relations activities that your company should do. Be sure to make them consistent with your branding and other promotions. In addition, write a plan for handling bad publicity. Bad publicity travels at lightspeed over the Internet and is much more of a challenge to an e-marketer. Check out **http://urbanlegends.about.com** to see how misinformation can travel the Internet and cause public relations nightmares for companies.

Short Case: IDEA CELLULAR

Prepared by
Dr. Dheeraj Sharma,
Indian Institute of Management, Ahmedabad

Idea Cellular advertisements have been known for its uniqueness and aggressiveness. When Idea was launched in India, it came up with fun and unusual advertisements telecasted on TV. It always used its mother-brand name (Idea) for the ads in a judicious way. Soon, the brand 'Idea Cellular' became known to everyone. The tag line it used then was "*An Idea Can Change Your Life*". Its advertisements focused on telling its customers about its ubiquitous coverage and cheap calling rates. Their advertising strategy worked for Idea. Its target was the urban population and soon it had a lot of subscribers in its kitty.

After Idea became a known telecom brand and had earned a good subscriber base, it changed its advertising strategy. It came up with "*What an idea, Sirji!*" campaign and appointed Abhishek Bachchan as the brand ambassador. There were many ads under this tagline. These ads were telecasted on TV, newspapers, radio, and digital media. This time, the ads focused on social issues, and how idea subscribers could overcome those using mobile phones. These campaigns addressed social issues like caste difference, language barriers, illiteracy, elections, global warming, and fitness. Decreasing tariff rates blended with its convincing ads enabled Idea to penetrate to the rural markets. About 40% of Ideas customers come from rural areas.[49] The "What an Idea Sirji" campaign became famous, and it did help Idea gain more subscribers. Anupama Ahluwalia, Senior Vice-President, Idea Cellular said to *The Economic Times* that the aforementioned marketing campaign *played an important role in the success of the Idea Brand.*[50]

Soon after the implementation of Mobile Number Portability (MNP) was announced, Idea came up with "*No Idea—Get Idea*" campaign. These ad campaigns were aggressive. The ads depicted customers using other networks with problems like no coverage in lifts, voice echo, inefficient customer services, etc., advising them to switch to Idea for a better service. Idea was first in the league to launch Mobile Number Portability ads. After MNP service was implemented in India, Idea received the most MNP requests to switch to Idea.[51] Today, Idea has the third largest subscriber base in India. It follows Bharti-Airtel and Vodafone in the league, and it only provides cellular services.

Continuing its trend, soon after it was announced that 3G services were to be launched, Idea was first to come up with ads that showed how Idea 3G services would make watching TV, videos, etc., quicker and easier. Recently, Idea came up with "3G pe Busy" ad campaign. This ad was much spoken as it promoted using a 3G connection to reduce the birth rate. The ad shows that the 3G services are so engaging that people will not really have time or interest in having babies. This ad has received both, a positive and negative response for its depiction.

Idea ads have been very well thought of and strategic. It has had a history of attracting its customers. It recently won EFFIES Gold and Silver 2011 awards for the campaigns '*No Idea—Get Idea*' and '*Break the language barrier*', respectively. Idea has time and again managed to create unique advertising and public relations strategies. Mr Himanshu Kapania, MD, Idea Cellular, said to *The Economic Times* that the marketing campaigns were able to get them a strong "rural footprint but with the option of MNP, the company also wanted to garner attention in metros and big cities".[52]

Questions

1. Do you think Idea advertisements are becoming redundant? Do you think Idea will continue to woo its customers with its advertising trends?
2. Do you think advertising has played a major role in attracting customers to Idea?

17 Advertising and Public Relations

KEY TERMS

LO 1

advertising response function a phenomenon in which spending for advertising and sales promotion increases sales or market share up to a certain level but then produces diminishing returns

LO 2

institutional advertising a form of advertising designed to enhance a company's image rather than promote a particular product

product advertising a form of advertising that touts the benefits of a specific good or service

advocacy advertising a form of advertising in which an organization expresses its views on controversial issues or responds to media attacks

pioneering advertising a form of advertising designed to stimulate primary demand for a new product or product category

competitive advertising a form of advertising designed to influence demand for a specific brand

comparative advertising a form of advertising that compares two or more specifically named or shown competing brands on one or more specific attributes

LO 3

advertising campaign a series of related advertisements focusing on a common theme, slogan, and set of advertising appeals

advertising objective a specific communication task that a campaign should accomplish for a specified target audience during a specified period

advertising appeal a reason for a person to buy a product

unique selling proposition a desirable, exclusive, and believable advertising appeal selected as the theme for a campaign

KEY CONCEPTS

LO 1

Discuss the effects of advertising on market share and consumers. Advertising helps marketers increase or maintain brand awareness as well as market share. Typically, more is spent to advertise new brands with a small market share than to advertise older brands. Brands with a large market share use advertising mainly to maintain their share of the market. Advertising affects consumers' daily lives as well as their purchases. Although advertising can seldom change strongly held consumer attitudes and values, it may transform a consumer's negative attitude toward a product into a positive one. Additionally, when consumers are highly loyal to a brand, they may buy more of that brand when advertising is increased. Lastly, advertising can also change the importance of a brand's attributes to consumers. By emphasizing different brand attributes, advertisers can change their appeal in response to consumers' changing needs or try to achieve an advantage over competing brands.

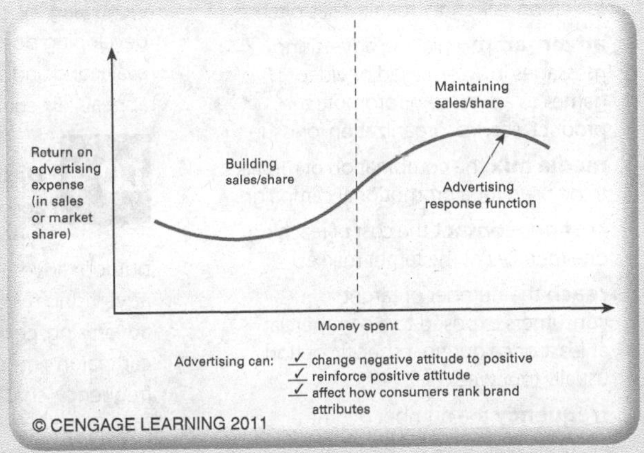

© CENGAGE LEARNING 2011

LO 2

Identify the major types of advertising. Advertising is any form of impersonal, paid communication in which the sponsor or company is identified. The two major types of advertising are institutional advertising and product advertising. Institutional advertising is not product oriented; rather, its purpose is to foster a positive company image among the general public, investment community, customers, and employees. Product advertising is designed mainly to promote goods and services, and it is classified into three main categories: pioneering, competitive, and comparative. A product's place in the product life cycle is a major determinant of the type of advertising used to promote it.

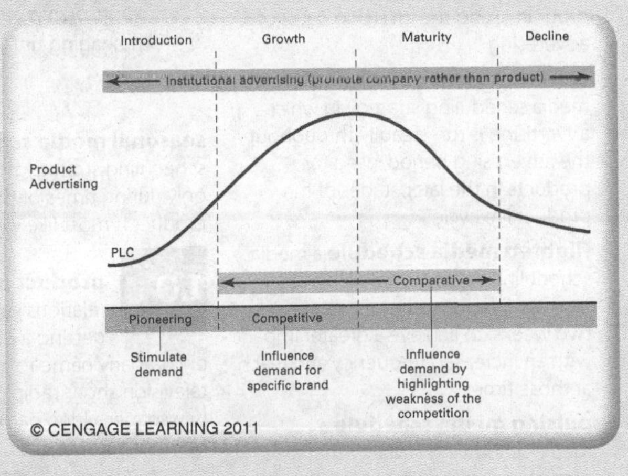

© CENGAGE LEARNING 2011

LO 4 **medium** the channel used to convey a message to a target market

media planning the series of decisions advertisers make regarding the selection and use of media, allowing the marketer to optimally and cost-effectively communicate the message to the target audience

cooperative advertising an arrangement in which the manufacturer and the retailer split the costs of advertising the manufacturer's brand

infomercial a 30-minute or longer advertisement that looks more like a television talk show than a sales pitch

advergaming placing advertising messages in Web-based or video games to advertise or promote a product, service, organization, or issue

media mix the combination of media to be used for a promotional campaign

cost per contact the cost of reaching one member of the target market

reach the number of target consumers exposed to a commercial at least once during a specific period, usually four weeks

frequency the number of times an individual is exposed to a given message during a specific period

audience selectivity the ability of an advertising medium to reach a precisely defined market

media schedule designation of the media, the specific publications or programs, and the insertion dates of advertising

continuous media schedule a media scheduling strategy in which advertising is run steadily throughout the advertising period; used for products in the later stages of the product life cycle

flighted media schedule a media scheduling strategy in which ads are run heavily every other month or every two weeks, to achieve a greater impact with an increased frequency and reach at those times

pulsing media schedule a media scheduling strategy that uses continuous scheduling throughout the year coupled with a flighted schedule during the best sales periods

LO 3 **Discuss the creative decisions in developing an advertising campaign.** Before any creative work can begin on an advertising campaign, it is important to determine what goals or objectives the advertising should achieve. The objectives of a specific advertising campaign often depend on the overall corporate objectives and the product being advertised. Once objectives have been defined, creative work can begin on the advertising campaign. Creative decisions include identifying the product's benefits, developing possible advertising appeals, evaluating and selecting the advertising appeals, executing the advertising message, and evaluating the effectiveness of the campaign.

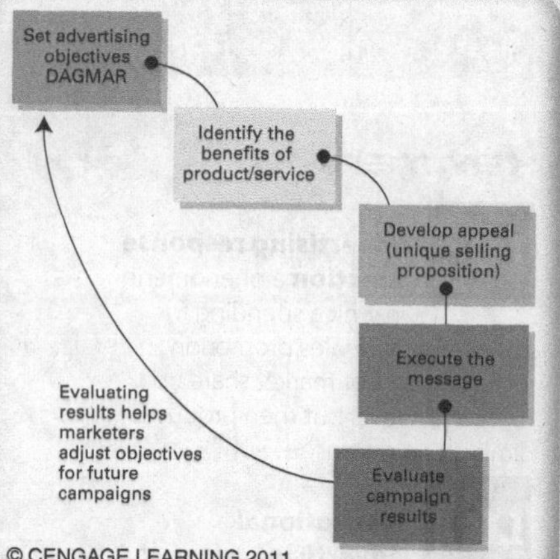

© CENGAGE LEARNING 2011

LO 4 **Describe media evaluation and selection techniques.** Media evaluation and selection make up a crucial step in the advertising campaign process. Major types of advertising media include newspapers, magazines, radio, television, outdoor advertising such as billboards and bus panels, and the Internet. Recent trends in advertising media include video shopping carts, computer screen savers, cinema and DVD advertising, cell phones, and videogames. Promotion managers choose the advertising campaign's media mix on the basis of the following variables: cost per contact, reach, frequency, characteristics of the target audience, flexibility of the medium, noise level, and the life span of the medium. After choosing the media mix, a media schedule designates when the advertisement will appear and the specific vehicles it will appear in.

LO 5 **Discuss the role of public relations in the promotional mix.** Public relations is a vital part of a firm's promotional mix. A company fosters good publicity to enhance its image and promote its products. Popular public relations tools include new-product publicity, product placements, consumer education, sponsorships, and Internet Web sites. An equally important aspect of public relations is managing unfavorable publicity to minimize damage to a firm's image.

seasonal media schedule a media scheduling strategy that runs advertising only during times of the year when the product is most likely to be used

LO 5 **product placement** a public relations strategy that involves getting a product, service, or company name to appear in a movie, television show, radio program, magazine, newspaper, video game, video or audio clip, book, or commercial for another product; on the Internet; or at special events

sponsorship a public relations strategy in which a company spends money to support an issue, cause, or event that is consistent with corporate objectives, such as improving brand awareness or enhancing corporate image

cause-related marketing a type of sponsorship involving the association of a for-profit company and a nonprofit organization; through the sponsorship, the company's product or service is promoted, and money is raised for the nonprofit

crisis management a coordinated effort to handle all the effects of unfavorable publicity or another unexpected unfavorable event

CHAPTER 18

Sales Promotion and Personal Selling

Learning Outcomes

- **LO 1** Define and state the objectives of sales promotion
- **LO 2** Discuss the most common forms of consumer sales promotion
- **LO 3** List the most common forms of trade sales promotion
- **LO 4** Describe personal selling
- **LO 5** Discuss the key differences between relationship selling and traditional selling
- **LO 6** List the steps in the selling process

Advertising offers the consumer a reason to buy; sales promotion offers an incentive to buy.

LO 1 Sales Promotion

In addition to using advertising, public relations, and personal selling, marketing managers can use sales promotion to increase the effectiveness of their promotional efforts. *Sales promotion* is marketing communication activities, other than advertising, personal selling, and public relations, in which a short-term incentive motivates consumers or members of the distribution channel to purchase a good or service immediately, either by lowering the price or by adding value.

consumer sales promotion sales promotion activities targeting the ultimate consumer

trade sales promotion sales promotion activities targeting a marketing channel member, such as a wholesaler or retailer

Advertising offers the consumer a reason to buy; sales promotion offers an incentive to buy. Sales promotion is usually cheaper than advertising and easier to measure. A major national television advertising campaign often costs ₹20 crore or more to create, produce, and place. In contrast, promotional campaigns using the Internet or direct marketing methods can cost less than half that amount. It is also very difficult to determine how many people buy a product or service as a result of radio or television ads. With sales promotion, marketers know the precise number of coupons redeemed or the number of contest entries.

Sales promotion is usually targeted toward either of two distinctly different markets. **Consumer sales promotion** is targeted to the ultimate consumer market. **Trade sales promotion** is directed to members of the marketing channel, such as wholesalers and retailers. Sales promotion expenditures have been steadily increasing over the past several years as a result of increased competition, the ever-expanding array of available media choices, consumers and retailers demanding more deals from manufacturers, and the continued reliance on accountable and

***Note:** All the figures in U.S. dollars are converted into rupee using the value $1 = ₹45.*

measurable marketing strategies. In addition, product and service marketers who have traditionally ignored sales promotion activities, such as power companies, have discovered the marketing power of sales promotion. In fact, annual expenditures on promotion marketing in the United States now exceed ₹18,00,000 crore. Direct mail is the most widely used promotional medium, accounting for 50 percent of annual promotional expenditures.[1]

The Objectives of Sales Promotion

Sales promotion usually has more effect on behavior than on attitudes. Immediate purchase is the goal of sales promotion, regardless of the form it takes. The objectives of a promotion depend on the general behavior of target consumers (see Exhibit 18.1). For example, marketers who are targeting loyal users of their product actually need to reinforce existing behavior or increase product usage. An effective tool for strengthening brand loyalty is the *frequent buyer program*, which rewards consumers for repeat purchases. Other types of promotions are more effective with customers prone to brand switching or with those who are loyal to a competitor's product. A rupee-off coupon, free sample, or eye-catching display in a store will often entice shoppers to try a different brand.

Once marketers understand the dynamics occurring within their product category and have determined the particular consumers and consumer behaviors they want to influence, they can then go about selecting promotional tools to achieve these goals.

LO 2 Tools for Consumer Sales Promotion

Marketing managers must decide which consumer sales promotion devices to use in a specific campaign. The methods chosen must suit the objectives to ensure success of the overall promotion plan. The popular tools for consumer sales promotion discussed in the following pages have also been easily transferred to online versions to entice Internet users to visit sites, purchase products, or use services on the Web.

EXHIBIT 18.1

Types of Consumers and Sales Promotion Goals

Type of Buyer	Desired Results	Sales Promotion Examples
Loyal customers People who buy your product most or all of the time	Reinforce behavior, increase consumption, change purchase timing	• Loyalty marketing programs, such as frequent buyer cards or frequent shopper clubs • Bonus packs that give loyal consumers an incentive to stock up or premiums offered in return for proofs of purchase
Competitor's customers People who buy a competitor's product most or all of the time	Break loyalty, persuade to switch to your brand	• Sampling to introduce your product's superior qualities compared to their brand • Sweepstakes, contests, or premiums that create interest in the product
Brand switchers People who buy a variety of products in the category	Persuade to buy your brand more often	• Any promotion that lowers the price of the product, such as coupons, price-off packages, and bonus packs • Trade deals that help make the product more readily available than competing products
Price buyers People who consistently buy the least expensive brand	Appeal with low prices or supply added value that makes price less important	• Coupons, price-off packages, refunds, or trade deals that reduce the price of the brand to match that of the brand that would have been purchased

SOURCE: From *Sales Promotion Essentials*, 2nd ed., by Don E. Schultz, William A. Robinson, and Lisa A. Petrison. Reprinted by permission of NTC Publishing Group, 4255 Touhy Ave., Lincolnwood, IL 60048.

© ISTOCKPHOTO.COM/THINKSTOCK

Coupons and Rebates

A **coupon** is a certificate that entitles consumers to an immediate price reduction when they buy the product. Coupons are a particularly good way to encourage product trial and repurchase. They are also likely to increase the amount of a product bought.

Distribution of coupons is a highly effective promotional scheme in the United States. Almost 30,000 crore coupons are distributed to U.S. households annually, and this does not include the crore of coupons increasingly available over the Internet and in stores. Intense competition in the consumer packaged goods category and the annual introduction of over 1,200 new products have contributed to this trend. Though coupons are often criticized for reaching consumers who have no interest in the product or for encouraging repeat purchase by regular users, recent studies indicate that coupons promote new-product use and are likely to stimulate purchases. However, companies must remember that customers' behaviour towards usage of coupons is not merely dependent on their desire to use coupons; the attractiveness of the coupons is equally important to induce usage.[2]

The market for coupons in India is relatively small in comparison with the developed economies; it is close to approximately ₹25 crore. Dining, personal care, and recreational activities are some of the categories driving the highest usage of coupons.[3] Nevertheless, Indian consumers are largely indifferent towards coupons as a tool of sales promotion and are more enticed by schemes like "buy one get one free" or a price discount. One reason for the unpopularity of coupons is that it requires active search on the part of the consumers, something that Indian consumers are not comfortable with. It is a kind of burden for them to collect coupons and carry them the next time they go out for purchasing. Also, the transaction utility is less in case of coupons as compared to price discounts since there is a time gap between the buying decision and actually getting the benefit of the deal.[4]

Freestanding inserts (FSIs), the promotional coupons inserts found in newspapers, have been the traditional way of circulating printed coupons. FSIs are used to distribute 85 percent of coupons. Internet coupons are gaining in popularity, with global market valued close to ₹22,500 crore and United States contributing more than 60 percent.[5] Coupon sites are growing rapidly in India as well, with 76 lakh visitors frequenting such sites in November 2011—equivalent to 16.5 percent of total online population in India. The traffic on coupon sites highlights an increase of 629 percent from the previous year, i.e., November 2010, when the number of visitors accessing such sites was just 10 lakh. Deal sites like SnapDeal.com, Mydala.com, and Crazeal.com are emerging as major coupon distribution outlets.[6] Digital coupons hold maximum popularity among the youth segment, consisting of 18–35 years old.[7]

coupon a certificate that entitles consumers to an immediate price reduction when they buy the product

Top 10 Coupon Sites by Total Unique Visitors (000)
November 2011
Total India – Visitors Age 15+ Home/Work Locations

	Total Unique Visitors (000)	% Reach
Total Internet : Total Audience	**46,390**	**100.0%**
Coupons	**7,647**	**16.5%**
Snapdeal.com	5,185	11.2%
Mydala.com	1,359	2.9%
Crazeal.com	989	2.1%
Dealsandyou.com	664	1.4%
Koovs.com	491	1.1%
Khojguru.com	239	0.5%
Coupondunia.in	117	0.3%
Sosasta.com	91	0.2%
Deals2buy.com	86	0.2%
Retailmenot.com	83	0.2%

*Excludes visits from public computers such as Internet cafes or access from mobile phones or PDAs

SOURCE: http://www.comscore.com/Press_Events/Press_Releases/2011/12/Online_Shopping_Takes_Off_in_India

In-store coupons have become popular because they are more likely to influence customers' buying decisions. Instant coupons on product packages, coupons distributed from on-shelf coupon-dispensing machines, and electronic coupons issued at the checkout counter now achieve much higher redemption rates because consumers are making more in-store purchase decisions.

As marketing tactics grow more sophisticated, however, coupons, digital and mobile both, are no longer viewed as a stand-alone tactic but as an integral component of a larger promotional campaign. Spencer's

rebate a cash refund given for the purchase of a product during a specific period

premium an extra item offered to the consumer, usually in exchange for some proof of purchase of the promoted product

loyalty marketing program a promotional program designed to build long-term, mutually beneficial relationships between a company and its key customers

frequent buyer program a loyalty program in which loyal consumers are rewarded for making multiple purchases of a particular good or service

Retail did a pilot test for mobile coupons in Bengaluru and Kolkata and realized a 20 percent redemption rate. Realizing the benefit of using coupons as a promotional tool, categories such as apparel, electronics, and liquor are also planning to foray into this scheme.[8]

Rebates are similar to coupons in that they offer the purchaser a price reduction; however, because the purchaser must mail in a rebate form and usually some proof of purchase, the reward is not as immediate. Manufacturers prefer rebates for several reasons. Rebates allow manufacturers to offer price cuts to consumers directly. Manufacturers have more control over rebate promotions because they can be rolled out and shut off quickly. Further, because buyers must fill out forms with their names, addresses, and other data, manufacturers use rebate programs to build customer databases. Perhaps the best reason of all to offer rebates is that although rebates are particularly good at enticing purchase, most consumers never bother to redeem them. The Federal Trade Commission in the United States estimates that only half of consumers eligible for rebates collect them.[9]

Premiums

A **premium** is an extra item offered to the consumer, usually in exchange for some proof that the promoted product has been purchased. Premiums reinforce the consumer's purchase decision, increase consumption, and persuade nonusers to switch brands. The best example of the use of premiums is McDonald's Happy Meal, which rewards children with a small toy.

Premiums can also include more product for the regular price, such as two-for-the-price-of-one bonus packs or packages that include more of the product. Several soap brands now come in bonus packs, with an offering of buy 3 get 1 free, enabling customers to get 4 soaps for the cost of 3.[10] Another possibility is to attach a premium to the product's package, such as a small sample of a complementary hair product attached to a shampoo bottle.

Loyalty Marketing Programs

Loyalty marketing programs, or **frequent buyer programs,** reward loyal consumers for making multiple purchases. The objective of loyalty marketing programs is to build long-term, mutually beneficial relationships between a company and its key customers.

There are more than 180 crore loyalty program memberships in the United States, with the average household signed up for 14 programs but actively participating in only 6 or 7 programs.[11] India, comparatively, is at a very nascent stage when it comes to loyalty program memberships, with close to 2 crore loyalty program members.[12] Popularized by the airline industry through frequent flyer programs, loyalty marketing enables companies to strategically invest sales promotion rupees in activities designed to capture greater profits from customers already loyal to the product or company. Some of the popular loyalty programs in India are "*The Inner Circle*" by Lifestyle, "*Club West*" by Westside, "*Book Rewards*" by Crossword, and "*Green Card*" by Pantaloons.[13] The *First Citizen* program by Shoppers' Stop gives its members the opportunity to attend exclusive previews of sale, select a specific day during the year to shop on discount instead of full price, and redeem points directly into cash.[14] The success of the program is highlighted in the fact that Shoppers' Stop has more than 20 lakh *First Citizen* members and derives as much as 73 percent of its sales from these members.[15]

Studies show consumer loyalty is on the decline in the development market. According to research conducted by Gartner in USA, more than 75 percent of consumers have more than one loyalty card that rewards them with redeemable points. Frequent shopper card programs offered by many retailers have exploded in popularity. Research from Forrester shows that 54 percent of primary grocery shoppers belong to two or more supermarket loyalty programs. Although this speaks to the popularity of loyalty cards in the USA, it also shows that customers are pledging "loyalty" to more than one store: 15 percent of primary grocery shoppers are cardholders in at least three programs. In India, loyalty cards are slowly increasing in prominence. *ClubMore,* the loyalty program of *More* stores operated by Aditya Birla Retail division, is one of the successful loyalty programs in grocery retail and has a subscribed customer base of 13 lakh customers nationwide.[16] Reliance Retail offers one loyalty card, *Reliance One*, that can be used across all its retail stores in nine different formats and has a membership base of 30 lakh customers. It is the first retail card that has a bar code and comes with a magnetic strip.[17] However, the loyalty cards of both Reliance and More stores are issued without any conditions and a single purchase of any amount makes one entitled to get a card.[18] There are other retail chains as well that have their own loyalty programs to reward their customers, such as Tanishq's *Anuttara* and Barista's *Beanoholic*.

Co-branded credit cards are an increasingly popular loyalty marketing tool. Big Bazaar, Lifestyle, Westside, Indian Oil, and Jet Airways are only a few of the companies sponsoring co-branded cards with ICICI Bank, Standard Chartered Bank, HSBC Bank, and Citibank respectively.

Through loyalty programs, shoppers receive discounts, alerts on new products, and other types of enticing offers. In exchange, retailers are able to build customer databases that help them better understand customer preferences.

Companies are increasingly using the Internet to build customer loyalty through e-mail and social media. Some customers feel that their rewards programs, especially hotel rewards programs, send too much spam e-mail. Hotel reward programs can greatly benefit the business, with an average loyalty member being twice as profitable as a nonmember and an elite member being up to 12 times as profitable as a nonmember. However, too much e-mail, overly complicated or restrictive programs, or rewards that aren't perceived as valuable can turn a loyal customer away from the program.[19] Some companies use social media sites to help customers earn rewards points. For example, Tasti D-Lite in New York has a TastiRewards card and encourages customers to link their card with their Twitter and Foursquare accounts. If they do, they earn additional points on each purchase, and their Twitter and Foursquare accounts are updated with the purchase when the card is swiped.[20] Some companies also encourage online transactions by rewarding the customers for the same. The State Bank of India launched a loyalty scheme, wherein the customers earned points for each online transaction they do. More the number of online transactions, more the points earned. For every transaction done online for more than ₹100, the customers could accumulate points. The customer could redeem the points earned in cash and every 400 points was equal to ₹100. This scheme required no registration and was open to all existing as well as new SBI customers.[21]

Contests and Sweepstakes

Contests and sweepstakes are generally designed to create interest in a good or service, often to encourage brand switching. *Contests* are promotions in which participants use some skill or ability to compete for prizes. A consumer contest usually requires entrants to answer questions, complete sentences, or write a paragraph about the product and submit proof of purchase. Winning a *sweepstakes*, on the other hand, depends on chance and participation is free. Sweepstakes usually draw about ten times more entries than contests do.

While contests and sweepstakes may draw considerable interest and publicity, generally they are not effective tools for generating long-term sales. To increase their effectiveness, sales promotion managers must make certain the award will appeal to the target market. Offering several smaller prizes to many winners instead of one huge prize to just one person often will increase the effectiveness of the promotion, but there's no denying the attractiveness of a jackpot-type prize.

FRITO LAYS "DILLICIOUS FLAVOUR" CONTEST

Frito Lays, the snack food division of PepsiCo, in order to engage its customers in co-creation, launched a campaign called "Give Us Your Dillicious Flavour." The campaign was divided in two phases. In the first phase, entries were invited from the consumers on what they thought must be the next flavour of Lays' potato chips. Of the total entries received, four entries were selected by a panel of judges as the winning entries. The second phase consisted of launch of the four winning flavours in the market, with the ultimate winner being decided by the consumers themselves through voting for the best flavour and the winning flavour then being officially launched. The four selected entries won an amount of ₹5 lakh each, while the ultimate winning flavour got ₹50 lakh and 1 percent of the sales turnover. The campaign was a massive hit among the consumers and generated 13 lakh flavour ideas and over 47 lakh votes.[23]

sampling a promotional program that allows the consumer the opportunity to try a product or service for free

point-of-purchase (P-O-P) display a promotional display set up at the retailer's location to build traffic, advertise the product, or induce impulse buying

Sampling

Sampling allows the customer to try a product risk-free. In a recent study of sampling in Costco, the largest warehouse membership club chain in the U.S., researchers found that sampling increased sales by an average of 88 percent. Expensive items benefited most from sampling, and items under ₹450, particularly beverages, benefited least from sampling.[22]

Samples can be directly mailed to the customer, delivered door-to-door, packaged with another product, or demonstrated or distributed at a retail store or service outlet. Sampling at special events is a popular, effective, and high-profile distribution method that permits marketers to piggyback onto fun-based consumer activities including sporting events, college fests, fairs and festival, and concerts.

Distributing samples to specific location types, such as health clubs, salons, or doctors' offices, is one of the most efficient methods of sampling. What better way to get consumers to try a product than to offer a sample exactly when it is needed most? If someone visits a health club regularly, chances are he or she is a good prospect for a health food product or vitamin supplement. Health club instructors can hand out not only these products but also body wash, deodorant, and face cloths to sweating participants at the end of class. Online sampling is gaining momentum as Web communities bring people together with common interests in trying new products, often using blogs to spread the word.

Point-of-Purchase Promotion

A **point-of-purchase (P-O-P) display** includes any promotional display set up at the retailer's location to build traffic, advertise the product, or induce impulse buying. P-O-P displays include shelf "talkers" (signs attached to store shelves), shelf extenders (attachments that extend shelves so products stand out), ads on grocery carts and bags, end-aisle and floor-stand displays, television monitors at supermarket checkout counters, in-store audio messages, and audiovisual displays. One big advantage of the P-O-P display is that it offers manufacturers a captive audience in retail stores. Another advantage is that between 70 and 80 percent of all retail purchase decisions are made in-store, so P-O-P displays can be very effective, increasing sales by as much as 65 percent. P-O-P displays essentially aid the customers' recall of a brand that is advertised in mass media. Point-of-purchase displays play multiple roles at the retail store like providing information, reminding, motivating, interactivity, and inducing product buying.[24]

Online Sales Promotion

Online sales promotions have expanded dramatically in recent years. Marketers are now spending crores of rupees annually on such promotions. Sales promotions online have proved effective and cost-efficient, generating response rates three to five times higher than off-line promotions. The most effective types of online sales promotions are free merchandise, sweepstakes, free shipping with purchases, and coupons.

Eager to boost traffic, Internet retailers are busy giving away free services or equipment, such as PCs and travel, to lure consumers not only to their own Web sites but to the Internet in general. Another goal is to add potential customers to their databases.

Marketers have discovered that online coupon distribution provides another vehicle for promoting their products. In addition, e-coupons can help marketers lure new customers. Online coupons often have a redemption rate of more than 20 percent, as much as ten times higher than for traditional coupons.[25] In fact, nearly 50 percent of consumers who make purchases online use coupons or discount promotional codes. With the speed of compiling data online, marketers can conduct tests in real time and measure the results in time to offer last-minute promotions and react to changing market conditions.[26]

Online versions of loyalty programs are also popping up, and although many types of companies have these programs, the most successful are those run by hotel and airline companies.

LO 3 Tools for Trade Sales Promotion

Whereas consumer promotions pull a product through the channel by creating demand, trade promotions *push* a product through the distribution channel (see Chapter 13). When selling to members of the distribution channel, manufacturers use many of the same sales promotion tools used in consumer promotions—such as sales contests, premiums, and P-O-P displays. Several tools, however, are unique to manufacturers and intermediaries.

- *Trade allowances:* A **trade allowance** is a price reduction offered by manufacturers to intermediaries such as wholesalers and retailers. The price reduction or rebate is given in exchange for doing something specific, such as allocating space for a new product or buying something during special periods. For example, a local Vijay Sales outlet could receive a special discount for running its own promotion on Sony new laptop range.
- *Push money:* Intermediaries receive **push money** as a bonus for pushing the manufacturer's brand through the distribution channel. Often the push money is directed toward a retailer's salespeople.
- *Training:* Sometimes a manufacturer will train an intermediary's personnel if the product is rather complex—as frequently occurs in the computer and telecommunications industries. For example, representatives of a television manufacturer like Toshiba may train salespeople in how to demonstrate the new features of the latest models of televisions to consumers.
- *Free merchandise:* Often a manufacturer offers retailers free merchandise in lieu of quantity discounts. Occasionally, free merchandise is used as payment for trade allowances normally provided through other sales promotions. Instead of giving a retailer a price reduction for buying a certain quantity of merchandise, the manufacturer may throw in extra merchandise "free" (i.e., at a cost that would equal the price reduction).
- *Store demonstrations:* Manufacturers can also arrange with retailers to perform an in-store demonstration. Food manufacturers often send representatives to grocery stores and supermarkets to let customers sample a product while shopping.
- *Business meetings, conventions, and trade shows:* Trade association meetings, conferences, and conventions are an important aspect of sales promotion and a growing, multi-crore-rupee market. At these shows, manufacturers, distributors, and other vendors have the chance to display their goods or describe their services to potential customers.

Companies participate in trade shows to attract and identify new prospects, serve current customers, introduce new products, enhance corporate image, test the market response to new products, enhance corporate morale, and gather competitive product information.

trade allowance
a price reduction offered by manufacturers to intermediaries, such as wholesalers and retailers

push money
money offered to channel intermediaries to encourage them to "push" products—that is, to encourage other members of the channel to sell the products

Williams-Sonoma, a high end retail company selling kitchenware, furnishing, and other house ware in United States and Canada, offers scheduled demonstrations of products, such as making the perfect cappuccino, in stores around the country. Stores also offer free technique classes every Sunday where culinary experts demonstrate how to use products and give recipes and samples to customers. All classes are free and allow store employees to interact with customers.[27]

© ISTOCKPHOTO.COM/DAVID CROCKETT

Trade promotions are popular among manufacturers for many reasons. Trade sales promotion tools help manufacturers gain new distributors for their products, obtain wholesaler and retailer support for consumer sales promotions, build or reduce dealer inventories, and improve trade relations. Car manufacturers annually sponsor dozens of auto shows for consumers. The shows attract lakhs of consumers, providing dealers with increased store traffic as well as good leads.

LO 4 Personal Selling

As mentioned in Chapter 16, *personal selling* is a purchase situation involving a personal, paid-for communication between two people in an attempt to influence each other. In a sense, all businesspeople are salespeople. An individual may become a plant manager, a chemist, an engineer, or a member of any profession and yet still have to sell. During a job search, applicants must "sell" themselves to prospective employers in an interview.

ADVANTAGES OF PERSONAL SELLING:

- Personal selling provides a detailed explanation or demonstration of the product. This capability is especially needed for complex or new goods and services.
- The sales message can be varied according to the motivations and interests of each prospective customer. Moreover, when the prospect has questions or raises objections, the salesperson is there to provide explanations. In contrast, advertising and sales promotion can only respond to the objections the copywriter thinks are important to customers.
- Personal selling can be directed only to qualified prospects. Other forms of promotion include some unavoidable waste because many people in the audience are not prospective customers.
- Personal selling costs can be controlled by adjusting the size of the sales force (and resulting expenses) in one-person increments. On the other hand, advertising and sales promotion must often be purchased in fairly large amounts.
- Perhaps the most important advantage is that personal selling is considerably more effective than other forms of promotion in obtaining a sale and gaining a satisfied customer.

EXHIBIT 18.2

Comparison of Personal Selling and Advertising/Sales Promotion

Personal selling is more important if . . .	Advertising and sales promotion are more important if . . .
The product has a high value.	The product has a low value.
It is a custom-made product.	It is a standardized product.
There are few customers.	There are many customers.
The product is technically complex.	The product is easy to understand.
Customers are concentrated.	Customers are geographically dispersed.
Examples: Insurance policies, custom windows, airplane engines	**Examples:** Soap, magazine subscriptions, cotton T-shirts

Personal selling offers several advantages over other forms of promotion. Personal selling may also work better than other forms of promotion given certain customer and product characteristics. Generally speaking, personal selling becomes more important as the number of potential customers decreases, as the complexity of the product increases, and as the value of the product grows (see Exhibit 18.2). For highly complex goods, such as business jets or private communication systems, a salesperson is needed to determine the prospective customer's needs, explain the product's basic advantages, and propose the exact features and accessories that will meet the client's needs. Some of the popular retailers in United States such as Macy's, Nordstrom, Saks Fifth Avenue, and Barneys New York offer free personal shopping, where consultants pull clothing they feel will fit the customer's style and specified need. This free service encourages customers to continue using personal shoppers and develop a relationship with the store.[28]

LO 5 Relationship Selling

Until recently, marketing theory and practice concerning personal selling focused almost entirely on a planned presentation to prospective customers for the sole purpose of making the sale. Marketers were most concerned with making a one-time sale and then moving on to the next prospect. Traditional personal selling methods attempted to persuade the buyer to accept a point of view or convince the buyer to take some action. Frequently, the objectives of the salesperson were at the expense of the buyer, creating a win-lose outcome. Although this type of sales approach has not disappeared entirely, it is being used less and less often by professional salespeople.

In contrast, modern views of personal selling emphasize the relationship that develops between a salesperson and a buyer. **Relationship selling**, or **consultative selling**, is a multistage process that emphasizes personalization and empathy as key ingredients in identifying prospects and developing them as long-term, satisfied customers. With relationship selling, the objective is to build long-term branded relationships with consumers and buyers, so the focus is on building mutual trust between the buyer and seller through the delivery of anticipated, long-term, value-added benefits to the buyer.

Relationship or consultative salespeople, therefore, become consultants, partners, and problem solvers for their customers. They strive to build long-term relationships with key accounts by developing trust over time. The emphasis shifts from a one-time sale to a long-term relationship in which the salesperson works with the customer to develop solutions for enhancing the customer's bottom line. Research has shown that positive customer–salesperson relationships contribute to trust, increased customer loyalty, and the intent to continue the relationship with the salesperson.[29] Thus, relationship selling promotes a win–win situation for both buyer and seller.

The end result of relationship selling tends to be loyal customers who purchase from the company time after time. A relationship selling strategy focused on retaining customers costs a company less than constantly prospecting and selling to new customers.

Relationship selling is more typical with selling situations for industrial-type goods, such as heavy machinery or computer systems, and services, such as airlines and insurance, than for consumer goods. Exhibit 18.3 lists the key differences between traditional personal selling and relationship or consultative selling. These differences will become more apparent as we explore the personal selling process later in the chapter.

relationship selling (consultative selling) a sales practice that involves building, maintaining, and enhancing interactions with customers in order to develop long-term satisfaction through mutually beneficial partnerships

sales process (sales cycle) the set of steps a salesperson goes through in a particular organization to sell a particular product or service

© COMSTOCK IMAGES/JUPITERIMAGES

LO 6 Steps in the Selling Process

Completing a sale requires several steps. The **sales process**, or **sales cycle**, is simply the set of steps a salesperson goes through to sell a particular product

EXHIBIT 18.3

Key Differences between Traditional Selling and Relationship Selling

Traditional Personal Selling	Relationship or Consultative Selling
Sell products (goods and services)	Sell advice, assistance, and counsel
Focus on closing sales	Focus on improving the customer's bottom line
Limited sales planning	Consider sales planning as top priority
Spend most contact time telling customers about product	Spend most contact time attempting to build a problem-solving environment with the customer
Conduct "product-specific" needs assessment	Conduct discovery in the full scope of the customer's operations
"Lone wolf" approach to the account	Team approach to the account
Proposals and presentations based on pricing and product features	Proposals and presentations based on profit impact and strategic benefits to the customer
Sales follow-up is short term, focused on product delivery	Sales follow-up is long term, focused on long-term relationship enhancement

SOURCE: Robert M. Peterson, Patrick L. Schul, and George H. Lucas Jr., "Consultative Selling: Walking the Walk in the New Selling Environment," *National Conference on Sales Management Proceedings*, March 1996.

lead generation (prospecting) identification of those firms and people most likely to buy the seller's offerings

referral a recommendation to a salesperson from a customer or business associate

networking a process of finding out about potential clients from friends, business contacts, coworkers, acquaintances, and fellow members in professional and civic organizations

or service. The sales process or cycle can be unique for each product or service, depending on the features of the product or service, characteristics of customer segments, and internal processes in place within the firm such as how leads are gathered.

Some sales take only a few minutes, but others may take much longer to complete. Sales of technical products like a Boeing or Airbus airplane and customized goods and services typically take many months, perhaps even years, to complete. On the other end of the spectrum, sales of less technical products like stationery are generally more routine and may take only a few days. Whether a salesperson spends a few minutes or a few years on a sale, there are seven basic steps in the personal selling process, outlined further in the following sections.

Seven Steps in the Personal Selling Process

1. Generating leads
2. Qualifying leads
3. Approaching the customer and probing needs
4. Developing and proposing solutions
5. Handling objections
6. Closing the sale
7. Following up

Like other forms of promotion, these steps of selling follow the AIDA concept discussed in Chapter 16. Once a salesperson has located a prospect with the authority to buy, he or she tries to get the prospect's attention. A thorough needs assessment turned into an effective sales proposal and presentation should generate interest. After developing the customer's initial desire (preferably during the presentation of the sales proposal), the salesperson seeks action in the close by trying to get an agreement to buy. Follow-up after the sale, the final step in the selling process, not only lowers cognitive dissonance (refer to Chapter 6) but also may open up opportunities to discuss future sales. Effective follow-up will also lead to repeat business in which the process may start all over again at the needs assessment step.

Traditional selling and relationship selling follow the same basic steps. They differ in the relative importance placed on key steps in the process. Traditional selling efforts are transaction oriented, focusing on generating as many leads as possible, making as many presentations as possible, and closing as many sales as possible. Minimal effort is placed on asking questions to identify customer needs and wants or matching these needs and wants to the benefits of the product or service. In contrast, salespeople practicing relationship selling emphasize an up-front investment in the time and effort needed to uncover each customer's specific needs and wants and meet them with the product or service offering. By doing their homework up front, salespeople create the conditions necessary for a relatively straightforward close. Look at each step of the selling process individually.

Step 1: Generating Leads

Initial groundwork must precede communication between the potential buyer and the salesperson. **Lead generation**, or **prospecting**, is the identification of those firms and people most likely to buy the seller's offerings. These firms or people become "sales leads" or "prospects."

Sales leads can be obtained in several different ways, most notably through advertising, trade shows and conventions, or direct mail and telemarketing programs. Favorable publicity also helps to create leads. Company records of past client purchases are another excellent source of leads. Many sales professionals are also securing valuable leads from their firm's Web site.

Another way to gather a lead is through a **referral**—a recommendation from a customer or business associate. The advantages of referrals over other forms of prospecting include highly qualified leads, higher closing rates, larger initial transactions, and shorter sales cycles. Referrals typically are as much as ten times more productive in generating sales than are cold calls. Unfortunately, although most clients are willing to give referrals, many salespeople do not ask for them. Effective sales training can help to overcome this reluctance to ask for referrals. To increase the number of referrals, some companies even pay or send small gifts to custom ers or suppliers that provide referrals.

Networking is using friends, business contacts, coworkers, acquaintances, and fellow members in professional and civic organizations to identify potential clients. Indeed, a number of national networking clubs have been started for the sole purpose of generating leads and providing valuable business advice. Increasingly, sales professionals are also using online networking sites such as LinkedIn to connect with targeted leads and clients around the world, 24 hours a day. Some of LinkedIn's estimated 3 crore users have reported response rates between 50 and 60 percent, versus 3 percent from direct marketing efforts.[30]

Before the advent of more sophisticated methods of lead generation, such as direct mail and telemarketing, most prospecting was done through **cold calling**—a form of lead generation in which the salesperson approaches potential buyers without any prior knowledge of the prospects' needs or financial status. Although cold calling is still used in generating leads, many sales managers have realized the inefficiencies of having their top salespeople use their valuable selling time searching for the proverbial "needle in a haystack." Passing the job of cold calling to a lower-cost employee, typically an internal sales support person, allows salespeople to spend more time and use their relationship-building skills on prospects who have already been identified.

Step 2: Qualifying Leads

When a prospect shows interest in learning more about a product, the salesperson has the opportunity to follow up, or qualify, the lead. Personally visiting unqualified prospects wastes valuable salesperson time and company resources. Many leads often go unanswered because salespeople are given no indication as to how qualified the leads are in terms of interest and ability to purchase. Unqualified prospects give vague or incomplete answers to a salesperson's specific questions, try to evade questions on budgets, and request changes in standard procedures like prices or terms of sale. In contrast, qualified leads are real prospects who answer questions, value your time, and are realistic about money and when they are prepared to buy. Salespeople who are given accurate information on qualified leads are more than twice as likely to follow up.[31]

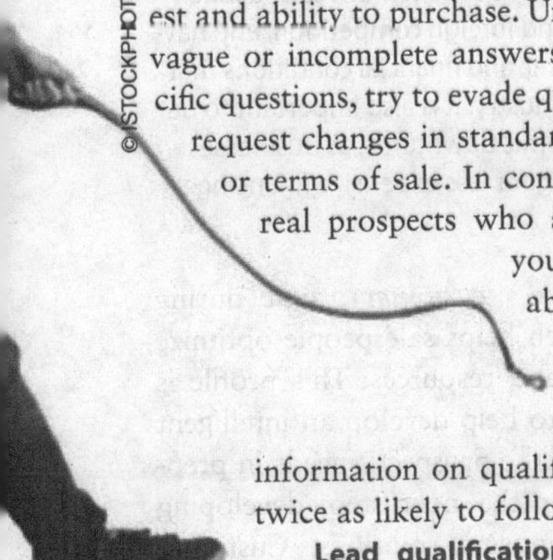

©ISTOCKPHOTO.COM/RYAN BALDERAS

Lead qualification involves determining whether the prospect has three things:

- *A recognized need:* The most basic criterion for determining whether someone is a prospect for a product is a need that is not being satisfied. The salesperson should first consider prospects who are aware of a need but should not disregard prospects who have not yet recognized that they have one. With a little more information about the product, they may decide they do have a need for it. Preliminary interviews and questioning can often provide the salesperson with enough information to determine whether there is a need.
- *Buying power:* Buying power involves both authority to make the purchase decision and access to funds to pay for it. To avoid wasting time and money, the salesperson needs to identify the purchasing authority and his or her ability to pay before making a presentation. Organizational charts and information about a firm's credit standing can provide valuable clues.
- *Receptivity and accessibility:* The prospect must be willing to see the salesperson and be accessible to the salesperson. Some prospects simply refuse to see salespeople. Others, because of their stature in their organization, will see only a salesperson or sales manager with similar stature.

Often the task of lead qualification is handled by a telemarketing group or a sales support person who *prequalifies* the lead for the salesperson. Prequalification systems free sales representatives from the time-consuming task of following up on leads to determine need, buying power, and receptiveness. Prequalification systems may even set up initial appointments with the prospect for the salesperson. The result is more time for the sales force to spend in front of interested customers. Software is increasingly being utilized in lead qualification.

Companies are increasingly using their Web sites to qualify leads. When qualifying leads online, companies want visitors to register, indicate the products and services they are interested in, and provide information on their time frame and resources. Leads from the Internet can then be prioritized (those indicating a short time frame, for instance, are given a higher priority) and then transferred to salespeople. Enticing visitors to register also enables companies to customize future electronic interactions.

Step 3: Approaching the Customer and Probing Needs

Before approaching customers, the salesperson should learn as much as possible about the prospect's organization and its buyers. This process, called the **preapproach**, describes the "homework" that must be done by the salesperson before contacting the prospect. This may include visiting company Web sites, consulting standard reference sources such as Moody's,

cold calling a form of lead generation in which the salesperson approaches potential buyers without any prior knowledge of the prospects' needs or financial status

lead qualification determination of a sales prospect's (1) recognized need, (2) buying power, and (3) receptivity and accessibility

preapproach a process that describes the "homework" that must be done by a salesperson before he or she contacts a prospect

needs assessment
a determination of the customer's specific needs and wants and the range of options the customer has for satisfying them

Standard & Poor's, or Dun & Bradstreet, or contacting acquaintances or others who may have information about the prospect. Another preapproach task is to determine whether the actual approach should be a personal visit, a phone call, a letter, or some other form of communication.

During the sales approach, the salesperson either talks to the prospect or secures an appointment for a future time in which to probe the prospect further as to his or her needs. Relationship selling theorists suggest that salespeople should begin developing mutual trust with their prospect during the approach. Salespeople must sell themselves before they can sell the product. Small talk that projects sincerity and some suggestion of friendship is encouraged to build rapport with the prospect, but remarks that could be construed as insincere should be avoided.

The salesperson's ultimate goal during the approach is to conduct a **needs assessment** to find out as much as possible about the prospect's situation. The salesperson should be determining how to maximize the fit between what he or she can offer and what the prospective customer wants. As part of the needs assessment, the consultative salesperson must know everything there is to know about the following:

© ISTOCKPHOTO/THINKSTOCK

- *The product or service:* Product knowledge is the cornerstone for conducting a successful needs analysis. The consultative salesperson must be an expert on his or her product or service, including technical specifications, the product's features and benefits, pricing and billing procedures, warranty and service support, performance comparisons with the competition, other customers' experiences with the product, and current advertising and promotional campaign messages. For example, a salesperson who is attempting to sell a Xerox copier to a doctor's office should be very knowledgeable about Xerox's selection of copiers, their attributes, capabilities, technological specifications, and postpurchase servicing.
- *Customers and their needs:* The salesperson should know more about customers than they know about themselves. That's the secret to relationship and consultative selling, where the salesperson acts not only as a supplier of products and services but also as a trusted consultant and adviser. The professional salesperson brings each client business-building ideas and solutions to problems. For example, if the Xerox salesperson is asking the "right" questions, then he or she should be able to identify copy-related areas where the doctor's office is losing or wasting money. The Xerox salesperson can act as a "consultant" on how the doctor's office can save money and time rather than just selling a copier.
- *The competition:* The salesperson must know as much about the competitor's company and products as he or she knows about his or her own company. *Competitive intelligence* includes many factors: who the competitors are and what is known about them, how their products and services compare, advantages and disadvantages, and strengths and weaknesses. For example, if the Canon copy machine is less expensive than the Xerox copier, the doctor's office may be leaning toward purchasing the Canon. But if the Xerox salesperson can point out that the cost of long-term maintenance and toner cartridges is lower for the Xerox copier, offsetting its higher initial cost, the salesperson may be able to persuade the doctor's office to purchase the Xerox copier.
- *The industry:* Knowing the industry involves active research on the part of the salesperson. This means attending industry and trade association meetings, reading articles published in industry and trade journals, keeping track of legislation and regulation that affect the industry, being aware of product alternatives and innovations from domestic and foreign competition, and having a feel for economic and financial conditions that may affect the industry. It is also important to be aware of economic downturns, as businesses may be looking for less expensive financing options.

Creating a *customer profile* during the approach helps salespeople optimize their time and resources. This profile is then used to help develop an intelligent analysis of the prospect's needs in preparation for the next step, developing and proposing solutions. Customer profile information is typically stored and manipulated using sales force automation software packages designed for use on laptop computers. Sales force automation software provides sales reps

THE **MORE** SALESPEOPLE **KNOW** ABOUT THEIR PROSPECTS, THE **BETTER THEY CAN MEET** THEIR NEEDS.

with a computerized and efficient method of collecting customer information for use during the entire sales process. Further, customer and sales data stored in a computer database can be easily shared among sales team members. The information can also be appended with industry statistics, sales or meeting notes, billing data, and other information that may be pertinent to the prospect or the prospect's company. The more salespeople know about their prospects, the better they can meet their needs.

A salesperson should wrap up the sales approach and need-probing mission by summarizing the prospect's need, problem, and interest. The salesperson should also get a commitment from the customer to some kind of action, whether it's reading promotional material or agreeing to a demonstration. This commitment helps qualify the prospect further and justify additional time invested by the salesperson. The salesperson should reiterate the action he or she promises to take, such as sending information or calling back to provide answers to questions. The date and time of the next call should be set at the conclusion of the sales approach as well as an agenda for the next call in terms of what the salesperson hopes to accomplish, such as providing a demonstration or presenting a solution.

Step 4: Developing and Proposing Solutions

Once the salesperson has gathered the appropriate information about the client's needs and wants, the next step is to determine whether his or her company's products or services match the needs of the prospective customer. The salesperson then develops a solution, or possibly several solutions, in which the salesperson's product or service solves the client's problems or meets a specific need.

These solutions are typically presented to the client in the form of a sales proposal presented at a sales presentation. A **sales proposal** is a written document or professional presentation that outlines how the company's product or service will meet or exceed the client's needs. The **sales presentation** is the formal meeting in which the salesperson has the opportunity to present the sales proposal. The presentation should be explicitly tied to the prospect's expressed needs. Further, the prospect should be involved in the presentation by being encouraged to participate in demonstrations or by exposure to computer exercises, slides, video or audio, flip charts, photographs, and the like. Technology has become an important part of presenting solutions for many salespeople.

sales proposal a formal written document or professional presentation that outlines how the salesperson's product or service will meet or exceed the prospect's needs

sales presentation a formal meeting in which the salesperson presents a sales proposal to a prospective buyer

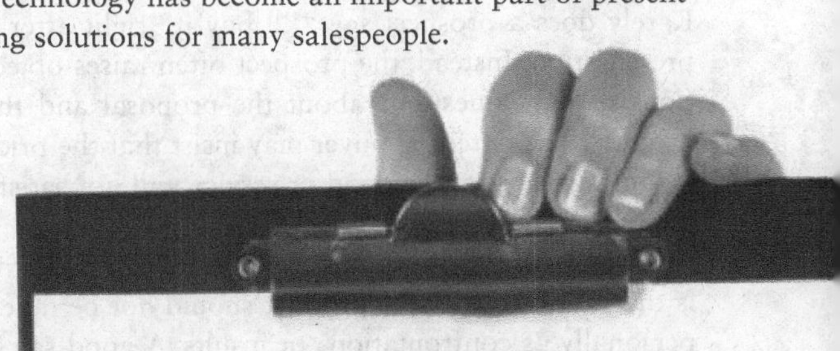

RELATIVE IMPORTANCE OF PRESENTATION BEHAVIORS

1. *Effective eye contact:* The most important factor. Scan the room throughout the presentation, beginning at the back of the room, and make quick individual eye contact.
2. *Use of visuals:* Visuals often overshadow the speaker. Always speak to the audience, not the visual, and avoid using PowerPoint slides as cue cards.
3. *Choice of language:* Word choice and organization of the presentation should be appropriate for the audience, without long sentences or inappropriate jargon.
4. *Speech:* Speak at a measured pace with appropriate inflection.
5. *Body movement:* Gestures and body position offer clues to the speaker's confidence.

SOURCE: Bill Rosenthal, "How to Use Your Eyes for Better Presenting," *Fast Company*, January 17, 2010, www.fastcompany.com.

negotiation the process during which both the salesperson and the prospect offer special concessions in an attempt to arrive at a sales agreement

Because the salesperson often has only one opportunity to present solutions, the quality of both the sales proposal and presentation can make or break the sale. Salespeople must be able to present the proposal and handle any customer objections confidently and professionally. For a powerful presentation, salespeople must be well prepared, use direct eye contact, ask open-ended questions, be poised, use hand gestures and voice inflection, focus on the customer's needs, incorporate visual elements that impart valuable information, know how to operate the audio/visual or computer equipment being used for the presentation, and make sure the equipment works.[32] Nothing dies faster than a boring presentation. Often customers are more likely to remember how salespeople present themselves than what they say.

Step 5: Handling Objections

Rarely does a prospect say "I'll buy it" right after a presentation. Instead, the prospect often raises objections or asks questions about the proposal and the product. The potential buyer may insist that the price is too high or that the good or service will not satisfy the present need.

One of the first lessons every salesperson learns is that objections to the product should not be taken personally as confrontations or insults. A good salesperson considers objections a legitimate part of the purchase decision. To handle objections effectively, the salesperson should anticipate specific objections such as concerns about price, fully investigate the objection with the customer, be aware of what the competition is offering, and, above all, stay calm. When Dell introduced its direct selling model, salespeople anticipated that customers would worry that they would not receive the same level of service and dedication as they would get from a reseller. As a result, the salespeople included assurances about service and support following the sale in their sales presentations.

Often salespeople can use objections to close the sale. If the customer tries to pit suppliers against each other to drive down the price, the salesperson should be prepared to point out weaknesses in the competitor's offer and stand by the quality in his or her own proposal.

Step 6: Closing the Sale

At the end of the presentation, the salesperson should ask the customer how he or she would like to proceed. If the customer exhibits signs that he or she is ready to purchase and all questions have been answered and objections have been met, then the salesperson can try to close the sale. Customers often give signals during or after the presentation that they are ready to buy or are not interested. Examples include changes in facial expressions, gestures, and questions asked. The salesperson should look for these signals and respond appropriately.

Closing requires courage and skill. A salesperson should keep an open mind when asking for the sale and be prepared for both a yes and a no. The typical salesperson makes several hundred sales calls a year, many of which are repeat calls to the same client in an attempt to make a sale. Building a good relationship with the customer is very important. Often, if the salesperson has developed a strong relationship with the customer, only minimal efforts are needed to close a sale.

Negotiation often plays a key role in the closing of the sale. **Negotiation** is the process during which both the salesperson and the prospect offer special concessions in an attempt to arrive at a sales agreement. For example, the salesperson may offer a price cut, free installation, or a trial order. Effective negotiators, however, avoid using price as a negotiation tool. Because companies spend lakhs on advertising and product development to create value, when salespeople give in to price negotiations too quickly, it decreases the value

OFTEN, IF THE SALES-PERSON HAS DEVELOPED A **STRONG** RELATIONSHIP WITH THE CUSTOMER, ONLY MINIMAL **EFFORTS** ARE NEEDED TO **CLOSE** **A SALE.**

of the product. Instead, effective salespeople should emphasize value to the customer, rendering price a nonissue. Salespeople should also be prepared to ask for trade-offs and try to avoid giving unilateral concessions. Moreover, if the customer asks for a 5 percent discount, the salesperson should ask for something in return, such as higher volume or more flexibility in delivery schedules.

More and more Indian companies are expanding their marketing and selling efforts into global markets. Salespeople selling in foreign markets should tailor their presentation and closing styles to each market. Different personalities and skills will be successful in some countries and absolute failures in others. For instance, if a salesperson is an excellent closer and always focuses on the next sale, doing business in Latin America might be difficult because people there want to take a long time building a personal relationship with their suppliers.

Step 7: Following Up

Salespeople's responsibilities do not end with making the sales and placing the orders. One of the most important aspects of their jobs is **follow-up**—the final step in the selling process, in which they must ensure delivery schedules are met, goods or services perform as promised, and buyers' employees are properly trained to use the products.

In the traditional sales approach, follow-up with the customer is generally limited to successful product delivery and performance. A basic goal of relationship selling is to motivate customers to come back, again and again, by developing and nurturing long-term relationships. Exhibit 18.4 depicts the time involved in the sales process and how those elements relate to the traditional and relationship selling approaches.

Most businesses depend on repeat sales, and repeat sales depend on thorough and continued follow-up by the salesperson. When customers feel abandoned, cognitive dissonance arises and repeat sales decline. Today, this issue is more pertinent than ever because customers are far less loyal to brands and vendors. Buyers are more inclined to look for the best deal, especially in the case of poor after-the-sale follow-up. Automated e-mail follow-up marketing—a combination of sales automation and Internet technology—is enhancing customer satisfaction as well as bringing in more business for some marketers. After the initial contact with a prospect, a software program automatically sends a series of personalized e-mail messages over a period of time.

follow-up the final step of the selling process, in which the salesperson ensures delivery schedules are met, goods or services perform as promised, and the buyers' employees are properly trained to use the products

The Impact of Technology on Personal Selling

Will the increasingly sophisticated technology now available at marketers' fingertips eliminate the need for salespeople? Experts agree that a relationship between the salesperson and customer will always be necessary. Technology, however, can certainly help to improve that relationship. Cell phones, laptops, pagers, e-mail, and electronic organizers allow salespeople to be more accessible to both clients and the company. Moreover, the Internet provides salespeople with vast resources of information on clients, competitors, and the industry. In fact, many companies are utilizing technology to stay more in touch with their own employees. For instance, when IBM held an electronic brainstorming session, a total

EXHIBIT 18.4

Relative Amount of Time Spent in the Key Steps of the Selling Process

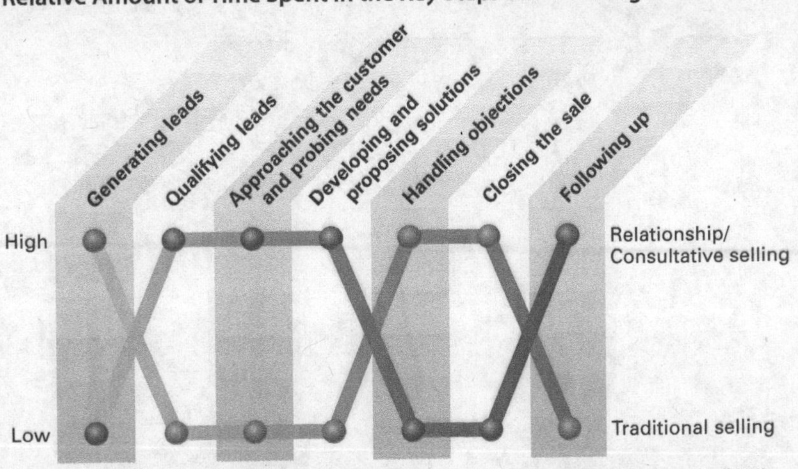

SOURCE: Robert Peterson, Patrick Schul, and George H. Lucas Jr., "Consultative Selling: Walking the Walk in the New Selling Enviroment," *National Conference on Sales Management Proceedings*, March 1996.

of 52,600 employees logged on to the event to discuss issues of employee retention, work efficiency, quality, and teamwork.[33]

E-business—buying, selling, marketing, collaborating with partners, and servicing customers electronically using the Internet—has had a significant impact on personal selling. Virtually all large companies and most medium and small companies are involved in e-commerce and consider it to be necessary to compete in today's marketplace. For customers, the Web has become a powerful tool, providing accurate and up-to-date information on products, pricing, and order status. The Internet also cost-effectively processes orders and services requests. Although on the surface the Internet might look like a threat to the job security of salespeople, the Web is actually freeing sales reps from tedious administrative tasks like shipping catalogs, placing routine orders, or tracking orders. This leaves them more time to focus on the needs of their clients.

PERSONAL SELLING WEB 2.0

Gary Vaynerchuk, an Internet celebrity in the U.S., knows wine. He knows social media. He also knows branding. The three combine to produce **Wine Library TV**, a daily webcast where Vaynerchuk very honestly tastes and talks wine to help drinkers develop more educated palates. Vaynerchuk answers every e-mail in his inbox personally and shoots his webcasts in one take. There is no gimmicky lighting or fancy production, just a man who knows wine and wants to share his knowledge. Vaynerchuk operated the family's wine retail shop, Wine Library, selling wine and growing the ₹18 crore business to ₹200 crore. He left the business to dedicate himself to selling variant types of wine through his webcast. Vaynerchuk uses social media, television, and all media avenues (including his book) to encourage drinkers to purchase new, unfamiliar wine.[34]

© 2010 WINE LIBRARY

Review And Applications

Define and state the objectives of sales promotion. Sales promotion consists of those marketing communication activities, other than advertising, personal selling, and public relations, in which a short-term incentive motivates consumers or members of the distribution channel to purchase a good or service immediately, either by lowering the price or by adding value. The main objectives of sales promotion are to increase trial purchases, consumer inventories, and repeat purchases. Sales promotion is also used to encourage brand switching and to build brand loyalty. Sales promotion supports advertising activities.

1.1 What is the primary factor that determines sales promotion objectives? Name some different types of sales promotion techniques, and explain the type of customer they are intended to influence.

1.2 You have recently been assigned the task of developing a promotional technique to introduce your company's new product, a garlic cheese sandwich. Advertising spending is limited, so the introduction will include only some low-budget sales promotion techniques. Write a sales promotion plan that will increase awareness of your new sandwich and allow your customer base to try it risk-free.

Discuss the most common forms of consumer sales promotion. Consumer forms of sales promotion include coupons and rebates, premiums, loyalty marketing programs, contests and sweepstakes, sampling, and point-of-purchase displays. Coupons are certificates entitling consumers to an immediate price reduction when they purchase a product or service. Coupons are a particularly good way to encourage product trial and brand switching. Similar to coupons, rebates provide purchasers with a price reduction, although it is not immediate. To receive a rebate, consumers generally must mail in a rebate form with a proof of purchase. Premiums offer an extra item or incentive to the consumer for buying a product or service. Premiums reinforce the consumer's purchase decision, increase consumption, and persuade nonusers to switch brands. Rewarding loyal customers is the basis of loyalty marketing programs. Loyalty programs are extremely effective at building long-term, mutually beneficial relationships between a company and its key customers. Contests and sweepstakes are generally designed to create interest, often to encourage brand switching. Because consumers perceive risk in trying new products, sampling is an effective method for gaining new customers. Finally, point-of-purchase displays set up at the retailer's location build traffic, advertise the product, and induce impulse buying.

2.1 Discuss how different forms of sales promotion can erode or build brand loyalty. If a company's objective is to enhance customer loyalty to its products, what sales promotion techniques will be most appropriate?

2.2 What forms of consumer sales promotion might induce impulse purchases? What forms of sales promotion are more effective at persuading consumers to switch brands?

2.3 Consider the different consumer sales promotion tools. Give an example of how each type of tool has influenced you to purchase—or purchase more of—a product or service.

2.4 Contests and sweepstakes are very common in the entertainment industry. Radio stations have contests almost daily; some television shows quiz viewers on trivia; even movies offer sweepstakes in conjunction with film previews and premiere nights. Think of a television or radio program unlikely to have contests or sweepstakes (things like *Emotional Atyachaar, Movers and Shakers,* or *We The People*, for example). Once you have chosen your program, design a contest or sweepstake to promote the show or the channel on which it airs. List the objectives and describe the rationale behind each part of your promotion.

List the most common forms of trade sales promotion. Manufacturers use many of the same sales promotion tools used in consumer promotions, such as sales contests, premiums, and point-of-purchase displays. In addition, manufacturers and channel intermediaries use several unique promotional strategies: trade allowances, push money, training programs, free merchandise, store demonstrations, and meetings, conventions, and trade shows.

3.1 How does trade sales promotion differ from consumer sales promotion? How is it the same?

3.2 What are the main forms of trade sales promotion? Which type might be most enticing to a grocery store manager? To a buyer for a major electronics chain?

3.3 Form a team of three to five students. As marketing managers, you are in charge of selling Yera glasses. Design a consumer sales promotion plan and trade sales promotion plan for your product. Incorporate at least three different promotion tools into each plan. Share your results with the other teams in the class.

Describe personal selling. Personal selling is direct communication between a sales representative and one or more prospective buyers in an attempt to influence each other in a purchase situation. Broadly speaking, all businesspeople use personal selling to promote themselves and their ideas. Personal selling offers several advantages over other forms of promotion. Personal selling allows salespeople to thoroughly explain and demonstrate a product. Salespeople have the flexibility to tailor a sales proposal to the needs and preferences of individual customers. Personal selling is more efficient than other forms of promotion because salespeople target qualified prospects and avoid wasting efforts on unlikely buyers. Personal selling affords greater managerial control over promotion costs. Finally, personal selling is the most effective method of closing a sale and producing satisfied customers.

4.1 Discuss the role of personal selling in promoting products. What advantages does personal selling offer over other forms of promotion?

4.2 What are the major advantages of personal selling to the company selling a product? What are the advantages to the person or company buying the product?

Discuss the key differences between relationship selling and traditional selling. Relationship selling is the practice of building, maintaining, and enhancing interactions with customers in order to develop long-term satisfaction through mutually beneficial partnerships. Traditional selling, on the other hand, is transaction focused. That is, the salesperson is most concerned with making onetime sales and moving on to the next prospect. Salespeople practicing relationship selling spend more time understanding a prospect's needs and developing solutions to meet those needs.

5.1 What are the key differences between relationship selling and traditional methods of selling? What types of products or services do you think would be conducive to relationship selling?

5.2 Based on the key differences between traditional and relationship selling, which type of sales approach would you use as a salesperson? Do the different approaches require different personal strengths or attributes?

List the steps in the selling process. The selling process is composed of seven basic steps: (1) generating leads, (2) qualifying leads, (3) approaching the customer and probing needs, (4) developing and proposing solutions, (5) handling objections, (6) closing the sale, and (7) following up.

6.1 You are a new salesperson for a well-known medical software company, and one of your clients is a large group of physicians. You have just arranged an initial meeting with the office manager. Develop a list of questions you might ask at this meeting to uncover the group's specific needs.

6.2 What does sales follow-up entail? Why is it an essential step in the selling process, particularly from the perspective of relationship selling? How does it relate to cognitive dissonance?

6.4 Consider each step in the selling process. Which steps could be conducted through technology (Internet, webinars, etc.)? Which are most important to handle "face-to-face"?

Exercises

APPLICATION EXERCISE

Have you ever waited forever to get a fast-food hamburger? Have you even been left to languish in a dressing room by a salesperson who left for a coffee break? If so, you already know that sales and customer service are integral parts of marketing. While you are working on this chapter, keep a journal of your personal sales and/or customer service experiences with local merchants. Don't ignore the details. Even such things as how crowded a store or restaurant is when you visit may affect your perceptions of the service you received.[35]

Activities

1. Keep your journal for a week, recording all sales and service transactions, if possible, on the day they occur.
2. At the end of the week, examine your journal, and pick the most noteworthy entry. Provide the basic information about the transaction:

company where it occurred, type of transaction (purchase, return, complaint, etc.), type of good or service involved, and so forth.

3. Once you have outlined the situation, evaluate the experience. Use the information about selling in this chapter as support for your evaluation. For example, did the salesperson seem to treat the situation as an individual, discrete transaction, or did he or she seem interested in building a relationship?

4. Finally, make recommendations as to how the company can improve its sales and/or service. Suggestions should be logical and achievable (meaning you have to consider the cost of implementing your suggestion).

ETHICS EXERCISE

Megha Ahuja works for Hi-Tech Electronics. Her responsibilities include selecting items to advertise in the Sunday newspaper inserts. One hot item is a 50-inch flat-panel plasma TV. The list price is INR 80,000, but her manager tells her to advertise it at INR 75,000, since customers can apply for a INR 5000 mail-in rebate. The advertised price has attracted many people to buy the TV; however, Megha has heard several complaints from customers who found the rebate process unusually complex and were denied a rebate because the manufacturer claimed they hadn't provided the required information. She would prefer to advertise the "real" list price, knowing that customers are not guaranteed to receive a rebate.

Questions

1. Is it unethical to advertise products at their post-rebate price in order to increase sales? Why or why not? What is another sales promotion method Hi-Tech Electronics could use to persuade customers to buy their plasma TV at the store?

2. Rebate programs are commonly used by electronics manufacturers because the rebates arouse consumers' interest in buying products; yet only half of purchasers ultimately claim their rebates. Is a rebate program itself unethical if the manufacturer knows consumers are unlikely to receive their money?

MARKETING PLAN EXERCISE

For the next stage of the strategic planning process you'll focus on your chosen company's sales promotion and personal selling decisions. Use the following exercises to guide you through the final elements of Part 5 of your strategic marketing plan:

1. Evaluate or create printed materials for your chosen company (such as data sheets, brochures, stationery, or rate cards). Does the literature sufficiently answer questions? Provide enough information for further contact? Effectively promote product features and customer service? Note a differential or competitive advantage.

2. Think about ways your promotions could turn a first-time customer or deal-hunter into a repeat, loyal customer. Which sales promotion tools should your company use? What trade shows could your firm attend? Explore the feasibility and costs of attending those trade shows.

3. What other sales promotion tools could your firm use? What are the costs? What is the impact of using these methods on pricing?

4. Will you need a sales force? Identify and justify the best type (internal or external) and structure (product, customer, geographic, etc.) for your firm's sales force. You may find that in e-marketing, a sales force is more of a customer service and customer relations management tool. True selling activities may be limited to selling and buying online media space and links. In many circumstances, forming strategic partnerships and distribution deals have replaced traditional sales in the Internet space. What types of alliances and partnerships will you pursue? Will you work with other online firms, offline firms, or both?

Short Case: AVON

Prepared by
Dr. Dheeraj Sharma,
Indian Institute of Management, Ahmedabad

The history of Avon cosmetics goes back to 1886. It came into existence with door-to-door selling of perfumes by Mr David H McConnell. Today, it is one of the largest cosmetic companies in the world. It only sells beauty products for women through the channel of direct-selling.

Avon started selling its products by appointing sales representatives (only women) to go *door-to-door selling* Avon products. The sales representatives not only sold beauty products to its customers, but also gave them beauty advises. Selling Avon products became a way through which women earned money and also got an opportunity to bond with other women on account of their common interest. Women no longer needed to travel to stores to make purchases for beauty products. They only had to invite an Avon representative and the customers got everything they needed at home. Soon, along with door-to-door selling, Avon came up with *workplace selling*. This made it easier for the customers to access the products. Representatives enjoyed selling and customers enjoyed the Avon purchasing experience. Avon marketing model brought an opportunity for the women to socialize with other women. Ever since then, Avon has played a major role in empowering women across the globe.

Avon was launched in India in 1996 and has established itself as one of the leading cosmetic brands. Today, Avon has more than 6.5 lakh representatives spread in more than 100 countries. Its representatives worldwide have a network of around 50 lakh sales representatives, and are still counting.[36] The Avon sales representatives believed in the products they sold and were satisfied with their work. The success of Avon lies in its marketing strategy that involves personal selling from its sales representatives.

Recently, to match with the current technology based marketing processes, Avon also started selling its products online. It not only promotes its products online, but also updates its customers with new product launches, schemes, discounts, etc. Online marketing proved to be successful for further growth of Avon. However, Avon's Group Vice President, North America Sales, Angie Rossi is quoted on Avon's website "*There will always be a space for relationship-based service to the consumer,*" indicating that nothing can replace direct marketing.[37]

Questions

1. Discuss the Avon model. Do you think this model is sustainable?
2. Given changes in the demographics and more and more people getting busier with work, do you think Avon can continue to be successful using the same model?

CHAPTER REV

18 Sales Promotion and Personal Selling

KEY TERMS

LO 1

consumer sales promotion sales promotion activities targeting the ultimate consumer

trade sales promotion sales promotion activities targeting a marketing channel member, such as a wholesaler or retailer

LO 2

coupon a certificate that entitles consumers to an immediate price reduction when they buy the product

rebate a cash refund given for the purchase of a product during a specific period

premium an extra item offered to the consumer, usually in exchange for some proof of purchase of the promoted product

loyalty marketing program a promotional program designed to build long-term, mutually beneficial relationships between a company and its key customers

frequent buyer program a loyalty program in which loyal consumers are rewarded for making multiple purchases of a particular good or service

sampling a promotional program that allows the consumer the opportunity to try a product or service for free

point-of-purchase (P-O-P) display a promotional display set up at the retailer's location to build traffic, advertise the product, or induce impulse buying

LO 3

trade allowance a price reduction offered by manufacturers to intermediaries, such as wholesalers and retailers

push money money offered to channel intermediaries to encourage them to "push" products that is, to encourage other members of the channel to sell the products

KEY CONCEPTS

LO 1 Define and state the objectives of sales promotion.

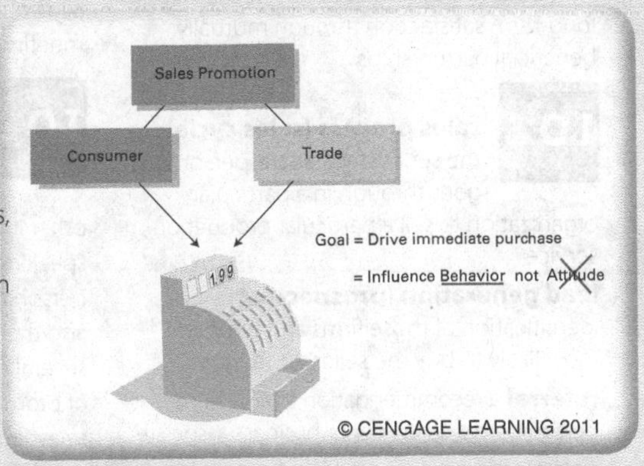

Sales promotion consists of those marketing communication activities, other than advertising, personal selling, and public relations, in which a short-term incentive motivates consumers or members of the distribution channel to purchase a good or service immediately, either by lowering the price or by adding value. The main objectives of sales promotion are to increase trial purchases, consumer inventories, and repeat purchases. Sales promotion is also used to encourage brand switching and to build brand loyalty. Sales promotion supports advertising activities.

LO 2 Discuss the most common forms of consumer sales promotion.

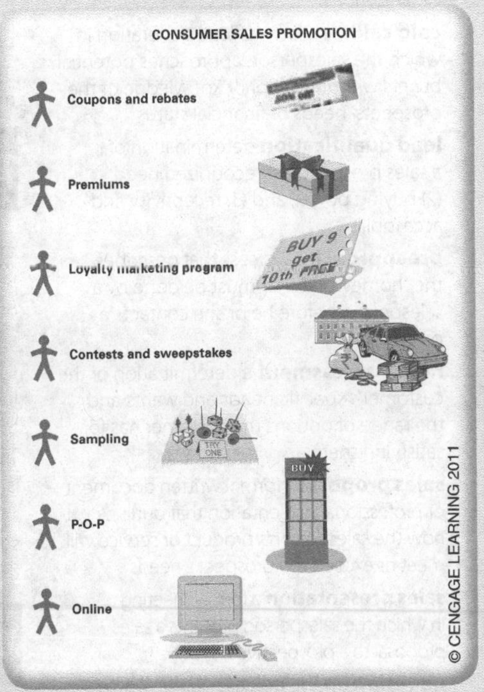

Consumer forms of sales promotion include coupons and rebates, premiums, loyalty marketing programs, contests and sweepstakes, sampling, and point-of-purchase displays. Coupons are certificates entitling consumers to an immediate price reduction when they purchase a product or service. Coupons are a particularly good way to encourage product trial and brand switching. Similar to coupons, rebates provide purchasers with a price reduction, although it is not immediate. To receive a rebate, consumers generally must mail in a rebate form with a proof of purchase. Premiums offer an extra item or incentive to the consumer for buying a product or service. Premiums reinforce the consumer's purchase decision, increase consumption, and persuade nonusers to switch brands. Rewarding loyal customers is the basis of loyalty marketing programs. Loyalty programs are extremely effective at building long-term, mutually beneficial relationships between a company and its key customers. Contests and sweepstakes are generally designed to create interest, often to encourage brand switching. Because consumers perceive risk in trying new products, sampling is an effective method for gaining new customers. Finally, point-of-purchase displays set up at the retailer's location build traffic, advertise the product, and induce impulse buying.

LO 5

relationship selling (consultative selling) a sales practice that involves building, maintaining, and enhancing interactions with customers in order to develop long-term satisfaction through mutually beneficial partnerships

LO 6

sales process (sales cycle) the set of steps a salesperson goes through in a particular organization to sell a particular product or service

lead generation (prospecting) identification of those firms and people most likely to buy the seller's offerings

referral a recommendation to a salesperson from a customer or business associate

networking a process of finding out about potential clients from friends, business contacts, coworkers, acquaintances, and fellow members in professional and civic organizations

cold calling a form of lead generation in which the salesperson approaches potential buyers without any prior knowledge of the prospects' needs or financial status

lead qualification determination of a sales prospect's (1) recognized need, (2) buying power, and (3) receptivity and accessibility

preapproach a process that describes the "homework" that must be done by a salesperson before he or she contacts a prospect

needs assessment a determination of the customer's specific needs and wants and the range of options the customer has for satisfying them

sales proposal a formal written document or professional presentation that outlines how the salesperson's product or service will meet or exceed the prospect's needs

sales presentation a formal meeting in which the salesperson presents a sales proposal to a prospective buyer

negotiation the process during which both the salesperson and the prospect offer special concessions in an attempt to arrive at a sales agreement

follow-up the final step of the selling process, in which the salesperson ensures delivery schedules are met, goods or services perform as promised, and buyers' employees are properly trained to use the products

LO 3 **List the most common forms of trade sales promotion.** Manufacturers use many of the same sales promotion tools used in consumer promotions, such as sales contests, premiums, and point-of-purchase displays. In addition, manufacturers and channel intermediaries use several unique promotional strategies: trade allowances, push money, training programs, free merchandise, store demonstrations, and meetings, conventions, and trade shows.

LO 4 **Describe personal selling.** Personal selling is direct communication between a sales representative and one or more prospective buyers in an attempt to influence each other in a purchase situation. Broadly speaking, all businesspeople use personal selling to promote themselves and their ideas. Personal selling offers several advantages over other forms of promotion. Personal selling allows salespeople to thoroughly explain and demonstrate a product. Salespeople have the flexibility to tailor a sales proposal to the needs and preferences of individual customers. Personal selling is more efficient than other forms of promotion because salespeople target qualified prospects and avoid wasting efforts on unlikely buyers. Personal selling affords greater managerial control over promotion costs. Finally, personal selling is the most effective method of closing a sale and producing satisfied customers.

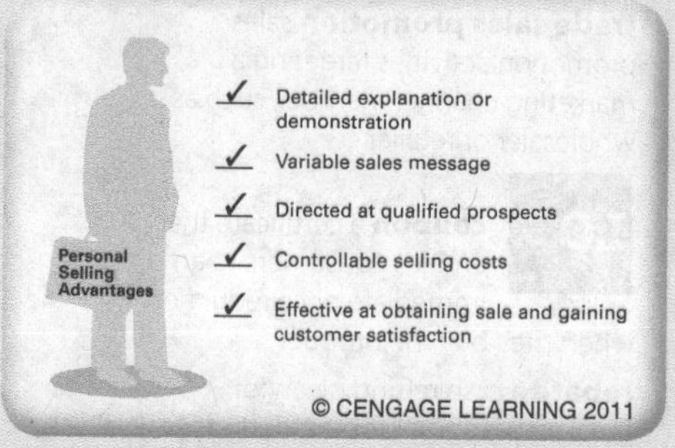

LO 5 **Discuss the key differences between relationship selling and traditional selling.** Relationship selling is the practice of building, maintaining, and enhancing interactions with customers in order to develop long-term satisfaction through mutually beneficial partnerships. Traditional selling, on the other hand, is transaction focused. That is, the salesperson is most concerned with making onetime sales and moving on to the next prospect. Salespeople practicing relationship selling spend more time understanding a prospect's needs and developing solutions to meet those needs.

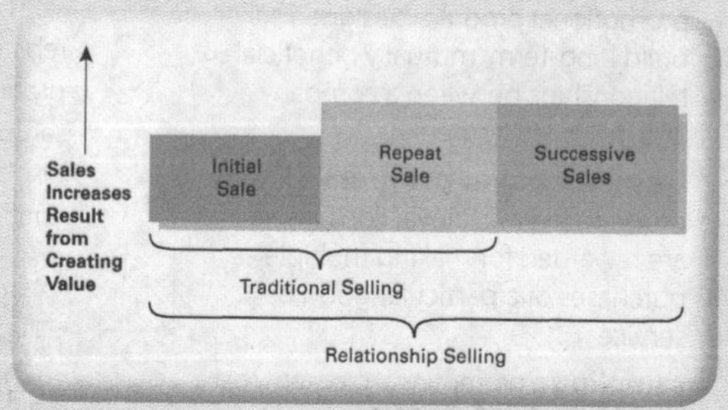

LO 6 **List the steps in the selling process.** The selling process is composed of seven basic steps: (1) generating leads, (2) qualifying leads, (3) approaching the customer and probing needs, (4) developing and proposing solutions, (5) handling objections, (6) closing the sale, and (7) following up.

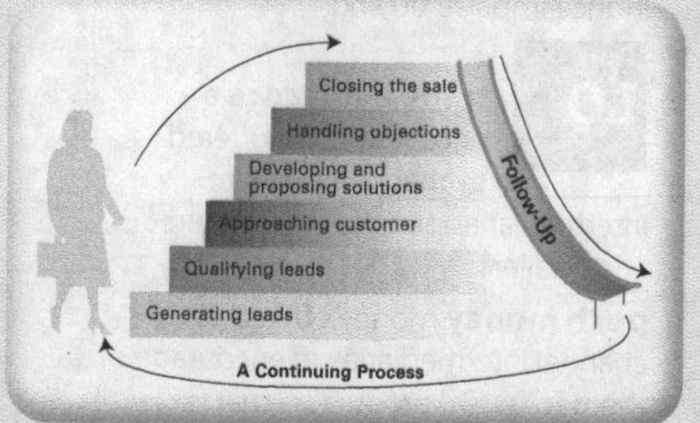

CASE 5 Jasmine— A Case Study

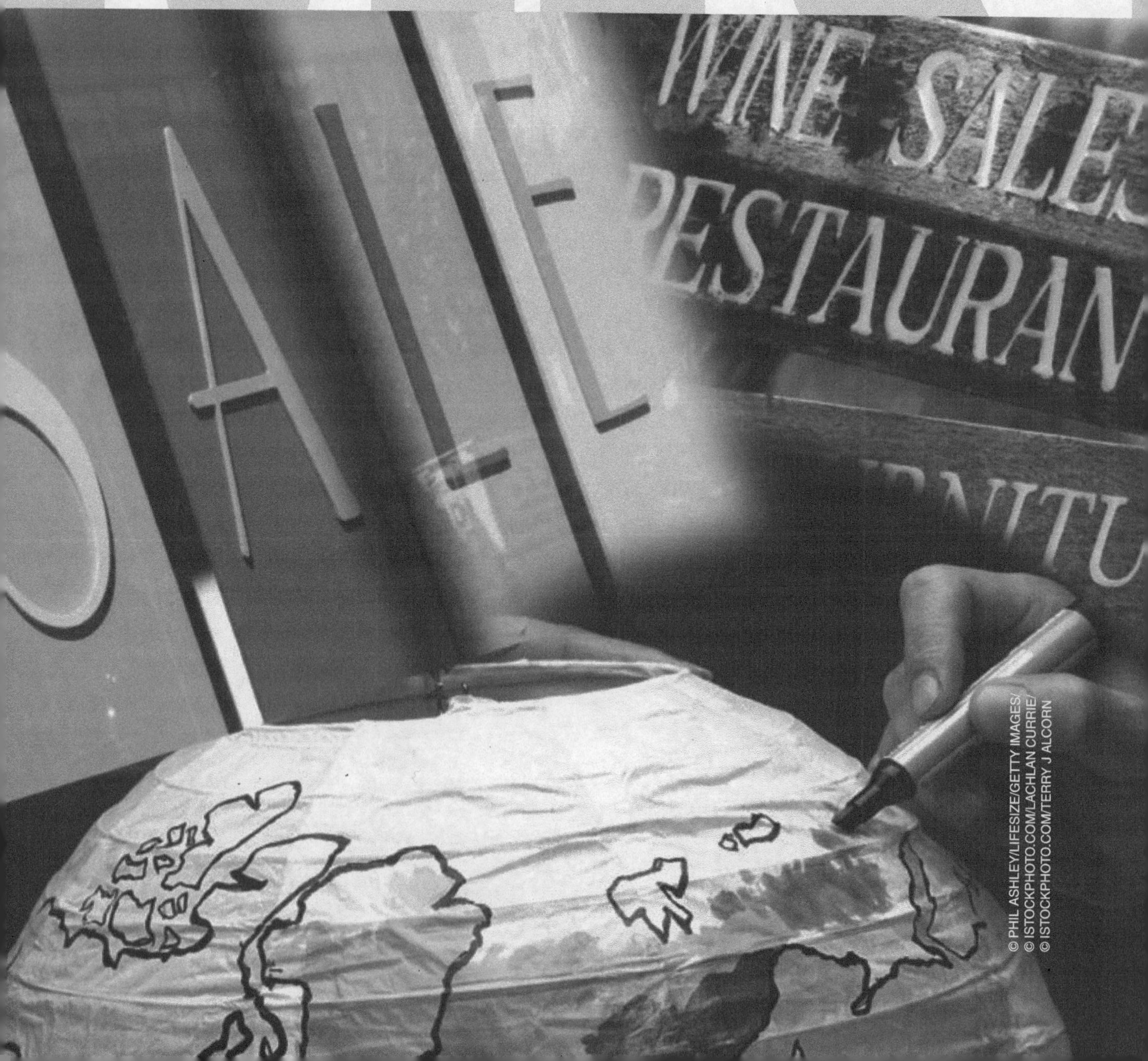

On an afternoon in early January 1996, Mr Peter Thomas, Senior Brand Manager of Biltek Tea (India) Limited (BTIL), was poring over the recent sales performance figures of *Jasmine*, a brand of premium dust tea that he was handling. The data for the fourth quarter of 1995 had just arrived, and the results were as depressing as they had been over the last few years. Although *Jasmine* was the market leader in the premium dust tea segment in southern India, the stagnant/low rate of growth was a cause for considerable concern to Mr Thomas. Being a significant contributor to the beverages profit center of BTIL, it was vital that *Jasmine* grew at a significant rate in the coming years to accelerate the beverages profitability.

In order to arrive at a reasonable understanding of the current situation and to obtain insights which would help in the process of decision making, the brand manager dug out the reports of several syndicated research and market research studies that he had commissioned in the recent past, Mr Thomas knew that a sound diagnosis of the situation was essential before deciding on the appropriate marketing strategy for the brand for 1996-97.

C5.1 Background

The popularity of tea in India owes its origin to the long British rule in the sub-continent. By 1995–96, 'black tea' was both the most popular and cheapest beverage in the country, accounting for a domestic consumption of 583,000 tons out of a national production of 780,000 tons. Though per capita consumption was low at 0.63 kg/year/capita, the domestic consumption had been growing slightly higher than the population growth rate of 2%. The overall tea production in the country had however remained more or less static over the last five years.

Tea in India was grown in three regions—Assam, North Bengal (Dooars), and the Nilgiris (Tamilnadu and Kerala). Assam had the largest acreage under cultivation and accounted for close to 60% of tea production in India. Black tea was manufactured using two processes : a) orthodox, and b) CTC (Crush, Tear, Curl) (Appendix I provides descriptions of these processes). CTC tea gave a stronger brew, and hence a

EXHIBIT C5.1
History of Tea Production, Exports and Domestic Sales (India)

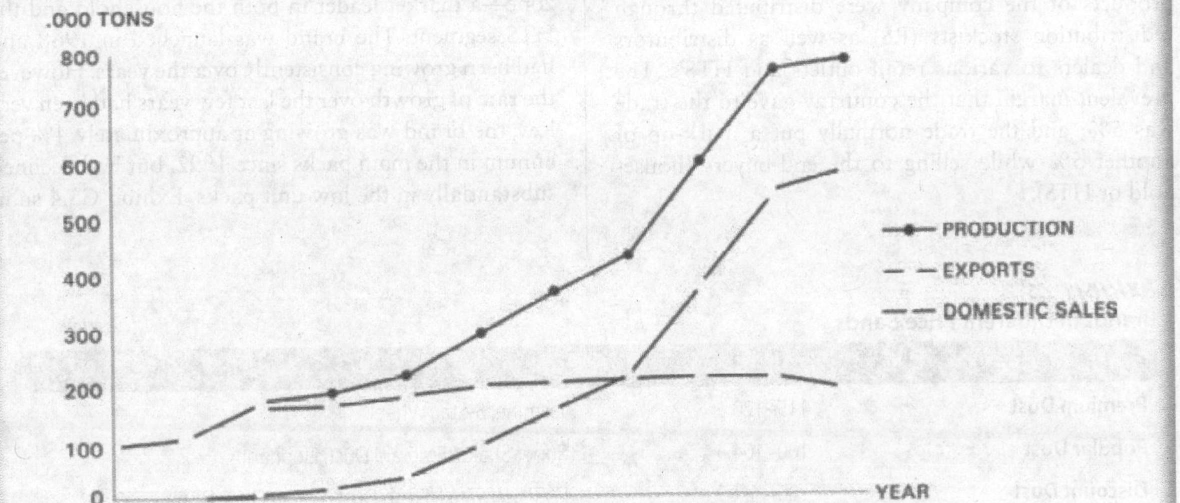

This case was prepared *by* Professor Bibek Banerjee of *Indian* Institute of Management, Ahmedabad, as *basis* for class discussion. The case is not meant to illustrate either effective or ineffective handling of administrative situation.

higher cuppage (number of cups per a certain quantity of tea). Currently, most Indian tea was manufactured using the above process. Orthodox teas were made using a less rigorous manufacturing process and hence were lighter, less astringent and more flavoury. Both CTC and Orthodox teas could be further classified as "leaf" and "dust" on the basis of the leaf size. Broadly, the northern, eastern and parts of western India consumed leaf tea while the entire south and some parts of western India consumed dust tea.

BTIL was a leading player in the branded processed food and hot beverages industry, with several years of experience in marketing a whole range of successful food and beverage products/brands. The beverages profit center of BTIL comprised of coffee and tea brands. The tea business of the company had several well-known national and regional brands catering to a variety of consumer segments.

The company was the biggest licensed buyer in the tea auction centers of India, where processed tea were brought from the tea-gardens for auctioning. Unlike Bata Tea, its formidable rival, BTIL did not own major tea gardens. However, the company had blending facilities where various grades of tea were blended and packaged for the various brands under the company's portfolio.

Generally, there were two broad segments in the tea industry, households and hot-tea-shops (HTS). The products of the company were distributed through redistribution stockists (RS) as well as distributors and dealers to various retail outlets and HTS's. The prevalent margin that the company gave to the trade was 5%; and the trade normally put a mark-up of another 5% while selling to the end-buyers (household or HTS).

C5.2 The Product

Jasmine was a blend of premium Assam CTC teas. The tea promised to deliver a rich golden colour, added strength and a superior taste and consequently a superior cuppage (Appendix 2 gives some details about blending operations in BTIL). *Jasmine* was packaged in a variety of pack sizes: a 1-kg stand pack; 500 gm and 250 gm carton packs; 100 gm, 50 gm and 25 gm soft packs in silver foil; and finally 2 gm, 4 gm and 7 grm polyester-poly and/or paper-poly pouches (termed as "paise-packs" or low-unit-price (LUP) packs). The 1 kg, 500gm and 50% of the 250 gm packs were normally consumed by the HTS's, and the rest by the households. The brand had a distinctive orange pack highlighting three white *jasmines* in a green circular background.

Jasmine: Brand History

The brand management team of BTIL categorised the dust-tea market in the southern part of India into three categories based on price: premium, popular and discount. The price bands and the brands which were present in each category are given in Exhibit C5.2. Exhibit C5.3 gives the rural-urban statewise split of the premium tea segment.

Jasmine was the largest tea brand in the south zone—a market leader in both the household and the HTS segment. The brand was launched in 1968 and had been growing consistently over the years. However the rate of growth over the last few years had been very low, the brand was growing at approximately 4% per annum in the main packs since 1992, but had declined substantially in the low unit packs. Exhibit C5.4 sum-

EXHIBIT C5.2
Brands in Different Price Bands

Category	Price Band (₹)	Brands
Premium Dust	115–120	Jasmine, 5-Star, Wheel*
Popular Dust	100–104	Super Shakti, Emerald Dust, Elephant*
Discount Dust	80–84	HVT®, HD Tea*, Fresh Dust, Yellow Dust, Disha
Premium Leaf	134–138	Qutab, Savvy∅
Popular Leaf	106–108	Orange, Fresh Leaf, Bata Leaf*

* Wheel (in guilt pack), Elephant (in carton), HD Tea (in pouch) & Bata Leaf are brands from the house of Bata Tea.
®, HVT Premium Tea (in pouch) is a brand from HV Tytler & Co.
∅Savvy is a brand from Bhasmukh Rai & Co.

marises some of the key facts and figures about the historical performance of *Jasmine* between 1989-1995.

The Market and Competition

Tea was the most popular form of beverage that was consumed across the length and breadth of the country, cutting across all income groups and social classes. According to ORG data, total packaged tea market in India had grown by 6.3% during 1993-94 and by 4.2% during 1994-95; with expected growth projected for 1996 being 1% for urban and 9% for rural areas. The ORG data also reported the split of packaged tea sales (as of 1994) to be 64% for urban and 36% for rural.

Over the recent years the packaged tea market had been witnessing a proliferation of brands. Traditional and established tea-parlours had also started packaging and marketing their own brands in areas where they had a strong franchise: for instance, Sharkan in Gujarat and Savvy in Bombay. Exhibit C5.5

EXHIBIT C5.3

Premium Packet Tea Market Size

	1993	1994	1995
AP - Premium			
Urban	2611	1591	2233
Rural	2975	2844	2213
Total	**5586**	**4435**	**4446**
TN - Premium			
Urban	3372	3456	3454
Rural	1713	1856	1851
Total	**5085**	**5312**	**5305**
KAR - Premium			
Urban	296	352	429
Rural	18	16	34
Total	**314**	**368**	**463**

EXHIBIT C5.4

Brand Trends—Jasmine Facts & Figures*

		1989	1990	1991	1992	1993	1994	1995
Volumes	Tons	15330	15624	17182	17118	17245	17525	16969
Net Proceeds	₹M	766.3	1035.4	1171.1	1169.7	1433.2	1471.3	1454.4
To Sales	₹/Kg	49.99	66.27	68.16	68,33	83.11	84.17	85.71
Support	₹/Kg	0.67	0.88	0.83	1.19	2.27	1.89	2.14
	% NPS	1.3	1.3	1.2	1.7	2.7	2.2	2.5

* Volumes are in main packs plus LUPs

EXHIBIT C5.5

Competition Scenario Statewise (Mains)

TAMIL NADU		A.P.	
WHEEL	30 TPW"	WHEEL	21 TPW (Coastal A.P.)
HVT	80 TPW (Mainly rural)	EMERALD	16 TPW
EMERALD	34 TPW	SUPER SHAKTI	14 TPW
SUPER SHAKTI	38 TPW	5-STAR	48 TPW
5-STAR	105 TPW	ELEPHANT	60 TPW
HD	20 TPW	ORANGE DUST	40 TPW (Mainly Hyderabad city)
		QUTAB	45 TPW (Coastal A.P.)
KARNATAKA		**KERALA**	
HD	70 TPW	FED	85 TPW
EMERALD	21 TPW	DISHA	30 TPW
SUPER SHAKTI	24 TPW	YELLOW DUST	20 TPW
ORANGE DUST	40 TPW (Mainly Bangalore city)	FRESH	18 TPW
QUTAB	10 TPW (Mainly Bangalore city)	HVT	45 TPW

"TPW : Tons Per Week

gives details regarding the brandwise-statewise sales of packaged tea (excluding LUPs).

The tea market in India had strong regional preferences across states and regions. This reflected in the statewise shares of each brand, as well as the market composition of packaged vis-a-vis loose tea. BTIL estimated that the volume of loose tea sales were to the tune of 80–100 TPW in Tamil Nadu, about 150 TPW in Andhra Pradesh and 300–350 TPW in Kerala.

Qutab had been growing steadily in coastal A.P. over the last five years, which seemed to indicate that some upgradation from premium dust to premium leaf was taking place. Maharashtra, Gujarat and Rajasthan in western India had pockets of 'dust' tea consumption. Orissa was another state which had a 'dust' market, with an estimated size of 130 TPW.

The pack-wise sales data for the brand *Jasmine* over the years 1993 to 1995 are given in Exhibits C5.6(A) and C5.6(B); and Exhibit C5.7 gives the packwise/statewise sales for 1995 along with the end consumer prices (ECPs). Exhibit C5.8 summarises the competitive scenario by depicting the statewise/quarterwise urban shares of major brands, while Exhibit C5.9 gives the quarterwise rural shares of the major brands between 1994-1995.

EXHIBIT C5.6(A)

Sales Trends In Kgs/Week (Jasmine)

	Pack sizes	AVG93	AVG94	AVG95
All India	Jasmine 1 KG	13224	15711	22212
	Jasmine 500 G	56349	60230	55114
	Jasmine 250 G	79177	83173	81229
	Jasmine 100 G	63914	67596	68790
	Jasmine 50 G	25514	30327	31749
	Jasmine 25 G	11339	13288	13040
	Jasmine 1/-	6135	9000	13345
	Jasmine 5OPP	19000	24711	16505
	Jasmine 25PP	57000	33000	21283
	TOTAL	**331652**	**337036**	**323267**

EXHIBIT C5.6(B)

Sales Trends in Kgs/Week (Jasmine)—State-wise

	Pack sizes	A VG93	AVG94	A VG95
Kerala	Jasmine 1 KG	361	468	500
	Jasmine 500 G	2652	2865	2692
	Jasmine 250 G	4954	5367	5096
	Jasmine 100 G	3974	4095	3750
	Jasmine 50 G	1184	1072	904
	Jasmine 25 G	630	706	500
	Jasmine I/-	329	182	77
	Jasmine SOPP	106	13	0
	Jasmine 25PP	16	4	0
	TOTAL	**14206**	**14772**	**13519**

EXHIBIT C5.6(B)

Sales Trends in Kgs/Week (Jasmine)—State-wise—(Continued)

Tamil Nadu	Jasmine 1 KG	11526	13605	19096
	Jasmine 500 G	36103	38711	35519
	Jasmine 250 G	33863	35016	35038
	Jasmine 100 G	32105	35874	38673
	Jasmine 50 G	15786	19495	21596 ,
	Jasmine 25 G	6041	8463	8288
	Jasmine 1/-	1933	4490	6769
	Jasmine SOPP	2392	3005	2962
	Jasmine 25PP	8732	1696	3173
	TOTAL	**148481**	**160335**	**171115**
Andhra Pradesh	Jasmine I KG		20	540
	Jasmine 500 G		11700	11480
	Jasmine 250 G		27600	27460
	Jasmine 1(X) G		18300	18290
	Jasmine 50 G		6600	6230
	Jasmine 25 G		3800	3540
	Jasmine 1/-		270	-1460
	Jasmine SOPP		3920	1620
	Jasmine 25PP		5600	2880
	TOTAL		**71810**	**73500**
Karnataka	Jasmine 1 KG	1104	14%	2000
	Jasmine 500 G	2391	3092	2885
	Jasmine 250 G	7506	10004	10808
	Jasmine 100 G	4982	7178	7173
	JasmiJ .2 50 G	1671	2570	2673
	Jasmine 25 G	750	657	635
	Jasmine II-	1469	3534	4/35
	Jasmine 50PP	8058	9257	8096
	Jasmine 25PP	14210	9231	5615
	TOTAL	**42141**	**47019**	**44020**

EXHIBIT C5.7

Linewise/Statewise Sales: 1995/Pack Ecp

Figs in Tons/WK

	Tamil Nadu	Andhra Pradesh	Karnataka	Maharashtra	Kerala	All India	PACK ECPs
1 KG	19.0	0.5	2.0	0.0	0.5	22.0	115.00
500 G	35.5	.11.5	3.0	2.5	3.0	55.5	59.00
250 G	35.0	27.5	11.0	2.8	5.0	81.3	30.00
100 G	39.0	18.0	7.0	0.9	4.0	68.9	12.50
50G	22.0	6.0	3.0	0.3	0.6	31.9	7.00
25 G	8.0	3.5	0.6	0.1	0.5	12.7	3.50J
MAINS	**158.5**	**67.0**	**26.6**	**6.6**	**13.64**	**272.6**	
Re 1	7.0	1.4	4.0	09		13.3	
50P	3.0	1.6	8.0	4.0		16.6	
25 P	3.0	3.0	6.0	9.0		21.0	
LUP	13.0	6.0	18.0	13.9	0.0	50.9	
TOTAL	**171.5**	**73.0**	**44.6**	**20.5**	**13.6**	**323.2**	

EXHIBIT C5.8

Urban Shares—South Zone

	1Q94	2 Q 94	3 Q94	4 Q94	1Q95	2Q95	3 Q 95	4 Q 95
Mina Nadu								
Jasmine	38.09	39.44	35.26	38.91	38.69	37.78	37.99	38.60
5-Star	23.72	22.5	27.94	22.40	21.90	24.69	23.32	24.02
Wheel	2.66	2.70	2.62	3.24	3.68	4.25	3.71	5.08
HVT	6.01	7.85	11.79	9.42	6.31	6.62	6.34	5.60
Andhra Pradesh								
Jasmine	18.93	18.46	19.21	17.54	21.87	23.49	20.04	18.87
5-Star	13.83	15.38	12.38	10.70	9.32	10.13	6.59	5.93
Wheel	—	—	—	—	1.29	3.70	4.38	4.44
Qutab	14.66	13.63	14.50	13.30	12.33	16.79	15.02	14.88
Orange, Dust	15.88	15.04	12.91	13.47	12.43	11.62	13.18	14.45
Elephant	16.34	18.32	22.15	22.79	19.49	18.57	21.63	19.43
Karnataka								
Jasmine	8.56	9.47	11.76	12.22	12.84	10.94	10.65	11.66
Qutab	9.26	10.83	9.69	8.43	8.54	9.24	8.12	8.26
Orange Dust	20.37	20.72	18.33	17.70	19.60	18.83	19.96	23.16
HD	25.61	26.09	23.24	23.70	24.86	25.61	23.69	23.75
Kerala								
Jasmine	9.59	7.71	7.94	6.82	7.21	7.12	5.48	4.61
HD	29.60	38.52	29.3	32.65	36.37	39.19	42.06	43.92
HVT	10.30	4.08	12.45	9.77	9.69	11.71	10.51	10.85
Disha	9.66	9.67	14.13	12.19	8.78	5.61	8.20	6.95

EXHIBIT C5.9
Rural Shares—South Zone

	1 Q'94	2 Q'94	3 Q'94	4 Q'94	1 Q'95	2 Q'95	3 Q'95	4 Q'95
Orange Dust	2.3	3.2	2.4	1.7	1.6	2.7	2.8	2.4
Fresh	0.6	0.5	0.7	1.3	0.9	1.4	1.4	0.6
Qutab	2.2	2.2	1.5	3.3	2.7	2.8	2.3	3.2
Jasmine	24.9	23.6	24.8	23.1	17.8	16.8	15.3	18.2
5-Star	12.1	10.4	9.8	5.1	12.4	7.6	7.8	7.5
Emerald Dust	13.6	13.1	13.4	7.3	16.4	12.1	9.3	7.7
Super Shakti	2.2	2.2	2.4	2.4	2.3	3.8	4.0	3.0
Elephant	16.8	19.5	16.7	21.4	18.1	13.0	13.3	10.4
HD	8.4	9.8	10.8	12.2	11.9	18.7	16.4	20.0
Wheel	0.0	0.1	0.8	1.2	0.5	0.4	0.3	0.6
HVT	9.9	9.3	12.0	13.8	10.4	13.9	14.8	12.5

Brand Positioning and Image Perceptions

In 1968, when the brand was launched, the intended positioning of *Jasmine* was on the dimension of 'taste'. It was repositioned in 1985 to "*Jasmine* for colour, taste and strength". The history of communication messages *of Jasmine* over the years were as follows:

1982-84:

Advertising Platform	:	*Jasmine* for taste
Creative Route	:	Natarajan the well known south Indian filmstar as spokesman
Media	:	Cinema and Radio

1985-90:

Advertising Platform	:	*Jasmine* for colour, taste and strength
Creative Route	:	Family situation
Media	:	Cinema and Radio

1991-92:

Advertising Platform	:	*Jasmine* for colour, taste and strength
Creative Route	:	Romance: strengthened link between Jasmine and the three benefits
Media	:	Television

1992 onward:

Advertising Platform	:	*Jasmine* for colour, taste and strength
Creative Route	:	Three ladies standing for three benefits offered by *Jasmine*
Media	:	Television

The advertising idea for the latest commercial which was being aired since 1992 was to create a link between the brand name *Jasmine* and the combination of the three qualities of colour, taste and strength for the perfect cup of tea using three ladies as metaphor. The three flowers in the *Jasmine* logo had been used as a mnemonic to symbolise the three properties of colour, taste and strength.

The brand management team at BTIL had been periodically doing market research (through specialised agencies) to keep in touch with the health and percieved image of the *Jasmine* brand among both its users as well as non-users. Some of the research findings were as follows:

Functional Benefits		Emotional Associations	
1991	1994	1991	1994
— taste — strength — aroma	— taste — strength — aroma — consistent quality — balance between taste, strength & aroma	— long-standing relationship — unquestioned loyalty — caring/nurturing — pride	— brand confidence — loyalty after discernment — pride in the brand — status enhancement — fits self image — aspirational

Exhibit C5.10 gives the research inputs which were available about the key elements of the brand's personality as discerned by the consumers of various brands of tea.

Consumer Behaviour and Mr Thomas' Dilemma

Mr Thomas knew that for him to be able to devise a marketing plan for the successful revival of the *Jasmine* brand, careful understanding of the consumer behaviour toward their disposition to the activity of tea-drinking was necessary. Exhibits C5.11(A)–C5.11(E) summarise some data available from various sources.

Mr Thomas was also wondering about the significance of two particularly discernible developments that had been taking place in the market place, i.e. the increasing presence of branded-tea as a percentage of the total market; and the growth of the rural segment as a major consumer of branded tea. Exhibits C5.12(A) and C5.12(B) furnish the details.

Furthermore, there were plenty of changes in the operating environment that were feeding on the minds of the *Jasmine* marketing team. In September 1995, the government allowed the addition of flavours in tea. The addition of natural ingredients like cardamom, ginger, lime etc. were common in some parts of the country like Gujarat but the marketing team was not sure whether the concept had relevance in the south where the *Jasmine* equity was strong.

The latest commercial with the three ladies had worked very well for the brand and the marketing team was wary of making any changes. The ad had been aired for the last four years and had very high recall and comprehension. However, the young brand manager and the agency team thought that a strong case could be made for revitalising the *Jasmine* brand attitude. They were keen to make a new commercial and leave their mark in the advertising arena. The wizened marketing director had however a word of caution—"There is something in this *Jasmine* mix which seems to be working—don't change it for the sake of changing it".

EXHIBIT C5.10
Brand Personality

	Jasmine Users	HD/HVT Users	5-Star Users
Jasmine	▸▸ young adult ▸▸ strong & healthy ▸▸ vital & active ▸▸ full of verve	▸▸ young adult ▸▸ boundless energy ▸▸ alert ▸▸ jolly	▸▸ prime of its life ▸▸ surging ahead ▸▸ competitive spirit ▸▸ involvedfmterested
HD	▸▸ teenager ▸▸ new entrant ▸▸ active & attention arresting ▸▸ yet to stabilise	▸▸ youth ▸▸ fresh & natural ▸▸ active ▸▸ attractive	▸▸ growing child ▸▸ active & alert
5-Star	▸▸ mature brand ▸▸ serious ▸▸ strong ▸▸ losing its grip	▸▸ mature but in good health ▸▸ strong ▸▸ active	▸▸ infant ▸▸ potential for growth ▸▸ not realised its full potential
Super Shakti	▸▸ aged ▸▸ infant	▸▸ dull ▸▸ senile	▸▸ old, but with vigour

EXHIBIT C5.11(A)
Consumption Habits (% Households)

	URBAN	RURAL	TOTAL
ALL INDIA			
Tea	97	93	94
Coffee	26	8	12
Dual Beverages	23	1	6
SOUTH			
Tea	83	70	74
Coffee	59	31	39
NORTH			
Tea	100	99	99
Coffee	15	2	5

EXHIBIT C5.11(B)
Attributes Considered Important—Tea CYO

	TOTAL	TAMIL NADU	DELHI
Taste	92	94	80
Aroma/Flavour	63	77	42
Good Quality	57	60	46
Strength	57	69	36
Freshness	54	53	48
Color of Decoction	50	42	35
Price	31	15	25
Color of leaf	23	13	32
Brand Name	17	22	9
Packaging	13	10	10

EXHIBIT C5.11(C)
Usage (Preparation Methods)

- Tea was usually boiled with water, milk and sugar (98%)
- Only 6% in Urban and 2% in Rural brew tea
- 99.4% add sugar and 99.7% add milk in their tea
- Majority of coffee consuming households prepare coffee by boiling, just like tea
- Only 26% in Rural India prepare coffee by decoction

EXHIBIT C5.11(D)
Tea-Triggers

- Tea consumption was inelastic with income. Other beverages were mostly in upper income groups.
- Average number of cups: 2.3 per person per day.
- Preference for packaged tea, leaf tea increases with income
- A ₹1000 increase in income leads to an increase of 1 cup per day.
- Taste, flavor, quality, freshness: key attributes in selecting tea.

EXHIBIT C5.11(E)
Consumer Habits

BLENDING

- Only 1.5% of the tea consuming households blended two types of tea - 2.5% in East and 2% in North.
- This practice increased with increase in household income (5% in ₹4000+)

FLAVORING

- Only 2% used flavour in their teas
  - — half of them used atleast once a week
  - — a quarter used almost daily
  - — major flavors used were cardamom (50%) and ginger (45%) - other flavours ranged between 3% to 7%
  - — usage of branded flavour was negligible

This set the marketing team thinking all over again. Here they had a powerful mix on *Jasmine*, an extremely strong brand equity and yet low growths in the last few years. "What should the strategy for the

EXHIBIT C5.12(A)

Tea-Scenario, 1985–1995

	1985	1990	1995
Tea consumption ('000 tons)	425	490	583
— Branded	107	160	215
— Loose	318	330	368
Share of Branded (%)	25	33	37

EXHIBIT C5.12(B)

Branded Tea (Urban-Rural Split), '000 Tons

	1985	1990	1995	2000 (Projected)
Urban	47	76	95	115
Rural	27	57	105	165
Total	74	133	200	280
Proportion of Rural to Total	36.5%	42.8%	52.5%	59%

brand be for 1996–97" wondered Mr Thomas, aware that any decision taken will have major implications on the current as well as the future destiny of this brand.

C5.3 Appendix 1: Tea Manufacturing Process

The tea that is popularly marketed and consumed in India is BLACK tea. It contains a little cafeine which acts as a stimulant. The manufacturing process helps develop *tannin* which makes tea a satisfying beverage. Besides black tea there are three other families of tea manufactured: GREEN, OOLONG and INSTANT. The green leaf or raw material is the same for all these varieties of tea.

In black tea processing, the purpose is to condition green leaf for fermentation, attain optimum fermentation and then arrest it. This is achieved by rupturing the leaf cells to release the enzymes and to expose them to oxygen. As soon as optimum fermentation is achieved, the leaf mass is passed through hot air which destroys the enzymes and thus arrests the process.

Two types of black tea are commonly manufactured—Orthodox and CTC. Orthodox or the traditional tea processing begins with 'withering' the freshly plucked leaf. Withering is the process of inducing (with the help of ambient or warm air) the leaf to lose about half its moisture in the course of 12–18 hours. At the end of this phase of manufacturing, the leaf is flaccid. The flaccid tea aid the next stage of tea making known as 'rolling'. It is achieved by rolling the leaf in a machine for one or two hours as if between the palms of two human hands, a process which sets of fermentation. To complete this process of fermentation the mass of rolled leaf is laid in a cool, humid atmosphere. The total time taken between the commencement of rolling and the achievement of optimum fermentation is 2-3 hours, after which the enzymes must be destroyed. At this point of time, the colour of the leaf is a bright gold.

To arrest fermentation, the mass of leaf if exposed to hot air by passing it though a chamber with perforated moving trays. The temperature of the air entering the chamber at its base ranges between 200°F to 250°F—a process known as 'firing'. It takes about half an hour and renders the leaf colour black. After the fired leaf is cooled to normal temperature, it is sorted and graded with a view to make tea widely marketable by offering it in uniform grades. After sorting, the tea is ready for packaging.

The CTC (Crush, Tear, Curl) process of manufacturing is similar to the one used for orthodox tea, except in the phase of rolling. This process is more severe: after a brief conditioning roll, the leaf is passed through a machine comprising two steel cylinders (normally 30 inches long and 8 inches in diameter) with fine toothlike sharp edges. When the leaf is consecutively passed through two or three machines, it is much reduced in size and most of its cells are ruptured. The object is to achieve accelerated as well as intensive fermentation. The result is that the liquor is much thicker and yields many more cups of drinking tea per kg. The dry tea leaves have a granulated appearance and are blackish brown in colour.

The single major achievement of the 20th century in the tea industry was the invention of the CTC machine in India in 1931 which doubled cuppage instantaneously. The Orthodox variety produces only 250 cups per kg of tea whereas CTC produces more than 500 cups per tea.

C5.4 Appendix 2: Blending Operation

Teas are stored in pallets at the **warehouse** portion of the blending units. Blenders located at the factories update their stocks book and prepare blend order sheets following

(a) the blendwise standards/specifications issued by the business and

(b) production plans.

A typical blend order sheet will have all the necessary information for each lot of teas (for say 30 lots) including garden name, broker name, sale no., number of chests, gross/nett weight, location, etc. Mechanical blend drums are used for blending teas from various gardens. After having fed the teas into the drums (as per blend order sheets) the drum is made to rotate on a horizontal axis for a specified number of rotation at a desired speed (so as to ensure that physical properties of tea leaves are not lost in the process) and then finally the blended teas are moved to the stationary hoppers above the packing machines. Iron and other foreign particles are also removed through magnetic separators or sieves before/after blending operation in order to comply with the stringent provisions of prevention of Food Adulteration Act.

CHAPTER 19 Pricing Concepts

Learning Outcomes

LO 1 Discuss the importance of pricing decisions to the economy and to the individual firm

LO 2 List and explain a variety of pricing objectives

LO 3 Explain the role of demand in price determination

LO 4 Understand the concept of yield management systems

LO 5 Describe cost-oriented pricing strategies

LO 6 Demonstrate how the product life cycle, competition, distribution and promotion strategies, customer demands, the Internet and extranets, and perceptions of quality can affect price

Trying to set the right price is one of the most stressful and pressure-filled tasks of the marketing manager.

LO 1 The Importance of Price

Price means one thing to the consumer and something else to the seller. To the consumer, it is the cost of something. To the seller, price is revenue—the primary source of profits. In the broadest sense, price allocates resources in a free-market economy. Marketing managers are frequently challenged by the task of price setting.

price that which is given up in an exchange to acquire a good or service

What Is Price?

Price is that which is given up in an exchange to acquire a good or service. Price plays two roles in the evaluation of product alternatives: as a measure of sacrifice and as an information cue. To some degree, these are two opposing effects.[1]

The Sacrifice Effect of Price Price is, again, "that which is given up," which means what is sacrificed to get a good or service. In India, the sacrifice is usually money, but it can be other things as well. It may also be time lost while waiting to acquire the good or service. Price might also include "lost dignity" for individuals who lose their jobs and must rely on charity.

The Information Effect of Price Consumers do not always choose the lowest-priced product in a category, such as shoes, cars or wine, even when the products are otherwise similar. One explanation of this, based upon research, is that we infer quality information from price.[2] That is, higher quality equals higher price. The information effect of price may also extend to favorable price perceptions by others

Note: All the figures in U.S. dollars are converted into rupee using the value $1 = ₹45.

revenue the price charged to customers multiplied by the number of units sold

profit revenue minus expenses

because higher prices can convey the prominence and status of the purchaser to other people. Thus, a Swatch and a Rolex both can accurately tell time but convey different meanings. The price–quality relationship will be discussed later in the chapter.

Value Is Based upon Perceived Satisfaction Consumers are interested in obtaining a "reasonable price." "Reasonable price" really means "perceived reasonable value" at the time of the transaction. The price paid is based on the satisfaction consumers *expect* to receive from a product and not necessarily the satisfaction they *actually* receive. Price can relate to anything with perceived value, not just money. When goods and services are exchanged, the trade is called *barter*.

The Importance of Price to Marketing Managers

Prices are the key to revenues, which in turn are the key to profits for an organization. **Revenue** is the price charged to customers multiplied by the number of units sold. Revenue is what pays for every activity of the company: production, finance, sales, distribution, and so on. What's left over (if anything) is **profit.** Managers usually strive to charge a price that will earn a fair profit.

© ISTOCKPHOTO.COM/MA-K

To earn a profit, managers must choose a price that is not too high or too low—a price that equals the perceived value to target consumers. If, in consumers' minds, a price is set too high, the perceived value will be less than the cost, and sale opportunities will be lost. Conversely, if a price is too low, the consumer may perceive it as a great value, but the firm loses revenue it could have earned.

Trying to set the right price is one of the most stressful and pressure-filled tasks of the marketing manager, as trends in the consumer market attest:

- Confronting a flood of new products, potential buyers carefully evaluate the price of each one against the value of existing products.
- The increased availability of bargain-priced private and generic brands has put downward pressure on overall prices.
- Many firms are trying to maintain or regain their market share by cutting prices.
- The Internet has made comparison shopping easier.
- The global economy, especially the United States, was in a recession from late 2007 until 2009.

In the business market, buyers are also becoming more price sensitive and better informed. Computerized information systems enable organizational buyers to compare price and performance with great ease and accuracy. Improved communication and the increased use of direct marketing and computer-aided selling have also opened up many markets to new competitors. Finally, competition in general is increasing, so some installations, accessories, and component parts are being marketed like indistinguishable commodities.

LO 2 Pricing Objectives

To survive in today's highly competitive marketplace, companies need pricing objectives that are specific, attainable, and measurable. Realistic pricing goals then require periodic monitoring to determine the effectiveness of the company's strategy. For convenience, pricing objectives can be divided into three categories: profit oriented, sales oriented, and status quo.

Profit-Oriented Pricing Objectives

Profit-oriented objectives include profit maximization, satisfactory profits, and target return on investment.

Profit Maximization *Profit maximization* means setting prices so that total revenue is as large as possible relative to total costs. Profit maximization does not always signify unreasonably high prices, however. Both price and profits depend on the type of competitive environment a firm faces, such as whether it is in a monopoly position (being the only seller) or in a much more competitive situation. Also, remember that a firm cannot charge a price higher than the product's perceived value. Many firms do not have the accounting data they need for maximizing profits.

Sometimes managers say that their company is trying to maximize profits—in other words, trying to make as much money as possible. Although this goal may sound impressive to stockholders, it is not good enough for planning.

In attempting to maximize profits, managers can try to expand revenue by increasing customer satisfaction, or they can attempt to reduce costs by operating more efficiently. A third possibility is to attempt to do both. Some companies may focus too much on cost reduction at the expense of the customer, or rely so heavily on customer satisfaction to increase revenue that costs creep up unnecessarily. However, a company can maintain or slightly cut costs while increasing customer loyalty through customer service initiatives, loyalty programs, and customer relationship management programs and allocating fewer resources to programs that are designed to improve efficiency and reduce costs. Both types of programs, of course, are critical to the success of the firm.

Satisfactory Profits Satisfactory profits are a reasonable level of profits. Rather than maximizing profits, many organizations strive for profits that are satisfactory to the stockholders and management—in other words, a level of profits consistent with the level of risk an organization faces. In a risky industry, a satisfactory profit may be 35 percent. In a low-risk industry, it might be 7 percent.

Target Return on Investment The most common profit objective is a target **return on investment (ROI)**, sometimes called the firm's return on total assets. ROI measures management's overall effectiveness in generating profits with the available assets. The higher the firm's ROI, the better off the firm is. Many companies use a target ROI as their main pricing goal. In summary, ROI is a percentage that puts a firm's profits into perspective by showing profits relative to investment.

© ISTOCKPHOTO.COM/ROB FRIEDMAN

return on investment (ROI) net profit after taxes divided by total assets

market share a company's product sales as a percentage of total sales for that industry

ROI is calculated as follows:

$$\text{ROI} = \frac{\text{Net profits after taxes}}{\text{Total assets}}$$

Assume that in 2008, Sun Microsystems had assets of ₹25 crore, net profits of ₹3 crore, and a target ROI of 10 percent. This was the actual ROI:

$$\text{ROI} = \frac{₹30000000}{₹250000000}$$
$$= 12 \text{ percent}$$

As you can see, the ROI for Sun Microsystems exceeded its target, which indicates that the company prospered in 2010.

Comparing the 12 percent ROI with the industry average provides a more meaningful picture, however. Any ROI needs to be evaluated in terms of the competitive environment, risks in the industry, and economic conditions. Generally speaking, firms seek ROIs in the 10- to 30-percent range. In some industries, such as the grocery industry, however, a return of under 5 percent is common and acceptable.

A company with a target ROI can predetermine its desired level of profitability. The marketing manager can use the standard, such as 10 percent ROI, to determine whether a particular price and marketing mix are feasible. In addition, however, the manager must weigh the risk of a given strategy even if the return is in the acceptable range.

Sales-Oriented Pricing Objectives

Sales-oriented pricing objectives are based either on market share or on dollar or unit sales.

Market Share **Market share** is a company's product sales as a percentage of total sales for that industry. Sales can be reported in rupees or in units of product. It is very important to know whether market share is expressed in revenue or units because the results may be different. Consider four companies competing in an industry with 2,000 total unit sales and total industry revenue of ₹4,000 (see Exhibit 19.1 on the next page). Company A has the largest unit market share at

EXHIBIT 19.1
Two ways to measure market share (units and revenue)

Company	Units sold	Unit price	Total revenue	Unit market share	Revenue market share
A	1000	₹1	₹1000	50	25
B	200	4	800	10	20
C	500	2	1000	25	25
D	300	4	1200	15	30
Total	2000		₹4000		

50 percent, but it has only 25 percent of the revenue market share. In contrast, company D has only a 15 percent unit share but the largest revenue share: 30 percent. Usually, market share is expressed in terms of revenue and not units.

Many companies believe that maintaining or increasing market share is an indicator of the effectiveness of their marketing mix. Larger market shares have indeed often meant higher profits, thanks to greater economies of scale, market power, and ability to compensate top-quality management. Conventional wisdom also says that market share and ROI are strongly related. For the most part they are; however, many companies with low market share survive and even prosper. To succeed with a low market share, companies need to compete in industries with slow growth and few product changes—for instance, industrial supplies. Otherwise, they must vie in an industry that makes frequently bought items, such as consumer convenience goods.

The conventional wisdom about market share and profitability isn't always reliable, however. Because of extreme competition in some industries, many market share leaders either do not reach their target ROI or actually lose money. Procter & Gamble switched from market share to ROI objectives after realizing that profits don't automatically follow from a large market share. Still, the struggle for market share can be all-consuming for some companies.

Nintendo's DS is the popular choice for handheld gaming, but Apple is vying for its share of the handheld market. The iPod Touch, iPhone, and iPad all have multi-touch screen function and a slew of inexpensive game applications that have earned Apple a 20 percent (and growing) share of the handheld game market. Nintendo hopes to regain some of those losses with the new 3D version of the DS that

ROUNDING UP PATENTS

© BRIAN HAGIWARA/BRAND X PICTURES/JUPITERIMAGES

Monsanto holds a patent on the gene that makes soybeans and corn immune to herbicides—specifically **Monsanto's Roundup.** That means farmers can plant Monsanto seed and then dust their fields with Roundup to kill weeds without damaging their crops. Because of the patent protection, Monsanto can charge farmers licensing fees to plant the seed. Since 1996, when Monsanto introduced the genetically modified and patented seed varieties, seed prices have nearly quadrupled. But farmers continue to pay the premium price because of the ease of chemically weeding their crops. Monsanto's patents expire in 2014, however. To prevent losing any of its 90-percent market share to generic versions of its seeds, Monsanto is encouraging farmers to switch to its newly patented second-generation seeds. With 90 percent of the market, Monsanto can control seed pricing, but recently the firm has come under antitrust investigation for its business practices, including pricing.[3]

doesn't require glasses to see the 3D effect. But 44 percent of the new apps being tested for the iPad are games, suggesting that Nintendo may have to fight for market share.[4]

Research organizations like the Nielsen Company and IMRB provide excellent market share reports for many different industries. These reports enable companies to track their performance in various product categories over time.

Sales Maximization Rather than strive for market share, sometimes companies try to maximize sales. A firm with the objective of maximizing sales ignores profits, competition, and the marketing environment as long as sales are rising.

If a company is strapped for funds or faces an uncertain future, it may try to generate a maximum amount of cash in the short run. Management's task when using this objective is to calculate which price–quantity relationship generates the greatest cash revenue. Sales maximization can also be effectively used on a temporary basis to sell off excess inventory.

Maximization of cash should never be a long-run objective because cash maximization may mean little or no profitability.

Status Quo Pricing Objectives

Status quo pricing seeks to maintain existing prices or to meet the competition's prices. This third category of pricing objectives has the major advantage of requiring little planning. It is essentially a passive policy.

Often firms competing in an industry with an established price leader simply meet the competition's prices. These industries typically have fewer price wars than those with direct price competition. In other cases, managers regularly shop competitors' stores to ensure that their prices are comparable.

LO 3 The Demand Determinant of Price

After marketing managers establish pricing goals, they must set specific prices to reach those goals. The price they set for each product depends mostly on two factors: the demand for the good or service and the cost to the seller for that good or service. When pricing goals are mainly sales oriented, demand considerations usually dominate. Other factors, such as distribution and promotion strategies, perceived quality, needs of large customers, the Internet, and the stage of the product life cycle, can also influence price.

status quo pricing a pricing objective that maintains existing prices or meets the competition's prices

demand the quantity of a product that will be sold in the market at various prices for a specified period

The Nature of Demand

Demand is the quantity of a product that will be sold in the market at various prices for a specified period. The quantity of a product that people will buy depends on its price. The higher the price, the fewer goods or services consumers will demand. Conversely, the lower the price, the more goods or services they will demand.

This trend is illustrated in the following graph of the demand per week for gourmet cookies at a local retailer at various prices. This graph is called a *demand curve* (Exhibit 19.2a). The vertical axis of the graph shows different prices of gourmet cookies, measured in rupees per package. The horizontal axis measures the quantity of gourmet cookies that will be demanded per week at each price. For example, at a price of ₹130, 40 packages will be sold per week; at ₹70, consumers will demand 100 packages—as the *demand schedule* (Exhibit 19.2b) shows.

Notice how the demand curve slopes downward and to the right, which indicates that more gourmet cookies are demanded as the price is lowered. In other words, if cookie manufacturers put a greater quantity on the market, then their hope of selling all

EXHIBIT 19.2

Demand curve and demand schedule for gourmet cookies

(a) Demand curve

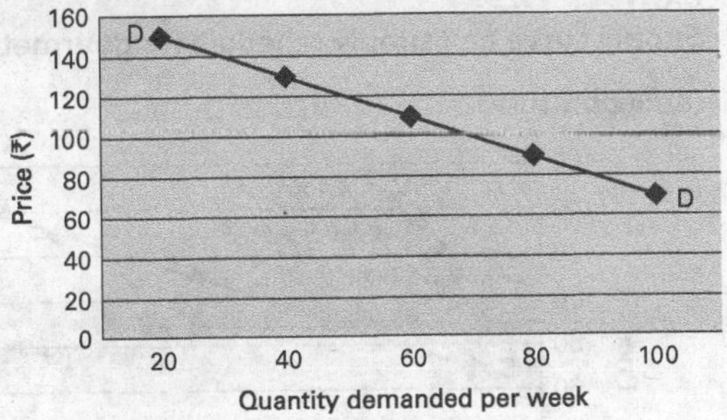

(b) Demand schedule

Price per package of gourmet cookies (₹)	Packages of gourmet cookies demanded per week
150	20
130	40
110	60
90	80
70	100

supply the quantity of a product that will be offered to the market by a supplier at various prices for a specified period

price equilibrium the price at which demand and supply are equal

of it will be realized only by selling it at a lower price.

One reason more is sold at lower prices than at higher prices is that lower prices bring in new buyers. With each reduction in price, existing customers may also buy extra.

Supply is the quantity of a product that will be offered to the market by a supplier or suppliers at various prices for a specified period. The graph below illustrates the resulting *supply curve* (Exhibit 19.3a) for gourmet cookies. Unlike the falling demand curve, the supply curve for gourmet cookies slopes upward and to the right. At higher prices, gourmet cookie manufacturers will obtain more resources (flour, eggs, chocolate) and produce more gourmet cookies. If the price consumers are willing to pay for gourmet cookies increases, producers can afford to buy more ingredients.

Output tends to increase at higher prices because manufacturers can sell more cookies and earn greater profits. The *supply schedule* in Exhibit 19.3b shows that at ₹90, suppliers are willing to place 40 packages of gourmet cookies on the market, but they will offer 100 packages at a price of ₹150.

How Demand and Supply Establish Prices At this point, combine the concepts of demand and supply to see how competitive market prices are determined. So far, the premise is that if the price is X, then consumers will purchase Y amount of gourmet cookies. The demand curve cannot predict consumption, nor can the supply curve alone forecast production. Instead, we need to look at what happens when supply and demand interact—as shown in Exhibit 19.4.

At a price of ₹150, the public would demand only 20 packages of gourmet cookies. However, suppliers stand ready to place 100 packages on the market at this price (data from the demand and supply schedules). If they do, they would create a surplus of 80 packages of gourmet cookies. How does a merchant eliminate a surplus? She lowers the price.

At a price of ₹70, 100 packages would be demanded, but only 20 would be placed on the market. A shortage of 95 units would be created. If a product is in short supply and consumers want it, how do they entice the dealer to part with one unit? They offer more money—that is, pay a higher price.

Now let's examine a price of ₹110. At this price, 60 packages are demanded and 60 are supplied. When demand and supply are equal, a state called **price equilibrium** is achieved. A temporary price below equilibrium—say, ₹70—results in a shortage because at that price the demand for gourmet cookies is greater than the available supply. Shortages put upward pressure on price. As long as demand and supply remain the same, however, temporary price increases or decreases tend to return to equilibrium. At equilibrium, there is no inclination for prices to rise or fall.

Prices may fluctuate during a trial-and-error period as the market for a good or service moves toward equilibrium. Sooner or later, however, demand and supply will settle into proper balance.

EXHIBIT 19.3

Supply curve and supply schedule for gourmet cookies

(a) Supply curve

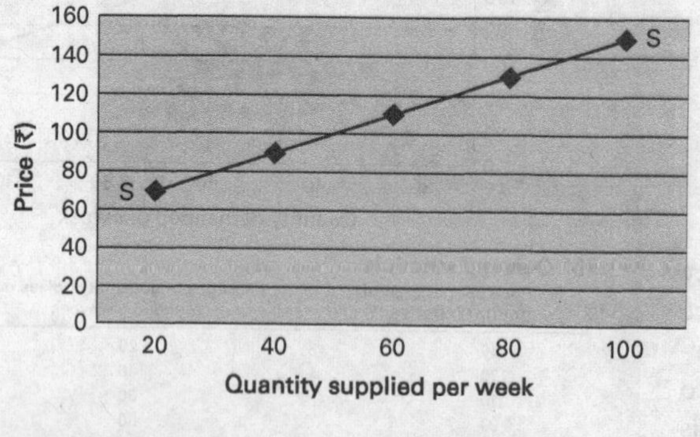

(b) Supply schedule

Price per package of gourmet cookies (₹)	Packages of gourmet cookies supplied per week
150	100
130	80
110	60
90	40
70	20

EXHIBIT 19.4
Equilibrium Price for Gourmet Cookies

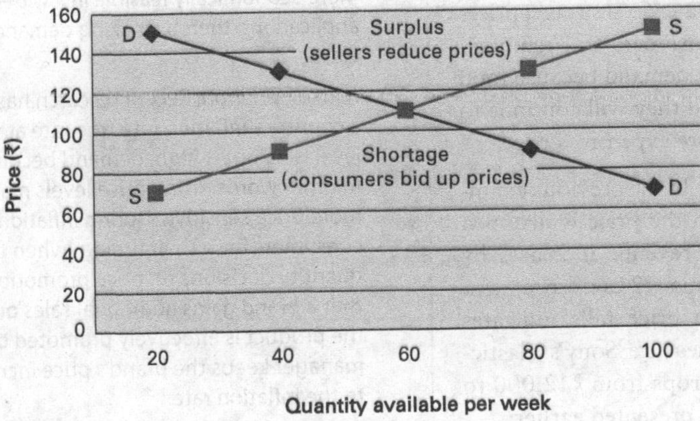

© CENGAGE LEARNING 2011

Elasticity of Demand

To appreciate demand analysis, you should understand the concept of elasticity. **Elasticity of demand** refers to consumers' responsiveness or sensitivity to changes in price. **Elastic demand** occurs when consumers buy more or less of a product when the price changes. Conversely, **inelastic demand** means that an increase or a decrease in price will not significantly affect demand for the product.

Elasticity over the range of a demand curve can be measured by using this formula:

$$\text{Elasticity } (E) = \frac{\text{Percentage change in quantity demanded of good A}}{\text{Percentage change in price of good A}}$$

If E is greater than 1, demand is elastic.

If E is less than 1, demand is inelastic.

If E is equal to 1, demand is unitary.

Unitary elasticity means that an increase in sales exactly offsets a decrease in prices, so total revenue remains the same.

Elasticity can be measured by observing these changes in total revenue:

- If price goes down and revenue goes up, demand is elastic.
- If price goes down and revenue goes down, demand is inelastic.
- If price goes up and revenue goes up, demand is inelastic.
- If price goes up and revenue goes down, demand is elastic.
- If price goes up or down and revenue stays the same, elasticity is unitary.

The demand curve for Sony DVD players is very elastic. Decreasing the price of one of these players from ₹12000 to ₹9000 increases sales from 18,000 units to 59,000 units. Revenue increases from ₹21.6 crore (₹12000 × 18,000) to ₹53.1 crore (₹9000 × 59,000). The price decrease results in a large increase in sales and revenue.

Inelastic Demand When price and total revenue fall, demand is inelastic. When demand is inelastic, sellers can raise prices and increase total revenue. Often, items that are relatively inexpensive but convenient tend to have inelastic demand. Crops such as wheat, soybeans, and corn have inelastic demand. When there is a particularly productive year (as 2010 was in the United States), excess or bumper crops cause the prices of these crops to fall.

elasticity of demand consumers' responsiveness or sensitivity to changes in price

elastic demand a situation in which consumer demand is sensitive to changes in price

inelastic demand a situation in which an increase or a decrease in price will not significantly affect demand for the product

unitary elasticity a situation in which total revenue remains the same when prices change

yield management systems (YMS) a technique for adjusting prices that uses complex mathematical software to profitably fill unused capacity by discounting early purchases, limiting early sales at these discounted prices, and overbooking capacity

But unless there is a drastic change in consumption rates, consumers won't readily buy greater amounts of grain, so revenue decreases with the price of the crops. If there is a crop shortage, prices escalate, but consumers still maintain the same level of demand because food is a necessity, and they will continue to purchase the more expensive crop.[6]

Elastic Demand In the previous example of Sony DVD players, when the price is dropped from ₹12,000 to ₹9,000, total revenue increases by ₹31.5 crore (₹53.1 crore minus ₹21.6 crore). An increase in total revenue when price falls indicates that demand is elastic. Let's measure Sony's elasticity of demand when the price drops from ₹12,000 to ₹9,000 by applying the formula presented earlier:

$$E = \frac{\text{Change in quantity/(Sum of quantities/2)}}{\text{Change in price/(Sum of prices/2)}}$$

$$E = \frac{(59{,}000 - 18{,}000)/[(59{,}000 + 18{,}000)/2]}{(₹12{,}000 - ₹9{,}000)/[(₹12{,}000 + ₹9{,}000)/2]}$$

$$E = \frac{41{,}000/38{,}500}{₹3{,}000/₹10{,}500}$$

$$E = \frac{1.065}{.3}$$

$$E = 3.55$$

Because E is greater than 1, demand is elastic.

Factors that Affect Elasticity Several factors affect elasticity of demand, including the following:

- *Availability of substitutes:* When many substitute products are available, the consumer can easily switch from one product to another, making demand elastic. The same is true in reverse: A person with complete renal failure will pay whatever is charged for a kidney transplant because there is no substitute.
- *Price relative to purchasing power:* If a price is so low that it is an inconsequential part of an individual's budget, demand will be inelastic.
- *Product durability:* Consumers often have the option of repairing durable products rather than replacing them, thus prolonging their useful life. In other words, people are sensitive to the price increase, and demand is elastic.
- *A product's other uses:* The greater the number of different uses for a product, the more elastic demand tends to be. If a product has only one use, as may be true of a new medicine, the quantity purchased probably will not vary as price varies. A person will consume only the prescribed quantity, regardless of price. On the other hand, a product like steel has many possible applications. As its price falls, steel becomes more economically feasible in a wider variety of applications, thereby making demand relatively elastic.
- *Rate of inflation:* Recent research has found that when a country's inflation rate (the rate at which the price level is rising) is high, demand becomes more elastic. In other words, rising price levels make consumers more price sensitive. During inflationary periods, consumers base their timing (when to buy) and quantity decisions on price promotions. This suggests that a brand gains additional sales or market share if the product is effectively promoted or if the marketing manager keeps the brand's price increases low relative to the inflation rate.[7]

LO 4 The Power of Yield Management Systems

When competitive pressures are high, a company must know when it can raise prices to maximize its revenues. More and more companies are turning to yield management systems to help adjust prices. First developed in the airline industry, **yield management systems (YMS)** use complex mathematical software to profitably fill unused capacity. The software employs techniques such as discounting early purchases, limiting early sales at these discounted prices, and overbooking capacity. YMS now are appearing in other services as well.

YMS are spreading beyond service industries as their popularity increases. The lessons of airlines and hotels aren't entirely applicable to other industries, however, because plane seats and hotel beds are perishable—if they go empty, the revenue opportunity is lost forever. So it makes sense to slash prices to move toward capacity if it's possible to do so without reducing the prices that other customers pay. Cars and steel aren't so perishable, but the capacity to make them is. An underused factory is a lost revenue opportunity. So it makes sense to cut prices to use up capacity if it's possible to do so while getting other customers to pay full price.

LO 5 The Cost Determinant of Price

Sometimes companies minimize or ignore the importance of demand and decide to price their products largely or solely on the basis of costs. Prices determined strictly on the basis of costs may be too high for the target market, thereby reducing or eliminating sales. On the other hand, cost-based prices may be too low, causing the firm to earn a lower return than it should. Nevertheless, costs should generally be part of any price determination, if only as a floor below which a good or service must not be priced in the long run.

The idea of cost may seem simple, but it is actually a multifaceted concept, especially for producers of goods and services. A **variable cost** is a cost that varies with changes in the level of output; an example of a variable cost is the cost of materials. In contrast, a **fixed cost** does not change as output is increased or decreased. Examples include rent and executives' salaries.

To compare the cost of production to the selling price of a product, it is helpful to calculate costs per unit, or average costs. **Average variable cost (AVC)** equals total variable costs divided by quantity of output. **Average total cost (ATC)** equals total costs divided by output. As the graph in Exhibit 19.5(a) on the next page shows, AVC and ATC are basically U-shaped curves. In contrast, average fixed cost (AFC) declines continually as output increases because total fixed costs are constant.

Marginal cost (MC) is the change in total costs associated with a one-unit change in output. Exhibit 19.5(b) shows that when output rises from seven to eight units, the change in total cost is from ₹640 to ₹750; therefore, MC is ₹110.

All the curves illustrated in Exhibit 19.5(a) have definite relationships:

- AVC plus AFC equals ATC.
- MC falls for a while and then turns upward, in this case with the fourth unit. At that point, diminishing returns set in, meaning that less output is produced for every additional rupee spent on variable input.
- MC intersects both AVC and ATC at their lowest possible points.
- When MC is less than AVC or ATC, the incremental cost will continue to pull the averages down. Conversely, when MC is greater than AVC or ATC, it pulls the averages up, and ATC and AVC begin to rise.
- The minimum point on the ATC curve is the least cost point for a fixed-capacity firm, although it is not necessarily the most profitable point.

Costs can be used to set prices in a variety of ways. Markup pricing is relatively simple. Profit maximization pricing and break-even pricing make use of the more complicated concepts of cost.

variable cost a cost that varies with changes in the level of output

fixed cost a cost that does not change as output is increased or decreased

average variable cost (AVC) total variable costs divided by quantity of output

average total cost (ATC) total costs divided by quantity of output

marginal cost (MC) the change in total costs associated with a one-unit change in output

PIZZA INDUSTRY CUTS PRICES TO INCREASE SALES

The pizza industry, in order to drive volumes and to reach out to a wider customer segment, has reduced the prices drastically to entice Indian consumers. With the price of a large pizza at Pizza Hut close to ₹600, the company has launched 4–5 inches pizzas at a price of just ₹29 each to offer greater value to the consumers. Domino's Pizza, the category leader, has also launched a range of pizzas under the name *pizza mania* at a price of ₹39 each. Pizza Corner, an Indian chain, too launched a pilot range of "my pizza" at Bengaluru at a price of ₹38 each for a 7-inch pizza.[8]

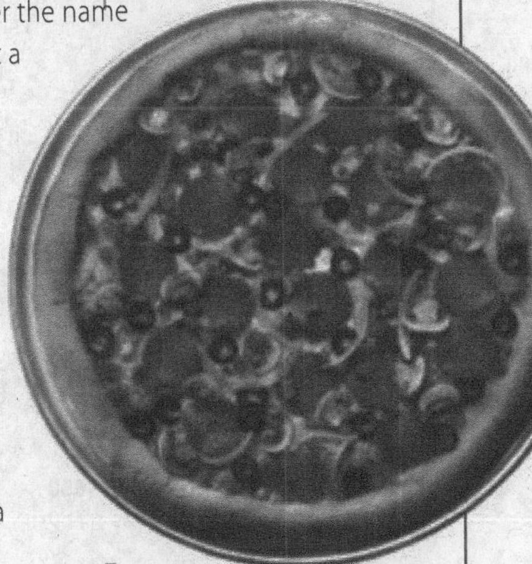

markup pricing the cost of buying the product from the producer, plus amounts for profit and for expenses not otherwise accounted for

Markup Pricing

Markup pricing, the most popular method used by wholesalers and retailers to establish a selling price, does not directly analyze the costs of production. Instead, **markup pricing** uses the cost of buying the product from the producer, plus amounts for profit and for expenses not otherwise accounted for. The total determines the selling price.

A retailer, for example, adds a certain percentage to the cost of the merchandise received to arrive at the retail price. An item that costs the retailer ₹80 and is sold for ₹100 carries a markup of ₹20, which is a markup of 25 percent of the cost (₹20/₹80). Retailers tend to discuss markup in terms of its percentage of the retail price—in this example, 20 percent (₹20/₹100). The difference between the retailer's cost and the selling price (₹20) is the gross margin.

EXHIBIT 19.5

Hypothetical Set of Cost Curves and a Cost Schedule

(a) Cost curves

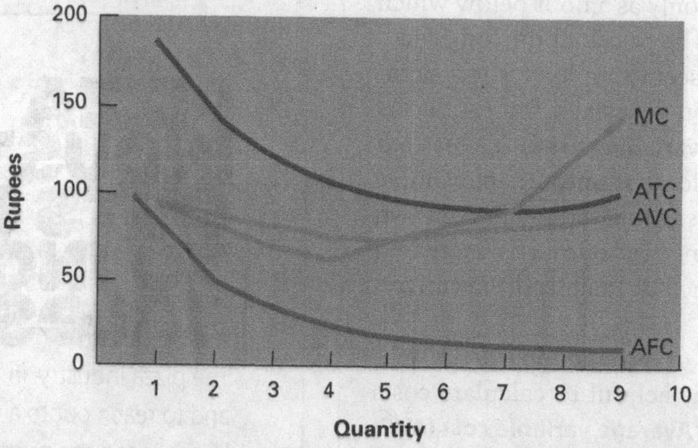

(b) Cost schedule

Total-cost data, per week				Average-cost data, per week			
(1) Total product (Q)	(2) Total fixed cost (TFC)	(3) Total variable cost (TVC)	(4) Total cost (TC)	(5) Average fixed cost (AFC)	(6) Average variable cost (AVC)	(7) Average total cost (ATC)	(8) Marginal cost (MC)
			$TC = TFC + TVC$	$AFC = \frac{TFC}{Q}$	$AVC = \frac{TVC}{Q}$	$ATC = \frac{TC}{Q}$	$(MC) = \frac{\text{change in TC}}{\text{change in Q}}$
0	₹100	₹ 0	₹ 100	—	—	—	—
1	100	90	190	₹100.00	₹90.00	₹190.00	₹ 90
2	100	170	270	50.00	85.00	135.00	80
3	100	240	340	33.33	80.00	113.33	70
4	100	300	400	25.00	75.00	100.00	60
5	100	370	470	20.00	74.00	94.00	70
6	100	450	550	16.67	75.00	91.67	80
7	100	540	640	14.29	77.14	91.43	90
8	100	650	750	12.50	81.25	93.75	110
9	100	780	880	11.11	86.67	97.78	130
10	100	930	1,030	10.00	93.00	103.00	150

The formula for calculating the retail price given a certain desired markup is as follows:

$$\text{Retail price} = \frac{\text{Cost}}{1 - \text{Desired return on sales}}$$

$$= \frac{₹80}{1.0 - 0.20}$$

$$= ₹100$$

If the retailer wants a 30 percent return, then:

$$\text{Retail price} = \frac{₹80}{1.0 - .30}$$

$$= ₹114$$

The reason that retailers and others speak of markups on selling price is that many important figures in financial reports, such as gross sales and revenues, are sales figures, not cost figures.

To use markup based on cost or selling price effectively, the marketing manager must calculate an adequate gross margin—the amount added to cost to determine price. The margin must ultimately provide adequate funds to cover selling expenses and profit. Once an appropriate margin has been determined, the markup technique has the major advantage of being easy to employ.

Markups are often based on experience. For example, many small retailers mark up merchandise 100 percent over cost. (In other words, they double the cost.) This tactic is called **keystoning**. Some other factors that influence markups are the merchandise's appeal to customers, past response to the markup (an implicit demand consideration), the item's promotional value, the seasonality of the goods, their fashion appeal, the product's traditional selling price, and competition. Most retailers avoid any set markup because of such considerations as promotional value and seasonality.

Profit Maximization Pricing

Producers tend to use more complicated methods of setting prices than distributors use. One is **profit maximization**, which occurs when marginal revenue equals MC. You learned earlier that MC is the change in total costs associated with a one-unit change in output. Similarly, **marginal revenue (MR)** is the extra revenue associated with selling an extra unit of output. As long as the revenue of the last unit produced and sold is greater than the cost of the last unit produced and sold, the firm should continue manufacturing and selling the product.

Exhibit 19.6 shows the MRs and MCs for a hypothetical firm, using the cost data from Exhibit 19.5(b). The profit-maximizing quantity, where MR = MC, is six units. You might say, "If profit is zero, why produce the sixth unit? Why not stop at five?" In fact, you would be right. The firm, however, would not know that the fifth unit would produce zero profits until it determined that profits were no longer increasing. Economists suggest producing up to the point where MR = MC. If MR is just one penny greater than MC, it will still increase total profits.

keystoning the practice of marking up prices by 100 percent, or doubling the cost

profit maximization a method of setting prices that occurs when marginal revenue equals marginal cost

marginal revenue (MR) the extra revenue associated with selling an extra unit of output or the change in total revenue with a one-unit change in output

break-even analysis a method of determining what sales volume must be reached before total revenue equals total costs

Break-Even Pricing

Now let's take a closer look at the relationship between sales and cost. **Break-even analysis** determines what sales volume must be reached before the company breaks even (its total costs equal total revenue) and no profits are earned.

The typical break-even model assumes a given fixed cost and a constant AVC. Suppose that Universal Confectionery, a hypothetical firm, has fixed costs of ₹2,000 and that the cost of labor and materials for each unit produced is 50 paise. Assume that it can sell up to 6,000 units of its product at ₹1 without having to lower its price.

Exhibit 19.7(a) illustrates Universal

EXHIBIT 19.6

Point of Profit Maximization

Quantity	Marginal Revenue	Marginal Cost	Cumulative Total Profit
0	—	—	—
1	₹140	₹ 90	₹ 50
2	130	80	100
3	105	70	135
4	95	60	170
5	85	70	185
*6	80	80	185
7	75	90	170
8	60	110	120
9	50	130	40
10	40	150	(70)

*Profit maximization.

Confectionery's break-even point. As Exhibit 19.7(b) indicates, Universal Confectionery's total variable costs increase by 50 paisa every time a new unit is produced, and total fixed costs remain constant at ₹2,000 regardless of the level of output. Therefore, for 4,000 units of output, Universal Confectionery has ₹2,000 in fixed costs and ₹2,000 in total variable costs (4,000 units × 0.50 paise), or ₹4,000 in total costs.

Revenue is also ₹4,000 (4,000 units × ₹1), giving a net profit of zero rupees at the break-even point of 4,000 units. Notice that once the firm gets past the break-even point, the gap between total revenue and total costs gets wider and wider because both functions are assumed to be linear.

The formula for calculating break-even quantities is simple:

$$\text{Break-even quantity} = \frac{\text{Total fixed costs}}{\text{Fixed cost contribution}}$$

Fixed cost contribution is the price minus the AVC. Therefore, for Universal Confectionery,

$$\text{Break-even quantity} = \frac{₹2{,}000}{(₹1.00 - ₹0.50 \text{ paise})}$$

$$= \frac{₹2{,}000}{0.50 \text{ paise}}$$

$$= 4{,}000 \text{ units}$$

The advantage of break-even analysis is that it provides a quick estimate of how much the firm must

EXHIBIT 19.7

Costs, Revenues, and Break-Even Point for Universal Confectionery

(a) Break-even point

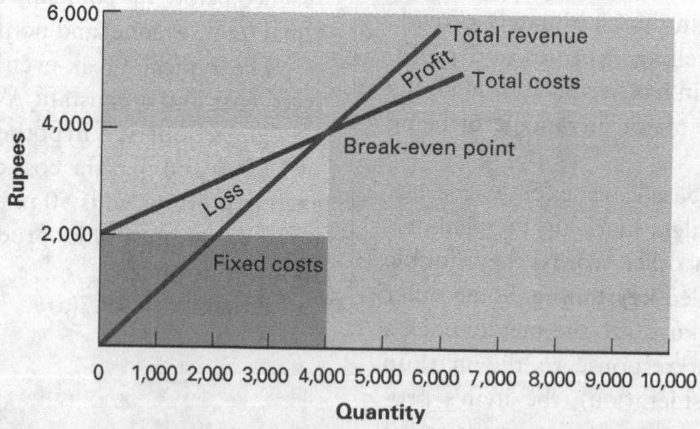

(b) Costs and revenues

Output	Total fixed costs	Average variable costs	Total variable costs	Average total costs	Average revenue (price)	Total revenue	Total costs	Profit or loss
500	₹2,000	₹0.50	₹ 250	₹4.50	₹1.00	₹ 500	₹2,250	(₹1,750)
1,000	2,000	0.50	500	2.50	1.00	1,000	2,500	(1,500)
1,500	2,000	0.50	750	1.83	1.00	1,500	2,750	(1,250)
2,000	2,000	0.50	1,000	1.50	1.00	2,000	3,000	(1,000)
2,500	2,000	0.50	1,250	1.30	1.00	2,500	3,250	(750)
3,000	2,000	0.50	1,500	1.17	1.00	3,000	3,500	(500)
3,500	2,000	0.50	1,750	1.07	1.00	3,500	3,750	(250)
*4,000	2,000	0.50	2,000	1.00	1.00	4,000	4,000	0
4,500	2,000	0.50	2,250	0.94	1.00	4,500	4,250	250
5,000	2,000	0.50	2,500	0.90	1.00	5,000	4,500	500
5,500	2,000	0.50	2,750	0.86	1.00	5,500	4,750	750
6,000	2,000	0.50	3,000	0.83	1.00	6,000	5,000	1,000

*Break-even point

sell to break even and how much profit can be earned if a higher sales volume is obtained. If a firm is operating close to the break-even point, it may want to see what can be done to reduce costs or increase sales. Moreover, in a simple break-even analysis, it is not necessary to compute MCs and MRs because price and average cost per unit are assumed to be constant. Also, because accounting data for marginal cost and revenue are frequently unavailable, it is convenient not to have to depend on that information.

Break-even analysis is not without several important limitations. Sometimes it is hard to know whether a cost is fixed or variable. If labor wins a tough guaranteed-employment contract, are the resulting expenses a fixed cost? More important than cost determination is the fact that simple break-even analysis ignores demand. How does Universal Confectionery know it can sell 4,000 units at ₹1? Could it sell the same 4,000 units at ₹2 or even ₹5? Obviously, this information would profoundly affect the firm's pricing decisions.

LO 6 Other Determinants of Price

Other factors besides demand and costs can influence price. For example, the stages in the product life cycle, the competition, the product distribution strategy, the promotion strategy, and the perceived quality can all affect pricing.

Stages in the Product Life Cycle

As a product moves through its life cycle (see Chapter 11), the demand for the product and the competitive conditions tend to change:

- *Introductory stage:* Management usually sets prices high during the introductory stage. One reason is that it hopes to recover its development costs quickly. In addition, demand originates in the core of the market (the customers whose needs ideally match the product's attributes) and thus is relatively inelastic. On the other hand, if the target market is highly price sensitive, management often finds it better to price the product at the market level or lower.
- *Growth stage:* As the product enters the growth stage, prices generally begin to stabilize for several reasons. First, competitors have entered the market, increasing the available supply. Second, the product has begun to appeal to a broader market, often lower-income groups. Finally, economies of scale are lowering costs, and the savings can be passed on to the consumer in the form of lower prices.
- *Maturity stage:* Maturity usually brings further price decreases as competition increases and inefficient, high-cost firms are eliminated. Distribution channels become a significant cost factor, however, because of the need to offer wide product lines for highly segmented markets, extensive service requirements, and the sheer number of dealers necessary to absorb high-volume production. The manufacturers that remain in the market toward the end of the maturity stage typically offer similar prices. At this stage, price increases are usually cost initiated, not demand initiated. Nor do price reductions in the late phase of maturity stimulate much demand. Because demand is limited and producers have similar cost structures, the remaining competitors will probably match price reductions.
- *Decline stage:* The final stage of the life cycle may see further price decreases as the few remaining competitors try to salvage the last vestiges of demand. When only one firm is left in the market, prices begin to stabilize. In fact, prices may eventually rise dramatically if the product survives and moves into the specialty goods category, as horse-drawn carriages and vinyl records have.

The Competition

Competition varies during the product life cycle, of course, and so at times it may strongly affect pricing decisions. Although a firm may not have any competi-

selling against the brand stocking well-known branded items at high prices in order to sell store brands at discounted prices

extranet a private electronic network that links a company with its suppliers and customers

tion at first, the high prices it charges may eventually induce another firm to enter the market.

Often, in hotly competitive markets, price wars break out. P&G launched a low priced variant of its Tide detergent, called Tide Naturals, in December 2009. The new variant was priced at ₹10 for 200 grams pack, ₹20 for 400 grams pack, and ₹50 for 1 kilogram pack. The prices of Tide Naturals were 30 percent cheaper than Tide and the detergent was aimed towards the mass-end of the market. The brand succeeded in garnering a market share of .6 percent within two months of its launch. HUL responded to P&G's strategy by slashing the prices of its Rin and Surf detergents by 10–30 percent. The price of 1 kilogram pack of Rin was reduced from ₹70 to ₹50 and that of 500 gram was brought down to ₹25 from ₹35. Similarly, the price of Surf Excel Blue was reduced by ₹2 and ₹7 for the 200 gram pack and 500 gram pack, respectively. P&G retaliated by increasing the volume of its Tide Naturals detergent by 25 percent, effectively offering the benefit of low prices to the consumers.[9]

Distribution Strategy

An effective distribution network can often overcome other minor flaws in the marketing mix.[10] For example, although consumers may perceive a price as being slightly higher than normal, they may buy the product anyway if it is being sold at a convenient retail outlet.

Adequate distribution for a new product can often be attained by offering a larger-than-usual profit margin to distributors. A variation on this strategy is to give dealers a large trade allowance to help offset the costs of promotion and further stimulate demand at the retail level.

Manufacturers have gradually been losing control within the distribution channel to wholesalers and retailers, which often adopt pricing strategies that serve their own purposes. For instance, some distributors are **selling against the brand:** They place well-known brands on the shelves at high prices while offering other brands—typically, their private-label brands, such as Food Bazaar's Tasty Treat instant noodles and Clean Mate floor cleaner—at lower prices. Of course, sales of the higher-priced brands decline.

Wholesalers and retailers may also go outside traditional distribution channels to buy gray-market goods. As explained previously, distributors obtain the goods through unauthorized channels for less than they would normally pay, so they can sell the goods with a bigger-than-normal markup or at a reduced price. Imports seem to be particularly susceptible to gray marketing. Although consumers may pay less for gray-market goods, they often find that the manufacturer won't honor the warranty.

Manufacturers can regain some control over price by using an exclusive distribution system, by franchising, or by avoiding doing business with price-cutting discounters. Manufacturers can also package merchandise with the selling price marked on it or place goods on consignment. The best way for manufacturers to control prices, however, is to develop brand loyalty in consumers by delivering quality and value.

The Impact of the Internet and Extranets

The Internet, **extranets** (private electronic networks), and wireless setups are linking people, machines, and companies around the globe—and connecting sellers and buyers as never before. These links are enabling buyers to quickly and easily compare products and prices, putting them in a better bargaining position. At the same time, the technology allows sellers to collect detailed data about customers' buying habits, prefer-

A signage displaying the Clean Mate product range at a Big Bazaar outlet

ences, and even spending limits so that sellers can tailor their products and prices.

Internet Auctions The Internet auction business is huge. Among the most popular consumer auction sites are the following:

- *www.ebay.com:* The most popular auction site
- *www.bidz.com:* Buys closeout deals in very large lots and offers them online in its no-reserve auctions

Even though consumers are spending billions on Internet auctions, business-to-business auctions are likely to be the dominant form in the future. Recently, Whirlpool began holding online auctions in the United States. Participants bid on the price of the items that they would supply to Whirlpool but with a twist: They had to include the date when Whirlpool would have to pay for the items. The company wanted to see which suppliers would offer the longest grace period before requiring payment. Five auctions held over five months helped Whirlpool uncover savings of close to ₹9 crore and more than doubled the grace period.

Whirlpool's success is a sign that the business-to-business auction world is shifting from haggling over prices to niggling over parameters of the deal. Warranties, delivery dates, transportation methods, customer support, financing options, and quality have all become bargaining chips.

Promotion Strategy

Price is often used as a promotional tool to increase consumer interest. The different types of price promotions used by marketers are price-off, coupons, refunds and rebates.[12] Indian customers are price sensitive by nature and hence, sales are driven by prices, with price promotions working its magic on the customers.[13] In a survey conducted by Nielsen Company, it was found that 91 percent are influenced by good value for money when it comes to selecting a grocery shop. 79 percent of the respondents associated a store with good value for money if it offered price discounts, regular promotions, and sold products at prices cheaper than that of competitors.[14] HLL (now HUL) ran a promotional campaign called *Ustaad's Challenge* for its Taj Mahal tea, wherein it invited customers to try the best tea in India—Taj Mahal tea—and if they were not satisfied with its taste, they could return the product and get their money back.[15] The weekly flyers sent out by grocery stores in the Sunday newspaper, for instance, advertise many products with special low prices.

Pricing can be a tool for trade promotions as well.

The Relationship of Price to Quality

As mentioned at the beginning of the chapter, when a purchase decision involves great uncertainty, consum-

PIZZA HUT'S PROMOTION PRICING

In an effort to reach to the youth of India, Pizza Hut launched the "Weekday Special" offer, giving the teenagers a chance to have a three-course meal at just ₹99 per person. The teenagers can choose from a mix of appetizers, beverages, and main course of pizzas and pastas to create their own three course meal. Through this promotion, it is trying to position itself as an "affordable" dining restaurant to the youngsters, who are always short of money and keep searching for economic deals.[16]

prestige pricing
charging a high price to help promote a high-quality image

ers tend to rely on a high price as a predictor of good quality. Reliance on price as an indicator of quality seems to occur for all products, but it reveals itself more strongly for some items than for others, particularly items geared toward the wealthy.[17] Among the products that benefit from this phenomenon are coffee, aspirin, salt, shampoo, clothing, furniture, perfumes, and many services. In the absence of other information, people typically assume that prices are higher because the products contain better materials, because they are made more carefully, or, in the case of professional services, because the provider has more expertise.

© AP IMAGES//DAMIAN DOVARGANE

Research has found that products that are perceived to be of high quality tend to benefit more from price promotions than products perceived to be of lower quality.[18] However, when perceived high- and lower-quality products are offered in settings where consumers have difficulty making comparisons, then price promotions have an equal effect on sales. Comparisons are more difficult in end-of-aisle displays, feature advertising, and the like.

Knowledgeable merchants take these consumer attitudes into account when devising their pricing strategies. **Prestige pricing** is charging a high price to help promote a high-quality image. A successful prestige pricing strategy requires a retail price that is reasonably consistent with consumers' expectations. No one goes shopping at a Gucci's store expecting to pay ₹1000 for a handbag. In fact, demand would fall drastically at such a low price. In fact, demand would fall drastically at such a low price. In addition to prestige pricing, research has found two other basic effects associated with the price quality relationship: *hedonistic* and *allocative effects*.[19] High purchase prices may create feelings of pleasure and excitement associated with consuming higher-priced products. This is the hedonistic effect. Hedonistic consumption refers to pursuing emotional responses associated with using a product, such as pleasure, excitement, arousal, good feelings, and fun.

The allocative effect refers to the notion that consumers must allocate their budgets across alternative goods and services. The more you spend on one product, the less you have to spend on all others. Consumers sensitive to the allocative effects likely prefer low prices. However, managers must be aware that setting low prices or lowering prices with a discount may lower perceptions of product quality, prestige value, and hedonistic value. This is because of the negative cues associated with lower selling prices.[20]

Some companies, wary of the consequences to their brand's images, are overly hesitant to lower prices. Some of the leading car manufacturers refused to enter into a price war when Maruti Udyog Limited announced to cut prices of some of its popular models. While Maruti slashed the prices of models like Maruti-800, Omni, and Wagon-R up to ₹25,000, others such as Tata Engineering, Hyundai Motor India, Fiat India, and Daewoo Motors India ruled out any revision of prices as such a move would hurt their brand image as well as consumers' interest.[21]

Some of the latest research on price–quality relationships has focused on consumer durable goods. The researchers first conducted a study to ascertain the dimensions of quality. These are (1) ease of use, (2) versatility (the ability of a product to perform more functions, or be more flexible), (3) durability, (4) serviceability (ease of obtaining quality repairs), (5) performance, and (6) prestige. The researchers found that when consumers focused on prestige and/or durability to assess quality, price was a strong indicator of perceived overall quality. Price was less important as an indicator of quality if the consumer was focusing on one of the other four dimensions of quality.[22]

Review And Applications

Discuss the importance of pricing decisions to the economy and to the individual firm. Pricing plays an integral role in the Indian economy by allocating goods and services among consumers, governments, and businesses. Pricing is essential in business because it creates revenue, which is the basis of all business activity. In setting prices, marketing managers strive to find a level high enough to produce a satisfactory profit.

1.1 Why is pricing so important to the marketing manager?

1.2 How does price allocate goods and services?

List and explain a variety of pricing objectives. Establishing realistic and measurable pricing objectives is a critical part of any firm's marketing strategy. Pricing objectives are commonly classified into three categories: profit oriented, sales oriented, and status quo. Profit-oriented pricing is based on profit maximization, a satisfactory level of profit, or a target return on investment. The goal of profit maximization is to generate as much revenue as possible in relation to cost. Often, a more practical approach than profit maximization is setting prices to produce profits that will satisfy management and stockholders. The most common profit-oriented strategy is pricing for a specific return on investment relative to a firm's assets. The second type of pricing objective is sales oriented, and it focuses on either maintaining a percentage share of the market or maximizing dollar or unit sales. The third type of pricing objective aims to maintain the status quo by matching competitors' prices.

2.1 Give an example of each major type of pricing objective.

2.2 Why do many firms not maximize profits?

Explain the role of demand in price determination. Demand is a key determinant of price. When establishing prices, a firm must first determine demand for its product. A typical demand schedule shows an inverse relationship between quantity demanded and price: When price is lowered, sales increase; and when price is increased, the quantity demanded falls. For prestige products, however, there may be a direct relationship between demand and price: The quantity demanded will increase as price increases.

Marketing managers must also consider demand elasticity when setting prices. Elasticity of demand is the degree to which the quantity demanded fluctuates with changes in price. If consumers are sensitive to changes in price, demand is elastic; if they are insensitive to price changes, demand is inelastic. Thus, an increase in price will result in lower sales for an elastic product and little or no loss in sales for an inelastic product. Inelastic demand creates pricing power.

3.1 Explain the role of supply and demand in determining price.

3.2 If a firm can increase its total revenue by raising its price, shouldn't it do so?

3.3 Explain the concepts of elastic and inelastic demand. Why should managers understand these concepts?

Understand the concept of yield management systems. Yield management systems use complex mathematical software to profitably fill unused capacity. The software uses techniques such as discounting early purchases, limiting early sales at these discounted prices, and overbooking capacity. These systems are used in service and retail businesses and are substantially raising revenues. The use of Internet cookies and targeting software enables online retailers to offer different pricing and promotional offers to online buyers based upon their online shopping and browsing habits.

4.1 Why are so many companies adopting yield management systems?

4.2 Explain the relationship between supply and demand and yield management systems.

4.3 Why is targeting technology so effective?

Describe cost-oriented pricing strategies. The other major determinant of price is cost. Marketers use several cost-oriented pricing strategies. To cover their own expenses and obtain a profit, wholesalers and retailers commonly use markup pricing: They tack an extra amount onto the manufacturer's original price. Another pricing technique is to maximize profits by setting price where marginal revenue equals marginal cost. Still another pricing strategy determines how much a firm must sell to break even and uses this amount as a reference point for adjusting price.

5.1 Your firm has based its pricing strictly on cost in the past. As the newly hired marketing manager, you believe this policy should change. Write the president a memo explaining your reasons.

5.2 Why is it important for managers to understand the concept of break-even points? Are there any drawbacks?

Demonstrate how the product life cycle, competition, distribution and promotion strategies, guaranteed price matching, customer demands, the Internet, and perceptions of quality can affect price. The price of a product normally changes as it moves through the life cycle and as demand for the product and competitive conditions change. Management often sets a high price at the introductory stage, and the high price tends to attract competition. The competition usually drives prices down because individual competitors lower prices to gain market share.

Adequate distribution for a new product can sometimes be obtained by offering a larger-than-usual profit margin to wholesalers and retailers. The Internet enables consumers to compare products and prices quickly and efficiently. Price is also used as a promotional tool to attract customers. Special low prices often attract new customers and entice existing customers to buy more. Price matching positions the retailer as a low price vendor. Firms that don't match prices are perceived as offering a higher level of service. Large buyers can extract price concessions from vendors. Such demands can squeeze the profit margins of suppliers.

Perceptions of quality can also influence pricing strategies. A firm trying to project a prestigious image often charges a premium price for a product. Consumers tend to equate high prices with high quality.

6.1 Divide the class into teams of five. Each team will be assigned a different grocery store from a different chain. (An independent is fine.) Appoint a group leader. The group leaders should meet as a group and pick 5 nationally branded grocery items. Each item should be specifically described as to brand name and size of the package. Each team will then proceed to its assigned store and collect price data on the 5 items. The team should also gather price data on 5 similar store brands and 5 generics, if possible.

Each team should present its results to the class and discuss why there are price variations between stores, national brands, store brands, and generics.

As a next step, go back to your assigned store and share the overall results with the store manager. Bring back the manager's comments and share them with the class.

6.2 How does the stage of a product's life cycle affect price? Give some examples.

Exercises

APPLICATION EXERCISE

Reliance on price as a predictor of quality seems to occur for all products. Does this mean that high-priced products are superior? Well, somctimes. Price can be a good predictor of quality for some products, but for others, price is not always the best way to determine the quality of a product or service before buying it. This exercise (and worksheet) will help you examine the price-quality relationship for a simple product: face cream.[23]

Activities

1. Take a trip to a local supermarket where you are certain to find multiple brands of liquid handwash. Pick and list five or six brands of liquid handwash in the following worksheet:

		Price				
(1) Brand	(2) Quality/Rank (y)	(3) Price/Weight	(4) Price per 100 grams	(5) Price Rank (x)	(6) d (y – x)	(7) d^2
Total						

2. Before going any further, rank the brands according to which you think is the highest quality (1) to the lowest quality (5 or 6, depending on how many brands you find). This ranking will be *y*.

3. Record the price and the volume of each brand. For example, if a 250 ml bottle cost ₹60, you would list ₹60/250 ml.

4. Translate the price per volume into price per 100 ml. Our 250 ml bottle cost ₹24 per 100 gram.
5. Now rank the price per 100 ml (we'll call it *x*) from the highest (1) to the lowest (5 or 6, again depending on how many brands you have).
6. We'll now begin calculating the coefficient of correlation between the price and quality rankings. The first step is to subtract *x* from *y*. Enter the result, *d*, in column 6.
7. Now calculate *d*2 and enter the value in column 7. Write the sum of all the entries in column 7 in the final row.
8. The formula for calculating a price-quality coefficient *r* is as follows:

   In the formula, r_s is the coefficient of correlation, 6 is a constant, and *n* is the number of items ranked.
9. What does the result of your calculation tell you about the correlation between the price and the quality of the canned vegetable or fruit you selected? Now that you know this, will it change your buying habits?

ETHICS EXERCISE

Advanced Bio Medics (ABM) has invented a new stem-cell-based drug that will arrest even advanced forms of lung cancer. Development costs were actually quite low because the drug was an accidental discovery by scientists working on a different project. To stop the disease requires a regimen of one pill per week for 20 weeks. There is no substitute offered by competitors. ABM is thinking that it could maximize its profits by charging ₹2.5 lakh per pill. Of course, many people will die because they can't afford the medicine at this price.

Questions

1. Should ABM maximize its profits?
2. Does the AMA Statement of Ethics address this issue? Go to **www.marketing power.com** and review the code. Then, write a brief paragraph on what the AMA Statement of Ethics contains that relates to ABM's dilemma.

MARKETING PLAN EXERCISE

In the last part of your strategic marketing plan you began the process of defining the marketing mix, starting with the components of product, distribution, and promotion. The next stage of the strategic planning process—pricing—completes the elements of the marketing mix.

In recent years, pricing has become a special challenge to the marketer because prices can be quickly and easily compared on the Internet. In any case, your goal should be to make pricing competitive and value-driven, as well as cover costs. Other features and benefits of your offering are likely to be more important than price. Use the following exercises to guide you through the pricing part of your strategic marketing plan:

1. List possible pricing objectives for your chosen firm. How might adopting different pricing objectives change the behavior of the firm and its marketing plans?
2. Gather information on tactics you decided on for the first parts of your marketing plan. What costs are associated with those decisions? Will you incur more or fewer costs by selling online? Will your marketing costs increase or decrease? Why? Calculate the break-even point for selling your offering. Can you sell enough to cover your costs? Try the break-even calculator at **http://connection.cwru.edu/mbac424/break-even/BreakEven.html.**
3. Pricing is an integral component of marketing strategy. Discuss how your firm's pricing can affect or be affected by competition, the economic environment, political regulations, product features, extra customer service, changes in distribution, or changes in promotion.
4. Is demand elastic or inelastic for your company's product or service? Why? What is the demand elasticity for your offering in an off-line world? Whatever the level, it is likely to be more elastic online. What tactics can you use to soften or reduce this on-line price sensitivity?

Short Case: IPHONE

Prepared by
Dr. Dheeraj Sharma,
Indian Institute of Management, Ahmedabad

The brand-name "Apple" tops in customer loyalty. It is one of the most trusted and demanded brands in the world, and iPhone is one of the most successful products of Apple. iPhone 4S model is sold in the U.S. at \$199 (₹10,150), \$299 (₹15,250), and \$399 (₹20,350) for the 16 GB, 32GB, and 64GB models, respectively. This price is charged if the user makes a contract with network carrier's, AT&T, Sprint, or Verizon. These phones are locked and can only be locked after the contract is over. The unlocked 16GB, 32GB, and 64GB IPhone 4 models are sold in the U.S. at \$649 (₹33,000), \$749 (₹38,000), and \$849 (₹43,200).

In India, the iPhones are not subsidized by network carriers, because of lack of profitability. However, the unlocked 16GB, 32GB, 64GB model of iPhone 4S are sold at ₹44,500, ₹50,900, and ₹57,500, respectively. Indians customers were quite upset with the price charged, as most of them could not afford it. The smartphone market in India is growing at fast rate. The number of smartphones sold in India increased from 1.7 million (17 lakh) units to 3 million (30 lakh) units from third quarter 2010 to third quarter 2011.[24] Smartphones are becoming substitutes for music players, computers, cameras, newspapers etc. Other smartphones also provide the same features, but the experience that Apple iPhone gives you makes it one of the most desired products world over.

The Price List

IPhone 4S Models	Price (₹) IPhone 4S in U.S. (locked)	Price (₹) of IPhone in U.S. (Unlocked)	Price (₹) of IPhone in India (Unlocked)
16 GB	10,150	33,000	44,500
32 GB	15,250	38,000	50,900
64 GB	20,350	43,200	57,500

Source: Economic Times and www.store.apple.com [25] [26]

Apple's share in the global mobile phone market is only 4.2%, yet it accounts for 52% of the total industry.[27] The question now stands is "Why are iPhones overpriced?" A report from *iSuppli* states that the actual cost of the iPhone 4S to Apple is only about ₹10,500(£ 130).[28] Apple is certainly the king of smartphones. A study reported that 93% of the iPhone users want to continue using an iPhone.[29] On the first week of its launch, Apple sold 1.7 million units of IPhone 4S in its first weekend. Apple has fierce loyal consumers, who are ready to buy its products even they are exorbitantly priced. In bargain, Apple has not been able to penetrate in to a large market segment. Many consumers prefer buying cheaper phones available in the market instead of Apple.

Questions

1. Do you think Apple will sustain its customer base, if it prices its phones at current rates?
2. The demand for smartphones in India is increasing. Given the strong following Apple has, should it charge a high price to maximize its profits, or should it decrease its price to capture a larger market share?

19 CHAPTER REVIEW

Pricing Concepts

KEY TERMS

LO 1

price that which is given up in an exchange to acquire a good or service

revenue the price charged to customers multiplied by the number of units sold

profit revenue minus expenses

LO 2

return on investment (ROI) net profit after taxes divided by total assets

market share a company's product sales as a percentage of total sales for that industry

status quo pricing a pricing objective that maintains existing prices or meets the competition's prices

LO 3

demand the quantity of a product that will be sold in the market at various prices for a specified period

supply the quantity of a product that will be offered to the market by a supplier at various prices for a specified period

price equilibrium the price at which demand and supply are equal

elasticity of demand consumers' responsiveness or sensitivity to changes in price

elastic demand a situation in which consumer demand is sensitive to changes in price

inelastic demand a situation in which an increase or a decrease in price will not significantly affect demand for the product

unitary elasticity a situation in which total revenue remains the same when prices change

KEY CONCEPTS

LO 1

Discuss the importance of pricing decisions to the economy and to the individual firm. Pricing plays an integral role in the Indian economy by allocating goods and services among consumers, governments, and businesses. Pricing is essential in business because it creates revenue, which is the basis of all business activity. In setting prices, marketing managers strive to find a level high enough to produce a satisfactory profit.

LO 2

List and explain a variety of pricing objectives. Establishing realistic and measurable pricing objectives is a critical part of any firm's marketing strategy. Pricing objectives are commonly classified into three categories: profit oriented, sales oriented, and status quo. Profit-oriented pricing is based on profit maximization, a satisfactory level of profit, or a target return on investment. The goal of profit maximization is to generate as much revenue as possible in relation to cost. Often, a more practical approach than profit maximization is setting prices to produce profits that will satisfy management and stockholders. The most common profit-oriented strategy is pricing for a specific return on investment relative to a firm's assets. The second type of pricing objective is sales oriented, and it focuses on either maintaining a percentage share of the market or maximizing dollar or unit sales. The third type of pricing objective aims to maintain the status quo by matching competitors' prices.

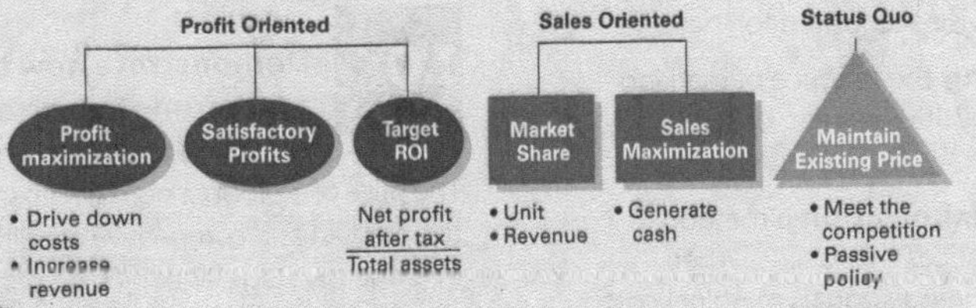

© CENGAGE LEARNING 2011

LO 3

Explain the role of demand in price determination. Demand is a key determinant of price. When establishing prices, a firm must first determine demand for its product. A typical demand schedule shows an inverse relationship between quantity demanded and price: When price is lowered, sales increase; and when price is increased, the quantity demanded falls. For prestige products, however, there may be a direct relationship between demand and price: The quantity demanded will increase as price increases.

Marketing managers must also consider demand elasticity when setting prices. Elasticity of demand is the degree to which the quantity demanded fluctuates with changes in price. If consumers are sensitive to changes in price, demand is elastic; if they are insensitive to price changes, demand is inelastic. Thus, an increase in price will result in lower sales for an elastic product and little or no loss in sales for an inelastic product. Inelastic demand creates pricing power.

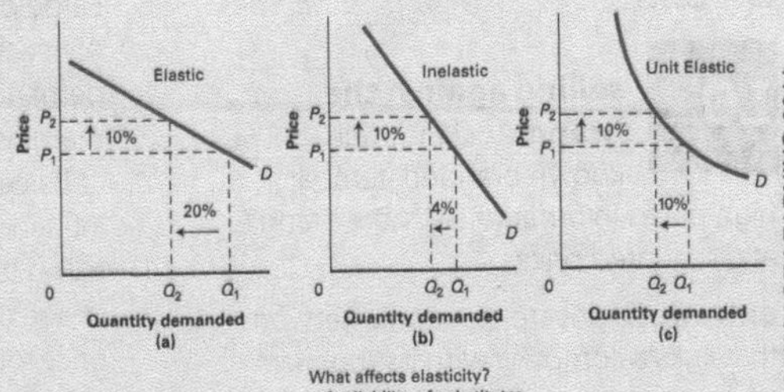

What affects elasticity?
- Availability of substitutes
- Price relative to purchasing power
- Product durability
- Product's other uses
- Inflation rate

© CENGAGE LEARNING 2011

LO 4 **yield management systems (YMS)** a technique for adjusting prices that uses complex mathematical software to profitably fill unused capacity by discounting early purchases, limiting early sales at these discounted prices, and overbooking capacity

LO 5 **variable cost** a cost that varies with changes in the level of output

fixed cost a cost that does not change as output is increased or decreased

average variable cost (AVC) total variable costs divided by quantity of output

average total cost (ATC) total costs divided by quantity of output

marginal cost (MC) the change in total costs associated with a one-unit change in output

markup pricing the cost of buying the product from the producer, plus amounts for profit and for expenses not otherwise accounted for

keystoning the practice of marking up prices by 100 percent, or doubling the cost

profit maximization a method of setting prices that occurs when marginal revenue equals marginal cost

marginal revenue (MR) the extra revenue associated with selling an extra unit of output or the change in total revenue with a one-unit change in output

break-even analysis a method of determining what sales volume must be reached before total revenue equals total costs

LO 6 **selling against the brand** stocking well-known branded items at high prices in order to sell store brands at discounted prices

extranet a private electronic network that links a company with its suppliers and customers

prestige pricing charging a high price to help promote a high-quality image

LO 4 **Understand the concept of yield management systems.** Yield management systems use complex mathematical software to profitably fill unused capacity. The software uses techniques such as discounting early purchases, limiting early sales at these discounted prices, and overbooking capacity. These systems are used in service and retail businesses and are substantially raising revenues. The use of Internet cookies and targeting software enables online retailers to offer different pricing and promotional offers to online buyers based upon their online shopping and browsing habits.

LO 5 **Describe cost-oriented pricing strategies. The other major determinant of price is cost.** Marketers use several cost-oriented pricing strategies. To cover their own expenses and obtain a profit, wholesalers and retailers commonly use markup pricing: They tack an extra amount onto the manufacturer's original price. Another pricing technique is to maximize profits by setting price where marginal revenue equals marginal cost. Still another pricing strategy determines how much a firm must sell to break even and uses this amount as a reference point for adjusting price.

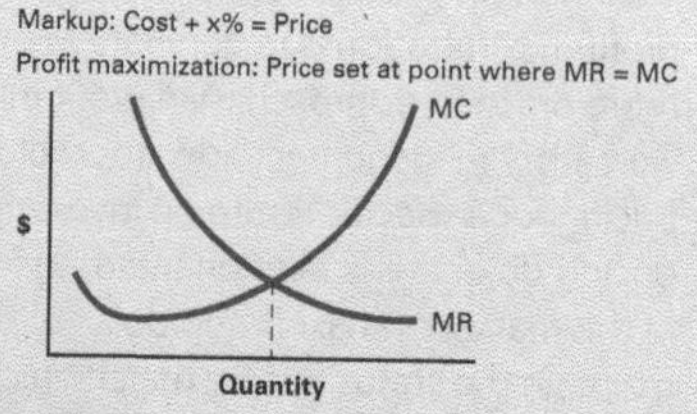

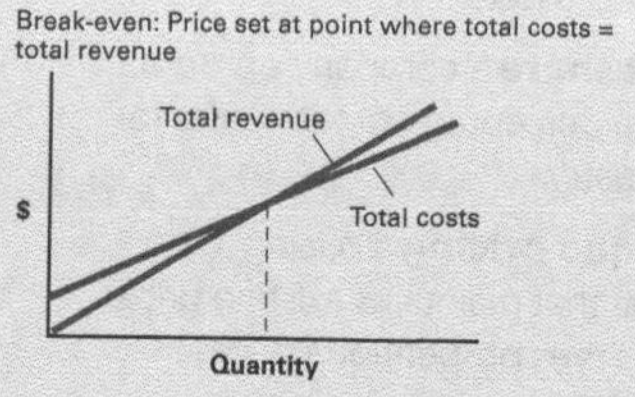

LO 6 **Demonstrate how the product life cycle, competition, distribution and promotion strategies, guaranteed price matching, customer demands, the Internet, and perceptions of quality can affect price.** The price of a product normally changes as it moves through the life cycle and as demand for the product and competitive conditions change. Management often sets a high price at the introductory stage, and the high price tends to attract competition. The competition usually drives prices down because individual competitors lower prices to gain market share.

Adequate distribution for a new product can sometimes be obtained by offering a larger-than-usual profit margin to wholesalers and retailers. The Internet enables consumers to compare products and prices quickly and efficiently. Price is also used as a promotional tool to attract customers. Special low prices often attract new customers and entice existing customers to buy more. Price matching positions the retailer as a low price vendor. Firms that don't match prices are perceived as offering a higher level of service. Large buyers can extract price concessions from vendors. Such demands can squeeze the profit margins of suppliers.

Perceptions of quality can also influence pricing strategies. A firm trying to project a prestigious image often charges a premium price for a product. Consumers tend to equate high prices with high quality.

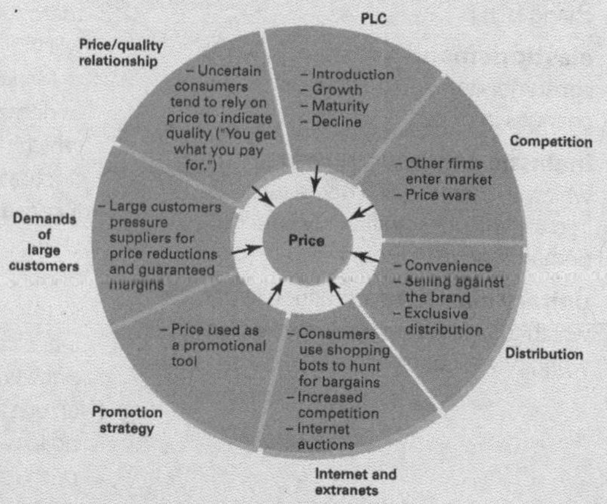

CHAPTER 20 Setting the Right Price

Learning Outcomes

LO 1 Describe the procedure for setting the right price

LO 2 Identify the legal and ethical constraints on pricing decisions

LO 3 Explain how discounts, geographic pricing, and other pricing tactics can be used to fine-tune the base price

LO 4 Discuss product line pricing

LO 5 Describe the role of pricing during periods of inflation and recession

All pricing objectives have trade-offs that managers must weigh.

LO1 How to Set a Price on a Product

Setting the right price on a product is a four-step process, illustrated in Exhibit 20.1 on the next page and discussed throughout this chapter:

1. Establish pricing goals.
2. Estimate demand, costs, and profits.
3. Choose a price strategy to help determine a base price.
4. Fine-tune the base price with pricing tactics.

Establish Pricing Goals

The first step in setting the right price is to establish pricing goals. Recall from Chapter 19 that pricing objectives fall into three categories: profit oriented, sales oriented, and status quo. These goals are derived from the firm's overall objectives. A good understanding of the marketplace and of the consumer can sometimes tell a manager very quickly whether a goal is realistic.

All pricing objectives have trade-offs that managers must weigh. A profit maximization objective may require a bigger initial investment than the firm can commit to or wants to commit to. Reaching the desired market share often means sacrificing short-term profit because without careful management, long-term profit goals may not be met. Meeting the competition is the easiest pricing goal to implement. But can managers really afford to ignore demand and costs, the life cycle stage, and other considerations? When creating pricing objectives, managers must consider these trade-offs in light of the target customer, the environment, and the company's overall objectives.

Note:* *All the figures in U.S. dollars are converted into rupee using the value $1 = ₹45.

price strategy a basic, long-term pricing framework that establishes the initial price for a product and the intended direction for price movements over the product life cycle

price skimming a pricing policy whereby a firm charges a high introductory price, often coupled with heavy promotion

EXHIBIT 20.1

Steps in Setting the Right Price on a Product

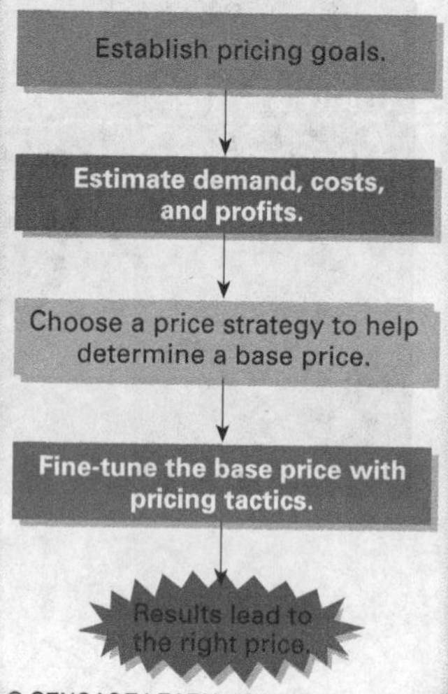

Estimate Demand, Costs, and Profits

Chapter 19 explained that total revenue is a function of price and quantity demanded and that quantity demanded depends on elasticity. The types of questions managers consider when conducting marketing research on demand and elasticity are key.

QUESTIONS FOR MARKET RESEARCH ON DEMAND AND ELASTICITY

- What price is so low that consumers would question its quality?
- What is the highest price at which the product would still be a bargain?
- What is the price at which the product is starting to get expensive?
- What is the price at which the product becomes too expensive to consider buying?[1]

After establishing pricing goals, managers should estimate total revenue at a variety of prices. Next, they should determine corresponding costs for each price. They are then ready to estimate how much profit, if any, and how much market share can be earned at each possible price. Managers can study the options in light of revenues, costs, and profits. In turn, this information can help determine which price can best meet the firm's pricing goals.

Choose a Price Strategy

The basic, long-term pricing framework for a good or service should be a logical extension of the pricing objectives. The marketing manager's chosen **price strategy** defines the initial price and gives direction for price movements over the product life cycle.

The price strategy sets a competitive price in a specific market segment, based on a well-defined positioning strategy. Changing a price level from premium to super premium may require a change in the product itself, the target customers served, the promotional strategy, or the distribution channels.

A company's freedom in pricing a new product and devising a price strategy depends on the market conditions and the other elements of the marketing mix. If a firm launches a new item resembling several others already on the market, its pricing freedom will be restricted. To succeed, the company will probably have to charge a price close to the average market price. In contrast, a firm that introduces a totally new product with no close substitutes will have considerable pricing freedom.

Despite its strategic value, pricing research is an underused tool. McKinsey & Company's Pricing Benchmark Survey estimated that only about 15 percent of companies do serious pricing research.[2]

Strategic pricing decisions tend to be made without an understanding of the likely buyer or the competitive response. Managers often make tactical pricing decisions without reviewing how they may fit into the firm's overall pricing or marketing strategy. Many companies make pricing decisions and changes without an existing process for managing the pricing activity. As a result, many of them do not have a serious pricing strategy and do not conduct pricing research to develop their strategy.[3]

Companies that do serious planning for creating a price strategy can select from three basic approaches: price skimming, penetration pricing, and status quo pricing.

Price Skimming **Price skimming** is sometimes called a "market-plus" approach to pricing because it denotes a high price relative to the prices of competing products. The term *price skimming* is derived from the phrase "skimming the cream off the top." Companies often use this strategy for new products when the product is perceived by the target market as having unique advantages. Often companies will use skimming and then lower prices over time. This is called "sliding down the demand curve." Hardcover book publishers, such as HarperCollins, lower the price when the books are re-released in paperback. Other manufacturers maintain skimming prices throughout a product's life cycle. A manager of the factory that produces Chanel purses (retailing for over ₹90,000 each) told one of your authors that it takes back unsold inventory and destroys it rather than selling it at a discount.

Price skimming works best when the market is willing to buy the product even though it carries an above-average price. When companies such as Sony, LG, and Samsung launched 29 inch television range, they were priced high to make them available to selected customers. Similarly, their current LCD and LED product range is also priced high to maintain exclusivity.[4] Firms can also effectively use price skimming when a product is well protected legally, when it represents a technological breakthrough, or when it has in some other way blocked the entry of competitors. Managers may follow a skimming strategy when production cannot be expanded rapidly because of technological difficulties, shortages, or constraints imposed by the skill and time required to produce a product. As long as demand is greater than supply, skimming is an attainable strategy.

A successful skimming strategy enables management to recover its product development costs quickly. Even if the market perceives an introductory price as too high, managers can lower the price. Firms often feel it is better to test the market at a high price and then lower the price if sales are too slow. Successful skimming strategies are not limited to products. Well-known athletes, lawyers, and hairstylists are experts at price skimming. Naturally, a skimming strategy will encourage competitors to enter the market.

Penetration Pricing Penetration pricing is at the opposite end of the spectrum from skimming. **Penetration pricing** means charging a relatively low price for a product as a way to reach the mass market. The low price is designed to capture a large share of a substantial market, resulting in lower production costs. If a marketing manager has made obtaining a large market share the firm's pricing objective, penetration pricing is a logical choice.

penetration pricing a pricing policy whereby a firm charges a relatively low price for a product initially as a way to reach the mass market

Penetration pricing does mean lower profit per unit, however. Therefore, to reach the break-even point, it requires a higher volume of sales than would a skimming policy. The recovery of product development costs may be slow. As you might expect, penetration pricing tends to discourage competition.

A penetration strategy tends to be effective in a price-sensitive market. Price should decline more rapidly when demand is elastic because the market can be expanded through a lower price. Also, price sensitivity and greater competitive pressure should lead to a lower initial price and a relatively slow decline in the price later to a stable low price.

Although Walmart is typically associated with penetration pricing, other chains have done an excellent job of following this strategy as well. Fast-food restaurants use rupee menus and low-priced foods to entice customers to visit one chain over another. McDonald's success is primarily because it offers a wide range of food at low-prices.

Another form of extreme penetration pricing that has dramatically increased sales during the recent economic downturn is salvage or surplus grocers. Salvage grocers sell "close-outs," which include products that manufacturers have discontinued, seasonal items that are outdated and goods that are near the date when manufacturers expect freshness to wane.

If a firm has a low fixed cost structure and each sale provides a large contribution to those fixed costs, penetration pricing can boost sales and provide large increases in profits—but only if the market size grows or if competitors choose not to respond. Low prices can attract additional buyers to the market. The increased sales can justify production expansion or the adoption of new technologies, both of which can reduce costs. And, if firms have excess capacity, even low-priced business can provide incremental notes toward fixed costs.

Penetration pricing can also be effective if an experience curve will cause costs per unit to drop significantly. The experience curve proposes that per-unit costs will go down as a firm's production experience

status quo pricing charging a price identical to or very close to the competition's price

price fixing an agreement between two or more firms on the price they will charge for a product

increases. Manufacturers that fail to take advantage of these effects will find themselves at a competitive cost disadvantage relative to others that are further along the curve.

The big advantage of penetration pricing is that it typically discourages or blocks competition from entering a market. The disadvantage is that penetration means gearing up for mass production to sell a large volume at a low price. If the volume fails to materialize, the company will face huge losses from building or converting a factory to produce the failed product.

Penetration pricing can damage an entire industry's profit cycle if customers expect deep discounts if products do not sell or there is overstock.

Status Quo Pricing The third basic price strategy a firm may choose is **status quo pricing**, also called meeting the competition or going rate pricing (see also Chapter 19). It means charging a price identical to or very close to the competition's price.

Although status quo pricing has the advantage of simplicity, its disadvantage is that the strategy may ignore demand or cost or both. If the firm is comparatively small, however, meeting the competition may be the safest route to long-term survival.

LO 2 The Legality and Ethics of Price Strategy

As we mentioned in Chapter 4, some pricing decisions are subject to government regulation. Among the issues that fall into this category are unfair trade practices, price fixing, price discrimination, and predatory pricing.

Unfair Trade Practices

The government has set up a Price Monitoring Cell (PMC) under the Department of Consumer Affairs for monitoring the prices of selected essential commodities. The cell monitors the retail and wholesale prices, analyses the price situation, and offers feedback for taking corrective measures to avoid any unwanted shortage in the availability of these essential commodities. However, the fixing of prices for these commodities is done entirely by wholesalers and retailers, with government having no control over profit margins earned. Recently, a Parliamentary Committee submitted a report, asking for a new law for controlling rise in prices of the essential commodities and to fix a limit on the profit margins of wholesalers, retailers, and other members in the supply chain up to a certain percentage.[5]

Price Fixing

Price fixing is an agreement between two or more firms on the price they will charge for a product. Suppose two or more executives from competing firms meet to decide how much to charge for a product or to decide which of them will submit the lowest bid on a certain contract. Such practices are illegal under the Competition Act. The offenders can be imposed with a penalty of 10 percent of turnover or three times the amount of profit derived from such agreement, whichever is higher. Price fixing is one area where lawmakers worldwide have developed clear laws, and enforcements of judiciary are quite vigorous. There are numerous instances where the price fixing offenders were handed penalties under the governing laws of the respective country. In May 2009, Asiana Airlines, a South Korean airline, pleaded guilty to fixing international cargo rates and passenger fares and agreed to pay a fine of ₹225 crore. In August, two former Asiana executives were indicted in United States for conspiring to fix economy-class prices for flights between the United States and South Korea. The maximum penalties for these charges are ten years in prison and ₹4.5 crore.[6]

International price fixing by private entities can be prosecuted under the antitrust laws of many countries. New Zealand filed allegations against six transportation companies for allegedly fixing prices in international freight forwarding services to New Zealand. The High Court is reviewing the allegations, but investigations have been ongoing since 2001 to develop a case against these companies. If found guilty, the company could incur penalties ranging from ₹45 crore to three times the company's net profit.[7] A few other examples are those of South Korea imposing a penalty of ₹175.5 crore on LG electronics and Samsung Electronics for fixing the prices of washing machines, flat panel TVs, and laptop computers[8], Panasonic was fined ₹46 crore in Europe for being involved in price fixing of refrigerator compressors[9], and fines totalling ₹2178 crore were meted out to P&G, Henkel AG, and Colgate-Palmolive Company for fixing soap prices in France[10].

Most price-fixing cases focus on high prices charged to customers. A reverse form of price fixing occurs when powerful buyers force their suppliers' prices down. Recently, bluberry growers in the state of Maine in the United States alleged that four big processors conspired to push down the price they would pay for fresh wild berries. A state court jury agreed and awarded crores in damages.[11] Some price-fixing accusations are less clear-cut.

Other Illegal Pricing

The Competition Act also carries provisions to prevent other forms of illegal pricing, such as price discrimination and predatory pricing. **Price discrimination** is the practice of charging different prices from different buyers. There are different ways in which price discrimination can be implemented. A seller can charge separate prices from separate customers based on their demand patterns; he can charge less prices from those who buy in large volumes; he can charge prices based on distribution channel used for purchasing—for example, soft drink companies charge different prices based on whether customer is buying it from fast-food outlet or a fine dining restaurant; he can charge based on time of purchase—for example, movie multiplexes have different prices for morning shows, afternoon shows, and evening shows; or he can charge based on location—for example, movie multiplexes charge different prices for different levels of seats (normally classified as silver, gold, and platinum).[12] **Predatory pricing** is the practice of charging a very low price for a product with the intent of driving competitors out of business or out of a market. Once the competitors have been driven out, the firm raises its prices.

price discrimination the practice of charging different prices from different buyers

predatory pricing the practice of charging a very low price for a product with the intent of driving competitors out of business or out of a market

base price the general price level at which the company expects to sell the good or service

LO 3 Tactics for Fine-Tuning the Base Price

After managers understand both the legal and the marketing consequences of price strategies, they should set a base price—the general price level at which the company expects to sell the good or service. The general price level is correlated with the pricing policy: above the market (price skimming), at the market (status quo pricing), or below the market (penetration pricing). The final step, then, is to fine-tune the base price.

Fine-tuning techniques are short-run approaches that do not change the general price level. They do, however, result in changes within a general price level. These pricing tactics allow the firm to adjust for com-

THERE MAY BE SUCH THING AS BAD PUBLICITY . . .

In San Francisco, California, a judge ruled that *San Francisco Weekly* sold advertising space at a steep discount to advertisers with the intent to injure a competing weekly newspaper. The *Bay Guardian* was awarded ₹72 crore in damages. California's laws differ from federal laws in that the *Bay Guardian* does not have to prove that *San Fransisco Weekly* will be able to recoup the losses incurred by selling the advertising space at below cost, which it would be required to do in a federal case. California hopes to demonstrate that actions discouraging or injuring competition are worthy of punishment.[13]

© COMSTOCK IMAGES/JUPITERIMAGES

quantity discount a price reduction offered to buyers buying in multiple units or above a specified dollar amount

cumulative quantity discount a deduction from list price that applies to the buyer's total purchases made during a specific period

noncumulative quantity discount a deduction from list price that applies to a single order rather than to the total volume of orders placed during a certain period

cash discount a price reduction offered to a consumer, an industrial user, or a marketing intermediary in return for prompt payment of a bill

functional discount (trade discount) a discount to wholesalers and retailers for performing channel functions

seasonal discount a price reduction for buying merchandise out of season

promotional allowance (trade allowance) a payment to a dealer for promoting the manufacturer's products

rebate a cash refund given for the purchase of a product during a specific period

value-based pricing setting the price at a level that seems to the customer to be a good price compared to the prices of other options

petition in certain markets, meet ever-changing government regulations, take advantage of unique demand situations, and meet promotional and positioning goals. Fine-tuning pricing tactics include various sorts of discounts, geographic pricing, and other pricing tactics.

Discounts, Allowances, Rebates, and Value-Based Pricing

A base price can be lowered through the use of discounts and the related tactics of allowances, rebates, low or zero-percent financing, and value-based pricing. Managers use the various forms of discounts to encourage customers to do what they would not ordinarily do, such as paying cash rather than using credit, taking delivery out of season, or performing certain functions within a distribution channel.[14] The following are the most common tactics:

- *Quantity discounts:* When buyers get a lower price for buying in multiple units or above a specified amount, they are receiving a **quantity discount**. A **cumulative quantity discount** is a deduction from list price that applies to the buyer's total purchases made during a specific period; it is intended to encourage customer loyalty. In contrast, a **noncumulative quantity discount** is a deduction from list price that applies to a single order rather than to the total volume of orders placed during a certain period. It is intended to encourage orders in large quantities.
- *Cash discounts:* A **cash discount** is a price reduction offered to a consumer, an industrial user, or a marketing intermediary in return for prompt payment of a bill. Prompt payment saves the seller carrying charges and billing expenses and allows the seller to avoid bad debt.
- *Functional discounts:* When distribution channel intermediaries, such as wholesalers or retailers, perform a service or function for the manufacturer, they must be compensated. This compensation, typically a percentage discount from the base price, is called a **functional discount** (or **trade discount**). Functional discounts vary greatly from channel to channel, depending on the tasks performed by the intermediary.
- *Seasonal discounts:* A **seasonal discount** is a price reduction for buying merchandise out of season. It shifts the storage function to the purchaser. Seasonal discounts also enable manufacturers to maintain a steady production schedule year-round.
- *Promotional allowances:* A **promotional allowance** (also known as a **trade allowance**) is a payment to a dealer for promoting the manufacturer's products. It is both a pricing tool and a promotional device. As a pricing tool, a promotional allowance is like a functional discount. If, for example, a retailer runs an ad for a manufacturer's product, the manufacturer may pay half the cost.
- *Rebates:* A **rebate** is a cash refund given for the purchase of a product during a specific period. The advantage of a rebate over a simple price reduction for stimulating demand is that a rebate is a temporary inducement that can be taken away without altering the basic price structure. A manufacturer that uses a simple price reduction for a short time may meet resistance when trying to restore the price to its original, higher level.
- *Zero-percent financing:* During the mid and late 2000s, new-car sales receded. To get people back into the automobile showrooms, manufacturers offered zero-percent financing, which enabled purchasers to borrow money to pay for new cars with no interest charge. The tactic created a huge increase in sales but not without cost to the manufacturers.

Value-Based Pricing **Value-based pricing**, also called *value pricing*, is a pricing strategy that has grown out of the quality movement. Instead of figuring prices based on costs or competitors' prices, it starts with the customer, considers the competition, and then determines the appropriate price. The basic assumption is that the firm is customer driven, seeking to understand the attributes customers want in the goods and services they buy and the value of that bundle of attributes to customers. Because very few firms operate in a pure monopoly, however, a marketer using value-based pricing must also determine the value of competitive offerings to customers. Customers determine the value of a product (not just its price) relative to the value of alternatives. In value-based pricing, therefore, the price of the product is set at a level that seems to the customer to be a good price compared with the prices of other options.

Peter England is a mid-priced apparel brand that offers quality and style at value for money prices.[15] Parle biscuits too offer value pricing on its product range—its biscuits are priced lower as compared to other companies for the same size pack. For example, while Parle bourbon is priced at ₹20 for 167 gram pack, Britannia Bourbon's 167 gram pack is priced at ₹22.[16] Frito Lay started offering its products at price points of ₹3 and ₹5 to capture the lower SEC customers, who are more value sensitive.[17]

Pricing Products Too Low Sometimes managers price their products too low, thereby reducing company profits. This seems to happen for two reasons. First, managers attempt to buy market share through aggressive pricing. Usually, however, these price cuts are quickly met by competitors. Thus, any gain in market share is short-lived, and overall industry profits end up falling. Second, managers have a natural tendency to want to make decisions that can be justified objectively.

The problem is that companies often lack hard data on the complex determinants of profitability, such as the relationship between price changes and sales volumes, the link between demand levels and costs, and the likely responses of competitors to price changes. In contrast, companies usually have rich, unambiguous information on costs, sales, market share, and competitors' prices. As a result, managers tend to make pricing decisions based on current costs, projected short-term share gains, or current competitor prices rather than on long-term profitability. A famous illustration proving this point is the ₹5 affordability strategy adopted by Coca Cola and Pepsi in 2002. The strategy proved to be a financial disaster for the companies. Though short term sales skyrocketed, the bottomline of both the cola giants was adversely impacted and volumes failed to justify the low price strategy. The strategy was rolled back two years later in 2004 and prices were hiked.[18]

The problem of "underpricing" can be solved by linking information about price, cost, and demand within the same decision support system. The demand data can be developed via marketing research. This will enable managers to get the hard data they need to calculate the effects of pricing decisions on profitability.

Geographic Pricing

Because many sellers ship their wares to a nationwide or even a worldwide market, the cost of freight can greatly affect the total cost of a product. Sellers may use several different geographic pricing tactics to moderate the impact of freight costs on distant customers. The following methods of geographic pricing are the most common:

- *FOB origin pricing:* **FOB origin pricing**, also called *FOB factory* or *FOB shipping point*, is a price tactic that

THE ADVERTISING CAMPAIGN FOR ₹5 COKE FEATURING BOLLYWOOD ACTOR AAMIR KHAN—THE AFFORDABLE PRICE STRATEGY DID NOT PROVE TO BE AFFORDABLE FOR THE COMPANY'S BOTTOMLINE

© ISTOCKPHOTO.COM/NICOLAS LORAN

© ISTOCKPHOTO.COM/NICOLAS LORAN

uniform delivered pricing a price tactic in which the seller pays the actual freight charges and bills every purchaser an identical, flat freight charge

zone pricing a modification of uniform delivered pricing that divides the United States (or the total market) into segments or zones and charges a flat freight rate to all customers in a given zone

freight absorption pricing a price tactic in which the seller pays all or part of the actual freight charges and does not pass them on to the buyer

basing-point pricing a price tactic that charges freight from a given (basing) point, regardless of the city from which the goods are shipped

single-price tactic a price tactic that offers all goods and services at the same price (or perhaps two or three prices)

flexible pricing (variable pricing) a price tactic in which different customers pay different prices for essentially the same merchandise bought in equal quantities

FOB origin pricing a price tactic that requires the buyer to absorb the freight costs from the shipping point ("free on board")

requires the buyer to absorb the freight costs from the shipping point ("free on board"). The farther buyers are from sellers, the more they pay, because transportation costs generally increase with the distance merchandise is shipped.

- *Uniform delivered pricing:* If the marketing manager wants total costs, including freight, to be equal for all purchasers of identical products, the firm will adopt uniform delivered pricing, or "postage stamp" pricing. With **uniform delivered pricing**, the seller pays the actual freight charges and bills every purchaser an identical, flat freight charge.
- *Zone pricing:* A marketing manager who wants to equalize total costs among buyers within large geographic areas—but not necessarily all of the seller's market area—may modify the base price with a zone-pricing tactic. **Zone pricing** is a modification of uniform delivered pricing.

  Rather than using a uniform freight rate for the entire market, the firm divides it into segments or zones and charges a flat freight rate to all customers in a given zone.
- *Freight absorption pricing:* In **freight absorption pricing**, the seller pays all or part of the actual freight charges and does not pass them on to the buyer. The manager may use this tactic in intensely competitive areas or as a way to break into new market areas.
- *Basing-point pricing:* With **basing-point pricing**, the seller designates a location as a basing point and charges all buyers the freight cost from that point, regardless of the city from which the goods are shipped. Thanks to several adverse court rulings, basing-point pricing has waned in popularity. Freight fees charged when none were actually incurred, called *phantom freight*, have been declared illegal.

Other Pricing Tactics

Unlike geographic pricing, other pricing tactics are unique and defy neat categorization. Managers use these tactics for various reasons—for example, to stimulate demand for specific products, to increase store patronage, and to offer a wider variety of merchandise at a specific price point. "Other" pricing tactics include a single-price tactic, flexible pricing, professional services pricing, price lining, leader pricing, bait pricing, odd–even pricing, price bundling, and two-part pricing.

Single-Price Tactic A merchant using a **single-price tactic** offers all goods and services at the same price (or perhaps two or three prices). My Dollar Store follows the single price strategy by charging a fixed price of ₹99 for its entire range of international products.[19]

Single-price selling removes price comparisons from the buyer's decision-making process. The retailer enjoys the benefits of a simplified pricing system and minimal clerical errors. However, continually rising costs are a headache for retailers following this strategy. In times of inflation, they must frequently raise the selling price.

Flexible Pricing **Flexible pricing** (or **variable pricing**) means that different customers pay different prices for essentially the same merchandise bought in equal quantities. This tactic is often found in the sale of shopping goods, specialty merchandise, and most industrial goods except supply items. Car dealers and many appliance retailers commonly follow the practice. It allows the seller to adjust for competition by meeting another seller's price. Thus, a marketing manager with a status quo pricing objective might readily adopt the tactic. Flexible pricing also enables the seller to close a sale with price-conscious consumers.

The obvious disadvantages of flexible pricing are the lack of consistent profit margins, the potential ill will of high-paying purchasers, the tendency for salespeople to automatically lower the price to make a sale, and the possibility of a price war among sellers.

Trade-Ins Trade-in is the pricing technique in which customers are offered a reduction on the price of a new product in exchange of an old one. Flexible pricing and trade-ins often go hand in hand. About 57 percent of all new car sales involve a trade-in.[20] Trade-ins occur for other products as well, such as musical instruments, jewellery, and consumer appliances. If a trade-in is involved, the consumer must negotiate two prices, one for the new product and one for the existing product. The existence of a trade-in raises several questions for the purchaser. For example, will the new product's price differ depending on whether there is a trade-in? Are consumers better off trading in their used product toward the purchase of the new one from the same retailer, or should they keep the two transactions separate by dealing with different retailers?

Recent research found that trade-in customers tend to care more about the trade-in value they receive than the price they pay for the new product. Thus, these buyers tend to pay more than purchasers without a trade-in. Analysis of data from the automobile market found that, on average, trade-in customers end up paying ₹20,000 more than customers who simply buy a new car from a dealer.[21]

Professional Services Pricing Professional services pricing is used by people with lengthy experience, training, and often certification by a licensing board—for example, lawyers, physicians, and family counselors. Professionals sometimes charge customers at an hourly rate, but sometimes fees are based on the solution of a problem or performance of an act (such as an eye examination) rather than on the actual time involved.

Those who use professional pricing have an ethical responsibility not to overcharge a customer. Because demand is sometimes highly inelastic, such as when a person requires heart surgery to survive, there may be a temptation to charge "all the traffic will bear."[22]

price lining the practice of offering a product line with several items at specific price points

leader pricing (loss-leader pricing) a price tactic in which a product is sold near or even below cost in the hope that shoppers will buy other items once they are in the store

Price Lining When a seller establishes a series of prices for a type of merchandise, it creates a price line. **Price lining** is the practice of offering a product line with several items at specific price points. Apple's iTunes has moved single-track purchases from a flat fee to a price line structure. The most popular tracks are ₹58 each, with less popular tracks priced at ₹44 or ₹31.

Price lining reduces confusion for both the salesperson and the consumer. The buyer may be offered a wider variety of merchandise at each established price. Price lines may also enable a seller to reach several market segments. For buyers, the question of price may be quite simple: All they have to do is find a suitable product at the predetermined price. Moreover, price lining is a valuable tactic for the marketing manager, because the firm may be able to carry a smaller total inventory than it could without price lines. The results may include fewer markdowns, simplified purchasing, and lower inventory carrying charges.

Price lines also present drawbacks, especially if costs are continually rising. Sellers can offset rising costs in three ways. First, they can begin stocking lower-quality merchandise at each price point. Second, sellers can change the prices, although frequent price line changes confuse buyers. Third, sellers can accept lower profit margins and hold quality and prices constant. This third alternative has short-run benefits, but its long-run handicaps may drive sellers out of business.

Leader Pricing **Leader pricing** (or **loss-leader pricing**) is an attempt by the marketing manager to attract customers by selling a product near or even below cost in the hope that shoppers will buy other items once they are in the store. This type of pricing appears weekly in the newspaper advertising of supermarkets. Leader pricing is normally used on well-known items that consumers can easily recognize as bargains. The trend of geo-social loss leader campaigns is growing in popularity as companies see how successful leader pricing is enticing people to buy. Retailers like Big Bazaar used this strategy effectively by highlighting best deals in its advertising to lure customers to visit its stores.

Advertisements highlighting great saving deals allure customers to walk into the store and end up purchasing even those products that have no offers on them.

Leader pricing is not limited to products. Health clubs offer a one-month free trial as a loss leader.

Bait Pricing In contrast to leader pricing, which is a genuine attempt to give the consumer a reduced price, bait pricing is deceptive. **Bait pricing** tries to get the consumer into a store through false or misleading price advertising and then uses high-pressure selling to persuade the consumer to buy more expensive merchandise. You may have seen this ad or a similar one:

> REPOSSESSED . . . Singer slant-needle sewing machine . . . take over 8 payments of INR 500 per month . . . ABC Sewing Center.

This is bait. When a customer goes in to see the machine, a salesperson says that it has just been sold or else shows the prospective buyer a piece of junk. Then the salesperson says, “But I've got a really good deal on this fine new model.” This is the switch that may cause a susceptible consumer to walk out with a ₹4,000 machine. Bait pricing is considered a deceptive act and has been banned in several countries.

Odd–Even Pricing **Odd–even pricing** (or **psychological pricing**) means pricing at odd-numbered prices to connote a bargain and pricing at even-numbered prices to imply quality. Bata is renowned for using odd pricing strategy and prices its shoes at ₹199, ₹249, and ₹499. This makes the consumers feel they are paying a lower price for the product. Even-numbered pricing is often used for “prestige” items, such as a fine perfume at ₹4,500 a bottle or a good watch at ₹3,000. The demand curve for such items would also be sawtoothed, except that the outside edges would represent even-numbered prices and, therefore, elastic demand.

Price Bundling **Price bundling** is marketing two or more products in a single package for a special price. For example, Microsoft offers “suites” of software that bundle spreadsheets, word processing, graphics, e-mail, Internet access, and groupware for networks of microcomputers. Price bundling can stimulate demand for the bundled items if the target market perceives the price as a good value.

Services like hotels and airlines sell a perishable commodity (hotel rooms and airline seats) with relatively constant fixed costs. Bundling can be an important income stream for these businesses because the variable cost tends to be low—for instance, the cost of cleaning a hotel room. Therefore, most of the revenue can help cover fixed costs and generate profits.

Bundling has also been used in the telecommunications industry. Companies offer local service, long distance, DSL Internet service, wireless, and even cable television in various menus of bundling. Telecom companies use bundling as a way to protect their market share and fight off competition by locking customers into a group of services. For consumers, comparison shopping may be difficult since they may not be able to determine how much they are really paying for each component of the bundle. A related price tactic is **unbundling**, or reducing the bundle of services that comes with the basic product. To help hold the line on costs, some stores require customers to pay for gift wrapping.

Clearly, price bundling can influence consumers' purchase behavior. But what about the decision to consume a particular bundled product or service? Some of the latest research has focused on how people consume certain bundled products or services. According to this research, the key to consumption behavior

bait pricing a price tactic that tries to get consumers into a store through false or misleading price advertising and then uses high-pressure selling to persuade consumers to buy more expensive merchandise

odd–even pricing (psychological pricing) a price tactic that uses odd-numbered prices to connote bargains and even-numbered prices to imply quality

price bundling marketing two or more products in a single package for a special price

unbundling reducing the bundle of services that comes with the basic product

is how closely consumers can link the costs and benefits of the exchange.[23] In complex transactions like a holiday package, it may be unclear which costs are paying for which benefits. In such cases, consumers tend to mentally downplay their up-front costs for the bundled product, so they may be more likely to forego a benefit that's part of the bundle, like a free dinner.

Similarly, when people buy season tickets to a concert series, sporting event, or other activity, the sunk costs (price of the bundle) and the pending benefit (going to see an event) become decoupled. This reduces the likelihood of consumption of the event over time.

Theatergoers who purchase tickets to a single play are almost certain to use those tickets. This is consistent with the idea that in a one-to-one transaction (i.e., one payment, one benefit), the costs and benefits of that transaction are tightly coupled, resulting in strong sunk cost pressure to consume the pending benefit.

A theater manager might expect a no-show rate of 20 percent when the percentage of season ticket holders is high, but a no-show rate of only 5 percent when the percentage of season ticket holders is low. With a high number of season ticket holders, a manager could oversell performances and maximize the revenue for the theater. The surge in petroleum prices in 2007–2008 forced airlines worldwide to unbundle in a dramatic fashion. Services like soft drinks, food, pillows, and blankets started coming at a price.

Though price bundling of services can result in a lower rate of total consumption of that service, the same is not necessarily true for products. Consider the purchase of an expensive bottle of wine. When the wine is purchased as a single unit, its cost and eventual benefit are tightly coupled. As a result, the cost of the wine will be important, and a person will likely reserve that wine for a special occasion. When purchased as part of a bundle (e.g., as part of a case of wine), however, the cost and benefit of that individual bottle of wine will likely become decoupled, reducing the impact of the cost on eventual consumption. Thus, in contrast to the price bundling of services, the price bundling of physical goods could lead to an increase in product consumption.

Two-Part Pricing **Two-part pricing** means establishing two separate charges to consume a single good or service. Health clubs charge a membership fee and a flat fee each time a person uses certain equipment or facilities.

Consumers sometimes prefer two-part pricing because they are uncertain about the number and the types of activities they might use at places like an amusement park. Also, the people who use a service most often pay a higher total price. Two-part pricing can increase a seller's revenue by attracting consumers who would not pay a high fee even for unlimited use. For example, a health club might be able to sell only 100 memberships at ₹12,000 annually with unlimited use of facilities, for a total revenue of ₹12,00,000. However, it could sell 400 memberships at ₹8,000 with a guarantee of using the swimming pool ten times a month. Every use over ten would require the member to pay a ₹200 fee. Thus, membership revenue would provide a base of ₹32,00,000, with some additional usage fees throughout the year.

two-part pricing a price tactic that charges two separate amounts to consume a single good or service

consumer penalty an extra fee paid by the consumer for violating the terms of the purchase agreement

Research has shown that when consumers are thinking of buying a good or service with two–part pricing, they may mentally process the base price, such as a membership fee, more thoroughly than the extra fee or surcharge (playing a game of tennis). Thus, they can underestimate the total price compared with when prices are not partitioned.[24] The researchers also found that low-perceived benefit components should be priced relatively low and vice versa. Consumers find a higher total price more acceptable when the high-benefit component is priced high than when the low-benefit component is priced high. For example, assume John joins a health club and swims at the club four times a month. John really enjoys working out and views being a member of the club as part of a healthy lifestyle (high value). He also swims after a workout once a week to unwind and relax. For John, swimming is not that important but is enjoyable (low value). If the club charges ₹1,600 a month dues and ₹200 per swim, John perceives this as acceptable. According to the research, John would find it less attractive if the monthly dues were ₹1,200 and each swim was ₹300. Yet the total cost is the same!

Consumer Penalties

More and more businesses are adopting **consumer penalties**—extra fees paid by consumers for violating the terms of a purchase agreement. Businesses impose consumer penalties for two reasons: They will allegedly (1) suffer an irrevocable revenue loss and/or (2) incur significant additional transaction costs

joint costs costs that are shared in the manufacturing and marketing of several products in a product line

product line pricing setting prices for an entire line of products

should customers be unable or unwilling to complete their purchase obligations. For the company, these customer payments are part of doing business in a highly competitive marketplace. With profit margins in many companies increasingly coming under pressure, organizations are looking to stem losses resulting from customers not meeting their obligations. However, the perceived unfairness of a penalty may affect some consumers' willingness to patronize a business in the future.

LO 4 Product Line Pricing

Product line pricing is setting prices for an entire line of products. Compared to setting the right price on a single product, product line pricing encompasses broader concerns. In product line pricing, the marketing manager tries to achieve maximum profits or other goals for the entire line rather than for a single component of the line.

Relationships among Products

The manager must first determine the type of relationship that exists among the various products in a line:

- If items are *complementary*, an increase in the sale of one good causes an increase in demand for the complementary product, and vice versa. For example, the sale of ski poles depends on the demand for skis, making these two items complementary.
- Two products in a line can also be *substitutes* for each other. If buyers buy one item in the line, they are less likely to buy a second item in the line.
- A *neutral* relationship can also exist between two products. In other words, demand for one of the products is unrelated to demand for the other.

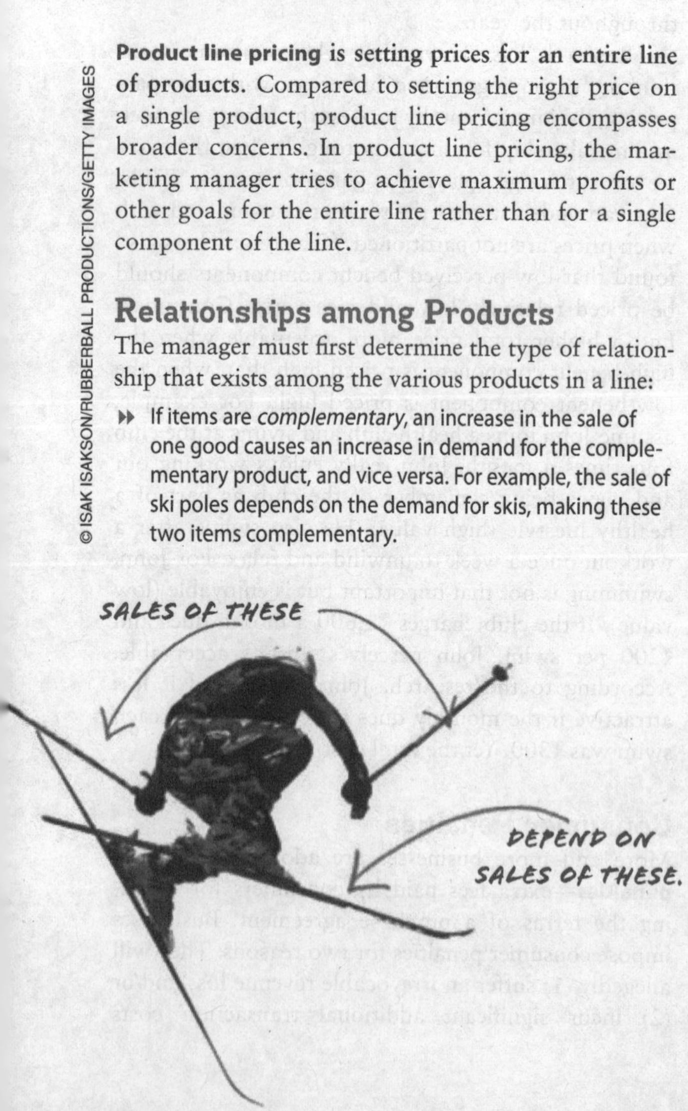

Joint Costs

Joint costs are costs that are shared in the manufacturing and marketing of several products in a product line. These costs pose a unique problem in product pricing (e.g., the production of CDs that combine photos and music).

Any assignment of joint costs must be somewhat subjective because costs are actually shared. Suppose a company produces two products, X and Y, in a common production process, with joint costs allocated on a weight basis. Product X weighs 500 kg, and product Y weighs 250 kg. Thus, costs are allocated on the basis of ₹100 for X for every ₹50 for Y. Gross margins (sales less the cost of goods sold) might then be as follows:

	Product X	Product Y	Total
Sales	₹20,000	₹6,000	₹26,000
Less cost of goods sold	15,000	7,500	22,500
Gross margin	₹ 5,000	(₹1,500)	₹ 3,500

This statement reveals a loss of ₹1,500 on product Y. However, the firm must realize that overall it earned a ₹3,500 profit on the two items in the line. Also, weight may not be the right way to allocate the joint costs. Instead, the firm might use other bases, including market value or quantity sold.

LO 5 Pricing during Difficult Economic Times

Pricing is always an important aspect of marketing, but it is especially crucial in times of inflation and recession. The firm that does not adjust to economic trends may lose ground that it can never make up.

Inflation

When the economy is characterized by high inflation, special pricing tactics are often necessary. They can be subdivided into cost-oriented and demand-oriented tactics.

Cost-Oriented Tactics One popular cost-oriented tactic is *culling products with a low profit margin* from the product line. However, this tactic may backfire for three reasons:

- A high volume of sales on an item with a low profit margin may still make the item highly profitable.
- Eliminating a product from a product line may reduce economies of scale, thereby lowering the margins on other items.
- Eliminating the product may affect the price-quality image of the entire line.

Another popular cost-oriented tactic is **delayed-quotation pricing**, which is used for industrial installations and many accessory items. Price is not set on the product until the item is either finished or delivered. Long production lead times force many firms to adopt this policy during periods of inflation. Builders of nuclear power plants, ships, airports, and office towers sometimes use delayed-quotation tactics.

Escalator pricing is similar to delayed-quotation pricing in that the final selling price reflects cost increases incurred between the time an order is placed and the time delivery is made. An escalator clause allows for price increases (usually across the board) based on the cost-of-living index or some other formula. As with any price increase, management's ability to implement such a policy is based on inelastic demand for the product. Often it is used only for extremely complex products that take a long time to produce or with new customers. Another tactic growing in popularity is to hold prices constant but add new fees.

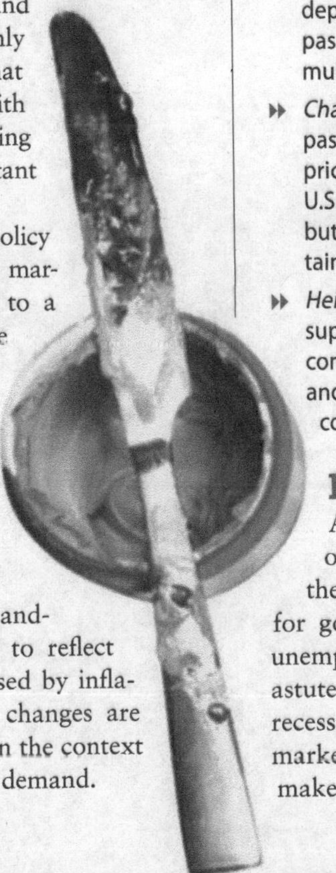

© MIKE KEMP/ RUBBERBALL/PHOTOLIBRARY

Any cost-oriented pricing policy that tries to maintain a fixed gross margin under all conditions can lead to a vicious circle. For example, a price increase will result in decreased demand, which in turn increases production costs (because of lost economies of scale). Increased production costs require a further price increase, leading to further diminished demand, and so on.

Demand-Oriented Tactics Demand-oriented pricing tactics use price to reflect changing patterns of demand caused by inflation or high interest rates. Cost changes are considered, of course, but mostly in the context of how increased prices will affect demand.

Price shading is the use of discounts by salespeople to increase demand for one or more products in a line. Often, shading becomes habitual and is done routinely without much forethought. To make the demand for a good or service more inelastic and to create buyer dependency, a company can use several strategies:

- *Cultivate selected demand:* Marketing managers can target prosperous customers who will pay extra for convenience or service. In cultivating close relationships with affluent organizational customers, marketing managers should avoid putting themselves at the mercy of a dominant firm. They can more easily raise prices when an account is readily replaceable. Finally, in companies where engineers exert more influence than purchasing departments do, performance is favored over price. Often a preferred vendor's pricing range expands if other suppliers prove technically unsatisfactory.
- *Create unique offerings:* Marketing managers should study buyers' needs. If the seller can design distinctive goods or services uniquely fitting buyers' activities, equipment, and procedures, a mutually beneficial relationship will evolve. By satisfying targeted buyers in a superior way, marketing managers can make them dependent. Cereal manufacturers have been able to pass along costs by marketing unique value-added or multi-ingredient cereals.
- *Change the package design:* Another way companies pass on higher costs is to shrink product sizes but keep prices the same. Skippy, a peanut butter brand in the U.S., added an inwardly curved bottom to its peanut butter packaging, reducing volume slightly, but maintaining the same price.[25]
- *Heighten buyer dependence:* Owens Corning Fiberglass supplies an integrated insulation service that includes commercial and scientific training for distributors and seminars for end users. This practice freezes out competition and supports higher prices.

Recession

As discussed in Chapter 4, a recession is a period of reduced economic activity, such as occurred in the United States in 2007–2009. Reduced demand for goods and services, along with higher rates of unemployment, is a common trait of a recession. Yet astute marketers can often find opportunity during recessions. A recession is an excellent time to build market share because competitors are struggling to make ends meet.

delayed-quotation pricing a price tactic used for industrial installations and many accessory items in which a firm price is not set until the item is either finished or delivered

escalator pricing a price tactic in which the final selling price reflects cost increases incurred between the time the order is placed and the time delivery is made

price shading the use of discounts by salespeople to increase demand for one or more products in a line

According to pricing strategy consultants Paul Hunt and Greg Thomas, using pricing research to adjust prices during a recession or difficult economic conditions can result in a profit improvement of 20 percent, sometimes more.[26]

Two effective pricing tactics to hold or build market share during a recession are value-based pricing and bundling. *Value-based pricing*, discussed earlier in the chapter, stresses to customers that they are getting a good value for their money.

Bundling or *unbundling* can also stimulate demand during a recession. If features are added to a bundle, consumers may perceive the offering as having greater value. Conversely, companies can unbundle offerings and lower base prices to stimulate demand.

Recessions are a good time for marketing managers to study the demand for individual items in a product line and the revenue they produce. Pruning unprofitable items can save resources to be better used elsewhere.

Prices often fall during a recession as competitors try desperately to maintain demand for their wares. Even if demand remains constant, falling prices mean lower profits or no profits. Falling prices, therefore, are a natural incentive to lower costs. During the past recession, companies implemented new technology to improve efficiency and then slashed payrolls. They also discovered that suppliers were an excellent source of cost savings; Specific strategies that companies use with suppliers include the following:

- *Renegotiating contracts:* Sending suppliers letters demanding price cuts of 5 percent or more; putting out for rebid the contracts of those that refuse to cut costs.
- *Offering help:* Dispatching teams of experts to suppliers' plants to help reorganize and suggest other productivity-boosting changes; working with suppliers to make parts simpler and cheaper to produce.
- *Keeping the pressure on:* To make sure that improvements continue, setting annual, across-the-board cost reduction targets, often of 5 percent or more a year.
- *Paring down suppliers:* To improve economies of scale, slashing the overall number of suppliers, sometimes by up to 80 percent, and boosting purchases from those that remain.

Review And Applications

Describe the procedure for setting the right price. The process of setting the right price on a product involves four major steps: (1) establishing pricing goals; (2) estimating demand, costs, and profits; (3) choosing a price policy to help determine a base price; and (4) fine-tuning the base price with pricing tactics.

A price strategy establishes a long-term pricing framework for a good or service. The three main types of price policies are price skimming, penetration pricing, and status quo pricing. A price-skimming policy charges a high introductory price, often followed by a gradual reduction. Penetration pricing offers a low introductory price to capture a large market share and attain economies of scale. Finally, status quo pricing strives to match competitors' price.

1.1 Ajay Shah, owner of a mid-priced dress shop, notes, "My pricing objectives are simple: I just charge what my competitors charge. I'm happy because I'm making money." React to Ajay's statement.

1.2 What is the difference between a price policy and a price tactic? Give an example.

Identify the legal and ethical constraints on pricing decisions. Government regulation helps monitor issues of pricing like price fixing, price discrimination, and predatory pricing. Appropriate provisions have been provided for keeping a check on such illegal pricing practices and protecting small businesses from large firms that operate efficiently on extremely thin profit margins. The Competition Act prohibits price fixing, which is an agreement between two or more firms on a particular price, price discrimination, which is the practice of charging different prices from different customers, and predatory pricing, in which a firm undercuts its competitors with extremely low prices to drive them out of business.

2.1 Have you ever been faced with any instance of price discrimination? If yes, share the incident with the rest of your batch mates.

Explain how discounts, geographic pricing, and other pricing tactics can be used to fine-tune the base price. Several techniques enable marketing managers to adjust prices within a general range in response to changes in competition, government regulation, consumer demand, and promotional and positioning goals. Techniques for fine-tuning a price can be divided into three main categories: discounts, allowances, rebates, and value-based pricing; geographic pricing; and other pricing tactics.

The first type of tactic gives lower prices to those that pay promptly, order a large quantity, or perform some function for the manufacturer. Value-based pricing starts with the customer, considers the competition and costs, and then determines a price. Additional tactics in this category include seasonal discounts, promotion allowances, rebates (cash refunds), zero percent financing, and markdown money.

Geographic pricing tactics—such as FOB origin pricing, uniform delivered pricing, zone pricing, freight absorption pricing, and basing-point pricing—are ways of moderating the impact of shipping costs on distant customers.

A variety of "other" pricing tactics stimulate demand for certain products, increase store patronage, and offer more merchandise at specific prices.

More and more customers are paying price penalties, which are extra fees for violating the terms of a purchase contract. The perceived fairness or unfairness of a penalty may affect some consumers' willingness to patronize a business in the future.

3.1 You are contemplating a price change for an established product sold by your firm. Write a memo analyzing the factors you need to consider in your decision.

3.3 Divide into teams of four persons. Each team should choose one of the following topics: skimming, penetration pricing, status quo pricing, price fixing, geographic pricing, adopting a single-price tactic, flexible pricing, or professional services pricing. Each team should then pick a retailer that it feels most closely follows the team's chosen pricing strategy. Go to the store and write down examples of the strategy. Interview the store manager and get his or her views on the advantages and disadvantages of the strategy. Each team should then make an oral report in class.

3.5 How is the "information age" changing the nature of pricing?

3.6 Have you ever paid a price penalty? How did it affect your attitude toward that company?

3.7 Imagine that you are a marketing manager for a mid-sized amusement park. You have attended an industry-wide meeting where a colleague gave a talk about new pricing strategies for amusement parks. You were very motivated by the seminar. On your return to work, write a memo to your boss outlining the pros and cons of the new pricing strategy. End your memo with a recommendation either for or against à la carte pricing of attractions (pricing each attraction separately rather than charging a single high entrance fee).

Discuss product line pricing. Product line pricing maximizes profits for an entire product line. When setting product line prices, marketing managers determine what type of relationship exists among the products in the line: complementary, substitute, or neutral. Managers also consider joint (shared) costs among products in the same line.

4.1 Develop a price line strategy for each of these firms:

a. a college bookstore

b. a restaurant

c. a video rental firm

Describe the role of pricing during periods of inflation and recession. Marketing managers employ cost-oriented and demand-oriented tactics during periods of economic inflation. Cost-oriented tactics include dropping products with a low profit margin, using delayed-quotation pricing and escalator pricing, and adding fees. Demand-oriented pricing methods include price shading and increasing demand through cultivating selected customers, creating unique offerings, changing the package size, and heightening buyer dependence.

To stimulate demand during a recession, marketers use value-based pricing, bundling, unbundling, and making strong promotional claims while avoiding discounting. Recessions are also a good time to prune unprofitable items from product lines. Managers strive to cut costs during recessions in order to maintain profits as revenues decline. Implementing new technology, cutting payrolls, and pressuring suppliers for reduced prices are common techniques used to cut costs. Companies also create new value-added products.

5.1 During a recession, what pricing strategies would you consider using to gain or maintain market share? Explain your answer.

5.2 The recent recession of 2008 took the world by surprise. Though the major impact was felt in the United States, India also felt the heat of this economic downturn. As a result, pricing became an issue for many consumers looking to save every possible penny. This was also true in areas where saving money isn't a common occurrence, like fashion retailers. Search the online archives of a business daily to find an article about pricing during a recession.

Exercises

APPLICATION EXERCISE

You read in the chapter about the dangers of pricing products too low. It seems so obviously wrong, but do companies really price their products so low that they won't make any money? After all, companies are in business to make money, and if they don't, they're probably not in business for very long. Let's take a deeper look at the effects of pricing products too low or creating too deep discounts during sale periods.[27]

Activity

1. The average markup for a produce department is 28 percent on selling price. When sold at 28 percent markup on selling price, bananas usually account for 25 percent of department sales and 25 percent of department markup. This week, because bananas were on special sale at the retailer's cost, the department sold twice as many dozen of bananas as usual. However, they were sold at zero markup. If all other things remain the same, what is the average markup on selling price for the entire produce department this week?

ETHICS EXERCISE

People feel better when they think they are getting a great bargain when they shop. Knowing this, some retailers mark up items above the traditional retail price and then offer a 60 percent discount. If they had simply discounted the normal retail price by 20 percent the resulting "sale price" would have been the same. One retailer says that he is just making shoppers happy that they got a great deal when he inflates the retail price before discounting.

Questions

1. What do you think?
2. Does the AMA Statement of Ethics address this issue? Go to **www.marketingpower.com** and review the statement. Then, write a brief paragraph summarizing what the AMA Code of Ethics contains that relates to retail pricing.

MARKETING PLAN EXERCISE

For continued general assistance on business plans and marketing plans, visit **www.bplans.com** or **http://www.businessplans.org**. You can also refer to Appendix 1 of Chapter 2 for marketing plan check-list items related to pricing decisions. Once you've worked through this marketing plan exercise, you can complete the Part 6 Marketing Planning Worksheet on your companion Web site at **www.cengage.com/international**. Continue the pricing stage of the strategic planning process for your chosen company with following exercises:

1. What price policy should your firm use? Are there any legal implications of this choice? Will there be differences in on-line versus off-line pricing policies? Are these differences related to your cost structure in the on-line environment? Why? Are these differences legal?
2. Note how easy it is to compare prices on the Internet. Check out price comparison sites such as **www.naaptol.com.** Given how products and prices are displayed, how can your offering show a differential advantage if there is a price difference? As prices reach parity on the Internet, how else will you differentiate your products or services?
3. What kinds of price discounts can your company offer? Should discounted prices be offered to online buyers that off-line buyers do not receive? Why might you charge your online customers less than your off-line customers?
4. As you work on the Internet component of your marketing plan, you must decide how to set geographic pricing policies. Will you appear as a nongeographic specific Internet provider and offer the same shipping costs to all, or will you have to charge more for longer distances? Will you market your product or services locally, regionally, or nationally? Just because you are on the Internet, does that mean you have to try to serve all markets? Explain.

Short Case: AKASH TABLET

Prepared by
Dr. Dheeraj Sharma,
Indian Institute of Management, Ahmedabad

The Cheapest Tablet in the World

Datawind, a British Company, unveiled the cheapest tablet in the world called Aakash on October 5, 2011, in India. Datawind manufactured this product as a tie-up with the Indian Government. Aakash was launched in collaboration with IIT Rajasthan, as a part of the HRD Ministry's National Mission on *Education Through Information and Communication Technology* (NME-ICT), under the governance of Minister Kapil Sibal. The Indian Government had floated tenders for low-cost ICT equipment, and it was won by Datawind.

Aakash boasts a 7-inch touchscreen, with a 2GB internal memory and an expandable memory of 32GB. This device provides Internet connection via GPRS or WiFi, based on Android OS 2.2, has a 3 hour battery life, and comes with a warranty of one year. The tablet does not have a camera and it can not facilitate making calls. The cost of Aakash tablet is low because the hardware components used are obtained at the cheapest prices possible. The hardware of Aakash/Ubislate Tablet has been assembled from South Korea, China, India, U.S., and a few other countries.

Aakash was sold to the Government at ₹2,250, which was further subsidized by the Government of India and made available to the students at ₹1,200. Indian Government promised Datawind a purchase of one lakh units of Aakash tablets. These tablets were to be made available to the students free of cost in the pilot phase. Simultaneously, Datawind also launched a commercial version of the tablet called Ubislate7 at ₹2,999 for other consumers. Datawind did set the right price for Aakash, but major drawbacks were notified by the customers. Complaints such as dim and unresponsive screen display, slow processor, short battery life, and heating up of the unit were made.[28]

The shortcomings of the tablet are an effect of the cheap hardware components. Datawind has announced that it is coming up with upgraded models, Aakash II and Ubislate7+ in the first quarter 2012, which will overcome issues found in the first model.[29]

Datawind did not introduce Aakash and Ubislate to compete with companies like Apple and Samsung that produced high-end PCs and tablets. Datawind's aim was to provide basic ITC equipment that would give Internet access to the people at the Bottom of the Pyramid. Akash was produced with an aim of bridging the digital divide between the rich and the poor. Aakash's target customers are those who cannot afford expensive ICT equipment.

Datawind, by setting the right price suitable to the Indian low income groups, has made itself a pioneer in the rural tablet/PC market. All the shortcomings in Aakash are significant, if one compares them with the high-end models. However, it is an introductory

OS to those who have not had access to a PC before. All of the above mentioned shortcomings don't really matter to them.

Mr Suneet Singh Tuli, CEO, Datawind said to *DNA News Daily*, "I am not competing with the high-end products in the market. I feel that by hitting the right price points we will be able to capture a larger market,"[30]

Questions

1. Should Datawind compromise on the quality of Aakash to provide it at a low price?
2. Should Aakash increase the price of its tablet and provide an upgraded model?
3. Do you think a higher priced and an upgraded version of Aakash/Ubislate will fetch more customers?

CHAPTER REVIEW

20 Setting the Right Price

KEY TERMS

LO 1

price strategy a basic, long-term pricing framework that establishes the initial price for a product and the intended direction for price movements over the product life cycle

price skimming a pricing policy whereby a firm charges a high introductory price, often coupled with heavy promotion

penetration pricing a pricing policy whereby a firm charges a relatively low price for a product initially as a way to reach the mass market

status quo pricing charging a price identical to or very close to the competition's price

LO 2

price fixing an agreement between two or more firms on the price they will charge for a product

price discrimination the practice of charging different prices from different buyers

predatory pricing the practice of charging a very low price for a product with the intent of driving competitors out of business or out of a market

LO 3

base price the general price level at which the company expects to sell the good or service

quantity discount a price reduction offered to buyers buying in multiple units or above a specified dollar amount

cumulative quantity discount a deduction from list price that applies to the buyer's total purchases made during a specific period

KEY CONCEPTS

LO 1 **Describe the procedure for setting the right price.** The process of setting the right price on a product involves four major steps: (1) establishing pricing goals; (2) estimating demand, costs, and profits; (3) choosing a price policy to help determine a base price; and (4) fine-tuning the base price with pricing tactics.

A price strategy establishes a long-term pricing framework for a good or service. The three main types of price policies are price skimming, penetration pricing, and status quo pricing. A price-skimming policy charges a high introductory price, often followed by a gradual reduction. Penetration pricing offers a low introductory price to capture a large market share and attain economies of scale. Finally, status quo pricing strives to match competitors' price.

LO 2 **Identify the legal and ethical constraints on pricing decisions.** Government regulation helps monitor issues of pricing like price fixing, price discrimination, and predatory pricing. Appropriate provisions have been provided for keeping a check on such illegal pricing practices and protecting small businesses from large firms that operate efficiently on extremely thin profit margins. The Competition Act prohibits price fixing, which is an agreement between two or more firms on a particular price, price discrimination, which is the practice of charging different prices from different customers, and predatory pricing, in which a firm undercuts its competitors with extremely low prices to drive them out of business.

LO 3 **Explain how discounts, geographic pricing, and other pricing tactics can be used to fine-tune the base price.** Several techniques enable marketing managers to adjust prices within a general range in response to changes in competition, government regulation, consumer demand, and promotional and positioning goals. Techniques for fine-tuning a price can be divided into three main categories: discounts, allowances, rebates, and value-based pricing; geographic pricing; and other pricing tactics.

The first type of tactic gives lower prices to those that pay promptly, order a large quantity, or perform some function for the manufacturer. Value-based pricing starts with the customer, considers the competition and costs, and then determines a price. Additional tactics in this category include seasonal discounts, promotion allowances, rebates (cash refunds), zero percent financing, and markdown money.

Geographic pricing tactics—such as FOB origin pricing, uniform delivered pricing, zone pricing, freight absorption pricing, and basing-point pricing—are ways of moderating the impact of shipping costs on distant customers.

A variety of "other" pricing tactics stimulate demand for certain products, increase store patronage, and offer more merchandise at specific prices.

More and more customers are paying price penalties, which are extra fees for violating the terms of a purchase contract. The perceived fairness or unfairness of a penalty may affect some consumers' willingness to patronize a business in the future.

LO 4 **Discuss product line pricing.** Product line pricing maximizes profits for an entire product line. When setting product line prices, marketing managers determine what type of relationship exists among the products in the line: complementary, substitute, or neutral. Managers also consider joint (shared) costs among products in the same line.

noncumulative quantity discount a deduction from list price that applies to a single order rather than to the total volume of orders placed during a certain period

cash discount a price reduction offered to a consumer, an industrial user, or a marketing intermediary in return for prompt payment of a bill

functional discount (trade discount) a discount to wholesalers and retailers for performing channel functions

seasonal discount a price reduction for buying merchandise out of season

promotional allowance (trade allowance) a payment to a dealer for promoting the manufacturer's products

rebate a cash refund given for the purchase of a product during a specific period

value-based pricing setting the price at a level that seems to the customer to be a good price compared to the price of other options

FOB origin pricing a price tactic that requires the buyer to absorb the freight costs from the shipping point ("free on board")

uniform delivered pricing a price tactic in which the seller pays the actual freight charges and bills every purchaser an identical, flat freight charge

zone pricing a modification of uniform delivered pricing that divides the United States (or the total market) into segments or zones and charges a flat freight rate to all customers in a given zone

freight absorption pricing a price tactic in which the seller pays all or part of the actual freight charges and does not pass them on to the buyer

basing-point pricing a price tactic that charges freight from a given (basing) point, regardless of the city from which the goods are shipped

single-price tactic a price tactic that offers all goods and services at the same price (or perhaps two or three prices)

LO 5 **Describe the role of pricing during periods of inflation and recession.** Marketing managers employ cost-oriented and demand-oriented tactics during periods of economic inflation. Cost-oriented tactics include dropping products with a low profit margin, using delayed-quotation pricing and escalator pricing, and adding fees. Demand-oriented pricing methods include price shading and increasing demand through cultivating selected customers, creating unique offerings, changing the package size, and heightening buyer dependence.

To stimulate demand during a recession, marketers use value-based pricing, bundling, unbundling, and making strong promotional claims while avoiding discounting. Recessions are also a good time to prune unprofitable items from product lines. Managers strive to cut costs during recessions in order to maintain profits as revenues decline. Implementing new technology, cutting payrolls, and pressuring suppliers for reduced prices are common techniques used to cut costs. Companies also create new value-added products.

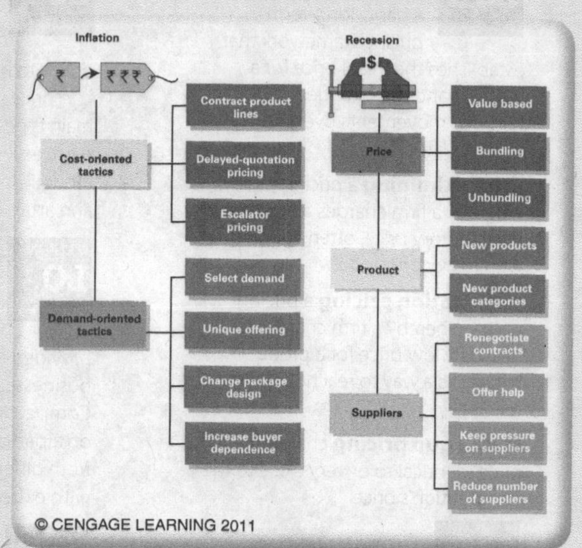

flexible pricing (variable pricing) a price tactic in which different customers pay different prices for essentially the same merchandise bought in equal quantities

price lining the practice of offering a product line with several items at specific price points

leader pricing (loss-leader pricing) a price tactic in which a product is sold near or even below cost in the hope that shoppers will buy other items once they are in the store

bait pricing a price tactic that tries to get consumers into a store through false or misleading price advertising and then uses high-pressure selling to persuade consumers to buy more expensive merchandise

odd–even pricing (psychological pricing) a price tactic that uses odd-numbered prices to connote bargains and even-numbered prices to imply quality

price bundling marketing two or more products in a single package for a special price

unbundling reducing the bundle of services that comes with the basic product

two-part pricing a price tactic that charges two separate amounts to consume a single good or service

consumer penalty an extra fee paid by the consumer for violating the terms of the purchase agreement

LO 4 **product line pricing** setting prices for an entire line of products

joint costs costs that are shared in the manufacturing and marketing of several products in a product line

LO 5 **delayed-quotation pricing** a price tactic used for industrial installations and many accessory items in which a firm price is not set until the item is either finished or delivered

escalator pricing a price tactic in which the final selling price reflects cost increases incurred between the time the order is placed and the time delivery is made

price shading the use of discounts by salespeople to increase demand for one or more products in a line

CASE 6

Modernization of Fair Price Shops: A Case of Gujarat

S K Nanda was evaluating the efforts on modernizing fair price shops (FPSs) in Gujarat. As Principal Secretary, Civil Supplies, Government of Gujarat, he had undertaken an initiative to make FPSs as the major retailing arm of the government. With 16,000 outlets in the state, they were by far the largest chain of stores that reached the grassroots that was not being serviced by any properly organized system. The exercise that began in 2004 had been implemented in 4,000 outlets across the state. The results were positive but all FPS stores were not performing as expected. Nanda was pondering over the report that highlighted the short comings. He was soon to be transferred to another department and hence he was also evaluating the sustainability of the changes brought about because of his initiative.

C6.1 Evolution of Public Distribution System (PDS)

The public distribution system (PDS) had its origins in rationing that was implemented by the British during the Second World War. The rationing and, subsequently PDS had played a crucial role in attaining a higher level of food security and completely eliminated the threats of famine. In the rationing system the British government distributed fixed quantity of cereals. The system was started in 1939 in Bombay and subsequently extended to other cities and towns. By the end of 1943, 13 cities had been brought under rationing and by 1946 as many as 771 cities/towns were covered. Some rural areas suffering from chronic food shortage were also included.

The Department of Food under the Government of India was created in 1942, which helped in food matters getting the serious attention of the government. When the war ended, India, like many other countries, decided to abolish the rationing system in 1943. However, just after independence, India was forced to reintroduce it in 1950 in the face of renewed inflationary pressures in the economy "which were accentuated by the already prevailing high global prices of food grains at the end of the War, which was around four times higher than the pre-war prices".[1] Public distribution of foodgrains was a well thought out social policy to smoothen the path of economic development. It was part of a plan to bring the poor and needy section of the society onto a path of growth and development through food security. While in the first five year plan the system was essentially urban, it was extended subsequently to all rural areas which suffered from chronic food shortages. There were two variants of the system. Firstly there were statutory rationing areas where foodgrains were supposed to be available through ration shops only. Secondly in non-statutory ration areas such shops supplemented open market availability. However, the system remained highly urban and by the end of the first five year plan it was losing its relevance due to adequate food stocks. This encouraged the government to abandon procurement of foodgrains and remove all restrictions on private trading. But the scenario changed quickly as production of foodgrains dropped and immediately, the government intervened to check its trading. Essential commodities like sugar, cooking coal, and kerosene were added to the basket. There was also a rapid increase in the number of ration shops (now being increasingly called fair price shops (**FPS**s). Their number went up from 18,000 in 1957 to 51,000 in 1961. By the end of the second five year plan, PDS had changed from a typical rationing system to a social safety system, making available foodgrains at a 'fair price' so that access of households to foodgrains could be improved and such distribution could keep a check on the speculative tendencies in the market.

The concept of bufferstocks was incorporated in the food policy and Food Corporation of India (FCI) and the Agricultural Prices Commission (APC) were created in 1965 to consolidate PDS. All through the ups and downs of Indian agriculture, PDS continued as a well thought out social policy of the government with the objectives of providing foodgrains and other essential items to vulnerable sections of the society at

Written by Professor Piyush Kumar Sinha, Indian Institute of Management, Ahmedabad, Dr. Sanjay Kumar Kar, GIPM, Gandhinagar and Siddharth Jaiswal, PGP-ABM (2006-08), Indian Institute of Management, Ahmedabad.

[1] B M Bhatia, *Food Security in South Asia,* Oxford & IBH 1985.

reasonable (subsidized) prices; having a moderating influence on the open market prices of cereals, the distribution of which constitutes a fairly big share of the total marketable surplus; and attempting socialization in the matter of distribution of essential commodities.[2]

Through PDS, the beneficiaries received two cereals (rice and wheat) and four essential commodities (sugar, edible oil, soft coke, and kerosene). However, the state governments had the option of adding other essential commodities like pulses, salt, candles, matchboxes, ordinary clothes, school textbooks/copies, and the like. In order to fasten supervision, the state governments had set up Civil Supplies Departments or Essential Commodities Corporations to provide such items at a subsidized rate through PDS. Making available essential commodities (rice, wheat, sugar, edible oil, soft coke, and kerosene oil) to state governments was the responsibility of the central government. (See Exhibit C6.1 for description of commodities made available through PDS.)

EXHIBIT C6.1

Essential Commodities Supply and Sales through PDS

Sugar	The central government, under the provisions of the Essential Commodities Act, fixes a levy percentage and accordingly every sugar factory has to deliver a percentage of production to the government. The state government lifts from the nominated factories at a pre-fixed price (which is based on the minimum support price paid by the factories to sugarcane farmers) and arranges to sell it through PDS. Non-levy or free sale sugar can be sold in the open market at the prevailing market price.
Edible Oil	In the early days of PDS, distribution of edible oil was important. But gradually with time, its usage by people has decreased considerably. However, the government has still retained the option of importing and supplying it through PDS if the situation so warrants. Of late, many states have started the distribution of fortified edible oil though PDS. Fortification could provide additional nutritional value and also indirectly could reduce or stop diversion.
Soft Coke	Soft coke was allotted to state governments from the stocks held by the public sector coal companies. As this was a cost effective medium for cooking for very poor households, it was sold at substantially subsidized rates. As and when the areas were covered by distribution of LPG, the allocation of soft coke to states was reduced.
Kerosene	Kerosene was used both as lighting and cooking medium by poor households in urban areas and as lighting material in interior rural areas. Supply to the state governments, on the basis of allocations made by the central government, was arranged by the public sector oil companies either from domestic production or through imports. It was also sold at subsidized rates. When large scale diversion of PDS kerosene was detected blue colour was added to it to differentiate it from kerosene sold in the open market.
Rice and Wheat	Food Corporation of India (FCI) was established to procure and distribute foodgrains such as rice and wheat. Foodgrains were largely procured from the domestic market. Imports were occasional and in small quantities. Stocks built by FCI were utilized both for allocations to state governments for distribution through PDS and maintaining a national buffer.

PDS in Gujarat

In order to reform and improve PDS by focusing on the poor and needy sections of society, the government launched of the targeted public distribution system (TPDS). The objective was to identify persons/families living below poverty line (BPL) and issue a distinct ration card for selling specified cereal items through PDS outlets at specially subsidized rates, viz. half the normal issue price under PDS. Under the scheme each BPL family was entitled to get 25 kg of foodgrains a month (See Exhibit C6.2 for the distribution of ration card holders in Gujarat).

The government of Gujarat (GoG) distributed wheat, rice, sugar, and edible oil in fixed quantum and at fixed prices through fair price shops to ration card holders. The government of India allotted wheat and

[2] http://www.fao.org/docrep/x0172e/x0172e06.htm#P1406_137724

EXHIBIT C6.2

Ration Cards in Gujarat (as of June 1, 2006)

	Name of District/City	BPL	AAY	APL	Total
1	Ahmedabad City	86061	17879	762221	866161
2	Ahmedabad Dist	95056	24267	450518	569841
3	Amreli	89643	27129	256213	372985
4	Banaskantha	140763	30895	343630	515288
5	Bharuch	113672	21790	171471	306933
6	Bhavnagar	143344	23974	457116	624434
7	Dang	27344	4518	8588	40450
8	Gandhinagar	60461	15809	203198	279468
9	Panchamahal	156707	28976	200248	385931
10	Junagadh	107077	29319	449154	585550
11	Jamanagar	93010	17777	375167	485954
12	Kheda	133315	42929	242748	418992
13	Kutch	137431	28963	230123	396517
14	Mehsana	65219	12262	363826	441307
15	Rajkot	129815	27276	813677	970768
16	Sabarkantha	212196	25385	220508	458089
17	Surat	259941	42999	824616	1127556
18	Surendranagar	105218	18791	277981	401990
19	Valsad	91871	24570	185801	302242
20	Vadodara	159700	47688	619693	827081
21	Patan	74941	16679	201663	293283
22	Anand	130246	27494	238451	396191
23	Dahod	52375	24862	158883	236120
24	Narmada	47477	16216	39007	102700
25	Navasari	102926	44534	120239	267699
26	Prbandar	35405	8489	97695	141589
	Total	**2851214**	**651470**	**8312435**	**11815119**

SOURCE: Food, Fuel and Fortification: Securing our Future, FCSCA, p.27

rice to the state for distribution under TPDS since June 1997. Foodgrains were lifted from Food Corporation of India (FCI) depots by the Gujarat State Civil Supplies Corporation on behalf of the state government and distributed under TPDS.

In order to provide maximum benefit to the targeted families, the state government implemented the Antyodaya Anna Yojana in July, 2001. All the beneficiaries were categorized into: Above Poverty Line (APL) families, having annual income above ₹11000; Below Poverty Line (BPL) families, having annual income of ₹11000 or less; and the poorest of poor families among BPL families (see Exhibit C6.3).

Above the Poverty Line (APL): There was a scheme of distributing foodgrains to families living above the poverty line during specific times and especially in times of natural disasters. Under this scheme, wheat was distributed at the rate of 5 kg per head and 25 kg maximum per card per month at ₹7.00 per kg. Rice was distributed at the rate of 2.5 kg per head and 10 kg maximum per card per month at ₹10.00 per kg

EXHIBIT C6.3

Level of Assistance

No	Scheme	Commodity	Distribution (Per Person) (Kg.)	Distribution (Per Card) (Kg.)	Distribution Price/Kg. (₹)
1.	Y	Wheat	9	28.0	2.00
		Rice	9	7.0	3.00
2.	BPL	Wheat	1.5	9.0	2.00
		Rice	1.0	3.5	3.00
		Sugar	0.5	9	13.50
3.	BPL (SP)	Wheat		5.0	5.00
		Rice		2.5	6.75
4.	PL	Wheat	5.0	25.0	7.00
		Rice	2.5	10.0	10.00

SOURCE: Department of Civil Supplies, GOG

to APL card holders. This scheme covered 74.95 lakh families in the state. Under this scheme during the year 2002-03, the state government distributed 23377 tons of wheat and 10,853 tons of rice, while during the year 2003–04 (April–November, 2003), the GoG had distributed 13,921 tons of wheat and 6,857 tons of rice in April–November 2003.

Below the Poverty Line (BPL): BPL ration cards were issued to families identified by the rural development and urban development department and issued by the concerned inspector/gram panchayat. Under this scheme, wheat was distributed at the rate of 1.5 kg per head and 9 kg maximum per card per month at ₹2 per kg. Rice was distributed at the rate of 1 kg per head and 3.5 kg maximum per card per month at ₹3 per kg to BPL card holders. This scheme covered 32.78 lakh families in the state. Under this scheme during 2002-03, the state government distributed 301580 tons of wheat and 131046 tonnes of rice at subsidized rates and in April–November 2003, the government distributed 188148 tons of wheat and 82089 tons of rice at subsidized rates.

Antyodaya Anna Yojana (AAY): This was a centrally sponsored scheme with special attention given to the poorest of the poor. The beneficiary families were entitled to 25 to 35 kg of rice per month at a highly subsidized rate. As per the directives of the government of India, the state government had identified 3.25 lakh families out of BPL families. The scheme was under implementation since July 2001 under which 28 kg wheat at ₹2 per kg and 7 kg rice at ₹3 per kg were distributed per card per month. Under this scheme, 48,930 tons of wheat and 12,104 tons of rice were distributed during year 2002–3 and 44,958 tons of wheat and 10,387 tonnes of rice during April–November 2003.

Commission Structure

Fair price shop owners lifted their allotted stocks from FCI godowns in their *taluka* and were paid commission based on the distance between their shop and the FCI godown. There was special commission, in addition to normal commission, for FPS operated by cooperative associations and tribal cooperatives. Exhibit C6.4 provides the commission structure of the Gujarat government for FPS. Turnover of FPSs had declined considerably because of the restrictions on sale of other types of products. There was hardly any scope to improve the business. This had threatened the economic viability of these shops. It was estimated that average earnings of an FPS not be more than ₹2,000 a month. Such low earning increased the possibility of malpractices by the owners and encouraged leakages and diversions of PDS commodities to the open market. Lack of assured supply and variety of goods and poor services also contributed to low satisfaction level of the customers. It was also inconvenient for the rural poor to travel to nearby town to get other items of necessity which are not sold by FPS.

EXHIBIT C6.4

Commission Paid to FPS in Gujarat [per 100 kg.]

Location of FPS shop and distance from the Godown	Wheat			Rice			Additional Commission (%)
	Retail Price (₹/Quintal)	Commission (₹/Quintal)	Godown Price (₹/Quintal)	Retail Price (₹/Quintal)	Commission (₹/Quintal)	Godown Price (₹/Quintal)	
Municipal Corporation Area	200	33.25	166.75	300	33.25	266.75	4.75
Shops in the Godown Village Area	200	31.5	168.5	300	31.5	268.5	4.5
10Km	200	35	165	300	35	265	5
11-25 Km	200	36.75	163.25	300	36.75	263.25	5.25
26-50Km	200	40.25	159.75	300	40.25	259.75	5.75
>50Km	200	42	158	300	42	258	6
Special Commission							
Cooperative association	200	1.75		300	1.75		0.5
Tribal cooperative	200	3.5		300	3.5		0.5

Note: Here retail price is the price at which BPL and AYY cardholders bought rice and wheat.
SOURCE: Deputy Collector, Kheda

Modernization of FPS in Gujarat

The public distribution network was believed to be the largest distribution machinery in the state with over 16,000 FPSs operating across Gujarat. It covered both rural and urban areas. Despite having a widespread network, the system could not achieve desirable outcomes. There were real concerns over the operational efficiency of the PDS machinery. There were discrepancies and irregularities in distribution of rationed products. One of the important and critical concerns was diversion of essential commodities from the FPS. The poor bore the brunt of an inefficient PDS. Nanda was confident that this huge network could play a more meaningful role if only the system was able to ensure availability of foodgrains and necessity articles for poor households.

The structure and operations of PDS needed revamping in order to make more efficient and effective. Foremost, there was an immediate need to bring changes in the regulations of PDS. Nanda was exploring the possibility of introducing innovative ideas such as modernizing FPS, fortification of items sold under FPS, introduction of smart cards, food credit/debit cards, and making FPS a brand.

Stop Large Scale Diversion One of the primary objectives of the revamping expense was to minimize the large scale diversion in PDS. According to a Planning Commission report, diversion at the national level was found to be of the order of 36 per cent in wheat, 31 per cent in rice, and 23 per cent in sugar. The diversion was more in northern, eastern, and north eastern regions compared to southern and western regions. Diversion was estimated to be as high as 64 per cent in rice in Bihar and Assam, while in the case of wheat the diversion went up to 100 per cent in Nagaland. Diversion was estimated to be less in the case of sugar. Diversion was much lower in Gujarat compared to states in the northern region. The Department of Civil Supplies, of the Gujarat government wanted to stop diversion by offering additional source of income to FPS owners.

Providing Financial Security for Owners In the emerging economic and social structure, it was felt that FPS owners were not able to make adequate money by strictly following legal means in their business. Earning more money through diversion was an easy carrot for them. So the department felt that by providing financial incentives at least a part of the diversion and large scale irregularities therein could be checked. The financial security would act as an incentive as well as a deterrent for carrying any further malpractices. Essentially there was a need for assuring the owners that they could stay in the business and earn a reasonable profit.

Improving Social Status Usually FPS owners were treated as inferior to independent shop owners in the same locality. The inferiority complex was a serious hindrance to their growth. The Department was determined to install confidence, belief, and above all the feeling of ownership among FPS owners. In a sense that would enhance their social acceptance.

Optimal Use of PDS PDS was a widely distributed system that connected each and every nook and corner of the state (see Exhibit C6.5). The state had over 14,131 FPSs which had the potential to become the largest retail network in the state with unparallel bargaining power. The network could easily be transformed into a chain of modern retail outlets (each outlet could be minimum 400 square feet) having total retail space of over 5.6 million square feet.

Capacity Building through Training It was necessary to build capability among the shop owners to upgrade and efficiently run FPSs. For this, employees/owners required basic training in retail store operations, customer management, and building fruitful relationship with suppliers. In the long run, training on information system management (MIS) and application of MIS would also be required for better management of their resources.

EXHIBIT C6.5

A Typical PDS Shop Before the Modernization Programme

C6.2 Model Fair Price Shops: Initiatives by the Government

The fortification initiative was in essence a risk mitigation drive to tackle political, socio-cultural, and economic risk associated with the system. Everyone knew about the leakages in the system. Fortification came as an easy conduit to minimize the leakages.

The Gujarat government started the fortification programme to address food quality and prevent malnutrition among the masses. Every year in India more than 24 lakh children and 132000 mothers die because of malnutrition, underweight, or poor nutrition. Productivity loss because of micro nutrient deficiency was calculated to be around US $900 million each year. The Prevention of Food Adulteration Act had no provision for micronutrient management for wheat flour or oil. Hence the only strategy left was to convert it into a national programme by implementation.

In oil, fortification was done by adding pre-mixed vitamins A and D in oil at 30 degrees temperature after crushing. It was then sold in packs from 500 g to 10 kg. Normal storage and cooking did not degrade the content and the cost of fortification was only 3 paise per kg according to the calculation of the Saurashtra Oil Millers Association. Oil was not a major commodity in PDS systems except during festivals.

In Gujarat, annual wheat consumption was about 4 lakh tons of which around 30,000 tons were routed through PDS. A Gujarat based company was asked to prepare the fortification mix which was then packed in sacks of 10 kg each by about 30 major and more than 40 mini flour mills by voluntary effort and support of district officials. Addition of 30 mg/kg of iron entailed an expenditure of ₹4 for every metric ton of wheat. The fortified wheat sacks displayed a new logo indicating fortified with pre-mixed iron and folic acid. As per the standards fixed by experts, 1 kg milled wheat yielded 970 grams of flour. The conversion cost per kg of wheat including sifting, cleaning, shifting, milling, packaging, and branding of fortified goods was 75 paise per kg. Wheat was distributed for government programmes like ICDS, MDM, Tribal Hostels, Social Welfare Institutions, and other government run nutrition programmes. It was estimated by the Civil Supplies Department that 1 kg of wheat could feed

15 children and 10 adults. The fortification cost came to around 6.3 paise per child and 10 paise per adult.

The effort yielded good results and Gujarat could reduce the diversion by a significant 50 per cent. Exhibit C6.6 shows the extent of diversion in various states and union territories. The department arranged workshops and fairs to create much needed awareness about the benefits of fortification. It also made a film starring Shahrukh Khan, a leading film actor, to promote the fortification programme.

EXHIBIT C6.6

State and National Level Diversion (After Fortification in Gujarat)

Name of State/UT	Estimated Diversion (%)		
	Wheat	Rice	Sugar
Northern Region			
Delhi	53	53	25
Haryana	53	44	28
Himachal Pradesh	47	18	8
Jammu & Kashmir	28	29	28
Punjab	69	40	6
Uttar Pradesh	46	49	36
Western Region			
Goa	23	28	6
Gujarat	23	21	18
Maharashtra	26	30	22
Madhya Pradesh	20	24	32
Rajasthan	31	36	17
Southeastern Region			
Andhra Pradesh	15	19	16
Karnataka	30	18	19
Kerala	28	23	25
Tamil Nadu	24	33	28
Eastern Region			
Bihar	44	64	47
Orissa	39	54	28
Sikkim	52	21	41
West Bengal	40	34	24
Northe Region			
Arunachal Pradesh	47	56	23
Assam	61	19	37
Manipur	48	19	37
Meghalaya	62	54	39
Mizoram	63	54	41
Nagaland	100	46	24
Tripura	27	33	13
Union Territories			
Chandigarh	24	12	35
Dadra & Nagar Haveli	18	7	26
Daman & Diu	40	38	13
Pondicherry	40	20	39
National Level	**36**	**31**	**23**

Source: Public Distribution System & Food Security, Chapter 8, Planning Commission

Setting up Model FPS The government had taken a decision to open one FPS for a population of 2000 in rural areas and 5000 in urban areas. While preparing the list, it ensured that a customer should not travel more than 3 km to visit a FPS. That meant these shops had to be easily accessible and convenient. The innovative concept of a Fair Price Shop Model Centre was introduced by the GoG to help shopkeepers improve and establish higher level of accountability and attract customers in larger numbers (see Exhibit C6.7). In order to facilitate the remodelling process of FPS, the Department of Civil Supplies took several critical and important initiatives. Some of those are presented below:

1. Changes in the succession laws were made so that the FPS licence could be passed on to the heir of the owner. This was expected to create a sense of belonging to FPS shopowners who till now were indifferent to refurbish and/or improve their shops.

EXHIBIT C6.7

Shelf Presentation at a Model FPS

2 Consumer products like cosmetics, non-subsidized gas cylinders, mobile phone recharge vouchers, SIM cards, postal supplies, fertilizers, certified seeds, toiletries, detergents, and courier facilities were proposed to be sold through FPSs. Even banks were tapped for spreading their credit net and use FPSs as links for financial products. In some cases, even fresh vegetables were allowed to be sold through FPS.

3 Selling these items not only ensured improved financial benefits for the owners but also ensured that shops were kept open throughout the year. These shops remained closed for most part of the month barring few days when foodgrains arrived.

4 To attract more customers, model FPSs required facelift. The restriction of a maximum space of 400 sq. ft was removed. They were required to follow certain practices such as electronic scale, exhibition of logo, provisioning of a separate space for STD/ISD, mobile cell recharge vouchers/coupons service, sale of fortified food items and display of stock price, entitlement of quota for PDS beneficiaries, and names of cardholders attached to the shops. National Institution of Design (NID), Ahmedabad, had been asked to develop uniform design and colour scheme for FPSs.

5 The Department of Civil Supplies took major initiatives in terms of establishing viable commercial relationship with prospective suppliers of various products to the FPS. The department wrote recommendation letters to leading telecom firms like Hutch[3] and BSNL to recruit the FPS as their dealers or retailers to sell a range of products such as mobile recharge vouchers, SIM cards, and handsets.

6 Oil marketing companies were contacted through formal letter to provide agency/distributorship of LPG/domestic cooking gas to FPS. In order to increase the portfolio, the chief post master general was requested to allow FPSs to sell some of the postal products as well.

7 Video conferences were held with district collectors and in many places they were allowed to deal directly with manufacturers and recommend FPSs in their area as distributors. All necessary measures were taken to promote the new FPS and install financial stability in the system.

Financing The Civil Supplies Department persuaded the State Bank of India (SBI) to provide loan to FPS owners to convert FPSs into model FPSs. Earlier it had asked Dena Bank to provide loans for modernization but it did not bring much success because Dena Bank had limited presence in the state.[4] SBI had strong presence in both rural and urban areas across the state. SBI agreed to be a part of the FPS modernization initiative and provided loans at priority lending rate (Exhibit C6.8). SBI also arranged loan *Melas* in various districts and the FPS owners were asked to attend them. SBI also identified a few interested FPS owners and gave them training for their selling its financial products.

Product Sourcing and Supply For product supply, either companies supplied their products directly to FPS through distributors or supplied to godowns from where FPS shop owners lifted their products. Payment terms were decided on a case to case basis. Some companies asked for cash on delivery while others gave credit. According to the store manager of Yogi Grahak Sahakari Mandali, a model FPS at Vasad, the store had no problem in product supply. This model shop usually sourced products like pulses, rice, and wheat from the local market. After grading and packing, these products were sold at a slightly higher price. Modern Dindayal Grahak Bhandar at Sarsaoni village sourced some of the products from Madhavpura and Jamalpur market yards in Ahmedabad. Many model shops followed multiple sourcing. Distributors of national brands visited the rural model shops less frequently, so these had to source products from the nearest wholesale market. Vegetables were either directly bought from farmers or from market yards. Rasik Chiman Bhai said "I order my requirements over telephone and the broker sends products from Madavpura." "Distributors of large FMCG companies visited the shop less frequently," he added. Therefore he had to source those products from Ahmedabad.

Margin and Promotional Support Different suppliers had different margin structures. In many cases the Department of Food and Civil Supplies was able to negotiate with suppliers/manufacturers to offer additional margin to model FPS compared to other retailers. Manufacturers like Emami which had a strong network were happy to be a part of this novel initiative. "Our range of product is tailormade to suit this channel. We will be honoured to be a part of this unique project of model FPS," said M. K. Dutta, All India Key Account Manager. Personal product companies offered 10–20 per cent margin on various products and their variants. Milk product companies offered 5–15 per cent margin on various products (Exhibit C6.9) and also offered special schemes from time to time. According to Mrs. Rita Joshi, she could sell 15

3. Now Vodafone
4. Interview with Mr. R. R. Chouhan, Director, Food, Civil Supplies and Consumer Affairs

EXHIBIT C6.8

Features of Loan Facility Provided by SBI

Target Group	Owner of FPSs holding govt. Licence
Purpose	Working capital for running the FPS, acquisition of fixed assets, and renovation of the shop
Type of Facility	Cash credit (if only working capital is considered), Composite loan (fixed asset and working capital combined)
Loan Amount	Up to maximum ₹1 lakh
Margin	NIL (for loan up to ₹25,000) and (4)20% for other loans
Processing Fee	Waived
Primary	Hypothecation for assets created out of loan
Collateral	NIL (for loan up to ₹25,000) and 25% for other loans
Insurance	Waived
Interest	Linked to SBAR Cash Credit for Working Capital Composite Loan
Up to ₹25,000	Upto 1.75% below BSAR
Over ₹25,000 and up to ₹1 lakh	Upto 0.75% below SBAR
Repayment Period	Upto 60 months
Moratorium	As required by cash flow-within the overall repayment period of 60 months
Other Conditions	Amount advanced for working capital purpose to be disbursed by way of deposit to govt. account though specified Challan against delivery of inventory by the DFACS. The replenishment to be done on a monthly basis after the sales proceeds for the previous month has been credited to the account by the shop owner.

Note: Benchmark Prime Lending Rate is referred as SBAR

SOURCE: Department of Civil Supplies, GOG

litre groundnut oil of a leading brand at a margin of ₹1 per litre easily.

Availability of Medicines and Family Planning Products The state government had instructed the fair price shops to provide contraceptives and medicines for malaria and iron deficiency. These were given to needy people free of cost. This was an initiative to enhance efficient demonstration of government schemes.

Roaming Ration Cards The Gujarat government recognized that many BPL and AAY farmers migrated from one village/city to another for work. Therefore, the government introduced roaming ration cards to them. To avail this facility, a ration card was issued offline to such families by the Mamlatdar at Taluka level and the Zonal Officer at zonal level. This card was in the form a booklet with details about family members registered in the card and attached to a shop. The applicant could receive the roaming ration card from the destination Taluka. All the fair price shops in the destination Taluka would have to honour the roaming card. Pilot implementation of roaming ration cards was successful in three districts. This programme needed system integration to achieve its fullest potential. This initiative was appreciated in many forums. Nanda was planning to introduce smart cards to replace roaming ration cards.

Monitoring In order to bring more transparency, accountability, and responsibility to the PDS and encourage people to actively participate, vigilance committees at various levels were formed. The Village Vigilance Committee (VVC) was one of them formed in the rural area. The Gujarat government had formed VVC in 7145 villages. A typical VVC was composed of the Sarpanch of the village two members from BPL card holders, two members from AAY card holders, one primary school teacher, and two women representatives.

VVC was entrusted to ensure transparent and effective functioning of PDS in rural areas. The Taluka Mamlatdar was the appointing authority of VVC.

EXHIBIT C6.9

Margin Offered by Mother Dairy

Brand	Product	Pack	MRP (₹)	% Margin on MRP
Dhara	Groundnut Oil	1 ltr pouch	74	6
Dhara		1 ltr tetra	77	6
Dhara		5 ltr jar	380	6
Dhara		15 ltr jar	1,100	6+
Dhara		15 ltr tin	1,120	6+
Dhara	Sunflower Oil	1 ltr pouch	65	6
Dhara		5 ltr jar	340	6
Dhara		15 ltr jar	1,050	6+
Dhara	Kachi Ghani Mustard Oil	1 ltr pouch	60	6
Dhara		1 ltr tetra	63	6
Dhara		5 ltr jar	325	6
Dhara	Refined Vegetable Oil	1 ltr tetra	60	6
Safal Juices	Orange, Mix Fruit, Mango Nectar	1 ltr	70	15
		200 ml	15	15
Mother Dairy	Butter	100g	16	8.4
	Butter	500g	77	8.4
	Cheese Cube	200g	50	8.4
	Cheese Slice	200g	56	8.4
	Cheese Spread	200g	35	8.4
	Pure Ghee	200ml	33	5.25
		500ml	80	5.25
		1 ltr Tin	165	5.25
Sugam	Full cream Milk	500ml	10	0.60/ltr
	Standardized Milk	1ltr	9	0.60/ltr
	Toned Milk	500ml	8.5	0.60/ltr
	Homogenized Toned Milk	1 ltr	16.5	0.60/ltr
	Butter Milk	500ml	4	0.60/ltr

SOURCE: Department of Food, Civil Supplies and Consumer Affairs

The primary function of this committee was to see that FPS managers worked within the guidelines of the government. The committee had to monitor complaints against FPS. As per the state government rule every month 20 per cent FPS in each Taluka had to be checked. There were supply inspectors to monitor functioning of the FPS. Apart from that a complaint register was kept at the Taluka level for card holders and VVC members to document their concerns and observations. There had been meetings of officers at state and district levels to review FPS performance. Documented feedbacks from the VVC were used for improvement. The state level organization structure is depicted in Exhibit C6.10.

Owner's Experience

The model FPS was liked by the owners. Sudhir Joshi, owner of a model FPS at Sarsaoni village said, "The model FPS has brought a refreshing change in my life and my profile has changed from a ration product dealer to a retailer. Initially when the D.S.O. of Kheda district gave me the idea to convert my old FPS to

EXHIBIT C6.10

Organizational Structure

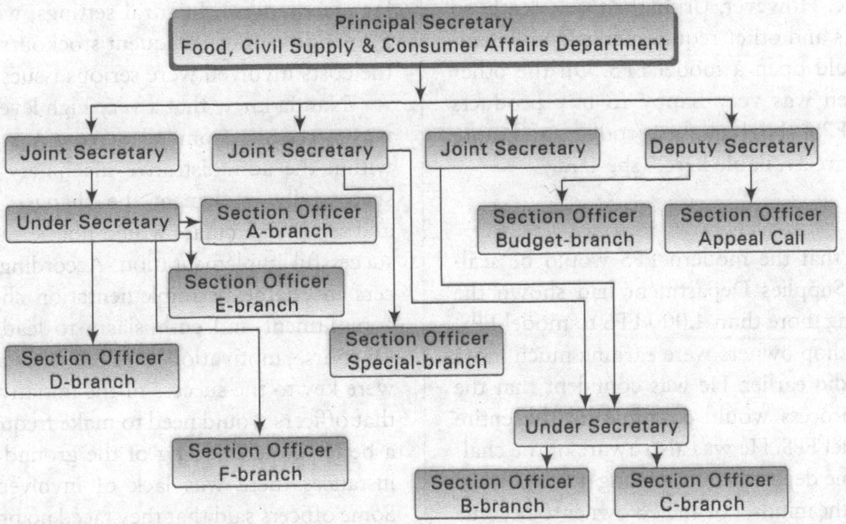

Source: Department of Civil Supplies, GOG

model FPS, it did not make sense to me. However, he convinced me to modernize the shop and I am very lucky that I heeded his advice."

The FPS in Sarsaoni village (population 5000) was turned into a model FPS on 13 August 2007 Joshi, spent ₹1 lakh for the makeover of the shop. The State Bank of India gave him a loan at 11.5 per cent interest. The monthly instalment came to ₹8,000. The margin money was paid by the government. He says that since his shop was turned into model FPS, the turnover is ₹1.25 lakh a month, giving him a monthly income of ₹15,000. He sold all items at less than MRP. He purchased vegetables from the wholesale market in Nadiad. People from nearby villages bought vegetables from him. Where other shops sold onions at ₹15 a kg, he sold them at ₹10 a kg. Vegetable sales alone fetched ₹2,500 daily. The shop remained open from 7 in the morning to 8.30 at night. He was thinking of getting a franchise of Amul, the largest dairy product company of the country, to further boost his sales.

Mrs. Joshi, a master's degree holder in Hindi, now worked with her husband to run their model FPS. "I am an entrepreneur now and am confident that I can beat anyone in this business in the village," said Mrs. Joshi. She looked after store operations and her husband was involved in sourcing and marketing activities. "Now our income has gone up and we can pursue our ambition," said Mrs. Joshi. According to her, the model FPS concept would offer many opportunities to the owners. Those who had converted expressed their happiness, while others had shown a strong desire to do so.

Rasiklal's model FPS in Haldaharva, a village with a population of 9,000, was renovated in 2006. The village is a buzzing market centre and trading activities takes place here. It caters to 25–30 surrounding villages. There were already other 45 shops in the area. But customers come to him because he sold items cheaper. Within six months his income had jumped to ₹15,000 a month. His daily turnover is ₹20,000. He has tied up with Amul and BSNL. He had spent ₹3 lakh for renovating the shop. He installed a computerized billing system and accepted credit cards. His shop was open from 6.00 am to 11.00 pm. Rasiklal paid income tax in 2006–7 for the first time! His experiences inspired many others to go for a makeover.

Customer Experience

Sudhaben never visited the Yogi Grahak Model FPS which was just about 200 meters from Kamlaben's shop from where she bought groceries. Many cardholders like Sudhaben did not want to buy from the model FPS as it was perceived to be expensive. On top of that the local kirana shop could provide the same kind of products at lower price along with credit facility. Urmilaben, a BPL card holder of Chandubhai FPS, had similar logic. However, Urmilaben was ready to buy her groceries and other requirements from Chandubhai if he could open a model FPS. On the other hand, Chandaben was very happy to buy products from the model FPS. "High quality products and more product variety are available here," she said.

Way Ahead

Nanda believed that the modern FPS would be scalable. The Civil Supplies Department had shown the way by converting more than 4,000 FPS to model FPS. All these model shop owners were earning much more than what they did earlier. He was confident that the modernization process would continue till the entire FPS became model FPS. He was also aware of the challenges faced by the department in scaling it fully. Raval said, "Changing the mindset of an FPS owner to become a model FPS owner proved to be the most challenging part of his job." Initially, the shop owners were indifferent and reluctant. But when things were explained to them in proper perspective, they were more than eager to come forward. Mr. Rajput, D.S.O. at Kheda, was very confident and sure about the success of the modernization process. In fact Kheda district was very successful in this initiative with a conversion rate of close to 63 per cent. He said, "Motivating FPS owners along with financial constraints prove to be the most challenging aspect of the modernization process." Self-motivation of the model shop owner could be extremely crucial for the long term sustainability of his business. According to R.R. Chouhan, Director at the Food and Civil Supplies Department, the financial condition of the model shop owners had improved a lot and the social status considerably had gone up. Training programmes were conducted from time to time to train these owners and install confidence in them. "The freedom and support that one receives from the polity is also a very important element in the success of such programmes. This was a programme initiated by the department and the Chief Minister came to know about it only when the report was being discussed in Delhi during the national PDS meeting. For a Chief Minister to allow a programme with such a big proportion and keep the polity out of till it has matured is a commendable support," said Nanda very emphatically.

Nanda was very confident that the initiative would be replicable in other parts of the country. But the results were varied. Increase in income ranged from ₹5,000 to ₹20,000 a month. The challenges for urban FPSs were different. The landscape was very competitive. There were several stores that sold similar merchandise. In rural settings, while the FPS had a clear advantage, frequent stockouts of products and the costs involved were serious issues.

Nanda knew that a very high level of commitment was necessary from all across. A strong motivation within the administrative machinery was required to successfully implement the changes. Modifying laws and sending circulars would not be sufficient to ensure successful implementation. According to Rajput, officers in charge of implementation should show their commitment and enthusiasm to lead from the front. Of course, motivation of FPS owners and their attitude were key to the success of the initiative. Rajput agreed that officers would need to make frequent visits to have a better understanding of the ground reality. In a few instances there was lack of involvement of officers. Some officers said that they faced no problems in implementing the model shop initiatives. However, they were neither able to meet the targets nor provide a reasonable explanation for performance. Besides motivation, expertise and capacity building were also important.

To supervise such a massive programme adequate manpower would be necessary. In some districts, with a stipulated requirement of 20 supervisors, the department was able to allocate only two, because, along with the modernization of FPS, there were other programmes that they had to look after. Implementation was very challenging. The officers were frequently transferred and this affected their attachment with the programme. In spite having agreements with companies and government departments to supply their products through FPS, supplies were not regular. For instance, one model shop owner said that he had to run from pillar to post in the postal department to procure postal supplies, despite the civil supplies department having a tie-up with the postal department. There was difficulty in getting loans from banks. More robust mechanism to track the progress of model FPS would have to be developed. However, Chouhan expressed confidence that these problems would be sorted out soon. In fact, Rajput was surprised to hear that in one of the model shops sales had gone down drastically. Nanda was aware of these issues and was sure that the state machinery would ensure implementation of the plans and monitor the progress. Initiatives taken to create nationwide awareness about the success of this programme would help in building confidence and easier scaling and replication.

EXHIBIT C6.11
Entry and Exit Point of a Model FPS

EXHIBIT C6.12
Cyber Café at a Model FPS

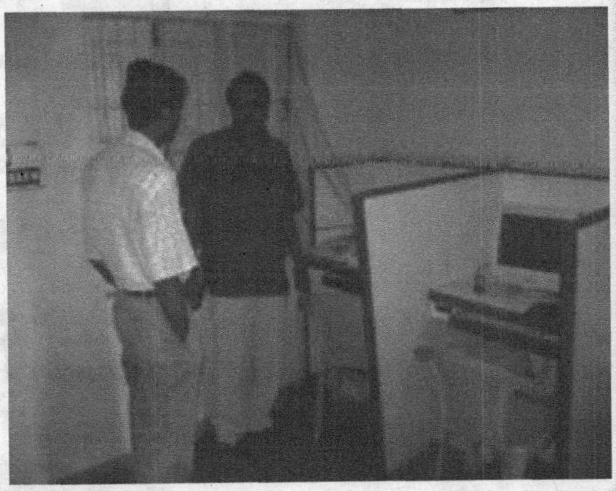

CHAPTER 21

Customer Relationship Management (CRM)

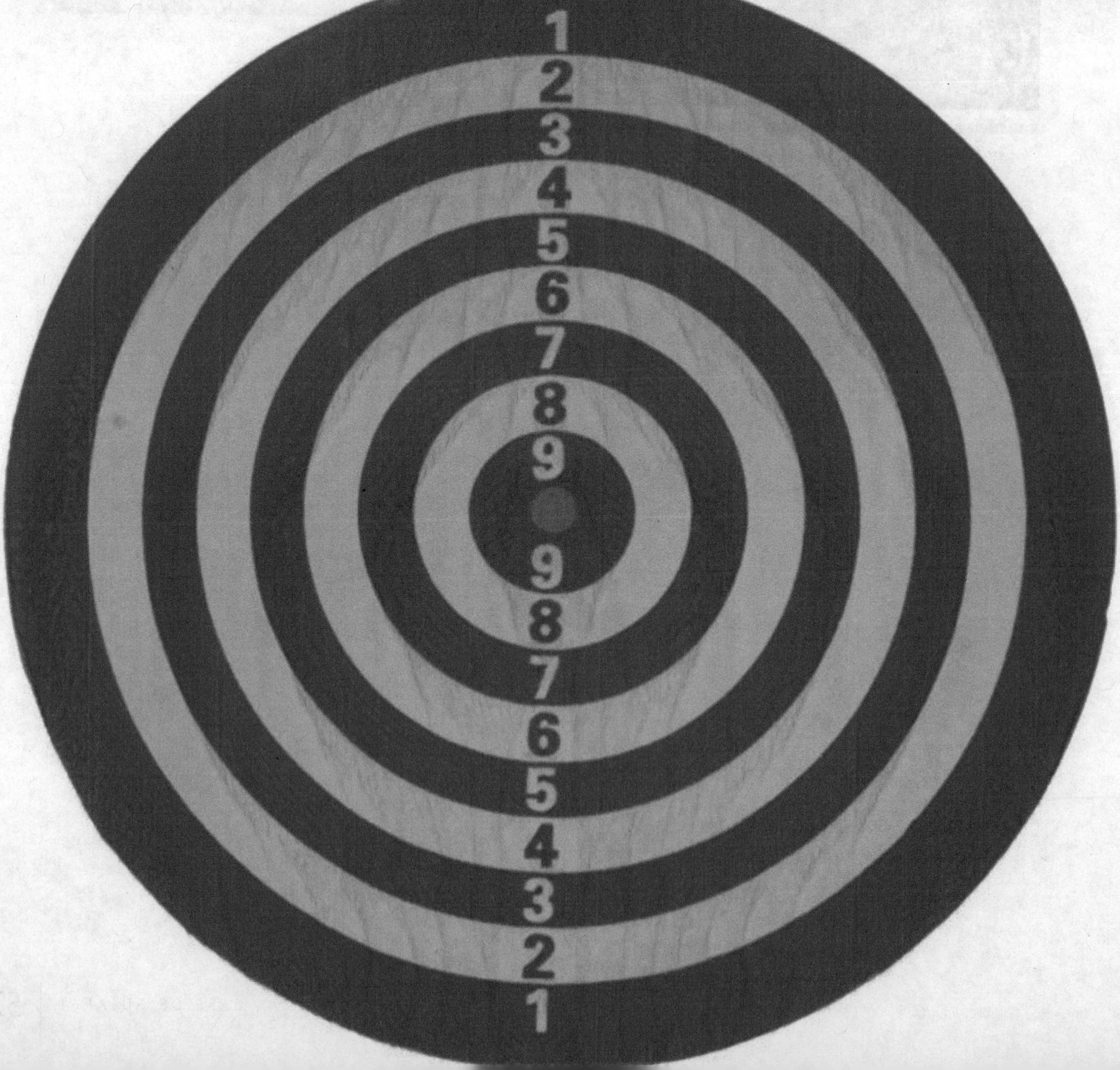

Learning Outcomes

LO 1 Define customer relationship management

LO 2 Explain how to identify customer relationships with the organization

LO 3 Understand interactions with the current customer base

LO 4 Outline the process of capturing customer data

LO 5 Describe the use of technology to store and integrate customer data

LO 6 Describe how to identify the best customers

LO 7 Explain the process of leveraging customer information throughout the organization

CRM is often described as a closed-loop system that builds relationships with customers.

LO 1 What Is Customer Relationship Management?

Customer relationship management is the ultimate goal of a new trend in marketing that focuses on understanding customers as individuals instead of as part of a group. To do so, marketers are making their communications more customer specific. This movement initially was popularized as one-to-one marketing. But CRM is a much broader approach to understanding and serving customer needs than is one-to-one marketing.

customer relationship management (CRM) a company-wide business strategy designed to optimize profitability, revenue, and customer satisfaction by focusing on highly defined and precise customer groups

Customer relationship management (CRM) is a company-wide business strategy designed to optimize profitability, revenue, and customer satisfaction by focusing on highly defined and precise customer groups. This is accomplished by organizing the company around customer segments, establishing and tracking customer interactions with the company, fostering customer-satisfying behaviors, and linking all processes of the company from its customers through its suppliers. The difference between CRM and traditional mass marketing can be compared to shooting a rifle and a shotgun. Instead of scattering messages far and wide across the spectrum of mass media (the shotgun approach), CRM marketers now are honing in on ways to effectively communicate with each customer (the rifle approach).

Note: All the figures in U.S. dollars are converted into rupee using the value $1 = ₹45.

The Customer Relationship Management Cycle

On the surface, CRM may resemble a simplistic customer service strategy. But, though customer service is part of the CRM process, it is only a small part of a totally integrated approach to building customer relationships. CRM is often described as a closed-loop system that builds relationships with customers. Exhibit 21.1 illustrates this closed-loop system, one that is continuous and circular with no predefined starting or end point.[1]

To initiate the CRM cycle, a company must *identify customer relationships with the organization.* This may simply entail learning who the customers are or where they are located, or it may require more detailed information about the products and services they are using. Indian Oil Corporation Ltd. (IOCL), an oil and gas company in India, wanted to venture into the polymer market. To achieve this, it installed a fully functional Customer Acquisition, Retention, and Enrichment (CARE) platform in collaboration with Microsoft in association with its partner Mahindra Satyam. The CARE solution consists a whole gamut of Microsoft business applications and helps the IOCL executives to view the same business information for gaining business insights and improving their decision making. For example, the sales force team of IOCL can view their distributor's interaction and details such as orders, credit, and inventory in a single dashboard. Such accurate and complete piece of information about sales and account gives insights to the sales managers about what is happening in the field and accordingly design their account strategies.[2]

Next, the company must *understand the interactions with current customers.* Companies accomplish this by collecting data on all types of communications a customer has with the company. Using this knowledge of its customers and their interactions, the company can *capture relevant customer data on interactions.* With the help of CARE solution, information like customer registration, orders, and credit data is available real time. It also enables the customers to view product information, order products, track delivery status, manage payments, and have interactions with IOCL's sales force and customer care. Such transparency and real-time insight simplifies the monitoring and managing of sales process, thereby increasing efficiency.[3] Using this knowledge of its customers and their interactions, the company then *captures relevant customer data on interactions.*

EXHIBIT 21.1
A Simple Flow Model of the Customer Relationship Management System

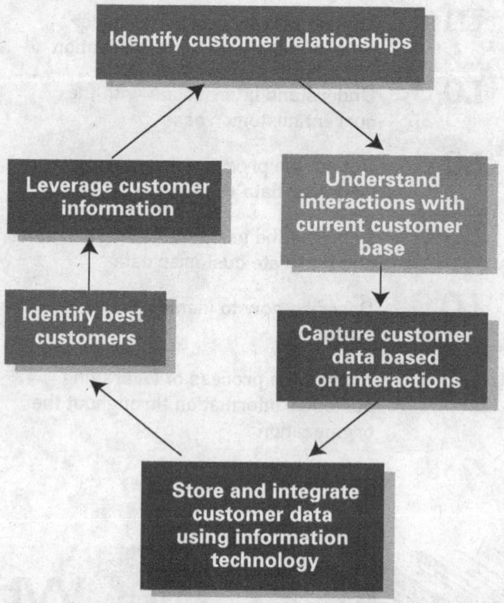

How can marketers realistically analyze and communicate with individual customers? The answer lies in how information technology is used to implement the CRM system. Fundamentally, a CRM approach is no more than the relationship cultivated by a salesperson with the customer. A successful salesperson builds a relationship over time, constantly thinks about what the customer needs and wants, and is mindful of the trends and patterns in the customer's purchase history. The salesperson may also inform, educate, and instruct the customer about new products, technology, or applications in anticipation of the customer's future needs or requirements.

This kind of thoughtful attention is the basis of successful CRM systems. Information technology is used not only to enhance the collection of customer data, but also to *store and integrate customer data* throughout the company and, ultimately, to "get to know" customers on a personal basis. Customer data are the firsthand responses that are obtained from customers through investigation or by asking direct questions. These initial data, which might include individual answers to questionnaires, responses on warranty cards, or lists of purchases recorded by electronic cash registers, have not yet been analyzed or interpreted.

The value of customer data depends on its consistency and on the system used to store it. Obtaining high-quality, actionable data from various sources is a key element in any CRM system. IOCL works with Microsoft in association with its partner Mahindra Satyam to maintain a well-organized CRM app, so the business managers in the field have the most relevant information to maintain customer relationships. Different kinds of database management software are available, from extremely high-tech, expensive, custom-designed databases to standardized programs.

Every customer wants to be a company's main priority. Yet not all customers are equally important in the eyes of a business. Consequently, the company must *identify its profitable and unprofitable customers*. Data mining is an analytical process that compiles actionable data about the purchase habits of a firm's current and potential customers. Essentially, data mining transforms customer data into customer information a company can use to make managerial decisions. For example, since CARE solution allows IOCL's partners and customers to have an online access of their credit and debit balances, the finance management task has been simplified since they have accurate information on how much payment is due.

Once customer data are analyzed and transformed into usable information, the information must be *leveraged*. The CRM system sends the customer information to all areas of a business because the customer interacts with all aspects of the business. Essentially, the company is trying to enhance customer relationships by getting the right information to the right person in the right place at the right time.

IOCL has found that getting timely customer information to its business managers has been profitable in several ways: time taken to complete order processing has been reduced from 3 days to less than 2 hours; with increased transparency, reconciliations and payments have become fast and accurate; and IOCL's total cost of ownership has reduced by 30 percent.[4]

Implementing a Customer Relationship Management System

Our discussion of a CRM system has assumed two key points. First, customers take center stage in any organization. Second, the business must manage the customer relationship across all points of customer contact throughout the entire organization. In the next sections, we examine how a CRM system is implemented and follow the progression depicted in Exhibit 21.1 as we explain each step in greater detail.

customer-centric a philosophy under which the company customizes its product and service offering based on data generated through interactions between the customer and the company

LO 2 Identify Customer Relationships

Companies that have a CRM system follow a customer-centric focus or model. Customer-centric is an internal management philosophy similar to the marketing concept discussed in Chapter 1. Under this philosophy, the company customizes its product and service offering based on data generated through interactions between the customer and the company. This philosophy transcends all functional areas of the business, producing an internal system where all of the company's decisions and actions are a direct result of customer information.

A customer-centric company builds long-lasting relationships by focusing on what satisfies and retains valuable customers. Taj Air Caterers, the airline catering division of the Taj Group of Hotels, has a nearly two decades old association with Singapore Air-

learning an informal process of collecting customer data through customer comments and feedback on product or service performance

knowledge management the process by which learned information from customers is centralized and shared in order to enhance the relationship between customers and the organization

empowerment delegation of authority to solve customers' problems quickly—usually by the first person the customer notifies regarding the problem

interaction the point at which a customer and a company representative exchange information and develop learning relationships

lines. What started as mere supply of inflight food and beverages has transformed over the years into a strong relationship. Taj is now an active participant in product designing that is in line with the preferences of the airline passengers. Realizing the popularity of Indian meals globally, Taj Chefs conduct annual workshops for worldwide caterers of Singapore Airlines on Indian cuisine. Such initiatives have helped in cementing the ties with Singapore Airlines.[5]

Customer-centric companies continually learn ways to enhance their product and service offerings. **Learning** in a CRM environment involves collecting customer information through comments and feedback on product and service performance.

Each unit of a business typically has its own way of recording what it learns and perhaps even its own customer information system. The departments' different interests make it difficult to pull all of the customer information together in one place using a common format. To overcome this problem, companies using CRM rely on knowledge management. **Knowledge management** is a process by which customer information is centralized and shared in order to enhance the relationship between customers and the organization. Information collected includes experiential observations, comments, customer actions, and qualitative facts about the customer.

As Chapter 1 explained, empowerment involves delegating authority to solve customers' problems. In other words, **empowerment** is the latitude organizations give their representatives to negotiate mutually satisfying commitments with customers. Usually, organizational representatives are able to make changes during interactions with customers through phone, fax, e-mail, Web communication, or face-to-face.

An **interaction** occurs when a customer and a company representative exchange information and develop learning relationships. With CRM, the customer—not the organization—defines the terms of the interaction, often by stating his or her preferences. The organization responds by designing products and services around customers' desired experiences. Starbucks implemented a Web site in United States specifically for customers to suggest ideas for new products, ways to modify the Starbucks experience, and new opportunities for community involvement. Many customers posted that the noise level made by the blenders in Starbucks stores was negatively affecting the otherwise welcoming atmosphere. In response, Starbucks rolled out new, quiet blenders to all its stores. Starbucks has also responded to the call for healthy breakfast items and fresh fruit with oatmeal cups, egg white sandwiches, and a selection of fruit.[6]

© ISTOCKPHOTO/THINKSTOCK

The success of CRM—building lasting and profitable relationships—can be directly measured by the effectiveness of the interaction between the customer and the organization. In fact, what further differentiates CRM from other strategic initiatives is the organization's ability to establish and manage interactions with its current customer base. The more latitude (empowerment) a company gives its representatives, the more likely the interaction will conclude in a way that satisfies the customer.

For example, if a flight experiences a delay or is re-routed, or if there are other anomalies, Southwest Airlines, a U.S. based low-cost airline, e-mails all the customers on the flight within 24 hours. Each e-mail has a brief sincere apology, a brief explanation, and a gift (usually a voucher). After a flight to Chicago was diverted to Milwaukee, Southwest sent an e-mail explaining that a sensor in the landing flaps went off, so the pilots needed to use a longer runway. Educating the customer and giving them an opportunity to learn why something happens has resulted in Southwest Airlines having the lowest customer complaint rate of all the major carriers. Delta Airlines, with the worst rating, had more than nine times as many complaints as Southwest.[7]

EXHIBIT 21.2
Customer-Centric Approach for Managing Customer Interactions

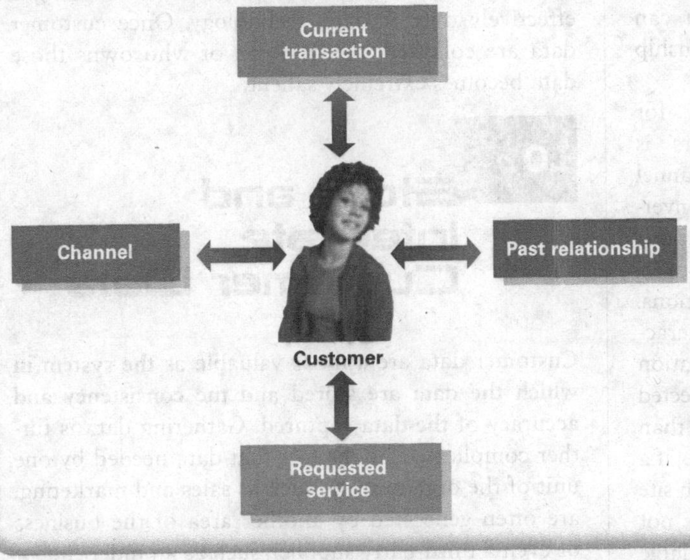

© IMAGE SOURCE/JUPITERIMAGES

LO 3 Understand Interactions of the Current Customer Base

The *interaction* between the customer and the organization is the foundation on which a CRM system is built. Only through effective interactions can organizations learn about the expectations of their customers, generate and manage knowledge about them, negotiate mutually satisfying commitments, and build long-term relationships.

Exhibit 21.2 illustrates the customer-centric approach for managing customer interactions. Following a customer-centric approach, an interaction can occur through a formal or direct communication channel, such as a phone, the Internet, or a salesperson. Any activity or touch point a customer has with an organization, either directly or indirectly, constitutes an interaction.

Companies that effectively manage customer interactions recognize that customers provide data to the organization that affect a wide variety of **touch points.** In a CRM system, touch points are all areas of a business where customers have contact with the company and data might be gathered. Touch points might include a customer registering for a particular service; a customer communicating with customer service for product information; a customer completing and returning the warranty information card for a product; or a customer talking with salespeople, delivery personnel, and product installers. Data gathered at these touch points, once interpreted, provide information that affects touch points inside the company. Interpreted information may be redirected to marketing research to develop profiles of extended warranty purchasers, to production to analyze recurring problems and repair components, and to accounting to establish cost-control models for repair service calls.

touch points all possible areas of a business where customers communicate with that business

point-of-sale interactions communications between customers and organizations that occur at the point of sale, normally in a store

Web-based interactions are an increasingly popular touch point for customers to communicate with companies on their own terms. Web users can evaluate and purchase products, make reservations, input preferential data, and provide customer feedback on services and products. Data from these Web-based interactions are then captured, compiled, and used to segment customers, refine marketing efforts, develop new products, and deliver a degree of individual customization to improve customer relationships.

Another touch point is through **point-of-sale interactions** in stores or at information kiosks. Many point-of-sale software programs enable customers to easily provide information about themselves without feeling violated. The information is then used for marketing and merchandising activities, and to accurately identify the store's best customers and the types of products they buy. Data collected at point-of-sale interactions is also used to increase customer satisfaction through the development of in-store services and customer recognition promotions.

LO 4 Capture Customer Data

Vast amounts of data can be obtained from the interactions between an organization and its customers.

data warehouse a central repository for data from various functional areas of the organization that are stored and inventoried on a centralized computer system so that the information can be shared across all functional departments of the business

database a collection of data, especially one that can be accessed and manipulated by computer software

response list a customer list that includes the names and addresses of individuals who have responded to an offer of some kind, such as by mail, telephone, direct response television, product rebates, contests or sweepstakes, or billing inserts

Therefore, in a CRM system, the issue is not how much data can be obtained, but rather what types of data should be acquired and how the data can effectively be used for relationship enhancement.

The traditional approach for acquiring data from customers is through channel interactions. Channel interactions include store visits, conversations with salespeople, interactions via the Web, traditional phone conversations, and wireless communications. In a CRM system, channel interactions are viewed as prime information sources based on the channel selected to initiate the interaction rather than on the data acquired. For example, if a consumer logs on to the Sony Web site to find out why a Sony device is not functioning properly and the answer is not available online, the consumer is then referred to a page where he or she can describe the problem. The Web site then e-mails the problem description to a company representative, who will research the problem and reply via e-mail. Sony continues to use the e-mail mode of communication because the customer has established this as the preferred method of contact.[8]

© ISTOCKPHOTO.COM/CRAFTVISION

Interactions between the company and the customer facilitate collection of large amounts of data. Companies can obtain not only simple contact information (name, address, phone number) but also data pertaining to the customer's current relationship with the organization—past purchase history, quantity and frequency of purchases, average amount spent on purchases, sensitivity to promotional activities, and so forth.

In this manner, a lot of information can be captured from one individual customer across several touch points. Multiply this by the thousands of customers across all of the touch points with an organization, and the volume of data can rapidly become unmanageable for company personnel. The large volumes of data resulting from a CRM initiative can be managed effectively only through technology. Once customer data are collected, the question of who owns those data becomes extremely salient.

LO 5 Store and Integrate Customer Data

Customer data are only as valuable as the system in which the data are stored and the consistency and accuracy of the data captured. Gathering data is further complicated by the fact that data needed by one unit of the organization, such as sales and marketing, are often generated by another area of the business or even a third-party supplier, such as an independent marketing research firm. Thus, companies must use information technology to capture, store, and integrate strategically important customer information. This process of centralizing data in a CRM system is referred to as data warehousing.

A **data warehouse** is a central repository (*database*) of customer data collected by an organization. Essentially, it is a large computerized file of all information collected in the previous phase of the CRM process—for example, information collected in channel, transaction, and product/service touch points. The core of the data warehouse is the **database**, a collection of data, especially one that can be accessed and manipulated by computer software. The CRM database focuses on collecting vital statistics on consumers, their purchasing habits, transactions methods, and product usage in a centralized repository that is accessible by all functional areas of a company. By utilizing a data warehouse, marketing managers can quickly access vast amounts of information required to make decisions.

When a company builds its database, usually the first step is to develop a list. A **response list** is based on customers who have indicated interest in a product or service, or who have responded to an offer of some kind, such as by mail, telephone, product rebates, contests or sweepstakes, or billing inserts. Response lists tend to be especially valuable because past behavior is a strong predictor of future behavior and because consumers who have indicated interest in the product or service are more prone to purchase. Companies may find it valuable to enhance their customer records with information about the customers' or prospective customers' demographics and lifestyle characteristics. They can often accomplish this by augmenting the records with compiled lists. **Compiled lists** are created by an outside company that has collected names and contact information for potential consumers. This information is usually obtained from telephone directories and membership rosters of various groups. Lists range from those owned by large list companies, such as Dun & Bradstreet for business-to-business data and Donnelley for consumer lists, to small groups or associations that are willing to sell their membership lists. Indeed, many lists are compiled from people who have opted in to the list after they have purchased a related product. Data compiled by large data-gathering companies usually are very accurate.

In this phase, companies are usually collecting channel, transaction, and product/service information such as store, salesperson, communication channel, contact information, relationship, and brands.

A customer database becomes even more useful to marketing managers when it is enhanced to include more than simply a customer's, or prospect's name, address, telephone number, and transaction history. Database enhancement involves purchasing information on customers or prospects to better describe their needs or determine how responsive they might be to marketing programs. Types of enhancement data typically include demographic, lifestyle, or behavioral information.

Database enhancement can increase the effectiveness of marketing programs. By learning more about their best and most profitable customers, marketers can maximize the effectiveness of marketing communications and cross-selling. Database enhancement also helps a company find new prospects.

Multinational companies building worldwide databases often face difficult problems when pulling together internal data about their customers. Differences in language, computer systems, and data-collection methods can be huge obstacles to overcome. Despite the challenges, many global companies are committed to building databases.

LO 6 Identify the Best Customers

compiled list a customer list developed by gathering names and addresses from telephone directories and membership rosters, usually enhanced with information from public records, such as census data, auto registrations, birth announcements, business start-ups, or bankruptcies

CRM manages interactions between a company and its customers. To be successful, companies must identify customers who yield high profits or potential profits. To do so, significant amounts of data must be gathered from customers, stored and integrated in the data warehouse, and then analyzed and interpreted for common patterns that can identify homogeneous customers who are different from other customer segments. Because not all customers are the same, organizations need to develop interactions that target *individual* customer needs and wants. Recall, from Chapter 8, the 80/20 principle—80 percent of a company's revenue is generated by 20 percent of its customers. Therefore, the question becomes, how do we identify the 20 percent of our customer base that contributes 80 percent of our revenue? In a CRM system, the answer is data mining.

Data Mining

Data mining is used to find hidden patterns and relationships in the customer data stored in the data warehouse. It is a data analysis approach that identifies

patterns of characteristics that relate to particular customers or customer groups. Although businesses have been conducting such analyses for many years, the procedures typically were performed on small data sets containing as few as 300 to 400 customers. Today, with the development of sophisticated data warehouses, millions of customers' shopping patterns can be analyzed.

When using data mining, it is important to remember that the real value is in the company's ability to transform its data from operational bits and bytes into information marketers need for successful marketing strategies. Companies must analyze the data to identify and profile the best customers, calculate their lifetime value, and ultimately predict purchasing behavior through statistical modeling. ICICI Bank implemented Siebel software to take care of its CRM process and to maintain customer database. The software helps the bank in keeping a track of its customers' activities, generating customized reports, and cross-selling products. For instance, the software facilitates the branch head to know if any customer starts withdrawing sizeable proportions of money from his or her bank account. The branch head can then try to understand the cause of such withdrawals and take appropriate actions; in case of any fault on the bank's part, rectification measures can be taken, and if the customer had been withdrawing for investment purposes, the bank can try to cross-sell its own investment products.[9]

Before the information is leveraged, several types of analysis are often run on the data. These analyses include customer segmentation, recency-frequency-monetary analysis, lifetime value analysis, and predictive modeling.

Customer Segmentation

Recall that *customer segmentation* is the process of breaking large groups of customers into smaller, more homogeneous groups. This type of analysis generates a "profile" or picture of the customers' similar demographic, geographic, and psychographic traits as well as their previous purchase behavior; it focuses particularly on the best customers. Profiles of the best customers can be compared and contrasted with other customer segments. For example, a bank could segment consumers on frequency of usage, credit, age, and turnover.

Once a profile of the best customer is developed using these criteria, it can be used to screen other potential consumers. Similarly, customer profiles can be used to introduce customers selectively to spe-

WHERE'S HOT?

Foursquare, a location-based social networking app, enables people to check in and let friends know where they are. Foursquare hopes to be able to mimic Twitter's success at letting everyone know "what's hot" by answering the question "where's hot?" Popular search engines may team up with Foursquare to show users where the most people have checked in around their area, showing the popular places using Foursquare's live data stream.[10]

© ISTOCKPHOTO.COM/DAN WILTON

cific marketing actions. For example, young customers with an open mind can be introduced to home banking. See Chapter 8 for a detailed discussion of segmentation.

Recency-Frequency-Monetary Analysis Customers who have purchased recently and often and have spent considerable money are more likely to purchase again. Recency-frequency-monetary analysis (RFM) identifies those customers most likely to purchase again because they have bought recently, bought frequently, or spent a specified amount of money with the firm. Firms develop equations to identify the "best customers" (often the top 20 percent of the customer base) by assigning a score to customer records in the database on how often, how recently, and how much they have spent. Customers are then ranked to determine which ones move to the top of the list and which ones fall to the bottom. The ranking provides the basis for maximizing profits because it enables the firm to use the information in its customer database to select those persons who have proved to be good sources of revenue.

Lifetime Value Analysis Recency, frequency, and monetary data can also be used to create a lifetime value model on customers in the database. Whereas RFM looks at how valuable a customer currently is to a company, **lifetime value analysis (LTV)** projects the future value of the customer over a period of years. One of the basic assumptions in any lifetime value calculation is that marketing to repeat customers is more profitable than marketing to first-time buyers. That is, it costs more to find a new customer in terms of promotion and gaining trust than to sell more to a customer who is already loyal.

Customer lifetime value has a number of benefits. It shows marketers how much they can spend to *acquire* new customers, it tells them the level of spending to *retain* customers, and it facilitates targeting new customers who look as though they will be profitable customers. Some marketers have taken CRM's lifetime value analysis one step further by implementing customer value management (or CVM) strategies. The goal is to determine which individual customers are most valuable so that their total lifetime purchasing can be maximized. CVM requires a series of "value exchanges" that reward customers for providing personal information and use the information to encourage customers to make additional purchases or renew ongoing services. Tata Steel launched a CVM initiative to develop close partnerships with some of its top customers, sell more to the chosen customers, and improvise the overall value chain. The CVM process lasted over 12 weeks during which a specifically constituted team worked in-tandem with the customer organization. The Tata Steel team first studied the whole steel deployment process in the customer organization, such as receipt of steel, its storage, reasons for rejection, usage pattern, and problems faced. This was followed by generation of ideas for improvement. The ideas generated were then thoroughly evaluated by teams from both Tata Steel and customer organization. The evaluation helped in arriving at the most promising ideas, which were further discussed upon and implementation plan for each idea was developed. The final stage of CVM process consisted of actual implementation and monitoring of the ideas. The CVM initiative turned out to be a win-win situation for both Tata Steel and its customers.[11]

lifetime value analysis (LTV) a data manipulation technique that projects the future value of the customer over a period of years using the assumption that marketing to repeat customers is more profitable than marketing to first-time buyers

predictive modeling a data manipulation technique in which marketers try to determine, based on some past set of occurrences, what the odds are that some other occurrence, such as a response or purchase, will take place in the future

campaign management developing product or service offerings customized for the appropriate customer segment and then pricing and communicating these offerings for the purpose of enhancing customer relationships

Predictive Modeling The ability to reasonably predict future customer behavior gives marketers a significant competitive advantage. Through **predictive modeling**, marketers try to determine, based on some past set of occurrences, what the odds are that some other occurrence, such as an Internet inquiry or purchase, will take place in the future. SPSS Predictive Marketing is one tool marketers can use to answer questions about their consumers. The software requires minimal knowledge of statistical analysis. Users operate from a prebuilt model, which generates profiles in three to four days. SPSS also has an online product that predicts Web site users' behavior.

LO 7 Leverage Customer Information

Data mining identifies the most profitable customers and prospects. Managers can then design tailored marketing strategies to best appeal to the identified segments. In CRM, this is commonly referred to as leveraging customer information to facilitate enhanced relationships with customers. Exhibit 21.3 on the next page shows some common CRM marketing database applications.

Campaign Management

Through campaign management, all areas of the company participate in the development of programs targeted to customers. **Campaign management** involves monitoring and leveraging customer interactions to sell a company's products and to increase customer service.

EXHIBIT 21.3
Common CRM Marketing Database Applications

Campaigns are based directly on data obtained from customers through various interactions. Campaign management includes monitoring the success of the communications based on customer reactions through sales, orders, callbacks to the company, and the like. If a campaign appears unsuccessful, it is evaluated and changed to better achieve the company's desired objective.

Campaign management involves developing customized product and service offerings for the appropriate customer segment, pricing these offerings attractively, and communicating these offers in a manner that enhances customer relationships. Customizing product and service offerings requires managing multiple interactions with customers, as well as giving priority to those products and services that are viewed as most desirable for a specifically designated customer. Even within a highly defined market segment, individual customer differences will emerge. Therefore, interactions among customers must focus on individual experiences, expectations, and desires.

Retaining Loyal Customers

If a company has identified its best customers, then it should make every effort to maintain and increase their loyalty. When a company retains an additional 5 percent of its customers each year, profits will increase by as much as 25 percent. What's more, improving customer retention by a mere 2 percent can decrease costs by as much as 10 percent.[12]

Loyalty programs reward loyal customers for making multiple purchases. The objective is to build long-term mutually beneficial relationships between a company and its key customers. Marriott, Hilton, and Starwood Hotels, for instance, reward their best customers with special perks not available to customers who stay less frequently. Travelers who spend a specified number of nights per year receive reservation guarantees, welcome gifts like fruit baskets and wine in their rooms, and access to concierge lounges. In addition to rewarding good customers, loyalty programs provide businesses with a wealth of information about their customers and shopping trends that can be used to make future business decisions.

Cross-Selling Other Products and Services

CRM provides many opportunities to cross-sell related products. Marketers can use the database to match product profiles and consumer profiles so that they can cross-sell customers products that match their demographic, lifestyle, or behavioral characteristics. CRM provides many opportunities to cross-sell related products. Marketers can use the database to match product profiles and consumer profiles so that they can cross-sell customers products that match their demographic, lifestyle, or behavioural characteristics. United Technologies, parent company of such powerful brands like Otis and Carrier, is planning to optimize cross sales across its three separate subsidiaries. It wants its three businesses in India—Carrier (air-conditioning line), Otis (elevator line), and UTC Fire & Security (fire and security products)—to work in concert. The parent company is of the view that these three product lines are bought by real estate developers for their projects. Hence, instead of selling the three products separately,

UTC's suite of companies can offer it all together.[13] DesignWorks NY, a graphic design and marketing communications firm in New York, sends a letter to each of its customers. That letter has a checklist of all the services offered by DesignWorks with the services already used by the customer checked off.

Internet companies use product and customer profiling to reveal cross-selling opportunities while a customer is surfing their site. Past purchases on a particular Web site and the site a surfer comes from give online marketers clues about the surfer's interests and what items to cross-sell.

Designing Targeted Marketing Communications

Using transaction and purchase data, a database allows marketers to track customers' relationships to the company's products and services and modify the marketing message accordingly.

Customers can also be segmented into infrequent users, moderate users, and heavy users. A segmented communications strategy can then be developed based on which group the customer falls into. Communications to infrequent users might encourage repeat purchases through a direct incentive such as a limited-time price discount for ordering again. Communications to moderate users may use fewer incentives and more reinforcement of past purchase decisions. Communications to heavy users would be designed around loyalty and reinforcement of the purchase rather than price promotions.

Reinforcing Customer Purchase Decisions

As you learned in Chapter 6, cognitive dissonance is the feeling consumers get when they recognize an inconsistency between their values and opinions and their purchase behavior. In other words, they doubt the soundness of their purchase decision and often feel anxious. CRM offers marketers an excellent opportunity to reach out to customers to reinforce the purchase decision. By thanking customers for their purchases and telling them they are important, marketers can help cement a long-term, profitable relationship.

Updating customers periodically about the status of their order reinforces purchase decisions. Postsale e-mails also afford the chance to provide more customer service or cross-sell other products.

Inducing Product Trial by New Customers

Although significant time and money are expended on encouraging repeat purchases by the best customers, a marketing database is also used to identify new custom-

REALITY MINING

Data mining compiles data from a variety of sources and crunches the numbers to reveal hidden patterns. Alexander Pentland, director of the Massachusetts Institute of Technology's Human Dynamics Laboratory, has developed research methods that add the real human element to data mining. Bank of America participated in a productivity study where 80 call center employees wore badges that recorded how fast they got through calls and who they talked to in the office and when. Workers who talked to more customers and worked through more calls actually had the same approval rating as the rest of the employees. Pentland's technology demonstrated that, when presented with more opportunities to share information, people become more productive. This sort of reality interaction data could be leveraged by marketers to target people who have the largest amounts of interactions in order to spread the word about their products or services. Having such specific data is another way to segment and target potential customers and to increase the number of touch points available to the marketing team.[14]

© ISTOCKPHOTO.COM/MAMMAMAART

ers. Because a firm using a marketing database already has a profile of its best customers, it can easily use the results of modeling to profile potential customers.

Marketing managers generally use demographic and behavioral data overlaid on existing customer data to develop a detailed customer profile that is a powerful tool for evaluating lists of prospects. For instance, if a firm's best customers are 35 to 50 years of age, live in suburban areas, and enjoy mountain climbing, then the company can find prospects already in its database or customers who currently are identified as using a competitor's product that match this profile.

Increasing Effectiveness of Distribution Channel Marketing

In Chapter 13, you learned that a marketing channel is a business structure of interdependent organizations, such as wholesalers and retailers, that move a product from the producer to the ultimate consumer. Most marketers rely on indirect channels to move their products to the end user. Thus, marketers often lose touch with the customer as an individual since the relationship is really between the retailer and the consumer. Marketers in this predicament often view their customers as aggregate statistics because specific customer information is difficult to gather.

With CRM databases, manufacturers now have a tool to gain insight into who is buying their products. Instead of simply unloading products into the distribution channel and leaving marketing and relationship building to dealers, auto manufacturers today are using Web sites to keep in touch with customers and prospects, learn about their lifestyles and hobbies, understand their vehicle needs, and develop relationships in the hope that these consumers will reward them with brand loyalty in the future. BMW and other vehicle manufacturers have databases with names of lakhs of consumers who have expressed an interest in their products.

With many brick-and-mortar stores setting up shop online, companies are now challenged to monitor purchases of customers who shop both in-store and online. This concept is referred to as multichannel marketing.

Companies are also using radio frequency identification (RFID) technology to improve distribution. The technology uses a microchip with an antenna that tracks anything from a soda can to a car. A computer can locate the product anywhere. The main implication of this technology is that companies will enjoy a reduction in theft and loss of merchandise shipments and will always know where merchandise is in the distribution channel. Moreover, as this technology is further developed, marketers will be able to gather essential information related to product usage and consumption.[16]

Improving Customer Service

CRM marketing techniques increasingly are being used to improve customer service. Amazon.com uses several Web site tools that get customers to return. For example, customers can build wish lists of items, much like a gift registry, so friends and family can make purchases for birthday and other occasions. Amazon also offers recommendations for products based on past purchase and search behavior. These recommendations are listed when a registered customer logs on to the site. Finally, Amazon stores all customer payment and shipping information so customers can make a purchase with one click and then track the shipment. Amazon makes the process of searching for and purchasing books and other products easy and efficient.

Privacy Concerns and CRM

Before rushing out to invest in a CRM system and build a database, marketers should consider consumers' reactions to the growing use of databases. Customers around the world are concerned about databases because of the potential for invasion of privacy. The sheer volume of information aggregated in databases makes it vulnerable to unauthorized access and use. A fundamental aspect of marketing using CRM databases is providing valuable services to customers based on knowledge of what customers really value. It is critical, however, that marketers remember that these relationships should be built on trust. Although database technology enables marketers to

In a recent study by Experian, the group most likely to act on direct mail is the one comprised of 15- to 24-year-olds. Companies that email offers with coupons, discounts, or free products to this group will see better responses to offers. This group is also the most likely to research products and companies before purchasing items. If a company or product has an unfavorable overall review, however, discounts are unlikely to benefit sales to the 15- to 24-year-old demographic.[15]

compile ever-richer information about their customers that can be used to build and manage relationships, if these customers feel their privacy is being violated, then the relationship becomes a liability.

The popularity of the Internet for e-commerce and customer data collection and as a repository for sensitive customer data has alarmed privacy-minded customers. Online users complain loudly about being "spammed," and Web surfers, including children, are routinely asked to divulge personal information to access certain screens or purchase goods or services. Many users are unaware of how personal information is collected, used, and distributed. The government actively sells huge amounts of personal information to list companies. Hospitals sell the names of women who just gave birth on their premises. Consumer credit databases are often used by credit card marketers to prescreen targets for solicitations. Online and off-line privacy concerns are growing and ultimately will have to be dealt with by businesses and regulators.

In 2007, Privacy International, a human rights research and campaign organization based in U.K., investigated the privacy practices of key Internet-based companies for six months. The results list the best and the worst performers across search, e-mail, e-commerce, and social networking sites. Amazon.com, AOL, Apple, eBay, Facebook, Google, and Yahoo! rank from notable lapses in privacy protection to being hostile to privacy. Privacy International considers its report an initial consultation and will continue soliciting input over several months before releasing a final report.[17]

Privacy policies for companies in the United States are largely voluntary, and regulations on how personal data are collected and used are being developed. But collecting data on consumers outside the United States is a different matter. For database marketers venturing beyond U.S. borders, success requires careful navigation of foreign privacy laws. For example, under the European Union's (EU) European Data Protection Directive, any business that trades with a European organization must comply with the EU's rules for handling information about individuals or risk prosecution. More than 50 nations have or are developing privacy legislation. Europe has the strictest legislation regarding the collection and use of customer data, and other countries are looking to that legislation when formulating their policies.

Review And Applications

Define customer relationship management. Customer relationship management (CRM) is a company-wide business strategy designed to optimize profitability, revenue, and customer satisfaction by focusing on highly defined and precise customer groups. This is accomplished by organizing the company around customer segments, encouraging and tracking customer interaction with the company, fostering customer-satisfying behaviors, and linking all processes of a company from its customers through its suppliers.

1.1 Identify the six components of the CRM process.

1.2 Form a team and identify several local businesses that would benefit from a CRM strategy. Select one business and outline a plan for implementing a CRM strategy for that business. You may want to visit the company and interview managers about their current initiatives. When you have completed your CRM plan, share it with the class—and the company.

1.3 General Motors installs the "OnStar" system in many of its vehicles. OnStar is a location, information, and communication system available to drivers who wish to subscribe to the service. Go to the OnStar Web site, **www.onstar.com,** and read about some of the services that are offered to consumers. Based on what you learn, write a short report describing the various ways that OnStar can be used as a CRM tool, specifically in the context of creating interactions, gathering customer data, and customizing service offerings to customers.

Explain how to identify customer relationships with the organization. Companies that implement a CRM system adhere to a customer-centric focus or model. A customer-centric company focuses on learning the factors that build long-lasting relationships with valuable customers and then builds its system on what satisfies and retains those customers. Building relationships through CRM is a strategic process that focuses on learning, managing customer knowledge, and empowerment.

2.1 Briefly explain the concept of a customer-centric focus. Why is this so important in a CRM process?

2.2 What is meant by knowledge management? Why is it so important in a CRM system?

Understand interactions with the current customer base. The interaction between the customer and the organization is considered to be the foundation on which a CRM system is built. Only through effective interactions can organizations learn about the expectations of their customers, generate and manage knowledge about them, negotiate mutually satisfying commitments, and build long-term relationships. Effective management of customer interactions recognizes that customers provide information to organizations across a wide variety of touch points. Consumer-centric organizations are implementing new and unique approaches for establishing interactions specifically for this purpose. They include Web-based interactions, point-of-sale interactions, and transaction-based interactions.

3.1 Develop a plan for establishing and managing interactions with a business's customers. In this plan, identify the key touch points for customers, explain how the data warehouse would be designed, and indicate the main interaction methods that would be promoted to the customer.

Outline the process of capturing customer data. Based on the interaction between the organization and its customers, vast amounts of information can be obtained. In a CRM system, the issue is not how much data can be obtained, but rather what type of data should be acquired and how those data can be used effectively for relationship enhancement. The channel, transaction, and product or service consumed all constitute touch points between a customer and the organization. These touch points represent possible areas within a business where customer interactions can take place and, hence, the opportunity for acquiring data from the customer.

4.1 Assume you are the manager for a department store. You have decided to provide your customers with a feedback form at the billing counter to gather information on their shopping experience. Your boss has asked you to design a questionnaire for the same. What aspects will you cover in the questionnaire to get a complete picture of customer shopping experience and how will this data help you in improving your customer relation management?

Describe the use of technology to store and integrate customer data. Customer data gathering is complicated because information needed by one unit of the organization (e.g., sales and marketing) is often generated by another area of the business or even a third-party supplier (e.g., an independent marketing research firm). Because of the lack of standard structure and interface, organizations rely on technology to capture, store, and integrate strategically important customer information. The process of centralizing data in a CRM system is referred to as data warehousing. A data warehouse is a central repository of customer information collected by an organization.

5.1 Briefly explain the concept of a data warehouse. In the context of a CRM framework, why is a data warehouse such an important tool?

5.2 What is being written about customer data in today's periodicals? Search your favorite database of articles using keywords like "customer data" and "data warehousing." Are certain industries better represented in the citation list generated by your search? Are certain issues more prevalent? Read a selection of at least three to four articles, and write a brief analysis of what is being discussed in the press regarding these CRM topics.

Describe how to identify the best customers. Customer relationship management, as a process strategy, attempts to manage the interactions between a company and its customers. To be successful, organizations must identify customers who yield high profitability or high potential profitability. To accomplish this task, significant amounts of information must be gathered from customers, stored and integrated in the data warehouse, and then analyzed for commonalities that can produce segments that are highly similar, yet different from other customer segments. A useful approach to identifying the best customers is recency-frequency-monetary (RFM) analysis. Data mining uses RFM, predictive modeling, and other approaches to identify significant relationships among several customer dimensions within vast data warehouses. These significant relationships enable marketers to better define the most profitable customers and prospects.

6.1 Explain the concept of data mining. Provide five examples of companies that are currently using data mining and explain why each is using it.

Explain the process of leveraging customer information throughout the organization. One of the benefits of a CRM system is the capacity to share information throughout the organization. This allows an organization to interact with all functional areas to develop programs targeted to its customers. This process is commonly referred to as campaign management. Campaign management involves developing customized product/service offerings for the appropriate customer segment and pricing and communicating these offerings for the purpose of enhancing customer relationships.

7.1 Campaign management is a benefit derived by an organization's ability to leverage and disseminate information throughout the company. Briefly define campaign management and explain how a business may apply it to its daily operations. In your answer, select a particular business as an example of effective campaign management.

7.2 What kind of product testing is currently going on at the Procter & Gamble Web site (**www.pg.com**)? Sign up to participate and find out how the company implements its one-to-one marketing plan through its Web site.

Exercises

APPLICATION EXERCISE

Understanding how companies use consumer information can be difficult if you have never had a job or internship that required you to use databases or customer profiles.[18]

Activities

1. Save all the direct-mail advertising that comes to your mailbox for at least a week. You may ask your parents or friends to collect direct mail that they receive as well.
2. Once you have your stack of mail, organize it according to the household that received it. For example, if friends and family helped you collect mail, then keep mail sent to each address together. Make a list of all material in each group.
3. To what kind of customer is each piece of mail targeted? What makes you think as you do?
4. Based on the content of the mail pieces, determine what kind of information the various companies have about you, your friends, or your

family in their databases. Are there indications on the mailers about what kind of interactions the recipient has had with the sender of the marketing piece?

5. Write out an aggregate profile for each address. If you were a direct marketer, what kind of products and services would you market to each? What kind of offers would you create?

ETHICS EXERCISE

By combining several of its databases of parental purchasing behavior and the results of its market research, Maxwell, Inc., believes it has the tools to launch one-to-one marketing messages for the six- to nine-year-old fans of its JoyMax educational toy products without violating the law. In spite of potential parental backlash, Maxwell believes the approach will help it customize new children's products and increase the company's share of these profitable young customers.

Questions

1. What do you think? Should Maxwell use one-to-one marketing tools to communicate with children?
2. Does the AMA Statement of Ethics address marketing to children? Go to **www.marketingpower.com** and review the statement. Then, write a brief paragraph on how the AMA Statement of Ethics relates to Maxwell's dilemma.

MARKETING PLAN EXERCISE

Your final strategic marketing plan exercise is to identify the ways in which your company will leverage the capabilities of database technology for implementation, evaluation, and control. A strategic plan is effective only when it is acted upon, so implementation guidelines should list specific action plans and a recommended time frame. Evaluation is needed to see if actual marketing activities are resulting in expected objectives. If not, control measures will need to take place. Use the following exercises to guide you through the additional technology aspects of a strategic marketing plan and then complete the Part 7 Marketing Plan Worksheet on your companion Web site at **www.cengage.com/international**

1. Specify how you will tailor your marketing strategies to reach and serve your most profitable customers and prospects
   - Identify the Best Customers
   - Retain Loyal Customers
   - Cross-Sell Other Products or Services
   - Target Marketing Communications
   - Reinforce Customer Purchase Decisions
   - Induce Product Trials
   - Increase Effectiveness of Channels
   - Improve Customer Service
2. Investigate the expansion of your marketing efforts to include a database marketing program. How will you collect data? How will you use it? What effect will the creation of the database have on your diverse marketing methods (mailings, catalogs, e-mailings, coupon distribution, product sample distribution, and so on)? How will this data be used? Write your online privacy policy.
3. Project management tools are the best way to set up your implementation, evaluation, and control program. Visit **www.allpm.com** to learn about project planning, alternative software tools, and free project information. For a free timeline utility tool, visit **www.smartdraw.com.** Decide whether the marketing or operations department will manage the implementation and control of the plan.
4. Make sure performance standards are set for each area of the marketing plan. Comparing performance against objectives is why objectives must be stated in numerical terms. What will your objectives be in terms of traffic (hits), sales, page views, visits per customer, and length of average visit (in minutes)? Which measurement is most important? Why?

Short Case: LOYALTY PROGRAM, WESTSIDE-CLUBWEST

Prepared by
Dr. Dheeraj Sharma,
Indian Institute of Management, Ahmedabad

Tata's retail arm Trent Ltd launched a lifestyle chain Westside in 1998 in Bangalore. In about a decade it made a good name for itself in the Indian retail market. The credit for the success of Westside chains can be attributed to the core company's values and commitment towards satisfying customers. The assortment of Westside range of products reflects the invaluable consumer insights that are taken into consideration. Affordability, style and good quality products are the pillars on which this chain has been expanding successfully. Another factor that contributes to Westside's popularity is that most of its products were made in-house (private labeled). This enables them to launch market-specific customized products keeping in sync with the regional diversities, in terms of consumer's taste and preference.

As Westside continues to garner a large consumer base, it has taken proactive steps to retain its customers by shifting from a "transactional approach" to a more "relational" approach through effective CRM since May 2001. Its customer loyalty program Clubwest offers unique ways to earn rewards and points to its customers. A complimentary membership, *ClubWest Classic* is given free of cost if one makes a purchase of more than ₹2000. Similarly, a complimentary membership, *ClubWest Gold is given free of cost,* if one makes a purchase of more than ₹5000. A part of this program membership cards can be sold at the billing counters at ₹150. Members earned reward points that could be redeemed in their subsequent purchase. Benefits and attractions also include like access to plenty of privileges and services through ties ups, intimating its members with exclusive shopping hours, seasonal sales, discounts, product launches, and promotions through direct mailers. Besides, these members can also avail gift vouchers, rebates on restaurants, holiday packages and home delivery of goods facility. Customers are allowed to return or exchange goods in a stipulated time, without any hassle. Great care was taken in addressing consumer grievances promptly and customers were made to fill specialized feedback forms. Feedback forms were a source through which they analyzed customers taste and suggestions.[19]

Such instruments and mechanisms have enabled a two way interaction between the firm and the consumers. It has helped Westside to attain emotionally loyal customers who not only make subsequent visits and purchases but enhance the brand image by word-of-mouth. Westside's work culture and ethics along with its efficient Customer loyalty program makes Westside one of the most trusted and preferred domestic stores in India.

Himanshu Chakrawarti, General Manager, Trent is quoted on Tata Group website "*Club West members are the major shoppers at Westside. The program, which has been running for the last two years, now has more than 1,60,000 members. The program is about building long-term relationships. We call it bonding; it is our glue.*"[20]

Questions

1. Over a period of time, different types of loyal consumers emerge. As the program is currently designed, it rewards customers based on the amount spent. This process does not differentiate between an infrequent user and a frequent user. Do you think Westside should continue with this loyalty program as it is; or it should segment its customers based on types of loyalty and make customized initiatives for different categories?
2. Should they treat Loyalty Customers differently, or should they follow a consistent program across all users?

21 Customer Relationship Management (CRM)

KEY TERMS

LO 1

customer relationship management (CRM) a company-wide business strategy designed to optimize profitability, revenue, and customer satisfaction by focusing on highly defined and precise customer groups

LO 2

customer-centric a philosophy under which the company customizes its product and service offering based on data generated through interactions between the customer and the company

learning an informal process of collecting customer data through customer comments and feedback on product or service performance

knowledge management the process by which learned information from customers is centralized and shared in order to enhance the relationship between customers and the organization

empowerment delegation of authority to solve customers' problems quickly—usually by the first person the customer notifies regarding the problem

interaction the point at which a customer and a company representative exchange information and develop learning relationships

LO 3

touch points all possible areas of a business where customers communicate with that business

point-of-sale interactions communications between customers and organizations that occur at the point of sale, normally in a store

KEY CONCEPTS

LO 1

Define *customer relationship management*. Customer relationship management (CRM) is a company-wide business strategy designed to optimize profitability, revenue, and customer satisfaction by focusing on highly defined and precise customer groups. This is accomplished by organizing the company around customer segments, encouraging and tracking customer interaction with the company, fostering customer-satisfying behaviors, and linking all processes of a company from its customers through its suppliers.

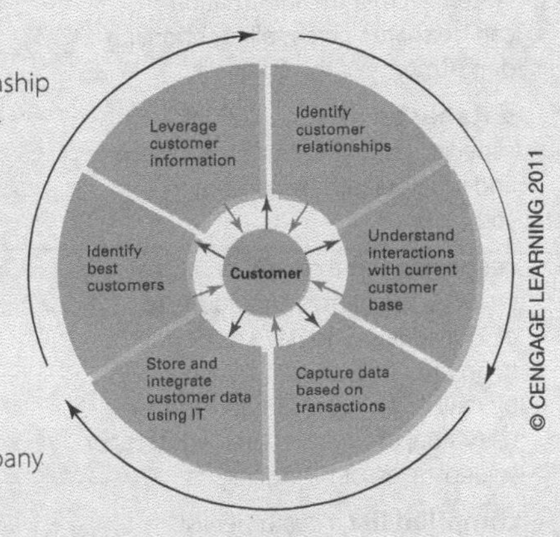

LO 2

Explain how to identify customer relationships with the organization. Companies that implement a CRM system adhere to a customer-centric focus or model. A customer-centric company focuses on learning the factors that build long-lasting relationships with valuable customers and then builds its system on what satisfies and retains those customers. Building relationships through CRM is a strategic process that focuses on learning, managing customer knowledge, and empowerment.

LO 3

Understand interactions with the current customer base. The interaction between the customer and the organization is considered to be the foundation on which a CRM system is built. Only through effective interactions can organizations learn about the expectations of their customers, generate and manage knowledge about them, negotiate mutually satisfying commitments, and build long-term relationships. Effective management of customer interactions recognizes that customers provide information to organizations across a wide variety of touch points. Consumer-centric organizations are implementing new and unique approaches for establishing interactions specifically for this purpose. They include Web-based interactions, point-of-sale interactions, and transaction-based interactions.

LO 4

Outline the process of capturing customer data. Based on the interaction between the organization and its customers, vast amounts of information can be obtained. In a CRM system, the issue is not how much data can be obtained, but rather what type of data should be acquired and how those data can be used effectively for relationship enhancement. The channel, transaction, and product or service consumed all constitute touch points between a

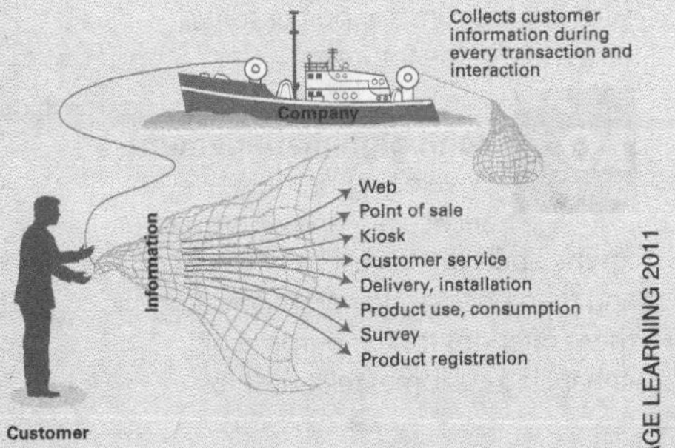

LO 5 **data warehouse** a central repository for data from various functional areas of the organization that are stored and inventoried on a centralized computer system so that the information can be shared across all functional departments of the business

database a collection of data, especially one that can be accessed and manipulated by computer software

response list a customer list that includes the names and addresses of individuals who have responded to an offer of some kind, such as by mail, telephone, direct response television, product rebates, contests or sweepstakes, or billing inserts

compiled list a customer list developed by gathering names and addresses from telephone directories and membership rosters, usually enhanced with information from public records, such as census data, auto registrations, birth announcements, business start-ups, or bankruptcies

LO 6 **lifetime value analysis (LTV)** a data manipulation technique that projects the future value of the customer over a period of years using the assumption that marketing to repeat customers is more profitable than marketing to first-time buyers

predictive modeling a data manipulation technique in which marketers try to determine, based on some past set of occurrences, what the odds are that some other occurrence, such as a response or purchase, will take place in the future

LO 7 **campaign management** developing product or service offerings customized for the appropriate customer segment and then pricing and communicating these offerings for the purpose of enhancing customer relationships

customer and the organization. These touch points represent possible areas within a business where customer interactions can take place and, hence, the opportunity for acquiring data from the customer.

LO 5 **Describe the use of technology to store and integrate customer data.** Customer data gathering is complicated because information needed by one unit of the organization (e.g., sales and marketing) is often generated by another area of the business or even a third-party supplier (e.g., an independent marketing research firm). Because of the lack of standard structure and interface, organizations rely on technology to capture, store, and integrate strategically important customer information. The process of centralizing data in a CRM system is referred to as data warehousing. A data warehouse is a central repository of customer information collected by an organization.

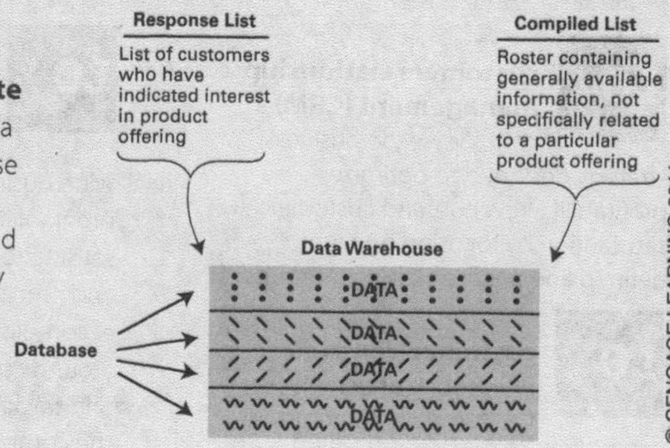

© CENGAGE LEARNING 2011

LO 6 **Describe how to identify the best customers.** Customer relationship management, as a process strategy, attempts to manage the interactions between a company and its customers. To be successful, organizations must identify customers who yield high profitability or high potential profitability. To accomplish this task, significant amounts of information must be gathered from customers, stored and integrated in the data warehouse, and then analyzed for commonalities that can produce segments that are highly similar, yet different from other customer segments. A useful approach to identifying the best customers is recency-frequency-monetary (RFM) analysis. Data mining uses RFM, predictive modeling, and other approaches to identify significant relationships among several customer dimensions within vast data warehouses. These significant relationships enable marketers to better define the most profitable customers and prospects.

LO 7 **Explain the process of leveraging customer information throughout the organization.** One of the benefits of a CRM system is the capacity to share information throughout the organization. This allows an organization to interact with all functional areas to develop programs targeted to its customers. This process is commonly referred to as campaign management. Campaign management involves developing customized product/service offerings for the appropriate customer segment and pricing and communicating these offerings for the purpose of enhancing customer relationships.

© CENGAGE LEARNING 2011

CHAPTER 22

Social Media and Marketing

Learning Outcomes

LO 1 Describe social media, how it is used, and its relation to integrated marketing communications

LO 2 Explain how to create a social media campaign

LO 3 Evaluate the various methods of measurement for social media

LO 4 Explain consumer behavior on social media

LO 5 Describe the social media tools in a marketer's toolbox and how they are useful

LO 6 Describe the impact of mobile technology on social media

For most people, social media is meant to be a social experience, not a marketing experience.

LO1 What Is Social Media?

social media any tool or service that uses the Internet to facilitate conversations

The most exciting thing to happen to marketing and promotion is the increasing use of online technology to promote brands, particularly social media. Social media has changed the way that marketers can communicate with their brands—from mass messages to intimate conversations. As marketing moves into social media, marketers must remember that for most people, social media is meant to be a social experience, not a marketing experience. In fact, social media is many things to different people, though most people think of it as digital technology. Brian Solis, of FutureWorks, defines **social media** as "any tool or service that uses the Internet to facilitate conversations."[1] However, social media can also be defined relative to traditional advertising like television and magazines in that traditional marketing media offers a mass media method of interacting with consumers, while social media offers more one-to-one ways to meet consumers. Social media also has more sophisticated methods of measuring how marketers meet and interact with consumers than traditional advertising. Currently, social media includes tools and platforms like social networks, blogs, microblogs, and media sharing sites, which can be accessed through a growing number of devices such as computers, laptops, Smartphones, e-readers, tablets, and netbooks. This technology changes daily, offering consumers new ways to experience social media platforms, which must constantly innovate to keep up with consumer demands.

***Note:* All the figures in U.S. dollars are converted into rupee using the value $1 = ₹45.**

At the basic level, social media consumers want to exchange information, collaborate with others, and have conversations. Social media has changed how and where conversations take place, making human interaction global through popular technology. Research shows that more than 73 percent of active online users have read a blog and more than half belong to at least one social network. Marketing consultant John Haydon said, "The real value of social media is that it exponentially leverages word-of-mouth."[2] Clearly, conversations are happening online; it is up to the marketer to decide if engaging in those conversations will be profitable and to find the most effective method of entering the conversation.

Marketers are interested in online communications because it is wildly popular; brands, companies, individuals, and celebrities promote their messages online. Today, Lady Gaga reigns as the queen of social media: She holds the record for the living person with the most Facebook fans; on Twitter she directly interacts with her millions of followers; the music video for the song "Bad Romance" holds the title of most viewed video ever on YouTube. Lady Gaga's celebrity is due in large part to being a highly effective brand—her messages resonate with audiences worldwide, and she makes her brand easily accessible through popular social media platforms. Her carefully crafted social media strategy has translated into real money; Lady Gaga recently debuted on the Forbes Celebrity 100 Power List for 2010 at number 4, earning more than ₹279 crore (including her corporate sponsorships and endorsements) in the past 12 months.[3] As far as brands go, very few marketers have leveraged social media to drive sales of core products better than Lady Gaga.[4]

© AP PHOTO/CHRIS PIZZELLO

How Consumers Use Social Media

Hoping to replicate some of Lady Gaga's social media success, many marketers are looking to get their message on the fastest-growing social media platform—Facebook. Facebook originated as a community for college students that opened to the general public as its popularity grew. There are hundreds of lakhs of users on Facebook. If Facebook were a country, it would be the third largest in the world. The largest area of growth in new profiles is the segment of people in the age group of late 40s to mid 60s, who use it as a way to connect with old friends and keep up with family. Other social networks, like MySpace and LinkedIn, offer alternative networks to other demographics. MySpace has a large music-oriented following, and many bands and musicians preview albums and music videos on MySpace pages. Videos are one of the most popular tools by which marketers reach consumers, and YouTube is by far the largest online video repository—it has more content than any major television network. Due to its connection with Google, YouTube offers a powerful search tool as well.[5] Flickr is a popular photo sharing site, where lakhs of people upload new photos daily. Twitter boasts hundreds of lakhs of registered users who average crores of tweets daily (just check out the Web site GigaTweet to see a running total). Technorati tracks hundreds of lakhs of blogs and indexes an estimated two lakhs new blog posts per day.[6] More than half of Technorati's active users have uploaded photos, and almost a quarter have uploaded videos. The bottom line, according to Universal McCann's Comparative Study on Social Media Trends, is that "if you are online, you are using social media."[7]

Increased usage of alternative platforms like Smartphones and tablet computers has further contributed to the proliferation of social media usage. In

India, there were 81.2 crore mobile telephone subscribers at the end of March 2011. Among this group, there were around 3.72 crore *claimed mobile Internet users*[8], and 2.63 crore *active mobile Internet users*[9]. The most used applications through mobile Internet are e-mail, chat, search , and social networking sites.[10] The ownership of mobile phones among the youth segment of India (8–24 years old) has witnessed a steady growth in recent times, increasing from 28 percent in 2008 to 37 percent in 2010. This is far ahead of the Asia regional average of 18 percent, thereby highlighting that mobile ownership of young Indians is highest as compared to their other Asian counterparts. The most popular mobile activities among the Indian youth are music (59 percent), messaging (58 percent), clicking pictures (51 percent), and playing games (46 percent).[11] In April 2010, Apple released the much anticipated iPad tablet computer. More than 8,500 native iPad apps (many of which connect to social networks) are available for download, and within the first two months of the tablet's release, 3.5 crore downloads had already been recorded.[12] The overall impact of tablet computing on social media (and thus the discipline of marketing) is yet to be seen, but given the incredible impact that the Smartphone has had in its short life span, tablets could prove to be game changing.

Social Commerce A new area of growth in social media is **social commerce**, which combines social media with the basics of e-commerce. Social commerce is a subset of e-commerce that involves the interaction and user contribution aspects of social online media to assist online buying and selling of products and services.[13] Basically, social commerce relies on user-generated content on Web sites to assist consumers with purchases. Social commerce sites often include ratings and recommendations (like Amazon) and social shopping tools (like Groupon). In general, social commerce sites are designed to help consumers make more informed decisions on purchases or services. Though the concept of group buying is extremely popular in the western markets, it is a superficial notion in India.[14]

Social Media and Integrated Marketing Communications

While marketers typically employ a social media strategy alongside traditional channels like print and broadcast, many budget pendulums are swinging toward social media. According to FICCI-KPMG report on media and entertainment industry in India, the Indian online advertising market was valued close to ₹1,000 crore in 2010, with paid search constituting up to 50 percent of this market. This market is expected to cross the ₹2,500 crore mark in 2014. The mobile advertising market also grew rapidly to reach around ₹40 crore in 2010 and is expected to attain the value of ₹1,000 crore by 2014-2015.[15]

social commerce
a subset of e-commerce that involves the interaction and user contribution aspects of social online media to assist online buying and selling of products and services

A unique consequence of social media is the widespread shift from one-to-many communication to many-to-many communication. Instead of simply putting a brand advertisement on television with no means for feedback, social media allows marketers to have conversations with consumers, forge deeper relationships, and build brand loyalty. Social media also allows consumers to connect with each other, share opinions, and collaborate on new ideas according to their interests. In June 2006, Sunsilk launched its online community called Gang of Girls exclusively for young girls. The community enabled the girls to express themselves as well as interact with others. The site became an instant hit—with registrations reaching the 2,50,000 mark, 25,000 "gangs" formed, 20 crore

crowdsourcing
using consumers to develop and market product

hits on the site, and about 1.2–1.3 crore page views per month—within 6 months of launch. Over the years, the site added several online tools like GOG TV, GOG chat, "life can't wait moment" tool, fashion content, blogs, and much more to keep alive the charm of Sunsilk. Enthused by the success of the community, HLL (now HUL) considered taking the Web site global.[16] With social media, the audience is often in control of the message, the medium, the response, or all three. This distribution of control is often difficult for companies to adjust to, but the focus of social marketing is unavoidably on the audience, and the brand must adapt to succeed. The interaction between producer and consumer becomes less about entertaining and more about listening, influencing, and engaging.

In 2009, Hewlett-Packard used social media to avert a public relations (PR) crisis after a video claiming that HP was racist garnered 20 lakhs views on YouTube. Because it was aware of its customers' social dialogues, HP learned about the groundswell early on and was able to quell the story before it gained too much momentum.[17] Mountain Dew's marketing team tested the limits of consumer control and the power of social media by moving the brand's advertising almost entirely online. The team tapped into the brand's core consumer demographic—18- to 39-year-old males with strong Facebook, MySpace, and You Tube presences—to build line extensions and help choose a marketing partner.

Using consumers to develop and market product is called **crowdsourcing**. Crowd-sourcing describes how the input of many people can be leveraged to make decisions that used to be based on the input of only a few people.[18] Companies get feedback on marketing campaigns, new product ideas, and other marketing decisions by asking customers to weigh in. Van Heusen used its community members' inputs to launch a new product line called *Eco Range*. The customers were directly involved in the product development process and the product range was built in line with youth's preference for eco-friendly products. The company also runs a program called *Coffee Mornings* during the weekends that enables interaction between the designing team of the brand and around 20 online community members. Similarly, *Will Lifestyle* from ITC is using sites like Facebook, wherein its fans can upload pictures and have forum discussions, to understand the latest trends among youth.[19]

LO 2 Creating and Leveraging a Social Media Campaign

Social media is an exciting new field, and its potential for expanding a brand's impact is enormous. Because its costs are often minimal and its learning curve is relatively low, some organizations are tempted to dive headfirst into social media. However, as with any marketing campaign, it is always important to start with a strategy. For most organizations, this means starting with a marketing or communications plan, as covered in Chapter 2.

The new communication paradigm created by a shift to social media marketing raises questions about categorization. In light of the convergence of traditional and digital media, researchers have explored

A young woman holds a glass of red wine during an online wine tasting. People from all parts of Germany regularly meet online to taste wine and exchange opinions via Twitter, generating earned media buzz for the winery whose wine they are drinking.

© Z1031/JAN WOITAS/DPA/CORBIS

different ways that interactive marketers can categorize media types. One such researcher, Sean Corcoran of Forrester Research, devised a distinction between owned, earned, and paid media. **Owned media** is online content that an organization creates and controls. Owned media includes blogs, Web sites, Facebook pages, and other social media presences. The purpose of owned media is to develop deeper relationships with customers. **Earned media** is a PR term connoting free media such as mainstream media coverage. In an interactive space, media is earned through word of mouth or online buzz about something the brand is doing. Earned media includes viral videos, retweets, comments on blogs, and other forms of customer feedback resulting from a social media presence. **Paid media** is content paid for by the company to be placed online. Paid media is similar to marketing efforts that utilize traditional media, like newspaper, magazine, and television advertisements. In an interactive space, paid media includes display advertising, paid search words, and other types of direct online advertising.[20]

To leverage all three types of media, marketers must follow a few key guidelines. First, they must maximize owned media by reaching out beyond their existing Web sites to create portfolios of digital touch points. This is especially true for brands with tight budgets, as the organization may not be able to afford much paid media. Second, marketers must recognize that aptitude at public and media relations no longer translates into earned media. Instead, markets must learn how to listen and respond to stakeholders. This will stimulate word of mouth. Finally, marketers must understand that paid media is not dead but should serve as a catalyst to drive customer engagement.[21] If balanced correctly, all three types of media can be powerful tools for interactive marketers.

The Listening System

The first action a marketing team should take when initiating a social media campaign is simple—it should just listen. Developing an effective listening system is necessary to both understanding and engaging an online audience. Marketers must not only hear what is being said about the brand, the industry, the competition, and the customer—they must pay attention to who is saying what. The specific ways that customers and noncustomers rate, rank, critique, praise, deride, recommend, snub, and generally discuss brands are all important. Negative comments and complaints are of particular importance, both because they can illuminate unknown brand flaws and because they are the comments that tend to go viral. Online tools such as Google Alerts, Google Blog Search, Twitter Search, SiteVolume, Social Mention and Socialcast are extremely helpful in the development of efficient, effective listening. In Exhibit 22.1, social media strategist Jeremiah Owyang outlines eight stages of effective listening. Listening to customers communicate about one's own brand can be very revealing, but social media is also a great way to monitor competitors' online presences, fans, and followers. Paying attention to the ways that competing brands attract and engage with their customers can be particularly enlightening for both small businesses and global brands.

owned media online content that an organization creates and controls

earned media a public relations term connoting free media such as mainstream media coverage

paid media content paid for by a company to be placed online

Social Media Objectives

After establishing a listening platform, the organization should develop a list of objectives for its social media team to accomplish. These objectives must be developed with a clear understanding of how social

BUILDING TRUST ONLINE

In order to succeed with any marketing campaign, customers' trust must be earned. Angie's List in U.S. is a great example of a Web site that consumers trust to guide them to reliable service providers. Here are some guidelines for earning customer trust:

- Online content must be up to date, easy to understand, and valuable. Be the translator for your customers as they wade through message after message.
- Make sure that your Web site is easy to navigate and gives customers quick access to the information and media they came for.
- Make your social space fun and interactive. Interactivity is all about forging relationships. Treat customers like people, not data, and they will treat you as a person, not junk mail.
- Follow contemporary design trends. Your audience will inevitably judge your book by its cover.[22]

EXHIBIT 22.1

Eight Stages of Effective Listening

Stage	Description	Resources Required	Purpose
Stage 1: Without Objective	The organization has established a listening system but has no goals.	Social media notification tools (Google Alerts)	Keep up with brand and competitor information.
Stage 2: Tracking brand mentions	The organization tracks mentions in social space but has no guidance on next steps.	A listening platform with key word report capabilities (Radian6)	Track discussions, understand sentiment, and identify influencers to improve overall marketing strategy.
Stage 3: Identifying market risks and opportunities	The organization seeks discussions online that may result in identification of problems and opportunities.	A listening platform with a large staff dedicated to the client (Converseon)	Staff seeks out discussions and reports to other teams, like product development and sales. These teams then engage the customers directly or conduct further research.
Stage 4: Improving campaign efficiency	The organization uses tools to get real-time data on marketing efficiency.	Web analytics software (Google Analytics)	See a wealth of information about consumers' behavior on their Web sites (and social media).
Stage 5: Measuring customer satisfaction	The organization collects information about satisfaction, including measures of sentiment.	Insight platforms that offer online focus group solutions	Measure impact of satisfaction or frustration during interaction.
Stage 6: Responding to customer inquiry	The organization identifies customers where they are (e.g., Twitter).	A customer service team is allowed to make real-time responses	Generate high sense of satisfaction for customer but generates public complaints.
Stage 7: Better understanding of customers	The organization adds social information to demographics and psychographics to gain a better profile.	Social customer relationship management (CRM) systems to sync data	Social CRM marries database and social media to create a powerful analytical tool. (See Chapter 21 for more on CRM.)
Stage 8: Being proactive and anticipating customer demands	The organization examines previous patterns of data and social behavior to anticipate needs.	Advanced customer database with predictive application (yet to be created)	Modify social media strategy to preempt consumer behavior modifications based on trends.

SOURCES: Jeremiah Owyang, "Web Strategy Matrix: The Eight Stages of Listening," Web Strategy, November 10, 2009, www.web-strategist.com/blog/2009/11/10/evolution-the-eight-stages-of-listening/; Jim Sterne, *Social Media Metrics* (Hoboken, NJ: John Wiley & Sons, 2010).

media changes the communication dynamic with and for customers. Remember—attempting to reach a mass audience with a static message will never be as successful as influencing people through conversation. Marketing managers must set objectives that reflect this reality. Here are some practical ideas that marketing managers should consider when setting social media objectives:

- *Listen and learn.* Monitor what is being said about the brand and competitors, and glean insights about audiences. Use online tools and do research to implement the best social media practices. If you have established a listening strategy, this objective should already be accomplished.
- *Build relationships and awareness.* Open dialogues with stakeholders by giving them compelling content across a variety of media. Engage in conversations, and answer customers' questions candidly. This will both increase Web traffic and boost your search engine ranking.
- *Promote products and services.* The clearest path to increasing the bottom line using social media is to get customers talking about products and services, which ultimately translates into sales.
- *Manage your reputation.* Develop and improve the brand's reputation by responding to comments and criticism that appear on blogs and forums. Additionally, organizations can position themselves as helpful

and benevolent by participating in other forums and discussions.

- *Improve customer service.* Customer comments about products and services will not always be positive. Use social media to search out displeased customers and engage them directly in order to solve their service issues.

LO 3 Evaluation and Measurement of Social Media

Social media has the potential to revolutionize the way organizations communicate with stakeholders. Given the relative ease and efficiency with which organizations can use social media, a positive return on investment (ROI) is likely for many—if not most—organizations. A Forrester Research report found that 95 percent of marketers planned to increase or maintain their investments in social media. However, though they understand that it is a worthwhile investment, most marketers have not been able to figure out how to measure the benefits of social media. As social media evolves, so do the measurements and metrics that track it.[23] Yet, as with traditional advertising, marketers lack hard evidence as to the relative effectiveness of these tools. Some marketers accept this unknown variable and focus on the fact that social media is less about ROI than about deepening relationships with customers; others work tirelessly to better understand the measurement of social media's effectiveness. While literally hundreds of metrics have been developed to measure social media's value, these metrics are meaningless unless they are tied to key performance indicators.[24] For example, a local coffee shop manager may measure the success of her social media presence by the raw number of friends on Facebook and followers on Twitter she has accumulated. But these numbers depend entirely on context. The rate of accumulation, investment per fan and follower, and comparison to similarly sized coffee shops are all important variables to consider. Without context, measurements are meaningless.

Facebook CEO Mark Zuckerberg introduces new features for Facebook during a one-day developer conference sponsored by Facebook. Behind him, you can see myriad ways social networking sites could interact.

THREE AREAS OF MEASUREMENT:

- *Social media measurement:* Ever-changing metrics that are used to determine the ROI of each tool. Social media measurement determines, for example, the conversion rate of a Facebook friend. Tools include Google Analytics, Social Mention, Twinfluence, Twitalyzer, and Klout, among others.[25]
- *Public relations measurement:* Since many modern PR campaigns entail social media, PR measurement exists to calculate the impact of social media on press coverage and other elements of PR. Tools include DIY Dashboard, Tealium, and Vocus, which quantizes information such as share of voice relative to competitors, stories by location, and a sentiment analysis for each press hit.

- *Social media monitoring:* Tools that are used less for campaign metrics and more for customer service improvement, brand management, and prospecting. Tools include BlogPulse, Technorati, Trendrr, Google Trends, Tweetdeck, Visible Technologies, and Trackur. Google News Alerts, a free online tool, leverages Google's search technology to report relevant news stories and blog posts about any topic or organization.

LO 4 Social Behavior of Consumers

blog a publicly accessible Web page that functions as an interactive journal, whereby readers can post comments on the author's entries

Once objectives have been determined and measurement tools have been implemented, it is important to identify the consumer. Who is using social media? What types of social media do they use? Does Facebook attract younger users? Do Twitter users retweet viral videos? These types of questions must be considered because they determine not only which tools will be most effective but also, more importantly, whether launching a social media campaign even makes sense for a particular organization.

Understanding an audience necessitates understanding how that audience uses social media. In *Groundswell*, Charlene Li and Josh Bernoff of Forrester Research identify six categories of social media users, which are listed below.

1. *Creators:* Those who produce and share online content like blogs, Web sites, articles, and videos
2. *Critics:* Those who post comments, ratings, and reviews of products and services on blogs and forums
3. *Collectors:* Those who use RSS feeds to collect information and vote for Web sites online
4. *Joiners:* Those who maintain a social networking profile and visit other sites
5. *Spectators:* Those who read blogs, listen to podcasts, watch videos, and generally consume media
6. *Inactives:* Those who do none of these things[26]

A 2009 study determined that 24 percent of social media users functioned as creators, 37 percent functioned as critics, 21 percent functioned as collectors, 51 percent functioned as joiners, and 73 percent functioned as spectators. While participation in each of these categories trended upward, inactives decreased from 44 percent in 2007 to only 18 percent in 2009.[27] However, recent Forrester research shows that the number of people who contribute content is slowing down. Participation in most categories fell slightly, prompting analysts to recommend that marketers re-examine how they are engaging with their customers online. Despite the apparent slowdown, research also shows that more social networking "rookies" are classified as joiners. Another bright spot is a new category, "conversationalists," or people who post status updates on social networking sites and microblogging services such as Twitter. Conversationalists represent 31 percent of users.[28]

LO 5 Social Media Tools: Consumer- and Corporate-Generated Content

A number of tools and platforms can be employed as part of an organization's social media strategy. Blogs, microblogs, social networks, media creation and sharing sites, social news sites, location-based social networking sites, review sites, and virtual worlds and online gaming all have their place in a company's social marketing plan. These are all tools in a marketing manager's toolbox, available when applicable to the marketing plan but not necessarily to be used all at once. Because of the breakneck pace at which technology changes, this list of resources will surely look markedly different five years from now. More tools emerge every day, and branding strategies must keep up with the ever-changing world of technology. For now, the resources highlighted in this section remain a marketer's strongest set of platforms for conversing and strengthening relationships with customers.

Blogs

Blogs have become staples in many social media strategies and are often a brand's social media centerpiece. A **blog** is a publicly accessible Web page that functions as an interactive journal, whereby readers can post comments on the author's entries. Some experts believe that every company should have a blog that speaks to current and potential customers, not as consumers, but as people.[29] Blogs allow marketers to create content in the form of posts, which ideally build trust and a sense of authenticity in customers. Once posts are made, audience members can provide feedback through comments. Because it opens a dialogue and gives customers a voice, the comments section of a blog post is one of the most important avenues of conversation between brands and consumers.

Blogs can be divided into two broad categories: corporate and professional blogs, and noncorporate blogs such as personal blogs. **Corporate blogs** are sponsored by a company or one of its brands and are maintained by one or more of the company's employees. They disseminate marketing-controlled information and are effective platforms for developing thought leadership, fostering better relationships with stakeholders, maximizing search engine optimization, attracting new customers, endearing the organization with anecdotes and stories about brands, and providing an active forum for testing new ideas. Because blogs are designed to be updated daily, corporate blogs are dynamic and highly flexible, giving marketers the opportunity to adapt their messages more frequently than any other communication channel.

Several brands use blogs effectively. GM's Fast-Lane Blog is considered a corporate best. It is packed with audio, video, and photos and is organized into categories that offer something for everyone. One of FastLane Blog's biggest draws is its high-quality writing. Each reader's comment is answered in a fun and pithy tone, encouraging participation and continued readership (http://fastlane.gmblogs.com). Cleartrip Blog, the official blog of cleartrip.com, offers information to its customers about its products and services and new features. It also uses its blog as a feedback mechanism tool to understand what changes and new features their customers are looking for (http://blog.cleartrip.com/). Infosys uses its blog to educate and spread awareness about flat world (http://www.infosysblogs.com/thinkflat/).[30]

In contrast, **noncorporate blogs** are independent and not associated with the marketing efforts of any particular company or brand. Because these blogs contain information not controlled by marketers, they are perceived to be more authentic than corporate blogs. Mommy bloggers, women who review children's products and discuss family related topics on their personal blogs, use noncorporate blogs. The goal of mommy blogs is to share parenting tips and experiences and become part of a community. Because of the popularity of these and other types of blogs, many bloggers receive products and/or money from companies in exchange for a review. Many bloggers disclose where they received the product or if they were paid, but an affiliation is not always clear. It is important for marketing managers to understand the rules behind complimentary products to bloggers as well as the high potential for social buzz. Even if a company does not have a formal social media strategy, chances are the brand is still out in the blogosphere, whether or not a marketing manager approached a blogger.

corporate blogs blogs that are sponsored by a company or one of its brands and maintained by one or more of the company's employees

noncorporate blogs independent blogs that are not associated with the marketing efforts of any particular company or brand

microblogs blogs with strict post length limits

Microblogs

Microblogs are blogs with strict post length limits. Twitter, the most popular microblogging platform, requires that posts be no more than 140 characters in length. However, there are several other platforms, including Jaiku, Tumblr, Plurk, and, of course, Facebook's status updates. Originally designed as a short messaging system used for internal communication, Twitter has gained global popularity and is now used as a communication and research tool by individuals and brands around the world. A large part of Twitter's success stems from the fact that the platform is extremely versatile: Posts and private messages can be sent and received via text messages, Smartphone apps, desktop clients, external Web sites, tablet computers, and e-mail, among others. Twitter posts, commonly called tweets, can be amended with photos, videos, and external links. Recently, Twitter has changed its interface to include visuals like video and photos and has added new products to try to monetize the site. It has also developed promoted tweets, which are ads that appear in search results and user feeds both on Twitter.com and third-party clients that access the service, such as TweetDeck, twhirl, TwitterBerry and Tweetie. Amitabh Bachchan, aka Big B, uses his Twitter page to keep his fans updated on his activities. His popularity on the micro-blogging is towering, with his account having 1850903 followers—the highest for any bollywood celebrity.[31]

Despite its strict character limit, Twitter has proven effective for disseminating breaking news, promoting longer blog posts and campaigns, sharing links, announcing events, and promoting sales. By following, retweeting, responding to potential customers' tweets, and by tweeting content that inspires customers

social networking sites Web sites that allow individuals to connect—or network—with friends, peers, and business associates

to engage the brand, corporate Twitter users can lay a foundation for meaningful two-way conversation quickly and effectively. Research has found that when operated correctly, corporate Twitter accounts are well respected and well received. MTV India used Twitter effectively to promote its reality series, *Roadies* 8, by running a contest that offered 50 of its fans a chance to exclusively preview the first episode of season 8 in MTV India's office one day prior to its broadcast on national television.[32] Twitter can be used to build communities; aid in customer service; gain prospects; increase awareness; and, in the case of nonprofits, raise funds.

The ways a business can use Twitter to successfully engage with customers are almost limitless. Dell was successful in generating sales worth ₹29.25 crore through its promotions on Twitter. About 15 lakh users get tweets from Dell and have direct interactions with the company.[33] Following the success of Dell on Twitter, Sony's European division too launched a campaign on Twitter, giving an opportunity to the customers to customize a Sony Vaio laptop and get a 10 percent discount on the final price. The limited period offer was exceptionally successful, generating sales of over ₹7.5 crore.[34]

Social Networks

Social networking sites allow individuals to connect—or network—with friends, peers, and business associates. Connections may be made around shared interests, shared environments, or personal relationships. Depending on the site, connected individuals may be able to send each other messages, track each other's activity, see each other's personal information, share multimedia, or comment on each other's blog and microblog posts. Depending on its goals, there are several social networks that a marketing team might engage as part of its social media strategy: Facebook is the largest and fastest-growing network; MySpace caters to younger audiences; LinkedIn is geared toward professionals and businesses who use it to recruit professionals; and niche networks like Instagram, Fab.com, Pinterest, and SoundCloud cater to specialized markets.[35] There is a niche social network for just about every demographic and interest. There is a niche social network for just about every demographic and interest. Beyond those already established, an organization may decide to develop a brand-specific social network or community. While all social networking sites are different, some marketing goals can be accomplished on any such site. Given the right strategy, increasing awareness, targeting audiences, promoting products, forging relationships, highlighting expertise and leadership, attracting event participants, performing research, and generating new business are attainable marketing goals on any social network.

Facebook is by far the largest social networking site. While individual Facebook users create profiles, brands, organizations, and nonprofit causes operate as pages. As opposed to individual profiles, all pages are public and are thus subject to search engine indexing. By maintaining a popular Facebook page, a brand not only increases its social media presence, it also helps to optimize search engine results. Pages often include photo and video albums, brand information, and links to external sites. The most useful page feature, however, is the Wall. The Wall allows a brand to communicate directly with fans via status updates, which enables marketers to build databases of interested stakeholders. When an individual becomes a fan of your organization or posts on your Wall, that information is shared with the individual's friends, creating a mini viral marketing campaign. Other Facebook marketing tools include groups, applications, and ads. Facebook is an extremely important platform for social marketers.

EXHIBIT 22.2
Facebook Lingo

Non-Individual (Usually Corporate)	Individual
Page	Profile
Fan of a page, tells fan's friends that the user is a fan, creates mini viral campaign	Friend a person, send private messages, write on the Wall, see friend-only content
Public, searchable	Privacy options, not searchable unless user enabled

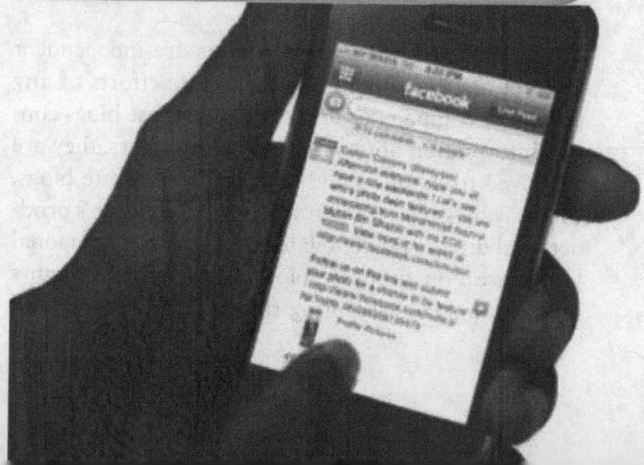

Facebook has proved to be fertile ground for new marketing ideas and campaigns. By creating a Facebook application called Real or Fake in U.S. and U.K., Adobe used the social network's built-in software platform to advertise student editions of the Photoshop photo editing software to college students. When users installed the Real or Fake application, they gained access to weekly images, which they were challenged to distinguish as authentic or digitally manipulated. After they took the challenge, users were directed to tutorials that demonstrated how the altered photos were manipulated using Photoshop. By the end of the campaign, Adobe had earned additional Facebook fans and had witnessed an increase in page views from 5,057 to 53,000 per week. More than 6 percent of Real or Fake users actually purchased the Photoshop software. Through this campaign, Adobe did not just establish a social media presence but also created a novel way to engage its fans.[36] Coca-Cola's Facebook Page, boasting 50 lakh fans, was developed by two individuals in California. Rather than assuming its management, Coca-Cola decided to work with fans to maintain the page. Again, to succeed in social media, organizations must learn to share control with the customer.

LinkedIn features many of the same services as Facebook (profiles, status updates, private messages, company pages, and groups) but is oriented around business and professional connections. Unlike Facebook, LinkedIn features a question-and-answer forum, where users can ask for advice and share expertise in specific fields, and a file hosting service, where users can upload intellectual property like slides, presentations, and other shared documents.[37] LinkedIn is used primarily by professionals who wish to build their personal brands online and businesses who are recruiting employees and freelancers.

media sharing sites Web sites that allow users to upload and distribute multimedia content like videos and photos

Media Sharing Sites

Media sharing sites allow users to upload and distribute multimedia content like videos and photos. Sites such as YouTube and Flickr are particularly useful to brands' social marketing strategies because they add a vibrant interactive channel on which to disseminate content. The distribution of user-generated content has changed markedly over the past few years. Today, organizations can tell compelling brand stories through videos, photos, and audio.

Photo sharing sites allow users to archive and share photos. Flickr, Picasa, Photobucket, Facebook, Zoomin, and Picsquare all offer free photo hosting services that can be utilized by individuals and businesses alike. For example, to strengthen its image of transparency and its relationship with potential donors, the American Red Cross maintained hundreds of Hurricane Katrina disaster photos and tracked sentiments about Red Cross services on Flickr throughout the crisis.[38]

Video creation and distribution have also gained popularity among marketers because of video's rich ability to tell stories. YouTube, the highest-trafficked video-based Web site and the sixth highest-trafficked site overall, allows users to upload and stream their videos to an enthusiastic and active community.[39] YouTube is not only large (in terms of visitors), it attracts a diverse base of users: Age and gender demographics are remarkably balanced.

Many entertainment companies and movie marketers have used YouTube as a showcase for new products, specials, and movie trailers. For example, Lions Gate Entertainment purchased ad space on the YouTube home page in 15 countries to promote the *Avatar* movie trailer. Sony Music released the video of the song *Kolaveri Di* on Youtube, which soon became a phenomenal hit and spread like a wildfire on the Internet.

A podcast, another type of user-generated media, is a digital audio or video file that is distributed serially for other people to listen to or watch. Podcasts can be streamed online, played on a computer,

These images were used as part of Adobe's Real or Fake game on Facebook. Can you tell which is real and which is fake? The chameleon is fake (those are goat horns imposed on its head), and the road is real (it's in Morocco).

© KENNETH JOW/© ISTOCKPHOTO.COM/ERIC ISSELÉE

social news sites Web sites that allow users to decide which content is promoted on a given Web site by voting that content up or down

location-based social networking sites Web sites that combine the fun of social networking with the utility of location-based GPS technology

uploaded to a portable media player (like an iPod), or downloaded onto a Smartphone (like HTC's Droid Incredible). Podcasts are like radio shows that are distributed through various means and not linked to a scheduled time slot. While they have not experienced the exponential growth rates of other digital platforms, podcasts have amassed a steadily growing number of loyal devotees. A good example of effective use of the medium is using podcasts in the field of medicine for offering virtual clinical education. Medical podcasts are already made available by a number of journals and universities across the globe.[40]

Social News Sites

Social news sites allow users to decide which content is promoted on a given Web site by voting that content up or down. Users post news stories and multimedia for the community to vote on crowd-sourced communities such as Reddit, Digg, and Yahoo! Buzz. The more interest from readers, the higher the story or video is ranked. Marketers have found that these sites are useful for promoting campaigns, creating conversations around related issues, and building Web site traffic.[41] If it is voted up, discussed, and shared enough to be listed among the most popular topics of the day, content posted to a crowd sourced site can go viral across other sites and, eventually, the entire Web. Social bookmarking sites are similar to social news sites but the objective of their users is to collect, save, and share interesting and valuable links. On these sites, users categorize links with short, descriptive tags. Users can search the site's database of links by specific tags or can add their own tags to others' links. In this way, tags serve as the foundation for information gathering and sharing on social bookmarking sites.[42] Examples of social bookmarking sites in India are Hotklix.com and Rambhai.com.

Location-Based Social Networking Sites

Considered by many to be the next big thing in social marketing, location sites can be an important tool in every marketer's radar. Essentially, **location-based social networking sites** combine the fun of social networking with the utility of location-based GPS technology. Foursquare, a popular location site in the United States, treats location-based micronetworking as a game: Users earn badges and special statuses based on their number of visits to particular locations. Users can write and read short reviews and tips about businesses, organize meet-ups, and see which Foursquare-using friends are nearby. Foursquare updates can also be posted to linked Twitter and Facebook accounts for followers and friends to see. Location sites such as Foursquare are particularly useful social marketing tools for local businesses, especially when combined with sales promotions like coupons, special offers, contests, and events. Location sites can be harnessed to forge lasting relationships with and deeply engrained loyalty in customers.[43] For example, a local restaurant can allow consumers to check in on Foursquare using their Smartphone and receive a coupon for that day's purchases. Since the location site technology is relatively new, many brands are still figuring out how best to utilize Foursquare. Facebook added Places to capitalize on this location-based technology, which allows people to "check in" and share their location with their online friends. It will be interesting to see how use of this technology grows over time.

Review Sites

Individuals tend to trust other people's opinions when it comes to purchasing. According to Nielsen Media Research, more than 70 percent of consumers said that they trusted online consumer opinions. This percentage is much higher than that of consumers who

trust traditional advertising. Based on the early work of Amazon and eBay to integrate user opinions into product and seller pages, countless Web sites allowing users to voice their opinions have sprung up across every segment of the Internet market. **Review sites** allow consumers to post, read, rate, and comment on opinions regarding all kinds of products and services. For example, Burrp, a local review directory on the web, combines customer critiques of local businesses with business information and elements of social networking to create an engaging, informative experience. On Burrp, users scrutinize local restaurants, gyms, salons, and other businesses, each of which has a detailed profile page. By giving marketers the opportunity to respond to their customers directly and put their businesses in a positive light, review sites certainly serve as useful tools for local and national businesses.

review sites Web sites that allow consumers to post, read, rate, and comment on opinions regarding all kinds of products and services

Virtual Worlds and Online Gaming

Virtual worlds and online gaming present additional opportunities for marketers to engage with consumers. These include online game sites like ibibo.com, zapak.com, and thegamebox.com. The Indian online gaming was estimated to be around ₹150 crore in 2010, accounting for 15 percent of the entire gaming market.[44] Online games are now being used for branding purposes in the form of in-game advertising or advergaming—virtual world environments are often fertile grounds for branded content. Several businesses, such as ITC's Bingo, Garnier, and Perk, have developed advergames to have direct customer engagement. While Bingo game required the users to help a man in saving his packet of chips, Perk game was about shooting Perk bars at pirate ships.[45] In fact, online gaming is also being used by film production houses for promoting their films. Several films like *Mission Impossible, Lara Croft: Tomb Raider, Ra.One, and Don 2* have used online gaming tool for connecting with movie-goers.[46] While unfamiliar to and even intimidating for many traditional marketers, the field of virtual worlds is an important, viable, and growing consideration for social media marketing.

One area of growth is social gaming. Nearly 25 percent of people play games within social networking sites like Facebook and MySpace. Women are most likely to play with real-world friends or relatives as opposed to strangers. Most play multiple times per week and more than 30 percent play daily. Facebook is by far the largest social network for gaming. The top five games on Facebook are Farmville, Bejeweled Blitz, Texas Hold'em Poker, Café World, and Mafia Wars. Because of the popularity of gaming with friends and relatives through these sites, marketers have to integrate their message based on the social network platforms and the demographic participating in social gaming.[47]

Another popular type of online gaming targets a different group—massive multiplayer online games (MMOGs) target the 18- to 34-yearold males. In these environments, thousands of people play simultaneously, and the games have revenues of more than ₹18,00,000 crore annually. Regardless of the type of experience, brands must be creative in how they integrate into games. Social and real-world–like titles are the most appropriate for marketing and advertising (as opposed to fantasy games), and promotions typically include special events, competitions, and sweepstakes. In some games (like *Sims*), having ads increases the authenticity. For example, Nike offers shoes in *Sims Online* that allow the player to run faster.

LO 6 Social Media and Mobile Technology

While much of the excitement in social media has been based on Web sites and new technology uses, much of the growth lies in new platforms. These platforms include the multitude of Smartphones like iPhones and BlackBerrys as well as netbooks and iPads. The major implications of new platforms mean consumers can access popular Web sites like Facebook, Mashable, Twitter, and Foursquare from their various platforms.

Mobile and Smartphone Technology

More than 25 percent of the world's population[48] and more than 50 percent of Indian population owns a mobile phone.[49] It is no surprise then that the mobile platform is such an effective marketing tool—especially when targeting a younger audience. In 2007, Fair & Lovely designed a mobile advertising campaign, promoted via Reliance Mobile, for its annual scholarship program for girls and generated close to 50,000 leads. In the 2008 presidential campaign, Barack Obama's staff utilized text messaging to raise funds and organize support from college students. Smartphones up the ante by allowing individuals to do nearly everything they can do with a computer—from anywhere. With a Smartphone in hand, reading a blog, writing an e-mail, scheduling a meeting, posting to Facebook, playing a multiplayer game, watching a video, taking a picture, using GPS, and surfing the Internet might all occur during one ten-minute car ride. Smartphone technology, often considered the crowning achievement in digital convergence and social media integration, has opened the door to modern mobile advertising as a viable marketing strategy.

According to research firm Gartner, mobile marketing revenues were expected to reach nearly ₹14,850 crore in 2011, a growth of over 100 percent from 2010 when revenues were ₹7,200 crore.[50] There are several reasons for the recent popularity of mobile marketing. First, an effort to standardize mobile platforms has resulted in a low barrier to entry. Second, especially given younger audiences, there are more consumers than ever acclimating to once-worrisome privacy and pricing policies. Third, because most consumers carry their Smartphones with them at all times, mobile marketing is uniquely effective at garnering consumer attention in real time. Fourth, mobile marketing is measurable: Metrics and usage statistics make it an effective tool for gaining insight into consumer behavior. Finally, mobile marketing's response rate is higher than that of traditional media types like print and broadcast advertisement. Some common mobile marketing tools include:

- *SMS (short message service):* 160-character text messages sent to and from cell phones. SMS is typically integrated with other tools.
- *MMS (multimedia messaging service):* Similar to SMS but allows the attachment of images, videos, ringtones, and other multimedia to text messages.
- *Mobile Web sites (MOBI and WAP Web sites):* Web sites designed specifically for viewing and navigation on mobile devices.
- *Mobile ads:* Visual advertisements integrated into text messages, applications, and mobile Web sites. Mobile ads are often sold on a cost-per-click basis.
- *Bluetooth marketing:* A signal is sent to Bluetooth-enabled devices, which allows marketers to send targeted messages to users based on their geographic locations.
- *Smartphone apps:* Software designed specifically for mobile and tablet devices. These apps include software to turn phones into scanners for various types of barcodes—including QR codes like those found at the ends of Chapters 1 and 2.

One example of mobile technology is offering banking services through a mobile phone—a convenient and eco-friendly way to add value to customers.

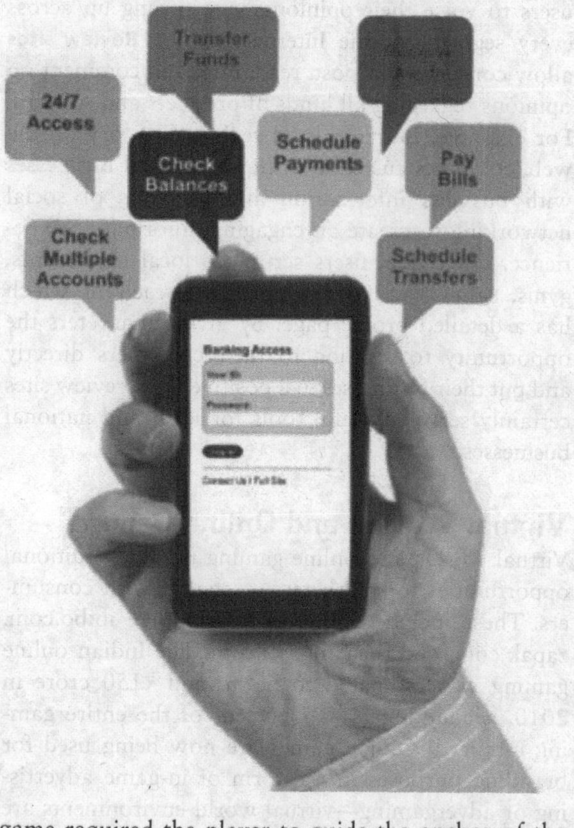

Thums Up Everest Challenge was the first ever mobile game in the world used for brand promotion. The game required the player to guide the anchor of the game in rock climbing, amidst various challenges. It offered a chance to the users to experience the thrill associated with an adventurous activity—the promotion tactic developed in sync with Thums Up strategy of association with extreme sports. Thums Up had always been associated with the proposition of thrill and adventure and was very popular among youth. The mobile game, thus, resonated well with this core proposition of the soft drink.[51]

Applications and Widgets

Given the widespread adoption of Apple's iPhone, RIM's BlackBerry line, Android-based phones, and other Smartphones, it's no surprise that lakhs of applications have been developed for the mobile market. Dozens of new and unique apps that harness mobile technology are added to mobile marketplaces every day. While many apps perform platform-specific tasks, others convert existing content into a mobile-ready format. Whether offering new or existing content, when an app is well branded and integrated into a

HUMANITARIAN TEXTING

In January 2010, a **7.0 earthquake** struck Port-au-Prince, Haiti, and the surrounding areas. By the time the dust settled, 230,000 people had died and 19 lakh more had been left homeless. Among the organizations that pledged aid, the American Red Cross's **text message-based donation campaign** proved to be the true breakthrough story of this crisis. By simply texting "HAITI" to 90999, individuals could make a $10 (₹450) donation to the American Red Cross that was charged to the donator's monthly mobile phone bill. More than three million individuals raised more than ₹144 crore for American Red Cross relief work throughout Haiti—simply by sending text messages.

A number of factors made the campaign successful. The major disaster inspired long-term news coverage, and the ease of texting a donation gave many people a way to help after being exposed to the tragedy. A televised public service announcement by First Lady Michelle Obama prompted a significant spike in donations, as did an NFL play-off game segment during which commentators discussed the Red Cross campaign.[52]

After the massive flooding in Pakistan displaced more than 1.4 crore people, the Disasters Emergency Committee set up a texting donation service similar to that used in Haiti. It is promoted here by the Boxer Amir Khan.

© ANTHONY UPTON/PA WIRE URN:9294569 (PRESS ASSOCIATION VIA AP IMAGES)

company's overall marketing strategy, it can create buzz and generate customer engagement.

One organization that used its Smartphone apps effectively was when Volkswagen Group of America introduced the 2010 GTI sedan in an app called VW Real Racing GTI, which it promoted through Facebook, Twitter, YouTube, and other traditional channels. VW Real Racing GTI is a racing game that allows players to enjoy competitive racing on their mobile devices. VW Real Racing GTI connected with players—it is one of the most talked about Apps from the Apple store, with nearly five million downloads.[53]

Web widgets, also known as gadgets and badges, are software applications that run entirely within existing online platforms. Essentially, a Web widget allows a developer to embed a simple application such as a weather forecast, horoscope, or stock market ticker into a Web site, even if the developer did not write (or does not understand) the application's source code. From a marketing perspective, widgets allow customers to display company information (such as current promotions, coupons, or news) on their own Web sites. Widgets are often cheaper than apps to develop, can extend an organization's reach beyond existing platforms, will broaden the listening system, and can make an organization easier to find.[54]

Allowing customers to promote up-to-date marketing material on their own blogs and Web sites is very appealing, but before investing in a marketing-oriented widget, a number of questions should be considered:

- Does my organization regularly publish compelling content, such as news, daily specials, or coupons, on its Web site or blog?
- Does my content engage individuals or appeal to their needs as customers?
- Is my content likely to inspire conversations with the company or with other customers? Will customers want to share my content with others?

If you can answer yes to these questions, a widget may be an effective tool for your organization.

The Changing World of Social Media

As you read through the chapter, some of the trends that are noted may already seem ancient to you. The rate of change in social media is astounding—usage statistics change daily for sites like Facebook and Twitter. Some things that are in the rumor mill as we write this may have exploded in popularity; others may have fizzled out without even appearing on your radar. In Exhibit 22.3, we've listed some of the items that seem to be on the brink of exploding on to the social media scene. Take a moment to fill in the current state of each. Have you heard of it? Has it come and gone? Maybe it is still rumored, or maybe it has petered out. This exercise highlights not only the speed with which social media changes but also the importance of keeping tabs on rumors. Doing so may result in a competitive advantage by being able to understand and invest in the next big social media site.

EXHIBIT 22.3
Social Media Trends

Site	Change	Where Is It Now?
Facebook	Threaded commenting, up/down voting comments.	
Twitter	Promoted tweets.	
Facebook/Bing	Linked searching in Bing. Search results include similar items liked by Facebook friends, and people searches pull information from your profile to find the correct person.	
Facebook Places/ Foursquare	Facebook Places is just introduced; Foursquare is gaining popularity away from major cities.	
Apple's Ping social music service	Released with iTunes 10, Ping allows users to like music, follow music stars and friends, post songs and albums, and find users with similar music tastes.	

Review And Applications

Describe social media, how it is used, and its relation to integrated marketing communications. Social media, commonly thought of as digital technology, is a way for marketers to communicate one-on-one with consumers and measure the effects of those interactions. Social media includes social networks, microblogs, and media sharing sites, all of which are used by the majority of adults. Smartphones and tablet computers have given consumers greater freedom to access social media on the go, which is likely to increase usage of social media sites. Many advertising budgets are allotting more money to online marketing, including social media, mobile marketing, and search marketing.

1.1 What are the benefits of marketing through social media as compared to traditional media?

1.2 Visit the profile pages of companies like Parle Agro, Aircel, and Axe deodorant on Facebook and ICICI, MTV India, and MSN India on Twitter. How are the companies using these sites for marketing activities?

Explain how to create a social media campaign. A social media campaign should take advantage of the three media categories: *owned media, earned media,* and *paid media.* To use these types of media in a social media campaign, first implement an effective listening system. Marketers can interact with negative feedback, make changes, and effectively manage their online presence. Paying attention to the ways that competing brands attract and engage with their customers can be particularly enlightening for both small businesses and global brands. Second, develop a list of objectives that reflects how social media dynamically communicates with customers and builds relationships.

2.1 As the marketing manager of Cadbury India, you have been asked to prepare a social media campaign for the newly launched *Oreo* biscuits. What do you think would be objectives of this campaign and what type of campaign will you design to attain your objectives?

Evaluate the various methods of measurement of social media. Hundreds of metrics have been developed to measure social media's value, but these metrics are meaningless unless they are tied to key performance indicators. The three areas of media measurement are social media measurement (track return on investment of each social media tool), public relations (PR) measurement (calculate the impact of social media on press coverage and other elements of PR), and social media monitoring (customer service improvement, brand management, and prospecting).

3.1 Is it actually possible to measure the effectiveness of social media? Are the number of followers on social networking sites actually reflective of success of social media?

Explain consumer behavior on social media. To effectively leverage social media, marketers must understand who uses social media and how they use it. If a brand's target market does not use social media, a social media campaign might not be useful. There are six categories of social media users: creators, critics, collectors, joiners, spectators, and inactives. A new category is emerging called "conversationalists," who post status updates on social networking sites or microblogs.

4.1 According to a recent article in *Times of India*, titled *India's saucy foodies*[55], food bloggers are increasingly using social media sites to keep their followers updated on what they are eating. Some of the highly successful blogs are Applemint, Finely Chopped, and former VJ Maria Goretti's personal blog. These blog pages attract thousands of views per month, with people eagerly waiting for the latest pictures or information. What does this trend of following food blogs indicate? How can it be helpful to the companies in the food industry? Can you classify the consumers as per the different categories of social media users?

Describe the social media tools in a marketer's toolbox and how they are useful. A marketer has many tools to implement a social media campaign. However, new tools emerge daily, so these resources will change rapidly. Some of the strongest social media platforms are blogs, microblogs, social networks, media creation, and sharing sites, social news sites, location-based social networking sites, and virtual worlds and online gaming. Blogs allows marketers to create content in the form of posts, which ideally build trust and a sense of authenticity in customers. Microblogs, like Twitter, allow brands to follow, retweet, respond to potential customers' tweets, and tweet content that inspires customers to engage the brand, laying a foundation for meaningful two-way conversation. Social networks allow marketers to increase awareness, target audiences, promote products, forge relationships, attract event participants, perform research, and generate new business. Media sharing sites give brands an interactive channel to disseminate content. Social news sites are useful to marketers to promote campaigns, create conversations, and build Web site traffic. Location-based social networking sites can forge lasting relationships and loyalty in customers. Review sites allow marketers to respond to customer reviews and comments about their brand. Virtual worlds are fertile ground for branded content, and online gaming allows marketers to integrate their message onto a game platform.

5.1 List the benefits of each of the social media platforms available to the marketers. Also give one illustration each to depict how these platforms are being effectively used by companies for marketing activities.

5.2 Would it be a good strategy to focus exclusively on social media for marketing campaign or should one opt for a mix of traditional and social media while designing the marketing campaign?

Describe the impact of mobile technology on social media. There are five reasons for the popularity of mobile marketing: (1) standardized mobile platforms, (2) fewer consumers concerned with privacy and pricing policies, (3) real-time advertising, (4) mobile marketing is measureable, and (5) there is a higher response rate than that with traditional advertising. Because of the rapid growth of Smartphones, well branded, integrated apps allow marketers to create buzz and generate customer engagement. Widgets allow customers to post a company's information to its site, are less expensive than apps, and broaden that company's exposure.

6.1 How has mobile marketing evolved in India? Which are the companies that are extensively using mobile marketing?

6.2 Elucidate the advantages of mobile marketing.

6.3 How are mobile marketing campaigns different from marketing on social networking sites?

Exercises

APPLICATION EXERCISE

With an increase in Internet proliferation in the country, use of social media has increased quite significantly among the Indian population. This has paved the way for marketers to leverage social media platforms to interact with their customers and build long-lasting customer relationships.

Activities

1. Identify such products/product categories that do not have a presence on social media. Can you assess the potential reasons as to why these products/categories are not present on social media?
2. In recent times, social media has been used effectively to raise awareness and voice opinions about social issues. List down five such social issues that became popular on social media and successfully created a public stir. Now try to identify five more such issues that you think can be voiced through social media and design a campaign for any one of them.

ETHICS EXERCISE

With the rise in popularity of social media, the number of people joining any of the social media platforms is also increasing rapidly. However, before joining any of these platforms, the users are required to submit their personal information to such sites. This makes the users vulnerable as the social media players can use the data collected to their advantage and sell it companies, who use it for predicting consumer behavior. This, at times, causes manipulation in advertising and communication on the part of the companies to win over customers' weakness.[56]

Questions

1. Is it ethically correct on the part of social media players to sell customer data to companies, thereby compromising their privacy?
2. By tweaking their communication campaign to win over customers' weakness and providing incorrect information, are the companies not trying to influence the customers improperly?

MARKETING PLAN EXERCISE

With online marketing witnessing a plethora of activities and participation from large number of companies, it would be disadvantageous if your chosen does not utilize this platform for promotions and customer engagement. Use the following exercises to guide you through the social media marketing part of your strategic marketing plan:

1. Identify the competitors who are using social media for the purpose of marketing and communication. Understand how they are building their brand online and what activities are they

performing to connect with their customers. If they are present in traditional media, then try to see if their online campaign has any linkage with the traditional one.

2. Design a social media campaign for your chosen company. List down which all platforms are you going to use for your online presence and what activities are you going to undertake to engage your customers. How will it help in differentiating you from your competitors?

3. How do you intend to measure the effectiveness of your social media campaign?

Short Case: FACEBOOK

Prepared by
Dr. Dheeraj Sharma,
Indian Institute of Management, Ahmedabad

Facebook was found in 2004 by Mark Zuckerberg in the United States. In 2011, the company's revenues amounted to $ 3.71 billion (₹16,695 crore), with advertising contributing as much as 85 percent of its revenues. The site had 845 million (84.5 crore) monthly active users worldwide in 2011, up by 39 percent as compared to 2010.[57] With more than 3.2 crore active users, India is the third biggest market for Facebook after United States and Indonesia.[58] Increasing Internet penetration due to cheaper access and proliferation of the Internet enabled phones, Facebook has been able to increase its activity in India rapidly. Given the trends in further increase in the interest in social networking Web sites, the popularity of Facebook is only expected to soar higher in the coming times. Due to the aforementioned reasons, many companies have now established their own pages on Facebook to connect with their customers. Companies from diverse fields like FMCG, automobiles, hospitality, retail, fashion labels, entertainment, and telecom use Facebook for advertising, communication and promotional activities.[59] According to a study by Socialbakers, the top 5 brands on Facebook in India are Tata Docomo, Kingfisher, Fastrack, Vodafone Zoozoos, and Pepsi India.[60] Apart from the big brands, smaller and relatively unknown brands have also used Facebook quite effectively to create awareness about themselves and build a fan following. Choco Tale, a Gurgaon based chocolate boutique run by a mother and daughter, was able to garner corporate orders pan-India after they reached out on Facebook.[61] Surprisingly, some of these small brands have even outperformed their bigger counterparts in terms of fan following and interactivity. Brands like Wildcraft are far stronger than some of the bigger names like Reebok and Idea Cellular.[62] Similarly, Cocoberry and Mad over Donuts are bigger than established brands such as Dominos Pizza and KFC India.[63] Wildcraft, Cocoberry, and Mad over Donuts are very popular in age group of 16–25 years. The success of the aforementioned brands indicates that social networking Web sites can create strong consumer following. Apart from the corporate brands, Facebook is also being used for promoting social causes or sports. Tata Tea used the medium for urging people to vote, while Aircel used it for promoting its "Save the Tiger Campaign." Similarly, companies such as Airtel and Volkswagen used the platform to promote soccer and polo, respectively.[64] Some of the possible reasons that can be attributed to the growing preference for digital media for marketing activities are no recurring costs, better customer engagement levels, improved visibility, and virility.[65] With the rising popularity of social media, companies have also increased their ad spend on this medium, allocating around 3040 percent of their overall marketing budget on social media.[66]

Questions

1. What are the reasons, according to you, that have led to this gigantic popularity of social networking sites like Facebook?

2. How does a company benefit by advertising on social networking sites?

3. Does advertising on social networking sites merely help in creating awareness or does it actually influence the consumption behaviour of the customers?

4. According to you, is this practice of advertising on social networking sites a current trend or a lone-term, sustainable strategy?

22 CHAPTER REVIEW

Social Media and Marketing

KEY TERMS

LO 1

social media any tool or service that uses the Internet to facilitate conversations

social commerce a subset of e-commerce that involves the interaction and user contribution aspects of social online media to assist online buying and selling of products and services

crowdsourcing using consumers to develop and market product

LO 2

owned media online content that an organization creates and controls

earned media a public relations term connoting free media such as mainstream media coverage

paid media content paid for by a company to be placed online

LO 5

blog a publicly accessible Web page that functions as an interactive journal, whereby readers can post comments on the author's entries

corporate blogs blogs that are sponsored by a company or one of its brands and maintained by one or more of the company's employees

noncorporate blogs independent blogs that are not associated with the marketing efforts of any particular company or brand

microblogs blogs with strict post length limits

social networking sites Web sites that allow individuals to connect—or network—with friends, peers, and business associates

media sharing sites Web sites that allow users to upload and distribute multimedia content like videos and photos

KEY CONCEPTS

LO 1 **Describe social media, how it is used, and its relation to integrated marketing communications.** Social media, commonly thought of as digital technology, is a way for marketers to communicate one-on-one with consumers and measure the effects of those interactions. Social media includes social networks, microblogs, and media sharing sites, all of which are used by the majority of adults. Smartphones and tablet computers have given consumers greater freedom to access social media on the go, which is likely to increase usage of social media sites. Many advertising budgets are allotting more money to online marketing, including social media, mobile marketing, and search marketing.

LO 2 **Explain how to create a social media campaign.** A social media campaign should take advantage of the three media categories: *owned media*, *earned media*, and *paid media*. To use these types of media in a social media campaign, first implement an effective listening system. Marketers can interact with negative feedback, make changes, and effectively manage their online presence. Paying attention to the ways that competing brands attract and engage with their customers can be particularly enlightening for both small businesses and global brands. Second, develop a list of objectives that reflects how social media dynamically communicates with customers and builds relationships.

LO 3 **Evaluate the various methods of measurement of social media.** Hundreds of metrics have been developed to measure social media's value, but these metrics are meaningless unless they are tied to key performance indicators. The three areas of media measurement are social media measurement (track return on investment of each social media tool), public relations (PR) measurement (calculate the impact of social media on press coverage and other elements of PR), and social media monitoring (customer service improvement, brand management, and prospecting).

LO 4 **Explain consumer behavior on social media.** To effectively leverage social media, marketers must understand who uses social media and how they use it. If a brand's target market does not use social media, a social media campaign might not be useful. There are six categories of social media users: creators, critics, collectors, joiners, spectators, and inactives. A new category is emerging called "conversationalists," who post status updates on social networking sites or microblogs.

LO 5 **Describe the social media tools in a marketer's toolbox and how they are useful.** A marketer has many tools to implement a social media campaign. However, new tools emerge daily, so these resources will change rapidly. Some of the strongest social media platforms are blogs, microblogs, social networks, media creation, and sharing sites, social news sites, location-based social networking sites, and virtual worlds and online gaming. Blogs allows marketers to create content in the form of posts, which ideally build trust and a sense of authenticity in customers. Microblogs, like Twitter, allow brands to follow, retweet, respond to potential

social news sites Web sites that allow users to decide which content is promoted on a given Web site by voting that content up or down

location-based social networking sites Web sites that combine the fun of social networking with the utility of location-based GPS technology

review sites Web sites that allow consumers to post, read, rate, and comment on opinions regarding all kinds of products and services

customers' tweets, and tweet content that inspires customers to engage the brand, laying a foundation for meaningful two-way conversation. Social networks allow marketers to increase awareness, target audiences, promote products, forge relationships, attract event participants, perform research, and generate new business. Media sharing sites give brands an interactive channel to disseminate content. Social news sites are useful to marketers to promote campaigns, create conversations, and build Web site traffic. Location-based social networking sites can forge lasting relationships and loyalty in customers. Review sites allow marketers to respond to customer reviews and comments about their brand. Virtual worlds are fertile ground for branded content, and online gaming allows marketers to integrate their message onto a game platform.

LO 6 **Describe the impact of mobile technology on social media.** There are five reasons for the popularity of mobile marketing: (1) standardized mobile platforms, (2) fewer consumers concerned with privacy and pricing policies, (3) real-time advertising, (4) mobile marketing is measureable, and (5) there is a higher response rate than that with traditional advertising. Because of the rapid growth of Smartphones, well branded, integrated apps allow marketers to create buzz and generate customer engagement. Widgets allow customers to post a company's information to its site, are less expensive than apps, and broaden that company's exposure.

CASE 7

Allegiance Corporation Bank:[1] Restructuring Private Banking

© ISTOCKPHOTO.COM/YUNUS ARAKON
© ISTOCKPHOTO.COM/VALERIE LOISELEUX /
© ISTOCKPHOTO.COM/TORSTEN LORENZ

C7.1 Incident One

Allegiance Corporation Bank, Nariman Point Branch, Mumbai, 30 June 2008, 11 am

An extremely well dressed customer hastily got out of his Mercedes and rushed inside the Allegiance Corporation Bank (ACB) Branch. The Branch was swarming with customers, with long queues at each counter. From the customer's puzzled expression, it seemed that this was his first visit to the branch. Helplessly, he looked at the "May I help you?" counter with a queue of almost twenty-five people. He needed to make a transfer of ₹15 lakh immediately via National Electronic Funds Transfer (NEFT)[2]; joining the queue did not seem to him to be a viable option.

He approached a branch staff who conveniently advised him to join the queue. He then looked for the branch manager, but his cabin seemed empty. With no quicker remedy in view, he found himself standing in the queue with the rest. When his turn came half an hour later, he explained his need to the lady at the counter who nonchalantly replied that he would have to meet the branch operations manager. When the customer asked the manager, he excused himself with, "Sorry Sir, but you will have to wait, as only the branch manger is authorised to run the NEFT process. Currently he is in a meeting with the newly-appointed sales staff."

After the customer waited for another hour—with a lunch break in-between—the branch manager arrived. It was 1.30 by then. He glanced at the irritated customer, and asked his peon to send him to his cabin. The frustrated customer mentioned his urgent need for the third time now! The branch manager checked out the customer's account, his balance was ₹20 lakh and his account code was "High Networth Individual-Private Banking Group".

Mindful of the customer's account details, the branch manager ordered a cold drink for him and explained, "Sir, I understand your anxiety, but as per the Reserve Bank rules, the NEFT requests are to be executed at fixed times, at 9.30 and 10.30 am, and at 12, 1, 3, 5 and 6 pm. Please bear with us. In the meanwhile, let me introduce our wealth manager for private banking Mr. Amit Sharma to you. Sir, you can wait in the AC lounge especially built for our private banking customers where Mr. Sharma will take care of you".

To this, the customer replied, "But I think, Mr. Dua is my wealth manager, I have been trying to reach him since yesterday. Isn't he here?" "No Sir, actually he has left the Bank," said the Branch Manager and gulped.

In the Lounge, Mr. Sharma grinningly greeted the customer, "Great to have you here, Sir! How may I help you"? He began to explain his need the fourth time...

C7.2 Incident Two

The Sapphire Conference Room, Grand Hyatt, Pacific Construction Group Meeting, 30 June 2008, 9 am

The Chief Executive Officer (CEO), Mr. Kapoor was addressing his team, and was interrupted by a call on his mobile. He ignored it since it was an unknown number. But it rang again, so this time he excused himself and took the call, "Good morning Sir, this is Sheetal from ACB. You are our most preferred customer, and we can give you a loan of ₹5 lakh without any guarantee or any processing charges", before the caller could say explain further, the CEO said, "Sorry Ma'm" and ended the call. Barely 20 minutes had passed and his mobile started buzzing again. He quickly took the call, "Good afternoon Sir, this is Bhupati calling from ACB, and because you are our preferred customer, we would like to offer you our new platinum credit card. Will you be interested, Sir?" "No!" boomed Mr. Kapoor and switched off the phone putting an end to his frustration.

At the end of the day, Mr. Kapoor decided to call the 24-hour helpline number of the ACB and put in a request for including his mobile number in the "Do Not Call List". He dialled the 10-digit helpline number, only to wait and get his line transferred to the correct person, almost thrice. When he finally got the right person on line, he was asked to give an application to the base branch, and told that the call centre

Written by Ms. Prachi Acharya, Academic Associate, Indian Institute of Management Ahmedabad, under the guidance of Professor Arindam Banerjee

1. The company name, characters names and the situations mentioned in the case are fictitious and are not related to any real life incident.

2. NEFT is a nationwide system that facilitates individuals, firms and corporates to electronically transfer funds from any bank branch to any individual, firm or corporate having an account with any other bank branch in the country. Definition taken from an RBI site: http://www.rbi.org.in/scripts/FAQView.aspx?Id=60

would not take up such requests. "But I am a preferred customer of your bank," exclaimed Mr. Kapoor. "Even then, Sir, I am unable to help you as our system doesn't allow us to enter such a request", was the reply.

An irate Mr. Kapoor summoned his accountant and asked him to end all his dealings with ACB immediately.

* * *

While the above incidents were taking place, Mr. Arpit Basu, Head, Private Banking, Allegiance Corporation Bank (ACB), was deliberating on new Customer Relationship Management (CRM) techniques to enhance the private banking group's (PBG) offerings, oblivious of customer grievances and poor delivery of services by the private banking group. He had just returned from a five-day long stint at the Asian Private Banking Conference in Bangkok and was full of insights, ideas and enthusiasm to bolster up the private banking functions at ACB.

At the same time, given the grim economic scenario, everyone in PBG expected the just–ended first quarter (April–June 08) of the new financial year to be a debacle. To confirm his own suspicion, Mr. Basu studied the comprehensive report on revenue contribution per wealth manager (WM) for the first quarter. The report corroborated his worst fears.

The revenue generation was 18% less than what it was during the same quarter last year (April–June 07). Economic slump and customers retreat from investments in market-linked products seemed to be the primary reasons, until Mr. Basu noticed employee turnover numbers. Out of 100 WMs recruited as senior officers in Jan 08, 26 had already left and 16 had requested for a change of profile.

Mr. Basu instantly called the four zonal managers, (North, East, South and West of the PBG) to put together the causes in a report for the quarter-end sales meet scheduled a few days later, from July 5–8 at the ACB's Head Office.

C7.3 Allegiance Corporation Bank: The Background

The ACB had been functioning as a major private sector bank in India since 1992 with total assets of ₹1,664.01 billion and ₹19.58 billion profit after tax for the year that ended on March 31, 2008. It had a network of 740 branches in India, and its equity shares were listed on the Bombay Stock Exchange and the National Stock Exchange of India Limited. The bank offered a wide range of banking products and financial services to corporate and retail customers through a variety of delivery channels and its specialised subsidiaries and affiliates in the areas of investment banking, life and non-life insurance, venture capital and asset management. The bank had its presence in Bangladesh, China, Hong Kong, Indonesia, Malaysia, Russia, Singapore, Sri Lanka, Thailand, and the United Kingdom. The bank had also stakes in its various subsidiaries (Annexure 1) ranged from general insurance to venture capital funding.

Private Banking

The ACB started investment offerings and selling third-party products in 2000, and then finally structured *private banking* in 2003. Initially the group functioned with coordination with the Retail Banking Group, but in mid of 2007, the group also started to coördinate with the Small and Medium Enterprises Group for expanding their business further. Since its inception, Arpit Basu had been heading the department. He strove hard to upscale it to make a significant impact on the bank's revenue earnings. Private Banking Group structure at the ACB is presented in Annexure 2.

The ACB's total domestic assets under management in private banking were about ₹60 billion in the Accounting Year 2007-08, and the revenue contribution by the group as a whole stood at 3% of total revenue earned by the bank in FY08 which was down by 1% compared to the previous year.

Customer Profile Private banking customers belonged to the high-income segment of the society. More specifically, the ACB termed a customer high net worth individual (HNI) if he/she maintained deposits amounting to ₹5 lakh in a saving account or had ₹10 lakh of assets in his/her personal investment portfolio handled by the bank. An HNI may well be a businessman, an entrepreneur, a self-employed person or may belong to the service echelon.

A typical High Net Worth Individual (HNI) enjoys all the privileges of a high-end life style and has social connections in opulent circles. He, usually owns a house, drives a premium segment car, has a club membership, is a globetrotter and spends heavily on

ANNEXURE 1

Organisation Structure of the ACB

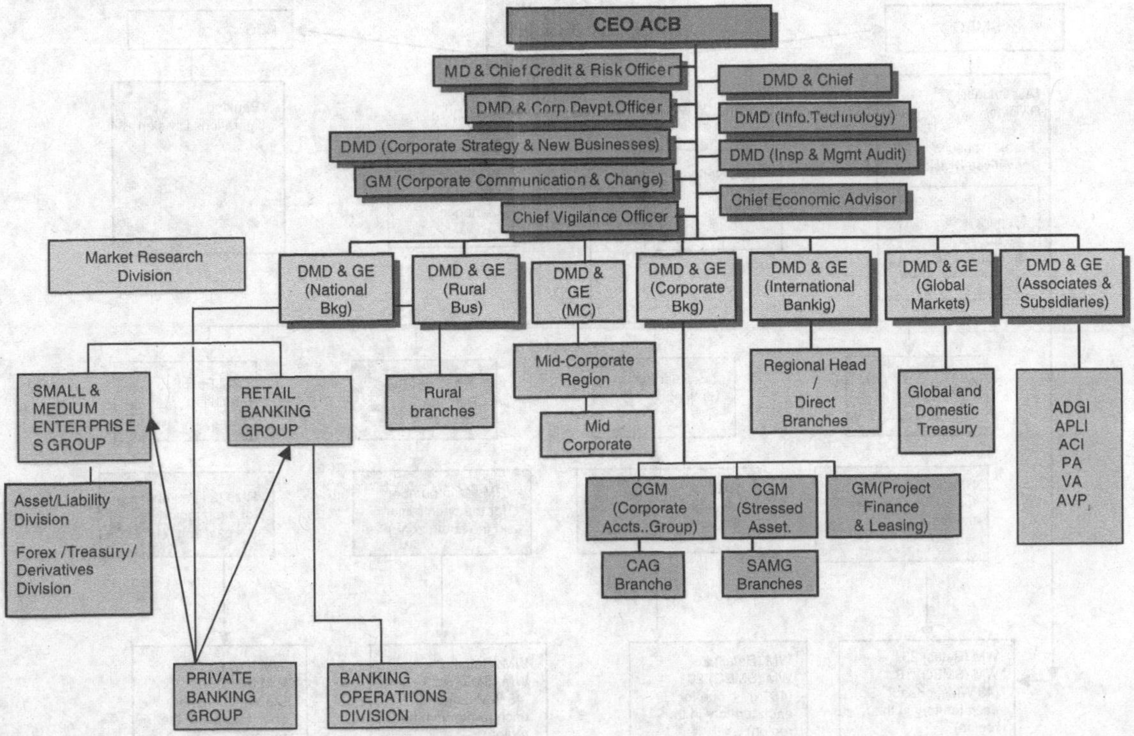

Key

ACI: Allegiance Corp Invest.com–The Online Demat Service Provider
ADGI: Allegiance Dutchinston General Insurance
APLI: Allegiance Prudent Life Insurance
AVP: Allegiance Vista Property
CAG: Corporate Assets Group
CGM: Chief General Manager
DMD: Deputy Managing Director
GE: Group Executive GM: General Manager PA-Prudent Allegiance: The Mutual Fund Arm
SAMG: Stressed-assets Management Group
SME: Small and Medium Enterprises
VA-Ventura Allegiance

his self-esteem needs. His general interests range from golfing to betting on horses, from making appearances in fashion events to hosting parties and clubbing, from art collection to participating in adventure tourism. He likes to be respected and admired for his achievements in life and looks for personalised services. When it comes to his financial needs, an HNI is keen on extracting high returns from his portfolio and is particular that expert professionals handle his portfolio. His investment interests range from investing in the stock market, property, and private equity placements to investing in gold. To fulfil his family obligations he buys sizeable life insurance policies and general insurance for his luxury cars, house, and jewellery and art collection. He is not a risk-averse person, but likes to have regular updates and information on his investment portfolio.

The Private Banking Group (PBG) wanted to tap this segment exclusively, and it appointed wealth managers (WMs) for the purpose. The WMs fell under two groups Retail Banking Group WMs and Small and Medium Enterprise Group WMs. Whereas the former

ANNEXURE 2
Private Banking Group Structure at ACB

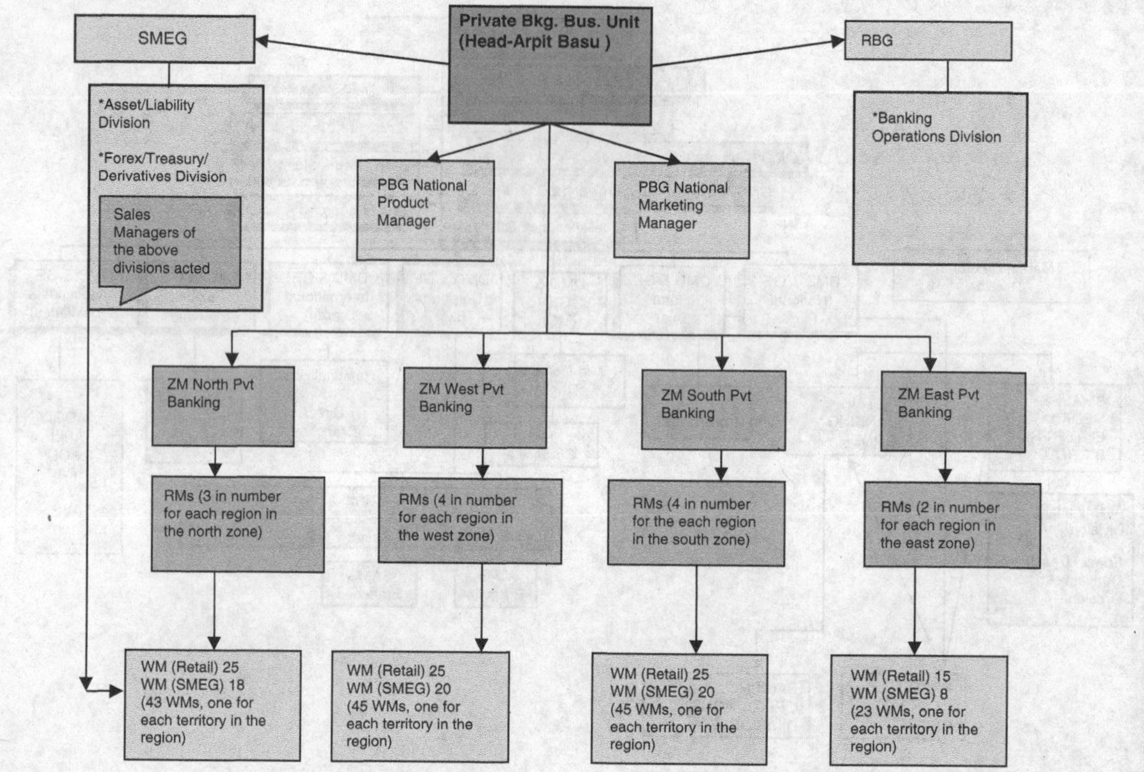

Key:
PBG: Private Banking Group
ZM: Zonal Manager
RM: Regional Manager
WM: Wealth Manager
SMEG: Small and Medium Enterprises Group

focused on HNIs irrespective of their mode of livelihood, the SMEG WMs mainly served businessmen who headed small or medium enterprise and who were already banking with the ACB for their business needs and hence in touch with the SMEG department of the bank. The SMEG, PBG, RBG were verticals under the National Banking Unit of ACB as shown in Annexure 1. All three divisions worked in coordination with each other for their business needs.

RBG was responsible for the entire banking operations and activities related to retail products and services like savings account, fixed deposits, clearances, locker services, mutual funds, personal loans etc. SMEG catered to business customers such as the owners of small and medium enterprises (with the turnover of less than ₹100 crore). The SMEG division earned its revenue by extending business products of the ACB such as roaming current accounts, term loans, small business loans, warehouse funding, mortgages, letters of credit, bank guarantees, working capital funding, forex, treasury services and insurance. Subsequently, they had a substantial base of customers who were wealthy and who believed in taking risks and diversifying funds by way of investments. The ACB-PBG took it up as an opportunity, and the heads of the SMEG and the PBG decided to work in coordination to generate revenues from such businessmen (and their families) under private banking function. Thus SMEG WMs were appointed in January 2008; they were relatively new recruits. The plan was that the sales managers of SMEG (handling SMEG products as listed above) should work as lead generators[3] of potential private banking clients and guide SMEG-WMs to close deals. However it was not yet decided whether PBG would also give any incentive to the lead generators (SMEG sales managers) for helping their SMEG Wealth Managers in PBG.

The Product The ACB offered private banking to the HNIs, providing expertise across wealth management disciplines to help them achieve their personal financial goals. For this purpose, the ACB keeps them informed of the availability of investment options duly focusing on risk-adjusted returns while tapping into tactical opportunities. The ACB has a robust market research division that brings out two fortnightly publications: "ACB MF Watch" and "ACB market.com" which are used as a mechanism to give quality financial advice. Details of ACB's exclusive offerings to its HNIs are given in Annexure 3.

ANNEXURE 3

ACB's Exclusive Offerings to Its High Net Worth Individual (HNWI) Customers

A typical HNWI customer of ACB would enjoy the following benefits:

1. A dedicated wealth manager
2. Preferential services:
    - Waiver of charges for non-maintenance of average quarterly balance
    - Discount/waiver on safety locker charges
    - Anywhere banking—complete waiver of charges
    - Demand draft/pay order—complete waiver of charges
    - Free multi-city cheque books
    - Foreign exchange services—American Express travellers cheques and ACB Travel Card, no load/reload charges on travel card, no commission charged on travellers cheques, preferential rate for sale and encashment of foreign currency
    - Credit assistance—home loans, personal loans and car loans at preferential rates
    - Personalised photo debit/credit cards
3. Exclusive wealth management zones in select ACB branches
4. Dedicated service helpline
5. Free subscription to ACB MF Watch, ACB Market .COM

Other privileges

Airport Pick-n-drop service, invitation to special events and customer meets of the bank, free tickets to movies and events, corporate gifts exclusively for private banking clients, invitation to golf events etc.

The Relationship Building Process at ACB-PBG A Private banking WM needs to work on

- Acquiring new clients
- Servicing existing high net worth customers
- Cross-selling to the first two above to meet his revenue targets

A professionally groomed WM was supposed to be the face of the bank for the HNI client and acted as a single point of contact for all his personal financial needs, queries and complaints. He had to be a personal guide of the HNI customers for all the products that the retail banking provides. In the process he needs to harness all the possibilities of wealth management and work closely with the client in achieving his financial goals.

When a private banking customer visited a branch, he would enjoy preferential treatment from the WM and would not need to stand in a queue. The private banking group WM had to call on the HNI customers to acquaint them with new products; he had to provide doorstep services to them.

The WMs were assisted by a customer service manager (at the call centre) to track his relationship with the customer and keep him posted about leads and customer appointments.

[3] In banking parlance, lead generator means a person who introduces the sales person to a potential customer.

Portfolio management services typically provided by the wealth manager are depicted in Annexure 4.

To be professionally competent, a WM was expected to track markets; know latest investment offerings; regularly study the client's risk profile, his current investments and risk appetite and then advise him on investments. He could consult ACB's research department on market trends and consult his seniors for their input in financial trends. In addition, he was expected to obtain two certifications: one from the Association of Mutual Funds of India (AMFI), mandatory for MF advisors, and the other from the Insurance Regulatory Authority of India (IRDA), required for insurance counselors.

At the end of each working day, the WM had to create an Excel sheet stating the number of leads generated on new client acquisition and cross-sell and update the status of the old leads. The report had to be sent across to his regional manager as a daily performance measure.

To add a personal touch to his customer relationship, the WM was required to know the client's family background, his business or occupation, his birthday, his anniversary, etc. He was expected to wish him on the occasion with bouquets or gifts. He may mail him seasonal greeting cards and send him invitations to specially organised investment seminars of his interest. As a part of organisational initiative, the PBG organised exclusive "High Net Worth Individual Meets" after each quarter at all locations, where the zonal and regional mangers arranged a grand dinner and discussed with them the latest financial happenings. The purpose of such events was to enhance existing customer relations.

ANNEXURE 4

Portfolio Management Services Provided by a Wealth Manager

- **Investment Planning:** Offering a suitable asset allocation plan based on client's investment goals, wealth requirements, tax plans, investment horizon, and age and risk profile. In addition, evaluating the existing investments frequently and realigning them.
- **Portfolio Construction:** Giving HNIs a tailor-made portfolio for their specific requirements, that includes investments in debt, equity, structured products and alternative asset classes as per the suggested asset allocation from a wide range of investment avenues.
- **Portfolio Maintenance and Review:** Monitoring investments and periodically suggest rebalancing the portfolio according to current market trends and aligning the portfolio according to the change in risk pattern.
- Fee-based Services: Providing individual product offerings that integrate the following:
  - **Mutual Funds** encompassing the entire universe of mutual funds of almost 15 fund houses apart from Prudent Allegiance,
  - **Alternate Asset Products** consisting of art funds, private equity funding, realty funds, and commercial property,
  - **Life Insurance and Retirement Solutions** covering Allegiance Prudent life insurance protection and pension covers,
  - **General Insurance** including Allegiance Dutchinston General Insurance's health, home, travel and car insurance, and
  - **Fixed Deposits** comprising fixed deposits, recurring deposit and floating rate deposits.

C7.4 Quarter-End Meet On PBG's Performance, July 5-8, 2009

(Responding to Mr. Basu's call of June 30, all the zonal sales managers had touched base with their regional managers, wealth managers and some esteemed customers and received comprehensive feedback on the deterrents to ACB's private banking progress. The exercise revealed a number of issues that needed to be dealt with right from the simple to the complex.)

Everyone from the private banking group had gathered in the Conference Room of the Worli Sea Face headquarters of the ACB, where Mr. Basu had called in the Head, Training and Support (Retail—Customer Service) as well as his National Product Manager and marketing manager.

The performance scenario was grim in almost every zone. The target vs. achievement ratio was low

("This is how the first quarter generally goes", was the undercurrent). But Mr. Basu was in no mood to relent. He strongly underlined the fact that the overall contribution by private banking had gone down last year and this year too the first quarter was no better. He said,

> I wonder whether the economic downturn is eating into your efforts or you have started relaxing in its wake. For us, it's time for a rebound—else soon we will all be out of business. So let's begin the review with the actual causes for our underperformance. You need to tell me what the people at the customer-contact point—our WMs, call centre staff, support staff, and branch employees—have to say on effectiveness of private banking. What problems do they face handling high net worth individuals, what do they need from us to convert leads, and what's the customers actual feedback? What actually do you intend to learn from the same?

The review began with the north zone manager who drew attention to the staff turnover issue. He had figured that it was greater in the SMEG-WM segment. The segment was newly placed. In his region alone, about six SMEG-WMs had resigned because they had to work on leads generated by SMEG managers; the latter did not provide enthusiastic support since there was no credit given to them as lead generators for the sales closed by the WM.

The second reason was that the WMs had to focus on businessmen and entrepreneurs to bring their and their family's deposits to the bank. But as one client rightly pointed out, "If my business is giving me more than 100% return if I re-invest in it, why should I block my money in the savings account or in an FD or an RD at 3–7%?" Thus mostly businessmen did not seem to believe that it was worthwhile putting money in saving instruments. What these customers preferred were *real* investments, products that they could touch and feel—commercial property, gold, art funds or private equity funding. But such deals were limited to Bangalore, Chennai, Delhi, and Mumbai through Ventura Allegiance and Allegiance Vista Properties. Commonly this state of affairs resulted in low lead generation, new customer acquisition and hence lower revenue and productivity.

The south zone manager said, "When I discussed PB with the call centre head, it seemed that existing and new WMs do not utilise call centre support effectively, which had actually been geared to generate private banking leads. The call centre reminds WMs of their appointments and subsequent follow-ups with prospective clients." Further, he pointed out that because there was no lead management and tracking system, the centre could neither track actual daily performance of its leads nor WMs' efficiency on closing them. Moreover, the recent poor performance of the stock market caused more problems for WMs since the customers were not keen on market-linked investment offerings which are a key contributor to a WM's revenue targets.

He emphasised, "Most of the High Net Worth Individuals find it rather hard to trust a new WM's ability to provide him investment advice or manage his ₹5–10 lakh portfolio, especially looking at the recent financial scandals cropping up across wealth management companies." He went on to say, "And even if our WM creates personalised investment reports for each of his clients, his difficulty will only be compounded since, on an average, there are 100 High Net Worth Individuals mapped to a single WM. Thus with lack of past reports on portfolio performance and investment advice, it becomes really difficult to convince new customers about WM's ability to provide credible investment advice."

Stressing the need for better customer orientation and preparedness, the east zone manager pointed out, "A High Net Worth Individual rarely visits a branch himself, and even if he does, there is no one to give him the so called preferential treatment, not until the staff takes a look at his account statistics. Further, it becomes all the more unpleasant if there is some urgent matter and the respective WM is not in the branch. Well, this isn't the case when he visits any of his other multinational banks—our competitors."

"Yes, I agree that the issues raised by you are important; similar complaints have come up in our region also. For instance, our customers get very agitated by multiple sales calls from ACB and its subsidiaries," said the west zone manager. He added, "Many of my wealth managers claim that most of the time they are preoccupied with resolving customer service issues, when they should actually be out in the field meeting prospects. They feel there should be one support staff to take care of such issues if the bank really wants them to achieve their revenue and deposit targets annually." Coming back to the issue of customer front, he added, "Our High Net Worth Individuals from non-metro locations like Nagpur, Indore, Surat, and Ahmedabad complain that certain preferential services listed in the private banking booklet such as quick currency exchange or airport call-and-drop are not available to them. In addition, most of them complain about not receiving issues of the *ACB MF Watch* or invitations to special events, which creates the impression that we are not able to fulfil our promises."

After this feedback session, Mr. Basu and his entire team felt that there was an urgent need for the private banking group to bring about a change—to work towards better revenue contribution and to improve its image.

"Consistent, timely and high quality service should be our focal point, and 'sales shall follow" suggested Mr. Basu, "Team! The first quarter has already gone, and we have not been able to achieve the stipulated targets. Further, we have to double up and make up for our last year's poor performance. Please remember, we need to increase private banking group's contribution to at least 4% this year." He added, "After hearing you out, what seems obvious is that we need to research extensively the relationship management area where we fall short, and renew our focus on our offerings and service quality that we earnestly promise to deliver."

He went on, "The first and foremost task is to solve the issue with the turnover of our new SMEG-WMs. Then we need to rethink our *customer orientation* and *wealth manager orientation*, and refurbish our backend support—whether it is the call centre or the lead management system."

He concluded, "Let us have a conference call after a week, with practical inputs from each of you. It should help us tackle existing issues and give a boost to our customer relations management."

With this, Mr. Basu went on to find out with the National Product Manager and National Marketing Manager, PBG on what they thought were the major challenges and the ways of meeting them.

C7.5 MR. ARPIT BASU'S OFFICE, JULY 15, 2008

Mr. Basu was looking at the "Major Customer Relations Management (CRM) Initiatives in Banking Sector", a report by the Federation of South Asian Banks (Annexure 5) and was wondering how he could use CRM effectively in ACB's private banking functions.

Should he consider reconciliation in private banking function with the basic CRM tools (which focus sharply on traditional customer orientation, satisfaction and retention approach) without seeking technological support? And if they adopt this option, what major initiatives should they take? For how long can manual monitoring and varying quality standards be sustained when the number of customers is increasing? Or should he go for the IT-enabled CRM approach which was discussed so extensively at the international conference in Bangkok?

For the past two weeks, Mr. Basu and his core team had been racking their brains about how they should go about reorganising product offerings, standardise quality in service, give speedier delivery, remain customer-focused, enable better co-ordination within and across departments—especially through delivery channels like the branch, allow and monitor sharing of information, provide for robust backend support, and improve accountability of lead management systems.

But with the experience that Mr. Basu had, he knew that the problem was more fundamental: it lay in the bank staff's inadequate understanding of the customers and their needs. A number of questions needed to be explored: Were they targeting the right customers? Were the targeted customers ready for such services? What did they expect from private banking, from their wealth managers? Are the wealth managers too young or too inexperienced to provide financial advice? Or are they not trained enough for the job?

He then thought, "Forget *products*, the key would be *service*: how to design service so that it strikes a chord with a typical Indian High Net Worth Individual?"

Eager to explore more, Mr. Basu could hardly wait for the conference call.

ANNEXURE 5

Major CRM Benefits

(Highlights taken from report—Major Customer Relations Management (CRM) Initiatives in Banking Sector, by the Federation of South Asian Banks—April 08; pg 32)

How a collaborative CRM-based technological upgrade can boost Wealth Management Division

- **Hassle-free Maintenance of Client Data:** Each and Every customer's information like his personal preferences on products, transactions, holdings, and communications history are captured and managed within a single interface. His personal details like E-mail ids, birthdays, anniversaries, family details, languages known, hobbies, interests, occupation, etc. are there on a single click. Alerts for special occasions for each client are directly sent to WMs' Mail/Mobile, to reach the customer without fail.
- **Comprehensive Lead Management System:** A unique proposition where all leads are entered by the WMs and the call centre executives, are updated and automatically produces reports to be sent to their bosses, removing hassles of consistent follow-ups. It tends to define key sales cycle and status criteria and automates sales cycle activities, such as call lists and plans, marketing activities, and follow-up actions or tasks required. Personalized Mobile alerts on daily appointments and pending updates are sent to WMs.
- **Sharing of Information across Teams:** Enables the bank to use extended functionality and features to grant permission and access to critical data of High Networth Individuals to specific members/allied groups of your organizations, and automate sales processes within the system. The solution allows users, belonging to different legal entities to work on a single system and database. This directly results in significantly lower implementation costs and ease of centralized reporting for the bank. Plus, this reduces inter-departmental conflicts, customer ownership issues and multiple calls to a single customer by the same Bank.
- **Generation of Exclusive Reports:** A CRM can enable WMs to auto-generate custom reports and summarize on sales and marketing activities. It provides Target v/s Achievements per WM on a daily basis, once updated. Also, on the customer front it allows WM to enhance his sales tools by providing rich and integrated insights about the HNWI client's investment portfolio. By using sophisticated analytics, relevant financial planning and asset allocation tools as a USP, a WM can leverage the opportunities to enhance his relationships with his clients and explore further prospects for cross-selling and fee-based personalized advice. The reports can be directly e-mailed to the customer individually, without exiting the CRM interface! These features give the WMs freedom from the traditional approach of creating individual portfolio reports in Excel.
- **Compliance Regulation and Security:** Enables use of sophisticated and high Level Security Enterprise Modules ensuring safety at each level wherever there is sharing of sensitive client data, while complying with industry regulations and privacy legislation. Execution of this ensures a successful update of all related data or a complete rollback in case of technical problems. Fully integrated and component-based, the wealth management solution guarantees consistency and reliability of data.
- **Enhancing Old-New Product Portfolio:** CRM based solutions are user-friendly and give flexibility to tailor solutions and create new product augmentations for emerging customer segments. It enables business users at the bank to add innovative functionalities and features to their offerings, without changing the source code of the application, synchronizing seamlessly with satellite and specialized systems. Hence it generally enhances the roll out of new products at the bank.
- **Higher Operational Efficiency:** Powerful integration framework is provided by the CRM solution to interface with the bank's core banking solution and external data sources, which helps minimize operational delays and ensures seamless transaction flow at the bank. Ultimately it provides faster services to High Networth Individuals in the best possible professional manner, giving him enhanced banking experience.

CHAPTER 23 | Bottom of the Pyramid

Learning Outcomes

LO 1 Understanding the BOP market

LO 2 Describe the characteristics and features of BOP market and BOP consumers

LO 3 Discuss the importance of investing in BOP market

LO 4 Discuss the challenges of marketing to BOP market and how they can be overcome

LO 5 Explain the socio-economic benefits of BOP marketing

80 percent of the world population falls in a category commonly referred as the Bottom of the Pyramid (BOP).

LO 1 The BOP Market

A recent working paper by UNICEF on income and inequality data states that 20 percent of world population enjoys more than 70 percent of world-income.[1] Thus, it is believed by many that 20 percent of the population may be classified as the affluent class, whereas the 80 percent of the world population falls in a category commonly referred as the Bottom of the Pyramid (BOP).

For years economists, anthropologists, NGO's, and government institutions have been trying to understand and cater to the needs of BOP sector in India. Several government and non-government initiatives for poverty alleviation, education for all, provision of micro-credits, etc., have been made. Needs of the BOP sector are being addressed by provision of subsidies, aids, and governments schemes like NREGA (National Rural Employment Guarantee Act),[2] *Swavlamban for LIC* (Pension Scheme for workers in the unorganized sector), Food Security Bills, etc.[3] However, the problems of the BOP sector still persist. Historically, the BOP sector has been looked as the deprived, the have not's.[4] In contemporary times, a new perception of the bottom of the pyramid has emerged. One of the key proponents of the concept of fortune at the bottom of the pyramid, Dr C. K. Prahlad contends that organizations should attempt to create a win–win situation by tapping into the BOP in a conscientious manner. Of late, there has been an emerging trend amongst business enterprises to find ways to positively exploit the potential in BOP market and embracing this new perception of BOP.

***Note:* All the figures in U.S. dollars are converted into rupee using the value $1 = ₹50.**

BOP markets referred as invisible and unorganized markets, annual income lies below ₹75,000

Bottom of the Pyramid: Status Quo

BOP is a group of people who form the base of the economic pyramid of the world (see Exhibit 23.1). The **BOP markets** are often referred as the *invisible markets* and the *unorganized markets*. It consists of more than 4 billion (400 crore) individuals whose annual incomes lie below $1500 (₹75,000). This includes a population of 2.6 billion (260 crore) which earns less than $2 (₹100) a day.[5] This section forms the largest and the poorest socio-economic group in the world.

Tier 1 of the pyramid depicts the high income group, whose annual incomes are above $20,000 (₹10,00,000). Tier 2–3 indicates the population whose annual per capita income lies between $1500–$20,000 (₹75,000–₹10,00,000). Tiers 1, 2, and 3 form the top of the pyramid (TOP) and tiers 4 and 5 depict the population whose annual per capita incomes are $1500 (₹75,000) or below, constituting the BOP. The purchasing power parity (PPP) of this segment is about ₹25,000 thousand crores and it accounts for nearly ₹75,000 thousand crores of the world's GDP.[6]

Most of the developing countries are emerging BOP markets. India, China, Brazil, Mexico, Turkey, Indonesia, Russia, South Africa, Nigeria, and Thailand alone have a GDP of ₹1,250 thousand crores and consist of a population over 3 billion (300 crore).[7] Asia and the Middle East countries together, constitute the largest BOP market in the world. It has a population of over 2.86 billion (286 crore—equivalent to 83 percent of the entire BOP population) with a PPP of ₹17,300 thousand crores (equivalent to 42 percent income of the total BOP income). The BOP market in the Eastern Europe has a population of over 254 million (25.4 crore) people with a PPP of ₹2,290 thousand crores. Latin America's BOP market has a population of 360 million (36 crore) people with a PPP of ₹2,545 thousand crores. Africa also has a large BOP market with a population of 486 million (48.6 crore) and with a PPP of ₹2,145 thousand crores.[8]

ISTOCKPHOTO/THINKSTOCK

India's BOP market has a population over 924 million (92.4 crore) with a PPP ₹6,550 thousand crores. There are 114 million (11.4 crore) households in India's BOP sector. This accounts for 76 percent of the rural population and about 60 percent of the total population of India. A study stated that 45 percent of the rural BOP population does not have access to electricity and about 85 percent of the rural BOP population still relies on the conventional energy resources (cow dung, firewood, etc.,) for cooking purposes.[9] India has the largest BOP housing market amongst all the Asian countries. The BOP population spends about ₹310.5 thousand crores on housing which is equal to 48 percent of the spending on India's national housing market.[10] Statistics indicate that a lot still needs to be done in this sector in India.

EXHIBIT 23.1
World Economic Pyramid

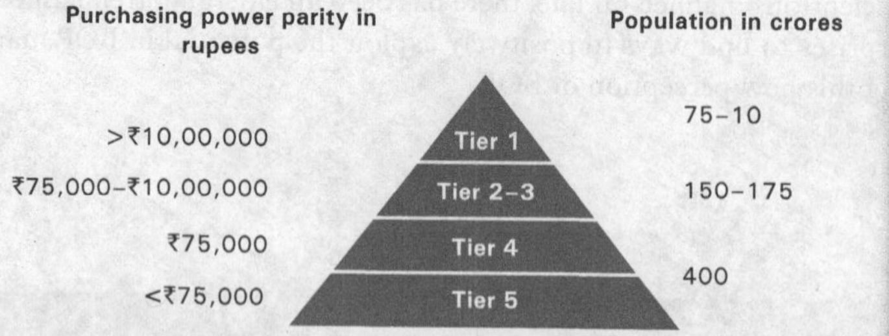

SOURCE: C.K Prahalad (2010). The Fortune at the Bottom of the Pyramid.

LO 2 Characteristics and Features of the BOP Market and BOP Consumers

The needs and wants of BOP market are unique and distinct from those of TOP market. Hence, the characteristics that define the BOP market are also significantly different. The BOP consumers have largely been the neglected segment of the market, with very few organizations modifying their marketing strategies to meet the needs of this segment. The consumers in this segment barely have enough resources to sustain themselves. Still, at times, they end up paying a higher price than the TOP consumers for availing the same goods or services. It is important for the organizations to understand that despite being price sensitive and value conscious, BOP consumers are equally brand conscious and it is imperative for the organizations to develop a separate strategy altogether for approaching this market.

Characteristics of the BOP market

Unmet Needs One could infer that some needs and wants of the BOP tier and the other tiers are similar, while some needs and wants of the BOP tier could be unique. For instance, BOP and all other tiers may have common needs for efficient transportation system, ICT (Information and Communication Technologies) equipment, banking services, water, electricity, health services, etc. However, need for electronics, apparel, entertainment, etc., may vary across people in BOP tiers and other tiers on the world economic pyramid. People at the BOP are willing to pay for it, but don't have access to it.

Subsistence Livelihood **Subsistence livelihood** can be explained as the minimum resources required to fulfill the basic needs necessary for one's survival. One may argue that subsistence livelihood is earning above the government determined poverty line or earning minimum wage prescribed by the government of India. The defined poverty line in India is ₹32 per day, per person for urban areas and ₹26 per day, per person for the rural areas.[11] Another measure to assess the subsistence livelihood of the people is the minimum wage. The power of establishing the minimum wage floor has now been given to the state government. Minimum wage starts from ₹100 per day, per person and goes up to ₹370 per day, per person, depending on the state policies, scheduled employment, and skill set of the workers.[12]

poverty penalty the excessive price paid by the poor segment of the population against the price paid by the rich for the same goods and services

subsistence livelihood the minimum resources required to fulfill the basic needs necessary for one's survival

Most constituents of BOP are dependent on the informal sector for their livelihood. Income generation activities in the informal sector mainly pertain to agriculture and allied activities. As the market for their goods and services, such as crops, handicrafts, labor, etc., is not organized, they are unable to fetch a fair price, thus live hand-to-mouth. They are also prone to losses on account of the seasonality of their occupation, perishabililty of their produce, dependency on free availability of natural resources, and occurrence of natural calamities.

It is widely believed that the profits of small businesses run of constituents of BOP are absorbed by the middlemen in most of the cases. In other words, it is believed that the middlemen procure products at a very low price and sell it in the organized markets at higher prices.

Poverty Penalty **Poverty penalty** can be explained as the excessive price paid by the poor segment of the population against the price paid by the rich for the same goods and services.[13] Despite the meager incomes and financial uncertainties inherent to the BOP, people in BOP tier often end up paying higher prices than people in the top tiers for same goods or services. For example, BOP tier constituents often obtain loans from money lenders because they do not have access to organized banking services. The rate of interest charged by these money lenders is much higher than the rate of interest charged by the banks[14]. Instances of people succumbing to the pressure created by informal lending practices are rampant across India. Many people end up committing suicide or end up repaying their loans for the rest of their lives.[15]

The aforementioned characteristics of the BOP market indicate that the rural population has reasonable financial resources and the potential to earn a better living. Not only there is scope for the private sector to provide to the BOP needs, but also the BOP segment can provide the TOP with various goods and services, thus creating a synergistic relationship between various tiers of the economic pyramid.

Consumers at BOP

Purchase decisions of the BOP consumers are essentially price-driven. Consequently, consumers in the BOP tier are believed to be price sensitive. Besides being price sensitive, BOP consumers are also brand and value conscious.[16] BOP consumers buy products which are more utilitarian in nature. They value the utility they derive from a product more than the consumers in the top tiers. BOP consumers expect that the utility they derive from the product should be more or at least equal to the price they have paid for it.

© ISTOCKPHOTO/THINKSTOCK

Characteristics of Consumers at the BOP

- *Price-sensitive:* Consumers in the BOP alter their purchases for priority goods with inferior goods if they derive the same utility from it. An example for this could be *Giffen Goods* such as, dalda and pucca rice.[17] People in the BOP prefer consuming dalda over ghee made from cow's milk because there is a significant price difference in the two. They derive the same utility from both the products. However, ghee is a superior good in terms of the nutrition and the taste it provides. Contrarily, dalda is considered as an unhealthy product. The purchase decisions of poor in the BOP are price driven and thus, they prefer to consume dalda instead of ghee.
- *Value-conscious:* A BOP consumer's consumption basket is relatively inelastic in certain situations. In other words, in several frequently used items a little change in price, quantity, or quality will affect their purchase decisions. For example, a bar of *Soap A* costs ₹3.5, and bar of *Soap B* costs ₹3.00. However, the bar of soap A is considered to last long and does not soften easily. A BOP consumer will typically prefer buying soap bar A, as he/she is getting better value for the product. Contrarily, a BOP consumer may prefer low quality washing powder due to its lower price as the consumer may not put too much importance on cleaning ability of the detergent. In other words, BOP consumers give a lot of importance to the utility they derive from a product. For example, when a new variant of Vim soap with a plastic coated bar was launched, its sale increased significantly and a major demand came from the BOP segment. This product helped the consumer save 30 percent of the soap which otherwise was wasted in flowing water.[18]
- *Brand-conscious:* It is a common misconception that people at the BOP tier don't pay heed to the brand of the products they purchase. A suitable example for this would be Lux beauty soap. Two brands prevalent in the bathing soap category in the BOP market are Lux (costing ₹18) and Lifebuoy (costing ₹16). Lux is more popular as a beauty product and is endorsed by Bollywood celebrities. On the other side, Lifebuoy is advertised as disinfectant toilet soap, endorsed by non-celebrities. It has been a general observation, that people in the BOP preferred buying Lux as a bathing soap, over Lifebuoy. It can be inferred that people at the BOP are brand-conscious when it comes to buying occasional luxury or beauty products.[19]

It is important for the organizations to have a better understanding of the customers in the BOP tier. The needs, wants, and attitude of the consumers at the BOP could be different from that of the consumers at the top of the pyramid, therefore requiring different strategies and tactics.

© ISTOCKPHOTO/THINKSTOCK

What Do People at the BOP Spend on?

People in the BOP spend their incomes prudently. Usually, BOP constituents do not have surpluses and spend their incomes in fulfilling the basic necessities. A significant portion of BOP consumer's income is spent on food. As per a study, consumers at the BOP spend about 60 percent of their income on food.[20] After spending on food, a major amount of their income is spent on energy, housing, transportation, health, and communication. BOP consumers also spend their income on luxury items.[21] It has been observed that many poor from the BOP stretch their means to spend on "positive goods" such as education, buffalo milk, ghee, etc. Similarly, BOP consumers also spend their incomes in buying "negative goods", such as cigarettes and alcohol. BOP consumers also follow an unconventional spending pattern during festivals and on entertainment. People in India spend a lot during festivals like Diwali, and also occasionally spend on entertainment sources, for example—TV, cable connection, and watching movies in theatres. The consumptions of consumers in the BOP are presented in Exhibit 23.2.

LO 3 Why Invest in BOP?

Investing in the BOP market is vital for overall development of the economy. Since government's reach to the entire BOP segment is limited, participation from the private sector is required for transforming the lives of the BOP customers. These customers do have the financial resources for buying the basic necessities; the need is to provide them with such products and services that are affordable and easily accessible. The advantages are multifold: the organizations can expand their customer base; they can generate additional revenue and profit; they can utilize their resources efficiently; considerable improvement in the standard of living of the BOP customers; and transition of customers from BOP to middle class.

© ISTOCKPHOTO/THINKSTOCK

BOP Has Financial Resources

According to poverty penalty concept explained above, it can be validated that people in the BOP do have money.[22] BOP constituents pay exorbitant prices for basic needs such as transportation, finance, and health services. In several cases, the price paid by the people at the BOP is higher than the prices paid by the people at the TOP. Private sector can tap the BOP market potential and gain a competitive advantage. Private sector can develop efficient marketing systems to not only expand their market into the BOP segment but can provide some price relief to the consumers in the BOP tier.

Limited Government Outreach

Government invests significantly in empowering the rural BOP sector. However, looking at the BOP

EXHIBIT 23.2

Consumption of Consumers in the BOP

Income Consuming Activities	Amount of Income Spent (₹Crore)	Income Spent (%)
Food	1,44,75,000	58
Energy	21,65,000	9
Housing	16,60,000	7
Transportation	8,95,000	4
Health	7,90,000	3
Information and Technology	$51 billion (₹510 crore) (Although the report estimates it could be double of this by the time it was printed given rapid growth rates).	1
Water	1,00,000	0.4
Other	46,60,000	18

SOURCE: Hammond, A.L., Kramer, W.J., Katz, R.S., Tran, J.T., and Walker, C., The Next 4 Billion (2007).

segment globally, it can be inferred that initiatives by the government alone cannot help in improving the standards of living of the BOP constituents. Thus, provide impetus for private sector participation. Business firms can enter the BOP sector as a Social Business Enterprises (SBE), which is a term coined for firms that make profits while creating a positive social impact in the operation areas.[23] When the government and the private sector work together for providing better access to products and services to this segment, its impact will be greater and the progress will be substantial, thus, creating a "win–win" situation for both industry and constituents of BOP tier.

Widening the Target Consumers

Most of the private sector firms focus on catering to the first 3 tiers, targeting the middle and higher income groups. Given the changes in international trade over the last few decades, the world is now a single global market. The private sector may be expected to experience market saturation by serving only to 200 crore consumers in the top tiers of the economic pyramid. Thus, it may be advantageous for the private sector firms to explore BOP segment for growth. Serving the BOP segment, will allow the firm operating in top tiers of the economic pyramid to obtain efficiencies by leveraging on economies of scale.

Reaching Economies of Scale

Many firms also have unutilized and under-utilized production capacities. These unutilized capacities can be used to produce goods or services that can be marketed to the BOP markets. Since, initial investments of creating infrastructure for developing products and service are already done, firms can simply use their excess capacity by diversifying their product portfolio targeting the BOP sector. For example, launching products in small packs (refer to the activity given at the end of the chapter). This will lead to optimum utilization of resources in whole, it will also help the firm reach its economies of scale and also render the rural markets with good quality products and services.

Increasing Aspirations of the People

It is believed that the BOP constituents are deprived of various commodities that could improve their standard of living. For example, people in the BOP tier don't have access to TVs which prevent them from being aware of the current events in the country and overseas. Further, access to communication equipment like mobile phones is also limited in areas that have high BOP consumers. The private sector can create goods and services that pique the aspirations of the BOP constituents, thus motivating them to consume. These goods and services prompt the BOP constituent's to ameliorate their standard of living by consuming various products and services.

© ISTOCKPHOTO/THINKSTOCK

Overcrowding in the Urban Areas

It is believed that people from the rural areas of the BOP migrate to the urban areas to meet their unsatisfied needs and aspirations. Participation of the private sector is necessary for provision of goods and services in BOP areas to prevent the urban areas from overcrowding. Additionally, private sector may need to focus on urban planning to take account of migration from rural areas. Intense migration and inappropriate urban planning may result in proliferation of slums. For instance, nearly 60 percent of the Mumbai population lives in slums.[24] These slums are ill-equipped with basic hygiene facilities and continue to remain in dilapidated state. Public-private partnership can play a vital role in uplifting the residents of these slums. Addressing the issue of overcrowding may lead to balanced development across rural and urban areas.

Transition from BOP to Middle Class

A study by The *Economist* states that "half the world can be categorized as the emerging middle income group". People from the lower income segments are gradually moving towards the middle income segments.[25]

A study by UN-Habitat states that 1,80,000 persons are being added to the urban sector each day. It is

EXHIBIT 23.3

Transition from the Pyramid to a Diamond

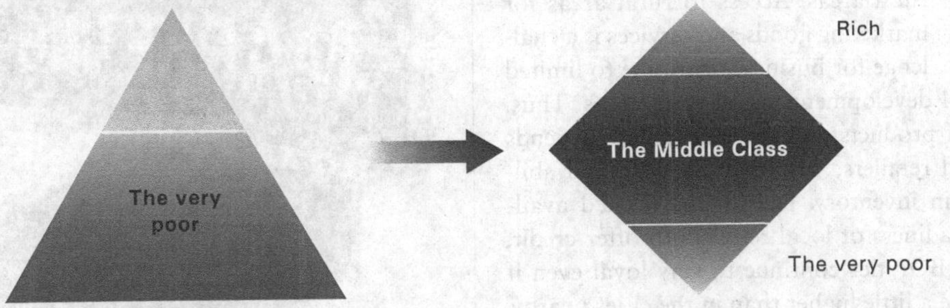

SOURCE: Prahalad K. C., The Fortune at the Bottom of the Pyramid, 2010.

anticipated that by 2030, 65 percent of the population will be living in the urban areas.[26] The growing urbanization indicates that there will be large accumulation of the BOP population in the urban areas, and this will make it easy for the private sector to target this segment. C. K. Prahalad mentions in his book *The Fortune at the Bottom of the Pyramid* that world economic pyramid is now shifting into diamond shaped structure (see Exhibit 23.3).

The above given transition indicates that a large population from the BOP will move upwards in the world economic pyramid, and reach the middle class segment.

LO 4 How Can Firms Reach the BOP?

It may be speculated that private sector will have to assess the business potential in BOP tier to invest in it. Managers will have to understand their needs of consumers, gauge the demand in the BOP market, and develop business models that support the product portfolios for the targeted segment.

Challenges of Marketing to BOP

Limited Purchasing Power Consumers in the BOP tier have limited purchasing power because of their subsistence livelihoods. They cannot buy a lot of things they may need. It is believed that BOP consumers are price sensitive and value conscious.[27] Thus, it can be inferred that BOP constituents will make a purchase that will be based on maximization of utility rather than purely hedonic reasons. According to C. K. Prahalad, some BOP consumers prefer purchasing durable and trustworthy brands. Thus, the private sector may need to create goods that are not only of good quality but also affordable for the BOP constituents.

Lack of Financial Services It is believed that majority of the consumers from the BOP don't have access to formal credit services. Further, they cannot attain loans because of lack of collateral securities. Many BOP constituents do not have bank accounts because of lack of guarantors and the required minimum balances. Plausibly, BOP constituents may not have any access to organized financial services industry posing a challenge to the private enterprises for sale of durables and white goods. Given that most consumers have little surplus money and limited access to credit, sale of durables to the BOP tier becomes a challenge.

© ISTOCKPHOTO/THINKSTOCK

Price Efficiency the degree to which stock prices of a good reflect the available information, timely and accurately

Inadequate Institutional Framework/ Undeveloped Market Structure Most of the BOP population lives in the rural areas. Access to rural areas for marketing goods and services is a challenge for business firms due to limited infrastructural development in the rural areas. Thus, availability of products and services largely depends on small local retailers, who may have limited ability to maintain inventory. Due to the limited availability and readiness of local retailers to offer credit, consumers in BOP tier continue to stay loyal even if their prices are a little higher than in the cities nearby. Most BOP consumers develop a relationship with the local retailers and the relationship thrives on serving each other's needs.[28] The BOP consumers are provided important products on credits by local retailers while enjoying continued retail patronage with high profit margin. Given the nature and type of transactions, firms will have to break through the aforementioned challenges caused by the insufficient market structure to be successful in the BOP tier.

Lack of Knowledge in Customers It is also believed that consumers in the BOP lack awareness of various products and services offering that are available in the market. Due to lack of consumer awareness, BOP constituents may not necessarily know the best prices to pay for goods and services purchased by them. Thus, for private enterprises to successfully venture into BOP tier, they will need to educate the consumers. Private companies along with selling their products will have to create awareness about the product usage by conducting demonstrations, providing free samples, mass media advertising, etc. It is believed that BOP tier is not very well connected with the other tiers of the economic pyramid because of insufficient infrastructure like transportation, telecommunication services, etc. Consequently, effective communication is very essential for both the private and public sector firms for better penetration and outreach into BOP tier.

Successful Marketing Strategies for BOP

Reaching out to the BOP It can be broadly classified along 3 A's (Availability, Affordability, and Accessibility).

- *Availability*: The first task for any firm to be successful in BOP tier is making available goods and services in a timely manner. Marketing strategy must entail proliferation of commodities into the slums, villages, informal settlements, and other remote areas. To make the goods available in the BOP tier, a distribution system that involves the BOP constituents must be created. Also, the goods and services must be made available as per requirements of the BOP constituents. In other words, goods should be made available in different sizes, prices, packaging, etc., to effectively reach the constituents of BOP tier.
- *Affordability:* Companies must offer products and services that correspond with the affordability of the BOP constituents. Therefore, companies may have to find cost efficient methods and distribution systems to reach the BOP tier. Majority of the purchasing decisions at the BOP are based on the price-efficiency of the commodity. **Price efficiency** of a good is the degree to which the stock prices reflect the available information, timely and accurately.[29] They carefully analyze the price performance of the goods and then make the purchase. In addition, there may be also a need for cheaper and efficient production processes to make the goods affordable to the lower income groups.
- *Accessibility:* It is often believed that economies of scale are difficult to achieve when working in BOP tier. In the BOP tier, there are a large number of consumers but consumption per head is small. Thus, cost of distribution per capita may be high. Consequently, some firms may find that although

© ISTOCKPHOTO/THINKSTOCK

the BOP segment is large, it is geographically dispersed. Furthermore, the BOP tier resides in areas that are not well connected by road and rail. Thus, a model that can overcome the constraints of low profitability because of the high cost involved in small transactions will have to be put in place. Thus, to be successful a firm must utilize a combination of mainstream and the informal distribution channels.

Creation of New Products and Services Products that are sold in the top tiers will not necessarily be in sync with the needs of the consumers in the BOP. Firms will have to analyze and understand the needs of the BOP tier separately and understand the price that the consumers are willing to pay to satisfy their needs. Thus, firms should come up with products that can provide better utility and performance at an affordable price for the constituents of BOP tier.

THE CASE OF COCA-COLA

© HEMERA/THINKSTOCK

In 2002, Coca-Cola came up with launching the ₹5 coke bottle. The launch was made after it was observed that a huge population in the rural area consumed coke. Many consumers bought one ₹10 coke bottle (300 ml) and then shared it between two.

This consumer behavior indicated that the rural consumers could not afford the entire bottle and also that half of that quantity was sufficient to quench their thirst. Soon, the ₹5 bottle (200 ml) was launched in summers to cater to the rural demands. The product was a great success. Coca-Cola sales for the ₹5 bottle shot up and it captured the entire rural market. This took care of the affordability of the product. To make the product easily available, Coca-Cola introduced the *own your asset scheme*, where in the retailer was able to purchase his own fridges at 50 percent cost price/half price. To meet the criterion of accessibility, Coca-Cola had placed its vending machines in many places. It also kept track of how many bottles were sold and how much stock was available. Accordingly, it upgraded the stocks. Also to promote the product in the rural area, it came up with the tag line "*Thanda Matlab Coca-Cola*" followed with a strong advertisements and brand endorsement by Bollywood actor, Amir Khan.[30]

The Coca-Cola case is a good example where an MNC took care of the affordability, accessibility, and the availability of the product while penetrating the rural market.

Creation of a New Business Model The existing business models will not necessarily prove to be efficient to reach the BOP sector. New business models should be established keeping in mind not only the utilization of a firm's capacity and the profit margin but also accessibility and the price sensitivity of the consumers

PROJECT URJA: SOLAR LANTERNS

© INDIATODAYIMAGES.COM

About 2 billion (200 crore) people in the world and 45 percent of the Indian rural population has no access to electricity. Electricity is one of the most important factors that affect one's productivity, be it work or household activities.

To address the concerns in the energy-scarce areas, SEWA Bank in collaboration with Selco formed a project called Urja in 2006. This project aimed at providing alternative cooking and lighting sources to the needy using the readily available natural resources. Selco was the technological partner and SEWA was the financial services partner in the project. Selco manufactured solar and bio-gas equipment and SEWA Bank provided financial support to people who wanted to invest in these devices.

To provide for the lighting needs, Selco came out with solar lanterns. These lanterns consisted of solar photovoltaic panels and a connecting cable. To charge the lantern, users only needed to place the lantern in sunlight, and the energy was stored in the device. The device could be used for about 4 hours and generated light equivalent to a 40 W incandescent lamp. It was also equipped with an LED screen that would indicate the status of the battery.[31] The lighting cost with this equipment was approximately ₹10 a day, cheaper than using kerosene lamps which costed around ₹15 a day.[32]

The rate of interest charged by SEWA Bank normally was 17 percent for a period of 12–18 months. However, under this project the rate of interest was charged between 5–10 percent for a period of 15–36 months to pull more consumers. To promote the product and to create awareness about its benefits, SEWA set up energy parks, training and demonstration centers, and participated in energy fairs. Not only did this project provide cheaper and better lighting services but the devices were also environment friendly, as it did not use CFL and did not give-out carbon emissions. Solar lanterns could be used for multiple uses, such as reading (specially for children), emergency lighting, cooking, etc. This project proved to be extremely helpful for the people with no access to electricity, particularly women and children.

in the BOP tier. A successful business model must find ways to engage the constituents of the BOP in synergistic manner. The business model should view the investment in BOP tier from a long term perspective. The investment in entering and penetrating the BOP tier may not result in instantaneous return. Thus, the business model should account for reasonable gestation period for return on investments.

GRAMEEN BANK MODEL

© INDIATODAYIMAGES.COM

Grameen Bank has been an initiative to provide the low income groups or the poor with credit services. Grameen Bank Model is a microcredit model propounded by Muhammad Yunus. This model has provided microcredit loans to more than 25 million (2.5 crore) people world over, and has made it possible to extend credit to the lowest-income groups.

Most of Grameen Bank's customers are poor and have no collateral securities. However, to obtain a loan, candidates have to make a proposal to apply for a loan. The application is then thoroughly evaluated by the bank authorities. Every loan is guaranteed/secured by five non-family members of the community. After providing the loans, a team from the bank is assigned to make regular visits to the villages for follow-ups on the projects undertaken by the borrowers.

This creates an interpersonal relationship between the bank and the customer. Also, obtaining loans in groups increases the responsibility and the credibility of the customers making the Grameen Bank Model successful. The Grameen Bank Model has been able to provide credit to 2.3 million (23 lakh) women and has reached more than 40,000 villages. Despite the high credit risk involved, the Grameen Bank Model has been able to achieve 95 percent repayment rate. This rate has not been achieved by any Indian bank, so far.[33]

New Distribution Channels Physical infrastructures accorded for marketing and distribution of products and services are dissimilar for the TOP and the BOP tiers. The BOP sector is more informal in nature, therefore, there will be a need to create new distribution channels that can formalize the process. Using the same distribution channels for both the tiers could increase the "per unit cost" of the product or service. To be successful, firms must develop distribution channels that capitalize on the strengths of BOP constituents, thus creating value for both the firm and the BOP tier.

Creating Local Ecosystems Firms will need to build a local network by tying up with the local BOP constituents, to accelerate the distribution and sale of the products. They will have to build local ecosystems through which firms and local markets conjoin to create a value-chain. Firms can approach the already existing retailers or create new retailers in the market to sell and distribute their products. In a country like India, which is multi-lingual and multi-cultural, local partners can communicate better with the consumers in their region and can understand their needs better. The participation of local constituents can assist in building ecosystems that will allow smooth, transparent, and efficient marketing of products and services in the BOP tier.

OPERATION I SHAKTI

© ISTOCKPHOTO/THINKSTOCK

Operation I Shakti was an initiative started by Hindustan Lever Ltd (HLL) in 2004. It's a public-private collaboration of HLL with Andhra Pradesh (AP) Government. Operation I shakti was an extension of Project Shakti, which was an HLL, where it worked closely with local and state governments, banks, NGOs, and self help groups (SHG's). Operation Shakti employed people to sell HLL products in the rural areas.

Operation I Shakti aimed at creating a rural information service network via use of computers. HLL developed I-Shakti Kiosks which were voice-based interactive systems. These kiosks provided information on agriculture, education, hygiene, health, and vocational training, along with building a new sales channel for its goods. All the content/information was made available in the local languages to the users. Experts from various fields were made available to the users through an online mailing query system. Queries were submitted by the user in the local language and the experts replied to them with appropriate solutions. With the implementation of this operation, not only were the consumers in the rural sector empowered with information and more variety of goods to choose from, but also HLL also found a cost-efficient way of distributing its products and understanding the needs of the rural market.[34]

Partnering with Other organizational Structures There are a large number of government organizations and NGO's already working in the BOP tier. Firms must not only partner with local constituent of the BOP tier but also with the existing government and non-government organizations. Firms should partner with government and non-government organizations to facilitate a smooth business process and to gain quicker results. The government has various development schemes running in the BOP sector. Private sector participation can prove to be an extension to the government initiatives. The combination of different organizational structures working together will bear holistic results.

ITC e-CHOUPAL

© INDIATODAYIMAGES.COM

ITC has come up with a very innovative model to meet its need for soybean from scattered farmers in Madhya Pradesh (MP). A Sanchalak is appointed who handles the assigned computer, which can be used by all the farmers. The farmers can compare the prices of the soya found in all the mandis and then sell their produce where ever they attain the highest price. This helps the farmers to get rid of the process of auctioning of goods where they are compelled to sell their produce at a price decided by the auctioneer, irrespective of the quality of the produce. This is a disincentive for the farmers as they get the same price for producing a good or an average quality of produce. The ITC e-Choupal model has proved to be an incentive to the soybean cultivators as they can assess the prices in all the mandis and then sell it at the best price/bid.[35]

The e-Choupal model has facilitated not only fair prices to the farmers but also accurate weighing and timely payments, and saving on external costs such as transportation and packaging costs. This model introduced IT with the rural sector and has made ITC e-Choupal an "electronic village meeting place".[36]

On the other hand, ITC had also benefited from this technological up-gradation. ITC has not only been able to easily source soybeans from widely scattered regions of MP, but it also has saved a considerable amount in the process.

OPERATION SAMURIDDHI—BASF

© ISTOCKPHOTO/THINKSTOCK

BASF was primarily involved in selling pesticides to farmers across the country. Over a period of time, BASF observed that farmer's productivity levels had not increased even after using its crop protection products. Therefore, in 2006, BASF came up with an operation called *Samuriddhi*. In this operation, various farmers were approached, and discussions and advices were given by the experts on how farmers could increase their productivity. This operation piloted with 30,000 soybean farmers. Agronomists were appointed to work with the farmers, and workshops and field-trials were also organized for them. Soon the participation of the farmers increased to 1,70,000 in 2010. To support the growth of this operation, a call center was created to provide assistance to the farmers from the experts in the field. Soon the government of Andhra Pradesh signed an MOU with BASF for carrying this operation in a few other regions. This operation not only increased the sales figures of the BASF's crop protection products by 60 percent, but it also showed a 24 percent growth in the farmers yields.[37]

Investing in the Best Technologies With the digitization of the world, one can remain connected to others from every nook and cranny of the world. Furthermore, technological costs have significantly reduced in last decades providing opportunity for further use of technology to attain greater efficiencies. Telecommunication industry in India is a suitable example for this. As on September 2011, the overall teledensity was 76%, and urban and rural teledensity was 167% and 37%, respectively.[38] Statistics indicate that the urban teledensity is close to saturation and the rural sector is the upcoming telecom market. Various reforms in the telecom sector have made it possible for the telecommunications firms to provide affordable services and telecom equipment to the rural sector. To increase the outreach of telecom services, cellular operators have come up with innovative features where customers can choose a vernacular/regional language for communication. This has made it easy for consumers from different regions to operate mobile phones, furthermore increasing its demand. Cellular operators have managed to surpass barriers such as illiteracy and have reached the rural segments.

ARAVIND eye HOSPITAL

© COMSTOCK/THINKSTOCK

Aravind Eye Hospital (AEH) specializes in eye care and has 50 surgeries performed each day on an average. AEH uses the best equipment in the world for their service provision. It charges nominal fees from the patients and also provides services free of cost for the needy. It has made no borrowings from the bank, but has kept employing its surplus' in the development of the hospital and other allied services in eye care. AEH's success can be determined from the fact that it has been consistently making profits and expanding. As against the national average of doctors performing 300 surgeries per year, doctors at AEH perform about 2000 surgeries per year on average. In the year 2007-08, AEH became the largest eye care provider in the world with 2,85,745 surgeries.[39]

LO 5 Socio-Economic Effect

Investing in the BOP sector will not only reap benefits for the business firms and the BOP sector, but it will also reap benefits for the economy as a whole. There is positive multiplier effect allied with the development of the BOP sector. Two long term positive effects of proliferation of the BOP markets are discussed here.

Poverty Alleviation

As discussed earlier, the private organized sector and local unorganized sector convergence will create a "win–win" situation for both. Increase in the economic activities will increase the incomes of the BOP population, increase employment, and stimulate the local economy. Access to more goods and services will improve the conditions of the poor, and may also promote entrepreneurship. Government's efforts to alleviate poverty alone have not and may not be sufficient. Thus, private sector participation in poverty alleviation effort is very important.

Boost to Entrepreneurship

The private sector firms can enter BOP sector by joining forces with the unorganized local entrepreneurs. It can be expected that the relationship between organized and unorganized sector will be synergistic resulting in superior ability to service the BOP market. As a result, the economic activities and transactions are expected to increase in both the sectors. Increased business activity may further create a need for small

local entrepreneurs to facilitate the business incumbents with more local services. Overall, synergies from the organized and unorganized sector may become a driving force for entrepreneurship and increased employment in BOP tier.

BOP is the way forward for a balanced economic and regional development across the world. With many firms realizing the potential in the BOP, we see developments of different business models, distribution and supply chains in various business horizons. With the help of right marketing strategies and an in-depth understanding of the BOP sector, businesses can expand by overcoming development barriers such as lack of infrastructure, skills, education, etc.

Review And Applications

Understanding the BOP market. Nearly 80 percent of the world population falls in the category called Bottom of the Pyramid (BOP). India's BOP market has a population over 924 million (92.4 crore) with a PPP ₹6550 thousand crores. There are 114 million (11.4 crore) households in India's BOP sector. Various subsidies, aids, and government schemes such as NREGA, *Swavlamban for LIC,* and Food Security Bills are provided to BOP sector. Dr. C. K. Prahlad, a key proponent of the concept of fortune at the BOP, was of the opinion that organizations should attempt to create a win–win situation by tapping into the BOP in a conscientious manner. BOP markets are referred to as invisible and unorganized markets and their annual income lies below ₹75,000. This section forms the largest and the poorest socio-economic group in the world. Asia and the Middle East countries together, constitute the largest BOP market in the world.

1.1 What are the most important challenges that you think firms will have to face to successfully manage business in the BOP tier?

1.2 Discuss the role government plays in the BOP market? Is government intervention required in SBE models? In last few years, newspapers have reported several financial scams involving the national government. Given the state of affairs of the nation, should government contribute more or less for the development of BOP tier?

Describe the characteristics and features of BOP market and BOP consumers. The characteristics that define the BOP market are unmet needs, subsistence livelihood, and poverty penalty. The aforementioned characteristics offer ample scope to the private sector to strive towards meeting the needs of BOP.

The BOP consumers have certain characteristics that make them distinct from the TOP consumers. BOP consumers are essentially price sensitive, value conscious, and brand conscious. They value the utility they derive from a product more than the consumers in the top tiers. Thus, in order to target the BOP consumers, organizations need to develop unique strategies.

2.1 What do you think are key similarities and dissimilarities between the consumption behavior of the constituents of BOP and other tiers on the economic pyramid?

Discuss the importance of investing in BOP market. There are several reasons that justify the importance of investing in BOP. They are availability of financial resources in the hands of BOP consumers, limited government outreach, a new target segment for the organizations to explore, optimum utilization of resources by organizations, improving the standard of living of BOP consumers by offering aspirational goods and services, rural development, and transformation of BOP consumers to middle class. All these reasons demonstrate the huge potential that remains untapped in BOP market.

3.1 Do you think firms should use consistent strategies through all tiers in the world economic pyramid or different strategies should be used?

3.2 Discuss the products and services that may have future potential in the BOP tier.

Discuss the challenges of marketing to BOP market and how they can be overcome. Some of the challenges of marketing to BOP are limited purchasing power of BOP customers, lack of financial services, undeveloped market structure, and lack of knowledge among the customers. These challenges may pose as roadblocks in reaching out to BOP market. However, there are certain strategies that can help in overcoming these challenges. Some key factors to focus on are availability, affordability, and accessibility of goods and services, creating new products and services for the BOP market, creating a new business model, developing new distribution channels, creating local ecosystems, partnering with other organizational structures, and investing in the best technologies.

4.1 What are some key challenges in the domain of logistics and distributions for entering and penetrating the BOP tier? What are some suitable logistics and distribution channel that will work efficiently and effectively in the BOP tier?

4.2 What type of marketing communication do you think will be most effective in the BOP sector? Discuss the most effective advertising strategies for the products and services targeted for the BOP consumers.

Explain the socio-economic benefits of BOP marketing. Investing in the BOP sector will not only reap benefits for the business firms and the BOP sector, but it will also reap benefits for the economy as a whole. Two long term positive effects of marketing to BOP are poverty alleviation and boost to entrepreneurship. With the help of right marketing strategies and an in-depth understanding of the BOP sector, businesses can expand by overcoming development barriers and lead to overall growth.

5.1 Do you think large business firms can compete with the local vendors (Kirana store)? Can a business firm co-exist with the Kirana store? What strategies should be adopted to compete with the Kirana store? What strategies should be adopted by the Kirana store operator to survive the onslaught of the large business firms entering the BOP tier?

Exercises

APPLICATION EXERCISE

Bottom of the Pyramid has become the new marketing concept that has caught the attention of the corporate world in recent times. With the developed urban markets getting saturated, organizations are now focusing their energies on the untapped rural markets. The benefit of targeting BOP market is two-fold—companies can earn profits and eradicate poverty. This has led to many organizations formulating separate strategies altogether for the BOP market.

Activities

1. Select an area close to yours that has a BOP population, visit it, and observe the consumption behavior of the residents. What are the different organizations that are currently serving this market? Select one organization that is serving the BOP residents in the selected area and illustrate the organization's business model. What are the strategies used by selected organization to remain in BOP market? Do you think the strategies used are suitable or should they be trying something else?
2. Select a product or a service that you believe is suitable for marketing in BOP tier. Develop an integrated marketing communication program for the selected product or service.
3. Form a group of five members and discuss the scope of the BOP sector as a goods or service provider for other tiers in the economic pyramid. What are the possible goods and services that can be efficiently offered by the BOP sector to the TOP sector?

ETHICS EXERCISE

Companies targeting BOP market have been criticized time and again for offering such products or services that the consumers do not really need, or that require some knowledge for proper product usage, or are very often beyond the purchasing capacity. Nestle faced severe protests in the late 1970s when it tried to sell its infant formula to the poor mothers in the developing countries. The company distributed free samples by dressing up their saleswomen in nurses' uniforms and did not even insure whether water was available to mix with the powder. These poor mothers were too vulnerable to understand how they would buy the product once the samples were exhausted. Casas Bahia, an appliance retailer in Brazil, is renowned for selling its products to the poor customers on credit. However, this has often led to customers purchasing products on debt, such as video game players or DVD players, for which they do not have a need. Similarly, companies involved in selling tobacco products or alcoholic beverages have often been condemned for targeting BOP market, where people do not even have sufficient funds to purchase even the most basic necessities for survival.[40]

Questions

1. Is it morally ethical on the part of the companies to sell their products or services to the BOP market which they do not really need or do not know how to use? Is it correct to burden them with buying costly products and services when they cannot even afford the basic requirements of life?
2. Targeting the BOP market—is it truly a CSR activity or just a profit maximization mechanism for the organizations?

MARKETING PLAN EXERCISE

BOP has emerged to be a lucrative market, offering tremendous potential for business innovation. With the segment remaining largely untapped, targeting it can be a fruitful proposition, especially in the absence of some stiff competition. Your chosen company must also reflect at the opportunity of reaching out to this market. The following exercises will help you in determining if the BOP can be prospective target market for your company:

1. Does the BOP market depict a need for your selected product or service? If yes, then describe the need, how your product/service satisfies that need, and what would be your overall marketing strategy for targeting the BOP market. If no, then explain as to how your product or service is different from the requirements of the BOP market. Is there any possibility of modifying the chosen product or service to meet the requirements of the BOP?
2. Assess the competition present in the BOP market and what is their marketing strategy for the BOP market.

Short Case: CHIK SHAMPOO

Prepared by
Dr. Dheeraj Sharma,
Indian Institute of Management, Ahmedabad

Years ago, using shampoo for washing hair was a practice staple to the high income groups. Shampoos were available in bottles in large quantities and thus, higher prices. People in the rural areas could not afford it and therefore, used cheap and readily available products like *shikakai* and *reetha* to wash their hair.

This practice changed when Cavin Care introduced Chik shampoo in small sachets. Cavin Care used innovative packaging, pricing, and distribution strategy and launched small sachets of Chik shampoo for ₹0.50 and ₹1. To promote the brand and to create its awareness in the rural areas, on-ground activities were taken up at individual village level. To promote Chik shampoo, demonstration counters were put up in rural areas. Villagers were shown live, how washing hair with Chik shampoo softened and improved the quality of their hair. Villagers were also taught how they should use the shampoo. This was accompanied with distribution of free samples of the sachets to the villagers. The free distribution strategy drove the consumers to use it the second time. The product was affordable and people began to use and recognize the product. As an advertising strategy, Cavin Care sponsored shows in which famous actor, Rajnikanth performed, and flashed its ads during breaks and other gaps.

Chik's excellent marketing strategy and forecasting enabled Chik to become one of the most trusted brands and the largest selling shampoo in South-India, particularly Andhra Pradesh and Tamilnadu. In no time, Chik became the second largest shampoo brand in India.

Today, Chik offers two product variants, Chik Hair Fall Control, and Chik Long and Strong ranging from ₹1 to ₹110. Chik shampoo is available in almost all stores across the country.[41]

Questions

1. Due its market positioning, Chik shampoo may be perceived to be a poor man's preference. On the other hand, Head & Shoulders, Pantene, and others have successfully catered to the demands of the upper tiers on the economic pyramid. Do you think Chik has limited its consumer base to the rural areas by virtue of its positioning?
2. Should Chik increase its product variants to compete with the high-end brands?
3. Do you think if Chik increases its price by ₹0.50, it will reduce its customer base?

23 Bottom of the Pyramid

KEY TERMS

LO 1 **BOP markets** referred as invisible and unorganized markets, annual income lies below ₹75,000

LO 2 **poverty penalty** the excessive price paid by the poor segment of the population against the price paid by the rich for the same goods and services

subsistence livelihood the minimum resources required to fulfill the basic needs necessary for one's survival

LO 4 **Price Efficiency** the degree to which stock prices of a good reflect the available information, timely and accurately

KEY CONCEPTS

LO 1 **Understanding the BOP market.** Nearly 80 percent of the world population falls in the category called Bottom of the Pyramid (BOP). India's BOP market has a population over 924 million (92.4 crore) with a PPP ₹6550 thousand crores. There are 114 million (11.4 crore) households in India's BOP sector. Various subsidies, aids, and government schemes such as NREGA, *Swavlamban for LIC*, and Food Security Bills are provided to BOP sector. Dr. C. K. Prahlad, a key proponent of the concept of fortune at the BOP, was of the opinion that organizations should attempt to create a win–win situation by tapping into the BOP in a conscientious manner. BOP markets are referred to as invisible and unorganized markets and their annual income lies below ₹75,000. This section forms the largest and the poorest socio-economic group in the world. Asia and the Middle East countries together, constitute the largest BOP market in the world.

LO 2 **Describe the characteristics and features of BOP market and BOP consumers.** The characteristics that define the BOP market are unmet needs, subsistence livelihood, and poverty penalty. The aforementioned characteristics offer ample scope to the private sector to strive towards meeting the needs of BOP.

The BOP consumers have certain characteristics that make them distinct from the TOP consumers. BOP consumers are essentially price sensitive, value conscious, and brand conscious. They value the utility they derive from a product more than the consumers in the top tiers. Thus, in order to target the BOP consumers, organizations need to develop unique strategies.

LO 3 **Discuss the importance of investing in BOP market.** There are several reasons that justify the importance of investing in BOP. They are availability of financial resources in the hands of BOP consumers, limited government outreach, a new target segment for the organizations to explore, optimum utilization of resources by organizations, improving the standard of living of BOP consumers by offering aspirational goods and services, rural development, and transformation of BOP consumers to middle class. All these reasons demonstrate the huge potential that remains untapped in BOP market.

LO 4 **Discuss the challenges of marketing to BOP market and how they can be overcome.** Some of the challenges of marketing to BOP are limited purchasing power of BOP customers, lack of financial services, undeveloped market structure, and lack of knowledge among the customers. These challenges may pose as roadblocks in reaching out to BOP market. However, there are certain strategies that can help in overcoming these challenges. Some key factors to focus on are availability, affordability, and accessibility of goods and services, creating new products and services for the BOP market, creating a new business model, developing new distribution channels, creating local ecosystems, partnering with other organizational structures, and investing in the best technologies.

LO 5 **Explain the socio-economic benefits of BOP marketing.** Investing in the BOP sector will not only reap benefits for the business firms and the BOP sector, but it will also reap benefits for the economy as a whole. Two long term positive effects of marketing to BOP are poverty alleviation and boost to entrepreneurship. With the help of right marketing strategies and an in-depth understanding of the BOP sector, businesses can expand by overcoming development barriers and lead to overall growth.

Endnotes

1

1. Announcement to the AMA Academic Council from Patricia K. Goodrich, Senior Director, Professional Development, American Marketing Association, October 25, 2007.
2. George Anderson, "Satisfied Workers Generate Greater Returns," *Retailwire*, January 16, 2008, www.retailwire.com.
3. Company website: http://www.tatasteel.com/corporate-citizenship/employer-of-choice.asp, (accessed December 12, 2011).
4. Philip Kotler and Kevin Lane Keller, *A Framework for Marketing Management*, 3rd ed. (Upper Saddle River, NJ: Prentice-Hall, 2007), 3.
5. "How to Reward Employees on a Budget," *Inc.*, April 19, 2010, www.inc.com/guides/2010/04/rewarding-employees-on-a-budget.html.
6. "Aggressive Deals Are Expected to Boost Toyota Sales 30 Percent in March," *Palm Beach Post*, March 12, 2010, www.palmbeachpost.com/money/aggressive-deals-are-expected-to-boost-toyota-sales-346358.html.
7. Woody Driggs, "Serving Up Customer Delight," *Customer Relationship Management*, April 2008, 14.
8. Ibid.
9. Press Trust of India, "Maruti tops JD Power customer satisfaction index chart," *The Economic Times*, October 31, 2011, http://articles.economictimes.indiatimes.com/2011-10-31/news/30342111_1_customer-satisfaction-jd-power-executive-director-mohit-arora.
10. Anya Kamenetz, "Cleaning Solution," *Fast Company*, September 2008, 121–124.
11. Ibid.
12. "U.S. Consumers Still Willing to Pay More for 'Green' Products," *environmentalleader.com*, March 29, 2010, www.environmentalleader.com/2010/03/29/u-s-consumers-still-willing-to-pay-more-for-green-products/.
13. Becky Ebenkamp, "Study: 'Green' Products Leave Consumers Puzzled," *Brandweek.com*, July 15, 2008, www.brandweek.com/bw/content_display/news-and-features/shopper-marketing/e3i26f4ff48c6b4dae290f1bbb4854e7b58.
14. Marc Gunther, "PET Project: Coke's Big Recycling Plant," January 14, 2009, GreenBiz.com, www.greenbiz.com/blog/2009/01/14/pet-project-cokes-big-recycling-plant.
15. Anonymous, "Here are some of India's leading 'green' companies," *Rediff Business*, June 3, 2011, http://www.rediff.com/business/slide-show/slide-show-1-world-environment-day-some-of-indias-leading-green-compa-nies/20110603.htm.
16. Tripathy, S., "Green Marketing," *Hindustan Times*, September 11, 2011, http://www.hindustantimes.com/business-news/ColumnsBusiness/Green-marketing/Article1-744451.aspx.
17. A. G. Lafley and Rom Charan, "The Consumer Is Boss," *Fortune*, March 17, 2008, 121–126.
18. Phred Dvorak, "Next in Line for Reinvention: The Art of Selling," *Wall Street Journal*, January 28, 2008, B3.
19. Karen Aho, "The Customer Service Hall of Shame," *MSN*, May 18, 2010, http://articles.moneycentral.msn.com/Investing/Extra/the-customer-service-hall-of-shame-2010.aspx.
20. Press Trust of India, "Maruti tops JD Power customer satisfaction index chart," *The Economic Times*, October 31, 2011, http://articles.economictimes.indiatimes.com/2011-10-31/news/30342111_1_customer-satisfaction-jd-power-executive-director-mohit-arora.
21. Jeffrey M. O'Brien, "A Perfect Season," *Fortune*, February 4, 2008, 61–66.
22. Samuel Fromartz, "Good Enough to Eat," *Fast Company*, September 2008, 29.
23. Lafley and Charan, "The Consumer Is Boss," 122.
24. Joshi, P., "Social media becomes critical for airlines," *Business Standard*, February 28, 2012, http://www.business-standard.com/india/news/social-media-becomes-critical-for-airlines/466084/.
25. http://censusindia.gov.in/.
26. Times News Network, "Family expenses on food decline in 20 years," *The Times of India*, July 10, 2011, http://articles.timesofindia.indiatimes.com/2011-07-10/india/29757590_1_consumption-expenditure-food-items-urban-areas.
27. The application exercises throughout the book are based on the winning entries in the "Best of the Great Ideas in Teaching Marketing" contest held in conjunction with the publication of the Eighth Edition of *Marketing*. Ideas came from marketing professors all across the country who teach many different sizes and types of marketing courses. Information on ways to implement these great ideas in the classroom can be found in the Instructor Manual that accompanies this text.
28. Times News Network, "Indian car market growth second fastest globally," *The Times of India*, January 12, 2012, http://articles.timesofindia.indiatimes.com/2011-01-12/india-business/28352452_1_global-auto-commercial-vehicles-indian-automobile-manufacturers.
29. Reuters, "India's flashy new rich drive luxury car boom," *The Times of India*, January 3, 2012, http://timesofindia.indiatimes.com/business/india-business/Indias-flashy-new-rich-drive-luxury-car-boom/articleshow/11351866.cms.

2

1. Corporate Web site: http://www.royalorchidhotels.com/common/about-ro-cms.asp (accessed January 7, 2012).
2. Connie Gugielmo and Aaron Ricadela, "Mulling Options, Dell Considers Going Private," *Bloomberg Businessweek*, June 21–June 27, 2010, 37–38.
3. Alex Schleifer and Jonathan Anderson, "Lessons from Ikea," *UX Magazine*, January 12, 2010, www.uxmag.com/strategy/lessons-from-ikea.
4. Rob Forbes, "Let's Rethink the Way We Get Around," *Public*, July 6, 2010, http://publicbikes.com/c/VISION.
5. Hesseldahl, "Why the Mac Is Still a Rock Star at Apple."
6. "Capcom's a Different Kind of Street Art," *Antenna*, Summer 2010, 81; "Super SFIV: Artist Series Campaign," Capcom Blog, April 1, 2010, www.capcom-unity.com/grant008/blog/2010/04/01/super_sfiv:_artist_series_campaign.
7. Gupta, S. D., "Meet India's king of retail," *Business Standard*, January 15, 2005, http://www.business-standard.com/india/news/meet-india%60s-kingretail/204526/.
8. Press Trust of India, "India's middle class population to touch 267 million in 5 years," *The Economic Times*, February 6, 2011, http://articles.economictimes.indiatimes.com/2011-02-06/news/28424975_1_middle-class-households-applied-economic-research.
9. Roy, S., "Emerging markets and blue ocean strategy," www.scip.org, 13(1), 14-17, January/March, 2010, http://www.tmtctata.com/Emerging_Markets_and_Blue_Ocean_Strategy.pdf.
10. Anonymous, "Tata Motors sales zoom 44 per cent, Nano sales improve in November," *Business Today*, December 1, 2011, http://businesstoday.intoday.in/story/tata-motors-nano-sales-november-auto-sales/1/20584.html.

3

1. Marianne M. Jennings, *Business Ethics*, 5th ed. (Mason, OH: Thomson Higher Education, 2006), 5–6.
2. Venkatraman, S., "Health drinks' 'tall' claims under the scanner," *NDTV*, July 17, 2010, http://www.ndtv.com/article/india/health-drinks-tall-claims-under-the-scanner-37975; Bhushan, R., "Product claims made by advertisers growing taller," *The Economic Times*, September 15, 2010, http://articles.economictimes.indiatimes.com/2010-09-15/news/27594953_1_health-drink-food-and-beverage-advertising-advertising-standards-council; Ghosh, A., "Food authority crackdown on ad claims," *The Indian Express*, February 10, 2012, http://www.indianexpress.com/news/food-author-ity-crackdown-on-ad-claims/910187/0.
3. Based on Edward Stevens, *Business Ethics* (New York: Paulist Press, 1979). Used with permission of Paulist Press.
4. Anusorn Singhapakdi, Skott Vitell, and Kenneth Kraft, "Moral Intensity and Ethical

Decision Making of Marketing Professionals," *Journal of Business Research*, 36, March 1996, 245–255; Ishmael Akaah and Edward Riordan, "Judgments of Marketing Professionals about Ethical Issues in Marketing Research: A Replication and Extension," *Journal of Marketing Research*, February 1989, 112–120. See also Shelby Hunt, Lawrence Chonko, and James Wilcox, "Ethical Problems of Marketing Researchers," *Journal of Marketing Research*, August 1984, 309–324; Kenneth Andrews, "Ethics in Practice," *Harvard Business Review*, September/October 1989, 99–104; Thomas Dunfee, Craig Smith, and William T. Ross, Jr., "Social Contracts and Marketing Ethics," *Journal of Marketing*, July 1999, 14–32; Jay Handleman and Stephen Arnold, "The Role of Marketing Actions with a Social Dimension: Appeals to the Institutional Environment," *Journal of Marketing*, July 1999, 33–48; and David Turnipseed, "Are Good Soldiers Good? Exploring the Link between Organizational Citizenship Behavior and Personal Ethics," *Journal of Business Research*, January 2002, 1–16.

5. "A Strong Ethical Culture Is Key to Cutting Misconduct on the Job," Ethics Resource Center, June 23, 2010, http://ethics.org/news/strong-ethical-culture-key-cutting-misconduct-job.

6. Ibid.

7. "Business Ethics: The Role of Culture and Values for an Ethical Workplace," Society for Human Resource Management, Fourth Quarter 2009, 5, www.shrm.org/Research/Articles/Documents/09-0711_RQ_4_2009_FINAL.pdf; Lauren Bloom, "Ring in the Year with Good Business Ethics—The Innovators," *TheStreet,* January 14, 2010, www.thestreet.com/story/10658690/2/ring-in-year-with-good-business-ethics--the-innovators.html.

8. Survey on Bribery and Corruption, *KPMG*, 2011.

9. Dexter Roberts and Justin Blum, "Bribery Is Losing Its Charm in China,"*Bloomberg Businessweek*, July 12–July 18, 2010, 11.

10. Marc Gunther, "Will Social Responsibility Harm Business?" *Wall Street Journal*, May 18, 2005, A2.

11. Anonymous, "Coca-Cola's 'toxic' India fertiliser," *BBC News*, July 25, 2003, http://news.bbc.co.uk/2/hi/south_asia/3096893.stm; Anonymous, "Supreme Court suspends mining in Bellary, Karnataka," *The Indian Express*, July 29, 2011, http://www.indianexpress.com/news/supreme-court-suspends-mining-in-bellary-karnataka/824300/0; Press Trust of India, "Alumina mining in Orissa causing health hazards: Report," *The Times of India*, February 9, 2010, http://articles.timesofindia.indiatimes.com/2010-02-09/pollution/28145453_1_niyamgiri-hills-alumina-refinery-dongria-kondh-tribe.

12. This section is adapted from Archie B. Carroll, "The Pyramid of Corporate Social Responsibility: Toward the Moral Management of Organizational Stakeholders," *Business Horizons*, July/August 1991, 39–48; see also Kirk Davidson, "Marketers Must Accept Greater Responsibilities," *Marketing News*, February 2, 1998, 6.

13. "Globally, Companies Are Giving Back," *HR Magazine*, June 1, 2007, 30.

14. "Americans Seek More Responsibility from Companies," *Daytona Beach News Journal*, May 26, 2007, 3B.

15. "Secretary-General Opens Global Compact Leaders Summit as Business, Government, Civil Society Leaders Rally for Corporate Citizenship," UNESCAP Press Release, July 5, 2007, Press Release No. L/38/2007.

16. Stanley Reed, "Why the U.S. Can't Turn Its Back on BP," *Bloomberg Businessweek*, June 23, 2010, www.businessweek.com/magazine/content/10_27/b4185013837191.htm.

17. Varma, S., "Bhopal Gas Tragedy: Endless Nightmare," *The Times of India*, December 3, 2009, http://articles.timesofindia.indiatimes.com/2009-12-03/india/28061521_1_compensation-gas-affected-persons-bhopal-gas-tragedy.

18. Gibson, O., "London 2012: Dow Chemical defends Olympic Stadium sponsorship deal," *The Guardian*, March 8 , 2012, http://www.guardian.co.uk/sport/2012/mar/08/dow-chemical-olympic-stadium.

19. American Marketing Association, www.marketingpower.com (accessed October 28, 2008).

20. "Marketing a Green Product," *BusinessWeek Online*, March 5, 2007, 13.

21. Ambwani, M.V., "Toyota Prius leads charge of green brigade," *The Economic Times*, January 8, 2010, http://articles.economictimes.indiatimes.com/2010-01-08/news/27572114_1_honda-civic-hybrid-electric-vehicle-green-cars; Nair, H. G., "Green Crusader: Toyota Prius," *The Economic Times*, May 23, 2010, http://articles.economictimes.indiatimes.com/2010-05-23/news/27583640_1_toyota-prius-hybrid-car-civic-hybrid; Anonymous, "Toyota launches new Prius," *The Indian Express*, January 7, 2012, http://www.indianexpress.com/news/toyota-launches-new-prius/897001/.

22. Company website: http://www.itcportal.com/itc-business/fmcg/cigarettes.aspx (accessed March 23, 2012).

23. Anonymous, "Guidelines for Law enforcers for effective implementation of tobacco control laws," *Ministry of Health and Family Welfare, Government of India* (2011c), May 18, 2003, http://whoindia.org/LinkFiles/Tobacco_Free_Initiative_Tobacco_Free_Initiative_Guidelines_for_Law_Enforcers_for_effective_implementation_of_tobacco_control_laws.pdf.

24. Das, P., "A Conceptual Review Of Advertising Regulation And Standards: Case Studies in The Indian Scenario," *International Marketing Conference on Marketing & Society, IIMK*, April 8-10, 2007, 746, http://asb-pgp.pbworks.com/f/KR-Ad-Ethics.pdf.

25. Reddy K. S., and Gupta P, C., "Report on Tobacco Control in India: Executive Summary", November 25, 2004, http://www.who.int/fctc/reporting/Annex6_Report_on_Tobacco_Control_in_India_2004.pdf.

26 Labbai, M.M., "Social responsibilities and ethics in marketing," *International Marketing Conference on Marketing & Society, IIMK*, April 8-10, 2007, http://dspace.iimk.ac.in/bitstream/2259/392/1/17-27.pdf.

27. Reddy K. S., and Gupta P, C., "Report on Tobacco Control in India: Executive Summary", November 25, 2004, http://www.who.int/fctc/reporting/Annex6_Report_on_Tobacco_Control_in_India_2004.pdf.

4

1. "Consumer Lifestyles—India", *Euromonitor International*, December 2010.

2. Press Trust of India, "Katrina Barbie doll to hit markets," *Livemint*, March 11, 2011, http://www.livemint.com/2011/03/11165849/Katrina-Barbie-doll-to-hit-mar.html.

3. "Quick Stats of Women Workers," June 17, 2010 www.dol .gov.

4. "First Steps to Digital Detox," *New York Times*, June 7, 2010, http://roomfordebate.blogs .nytimes.com/2010/06/07/first-steps-to-digital-detox.

5. Anonymous, "India's population to surpass China's by 2025," *The Hindu*, April 16, 2011, http://www.thehindu.com/news/national/article1701790.ece.

6. "Consumer Lifestyles–India", *Euromonitor International*, December 2010.

7. Population projections for India and States 2001-2026, National Commission on Population, May 2006.

8. "Cities Grow at Suburbs' Expense during Recession," *Wall Street Journal*, July 1, 2009, A5.

9. "Consumer Lifestyles—India", *Euromonitor International*, December 2010, 9.

10. Ibid., 10.

11. Ibid.

12. Ibid., 11.

13. Ibid., 12.

14. Ibid., 14.

15. Ibid.

16. Ibid., 15.

17. Desai, S.B. et, al., "Human Development in India", Oxford University Press, 2010, 25.

18. Ibid., 13.

19. David Wessel, "Did 'Great Recession' Live Up to Its Name?" *Wall Street Journal*, April 8, 2010, http://online.wsj.com/article/SB100014240527023035912045751696931663 52882.html.

20. "At the Supermarket Checkout, Frugality Trumps Brand Loyalty," *Wall Street Journal*, November 6, 2008, D1.

21. "Ben Franklin, Where Are You?" *Bloomberg Businessweek*, January 4, 2010, 29.

22. Partially adopted from John Bessant, Kathrin Moslein, and Bettina Von Stamm, "In Search of Innovation," *Wall Street Journal*, June 22, 2009, R4.

23. "The 50 Most Innovated Companies 2010," *Bloomberg Businessweek*, April 15, 2010, www.businessweek.com/interactive_reports/innovative_companies_2010.html.

24. "Creativity Pays. Here's How Much," *BusinessWeek*, April 24, 2006, 45.

25. "Yes, Innovations Do Pay Off, Study Finds," *International Herald Tribune*, August 30–31, 2008, 15.

26. Company website: http://fcamin.nic.in/index.asp.

27. Company website: http://www.fssai.gov.in/AboutFssai/Introduction.aspx?RequestID=thsk01MhHE11H1iiS8k_doAction=True.

28. Company website: http://www.bis.org.in/.

29. Emily Steel and Justin Scheck, "Smartphone Trackers Raise Privacy Worries," *Wall Street Journal*, June 14, 2010, http://online.wsj.com/article/SB100014240527487040675045753046431345 31922.html.

30. Anonymous, "India facing obesity epidemic: experts," *The Hindu*, October 12, 2007, http://hindu.com./2007/10/12/stories/2007101260940600.htm.

5

1. William Wrigley Jr. Company, news release, July 2, 2007.

2. "India: Foreign Trade Policy, International Economics and Trade in South Asia, *World*

Bank", http://web.worldbank.org/WBSITE/EXTERNAL/COUNTRIES/SOUTHASIAEXT/EXTSARREGTOPINTECOTRA/0,,contentMDK:20592520~menuPK:579454~pagePK:34004173~piPK:34003707~theSitePK:579448,00.html.

3. "Trends in India's Foreign Trade, Annual Report 2010-11", *Department of Commerce, India*, http://commerce.nic.in/publications/anualreport_chapter2-2010 11.htm.

4. Anonymous, "Exports emerging as source of job creation," *The Financial Express*, April 8, 2006, http://www.financialexpress.com/news/exports-emerging-as-source-of-job-creation/85601/.

5. "Trends in India's Foreign Trade, Annual Report 2010-11", *Department of Commerce, India*, http://commerce.nic.in/publications/anualreport_chapter2-2010-11.htm.

6. MSME Annual Report 2010-11, 13, http://msme.gov.in/MSME-Annual-Report-2010-11-English.pdf.

7. "Globalization's Gains Come with a Price," *Wall Street Journal*, May 24, 2007, A1, A12.

8. Anonymous, "The TATA Group-Out of India," *The Economist*, March 3, 2011, http://www.economist.com/node/18285497.

9. Raj, R., "Foreign forays fuel ascent of Indian MNCs," *The Indian Express*, January 28, 2011, http://www.indianexpress.com/news/foreign-forays-fuel-ascent-of-indian-mncs/743031/0.

10. Li Qiaoyi, "US Tries to Block Angang Steel's Investment," *Global Times*, July 4, 2010, http://business.globaltimes.cn/industries/2010-07/548180.html.

11. Theodore Levitt, "The Globalization of Markets," *Harvard Business Review*, May/June 1983, 92–100.

12. "Ford Chief Bets on One Global Car," *International Herald Tribune*, January 22, 2010, 1, 16.

13. Ellen Gamerman, "Exporting Broadway," *Wall Street Journal*, July 16, 2010, W1–W2.

14. "Gross National Income Per Capita 2008, Atlas Method and PPP," *World Development Indicators Database*, World Bank, October 7, 2009, http://siteresources.worldbank.org/DATASTATISTICS/Resources/GNIPC.pdf; "Gross National Income 2008, Atlas Method," *World Development Indicators Database*, World Bank, October 7, 2009, http://siteresources.worldbank.org/DATASTATISTICS/Resources/GNI.pdf.

15. Vanessa Wong, "Cities Where the Dollar Is Weakest," *Bloomberg Businessweek*, June 22, 2010, www.businessweek.com/lifestyle/content/jun2010/bw20100622_768389.htm.

16. Anil K. Gupta and Haiyan Wang, "How to Get China and India Right," *Wall Street Journal*, April 28–29, 2007, R9. Reprinted with permission of *Wall Street Journal* © 2007 Dow Jones & Company, Inc. All Rights Reserved Worldwide.

17. Peter Coy, "Five Ways Forward with China," *Bloomberg Businessweek*, June 28–July 4, 2010, 4–5; Arnold J. Karr, "Study: China Top Market for Retail Development," *Women's Wear Daily*, June 23, 2010, 2.

18. "Doing Business 2008," *The World Bank*, www.doingbusiness.org/.

19. Mark Lee, "China Unicom Boycott of Google May Signal Fallout Is Spreading," *Bloomberg Businessweek*, March 25, 2010, www.businessweek.com/news/2010-03-25/china-unicom-boycott-of-google-may-signal-fallout-is-spreading.html.

20. David Wessel, "Free-Trade Winds May Be Blowing Again," *Wall Street Journal*, July 1, 2010, http://online.wsj.com/article/SB10001424052748704334604575338793673236632.html.

21. Tom Barkley, "U.S. Chamber Kicks Up Campaign for Free Trade," *Wall Street Journal*, May 14, 2010, http://online.wsj.com/article/SB10001424052748703460404575244170961738574.html.

22. "Refighting NAFTA," *BusinessWeek*, March 31, 2008, 56–59; also see "Make the World Go Away," *Fortune*, February 4, 2008, 105–107.

23. Barkley, "U.S. Chamber Kicks Up Campaign for Free Trade."

24. "U.S. Central America-Dominican Republic Free Trade Agreement (CAFTA-DR) Analysis," (Washington, DC: International Trade Association), Summer 2008, 12.

25. www.eurunion.org (accessed July 20, 2010).

26. Natascha Gewaltig, "Greece's Painful Choice," *Bloomberg Businessweek*, February 19, 2010, www.businessweek.com/investor/content/feb2010/pi20100218_722508.htm; Stephen Fidler and Charles Forelle, "World Races to Avert Crisis in Europe," *Wall Street Journal*, May 10, 2010, http://online.wsj.com/article/SB10001424052748703880304575235632618569478.html; Katie Martin, "Emergency Lenders Play It Straight," *Wall Street Journal*, July 19, 2010, http://blogs .wsj.com/source/2010/07/19/emergency-lenders-play-it-straight.

27. "European Union's Kroes Says U.S. Criticism of Microsoft Ruling Is Unacceptable," *Associated Press Newswires*, September 19, 2007.

28. Jonathan Bensky, "World's Biggest Market: European Union Offers Great Opportunities for U.S. Companies, But There Are Also Plenty of Challenges," *Shipping Digest*, July 30, 2007.

29. Elliot Blair Smith, Eltaf Najafizada, and James Rupert, "Afghan Mineral Wealth: No Easy Road for Westerners," *Bloomberg Businessweek*, June 21–June 27, 2010, 11–12.

30. Gamerman, "Exporting Broadway," W1–W2.

31. Franchising Industry—An anonymous contributor to SME growth, *FraNews, Indian Franchise Association Newsletter*, February 2011, http://www.franchiseindia.org/pdf/feb_issue.pdf.

32. Press Trust of India, "India Inc's FDI outflow dips 36pc in FY10: RBI," *The Economic Times*, July 13, 2010, http://articles.economictimes.indiatimes.com/2010-07-13/news/27601240_1_preferred-destination-singapore-top-destinations.

33. Anonymous, "FDI inflow to India dips to $25.89 bn," *Rediff Business*, May 4, 2010, http://business.rediff.com/report/2010/may/04/fdi-inflow-to-india-dips.htm.

34. Kenneth Hein, "Emerging Markets Still Like U.S. Brands," *BrandWeek*, April 16, 2007, 4. Used by permission of Aegis Group, plc.; also see "Best Global Brands," September 29, 2008, 52–57.

35. Goyal, M. and Jaiswal, K. "How Nokia fell from dominance and got pinned down by competitors," *The Economic Times*, May 27, 2011, http://articles.economictimes.indiatimes.com/2011-03-27/news/29194836_1_nokia-india-ceo-stephen-elop-nokia-c7.

36. Will Connors and Sarah Childress, "Africa's Local Champions Begin to Spread Out," *Wall Street Journal*, May 26, 2010, B8.

37. Linda Blake, "Floating Supermarket Cater to Indian Villagers," *Wall Street Journal*, May 3, 2010, http://online.wsj.com/video/floating-supermarket-caters-to-indian-villagers/AF2D474B-97BE-4661-AF30-9236E410A7B9.html.

38. "100 Best Global Brands," *BusinessWeek*, September 28, 2009, 50.

39. "The Coca-Cola System," http://www.thecoca-colacompany.com/sustainabilityreport/in-our-company/the-coca-cola-system.html (accessed March 22, 2012).

40. Chamokutti, P., "Not so cool anymore: Will the Coca-Cola ad be able to get the fizz back?" *The Economic Times*, March 21, 2012, http://articles.economictimes.indiatimes.com/2012-03-21/news/31220052_1_thanda-matlab-coca-cola-coca-cola-india-limca.

41. Anonymous, "Coca-Cola launches global ads for London 2012 Olympic games starring Mark Ronson," The Coca-Cola Company, February 15, 2012, http://www.thecoca-colacompany.com/dynamic/press_center/2012/02/global-ads-for-london-2012-olympic-games.html.

42. Sharma, S., "Coca-Cola cuts prices, Pepsi may follow suit," *The Economic Times*, February 15, 2012, http://articles.economictimes.indiatimes.com/2012-02-15/news/31063326_1_coca-cola-cola-segment-pet-bottles.

6

1. "LG Electronics: Rural Is the Future," *Wall Street Journal*, May 6, 2010, http://online.wsj.com/article/SB127313731105787137.html.

2. Anonymous, "Indians Now Spend More Time on Social Media Sites than on Personal Email," *Nielsenwire*, May 25, 2011, http://blog.nielsen.com/nielsenwire/global/indians-now-spend-more-time-on-social-media-sites-than-on-personal-email/.

3. Anonymous, "Indians Now Spend More Time on Social Media Sites than on Personal Email," *Nielsenwire*, May 25, 2011, http://blog.nielsen.com/nielsenwire/global/indians-now-spend-more-time-on-social-media-sites-than-on-personal-email/.

4. Allen Weiss, Nicholas Lurie, and Deborah MacInnis, "Listening to Strangers: Whose Responses Are Valuable, How Valuable Are They, and Why?" *Journal of Marketing Research*, August 2008, 450–461.

5. Jeffrey Inman and Russell Winer, "Impulse Buys," *Wall Street Journal*, April 15, 1999, A1; David Silvera, Anne Lavack, and Fredric Kropp, "Impulse Buying: The Role of Affect, Social Influence, and Subjective Well-Being," *Journal of Consumer Research*, 25, no. 1, 2008, 23–33.

6. India Infoline News Service, "P&G's Shiksha building 20+ schools across India," *India Infoline*, May 5, 2011, http://www.indiainfoline.com/Markets/News/PandGs-Shiksha-building-20plus-schools-across-India/5147215227.

7. Mandal, P., "Fashion and You raises $40 mn in venture funding," *Business Standard*, November, 15, 2011, http://business-standard.com/india/news/fashionyou-raises-40-mn-in-venture-funding-/455528/.

8. Corporate Web site, http://newms.fashionandyou.com/FaqHelp/aboutus.html (accessed January 28, 2012).

9. Krishnakumar, PK., "South India accounts for 40% of gold purchases," *The Economic Times*, December 29, 2011, http://articles.economictimes.indiatimes.com/2011-12-29/news/30568918_1_gold-demand-gold-jewellery-gold-purchases.

10. Ghosal, A., "Special: national brands with regional tongue," *Afaqs*, July 12, 2010, http://www.afaqs.com/news/story.html?sid=27648.

11. Ghosal, A., "Special: national brands with regional tongue," *Afaqs*, July 12, 2010, http://www.afaqs.com/news/story.html?sid=27648.
12. CNBC-TV18, "IPL 5: Why are sponsors logging on to internet," *Moneycontrol*, arch 31, 2012, http://www.moneycontrol.com/news/special-videos/ipl-5-whysponsors-loggingto-internet_687313.html; Bhushan, R., "Parle ropes in Ravi Kishan and Rituparna Sengupta as brand ambassadors," The *Economic Times*, January 10, 2010, http://articles.economictimes.indiatimes.com/2011-01-10/news/28428741_1_brand-ambassadors-parle-products-ravi-kishan.
13. BIjapurkar, R., "Calibrating SEC Classifications In Terms Of Relative Purchasing Power," http://www.bijapurkar.com/demanddrivers/dsds_calibrating.php.
14. "Socio-Economic Classification," *The Market Research Society of India*, http://mrsi.in/sec.html; "Marketing Funda: Socio Economic Classification," http://marketingpractice.blogspot.in/2007/02/marketing-funda-socio-economic.html.
15. "TJX: Dressed to Kill for the Downturn," *BusinessWeek*, October 27, 2008, 60.
16. Orth and Kahle, "Intrapersonal Variation in Consumer Susceptibility to Normative Influence: Toward a Better Understanding of Brand Choice Decisions," 429.
17. Ronald Clark, James Zboja, and Ronald Goldsmith, "Status Consumption and Role-Relaxed Consumption: A Tale of Two Retail Consumers," *Journal of Retailing and Consumer Services*, January 2007, 45–59.
18. Chenting See, Kevin Zheng Zhou, Nan Zhou, and Julie Juan Li, "Harmonizing Conflict in Husband-Wife Purchase Decision-Making: Perceived Fairness and Spousal Influence Dynamics," *Journal of the Academy of Marketing Science* (Fall 2008), 378–394; also see Michel Laroche, Zhiyong Yang, Kim Chankon, and Marie-Odile Richard, "How Culture Matters in Children's Purchase Influence: A Multi-level Investigation," *Journal of the Academy of Marketing Science* (Spring 2007), 113–116.
19. Derek Gale, "Who's the Boss?" *Restaurants & Institutions*, 117, no. 2, February 1, 2007, 50.
20. Ira Mayer, "New Report: Teen Spending and Influence," Publicity e-mail, June 16, 2010.
21. Karin Ekstrom, "Parental Consumer Learning or 'Keeping Up with Their Children,'" *Journal of Consumer Behavior*, July/August 2007, 203–217.
22. Steve McClellan, "Are Demographics Dead?" *AdWeek*, February 23, 2010, www.adweek.com.
23. Anil Mathur, George Moschis, and Euehun Lee, "A Longitudinal Study of the Effects of Life Style Status Changes on Changes in Consumer Preferences," *Journal of the Academy of Marketing Sciences*, Summer 2008, 234–246.
24. www.ampacet.com, December 28, 2007.
25. Laura Petrecca, "Axe Ads Turn Up the Promise of Sex Appeal," *USA Today*, April 17, 2007.
26. Elizabeth J. Wilson, "Using the Dollar-metric Scale to Establish the Just Meaningful Difference in Price," in 1987 AMA *Educators' Proceedings*, ed. Susan Douglas et al. (Chicago: American Marketing Association, 1987), 107.
27. Kenneth Hein, "Teens Schizophrenic about Their Brands: Millennials Have Complex Feelings about Brands Unless, of Course, It's Apple," *Brandweek*, June 18, 2007.
28. Katherine Boehret, "Making Hotmail Hot Again," *Wall Street Journal*, June 9, 2010, http://online.wsj.com/article/SB10001424052748703302604575294700105749996.html.
29. Jyothi Datta, "Aspartame: Bitter Truth in Artificial Sweeteners?" *Business Line*, www.thehindubusinessline.com/2005/10/04/stories/2005100404220300.htm (accessed September 14, 2007).
30. Rajpal, U., "Consumer Electronics Industry will be at Rs. 350 billion in 2012," *EFY Times News Network*, February 7, 2012, http://www.efytimes.com/e1/fullnews.asp?edid=78373.
31. Anonymous, "Booming Consumer electronic market in India," *Research and Markets*, August 2011, http://www.researchandmarkets.com/reports/660076/booming_consumer_electronics_market_in_india.
32. Company website: http://www.videoconworld.com/index.php?option=com_content&view=article&id=3&Itemid=5 (accessed March 22, 2012).
33. Anonymous, "Videocon Industries Ltd," *India Infoline*, http://www.indiainfoline.com/Markets/Company/Fundamentals/Management-Discussions/Videocon-Industries-Ltd/511389 (accessed March 23, 2012).
34. Rajpal, U., "Consumer Electronics Industry will be at Rs. 350 billion in 2012," *EFY Times News Network*, February 7, 2012, http://www.efytimes.com/e1/fullnews.asp?edid=78373.

7

1. Michael D. Hutt and Thomas W. Speh, *Business Marketing Management: B2B*, 9e. (Cincinnati, OH: Thomson, 2007), 4.
2. "BtoB's Best Marketers," *BtoB Magazine*, October 11, 2010, www.btobonline.com/section/best2010marketers.
3 Sengupta, S., "The roll out continues," *Outlook Business*, May 31, 2008, http://business.outlookindia.com/article.aspx?101183.
4. Hutt and Speh, *Business Marketing Management*, 315.
5. Mary E. Morrison, "Industrial Buyers Shopping Online," *BtoB Magazine*, October 13, 2008, 19.
6. Karen J. Bannan, "10 Great b2b Sites," *BtoB Magazine*, September 13, 2010, www.btobonline.com/article/20100913/FREE/309139988/10-great-b-to-b-sites.
7. "Survey Says! Recent BtoB Webcast Audience Poll Results," *BtoB Magazine*, November10, 2008, 8.
8. NetGenesis, E-Metrics: Business Metrics for the New Economy, www.spss.com.
9. Morrison, "Industrial Buyers Shopping Online."
10. Karen Bannan, "How RSS Can Complement eMail Marketing," *BtoB Magazine*, September 28, 2009, www.btobonline.com/apps/pbcs.dll/article?AID=/20090928/FREE/309289985.
11. "Disintermediation," *marketingterms.com*, www.marketingterms.com/dictionary/disintermediation/.
12. Christopher Hosford, "'BtoB' Leading Edge Attendees Urged to 'Flip the Funnel' Towards Retention," *BtoB Magazine*, June 23, 2010, www.btobonline.com/apps/pbcs.dll/article?AID=/20100623/FREE/100629964.
13. "About Inc.com," *Inc.*, December 21, 2008, www.inc.com/about/index.html (accessed July 26, 2010).
14. Seth Goldman, "The Big Brewer" *Inc.*, April 21, 2010, www.inc.com/seth-goldman/the-big-brewer.html.
15. Harish, M., "Customer Service: A Culture and A Habit" *India Retail Report 2011*, pp.161 (Images Group Publication, India); Anonymous, "TATA Coffee brings Starbucks to India," *Business Standard*, January 14, 2011, http://www.business-standard.com/india/news/tata-coffee-brings-starbucks-to-india/421757/.
16. Steven Reinberg, "The Issue: DHL Turns to Rival UPS," *BusinessWeek*, June 11, 2008, www.businessweek.com/managing/content/jun2008/ca20080611_101915.htm.
17. Anonymous, "Airtel, SKS Microfinance tie up to offer package," *The Hindu*, July 18, 2008, http://www.hindu.com/2008/07/18/stories/2008071853700500.htm.
18. Robert M. Morgan and Shelby D. Hunt, "The Commitment-Trust Theory of Relationship Marketing," *Journal of Marketing*, 58, no. 3, 1994, 23.
19. Ibid.
20. "Suzuki-VW Alliance to Include Hybrids, Management," *Bloomberg Businessweek*, January 15, 2010, www.businessweek.com/news/2010-01-15/suzuki-vw-alliance-to-include-hybrids-management-update1-.html.
21. Amir Efrati, "Microsoft, Google Vie to Sell U.S. Cloud Mail," *Wall Street Journal*, July 26, 2010, http://online.wsj.com/article/SB10001424052748704719104575388374158004334.html.
22. For a complete listing of all NIC codes, see http://mospi.nic.in/Mospi_New/upload/nic_2008_17apr09.pdf.
23. Daniel Michaels, "Rivals Race for Tanker Deal," *Wall Street Journal*, July 23 2010, http://online.wsj.com/article/SB10001424052748704421304575383132903915038.html.
24. Chatterjee, P. and R. P. Nair, "Warburg Pincus in talks with IndiaMart for Rs 150 crore investment," *The Economic Times*, May 7, 2011, http://articles.economictimes.indiatimes.com/2011-05-07/news/29520564_1_private-equity-intel-capital-indiamart.
25. Peter Sanders, "Boeing 787 Lands in Farnborough," *Wall Street Journal*, July 19, 2010, http://online.wsj.com/article/SB10001424052748704196404575374693695488042.html.
26. Marshall Lager, "Listen Up," *Customer Relationship Management*, March 2007, 24–27.
27. *Inc.* Staff, "How to Sell to Northrop Grumman," *Inc.*, April 5, 2010, www.inc .com/magazine/20100401/how-to-sell-to-northrop-grumman.html; *Inc.* Staff, "How to Sell to Dell," *Inc.*, April 5, 2010, www.inc.com/magazine/20100401/how-to-sell-to-dell.html; *Inc.* Staff, "How to Sell to Coca-Cola," *Inc.*, April 5, 2010, www.inc.com/magazine/20100401/how-to-sell-to-coca-cola.html.
28. "Right-Channeling: Making Sure Your Best Customers Get Your Best Service," Right Now Technologies, June 3, 2009, http://jobfunctions.bnet.com/abstract.aspx?docid=132740.
29. This application exercise is based on the contribution of Gregory B. Turner (College of Charleston) to *Great Ideas in Teaching Marketing*, a teaching supplement that accompanies Lamb, Hair, and McDaniel's *Marketing*. Professor Turner's entry titled "Student Ethics versus Practitioner Ethics" received an Honorable Mention in the "Best of the Great Ideas in Teaching Marketing" contest held in conjunction with the publication of the eighth edition of *Marketing*.
30. Company website: http://www.hp.com/ (accessed March 22, 2012).
31. Company Website: http://www8.hp.com/us/en/business-services/it-services.

html?compURI=1077422 (accessed March 27, 2012).
32. Company Website: http://h20271.www2.hp.com/SMB-AP/cache/275302-0-0-101-121.html (accessed March 27, 2012).
33. Company Website: http://www8.hp.com/in/en/contact-hp/contact.html# (accessed March 27, 2012).
34. Anonymous, "Be Print Happy with Creative Studio," *HP Website*, September 06, 2011, http://hpwriteandread.com/Be-Print-Happy-With-HP-Creative-Studio.php.
35. Chadha, P., "HP India launched 'Trade In Trade Out' Program in India," *Cyber Media*, September 9, 2009, http://www.ciol.com/Channel-News/News-Reports/HP-India-launches-Trade-In-Trade-Out-program-in-India/9909124810/0/.
36. Anonymous, "HP to roll out cloud computing solutions for key verticals," *The Economic Times*, July 7, 2010, http://articles.economictimes.indiatimes.com/2010-07-07/news/27616749_1_hp-india-smb-segment-san-tanu-ghose.
37. Anonymous, "Hewlett Packard India launches new monochrome, color laser jet," *Business Line*, February 09, 2012, http://www.thehindubusinessline.com/industry-and-economy/info-tech/article2875522.ece?homepage=true&ref=wl_home.
38. Anonymous, "Acer pips HP to become no.2 PC seller in India," *Business Standard*, August 18, 2011, http://www.business-standard.com/india/news/acer-pips-hp-to-become-no-2-pc-seller-in-india/446200/.
39. Anonymous, "IT's business as usual at HP's India PSG unit," *Business Standard*, August 25, 2011, http://www.business-standard.com/india/news/it%5Cs-business-as-usual-at-hp%5Cs-india-psg-unit/446978/.
40. Goldman, D., "HP decides to keep its PC business," *CNN Money*, October 27, 2011, http://money.cnn.com/2011/10/27/technology/hp_keeps_pcs/index.htm?iid=EAL.
41. Goldman, D., "HP lumps printers unit with PC business," *CNN Money*, March 21, 2012, http://money.cnn.com/2012/03/21/technology/hewlett-packard-printers/.
42. Sharma, V., "Small Business Service Ltd. HP to click on small - town SMEs," *The Economic Times*, April 18, 2008, http://articles.economictimes.indiatimes.com/2008-04-18/news/27716284_1_channel-partners-smes-travel-agents.

8

1. Goran Mijuk, "Nestlé Bets on Emerging Markets," *Wall Street Journal*, June 22 2010, http://online.wsj.com/article/SB10001424052748704853404575322382547240528.html.
2. "Rural Calling: Can Nokia Sustain Its First-mover Advantage?" *Wall Street Journal*, May 4, 2010, http://online.wsj.com/article/SB127296947929886511.html.
3. "Consumer Lifestyles—India," *Enromonitor International*, December 2010.
4. Ibid.
5. Ibid.
6. Ibid.
7. Ibid.
8. Chauhan, C.P. and L. Philip, "Scooter makers gear up to meet record demand; sales grow 39% year-on-year," *The Economic Times*, December 14, 2011, http://economictimes.indiatimes.com/news/news-by-industry/auto/two-wheelers/scooter-makers-gear-up-to-meet-record-demand-sales-grow-39-year-on-year/articleshow/11099885.cms?curpg=1.
9. Men's grooming in India, Euromonitor International, August 2011.
10. "Luxury Brands: Marketing the Upscale during a Downturn," November 13, 2008, http://knowledge.wharton.upenn.edu/article.cfm?articleid=2091.
11. Anonymous, "Tata Swach launched in state market," *Business Standard*, March 30, 2011, http://business-standard.com/india/news/tata-swach-launched-in-state-market/430235/.
12. Emily Steel, "Marketers Tie Ads to Bollywood," *Wall Street Journal*, May 20, 2009, http://online.wsj.com/article/SB124278296830537521.html.
13. Consumer lifestyles – India, Euromonitor International, 2011, 18.
14. Emily Steel, "Exploring Ways to Build a Better Consumer Profile," *Wall Street Journal*, March 15, 2010, http://online.wsj.com/article/SB10001424052748703447104575117972284656374.html.
15. Ann Zimmerman, "Home Depot Learns to Go Local," *Wall Street Journal*, October 7, 2008, B1.
16. George Stalk Jr., "In Praise of the Heavy Spender," *Globe and Mail*, May 21, 2007, www.theglobeandmail.com/report-on-business/.
17. Niraj Sheth and Yukari Iwatani Kane, "Smart-Phone Makers Call the Doctor," *Wall Street Journal*, October 8, 2009, http://online.wsj.com/article/SB125487806705169673.html.
18. Anonymous, "GSK Consumer launches Women's Horlicks," *Business Standard*, January 29, 2008, http://www.business-standard.com/india/news/gsk-consumer-launches-womens-horlicks/311977/; Subramanian, S., "Horlicks stretches out," *Business Standard*, July 14, 2009, http://www.business-standard.com/india/news/horlicks-stretches-out/363790/.
19. Jennifer Valentino-DeVries, "Is the iPad Cannibalizing Other Apple Products?" *Wall Street Journal*, May 17, 2010, http://blogs.wsj.com/digits/2010/05/17/is-the-ipad-cannibalizing-other-apple-products.
20. Available at company's website: http://www.madurafnl.com/brands/madura_fashion_lifestyle.html.
21. Jenny McTaggart, "Taking a Bite Out of Baggers," *Brandweek*, June 27, 2005, 42–45.
22. This application exercise is based on the contribution of Kim McKeage (University of Maine) to *Great Ideas in Teaching Marketing*, a teaching supplement that accompanies Lamb, Hair, and McDaniel's *Marketing*. Professor McKeage's entry, titled "Students Practice Making Market/Product Grids on Themselves," received an Honorable Mention in the "Best of the Great Ideas in Teaching Marketing" contest held in conjunction with the publication of the eighth edition of *Marketing*.
23. Pandey, M, "Segmentation, Targeting and Positioning," *In Contemporary Indian Cases in marketing*, (New Delhi, IND: Dreamtech Press, 2006-07), 73–76.
24. http://www.zeetelevision.com.

9

1. Ellen Byron, "Wash Away Bad Hair Days," *Wall Street Journal*, June 30, 2010, D1.
2. Ibid.
3. "Second Half of '09 Could Set Research in Motion," *Quirks Marketing Research Review*, July 2009, 80–81.
4. "Be Mindful of Cellphone Interviews," *Marketing Research*, Summer 2009, 4.
5. "Marketers Watch As Friends Interact Online," *Wall Street Journal*, April 15, 2010, B5.
6. Raymond R. Burke, "Virtual Shopping: Breakthrough in Marketing Research," *Harvard Business Review*, March/April 1996, 120–131.
7. Kuruvilla, S.J. and N. Joshi, "Influence of demographics, psychographics, shopping orientation, mall shopping attitude and purchase patterns on mall patronage in India," *Journal of Retailing and Consumer Services*, 2010, Vol. 17 (4), 259–269.
8. "Research in a Petri Dish: Learning from Communities," *Marketing News*, September 3, 2009, 22.
9. Rai, A. "Companies heed the online message," *Livemint*, August 3, 2008, http://www.livemint.com/2008/08/03235151/Companies-heed-the-online-mess.html.
10. "About Consumer-Generated Media (CGM)," Nielsen, http://www.nielsen-online.com/resources.jsp?section=about_cgm (accessed October 25, 2010).
11. "BuzzMetrics," Nielsen, (accessed October 25, 2010), http://en-us.nielsen.com/content/nielsen/en_us/product_families/nielsen_buzzmetrics.html.
12. Products and Solutions: InfoScan Tracking Service, Information Resources, Inc., www.usa.infores.com/ProductsSolutions/AllProducts/AllProductsDetail/tabid/159/productid/83/Default.aspx, (accessed December 1, 2008).
13. Byron, "Wash Away Bad Hair Days."
14. Sahay, A., N. Sharma, and K. Mehta, "Role of affect and cognition in consumer brand relationship: exploring gender differences", *Journal of Indian Business Research*, Vol. 4 Iss: 1, 36–60.
15. Parmeshwaran M.G., "Brand Building Consumer Product Advertising," *In FCB-ULKA Brand Building Advertising Concepts and Cases*, (New Delhi, IND: Tata McGraw Hill Publishing Company Limited, 2002), 11–23.
16. PTI, "Wipro to relaunch brand Santoor," *The Economic Times*, March 28, 2012, http://articles.economictimes.indiatimes.com/2012-02-08/news/31037775_1_santoor-wccl-brand-ambassador.
17. BestMediaInfo Bureau, "Draftfcb Ulka gives a contemporary makeover to Santoor," *Best Media Info* (2012), March 28, 2012, http://www.bestmediainfo.com/2012/03/draftfcb-ulka-gives-a-contemporary-makeover-to-santoor/.

10

1. Darren Murph, "LG Debuts Optimus Smartphone Series, Froyo-powered 'One' and 'Chic' Arriving First," Engadget, July 5, 2010, www.engadget.com/2010/07/05/lg-debuts-optimus-smartphone-series-froyo-powered-one-and-ch.
2. Roger Cheng, "Apartments Get TV Focus," *Wall Street Journal*, July 4, 2010, B5.
3. Company website: http://www.tata.com/media/releases/inside.aspx?artid=NA9Z1kWIGYM=.
4. Gren Manuel, "Scrabble Rules Are Not Being Changed," *Wall Street Journal*, April 7,

2010, http://blogs.wsj.com/source/2010/04/07/scrabble-rules-are-not-being-changed/.
5. Ellen Byron, "Wash Away Bad Hair Days," *Wall Street Journal*, June 30, 2010, http://online.wsj.com/article/SB10001424052748704911704575327141935381092.html.
6. Khandelwal, P., *A Private Affair*, 2011, http://www.financialexpress.com/news/a-private-affair/878843/0.
7. Nirmalya Kumar and Jan-Benedict E. M. Steenkamp, "Premium Store Brands: The Hottest Trend in Retailing," www.marketingprofs.com, March 20, 2007.
8. Anonymous, "Private labels dent established FMCG brand share," *Rediff Business*, August 26, 2009, http://business.rediff.com/special/2009/aug/26/private-labels-dent-established-fmcg-brand-shares.htm.
9. Elaine Wong, "Retailers Rally Behind Their 'Captive Brands,'" *Brandweek.com*, September 29, 2008.
10. ET Bureau, "Indian FMCG companies tie up with Hollywood to co-brand products," *The Economic Times*, October 8, 2011, http://articles.economictimes.indiatimes.com/2011-10-08/news/30258138_1_tintin-brands-funskool-india.
11. Deborah L. Vence, "Product Enhancement," *Marketing News*, May 1, 2005, 19.
12. TNN, "Amul wins trademark case in Gujarat HC," *The Times of India*, September 26, 2007, http://timesofindia.indiatimes.com/business/india-business/Amul-wins-trademark-case-in-Gujarat-HC/articleshow/2402952.cms.
13. Krishna, S., "Partner may face $30 mn Hitch," *The Economic Times*, August 8, 2007, http://articles.economictimes.indiatimes.com/2007-08-08/news/27673674_1_hitch-indian-films-bollywood.
14. Madhukar, S., "Flavour of India," 2009, http://www.tata.com/pdf/tata_review_oct_09/business_flavour_of_india.pdf.
15. Sayal, S., "Fanta:delivering a new 'orangy 'blast," *Afaqs*, February 28, 2008, http://www.afaqs.com/news/story.html?sid=20481.
16. Srinivasan, L., "*HUL partners with Disney for packaging initiative*," 2008, http://www.financialexpress.com/news/hul-partners-with-disney-for-packaging-initiative/348608/0.
17. Cecily Hall, "The High Stakes of Repackaging," *Women's Wear Daily*, April 8, 2009, 12.
18. Deborah Ball, "The Perils of Packaging: Nestlé Aims for Easier Openings" *Wall Street Journal*, November 17, 2005, B1.
19. Anonymous, "Maggi Cuppa Mania: Nestle launches instant noodles," *Live Mint*, April 1, 2008, http://www.livemint.com/2008/04/01193846/Maggi-Cuppa-Mania-Nestle-laun.html.
20. "Environmentally Responsible Packaging: Convenience vs. Conscience," www.retailwire.com, April 30, 2008.
21. Kate Galbraith, "A Compostable Chips Bag Hits the Shelves," *New York Times*, March 16, 2010, http://green.blogs.nytimes.com/2010/03/16/a-compostable-chips-bag-hits-the-shelves; "The Compostable Label," Biodegradable Products Institute, www.bpiworld.org/BPI-Public/Program.html.
22. Anonymous, "59% Indian consumers study nutrition labels: Nielsen," *Business Standard*, August 12, 2008, http://www.business-standard.com/india/news/59-indian-consumers-study-nutrition-labels-nielsen/331133/.
23. Darren Rovell, "One-on-One with Nike Brand President Charlie Denson," CNBC, June 9, 2010, www.cnbc.com/id/37600508/One_on_One_with_Nike_Brand_President_Charlie_Denson.
24. Gwendolyn Bounds, "As Eco-Seals Proliferate, So Do Doubts," *Wall Street Journal*, April 2, 2009, http://online.wsj.com/article/SB123862823846680371.html.
25. "Garnier Fructis Shampoo +Oil 2 in 1 shampoo," http://www.garnier.in/_en/_in/our_products/product-struct.aspx?tpcode=OUR_PRODUCTS^PRD_HAIRCARE^FRUCTIS^FRUCTIS_DISCOVER^FRUCTIS_OIL_REPAIR (accessed March 22, 2012).

11

1. Reena Jana, "In Data," *BusinessWeek*, September 22, 2008, 48.
2. "The 50 Most Innovative Companies 2010," *Bloomberg Businessweek*, August 11, 2010, www.businessweek.com/interactive_reports/innovative_companies_2010.html.
3. Jana, "In Data."
4. Mukherjee, W., "ITC plans launching one or more mass products to grow personal care and food businesses," *The Economic Times*, May 9, 2011, http://articles.economictimes.indiatimes.com/2011-05-09/news/29524975_1_itc-plans-premium-brand-fiama-di-wills.
5. Ghosal, A., "Surf Excel Matic: Offering a helping hand," *Afaqs*, July 7, 2010, http://www.afaqs.com/news/story.html?sid=27606.
6. Bhattacharyya, A., "Airtel dons a new look, plans to be closer to consumers across the globe," *Afaqs*, November 19, 2010, http://www.afaqs.com/news/story.html?sid=28828.
7. Joel Rubinson, "Innovating Innovation: The Best Ideas Can Come from Anywhere," *Fast Company*, June 17, 2009, www.fastcompany.com/blog/joel-rubinson/brave-new-marketing/innovating-innovation-best-ideas-can-come-anywhere.
8. Melanie Warner, "P&G's Chemistry Test," *Fast Company*, July/August 2008, 71.
9. Khicha, P., "Consumers lead the way," *Business Standard*, September 21, 2011, http://www.business-standard.com/india/news/consumers-leadway/449907/.
10. Michael Arndt and Brice Einhorn, "The 50 Most Innovative Companies," *Bloomberg Businessweek*, April 15, 2010, www.businessweek.com/magazine/content/10_17/b4175034779697.htm.
11. Tom Ryan, "Finding Sources of Innovation," *RetailWire*, July 18, 2008, online.
12. Ibid.
13. John Karolefski, "CPG Matters: P&G Changes Rules for Product Development," *RetailWire*, February 19, 2008, online.
14. Spence Ante and Nathan Becker, "IBM to Open Research Lab in Brazil," *Wall Street Journal*, June 9, 2010, http://online.wsj.com/article/SB10001424052748703302604575294820196514024.html.
15. William Bulkeley, "MIT Unveils New Digital Sandbox," *Wall Street Journal*, March 5, 2010, http://blogs.wsj.com/digits/2010/03/05/mit-unveils-new-digital-sandbox/.
16. Andrew Marton, "2006: A Face Odyssey," *Fort Worth Star-Telegram*, February 16, 2006, E1, E8.
17. Pete Engardio, "Scouring the Planet for Brainiacs," *BusinessWeek*, October 11, 2004, 106.
18. Allison Enright, "P&G Looks Outside for Innovative Solutions," *Marketing News*, March 1, 2007, 20–21.
19. Firstbrook, C. and R. Wollan, "Harnessing the power of social media," Accenture website, February 2011, http://www.accenture.com/us-en/outlook/pages/outlook-journal-2011-harnessing-power-social-media.aspx.
20. Vasudevan, V., "What is the ISI mark all about," *Livemint*, April 29, 2011, http://www.livemint.com/2011/04/28230233/What-is-the-ISI-mark-all-about.html.
21. Associated Press, "1962 Glass Could Be Corning's Next Bonanza Seller," *Wall Street Journal*, August 2, 2010, http://online.wsj.com/article/APfbe39da1528b4a81bdf18dc4ff0277fe.html.
22. Chandrasekaran, A., "GSK tests cheaper Horlicks avatar for rural India consumers," *Live Mint*, December 9, 2009, http://www.livemint.com/2009/12/09001518/GSK-tests-cheaper-Horlicks-ava.html.
23. "Think Big with a Gig: Our Experimental Fiber Network," The Official Google Blog, February 2, 2010, http://googleblog.blogspot.com/2010/02/think-big-with-gig-our-experimental.html; Nancy Gohring, "Majority of US States Request Google Broadband Fibre Network," *TechWorld*, July 15, 2010, http://news.techworld.com/networking/3232059/majority-of-us-states-request-google-broadband-fibre-network/; John Sutter, "Topeka 'Renames' Itself, 'Google, Kansas,'" CNN, March 2, 2010, www.cnn.com/2010/TECH/03/02/google.kansas.topeka/index.html.
24. David Kesmodel, "Smokeless Products Are Tough Test for Reynolds," *Wall Street Journal*, March 26, 2010, http://online.wsj.com/article/SB10001424052748703523204575129633103406778.html.
25. "PG.com—All P&G Products," Proctor & Gamble, www.pg.com/en_US/products/all_products/index.shtml (accessed October 20, 2008).
26. Mark Phelan, "Lessons from the Tiny Nano," Free Press, March 28, 2010, www.freep.com/article/20100328/COL14/3280499/1014/BUSINESS01/Lessons-from-the-tiny-Nano.
27. Robert Scoble, "PassionPlay," *Fast Company*, November 2008, 90.
28. Kevin J. Clancy and Peter C. Krieg, "Product Life Cycle: A Dangerous Idea," *Brandweek*, March 1, 2004, 26.
29. Ross Tucker, "Stretch Jeans Expand Appeal," *Women's Wear Daily*, May 20, 2010, 32.
30. Hitting The High Notes, FICCI-KPMG Indian Media and Entertainment Industry Report 2011, pp. 86–88.
31. Ronald J. Baker, *Pricing on Purpose: Creating and Capturing Value* (Hoboken, NJ: John Wiley & Sons, 2006), 338.
32. This application exercise is based on the contribution of Karen Stewart (Richard Stockton College of New Jersey) to *Great Ideas in Teaching Marketing*, a teaching supplement that accompanies Lamb, Hair, and McDaniel's *Marketing*. Professor Stewart's entry titled "New-product development" was a winner in the "Best of the Great Ideas in Teaching Marketing" contest held in conjunction with the publication of the eighth edition of *Marketing*.
33. http://www.kelloggcompany.com/company.aspx?id=32 (accessed March 22, 2012).

34. "Kellogg's to focus more on taste, health benefits," March 22, 2012, http://articles.economictimes.indiatimes.com/2011-02-17/news/28555030_1_chocos-health-benefits-cereal.
35. "KELLOGG INDIA," http://www.ibef.org/download/Kellogg_India.pdf (accessed March 22, 2012).
36. "Kellogg's nutrition overview," http://www.kelloggs.com/en_US/SpecialK.pt-Cereal*.pc-null.desc-null.html (accessed March 22, 2012).
37. "Kellogg's Special K, Products," https://www.specialk.co.in/products.aspx (accessed March 22, 2012).
38. "Beyond Breakfast," *Business Standard*, http://www.business-standard.com/india/news/beyond-breakfast/312528/ (accessed March 22, 2012).

12

1. Press Trust of India, "Services sector growth pegged at 9.6%, lower than FY10," *Business Standard*, February 25, 2011, http://www.business-standard.com/india/news/services-sector-growth-pegged-at-96-lower-than-fy10/126949/on.
2. Spence Morgan, "Scent Branding Sweeps the Fragrance Industry," *Bloomberg Businessweek*, June 21–27, 2010, 86–87.
3. Alexandra Berzon, "Independent Hotels Sign On with Marrriott," *Wall Street Journal*, January 24, 2010, http://online.wsj.com/article/SB10001424052748703415804575023274246886214.html.
4. Valarie Zeithaml, Mary Jo Bitner, and Dwayne Gremler, *Services Marketing* (New York: McGraw-Hill, 2006).
5. Ibid.
6. Much of the material in this section is based on Christopher H. Lovelock and Jochen Wirtz, *Services Marketing*, 5th ed. (Upper Saddle River, NJ: Prentice Hall, 2004); Christian Gronroos, *Service Management and Marketing: Customer Management in Service Competition*, 3rd ed. (Hoboken, NJ: John Wiley & Sons, 2007).
7. Anonymous, "Mass customisation," *The Economist*, October 22, 2009, http://www.economist.com/node/14299807.
8. Larry Magid, "Control Facebook Instant Personalization & Other Privacy Settings," *Huffington Post*, May 17, 2010, www.huffingtonpost.com/larry-magid/new-video control-faceboo_b_578148.html.
9. Denise Power, "Brands Expand Mobile and Social Marketing," *Women's Wear Daily*, June 16, 2010, 9.
10. Customer Centricity, *Technopak retail and consumer goods, Outlook*, September 2011.
11. Preetha, M.S., "Future Generali registers growth," *The Hindu*, March 13, 2010, http://www.hindu.com/2010/03/13/stories/2010031352220700.htm.
12. Lovelock and Wirtz, *Services Marketing*; Gronroos, *Service Management and Marketing*.
13. Ibid.
14. Much of the material in this section is based on Leonard L. Berry and A. Parasuraman, *Marketing Services* (New York: Free Press, 1991), 132–150.
15. Anonymous, "Cricket Dominates India's Cable and Satellite Networks in 2010," *IAS Media*, February 2, 2011, http://iasmedia.com/news_detail.asp?newsid=25.
16. Anonymous, "NEO cricket contests,", *BlogSpot*, June 15, 2010, http://onlyonlinecontests.blogspot.in/2010/06/neo-cricket-contests.html.
17. Alaina Love, "The Passion and Power of Giving Back," *BusinessWeek*, July 28, 2009, www.businessweek.com/managing/content/jul2009/ca20090728_516144.htm.
18. Service Sector, 2010-11, http://indiabudget.nic.in/es2010-11/echap-10.pdf.
19. This exercise is based on the contribution of Stacia Wert-Gray (University of Central Oklahoma) and Gordon T. Gray (Oklahoma City University) to Great Ideas in Teaching Marketing, a teaching supplement that accompanies Lamb, Hair, and McDaniel's *Marketing*.
20. www.tajhotels.com.
21. www.hotelsinindia.com.

13

1. Simon Zekaria, "Burberry Has Reasons to Be Bullish," *Wall Street Journal*, July 13, 2010, http://blogs.wsj.com/source/2010/07/13/why-burberry-has-reasons-to-be-bullish.
2. A dish in south India, made of vegetables in a tamarind and lentil soup base.
3. A thick sauce of Indian origin, essentially used for enhancing a food's flavor, made of vegetables or fruits, vinegar, spices, sugar, and other herbs.
4. Daisuke Wakabayashi and Jung-Ah Lee, "Gadget Appetite Strains Suppliers," *Wall Street Journal*, July 14, 2010, http://online.wsj.com/article/SB10001424052748703792704575367003265429096.html.
5. Lauren Schuker, "'Eat, Pray, Love'—and Shop at HSN," *Wall Street Journal*, August 5, 2010, http://online.wsj.com/article/SB10001424052748704499604575407460346870810.html.
6. Banerjee, D., "Eat, Pray, Love promotes tourism to India," *The Indian Express*, August 16, 2010, http://www.indianexpress.com/news/eat-pray-love-promotes-tourism-to-india/660833/.
7. Sweney, M., "*YouTube confirms worldwide deal for live Indian Premier League cricket*," 2010, http://www.guardian.co.uk/media/2010/jan/20/youtube-live-indian-premier-league.
8. Anjali Cardeiro, "After Buying Its Bottlers, Pepsi Cozies Up to Stores," *Wall Street Journal*, June 21, 2010, B6.
9. Vyas, M., "Fast food joints cash in on new-age transit locations," *The Economic Times*, March 29, 2010, http://articles.economictimes.indiatimes.com/2010-03-29/news/28458594_1_fast-food-amit-jatia-airports.
10. Afaqs news bureau, "Coca-Cola launches energy drink, Burn," *Afaqs*, December 2, 2009, http://www.afaqs.com/news/story.html?sid=25657.
11. Ojha, A. and S. Agarwal, "Recognizing firms tapping social media's potential," *Livemint*, September 21, 2011, http://www.livemint.com/2011/09/21230222/Recognizing-firms-tapping-soci.html.
12. Sharma, S., "L'Oreal says sticking real close to consumers is the key to the India game," *DNA India*, September 9, 2011, http://www.dnaindia.com/money/report_loreal-says-sticking-real-close-to-consumers-is-the-key-to-the-india-game_1584924.
13. This application exercise is based on the contribution of John Beisel (University of Pittsburgh) to *Great Ideas in Teaching Marketing*, a teaching supplement that accompanies Lamb, Hair, and McDaniel's *Marketing*. The entry by Professor Beisel was a runner-up in the "Best of the Great Ideas in Teaching Marketing" contest held in conjunction with the publication of the 8th Edition of *Marketing*.
14. "A tale of two airlines: Kingfisher vs IndiGo," February 21, 2012, http://www.business-standard.com/taketwo/news/a-taletwo-airlines-kingfisher-vs-IndiGo/465252/(accessed March 22, 2012).
15. "GoIndiGo Airlines," March 22, 2012, http://www.goIndiGoairlines.co.in/.
16. "Aviation," March 22, 2012, http://www.ibef.org/industry/aviation.aspx.
17. "Indian Aviation Industry: Through turbulent times, FDI relaxation alone not a game changer March 2012, http://www.icra.in/Files/ticker/Indian%20Aviation%20Industry%20(NEW).pdf.
18. "The Airline IT Trends Survey Executive summary 2011," (accessed March 22, 2012).
19. "Integrated Company Analysis," JetBlue Airways, March 22, 2012, http://business.library.wisc.edu/resources/kavajecz/10_Fall/JetBlue_Report.pdf.

14

1. "2011 Ford Fiesta Build Your Own," http://bp2.forddirect.fordvehicles.com/2011-Ford-Fiesta.
2. Yang, J.L., "Veggie Tales," *CNN Money*, May 27, 2009, http://money.cnn.com/2009/05/26/technology/yang_sysco.fortune/index.htm.
3. Much of this section is based on material adapted from *21st Century Logistics: Making Supply Chain Integration a Reality*, by Donald J. Bowersox, David J. Closs, and Theodore P. Stank, Council of Logistics Management, Oak Brook, IL.
4. Much of this and the following sections is based on material adapted from the edited volume, *Supply Chain Management: Processes, Partnerships, Performance*, ed. Douglas M. Lambert, 2004, Supply Chain Management Institute, Sarasota, FL.
5. Paul Ziobro, "Smoothie Hype Cools, for Now," *Wall Street Journal*, July 2, 2010, B7.
6. Banker, "General Mills and Tesco."
7. Anjali Cordeiro, "After Buying Its Bottlers, Pepsi Cozies Up to Stores," *Wall Street Journal*, June 21, 2010, B6.
8. David Hannon, "Land Rover Leverages RFID for Streamlined Logistics," *Purchasing Magazine*, April 2008, 20; Thomas Craig, "Lean Supply Chain Management," at **www.webpronews.com**, June 18, 2004; Marcia McLeod, "Treat Them Lean," *Automotive Logistics*, November/December 2005.
9. Stacy Meichtry, "Benetton Picks Up the Fashion Pace," *The Wall Street Journal*, April 10, 2007, B1.
10. "BMW to Push Build-to-Order for X3," Autoweek.com, May 14, 2010, www.autoweek.com/article/20100514/CARNEWS/100519923.
11. Elizabeth Holmes, "Tug-of-War in Apparel World," *Wall Street Journal*, July 16, 2010, http://online.wsj.com/article/SB10001424052748703722804575369392983459752.html.
12. Geoffrey A. Fowler and Rachel Dodes, "Retailers Tap Stores to Speed Online Orders," *Wall Street Journal*, May 20, 2010, http://online.wsj.com/article/SB10001424052748703565804575238542925807102.html.

13. www.balancedscorecard.org. (accessed November 30, 2007).
14. Barr, A., "Amazon setting up first "fulfillment center" in India," *Livemint, January* 21, 2012, http://www.livemint.com/2012/01/21152937/Amazon-setting-up-first-8220.html.
15. Robert Hardman, "Santa's Not so Little Helper," *Mail* Online, December 8, 2009, www.dailymail.co.uk/news/article-1233766/Santas-little-helper-Todays-busiest-online-shopping-day-year-So-ready-biggest-grotto-Lapland.html.
16. Miguel Bustillo, "Wal-Mart Radio Tags to Track Clothing," *Wall Street Journal*, July 23, 2010, http://online.wsj.com/article/SB10001424052748704421304575383213061198090.html.
17. Rivenburg, R., "FedEx, Amazon Offer 'Harry Potter' Deal," Los *Angeles Times*, June 22, 2000, http://articles.latimes.com/2000/jun/22/news/cl-43456.
18. Company website: http://www.rkfoodland.com/big-mac-adds-bite-to-suppliers-kitty.html
19. Mukherjee, A., "It's Mac, The Desi Snack," *Outlook India*, July 20, 1998, http://www.outlookindia.com/article.aspx?205872.
20. John Wasik, "The Surprising Success of the Green Supply Chain," *Fortune*, August 13, 2010, http://money.cnn.com/2010/08/13/news/companies/corporate_sustainability.fortune/index.htm.
21. Reference: Indian 'slave' children found making low-cost clothes destined for Gap http://www.guardian.co.uk/world/2007/oct/28/ethicalbusiness.retail.
22. William Hoffman, "Dell Chief Targets Supply-Chain Gaps," *Shipping Digest*, March 12, 2007; Clay Risen, "Dell Takes on India," *World Trade Magazine*, September 2006; David Hannon, "Dell Flies in the Right Direction," *Purchasing*, November 17, 2005.

15

1. "Retailing in India," *Euromonitor International*, March 2011.
2. "The Indian Retail Market," India Retail Report 2011, Images Group Publication, India.
3. Kapany, D., "The new Indian consumer," India Retail Report 2011, Images Group Publication, India.
4. "The Indian Retail Market," India Retail Report 2011, Images Group Publication, India.
5. Press Trust of India, "Hidesign to enter luxury mkt; to bring Ciaschini bags," *The Economic Times*, September 25, 2011, http://articles.economictimes.indiatimes.com/2011-09-25/news/30200858_1_luxury-segment-exclusive-stores-manufacturing-plant.
6. Sinha, P. K. and D. P. Uniyal, *Managing Retailing*, (Oxford University Press, India 2008), 436.
7. Pradhan, S., *Retailing Management*, 2nd, ed., (Tata-McGraw Hill, India 2007), 66.
8. Holly Haber, "Military Retail Giant Sees Opportunities for Expansion," *Women's Wear Daily*, January 5, 2010, 13; "Fact Sheet," AAFES, June 2010, www.aafes.com/pa/factsheet19.pdf.
9. Sangeeta, G., "The loot is on," *India Today*, February 12, 2011, http://indiatoday.intoday.in/story/the-loot-is-on/1/129460.html.
10. Kamath, R., "Megamart, Loot bet big on aspirant shoppers," *Business Standard*, November 25, 2010, http://www.business-standard.com/india/news/megamart-loot-bet-bigaspirant-shoppers/416018/
11. Gupta, S., H. W. Kim, and M. Sharma, "Customer Switching to Organized Retail in Semiurban Markets: A Study in an Indian Context," *Journal of International Consumer Marketing 2011*, Vol. 23 (5), 314–328.
12. Sinha, P. K. and D. P. Uniyal, *Managing Retailing*, (Oxford University Press, India 2008), 124–125.
13. 'Formatting Indian Retail,' *India Retail Report 2011*, Images Group Publication, India, 218.
14. Pradhan, S., *Retailing Management*, 2nd ed., (Tata-McGraw Hill, India, 2007), 63.
15. 'Food Services,' *India Retail Report 2011*, Images Group Publication, India, pp. 93
16. Jeffrey Ball, "In Digital Era, Marketers Still Prefer a Paper Trail," *Wall Street Journal*, October 16, 2009, A13.
17. "Online Retail," *India Retail Report 2011*, Images Group Publication, India, 222–225.
18. "Purchasing Your Franchise," About McDonald's, February 12, 2009, www.aboutmcdonalds.com/mcd/franchising/us_franchising/purchasing_your_franchise.html.
19. Vijayraghavan, K., "Godrej hives off Nature's Basket," *The Economic Times,* March 6, 2009, http://articles.economictimes.indiatimes.com/2009-03-06/news/28461897_1_retailing-health-and-nutrition-awareness-godrej-group; Srivastava, S., "Nature's Basket: Double Take," *Forbes India,* February 10, 2012, http://forbesindia.com/printcontent/32204.
20. France-Presse, A., "Amazon enters India with junglee.com," *NDTV Gadgets*, February 8, 2012, http://gadgets.ndtv.com/shownews.aspx?Sec=NEWS&id=GADEN20120194019.
21. Company website: http://corporate.shoppersstop.com/uploaded_files/3521011-aa84.pdf.
22. "Matcha Box Pop-Up Stores in NYC," *Matcha Source*, www.matchasource.com/as-seen-in-s/86.htm.
23. http://www.indiaprwire.com/businessnews/20080303/101651.htm.
24. "USA Technologies: ePort," USA Technologies, www.usatech.com/eport/index.php; "VeriSign Enables Coca-Cola Vending Machine Purchases via Mobile Phones," VeriSign, http://press.verisign.com/easyir/customrel.do?easyirid=AFC0FF0DB5C560D3&version=live&prid=181452&releasejsp=custom_97.
25. Kaila Krayewski, "The M-Commerce Revolution Begins: Consumers Use Their Mobile Phones for Online Shopping," ISEdb.com, January 21, 2010, http://isedb.com/20100121-2947.php.
26. Chris Foresman, "Wireless Survey: 91% of Americans Use Cell Phones," Ars Technica, March 2010, http://arstechnica.com/telecom/news/2010/03/wireless-survey-91-of-americans-have-cell-phones.ars.
27. Press Trust of India, "Bharti Airtel launches airtel money across India," *Hindustan Times*, February 23, 2012, http://www.hindustantimes.com/Technology/technology-update-personaltech/Bharti-Airtel-launches-airtel-money-across-India/SP-Article1-815838.aspx; Company website: http://www.bharti.com/wps/wcm/connect/BhartiPortal/bharti/home/media_centre/press_releases/fy2010-2011/now+pay+your+easyday+store+bills+using+airtel+money.
28. Peter Eichenbaum and Margaret Collins, "AT&T, Verizon to Target Visa, MasterCard with Smartphones," *Bloomberg*, August 2, 2010, www.bloomberg.com/news/2010-08-02/at-t-verizon-said-to-target-visa-mastercard-with-smartphones.html.
29. This application exercise is based on the contribution of Amy Hubbert (University of Nebraska at Omaha) to *Great Ideas in Teaching Marketing*, a teaching supplement that accompanies Lamb, Hair, and McDaniel's *Marketing*. Professor Hubbert's entry titled "Discovery of Strategic Retailing Factors" was a winner in the "Best of the Great Ideas in Teaching Marketing" contest conducted in conjunction with the publication of the eighth edition of *Marketing*.
30. "Tanishq: Honest and transparent glitter," 2002, http://www.tata.com/article.aspx?artid=t9a/ZefiVik=(accessed March 20, 2012).
31. "Tanishq eyes 35 40% growth this fiscal," 2011, http://articles.economictimes.indiatimes.com/2011-12-15/news/30520469_1_tanishq-eyes-large-format-large-format-retail-stores (accessed March 20, 2012).
32. Lather A., and Khatri P., "Tata GoldPlus: The Success Story of the 'Nano' of the Jewellery Market" July–September 2011, Volume 36, No 3 http://www.vikalpa.com/pdf/articles/2011/Pages-from-Vikalpa36-3-119-130.pdf (accessed March, 22, 2012).
33 "Goldplus Launches Diamantine™ In India," http://goldplus.in/goldplus-launches-diamantine-india (accessed March, 22, 2012).

16

1. Eric Clemons, Paul Nunes, and Matt Reilly, "Six Strategies for Successful Niche Marketing," *Wall Street Journal*, May 24, 2010, http://online.wsj.com/article/SB10001424052748704130904574644084205858424.html.
2. Pinto, S. J., "TOI leads India to the classroom with Teach India," *Afaqs*, July 9, 2008, http://www.afaqs.com/media/story.html?sid=21601.
3. Anonymous, "Twitter Buzz: ZNMD," *Hindustan Times*, July 15, 2011, http://www.hindustantimes.com/Entertainment/Bollywood/Twitter-Buzz-ZNMD/Article1-721468.aspx; Zindagi Na Milegi Dobara - Twitter Reviews, http://wogma.com/movie/zindagi-na-milegi-dobara-wtwit/.
4. "Agent Vinod - Twitter Reviews," http://wogma.com/movie/agent-vinod-wtwit/.
5. Anonymous, "Ishaqzaade's first trailer a hit on Twitter," *Hindustan Times*, March 15, 2012, http://www.hindustantimes.com/entertainment/bollywood/ishaqzaade-s-first-trailer-a-hit-on-twitter/article1-825898.aspx.
6. Joseph De Avila, "Who Could Eat All This?" *Wall Street Journal,* March 17, 2010, D1–D2.
7. Ellen Byron, "An Old Dice Game Catches On Again, Pushed by P&G," *Wall Street Journal*, January 30, 2007, A1, A13.
8. Based on a case study "Britannia Khao World Cup Jao" by Dr. Preeta Vyas and Ms. Sonal Kureshi, IIM Ahmedabad, 2000.
9. The AIDA concept is based on the classic research of E. K. Strong, Jr., as theorized in *The Psychology of Selling and Advertising* (New York: McGraw-Hill, 1925) and "Theories of Selling," *Journal of Applied Psychology*, 9, 1925, 75–86.
10. Thomas E. Barry and Daniel J. Howard, "A Review and Critique of the Hierarchy of Effects in Advertising," *International Journal of Advertising*, 9, 1990, 121–135.

11. Lauren Schuker, "'Eat, Pray, Love,'—and Shop at HSN," *Wall Street Journal*, August 5, 2010, B8; Shahnaz Mahmud, "HSN, Sony Promote 'Eat Pray Love' Movie with Direct Mail, Integrated Effort," DMNews, July 8, 2010, www.dmnews.com/hsn-sony-promote-eat-pray-love-movie-with-direct-mail-integrated-effort/article/174207; "Rotten Tomatoes, Weekend Box Office Results," Rotten Tomatoes, August 14–16, 2010, www.rottentomatoes.com/movie/box_office.php.

12. Anjali Cordeiro, "Promotions Boost Sales for Food and Beverage Makers," *Wall Street Journal*, July 14, 2010, B5.

13. Anonymous "Big Bazaar 'Sabse Saste 4 Din' from Jan. 23," The Hindu, January 21, 2010, http://www.hindu.com/2010/01/21/stories/2010012151730200.htm.

14. KBR, U., "The original 'angry man' is back," *Mid Day*, May 13, 2011, http://www.mid-day.com/entertainment/2011/may/130511-Bbuddah-Hoga-Terra-Baap-Amitabh-Bachchan-angry-man-back.htm.

15. Bhat, V., "Don 2 bets big on new media for promotions," *Business Standard*, December 20, 2011, http://www.business-standard.com/india/news/don-2-bets-bignew-media-for-promotions/459093/.

16. This application exercise is based on the contribution of Lyn R. Godwin (University of St. Thomas) to *Great Ideas in Teaching Marketing*, a teaching supplement that accompanies Lamb, Hair, and McDaniel's *Marketing*. Professor Godwin's entry titled "Taboo or Not Taboo: That Is the Question" was a runner-up in the "Best of the Great Ideas in Teaching Marketing" contest held in conjunction with the publication of the eighth edition of *Marketing*.

17. This application exercise is based on the contribution of David M. Blanchette (Rhode Island College) to *Great Ideas in Teaching Marketing*, a teaching supplement that accompanies Lamb, Hair, and McDaniel's *Marketing*. Professor Blanchette's entry titled "Applying Semiotics in Promotion" was a runner-up in the "Best of the Great Ideas in Teaching Marketing" contest held in conjunction with the publication of the eighth edition of *Marketing*.

18. "Hero-Honda split likely to kick-start price war," *The Economic Times* (December 17, 2010, http://articles.economictimes.indiatimes.com/2010-12-17/news/28407673_1_hero-honda-motorcycle-market-honda-motorcycle (accessed March 22, 2012).

19. "Hero, Honda split after 26 years," December 17, 2010, http://www.dnaindia.com/money/report_hero-honda-split-after-26-years_1482149 (accessed March 23, 2012).

20. "Hero MotoCorp named Title Sponsor for India Olympic Qualifiers," http://www.fih.ch/en/news-3551-hero-motocorp-named-title-sponsor-for-india.

21. "Honda aims to challenge market leader Hero MotoCorp with China made models," *The Economic Times*, January 6, 2011, http://articles.economictimes.indiatimes.com/2012-01-06/news/30597709_1_super-splendor-hero-honda-scooter-market (accessed March 223, 2012); "Hero Honda changes name, becomes Hero MotoCorp," http://businesstoday.intoday.in/story/hero-honda-changes-name-becomes-hero motocorp/1/17431.html (accessed March 22, 2012).

17

1. "Hitting the High Notes," *FICCI-KPMG Indian Media and Entertainment Industry Report 2011*, 5.

2. Press Trust of India, "India's ad spend growth highest in AsiaPac, touches $6.7 billion," *The Economic Times*, October 29, 2010, http://articles.economictimes.indiatimes.com/2010-10 29/news/27592341_1_ad-newspaper-magazine.

3. "India Entertainment and Media Outlook 2011," *PricewaterhouseCoopers India*, 32.

4. Ghaswalla, A. N. and N. Singh, "HUL retails WPP as partner," *The Times of India*, February 10, 2010, http://articles.timesofindia.indiatimes.com/2010-02-10/india-business/28138985_1_global-media-hul-indian-subsidiary-hindustan-unilever.

5. Michael R. Solomon, *Consumer Behavior*, 6th ed. (Upper Saddle River, NJ: Prentice Hall, 2004), 275.

6. Tom Duncan, *Integrated Marketing Communications* (Burr Ridge, IL: McGraw-Hill, 2002), 257.

7. Challapalli, S., "Frooti's 'reality TV' ads aim to shock and awe," *Business Line*, April 28, 2010, http://www.thehindubusinessline.com/todays-paper/tp-marketing/article990512.ece.

8. Singh, P., "Glaxo sets teeth on dental opening," *Business Standard*, January 6, 2011, http://business-standard.com/india/news/glaxo-sets-teethdental-opening/420937/.

9. Khicha, P., "For a bigger bite," *Business Standard*, June 27, 2011, http://www.business-standard.com/india/news/forbigger-bite/440464/.

10. Khicha, P., "For a bigger bite," *Business Standard*, June 27, 2011, http://www.business-standard.com/india/news/forbigger-bite/440464/.

11. Pathak, A., "Comparative Advertising in India: Need to Strengthen Regulations," *Vikalpa*, 2005, Vol. 30 No. 1 (Jan-March), 67–75.

12. Pathak, A., "Comparative Advertising in India: Need to Strengthen Regulations," *Vikalpa*, 2005, Vol. 30 No. 1 (Jan-March), 67–75; Annuncio, C., "With fangs bared," *Outlook India*, November 24, 1997, http://www.outlookindia.com/article.aspx?204602.

13. Company website: https://www.specialk.co.in/products.aspx.

14. Sangameshwaran, P., "Beyond breakfast," *Business Standard*, February 5, 2008, http://www.business-standard.com/india/news/beyond-breakfast/312528/.

15. Laura Q. Hughes and Wendy Davis, "Revival of the Fittest," *Advertising Age*, March 12, 2001, 18–19.

16. Geoffrey Fowler, "For P&G in China, It's Wash, Rinse, Don't Repeat," *Wall Street Journal*, April 7, 2006.

17. Press Trust of India, "Incredible India attracts 4.2 lakh foreigners in August," *The Economic Times*, September 13, 2011, http://articles.economictimes.indiatimes.com/2011-09-13/news/30149452_1_tourist-arrivals-foreign-tourists-foreign-exchange-earnings.

18. Singh, S., "Brand India," *Hindustan Times*, June 25, 2011, http://www.hindustantimes.com/News-Feed/Travel/Brand-India/Article1-713809.aspx.

19. Ty McMahan, "Goom Radio Hopes to Avoid Same Sad Song," *Wall Street Journal*, April 15, 2009, http://blogs.wsj.com/venturecapital/2009/04/15/goom-radio-hopes-to-avoid-same-sad-song.

20. Tanwar, S., "It's not a war of nerves during non-prime time," *Afaqs*, July 8, 2010, http://www.afaqs.com/media/story.html?sid=27622.

21. Nautiyal, R. and P. M. Dasgupta, "A Perfect Pitch," *Financial Express*, April 12, 2011, http://www.financialexpress.com/news/a-perfect-pitch/774923/0.

22. Suzanne Vranica, "Tallying Up Viewers," *Wall Street Journal*, July 26, 2010, http://online.wsj.com/article/SB10001424052748704249004575385680793742048.html.

23. Associated Press, "TV's New Attempt at Keeping Viewers Tuned In," *New Jersey Business*, October 5, 2009, www.nj.com/business/index.ssf/2009/10/post_10.html.

24. PricewaterhouseCoopers, "IAB Internet Advertising Revenue Report," Interactive Advertising Bureau, April 2010, www.pwc.com/us/en/industry/entertainment-media/assets/IAB-Ad-Revenue-Full-Year-2009.pdf; Teddy Wayne, "A Milestone for Internet Ad Revenue," *New York Times*, April 25, 2010, www.nytimes.com/2010/04/26/business/media/26drill.html.

25. "Google Talks about Android, Personalized Ads and New Hires," *Wall Street Journal*, July 15, 2010, http://blogs.wsj.com/digits/2010/07/15/live-blogging-google-on-its-earnings.

26. PricewaterhouseCoopers, "IAB Internet Advertising Revenue Report."

27. Addy Dugdale, "Chevy Volt and Microsoft Kinect Join for Virtual Test Drive Advergame," *Fast Company*, June 22, 2010, www.fastcompany.com/1662575/this-is-not-a-tired-marketing-campaign-chevy-volt-and-microsoft-kinect-connect.

28. Andrew LaValle, "Start-Ups Find Revenue Source on Hold," *Wall Street Journal*, June 11, 2008, B9.

29. "Massive Incorporated: Video Game Advertising," www.massiveincorporated.com; "Massive Inc. and comScore Prove In-Game Advertising ROI for Bing," Microsoft News Center, May 20, 2010, www.microsoft.com/presspass/press/2010/may10/05-20ingameadroipr.mspx.

30. Paul Korzeniowski, "Technology News: Wireless: Cell Phones Emerge as New Advertising Medium," *ECT News Network*, www.technewsworld.com/story/46630.html (accessed October 21, 2008); "Media Planning Instala En Barcelona La Primera Lona Con Bluethooth De Europa," www.marketingdirecto.com/noticias/noticia.php?idnoticia=16532.

31. Anonymous, "India now the largest mobile advertising market in Asia Pacific," *Inmobi*, January 6, 2011, http://www.inmobi.com/press-releases/2011/01/06/india-now-the-largest-mobile-advertising-market-in-asia-pacific/.

32. Anonymous, "India leads in Asian mobile ad impressions: InMobi," *Inmobi*, November 22, 2010, http://www.inmobi.com/press-releases/2010/11/22/india-leads-in-asian-mobile-ad-impressions-inmobi/.

33. "India Entertainment and Media Outlook 2011," *PricewaterhouseCoopers India*, 34.

34. Andrew Hampp, "Cross-Platform Ads: What's Working?" *Advertising Age*, June 26, 2008, http://adage.com.mediaworks/article?article_id=128029.

35. "'Lost' Finale Finds Above Average Ad Engagement," Nielsenwire, June 1, 2010, http://blog.nielsen.com/nielsenwire/online_mobile/lost-finale-finds-above-average-ad-engagement.

36. Ohri, K., "ZooZoos hijack the online world," *Afaqs*, May 6, 2009, http://www.afaqs.com/news/story.html?sid=23957.
37. Williams, K., et. al., "Product placement effectiveness: revisited and renewed," *Journal of Management & Marketing Research*, March 2011, Vol. 7, 1–24.
38. "Indian entertainment & media outlook 2010," *PricewaterhouseCoopers*, 10.
39. Klayman, B., "Global sponsorship spending to rise 5.2 pct in 2011," *Reuters*, January 11, 2011, http://www.reuters.com/article/2011/01/11/ieg-sponsorship-idUSN1125970320110111.
40. Anonymous, "Sponsorship Spending: 2010 Proves Better Than Expected; Bigger Gains Set For 2011," *IEG*, January 6, 2011, http://www.sponsorship.com/About-IEG/Press-Room/Sponsorship-Spending--2010-Proves-Better-Than-Expe.aspx.
41. Patricia Odell, "Sponsorship Spending Struggles to Recover," *Promo*, January 28, 2010, http://promomagazine.com/news/sponsorship-spending-struggles-0128/.
42. "Information on Select Cause Marketing Campaigns," Breast Cancer Action, http://thinkbeforeyoupink.org/?page_id=13; *Business in the Community*, www.bitc.org.uk/.
43. "PlayStation®—PS3™, PS2™, PSP® & PSP®go Systems, Games, & PlayStation®Network" Sony Computer Entertainment America, www.playstation.com.
44. "Kraft Foods—Great Recipes and Meal Ideas from Kraft Foods," Kraft, www.kraftrecipes.com/home.aspx.
45. "Blogs Can Offer a Big Advantage to Brands—If They're Honest," *New Age Media*, March 23, 2006, 15.
46. Geoffrey Fowler, Ian Sherr, and Niraj Sheth, "A Defiant Steve Jobs Confronts 'Antennagate,'" *Wall Street Journal*, July 16, 2010, http://online.wsj.com/article/SB10001424052748704913304575371131458273498.html.
47. This application exercise is based on the contribution of S. J. Garner (Eastern Kentucky University) to *Great Ideas in Teaching Marketing*, a teaching supplement that accompanies Lamb, Hair, and McDaniel's *Marketing*. Professor Garner's entry titled "Creating Advertising for Illegal Products/Services" was a runner-up in the "Best of the Great Ideas in Teaching Marketing" contest conducted in conjunction with the publication of the eighth edition of *Marketing*.
48. This application exercise is taken from Chuck Williams, *Management*, 3rd ed. (Cincinnati: South-Western, 2005). The idea to include a crisis management exercise in this chapter came from a contribution by Jack K. Mandel (Nassau Community College) to *Great Ideas in Teaching Marketing*, a teaching supplement that accompanies Lamb, Hair, and McDaniel's *Marketing*. Professor Mandel's entry titled "Putting Students in the Line of Fire to Learn Crisis Management Techniques" received an honorable mention in the "Best of the Great Ideas in Teaching Marketing" contest held in conjunction with the publication of the eighth edition of *Marketing*.
49. "The rural bet: Idea Cellular on the 3G turf," *The Economic Times*, May 21, 2010, http://articles.economictimes.indiatimes.com/2010-05-21/news/27600864_1_rural-markets-circles-3g.
50. "Idea Cellular network's campaign, like its brand ambassador, is losing out on fans," *The Indian Express*, November 14, 2010, http://www.indianexpress.com/news/old-idea-sirji/710716/ (accessed March 22, 2012).
51. "Idea gains maximum subscribers via MNP," November 31, 2011, http://www.ciol.com/News/News/News-Reports/Idea-gains-maximum-subscribers-via-MNP/157236/0/ (accessed March 22, 2012).
52. "Vodafone Essar, Airtel, Idea Cellular still a hit in MNP regime," *The Economic Times*, February 23, 2011, http://articles.economictimes.indiatimes.com/2011-02-23/news/28625748_1_mnp-rcom-vodafone-essar (accessed March 22, 2012).

18

1. http://promomagazine.com, October 2008 report.
2. Bawa, K., S. S. Srinivasan, and R. K. Srivastava, "*Coupon Attractiveness and* Coupon Proneness: A Framework for Modeling Coupon Redemption," *Journal of Marketing Research*, 1997, Vol. 34 No. 4, 517–525.
3. TNN, "Digital coupons: the new sales tool," The *Times of India*, September 1, 2010, http://articles.timesofindia.indiatimes.com/2010-09-01/strategy/28267752_1_coupons-retail-outlets-discount.
4. Mittal, M., and P. Sethi, "The Effectiveness of Sales Promotion Tools among Indian Consumers: An Empirical Study," *Journal of Promotion Management*, 17:2, 165–182.
5. TNN, "*Digital coupons: the new sales tool*," The *Times of India*, September 1, 2010, http://articles.timesofindia.indiatimes.com/2010-09-01/strategy/28267752_1_coupons-retail-outlets-discount.
6. Anonymous; "Online Shopping Takes Off in India: Retail Web Audience Grows 18 Percent in the Past Year as Nearly 3 of Every 5 Internet Users Now Shop Online. comScore," December 22, 2011, http://www.comscore.com/Press_Events/Press_Releases/2011/12/Online_Shopping_Takes_Off_in_India.
7. TNN, "*Digital coupons: the new sales tool*," The *Times of India*, September 1, 2010, http://articles.timesofindia.indiatimes.com/2010-09-01/strategy/28267752_1_coupons-retail-outlets-discount.
8. TNN, "*Digital coupons: the new sales tool*," The *Times of India*, September 1, 2010, http://articles.timesofindia.indiatimes.com/2010-09-01/strategy/28267752_1_coupons-retail-outlets-discount.
9. Bruce Mohl, "Retailers Simplify the Rebate Process," *Boston Globe*, November 7, 2004; FTC Consumer Alert, "Taking the 'Bait' Out of Rebates," www.ftc.gov/bcp/edu/pubs/consumer/alerts/alt059.shtm.
10. Dang, P. J. and A. Koshy, "An emperical view of the different types of consumer promotions in India", IIMA working paper, March 3, 2004.
11. Convenience Store News Staff, "Loyalty Rewards Membership on the Rise," *Brandweek*, April 17 2009, www.brandweek.com/bw/content_display/news-and-features/direct/e3i76c769b73ce851586daedf100023fcf1.
12. Jacob, S., and P. Mamgain, "Retailers make loyalty programmes more attractive," *The Economic Times*, January 17, 2011, http://articles.economictimes.indiatimes.com/2011-01-17/news/28431895_1_loyalty-programmes-loyalty-cards-big-retail-chains.
13. Vyas, P. H., "Sales Promotion Practices in Apparel Retail Sector and Challenges Ahead," Research and Publications, Indian Institute of Management Ahmedabad, W. P. No. 2007-11-02, November 2007, 1–13; "*The 20 years of start something new*, Shoppers Stop Annual Report 2010-11, 25.
14. Jacob, S., and P. Mamgain, "Retailers make loyalty programmes more attractive," *The Economic Times*, January 17, 2011, http://articles.economictimes.indiatimes.com/2011-01-17/news/28431895_1_loyalty-programmes-loyalty-cards-big-retail-chains.
15. *The 20 years of start something new*, Shoppers Stop Annual Report 2010–11, 24
16. Ganguly, P., "In terms of operating costs, ours is the lowest," *Moneylife*, July 14, 2010, http://www.moneylife.in/article/4/7120.html.
17. Press Trust of India, "Reliance Retail gets one loyal customer on every square foot," *Livemint*, February 10, 2008, http://www.livemint.com/2008/02/10134815/Reliance-Retail-gets-one-loyal.html.
18. Vyas, P. H., and P. K. Sinha, "Loyalty Programmes: Practices, Avenues and Challenges," *Research and Publications-Indian Institute of Management Ahmedabad*, W.P. No.2008-12-01.
19. Barbara De Lollis, "Loyalty Programs: Study Reveals Top Complaints; Spam Tops List," *USA Today*, February 8, 2010, http://travel.usatoday.com/hotels/legacy/2010/02/marriott-rewards-hilton-hhonors-intercontinental-priority-club-rewards-choice-wyndham-loyalty/1.
20. Jennifer Van Grove, "Twitter and Foursquare Become the New Loyalty Program at Tasti D-Lite," *Mashable*, January 2010, http://mashable.com/2010/01/13/tasti-d-lite-tastirewards/.
21. http://freeworking.hubpages.com/hub/STATE-BANK-OF-INDIA-LOYALTY-SCHEME.
22. John Wu, "Effects of In-Store Sampling on Retail Sales: Case Study of a Warehouse Store," *FindArticles.com*, Spring 2010, http://findarticles.com/p/articles/mi_hb6054/is_201004/ai_n53928748/.
23. Das, B., "Lays calls for flavour ideas from consumers in new campaign," *Afaqs*, October 29, 2009, http://www.afaqs.com/news/story.html?sid=25339; Times News Network, "The winner of Lays is .....," *The Times of India*, July 19, 2010, http://articles.timesofindia.indiatimes.com/2010-07-19/tv/28322830_1_flavour-frito-lay-india-consumers.
24. Sinha, P. K., and D. P. Uniyal, 'Point of purchase communication', *Managing Retailing* (Oxford University Press, India 2007), 406.
25. "Point-of-Purchase: $17 Billion," *PROMO Magazine*, October 29, 2001, 3; "In Praise of Promotion," *PROMO Xtra*, http://promomagazine.com.
26. "Internet," CMS, www.couponinfonow.com/Couponing/Internet.cfm.
27. "Free Culinary Demonstrations from Williams-Sonoma," Willams-Sonoma, http://edm.williams-sonoma.com/ws/2008/noimage/sept_storedemo_all_082708.html.
28. Peter King, "Personal Shoppers Find Clothes to Make the Man," *Wall Street Journal*, August 12, 2010, http://online.wsj.com/article/SB10001424052748704164904575421373622725304.html.
29. Michael Beverland, "Contextual Influences and the Adoption and Practice of Relationship

Selling in a Business-to-Business Setting: An Exploratory Study," *Journal of Personal Selling & Sales Management*, 21, no. 3, Summer 2001, 207; Gabriel R. Gonzalez, K. Douglas Hoffman, and Thomas N. Ingram, "Improving Relationship Selling through Failure Analysis and Recovery Efforts: A Framework and Call to Action," *Journal of Personal Selling & Sales Management*, 25, no. 1, Winter 2005, 57.

30. Catherine Seda, "The Meet Market," *Entrepreneur*, August 2004, 68; Jim Dickie, "Is Social Networking an Overhyped Fad or a Useful Tool?" *Destination CRM*, January 21, 2005; Kristina Dell, "What Are Friends For?" *Time*, September 21, 2004; Media Releases, www.linkedin.com, December 3, 2007; "About Us," www.linkedin.com/static?key=company_info.

31. Barton Weitz, Stephen Castleberry, and John Tanner, *Selling: Building Partnerships* (Burr Ridge, IL: McGraw-Hill/Irwin, 2004), 198–201.

32. "Effective Business Presentation—Sales Presentation—Effective Presentation Skill," *Nielsen Business Media*, www.presentations.com.

33. Kathleen Cholewka, "E-Market Stats," *Sales & Marketing Management*, September 2001, 21; Jamie Smith Hopkins, "Corporations Podcast Their Marketing Nets," *Baltimore Sun*, December 11, 2005.

34. "About Winelibrary TV," Wine Library TV, http://tv.winelibrary.com/about.

35. This application exercise is based on the contribution of John Ronchetto (University of San Diego) to *Great Ideas in Teaching Marketing*, a teaching supplement that accompanies Lamb, Hair, and McDaniel's *Marketing*. Professor Ronchetto's entry titled "Sales and Customer Service Experiential Journal and Paper" was a winner in the "Best of the Great Ideas in Teaching Marketing" contest held in conjunction with the publication of the eighth edition of *Marketing*.

36. "Avon the Company," March 22, 2011, http://www.in.avon.com/PRSuite/careers.page.

37. "Little Dot" to Dot-Coms: the Evolution of Direct Selling at Avon," http://www.avoncompany.com/aboutavon/history/avon_direct_sell_history.html.

19

1. Franziska Volckner, "The Dual Role of Price: Decomposing Consumers' Reactions to Price," *Journal of the Academy of Marketing Science*, 36, no. 3, Fall 2008, 359–377.

2. Ibid.

3. Scott Kilman, "Monsanto Draws Antitrust Scrutiny," *Wall Street Journal*, March 11, 2010, B8.

4. Kit Eaton, "Nintendo Announces 3-D Handheld—But Can It Steal Back Apple's Gaming Market Shares?" *Fast Company*, March 23, 2010, www.fastcompany.com/1594735/nintendo-ds-3d-ipad-iphone-apple-gaming-portable-handheld-mobile.

5. David Goldman, "Why All Smartphones Are $199," *CNNMoney*, September 1, 2010, http://money.cnn.com/2010/09/01/technology/smartphone_price.

6. Edward Lotterman, "Why a Great Crop Year Like 2010 Can Be Bad News for U.S. Farmers," *Idaho Statesman*, August 15, 2010, www.idahostatesman.com/2010/08/15/1302125/ed-lotterman-why-a-great-crop.html.

7. Tammo H. A. Bijmolt, Harald J. Van Heerde, and Rik G. M. Pieters, "New Empirical Generalizations on the Determinants of Price Elasticity," *Journal of Marketing Research*, 42, May 2005, 141–156; Christian Homburg, Wayne Hoyer, and Nicole Koschate, "Customers' Reactions to Price Increases: Do Customer Satisfaction and Perceived Motive Fairness Matter?" *Journal of the Academy of Marketing Science*, 33, no. 1, Winter 2005, 35–49; Gadi Fibich, Arieh Gavious, and Oded Lowengart, "The Dynamics of Price Elasticity of Demand in the Presence of Reference Price Effects," *Journal of the Academy of Marketing Science*, 33, no. 1, Winter 2005, 66–78.

8. Bhushan, R. and S. Jacob, "Pizza makers Pizza Hut, Domino's Pizza and others cut prices for higher sales," *The Economic Times*, April 30, 2012, http://articles.economictimes.indiatimes.com/2012-04-30/news/31508319_1_pizza-corner-domino-s-pizza-pizza-makers.

9. Pinto, V. S., "HUL, P&G slug it out over detergents," Business Standard, February 5, 2010, http://www.business-standard.com/india/news/hul-pg-slug-it-out-over-detergents/384697/; Sharma, S., "Hindustan Unilever cuts Rin price by 30%," *Daily News and Analysis*, January 29, 2010, http://www.dnaindia.com/money/report_hindustan-unilever-cuts-rin-price-by-30pct_1340489; Agarwal, S., "P&G raises weight of Tide Naturals by 25%," *Livemint*, March 10, 2010, http://www.livemint.com/2010/03/10235922/PampG-raises-weight-of-Tide.html.

10. Joseph Cannon and Christian Homburg, "Buyer-Supplier Relationships and Customer Firm Costs," *Journal of Marketing*, 65, January 2001, 29–43.

11. "How Shopping Bots Really Work," *MSN Money*, July 11, 2005, http://moneycentral.msn.com.

12. Dang, P. J. and A. Koshy, "An emperical view of the different types of consumer promotions in India", IIMA working paper, March 3, 2004.

13. Press Trust of India, "Good value for money influence Indian consumers," *The Economic Times*, January 8, 2008, http://articles.economictimes.indiatimes.com/2008-01-08/news/27736593_1_indian-consumers-grocery-shop-promotions.

14. Press Trust of India, "Good value for money influence Indian consumers," *The Economic Times*, January 8, 2008, http://articles.economictimes.indiatimes.com/2008-01-08/news/27736593_1_indian-consumers-grocery-shop-promotions.

15. Anonymous, "HLL announces Ustaad's Challenge to promote Taj Tea," *Financial Express*, July 13, 2000, http://www.financialexpress.com/old/fe/daily/20000713/fst13021.html.

16. Company website: http://www.pizzahut.co.in/dinein/pdf/Weekdays%20Special%20-%20Product%20Release.pdf; Prayag, A., "Pizza Hut outlets to get larger," *The Hindu Business Line*, June 28, 2011, http://www.thehindubusinessline.com/industry-and-economy/marketing/article2142207.ece.

17. Vicki Young, "Cautions for Luxury: Survey Finds Wealthy Less Keen on Category," *Women's Wear Daily*, September 22, 2009, 20.

18. Katherine Lemon and Stephen Nowlis, "Developing Synergies between Promotions and Brands in Different Price-Quality Tiers," *Journal of Marketing Research*, 39, May 2002, 171–185; also see Valerie Taylor and William Bearden, "The Effects of Price on Brand Extension Evaluations: The Moderating Role of Extension Similarity," *Journal of the Academy of Marketing Science*, 30, no. 2, Spring 2002, 131–140; and Raj Sethuraman and V. Srinivasan, "The Asymmetric Share Effect: An Empirical Generalization on Cross-Price Effects," *Journal of Marketing Research*, 39, no. 3, August 2002, 379–386.

19. Volckner, "The Dual Role of Price"

20. Ibid.

21. EEB & Agencies, "Car manufacturers rule out any price war," *Indian Express*, June 29, 2000, http://www.indianexpress.com/Storyold/154820/.

22. Merrie Brucks, Valarie Zeithaml, and Gillian Naylor, "Price and Brand Name as Indicators of Quality Dimensions for Consumer Durables," *Journal of the Academy of Marketing Science*, 28, no. 3, Summer 2000, 359–374; Wilford Amaldoss and Sanjay Jain, "Pricing of Conspicuous Goods: A Competitive Analysis of Social Effects," *Journal of Marketing Research*, 42, February 2005, 30–42; and also see Margaret Campbell, "Says Who?! How the Source of Price Information and Affect Influence Perceived Price (UN)fairness," *Journal of Marketing Research*, 44, no. 2, May 2007, 261–271.

23. This application exercise is based on the contribution of Vaughn C. Judd (Auburn University, Montgomery) to Great Ideas in Teaching Marketing, a teaching supplement and accompanies Lamb, Hair, and McDaniel's *Marketing*. Professor Judd's entry, titled "Analyzing the Price-Quality Relationship," was a winner in the "Best of the Great Ideas in Teaching Marketing" contest held in conjunction with the publication of the eighth edition of *Marketing*.

24. "Google survey: India tops US in using smartphone to go online," http://www.thehindubusinessline.com/industry-and-economy/info-tech/article2939038.ece.

25. "Indians slam Apple for launching iPhone 4S at much higher price than its US retail cost," *The Economic Times*, November 21, 2011, http://articles.economictimes.indiatimes.com/2011-11-21/news/30424680_1_iphone-canalys-latest-smartphone (accessed March 22, 2012).

26. "Apple Store," March 22, 2012, http://store.apple.com/us/browse/home/shop_iphone/family/iphone/iphone4s.

27. "Apple iPhone accounts for just 4% of the mobile market ... but rakes in an impressive 52% of the industry's profits," *Daily Mail*, November 7, 2011, http://www.dailymail.co.uk/news/article-2058406/Apple-iPhone-accounts-just-4-mobile-market---rakes-impressive-52-industrys-profits.html#ixzz1qDXUVTs1 (accessed March 22, 2012).

28. "Apple's £499 iPhone 4S only costs £130 to make, say experts," *Daily Mail*, March 22, 2012, http://www.dailymail.co.uk/sciencetech/article-2051851/Apples-499-iPhone-4S-costs-130-make-say-experts.html#ixzz1qDnnRUCU.

29. "Apple Beats HTC as Nokia Customer Loyalty Falls for First Time," March 22, 2012, http://www.bloomberg.com/news/2011-10-05/apple-beats-htc-samsung-as-nokia-s-customer-loyalty-falls-for-first-time.html.

20

1. Keith Chrzan, "An Overview of Pricing Research," *Quirk's Marketing Research Review*, July/August 2006, 24–29.

2. Kent Monroe and Jennifer Cox, "Pricing Practices that Endanger Profits," *Marketing Management*, September/October 2001, 42–46.

3. Ibid.

4. Paul, J. and R. Kapoor, "Pricing Strategy and Decision for International Marketing," *International Marketing*, (Tata-McGraw Hill, India, 2008), 224.

5. Press Trust of India, "Govt told to frame law to control retail food prices," *Business Standard*, November 22, 2010, http://www.business-standard.com/india/news/govt-told-to-frame-law-to-control-retail-food-prices/116806/on.

6. Sookyung Seo, "Ex-Asiana Executives Indicted in U.S. on Price-Fixing," *Bloomberg Businessweek*, August 27, 2010, www.businessweek.com/news/2010-08-27/ex-asiana-executives-indicted-in-u-s-on-price-fixing.html.

7. Liam Baldwin, "Freight Price Fixing Cartel Charged," *National Business Review*, September 2, 2010, www.nbr.co.nz/article/freight-price-fixing-cartel-charged-129366.

8. Anonymous, "Samsung and LG fined by regulator for price fixing," *BBC News*, January 13, 2012, http://www.bbc.co.uk/news/business-16540678.

9. Anonymous, "Panasonic fined in European price fixing case," *The Economic Times*, December 8, 2011, http://economictimes.indiatimes.com/news/international-business/panasonic-fined-in-european-price-fixing-case/articleshow/11029058.cms.

10. Colchester, M., and C. Passariello, "Dirty Secrets in Soap Prices," *The Wall Street Journal*, December 9, 2011, http://online.wsj.com/article/SB10001424052970203413304577086251676539124.html.

11. "How Driving Prices Lower Can Violate Antitrust Statutes," *Wall Street Journal*, January 24, 2004, A1, A11.

12. Kotler, P., K. L. Keller, A. Koshy, and M. Jha, Developing pricing strategies and programs. *Marketing Management—A South Asian Perspective*, 13th ed (Pearson Education, India, 2009) 392–393.

13. Kenneth Ofgang, "C.A. Upholds $16 Million Predatory Competition Judgment," *Metropolitan News-Enterprise*, August 12, 2010, www.metnews.com/articles/2010/bayy081210.htm.

14. Bruce Alford and Abhijit Biswas, "The Effects of Discount Level, Price Consciousness, and Sale Proneness on Consumers' Price Perception and Behavioral Intention," *Journal of Business Research*, 55, no. 9, September 2002, 775–778; also see V. Kumar, Vibhas Madan, and Srinin Srinivasan, "Price Discounts or Coupon Promotions: Does It Matter?" *Journal of Business Research*, 57, no. 9, September 2004, 933–941.

15. Company website: http://www.adityabirlanuvo.com/media/press_releases/pressrelease.aspx?ID=AEsQir6u0NU=.

16. Sharan, A., and R. Vats, "Low and behold," *Hindustan Times*, November 16, 2009, http://www.hindustantimes.com/News-Feed/Business/Low-amp-behold/Article1-476783.aspx.

17. Bhushan, R., "Lay's, Kurkure love marks with snackers," *The Economic Times*, November 2, 2009, http://articles.economictimes.indiatimes.com/2009-11-02/news/27635892_1_kurkure-core-brands-snacks.

18. Kaul, P., "Oops! You've missed it," *Outlook Business*, September 20, 2006, http://business.outlookindia.com/article.aspx?101083; Chakravarty, C., "Coke, Pepsi to can ₹5 strategy, hike prices," *The Economic Times*, August 2, 2004, http://articles.economictimes.indiatimes.com/2004-08-02/news/27404872_1_neville-isdell-hike-prices-pepsi-and-coca-cola.

19. Company website: http://www.mydollarstoreindia.com/.

20. Rui (Juliet) Zhu, Xinlei (Jack) Chen, and Srabana Dasgupta, "Can Trade-Ins Hurt You? Exploring the Effect of a Trade-In on Consumers' Willingness to Pay for a Product," *Journal of Marketing Research*, 45, no. 2, April 2008, 159–170.

21. Ibid.

22. To learn more about pricing fairness, see Lan Xia, Kent Monroe, and Jennifer Cox, "The Price Is Unfair! A Conceptual Framework of Price Fairness Perceptions," *Journal of Marketing*, 68, no. 4, October 2004, 1–15.

23. Dilip Soman and John Gourville, "Transaction Decoupling: The Effects of Price Bundling on the Decision to Consume," MSI Report, 2002, 98–131; Stefan Stremersch and Gerard J. Tellis, "Strategic Bundling of Products and Prices: A New Synthesis for Marketing," *Journal of Marketing*, 66, no. 1, January 2002, 55–71; "Forget Prices and Get People to Use the Stuff," *Wall Street Journal*, June 3, 2004, A2.

24. Rebecca Hamilton and Joydeep Srivastava, "When 2+2 Is Not the Same as 1+3: Variations in Price Sensitivity across Components of Partitioned Prices," *Journal of Marketing Research*, 45, no. 4, August 2008, 450–461.

25. Sean Cole, "Less Product, Same Price," American Public Media, January 8, 2009, http://marketplace.publicradio.org/display/web/2009/01/08/pm_deceptive_packaging/.

26. Paul Hunt and Greg Thomas, "Scoring Birdies instead of Bogies," *Pricing Solutions Newsletter*, 2, no. 2, Winter 2009, www.pricingsolutions.com.

27. This application exercise is based on the contribution of William H. Brannen (Creighton University) to *Great Ideas in Teaching Marketing*, a teaching supplement that accompanies Lamb, Hair, and McDaniel's *Marketing*. Professor Brannen's entry titled "Can Your Marketing Students Solve the Banana Problem? Can You?" was a runner-up in the "Best of the Great Ideas in Teaching Marketing" contest held in conjunction with the publication of the eighth edition of *Marketing*.

28. "Aakash tablet to be available on rent in college libraries" http://indiatoday.intoday.in/story/aakash-tablet-to-be-available-on-rent-in-college-libraries/1/168313.html (accessed March 22, 2012).

29. "Aakash and Ubislate Tablets," http://www.akashtablet.com/(accessed March 22, 2012).

30. "With low-cost tablet Aakash, sky is the limit for students," http://www.dnaindia.com/india/report_with-low-cost-tablet-aakash-sky-is-the-limit-for-students_1630779 (accessed March 22, 2012).

21

1. Joseph Hair, Robert Bush, and David Ortinau, *Marketing Research: Within a Changing Information Environment*, 3rd ed. (Burr Ridge, IL: McGraw-Hill/Irwin, 2006), 114.

2. Anonymous, "India's largest oil company reduces total cost of ownership by 30 percent," *Microsoft Case Studies*, May 17, 2011, http://www.microsoft.com/india/casestudies/microsoft-dynamics-crm-4.0/indian-oil-corporation-limited/india-s-largest-oil-company-reduces-total-cost-of-ownership-by-30-percent/4000009980.

3. Anonymous, "India's largest oil company reduces total cost of ownership by 30 percent," *Microsoft Case Studies*, May 17, 2011, http://www.microsoft.com/india/casestudies/microsoft-dynamics-crm-4.0/indian-oil-corporation-limited/india-s-largest-oil-company-reduces-total-cost-of-ownership-by-30-percent/4000009980.

4. Anonymous, "India's largest oil company reduces total cost of ownership by 30 percent," *Microsoft Case Studies*, May 17, 2011, http://www.microsoft.com/india/casestudies/microsoft-dynamics-crm-4.0/indian-oil-corporation-limited/india-s-largest-oil-company-reduces-total-cost-of-ownership-by-30-percent/4000009980.

5. Sheth, J. N., "Building customer relationships—The Taj Air Caterers experience," *Customer Relationship Management: Emerging Concepts, Tools, and Applications*, (Tata-McGraw Hill Education 2001), 379–387.

6. "My Starbucks Idea," Starbucks, http://mystarbucksidea.force.com/.

7. Terry Maxon, "For Southwest Airlines Team, Work Means Always Having to Say You're Sorry," *Dallas Morning News*, August 15, 2010, www.dallasnews.com/sharedcontent/dws/bus/stories/DN-swapology_15bus.ART0.State.Edition1.26cd7a0.html.

8. SAP Customer Success Story, "Playstation.com Chooses mySAP CRM," http://h20338.www2.hp.com/enterprise/downloads/playstation.pdf.

9. Rai, A. K., 'CRM – practice and application in select service companies'. *Customer Relationship Management: Concepts and Cases*, (PHI Learning Private Limited, New Delhi 2008), 199.

10. Nick Saint, "Foursquare in Partnership Talks with Google, Microsoft, and Yahoo," *Business Insider*, July 19, 2010, www.businessinsider.com/foursquare-looking-to-sell-check-in-data-to-search-engines-2010-7.

11. Muthuraman, B., et. al., "Understanding the Process of Transitioning to Customer Value Management." *Vikalpa*, 2006, Vol. 31 No. 2, 1–27.

12. Barton Weitz, Stephen Castleberry, and John Tanner, *Selling: Building Partnerships* (Burr Ridge, IL: McGraw-Hill/Irwin, 2004), 184–185.

13. Srinivasan, S., "United Technologies is Quickening its Steps in India," *Forbes India*, April 30, 2011, http://forbesindia.com/printcontent/24442; Bhandari, B., "United we stand," *Business Standard*, September 6, 2010, http://www.business-standard.com/india/news/united-we-stand/407042/.

14. Andy Greenberg, "Mining Human Behavior at MIT," *Forbes*, August 12, 2010, www.forbes.com/forbes/2010/0830/e-gang-mit-sandy-pentland-darpa-sociometers-mining-reality_2.html.

15. "Young Adults 'More Receptive to Direct Mail,'" Equi Media, September 8, 2010, www.equimedia.co.uk/index.php?id=98&article=800056175.

16. Miguel Bustillo, "Wal-Mart Radio Tags to Track Clothing," *Wall Street Journal*, July 23,

2010, http://online.wsj.com/article/SB100014240 52748704421304575383213061198090.html.
17. Privacy International, "Consultation Report: Race to the Bottom? 2007," June 9, 2007, www .privacyinternational.org/issues/internet/ interimrankings.pdf.
18. This application exercise is based on the contribution of Kenneth J. Radig (Medaille College) to *Great Ideas in Teaching Marketing*, a teaching supplement that accompanies Lamb, Hair, and McDaniel's *Marketing*. Professor Radig's entry titled "Direct Mail Assignment" was a runner-up in the "Best of the Great Ideas in Teaching Marketing" contest held in conjunction with the publication of the eighth edition of *Marketing*.
19. Levy Michael, Weitz Baeton, Pandit Ajay, *Retailing Management*, 6th ed, (New York: Tata McGraw-Hill, 2008).
20. "Shopping without stopping," March 22, 2012, http://www.tata.com/company/Articles/ inside.aspx?artid=LbPZERYdRd4=.

22

1. Brian Solis, *Engage: The Complete Guide for Brands and Businesses to Build, Cultivate and Measure Success in the New Web* (Hoboken, NJ: John Wiley & Sons, 2010), 37.
2. "Social Media for Non Profits," *Primalmedia*, February 18, 2009, www.primalmedia.com/blog /social-media-non-profits.
3. Salma Jafri, "Lady Gaga's Social Media Success and Strategy," Suite101.com, June 5, 2010, http://marketingpr.suite101.com/article .cfm/lady-gagas-social-media-success-and-strategy; Dorothy Pomerantz, "Lady Gaga Leads List of Celeb 100 Newcomers," *Forbes*, June 28, 2010, www.forbes.com/2010/06/22/lady-gaga-kristin-stewart-business-entertainment-celeb-100-10-newcomers.html.
4. Andrew Hampp, "Gaga, Oooh La La: Why the Lady Is the Ultimate Social Climber," *Advertising Age*, February 22, 2010, http://adage .com/digitalalist10/article?article_id=142210.
5. Solis, *Engage*.
6. Ibid.
7. Universal McCann, "Power to the People–Wave3 Study on Social Media Trends," March 2008, www.slideshare.net/mickstravellin/ universal-mccann-international-social-media -research-wave-3.
8. Claimed mobile Internet users are those who have accessed internet through their mobile phones at least once in the past.
9. Active mobile Internet users are those who access internet through their mobile phones at least once a month.
10. "Mobile Internet in India 2011," IMRB International and IAMAI , August 2011.
11. Anonymous, "Television continues to rule the hearts of young Indians, though mobile phone usage shows potential to grow," Synovate Research, August 27, 2010, http://www.synovate. com/news/article/2010/08/television-continues-to-rule-the-hearts-of-young-indians-though-mobile-phone-usage-shows-potential-to-grow.html.
12. Shane Snow, "iPad by the Numbers," *Mashable*, July 2010, http://mashable .com/2010/06/07/ipad-infographic-2.
13. Paul Marsden, "Simple Definition of Social Commerce," *Social Commerce Today*, June 2010, http://socialcommercetoday.com/social-commerce-definition-word-cloud-definitive-definition-list.
14. Madhavan, N., "Social commerce awaits big revolution," *Hindustan Times*, October 30, 2011, http://www.hindustantimes.com/business-news/ ColumnsBusiness/Social-commerce-awaits-big-revolution/Article1-762934.aspx.
15. "Hitting the High Notes," FICCI-KPMG Indian Media and Entertainment Industry Report 2011, 103–122.
16. Coutinho, A., "Sunsilk's Gang of Girls goes global," *The Economic Times*, November 17, 2006, http://articles. economictimes.indiatimes.com/2006-11-17/ news/27427176_1_spread-awareness-girls-website; Sachdev, H., "Brave New World of Web Marketing," *The Economic Times*, June 8, 2010, http://economictimes.indiatimes. com/tech/ites/the-brave-new-world-of-web-marketing/articleshow/6021636.cms.
17. *Marketing News* Staff, "Digital Dozen: Step Up to The Bar," *Marketing News*, March 15, 2010, www.marketingpower. com/ResourceLibrary/Publications/ MarketingNews/2010/3_15_10/Digital Dozen. pdf.
18. Jeff Howe, *Crowdsourcing: Why the Power of the Crowd Is Driving the Future of Business* (New York, NY: Three Rivers Press, 2009), 32.
19. Ghosh, D., "Apparel brands chase new design trends on Facebook, Twitter," *The Economic Times*, April 13, 2010, http://economictimes. indiatimes.com/news/news-by-industry/cons-products/garments-/-textiles/apparel-brands-chase-new-design-trends-on-facebook-twitter/ articleshow/5789684.cms.
20. Sean Corcoran, "Defining Earned, Owned and Paid Media," Forrester Blogs, December 16, 2009, http://blogs.forrester.com/interactive_ marketing/2009/12/defining-earned-owned-and-paid-media.html; Brian Solis, "Why Brands Are Becoming Media," *Mashable*, February 11, 2010.
21. Ibid.
22. Jonathon Hensley, "How to Build Trust Online," *Marketing News*, March 15, 2010.
23. Erik Bratt, "Social Media ROI Success Stories," *MarketingProfs*, 2009, www .marketingprofs.com/store/product/27/ social-media-roi-success-stories.
24. David Berkowitz, "100 Ways to Measure Social Media," *Inside the Marketers Studio*, November 17, 2009, www.marketersstudio.com/ 2009/11/100-ways-to-measure-social-media-.html.
25. Jim Sterne, *Social Media Metrics* (Hoboken, NJ: John Wiley & Sons, 2010).
26. Charlene Li and Josh Bernoff, *"Groundswell": Winning in a World Transformed by Social Technologies,* (Boston, MA: Harvard Business Press, 2009).
27. *North American Technographics Interactive Marketing Online Survey*, Forrester Research, June 2009, www.forrester.com/ER/Research /Survey/Excerpt/1,10198,726,00.html.
28. Juan Carlos Perez, "Forrester Notes Social Media Contributor Slowdown," *Computerworld*, September 28, 2010, www.computerworld.com/s/ article/9188538/Forrester_notes_social_media_ contributor_slowdown.
29. Dan Zarella, *The Social Media Marketing Book* (Beijing, China: O'Reilly, 2010).
30. Bhatt, K., "A different blogosphere in India," *The Financial Express*, March 30, 2008, http://www.financialexpress.com/ news/a-different-blogosphere-in-india/290028/0.
31. Press Trust of India, "Amitabh Bachchan most followed Bollywood celeb on Twitter," *Deccan Chronicle*, January 2, 2012, http:// www.deccanchronicle.com/channels/showbiz/ bollywood/amitabh-bachchan-most-followed-bollywood-celeb-twitter-289.
32 Shah, S., "How MTV India's Twitter campaign became a trending topic," *TechinAsia*, January 26, 2011, http://www.techinasia.com/ mtv-india-twitter-marketing/.
33. Guglielmo, C., "Dell Rings Up $6.5 Million in Sales Using Twitter," *Bloomberg*, December 8, 2009, http://www.bloomberg.com/apps/news?pid =newsarchive&sid=akXzD_6YNHCk.
34. Warner, B. , "Selling via Twitter: now it's Sony's turn," *Social Media Influence*, March 18, 2010, http:// socialmediainfluence.com/2010/03/18/ selling-via-twitter-now-its-sonys-turn/.
35. Sathe, G. "Social Media | The new niche networker," *Livemint*, January 6, 2012, http:// www.livemint.com/2012/01/06211129/Social-Media--The-new-niche-n.html.
36. Marketing Profs, "Adobe Systems," *Facebook Success Stories*, 2009, www.marketingprofs.com/ store/product/35/facebook-success-stories.
37. Marketing Profs, *LinkedIn Success Stories*, 2009, www.marketingprofs.com/store/product/ 37/linkedin-success-stories.
38. Solis, *Engage*, 64.
39. Ramya Raghavan, "Using Video to Connect with Your Donors and Prospects," International Fundraising eConference, May 12–14, 2009.
40. Sethi, S. K., "Podcasting: Emerging Form of Virtual Clinical Education," *Indian Pediatrics*, 2008, Vol. 45, 165.
41. Zarella, *The Social Media Marketing Book*.
42. Solis, *Engage*, 54.
43. Solis, *Engage*, 97.
44. "Hitting the High Notes," FICCI-KPMG Indian Media and Entertainment Industry Report 2011, 114.
45. Khan, T., "The game is changing for brands," *Afaqs*, July 7, 2008, http://www.afaqs.com/news/ story.html?sid=21579_The+game+is+changing+fo r+brands.
46. Menon, N., "Bollywood loves online gaming," *Afaqs*, December 22, 2011, http:// www.afaqs.com/news/story.html?sid=32534_ Bollywood+loves+online+gaming.
47. "Social Gaming Integral to Social Networking," *Marketing Profs*, February 19, 2010, www. marketingprofs.com/charts/2010/3425/ social-gaming-integral-to-social-networking.
48. Lon Safko and David K. Brake, *The Social Media Bible: Tactics, Tools & Strategies for Business Success* (Hoboken, NJ: John Wiley & Sons, 2009).
49. Anonymous, "India census: Half of homes have phones but no toilets," *BBC*, March 14, 2012, http://www.bbc.co.uk/news/ world-asia-india-17362837.
50. Anwar, J., "Mobile advertising revenue to reach $3.3bn in 2011," *The Times of India*, June 16, 2011, http://articles.timesofindia.indiatimes. com/2011-06-16/india-business/29664913_1_ mobile-advertising-revenue-smartphones.
51. Anonymous, "Paradox Studios releases the 'Thums Up Everest Challenge' mobile game," Afaqs, March 17, 2005,http://www.afaqs.com/ news/company_briefs/index.html?id=4082_Parad ox+Studios+releases+the+Thums+Up+Everest+Ch allenge+mobile+game.
52. Michael Bush, "Red Cross Delivers Real Mobile Results for a Real Emergency"

Advertising Age, February 22, 2010, http://adage.com/digitalalist10/article?article_id=142204; Nicole Wallace and Ian Wilhelm, "Charities Text Messaging Success Shakes Up the Fundraising World," *Chronicle of Philanthropy*, February 11, 2010, 7.

53. "Real Racing GTI," Volkswagen, www.vw.com/realracinggti/en/us (accessed October 14, 2010).

54. Beth Kanter, "Screencast: Using Widgets to Build Community on Blogs Featured on NTEN Blog," *Beth's Blog*, March 20, 2007, http://beth.typepad.com/beths_blog/2007/03/screncast_using.html.

55. Tahseen, I., "India's saucy foodies," *The Times of India*, April 29, 2012, http://articles.timesofindia.indiatimes.com/2012-04-29/food-reviews/31475772_1_bloggers-dishes-julie-julia.

56. The ethics exercise was prepared on the basis of an article, "Ethical brandwagon," contributed by Tirna Ray in *The Times of India*. http://articles.timesofindia.indiatimes.com/2012-04-16/news/31349503_1_social-media-consumer-marketing.

57. Anonymous, "10 big stats from Facebook's IPO documents," *NDTV Gadgets*, February 7, 2012, http://gadgets.ndtv.com/shownews.aspx?id=GADEN20120193984&Sec=NEWS&nid=174169.

58. Gokhale, K., "Facebook popularity rises with cheaper Internet," *Hindustan Times*, August 8, 2011, http://www.hindustantimes.com/Technology/technology-industrytrends/Facebook-popularity-rises-with-cheaper-Internet/SP-Article1-730831.aspx.

59. Anonymous, "Auto firms like Maruti Suzuki, Hyundai, Tata Motors make efforts to tap customers on Facebook, Twitter," *The Economic Times*, January 22, 2012, http://articles.economictimes.indiatimes.com/2012-01-22/news/30652751_1_social-media-social-networking-sites-e-mail-marketing;Anonymous, "India can be no. 1 market in coming years: Facebook," *Business Today*, November 9, 2011, http://businesstoday.intoday.in/story/facebook-expects-user-base-to-grow-in-coming-years/1/19923.html; Rastogi, A., "How well are Indian brands leveraging Facebook today?" *Trak.in*, July 30, 2010, http://trak.in/tags/business/2010/07/30/indian-brands-facebook-use/.

60. Anonymous, "Facebook brand statistics in India," *Socialbakers*, http://www.socialbakers.com/facebook-pages/brands/india/ (accessed on May 1, 2012).

61. Mitra, M., "Companies increasingly using Facebook to promote business," *The Economic Times*, March 25, 2011, http://articles.economictimes.indiatimes.com/2011-03-25/news/29188680_1_frooti-parle-agro-nadia-chauhan.

62. Ohri, K., "Facebook: Surprise Factor," *Afaqs*, August 26, 2010, http://www.afaqs.com/news/story.html?sid=28054_Facebook:+Surprise+Factor.

63. Ohri, K., "Facebook: Surprise Factor," *Afaqs*, August 26, 2010, http://www.afaqs.com/news/story.html?sid=28054_Facebook:+Surprise+Factor.

64. Mitra, M., "Companies increasingly using Facebook to promote business," *The Economic Times*, March 25, 2011, http://articles.economictimes.indiatimes.com/2011-03-25/news/29188680_1_frooti-parle-agro-nadia-chauhan/2.

65. Chopra, P., "The 'cost' of Facebook marketing," *The Wall Street Journal*, July 12, 2010, http://blogs.wsj.com/india-chief-mentor/2010/07/12/the-cost-of-facebook-marketing/.

66. Anonymous, "India Inc spends ₹1,200 cr on social media," *Business Today*, October 5, 2011, http://businesstoday.intoday.in/story/india-inc-spends-rs-1200-cr-on-social-media/1/19124.html.

23

1. Ortiz I., Cummins M., "Global Inequality: Beyond the Bottom Billion", Social and Economic Policy Working Paper, April 2011, http://www.unicef.org/socialpolicy/files/Global_Inequality_Revised_-_5_July.pdf (accessed March 22, 2012).

2. 10th Five year Plan 2002-2007, Poverty Alleviation in Rural Areas: Strategies and Programs, Chapter 3.2, http://planningcommission.nic.in/plans/planrel/fiveyr/10th/volume2/10th_vol2.pdf, (accessed March 22, 2012).

3. Budget Speech 2010-11, 2011-12, *indiabudget.nic.in/ub2011-12/bs/bs.doc* (accessed March 22, 2012).

4. Prahalad, C. K., *The Fortune at the Bottom of the Pyramid*, (Dorling Kindersley Pvt Ltd, India, 2010).

5. Schuster T., Holtbrugge D., "Market entry of multinational companies in markets at the bottom of the pyramid: A learning perspective", Elsevier International Business Review, September 14, 2010.

6. Prahalad, C. K., *The Fortune at the Bottom of the Pyramid*, (Dorling Kindersley Pvt Ltd, India, 2010).

7. Ibid.

8. Hammond, A.L., Kramer, W.J., Katz, R.S., Tran, J.T., and Walker, C., The Next 4 Billion: Market Size and Business Strategy at the Base of The Pyramid, World Resources Institute/International Finance Corporation, 2007.

9. Bairiganjan, S., Cheung R., Delio A E, Fuente D., Lall S., and Singh S., Power To The People: Investing in Clean Energy for the Base of the Pyramid in India, 2010, http://pdf.wri.org/power_to_the_people.pdf (accessed March 22, 2012).

10. "The Housing Market", The Next 4 Billion. World Resources Institute, 2007, http://pdf.wri.org/n4b_chapter6.pdf (accessed March 22, 2012).

11. Ahluwalia Montek Singh, " ₹32 per day poverty line not all that 'ridiculous'":. http://articles.economictimes.indiatimes.com/2011-10-11/news/30266895_1_poverty-line-urban-areas-indian-conditions (accessed March 22, 2012).

12. Minimum Wages in the States, February 2011, http://labour.nic.in/wagecell/minwages.htm (accessed March 22, 2012).

13. Prahalad, C. K., *The Fortune at the Bottom of the Pyramid*, (Dorling Kindersley Pvt Ltd, India, 2010).

14. Ibid.

15. Wakude S M., Suicide of Farmers in Maharashtra–Causes & Remedies, http://www.nabard.org/databank/IARD percent20Web/csidfiles/Suicide percent20of percent20Farmers percent20in percent20Maharashtra.pdf (accessed March 22, 2012).

16. Prahalad, C. K., *The Fortune at the Bottom of the Pyramid*, (Dorling Kindersley Pvt Ltd, India, 2010).

17. Varian H. Intermediate Microeconomics: A Modern Approach, Affiliated East-West Press Pvt Ltd, 2006.

18. Prahalad, C. K., *The Fortune at the Bottom of the Pyramid*, (Dorling Kindersley Pvt Ltd, India, 2010).

19. Subhramanyan S., Gomez-Arias T., Journal of Consumer Marketing Emerald Article: Integrated approach to understanding consumer behavior at bottom of pyramid, http://dx.doi.org/10.1108/07363760810915617 (accessed March 22, 2012).

20. Braun J.V., "Rising food prices: what should be done?", IFPRI Policy Brief, 2008, www.ifpri.org/themes/foodprices/foodprices.asp (accessed March 22, 2012).

21. Belk, R.W., "Leaping luxuries and transitional consumers", Transition Newsletter, The World bank Group, www.worldbank.org/html/prddr/trans/so99/pgs24-26.htm (accessed March 22, 2012).

22. Prahalad, C. K., *The Fortune at the Bottom of the Pyramid*, (Dorling Kindersley Pvt Ltd, India, 2010).

23. Yunus M., "Creating a World Without Poverty: Social Business and Future of Capitalism", Public Affairs, USA, 2007.

24. 6"2% of Mumbai lives in slums: Census", The *Hindustan Times*, October 17, 2010, http://www.hindustantimes.com/India-news/Mumbai/62-of-Mumbai-lives-in-slums-Census/Article1-614027.aspx.

25. Burgeoning Bourgeoisie, *The Economist*, http://www.economist.com/node/13063298 (accessed March 22, 2012).

26. UN-HABITAT - WORKING GROUP A, Bottom of the Pyramid Approaches for Urban Sustainability, 2008, Background Paper – Draft 0

27. Prahalad, C. K., *The Fortune at the Bottom of the Pyramid*, (Dorling Kindersley Pvt Ltd, India, 2010).

28. Wood R V., Pitta A D, Franzak J F., "Successful marketing by multinational firms to the bottom of the pyramid: connecting share of heart, global 'umbrella brands', and responsible marketing", 2008, http://dx.doi.org/10.1108/07363760810915635 (accessed March 22, 2012).

29. Sigurdsson K., Saffi A. C. P., "Price Efficiency and Short Selling", April 2008, http://www.iese.edu/research/pdfs/DI-0748-E.pdf (accessed March 22, 2012).

30. "Coca-Cola India's Thirst for the Rural Market", http://www.icmrindia.org/free percent20resources/casestudies/Coca percent20Cola percent20India percent20Thirst percent20for percent20the percent20Rural percent20Market3.htm (accessed March 14, 2012).

31. "Project Urja—An initiative by SEWA Bank", 2007, http://nexus.som.yale.edu/design-selco/sites/nexus.som.yale.edu.design-selco/files/imce_imagepool/Project percent20Urja.pdf (accessed March 22, 2012).

32. SEWA, UN to set energy park in Gujarat, February 2007, http://www.business-standard.com/india/news/sewa-un-to-set-energy-park-in-gujarat/275630/ (accessed March 22, 2012).

33. Prahalad C.K. and Stuart L. Hart, "The Fortune at the Bottom of the Pyramid", Strategy + Business, 2002, Issue 26.

34. "HLL Launches I-Shakti Rural Information Service In Association With Andhra Pradesh Government", (November 03, 2004), http://www.hul.co.in/mediacentre/news/2004/HLLLaunchesIShakti RuralInfoServiceIn Association With APGovt.aspx (accessed March 14, 2012).

35. "E-Choupal, Empowering Indian Farmers", http://www.itcportal.com/sustainability/lets-put-india-first/echoupal.aspx (accessed March 22, 2012).
36. Prahalad, C. K., *The Fortune at the Bottom of the Pyramid*, (Dorling Kindersley Pvt Ltd, India, 2010).
37. "Samruddhi—A farmer training project for sustainable agriculture in India", http://www.agro.basf.com/agr/APInternet/en/content/sustainability/best_practices/samruddhi/india-agriculture-project (accessed March 14 2012).
38. Telecom Regulatory Authority of India (TRAI). (January 2012) The Indian Telecom Services Performance Indicator Reports. September 31, 2011.
39. Prahalad, C. K., *The Fortune at the Bottom of the Pyramid*, (Dorling Kindersley Pvt Ltd, India, 2010).
40. The ethics exercise was prepared on the basis of a research paper, "Ethical concerns at the bottom of the pyramid: where CSR meets BOP," published by Kirk Davidson in *Journal of International Business Ethics*, Vol. 2 (1), 2009.
41. Cavin Care, Chik Shampoo, http://www.cavinkare.com/chikshampoo.html?reload (accessed March 22, 2012).

Index

T

U

V

W

Y

Z